THE
INTERNET
DIRECTORY
Version 2.0

THE
INTERNET
DIRECTORY
Version 2.0

ERIC BRAUN

WITH

MARK LEGER

Fawcett Columbine • New York

A Fawcett Columbine Book
Published by Ballantine Books

Copyright © 1996 by Eric Harris-Braun

All rights reserved under International and Pan-American Copyright Conventions. Published in the United States by Ballantine Books, a division of Random House, Inc., New York, and simultaneously in Canada by Random House of Canada Limited, Toronto.

http://www.randomhouse.com

Library of Congress Catalog Card Number: 96-96214

ISBN: 0-449-98370-6

Cover design by David Stevenson
Cover photo © FPG International

Manufactured in the United States of America

First Edition: April 1996

10 9 8 7 6 5 4 3 2 1

This book is for Ellen
(about whom most everything I want to
say is very, very sappy).

This book is also for every librarian
there ever was, because since I took on
the crazy task of trying to categorize the
Internet, I have come to regard them
and their job with a not insignificant
amount of awe.

ACKNOWLEDGMENTS

BUSINESS

PARTNERSHIPS

➤ **Mark Leger:** for tremendous amounts of work and for going well above and beyond the call of duty (see title page for full listing)

PUBLISHING, FREELANCING

1 **Jeff Kleinbard:** for Usenet & e-journal indexing
2 **Brian Canivan:** for OPAC verification
3 **Lynda Gibson:** for resource verification

PUBLISHING, PROOFREADING

4 **Josh Karpf:** for copy-editing the entire book and proofing its index

PUBLISHING, DESIGN

5 **Alex Klapwald:** for a great book design

PUBLISHING, VARIOUS

6 **Owen Lock:** for urging Eric to do this project in the first place

COMPUTERS

DATABASES, PROGRAMMING

7 **Shelley Valfer:** for designing and coding an excellent database and for putting up with lots of hassle

INTERNET, INFORMATION SOURCES

8 **Marty Hoag:** for his New-List mailing list which kept us up to date on mailing lists
9 **David Lawrence:** for allowing us to reprint his Usenet newsgroups descriptions
10 **Peter Scott:** for permission to use portions of the Hytelnet database
11 **Ann Okerson:** for permission to use portions of the ARL Directory of Electronic Journals
12 **A.J. Wright:** for his anesthesiology and medical resources
13 **John December:** for his resources on computer-mediated communications
14 **Sarah Nesbeitt & Munn Heydorn:** for their non-profit related resources
15 **Sheila Webber:** for her business-related resources
16 **Denis Anthony:** for his midwifery resources
17 **Ken McCoy :** for his theater resources

LIVING

GETTING TOGETHER, RELATIONSHIPS

➤ **Ellen Key Harris-Braun:** for everything (see dedication for full listing)
18 **Chris Cochrane:** who put up with Mark's keyboard tapping late into the night and kept the music playing (tho' a little heavy on the Beatles)
19 **Adam King:** for yet again not complaining while Eric wasn't working on Snap Mail!
20 **Natalie & Lucas:** for being understanding when Eric couldn't play because he had to work on this book

SOCIAL ISSUES

UTOPIA, DYSTOPIA & FUTURISM

21 **All cyber-rads, paradigm shifters, technoshamans, and free thinkers:** The Internet is our medium—let's liberate the planet!

TABLE OF CONTENTS

INTRODUCTION

Welcome to *The Internet Directory v2.0*. In the fall of 1993, when version 1.0 was published, there were *no* other comprehensive directories to the Internet, either hard copy or online. Now there are many of both. At that time many people hadn't even heard of the Internet. Now it's a household word. "Roadkill on the information superhighway" was a new joke (and even a little bit funny). Since the publishing of version 1.0, the Internet has undergone an amazing transformation. From being a place populated mostly by computer hobbyists, academics, and high-tech businesspeople, it is fast becoming a place where citizens of all kinds carry out a whole range of daily activities. What was then a fledgling experiment called the World Wide Web has now exploded into one of the main venues of information transfer on the Internet.

So now it is even more important to have a good directory to the information in this burgeoning medium. I hope that's exactly what you'll find on the pages of this book (and in the bytes on its companion CD-ROM). I certainly don't claim that it's a *complete* directory—the Internet changes too quickly and is to large for any guide to be that—but I have done my best to provide a *good* directory. All the entries have been verified, and they have all been categorized and indexed and cross-referenced by real people, not by computers, so you should be able to find quickly things that you are interested in.

HOW TO BECOME A NET CITIZEN

First, you need to learn what the Internet is—what services it provides and what tools you need to access those services. The next section of this introduction, "An Internet Refresher," provides a brief overview for those who have a nodding acquaintance with the information services that the Internet provides. If terms like *telnet*, *FTP*, *gopher*, *URL*, and *World Wide Web* are new to you, then you need a how-to guide, of which there seem to be hundreds in most bookstores.

Second, you need to learn the conventions of proper behavior on the Internet. This is called *netiquette*, and observing it is extremely important if you want to be successful and productive in your use of the Internet. Unless you have been using the Internet for a long time, make sure you read the section "Netiquette and Internet Culture," an introduction to proper behavior on the Internet and to issues of net citizenship. There are no Internet police as yet, and none are needed because the proper observation of netiquette by most Internet visitors makes the Internet a nice "small town" place to be, despite the fact that millions of people "live" in it. Let's keep it this way.

Third, you need to learn where to go! This book is full of lists that direct you to the tens of thousands of places to go and things to see on the Internet. Use the table of contents to browse the lists by subject, and use the index to find listings by key words.

A FEW WORDS ABOUT CHANGE

By its nature the Internet is ephemeral. It changes and grows by the second. From the time I stop adding information to the manuscript of *The Internet Directory v2.0* to the earliest opportunity for the finished book to reach your hands (approximately one month), thousands of new people will have joined the Internet, new Web sites will have come online, mailing lists will have changed addresses, and so on. This book is clearly not the final word—you have to get online for that. But even when you *are* online, remember that even the most up-to-date resources will contain errors. Much of the information for this book was derived from the most up-to-date lists of resources available and then verified for accuracy. Because of the phenomenal growth of the Internet, it was impossible for us to include every resource we know about. Verifications and new information arrive in our mailbox all the time, so we had to set a cutoff date after which any new information would appear in the next edition. This book most certainly has some errors in it, and just as certainly doesn't list a few important resources. If you find a mistake or if you are the owner of a resource that you would like to see listed, drop us a note. The e-mail address for updates and corrections is tid@randomhouse.com

HOW THIS BOOK IS ORGANIZED

The main body of the book is a list of mailing lists, newsgroups, electronic journals and magazines, World Wide Web sites, gopher servers, anonymous FTP archives, and telnet resources, all categorized by topic. Many of these entries are cross-listed under various other topics, where you will find brief mentions pointing you to the main listings for those entries. Each entry has been carefully indexed so that you can find items just by looking for key words in the index. So, when you are looking for items about a broad subject (mathematics, for example), browse the table of contents to find the subject, and look at the items in that section. If you are looking for something more specific (the Mathematica symbolic-math software, for example) turn to the index and look for its name.

You will notice that each entry has a number in front of it, and that the first and last entry numbers on each page appear on the top corners of that page. That way, when you look something up in the index, you can flip directly to the exact item that interests you. Cross references show an arrow like this: ➤ instead of a number. Also, you will notice that the first few entries in many of the topics are underlined. These entries are "meta" entries, or collections of pointers to other resources on the Internet about the particular topic.

The book also has an appendix, which is a listing of OPACs (online library card catalogs) and how to get access to them.

HOW THIS BOOK WAS COMPILED

The guiding philosophy behind the *Directory* is to list as much information of absolutely any sort as can be located, so long as we could verify, with the resource owner or maintainer, the address, accessibility, and procedures for using it. There are many compilations of Internet resources on the Internet, as well as mailing lists that people use to send out announcements of new resources. We were given permission to publish many compilations put together by other people; one prominent example is the descriptions of almost all of the Usenet newsgroups, which are taken from David Lawrence's compilation. (See the Acknowledgments section for a complete list.) We also subscribed to the various announcement mailing lists. Of course, we also just went out exploring, and added the interesting things we found to our database.

AN INTERNET REFRESHER

WHAT IS THE INTERNET?

This is a much-discussed question to which there is no one answer. Nor is there a single answer to the more sticky question of what it means to be "on" the Internet. This question is typically answered in terms of what kind of data-transport protocol a computer uses to communicate with other computers, the one called "TCP/IP" being what definitely puts you on the Internet. But I offer a different definition of the Internet:

The Internet is the collection of information services publicly available on the interconnected computer networks that span the globe.

From my point of view, the more access you have to the different services the Internet provides, the more "on" the Internet you are. I emphasize the services, not the data-transport protocol used. True, many of the services to which this book is a directory are currently available only to those computers that communicate via the TCP/IP protocol. But others, like e-mail, are available on practically all networks. So I would say that any computer that can take advantage of internetwork e-mail is at least partially on the Internet.

Most of this book is a directory to what is accessible via the Internet's information services: data, computers, interest groups, and more. These services can be grouped into three categories: communication services, connection services, and data-access services. We'll look at each separately.

COMMUNICATION SERVICES

Communication services allow people to send messages to each other. The Internet provides two main communication services: electronic mail (e-mail) and newsgroups (the so-called Usenet). E-mail is much like regular mail, but with a few added conveniences and much faster delivery. In fact, users have come to refer to the regular postal service as *snail mail* (commonly abbreviated *s-mail*). Newsgroups, on the other hand, don't have much to do with news as we know it—a one-way communication service from reporter to audience. On the Internet, newsgroups are a true two-way, interactive communication service, perhaps best thought of as discussion groups in which anybody can "publish" articles relevant to the interests of the particular newsgroup.

E-mail

A sample e-mail message:

```
From: anansi@jungle.com (Anansi T. Spider)        ← The header starts here
To: brother.tiger@forest.com
Subject: Where can I find fly databases?
Date: Wed, 31 Jan 96 11:29:59 PDT
Reply-To: anansi@jungle.com
Content-Type: TEXT/PLAIN; charset=US-ASCII
X-Mailer: uAccess - Macintosh Release: 1.6v2


Brother Tiger,                                   ← the body starts here
>                               ← ">" indicates a quote from earlier e-mail
> I've got some info but I'm swamped.
> Can I get it to you later this month?
>
That's fine ... I'm in no major hurry at the moment.
cheers ... -Anansi


Anansi T. Spider    Trickster Supreme    anansi@jungle.com ← signature
```

The header: The e-mail header contains `From:` and `To:` addresses and the subject and date of the message as well as other, sometimes cryptic information. This information is in a standardized format because it must be interpreted by the software responsible for routing the e-mail to its destination. You can read more about these standards in the Request For Comment (RFC) documents 822, 1049, and 1341 (please see entries 2913 and 2914 in the main body of the book for pointers to RFC repositories).

The body: The body of a piece of e-mail is usually just the message typed in by the sender. Sometimes the body will contain a few other things. For example, if the e-mail has been forwarded or returned, the beginning of the body will be the header of the forwarded or returned piece of mail. Also, the body will sometimes contain an attachment. With the advent of MIME, the Multipurpose Internet Mail Extensions standard (see RFC 1341), the body of an e-mail message can even contain encoded pictures and audio.

People often append a "signature" to the body of their e-mail. This makes it easy for the recipient to find information on the sender, such as a return e-mail address. A signature can be very useful because the `From:` address in the header can be garbled by some mail-forwarding software. This is especially true for people who send e-mail to the Internet via some other connected network or the UUCP data-transmission protocol.

E-mail Addressing

Addressing on the Internet can get quite complicated if you delve into its depths, and there are whole books devoted to the topic. But basically, what you need to know is that an e-mail address is of the form *user@host*, where *user* is the login name of the person you are sending mail to, and *host* is either the domain name or IP number (more about these below) of the computer where that person has an account. Addressing e-mail to people on non-TCP/IP networks is often just the same as addressing e-mail to someone directly on the Internet because "alias" domain names have been set up. In such cases your e-mail sending software may be able to translate the e-mail address for you. Sometimes, however, this does not work.

IP Numbers and Domain Names

Any computer directly on the TCP/IP portion of the Internet has a numerical address assigned to it, and you can always use that number to reference it. For example, if you wanted to send e-mail to `tiger@forest.com` and `forest.com` had the IP number `198.7.1.7`, you could send your e-mail to `tiger@[198.7.1.7]`. Notice that in an e-mail address the IP number must be put in brackets.

Using a domain name is a much more convenient way of referring to a host, since words are more easily remembered than numbers. Domain names are translated to IP addresses by special computers called domain-name servers. The software of the originating computer substitutes the IP address to send its e-mail. (For more details on this process, see RFCs 1034 and 1035.)

Another thing to keep in mind about domain names is that, as previously noted, many hosts that are on other networks and are never directly connected to the TCP/IP portion of the Internet are still assigned domain names. Mail sent to those domains gets translated into an address that the gateway computer to the given network can understand. For example, if Mr. Anansi T. Spider had an account on the Bitnet node JUNGL, you could send him e-mail to `anansi@jungl.bitnet`. This address gets translated by the name servers to `anansi%jungl.bitnet@cunyvm.cuny.edu`. The new domain name `cunyvm.cuny.edu` is a gateway computer that is on both the Internet and Bitnet and will forward the mail to the proper Bitnet node and user by examining the user portion of the e-mail address, `anansi%jungl.bitnet`.

It is often the case, especially for larger institutions, that you don't need to specify the full domain name of a host when addressing e-mail. This is because people often have accounts on many hosts, and hosts appear and disappear as people and computers move around. For example, you could send mail for the computer-science professor Anansi Spider at Yale University to the address `anansi@cs.yale.edu`. Even though there is no single host `cs.yale.edu` the name server will translate the `cs.yale.edu` domain name to the host that Yale's computer-science department has registered as being responsible for forwarding mail to the proper destination.

Bounced Mail

A piece of e-mail will undoubtedly be returned to you at some point or another. Examining a piece of returned mail to figure out what happened can be tricky. Below are some examples of session transcripts for e-mail that has been returned for some of the more common reasons, as well as explanations of what happened and what you can do about it, if anything.

Host Unknown
```
-- Transcript of session follows --
554 pipkins@vicstoy.oua.org... 550 Host unknown (Authoritative answer
from name server)
```

The domain name `vicstoy.oua.org` does not exist. Usually you get this as a result of a misspelling. Check the spelling of the domain name to make sure you got it right. Occasionally the domain name server (the computer that is responsible for translating domain names into a computer's IP number) loses track of some domain names. If you are sure that the domain name exists, just try sending the mail again later and it should go through.

User Unknown
```
-- Transcript of session follows --
While connected to gps1 [129.11.128.109] (ether):
```

```
>>> RCPT To:<TEX5HAD%cms1.ucs.leeds.ac.uk@leeds.ac.uk>
<<< 550 <TEX5HAD%cms1.ucs.leeds.ac.uk@leeds.ac.uk>... User unknown
550 <TEX5HAD@cms1.ucs.leeds.ac.uk>... User unknown
```

TEX5HAD is not a person who has an account on that computer. Again you will see this most often due to typos.

Connection Timed Out

```
-- Transcript of session follows --
421 csd-reserved2.Stanford.EDU (TCP)... Deferred: Connection timed out
during user open with csd-reserved2.Stanford.EDU
```

Though the host name is known, a connection could not be established with it after several retries. Usually the Subject: heading will tell you for how many days delivery was attempted.

Service Unavailable

```
-- Transcript of session follows --
Connected to mailhost:
>>> DATA
<<< 554 sendall: too many hops 27 (25 max): from , to (null)
554 <salim@mesis.esrin.esa.it>... Service unavailable
```

This error can occur for a number of reasons, and it will usually be explained in the transcript. In this particular case, the problem is that the mail was forwarded too many times. Each time it gets forwarded to a different computer, a "hop count" register gets increased by one. If the hop count gets too big, mail will be sent back to you. This prevents mail from bouncing around the Internet forever trying to get to its destination. Another frequent reason for the Service unavailable message is that though the message was delivered to the proper address, it couldn't actually be added to the user's mailbox for one reason or another—for example, the maximum allowable disk space assigned to the user had been exceeded.

In all such cases you can try to send the mail again and see if it gets through. It's a good idea to wait a day or two for the problem to get cleared up.

Unknown Error

```
-- Transcript of session follows --
554 <aidsnews@aol.com>... unknown mailer error 1
```

This type of error usually occurs when the destination computer crashes or has a problem during transmission. Try sending the mail again.

Mailing Lists

Mailing lists are a very important extension of the communication services provided by e-mail. This directory lists thousands of interest groups that use mailing lists to carry out their discussions. A mailing list is just a group of e-mail addresses maintained either manually, by some person who takes on the responsibility of forwarding mail to all the people on the list, or automatically, by a computer program. Such a computer program is called a mail reflector. Mail reflectors usually have two address-es: the address to which all mail is sent that is to be distributed to everybody on the list, and the address to which changes to the mailing list are sent.

Mailing lists have usually been divided into two classes, Internet and Bitnet, but this distinction is becoming less and less important as e-mail flows freely between the Internet and Bitnet. There are a few things you should be aware of regarding the dif-ferences between the two kinds of list, however. Bitnet mailing lists are almost all han-dled by a program called listserv. For more information on how to use a Bitnet listserv, simply send e-mail with `help` as the body of the message to any Bitnet listserv (for example, `listserv@bitnic.educom.com`). Mailing lists on the Internet, however, are handled in a variety of ways. Many of them are processed by people who keep track of all the addresses of subscribers and forward all submissions manually. There are also a number of different programs that handle Internet mailing lists—majordomo, Unix listserv, LISTPROC, and Mail-serv, to name a few. Each of these works slightly differently, but you can find out about all of them by sending them e-mail with the sin-gle word `help` as the body of the message. Please note that in the main section of this book, the addresses listed after the symbol ± in the form "list-name-request@host.domain" are sometimes aliases for people and sometimes aliases for one of the programs listed above. If the list is being run by a computer, the entry will include exact directions on what to send in a subscription request. Otherwise there are no instructions; send a personal request, as it will be read by a person.

Usenet Newsgroups

Usenet newsgroups are, after e-mail and mailing lists, the Internet's most widely used communication service. Theoretically, Usenet provides the same type of service as is provided by e-mail mailing lists—discussion groups. In practice, however, Usenet is a much more robust service because, unlike e-mail, it was specifically designed to pro-vide discussion-group services. Just imagine what would happen if all newspaper reporters worked freelance and mailed you copies of their stories every day instead of having them published in a newspaper. Pretty soon your mailbox would be impossi-bly full. Usenet is the Internet's mechanism for organizing the thousands of messages on hundreds of topics that are sent every day. Perhaps for the first time in history, free-dom of the press is not contingent upon owning a press; you can simply publish your ideas on Usenet.

The newsgroups listed in this book are taken from a recent compilation of all the newsgroups that are distributed worldwide. Many of these newsgroups are not avail-able to everyone, since it is up to the system administrator of each host computer to determine which newsgroups that computer will process. This is usually determined by how much extra processing power and disk space is available, since some of the newsgroups considered "optional" by administrators take up large amounts of disk space. Also, you will probably find a number of local-area interest groups available on your system that are not published in the *Directory*.

Other Communication Services

The Internet also provides some direct communication services that allow people to communicate in real time, as if over a telephone. The two main services of this type are Talk and Internet Relay Chat (IRC).

Talk

Talk is a two-person communication service. When you run Talk, you specify the address of the person to whom you wish to speak. A message is sent to that person indicating your talk request. Once your request is acknowledged, you can "talk" simply by typing. The software splits your screen into two portions: in one you see what you type and in the other you see what the other person types. Talk is an interesting mode of communication in that you see each character as it is being typed. Because people generally type more slowly than they talk, multiple lines of conversation take place at the same time. Try it—it's a strange experience!

Internet Relay Chat

Internet Relay Chat (IRC) is the citizens-band radio of the Internet. This communication service is different from Talk in the same way Usenet is different from e-mail: it is designed for group discussions. When you log on to an IRC server, you will be presented with a large number of channels on which people are chatting. A channel's name usually describes the general thrust of the conversation, or at least the language being used (remember that the Internet is a worldwide entity). When you join a channel, you immediately begin receiving messages sent by others on that channel. IRC differs from Talk in that you compose an entire line of text before sending it off.

CONNECTION SERVICES

The Internet's connection services provide access to its destinations, the millions of computers interconnected by it. Using a connection service, you can log on to practically any computer on the Internet and use it just as if you were sitting at a terminal right next to it (provided, of course, that you have an account and know the password to the computer!)

Telnet

Telnet is the most widely used connection service on the Internet. You can think of telnet simply as a "virtual" terminal. You provide telnet with the host name of the computer you want to connect to (see the section on e-mail addressing above), and it sets up a connection, sends to the computer the keystrokes you type, and displays on your screen the characters the computer sends back. That's all there is to it. Telnet is used most often along with a resource provided by some institution, such as the computerized card catalog of a library. On the Internet, online library catalogs are called OPACs (for Online Public Access Catalogs). This book's appendix is a directory to most of the OPACs in the world that are accessible via telnet.

DATA-ACCESS SERVICES

Data-access services are a bit more complicated and more varied than the communication services, simply because accessing data is a much less well-structured activity. Also, like most everything else on the Internet, databases and the tools to access them have been added continually throughout the Internet's evolution.

The Client-Server Model

To understand the Internet's major data-access services, you need to understand what is known as the client-server model of software design. Client-server software was developed to increase the efficiency of network information services. It does this by separating a service's software into two parts: the user-interface software (the client) and the data-handling software (the server).

The problems of efficiently providing information services between computers connected by networks are clearly shown by examining what happens when you log on to a library catalog using a connection service like telnet (see above). Every aspect of that service, from performing searches in the card catalog to displaying characters on the screen, is controlled by the library's computer. Telnet is acting only as a dumb terminal. This is inefficient for two reasons: (1) the library's computer is wasting its processing time by sending to your computer commands that draw the screen and by processing each keystroke that you type, and (2) sending these commands across a network adds unnecessary traffic. If telnet could be made smarter—that is, if it could take on some of the tasks, such as displaying entire menus or interpreting your keystrokes—then the library's computer could spend more of its time answering search requests (i.e., providing its service), and network traffic would be decreased. Such an enhanced telnet would become the *client* of a library-service *server*.

Client-server software is usually designed so that many clients can be connected to one server. Telnet itself is actually based on the client-server model, but only for the relatively simple connection service. The data-access services described below provide more extensive client-server interactions.

FTP and Archie

The first widely used data-access service on the was the File Transfer Protocol (FTP), a network-wide client-server standard for sending files from one computer to another. Software that implements both the client and the server portions of FTP exists for virtually every kind of computer that can communicate using TCP/IP. FTP allows users to connect to any other computer (given, of course, that they have an account and know the password) and transfer files.

Many computers on the Internet have been set up as file archives with special "anonymous" accounts so that, by means of FTP, users who have no routine access to such computers can still make use of the huge number of interesting and useful files that they contain. FTP archives store a huge range of files, from computer programs for the home computer to text files containing all the recent decisions of the Supreme Court.

Using FTP

When using an FTP client, you first establish a connection with a computer running an FTP server by specifying a valid account and password. When accessing an anonymous-FTP archive, you simply type `anonymous` at the computer's request for a user name, and type your e-mail address when prompted for a password. Once you are connected, you can issue various commands to list files or transfer them to or from the computer you have connected to. Exactly how you will issue these command depends on the client you are using. The most primitive clients use commands based on the Unix command set. Some of these are:

- `cd [dir]`   change directory on remote machine
- `ls`   list contents of remote directory
- `get [file]`   transfer the remote file
- `mget [files]`   transfer many remote files (you can use patterns, e.g., *.txt)
- `binary`   set file-transfer mode to binary (for compressed files, programs, etc.)
- `ascii`   set file-transfer mode to text
- `help`   get a list of commands

Most World Wide Web browsers let you access data via the FTP protocol. You simply specify the computer, login information, directory, and file name in a URL (Uniform Resource Locator). For example, Anansi Spider wants to get the file `my_stuff.txt` from the directory `my_junk`, on the computer `jungle.com` where he has an account, `anansi`. As we all know, his password is `lotsayams`. So he would enter the following URL into his Web browser:

```
ftp://anansi:lotsayams@jungle.com/my_junk/my_stuff.txt
```

If you are getting files from a computer that allows anonymous login, you don't need to specify the user or a password; the Web browser will take care of that for you. Also, you need not specify a particular file name in the URL if you just want a listing of the files in a particular directory.

Archie

Although FTP programs provide you with access to the data archives at anonymous-FTP sites, there remains the problem of finding the data you want in the mountains of files stored in those archives, and across the many archives that exist. Archie is a program that solves this problem by providing indexing of FTP archives. This is how it works: periodically, anonymous-FTP sites send information on the contents of their archives to a few computers on the Internet. These computers run the Archie server software. If your host computer has Archie client software, you can use it to send queries to the server software about files in the participating archives. The server software searches its database and sends back descriptions and locations of materials that match your query. For people who don't have Archie client software on their host computers, there are World Wide Web Archie gateways available at:

```
http://hoohoo.ncsa.uiuc.edu/archie.html
http://www.earn.net/gnrt/archie.html
```

Also, the computers where the archie data is stored also allow public access via telnet (login as `archie`). These computers are:

Host	Country
archie.au	Australia
archie.aco.ne	Austria
archie.cs.mcgill.ca	Canada
archie.uqam.ca	Canada
archie.funet.fi	Finland
archie.univ-rennes1.fr	France
archie.th-darmstadt.de	Germany
archie.ac.il	Israel
archie.unipi.it	Italy
archie.kyoto-u.ac.jp	Japan
archie.wide.ad.jp	Japan
archie.hana.nm.kr	Korea
archie.sogang.ac.kr	Korea
archie.nz	New Zealand
archie.uninett.no	Norway
archie.rediris.es	Spain
archie.luth.se	Sweden
archie.switch.ch	Switzerland
archie.ncu.edu.tw	Taiwan

`archie.twnic.net`	Taiwan
`archie.doc.ic.ac.uk`	United Kingdom
`archie.hensa.ac.uk`	United Kingdom
`archie.ans.net`	USA
`archie.internic.net`	USA
`archie.rutgers.edu`	USA
`archie.sura.net`	USA
`archie.unl.edu`	USA

FTP by mail

For computers that don't have access to the FTP data service but do have e-mail, a special computer has been set up by DEC (Digital Equipment Corporation) to which you can send e-mail requesting a particular file from a particular computer. The DEC computer will make an FTP connection for you and then e-mail the file to you. (If the file is large, it may be sent to you in convenient segments—you are responsible for putting it back together.) For further information, send e-mail to `ftpmail@decwrl.dec.com` with `help` as the body of the message. Use this resource sparingly or it will disappear! Remember, it is only one computer for thousands of users across the entire Internet.

Gopher and Veronica

Gopher is a later addition to the Internet. The idea behind gopher was to provide an organized, user-friendly way of getting access to information on the Internet. What makes gopher unique is the fact that it is menu driven. Gopher servers send clients a list of menu items to display to the user. These menu items can be data resources (e.g., text files or sounds), the names of other menus, or links to other gopher servers. This last item was the conceptual breakthrough first provided by the gopher data service because it allows for a decentralized database system that looks well organized to the user. The conglomerate of all gopher menus is called *gopherspace*, and it is indeed a kind of space that you will wander through as you look for information on the Internet.

Veronica

Veronica is to gopher as Archie is to FTP. It provides an indexing service for the many menus of gopherspace. As the number of gopher servers grows, finding the particular gopher server with the information you want becomes a big problem—though not impossible, since you could just "tunnel" around from gopher to gopher looking for it. However, a solution similar to Archie was created for gophers, and not surprisingly it was called Veronica. But Veronica is a bit more sophisticated than Archie, and is also directly available from within gopher. It works like this: Periodically, gopher servers send information on what is in their gopher databases to the Veronica database. The Veronica database has an entry for almost every word of every menu item in every gopher database, so it is extremely useful for performing broad searches. The problem is usually to make the searches specific enough to yield a reasonably small number of matches.

The beauty of the gopher concept is that Veronica (unlike Archie) forms links to the actual menu items you want, rather than just displaying their locations. The gopher-client software thus builds a custom menu of all of these items. When you select one, your gopher client will reach out to the gopher server where that information is stored. One problem with this, however, is that sometimes the Veronica database is out of date and lists an entry that has been removed from its gopher server. When you attempt to access that little gem, you find out it is no longer there. But such is the nature of a changing universe.

WAIS

WAIS stands for Wide Area Information Server. It is a particular implementation of the Z39.50 protocol, which provides yet another data-access service over the Internet. Unlike FTP and gopher (which require the use of Archie and Veronica for doing searches), this protocol directly addresses the problem of searching for the information you want. It works like this: If you have data—for example, text files containing Supreme Court decisions—to which you want to provide access, you use special indexing software to create an index of the files' contents. Then you set up a WAIS server to provide the access to this resource. A user can then search for all the Supreme Court decisions that have anything to do with, for instance, abortion by utilizing a WAIS client to query your resource. The client will return a "hit list" of all the files that match the query, and from that list the user can request the actual files.

WAIS clients and servers for many computer platforms are available free on various FTP archives, and the WAIS software is utilized by many Internet resources that provide searchable contents.

WWW

WWW stands for World Wide Web. The first version of this book contained very little information on the Web because in 1993 the Web was so new that there really weren't very many Web resources. However, the current rapid expansion of the Internet is now largely in the area of Web resources. The World Wide Web is perhaps the most interesting of all the information services available because it conceptually encompasses all the others. Like gopher, it links servers transparently, yet the interface is not a menu of items to choose from, but a hypertext page of text or graphics with "live" cross-links that you can select. The links can be to anything: other hypertext pages, indexes of the information on a particular WWW server, text files, graphics, sounds, etc.

The World Wide Web is based on the HyperText Transfer Protocol (HTTP), which is the set of rules that govern communication between the Web client (your browser software, like Netscape or Mosaic) and the Web server, which provides the documents that are displayed by the browser. The documents themselves are in a special format called the HyperText Markup Language (HTML). This language is simply a set of rules for adding tags to plain old text documents that client software interprets to display the documents in an enhanced way. These tags include formatting elements that might, for example, mark a given part of the document to be in italics. They also include tags that cause the browser to display the graphic from another file in the place of the tag, which allows documents to be a bit more attractive. But most importantly, there are tags that mark a given bit of the text as a "hot link" to a different document anywhere else on the Internet. When the you click on that bit of text, the browser loads the new document specified in the tag. That feature is why this information service is called the Web: documents are linked to documents which are in turn linked to other documents, and so on in a huge, complex web of interconnected information. Furthermore, most WWW client programs can also speak gopher and FTP protocols, so links can be to documents stored on FTP archives and gopher servers. In fact, many Web browsers also let you send e-mail and read Usenet news! Thus Web browsers have come to be the preferred way to access information from information servers on the Internet. So even though the Web is just one of the data-access services, Web browsers have become multipurpose clients that can use many of the data-transfer protocols on the Internet.

NETIQUETTE AND INTERNET CULTURE

All technology requires wisdom in its wielding. The Internet requires it doubly since it is a social technology, not an instrumental one. What follows are some of the dos and don'ts and ways of looking at the Internet that I have picked up over the years I have been a part of it. They are the sorts of conventions that any social group might develop, so think of this section as an orientation to a different culture.

CITIZENSHIP VERSUS CONSUMERISM

Don't look at your relationship to the Internet as that of a consumer. Though this book is a directory to the resources on the Internet, it must not be viewed simply as a catalog that you can use for your shopping. A much better analogy is that of a phone book that can put you in touch with your fellow net citizens. Consider yourself a citizen of the Internet, and remember that most of the resources listed in this book were created by people in their spare time purely because they had some special interest. This, too, is how you should approach the Internet: What can you do to add richness and depth to this community?

The Internet is not a commercial service. Even though you may be paying an access provider, what you are paying for is the use of the provider's hardware and software, just as you might pay a car-rental agency for use of a car that makes your access to the highways of the nation possible. And while everyone with a car has the right to use the highways, everyone also has responsibilities and a set of rules to follow. It's the same with the Internet. So when you are out there on the network's roads, think of yourself as a citizen.

CORRECT MANNERS WHEN USING RESOURCES (JUST PLAIN UNCOMMON SENSE)

Each of the Internet's information services has different requirements for the proper approach to take when using it, so below I have provided netiquette pointers for each of them. But there are a few items that generally apply across the board:

The Categorical Imperative

Always remember that the person on the other end of the line is exactly that, a person. There is a great temptation to begin to think of people as resources, especially because, on the many newsgroups and mailing lists, it is so easy just to ask a question and get an answer from someone very knowledgeable. But don't treat people as means to your ends. A good way to make sure you don't do this is to give as much as you receive. There is probably a newsgroup or mailing list where you can provide answers to other people's questions. Subscribe.

The Tragedy of the Commons

Always keep in mind the problems that arise from what is called the tragedy of the commons. The tragedy is illustrated by the following story: There was once a village with a beautiful commons. There came a time of drought, and all the villagers' local pasturelands dried up, so they had to take their cows far and wide to provide them with enough pasture. No cows were allowed to graze on the commons, but one day a villager who was generally a hard worker was just a bit too tired take his cow to the distant pastures. So he thought to himself that if he let his cow graze on the commons, well, it wouldn't hurt the commons at all—after all, it was just one cow. So "just this once" he let his cow graze on the commons, and then called it back in the evening. The only problem was that the next day all the other villagers had the same thought, and in a week or so the commons was ruined. If only the one villager had broken the rules "just this once" no harm would have been done. But all the villagers kept telling themselves "just this once" and their commons was destroyed.

Like our natural environment, the Internet is a delicately balanced system that can only take so much abuse before it shuts down. So remember that the computers you connect to are finite resources—they have only a certain amount of processing power and disk space. Many provide specific instructions on how and when you should connect to them. Follow those rules. Also, in many cases resources have been mirrored around the world. If a local version of the resource is busy, wait for it to be freed up. *Don't* use the one on a different continent unless you absolutely must, especially if what you want to do is download large files. The transcontinental links are limited resources. Sure, you could do it "just this once," but don't.

The Signal-to-Noise Ratio

It's very easy to blabber on the Internet. In e-mail this is fine—after all, e-mail is (or should be) private communication. But on newsgroups and mailing lists, the so-called signal-to-noise ratio becomes very important. Messages you send to such forums can be propagated to hundreds of thousands of people (and, in a few years, perhaps millions). Thus, it is very important that all of what you say be meaningful. Add quality, not quantity, to any discussion. Don't be tempted by how easy it is to join into a conversation. Adding your two cents' worth is probably a bad idea—wait till it's at least a buck's worth!

Another source of noise in communication is excessively long signatures. Keep your signature to a minimum. A large, cutesy signature is cute only the first time someone sees it. After that it gets annoying. And it takes up bandwidth.

The Flame

It is very easy to rant and rave on the Internet. This is called *flaming*. People on the Internet sometimes say what sound like odd things, but before you fire off a response, try to remember that the Internet is by far the most diverse human environment you can take part in. People's "crazy" ideas are usually just ideas that are different from your own. So if you must respond to something you strongly disagree with, be civil. And remember that keeping an open mind is a crucial part of being a good net citizen.

One of the major sources of flaming on the is misunderstood irony or sarcasm. In speech we rely on our tone of voice, facial expression, and body language to convey the message that we are being ironic. On the Internet, we often can't do this; we must write what we think explicitly or mark what we write as ironic. The convention for doing this is to add a "smiley" after the ironic part of a message. The smiley is sideways and it shows up as `:-)` or `:)` —a colon followed by a close parenthesis, with the hyphen optional. So, for example, in a recent piece of mail I wrote: `That sounds like` a dodge if I ever heard one! :-) I included the smiley to make sure that the tone of my message was not accusatory. Remember also that to many people on the Internet, English is a foreign language. Detecting irony is even more difficult for people writing and reading in a language not their own.

NETIQUETTE POINTS FOR SPECIFIC SERVICES

Each of the information services on the Internet, especially the communication services, has rules that everybody generally plays by to keep that information service running smoothly. Below is my codification of those rules.

Mailing List Netiquette

Most mailing lists are completely public forums (and many are gated with newsgroups, so be sure also to read the netiquette section on Usenet news below), so remember, even though you are typing your words in the privacy of your own home, they are going out into a public space. Most mailing lists also have a charter (usually sent to you when you subscribe to the mailing list) that details acceptable topics and conventions used by that particular mailing list.

Here is a general list of things to keep in mind when submitting articles to any mailing list:

- Remember, the net is made up of *people*. Don't say anything you wouldn't in a face-to-face setting. If you disagree with someone, be civil, and when someone is rude and doesn't follow common netiquette (which does happen, unfortunately) *don't* respond in kind.
- Familiarize yourself with a mailing list before you submit e-mail to it. Each list has its own rules of order and limits as to what is appropriate to discuss. Follow these rules.
- Follow up via personal e-mail, not by submitting to the list—unless you are absolutely sure that the follow-up is relevant to all (or at least most) members of the list.
- Keep the signal-to-noise ratio low:
  - When quoting, quote only relevant portions, not the whole message, and especially not the header or signature of a message. You have a text editor; use it!
  - Single-line submissions of the "Me, too" and "Yes" variety are usually inappropriate. You should be adding substance to a discussion, not bulk.
  - All administrative requests should go to the administrative address, not the submissions address. When you subscribe you will receive the submissions address. You should *never* post any subscription, unsubscribe, or other administrative messages to that address. If you do so, everyone in the list will needlessly have to read your request and you will look like a fool.

- Remember that mailing lists are extremely varied. Some are purely for entertainment; others are places where real work gets done. What may be appropriate on one list won't be on another.

Usenet News Netiquette

Net news is a public forum. Anything you post will be read by hundreds, if not thousands, of people. Chris Anderson wrote the following in his article on net-news etiquette: "Imagine a stadium with every seat filled. Now imagine that you have to get up in front of this crowd and that you have to read *out loud* anything you post in news. Would that make you nervous? Would you be willing to stand by your words under that scrutiny? No? Then don't post the article to Netnews. E-mail it instead."

Net news provides true freedom of the press. For the first time in history you don't have to own a press to publish. But any freedom entails a complementary set of responsibilities. Below is a list of some of the things you should keep in mind when posting to the newsgroups. Many of these points are taken directly from the article "A Primer on How to Work With the Usenet Community" by Chuq Von Rospach, which is posted monthly to the `news.newusers` newsgroup. Make sure to read his entire article before posting an article on net news.

- Never forget that the person on the other side is human.
- Be careful what you say about others; your voice may be louder than you expect.
- Be brief.
- Your postings reflect upon you; be proud of them, from content to spelling.
- Use descriptive titles.
- Think about your audience.
- Be careful with humor and sarcasm.
- Check the FAQ (Frequently Asked Questions) file before you post a question.
- Post a message only once.
- Please scramble (rotate) material with questionable content.
- Summarize what you are following up. Don't quote the whole article.
- Use e-mail; don't post a follow-up.
- Read all follow-ups and don't repeat what has already been said.
- Double-check follow-up newsgroups and distributions to prevent spurious reposting.
- E-mail is private; don't post someone else's without explicit permission.
- Be careful about copyrights and licenses.
- Cite appropriate references.
- Mark or rotate answers or spoilers.
- Spelling flames are considered harmful. Many contain spelling errors themselves!

- Don't overdo signatures; it's a waste of bandwidth. Three lines or less is nice.
- Don't flame. If you disagree with someone, be civil.
- When someone does flame, *don't* respond in kind.
- Familiarize yourself with a group before you post articles to it. Each group has its own rules of order and its own limits as to what is appropriate to discuss. Follow these rules.

Anonymous FTP Archive Netiquette

Most anonymous FTP archives exist purely by the goodwill of their hosting institutions. Usually they are maintained by volunteers and are run on computers that are also used for "real work." So if use of the archives begins to affect the performance of the host computers, the archives will be discontinued. This means you should follow some simple rules:

- Keep connection times short! (Note that if you use a Web browser to access FTP servers you really don't have to worry about this because the browser logs in and then right back out again once it gets the file or directory listing).
- Search for what you want with Archie first, then go and get it directly, so that you don't have to spend lots of time browsing.
- If you do need to browse, then download the index file, disconnect from the FTP archive, and reconnect later once you have found what you want in the index.
- Do your downloading after hours (and remember to take into account time-zone changes).
- Download files from a mirror archive close to you. Mirrors are almost always less busy than the source archives. Use them and you'll be less likely to have your connection refused!

INTERNET HOAXES

There are a few Internet hoaxes of which you should be aware. One particularly nasty one, since it is very wasteful of bandwidth, is the chain letter. Some chain letters have seemingly good intentions, like e-mail to a terminally ill boy who wants to break the world record for get-well messages. But even these have disastrous consequences like bringing the poor boy's e-mail account to its knees because of a flood of messages. So ignore them all! Most commercial Internet access providers have rules to the effect that anybody caught participating in a chain letter will be kicked off the system. This is a good rule.

Some of the more devious hoaxes involve hackers who are trying to learn passwords to break into computer systems. It is not too difficult on the Internet to send e-mail that impersonates someone else. Occasionally e-mail is sent that purports to be from your system manager asking you for your password for some seemingly innocuous reason. Don't e-mail your password to anyone for any reason. If you absolutely have to give someone your password, do it over the phone, or in person.

So, after all that, welcome to the Internet. It's an exciting place to be.

ARTS & ENTERTAINMENT

1 `rec.arts.misc` Discussions about the arts not in other groups. *Moderated newsgroup*

ADVENTURE

2 `alt.binaries.sounds.misc` Digitized audio adventures. *Newsgroup*

3 `alt.fan.doc-savage` The man of bronze. *Newsgroup*

4 `alt.fan.james-bond` On His Majesty's Secret Service (and secret linen too). *Newsgroup*

5 **SUPERGUY:** For participants in SUPERGUY, a multiauthor, shared multiverse that focuses on humorous super-hero-genre stories, but includes serious superhero, science-fiction, and related stories. *Mailing List*
± `listserv@ucf1vm.cc.ucf.edu` [body = SUBSCRIBE SUPERGUY first-name last-name]
INFO OWNER `simmons@ucf1vm.cc.ucf.edu` (Tad Simmons)
ARCHIVES
`listserv@ucf1vm.cc.ucf.edu`
`http://www.halcyon.com/superguy/`
Gated: `bit.listserv.superguy`
Comments: Users on systems that have stringent limits on the amount of mail you can have should consider using the Usenet echo `bit.listserv.superguy`

AMUSEMENT PARKS

6 `alt.fairs.renaissance` Discussions of Renaissance faires and festivals. *Newsgroup*

➤ **Carousel!:** Carousel is a center for the appreciation of carousel art, history, and magic, featuring the grand works of the Golden Age of Carousels. (See entry 252 for full listing.)

7 `rec.arts.disney` Discussion of any Disney-related subjects. *Newsgroup*

8 `rec.arts.disney.announce` FAQs, lists, information, announcements. *Moderated newsgroup*

9 `rec.arts.disney.misc` General topics pertinent to the Disney Company. *Newsgroup*

10 `rec.arts.disney.parks` Parks, resorts, dining, attractions, vacations. *Newsgroup*

11 `rec.parks.theme` Entertainment theme parks. *Newsgroup*

12 `rec.roller-coaster` Roller coasters and other amusement park rides. *Newsgroup*

ANIMATION & ANIME

13 `alt.aeffle.und.pferdle` German television cartoon characters das Aeffle und das Pferdle. *Newsgroup*

14 `alt.animation.spumco` The Danes call it Quality. *Newsgroup*

15 `alt.animation.warner-bros` Discussions about Warner Brothers cartoons. *Newsgroup*

16 `alt.binaries.pictures.anime` Images from Japanese animation. *Newsgroup*

17 `alt.binaries.pictures.cartoons` Images from animated cartoons. *Newsgroup*

18 `alt.binaries.pictures.erotica.anime` Anime erotica—"Ecchi"/"Hentai"/"H. *Newsgroup*

19 `alt.binaries.sounds.cartoons` Sounds from copyrighted animated shows. *Newsgroup*

20 `alt.cartoon.reboot` Don't like the current animation? Ctrl-alt-del. *Newsgroup*

21 `alt.fan.disney.afternoon` Disney Afternoon characters and shows. *Newsgroup*

22 `alt.fan.lion-king` Discussion of Disney's *The Lion King*. *Newsgroup*

23 `alt.fan.mike-jittlov` Electronic fan club for animator Mike Jittlov. *Newsgroup*

24 `alt.fan.pocahontas` Discussion group for Disney's *Pocahontas* film. *Newsgroup*

25 `alt.fan.ren-and-stimpy` For folks who couldn't find `alt.tv.ren-n-stimpy`. *Newsgroup*

➤   **alt.fan.robotech:** Discussing all things relating to Robotech. *Newsgroup*

26   **alt.fan.sailor-moon** Sailor Moon animation, manga, and merchandise. *Newsgroup*

27   **alt.religon.beavis-n-butthead** Worshiping two teen morons. *Newsgroup*

28   **alt.tv.animaniacs** Steven Spielberg's Animaniacs! *Newsgroup*

29   **alt.tv.animaniacs.pinky-brain** Discussing *Pinky and the Brain* cartoons (Narf). *Newsgroup*

30   **alt.tv.beavis-n-butthead** Uh huh huh huh uh uh huh uh huh. *Newsgroup*

31   **alt.tv.casper** For discussing Casper, in comics, on TV, or the big screen. *Newsgroup*

32   **alt.tv.duckman** The *Duckman* animated sitcom. *Newsgroup*

33   **alt.tv.liquid-tv** Animated variety. *Newsgroup*

34   **alt.tv.reboot** Convincing 3-D animation. *Newsgroup*

35   **alt.tv.ren-n-stimpy** Some change from Lassie, eh? *Newsgroup*

36   **alt.tv.robotech** The *Robotech* animated sf TV series. *Newsgroup*

37   **alt.tv.simpsons** Don't have a cow, man! *Newsgroup*

38   **alt.tv.simpsons.itchy-scratchy** The cartoon-within-a-cartoon. *Newsgroup*

39   **alt.tv.taz-mania** The Tazmanian Devil's show. *Newsgroup*

40   **alt.tv.the-critic** Fox's animated series with Jon Lovmyself. *Newsgroup*

41   **alt.tv.tiny-toon** Discussion about the *Tiny Toon Adventures* show. *Newsgroup*

42   **alt.tv.tiny-toon.fandom** Apparently one fan group could not bind them all. *Newsgroup*

43   **alt.tv.tiny-toon.sex** Careful with that cel! *Newsgroup*

44   **The Anime Picture Archive:** A large archive of anime/manga images. It also contains information about the different series and links to other places.
http://www.lysator.liu.se/
INFO neotron@lysator.liu.se (David Hedbor)

45   **Bedrock Online (The Flintstones Mailing List):** On the *Flintstones* television series. (Where's Pebbles?) *Mailing List*
± listserv@netcom.com [body = subscribe bedrock-list]
OWNER mdb@cunyvms1.gc.cuny.edu (Marc Barnhill)
ARCHIVE mdb@cunyvms1.gc.cuny.edu (Marc Barnhill)

46   **fj.rec.animation** Discussion about animated movies. *Newsgroup*

➤   **Infini-D:** On Infini-D, a 3-D and animation software package for Macintosh. (See entry 2471 for full listing.)

47   **NAUSICAA:** For discussing the anime (Japanese animation) and manga (Japanese comics) of Hayao Miyazaki, the anime of Isao Takahataand the anime by other directors which are of a quasi-serious and/or progressive nature. *Mailing List*
± listserv@brownvm.brown.edu [body = SUBSCRIBE NAUSICAA first-name last-name]
INFO nausicaa-request@brownvm.brown.edu
INFO raub@kushana.aero.ufl.edu (Mauricio Tavares)
OWNER msj@u.washington.edu (Michael S. Johnson)
OWNER dmt@u.washington.edu (John Blankenship)
OWNER quark@u.washington.edu (Theo Hua)
OWNER ar402004@brownvm.brown.edu (Steven Feldman)
ARCHIVES
ftp://ftp.tcp.com/pub/nausicaa/
http://www.tcp.com/~miyazaki/NAUSICAA/
listserv@brownvm.brown.edu [body = INDEX NAUSICAA]
Please Note: Subscription by approval only.

Comments: Discussion is not about anime in general - see `rec.arts.anime` for that. Owners prefer that new subscribers monitor the discussion for a couple weeks before participating.

48 `rec.arts.animation` Discussion of various kinds of animation. *Newsgroup*

49 `rec.arts.anime` Japanese animation fen discussion. *Newsgroup*

50 `rec.arts.anime.info` Announcements about Japanese animation. *Moderated newsgroup*

51 `rec.arts.anime.marketplace` Things for sale in the Japanese animation world. *Newsgroup*

52 `rec.arts.disney.animation` Animated features, cartoons, short subjects. *Newsgroup*

53 `relcom.comp.animation` Discussions on computer animation programs. *Newsgroup*

ARCHITECTURE

54 **Architecture And Building Internet Resources:** Comprehensive collection of architecture- and building-related Internet resources.
`http://www.unlv.edu/library/ARCH/index.html`
`ftp://una.hh.lib.umich.edu/inetdirsstacks/archi%3Abrown`
INFO `jeanneb@nevada.edu`
MIRROR `http://www.tue.nl/lava/other/brown/`

➤ **Building Industry Exchange (BIX):** BIX is a nonprofit clearinghouse and search index of educational, communication, and information resources for the building industry. (See entry 1825 for full listing.)

➤ **BuildNet:** This site provides links, resources, and opportunities for all the members of the construction industry, including architects, contractors, and engineers. (See entry 1826 for full listing.)

55 **Planning and Architecture Internet Resource Center (SUNY Buffalo):** Collection of architecture and building and planning resources on the Internet.
`http://www.arch.buffalo.edu/pairc/`
INFO `tasman@acsu.buffalo.edu` (Dan Tasman) (Dan Tasman)

56 `alt.architecture` Building design/construction and related topics. *Newsgroup*

57 `alt.architecture.alternative` Nontraditional building designs. *Newsgroup*

58 `alt.architecture.int-design` Interior design of man-made spaces. *Newsgroup*

59 `alt.building.architecture` Building industry architecture. *Newsgroup*

60 `alt.landscape.architecture` Landscape design and planning. *Newsgroup*

61 **Architronic: The Electronic Journal of Architecture:** Scholarly and critical ideas about architecture. *E-Journal, moderated*
± `listserv@kentvm.kent.edu` [body = SUBSCRIBE ARCHITRON first-name last-name]
ARCHIVES
`http://www.kent.edu/Architronic/`
`gopher://gopher.kent.edu`
Frequency: three times per year

➤ **Built-environment:** On the built environment: architecture, civil engineering, surveying. (See entry 4566 for full listing.)

62 **The DuPont Building, Burlington, Vermont:** Joanna Oltman's historic preservation project traces the history of the classic DuPont Building on the waterfront in Burlington, Vermont.
`http://moose.uvm.edu/~joltman`
`http://moose.uvm.edu/~joltman/duponthist.html`
INFO `joltman@moose.uvm.edu`

63 `fj.engr.arch` Topics about architecture. *Newsgroup*

➤ **Isfahan Online:** Architectural guide and "walking tour" of the city of Isfahan, Iran. (See entry 8792 for full listing.)

64 **The Ladies Pavilion, Central Park, New York City:** Joanna Oltman's historic preservation project traces the history of one of Central Park's architectural gems, the Ladies' Pavilion.

```
http://moose.uvm.edu/~joltman
http://moose.uvm.edu/~joltman/ladies.html
```
INFO joltman@moose.uvm.edu

65 **LArch-L:** On landscape architecture. *Mailing List*
± listserv@listserv.syr.edu [body = SUBSCRIBE LARCH-L first-name last-name]
INFO zooey@mailbox.syr.edu
ARCHIVE http://www.clr.toronto.edu:1080/ARCHIVES/larchl.html

66 **Robinson Green Beretta Corporation:** RGB is the largest architectural, engineering, and interior design firm in Rhode Island.
http://www.rgb.net/rgb/
INFO rgb@rgb.net

67 **tnn.architect** Discussions about architecture. *Newsgroup*

ART HISTORY

68 **Art History Virtual Library:** Comprehensive list of art history links maintained by the History of Art Department of Birkbeck College, University of London.
```
http://www.hart.bbk.ac.uk/VirtualLibrary.html
```
INFO kirk@giorgio.hart.bbk.ac.uk

69 **alt.surrealism** Surrealist ideologies and their influences. *Newsgroup*

➤ **ARCO:** On art and literature, psychology and communication. (See entry 278 for full listing.)

➤ **C18-L:** For interdisciplinary discussion of the 18th century. (See entry 5240 for full listing.)

70 **NAHIA-L:** For North American historians of Islamic art. *Mailing List*
± listserv@msu.edu [body = SUBSCRIBE NAHIA-L first-name last-name]
INFO alan@ah2.cal.msu.edu (Alan Fisher)
ARCHIVE listserv@msu.edu

ART JOURNALS

71 **Enterzone:** A hyperzine of writing, art, and new media. It features criticism, fiction, philosophy, hypertexts, computer graphics, interactive art forms, scanned photography, and drawings. *E-Zine*
```
http://enterzone.berkeley.edu/enterzone.html
```
± http://enterzone.berkeley.edu/ez/subscr.html
INFO xian@pobox.com (Christian T. S. Crumlish)
ARCHIVE http://enterzone.berkeley.edu/ez/anthology.html
FAQ http://enterzone.berkeley.edu/ez/howto.html
Frequency: quarterly

72 **Plexus:** Online gallery, journal, and selected archive of art, video, criticism, theory, poetry, and literature. The site is always under construction, frequently updated with new works from artists and writers. *E-Journal*
```
http://www.plexus.org/
```
INFO kim@plexus.org (Director: Yu Yeon Kim)
INFO scp@plexus.org (Editor/Technical Admininistrator: Stephen Pusey)
EDITOR sub@plexus.org
Frequency: monthly

73 **think:** A newspaper of literary and visual art. *Magazine*
```
http://think.ucdavis.edu/
```
± listproc@ucdavis.edu [body = SUBSCRIBE THINK-REMINDER first-name last-name]
INFO info@think.ucdavis.edu
OWNER think-exec@ucdavis.edu

ARCHIVE `http://think.ucdavis.edu/index.html`
Frequency: bimonthly

74 **The Unit Circle:** A journal of art, music, prose, commentary, and poetry. *E-Journal*
`http://www.etext.org/Zines/UnitCircle/`
± `unitcircle-list-request@netcom.com`
± INFO `zine@unitcircle.org` (Kevin Goldsmith)
ARCHIVES
`ftp://ftp.etext.org/pub/Zines/UnitCircle/`
`gopher://fir.cic.net/00/Zines-by-subject/Graphic_Art/UnitCircle/`
FAQ `http://www.etext.org/Zines/UnitCircle/generalinfo.html`
Frequency: quarterly

75 **Whisper:** Whisper is a poetry, fiction, art, photography, and review magazine. *E-Zine*
`http://www.crl.com/~whisper/SPhome.html`
INFO OWNER `whisper@crl.com` (Anthony Boyd)
ARCHIVE `http://www.crl.com/~whisper/SPhome.html`
Frequency: 3 times a year

ARTS EDUCATION

76 `alt.art.colleges` An art forum for colleges. *Newsgroup*

➤ `can.schoolnet.arts.drama:` Drama studies in elementary/secondary schools. *Newsgroup*

77 **CSEA-L:** On visual-arts education in Canada. *Mailing List*
± `listserv@unb.ca` [body = SUBSCRIBE CSEA-L first-name last-name]
INFO `dsoucy@unb.ca` (Don Soucy)
ARCHIVES
`http://cnet.unb.ca/c-arts/`
`listserv@unb.ca` [body = INDEX CSEA-L]
Language: English, French

78 **INSEA-L:** On international education through the arts. *Mailing List*
± `listserv@unb.ca` [body = SUBSCRIBE INSEA-L first-name last-name]
INFO `dsoucy@unb.ca` (Don Soucy)

➤ `k12.ed.art:` Arts and crafts curricula in K-12 education. *Newsgroup*

➤ `k12.ed.music:` Music and performing arts curriculum in K-12 education. *Newsgroup*

➤ **PhotoForum:** On photography and imaging education. (See entry 1244 for full listing.)

79 **Seneca Information Service:** This is the CWIS of Seneca College of Applied Arts and Technology, Toronto, Canada.
`http://www.senecac.on.ca/`
`gopher://www.senecac.on.ca`
INFO `webmaster@mars.senecac.on.ca`

80 **UNL College of Fine and Performing Arts:** An online guide to the University of Nebraska-Lincoln College of Fine and Performing Arts, including programs, calendar of events, and more.
`http://www.unl.edu/finearts`
INFO `kanderse@unlinfo.unl.edu`

ARTS NEWS

81 `alt.art.scene` Making a spectacle of yourself in the art world. *Newsgroup*

82 `clari.living.arts` News of the arts. *Moderated newsgroup*

AUDIO-VISUAL EQUIPMENT

83 **aus.hi-fi** Hi-fi issues. *Newsgroup*

84 **fj.rec.av** High-fidelity audio and video components. *Newsgroup*

85 **rec.audio.high-end** High-end audio systems. *Moderated newsgroup*

86 **rec.audio.marketplace** Buying and selling of home audio equipment. *Newsgroup*

87 **rec.audio.misc** Post about audio here if you can't post anywhere else. *Newsgroup*

88 **rec.audio.opinion** Everybody's two bits on audio in your home. *Newsgroup*

89 **rec.audio.pro** Professional audio recording and studio engineering. *Newsgroup*

90 **rec.audio.tech** Theoretical, factual, and DIY topics in home audio. *Newsgroup*

91 **rec.audio.tubes** Electronic audio circuits which use vacuum tubes. *Newsgroup*

92 **relcom.commerce.audio-video** Audio and video equipment. *Newsgroup*

93 **relcom.fido.ru.strack** FIDOnet, digitized sound. *Newsgroup*

BODY ART

94 **alt.art.bodypainting** Discussions about temporary body painting. *Newsgroup*

95 **alt.binaries.pictures.bodyart** Graphics of body stylings. *Newsgroup*

96 **Body Modification ezine (BME):** All about piercing, tattoing, and other things you can do to your body for fun.
http://www.io.org/~bme/
INFO bme@io.org

97 **Jesster's Tattoo Page:** Collection of tattoo images and pointers to other tattoo resources.
http://www.wpi.edu/~jesster/tattoo.html
INFO jesster @wpi.edu (Jesse Parent)

98 **rec.arts.bodyart** Tattoos and body-decoration discussions. *Newsgroup*

BOOKS

99 **BookWire:** Book information galore. It includes information on publishers, bookstores, book events, and a "BookIndex" of book-related Internet resources.
http://www.bookwire.com/
INFO www@bookwire.com

100 **Digital BookWorld:** A Web site about books: includes information on new books, backlist books, authors, booksellers, and publishers. Also provides excerpts, reviews, and interviews.
http://www.digitalbookworld.com/
INFO gerrydunn@eworld.com

101 **The Internet Book Information Center:** This site includes: a guide to book-related resources on the Internet, The IBIC Journal (reviews of current and classic books), and more book-related goodies.
http://sunsite.unc.edu/ibic/
INFO ibic@sunsite.unc.edu

102 **alt.books.reviews** "If you want to know how it turns out, read it!". *Newsgroup*

103 **alt.books.technical** Discussion of technical books. *Newsgroup*

104 **Bookport:** Online editions of current books. Can be sampled, purchased, unlocked, and read online, or ordered from the publishers.
http://www.bookport.com/welcome/bookport/rhidbook
INFO info@bookport.com

105   **BookWeb:** All sorts of book information, brought to you by the American Booksellers Association. Includes book news, author tour information, a directory of bookstores, a monthly contest, information on how to open a bookstore, and more.

http://www.bookweb.org/bookweb/
INFO martha@ambook.org (Martha Schulze)
INFO wexler@ambook.org

106   clari.living.books News about books and authors. *Moderated newsgroup*

➤   **Clue Lass Home Page—A Mystery Newsletter:** A newsletter about mystery fiction. (See entry 1214 for full listing.)

107   fj.books Books of all genres, shapes, and sizes. *Newsgroup*

108   misc.books.technical Discussion of books about technical topics. *Newsgroup*

109   pdx.books Information about various books. *Newsgroup*

➤   **Publishers' Catalogues Home Page :** A comprehensive list of publishers from around the entire world. (See entry 1929 for full listing.)

110   rec.arts.books Books of all genres, and the publishing industry. *Newsgroup*

111   rec.arts.books.marketplace Buying and selling of books. *Newsgroup*

112   rec.arts.books.reviews Book reviews. *Moderated newsgroup*

113   relcom.fido.su.books FIDOnet, for book readers and lovers. *Newsgroup*

114   tnn.books Topics and information about books. *Newsgroup*

115   tnn.books.new Topics and information about newly released books. *Newsgroup*

BOOKS—BOOKSTORES

116   **Bolen Books:** Bolen Books is an independent bookstore whose Web site offers online ordering and pages of interesting forthcoming new titles and new arrivals.

http://www.bolen.bc.ca/books/
INFO books@bolen.bc.ca

117   **D-Pendable Books & Products:** D-Pendable Books & Products catalog features books and other odds and ends.

http://www.parentsplace.com/shopping/soother/
http://www.worldprofit.com/madpent.htm
INFO dherman@cln.etc.bc.ca

➤   eug.hungryhead: Books/events at Hungry Head Bookstore. *Newsgroup*

➤   **Future Fantasy Bookstore:** A bookstore of science fiction, fantasy, and mysteries. (See entry 1324 for full listing.)

118   **House of Speculative Fiction:** Ottowa-based bookseller of science-fiction and fantasy books.

http://www.cyberus.ca/specfic/
INFO specfic@cyberus.ca
INFO rturner@cyberus.ca

119   **Open Book Systems (OBS):** An online publisher and bookstore in English, German, French, and Romanian.

http://www.obs-us.com/
INFO info@obs-us.com
FAQ http://www.obs-us.com/obs/english/about/top.htm
MIRROR http://www.obs-europa.de/ (Germany)

120   **Village Books:** A community-based bookstore located in Bellingham, Washington. This site includes event listings, author comments about the store, and links to other interesting book-related sites.

http://www.fairhaven.com/villagebooks/
INFO villagebks@aol.com

121 **WordsWorth Books:** WordsWorth Books is a large independent bookstore with a complete search-and-order Web site.

http://www.wordsworth.com/
gopher://gopher.wordsworth.com
telnet://wordsworth.com
INFO sanj@wordsworth.com
INFO info@wordsworth.com

CARTOONS, COMICS & MANGA

122 `alt.comics.2000ad` Discussing British comic *2000 A.D.* and related issues. *Newsgroup*

123 `alt.comics.alan-moore` Quis custodiet ipsos custodes? *Newsgroup*

124 `alt.comics.alternative` You could try a book without pictures, for example. *Newsgroup*

125 `alt.comics.batman` Marketing mania. *Newsgroup*

126 `alt.comics.classic` For the discussion of golden- and silver-age comic books. *Newsgroup*

127 `alt.comics.dilbert` Scott Adams's intrepid engineer. *Newsgroup*

128 `alt.comics.elfquest` W. & R. Pini's ElfQuest series. *Newsgroup*

129 `alt.comics.fan-fiction` Original works using existing comic characters. *Newsgroup*

130 `alt.comics.image` What would a comic be without an image? *Newsgroup*

131 `alt.comics.joe-the-circle` Discussing *Joe the Circle* comics. *Newsgroup*

132 `alt.comics.lnh` Interactive net.madness in the superhero genre. *Newsgroup*

133 `alt.comics.peanuts` For the discussion of the *Peanuts* comic strip. *Newsgroup*

134 `alt.comics.superman` No one knows it is also alt.clark.kent. *Newsgroup*

135 `alt.fan.hello-kitty` I have no damn mouth! *Newsgroup*

136 `alt.fan.neil-gaiman` The Sandman. *Newsgroup*

137 `alt.fan.peter-david` For fans of comic and sf writer Peter David. *Newsgroup*

138 `alt.rodney.dangerfield` Still not getting any respect. *Newsgroup*

➤ `alt.sex.hello-kitty:` Why are there so few hot, exhibitionist, S & M pussies? *Newsgroup*

➤ **The Anime Picture Archive:** A large archive of anime/manga images. It also contains information about the different series and links to other places. (See entry 44 for full listing.)

139 **Business Cartoons by Goff:** Teamwork, safety, management, sales, and technology cartoons for in-house newsletters, training manuals, presentations, advertising, brochures, and other publications, by professional cartoonist Ted Goff.

http://www.tfs.net/personal/tgoff/main.html
INFO tedgoff@aol.com

140 `clari.editorial.cartoons.toles` Editorial cartoons from Tom Toles. *Moderated newsgroup*

141 `clari.editorial.cartoons.worldviews` Views of the World editorial cartoons. *Moderated newsgroup*

142 `clari.feature.bizarro` *Daily Bizarro* comic panel by Dan Piraro. *Moderated newsgroup*

143 `clari.feature.dilbert` The daily comic strip *Dilbert* (MIME/uuencoded GIF). *Moderated newsgroup*

144 `clari.feature.doonesbury` Garry Trudeau's Doonesbury. *Newsgroup*

145 `clari.feature.forbetter` Lynn Johnston's For Better or For Worse comic. *Newsgroup*

146 `clari.feature.foxtrot` Bill Amend's FoxTrot comic. *Newsgroup*

147 `clari.feature.toles` Tom Toles' editorial cartoons. *Newsgroup*

148 `clari.feature.worldviews` Views of the World: international editorial cartoons. *Moderated newsgroup*

149   `clari.living.comics.bizarro` Dan Piraro's bizarre comic panel. *Moderated newsgroup*

150   `clari.living.comics.cafe_angst` Comic by Hans Bjordahl & Holley Irvine. *Moderated newsgroup*

151   `clari.living.comics.doonesbury` Garry Trudeau's classic political comic. *Moderated newsgroup*

152   `clari.living.comics.forbetter` Lynn Johnston's *For Better or For Worse*. *Moderated newsgroup*

153   `clari.living.comics.foxtrot` Bill Amend's *Foxtrot*. *Moderated newsgroup*

154   `clari.living.comics.ozone_patrol` Holley Irvine's unique *Ozone Patrol*. *Moderated newsgroup*

155   **COMICW-L:** The Comic Writers Workshop. *Mailing List*
± `listserv@unlvm.unl.edu` [body = SUBSCRIBE COMICW-L first-name last-name]
EDITOR `jrd@frame.com` (James Drew)
Please Note: Subscription by approval only.

156   **comix:** On nonmainstream and independent comic books. Little about superheroes and nothing about Marvel Mutants. *Mailing List*
± `comix-request@world.std.com` (Elizabeth Lear Newman)
INFO OWNER `owner-comix@world.std.com`

157   `fj.rec.comics` The funnies, old and new. *Newsgroup*

158   **Modesty Blaise:** Discussion and information exchange about Peter O'Donnell's *Modesty Blaise* books and comics. *Mailing List*
`http://www.cs.umu.se/~dvlkhh/modesty.html`
± `majordomo@ifi.uio.no` [body = subscribe mb]
INFO OWNER `thomasg@ifi.uio.no` (Thomas Gramstad)
FAQ `majordomo@ifi.uio.no` [body = info mb]

159   `rec.arts.anime.stories` All about Japanese comic fanzines. *Moderated newsgroup*

160   `rec.arts.comics.alternative` Alternative (non-mainstream) comic books. *Newsgroup*

161   `rec.arts.comics.creative` Encouraging good superhero-style writing. *Newsgroup*

162   `rec.arts.comics.dc.lsh` The Legion of Super-Heroes and related characters. *Newsgroup*

163   `rec.arts.comics.dc.universe` DC Comics shared universe and characters. *Newsgroup*

164   `rec.arts.comics.dc.vertigo` Comics from the Vertigo imprint. *Newsgroup*

165   `rec.arts.comics.elfquest` The Elfquest universe and characters. *Newsgroup*

166   `rec.arts.comics.info` Reviews, convention information, and other comics news. *Moderated newsgroup*

167   `rec.arts.comics.marketplace` The exchange of comics and comic related items. *Newsgroup*

168   `rec.arts.comics.marvel.universe` Marvel Comics shared universe and characters. *Newsgroup*

169   `rec.arts.comics.marvel.xbooks` The mutant universe of Marvel Comics. *Newsgroup*

170   `rec.arts.comics.misc` Comic books, graphic novels, sequential art. *Newsgroup*

171   `rec.arts.comics.other-media` Comic book spinoffs in other media. *Newsgroup*

172   `rec.arts.comics.strips` Discussion of short-form comics. *Newsgroup*

173   `rec.arts.manga` All aspects of the Japanese storytelling art form. *Newsgroup*

CELEBRITIES

174   `alt.binaries.nude.celebrities` Willard Scott nekkid and other natural wonders. *Newsgroup*

175   `alt.binaries.pictures.celebrities` Unrated pictures of famous people. *Newsgroup*

176   `alt.binaries.pictures.teen-idols` Pictures of the hunks of tomorrow. *Newsgroup*

177   `alt.binaries.pictures.teen-starlets` Pictures of starlets. *Newsgroup*

178   `alt.celebrities` Famous people and their sycophants. *Newsgroup*

179 `alt.collecting.autographs` *wow!* You got Pete Rose's? What about Kibo's? *Newsgroup*

180 `alt.fan.actors` Discussion of actors, male and female. *Newsgroup*

➤ `alt.fan.alicia-slvrstone:` For discussion of and about Alicia Silverstone. *Newsgroup*

181 `alt.fan.brad-pitt` A young actor the women seem to be crazy about. *Newsgroup*

182 `alt.fan.bruce-campbell` From *The Evil Dead* to *Brisco County, Jr.. Newsgroup*

183 `alt.fan.chris-elliott` Get a life, you Letterman flunky. *Newsgroup*

184 `alt.fan.conan-obrien` *Late Night* with a big red pompadour. *Newsgroup*

185 `alt.fan.crispin-glover` Discussion of actor Crispin Glover. *Newsgroup*

186 `alt.fan.david-bowie` The man who fell to earth. *Newsgroup*

187 `alt.fan.fabio` A hunk of pecs. *Newsgroup*

188 `alt.fan.harrison-ford` From *Blade Runner* to Indiana Jones to Clancy stories. *Newsgroup*

189 `alt.fan.heather-locklear` T. J. Hooker's hottest cop. *Newsgroup*

➤ `alt.fan.jodie-foster:` Jodie Foster fandom. *Newsgroup*

190 `alt.fan.karl-malden.nose` Forget the rest of him, ya gotta love the nose. *Newsgroup*

191 `alt.fan.keanu-reeves` People who love Keanu Reeves, in all his blandness. *Newsgroup*

192 `alt.fan.kenya-moore` Discussion of the former Miss USA (of all time). *Newsgroup*

193 `alt.fan.meg-ryan` For the general discussion of Meg Ryan and all her acting work. *Newsgroup*

194 `alt.fan.pam-anderson` Playmate and *Baywatch* lifeguard. *Newsgroup*

195 `alt.fan.phoebe-cates` Princess Caraboo. *Newsgroup*

196 `alt.fan.pj-orourke` P. J. O'Rourke's dramatic displays. *Newsgroup*

197 `alt.fan.ralph.fiennes` For fans of actor Ralph Fiennes. *Newsgroup*

198 `alt.fan.ricci.christina` Fans of actress Christina Ricci. *Newsgroup*

199 `alt.fan.sandra-bullock.binaries` Use `alt.binaries.pictures.celebrities` instead. *Newsgroup*

200 `alt.fan.schwarzenegger` Ahrnold, MacArthur at twice the mass. *Newsgroup*

201 `alt.fan.teen.idols` Boys and men that teenagers worship. *Newsgroup*

202 `alt.fan.teen.starlets` Girls and women that teenagers worship. *Newsgroup*

203 `alt.fan.vic-reeves` Britain's top light entertainer and formation mollusk. *Newsgroup*

204 `alt.fan.winona-ryder` Generation X's gorgeous, elfin, brainy goddess actress. *Newsgroup*

➤ `alt.fandom.cons:` Announcements of conventions (sf and others). *Newsgroup*

205 `alt.fandom.misc` General topics of fandom. *Newsgroup*

206 `alt.gossip.royalty` Rumors plaguing the crown. *Newsgroup*

207 `alt.movies.chaplin` Discussion of Charlie Chaplin's life and art. *Newsgroup*

➤ `alt.politics.usa.newt-gingrich:` Discussion of House Speaker Gingrich. *Newsgroup*

208 `alt.showbiz.gossip` A misguided attempt to centralize gossip. *Newsgroup*

209 `alt.supermodels` Discussing famous and beautiful models. *Newsgroup*

210 `alt.talk.royalty` Discussion of royalty and nobility. *Newsgroup*

➤ `alt.tv.xuxa:` That Connie Dobbs clone, her TV show, and her double Xs. *Newsgroup*

➤ **Beatles, Beatles, Beatles!:** For the Beatles fan. Many links to the Beatles here! (See entry 1015 for full listing.)

211 `clari.living.celebrities` Famous people in the news. *Moderated newsgroup*

212 `clari.living.royalty` The world's royal families. *Moderated newsgroup*

213 **Hot Hollywood Gossip:** Weekly humor newsletter of biting satire and commentary relating to popular television shows, movies, actors, actresses, Kennedys, and other public figures.
http://members.aol.com/editorman/gossip.html
INFO editorman@aol.com

214 **The Kenneth Branagh Page:** Dedicated to the British actor/director/writer Kenneth Branagh. This page contains links to photographs of Kenneth Branagh and information on his career and films, as well as links to other Kenneth Branagh resources.
http://www.inforamp.net/~billie/ken.html
INFO billie@inforamp.net

215 `alt.current-events.oj-simpson.boycott` Discussion of post-verdict boycott. *Newsgroup*

216 `alt.fan.oj-simpson` Juice! Juice! Juice! *Newsgroup*

217 `alt.fan.oj-simpson.die.die.die` People who've decided he's guilty. *Newsgroup*

218 `alt.fan.oj-simpson.gas-chamber` More people who've decided he's guilty. *Newsgroup*

219 **SANDRA-FAN:** A resource for fans of actress Sandra Bullock to discuss her and her work. *Mailing List*
http://www.penguin.net/sandra.html
± listproc@lists.penguin.net [body = SUBSCRIBE SANDRA-FAN first-name last-name]
INFO EDITOR OWNER list-mgr@lists.penguin.net (Ron Fitzherbert)

CHILDREN'S ART

220 `alt.tv.sesame-street` Sunny day. *Newsgroup*

221 **Good Green Fun!-Children's Music and Forest Ecology:** Educational activities, ecology questions, Web links, sound samples, chords, and lyrics to this 1995 Parents' Choice Award-winning children's music recording.
http://www.efn.org/~dharmika
INFO dharmika@efn.org

222 **Notes from the Windowsill (Formerly The WEB Online Review):** Reviews of new and reprinted children's books (all ages) for parents, educators, and children's literature enthusiasts. *Newsletter*
http://www.armory.com/~web/notes.html
gopher://lib.nmsu.edu
ftp://ftp.armory.com/pub/user/web
± kidsbooks@armory.com
INFO EDITOR web@armory.com (Wendy E. Betts, Editor)
Frequency: irregular

223 `rec.arts.books.childrens` All aspects of children's literature. *Newsgroup*

COMEDY

224 `alt.comedy.british` Discussion of British comedy in a variety of media. *Newsgroup*

225 `alt.comedy.british.blackadder` The *Blackadder* program. *Newsgroup*

226 `alt.comedy.firesgn-thtre` Firesign Theatre in all its flaming glory. *Newsgroup*

227 `alt.comedy.improvisation` Group improvisational comedies. *Newsgroup*

228 `alt.comedy.laurel-hardy` The Laurel and Hardy comedy team. *Newsgroup*

229 `alt.comedy.slapstick` Slapstick: comedy stressing farce and horseplay. *Newsgroup*

230 `alt.comedy.slapstick.3-stooges` Hey, Moe! *Newsgroup*

231 `alt.comedy.standup` Discussion of stand-up comedy and comedians. *Newsgroup*

232 `alt.comedy.vaudeville` Vaudeville and its descendants. *Newsgroup*

233 `alt.fan.ben-elton` British comic Ben Elton's plays and other writings. *Newsgroup*

234   `alt.fan.dennis-miller` Comedian Dennis Miller. *Newsgroup*

235   `alt.fan.goons` Careful, Neddy, it's that dastardly Moriarty again. *Newsgroup*

236   `alt.fan.jim-carrey` Wild and wacky comedian Jame Carrey. *Newsgroup*

237   `alt.fan.mel-brooks` Comedic great Mel Brooks. *Newsgroup*

238   `alt.tv.ab-fab` Discussion of the BBC TV comedy *Absolutely Fabulous*. *Newsgroup*

239   `alt.tv.comedy-central` Just what the hell is going on here? *Newsgroup*

240   `alt.tv.kids-in-hall` *The Kids in the Hall* comedy skits. *Newsgroup*

➤   `alt.tv.mst3k:` Hey, you robots! Down in front! *Newsgroup*

➤   `alt.tv.roseanne:` In all her glory. *Newsgroup*

➤   `alt.tv.seinfeld:` A funny guy. *Newsgroup*

241   `alt.tv.snl` *Saturday Night Live*, older but not better. *Newsgroup*

242   **Comedy Central Online:** Irreverent, topical comedy from the Comedy Central cable network, together with program and schedule information.
      `http://www.comcentral.com/`
      INFO `clucas@comcentral.com`

243   **The Comedy Page:** Information on comedy clubs, comedians, angencies, comedy on TV, and even how to become a comedian.
      `http://comedypage.com/`
      INFO `comedy@comedypage.com`

244   **GOODIES-L:** On the British television comedy show *The Goodies*. *Mailing List*
      `http://www.cathouse.org/BritishComedy/Goodies/FanClub/`
      ± `listserv@listserv.aol.com` [body = SUBSCRIBE GOODIES-L first-name last-name]
      OWNER `goodies@badger.idiscover.co.uk` (Melinda Casino)

➤   **Los Angeles After Dark:** Features live and prerecorded over-the-Internet broadcasts of bands, comedy, and entertainment-oriented programming. Also featuring audio and video on demand of various shows and music. Some artists will be actually debuting their CDs and singles here prior to release. (See entry 1227 for full listing.)

245   `rec.arts.tv.uk.comedy` Regarding U.K.-based comedy shows. *Newsgroup*

➤   `rec.music.dementia:` Discussion of comedy and novelty music. *Newsgroup*

COMPUTER-GENERATED ART

246   `alt.ascii-art` Pictures composed of ASCII characters. *Newsgroup*

247   `alt.ascii-art.animation` Movies composed of ASCII characters. *Newsgroup*

248   `alt.binaries.gothic` Mournful and dark binaries. *Newsgroup*

249   `alt.binaries.pictures.fine-art.graphics` Art created on computers. *Moderated newsgroup*

250   `alt.binaries.pictures.fractals` Cheaper to send just the program parameters. *Newsgroup*

➤   **Biohazard:** A site ostensibly designed to foster collaboration among Bay Area artists, its front page is introduced by a collage made from text and links that betray Biohazard's unique aesthetic and nonlinear sense of humor. (See entry 1636 for full listing.)

251   **Paramind:** On computer-generated writing, esp. related to "telical exhaustion." *Mailing List*
      ± `paramind-request@eskimo.com`
      OWNER `telical@eskimo.com` (Robert Pearson)

CONSERVATION

➤   **Internet Resources for Heritage Conservation, Historic Preservation, Archeology:** Resources for professionals in the fields of restoration architecture, historic preservation, and archaeology; and all others interested in identification, protection, and management of cultural resources. Maintained by the National Center for Preservation Technology and Training, National Park Service. (See entry 5133 for full listing.)

252 **Carousel!:** Carousel is a center for the appreciation of carousel art, history, and magic, featuring the grand works of the Golden Age of Carousels.

`http://www.access.digex.net/~rburgess`
`http://users.aol.com/rburgessjr`
INFO `rburgess@digex.net`

➤ **The DuPont Building, Burlington, Vermont:** Joanna Oltman's historic preservation project traces the history of the classic DuPont Building on the waterfront in Burlington, Vermont. (See entry 62 for full listing.)

➤ **The Ladies Pavilion, Central Park, New York City:** Joanna Oltman's historic preservation project traces the history of one of Central Park's architectural gems, the Ladies' Pavilion. (See entry 64 for full listing.)

CRAFTS

253 `alt.crafts.plastic-canvas` Using plastic and canvas in artful creations. *Newsgroup*

254 `alt.crafts.professional` Professional craftsmen. *Newsgroup*

255 `bit.listserv.clayart` Ceramics discussions. *Moderated newsgroup*

256 **The CraftWeb Project:** An online community for professional craftspeople, craft organizations, and people interested in crafts to meet, share information, and promote fine crafts worldwide.

`http://www.craftweb.com/`
INFO `kmcmahon@craftweb.com`

➤ **Japan from the View of a Frog - an Art Journey:** Explore a less known—and humorous—side of Japan through a journey of the world of Japanese arts and crafts. (See entry 7428 for full listing.)

257 **MARBLE:** On marbling paper & fabric with colored ink floated on water baths. *Mailing List*

± `majordomo@southwind.net` [body = `subscribe marble` e-mail-address]
INFO EDITOR `http://www.southwind.net/~rjones/marble.html`
OWNER `rjones@southwind.net` (Russ Jones)
ARCHIVE `http://www.southwind.net/~rjones/marble.html`

➤ `pei.crafts:` Crafts in the Prince Edward Island (Canada) area. *Newsgroup*

258 `rec.crafts.beads` Making, collecting, and using beads. *Newsgroup*

259 `alt.beadworld` We must appease the bead gods. *Newsgroup*

260 `rec.crafts.glass` All aspects of glassworking and glass. *Newsgroup*

261 `rec.crafts.jewelry` All aspects of jewelry making and lapidary work. *Newsgroup*

262 `rec.crafts.marketplace` Small-scale ads for craft products of all kinds. *Newsgroup*

263 `rec.crafts.metalworking` All aspects of working with metal. *Newsgroup*

264 `rec.crafts.misc` Handiwork arts not covered elsewhere. *Newsgroup*

265 `rec.crafts.polymer-clay` Techniques and resources relating to polymer clay crafts. *Newsgroup*

266 `rec.crafts.pottery` The ancient art of making clay pots. *Newsgroup*

267 `rec.crafts.textiles.misc` Fiber and textile crafts not covered elsewhere. *Newsgroup*

268 `rec.crafts.textiles.needlework` Any form of decorative stitching done by hand. *Newsgroup*

269 `rec.crafts.textiles.sewing` Sewing: clothes, furnishings, costumes, etc. *Newsgroup*

270 `rec.crafts.textiles.yarn` Yarn making and use: spin, dye, knit, weave, etc. *Newsgroup*

➤ `uk.rec.crafts:` Newsgroup for craft-related topics in the U.K. . *Newsgroup*

271 **WOODWORK:** On woodworking. *Digest & Reflector*

± `listserv@vmb.ipfw.indiana.edu` [body = `SUBSCRIBE WOODWORK` first-name last-name]

INFO OWNER rondot@vmb.ipfw.indiana.edu (Larry Rondot)

ARCHIVE listserv@vmb.ipfw.indiana.edu [body = INDEX WOODWORK]

Gated: rec.woodworking

272 **rec.woodworking** Hobbyists interested in woodworking. *Newsgroup*

CREATIVITY

273 **BUZAN:** On virtual study skills and creativity—based on the work of Tony Buzan. *Mailing List*

± listserv@sjuvm.stjohns.edu [body = SUBSCRIBE BUZAN first-name last-name]

OWNER i.pitchford@sheffield.ac.uk

ARCHIVE listserv@sjuvm.stjohns.edu [body = INDEX BUZAN]

274 **CREA-CPS:** On creativity and creative problem solving. *Mailing List*

± listserv@nic.surfnet.nl [body = SUBSCRIBE CREA-CPS first-name last-name]

INFO m.tassoul@io.tudelft.nl (Marc Tassoul)

➤ **DEBONO:** On the work of Edward de Bono on lateral thinking and practical creativity. (See entry 9519 for full listing.)

275 **Imagination:** On exploring imagination—initialized by students at Bogazici University in Turkey and developed by international contributors. *Mailing List*

http://www.busim.ee.boun.edu.tr/imagination

± **OWNER** beyret@boun.edu.tr (Ersin Beyret, Editor)

INFO mindeb@ix.netcom.com (Deborah S.)

276 **misc.creativity** Promoting the use of creativity in all human endeavors. *Newsgroup*

CRITICISM

277 **alt.postmodern** Postmodernism, semiotics, deconstruction, and the like. *Newsgroup*

278 **ARCO:** On art and literature, psychology and communication. *Mailing List*

± listserv@sjuvm.stjohns.edu [body = SUBSCRIBE ARCO first-name last-name]

OWNER quadrant@iol.it (Danilo Curci)

279 **ARTCRIT:** On visual-art criticism: postmodernism, Marxism, feminism, curatorial practices, funding, and any issue that affects artists, critics, and art viewers. *Mailing List*

listserv@yorku.ca

± listserv@yorku.ca [body = SUBSCRIBE ARTCRIT first-name last-name]

INFO macal@nexus.yorku.ca (Michele Macaluso)

Gated: bit.listserv.artcrit

➤ **EJournal:** Electronic networks and "texts"; theory and practice; social, psychological, economic, artistic implications and more. Peer-reviewed. (See entry 5171 for full listing.)

➤ **The Electronic Visual Arts Magazine:** Dedicated to the exploration of the visual arts in all their complexities: artistic, political, philosophical, technical, and conceptual. (See entry 458 for full listing.)

➤ **Paglia-L:** On the writings and ideas of Dr. Camille Paglia. (See entry 10161 for full listing.)

➤ **POLANYI:** On the thought of Michael Polanyi: "post-critical" thought. (See entry 5341 for full listing.)

➤ **POPCULT:** For analytical discussion of popular culture. (See entry 1265 for full listing.)

280 **POSTCOLONIAL:** On culture affected by the imperial process: loss, agency, and recovery; on the political and cultural situation of the so-called "Third World." *Mailing List*

± majordomo@lists.village.virginia.edu

INFO http://jefferson.village.virginia.edu/~spoons

OWNER spoons@jefferson.village.virginia.edu (Spoon Collective)

ARCHIVE http://jefferson.village.virginia.edu/~spoons

➤ **PSYART:** On the psychological study of the arts, especially literature. (See entry 9523 for full listing.)

➤ **PURTOPOI:** On rhetoric, language, and professional writing. (See entry 4549 for full listing.)

DANCE

281 **DanceLinks:** Savvy and well-organized compilation of dance resources on the net.
`http://bohr.physics.purdue.edu/~jswhite/dance_links.html`
INFO `jswhite@physics.purdue.edu`

➤ **ADTA:** A discussion list related to matters of concern to dance/movement therapy. (See entry 5072 for full listing.)

282 `alt.arts.ballet` All aspects of ballet and modern dance as performing art. *Newsgroup*

➤ `alt.music.dance`: Music to dance to. *Newsgroup*

283 **Dance Ink:** A nonprofit quarterly devoted to essays, both photographic and written, on movement ideas. *Magazine*
`http://www.webcom.com/~ink/`
± INFO `inkmag@aol.com`
INFO OWNER `ink@webcom.com` (Jenny Carchman)
ARCHIVE `http://www.webcom.com/~ink`
Frequency: quarterly

284 **DANCE-L:** On international folk and traditional dance. *Mailing List*
± INFO `listserv@hearn.nic.surfnet.nl` [body = SUBSCRIBE DANCE-L first-name last-name]
INFO OWNER `l.a.m.vanderheijden@ab.dlo.nl` (Leo A.M. van der Heijden)
ARCHIVE `listserv@hearn.nic.surfnet.nl`

285 **Folk Dancing:** On folk dancing: international, contra, square, cajun, barn, and more. The Folk Dancing mailing list is for those who do not have access to Usenet and the `rec.folk-dancing` newsgroup. *Mailing List*
± INFO `tjw+@pitt.edu`
Gated: `rec.folk-dancing`
Comments: Those who have access to Usenet are asked to use the newsgroup.

286 **North Alabama Country Dance Newsletter:** This newsletter includes a schedule of opportunities for participatory dance, especially contra, Appalachian squares, and traditional round dances, within reasonable driving distance of Huntsville, Alabama. *Newsletter*
`http://www.cici.com/~bwalls/`
`ftp://ftp.std.com/pub/dance/americas/usa/AL/N-AL-country.nwl`
`http://www.cici.com/~bwalls/NACDS.html`
± INFO `bwalls@cici.com` (Bryan Walls)
EDITOR `rocoupla@hsv24.pcmail.ingr.com` (Katrina Coupland)
Gated: `rec.folk-dancing`
Frequency: monthly

287 `phl.dance` Dance events, reviews, and discussions. *Newsgroup*

288 `rec.arts.dance` Any aspects of dance not covered in another newsgroup. *Newsgroup*

289 `rec.folk-dancing` Folk dances, dancers, and dancing. *Newsgroup*

290 `tnn.rec.dance` Topics related to dance. *Newsgroup*

DESIGN

291 `alt.design.graphics` Discussion of graphics design. *Newsgroup*

292 **Digital Directions:** A guide for art directors and designers to new media and design technology. *Magazine*
`http://www.lawler.com/directions/`
INFO `directions@lawler.com` (Elizabeth Lawler)
Frequency: bimonthly

293   **humanities.design.misc**   Theory, practice, history, and aesthetic issues in design. *Newsgroup*

➤   **IDFORUM:** On industrial/product design and design education. (See entry 9357 for full listing.)

294   **NDDESIGN:** For graphic and industrial design educators. *Mailing List*
± listserv@vma.cc.nd.edu [body = SUBSCRIBE NDDESIGN first-name last-name]
INFO nddesign-request@vma.cc.nd.edu
ARCHIVE listserv@vma.cc.nd.edu [body = INDEX NDDESIGN]

295   **TYPO-L:** On typography, type, and typographic design. *Mailing List*
± listserv@irlearn.ucd.ie
 [body = SUBSCRIBE TYPO-L first-name last-name]
INFO pflynn@curia.ucc.ie (Peter Flynn)

ENTERTAINMENT NEWS

296   **clari.apbl.entertainment**   Entertainment news. *Moderated newsgroup*

297   **clari.biz.industry.media.entertainment**   Film, TV, other entertainment. *Moderated newsgroup*

298   **clari.biz.industry.media.entertainment.releases**   Entertainment news releases. *Moderated newsgroup*

299   **clari.living.entertainment.briefs**   Entertainment news summaries. *Moderated newsgroup*

300   **clari.living.entertainment.misc**   Miscellaneous entertainment news. *Moderated newsgroup*

301   **The Hollywood Reporter:** The Hollywood Reporter Web site provides an exclusive look at the next day's headlines and news briefs prior to press time, highlighting breaking film, television, music, and other entertainment industry news.
http://www.hollywoodreporter.com/
INFO hittle@hollywoodreporter.com

EROTICA

302   **alt.amazon-women.admirers**   Worshiping women you have to look up to. *Newsgroup*

303   **alt.binaries.erotica.fetish**   Fetish-oriented binary erotica. *Newsgroup*

304   **alt.binaries.multimedia.erotica**   Moving pictures of a prurient nature. *Newsgroup*

305   **alt.binaries.pictures.boys.barefoot**   The institute for studies in pedophilia. *Newsgroup*

306   **alt.binaries.pictures.erotica**   Gigabytes of copyright violations. *Newsgroup*

307   **alt.binaries.pictures.erotica.amateur.d**   Amateur subjects/photographers. *Newsgroup*

308   **alt.binaries.pictures.erotica.amateur.female**   Amateur subjects/photographers. *Newsgroup*

309   **alt.binaries.pictures.erotica.amateur.male**   Amateur subjects/photographers. *Newsgroup*

310   **alt.binaries.pictures.erotica.animals**   Bestial binaries. *Newsgroup*

➤   **alt.binaries.pictures.erotica.anime:**   Anime erotica—"Ecchi"/"Hentai"/"H. *Newsgroup*

311   **alt.binaries.pictures.erotica.art.pin-up**   Nonphotographic realistic art. *Newsgroup*

312   **alt.binaries.pictures.erotica.bears**   Very hairy men. *Newsgroup*

313   **alt.binaries.pictures.erotica.bestiality**   Pictures of sex with animals. *Newsgroup*

314   **alt.binaries.pictures.erotica.black.females**   Sexy ebony women. *Newsgroup*

315   **alt.binaries.pictures.erotica.black.male**   Tall, dark, and handsome black men. *Newsgroup*

316   **alt.binaries.pictures.erotica.blondes**   Copyright violations featuring blondes. *Newsgroup*

317   **alt.binaries.pictures.erotica.bondage**   Bondage and S & M-related erotic images. *Newsgroup*

318   **alt.binaries.pictures.erotica.breasts**   Pictures of mammalian protruberances. *Newsgroup*

319 `alt.binaries.pictures.erotica.butts` Erotic butts come into view. *Newsgroup*

320 `alt.binaries.pictures.erotica.cartoons` Copyright violations featuring toons. *Newsgroup*

321 `alt.binaries.pictures.erotica.cheerleaders` Gimme a B . . . R . . . E . . . A . . . K. *Newsgroup*

322 `alt.binaries.pictures.erotica.d` Discussing erotic copyright violations. *Newsgroup*

323 `alt.binaries.pictures.erotica.female` Copyright violations featuring females. *Newsgroup*

324 `alt.binaries.pictures.erotica.female.anal` Women's poop chutes. *Newsgroup*

325 `alt.binaries.pictures.erotica.fetish` Fetishistic, exotic, erotic images. *Newsgroup*

326 `alt.binaries.pictures.erotica.fetish.feet` Erotic visual foot action. *Newsgroup*

327 `alt.binaries.pictures.erotica.fetish.hair` Binary pictures of hair erotica. *Newsgroup*

328 `alt.binaries.pictures.erotica.fetish.latex` Sexy pictures of people wearing latex. *Newsgroup*

329 `alt.binaries.pictures.erotica.fetish.leather` Sexy pictures of people wearing leather. *Newsgroup*

330 `alt.binaries.pictures.erotica.furry` Erotic furry images. *Newsgroup*

331 `alt.binaries.pictures.erotica.gaymen` Explicit pictures of gay men. *Newsgroup*

332 `alt.binaries.pictures.erotica.high-heels` For pictures of women's high heels. *Newsgroup*

333 `alt.binaries.pictures.erotica.interracial` Binaries of interracial erotica. *Newsgroup*

334 `alt.binaries.pictures.erotica.latina` Latina women. *Newsgroup*

335 `alt.binaries.pictures.erotica.male` Copyright violations featuring males. *Newsgroup*

336 `alt.binaries.pictures.erotica.male.anal` Men's poop chutes. *Newsgroup*

337 `alt.binaries.pictures.erotica.mardi-gras` Memorable carnival moments. *Newsgroup*

338 `alt.binaries.pictures.erotica.midgets` Binary erotica concerning small people. *Newsgroup*

339 `alt.binaries.pictures.erotica.oral` Images of oral sex. *Newsgroup*

340 `alt.binaries.pictures.erotica.orientals` Copyright violations featuring Asians. *Newsgroup*

341 `alt.binaries.pictures.erotica.pornstar` Copyright violations of porn stars. *Newsgroup*

342 `alt.binaries.pictures.erotica.pre-teen` Binary erotica of preadolescents. *Newsgroup*

343 `alt.binaries.pictures.erotica.pregnant` Pregnant women in sexual situations. *Newsgroup*

344 `alt.binaries.pictures.erotica.redheads` Erotic images of redheads. *Newsgroup*

345 `alt.binaries.pictures.erotica.spanking` Spanking pictures and images. *Newsgroup*

346 `alt.binaries.pictures.erotica.teen` Teens, should be above age of consent. *Newsgroup*

347 `alt.binaries.pictures.erotica.teen.d` Teens, should be above age of consent. *Newsgroup*

348 `alt.binaries.pictures.erotica.teen.female` Teens, should be above age of consent. *Newsgroup*

349 `alt.binaries.pictures.erotica.teen.fuck` Teens, above age of consent, having sex. *Newsgroup*

350 `alt.binaries.pictures.erotica.teen.male` Teens, should be above age of consent. *Newsgroup*

351 `alt.binaries.pictures.erotica.transvestites` Sexy pictures of men dressed as female penguins. *Newsgroup*

352 `alt.binaries.pictures.erotica.urine` New dimensions in water photography. *Newsgroup*

353 `alt.binaries.pictures.erotica.voyeurism` Views for the viewers. *Newsgroup*

354 `alt.binaries.pictures.girlfriends` Commercially controversial group. *Newsgroup*

355 `alt.binaries.pictures.girls` GIFs, JPEGs, etc. of girls. *Newsgroup*

356 `alt.binaries.pictures.groupsex` Menage a trois and orgies. *Newsgroup*

357 `alt.binaries.pictures.lesbians` Images of women who love women. *Newsgroup*

358 `alt.binaries.pictures.lingerie` As if Victoria's Secret isn't frequent enough. *Newsgroup*

359 `alt.binaries.pictures.nude.celebrities` Images of normally clothed famous folk. *Newsgroup*

360 `alt.binaries.pictures.nudism` Images featuring nudists. *Newsgroup*

361 `alt.binaries.pictures.pantyhose` Pantyhose-oriented binary erotica. *Newsgroup*

362 `alt.binaries.pictures.supermodels` Yet more copyright violations. *Newsgroup*

363 `alt.binaries.pictures.voyeurism` Voyeur pictures. *Newsgroup*

364 `alt.binaries.sounds.erotica` Uhh uhh uhh uhhhhhhhhhhhh. Ooh. *Newsgroup*

➤ `alt.books.poppy-z-brite:` Horror and fantasy by author Poppy Z. Brite. *Newsgroup*

365 `alt.dead.porn.stars` And the diseases that killed them, next on *Geraldo. Newsgroup*

366 `alt.fan.cock-sucking` Fans of fellatio. *Newsgroup*

367 `alt.polyamory` For those with multiple loves. *Newsgroup*

368 `alt.religion.sexuality` The politics of sexuality and religion. *Newsgroup*

369 `alt.seduction.fast` The story of television. *Newsgroup*

370 `alt.sex` Postings of a prurient nature. *Newsgroup*

371 `alt.sex.aliens` Extraterrestial erotica. *Newsgroup*

372 `alt.sex.anal` Sexual acts involving the anus. *Newsgroup*

373 `alt.sex.bears` Hairy homosexual men. *Newsgroup*

374 `alt.sex.bestiality` Happiness is a warm puppy. *Newsgroup*

375 `alt.sex.bondage` Tie me, whip me, make me read the net! *Newsgroup*

376 `alt.sex.boredom` Excuse me while I turn the page. *Newsgroup*

377 `alt.sex.breast` Discussions about female breasts—big and small. *Newsgroup*

378 `alt.sex.brothels` All about cathouses. *Newsgroup*

379 `alt.sex.enemas` Cleansing the bowels as an erotic act. *Newsgroup*

380 `alt.sex.erotica.marketplace` The business of sex. *Newsgroup*

381 `alt.sex.escorts.ads` Looking for personal escorts. *Newsgroup*

382 `alt.sex.escorts.ads.d` Discussion of personal escort advertisements. *Newsgroup*

383 `alt.sex.exhibitionism` So you want to be a star. *Newsgroup*

384 `alt.sex.fat` Rollin' with the roly-poly. *Newsgroup*

385 `alt.sex.femdom` Discussions about female-dominant relationships. *Newsgroup*

386 `alt.sex.fetish.amputee` Sexual attraction to missing body parts. *Newsgroup*

387 `alt.sex.fetish.boyfeet` Worshiping the feet of male children (pedal pederasty). *Newsgroup*

388 `alt.sex.fetish.diapers` They're dry and secure all day, too. *Newsgroup*

389 `alt.sex.fetish.drew-barrymore` Keen on ET's star child, all grown up. *Newsgroup*

390 `alt.sex.fetish.fa` Rollin' with the roly-poly. *Newsgroup*

391 `alt.sex.fetish.fashion` Rubber, leather, chains, and other fetish clothing. *Newsgroup*

392 `alt.sex.fetish.feet` Kiss them. Now. *Newsgroup*

393 `alt.sex.fetish.hair` Hair, hair, everywhere. Palms, even. *Newsgroup*

394 `alt.sex.fetish.jello` Sticky and almost fluid . . . hmm. *Newsgroup*

395 `alt.sex.fetish.motorcycles` Motorcycles as sex objects. *Newsgroup*

396 `alt.sex.fetish.orientals` The mysteries of Asia are a potent lure. *Newsgroup*

397   `alt.sex.fetish.robots` This is for you robot types. *Newsgroup*

398   `alt.sex.fetish.scat` People excited by excrement. *Newsgroup*

399   `alt.sex.fetish.size` For discussion and posting of fantasies related to size. *Newsgroup*

400   `alt.sex.fetish.smoking` Discussion of smoking as a sexual fetish. *Newsgroup*

401   `alt.sex.fetish.sportswear` For those with a fetish about sports clothes. *Newsgroup*

402   `alt.sex.fetish.tickling` Laughter is the best foreplay. *Newsgroup*

403   `alt.sex.fetish.trent-reznor` Trent "NIN" Reznor's screaming slaves. *Newsgroup*

404   `alt.sex.fetish.waifs` Arousal by young, underweight people. *Newsgroup*

405   `alt.sex.fetish.watersports` They don't mean hot-tub polo. *Newsgroup*

406   `alt.sex.fetish.wet-and-messy` Sploshing, food, mud, and other messy fetishes. *Newsgroup*

407   `alt.sex.fetish.white-mommas` People who dig covering a women with White-Out. *Newsgroup*

408   `alt.sex.fetish.wrestling` Roughhousing for sexual kicks. *Newsgroup*

409   `alt.sex.first-time` What was your first time like? *Newsgroup*

410   `alt.sex.guns` Fuel for the pornography-incites-violence debate. *Newsgroup*

411   `alt.sex.hello-kitty` Why are there so few hot, exhibitionist, S & M pussies? *Newsgroup*

412   `alt.sex.homosexual` Homosexual relations. *Newsgroup*

413   `alt.sex.intergen` Robbing the cradle and the grave. *Newsgroup*

414   `alt.sex.masturbation` Where one's SO is oneself. *Newsgroup*

415   `alt.sex.motss` Jesse Helms would not subscribe to this group. *Newsgroup*

416   `alt.sex.necrophilia` Dead people as stimulus. *Newsgroup*

417   `alt.sex.oral` Not involving sound. Void where prohibited by law. *Newsgroup*

418   `alt.sex.orgy` Discussion of orgies and group sex. *Newsgroup*

419   `alt.sex.pedophilia` Discussing the issues around attraction to children. *Newsgroup*

420   `alt.sex.pictures` Gigabytes of copyright violations. *Newsgroup*

421   `alt.sex.pictures.d` Discussion of gigabytes of copyright violations. *Newsgroup*

422   `alt.sex.pictures.female` Copyright violations featuring mostly females. *Newsgroup*

423   `alt.sex.pictures.male` Copyright violations featuring mostly males. *Newsgroup*

424   `alt.sex.plushies` Plush sex: strategically placed holes. *Newsgroup*

425   `alt.sex.prostitution` The oldest profession. *Newsgroup*

426   `alt.sex.safe` For the discussion and encouragement of safe sex. *Newsgroup*

427   `alt.sex.services` The oldest profession. *Newsgroup*

428   `alt.sex.sgml` Markup languages as a sexual tool. *Newsgroup*

429   `alt.sex.sm.fig` Sadism and masochism with mulberries. *Newsgroup*

430   `alt.sex.sounds` Noises from the heat of passion. *Newsgroup*

431   `alt.sex.spanking` Bondage for beginners. *Newsgroup*

432   `alt.sex.stories` For those who need it *now*. *Newsgroup*

433   `alt.sex.stories.d` For those who talk about needing it *now*. *Newsgroup*

434   `alt.sex.stories.gay` Erotic tales involving homosexuals. *Newsgroup*

435   `alt.sex.stories.hetero` Stories featuring heterosexual sex. *Newsgroup*

436   `alt.sex.stories.moderated` Stories with sexual content. *Moderated newsgroup*

437 `alt.sex.strip-clubs` Discussion of strip clubs, exotic dancers, etc. *Newsgroup*

438 `alt.sex.super-size` Sex talk for very large people and their admirers. *Newsgroup*

439 `alt.sex.swingers` The promiscuous crowd. *Newsgroup*

440 `alt.sex.telephone` Discussion of phone sex services. *Newsgroup*

441 `alt.sex.trans` Sex lives of transsexuals. *Newsgroup*

442 `alt.sex.ugly` Not all girls are beautiful, but we love the ugly too. *Newsgroup*

443 `alt.sex.voyeurism` A lot of lurkers in this group. *Newsgroup*

444 `alt.sex.wanted` Requests for erotica, either literary or in the flesh. *Newsgroup*

445 `alt.sex.wanted.escorts.ads` Looking for escorts. *Newsgroup*

446 `alt.sex.watersports` Not quite coed naked water polo. *Newsgroup*

447 `alt.sex.weight-gain` Exploring the eroticism of feeding and being fed. *Newsgroup*

448 `alt.sex.wizards` Questions for only true sex wizards. *Newsgroup*

449 `alt.sexy.bald.captains` More Star Drek. *Newsgroup*

450 `alt.support.disabled.sexuality` Sexual issues relating to disabled people. *Newsgroup*

451 `aus.sex` Australian discussion of matters sexual. *Newsgroup*

452 `rec.arts.erotica` Erotic fiction and verse. *Moderated newsgroup*

ETHNIC ART

➤ **NAHIA-L:** For North American historians of Islamic art. (See entry 70 for full listing.)

FINE ARTS

453 <u>Art Planet</u>: Art Planet is the Internet directory designed exclusively for fine-art sites.
http://www.artplanet.com/
INFO findit@artplanet.com

454 `alt.binaries.pictures.fine-art.d` Discussion of the fine-art binaries. *Moderated newsgroup*

455 `alt.binaries.pictures.fine-art.digitized` Art from conventional media. *Moderated newsgroup*

456 `alt.binaries.pictures.fine-art.misc` Binary pictures from the fine arts. *Newsgroup*

457 **Art Cellar Exchange:** Art Cellar Exchange is an international fine-art brokerage specializing in buying and selling art on the secondary market.
http://www.artcellarex.com/~ace/
INFO ace@artcellarex.com

458 **The Electronic Visual Arts Magazine:** Dedicated to the exploration of the visual arts in all their complexities: artistic, political, philosophical, technical, and conceptual. *E-Journal*
http://www.uwo.ca/visarts/eva.html
± listserv@bosshog.arts.uwo.ca [body = subscribe <name>]
INFO EDITOR eva@bosshog.arts.uwo.ca (Mickey Meads and Samuel Gerszon, Editors)
Frequency: irregular but roughly three per year

459 `fj.rec.fine-arts` Topics about fine arts which are visual arts. *Newsgroup*

460 **Laboratory for Extended Media of the University of Victoria Faculty of Fine Arts:** This is a CWIS for the Faculty of Fine Arts, University of Victoria, Canada, as well as a place to view the works of students and faculty. The site includes various galleries, a music archive, and more.
http://kafka.uvic.ca/
gopher://kafka.uvic.ca
INFO mhuston@finearts.uvic.ca

461 **Masterprints Gallery Shop:** Sales of fine-art posters of Monet, Matisse, Rembrandt, Renoir, Van Gogh, Picasso, Degas, and other Master artists, of "museum reproduction" quality.
http://www.rams.com/masterprints/
INFO masterp@isomedia.com

462 **PRINTS-L:** On fine art prints and multiples. *Mailing List*
± listserv@ukanvm.cc.ukans.edu
OWNER goddard@falcon.cc.ukans.edu (Stephen Goddard)
ARCHIVE http://www.ukans.edu/~sma/prints.html
FAQ http://www.ukans.edu/~sma/prints.html

463 **rec.arts.fine** Fine arts and artists. *Newsgroup*

FOLKLORE

➤ **alt.arts.storytelling:** Discussion of storytelling in all its forms. *Newsgroup*

464 **alt.folklore.info** Current urban legends and other folklore. *Moderated newsgroup*

465 **alt.folklore.suburban** Serious discussion of urban legends. *Moderated newsgroup*

466 **alt.folklore.urban** Urban legends, la Jan Harold Brunvand. *Newsgroup*

467 **alt.legend.king-arthur** Legends and history of Arthur, king of the Britons. *Newsgroup*

468 **alt.mythology** Zeus rules. *Newsgroup*

469 **alt.mythology.mythic-animals** Creatures of myth, fantasy, and imagination. *Newsgroup*

➤ **HORROR:** On horror films and fiction. (See entry 1325 for full listing.)

470 **Nerdnosh:** For virtual storytelling: family fables, yarns, campfire tales. *Daily Digest*
http://www.corcom.com/reloj/Nerdnosh.html
± listserv@nerdnosh.org [body = join NERDNOSH]
INFO urder@nerdnosh.org (Nerdnosh Nanny)
OWNER tcbowden@nerdnosh.org (Tim Bowden)
ARCHIVES
http://www.netins.net/showcase/dmorris/nerdnosh.html
ftp://ftp.infonet.net
FAQ info@nerdnosh.org (infobot)
Comments: The nature of a neighborly campfire where personal stories be shared requires a more refined environment than you might find on the net in general. Nerdnosh is open enrollment, but there are no reservations about disinviting those who pollute the campfire. Nerdnosh is produced daily in digest format as articles are submitted and sent out after 9:10 Pacific U.S. time.

HARD TO BELIEVE

471 **alt.fan.ed-wood** Ed Wood. *Newsgroup*

472 **clari.living.bizarre** Unusual or funny news stories. *Moderated newsgroup*

473 **clari.tw.columns.imprb_research** The Annals of Improbable Research. *Moderated newsgroup*

474 **This is True:** Bizarre-but-true news items from the world's legitimate press (no tabloid material), with off-the-wall commentary by Randy Cassingham. *Newsletter*
± listserv@netcom.com [body = subscribe this-is-true]
INFO trueinfo@freecom.com [body = blank]
EDITOR arcie@netcom.com (Randy Cassingham)
ARCHIVE http://freecom.com/truehome
Frequency: weekly

HUMOR, FUN & BIZARRE

➤ **"I Just Want To Be Friends":** "Joelogon's Foolproof Guide to Making Any Woman Your Platonic Friend." (See entry 5945 for full listing.)

475 **A groovy distraction... MADworks' HeadShop:** Pure wicked fun. Lots of free original movies, sounds, poster art, and other pop art pretties. Guess what? Guess the clown's name and win stuff.
http://www.madworks.com/
INFO ma@madworks.com

476 `alt.binaries.pictures.tasteless` Eccchh, that last one was *sick*. *Newsgroup*

477 `alt.fan.art-bell` For fans of old AT&T logos. *Newsgroup*

478 `alt.fan.cecil-adams` The brother Douglas Adams never talks about. *Newsgroup*

479 `alt.fan.cult-dead-cow` Fans and files from cDc Communications. *Newsgroup*

480 `alt.fan.dave_barry` Electronic fan club for humorist Dave Barry. *Newsgroup*

481 `alt.fan.jerky-boys` Phone pranks 'r' us. *Newsgroup*

482 `alt.fan.wodehouse` Discussion of the works of humor author P. G. Wodehouse. *Newsgroup*

483 `alt.fan.woody-allen` The diminutive neurotic. *Newsgroup*

484 `alt.humor.bluesman` Humor from the 105th St. BluesMan's world. *Newsgroup*

485 `alt.humor.puns` Not here. *Newsgroup*

486 `alt.jokes.limericks` There once was a group in `alt`. *Newsgroup*

487 `alt.jokes.pentium` Playing with the problems plaguing Pentium. *Newsgroup*

488 `alt.music.weird-al` Parodies 'R' us. *Newsgroup*

489 `alt.quotations` Quotations, quips, .sig lines, witticisms, et al. *Newsgroup*

490 `alt.random.noise` Bitstream Underground's Random Noise. *Newsgroup*

491 `alt.shenanigans` Practical jokes, pranks, randomness, etc. *Newsgroup*

492 `alt.tasteless.jokes` Sometimes insulting rather than disgusting or humorous. *Newsgroup*

493 `alt.wonderment.bgjw` Making up urban legends at McGill U. and other places. *Newsgroup*

494 `aus.jokes` Jokes, humor, and boring trivia. *Newsgroup*

➤ **BOB©WEB:** An eclectic mix of arts- and popular-culture-related links. BOB©WEB is also the home of BOB©NET, the Club BOB© (a nonprofit Internet arts organization). (See entry 1263 for full listing.)

495 **The Borderline Humor Netazine:** Original humor, daily cartoon, and political satire. *E-Journal*
http://www.cts.com/~borderln/
INFO borderln@cts.com (Gabe Martin)
ARCHIVE http://www.cts.com/~borderln/
Frequency: daily cartoon, monthly features

496 **BRETTnews:** "The peppy zine for active people." Brush your teeth.
INFO bretts@brettnews.com (Brett Leveridge)
ARCHIVE http://www.brettnews.com/~brettnews
Frequency: quarterly

497 `chile.humor` Humor :-). *Newsgroup*

498 **Citizen Poke:** An Internet magazine of humor and satire. *E-Journal*
http://www.amherst.edu/~poke
ftp://unix.amherst.edu/pub/poke
INFO jakoppel@amherst.edu (Josh Koppel)
Frequency: monthly

499   `clari.feature.dave_barry` Columns of humorist Dave Barry. *Moderated newsgroup*

500   `clari.feature.imprb_research` Excerpts from the Annals of Improbable Research. *Newsgroup*

501   `clari.feature.joebob` *Joe Bob Briggs Goes to the Drive-In. Moderated newsgroup*

502   `clari.feature.miss_manners` Judith Martin's humorous etiquette advice. *Moderated newsgroup*

503   `clari.living.columns.lipton` Columns of humorist Eric F. Lipton. *Moderated newsgroup*

➤   `clari.living.columns.miss_manners`: Etiquette advice from Miss Manners. *Moderated newsgroup*

➤   `clari.tw.columns.imprb_research`: The Annals of Improbable Research. *Moderated newsgroup*

➤   **The Creative Internet Home Page:** A collection of fun and useful resources. (See entry 2730 for full listing.)

504   **The Creep of the Week:** A weekly description of the person or persons most deserving of the title: The Creep of the Week.
      `http://www.servtech.com/public/montgome/cotw.htm`
      INFO `montgome@servtech.com`

505   **Culture Time:** Short, periodic postings of humorous messages. *Distribution List, moderated*
      `http://www.cybernothing.org/jdfalk/html/culture-time.html`
      ± `culture-time-request@lists.cybernothing.org` [body = `subscribe`]

506   **Culture Time: 20 PAST MIDNIGHT:** Daily message includes "fortune" and historical calendar. *Mailing List, moderated*
      `http://www.cybernothing.org/jdfalk/html/culture-time.html`
      ± `20-past-request@lists.cybernothing.org` [body = `subscribe`]
      INFO `20-past-owner@cybernothing.org`
      ARCHIVE `http://www.cybernothing.org/jdfalk/html/culture-time.html`
      Gated: `alt.motd`
      Comments: Additions to calendar always gratefully accepted.

➤   **The Cyber Maze:** An online compilation of the *PPSA Magazine*. Topics include: real-life stories and road trips, humor, photos and art, editorials and commentary on social issues and current events. (See entry 7829 for full listing.)

507   **Doctor Fun Page:** A daily Internet cartoon.
      `http://www.unitedmedia.com/comics/drfun/`
      INFO `d-farley@tezcat.com` (David Farley)
      MIRRORS
      `http://www.ctrl-c.liu.se/dr-fun/`
      `ftp://ftp.dei.uc.pt/pub/fun/images/dr-fun`
      `http://sunsite.doc.ic.ac.uk/packages/Dr-Fun/html/`
      `http://www.mcc.ac.uk/Dr-Fun/drfun.html`
      `http://www.cs.ualberta.ca/~cdshaw/Dr-Fun/drfun.html`
      `http://sunsite.unc.edu/Dave/drfun.html`
      `http://www.oslonett.no/drfun/drfun.html`
      `http://www.funet.fi/DoctorFun/drfun.html`

508   `eunet.jokes` Jokes only Europeans can (do?) understand . . . :-). *Newsgroup*

509   `fj.jokes` Jokes and humor. *Newsgroup*

510   `fj.jokes.d` Discussion about jokes. *Newsgroup*

➤   **FREAKS:** On freaks on the Internet: snide discussion on twisted writing. (See entry 2847 for full listing.)

511   **George Jr. magazine:** A monthly magazine (with daily updates) of culture, books, art, music, and software for the wired.
      `http://www.webroi.com/greenhouse/georgejr/georgejr.html`
      INFO `gmyers@coil.com`

512 **Good quotes by famous people:** This page contains a growing list of good, often humorous quotes by famous people; it is updated regularly.
http://www.cs.virginia.edu/~robins/quotes.html
INFO robins@cs.virginia.edu

513 **han.rec.humor** Humorous or funny stories, jokes. *Newsgroup*

514 **HIP Webzine:** Humorous commentary on everyday stuff. *E-Zine*
http://www.hip.com/
± admin@hip.com
INFO dick_hardt@hip.com (Dick Hardt)
EDITOR editor@hip.com
Frequency: monthly and weekly

515 **HUMOR:** Funny things (warning required for risqué content). *Digest & Reflector, moderated*
± listserv@uga.cc.uga.edu [body = SUBSCRIBE HUMOR first-name last-name]
INFO OWNER bedwards@uga.cc.uga.edu (Bill Edwards)
ARCHIVE listserv@uga.cc.uga.edu
FAQ listserv@uga.cc.uga.edu [body = GET HUMOR GUIDE]
Comments: HUMOR is a rule-governed list. Contributors, who apply separately for that status, agree to be guided by our goals and rules. They have a monitor who enforces the rules.

516 **LeClub:** For members of LeClub, a group to promote the lighter side of computing. *Mailing List, moderated*
± leclub@yucc.yorku.ca
EDITOR OWNER savundra@yorku.ca (Thomas Savundranayagam)
ARCHIVE http://yucc.yorku.ca/home/leclub/archives.html
Please Note: Subscription by approval only.

517 **LOTD:** LaughWEB's Laugh Of The Day. *Distribution List*
http://www.misty.com/laughweb/
± majordomo@world.std.com [body = subscribe lotd e-mail-address]
OWNER owner-lotd@world.std.com

518 **MANIC MOMS "A humorous newsletter for crazed mothers.":** The purpose of this newsletter is to find the humor in daily struggles with children (or the people who behave like children) and to comfort manic moms everywhere that they are not alone.
http://www.parentsplace.com/readroom/manicmoms
INFO pswx76a@prodigy.com

➤ **NET.SCANDAL:** A world repository of irritainment. (See entry 3729 for full listing.)

519 **Personalized/Vanity/Environmental License Plates:** A collection of over 10,000 great-looking personalized/vanity/environmental license plate "numbers." Here are some examples: EX N TRNK, O I C U 8 N 8, LIFE M8S, WED 2 GLF, WARP SPD, SOM 1 2 LV, PEGASUS, and SPD GZLS. Check it out!
http://licplate.andhra.com/
INFO plate@ix.netcom.com

520 **rec.humor** Jokes and the like. May be somewhat offensive. *Newsgroup*

521 **rec.humor.d** Discussions on the content of rec.humor articles. *Newsgroup*

522 **rec.humor.funny** Jokes that are funny (in the moderator's opinion). *Moderated newsgroup*

523 **rec.humor.oracle** Sagacious advice from the Usenet Oracle. *Moderated newsgroup*

524 **rec.humor.oracle.d** Comments about the Usenet Oracle's comments. *Newsgroup*

➤ **REHU-L:** For religious humor—a spinoff of ECCHST-L (Ecclesiastical History). (See entry 8865 for full listing.)

525 **relcom.humor** Ha-ha-ha. Jokes, you know them, funny. *Newsgroup*

526 **relcom.humor.lus** Moderated humor and jokes. *Moderated newsgroup*

527 `sanet.fun` General humor conference. *Newsgroup*

➤ **Science Jokes:** Poking fun at mathematics, chemistry, biology, and more. (See entry 9355 for full listing.)

528 **SNUFFIT-L:** The Church of Euthanasia. *Mailing List*
± `listserv@netcom.com` [body = SUBSCRIBE snuffit-l]
INFO `lamorte@deeptht.armory.com`
EDITOR `coe@paranoia.com`
OWNER `coe@netcom.com` (Rev. Chris Korda)
ARCHIVES
`ftp://ftp.etext.org/pub/Zines/Snuffit`
`gopher://gopher.etext.org/Zines/Snuffit`
`http://www.paranoia.com/coe/`

529 `talk.bizarre` The unusual, bizarre, curious, and often interesting. *Newsgroup*

530 **The Useless Pages:** "America's Funniest Home Hypermedia," a collection of strange, trivial, bizarre, unusual, and weird WWW pages, collected by Paul Phillips and Steve Berlin.
`http://www.primus.com/staff/paulp/useless.html`
INFO `useless@primus.com`

531 **usenet-oracle:** An active, cooperative effort for creative humor. The Usenet Oracle answers any questions posed to it. *Mailing List, moderated*
± `oracle-request@cs.indiana.edu`
INFO `oracle@cs.indiana.edu` [subject = help]
EDITOR OWNER `oracle-admin@cs.indiana.edu` (Steve Kinzler)
ARCHIVES
`ftp://ftp.cs.indiana.edu/pub/oracle`
`mailserv@cs.indiana.edu` [body = help]
FAQ `ftp://ftp.cs.indiana.edu/pub/oracle/help`
Gated: `rec.humor.oracle`

532 **WEIRD-L:** For disturbing/bizarre/offensive short stories, poetry, and ramblings. Not for humor or jokes. Only postings original with the submitter will be accepted. *Mailing List, moderated*
± `listserv@brownvm.brown.edu` [body = SUBSCRIBE WEIRD-L first-name last-name]
INFO `http://www.cyborganic.com/people/uke/lists/weird/`
ARCHIVE `listserv@brownvm.brown.edu`

533 **WRIGHT-QUOTE:** Distribution of a single Steven Wright quote each day: deadpan one liners. *Distribution List, moderated*
± `listproc@listproc.gcnet.com` [body = SUB WRIGHT-QUOTE first-name last-name]
OWNER `owenc@gcnet.com` (Chris Owen)

534 **Your MoM:** Funny, wacky goodness with an easy carryall handle. *E-Journal*
`http://bird.taponline.com/yourmom` (Humor Site of the Every Other Day)
`http://bird.taponline.com/yourmom/HSotEOD.html` (Humor Site of the Every Other Day)
INFO `emj5@columbia.edu` (Evan Jacover)
EDITOR `jacover@taponline.com`
ARCHIVE `http://bird.taponline.com/yourmom/archives/` (Humor Site of the Every Other Day)

HUMOR, FUN & BIZARRE—USENET ODDITIES

535 `alt.binaries.slack` Sounds and pictures of J. R. "Bob" Dobbs. *Newsgroup*

536 `alt.bitterness` No matter what it's for, you know how it'll turn out. *Newsgroup*

537 `alt.bored` What people do when they are bored. *Newsgroup*

538 `alt.devilbunnies` Probably better left undescribed. *Newsgroup*

539 `alt.discordia` All hail Eris, etc. *Newsgroup*

540 `alt.evil` Tales from the dark side. *Newsgroup*

541 `alt.fan.dr-bronner` "ALL-ONE!" apparently means something here. *Newsgroup*

542 `alt.fan.lightbulbs` Luminescence in a glass case. *Newsgroup*

543 `alt.fan.longest-thread` Fans of the longest thread ever. *Newsgroup*

544 `alt.fan.piers` Like `alt.fan.piers-anthony`, but for anyone named Piers. *Newsgroup*

545 `alt.flame` Alternative, literate, pithy, succinct screaming. *Newsgroup*

546 `alt.flame.spelling` Usenet's favourite fallacious argoomint. *Newsgroup*

547 `alt.folklore.kooks` The outer limits of human belief. *Newsgroup*

548 `alt.happy.birthday.to.me` Exploding egoism. *Newsgroup*

549 `alt.insults.gangbang` Group taunting. *Newsgroup*

550 `alt.lifestyle.barefoot` Discussions related to going barefoot. *Newsgroup*

551 `alt.misanthropy` People who hate people. *Newsgroup*

552 `alt.motd` The messages of the day. *Newsgroup*

553 `alt.pave.the.earth` Damn the environmentalists, full speed ahead! *Newsgroup*

554 `alt.pens.bic` Discussion of Bic pens. *Newsgroup*

555 `alt.pens.montblanc` Discussion of Mont Blanc pens. *Newsgroup*

556 `alt.religion.kibology` He's Fred, Jim. *Newsgroup*

557 `alt.sex.bestiality.barney` For people with big, purple newt fetishes. *Newsgroup*

558 `alt.silly.group.names.d` Eponymy. *Newsgroup*

559 `alt.slack` Posting relating to the Church of the Subgenius. *Newsgroup*

560 `alt.stupidity` Discussion about stupid newsgroups. *Newsgroup*

561 `alt.sysadmin.recovery` Getting over the trauma of system administration. *Newsgroup*

562 `alt.tasteless` Truly disgusting. *Newsgroup*

563 `alt.usenet.kooks` I have a theory about why we have such crazy theories. *Newsgroup*

LITERARY JOURNALS & MAGAZINES

➤ **Poet's Park:** A WWW-based literary digizine. Subtitled "A Resting Spot on the Superhighway," presents art, graphics, poetry, and short stories—also a links page to well over 50 of the best poetry sites on the Web. (See entry 623 for full listing.)

564 **Atmospherics:** A literary journal dedicated to new writers. Accepts short fiction, poetry, literary essays, and literary reviews. *E-journal*
`http://www.inforamp.net/~billie`
± OWNER `keeping@library.utoronto.ca`
ARCHIVE `gopher://locust.cic.net/11/Zines/Atmospherics`
Frequency: quarterly

565 **BEATRICE WWW:** Fiction, articles, poetry, and reviews with a sophisticated, slightly Gen-X bent. *E-Journal*
`http://www.primenet.com/~grifter/beatrice.html`
INFO `grifter@primenet.com` (Ron Hogan)
Frequency: irregular

566 **The Blue Penny Quarterly:** Fine literary fiction, poetry, and creative nonfiction. Also includes artwork. *E-Journal*
INFO `http://ebbs.english.vt.edu/olp/bpq/front-page.html`
EDITOR `dlawson@ebbs.english.vt.edu` (Doug Lawson)

ARCHIVE http://ebbs.english.vt.edu/olp/bpq/front-page.html

Frequency: quarterly

567   **Cyberkind: Poetics and Prosaics for a Wired World:** Net-related poetry, fiction, nonfiction, and art published solely on the World Wide Web. *E-Journal*

http://sunsite.unc.edu/ckind/title.html

INFO shannon@sunsite.unc.edu (Shannon Turlington)

ARCHIVE http://sunsite.unc.edu/ckind/title.html

Frequency: irregular but leaning toward monthly

➤   **darpan:** A literary magazine devoted to reflections on India, published by students at the University of Illinois at Urbana-Champaign. (See entry 614 for full listing.)

568   **Downstate Story:** Magazine of short fiction, illustrated. *Magazine*

http://www.wiu.bgu.edu/users/mfgeh/dss

INFO OWNER ehopkins@prairienet.org (Elaine Hopkins)

Frequency: new story each month on the Web

Archive: by mail only

569   **The Edifice or Writing and Literature:** Features solid writers and stories of a culturally relevant international flavor, not hipness or esoterica. *Magazine*

http://www-leland.stanford.edu/~lmgorbea/

INFO OWNER 72774.124@compuserve.com (James O'Malley)

ARCHIVE http://www-leland.stanford.edu/~lmgorbea/

Frequency: monthly

570   **The Fryburger:** Freiburg's English-language magazine. Our focus is fiction, that is, short stories, poetry, interviews with various authors, reviews, and of course also the occasional piece of nonfiction. *E-Journal*

http://www.uni-freiburg.de/borsch/fryburger/fryburger.html

INFO borsch@mibm.ruf.uni-freiburg.de (Frank Borsch)

INFO casagran@mibm.ruf.uni-freiburg.de (Sabina Casagrande)

571   **In Vivo:** Intelligent, eclectic, involved. *E-Journal*

http://freenet3.scri.fsu.edu:81/users/jtillman/titlepage.html

INFO jtillman@freenet.scri.fsu.edu (James Tillman)

572   **InterText:** For materials ranging from mainstream stories to fantasy to horror to science fiction to humor. *E-Journal*

± subscriptions@intertext.com [subject = SUBSCRIBE INTERTEXT followed by one of ascii, ps, notification or pdf]

INFO intertext@intertext.com

EDITOR jsnell@intertext.com (Jason Snell, Editor)

EDITOR geoff@intertext.com (Geoff Duncan, Assistant Editor)

EDITOR susan@intertext.com (Susan Grossman, Assistant Editor)

EDITOR editors@intertext.com

ARCHIVES

ftp://ftp.etext.org/pub/Zines/InterText/

http://www.etext.org/Zines/InterText/

ftp://network.ucsd.edu/intertext/

Frequency: bimonthly

Available in ASCII, PostScript, PDF, and HTML formats

573   **NWHQ:** Contemporary art and literature with a particular emphasis on hypertexted fiction. *E-Journal*

http://www.knosso.com/NWHQ/

INFO nwhq@wimsey.com (Elizabeth Fischer)

EDITOR efischer@wimsey.com (Elizabeth Fischer)

Frequency: quarterly

574 **Open Scroll:** Periodic poetry, prose, and political magazine dedicated to the pursuit of passion, brilliance, and insanity. *Magazine*
http://www.hooked.net/users/toconnor/
INFO scroll@hooked.net (The Open Scroll)
ARCHIVE http://www.hooked.net/users/toconnor/
Frequency: monthly

575 **Oyster Boy Review:** An independent literary magazine of fiction and poetry published quarterly in Chapel Hill, North Carolina. *E-Journal*
http://sunsite.unc.edu/ob/cotton_gin/cg.html
http://sunsite.unc.edu/ob
INFO damon_sauve@unc.edu (Damon Sauve, editor/publisher)
ARCHIVES
http://sunsite.unc.edu/ob/crews/crews.html
http://ruby.ils.unc.edu/oyster_boy/
Frequency: quarterly

576 **Parthenogenesis:** Short fiction. *Distribution List*
± INFO dherrick@nyx.cs.du.edu (Dan Herrick)
ARCHIVE ftp://etext.archive.umich.edu/pub/Zines/Parthenogenesis/
Frequency: irregular

577 **PATCHWORK:** Original literary works, including poetry, prose, quotations, ASCII art. *Mailing List*
± patchwork-request@nox.cs.du.edu
OWNER owner-patchwork@nox.cs.du.edu
OWNER tsitzlar@nyx.cs.du.edu (Travis E. Sitzlar)
ARCHIVES
ftp://ftp.cdc.net/pub/users/tsitzlar/patchwork
http://www.cdc.net/~tsitzlar

➤   **Pen and Sword:** Imaginative art and writing for the gay, lesbian, and diverse community. (See entry 9971 for full listing.)

578 **The Red Dog Journal:** "The anthology of the imagination" includes poetry and prose of all genres (science fiction and speculative, mainsteam, and experimental), visual arts, and new thought in various fields such as politics and science. *E-Journal*
gopher://indirect.com
http://www.indirect.com/user/informa/reddog.html
INFO OWNER informa@indirect.com (Stephen Barnes)
Language: English, Spanish
Frequency: irregular updates

579 **RPOETIK:** For REALPOETIK, the little magazine of the Internet. *Mailing List*, moderated
http://www.wln.com/~salasin/rp94.html
± listserv@wln.com [body = SUBSCRIBE RPOETIK first-name last-name]
OWNER salasin@wln.com (Sal Salasin)

580 **TextureMagazine:** Texture, an online monthly literary magazine, adds texture to what is otherwise mere text, publishing innovative fiction, humor, essays, and poetry. *Magazine*
http://catalog.com/texture/index.htm
INFO OWNER mbleich@ix.netcom.com (Matthew L. Bleich)
ARCHIVE http://catalog.com/texture/index.htm
Frequency: monthly

➤ **WEIRD-L:** For disturbing/bizarre/offensive short stories, poetry, and ramblings. Not for humor or jokes. Only postings original with the submitter will be accepted. (See entry 532 for full listing.)

LITERATURE

➤ **BookWire:** Book information galore. It includes information on publishers, bookstores, book events, and a "BookIndex" of book-related Internet resources. (See entry 99 for full listing.)

➤ **Digital BookWorld:** A Web site about books: includes information on new books, backlist books, authors, book-sellers, and publishers. Also provides excerpts, reviews, and interviews. (See entry 100 for full listing.)

➤ **The Internet Book Information Center:** This site includes: a guide to book-related resources on the Internet, The IBIC Journal (reviews of current and classic books), and more book-related goodies. (See entry 101 for full listing.)

581 `alt.arts.storytelling` Discussion of storytelling in all its forms. *Newsgroup*

582 `alt.fan.pooh` Winnie-the-Pooh and Piglet too. *Newsgroup*

583 `alt.pulp` Paperback fiction, newsprint production, orange juice. *Newsgroup*

584 `bit.listserv.literary` Discussions about literature. *Newsgroup*

➤ **GUTNBERG:** On Project Gutenberg, an effort to create large numbers of publically accessible texts on-line. (See entry 5675 for full listing.)

585 **In Some Unrelated Land:** An online novel with art by the author.
`http://www.syx.com/pilgrim/land.html`
INFO `conway@syx.com`

➤ **New York University School of Medicine Medical Humanities Pages:** Database of literature and medicine, medical humanities directory and syllabi, archives of the lit-med discussion group messages, and pointers to related resources. (See entry 4914 for full listing.)

➤ **Project Runeberg:** Project Runeberg publishes free electronic editions of classic Nordic literature and art over the Internet since 1992. (See entry 5679 for full listing.)

586 `rec.arts.books.hist-fiction` Historical fictions (novels) in general. *Newsgroup*

587 `rec.arts.int-fiction` Discussions about interactive fiction. *Newsgroup*

588 `relcom.arts.epic` Literary arts of epical kind (more then 10 kilobytes). *Newsgroup*

589 `relcom.arts.qwerty` Literary arts of small forms (less then 10 kilobytes). *Newsgroup*

➤ **SALON:** An online interactive magazine of culture, books, arts, and ideas. (See entry 653 for full listing.)

➤ **SF-LIT:** The Literary Science Fiction & Fantasy Discussion Forum: from the Library of Congress, the literary side of science fiction & fantasy. (See entry 1343 for full listing.)

590 `tnn.literature` Discussions in literature. *Newsgroup*

LITERATURE—AUTHORS

591 **Abbey's Web:** This site is devoted to the life and works of the environmental writer Edward Abbey. It includes a biography, a bibliography, quotes, reader contributions, a discussion group, links to related information, and more.
`http://www.abalon.se/beach/aw/abbey.html`
INFO `clindh@abalon.se` (Christer Lindh)

592 **AbbeyWeb:** Discussions about author Edward Abbey. *Mailing List*
± `abbeyweb-request@abalon.se`
OWNER `clindh@abalon.se` (Christer Lindh)
ARCHIVES
`abbeyweb-request@abalon.se`
`http://www.abalon.se/beach/aw/abbey.html`

593 `alt.books.bukowski` Discussion on the works and life of Charles Bukowski. *Newsgroup*

594 `alt.books.kurt-vonnegut` Discussion of Kurt Vonnegut's works. *Newsgroup*

595 `alt.books.robert-rankin` For the discussion of the books of Robert Rankin. *Newsgroup*

➤ `alt.fan.cecil-adams`: The brother Douglas Adams never talks about. *Newsgroup*

596 `alt.fan.eddings` The works of writer David Eddings. *Newsgroup*

597 `alt.fan.hofstadter` Douglas Hofstadter and Godel, Escher, Bach. *Newsgroup*

598 `alt.fan.tom-robbins` 31 flavors for readers. *Newsgroup*

599 **Blake:** On the works and influence of William Blake (1757-1827). *Mailing List*
   ± `blake-request@albion.com`
   OWNER `seth@albion.com` (Seth Ross)
   ARCHIVE `http://www.bookport.com/Albion/`

600 `humanities.lit.authors.shakespeare` Poetry, plays, history of Shakespeare. *Newsgroup*

➤ **J. V. Jones Website:** This is the author Web page of the number-one national bestselling sf trade paperback novel *The Baker's Boy*. The site combines stylish graphics, humor, and lots of custom-written material. (See entry 1446 for full listing.)

601 **JAMESF-L:** On the James family (Alice, William, Henry, and Henry Sr.) *Mailing List*
   ± `listserv@wvnvm.wvnet.edu`
   OWNER `torsney@wvnvm.wvnet.edu` (Cheryl Torsney)
   OWNER `pmb@cunyvms1.gc.cuny.edu` (Marc Bousquet)

602 **MERELEWIS:** On the life, works, and influence of C. S. Lewis. *Daily Digest, moderated*
   ± `listserv@listserv.aol.com` [body = SUBSCRIBE MERELEWIS first-name last-name]
   INFO `dwalheim@aol.com` (Debra Walheim)
   ARCHIVES
   `http://sleepy.usu.edu/~slq9v/cslewis/index.html` (Mere Lewis link)
   `ftp://cc.usu.edu/DISK$USR5:[Q.SLQ9V.WWW.CSLEWIS.MERELEWIS]` (vol*.html)
   `listserv@listserv.aol.com` [body = INDEX MERELEWIS]
   Frequency: daily

603 **NABOKV-L:** For scholarly discussion on the English and Russian writings of Vladimir Nabokov. *Mailing List, moderated*
   ± `listserv@ucsbvm.ucsb.edu` [body = SUBSCRIBE NABOKV-L first-name last-name]
   INFO `chtodel@humanitas.ucsb.edu` (D. Barton Johnson)
   ARCHIVE `listserv@ucsbvm.ucsb.edu` [body = INDEX NABOKV-L]

604 **The Official Nicola Griffith Page:** Information on Nicola Griffith, author of the novels *Ammonite* and *Slow River* and the collection *Women and Other Aliens* (forthcoming).
   `http://www.america.net/~daves/ng/`
   INFO `daves@america.net`

➤ **SHAKSPER:** For discussion of the works of William Shakespeare. (See entry 1630 for full listing.)

605 **Thoreau Quarterly:** Quarterly-reissued hypertextspace centering upon the life and times and literary productions of Henry David Thoreau. *E-Journal*
   ± INFO OWNER `r2chow@uci.edu` (Austin Meredith)
   Frequency: quarterly

606 **The Tolkien Timeline:** This compilation is a chronological list of important events relating to Tolkien's life, career, and scholarly pursuits, and attempts to provide a more clear picture of this astounding man.
   `http://www.lights.com/tolkien/timeline.html`
   INFO `darryl.friesen@lights.com`

607 **Trollope:** Life and works of Anthony Trollope. *Mailing List*
   ± `majordomo@world.std.com` [body = subscribe trollope]

OWNER `libmgmt@world.std.com` (Elizabeth Thomsen)

608   **TWAIN-L:** The Mark Twain Forum: for scholarly discussion of the life and writings of Mark Twain. *Mailing List*
`http://www.netspace.org/cgi-bin/lwgate/TWAIN-L/`
± `listserv@yorku.ca` [body = SUBSCRIBE TWAIN-L first-name last-name]
INFO `troberts@mit.edu` (Taylor Roberts)

LITERATURE—CULTURES & MOVEMENTS

609   `alt.books.beatgeneration`   Beat authors, Burroughs, Kerouac, etc. *Newsgroup*

610   `alt.language.urdu.poetry`   Poetry in the Indic Urdu language. *Newsgroup*

611   **AMLIT-L:** Academic discussions and announcements concerning American literature. *Mailing List*
± `listserv@mizzou1.missouri.edu` [body = SUBSCRIBE AMLIT-L first-name last-name]
INFO `engmo@mizzou1.missouri.edu` (Michael O'Conner)
ARCHIVE `listserv@mizzou1.missouri.edu` [body = INDEX AMLIT-L]

➤   **ANSAX-L:** Scholarly discussions on topics in Anglo-Saxon studies (7th to 11th centuries). (See entry 5235 for full listing.)

612   **APPLIT:** On Appalachian literature, and history as it informs the literature. *Mailing List, moderated*
± `listserv@msuacad.morehead-st.edu` [body = subscribe applit first-name last-name]
INFO EDITOR OWNER `jfrazier@morehead-st.edu` (Jill LeRoy-Frazier)
INFO `frazier@morehead-st.edu` (David Frazier)

613   **AUSTLIT:** On Austrian literature: scholarly discussion and teaching approaches. *Mailing List*
± `listserv@vm1.nodak.edu` [body = SUBSCRIBE AUSTLIT first-name last-name]
OWNER `blaman@dsu1.dsu.nodak.edu` (Barbara Laman)
Language: English & German

614   **darpan:** A literary magazine devoted to reflections on India, published by students at the University of Illinois at Urbana-Champaign.
`http://www.exclamation.com/darpan/`
INFO `darpan@uiuc.edu`

➤   **DE PROVERBIO:** An electronic journal of international proverb studies. (See entry 5183 for full listing.)

615   **EARAM-L:** On early American literature and history, i.e., before circa 1820, including Native Americans, "discovery" documents, colonial and federal materials. *Mailing List*
± `listserv@kentvm.kent.edu` [body = SUBSCRIBE EARAM-L first-name last-name]
INFO `rcraig2@kentvm.kent.edu` (Ray Craig)
ARCHIVE `listserv@kentvm.kent.edu` [body = INDEX EARAM-L]

616   **The Jolly Roger:** A monthly journal of conservative thought which publishes contemporary literature written in the context of the Western canon. *E-Journal*
`http://jollyroger.com/`
± `jollyroger@jollyroger.com`
INFO `info@jollyroger.com`
OWNER `mcgucken@jollyroger.com`
ARCHIVE `http://jollyroger.com/beaconway/jollyroger.html`
Frequency: monthly

617   **MEDEVLIT:** For open discussion of medieval English literature. *Mailing List*
± `listserv@siucvmb.bitnet` [body = SUBSCRIBE MEDEVLIT first-name last-name]
INFO `medevlit-request@siucvmb.bitnet`
ARCHIVE `listserv@siucvmb.bitnet` [body = INDEX MEDEVLIT]

➤   **MGSA-L:** For scholars of modern Greek culture, society and literature—of special interest to graduate students in Modern Greek studies. (See entry 7316 for full listing.)

618   ModBrits: On modern British and Irish literature from 1895 to 1955. *Mailing List, moderated*

± `listserv@kentvm.kent.edu` [body = SUBSCRIBE ModBrits first-name last-name]

INFO `modbreds@kentvm.bitnet`

INFO OWNER `sreid@kentvm.bitnet` (S. W. Reid)

ARCHIVE `listserv@kentvm.kent.edu` [body = INDEX ModBrits]

Please Note: Subscription by approval only.

619   NASSR-L: For members of the North American Society for the Study of Romanticism (NASSR). Scholarly discussions on Romantic literature. *Mailing List*

± `listserv@wvnvm.wvnet.edu` [body = SUBSCRIBE NASSR-L first-name last-name]

INFO `dcstewa@wvnvm.bitnet` (David C. Stewart)

620   NEDER-L: An e-journal for the study of Dutch language and literature. *E-journal, moderated*

± `listserv@nic.surfnet.nl` [body = SUBSCRIBE NEDER-L first-name last-name]

INFO `b.salemans@let.kun.nl` (Ben Salemans)

ARCHIVE `gopher://hearn.nic.surfnet.nl/11/1.%20LISTSERVs%20public%20archives%20on%20%hearn.nic.surfnet.nl/Neder-L`

FAQ `listserv@nic.surfnet.nl` [body = get neder-l info]

Language: Dutch

Gated: `bit.lang.neder-l`

➤   **Pen and Sword:** Imaginative art and writing for the gay, lesbian, and diverse community. (See entry 9971 for full listing.)

➤   **SEELANGS:** On Slavic and eastern European languages and literatures. (See entry 5305 for full listing.)

621   T-AMLIT: On teaching a radically expanded literature of the United States. *Mailing List, moderated*

± `listproc@list.cren.net` [body = SUBSCRIBE T-AMLIT first-name last-name]

INFO `tamlit@gusun.georgetown.edu`

INFO `http://www.georgetown.edu/tamlit/`

EDITOR OWNER `rbass@guvax.acc.georgetown.edu` (Randy Bass)

ARCHIVE `http://www.cren.net/`

622   WIG-L: On the feminist study of German literature. *Mailing List*

± `listserv@cmsa.berkeley.edu` [body = SUBSCRIBE WIG-L first-name last-name]

OWNER `wiggle@violet.berkeley.edu` (Women's Caucus)

Language: English & German

LITERATURE—POETRY

623   Poet's Park: A WWW-based literary digizine. Subtitled "A Resting Spot on the Superhighway," presents art, graphics, poetry, and short stories—also a links page to well over 50 of the best poetry sites on the Web. *Magazine*

`http://www.soos.com/poetpark`

INFO `soos@soos.com`

➤   `alt.language.urdu.poetry:` Poetry in the Indic Urdu language. *Newsgroup*

➤   **Blake:** On the works and influence of William Blake (1757-1827). (See entry 599 for full listing.)

➤   `christnet.poetry:` Christian poetry. *Newsgroup*

➤   **Cross Way Publications:** Publishers of poetic works focusing on Christianity. (See entry 8719 for full listing.)

624   Georgian Blue Poetry Society: Society promoting the Poetic Arts. Submissions of unpublished poetry for the 1996 Annual Poetry Contest are invited.

`http://www.freudeman.com/poetry.htm`

INFO `frudeman@maple.net`

625   Grist On-line: Online publisher of language arts. First publication of individual works and complete book-length texts, as well as archives of poetry, visual poetry, prose, essays, and reviews. *E-Journal*

http://www.phantom.com/~grist
EDITOR fowler@phantom.com (John Fowler)
EDITOR f.doctor@digiweb.com (Fabio DOCTOROVICH, "Postypographika", Participating Editor and Publisher)
Frequency: irregular

626 **Poetica Dementia:** Poetica Dementia is a site of original poetry and photography and abstract art.
http://value.net/~rasumovski/
INFO rasumovski@value.net

➤ **Progression: The Future of Arts and Music:** Arts, music, and culture magazine. Incorporating the poetry magazine *Tandem*. (See entry 770 for full listing.)

627 **RIF/T : An Electronic Space for New Poetry, Prose, and:** Experimental work from young and established writers. In cooperation with the Electronic Poetry Center (Buffalo). *E-Journal*
ftp://ubvm.cc.buffalo.edu/e-poetry
gopher://wings.buffalo.edu
± listserv@ubvm.cc.buffalo.edu [body = sub e-poetry first-name last-name e-mail-address]
INFO e-poetry@ubvm.cc.buffalo.edu (Kenneth Sherwood)
INFO lolpoet@ubvm.cc.buffalo.edu (Loss Glazier)
ARCHIVE ftp://ubvm.cc.buffalo.edu/e-poetry
Frequency: quarterly

628 **SCRNFUL:** The Occasional Screenful: short poetry, generally rhymed and metered. *E-Zine*
± maiser@humnet.ucla.edu
OWNER volokh@law.ucla.edu (Eugene Volokh)

➤ **scruz.poetry:** Poetry and poets in the Santa Cruz, California (USA) area. *Newsgroup*

629 **So It Goes...:** WWW digizine devoted exculsively to poetry in all genres, from any submitting poet. *E-Zine*
http://info.pitt.edu/~soitgoes
http://www.pitt.edu/~soitgoes
INFO OWNER soitgoes@pitt.edu (Andrew Cooper)
INFO OWNER alcst20@pitt.edu
INFO OWNER geek@pitt.edu
ARCHIVE http://www.pitt.edu/~soitgoes
Frequency: bimonthly

630 **Stream-of-Consciousness:** Poetry meets image, plus some "art" thrown in. *E-Journal*
http://kzsu.stanford.edu/uwi.html
INFO jon@kzsu.stanford.edu
Frequency: irregular (approximately quarterly)

631 **We Magazine:** A poetic arts journal that has appeared on compact disc, casette, and video—and now the Internet. Multidimensional endeavors and distribution through an international "grassroots" approach. *E-Journal*
gopher://wings.buffalo.edu/11/internet library/e-journals/ub/rift
± INFO cf2785@albnyvms.bitnet
INFO scope@cats.ucsc.edu (Stephen Cope)
ARCHIVES
gopher://wings.buffalo.edu/11/internet library/e-journals/ub/rift
cf2785@albnyvms.bitnet
Frequency: irregular

LITERATURE—WRITER'S WORKSHOPS & RESOURCES

632   Poet Warrior Press Writer's Resource Center: A guide to Internet resources for writers, including many areas such as fiction, journalism, screenwriting, and publishers. Includes several articles.

http://www.azstarnet.com/~poewar
http://www.azstarnet.com/~poewar/writer/writer.html
INFO poewar@azstarnet.com

633   Writers' Resources: Interesting list of useful links for writers. Special focus on science fiction and the Pacific Northwest.

http://www.seanet.com/Users/warlock/ (Science Fiction Conventions Northwest)
http://www.seanet.com/Users/warlock/writers.html (Writers' Resources)
INFO warlock@warlock.seanet.com

634   alt.anagrams Playing with words. *Newsgroup*

➤   **christnet.writers:** Discussion group for Christian writers. *Newsgroup*

635   Critters Workshop: Online workshop/critique group for serious science-fiction/fantasy/horror writers.

http://www.cs.du.edu/users/critters/
INFO critters@cs.du.edu

➤   **DargonZine:** DargonZine is an electronic magazine that prints original amateur fantasy fiction by aspiring Internet writers. All stories in the anthology take place in a common shared setting. (See entry 1317 for full listing.)

636   ECRIVAINS: A French-language writers' workshop allowing authors to exchange and critique works in progress and to discuss writing issues. *Mailing List*

± listserver@uquebec.ca [body = SUBSCRIBE ECRIVAINS first-name last-name]
INFO OWNER nadeau@nortel.ca (Rhéal Nadeau)
INFO OWNER jean-claude_boudreault@uqtr.uquebec.ca (Jean-Claude Boudreault)
Language: French

637   Straycat's Writers Workshop: For response to stories or poems posted to Web site.

http://www.generation.net/~straycat/workshop.html
INFO straycat@generation.net

638   WRITERS: On the art and craft of writing and for the sharing of works in progress. *Mailing List*

± listserv@mitvma.mit.bitnet [body = SUBSCRIBE WRITERS first-name last-name]
OWNER mbarker@mit.edu (Mike Barker)

639   Writing Workshop: A collection of lists (Fiction, NFiction, Novels-L, Poetry-W, and Writing) where people who are interested in writing professionally can share and critique works in progress and discuss the art and craft of writing. *Daily Digest*

± listserv@psuvm.psu.edu [body = SUBSCRIBE followed by one of Writing, Fiction, NFiction,
  Novels-L, Poetry-W or Writing followed by *first-name last-name*]
INFO writing-request@psuvm.psu.edu (Writing Workshop)
OWNER workshop@nortel.ca (Rhéal Nadeau)
Please Note: Subscription by approval only.

MAGAZINES

640   alt.mag.playboy Four decades of appreciation or degradation. Your pick. *Newsgroup*

641   alt.motherjones *Mother Jones* magazine. *Newsgroup*

642   alt.sex.magazines Discussions of magazines with sticky pages. *Newsgroup*

643   alt.zines Small magazines, mostly noncommercial. *Newsgroup*

644   alt.zines.samizdat Kein vernugen ohne gefahr. *Newsgroup*

645   ChipNet: ChipNet topics include computer chat, sports, cooking and travel, video games, general interests, opinions, advice, humor, and more. *Magazine*

http://www.win.net/~tybeelytes/chipnet/index.html

http://www.tybee.com/~tybeelytes/chipnet/index.html

INFO OWNER chipnet@aol.com (John Peck, President)

Frequency: monthly

➤ **The Cyber Maze:** An online compilation of the *PPSA Magazine*. Topics include: real-life stories and road trips, humor, photos and art, editorials and commentary on social issues and current events. (See entry 7829 for full listing.)

➤ **DARK PLANET:** DARK PLANET is an electronic magazine of science fiction, fantasy, horror, and genre-related poetry, artwork, nonfiction, and reviews. (See entry 1318 for full listing.)

646 **FEED:** An online-only magazine of politics, culture, and technology.

http://www.feedmag.com/

INFO feed@feedmag.com

➤ **George Jr. magazine:** A monthly magazine (with daily updates) of culture, books, art, music, and software for the wired. (See entry 511 for full listing.)

647 **Glow:** A New York-based, general-interest multimedia publication with a focus on culture and the human side of world events. *Magazine*

http://www.vyne.com/glow/

INFO OWNER sherrard@interramp.com (Geoffrey G. Sherrard)

POST glowmag@aol.com

Frequency: quarterly (initially)

648 **Hawaii Hypermedia, Inc.:** Hawaii Hypermedia is the publisher/host of many of Hawaii's online publications, including Surf News Network Hawaii, Brew Hawaii, PC Currents, PennySaver, and more.

http://hypermedia.net/

INFO sean@hypermedia.net

FAQ http://hypermedia.net/faq.htm

➤ **HotWired:** Online sister of *Wired* magazine. Contains articles, discussion forums, and lots more for net hipsters and newbies alike. "Mainstream Culture for the 21st Century." (See entry 9826 for full listing.)

➤ **InfoZine:** Kansas City's Digital Publishing Company. (See entry 8138 for full listing.)

649 **International Teletimes:** General-interest culture magazine with varying monthly themes such as education, history, and travel. Regular columns include "Cuisine," "Keepers of the Light" (photography), and "The Wine Enthusiast." *E-Journal*

editor@teletimes.com [body = e-mail-address computer-type] (Ian Wojtowicz)

ARCHIVE http://www.teletimes.com/

Language: English, French, Esperanto, Spanish, German, Others

Frequency: bimonthly

650 **Loci:** An online magazine by and for college students. Includes entertainment information, games, chat forums, and more. Sponsored by Barnes & Noble booksellers.

http://www.loci.com/

INFO chiefeditor@loci.com

651 **Multiworld Magazine:** Multiworld is a bimonthly, multilingual, multimedia magazine distributed via the Web. It mainly carries the experiences of contributors relating to nature, wildlife, culture, people, and art.

http://www.jnw.com/mw/index.html

INFO mw_publisher@garnet.berkeley.edu

ARCHIVE http://www.jnw.com/mw/index.html

POST mw_submit@garnet.berkeley.edu

Language: Chinese, English, French

Frequency: bimonthly

➤ **Pathfinder:** Web outlet of the Time Warner entertainment conglomerate. As well as shopping and news, this site contains content from and promotions for magazines, books, TV and cable, music, movies, and more. (See entry 6129 for full listing.)

➤ **Progression: The Future of Arts and Music:** Arts, music, and culture magazine. Incorporating the poetry magazine *Tandem*. (See entry 770 for full listing.)

652   `rec.mag` Magazine summaries, tables of contents, etc. *Newsgroup*

653   **SALON:** An online interactive magazine of culture, books, arts, and ideas.

     `http://www.salon1999.com/`

     INFO `feedback@salon.batnet.com`

➤ **Science On-Line:** Science On-Line includes: *Science* magazine, current and back issues; Science's Next Wave, an electronic network for young scientists; Classified Advertising, including career opportunities; Beyond the Printed Page, interactive projects and additional data; and Electronic Marketplace, with the latest new product information. (See entry 9442 for full listing.)

654   **Suck:** Suck is "an experiment in provocation, mordant deconstructionism, and buzz-saw journalism," or, to quote Brock Meeks, "a kind of de facto Web 'Ombudsmen' with Attitude."

     `http://www.suck.com/`

     INFO `sucksters@www.suck.com`

655   **Super AM Magazine:** The Journal founded by the enlightened. Super AM is to information in the nineties what A.M. radio was to information in the thirties. Global and undefinable. How will you find it? *Magazine*

     `http://www.superam.com/`

     INFO OWNER `tompaul@earthlink.net` (Tom Wilson)

     Frequency: monthly

656   `tnn.books.magazine` Topics and information about magazines. *Newsgroup*

657   **Triangle Online:** More than a magazine, more than an online guide to the Triangle Area, and more than just another Web page in cyberspace; not just be published once a month, it's a living document. *Magazine*

     `http://www.trinet.com/online.html`

     INFO EDITOR `ftaylor@trinet.com` (Frank Taylor, Editor)

658   **Tristero:** The online magazine of creative arts and entertainment. *Newsletter*

     `http://superlink.com/tristero`

     INFO OWNER `tristero@superlink.com`

     INFO EDITOR OWNER `cristoph@superlink.com` (Christopher Kienle, Editor/Webmaster)

     ARCHIVE `http://superlink.com/tristero`

     Frequency: seasonal, soon to be monthly

659   **Venue Magazine:** A venture committed to maintaining a freer, more interactive channel for expression and creation in music, politics, and literature. *E-Zine*

     `http://www.interlog.com/~venue/`

     INFO `venue@interlog.com`

MAGIC

660   **The Magic Page:** A good collection of magic resources. Includes documents on magic, links to other magic pages on the Web organized by magician, shopping, and places.

     `http://www.daimi.aau.dk/~zytnia/eg.html`

     INFO `zytnia@daimi.aau.dk`

661   `alt.fan.penn-n-teller` The magicians Penn Jillette and Teller. *Newsgroup*

662   `alt.magic` For discussion about stage magic. *Newsgroup*

663   `alt.magic.secrets` The butler did it, with mirrors, to Colonel Mustard. *Newsgroup*

664   **The Encore Magic Page:** All sort of magic information. Includes listings of magic books, companies, clubs and societies, as well as a Swap Shop and magic clip art.

```
http://user.itl.net/~encore/index.html
```
INFO encore@itl.net

665 **Magician's WWW Repository:** A place for magicians to check out a library of magical effects and more. Password required.
```
http://corona.unomaha.edu/~choman/magic/
```
INFO choman@unomaha.edu

MOVIES & FILMS

➤ <u>MEGA-MEDIA LINKS index @ OMNIBUS:EYE:</u> A searchable index of thousands of film/TV/radio/multimedia/new-media/cinema links subcategorized into over 60 helpful areas. (See entry 6055 for full listing.)

666 **12 Monkeys:** A fully navigable world, without the text, links you to the strange mystery of *12 Monkeys*, the Terry Gilliam movie.
```
http://www.mca.com/universal_pictures/12
```
INFO tracyg123@aol.com

667 `alt.asian-movies` Movies from Hong Kong, Taiwan, and the Chinese mainland. *Newsgroup*

668 `alt.binaries.sounds.movies` Sounds from copyrighted movies. *Newsgroup*

669 `alt.cult-movies` Movies with a cult following. *Newsgroup*

670 `alt.cult-movies.evil-deads` The Evil Dead movie series. *Newsgroup*

671 `alt.cult-movies.rocky-horror` Virgin! *Newsgroup*

672 `alt.fan.alicia-slvrstone` For discussion of and about Alicia Silverstone. *Newsgroup*

673 `alt.fan.blues-brothers` Jake and Elwood ride again! *Newsgroup*

674 `alt.fan.james.cameron` For fans of sf movies by director James Cameron. *Newsgroup*

675 `alt.fan.jodie-foster` Jodie Foster fandom. *Newsgroup*

➤ `alt.fan.keanu-reeves:` People who love Keanu Reeves, in all his blandness. *Newsgroup*

➤ `alt.fan.mandy-patinkin:` For fans of actor Mandy Patinkin ("My name is Inigo Montoya..."). *Newsgroup*

➤ `alt.fan.meg-ryan:` For the general discussion of Meg Ryan and all her acting work. *Newsgroup*

➤ `alt.fan.mst3k:` I thought people hated jerks who talked in theaters. *Newsgroup*

➤ `alt.fan.ralph.fiennes:` For fans of actor Ralph Fiennes. *Newsgroup*

676 `alt.fan.sam-raimi` Fans of the talented horror/comedy movies director. *Newsgroup*

677 `alt.fan.sandra-bullock` The Speed-ing babe from Arlington, Virginia. *Newsgroup*

678 `alt.fan.spinal-tap` The newsgroup that goes to 11. *Newsgroup*

679 `alt.fan.tarantino` Filmmaker Quentin Tarantino. *Newsgroup*

680 `alt.movies.branagh-thmpsn` Films of Kenneth Branagh and Emma Thompson. *Newsgroup*

➤ `alt.movies.chaplin:` Discussion of Charlie Chaplin's life and art. *Newsgroup*

681 `alt.movies.hitchcock` The films of Alfred Hitchcock. *Newsgroup*

682 `alt.movies.independent` Films put out by independent producers. *Newsgroup*

683 `alt.movies.indian` Films from India and the Indian subcontinent. *Newsgroup*

684 `alt.movies.joe-vs-volcano` Fans discuss the movie *Joe versus the Volcano*. *Newsgroup*

685 `alt.movies.kubrick` For the discussion of Stanley Kubrick's movies. *Newsgroup*

686 `alt.movies.scorsese` Are you talking to me? You think I'm funny? *Newsgroup*

687 `alt.movies.silent` Shhhhhhhhhhh! *Newsgroup*

688 `alt.movies.spielberg` Films of blockbuster director Steven Spielberg. *Newsgroup*

689   `alt.movies.tim-burton` The brooding works of Tim Burton. *Newsgroup*

690   `alt.movies.visual-effects` Discussion of visual f/x for movies and TV. *Newsgroup*

691   `alt.sex.movies` Discussing the ins and outs of certain movies. *Newsgroup*

692   `alt.video.tape-trading` Trading of legally copied videos. *Newsgroup*

693   `bit.listserv.cinema-l` Discussions on all forms of cinema. *Newsgroup*

694   `bit.listserv.movie.memorabilia` Movie poster list. *Newsgroup*

➤   `bit.listserv.screen-l`: Film and television discussion list. *Moderated newsgroup*

➤   **Chicago Moving Image Scene:** The online resource and directory for Chicagoland producers of film, video, and multimedia. Free professional listings. (See entry 8112 for full listing.)

695   `chile.cine` Chileans discuss movies. *Newsgroup*

696   **CINEMA-L:** Discussions about all aspects of cinema. *Mailing List*
    `ftp://listserv.american.edu/pub/cinema/archives`
    ± `listserv@american.edu` [body = SUBSCRIBE CINEMA-L first-name last-name]
    INFO `mike@wvnvm.wvnet.edu` (Mike Karolchik)
    ARCHIVE `listserv@american.edu` [body = SUBSCRIBE CINEMA-L first-name last-name]
    POST `cinema-l@american.edu`
    Gated: `bit.listserv.cinema-l`

697   `clari.apbl.movies` News on movies and filmmaking. *Moderated newsgroup*

698   `clari.living.columns.joebob` Joe Bob Briggs: drive-in movie critic. *Moderated newsgroup*

699   `clari.living.movies` News of film and movies. *Moderated newsgroup*

700   **DRIVE-INS:** On drive-in movie theaters and classic indoor bijous. *Mailing List*
    `http://www.brettnews.com/~brettnews`
    ± `listproc@echonyc.com` [body = SUBSCRIBE DRIVE-INS first-name last-name]
    OWNER `brett@echonyc.com` (Brett Leveridge)

701   **exhibitionists:** Aimed at people working in the motion picture exhibition industry (cinemas, film societies, etc.), but open to all interested parties. *Mailing List*
    ± INFO `exhibitionists-request@jvnc.net`

702   **filmmakers:** On all aspects of motion picture (not video) production, with an emphasis on technical issues, especially construction and design issues for those working on tight budgets. *Mailing List*
    ± INFO `filmmakers-request@power.net`

➤   **FILMUS-L:** Discussion on film music. (See entry 758 for full listing.)

703   `fj.rec.movies` Reviews and discussions of movies. *Newsgroup*

704   **Journal of Criminal Justice and Popular Culture:** Reviews of movies with a criminal-justice theme, and refereed papers on criminal justice and popular culture. *E-journal*
    `http://www.scj.albany.edu:90/jcjpc/index.htm`
    ± `listserv@cnsibm.albany.edu` [body = SUBSCRIBE CJMOVIES first-name last-name]
    INFO `sunycrj@cnsibm.albany.edu` (Graeme Newman)
    EDITOR `br5566@cnsunix.albany.edu` (Brian Renauer)
    EDITOR `jr0280@cnsunix.albany.edu` (Jack Reed)
    ARCHIVE `listserv@cnsibm.albany.edu` [body = INDEX CJMOVIES]

705   `kw.movies` Film reviews. *Newsgroup*

➤   `misc.writing.screenplays`: Aspects of writing and selling screenplays. *Newsgroup*

706   **MovieLink:** Movie information for major metropolitan areas in the U.S. Includes listings, showtimes, and ticket purchasing.
    `http://www.movielink.com/`

INFO `comments@moviefone.com`

707 **Movies-seivoM:** On self-referential movies that "break the fourth wall." *Mailing List, moderated*

± `movies-seivom@kinexis.com` [subject = `subscribe`]

OWNER `barbara@kinexis.com` (Barbara Bernstein)

ARCHIVES

`gopher://kserver.kinexis.com`

`http://www.kinexis.com/movies-seivom.html`

`ftp://ftp.kinexis.com/movies`

➤ **Pathfinder:** Web outlet of the Time Warner entertainment conglomerate. As well as shopping and news, this site contains content from and promotions for magazines, books, TV and cable, music, movies, and more. (See entry 6129 for full listing.)

708 `rec.arts.movies.announce` Newsworthy events in the movie business. *Moderated newsgroup*

709 `rec.arts.movies.current-films` The latest movie releases. *Newsgroup*

710 `rec.arts.movies.lists+surveys` Top-n lists and general surveys. *Newsgroup*

711 `rec.arts.movies.misc` General aspects of movies not covered by other groups. *Newsgroup*

712 `rec.arts.movies.movie-going` Going-to-movies experiences. *Newsgroup*

713 `rec.arts.movies.past-films` Past movies. *Newsgroup*

714 `rec.arts.movies.people` People in the movie business. *Newsgroup*

715 `rec.arts.movies.production` Filmmaking, amateur and professional. *Newsgroup*

716 `rec.arts.movies.reviews` Reviews of movies. *Moderated newsgroup*

717 `rec.arts.movies.tech` Technical aspects of movies. *Newsgroup*

➤ `rec.music.artists.danny-elfman`: Composer Danny Elfman's music. *Newsgroup*

➤ `rec.music.movies`: Music for movies and television. *Newsgroup*

718 `rec.video.releases` Prerecorded video releases on laser disc and videotape. *Newsgroup*

➤ **SALON:** An online interactive magazine of culture, books, arts, and ideas. (See entry 653 for full listing.)

719 `triangle.movies` Movies discussions in North Carolina. *Newsgroup*

➤ **TV-film-video:** Vortex Technology's collection of materials relating to television, film, and video, including "Professor Neon's TV & Movie Mania" and other topic areas. (See entry 6069 for full listing.)

MUSEUMS

720 **ARGUS-L:** For users of ARGUS, a Unix-based collections-management system used in art, ethnographic, and natural history museums. *Mailing List*

± `listserv@yalevm.ycc.yale.edu` [body = `SUBSCRIBE ARGUS-L` first-name last-name]

INFO `lawrence.gall@yale.edu` (Larry Gall)

721 **CIDOC-L:** On documentation and information management at museums. *Mailing List*

± `listserv@nrm.se` [body = `SUBSCRIBE CIDOC-L` first-name last-name]

OWNER `cidoc-l-request@nrm.se`

➤ **CIMCIM-L:** On musical-instrument museums: curation, conservation, research. (See entry 894 for full listing.)

➤ **Exploratorium:** A collection of 650 interactive exhibits in the areas of science, art, and human perception. (See entry 4301 for full listing.)

722 **ICOM-Announce:** For information from the International Council of Museums (ICOM). *Distribution List*

± `listserv@doc.nrm.se` [body = `SUBSCRIBE ICOM-ANNOUNCE` first-name last-name]

OWNER `icom-announce-request@nrm.se`

723 **ICOM-SWEDEN:** On providing and accessing Internet services through museums. *Mailing List*

± `listserv@nrm.se` [body = SUBSCRIBE ICOM-SWEDEN first-name last-name]
OWNER `icom-sweden-request@nrm.se`

724   **Museum-L:** Discussion group about museums. *Mailing List*
± `listserv@unmvma.unm.edu` [body = SUBSCRIBE MUSEUM-L first-name last-name]
INFO OWNER `chadwick@nmmnh-abq.mus.nm.us` (John Chadwick)
ARCHIVE `gopher://ucmp1.berkeley.edu`
FAQS
`http://www.aps.edu/HTMLPages/museum-l.html`
`ftp://198.59.157.5/misc/museum-l-faq.txt`
Gated: `bit.listserv.museum-l`

725   **The Smithsonian Institution:** Online guide and tour to the museums and programs of the Smithsonian Institution in Washington, D.C.
`http://www.si.edu/` (Smithsonian Institute)
INFO `webmaster@si.edu`
MIRROR `http://www.si.sgi.com/sgi.htm`

MUSIC

726   <u>**List of Music Lists:**</u> For an e-mail infobot providing a regularly updated, comprehensive list of music-related mailing lists on the net.
± `majordomo@edmonds.home.cs.ubc.ca` [body = get faq lomml.txt] (Infobot)
± `avalon-request@dfw.net` [body = send lomml] (Infobot)

727   **ALLMUSIC:** Discussions about all aspects of music. *Distribution List*
`ftp://listserv.american.edu/pub/allmusic/archives`
± `listserv@american.edu` [body = SUBSCRIBE ALLMUSIC first-name last-name]
INFO `mike@wvnvm.wvnet.edu` (Mike Karolchik)
Gated: `bit.listserv.allmusic`

728   `alt.binaries.sounds.music` Music samples in MOD/669 format. *Newsgroup*

729   `alt.collecting.8-track-tapes` Fans of the endless-loop cartridge. *Newsgroup*

730   `alt.exotic-music` Exotic music discussions. *Newsgroup*

731   `alt.gothic` The gothic movement: things mournful and dark. *Newsgroup*

732   `alt.gothic.fashion` Discussion on pointy boots, hair dye, and makeup tips! *Newsgroup*

733   `alt.music.4-track` People who need to get out more often. *Newsgroup*

734   `alt.music.4ad` Artists on the 4 A.D. music label. *Newsgroup*

735   `alt.music.banana-truffle` Bananananana Truffle. *Newsgroup*

736   `alt.music.bootlegs` People pirating music performances. *Newsgroup*

737   `alt.music.canada` Oh, Canada, eh? *Newsgroup*

738   `alt.music.dance` Music to dance to. *Newsgroup*

739   `alt.music.independent` Soloists without contracts with the major labels. *Newsgroup*

740   `alt.music.karaoke` Givin' it from the (usually drunken) heart. *Newsgroup*

741   `alt.music.lyrics` Discussion of song lyrics. *Newsgroup*

742   `alt.music.makers.dj` About DJs, their music and lives. *Newsgroup*

743   `alt.music.producer` Discussion about record production and A & R. *Newsgroup*

744   `alt.music.techno` Bring on the bass! *Newsgroup*

745   `alt.music.texas` Janis Joplin to ZZ Top, Willie Nelson to Pantera. *Newsgroup*

746 `alt.music.video-games` Music that appears in video games. *Newsgroup*

747 `alt.niteclub.alternative` Alternative-music nightclubs. *Newsgroup*

748 `alt.thrash` Thrash life. *Newsgroup*

749 `aus.music` Music and related issues. *Newsgroup*

➤ `austin.music:` Music around Austin, Texas. *Newsgroup*

➤ `bit.listserv.mla-l:` Music Library Association. *Newsgroup*

750 **CDnow:** Comprehensive online music store. Includes album reviews and musician discographies as well. CDnow may be the Web's most popular music retailer and information source. They offer more than 165,000 domestic and imported CDs, cassettes, T-shirts, videos, and laserdiscs.

`http://cdnow.com/`

INFO `manager@cdnow.com`

751 `clari.apbl.music` News on music and the music industry. *Moderated newsgroup*

752 `clari.living.music` News of the music scene. *Moderated newsgroup*

753 **COMMUNITY-MUSIC:** On community bands and orchestras: musicians, conductors, fundraising, publicity. *Digest & Reflector*

± `majordomo@mpd.tandem.com`

INFO `http://www.io.com/~rboerger/community.html`

OWNER `owner-community-music@mpd.tandem.com` (Ron Boerger)

ARCHIVE `http://www.io.com/~rboerger/community.html`

FAQ `http://www.io.com/~rboerger/community.html`

754 `comp.music` Applications of computers in music research. *Newsgroup*

755 **The Concert Connection:** A concert tour information interactive resource. The site includes tour and news updates on over 600 bands and 5,000 venues worldwide. Updated weekly.

`http://cconnection.com/`

INFO `jgreene@cdnow.com`

756 **Consumable:** Music reviews primarily in the "alternative" genre, but also pop, rock, and other musical formats. *E-Zine*

`http://www.westnet.com/consumable/Consumable.html`

INFO `gajarsky@pilot.njin.net` (Bob Gajarsky)

ARCHIVES

`http://www.westnet.com/consumable/Consumable.html`

`gopher://diana.zems.etf.hr:70/11/eng/Music/Consumable`

`ftp://ftp.etext.org/pub/Zines/Consumable`

➤ `dc.music:` Music-related issues in the D.C. area. *Newsgroup*

757 **The Eyesore Database:** This is the Web page for the Eyesore Database, a comprehensive listing of music released on the 4ad record label.

`http://www.evo.org/eyesore.html`

INFO `webmaster@evo.org`

758 **FILMUS-L:** Discussion on film music. *Digest & Reflector*

`http://www.netspace.org/cgi-bin/lwgate/FILMUS-L/`

± `listserv@iubvm.ucs.indiana.edu` [body = SUBSCRIBE FILMUS-L first-name last-name]

INFO OWNER `c60hsw1@corn.cso.niu.edu` (H. Stephen Wright, Principal Owner)

INFO `papakhi@iubvm.bitnet` (A. Ralph Papakhian, Associate Owner)

ARCHIVE `listserv@iubvm.indiana.edu` [body = INDEX FILMUS-L]

FAQ `listserv@iubvm.indiana.edu` [body = GET FILMUS-L WELCOME]

759   **firefly:** This "personal music recommendation agent" matches your musical tastes with those of other people who have left their music profiles on the system.

     `http://www.agents-inc.com/`

     INFO `firefly@agents-inc.com`

     MIRROR `http://www.ffly.com/`

760   `fj.rec.music` Discussion about music. *Newsgroup*

761   **funky-music:** On funk music, as well as rap, hip-hop, soul, rhythm and blues, and related varieties. Discussions of zydeco, reggae, salsa, soca, and similar gutsy street music are also welcome. *Digest & Reflector*

     ± INFO `funky-music-request@athena.mit.edu`

762   **Harmony Music List:** A comprehensive list of over 2,200 music-related Internet resources. Covers artists, classical music, cultures, discographies, events, instruments and equipment, jazz, labels, general music lists, magazines, people's pages, places, radio stations, music research, studios, and styles.

     `http://www.ucsd.edu/harmony`

     INFO `webmaster@ucsd.edu`

➤   `houston.music:`   Musical happenings and discussions in Houston, Texas. *Newsgroup*

763   **The Internet Jukebox:** The Internet Jukebox is designed to enhance the musical experience for all Web surfers. The Internet Jukebox contains music in six different genres and plays entire songs and albums through the use of RealAudio 2.0.

     `http://interjuke.com/`

     INFO `jgreene@cdnow.com`

➤   **The Lighthouse:** A monthly Christian music (all genres) magazine featuring an upcoming album list, album reviews, artist interviews, industry press releases, brief reviews of all new products, and an indie section. Rated top 5% Web site. (See entry 8725 for full listing.)

764   **LiSTeN Up MAGaZINE:** Uses real-audio technology to provide real-time access to oral album reviews with music samples within the review. Also, contains interviews with artists, bands, and music-industry personnel. *Magazine*

     `http://www.interport.net/~anthem/`

     INFO OWNER `anthem@interport.net` (Greg Karr)

     ARCHIVE `http://www.interport.net/listenup`

➤   **Los Angeles After Dark:** Features live and prerecorded over-the-Internet broadcasts of bands, comedy, and entertainment-oriented programming. Also featuring audio and video on demand of various shows and music. Some artists will be actually debuting their CDs and singles here prior to release. (See entry 1227 for full listing.)

➤   **The LP Lover's Guide to San Francisco:** For descriptions and ratings of the best used record stores throughout the San Francisco Bay Area, visit The LP Lover's Guide to San Francisco. (See entry 8024 for full listing.)

765   **Musi-Cal:** A calendar that provides access to worldwide live music information: concerts, festivals, gigs, and other musical events.

     `http://www.automatrix.com/concerts/`

     INFO `concerts@calendar.com` (e-mail access)

     INFO `concertmaster@automatrix.com`

766   **Network-Audio-Bits:** Reviews of and information about current rock, pop, new age, jazz, funk, folk, and other musical genres. *E-Zine*

     ± INFO `n-audio@maine.maine.edu` (Network Audio Bits)

     ± INFO `murph@maine.maine.edu` (Michael A. Murphy)

     INFO `http://maine.maine.edu/~n-audio`

767   **The Official Online Guide to Canada's West Coast Music Industry:** The most comprehensive guide to Vancouver and British Columbia's music industry. Free listings for businesses and musicians. Also includes classified ads.

     `http://www.smartt.com/worldone.com/`

     INFO `worldone@smartt.com`

768   `okinawa.rec.music` Discussion about music. *Newsgroup*

➤ `pdaxs.services.music:` Learn to play the tuba! *Newsgroup*

769 `phl.misc` Miscellaneous postings. *Newsgroup*

770 **Progression: The Future of Arts and Music:** Arts, music, and culture magazine. Incorporating the poetry magazine *Tandem. Magazine*
http://www.gold.net/users/ex14/
INFO OWNER wing@cityscape.co.uk (Mark Wingfield)
INFO carl@mitt.demon.co.uk (Carl Homer)
Frequency: monthly

771 **Quadraverb:** Discussion of the Alesis Quadraverb effects boxes. *Mailing List*
± INFO qv-request@neato.org
ARCHIVE http://www.neato.org/qv/

➤ `rec.arts.marching.band.college:` College marching bands. *Newsgroup*

➤ `rec.arts.marching.band.high-school:` High-school marching bands. *Newsgroup*

➤ `rec.arts.marching.drumcorps:` Drum and bugle corps. *Newsgroup*

772 `rec.music.a-cappella` Vocal music without instrumental accompaniment. *Newsgroup*

773 `rec.music.cd` CDs—availability and other discussions. *Newsgroup*

774 `rec.music.christian` Christian music, both contemporary and traditional. *Newsgroup*

775 `rec.music.collecting.cd` Compact discs of collector value. *Newsgroup*

776 `rec.music.collecting.misc` Music collecting other than vinyl or CD. *Newsgroup*

777 `rec.music.collecting.vinyl` Collecting vinyl records. *Newsgroup*

778 `rec.music.dementia` Discussion of comedy and novelty music. *Newsgroup*

779 `rec.music.funky` Funk, soul, rhythm and blues, and related. *Newsgroup*

780 `rec.music.info` News and announcements on musical topics. *Moderated newsgroup*

781 `rec.music.makers.choral` Choral groups and choral music. *Newsgroup*

782 `rec.music.marketplace.cd` Buying and selling collectible compact discs. *Newsgroup*

783 `rec.music.marketplace.misc` Buying and selling non-vinyl/CD music. *Newsgroup*

784 `rec.music.marketplace.vinyl` Buying and selling collectible vinyl records. *Newsgroup*

785 `rec.music.misc` Music lovers' group. *Newsgroup*

786 `rec.music.movies` Music for movies and television. *Newsgroup*

787 `rec.music.promotional` Information and promo materials from record companies. *Moderated newsgroup*

788 `rec.music.ragtime` Ragtime and related music styles. *Newsgroup*

789 `rec.music.reviews` Reviews of music of all genres and mediums. *Moderated newsgroup*

790 `relcom.music` Music lovers. *Newsgroup*

➤ `sat.music:` Music around San Antonio, Texas. *Newsgroup*

➤ `sdnet.music:` San Diego concert/performance reviews and comments. *Newsgroup*

791 **soundout:** Online magazine of contemporary music. *E-Zine*
http://www.tmn.com/0h/Community/juechi/soundout.html
INFO OWNER juechi@tmn.com (Jason Uechi)
ARCHIVE http://www.tmn.com/0h/Community/juechi/soundout.html
Frequency: irregular

792 `tnn.music` Topics and discussions about music. *Newsgroup*

793 `tnn.music.players` Music and instruments for music players. *Newsgroup*

794 `tnn.music.techno` Topics and discussions about techno music. *Newsgroup*

795 `uk.music.misc` General discussion of U.K. music. *Newsgroup*

796 `uk.music.rave` Discussion of U.K. rave music and the U.K. rave scene. *Newsgroup*

MUSIC—ALTERNATIVE

797 `alt.fan.laurie.anderson` Will it be a music concert or a lecture this time? *Newsgroup*

798 `alt.music.alternative` For groups having two or less platinum-selling albums. *Newsgroup*

799 `alt.music.alternative.female` Discussing alternative music by female artists. *Newsgroup*

800 `alt.music.mazzy-star` Discussions of the Band Mazzy Star. *Newsgroup*

801 `alt.music.ween` Marble Tulip Juicy Tree. *Newsgroup*

MUSIC—BLUES

802 `bit.listserv.blues-l` Blues music list. *Moderated newsgroup*

803 `rec.music.bluenote.blues` The blues in all forms and all aspects. *Newsgroup*

804 `uk.music.rhythm-n-blues` U.K. newsgroup for discussing rhythm-and-blues music. *Newsgroup*

MUSIC—CLASSICAL

805 **Classical Net:** A wide array of informational files about all types of classical music, as well as pointers to other classical-music Web sites, mailing lists, and newsgroups. Includes a basic repertoire list, recommended CDs, information on classical CD buying, composer biographies, CD reviews, and articles on related topics. The site is fully searchable using keywords, and includes a master index to on-site information on over 255 composers.

   `http://www.classical.net/music/`

   INFO `lampson@wco.com`

806 `alt.fan.shostakovich` Fans of the music of Shostakovich. *Newsgroup*

807 `alt.music.philip-glass` The American composer Philip Glass. *Newsgroup*

808 **Austin Symphony Home Page:** The Austin Symphony Orchestra's Web site posts all recent press releases and the season schedule.

   `http://www.quadralay.com/Austin/FineArts/Symphony/symphony.html`

   INFO `greening@quadralay.com`

809 **Classical Music Online®:** Classical Music Online® is an online resource dedicated exclusively to classical music. Weekly updates, current news, live discussions, emerging new classical artists, and links to the top ten classical-music sites on the Web.

   `http://www.onworld.com/`

   INFO `jeff@onworld.com`

810 **CLASSM-L:** On classical music. *Mailing List*

   ± `listserv@brownvm.brown.edu` [body = SUBSCRIBE CLASSM-L first-name last-name]

   INFO OWNER `catherine_yang@brown.edu` (Catherine Yang)

   ARCHIVE `listserv@brownvm.brown.edu` [body = INDEX CLASSM-L]

811 **FINLANDIA:** On Finnish classical music: composers, performances, recordings. *Mailing List*

   ± `majordomo@lists.oulu.fi`

   OWNER `finlandia-owner@phoenix.oulu.fi` (Marko Hotti)

812 `fj.rec.music.classical` Talk about classical music. *Newsgroup*

813 **Gustav Mahler web page:** Biography, works list, timeline, and pointers to other Mahler-related resources on the net. Also contains archive of posts to mahler-list, the Mahler mail list.

   `http://www.netaxs.com/~jgreshes/mahler`

   INFO `jgreshes@netaxs.com`

814 **Maestronet:** This site sports a database providing listings of stringed instruments and bows for sale from dealers around the world. It also has a searchable database of string instrument price histories and a worldwide listing of stolen instruments. Its Conservatory division includes downloadable sheet music and MIDI files.

http://www.maestronet.com/

INFO admin@maestronet.com

815 **mahler-list:** For discussion of Gustav Mahler, his life, works, and recordings of his works. *Mailing List*

http://www.netaxs.com/~jgreshes/mahler

± majordomo@eskimo.com [body = SUBSCRIBE MAHLER-LIST]

INFO OWNER jgreshes@netaxs.com

ARCHIVE http://www.netaxs.com/~jgreshes/mahler

816 **Midsummer Mozart Festival:** The Midsummer Mozart Festival gives concerts of the works of Wolfgang Amadeus Mozart and his contemporaries. These concerts take place in the San Francisco Bay Area in the summer. A 41-piece orchestra is conducted by maestro George Cleve.

http://www.webcom.com/mozart/

INFO wwrider@cats.ucsc.edu

817 `rec.music.classical` Discussion about classical music. *Newsgroup*

818 `rec.music.classical.guitar` Classical music performed on guitar. *Newsgroup*

819 `rec.music.classical.performing` Performing classical (including early) music. *Newsgroup*

820 `rec.music.classical.recordings` Classical music on CD, vinyl, cassette, etc. *Newsgroup*

821 `rec.music.early` Discussion of pre-classical European music. *Newsgroup*

822 **TML-L:** A full-text database of Latin music theory, including graphics. *Mailing List*

± listserv@iubvm.ucs.indiana.edu [body = SUBSCRIBE TML-L first-name last-name]

INFO mathiese@iubvm.ucs.indiana.edu

ARCHIVES

listserv@iubvm.ucs.indiana.edu

gopher://iubvm.ucs.indiana.edu/11/TML

Language: Latin

MUSIC—COMPOSITION

823 **Composer's Pages on the Web:** A collection of links to Web pages of composers.

http://molbiol2.anu.edu.au/DixonGroup/Cameron/Composers.html

INFO cam@rschp1.anu.edu.au (Cameron Neylon)

Comments: This collection is irregularly posted to `rec.music.compose`

824 **Contemporary Music Info-Junction:** All sorts of information for the contemporary composer and music theorist. Covers composition and theory, orchestration and media, reviews, discussions, and information on particular composers, and much more. Also includes a Music Meta-Index, a list of other music-related sites on the Web.

http://www.thoughtport.com/CMIJ/

INFO cmij@thoughtport.com

825 `alt.music.complex-arrang` Too complex for *your* simple mind. *Newsgroup*

826 `comp.music.research` The use of computers in music research and composition. *Moderated newsgroup*

827 `rec.music.compose` Creating musical and lyrical works. *Newsgroup*

828 `rec.music.makers.songwriting` All about songwriting. *Newsgroup*

829 **SCION/SCI Online News:** Information for members of the Society of Composers, an organization for composers of contemporary classical music: calls for scores and tapes, competitions, festivals, conferences, recordings, funding, employment, and publications. *Newsletter*

± sci@vaxa.weeg.uiowa.edu [body = *for members in good standing:* request to be added to the distribution list first-name last-name e-mail-address postal-address *for all others:* request a sample copy of SCION]

INFO EDITOR `weidenaa@pilot.njin.net` (Reynold Weidenaar, Editor)

INFO `sci@vaxa.weeg.uiowa.edu`

Frequency: monthly

MUSIC—COUNTRY WESTERN & BLUEGRASS

830   **Wayne's Country Music Page:** A wealth of resource pointers for country music and the country life.
      `http://www.tpoint.net/~wallen/country/country.html`
      INFO `wallen@tpoint.net`

831   **BGRASS-L:** For discussion of bluegrass music and old-time music. *Mailing List*
      ± `listserv@ukcc.uky.edu` [body = SUBSCRIBE BGRASS-L first-name last-name]
      INFO OWNER `uka016@ukcc.uky.edu` (Frank Godbey)
      ARCHIVE `listserv@ukcc.uky.edu`
      POST `bgrass-l@ukcc.uky.edu`
      Gated: `bit.listserv.bgrass-l`

832   `bit.listserv.bgrass-l` Bluegrass music list. *Moderated newsgroup*

833   **chelyfan:** For topics related to Chely Wright and her music. *Mailing List, moderated*
      ± `majordomo@grendel.mo.net`
      OWNER `bill@grendel.mo.net` (Bill Bowman)

834   **country-music:** On country music and artists. *Digest & Reflector*
      ± `country-music-request@world.std.com` [body = subscribe]
      OWNER `jhodgson@ultranet.com` (Jeff Hodgson)

835   **Cybergrass:** On bluegrass music. *Magazine*
      INFO `cherry@banjo.com`
      EDITOR `http://www.banjo.com/bc_intro.html`
      ARCHIVES
      `http://www.banjo.com/BG/`
      `ftp://ftp.info.net/pub/BG/`
      Frequency: usually daily

836   **Kathy:** For fans of country music singer Kathy Mattea. *Mailing List, moderated*
      ± **OWNER** `michaelb@ksgrsch.harvard.edu` (Michael Blackmore)
      OWNER `michael_blackmore@harvard.edu`

837   **kathys-clowns:** For fans of country-music singer Kathy Mattea. *Digest & Reflector, moderated*
      ± `majordomo@world.std.com` [body = subscribe kathys-clowns or kathys-clowns-digest]
      OWNER `michaelb@ksgrsch.harvard.edu` (Michael Blackmore)
      OWNER `michael_blackmore@harvard.edu`

838   `rec.music.country.old-time` Southern fiddle/banjo music and beyond. *Newsgroup*

839   `rec.music.country.western` C & W music, performers, performances, etc. *Newsgroup*

840   **Starr Lyn:** All about the recent addition to the Southeast Texas Circuit of country singers.
      `http://www.sat.net/~block/dnl.htm`
      `http://www.sat.net/~block/dnl1.htm`
      INFO `starr@sat.net`

MUSIC—EDUCATION

841   `alt.music.band-director` Band directors' forum. *Newsgroup*

842   **Association for Technology in Music Instruction:** For discussions of the use of technology in music instruction. *Mailing List, moderated*
± `atmi-request@list.uiowa.edu` [body = `subscribe`]
INFO EDITOR OWNER `paul-soderdahl@uiowa.edu` (Paul Soderdahl)

843   **ASTA-L:** For the American String Teachers Association. *Mailing List*
± `listserv@cmsuvmb.cmsu.edu` [body = `SUBSCRIBE ASTA-L first-name last-name`]
OWNER `mb0458@cmsuvmb.cmsu.edu` (Michael Bersin)

844   `can.schoolnet.arts.music`   Music studies in elementary/secondary schools. *Newsgroup*

845   **MUSPRF-L:** On music performance and pedagogy. *Mailing List*
± `listserv@cmsuvmb.cmsu.edu` [body = `SUBSCRIBE MUSPRF-L first-name last-name`]
OWNER `mb0458@cmsuvmb.cmsu.edu` (Michael Bersin)
OWNER `mcadams@cmsuvmb.cmsu.edu` (Charles McAdams)

846   **PIANO-L:** For pianists and piano teachers, including literature, techniques, performance. *Mailing List*
± `piano-l-request@uamont.edu`
OWNER `becker@uamont.edu` (Paul Becker)
OWNER `beeson@uamont.edu` (Patrick Beeson)

847   **SINFONIA:** For members of Phi Mu Alpha Sinfonia, a music fraternity. *Digest & Reflector*
± `listserv@asuvm.inre.asu.edu` [body = `SUBSCRIBE SINFONIA first-name last-name`]
INFO `robert.d.reynolds@asu.edu`

MUSIC—EXPERIMENTAL & ELECTRONIC

848   `alt.binaries.sounds.midi`   MIDI binaries. *Newsgroup*

849   `alt.binaries.sounds.mods`   MODs and related sound formats. *Newsgroup*

850   `alt.emusic`   Ethnic, exotic, electronic, elaborate, etc. music. *Newsgroup*

851   `alt.music.bela-fleck`   Bela and the Flecktones. *Newsgroup*

852   `alt.music.ebm`   Electronic (or not?) body music. *Newsgroup*

853   `alt.music.ecto`   Happy Rhodes and other music by plasms. *Newsgroup*

854   `alt.music.makers.electronic`   The art of creating techno, ambient, etc. *Newsgroup*

855   `alt.music.makers.theremin`   Lothar and the Hand People played one. *Newsgroup*

856   `alt.music.midi`   Music from MIDI devices. *Newsgroup*

857   `alt.music.orb`   For fans of the ambient techno music group the Orb. *Newsgroup*

858   `bit.listserv.emusic-l`   Electronic-music discussion list. *Newsgroup*

859   **Chaos Control:** A guide to electronic and experimental music, featuring interviews with both major-label and underground artists. *E-Journal*
`http://www.ids.net/~chaos/`
`ftp://obi.std.com/obi/zines/chaos.control`
± `majordomo@world.std.com` [body = `subscribe chaoscontrol`]
INFO `rsgour@aol.com` (Bob Gourley)
ARCHIVE `ftp://obi.std.com/obi/zines/chaos.control`
Frequency: Hypercard: bimonthly. ASCII: irregular

860   **emdreams:** On the progressive electronic music of artists/groups such as Tangerine Dream, Jean-Michel Jarre, Klaus Schulze, and Vangelis. *Digest & Reflector*
± INFO `elana@netcom.com` (Elana Mell Beach)
ARCHIVE `ftp://ftp.uwp.edu`
Comments: To join this list, you must first become a paid member of Electronic Dreams—e-mail owner for more

information.

861 `fj.comp.music` Topics about computers and music. *Newsgroup*

➤ `rec.music.makers.synth:` Synthesizers and computer music. *Newsgroup*

MUSIC—FOLK

862 `alt.fan.john-denver` Please, take him home to the place where he belongs. *Newsgroup*

863 `alt.fan.liz-phair` Liz Phair, one non-blonde, sorta. *Newsgroup*

864 `alt.music.filk` Sf/fantasy-related folk music. *Newsgroup*

865 `alt.music.guthrie` Discussion of folksingers Arlo and Woody Guthrie. *Newsgroup*

866 `alt.music.harry-chapin` Taxi! *Newsgroup*

867 `alt.music.leonard-cohen` The music of Leonard Cohen. *Newsgroup*

868 `alt.music.lightfoot` Discussion about the music of Gordon Lightfoot. *Newsgroup*

869 `alt.music.lor-mckennitt` Discussion of Loreena McKennit. *Newsgroup*

870 **Digital Tradition Folk Song Server:** A data base containing the words and music to thousands of folk songs.
`http://pubweb.parc.xerox.com/docs/DigiTrad/AboutDigiTrad.html`
INFO `putz@parc.xerox.com`

➤ **Folk Dancing:** On folk dancing: international, contra, square, cajun, barn, and more. The Folk Dancing mailing list is for those who do not have access to Usenet and the `rec.folk-dancing` newsgroup. (See entry 285 for full listing.)

871 **Folk Music:** On new American folk music. *Mailing List, moderated*
`ftp://ftp.nysernet.org/listserv/folk_music/`
`http://www.cgrg.ohio-state.edu/folkbook/`
± `listserv@nysernet.org` [body = SUBSCRIBE folk_music e-mail-address]
± `ftp://ftp.nysernet.org/listserv/folk_music/faq/fm.html`
INFO `alanr@nysernet.org` (Alan Rowoth)
ARCHIVE `http://www.hidwater.com/fmd/`
FAQS
`listserv@nysernet.org` [body = INFO FOLK_MUSIC]
`ftp://ftp.nysernet.org/listserv/folk_music/faq/fm.faq.pt1`

872 **folkdj-l:** For folk/bluegrass/Celtic DJs. *Mailing List*
± `listserv@psuvm.psu.edu` [body = SUBSCRIBE FOLKDJ-L first-name last-name]
OWNER `tmh1@psuvm.psu.edu` (Tina Hay)

873 **folkvenu:** For folk-music presenters. *Mailing List*
± `listserv@psuvm.psu.edu` [body = SUBSCRIBE FOLKVENU first-name last-name affiliation]
OWNER `s.jerrett1@genie.geis.com`
(Steve Jerrett)

➤ `alt.music.indigo-girls:` The musical duo Indigo Girls. *Newsgroup*

874 **IRTRAD-L:** On Irish traditional music. *Digest & Reflector*
± `listserv@irlearn.ucd.ie` [body = SUBSCRIBE IRTRAD-L first-name last-name]
INFO `irtrad-l-request@irlearn.ucd.ie`
ARCHIVE `listserv@irlearn.ucd.ie` [body = INDEX IRTRAD-L]

875 `rec.music.celtic` Traditional and modern music with a Celtic flavor. *Newsgroup*

876 `rec.music.folk` Folks discussing folk music of various sorts. *Newsgroup*

➤ **RootsWorld:** A magazine of world music, folk, and jazz, RootsWorld focuses on the lesser-known traditions and the uncommon ground in the world's music. (See entry 1205 for full listing.)

877 **stormcock:** For discussion and news on the music of folk rocker Roy Harper. *Mailing List*
± majordomo@bilpin.co.uk [body = SUBSCRIBE STORMCOCK e-mail-address]
OWNER pd@bilpin.co.uk (Paul Davison)
ARCHIVE http://www.bilpin.co.uk/stormcock

878 **Timothy O'Connor (aka Kerouac):** The author/folksinger's Web page.
http://www.nashville.com/"timothy.o'connor"/moogoo.html
INFO timothy.o'connor@nashville.com

879 **WATERFALL:** On singer/songwriter Linda Waterfall. *Mailing List*
± majordomo@world.std.com [body = subscribe waterfall]
OWNER tneff@panix.com (Tom Neff)
ARCHIVE http://www.panix.com/~tneff/linda/

MUSIC—INSTRUMENTS

880 **alt.banjo** Someone's in the kitchen with Dinah. *Newsgroup*

881 **alt.banjo.clawhammer** Technique and tricks from the masters of banjo. *Newsgroup*

882 **alt.guitar** You axed for it, you got it. *Newsgroup*

883 **alt.guitar.amps** Discussion of guitar amplifiers. *Newsgroup*

884 **alt.guitar.bass** Bass guitars. *Newsgroup*

885 **alt.guitar.lap-pedal** Pedal steel guitar discussion group. *Newsgroup*

886 **alt.guitar.tab** Discussions about guitar tablature music. *Newsgroup*

887 **alt.music.harmonica** Lip music. *Newsgroup*

888 **alt.music.makers.woodwind** People who play woodwind instruments. *Newsgroup*

889 **alt.music.saxophone** Making the music and/or listening to it. *Newsgroup*

890 **alt.music.synth.roland.u20** The Roland U20 synthesizer. *Newsgroup*

891 **bagpipe:** Reflection of rec.music.makers.bagpipe: on bagpipes—all styles of instrument and music. *Daily Digest*
± INFO bagpipe-request@cs.dartmouth.edu
Gated: rec.music.makers.bagpipe

892 **bass-digest:** The Bottom Line: bass players' digest. *Mailing List*
± majordomo@magpie.com [body = subscribe bass-digest]
INFO majordomo@magpie.com [body = subscribe bass-digest]
OWNER bassmgr@uwplatt.edu

893 **brass:** About brass musical performance and related topics, especially small musical ensembles of all kinds. *Mailing List*
± brass-request@gly.fsu.edu (Ted Zateslo)

894 **CIMCIM-L:** On musical-instrument museums: curation, conservation, research. *Mailing List, moderated*
http://www.icom.nrm.se/ICOM/CIMCIM/
± listserv@nrm.se [body = SUBSCRIBE CIMCIM-L first-name last-name]
OWNER cimcim-l-request@nrm.se

895 **Doublereed-l:** On bassoons, oboes, and all other double reed instruments. *Mailing List*
± listserv@acc.wuacc.edu
OWNER zzboyr@acc.wuacc.edu (Rodney Boyd)
ARCHIVE http://www.wuacc.edu/acc/doublereed-L/

896 **FLUTE-M:** On flutes and flute playing. *Mailing List*
± majordomo@unixg.ubc.ca

OWNER camcastl@unixg.ubc.ca (Cara Camcastle)

897 **HPSCHD-L:** On early stringed keyboard instruments: harpsichords, clavichords, fortepianos . *Mailing List*
± listserv@albany.edu [body = SUBSCRIBE HPSCHD-L first-name last-name]
OWNER dkelzenb@blue.weeg.uiowa.edu (Dave Kelzenberg)
OWNER bec@albany.edu (Ben Chi)
ARCHIVE listserv@albany.edu [body = INDEX HPSCHD-L]

898 **korg-m1-l:** On Korg's M1, M3, T1-3 series synthesizers. *Mailing List*
± korg-m1-l-request@io.org
OWNER noise@io.org (noise)

899 **lute:** For lute players and researchers of lute music. *Mailing List*
http://www.cs.dartmouth.edu/~wbc/lute.html
± INFO lute-request@cs.dartmouth.edu (Wayne B. Cripps)
ARCHIVE ftp://ftp.cs.dartmouth.edu/pub/lute

➤ **PIANO-L:** For pianists and piano teachers, including literature, techniques, performance. (See entry 846 for full listing.)

900 **PIPORG-L:** On pipe organs and related topics. *Mailing List*
http://albany.edu/~piporg-l/
± listserv@albany.edu [body = SUBSCRIBE PIPORG-L first-name last-name]
INFO dkelzenb@blue.weeg.uiowa.edu (Dave Kelzenberg)
INFO bec@albany.edu (Ben Chi)
ARCHIVE http://albany.edu/~piporg-l/htbin/match?piporg-l.log*/1995_PIPORG-L_Archives
FAQ http://albany.edu/~piporg-l/pipguide.html

901 rec.music.makers For performers and their discussions. *Newsgroup*

902 rec.music.makers.bagpipe Music and playing of all types of bagpipes. *Newsgroup*

903 rec.music.makers.bands For musicians who play in groups with others. *Newsgroup*

904 rec.music.makers.bass Upright bass and bass guitar techniques and equipment. *Newsgroup*

905 rec.music.makers.bowed-strings Violin family (current and old) performance. *Newsgroup*

906 rec.music.makers.builders Design, building, repair of musical instruments. *Newsgroup*

907 rec.music.makers.dulcimer Dulcimers and related instruments. *Newsgroup*

908 rec.music.makers.french-horn About horn players and playing. *Newsgroup*

909 rec.music.makers.guitar Electric and acoustic guitar techniques and equipment. *Newsgroup*

910 rec.music.makers.guitar.acoustic Discussion of acoustic guitar playing. *Newsgroup*

911 rec.music.makers.guitar.tablature Guitar tablature/chords. *Newsgroup*

912 rec.music.makers.marketplace Buying and selling used music-making equipment. *Newsgroup*

913 rec.music.makers.percussion Drum and other percussion techniques and equipment. *Newsgroup*

914 rec.music.makers.piano Piano music, performing, composing, learning, styles. *Newsgroup*

915 rec.music.makers.squeezebox Accordions, concertinas, and related free reeds. *Newsgroup*

916 rec.music.makers.synth Synthesizers and computer music. *Newsgroup*

917 rec.music.makers.trumpet The exchange of trumpet-related information. *Newsgroup*

918 tnn.music.early.lute Topics and information about lute. *Moderated newsgroup*

919 **VOCALIST:** Discussion on singing: technique, voice care, performance, recording. *Digest & Reflector*
± majordomo@lists.oulu.fi
INFO http://phoenix.oulu.fi/~mhotti/vocalist/

OWNER mhotti@paju.oulu.fi (Marko Hotti)

ARCHIVE http://phoenix.oulu.fi/~mhotti/vocalist/

MUSIC—JAZZ

920 **alt.music.pat-metheny** Free discussion of Pat Metheny and his group. *Newsgroup*

921 **dixielandjazz:** On Dixieland jazz. *Mailing List*
± dixielandjazz-request@islandnet.com [subject = subscribe]
INFO http://islandnet.com/~peter
OWNER peter@islandnet.com (Peter Lovric)

922 **Jazz-L:** For lovers of jazz music. *Mailing List*
± listserv@brownvm.brown.edu [body = SUBSCRIBE JAZZ-L first-name last-name]
OWNER jazz-l-request@brownvm.brown.edu
Comments: Please, no commercial notices without talking to the listowner first!

923 **MILES:** For discussing jazz trumpeter Miles Davis. *Mailing List*
± listserv@hearn.nic.surfnet.nl [body = SUBSCRIBE MILES first-name last-name]
INFO miles-request@hearn.bitnet
OWNER gmeltzer@gordon.isdn.net (Gordon Meltzer)
ARCHIVE listserv@hearn.nic.surfnet.nl [body = INDEX MILES]

924 **MUSICA:** Advanced music discussion from Pantheon, a leading Italian recording studio. *Mailing List, moderated*
± majordomo@pantheon.it [body = SUBSCRIBE MUSICA]
INFO staff@pantheon.it
OWNER dario@pantheon.it (Dario Centofanti)
Language: Italian and/or English

925 **rec.music.bluenote** Discussion of jazz, blues, and related types of music. *Newsgroup*

➤ **RootsWorld:** A magazine of world music, folk, and jazz, RootsWorld focuses on the lesser-known traditions and the uncommon ground in the world's music. (See entry 1205 for full listing.)

926 **SATURN:** On jazz composer and musician Sun Ra and his Arkestra. *Mailing List*
± listserv@hearn.nic.surfnet.nl [body = SUBSCRIBE SATURN first-name last-name]
INFO saturn-request@hearn.bitnet
ARCHIVE listserv@hearn.nic.surfnet.nl

927 **tnn.music.jazz-fusion** Jazz and fusion music and instruments. *Newsgroup*

MUSIC—MUSICAL THEATER

928 **alt.fan.mandy-patinkin** For fans of actor Mandy Patinkin ("My name is Inigo Montoya..."). *Newsgroup*

929 **alt.music.lloyd-webber** Life and music of Andrew Lloyd Webber. *Newsgroup*

930 **alt.music.sondheim** Life and music of Stephen Sondheim. *Newsgroup*

➤ **COLLAB-L:** On collaboration among playwrights, directors, techies, composers, and librettists. (See entry 1618 for full listing.)

931 **musicals:** Forum for general discussions on musical theater. *Mailing List*
ftp://ftp.std.com/archives/RAT-archive/
± musicals-request@world.std.com
INFO OWNER owner-musicals@world.std.com
Gated: rec.arts.theatre.musicals

932 **rec.arts.theatre.musicals** Musical theater around the world. *Newsgroup*

➤ **SavoyNet:** On Gilbert and Sullivan and their operettas. (See entry 939 for full listing.)

MUSIC—NEW AGE

933 `alt.music.j-s-bach` Discussions about J. S. Bach (1685-1750). *Newsgroup*

934 **direct:** On the musical artist Vangelis. *Digest & Reflector*
± **INFO** `direct-request@celtech.com`
ARCHIVE `ftp://ftp.uwp.edu/pub/music/lists/direct`

935 `rec.music.ambient` Ambient music and artists. *Newsgroup*

936 `rec.music.newage` New Age music discussions. *Newsgroup*

MUSIC—OPERA

937 **OPERA-L:** Discussion of opera and related topics. *digest & reflector*
± `listserv@cunyvm.cuny.edu` [body = sub `opera-l` first-name last-name]
OWNER `rjkgc@cunyvm.cuny.edu` (Bob Kosovsky)

938 `rec.music.opera` All aspects of opera. *Newsgroup*

939 **SavoyNet:** On Gilbert and Sullivan and their operettas. *Mailing List*
± `listserv@bridgewater.edu` [body = subscribe `savoynet` first-name last-name]
INFO `rmacphai@bridgewater.edu` (Ralph MacPhail, Jr.)

MUSIC—POPULAR

940 `alt.fan.barry-manilow` Discussion group for fans of Barry Manilow. *Newsgroup*

941 `alt.fan.debbie.gibson` Thwarter of the supervillain Tiffany. *Newsgroup*

942 `alt.fan.jimmy-buffett` A white sports coat and a pink crustacean. *Newsgroup*

943 `alt.fan.madonna` Nice tits, eh . . . and how about that puppy? *Newsgroup*

944 `alt.fan.michael-bolton` Fear for his bad hair days. *Newsgroup*

945 `alt.fan.samantha-fox` For fans of the famous page 3 girl/pop singer. *Newsgroup*

946 `alt.fan.tlc` Discussion of TLC rap/hip-hop group. *Newsgroup*

947 `alt.music.abba` Swedish pop. *Newsgroup*

948 `alt.music.amy-grant` Discussion about Amy Grant and her music. *Newsgroup*

949 `alt.music.bee-gees` The soulful stylings of the Brothers Gibb. *Newsgroup*

950 `alt.music.big-band` Sounds from the Big Band era. *Newsgroup*

951 `alt.music.billy-joel` Discussion of Billy Brinkley, er, Joel. *Newsgroup*

952 `alt.music.boyz-2-men` The harmonizing tunes of Boyz II Men. *Newsgroup*

953 `alt.music.enya` Gaelic set to spacey music. *Newsgroup*

954 `alt.music.erasure` Erasure's fan following. *Newsgroup*

955 `alt.music.kylie-minogue` Music of Kylie Minogue. *Newsgroup*

956 `alt.music.mariah.carey` Able to break glasses with a single boundless high note. *Newsgroup*

957 `alt.music.michael-jackson` The enigmatic Michael Jackson. *Newsgroup*

958 `alt.music.pet-shop-boys` The music of the Pet Shop Boys. *Newsgroup*

959 `alt.music.polkas` Weird Al or not, polka is popular to some folks. *Newsgroup*

960 `alt.music.s-mclachlan` A Touch of Solace in Ecstasy. *Newsgroup*

961 `alt.music.soul` Discussion of sweet soul music. *Newsgroup*

962 `alt.music.swedish-pop` ABBA and beyond. *Newsgroup*

963 `alt.music.synthpop` Depeche Mode, Erasure, Pet Shop Boys, and much more! *Newsgroup*

➤   `alt.music.weird-al:`   Parodies 'R' us. *Newsgroup*

964   **Bobs:** The Bobs, an alternative a cappella quartet from the San Francisco Bay Area. "The Bobs sing like (Gary) Larson draws."—*The Seattle Daily Times Mailing List*
`http://www.bobs.com//`
INFO `info@bobs.com`

965   **Mariah Carey:** On Mariah's music and musical projects, and to share information about concerts and paraphernalia. *Mailing List*
`http://biodec.wustl.edu/audio/mariah.html`
INFO `vision-dude@biodec.wustl.edu`
ARCHIVE `http://biodec.wustl.edu/0h/audio/mariah_carey/mail`

966   `rec.music.artists.danny-elfman`   Composer Danny Elfman's music. *Newsgroup*

967   `rec.music.artists.debbie-gibson`   The music of Deborah Gibson. *Newsgroup*

968   **Sinatra:** For fans of the music of Frank Sinatra: recordings, composers, lyrics, movies. *Mailing List*
± `listserv@vm.temple.edu` [body = `SUBSCRIBE SINATRA` first-name last-name]
OWNER `v2153a@vm.temple.edu` (Eleanor M. Cicinsky)

MUSIC—ROCK & HIP-HOP

969   **Addicted to Noise:** Sound/opinion/image/art/text/news/video/reviews/chaos information about rock and roll. *E-Zine*
`http://www.addict.com/ATN/`
INFO `atn-support@addict.com`
ARCHIVE `http://www.addict.com/ATN/`
Frequency: monthly, plus daily updated rock news section, "Music News of the World."

970   `alt.music.black-metal`   Iron instruments. *Newsgroup*

971   `alt.music.hardcore`   Could be porno set to music. *Newsgroup*

972   `alt.music.modern-rock`   Discussion of current rock and pop music. *Newsgroup*

973   `alt.music.progressive`   Yes, Marillion, Asia, King Crimson, etc. *Newsgroup*

974   `alt.music.psychedelic`   All types of psychedelic music. *Newsgroup*

975   `alt.music.rockabilly`   Rockabilly. *Newsgroup*

976   `alt.punk`   Punk rock and its surrounding culture. *Newsgroup*

977   `alt.punk.europe`   The punk rock scene in Europe. *Newsgroup*

978   `alt.punk.straight-edge`   Not shaving eyebrows, but the sXe movement. *Newsgroup*

979   `alt.rap.lyrics`   Rap music lyrics. *Newsgroup*

980   `alt.rap.sucks`   The anti-rap crowd sounds off. *Newsgroup*

981   `alt.rock-n-roll`   Counterpart to `alt.sex` and `alt.drugs`. *Newsgroup*

982   `alt.rock-n-roll.classic`   Classic rock, both the music and its marketing. *Newsgroup*

983   `alt.rock-n-roll.hard`   Music where stance is everything. *Newsgroup*

984   `alt.rock-n-roll.metal`   For the head-bangers on the net. *Newsgroup*

985   `alt.rock-n-roll.metal.death`   "death metal" and new-group overkill. *Newsgroup*

986   `alt.rock-n-roll.metal.gnr`   "Axl Rose" is an anagram for "oral sex". *Newsgroup*

987   `alt.rock-n-roll.metal.heavy`   Non-sissy-boy metal bands. *Newsgroup*

988   `alt.rock-n-roll.metal.progressive`   Slayer teams up with Tom Cora. *Newsgroup*

989   `alt.rock-n-roll.oldies`   Discussion of rock and roll music from 1950 to 1970. *Newsgroup*

990   **Chronicles of Chaos:** On all forms of death/thrash/black metal and other forms of brutal music. *E-Zine*

± `listproc@lists.colorado.edu` [body = SUBSCRIBE `coc-ezine` first-name last-name]

INFO `ginof@io.org` (Gino Filicetti)

ARCHIVE `http://www.io.org/~ginof/coc.html`

Frequency: monthly

991   **European Top 20 Charts:** Distribution of the MTV European Top 20 charts. *Distribution List*

± `euro20-request@gnu.ai.mit.edu`

INFO `a3@a3.xs4all.nl` (Adri Verhoef)

INFO `rnovak@indyramp.com` (Robert Novak)

Gated: `rec.music.info`

992   `fj.rec.music.progressive` Talk about progressive rock. *Newsgroup*

993   **GRUNGE-L:** On grunge rock. *Mailing List*

`http://www.mcs.net/~phredd/grunge.html`

± `listserv@ubvm.cc.buffalo.edu` [body = SUBSCRIBE `GRUNGE-L` first-name last-name]

INFO `phredd@mcs.net` (Blaine Thompson)

994   `han.rec.artrock` Lovers of art-rock music. *Newsgroup*

995   **HardC.O.R.E.:** The electronic magazine of hip-hop music and culture, brought to you as a service of the Committee of Rap Excellence. *Newsletter*

`gopher://gopher.etext.org/Zines/HardCORE`

`http://www.public.iastate.edu/~krs_one`

± `hardcore-l@vnet.net` [body = subscribe `hardcore-l` e-mail-address]

INFO `davidj@vnet.net` (David J. Warner, Director of Network Distribution)

INFO `krs_one@iastate.edu` (Steve Juon, Chief Editor and Publisher)

EDITOR `rapotter@colby.edu` (Russell A. Potter, Managing Editor)

ARCHIVE `ftp://ftp.etext.org/pub/Zines/HardCORE`

Gated: `rec.music.hip-hop`

Frequency: bimonthly

996   **INDIE-BRASIL:** From Brazil, a list on indie pop rock culture. *Mailing List*

`http://www.dcc.ufba.br/~deus`

± `listproc@ufba.br` [body = SUBSCRIBE `INDIE-BRASIL` first-name last-name]

OWNER `messias@ufba.br` (Messias Guimaraes Bandeir)

997   `rec.music.hip-hop` Hip-hop music and culture in general. *Newsgroup*

998   `rec.music.industrial` Discussion of all industrial-related music styles. *Newsgroup*

999   `rec.music.progressive` Symphonic rock, art rock, fusion, Canterbury, RIO, etc. *Newsgroup*

1000   `rec.music.video` Discussion of music videos and music-video software. *Newsgroup*

1001   **WESTCANALTER:** On alternative music in Western Canadian: grunge and such. *Mailing List*

± `listserv@age.cuc.ab.ca`

OWNER `kpierce@age.cuc.ab.ca` (Ken Pierce)

MUSIC—ROCK & HIP-HOP—BANDS & PERFORMERS

1002   `alt.rock-n-roll.acdc` Dirty deeds done dirt cheap. *Newsgroup*

1003   `alt.rock-n-roll.aerosmith` Lead singer looks like an ugly lady. *Newsgroup*

1004   **SickThings:** On the rock group Alice Cooper. *Mailing List*

INFO `mxserver@wkuvx1.wku.edu` (Hunter Goatley)

INFO `goathunter@loki.com` (Hunter Goatley)

OWNER goathunter@wkuvx1.wku.edu (Hunter Goatley)

1005 **alt.music.aliceinchains** One of Seattle's finest. *Newsgroup*

1006 **allman:** On the Allman Brothers, players of rock, blues, jazz, and southern rock. *Mailing List*
± INFO allman-request@world.std.com
± INFO allman-request@netspace.org
OWNER http://www.netspace.org/users/budke
ARCHIVE http://www.netspace.org/allmans

1007 **alt.fan.allman-brothers** Fans of the Allman Brothers' music. *Newsgroup*

1008 **alt.music.america** Discussion of the pop-rock group America. *Newsgroup*

1009 **rec.music.tori-amos** Discussion of the female singer/songwriter Tori Amos. *Newsgroup*

1010 **alt.music.live.the.band** Talk about the Band. *Newsgroup*

1011 **alt.music.the-band** The music and fans of the Band. *Newsgroup*

1012 **alt.music.barenaked-ladies** Kraft Dinner at its finest. *Newsgroup*

1013 **rec.music.artists.beach-boys** The Beach Boys' music and the effect they've had. *Newsgroup*

1014 **alt.music.beastie-boys** The Beastie Boys. *Newsgroup*

1015 **Beatles, Beatles, Beatles!:** For the Beatles fan. Many links to the Beatles here!
http://www.sonic.net/~custom/beat.html
INFO custom@sonic.net

1016 **rec.music.beatles** Postings about the Fab Four and their music. *Newsgroup*

1017 **Bel Canto:** On all aspects of the pop group Bel Canto. *Mailing List*
± INFO dewy-fields-request@ifi.uio.no
ARCHIVES
ftp://ftp.ifi.uio.no/pub/bel-canto
http://www.math.uio.no/music/bel-canto/
FAQ http://www.math.uio.no/music/bel-canto/

1018 **alt.music.bjork** For fans of Bjork and the late Sugarcubes. *Newsgroup*

1019 **alt.music.black-sabbath** The band Black Sabbath and their music. *Newsgroup*

1020 **alt.music.blues-traveler** For "all fellow travelers". *Newsgroup*

1021 **alt.music.blur** Fandom of the uniquely British group Blur. *Newsgroup*

1022 **boc-l:** On the rock bands Blue Oyster Cult and Hawkwind. *Mailing List*
ftp://spcvxa.spc.edu/boc-l/
± INFO boc-request@listserv.spc.edu
ARCHIVE ftp://spcvxa.spc.edu/boc-l/
FAQ ftp://spcvxa.spc.edu/boc-l/boc_faq-2_0.txt

1023 **alt.music.blueoystercult** BOC—Godzilla's gonna get ya. *Newsgroup*

1024 **rec.music.artists.bruce-hornsby** The music of Bruce Hornsby. *Newsgroup*

1025 **BUFFETT:** On Jimmy Buffett: music, concerts, books, and generally the Parrothead lifestyle. *Mailing List*
± listserv@miamiu.acs.muohio.edu [body = SUBSCRIBE BUFFETT first-name last-name]
INFO http://www.io.com/~12vman/buffett/listserv.html
OWNER lackwe@muohio.edu (Bill Lack)
OWNER 12vman@io.com (W. Jarrett Campbell)
FAQ http://www.io.com/~12vman/buffett/jbfaq.html

1026 **Love-Hounds:** On Kate Bush and related musicians. *Mailing List*
± love-hounds-request@uunet.uu.net

INFO wisner@uunet.uu.net (Bill Wisner)

ARCHIVE ftp://ftp.uu.net/usenet/rec.music.gaffa/archives

Gated: rec.music.gaffa

1027 **rec.music.gaffa** Discussion of Kate Bush and other alternative music. *Moderated newsgroup*

1028 **alt.music.butholesurfers** The Butthole Surfers. *Newsgroup*

1029 **alt.music.byrds** The music and fans of the Byrds. *Newsgroup*

1030 **alt.fan.capt-beefheart** Some musician guy I've never heard of. *Newsgroup*

1031 **alt.music.chapel-hill** You might think hymnals and chants, but you'd be wrong. *Newsgroup*

1032 **alt.music.cheap-trick** Discussion of the pop-rock band Cheap Trick. *Newsgroup*

1033 **alt.music.chicago** Discussion of the band Chicago. *Newsgroup*

1034 **alt.music.clash** Anything about the musical group the Clash. *Newsgroup*

1035 **Elvis Costello:** Discussions and news of the music of Declan Patrick Aloysius MacManus, better known as Elvis Costello. Topics about the King (of America) are always welcomed, as are other artists and music. *Mailing List*

http://east.isx.com/~schnitzi/elvis.html

± costello-request@gnu.ai.mit.edu (Danny Hernandez)

INFO djh@en.com

1036 **alt.fan.elvis-costello** Fans of the singer Elvis Costello. *Newsgroup*

1037 **alt.music.counting-crows** In my day, we used to count sheep. *Newsgroup*

1038 **cranberry-saw-us:** On the Irish rock group the cranberries. *Mailing List*

± majordomo@ocf.berkeley.edu [**body** = subscribe cranberry-saw-us e-mail-address]

OWNER cranberry-saw-us-owner@ocf.berkeley.edu

1039 **alt.music.cranberries** The musical group the cranberries. *Newsgroup*

1040 **alt.music.ct-dummies** Discussion of the musical group Crash Test Dummies. *Newsgroup*

1041 **MINESTRONE:** On 10 cc, Godley, and Creme rock groups. *Digest & Reflector*

± **INFO OWNER** capnbizr@interaccess.com (TJ Thurston)

OWNER mikes@pacifier.com (Michael Stroup)

1042 **Crowded House:** On Crowded House, Split Enz rock group and related rock groups (Finn, Schnell Fenster, ALT, etc.). *Digest & Reflector*

http://www.etext.org/Mailing.Lists/house

± listproc@listproc.wsu.edu [**body** = subscribe ch or ch-digest first-name last-name]

INFO marck@nwu.edu (Marck L. Bailey)

INFO ch-adm@listproc.wsu.edu (Crowded House list administrators)

INFO magritte@nwu.edu (Elizabeth Wasserman)

INFO zenyatta@wsu.edu (Tricia Cox)

ARCHIVE ftp://jater.acns.nwu.edu/Pub/crowded-house/ (includes lyrics, chords and tablature of all songs)

1043 **alt.fan.jester** An industrial band named the Cult of Jester. *Newsgroup*

1044 **babble:** For discussion about the band The Cure. *Mailing List*

http://miso.wwa.com/~anaconda/cure2.html

± babble-request@anthrax.ecst.csuchico.edu

INFO owner-babble@anthrax.ecst.csuchico.edu

ARCHIVE ftp://anthrax.ecst.csuchico.edu/babble-m/

1045 **alt.music.thecure** The band the Cure. *Newsgroup*

1046 **alt.music.danzig** Discussion of the works of Glenn Danzig. *Mother!*. *Newsgroup*

1047 `alt.music.dave-matthews` The Dave Matthews Band. *Newsgroup*

1048 `alt.music.dead-kennedys` Art is not bound by the limits of tastefulness. *Newsgroup*

1049 `alt.fan.jello-biafra` The Dead Kennedys' lead singer. *Newsgroup*

1050 `alt.music.deep-purple` Discussions about Deep Purple and related artists. *Newsgroup*

1051 `alt.music.def-leppard` Discussion about the rock group Def Leppard. *Newsgroup*

1052 `alt.fan.depeche-mode` A pop-music group. *Newsgroup*

1053 `alt.music.detox` Getting off a bad habit. *Newsgroup*

1054 `alt.fan.devo` Funny hats do not a band make. *Newsgroup*

1055 `alt.music.dio` For discussion about Ronnie James Dio. *Newsgroup*

1056 **Dokken/Lynch Mob:** Articles, questions, and discussions on the Dokken and Lynch Mob pop music groups. *Mailing List*
  ± INFO `kirsten@mik.uky.edu`
  ± INFO `kirsten@pa.uky.edu`
  ARCHIVE `ftp://einstein.fallon.com/dokken`

1057 `alt.music.the-doors` A rider on the storm no more. *Newsgroup*

1058 `alt.music.dream-theater` Is "progressive metal" an accepted label? *Newsgroup*

1059 **HWY61-L:** On Bob Dylan. *Digest & Reflector*
  ± `listserv@ubvm.cc.buffalo.edu` [body = SUBSCRIBE HWY61-L first-name last-name]
  INFO `hwy61-l-request@ubvm.cc.buffalo.edu`
  OWNER `turning_pt@umbsky.cc.umb.edu` (Maureen LeBlanc)
  ARCHIVE `http://www.netspace.org/cgi-bin/lwgate/hwy61-l`
  Gated: `rec.music.dylan`

1060 `rec.music.dylan` Discussion of Bob's works and music. *Newsgroup*

1061 `alt.music.eagles` Discussion of the band. *Newsgroup*

1062 `alt.music.elo` The Electric Light Orchestra. *Newsgroup*

1063 `alt.elvis.king` Fat and dead, too. Pretty useless king. *Newsgroup*

1064 `alt.fan.elvis-presley` The late, great Elvis the Pelvis. *Newsgroup*

1065 `alt.music.enigma-dcd-etc` Enigma and similar bands. *Newsgroup*

1066 `alt.music.brian-eno` Apparently too popular to warrant further description. *Newsgroup*

1067 `alt.music.faith-no-more` Discussion of the musical group Faith No More. *Newsgroup*

1068 `alt.music.fates-warning` Fates Warning. *Newsgroup*

1069 `alt.music.fleetwood-mac` Rock group Fleetwood Mac and its members. *Newsgroup*

1070 `alt.music.peter-gabriel` So, it's the music of Peter Gabriel, sans frontier. *Newsgroup*

1071 `alt.music.genesis` Genesis, in all their incarnations. *Newsgroup*

1072 `rec.music.gdead` A group for (Grateful) Deadheads. *Newsgroup*

1073 `alt.rap-gdead` Fans of the Grateful Dead and rap. Really. *Newsgroup*

1074 `alt.music.green-day` The band Green Day. *Newsgroup*

1075 `alt.music.gwar` Gwarrrrr! *Newsgroup*

1076 **Deborah Harry/Blondie Information Service:** A mailing list for current information on Deborah Harry and Blondie. *Mailing List, moderated*
  ± INFO `lab@primenet.com` (Louis A. Bustamante)
  ARCHIVE `http://www.primenet.com/~lab/DHDeborahHarry.html`

1077 **alt.music.sophie-hawkins** News and discussions on Sophie B. Hawkins. *Newsgroup*

1078 **hey-joe:** For fans of Jimi Hendrix and his music. *Mailing List*
± INFO `hey-joe-request@ms.uky.edu`
OWNER `hey-joe-owner@ms.uky.edu`
OWNER `abbott@ms.uky.edu`
ARCHIVES
`ftp://ftp.ms.uky.edu/pub/mailing.lists/hey-joe`
`http://www.ms.uky.edu/hey-joe.html`

1079 **alt.music.jimi.hendrix** 'Scuse me while I kiss the sky. *Newsgroup*

1080 **alt.fan.jimi-hendrix** Fans of the late great guitarist Jimi Hendrix. *Newsgroup*

1081 **Dan Hicks:** On Dan Hicks (Hot Licks, Acoustic Warriors), past and present. *Mailing List*
`http://www.ns.net/~chaler/hicks.html`
± INFO `sramirez@sedona.intel.com` (Steve Ramirez)
± `majordomo@sedona.intel.com`

1082 **fegmaniax:** Discussion, news, and whatnot about Robyn Hitchcock and associated bands (Soft Boys, Egyptians, etc.) with tenuous ties to the ex-official Robyn Hitchcock ex-fan club Fegmaniax. *Mailing List*
`http://remus.rutgers.edu/~woj/fegmaniax/`
± `majordomo@nsmx.rutgers.edu` [body = subscribe `fegmaniax`]
INFO OWNER `woj@remus.rutgers.edu`
INFO OWNER `owner-fegmaniax@nsmx.rutgers.edu`
ARCHIVE `http://archive.uwp.edu/pub/music/lists/fegmaniax/`

1083 **alt.music.iggy-pop** Discussing Iggy Pop, his life and work. *Newsgroup*

1084 **alt.music.indigo-girls** The musical duo Indigo Girls. *Newsgroup*

1085 **alt.music.inxs** Get it? "In Excess." In the words of Nelson, "Ha ha". *Newsgroup*

1086 **alt.rock-n-roll.metal.ironmaiden** Sonic torture methods. *Newsgroup*

1087 **Joe-Jackson:** On the music of Joe Jackson. *Mailing List*
± `majordomo@primenet.com` [body = subscribe `joe-jackson`]
OWNER `joe-jackson-approval@primenet.com` (Brad Waddell)
OWNER `bradw@aztec.asu.edu` (Brad Waddell)
ARCHIVES
`http://www.megatoon.com/~chris/JJ/index.html`
`http://www.cryst.bbk.ac.uk/~ubcg5ab/JJ/joe.html`

1088 **alt.music.janes-addictn** The music of Jane's Addiction and its members. *Newsgroup*

1089 **Jethro Tull Digest:** On the music of the Jethro Tull rock group. *Digest*
± INFO `jtull-request@remus.rutgers.edu`
ARCHIVE `http://jtull.rutgers.edu/JethroTull/`
Gated: `info.jethro-tull`

1090 **alt.music.jethro-tull** Ironman sitting on a park bench. *Newsgroup*

1091 **alt.fan.elton-john** The music and antics of Elton John. *Newsgroup*

1092 **Journey-L:** On the rock group Journey. *Mailing List*
± `mxserver@wkuvx1.wku.edu` (Hunter Goatley)
OWNER `goathunter@loki.com` (Hunter Goatley)

1093 **alt.music.bon-jovi** For fans of Jon and the gang. *Newsgroup*

1094 **Elephant Talk:** For Robert Fripp and King Crimson enthusiasts. *Digest & Reflector, moderated*
`http://www.cs.man.ac.uk/aig/staff/toby/elephant-talk.html`

± **INFO** `toby@cs.man.ac.uk` (Toby Howard)
ARCHIVE `http://www.cs.man.ac.uk/aig/staff/toby/et/archives.html`

1095 `alt.fan.kinks` Come dancing. *Newsgroup*

1096 **Strange Ways:** Devoted to the hottest band in the land . . . KISS! *Newsletter*
`http://www.pitt.edu/~zucker/strange-ways.html`
INFO `azeeeman@aol.com` (Adam Zucker)
ARCHIVE `gopher://gopher.wku.edu`
Frequency: bimonthly

1097 `alt.music.led-zeppelin` Discussion about Led Zeppelin and their music. *Newsgroup*

1098 **HOYHOY:** On the band Little Feat. *Mailing List*
± **OWNER** `amygoode@ultranet.com` (Amy Goode)
OWNER `fmiller@it.berklee.edu` (Red Miller)
ARCHIVE `http://www.ultranet.com/~hoyhoy/`

1099 `alt.music.marillion` A progressive band. *The Silmarillion* is a book. *Newsgroup*

1100 `alt.music.marilyn-manson` You've been a good little boy! *Newsgroup*

1101 `alt.rock-n-roll.metal.megadeth` The band Megadeth. *Newsgroup*

1102 `alt.rock-n-roll.metal.metallica` Sort of like Formica with more hair. *Newsgroup*

1103 **powderworks:** On the musical group Midnight Oil: socially and environmentally aware—and danceable. *Mailing List*
± `majordomo@cs.colorado.edu` [body = SUBSCRIBE POWDERWORKS e-mail-address]
INFO `powderworks-owner@cs.colorado.edu` (Tim Hunter)
ARCHIVE `ftp://refuge.colorado.edu/pub/powderworks`

1104 `alt.music.ministry` Perhaps not the music you would expect. *Newsgroup*

1105 **Monkees:** Hey Hey We're the Monkees: Wacky TV Rock Stars. *Mailing List*
± `majordomo@primenet.com` [body = subscribe monkees]
OWNER `monkees-approval@primenet.com` (Brad Waddell)
OWNER `bradw@aztec.asu.edu` (Brad Waddell)
ARCHIVE `http://www.primenet.com/~flex/monkees.html`
Gated: `alt.music.monkees`

1106 `alt.music.monkees` Hey, hey, they were the Monkees. *Newsgroup*

1107 **lost-chords:** On the Moody Blues rock group. *Digest & Reflector*
± **INFO** `lost-chords-request@mit.edu`
ARCHIVE `ftp://ftp.uwp.edu/pub/music/lists/moody.blues`

1108 `alt.music.moody-blues` Still In Search of the Lost Chord. *Newsgroup*

1109 **VAN-L:** On the rock musician Van Morrison. *Mailing List*
± `listserv@nic.surfnet.nl` [body = SUBSCRIBE VAN-L first-name last-name]
INFO `hlrutten@ped.kun.nl` (Henk Rutten)
ARCHIVE `listserv@nic.surfnet.nl` [body = INDEX VAN-L]
POST `van-l@nic.surfnet.nl`

1110 `alt.music.morrissey` Morrissey's career and music. *Newsgroup*

1111 `alt.rock-n-roll.metal.motley-crue` The music of Mötley Crüe. *Newsgroup*

1112 `alt.music.moxy-fruvous` Discussions of the band Moxy Fruvous. *Newsgroup*

1113 `alt.music.new-order` The music of New Order and its members. *Newsgroup*

1114 `alt.music.nin` Nine Inch Nails. *Newsgroup*

1115 **alt.music.nin.creative** Works for Reznor's Nine Inch Nails. *Newsgroup*

1116 **alt.music.nirvana** Generation X's Seattle leaders, leaderless. *Newsgroup*

1117 **Jump in the River (JITR):** On the music and work of the Irish musician and social activist Sinead O'Connor. *Mailing List*
± `majordomo@server.postmodern.com` [body = SUBSCRIBE JITR]
INFO `jitr-approval@server.postmodern.com`
ARCHIVE `http://www.postmodern.com/~mcb/jitr/`

1118 **alt.music.oasis** Discussions of the band oasis. *Newsgroup*

1119 **O'Boingo Electronic Newsletter (OBEN):** Official periodic electronic newsletter of Oingo Boingo (Boingo); also Danny Elfman, the Allstars, Doug and the Mystics, and other (related) projects. *Newsletter*
`http://www.boingo.com/boingo`
± `oben@boingo.com`
INFO `elnppr@ritvax.isc.rit.edu` (Eric L. Neumann)
INFO `boingonews`
INFO `boingonews@aol.com`
Please Note: Subscription by approval only.

1120 **alt.fan.oingo-boingo** Have you ever played ping-pong in Pago Pago? *Newsgroup*

1121 **alt.music.ozzy** Blizzard of Osbourne. *Newsgroup*

1122 **alt.music.pantera** I'm broken. *Newsgroup*

1123 **Graham-Parker:** On the music of Graham Parker. *Mailing List*
± `majordomo@primenet.com` [body = subscribe graham-parker]
OWNER `graham-parker-approval@primenet.com` (Brad Waddell)
OWNER `bradw@aztec.asu.edu` (Brad Waddell)
ARCHIVE `http://reality.sgi.com/employees/howells/gparker.html`

1124 **alt.music.pearl-jam** The music of the alternative rock band Pearl Jam. *Newsgroup*

1125 **rec.music.phish** Discussing the musical group Phish. *Newsgroup*

1126 **echoes:** Information and commentary on the musical group Pink Floyd as well as other projects members of the group have been involved with. *Mailing List*
± `echoserv@fawnya.tcs.com`
INFO `echoes-request@fawnya.tcs.com`

1127 **alt.music.pink-floyd** Sold-out shows everywhere. *Newsgroup*

1128 **alt.music.roger-waters** To Pink or not to Pink. *Newsgroup*

1129 **alt.music.planet-gong** History and mystery of the Planet Gong. *Newsgroup*

1130 **alt.music.the.police** If you play it too loud, they bust your party. *Newsgroup*

1131 **alt.music.pop-eat-itself** Musical group Pop Will Eat Itself. *Newsgroup*

1132 **alt.music.primus** Discussions related to the music group Primus. *Newsgroup*

1133 **alt.music.prince** So my Prince came. Make him go away. *Newsgroup*

1134 **alt.music.pulp** Fandom of the British band Pulp. *Newsgroup*

1135 **alt.music.queen** The band Queen and related solo acts. *Newsgroup*

1136 **Screaming in Digital:** Queensryche's Internet Magazine *E-Zine*
± INFO `queensryche@pilot.njin.net` (Dan "Shag" Birchall)
INFO `http://www.ios.com/~qryche/about.html`
OWNER `birchall@pilot.njin.net` (Dan "Shag" Birchall)
ARCHIVE `http://www.ios.com/~qryche/archives.html`

Gated: `rec.music.artists.queensryche`
Frequency: monthly

1137 `rec.music.artists.queensryche` The thinking mind's metal band. *Newsgroup*

1138 `alt.music.ramones` For discussion of the kings of punk rock. *Newsgroup*

1139 `alt.music.lou-reed` Lou Reed. *Newsgroup*

1140 `rec.music.rem` The musical group REM. *Newsgroup*

1141 `alt.music.replacements` Jesus rides beside us. *Newsgroup*

1142 `alt.music.paul-westerberg` Discussion of Paul and the Replacements. *Newsgroup*

1143 `alt.fan.henry-rollins` Fans of the Henry Rollins Band. Mother! *Newsgroup*

1144 **awizard:** On Todd Rundgren. *Mailing List*
± `awizard-request@planning.ebay.sun.com`
± `http://www.roadkill.com/todd/join-awizard.pl`
INFO `ed.grieze@ebay.sun.com` (Ed Grieze)
ARCHIVE `http://www.roadkill.com/todd/trconn`

1145 `alt.music.todd-rundgren` Todd Rundgren music fandom. *Newsgroup*

1146 `alt.music.rush` For Rushheads. *Newsgroup*

1147 `alt.music.seal` Aquatic creatures playing cymbals and the horn stand. *Newsgroup*

1148 `alt.music.shonen-knife` Ultimate Japanese girl group. *Newsgroup*

1149 `alt.music.paul-simon` Discussion of Paul Simon's music. *Newsgroup*

1150 **dominion:** On the Sisters of Mercy rock group and related music. *Mailing List*
± `dominion-request@ohm.york.ac.uk`
INFO `pete@ohm.york.ac.uk`
ARCHIVE `ftp://ftp.caprica.com/pub/users/briansin`

1151 **slade:** On the English glam-rock group Slade. *Mailing List*
`http://www.sojourn.com/~mcutler/slade.html`
± `slade-request@a3.xs4all.nl`
INFO `a3@a3.xs4all.nl` (Adri Verhoef)

1152 `alt.music.smash-pumpkins` The Smashing Pumpkins. *Newsgroup*

1153 `alt.music.smiths` Discussion about the Smiths and related solo projects. *Newsgroup*

1154 `alt.music.sonic-youth` Loud enough to make you deaf. *Newsgroup*

1155 `alt.music.soundgarden` The band Soundgarden. *Newsgroup*

1156 **mael-list:** On the rock band Sparks. *Mailing List*
± `mael-list-request@wopr.gsm.uci.edu`
INFO `nraggett@wopr.gsm.uci.edu`
OWNER `owner-mael-list@wopr.gsm.uci.edu`

1157 `alt.music.bruce-springsteen` New Jersey's finest. *Newsgroup*

1158 **LuckyTown:** For fans of Bruce Springsteen's music. *Daily Digest, moderated*
`http://www.mcs.net/~kvk/luckytown.html`
± INFO `luckytown-request@netcom.com` (Kevin Kinder)
Comments: Mailing list used to be named BackStreets.

1159 `rec.music.artists.springsteen` Forum for fans of Bruce Springsteen's music. *Newsgroup*

1160 `alt.music.squeeze` Discussion of the Brit-pop combo Squeeze. *Newsgroup*

1161 `alt.music.steely-dan` Discussing the band Steely Dan. *Newsgroup*

1162 al-stewart: On the musician Al Stewart. *Mailing List*
  ± `al-stewart-request@death.corp.sun.com`
  OWNER `zen@fish.com`
  ARCHIVE `http://www.fish.com/music/al_stewart/digest_archives`
  FAQ `http://www.fish.com/music/al_stewart/digest_archives`

1163 `alt.fan.sting` See alt.sex.bestiality.with-bees. *Newsgroup*

1164 roses-list: On the U.K. band The Stone Roses. *Mailing List*
  ± `majordomo@best.com`
  OWNER `owner-roses-list@lists.best.com` (Eric Thompson)
  ARCHIVE `http://www.freestyle.com/roses/`

1165 `alt.music.stone-roses` No smell, sweet or nothin'. *Newsgroup*

1166 `alt.rock-n-roll.stones` Gathering plenty of moss by now. *Newsgroup*

1167 `alt.music.stone-temple` The band Stone Temple Pilots. *Newsgroup*

1168 `alt.music.suede` Yeah right, you've never . . . . *Newsgroup*

1169 `alt.music.james-taylor` J. T.! *Newsgroup*

1170 tears4-fears: Discussion of the music group Tears for Fears. *Mailing List*
  `http://www.ms.uky.edu/tears4-fears.html`
  ± INFO `tears4-fears-request@ms.uky.edu`
  ARCHIVE `ftp://ftp.ms.uky.edu/pub/mailing.lists/tears4-fears`

1171 `alt.music.tmbg` They Might Be Giants. *Newsgroup*

1172 `alt.music.tool` Tool is so . . . out there, man. *Newsgroup*

1173 `alt.music.tragically-hip` The rock band the Tragically Hip. *Newsgroup*

1174 `alt.music.u2` Another group for the band U2. *Newsgroup*

1175 `alt.fan.u2` The Irish rock band U2. *Newsgroup*

1176 ph7: On Van Der Graaf Generator, Peter Hammill, and related rock groups. *Mailing List*
  ± INFO `ph7-request@arastar.com` [subject = `asdf`] (subject = asdf)
  OWNER `ph7-owner@arastar.com`

1177 `alt.music.van-halen` For discussion of topics related to Van Halen. *Newsgroup*

1178 `alt.music.tom-waits` Discussion of works of artist Tom Waits. *Newsgroup*

1179 `alt.music.who` Enduring megagroup. *Newsgroup*

1180 Notes From The Edge: Newsletter on the Yes rock group, Anderson-Bruford-Wakeman-Howe, and band-member-related news. Includes interviews. *Newsletter*
  `http://www.wilmington.net/yes`
  ± INFO `nfte@cms.uncwil.edu`
  OWNER `hunnicutt@uncwil.edu` (Jeff Hunnicutt)
  Frequency: every two weeks, on average

1181 `alt.music.yes` The progressive band Yes. *Newsgroup*

1182 `alt.fan.frank-zappa` Is that a Sears poncho? *Newsgroup*

1183 `alt.music.zevon` Warren Zevon's music. *Newsgroup*

MUSIC—WORLD

1184 ACMR-L: For members of the Association for Chinese Music Research. *Mailing List*
  ± `listserv@uhccvm.its.hawaii.edu` [body = SUBSCRIBE ACMR-L first-name last-name]
  INFO `acmr-l-request@uhccvm.its.hawaii.edu`

ARCHIVE `listserv@uhccvm.its.hawaii.edu` [body = INDEX ACMR-L]

1185 **alt.music.african** African music. *Newsgroup*

1186 **alt.music.arabic** Arabic music. *Newsgroup*

1187 **alt.music.carnival** Soca, calypso, and steel pan. *Newsgroup*

1188 **alt.music.celine-dion** The music and art of the international star Celine Dion. *Newsgroup*

1189 **alt.music.france** Melodies from the French. *Newsgroup*

1190 **alt.music.hawaiian** The music of the Hawaiian islands. *Newsgroup*

1191 **alt.music.jewish** Music from the Jewish heritage. *Newsgroup*

1192 **alt.music.mexican** Mexican-influenced music. *Newsgroup*

1193 **alt.music.ska** Discussions of ska (skank) music, bands, and suchlike. *Newsgroup*

1194 **alt.music.uk** Music from the British Isles. *Newsgroup*

1195 **alt.music.world** Music from around the world (no "pop" or "rock"). *Newsgroup*

1196 **The Global Link:** Newsletter of the Music of the World record label. *Newsletter*
    `http://kiwi.futuris.net/rw/motw/`
    ± INFO OWNER `motw1@aol.com` (Martha Lorentos)
    Frequency: 3 to 4 times per year

➤   **IRTRAD-L:** On Irish traditional music. (See entry 874 for full listing.)

1197 **LATAMMUS:** For discussion of all aspects and styles of music in Latin American countries. *Mailing List*
    ± `listserv@asuvm.inre.asu.edu` [body = SUBSCRIBE LATAMMUS first-name last-name]
    INFO `latammus-request@asuvm.inre.asu.edu`
    ARCHIVE `listserv@asuvm.inre.asu.edu` [body = INDEX LATAMMUS]
    Please Note: Subscription by approval only.

1198 **rec.music.afro-latin** Music with Afro-Latin, African, and Latin influences. *Newsgroup*

1199 **rec.music.brazilian** All aspects of Brazilian music. *Newsgroup*

1200 **rec.music.filipino** All types and forms of Filipino music. *Newsgroup*

1201 **rec.music.indian.classical** Hindustani and Carnatic Indian classical music. *Newsgroup*

1202 **rec.music.indian.misc** Discussing Indian music in general. *Newsgroup*

1203 **rec.music.iranian** Discussion of Iranian music. *Newsgroup*

1204 **rec.music.reggae** Roots, rockers, dancehall reggae. *Newsgroup*

1205 **RootsWorld:** A magazine of world music, folk, and jazz, RootsWorld focuses on the lesser-known traditions and the uncommon ground in the world's music.
    `http://www.rootsworld.com/rw/`
    INFO `cliff@rootsworld.com`

1206 **Scandinavian Indie:** The place for independent music coming from any Scandinavian country, plus the Baltic countries.
    `http://sf.www.lysator.liu.se/~chief/scan.html`
    `http://www.lysator.liu.se/~chief/scan.html`
    `ftp://ftp.lysator.liu.se/pub/texts/uxu/SID/`
    INFO `scan-indie-request@lysator.liu.se` [subject = info]
    INFO `chief@lysator.liu.se` (Erik Soderstrom)
    Comments: Mailing list is also available, see contact address for information.

1207 **ZapMama:** On the world music group Zap Mama. *Mailing List*
    `http://www.tyrell.net/~dave/zapmama.html`
    ± OWNER `dave@tyrell.net` (Dave Bales)

ARCHIVE dave@tyrell.net (Dave Bales)

MYSTERIES & THRILLERS

1208 **alt.books.chesterton** Books by G. K. Chesterton. *Moderated newsgroup*

1209 **alt.books.tom-clancy** The group for discusson of Mr. Techno-Thriller. *Newsgroup*

1210 **alt.fan.holmes** Elementary, my dear Watson. Like he ever said that. *Newsgroup*

1211 **alt.fan.inspector-morse** For fans of Inspector Morse books and TV show. *Newsgroup*

1212 **alt.fan.rumpole** Rumpole of the Bailey. *Newsgroup*

1213 **bit.listserv.dorothyl** Mystery-literature lovers. *Moderated newsgroup*

1214 **Clue Lass Home Page—A Mystery Newsletter:** A newsletter about mystery fiction.
http://www.slip.net/~cluelass/
FAQ http://www.slip.net/~cluelass/FAQ.html

1215 **DOROTHYL:** On mystery literature. *Digest*
listserv@kentvm.kent.edu
± listserv@kentvm.kent.edu [body = SUBSCRIBE DOROTHYL first-name last-name]
OWNER diane@kovacs.com (Diane Kovacs)
OWNER krobinso@kentvm.kent.edu (Kara Robinson)

1216 **fj.rec.mystery** Talk about mysteries. *Newsgroup*

➤ **Future Fantasy Bookstore:** A bookstore of science fiction, fantasy, and mysteries. (See entry 1324 for full listing.)

1217 **LAW-AND-ORDER:** On the television show *Law and Order. Mailing List, moderated*
http://users.aol.com/lomail
± listserv@listserv.aol.com [body = SUBSCRIBE LAW-AND-ORDER first-name last-name]
INFO OWNER dwalheim@aol.com (Debra Walheim)
ARCHIVES
listserv@listserv.aol.com [body = INDEX LAW-AND-ORDER]
ftp://users.aol.com/lomail
Frequency: daily

➤ **Modesty Blaise:** Discussion and information exchange about Peter O'Donnell's *Modesty Blaise* books and comics. (See entry 158 for full listing.)

1218 **Murder on the Internet:** Features descriptions of mystery titles from the Ballantine Publishing Group, articles by authors and editors, upcoming titles, author tour information, and excerpts. *Newsletter*
± majordomo@www.randomhouse.com [body = SUBSCRIBE MOI-dist e-mail-address first-name last-name]
INFO EDITOR OWNER srandol@randomhouse.com (Susan Randol, Editor)
ARCHIVE http://www.randomhouse.com/BB/mysterydex.html
Frequency: monthly

1219 **The Mysterious Homepage:** An extensive collection of pointers to newsgroups, mailing lists, and Web sites that have mystery and crime fiction content.
http://www.db.dk/dbaa/jbs/homepage.htm
INFO jbs@db.dk
MIRROR http://users.aol.com/bchrcon97/mysteris.htm

1220 **Mystery Connection:** Access to The Magnifying Glass mystery newsletter and to Over My Dead Body!, a mystery magazine and BBS. This site also includes reviews, mystery event listings, information on authors, and links to other mysterious sites.
http://emporium.turnpike.net/~mystery/index.html
INFO omdb@aol.com

1221 The PAPER CHASE: a newsletter on mystery paperbacks: The PAPER CHASE is a four-times-a-year newsletter and buyers' guide to crime literature in paperback. Features full list of new titles/season, reviews, recommendations, and articles.

http://www.av.qnet.com/~supak/pprchs.htm

INFO anthony_pascal@rand.org

Comments: The PAPER CHASE is available by snailmail subscrip. (soon to be available by fax and online) for $10 to 11693 San Vicente #158, L.A. CA 90049

1222 rec.arts.mystery Mystery and crime books, plays, and films. *Newsgroup*

ONLINE ENTERTAINMENT

1223 Bounty Hunters Online: The bounty-hunting story of the month, toys, links, professional services, live forums, how to become one.

http://www.onworld.com/BHO/

INFO submit@onworld.com

1224 Ferndale: Log on to Ferndale, a live interactive soap opera that hit the Web on January 15. It's *Twin Peaks* meets *Soap*, with intrigue, drama, romance, and mystery.

http://www.ferndale.com/

INFO lindad@songline.com

1225 The Foresight Exchange (FX): The Foresight Exchange is a market that is designed to ascertain the probabilities of specific advances in science and technology. It is a "futures" market about the future. The subject matter dealt with by this market varies from politics and current events to science and technology to popular culture.

http://www.ideafutures.com/

telnet://lucifer.com:7002

INFO fxmail@lucifer.com

INFO info@ideosphere.com

1226 Internet Charts: The Internet Charts are compiled from votes from Internet users. There are weekly charts containing the most popular PC games, movies, and albums in the world. They are the most professional source of information for all who are interested in the most popular entertainment products on this planet.

http://www.xs4all.nl/~jojo

INFO jojo@xs4all.nl

1227 Los Angeles After Dark: Features live and prerecorded over-the-Internet broadcasts of bands, comedy, and entertainment-oriented programming. Also featuring audio and video on demand of various shows and music. Some artists will be actually debuting their CDs and singles here prior to release.

http://world-wide.com/LAAfterDark/

INFO farpoint@world-wide.com

1228 ON World: Incredible 3-D scapes full of entertainment. From Bounty Hunters Online to the Astronomy Scape, ON World has hours of top-rated entertainment.

http://www.onworld.com/

INFO submit@onworld.com

➤ **Traders' Connection BBS:** This BBS, accessible through the World Wide Web, provides e-mail, 1.5 million classified ads, over 80 multiplayer games, the Official Internet MUD (games) List, thousands of downloadable files, technical help, online publications, moderated special interest groups, Internet and Web services, personal Web pages, and more. (See entry 2205 for full listing.)

PERFORMING ARTS

➤ **ARTS-MD:** On physicians who are also performing artists. (See entry 4823 for full listing.)

1229 rec.arts.marching.band.college College marching bands. *Newsgroup*

1230 rec.arts.marching.band.high-school High-school marching bands. *Newsgroup*

1231 rec.arts.marching.colorguard Competitive color guard activity. *Newsgroup*

1232 `rec.arts.marching.drumcorps` Drum and bugle corps. *Newsgroup*

1233 `rec.arts.marching.misc` Marching-related performance activities. *Newsgroup*

1234 `rec.juggling` Juggling techniques, equipment, and events. *Newsgroup*

PHOTOGRAPHY

1235 **12hr-ISBN-JPEG:** Irregular announcements concerning The 12hr-ISBN-JPEG Project: continuously posted, sequenced, hypermodern photo-art by Brad Brace—available via FTP, WWW, Usenet. *Distribution List*
± `listserv@netcom.com` [body = `SUBSCRIBE 12hr-isbn-jpeg`]
OWNER `bbrace@netcom.com` (brad brace)
ARCHIVES
`ftp://ftp.netcom.com/pub/bbrace/books`
`http://www.teleport.com/~bbrace/bbrace.html`
FAQ `ftp://ftp.netcom.com/pub/bbrace/books`

1236 `alt.binaries.pictures.fine-art.photos` Binary pictures of fine-art photos. *Newsgroup*

1237 `aus.photo` Photography, video, etc. *Newsgroup*

1238 `clari.sports.photos` Sports photographs. *Moderated newsgroup*

1239 **Custom Medical Stock Photos Online:** This site is maintained by the Chicago, Illinois, company that offers access to more than 250,000 medical and scientific images.
`http://www.cmsp.com/`
INFO `admin@cmsp.com`

1240 `fj.rec.photo` Topics about cameras and photographs. *Newsgroup*

1241 **Fox Studio Limited:** A full-service commercial photography studio in Minneapolis, MN.
`http://www.webcom.com/foxstu`
INFO `patrick@foxstudio.com`

➤ **In Some Unrelated Land:** An online novel with art by the author. (See entry 585 for full listing.)

1242 **Kilgore Photography:** A portfolio page of photographs (made without the assistance of a computer), by Pat Kilgore.
`http://www.tiac.net/users/palito`
INFO `palito@tiac.net` (Pat Kilgore)

1243 **Leo's Gallery:** Leo's collection of pictures from all around the world.
`http://www.lance.colostate.edu/optical/Leo/Pictures/`
INFO `irakliot@lance.colostate.edu`

1244 **PhotoForum:** On photography and imaging education. *Mailing List*
± `listserv@listserver.isc.rit.edu`
EDITOR `rckpph@rit.edu` (Russell Kraus)
EDITOR `andpph@rit.edu` (Andrew Davidhazy)
ARCHIVE `ftp://vmsftp.rit.edu/pub/ritphoto/photoforum`

1245 **PHOTON:** The World Wide Web photo magazine. *E-Magazine*
`http://www.scotborders.co.uk/photon/`
INFO `davidkilpatrick@photon.scotborders.co.uk` (David Kilpatrick)
ARCHIVES
`http://www.photonpub.co.uk/photon/`
`http://www.photonpub.co.uk/photon/netindex.html`

➤ **Poetica Dementia:** Poetica Dementia is a site of original poetry and photography and abstract art. (See entry 626 for full listing.)

1246 `rec.photo.darkroom` Developing, printing, and other darkroom issues. *Newsgroup*

1247 `rec.photo.digital` Digital cameras, scanners, printers, software, photo CD. *Newsgroup*

1248 `rec.photo.equipment.35mm` 35-mm cameras and lenses. *Newsgroup*

1249 `rec.photo.equipment.large-format` Large-format cameras and lenses. *Newsgroup*

1250 `rec.photo.equipment.medium-format` Medium-format cameras and lenses. *Newsgroup*

1251 `rec.photo.equipment.misc` Other formats, tripods, projectors, bags, etc. *Newsgroup*

1252 `rec.photo.film+labs` Film and commercial photofinishing. *Newsgroup*

1253 `rec.photo.help` Beginners' questions about photography (and answers). *Newsgroup*

1254 `rec.photo.marketplace` Trading of personal photographic equipment. *Newsgroup*

1255 `rec.photo.misc` General issues related to photography. *Newsgroup*

1256 `rec.photo.moderated` The art and science of photography. *Moderated newsgroup*

1257 `rec.photo.technique.art` Issues of fine art, framing, display. *Newsgroup*

1258 `rec.photo.technique.misc` Other non-equipment posts about technique. *Newsgroup*

1259 `rec.photo.technique.nature` Wildlife, landscapes, travel tips, etc. *Newsgroup*

1260 `rec.photo.technique.people` Portraits, figure studies, weddings etc. *Newsgroup*

1261 **STOCKPHOTO:** For professional discussion within the stock photography industry. *Mailing List*
± `listproc@info.curtin.edu.au` [body = SUBSCRIBE STOCKPHOTO first-name last-name]
INFO `http://www.curtin.edu.au/curtin/dept/design/STOCKPHOTO`
OWNER `sdayj@cc.curtin.edu.au` (Joel Day)
ARCHIVE `http://www.curtin.edu.au/curtin/dept/design/STOCKPHOTO`
FAQ `http://www.curtin.edu.au/curtin/dept/design/STOCKPHOTO`

POPULAR CULTURE

1262 `alt.graffiti` The writing is on the wall. *Newsgroup*

1263 **BOB©WEB:** An eclectic mix of arts- and popular-culture-related links. BOB©WEB is also the home of BOB©NET, the Club BOB© (a nonprofit Internet arts organization).
`http://www4.ncsu.edu/unity/users/a/asdamick/www/`
INFO `asdamick@unity.ncsu.edu`

➤ **DRIVE-INS:** On drive-in movie theaters and classic indoor bijous. (See entry 700 for full listing.)

1264 **POPCULIB:** On popular culture resources in libraries. *Mailing List*
± `listserv@kentvm.kent.edu` [body = SUBSCRIBE POPCULIB first-name last-name]
OWNER `krobinso@kentvm.kent.edu` (Kara Robinson)
ARCHIVE `listserv@kentvm.kent.edu` [body = INDEX POPCULIB]

1265 **POPCULT:** For analytical discussion of popular culture. *Mailing List*
± `mailserv@camosun.bc.ca` [body = SUBSCRIBE POPCULT]
OWNER `montgomery@camosun.bc.ca` (Peter Montgomery)

➤ **ROADSIDE:** On roadside attractions: alligator ranches, coffeepot-shaped restaurants, and the like. (See entry 7845 for full listing.)

QUILTING

1266 **Judy's Hotlist:** This site lists the best quilting resources on the Web.
`http://www.geocities.com/TheTropics/2063/`
INFO `judyqltz@nando.net`

1267 **InterQuilt:** On quilting. *Mailing List*
OWNER `mbishop@needles.com` (Melissa Bishop)

Comments: Subscription fee. $7.50 three-month trial.

1268 **QUILTART-LIST:** On art quilting: design, technique, books, software, and other resources. *Mailing List*
± `listserv@netcom.com` [body = SUBSCRIBE quiltart-list]
OWNER `jlsmith@netcom.com` (Judy Smith)
OWNER `judysmith@genie.com` (Judy Smith)

1269 `rec.crafts.textiles.quilting` All about quilts and other quilted items. *Newsgroup*

RADIO

1270 **Airwaves Radio Journal:** Information and discussion pertaining to domestic broadcast radio (radio broadcasting that is primarily for reception within the same country from which it originates). *E-Journal, moderated*
`http://radio.aiss.uiuc.edu/~airwaves/online.html` (Current Issues)
± `subscribe@airwaves.com`
INFO `info@airwaves.com` (InfoBot)
INFO `wdp@wwa.com` (Emergency only)
EDITOR `editor@airwaves.com` (William Pfeiffer)
ARCHIVES
`ftp://deja-vu.aiss.uiuc.edu/misc/rec.radio.b-cast`
`http://radio.aiss.uiuc.edu/~rrb/` (Current Issues)
`ftp://radio.aiss.uiuc.edu/pub/AIRWAVES/`
Gated: `rec.radio.broadcasting`

1271 `alt.fan.cfny` For listeners and fans of New York radio station CFNY. *Newsgroup*

1272 `alt.fan.don-imus` Fans of radio host Imus. *Newsgroup*

1273 `alt.fan.don-n-mike` Two radio guys. *Newsgroup*

1274 `alt.fan.greaseman` Fans of Doug Tracht, the DJ. *Newsgroup*

1275 `alt.fan.howard-stern` Fans of the abrasive radio and TV personality. *Newsgroup*

1276 `alt.fan.kroq` LA radio station KROQ, FM 106.7. Great monster name. *Newsgroup*

1277 `alt.fan.mark-brian` Discussion of the Mark and Brian radio program. *Newsgroup*

➤ `alt.fan.rush-limbaugh:` Derogation of others for fun and profit. *Newsgroup*

➤ `alt.flame.rush-limbaugh:` The opposition's version of `alt.fan.rush-limbaugh`. *Newsgroup*

1278 `alt.radio.networks.npr` U.S. National Public Radio: shows, stories, hosts, etc. *Newsgroup*

1279 `alt.radio.online-tonight` OnLine Tonight radio show discussion. *Newsgroup*

1280 `alt.radio.talk` Radio talk and call-in shows. *Newsgroup*

➤ `alt.rush-limbaugh:` Fans of the conservative activist radio announcer. *Newsgroup*

1281 **B-1000 Radio Brunel:** B-1000 Radio Brunel. Student Radio for Brunel University.
`http://b1000.brunel.ac.uk:4040/`
INFO `b1000@brunel.ac.uk`

1282 `fj.rec.radio` Talk about radio broadcasting and its programs. *Newsgroup*

➤ **PBS Online®:** This site provides listings of PBS's programs, such as science and nature, documentaries, history, biography, how-to, and instructional television. Also included on this site is information about your local PBS station, the PBS store, learning services, and an online news service. (See entry 6067 for full listing.)

➤ `phl.scanner:` Scanning the airwaves in Philadelphia. *Newsgroup*

1283 **Radio Resistor's Bulletin:** A conduit for the voices, ideas, and concerns of those who care passionately about the state of noncommercial radio, including community radio, public radio, college radio, pirate radio, and short-wave. *Newsletter*
`http://www.hear.com/rw/feature/rrb.html`

± **INFO OWNER** haulgren@well.com (Frank Haulgren)

Frequency: 4-5 times peryear

1284 **rec.arts.wobegon** *A Prairie Home Companion* radio show discussion. *Newsgroup*

1285 **rec.radio.broadcasting** Discussion of global domestic broadcast radio. *Moderated newsgroup*

1286 **rec.radio.info** Informational postings related to radio. *Moderated newsgroup*

1287 **rec.radio.noncomm** Topics relating to noncommercial radio. *Newsgroup*

1288 **rec.radio.swap** Offers to trade and swap radio equipment. *Newsgroup*

1289 **SNDPRINT:** On the public radio documentary series *Soundprint. Mailing List*
± listserv@soundprint.org [body = SUBSCRIBE SNDPRINT]
OWNER beth@soundprint.org (Beth Lewand)

➤ **SunSITE Internet Talk Radio Archives:** Archives of the Internet Talk Radio shows. (See entry 2701 for full listing.)

1290 **SWL$L:** For shortwave-radio listeners. *Mailing List*
± listserv@cuvmb.columbia.edu [body = SUBSCRIBE SWL$L first-name last-name]
INFO swl$l-request@cuvmb.columbia.edu

1291 **tnn.radio.life** Discussions about daily life with radio technology. *Newsgroup*

1292 **uk.media.radio.archers** Discussion of the BBC radio soap opera *The Archers. Newsgroup*

➤ **United States Public Broadcasting Service (PBS):** PBS Online™ provides listings of their programs, in categories such as science and nature, documentaries, history, biography, how-to, and instructional television. Also included on this site is information about your local PBS station, the PBS store, learning services, and an online news service. (See entry 6071 for full listing.)

RAVES

1293 **alt.rave** Technoculture: music, dancing, drugs, dancing, etc. *Newsgroup*

1294 **ne-raves:** High-volume discussion list covering the northeastern rave scene. *Mailing List*
± danarchy@hyperreal.com
INFO EDITOR freelove@access.digex.net
OWNER anarchy@glue.umd.edu
ARCHIVE http://taz.hyperreal.com/raves/ne/archives/ne-faq.txt

RESOURCES

1295 **ArtsUSA:** Award-winning Web site of the American Council for the Arts, providing arts education and advocacy information (congressional committees, how to contact members, current legislation regarding arts funding, and more).
http://www.artsusa.org/
INFO webmaster@artsusa.org

1296 **alt.art.marketplace** Art and art supplies wanted and for sale. *Newsgroup*

1297 **alt.artcom** Artistic community, arts and communication. *Newsgroup*

1298 **Arts Wire:** A networking and communications resource for artists. Includes arts news and information, as well as discussion groups and more.
http://artswire.org/Artswire/www/awfront.html
gopher://gopher.tmn.com/11/Artswire
INFO artswire@artswire.org

1299 **ArtsNet:** For services and information relating to arts management and cultural resources on the Internet.
http://artsnet.heinz.cmu.edu/
INFO mamprog@andrew.cmu.edu

1300 **C-ARTS:** On arts resources on the Internet; associated with a database (C-ARTSdb). *Mailing List, moderated*

```
http://cnet.unb.ca/c-arts/
```
± `listserv@unb.ca` [body = SUBSCRIBE C-ARTS first-name last-name]
INFO `c-arts-request@unb.ca`
OWNER `s6sa@unb.ca` (Michael McEwing)
OWNER `ryana@unb.ca` (Anne Ryan)
OWNER `dsoucy@unb.ca` (Don Soucy)
FAQ `listserv@unb.ca` [body = GET C-ARTS FAQ]

1301 **kspace-list:** On the independent artists and musicians affiliated with Kaleidospace, an online art mall: profiles, a technical section, announcements of concerts/exhibitions/chat sessions/free tickets. *Mailing List, moderated*
```
gopher://gopher.kspace.com
ftp://ftp.kspace.com
http://kspace.com/
```
± `majordomo@kspace.com` [body = subscribe kspace-list]
OWNER `editors@kspace.com`
Comments: Fee based.

ROMANCE

1302 `bit.listserv.rra-l` Romance Readers Anonymous. *Moderated newsgroup*

1303 **RRA-L:** Romance Readers Anonymous. *Mailing List, moderated*
INFO `lhaas@kentvm.kent.edu` (Leslie Haas)
ARCHIVE `listserv@kentvm.kent.edu`

SCIENCE FICTION, FANTASY & HORROR

1304 <u>Linkoping Science Fiction & Fantasy Archive</u>: The Linkoping Science Fiction & Fantasy Archive collects information on science fiction and fantasy. This includes book and movie reviews, biographies, bibliographies, listings of different kinds, and original artwork.
```
http://sf.www.lysator.liu.se/
gopher://gopher.lysator.liu.se/11/lysator-Science_Fiction_Archive
```
INFO `matoh@lysator.liu.se`
FAQ `http://sf.www.lysator.liu.se/sf_archive/faq/`

➤ <u>Writers' Resources</u>: Interesting list of useful links for writers. Special focus on science fiction and the Pacific Northwest. (See entry 633 for full listing.)

1305 **800-TREKKER:** An online source for science-fiction gifts and apparel.
```
http://www.scifi.com/trader/trekker/trekker.html
```
INFO `feedback@usanetworks.com`

1306 `alt.fandom.cons` Announcements of conventions (sf and others). *Newsgroup*

1307 `alt.horror` The horror genre. *Newsgroup*

1308 `alt.horror.creative` Original horror fiction, poems, pictures. *Newsgroup*

1309 `alt.horror.werewolves` They were wolves, now they're something to be wary of. *Newsgroup*

1310 `alt.movies.monster` Godzilla! The Wolfman! The Thing! Aiiieee! *Newsgroup*

1311 `alt.necronomicon` Big time death wish. *Newsgroup*

1312 `alt.shared-reality.sf-and-fantasy` Worlds Beyond shared universe. *Newsgroup*

1313 `alt.vampyres` Discussion of vampires and related writings, films, etc. *Newsgroup*

➤ **The Anime Picture Archive:** A large archive of anime/manga images. It also contains information about the different series and links to other places. (See entry 44 for full listing.)

1314 **Ansible:** Science fiction (and sf fandom) news/gossip. Received 1995 Hugo award for best science-fiction fanzine. *E-Journal*

± `ansible-request@dcs.gla.ac.uk` [body = SUBSCRIBE]

INFO `ansible@cix.compulink.co.uk` (David Langford)

ARCHIVES

`http://www.dcs.gla.ac.uk/SF-Archives/Ansible`

`ftp://ftp.dcs.gla.ac.uk/pub/SF-Archives/Ansible`

Gated: `rec.arts.sf.fandom`

Frequency: monthly

In the archive, both plain ASCII and HTML versions are stored. For instance, issue 100 is `Ansible.100` in ASCII, and `a100.html` in HTML.

1315 `aus.sf` Australian discussion of sf & f literature, media, fandom. *Newsgroup*

1316 `chile.ciencia-ficcion` Science-fiction discussion. *Newsgroup*

➤ **Critters Workshop:** Online workshop/critique group for serious science-fiction/fantasy/horror writers. (See entry 635 for full listing.)

1317 **DargonZine:** DargonZine is an electronic magazine that prints original amateur fantasy fiction by aspiring Internet writers. All stories in the anthology take place in a common shared setting. *E-Zine*

± INFO `dargon@wonky.boston.ma.us` [body = *Please specify whether you wish to receive entire issues via e-mail, or merely notifications when new issues are distributed*]

EDITOR `ornoth@wonky.boston.ma.us`

ARCHIVES

`http://www.shore.net/~dargon`

`ftp://ftp.etext.org/pub/Zines/DargonZine`

Gated: `rec.mag.dargon`

Comments: Writers who are interested in joining the Dargon Project should send email to `dargon@wonky.boston.ma.us`, requesting the DargonZine Writers' FAQ. That document describes the requirements for participation in the project as a contributing writer.

1318 **DARK PLANET:** DARK PLANET is an electronic magazine of science fiction, fantasy, horror, and genre-related poetry, artwork, nonfiction, and reviews.

`http://nickel.ucs.indiana.edu/~lusnyde/cover.html`

INFO `lusnyde@indiana.edu`

Comments: DARK PLANET accepts stories and poems that have been previously published in print-only magazines as well as unpublished work. Shorter stories are preferred, but DP accepts stories up to 10,000 words. Please request submission guidelines before submitting work.

1319 **Darklava:** Darklava: The marvelous world of the fantastic is news from editors of science-fiction, fantasy, and horror books recent and upcoming in Italy.

`http://www.sira.it/darklava/darklava.htm`

INFO `gioleo@sira.it`

1320 **Del Rey Books Internet Newsletter (DRIN):** Monthly promotional electronic publication of Del Rey Books, publisher of science fiction and fantasy since 1977. *Newsletter*

`http://www.randomhouse.com/delrey/drindex/`

± `majordomo@www.randomhouse.com` [body = SUBSCRIBE DRIN-dist e-mail-address first-name last-name]

INFO `delrey@randomhouse.com`

EDITOR OWNER `eharris@randomhouse.com` (Ellen Key Harris)

ARCHIVES

`http://www.randomhouse.com/delrey/drindex/`

`gopher://gopher.panix.com/Del Rey Books`

`delrey@tachyon.com` [body = help]

Frequency: monthly

1321 Delos Cyberzine: Science-fiction monthly magazine. Interviews, news, columns, short stories. *E-Zine*
http://www.mclink.it/n/delos
http://www.cyberg.it/delos (International Edition)
http://www.mclink.it/n/delos/intlhome.html
http://www.cyberg.it/delos/intlhome.html (International Edition)
INFO delos@pobox.com
INFO silvio.sosio@pobox.com
INFO luigi.pachi@iol.it
Language: Italian & English (International Edition)
Frequency: monthly

1322 The Dominion: Sci-Fi Channel.
http://www.scifi.com/
INFO feedback@usanetworks.com
FAQ http://www.scifi.com/feedback/FAQ1.html

1323 fj.rec.sf Discussion about science fiction. *Newsgroup*

1324 Future Fantasy Bookstore: A bookstore of science fiction, fantasy, and mysteries.
http://futfan.com/
INFO futfan@netcom.com

1325 HORROR: On horror films and fiction. *Mailing List*
± listserv@iubvm.ucs.indiana.edu [body = SUB HORROR first-name last-name]
OWNER mlperkin@indiana.edu (Mildred Perkins)
OWNER rshepard@indiana.edu (Randal Shepard)
ARCHIVE listserv@iubvm.ucs.indiana.edu [body = INDEX HORROR]

➤ **House of Speculative Fiction:** Ottowa-based bookseller of science-fiction and fantasy books. (See entry 118 for full listing.)

1326 IAFA-L: For scholarly discussion of fantastic literature. *Mailing List*
http://ebbs.english.vt.edu/iafa/iafa.home.html
± listserv@vtvm1.cc.vt.edu [body = SUBSCRIBE IAFA-L first-name last-name]
INFO lhat@ebbs.english.vt.edu (Len Hatfield)
ARCHIVE listserv@vtvm1.cc.vt.edu [body = INDEX IAFA-L]

➤ **InterText:** For materials ranging from mainstream stories to fantasy to horror to science fiction to humor. (See entry 572 for full listing.)

1327 NIGHT-L: On supernatural creatures (ghosts, demons, vampires, etc.). *Mailing List*
± listproc@unicorn.acs.ttu.edu [body = SUBSCRIBE NIGHT-L first-name last-name]
OWNER raven@kehleyr.phys.ttu.edu (Morgan Bottrell)

1328 Nightstalkers: On the night—from vampires and werewolves to phases of the moon and things that go bump. *Mailing List*
± majordomo@world.std.com [body = subscribe nightstalkers]
OWNER chaotic@world.std.com (Chaos)
OWNER pse178@delphi.com (wraith)
OWNER fraser@library.utoronto.ca (Baron Gideon)

1329 ont.sf-lovers Science-fiction lovers in Ontario, Canada. *Newsgroup*

➤ **Pen and Sword:** Imaginative art and writing for the gay, lesbian, and diverse community. (See entry 9971 for full listing.)

1330 rec.arts.sf.announce Major announcements of the sf world. *Moderated newsgroup*

1331 rec.arts.sf.fandom Discussions of sf fan activities. *Newsgroup*

1332 `rec.arts.sf.marketplace` Personal forsale notices of sf materials. *Newsgroup*

1333 `rec.arts.sf.misc` Science-fiction lovers' newsgroup. *Newsgroup*

1334 `rec.arts.sf.movies` Discussing sf motion pictures. *Newsgroup*

1335 `rec.arts.sf.reviews` Reviews of science-fiction/fantasy/horror works. *Moderated newsgroup*

1336 `rec.arts.sf.science` Real and speculative aspects of sf science. *Newsgroup*

1337 `rec.arts.sf.tv` Discussing general television sf. *Newsgroup*

1338 `rec.arts.sf.written` Discussion of written science fiction and fantasy. *Newsgroup*

1339 `rec.mag.dargon` DargonZine fantasy fiction e-mag issues and discussion. *Newsgroup*

1340 **Science Fiction Conventions Northwest:** This site is an open-ended resource for fans of science fiction in the Pacific Northwest. There are areas dealing with conventions, resources for writers, a listing of clubs and organizations in the region, and links to other resources that range across the world, as well as an opportunity to leave messages for others.
`http://www.seanet.com/Users/warlock/`
INFO `warlock@warlock.seanet.com`

1341 **Science Fiction Weekly:** For science-fiction news, reviews, and short stories. *Magazine*
INFO EDITOR OWNER `70334.2433@compuserve.com` (Craig Engler, Editor)
ARCHIVE `http://www.scifiweekly.com/sfw/`
Frequency: weekly

1342 **Science Fiction Weekly:** An online science-fiction magazine with all sorts of information and news on and about the science-fiction world. Includes reviews of books, games, movies, toys, other Web sites, and just about anything else related to the genre. Also contains interactive celebrity interviews, original artwork, short stories, and more.
`http://www.scifiweekly.com/`
INFO `70334.2433@compuserve.com` (Craig Engler, Editor)

1343 **SF-LIT:** The Literary Science Fiction & Fantasy Discussion Forum: from the Library of Congress, the literary side of science fiction & fantasy. *Mailing List, moderated*
± `listproc@loc.gov` [body = SUBSCRIBE SF-LIT first-name last-name]
EDITOR `cstu@loc.gov` (Colleen Stumbaugh)
EDITOR `eaj@loc.gov` (Eric A. Johnson)
ARCHIVE `gopher://marvel.loc.gov/11/.listarch/sf-lit`

1344 **sf-lovers:** On all topics in science fiction and fantasy in general, including sf and fantasy books, sf movies, and sf conventions, reviews of books, movies, television shows, and more. *Digest & Reflector, moderated*
`http://sflovers.rutgers.edu/`
± **INFO** `sf-lovers-request@rutgers.edu` (Saul Jaffe)
ARCHIVE `ftp://sflovers.rutgers.edu`
Comments: Owner also operates lists on specialized aspects of science fiction: written sci fi, Babylon Five, sci fi on television and sci fi in movies.

1345 `soc.history.what-if` Alternate history. *Newsgroup*

1346 **Twilight World:** Fiction-only online magazine, published every two months, containing mostly fantasy fiction, science fiction, and humorous fiction. *E-Journal*
± **INFO** `r.c.karsmakers@stud.let.ruu.nl` (Richard Karsmakers)
ARCHIVES
`ftp://atari.archive.umich.edu`
`ftp://etext.archive.umich.edu`
Frequency: bimonthly

1347 **UD-L:** For the Ultimate Dungeon fantasy collective, where the overworked make up questionnaires—a fantasy-spinning collective. *Mailing List*
± `listserv@uriacc.uri.edu` [body = SUBSCRIBE UD-L first-name last-name]

INFO opus@uriacc.uri.edu (Mark Oliver)
ARCHIVE listserv@uriacc.uri.edu [body = INDEX UD-L]
Please Note: Subscription by approval only.

1348   **UK-SF:** On televisual science fiction in the United Kingdom. *Daily Digest*
http://www.lists.pipex.com/people/chuck/sf
± listproc@lists.pipex.com [body = SUBSCRIBE UK-SF first-name last-name]
INFO admin-uk-sf@lists.pipex.com
ARCHIVE http://www.lists.pipex.com/cgi-bin/listproc/digests?list=uk-sf
FAQ http://www.lists.pipex.com/people/chuck/sf/lists/uk-sf-faq.html

1349   **UK-SF-BOOKS:** From the U.K., on science-fiction and fantasy authors and books. *Mailing List*
http://www.pipex.net/people/chuck/sf/authors
± listproc@lists.pipex.com [body = subscribe uk-sf-books first-name last-name]
INFO OWNER admin-uk-sf-books@lists.pipex.com
ARCHIVE http://www.lists.pipex.com/cgi-bin/listproc/digests?list=uk-sf-books
FAQ http://www.pipex.net/people/chuck/sf/lists/uk-sf-books-faq.html

1350   uk.media.tv.sf.misc   General discussion of science fiction on U.K. television. *Newsgroup*

SCIENCE FICTION, FANTASY & HORROR—STAR TREK

1351   alt.binaries.startrek   Various binaries related to *Star Trek*. *Newsgroup*

1352   alt.ensign.wesley.die.die.die   We just can't get enough of him. *Newsgroup*

1353   alt.fan.q   Omnipotent being from either *Star Trek* or James Bond. *Newsgroup*

1354   alt.fan.surak   That wild and crazy Vulcan. *Newsgroup*

1355   alt.org.starfleet   The "Starfleet" Star Trek fan organization. *Newsgroup*

1356   alt.sex.fetish.startrek   Illogical yet fascinating *Star Trek* lust. *Newsgroup*

1357   alt.shared-reality.startrek.cardassian   Role-play Cardassians. *Newsgroup*

1358   alt.shared-reality.startrek.klingon   Klingons: blood, honor, and tribbles. *Newsgroup*

1359   alt.starfleet.rpg   Starfleet role-playing games. *Newsgroup*

1360   alt.startrek.bajoran   Discussion on the Star Trek alien race known as the Bajorans. *Newsgroup*

1361   alt.startrek.borg   Galactic spam. *Newsgroup*

1362   alt.startrek.cardassian   Cardassians in the Star Trek universe. *Newsgroup*

1363   alt.startrek.creative   Stories and parodies related to Star Trek. *Newsgroup*

1364   alt.startrek.creative.erotica   Star Trek lust. *Newsgroup*

1365   alt.startrek.klingon   Ack! What is that thing on your head? *Newsgroup*

1366   alt.startrek.romulan   Romulans in the Star Trek universe. *Newsgroup*

1367   alt.startrek.uss-amagosa   The Internet Star Trek Society. *Newsgroup*

1368   alt.startrek.vulcan   Vulcans in the Star Trek universe. *Newsgroup*

1369   alt.tv.star-trek.ds9   *Deep Space 9*. *Newsgroup*

1370   alt.tv.star-trek.tos   The original *Star Trek* series. *Newsgroup*

1371   alt.tv.star-trek.voyager   Another Star Trek universe show: *Voyager*. *Newsgroup*

1372   alt.wesley.crusher.die.die.die   Ensigns just get no respect. *Newsgroup*

1373   aus.sf.star-trek   Australian discussions of Star Trek, in all its forms. *Newsgroup*

1374   **The Babylon 5 Reviews Electronic Forum:** A dissemination point for critical opinion about the Babylon 5 television show series. Reviews are distributed to the list as soon as possible after receipt. *Newsletter*

listproc@cornell.edu [body = SUBSCRIBE B5-REVIEW-L first-name last-name]
INFO mss1@cornell.edu (Michael Shappe)
Frequency: irregular

1375 **Dateline: Starfleet:** News and commentary on the various Star Trek TV series and motion pictures. *E-Journal*
± datelined@aol.com
INFO data1701d@aol.com (Bill Mason)
Frequency: monthly

1376 **fj.rec.sf.startrek** Discussion on Star Trek (in Japanese). *Newsgroup*

1377 **rec.arts.startrek.current** New Star Trek shows, movies, and books. *Newsgroup*

1378 **rec.arts.startrek.fandom** Star Trek conventions and memorabilia. *Newsgroup*

1379 **rec.arts.startrek.info** Information about the universe of Star Trek. *Moderated newsgroup*

1380 **rec.arts.startrek.misc** General discussions of Star Trek. *Newsgroup*

1381 **rec.arts.startrek.reviews** Reviews of Star Trek books, episodes, films, etc. *Moderated newsgroup*

1382 **rec.arts.startrek.tech** Star Trek's depiction of future technologies. *Newsgroup*

1383 **Romulan International Empire Homepage:** The Romulan International Empire is a Star Trek fan organization.
http://unix.mclv.net/staff/death/rie.html
INFO death@unix.mclv.net

1384 **Trek-cochavim:** On Star Trek from a Jewish perspective. *Mailing List, moderated*
± listserv@shamash.nysernet.org [body = SUB TREK-COCHAVIM first-name last-name]
INFO mrand@dorsai.org (Michael Rand)

1385 **TREKWHO-L:** On *Star Trek* and *Doctor Who*: Malta's first publically accessible mailing list. *Mailing List*
± majordomo@jaguar.is.unimt.mt [body = SUBSCRIBE TREKWHO-L]
INFO cmeli@jaguar.is.unimt.mt (Clyde Meli, B.Sc.)

1386 **TREKWRTR:** Submitting and discussing *Star Trek* episodes from a writer's—not a fan's—viewpoint, plus other script-writing issues. *Mailing List*
± majordomo@stargame.org [body = subscribe trekwrtr]
OWNER kaseyc@discopy.com (Kasey Chang)

1387 **U.S.S. Columbia II:** The U.S.S. Columbia II is a fan chapter of the UFPI, a Star Trek fan orginization.
http://unix.mclv.net/columbia/home.html
INFO death@unix.mclv.net

1388 **uk.media.tv.sf.startrek** For discussion of Star Trek relevant to the U.K. *Newsgroup*

SCIENCE FICTION, FANTASY & HORROR—WORKS & AUTHORS

1389 **alt.books.anne-rice** The Vampire Thermostat. *Newsgroup*

1390 **alt.books.arthur-clarke** The writings of sf writer Arthur C. Clarke. *Newsgroup*

1391 **alt.books.brian-lumley** Books by Brian Lumley. *Newsgroup*

1392 **alt.books.clive-barker** Discussion of the writings of Clive Barker. *Newsgroup*

1393 **alt.books.cs-lewis** Narnia and other C. S. Lewis tales. *Newsgroup*

1394 **alt.books.dean-koontz** Discussion of the writings of Dean R. Koontz. *Newsgroup*

1395 **alt.books.deryni** Katherine Kurtz's books, especially the Deryni series. *Newsgroup*

1396 **alt.books.isaac-asimov** Fans of the late sf/science author Isaac Asimov. *Newsgroup*

1397 **alt.books.larry-niven** Discussion of the works of sf writer Larry Niven. *Newsgroup*

1398 **alt.books.moorcock** Discussions about the writings of Michael Moorcock. *Newsgroup*

1399 `alt.books.phil-k-dick` Discussion about the works of Philip K. Dick. *Newsgroup*

1400 `alt.books.poppy-z-brite` Horror and fantasy by author Poppy Z. Brite. *Newsgroup*

1401 `alt.books.raymond-feist` Fantasy author Raymond Feist and the Midkemia series. *Newsgroup*

1402 `alt.books.sf.melanie-rawn` The author of the Dragon Star and Dragon Prince series. *Newsgroup*

1403 `alt.cult-movies.alien` The Alien series of films. *Newsgroup*

1404 `alt.fan.addams.wednesday` She's deadpan and she's homicidal / the Addams Family. *Newsgroup*

1405 `alt.fan.authors.stephen-king` Modern master of the spooky story. *Newsgroup*

1406 `alt.fan.bgcrisis` Priss, the Replicants, the ADP, and Bubblegum Crisis. *Newsgroup*

1407 `alt.fan.blade-runner` The movie *Blade Runner*. *Newsgroup*

1408 `alt.fan.douglas-adams` Author of *The Meaning of Life* and other fine works. *Newsgroup*

1409 `alt.fan.dragonlance` For fans of the fantasy Dragonlance™ series. *Newsgroup*

1410 `alt.fan.dragons` People just love automobiles at Pennsic. *Newsgroup*

1411 `alt.fan.dune` Herbert's drinking buddies. *Newsgroup*

➤ `alt.fan.eddings:` The works of writer David Eddings. *Newsgroup*

1412 `alt.fan.harlan-ellison` For the discussion of the works of Harlan Ellison. *Newsgroup*

1413 `alt.fan.heinlein` Fans of sf author Robert Heinlein grok this group. *Newsgroup*

➤ `alt.fan.mst3k:` I thought people hated jerks who talked in theaters. *Newsgroup*

1414 `alt.fan.nathan.brazil` The Well of Souls and all things Markovian. *Newsgroup*

➤ `alt.fan.neil-gaiman:` The Sandman. *Newsgroup*

1415 `alt.fan.pern` Anne McCaffrey's sf oeuvre. *Newsgroup*

➤ `alt.fan.peter-david:` For fans of comic and sf writer Peter David. *Newsgroup*

1416 `alt.fan.philip-dick` The greatest sf mind on any planet. *Newsgroup*

1417 `alt.fan.piers-anthony` For fans of the sf author Piers Anthony. *Newsgroup*

1418 `alt.fan.power-rangers` Discussion of important Power Rangers facts. *Newsgroup*

1419 `alt.fan.pratchett` For fans of Terry Pratchett, sf humor writer. *Newsgroup*

1420 `alt.fan.pratchett.announce` Announcements about pubic wigs and book signings. *Moderated newsgroup*

1421 `alt.fan.robotech` Discussing all things relating to Robotech. *Newsgroup*

1422 `alt.fan.tank-girl` No, she doesn't make noises like a squirrel. Really. *Newsgroup*

1423 `alt.fantasy.conan` People dreaming about O'Brien. *Newsgroup*

1424 `alt.galactic-guide` Hitchhiker's guide to the Known Galaxy Project. *Newsgroup*

1425 `alt.horror.cthulhu` Campus Crusade for Cthulhu, Ctulhu, Ctulu, and the rest. *Newsgroup*

1426 `alt.illuminati` See alt.cabal. *Newsgroup*

➤ `alt.tv.highlander:` There was only one, then a bad sequel, now a TV show. *Newsgroup*

➤ `alt.tv.lois-n-clark:` The new adventures of the man from Krypton, Superman. *Newsgroup*

1427 `alt.tv.lost-in-space.danger.will-robinson.danger.danger.danger` Lost in Space. *Newsgroup*

➤ `alt.tv.mst3k:` Hey, you robots! Down in front! *Newsgroup*

1428 `alt.tv.seaquest` Deep-sea adventures in the future. *Newsgroup*

1429 `alt.tv.sentai` Live-action Asian sf/fantasy discussion, etc. *Newsgroup*

1430 `alt.tv.space-a&b` Discussion of the television show *Space: Above and Beyond*. *Newsgroup*

1431 `alt.tv.tekwar` A discussion of the television TekWar series. *Newsgroup*

1432 `alt.tv.time-traxx` Back from the future in *Time Traxx*. *Newsgroup*

1433 `alt.tv.v` Discussion of the sf phenomenon V. *Newsgroup*

1434 `rec.arts.sf.tv.babylon5` *Babylon 5* creators meet *Babylon 5* fans. *Newsgroup*

1435 `uk.media.tv.sf.babylon5` Babylon 5 TV show. *Newsgroup*

1436 `aus.sf.babylon5` The science-fiction television show Babylon 5. *Newsgroup*

1437 `rec.arts.sf.tv.babylon5.info` Announcements about TV show *Babylon 5. Moderated newsgroup*

➤ **Belior Rising MUSH:** Belior Rising is a small MUSH (Multiple User Shared Hallucination) based on Anne McCaffrey's Dragonriders of Pern series. It is a venue for those who love the world and for those who love to role-play. (See entry 3178 for full listing.)

1438 **The Cabinet of Dr. Casey - The Horror Web Page:** A tribute to the horror genre. The Cabinet has information on both movies and literature, plus graphics, audio files, a timeline of horror, the Horror Atlas, and even a section where amateur authors can post their stories.

   `http://www.cat.pdx.edu/~caseyh/horror/index.html`

   INFO `caseyh@ee.pdx.edu`

➤ **Coven Pride:** Semi-literary map of the Coptic, neo-Goth city of Coven Pride. It's all about love, labor, and traversing one's days over a landscape of pain. It lets in unsolicited submissions and keeps out only academes and homophobes. (See entry 1639 for full listing.)

1439 `rec.arts.drwho` Discussion about Dr. Who. *Newsgroup*

1440 **drwho-l:** On the U.K. fantasy/science-fiction series Dr. Who. *Mailing List*

   `http://www.pipex.net/people/chuck/sf/drwho`

   ± `listproc@lists.pipex.com` [body = SUBSCRIBE DRWHO-L first-name last-name]

   INFO OWNER `admin-drwho-l@lists.pipex.com`

   ARCHIVE `http://www.pipex.net/cgi-bin/listproc/digests?list=drwho-l`

   FAQ `http://www.pipex.net/people/chuck/sf/lists/drwho-l-faq.html`

➤ **Who-RPG-L:** Discussion of role-playing in the universe of Dr. Who. (See entry 6522 for full listing.)

1441 `rec.arts.drwho.info` Information about Doctor Who. *Moderated newsgroup*

1442 `alt.drwho.creative` Writing about long scarves and time machines. *Newsgroup*

1443 **FAB-L:** On Gerry Anderson and his "tele-fantasy" work. *Mailing List*

   ± `listproc@lists.pipex.com` [body = SUBSCRIBE FAB-L first-name last-name]

   INFO `admin-fab-l@lists.pipex.com`

   INFO `listmaster@lists.pipex.com` (technical problems)

1444 **FAB-UFO:** The *UFO* TV series mailing list. *Mailing List*

   ± `listproc@lists.pipex.com` [body = SUBSCRIBE FAB-UFO first-name last-name]

   INFO `listmaster@lists.pipex.com` (technical problems)

   OWNER `admin-fab-ufo@lists.pipex.com` (Marc Martin)

   ARCHIVE `http://www.lists.pipex.com/cgi-bin/listproc/digests?list=FAB-UFO`

1445 **GARGOYLES:** On the animated series *Gargoles* from Disney. *Mailing List*

   ± `majordomo@lists.mv.net` [body = subscribe gargoyles]

   OWNER `raven@kehleyr.phys.ttu.edu` (Morgan Bottrell)

1446 **J. V. Jones Website:** This is the author Web page of the number-one national bestselling sf trade paperback novel *The Baker's Boy*. The site combines stylish graphics, humor, and lots of custom-written material.

   `http://www.imgnet.com/auth/jjones.html`

   INFO `http://www.imgnet.com/auth/jjfrm.html`

1447 **MERCEDES-LACKEY:** On work of fantasy author Mercedes Lackey. *Mailing List*

   ± `listproc@herald.co.uk` [body = SUBSCRIBE MERCEDES-LACKEY first-name last-name]

   OWNER `lackey-owner@herald.co.uk` (Melanie Dymond Harper)

ARCHIVES

```
ftp://ftp.herald.co.uk/pub/lists/lackey-archives
http://ftp.herald.co.uk/pub/lists/lackey-archives
```

1448 `alt.books.m-lackey` Author Mercedes Lackey and her books. *Newsgroup*

➤ **The Official Nicola Griffith Page:** Information on Nicola Griffith, author of the novels *Ammonite* and *Slow River* and the collection *Women and Other Aliens* (forthcoming). (See entry 604 for full listing.)

1449 `rec.arts.sf.tv.quantum-leap` *Quantum Leap* TV, comics, cons, etc. *Newsgroup*

1450 `rec.arts.sf.written.robert-jordan` Books by author Robert Jordan. *Newsgroup*

1451 `rec.arts.tv.mst3k.announce` *Mystery Science Theater 3000* announcements. *Moderated newsgroup*

1452 `rec.arts.tv.mst3k.misc` For fans of *Mystery Science Theater 3000. Newsgroup*

1453 **REDDWARF:** On Red Dwarf, the U.K. fantasy/science-fiction TV series. *Mailing List*
± `listproc@lists.pipex.com` [body = SUBSCRIBE REDDWARF first-name last-name]
INFO `admin-reddwarf@lists.pipex.com`
INFO `listmaster@lists.pipex.com` (technical problems)
ARCHIVE `http://www.pipex.net/people/chuck/sf/reddwarf`

1454 `alt.tv.red-dwarf` The British sf/comedy show1. *Newsgroup*

1455 **SFYNX-RA3:** Logs of J. D. Flora: A sci-fi/New-Age e-mail sequel. *Distribution List*
± `logs-admin@newciv.org`
OWNER `jhs@newciv.org` (Joachim H. Steingrubner, PhD)
ARCHIVE `http://www.newciv.org/sfra3/`

1456 **shadows:** On the late sixties ABC daily soap opera *Dark Shadows. Mailing List*
± `majordomo@sunee.uwaterloo.ca` [body = subscribe shadows]
INFO `shadows-request@sunee.uwaterloo.ca`

1457 `rec.arts.sf.starwars.games` Star Wars games: RPG, computer, card, etc. *Newsgroup*

1458 `rec.arts.sf.starwars.collecting` Topics relating to Star Wars collecting. *Newsgroup*

1459 `alt.binaries.starwars` Images and sounds from the Star Wars movies. *Newsgroup*

1460 `rec.arts.sf.starwars.info` General information pertaining to Star Wars. *Moderated newsgroup*

1461 `rec.arts.sf.starwars.misc` Miscellaneous topics pertaining to Star Wars. *Newsgroup*

1462 `alt.books.stephen-king` The works of horror writer Stephen King. *Newsgroup*

1463 `alt.fan.tolkien` Mortal men doomed to die. *Newsgroup*

1464 `rec.arts.books.tolkien` The works of J. R. R. Tolkien. *Newsgroup*

1465 `relcom.fido.su.tolkien` FIDOnet, creations of J.R.R Tolkien. *Newsgroup*

➤ **The Tolkien Timeline:** This compilation is a chronological list of important events relating to Tolkien's life, career, and scholarly pursuits, and attempts to provide a more clear picture of this astounding man. (See entry 606 for full listing.)

1466 **TolkLang:** On the linguistic aspects (from Elvish vocabulary and grammar to the use of Old English) in J. R. R. Tolkien's works. *Mailing List, moderated*
± INFO `tolklang-request@dcs.ed.ac.uk`
ARCHIVES
```
ftp://ftp.dcs.ed.ac.uk/export/TolkLang
http://www.dcs.ed.ac.uk/misc/local/TolkLang
```

1467 **X-Files:** On the television show *X-Files. Mailing List*
± `listproc@lists.pipex.com` [body = SUBSCRIBE X-FILES first-name last-name]
INFO `listmaster@lists.pipex.com` (technical problems)

INFO http://www.pipex.net/people/chuck/sf/x-files

OWNER admin-x-files@lists.pipex.com

FAQ http://www.pipex.net/people/chuck/sf/x-files

1468 `alt.binaries.x-files` Binary images from the popular tv show. *Newsgroup*

1469 `alt.tv.x-files` Extraterrestrial cover-up conspiracies. *Newsgroup*

1470 `alt.tv.x-files.creative` Creative writings for the the *X Files*. *Newsgroup*

1471 `uk.media.tv.sf.x-files` A group for all you U.K. *X Files*. *Newsgroup*

1472 `aus.tv.x-files` The paranormal suspense drama: The X Files. *Newsgroup*

TECHNOLOGY & ART

➤ **ACTLab (Advanced Communication Technologies Laboratory):** Information on issues of human-computer interfaces, interaction, and agency. (See entry 9358 for full listing.)

1473 `alt.art.video` Artistic expression using video as a medium. *Newsgroup*

1474 `alt.arts.nomad` Shifting, searching, belonging, place, identity, power? *Newsgroup*

1475 **ArtCompas Amsterdam:** ArtCompas, created by Dutch artist Francis Horbach, is a personalized view on quality and meaning in art. ArtCompas wants to explore origins and visions of creative imagination. Works of art are exhibited and links are made to art sources.

http://www.euronet.nl/users/artcompas/index.html

INFO artcompas@euronet.nl

➤ **Exploratorium:** A collection of 650 interactive exhibits in the areas of science, art, and human perception. (See entry 4301 for full listing.)

➤ **Fractal Explorer:** A nifty Web interface to viewing many different kinds of fractals (including Mandelbrot, Julia, Lyapunov, Magnet, and more). (See entry 9126 for full listing.)

1476 **Interface:** The creative person's technology magazine. *Newsletter*

INFO interface@vvv.com (Robert McCourty)

EDITOR editor@vvv.com (Robert McCourty)

ARCHIVE http://www.vvv.com/interface

1477 **Leonardo World Wide Web Site:** Published by Leonardo/ISAST, this Web site contains articles, galleries, artists' Web works, sound files, and a members' directory created for the Web site, as well as sections linked to the journal *Leonardo*, such as Words on Works (short illustrated texts written by artists about their own work), member services, *Leonardo* calls for papers, product evaluations and reviews of books, magazines, CDs, CD-ROMs, and exhibits.

http://www-mitpress.mit.edu/Leonardo/home.html

INFO isast@sfsu.edu (Pat Bentson)

1478 **Leonardo Electronic Alamanac:** An international and interdisciplinary forum on the use of new media in artistic expression, especially involving twentieth-century science and technology. Published on the Internet for Leonardo, the International Society for the Arts, Sciences, and Technology (ISAST). *E-Journal, moderated*

http://www-mitpress.mit.edu/jrnls.-catalog/leonardo-almanac.html

± INFO journals-orders@mit.edu

INFO journals-info@mit.edu

EDITOR harri067@maroon.tc.umn.edu (Craig Harris)

ARCHIVE http://www-mitpress.mit.edu/LEA/home.html

Frequency: continuous

➤ **Super AM Magazine:** The Journal founded by the enlightened. Super AM is to information in the nineties what A.M. radio was to information in the thirties. Global and undefinable. How will you find it? (See entry 655 for full listing.)

TELEVISION

➤ <u>**MEGA-MEDIA LINKS index @ OMNIBUS:EYE**</u>: A searchable index of thousands of film/TV/radio/multimedia/new-media/cinema links subcategorized into over 60 helpful areas. (See entry 6055 for full listing.)

1479 **TV Net:** Web Homes for Television and Cable Stations throughout the U.S. and the world. Includes listings of TV shows and cable programming, as well as TV discussion forums.
     http://www.tvnet.com/
     INFO david@tvnet.com

1480 **AGOTHIC:** On the CBS television show *American Gothic. Digest & Reflector*
     ± majordomo@stargame.org [body = subscribe agothic or agothic-digest]
     OWNER brianh@hq.stargame.org (Brian Hartsfield)

1481 **alt.computer.workshop.live** Interactive TV. *Newsgroup*

1482 **alt.tv.commercials** Keep them on the boob tube and off the net. *Newsgroup*

1483 **alt.tv.infomercials** 30 minutes to sell you a vacuum haircutting system. *Newsgroup*

1484 **alt.tv.networks.cbc** Shows on the Canadian Broadcasting Corporation (CBC). *Newsgroup*

1485 **alt.tv.nickelodeon** The first network for kids. *Newsgroup*

1486 **alt.tv.public-access** Public access and community television. *Newsgroup*

1487 **Arlington Community Television's Homepage:** Home page for Channel 33—Arlington, Virginia's community access cable station. This home page offers information about ACT and access in general, contact information, and examples of the type of progams produced through the facilities.
     http://www.channel33.org/
     INFO paul@channel33.org

1488 **aus.tv.community** Discussions relating to community television. *Newsgroup*

➤ **be.tv:** About television programs in Belgium. *Newsgroup*

1489 **bit.listserv.screen-l** Film and television discussion list. *Moderated newsgroup*

➤ **C-SPAN:** Cable-Satellite Public Affairs Network's Web and gopher sites to information about C-SPAN, job opportunities, reports, articles, press releases, historic documents and speeches, and more. (See entry 5508 for full listing.)

1490 **CBS:** Eye on the Net @ CBS; contains links to sites like CBS Sports, Late Show with David Letterman, and CBS News, among others.
     http://www.cbs.com/faq
     http://www.cbs.com/
     INFO marketing@cbs.com

1491 **chile.tv** Discussions about TV. *Newsgroup*

1492 **clari.apbl.tv** News on television and broadcasting. *Moderated newsgroup*

1493 **clari.living.tv** News of television programs and events. *Moderated newsgroup*

1494 **clari.nb.broadcast** Newsbytes: interactive television, cable TV. *Moderated newsgroup*

➤ **Court TV Law Center:** This site offers basic legal guidance on everything from family law to small-business issues. There are seminars, games, discussion forums, and an "Ask the Laywers" section where you can submit legal questions via e-mail. (See entry 5525 for full listing.)

➤ **The Dominion:** Sci-Fi Channel. (See entry 1322 for full listing.)

1495 **fj.rec.tv** Talk about television and its shows. *Newsgroup*

1496 **fj.rec.tv.cm** Information and discussions on TV commercials. *Newsgroup*

➤ **Inquisitor Mediarama:** The adjunctive Web site to *Inquisitor* magazine, a quarterly journal of art, technology, and culture. (See entry 9827 for full listing.)

1497 **ITFS-L:** On educational television using FCC designated microwave frequencies. *Mailing List*
     ± maiser@enm.uma.maine.edu
     OWNER hurst@enm.uma.maine.edu (Fred Hurst)

➤ **PBS Online®:** This site provides listings of PBS's programs, such as science and nature, documentaries, history, biography, how-to, and instructional television. Also included on this site is information about your local PBS station, the PBS store, learning services, and an online news service. (See entry 6067 for full listing.)

➤ **Possum-Lodge:** Discussion about the [New] Red Green Show. Quotes from the shows and duct tape are likely to be discussed. (See entry 6045 for full listing.)

1498 `rec.arts.tv` The boob tube, its history, and past and current shows. *Newsgroup*

1499 `rec.arts.tv.interactive` Developments in interactive television. *Newsgroup*

1500 `rec.arts.tv.soaps.abc` Soap operas produced by or for the ABC network. *Newsgroup*

1501 `rec.arts.tv.soaps.cbs` Soap operas produced by or for the CBS network. *Newsgroup*

1502 `rec.arts.tv.soaps.misc` Postings of interest to all soap operas viewers. *Newsgroup*

1503 `rec.arts.tv.uk.misc` Miscellaneous topics about U.K.-based television. *Newsgroup*

1504 `rec.video.cable-tv` Technical and regulatory issues of cable television. *Newsgroup*

1505 `rec.video.satellite.europe` European satellite broadcasting. *Newsgroup*

1506 `rec.video.satellite.tvro` "large dish" ("BUD") systems and technologies. *Newsgroup*

➤ **SALON:** An online interactive magazine of culture, books, arts, and ideas. (See entry 653 for full listing.)

1507 `sci.engr.television.advanced` HDTV/DATV standards, equipment, practices, etc. *Newsgroup*

1508 `sci.engr.television.broadcast` Broadcast facility equipment and practices. *Newsgroup*

➤ **srg.tvdrs:** Swiss TV-related information; sources: ELSA and SRG. *Newsgroup*

➤ **TV-film-video:** Vortex Technology's collection of materials relating to television, film, and video, including "Professor Neon's TV & Movie Mania" and other topic areas. (See entry 6069 for full listing.)

1509 `uk.media.tv.misc` Discussion of all aspects of TV in the U.K. *Newsgroup*

➤ **United States Public Broadcasting Service (PBS):** PBS Online™ provides listings of their programs, in categories such as science and nature, documentaries, history, biography, how-to, and instructional television. Also included on this site is information about your local PBS station, the PBS store, learning services, and an online news service. (See entry 6071 for full listing.)

➤ **WHNT 19 News:** From Huntsville, Alabama: a prototype TV news presence on the Web. (See entry 6139 for full listing.)

TELEVISION—SHOWS

1510 `alt.barney.dinosaur.die.die.die` "There's enough hatred of Barney for everyone!". *Newsgroup*

1511 `alt.binaries.sounds.tv` Sounds from copyrighted television shows. *Newsgroup*

1512 `alt.fan.bill-nye` Bill Nye, the Science Guy (TV show). *Newsgroup*

1513 `alt.fan.gene-scott` Some TV preacher and horse breeder. *Newsgroup*

1514 `alt.fan.greg-kinnear` The host of *Talk Soup* on the E! Entertainment Channel. *Newsgroup*

1515 `alt.fan.hawaii-five-o` Book 'em, Danno. *Newsgroup*

1516 `alt.fan.jay-leno` Fans of the *Tonight Show* with Jay Leno. *Newsgroup*

1517 `alt.fan.jen-aniston` Discussing the popular "Friends" star. *Newsgroup*

1518 `alt.fan.letterman` One of the top ten reasons to get the `alt` groups. *Newsgroup*

1519 `alt.fan.letterman.guests.female` Dave's babes. *Newsgroup*

1520 `alt.fan.letterman.top-ten` Top ten lists from the Letterman show. *Moderated newsgroup*

1521 `alt.fan.michaela.strachan` British children's TV presenter. *Newsgroup*

1522 `alt.fan.monty-python` Electronic fan club for those wacky Brits. *Newsgroup*

1523 `alt.fan.mst3k` I thought people hated jerks who talked in theaters. *Newsgroup*

1524 `alt.fan.televisionx` Forum for adult discussion relevant to *Television X*. *Newsgroup*

1525 `alt.fan.televisionx.charmaine` Fans of *Television X*'s Charmaine Sinclair. *Newsgroup*

1526 `alt.fan.televisionx.sammi` Fans of *Television X*'s Sammi Jessop. *Newsgroup*

1527 `alt.philosophy.no-dogs` Items in TV show *No Dogs or Philosophers Allowed*. *Newsgroup*

1528 `alt.ql.creative` *Quantum Leap* fiction for the typographically challenged. *Newsgroup*

1529 `alt.supermodels.cindy-crawford` House of Style's overexposed host. *Newsgroup*

➤ `alt.tv.ab-fab`: Discussion of the BBC TV comedy *Absolutely Fabulous*. *Newsgroup*

1530 `alt.tv.air-farce` Royal Canadian Air Farce. *Newsgroup*

1531 `alt.tv.amer-gothic` Discussion of the TV show *American Gothic*. *Newsgroup*

1532 `alt.tv.barney` He's everywhere. Now appearing in several `alt` groups. *Newsgroup*

1533 `alt.tv.baywatch` Discussing the world's #1 show! *Newsgroup*

1534 `alt.tv.beakmans-world` Some sort of science and comedy show. *Newsgroup*

1535 `alt.tv.bh90210` Fans of *Beverly Hills 90210* TV show. *Newsgroup*

1536 `alt.tv.billnye` The science guy. *Newsgroup*

1537 `alt.tv.brady-bunch` Here's the story of a lovely lady. *Newsgroup*

1538 `alt.tv.brisco-county` A western comedy adventure. *Newsgroup*

1539 `alt.tv.chicago-hope` Discussion of the TV show *Chicago Hope*. *Newsgroup*

➤ `alt.tv.comedy-central`: Just what the hell is going on here? *Newsgroup*

1540 `alt.tv.dark_shadows` For the fans that refuse to die. *Newsgroup*

1541 `alt.tv.dinosaurs` A live-action animated sitcom. *Newsgroup*

1542 `alt.tv.dinosaurs.barney.die.die.die` Squish the saccharine newt. *Newsgroup*

1543 `alt.tv.discovery.canada` The Discovery Channel Canada discussion group. *Newsgroup*

1544 `alt.tv.due-south` For the discussion of CTV's *Due South*. *Newsgroup*

1545 `alt.tv.dweebs` *Dweebs* sitcom on CBS. *Newsgroup*

1546 `alt.tv.earth2` Discussion of *Earth 2* television series. *Newsgroup*

1547 `alt.tv.eek-the-cat` Fans of the television show *Eek the Cat*. *Newsgroup*

1548 `alt.tv.er` Discussion of the television show *ER*. *Newsgroup*

1549 `alt.tv.forever-knight` The *Forever Knight* television programme. *Newsgroup*

1550 `alt.tv.frasier` Kelsey Grammer as Frasier. *Newsgroup*

1551 `alt.tv.friends` Discussion of NBC's comedy *Friends*. *Newsgroup*

1552 `alt.tv.game-shows` Just look at these wonderful prizes. *Newsgroup*

1553 `alt.tv.hercules-legendary-journeys` *Hercules: the Legendary Journeys*. *Newsgroup*

1554 `alt.tv.hermans-head` Fans of those inside (and outside) of *Herman's Head*. *Newsgroup*

1555 `alt.tv.highlander` There was only one, then a bad sequel, now a TV show. *Newsgroup*

1556 `alt.tv.home-imprvment` Discussions on the hit ABC sitcom *Home Improvement*. *Newsgroup*

1557 `alt.tv.homicide` A shotgun does an impressive job of destroying a TV. *Newsgroup*

1558 `alt.tv.knight-rider` Discussions about *Knight Rider*. *Newsgroup*

1559 `alt.tv.kungfu` *Kung-fu* and *Kung-fu: The Legend Continues*. *Newsgroup*

1560 `alt.tv.la-law` *LA Law*'s evening soap opera. *Newsgroup*

1561 `alt.tv.law-and-order` The "Law and Order" television program. *Newsgroup*

1562 `alt.tv.lois-n-clark` The new adventures of the man from Krypton, Superman. *Newsgroup*

1563 `alt.tv.lois-n-clark.fanfic` Posting and discussion of fan fiction works. *Newsgroup*

1564 `alt.tv.mad-about-you` Some people really love their televisions. *Newsgroup*

1565 `alt.tv.mad-tv` Alfred E. Neuman's *own* TV show. *Newsgroup*

1566 `alt.tv.magnum-pi` Your chest hair is showing! *Newsgroup*

1567 `alt.tv.man-from-uncle` The classic *Man from U.N.C.L.E.* series. *Newsgroup*

1568 `alt.tv.mash` Nothing like a good comedy about war and dying. *Newsgroup*

1569 `alt.tv.max-headroom` Blipverts will kill ya. *Newsgroup*

1570 `alt.tv.melrose-place` Catfights and sleaziness, Wednesdays on Fox. *Newsgroup*

1571 `alt.tv.models-inc` A spinoff of *Melrose Place*. *Newsgroup*

1572 `alt.tv.mst3k` Hey, you robots! Down in front! *Newsgroup*

1573 `alt.tv.mtv` I want my MTV. *Newsgroup*

1574 `alt.tv.muppets` Miss Piggy on the tube. *Newsgroup*

1575 `alt.tv.murder-one` Discussion of the TV series *Murder One*. *Newsgroup*

1576 `alt.tv.mwc` *Married . . . With Children*. *Newsgroup*

1577 `alt.tv.my-s-c-life` *My So-Called Life* and Operation Life Support. *Newsgroup*

1578 `alt.tv.news-shows` Tabloid journalism on the television. *Newsgroup*

1579 `alt.tv.newsradio` Discussion of the NBC sitcom *Newsradio*. *Newsgroup*

1580 `alt.tv.northern-exp` For the TV show with moss growing on it. *Newsgroup*

1581 `alt.tv.nowhere-man` The TV show *Nowhere Man* on U.S. UPN stations. *Newsgroup*

1582 `alt.tv.nypd-blue` For fans of the *NYPD Blue* TV show. *Newsgroup*

1583 `alt.tv.party-of-five` Fans of Fox's *Party of Five*. *Newsgroup*

1584 `alt.tv.picket-fences` The *Picket Fences* show. *Newsgroup*

1585 `alt.tv.prisoner` *The Prisoner* television series from years ago. *Newsgroup*

1586 `alt.tv.quantum-leap.creative` Fan fiction relating to the show *Quantum Leap*. *Newsgroup*

1587 `alt.tv.real-world` Discussion of the MTV program *The Real World*. *Newsgroup*

1588 `alt.tv.road-rules` *Road Rules* MTV series. *Newsgroup*

1589 `alt.tv.rockford-files` But he won't do windows. *Newsgroup*

1590 `alt.tv.roseanne` In all her glory. *Newsgroup*

1591 `alt.tv.saved-bell` *Saved by the Bell*, a sitcom for teens. *Newsgroup*

1592 `alt.tv.sctv` SCTV (Second City TV) and alumni discussions. *Newsgroup*

1593 `alt.tv.seinfeld` A funny guy. *Newsgroup*

➤ `alt.tv.sesame-street:` Sunny day. *Newsgroup*

1594 `alt.tv.silk-stalkings` USA's *Silk Stalkings* murder-mystery show. *Newsgroup*

1595 `alt.tv.sliders` Fox's *Sliders*. *Newsgroup*

1596 `alt.tv.sliders.creative` Writing stories in the *Sliders* show environment. *Newsgroup*

1597 `alt.tv.strange-luck` Discussion of the television show *Strange Luck*. *Newsgroup*

1598 `alt.tv.talkshows.daytime` Babble. *Newsgroup*

1599 `alt.tv.talkshows.late` Late-night wars on the major networks. *Newsgroup*

1600 `alt.tv.the-tick` *Spooon!*. *Newsgroup*

1601   `alt.tv.tv-nation`   Some show called *TV Nation*. *Newsgroup*

1602   `alt.tv.twin-peaks`   Discussion about the popular (and unusual) TV show. *Newsgroup*

1603   `alt.tv.upstairs-downstairs`   Discussing *Upstairs, Downstairs*. *Newsgroup*

1604   `alt.tv.vr5`   *VR 5*. *Newsgroup*

1605   `alt.tv.weird-science`   *Weird Science*. *Newsgroup*

1606   `alt.tv.wings`   For Sandpiper Air frequent flyers. *Newsgroup*

1607   `alt.tv.wiseguy`   A wise guy. *Newsgroup*

1608   `alt.tv.xuxa`   That Connie Dobbs clone, her TV show, and her double Xs. *Newsgroup*

➤   `alt.video.tape-trading`:   Trading of legally copied videos. *Newsgroup*

➤   **Bedrock Online (The Flintstones Mailing List):** On the *Flintstones* television series. (Where's Pebbles?) (See entry 45 for full listing.)

➤   **Comedy Central Online:** Irreverent, topical comedy from the Comedy Central cable network, together with program and schedule information. (See entry 242 for full listing.)

1609   `rec.arts.tv.uk.coronation-st`   Regarding the U.K. based show *Coronation Street*. *Newsgroup*

1610   `rec.arts.tv.uk.eastenders`   Regarding the U.K. based show *Eastenders*. *Newsgroup*

➤   `alt.tv.red-dwarf`:   The British sf/comedy show1. *Newsgroup*

THEATER

➤   `alt.comedy.vaudeville`:   Vaudeville and its descendants. *Newsgroup*

➤   `alt.fan.ralph.fiennes`:   For fans of actor Ralph Fiennes. *Newsgroup*

1611   `alt.home-theater.marketplace`   Home theater equipment wanted and for sale. *Newsgroup*

1612   `alt.home-theater.misc`   Discussing all aspects of home theater systems. *Newsgroup*

1613   `alt.stagecraft`   Technical theater issues. *Newsgroup*

1614   **Applied and Interactive Theater guide:** Information on and links to psychodrama, drama therapy, sociodrama, playback theater, Boal centers and practitioners, community-issues groups, and training and development specialists. Maintained by Joel Plotkin.
     `http://csep.sunyit.edu/~joel/guide.html`
     INFO `joel@sunyit.edu`

1615   **ASTR-L:** On theater history (American Society for Theatre Research). *Mailing List*
     `http://www.uiuc.edu/providers/kcpa/astr/`
     ± `listserv@postoffice.cso.uiuc.edu` [body = SUBSCRIBE ASTR-L first-name last-name]
     INFO `padavis@ux1.cso.uiuc.edu` (Peter Davis)

➤   **The Audio Description Home Page:** Provides information and resources for audio description techniques for people who are seeing-impaired. (See entry 9885 for full listing.)

1616   `can.schoolnet.arts.drama`   Drama studies in elementary/secondary schools. *Newsgroup*

1617   **Candrama:** For research of Canadian theater. *Mailing List*
     `http://www.lib.unb.ca/UNB/theatre/`
     ± `listserv@unb.ca` [body = SUBSCRIBE CANDRAMA first-name last-name]
     INFO `mullaly@unb.ca` (Edward Mullaly)
     ARCHIVE `listserv@unb.ca` [body = INDEX Candrama]

1618   **COLLAB-L:** On collaboration among playwrights, directors, techies, composers, and librettists. *Mailing List*
     ± OWNER `sas14@psu.edu` (Stve Schrum)
     ARCHIVE `http://k302.hn.psu.edu/COLLABL/Collab-l.html`

1619   **COMEDIA:** On Spanish Golden Age theater. *Mailing List*

```
http://listserv.arizona.edu/comedia.html
```
± `listserv@arizvml.ccit.arizona.edu` [body = SUBSCRIBE COMEDIA first-name last-name]
INFO `jabraham@ccit.arizona.edu`
ARCHIVE `listserv@arizvml.ccit.arizona.edu`

1620 **Didaskalia: Ancient Theater Today:** Listings, reviews, and features on Greek and Roman drama in performance. *E-Journal*
```
http://www.warwick.ac.uk/didaskalia/didaskalia.html
```
± INFO `didaskalia@csv.warwick.ac.uk`
INFO `tssac@csv.warwick.ac.uk` (Sallie Goetsch)
ARCHIVES
```
ftp://ftp.csv.warwick.ac.uk/pub/journals/didaskalia/
gopher.csv.warwick.ac.uk
```
Frequency: bimonthly

1621 `fj.rec.play` Topics about plays and theater. *Newsgroup*

1622 `kw.theatre` Theater reviews, etc. *Newsgroup*

1623 **Playbill On-Line:** Online theater resource, including worldwide listings, news, and features.
```
http://www.playbill.com/
```
INFO `webmaster@playbill.com`

1624 **Queatre:** On theater in Quebec. *Mailing List, moderated*
± `listproc@uqam.ca`
OWNER `bourassa.andre_g@uqam.ca` (Andre Bourassa)
ARCHIVE `http://www.er.uqam.ca/nobel/c2545/theatral.html`
Language: French
Please Note: Subscription by approval only.

1625 `rec.arts.puppetry` For discussion of puppets in any form or venue. *Newsgroup*

1626 `rec.arts.theatre.misc` Miscellaneous topics and issues in theatre. *Newsgroup*

1627 `rec.arts.theatre.plays`. Dramaturgy and discussion of plays. *Newsgroup*

1628 `rec.arts.theatre.stagecraft` Issues in stagecraft and production. *Newsgroup*

1629 **REED-L:** For discussion of early English drama. *Mailing List*
± `listserv@vm.utcc.utoronto.ca` [body = SUBSCRIBE REED-L first-name last-name]
INFO `reed@epas.utoronto.ca` (Dr. Abigail Young)
ARCHIVE `listserv@vm.utcc.utoronto.ca` [body = INDEX REED-L]
Please Note: Subscription by approval only.

➤ **SavoyNet:** On Gilbert and Sullivan and their operettas. (See entry 939 for full listing.)

1630 **SHAKSPER:** For discussion of the works of William Shakespeare. *Mailing List, moderated*
± `listserv@ws.bowiestate.edu` [body = SUBSCRIBE SHAKSPER first-name last-name]
INFO `hmcook@boe00.minc.umd.edu` (Hardy Cook)
Please Note: Subscription by approval only.
Comments: Potential subscribers are requested to submit a brief biography to the list owner prior admission to the list.

➤ **SpiGopher at Iowa State University:** This is the Computation Center at Iowa State. The server itself is located on the ISUMVS system (WYLBUR) at Iowa State and primarily uses the SPIRES database facility. It includes a play concordance of eight fully indexed plays. (See entry 4449 for full listing.)

1631 **stagecraft:** On all aspects of stage work (special effects, sound effects, stage management, set design, lighting, hall management, show production, etc.). *Mailing List*
```
http://www.ffa.ucalgary.ca/citt/clbd/wais.html
```

± **INFO** stagecraft-request@jaguar.cs.utah.edu (Brad Davis)

INFO OWNER bdavis@zinc.com (Brad Davis)

ARCHIVE ftp://ftp.ffa.ucalgary.ca/pub/stagecraft

POST stagecraft@zinc.com

1632 UK Theatre Web: A guide to professional and amateur theatre in the U.K. Covers opera, plays, musicals, dance, theatre news, and more. This site is the only online theatre guide to cover the whole of the U.K.

http://www.uktw.co.uk/

INFO webmaster@uktw.co.uk

INFO info@uktw.co.uk

ZINES

1633 e-zine-list: A directory of electronic magazines (e-zines, for short). Most of the zines listed are esoteric, bizarre, and/or personal.

http://www.meer.net/~johnl/e-zine-list/

ftp://ftp.etext.org/pub/Zines/e-zine-list

gopher://gopher.etext.org/11/Zines/e-zine-list

INFO johnl@meer.net (John Labovitz)

1634 FactSheet Five - Electric: Central clearinghouse of information about zines, which are small-press magazines published by individuals or groups of people who need to communicate with others about subjects of intense, passionate interest.

ftp://ftp.etext.org

http://www.well.com/~Publications/F5/Reviews/

gopher://gopher.well.com

± **INFO** jerod23@well.sf.ca.us (Jerod Pore)

Frequency: quarterly

Maintains an archive of over 100 e-zines, and links to 1,000 electronic publications.

1635 Zine.Net: A guide to a vast assortment of independent, self-published zines: the goal is to generate sales for printed (hard-copy) zines.

http://www.zine.net/

INFO roy@zine.net

1636 Biohazard: A site ostensibly designed to foster collaboration among Bay Area artists, its front page is introduced by a collage made from text and links that betray Biohazard's unique aesthetic and nonlinear sense of humor.

http://www.biohazard.org/www/

INFO jennings@biohazard.org

Comments: Unrelated to the punk band of the same name.

➤ **BRETTnews:** "The peppy zine for active people." Brush your teeth. (See entry 496 for full listing.)

1637 buzznet: Online zine for the counterculture. Music, politics, action, tech, comics, lit, sci-fi and fun. Killer graphics make the experience most user friendly. :) *E-Zine*

http://www.buzznet.com/

INFO OWNER editor@buzznet.com (Marc Brown)

INFO info@buzznet.com (Marc Brown & Alistair Jeffs)

ARCHIVE http://www.buzznet.com/annex/archive

Frequency: monthly

1638 Carolyn's Diary: The continuing diary of Carolyn L Burke, a 30-year-old woman living in Toronto.

http://carolyn.org/~clburke/Diary.html#today

INFO clburke@carolyn.org

1639 Coven Pride: Semi-literary map of the Coptic, neo-Goth city of Coven Pride. It's all about love, labor, and traversing one's days over a landscape of pain. It lets in unsolicited submissions and keeps out only academes and homophobes. *E-Journal*

`http://www.brown.edu/Departments/MCM/Rabyd/Coven_Pride_814.html`

INFO `rabyd@brownvm.brown.edu` (Vera Rabyd)

Frequency: weekly

1640 Cropduster: Zine of cultural underachievers, featuring vendettas, spelling mistakes, stubborness, and vulgarity. *E-Zine*

± `ftp://etext.archive.umich.edu/pub/Zines/Cropduster`

INFO `ad522@freenet.carleton.ca` (Steven Meece)

INFO `cwoodill@interlog.com` (Chris Woodhill)

ARCHIVES

`ftp://etext.archive.umich.edu/pub/Zines/Cropduster`

`http://chat.carleton.ca/~smeece`

Frequency: annually (for right now)

➤ **Cyborganics:** The first step in a grand plan to build a funky, friendly place that exists on both sides of the screen. (See entry 9821 for full listing.)

1641 dEPARTURE fROM nORMAL: A free zine of art works. *E-Zine*

`http://www.teleport.com/~xwinds/dfn`

1642 Drain e-Zine: News and happenings otherwise unattainable through normal media processes. *E-Zine*

± INFO `sfarrug@caticsuf.csufresno.edu` [body = `Please add my name to the Drain e-Zine mailing list` e-mail-address] (Shaun Farrugia)

ARCHIVE `gopher://etext.archive.umich.edu/Zines/`

Frequency: irregular

➤ **DRIVE-INS:** On drive-in movie theaters and classic indoor bijous. (See entry 700 for full listing.)

1643 E-Text E-Zines: Extensive archive of electronic magazines in ASCII, PDF, and other formats, plus hypertext zines on Web server.

`http://www.etext.org/Zines/`

`ftp://ftp.etext.org/pub/Zines/`

INFO `www@etext.org`

1644 et Cetera: the zine of everything and nothing. et Cetera is exactly what it says . . . "and other things" if i'm not mistaken. it will conduct interviews on random topics (we'll try to cover *everything* at least once!). *E-Zine*

`ftp://etext.archive.umich.edu`

`http://www.cs.andrews.edu/~adap/etcetera/`

INFO `lees@andrews.edu` (Steve Lee)

Frequency: irregular

1645 F.U.C.K.: Good writing. Punk. Sorta. Check it out. *E-Zine*

INFO `jericho@netcom.com` (Damien Sorder)

ARCHIVE `ftp://ftp.netcom.com/pub/je/jericho/jericho.html`

➤ **Fat City News:** The world's lone repository of outlandish and gonzo journalism. (See entry 6092 for full listing.)

➤ **FringeWare:** Fringe culture dispersed through design and undesign, community, humor, the marketplace, the net. (See entry 9824 for full listing.)

1646 Hallucinet: Southern California's "koolest, neato-est, freakiest zine/site/good karma meeting place." Site for Lethal Records, Cleopatra Records, Retail Slut, and several zines including Caffeine, Underscope, Asylum, and more.

`http://www.hallucinet.com/`

INFO `fuligin@aol.com`

1647 **ICS Electrozine:** Information, Control, Supply—stories, articles, editorials, letters, etc. on topics including the unknown, the Internet, society, philosophy, music, role-playing games, and science. *E-Zine*

http://www.western.edu/happen/welcome.html

± INFO org_zine@wsc.colorado.edu

Frequency: every two weeks

➤ **Inquisitor Mediarama:** The adjunctive Web site to *Inquisitor* magazine, a quarterly journal of art, technology, and culture. (See entry 9827 for full listing.)

1648 **Interesting! On Line:** A compilation of things that Rich Sagall finds interesting. *E-Zine*

http://www.agate.net/~richs/interesting.html

± interesting@pobox.com

OWNER rich.sagall@pobox.com (Rich Sagall)

ARCHIVE http://www.agate.net/~richs/interesting.html

➤ **kulturCHOCK!:** A Swedish-American journal of being neither here nor there. Information and commentary for the Swede living in the U.S. and the American living in Sweden. (See entry 7616 for full listing.)

➤ **Line Noiz:** Line Noiz is a cyberpunk-related e-zine featuring articles on cyberpunk, cyberpunk science fiction, the Internet, and other associated themes. (See entry 9828 for full listing.)

➤ **Suck:** Suck is "an experiment in provocation, mordant deconstructionism, and buzz-saw journalism," or, to quote Brock Meeks, "a kind of de facto Web 'Ombudsmen' with Attitude." (See entry 654 for full listing.)

➤ **TAO:** As "freedom and independent consciousness face the threat of cyber-design and virtual reality," this site provides a wise and impassioned response. (See entry 5594 for full listing.)

1649 **TikiZine:** A biweekly electronic magazine housed on the World Wide Web, dedicated to informal discussion of things great and small; entertainment, pop culture, current events, etc. *E-Zine*

http://www.students.uiuc.edu/~cricket/tikizine/

EDITOR editor@tikizine.com (Dan Kast, Editor-in-Chief)

ARCHIVE ftp://crh0495.urh.uiuc.edu/tikizine/

Frequency: bimonthly

1650 **uXu: Underground eXperts United:** Swedish-based series written in English, containing, but not limited to, anything ranging from fiction and bizarre experiences to how-to descriptions. Readers are welcome to send their own work. *E-Zine*

http://www.lysator.liu.se/~chief/

± INFO uxu-info-request@lysator.liu.se [subject = subscribe uxu]

INFO chief@lysator.liu.se (Erik Soderstrom)

ARCHIVES

uxu-info-request@lysator.liu.se [body = SUB UXU first-name last-name]

ftp://etext.archive.umich.edu/pub/Zines/UXU

ftp://ftp.lysator.liu.se/pub/texts/uxu

gopher://gopher.cic.net/11/e-serials/alphabetic/u/uxu/

gopher://etext.archive.umich.edu/11/Zines/

gopher://locust.cic.net/11/Zines/UXU

http://www.algonet.se/~daba/

Frequency: irregular (monthly, if possible)

BUSINESS & INDUSTRY

1651 <u>Business Sources on the Internet</u>: This site lists business sources available on the Internet. Resources listed include: Web and gopher servers, telnet services, mailing lists, lists and directories of commercial sites, company and financial information, country-specific business resources, government, statistical, economic, market and industry-specific resources, and a list of news sources.

    `http://www.dis.strath.ac.uk/business/`

    INFO `sheila@dis.strath.ac.uk`

1652 `alt.business.misc` All aspects of commerce. *Newsgroup*

1653 `biz.general` Dialogue related to business operations and offerings. *Newsgroup*

1654 `biz.marketplace.services.discussion` Discussion of business services. *Newsgroup*

➤ **H-Business:** On business history. (See entry 5204 for full listing.)

1655 `misc.business.facilitators` Discussions for all types of facilitators. *Newsgroup*

ACCOUNTING

1656 **accounting:** For news, notices, announcements, and standards of interest to public accountants. *Distribution List*

    ± `listproc@financenet.gov` [body = SUBSCRIBE ACCOUNTING first-name last-name]

    OWNER `support@financenet.gov`

    Gated: `fnet.accounting`

    Comments: Part of Al Gore's FinanceNet

1657 **AEthics-L:** On the ethical dimension of accounting and auditing. *Mailing List*

    ± `listproc@scu.edu.au` [body = SUBSCRIBE AETHICS-L first-name last-name]

    INFO `http://anet.scu.edu.au/anet/lists/`

    EDITOR `rpm@milton.bus.bond.edu.au` (Prof. Ray McNamara)

    OWNER `anetadm@anet.scu.edu.au` (ANet)

    ARCHIVE `listproc@scu.edu.au`

➤ **AGA:** List for members of the Association of Government Accountants. (See entry 5413 for full listing.)

1658 **AIntAcc-L:** On all aspects of international accounting. *Mailing List*

    `http://anet.scu.edu.au/ANetHomePage.html`

    ± `listproc@scu.edu.au` [body = SUBSCRIBE AINTACC-L first-name last-name]

    EDITOR `ieddie@metz.une.edu.au` (Ian Eddie)

    OWNER `anetadm@anet.scu.edu.au` (ANet)

    ARCHIVE `listproc@scu.edu.au` [body = index AIntAcc-L]

1659 `alt.business.internal-audit` Discussion of internal auditing. *Newsgroup*

1660 `alt.payroll` Payroll—taxes—labor relations—human resources. *Newsgroup*

1661 `biz.comp.accounting` Dialogue specific to the accounting software industry. *Newsgroup*

1662 **WACCNET-L:** For accountants in the state of Washington. *Mailing List, moderated*

    ± `listserv@eskimo.com` [body = SUBSCRIBE WACCNET-L first-name last-name]

    OWNER `earl@eskimo.com` (Earl Hall, CPA)

    Please Note: Subscription by approval only.

BANKS & BANKING

1663 `clari.biz.industry.banking` Banks and S & Ls. *Moderated newsgroup*

1664 `clari.biz.industry.banking.releases` News releases: banks and S & Ls. *Moderated newsgroup*

➤ **CommunityDevelopmentBanking-L:** On community reinvestment. (See entry 9760 for full listing.)

1665 **CU-TALK:** On credit union management issues. *Mailing List*

± `listserv@usa.net` [body = SUBSCRIBE CU-TALK first-name last-name]

OWNER `philk@ucg.com` (Phil Kemelor)

1666 **Minority Bank Monitor:** The site provides information on every women- or minority-owned financial institution in the U.S.

`http://www2.ari.net/cirm/`

INFO `cirm@ari.net`

1667 `relcom.banktech` Discussions on banking technologies. *Newsgroup*

1668 `relcom.commerce.money` Credits, deposits, currency. *Newsgroup*

➤ **The World Bank:** This site contains information about the World Bank, its press releases, country and project Information, regional information, publications, and research studies. (See entry 5446 for full listing.)

CLASSIFIEDS

1669 `alt.marketplace.funky-stuff.forsale` Miscellaneous and offbeat items on offer. *Newsgroup*

➤ **The Beer Classifieds:** A place for providers of beer-related products and services to announce their wares. (See entry 5874 for full listing.)

➤ `biz.marketplace.computers.other:` Other computer hardware/software. *Newsgroup*

1670 `biz.marketplace.non-computer` Noncomputer merchandise offered/wanted. *Newsgroup*

➤ `biz.marketplace.services.computers:` Computer services offered/wanted. *Newsgroup*

1671 `biz.marketplace.services.non-computer` Noncomputer services offered/wanted. *Newsgroup*

1672 **The Business Page International:** Professional business advertising. Includes listings on businesses wanted and for sale, real estate, trade opportunities, and more.

`http://www.sgn.com/`

INFO `hostmaster@sgn.com`

1673 **Classified Advertising Network:** Classified Advertising Network is a 56-newspaper group under Donrey Media. One purchase can place your classified ad in the hands of over one million readers nationwide.

`http://texoma.com/donrey/classified/newspaper/advertising`

INFO `can@texoma.com`

INFO `http://texoma.com/donrey`

1674 `demon.adverts` Personal and commercial advertisements by Demon members. *Newsgroup*

1675 `demon.adverts.d` Discussion area for demon.adverts. *Newsgroup*

➤ `fj.fleamarket.*:` Japanese for-sale groups. *Newsgroup*

➤ `fj.wanted:` Requests for things that are needed. *Newsgroup*

➤ `han.misc.forsale:` Things for sale, wanted to buy. *Newsgroup*

➤ `hsv.forsale:` Items for sale in Huntsville, Alabama. *Newsgroup*

1676 **Instant Connections:** Large classified advertising resource. Source of sites and products from around the world.

`http://webcom.net/~peak/classdir.html`

INFO `abelynx@globedirect.com`

➤ `israel.lists.il-ads:` Israel bulletin board for advertisements. *Newsgroup*

➤ `kc.forsale:` Goods and services for sale in the Kansas City area. *Newsgroup*

➤ `li.forsale:` Things for sale in the Long Island, NY (USA) area. *Newsgroup*

➤ `li.wanted:` Long Island's most-wanted list (classifieds). *Newsgroup*

1677 `misc.forsale.computers.discussion` Discussions only about items for sale. *Newsgroup*

1678 `misc.forsale.non-computer` Noncomputer items for sale and wanted. *Newsgroup*

1679 `misc.wanted` Requests for things that are needed (*not* software). *Newsgroup*

1680 `ne.forsale` Short postings on items for sale in New England. *Newsgroup*

➤ **The Official Online Guide to Canada's West Coast Music Industry:** The most comprehensive guide to Vancouver and British Columbia's music industry. Free listings for businesses and musicians. Also includes classified ads. (See entry 767 for full listing.)

1681 `relcom.ads` Non-commercial ads. *Newsgroup*

1682 `relcom.commerce.jobs` Jobs offered/wantedy. *Newsgroup*

1683 `relcom.commerce.orgtech` Office equipment. *Newsgroup*

➤ `sac.swap:` Sacramento for-sale group. *Newsgroup*

1684 **SOC:** Selected Online Classifieds: ads in categories selected by subscriber. *Mailing List*

± soc@pangaea.texas.net

INFO doug@pangaea.texas.net

OWNER douggurich@aol.com (Doug Gurich)

1685 `tnn.cm.new-product` Commercial messages and advertisements of new products. *Newsgroup*

1686 **Traders' Connection - Classified Ads:** Subscription-based service for over 1.5 million ads for automobiles, motorcycles, furniture, collectibles, computers, antiques, and more, plus value guides, search tools, and AdWatch(tm), which seeks specific items and reports results by way of pager, fax, or e-mail.

http://www.trader.com/ads

telnet://trader.com

1687 **TradeSafe:** This site provides a listing of classified-ad Web sites as well as a unique escrow service to help you purchase items safely from them.

http://www.tradesafe.com/tradesafe

INFO tradesafe@tradesafe.com

1688 **The Trading Post:** Free WWW classified advertising site.

http://www.tradingpost.com/

INFO posse@tradingpost.com

FAQ http://www.tradingpost.com/faq.html

1689 **The Usenet Marketplace FAQ:** This web page is an organized interface to the large number of Usenet classifieds newsgroups.

http://www.phoenix.net/~lildan/FAQ/

INFO lildan@phoenix.net

1690 **World-Wide Classifieds™:** Need a car? Want to sell that old ten-speed bicycle in the garage? This is the nickel want ads for the Information Highway. Browse ads by keyword, location, or classification. Enter your own ads online.

http://www.world-wide.com/wwa/

INFO wwcinfo@world-wide.com

FAQS

http://www.world-wide.com/wwa/queryex.htm

http://www.world-wide.com/wwa/placeex.htm

CORPORATIONS

1691 `clari.biz.industry.conglomerates` Conglomerates and holding companies. *Moderated newsgroup*

1692 `clari.biz.stocks.corporate_news` Corporate stocks, dividends. *Moderated newsgroup*

1693 **Federal Express:** Get tracking data on that package that's coming to you!

http://www.fedex.com/

INFO webmaster@fedex.com

DIRECTORIES

➤ **BizWeb:** A subject-oriented directory of companies on the Web. (See entry 2755 for full listing.)

➤ **The Canadian Internet Business Directory:** Search businesses and government and educational institutions in Canada by company, name, province, or type. (See entry 7126 for full listing.)

➤ **Chicago Moving Image Scene:** The online resource and directory for Chicagoland producers of film, video, and multimedia. Free professional listings. (See entry 8112 for full listing.)

➤ **Global Recycling Network:** GRN is the most comprehensive recycling information resource available on the Internet. Its goal is to offer a one-stop solution to the recycling information needs of business users, consultants, researchers, students, and consumers alike, while helping to develop the international trade of recyclable goods. (See entry 4628 for full listing.)

1694 **IOMA Business page:** A directory of business-related Internet resources listed alphabetically by topic from the Institute of Management and Administration (IOMA).

http://starbase.ingress.com/ioma/

INFO kathie@ingress.com

Comments: The site also includes articles from all the IOMA publications offering useful information to professionals from virtually all industries.

➤ **ShopDNet:** A list of virtual marketplaces, from Blake and Associates, Internet Marketing Consultants. (See entry 1711 for full listing.)

➤ **U.S. Securites & Exchange Commission (SEC):** Access to the EDGAR database and other information from the SEC. (See entry 1783 for full listing.)

➤ **Who's Who Online:** Biographical and professional data about people of accomplishment who are part of the worldwide Internet community. Currently searchable by name, with geographic, nature of work, and language-capability searches to be added in 1996. (See entry 2769 for full listing.)

EDUCATION

1695 `alt.business.seminars` Business seminars. *Newsgroup*

1696 **ASACNET:** On business studies from a Canadian perspective. *Mailing List*

± listserv@pdomain.uwindsor.ca [body = SUBSCRIBE ASACNET first-name last-name]

OWNER templer@uwindsor.ca (Andrew Templer, Windsor)

OWNER apetit@adm.usherb.ca (Andre Petit, Sherbrooke-francophone)

Language: English & French

1697 `bit.listserv.mba-l` MBA student curriculum discussion. *Newsgroup*

1698 **Business Education Network:** A non-profit-making organization promoting business education through the production of high-quality teaching/learning materials and the delivery of highly effective training courses; subjects covered include bookkeeping/accounting, economics, information technology, management, and office/administration skills.

http://www.norcol.ac.uk/business/index.html

INFO ben.enquiries@norcol.ac.uk

INFO j.d.grant@norcol.ac.uk

1699 **Education, Training and Development Resource Center for Business and Industry:** A central, free access database where people in business and industry can find, apply online to register, purchase, view multimedia demos, or ask for more information on training, development, and education-related resources, when, where, in the form, and by the providers of their choice.

http://www.tasl.com/tasl/home.html

INFO mms@tasl.com (Margie Sweeny)

1700 **IBSCG:** For members of International Business Schools Computing Association. *Mailing List*

± listserv@miamiu.acs.muohio.edu [body = SUBSCRIBE IBSCG first-name last-name]

INFO rajkumar@miamiu.bitnet (Rajkumar)

ARCHIVE listserv@miamiu.acs.muohio.edu

➤ `k12.ed.business`: Business education curricula in grades K-12. *Newsgroup*

➤ **Masters in Telecommunications Management:** Information on the master of science in telecommunications management program at Oklahoma State University. (See entry 9634 for full listing.)

1701 `soc.college.org.aiesec` The International Association of Business and Commerce Students. *Newsgroup*

1702 **Syllabits - Business Educational Materials:** Syllabits is a collection of business-school course materials including syllabi and lecture notes. Topics included are economics, marketing, finance, accounting, real estate, management, statistics, information systems, business law, and hospitality administration.
 `http://nsns.com/Syllabits/`
 INFO `chofack@nsns.com`

ELECTRONIC COMMERCE

1703 **Meta Network:** This is the public information space for organizations hosted by the Meta Network.
 `http://www.tmn.com/`
 `gopher://gopher.tmn.com`
 INFO `info@tmn.com`
 FAQ `http://www.tmn.com/MetaNet/metanetfaq.html`

➤ **800-TREKKER:** An online source for science-fiction gifts and apparel. (See entry 1305 for full listing.)

➤ **Advertising Blacklist:** A compendium of advertisers who have misused Net access, compiled by Axel Boldt. (See entry 2680 for full listing.)

1704 `alt.internet.commerce` Doing business on the Internet. *Newsgroup*

1705 `biz.marketplace.discussion` Discussion of biz.marketplace discussion issues. *Newsgroup*

➤ **BizOpList:** For announcements of new business opportunities & self-employment opportunities. (See entry 2064 for full listing.)

1706 `can.com.misc` Miscellaneous net commerce discussions in Canada. *Newsgroup*

1707 **Commercial InfoList:** For announcements of a commercial nature. *Distribution List, moderated*
 ± `automailer@teletron.com`
 INFO EDITOR OWNER `sysop@teletron.com` (Howard Barton)

➤ **FringeWare:** Fringe culture dispersed through design and undesign, community, humor, the marketplace, the net. (See entry 9824 for full listing.)

➤ **Global Information and Improvement Network:** Commercial advertising Web site for small business. Accept checks online, order online, free software and products. (See entry 1810 for full listing.)

1708 **IMALL-CHAT:** On shopping on the Internet and the "Internet Mall™." *Mailing List*
 ± `listserv@netcom.com` [body = SUBSCRIBE imall-chat]
 OWNER `taylor@intuitive.com` (Dave Taylor)

➤ **The Internet Advertising Resource Guide:** Contains links to select sources of information about advertising and marketing on the Internet. (See entry 1811 for full listing.)

1709 **Internet Business News (IBN):** A monthly newsletter that covers the commercial activities and benefits of the Internet.
 `http://www.m2.com/`
 INFO `ibn-edit@m2.com`

➤ **Internet Economics Collection:** The economics of the Internet, information goods, intellectual property, and related issues. (See entry 5205 for full listing.)

1710 **JunkMailList:** For junque mail—in case you've been missing it. *Distribution List, moderated*
 ± `junkbot@teletron.com`
 EDITOR `sysop@teletron.com` (Howard Barton)
 Comments: List is not rented or shared.

➤ **LithoBid:** Global tendering system for printing. (See entry 1911 for full listing.)

➤ **Netcast Global Communications:** Internet broadcasting, consultation, and audio/video information provider. (See entry 6066 for full listing.)

➤ **Open Book Systems (OBS):** An online publisher and bookstore in English, German, French, and Romanian. (See entry 119 for full listing.)

➤ **procurement:** List for government procurement, acquisition, and electronic commerce. (See entry 5429 for full listing.)

1711 **ShopDNet:** A list of virtual marketplaces, from Blake and Associates, Internet Marketing Consultants.

http://www.neosoft.com/citylink/blake/malls.html

INFO blake@neosoft.com

➤ **Sybase New Media:** Visitors to http://www.newmedia.sybase.com can exchange ideas about Web-site design and electronic commerce, learn about (and download) Sybase and Powersoft products, and see how leading developers are using Sybase products to conduct business on the Internet and create Web sites. (See entry 3026 for full listing.)

➤ **Tradewinds:** A monthly roundup of Internet coverage in trade and industry periodicals. (See entry 2885 for full listing.)

EMPLOYMENT

1712 **Employment Opportunities and Job Resources on the Internet:** Includes resources for job listings and other job-related information on the Internet that can be accessed at no additional cost to the job hunter. Links to additional job-hunting guides and collected links are included.

http://www.wpi.edu/~mfriley/jobguide.html

http://www.jobtrak.com/jobguide/

INFO mfriley@jobtrak.com (Margaret F. Riley)

MIRRORS

http://www.lib.umich.edu/chhome.html

http://www.wpi.edu/Academics/IMS/Library/jobguide/

1713 **Job Search Sites:** This site lists serveral sites that offer job search information and resume posting services. Most of these sites have free services.

http://www.geocities.com/TheTropics/2063/jobs.html

INFO jmkizer@nando.net

➤ **ab.jobs:** Jobs in Alberta, Canada. *Newsgroup*

1714 **alt.building.jobs** Building industry jobs. *Newsgroup*

1715 **alt.computer.consultants** The business of consulting about computers. *Newsgroup*

1716 **alt.computer.consultants.ads** Soliciting for computer consultants. *Newsgroup*

1717 **ba.jobs.contract** Listings of Bay Area (USA) contract job opportunites. *Newsgroup*

1718 **biz.jobs.offered** Position announcements. *Newsgroup*

1719 **Career Mosaic:** A career information site; includes a searchable job posting index, information about potential employers, information for college students and recent graduates, information about online job fairs, a new resume-posting service, and helpful advice about resumes and cover letters.

http://www.careermosaic.com/cm/

INFO feedback@pa.hodes.com

➤ **CJI:** Listings of computer jobs in Israel. (See entry 7363 for full listing.)

1720 **clari.news.labor.employment** Layoffs, hiring, and employment statistics. *Moderated newsgroup*

1721 **GET A JOB!:** GET A JOB! shortens the searching process for you and offers one of the best collections of employment sites and resources available on the Web today.

http://www.getajob.com/

INFO esargent@getajob.com

➤ `hepnet.jobs`: High Energy Physics job announcements and discussions. *Newsgroup*

1722 `ie.jobs` Job offerings in Ireland. *Newsgroup*

1723 **Internet Profesional Association (IPA):** Virtual Association of over 1,300 recruiters, employment agenices worldwide. Online listing of members, free resume uploads, career advice.
`http://www.ipa.com/opa/`
`http://www.ipa.com/ipa/`
INFO `billvick@ipa.com`

1724 **JobPlace:** On self-directed job-search training and placement: for trainers, educators, researchers. *Mailing List*
`http://www.jobweb.org/`
± `listserv@news.jobweb.org` [body = SUBSCRIBE JOBPLACE first-name last-name]
± `http://news.jobweb.org/cgi-bin/lwgate/JOBPLACE`
INFO `josh@news.jobweb.org` (Josh Renzema)
ARCHIVE `http://www.jobweb.org/`

➤ `li.jobs`: Employment in the Long Island, New York region. *Newsgroup*

➤ `misc.jobs.contract`: Discussions about contract labor. *Newsgroup*

1725 `misc.jobs.offered` Announcements of positions available. *Newsgroup*

1726 `misc.jobs.offered.entry` Job listings only for entry-level positions. *Newsgroup*

1727 `misc.jobs.resumes` Postings of resumes and "situation wanted" articles. *Newsgroup*

➤ `nj.jobs`: Employment in the New Jersey area. *Newsgroup*

➤ `tor.jobs`: Jobs in Toronto, Canada. *Newsgroup*

➤ `uk.jobs.d`: Discussions about situations vacant and wanted. *Newsgroup*

➤ `vmsnet.employment`: Jobs sought/offered, workplace- and employment-related issues. *Moderated newsgroup*

➤ **Women in Technology Directory:** A professional directory for women in technological fields designed to facilitate and encourage women's ability to network with one another via e-mail. (See entry 9582 for full listing.)

FINANCE

1728 `alt.business.offshore` About taxhaven/offshore/datahaven corporations & trusts. *Newsgroup*

1729 **BerBiz:** On the international business sector of Bermuda. *Newsletter*
`http://www.webcom.com/~wrsl`
± `berbiz-request@webcom.com`
OWNER `wrsl@ibl.bm` (Bill Storie, President)
Frequency: monthly

1730 `clari.apbl.reports.finance` Reports on the money supply. *Moderated newsgroup*

1731 `clari.biz.finance` Finance, currency, corporate finance. *Moderated newsgroup*

1732 `clari.biz.mergers` Mergers and acquisitions. *Moderated newsgroup*

1733 `comp.os.ms-windows.apps.financial` MS Windows financial and tax software. *Newsgroup*

1734 **eFINANCE:** For academic researchers in finance. *E-journal*
± `listserv@vm.temple.edu` [body = SUBSCRIBE FINANCE first-name last-name]
INFO `jfried@vm.temple.edu` (Dr. Joseph Friedman)
ARCHIVE `listserv@vm.temple.edu`

1735 `misc.business.credit` Domestic and international business credit. *Moderated newsgroup*

➤ **Money Issues:** Canada's first regular financial-planning magazine, available simultaneously in print and in electronic form. (See entry 6052 for full listing.)

1736 `uk.finance` U.K. financial issues. *Newsgroup*

FINANCIAL MARKETS & INVESTING

➤ **Business Sources on the Internet:** This site lists business sources available on the Internet. Resources listed include: Web and gopher servers, telnet services, mailing lists, lists and directories of commercial sites, company and financial information, country-specific business resources, government, statistical, economic, market and industry-specific resources, and a list of news sources. (See entry 1651 for full listing.)

1737 **Allegis Investment Management:** Providing global equity management services, Allegis brings together a systematic and fundamental stock valuation process, tempered with a solid investment philosophy of active risk management and strict buy/sell disciplines.

http://www.allegis.com/
INFO rdelyons@allegis.com

1738 `alt.invest.penny-stocks` Investing in low-cost stocks. *Newsgroup*

1739 `aus.invest` Investment and other financial matters. *Newsgroup*

1740 `bermuda.business.financial` Information about Bermuda's financial sector. *Newsgroup*

1741 `clari.apbl.stocks` General stock market reports. *Moderated newsgroup*

1742 `clari.apbl.stocks.analysis` Market analysis from the insiders. *Moderated newsgroup*

1743 `clari.apbl.stocks.dow` Dow Jones averages. *Moderated newsgroup*

1744 `clari.apbl.stocks.tech` ClariNews TechWire stock reports. *Moderated newsgroup*

1745 `clari.biz.currencies.misc` World currency news, interest rates. *Moderated newsgroup*

1746 `clari.biz.currencies.us_dollar` U.S. currency news, interest rates. *Moderated newsgroup*

1747 `clari.biz.earnings` Businesses' earnings, profits, losses. *Moderated newsgroup*

1748 `clari.biz.earnings.releases` News releases: earnings, profits, losses. *Moderated newsgroup*

1749 `clari.biz.market.commodities` Commodity reports. *Moderated newsgroup*

1750 `clari.biz.market.misc` Bonds, money market funds, other instruments. *Moderated newsgroup*

1751 `clari.biz.market.news` News affecting the financial markets. *Moderated newsgroup*

1752 `clari.biz.market.report` General market reports, S & P, etc. *Moderated newsgroup*

1753 `clari.biz.market.report.asia` Asian market reports. *Moderated newsgroup*

1754 `clari.biz.market.report.europe` European market reports. *Moderated newsgroup*

1755 `clari.biz.market.report.top` Overview of the markets. *Moderated newsgroup*

1756 `clari.biz.market.report.usa` U.S. market reports. *Moderated newsgroup*

1757 `clari.biz.market.report.usa.nyse` New York Stock Exchange reports. *Moderated newsgroup*

1758 `clari.biz.stocks.dividend.releases` Dividend announcements. *Moderated newsgroup*

1759 `clari.biz.stocks.report.asia` Asian stock market reports. *Moderated newsgroup*

1760 `clari.biz.stocks.report.elsewhere` International stock market reports. *Moderated newsgroup*

1761 `clari.biz.stocks.report.europe.eastern` Eastern European stock reports. *Moderated newsgroup*

1762 `clari.biz.stocks.report.europe.western` Western European stock markets reports. *Moderated newsgroup*

1763 `clari.biz.stocks.report.top` Overview of the stock markets. *Moderated newsgroup*

1764 `clari.biz.stocks.report.usa.misc` U.S. stock market reports. *Moderated newsgroup*

1765 `clari.biz.stocks.report.usa.nyse` New York Stock Exchange reports. *Moderated newsgroup*

1766 `clari.tw.stocks` Regular reports on computer and technology stock prices. *Moderated newsgroup*

1767 **George Chelekis' Hot Stocks Review:** Features emerging company stocks, often traded on international exchanges, with the potential high-growth, home-run returns. *Newsletter*

http://www.gate.net/hotstocks-review/

± **INFO** hotstock@gate.net (Sheila Estrada, Vice President On-Line Services)

ARCHIVE http://www.gate.net/hotstocks-review

➤ **Journal of Financial Abstracts:** Abstracts of major working and accepted papers in financial economics, organized into five categories: corporate finance, real estate, derivatives, banking and economics, and capital markets. (See entry 5206 for full listing.)

1768 `misc.invest` Investments and the handling of money. *Newsgroup*

1769 `misc.invest.canada` Investing in Canadian financial markets. *Newsgroup*

1770 `misc.invest.funds` Sharing information about bond, stock, real estate funds. *Newsgroup*

1771 `misc.invest.futures` Physical commodity and financial futures markets. *Newsgroup*

1772 `misc.invest.stocks` Forum for sharing info about stocks and options. *Newsgroup*

1773 `misc.invest.technical` Analyzing market trends with technical methods. *Newsgroup*

1774 **OFFSHORE:** On international asset protection, financial planning, wealth conservation, offshore banking, corporations, and trusts. *Mailing List, moderated*

http://www.law.vill.edu/~mquarles/offshore/osindex/html

http://www.euro.net/innovation/

± **INFO** offshore@dnai.com

± **EDITOR** arniec@hopf.dnai.com (Arnold L. Cornez, J.D.)

Comments: *Offshore2//Extra*, an advance e-journal, by paid subscription only.

1775 **PRAGUE-FM:** For the Prague Financial Monitor: on financial markets in the Czech Republic. *Newsletter*

http://www.eunet.cz/

± prague-fm-request@eunet.cz

OWNER hewes@traveller.cz (Cameron M. Hewes)

OWNER wordup@traveller.cz (Cameron M. Hewes)

ARCHIVES

prague-fm-request@eunet.cz

gopher://gopher.eunet.cz/11/Journals/prague-fm/

Frequency: weekly.

1776 **Quote-Page:** For daily futures quotes on commodity futures. *Distribution List*

http://www.geopages.com/WallStreet/1295/

± listserv@pitstar.com [body = SUBSCRIBE QUOTE-PAGE e-mail-address]

OWNER sysop@pitstar.com (Patrick Smith)

OWNER pady.smith@pitstar.com (Patrick Smith)

1777 **Quote.Com:** All sorts of financial market data including current quotes on stocks, options, commodity futures, mutual funds, and bonds; also, business news and market analysis.

http://www.quote.com/

INFO staff@quote.com

1778 `relcom.commerce.stocks` Stocks and bonds. *Newsgroup*

1779 `relcom.infomarket.talk` Discussion on security market development. *Moderated newsgroup*

➤ **The Securities Law Home Page:** This Web site is designed to provide information to the Internet community regarding the law as it relates to the United States financial markets, and those who participate in those markets—stockbrokers and investors. (See entry 5533 for full listing.)

1780 **SRB:** On socially responsible business and investing. *Mailing List*

± listproc@mail.together.net [body = SUBSCRIBE SRB first-name last-name]

OWNER jason.jepsen@together.org (Jason Jepsen)

ARCHIVE http://www.together.org/srb/

1781 **STOCK-PICKING:** On selecting common stock and investment strategies. *Mailing List*

± `majordomo@listserv.nashville.net`
INFO `majordomo-owner@listserv.nashville.net`
OWNER `doug@telalink.net` (Doug Schroeder)

1782 Studies in Nonlinear Dynamics and Econometrics: The SNDE is formed in recognition that advances in statistics and dynamical systems theory may increase our understanding of economic and financial markets. The journal seeks both theoretical and applied papers. *E-Journal*
`http://www-mitpress.mit.edu/SNDE/WWW/journal/demo.html`
± `journals-info@mit.edu`
INFO OWNER `fisher@mitvma.mit.edu` (Janet Fisher)
EDITOR `mizrach@rci.rutgers.edu` (Bruce Mizrach)
ARCHIVE `ftp://mitpress.mit.edu/pub/SNDE/`
Frequency: quarterly

1783 U.S. Securites & Exchange Commission (SEC): Access to the EDGAR database and other information from the SEC.
`http://www.sec.gov/`
INFO `webtech@sec.gov` (Technical Questions)
INFO `webmaster@sec.gov`
FAQ `http://www.sec.gov/oursite/faq.htm`
Comments: This site also supports FTP and Gopher access.

1784 Wall Street Journal Money and Investing Update: Continually updated coverage of global markets and the top stories in business and finance worldwide.
`http://update.wsj.com/`
INFO `info@update.wsj.com`
MIRROR `http://interactive.wsj.com/`

1785 WallStreet: Resources for traders of financial instruments and investors. *Digest & Reflector*
`http://www.wsdinc.com/`
`http://www.wsdinc.com/pgs_idx/subscrib.shtml`
± `http://www.wsdinc.com/pgs_idx/subscrib.shtml`
± `majordomo@shore.net` [body = `subscribe wsd`]
OWNER `wallst@cts.com` (Steve Schulman)

FOREIGN TRADE & INTERNATIONAL

➤ **A & G Information Services:** Business news and information about Russia and St. Petersburg. (See entry 7588 for full listing.)

1786 `alt.business.import-export` Business aspects of international trade. *Newsgroup*

1787 `alt.business.import-export.computer` Computer import-export business. *Newsgroup*

1788 `alt.business.import-export.raw-material` Raw materials import-export business. *Newsgroup*

1789 `alt.business.import-export.services` Import-export business. *Newsgroup*

1790 Arab Trade: A group of companies helping businesses worldwide increase their business in the Arabian Gulf and the Middle East by finding agents, partners, and distributors for their products.
`http://www.arab-trade.com/intergulf`
INFO `intergulf@arab-trade.com`

➤ `bit.listserv.e-europe`: Eastern Europe business network. *Moderated newsgroup*

1791 `biz.marketplace.international` International commerce opportunities. *Newsgroup*

1792 `biz.marketplace.international.discussion` Talk of international commerce. *Newsgroup*

➤ **Cargo-L:** On international cargo transportation and shipping. (See entry 1963 for full listing.)

1793 CEINEWS: For China Economic Information—daily business news for Canadians only. *Distribution List* http://www.attaina.com/

± ceinews-request@attaina.com [body = SUBSCRIBE CEINEWS]

INFO cei@attaina.com

OWNER eleung@attaina.com (Eric Leung)

Please Note: Subscription by approval only.

1794 **china-link:** Weekly newsletter of import/export business with China. *Newsletter*

http://www.crl.com/~cnlink

± listserv@ifcss.org [body = SUBSCRIBE CHINA-LINK first-name last-name]

OWNER cnlink@world.std.com (China Link Club)

Frequency: biweekly

1795 `clari.biz.world_trade` GATT, free trade, trade disputes. *Moderated newsgroup*

1796 **eeurope-business:** For doing business in eastern Europe. *Digest & Reflector*

± listmanager@hookup.net

INFO OWNER naafetee@hookup.net (Ross Hedvicek)

1797 **GINLIST:** For Global Interact Network: a network of international business and marketing professionals (both educators and practitioners). *Mailing List*

± listserv@msu.edu [body = SUBSCRIBE GINLIST first-name last-name]

OWNER ciber@msu.edu (International Business Center, Michigan State University)

ARCHIVE http://ciber.bus.msu.edu/ginlist/

FAQ http://ciber.bus.msu.edu/ginlist/

Please Note: Subscription by approval only.

➤ **International Trade Law Project (ITLP):** Network resources for legal research and education in the field of international trade law. (See entry 5567 for full listing.)

➤ **Internet CZ - EUnet Czech Republic:** WWW server that offers commercial, business, and finance information not only about the Czech Republic but also about central Europe, including the Prague stock exchange, exchange rates, statistical information, databases of Czech commercial subjects involved in the Czech Coupon Privatization, municipal information, bus and train timetables, Czech firms' advertisements, news and journals, and so on. Other important databases and resources are in progress. (See entry 7266 for full listing.)

1798 **PCBR-L:** For members of Paciber, an organization interested in research and development of business activities that span the Pacific basin. *Mailing List, moderated*

± listserv@uhccvm.uhcc.hawaii.edu [body = SUBSCRIBE PCBR-L first-name last-name]

INFO morton@hawaii.edu

1799 `relcom.wtc` Commercial proposals of World Trade Centers. *Newsgroup*

1800 **TradeNet:** For international trade contacts, products, and services from around the world. *Mailing List, moderated*

http://www.tradenet.org/

± list@tradenet.org

OWNER admin@tradenet.org (TradeNet World Service)

OWNER berkeley@tradenet.org

ARCHIVE http://www.tradenet.org/

FAQ faq@tradenet.org

1801 **United States Trade Representatives Homepage:** Home page for the United States Trade Representative. Providing information related to the office and activities of the USTR.

http://www.ustr.gov/

INFO webmaster@www.ustr.gov

1802 **Worldwide Business Practices Report:** International business practices, customs, negotiating tactics, marketing strategies, safety, and travel tips. Information on just about everything executives need to know to do business abroad successfully. *Newsletter*

http://www.worldbiz.com/

INFO ice@mercury.mcs.com

Frequency: monthly

HUMAN RESOURCES

➤ `alt.payroll`: Payroll—taxes—labor relations—human resources. *Newsgroup*

1803 `clari.biz.personnel.releases` Press releases: personnel changes, layoffs. *Moderated newsgroup*

➤ **DIVERSITY-FORUM:** On human resource management of diversity in business, education & social work. (See entry 9892 for full listing.)

1804 **EAP:** On employee assistance counseling and psychological intervention at the workplace. *Mailing List*

± ea-request@webcom.com

± majordomo@pinsight.com

OWNER bfleming@pinsight.com (From: Bob Fleming)

ARCHIVES

http://www.webcom.com/~eap/

ftp://ftp.webcom.com/pub1/eap

1805 **FAXNEWZ:** A one-page newsletter on matters relating to personnel security, produced every six weeks by The Integrity Center, Inc., a preemployment screening agency. *Newsletter*

± INFO info@integctr.com

INFO jallan@integctr.com (Dr. John Allan)

ARCHIVES

info@integctr.com

jallan@integctr.com (Dr. John Allan)

http://www.integctr.com/

Frequency: every six weeks

➤ **INFAQ Criminal History Research Page:** INFAQ, a criminal history research firm, offers criminal history checks to the general public through this Web site. Order online and get results through e-mail. (See entry 1915 for full listing.)

1806 `misc.jobs.misc` Discussion about employment, workplaces, careers. *Newsgroup*

INDUSTRIES

INDUSTRIES—ADVERTISING

➤ **Advertising Blacklist:** A compendium of advertisers who have misused Net access, compiled by Axel Boldt. (See entry 2680 for full listing.)

1807 **The Advertising Law Internet Site:** This site points to numerous resources regarding advertising and marketing law.

http://www.arentfox.com/

http://www.webcom.com/~lewrose/home.html

INFO lewrose@netcom.com (Lewis Rose)

1808 **BackChannel:** The interactivity newsletter of the American Association of Advertising Agencies. *Newsletter*

http://www.commercepark.com/AAAA/bc.html

EDITOR tforbes@tforbes.com (Thom Forbes)

ARCHIVE http://www.commercepark.com/AAAA/bc/back_issues/back_issues.html

Frequency: irregular

1809 **BluFire Model & Talent Registry:** Fashion and commercial print models, actors and children.

http://www.sapphire.com/blufire/

INFO blufire@sapphire.com

➤ `can.com.ad-agencies`: Ad agency discussions in Canada. *Newsgroup*

1810 Global Information and Improvement Network: Commercial advertising Web site for small business. Accept checks online, order online, free software and products.

`http://www.giin.com/giin/`

INFO `rklein@iquest.net`

1811 The Internet Advertising Resource Guide: Contains links to select sources of information about advertising and marketing on the Internet.

`http://www.missouri.edu/internet-advertising-guide.html`

INFO `jourli@showme.missouri.edu`

1812 M2 NewsWEB: NewsWEB is an online service from M2 Communications, which provides permanent access to your company's news and background information to users of the Internet, wherever they are in the world and whenever they want it.

`http://www.m2.com/nw`

INFO `di@m2.com`

➤   **Magazine and Newsletter Editors' Resource List:** This no-graphics page has easy-to-follow links to sites regarding shipping, circulation, advertising, associations, going electronic, the Pulitzer Prize, and much more. (See entry 6093 for full listing.)

➤   **McSpotlight:** An online library of detailed, accurate, up-to-date information about the McDonald's Corporation, its business practices, and its effects on the world. Everything you could ever need to know about the "McLibel Trial" and worldwide opposition and resistance to the company (and others like them) can be found on this Web site. Possibly the most comprehensive and damning collection of material on a multinational corporation ever assembled. (See entry 9782 for full listing.)

1813 World-Wide Business Pages™: Mall fronts for various product and service categories to make it easy to find what you want.

`http://world-wide.com/wwbus/`

INFO `wwcinfo@world-wide.com`

➤   **World-Wide Classifieds™:** Need a car? Want to sell that old ten-speed bicycle in the garage? This is the nickel want ads for the Information Highway. Browse ads by keyword, location, or classification. Enter your own ads online. (See entry 1690 for full listing.)

INDUSTRIES—AVIATION & AEROSPACE

➤   **AIRCRAFT:** On fixed-wing and rotary-wing aircraft, modern, classic, and antique, including listings of air shows and similar events. (See entry 6259 for full listing.)

1814 `alt.disasters.aviation` Plane lands safely at airfield, film at eleven. *Newsgroup*

1815 `alt.flame.airlines` Problems and complaints with the airlines. *Newsgroup*

1816 AV-JOBS: For posting of job openings in the general aviation industry. *Mailing List, moderated*

± `listserv@rotor.com` [body = SUBSCRIBE `AV-JOBS` first-name last-name]

OWNER `david.lutes@rotor.com`

1817 AV-ROTOR: On civil helicopters: their uses, and related legislation and regulations. *Mailing List*

`http://www.rotor.com/`

± `listserv@rotor.com` [body = SUBSCRIBE `AV-ROTOR` first-name last-name]

OWNER `david.lutes@rotor.com` (David Lutes)

➤   **AvMail:** On aviation issues from a gay & lesbian perspective. (See entry 9951 for full listing.)

1818 `clari.biz.industry.aviation` Airlines and airports. *Moderated newsgroup*

1819 `clari.biz.industry.aviation.releases` News releases: airlines and airports. *Moderated newsgroup*

1820 `clari.tw.aerospace` Aerospace industry and companies. *Moderated newsgroup*

1821 `clari.tw.aerospace.cbd.components` Aircraft components. *Moderated newsgroup*

1822 `clari.tw.aerospace.cbd.misc` Space vehicles, miscellaneous aircraft equipment. *Moderated newsgroup*

1823 `clari.tw.aerospace.releases` Releases covering the aerospace industry. *Moderated newsgroup*

1824 `eunet.aviation` European aviation rules, means and methods. *Newsgroup*

➤ **FlightMed:** For air medical professionals: flight nurses & paramedics, pilots, physicians. (See entry 5077 for full listing.)

➤ `misc.transport.air-industry`: Airlines, airports, commercial aircraft. *Moderated newsgroup*

➤ `rec.travel.air`: Airline travel around the world. *Newsgroup*

INDUSTRIES—CONSTRUCTION

1825 **Building Industry Exchange (BIX):** BIX is a nonprofit clearinghouse and search index of educational, communication, and information resources for the building industry.
`http://www.building.org/`
INFO `webmaster@building.org`

1826 **BuildNet:** This site provides links, resources, and opportunities for all the members of the construction industry, including architects, contractors, and engineers.
`http://www.abuildnet.com/`
INFO `postmaster@abuildnet.com`

1827 **Accurate New Home Builder Web Guide:** This Web site lists new home builder pages that contain valuable information. Items such as location maps, floor plans, photos, and renderings are important to new home buyers.
`http://www.insync.net/~laura/accurate.html`
INFO `laura@insync.net`

1828 `alt.building.construction` Building-industry construction. *Newsgroup*

1829 `alt.building.consulting-specialty` Building-industry consulting and specialty. *Newsgroup*

1830 `alt.building.distributor-dealer` Building-industry distributor-dealer. *Newsgroup*

1831 `alt.building.education` Building-industry education. *Newsgroup*

1832 `alt.building.finance` Building-industry finance. *Newsgroup*

1833 `alt.building.gov-issues` Building-industry government issues. *Newsgroup*

1834 `alt.building.health-safety` Building-industry health-safety. *Newsgroup*

1835 `alt.building.insurance-bonding-surety` Building-industry insurance, bonding, and surety. *Newsgroup*

1836 `alt.building.interior-design` Building-industry interior design. *Newsgroup*

1837 `alt.building.landfill` Building-industry landfill. *Newsgroup*

1838 `alt.building.law` Building-industry law. *Newsgroup*

1839 `alt.building.planning-preservation` Building-industry planning and preservation. *Newsgroup*

1840 `alt.building.survey-mapping` Building-industry surveying and mapping. *Newsgroup*

1841 `alt.building.union-assn-society` Building-industry union, association, and society. *Newsgroup*

1842 **Build.com:** This site is an online resource and directory for building and home improvement products and information.
`http://www.build.com/`
INFO `build@build.com`

➤ **Built-environment:** On the built environment: architecture, civil engineering, surveying. (See entry 4566 for full listing.)

1843 `clari.biz.industry.construction` The construction industry. *Moderated newsgroup*

1844 `clari.biz.industry.construction.cbd.acquisition` Purchasing facilities. *Moderated newsgroup*

1845 `clari.biz.industry.construction.cbd.architect+eng` Architecture, engineering. *Moderated newsgroup*

1846   `clari.biz.industry.construction.cbd.hardware`   Hardware and abrasives. *Moderated newsgroup*

1847   `clari.biz.industry.construction.cbd.maintenance`   Maintenance, alteration. *Moderated newsgroup*

1848   `clari.biz.industry.construction.cbd.misc`   Building structures or facilities. *Moderated newsgroup*

1849   `clari.biz.industry.construction.cbd.supplies`   Tools, other supplies. *Moderated newsgroup*

1850   **Construction Site:** This site is a place is where people who need a service or product can make a connection with the people who want to provide such commodities. It is also a place to stay "in the know" about industry trends, upcoming events, and business opportunities, as well as new rules and regulations.
http://www.constructionsite.com/
INFO webmaster@rezn8.com

1851   **ConstructionNet:** This site features a periodicals library, a product and service directory, and lists of other Internet construction resources.
http://www.constructnet.com/
INFO constrnet@aol.com

1852   `relcom.commerce.construction`   Construction materials and equipment. *Newsgroup*

INDUSTRIES—DRY GOODS

1853   `clari.biz.industry.dry_goods`   Consumer goods, clothing, furniture. *Moderated newsgroup*

1854   `clari.biz.industry.textiles`   Textile industry. *Moderated newsgroup*

1855   `clari.biz.industry.textiles.cbd`   Textiles, leather, fur, clothing. *Moderated newsgroup*

INDUSTRIES—ELECTRONICS

1856   `alt.electronics.manufacture.circuitboard`   Discussion of circuit-board manufacture. *Newsgroup*

1857   `clari.tw.electronics`   Electronics makers and sellers. *Moderated newsgroup*

1858   `clari.tw.electronics.cbd`   Electrical and electronic equipment, components. *Moderated newsgroup*

1859   `clari.tw.electronics.releases`   News releases: electronics industry. *Moderated newsgroup*

1860   **Electronix Corp:** Distributor of electronic replacement parts and producer of instructional video and service software for electronic service/repair.
http://www.electronix.com/elexcorp
INFO elexcorp@erinet.com

1861   `misc.industry.electronics.marketplace`   Electronics products and services. *Newsgroup*

➤   **PCI-SIG:** On PCI (Peripheral Component Interconnect) bus, as defined by the PCI-SIG group. (See entry 3776 for full listing.)

INDUSTRIES—HOTEL, CATERING & FOOD SERVICE

➤   **Aarons's Catalog Listings:** A large directory to motels and hotels all over the United States. (See entry 7819 for full listing.)

➤   **AccomoDATA:** A resource with listings of hotels, bed and breakfasts, cottage rentals, and boat rentals in England, Wales, Scotland, Ireland, and France, plus the rest of Europe. You can make direct bookings from this site. (See entry 7820 for full listing.)

1862   `alt.business.hospitality`   Hotel, resort, tour, and restaurant businesses. *Newsgroup*

1863   `aus.foodtech`   Food science and technology. *Newsgroup*

1864   `clari.biz.industry.food`   Food processing, markets, restaurants. *Moderated newsgroup*

1865   `clari.biz.industry.food.cbd`   Food and agricultural supplies. *Moderated newsgroup*

1866   `clari.biz.industry.food.releases`   News releases: food processing and products. *Moderated newsgroup*

1867 `clari.biz.industry.food.retail.releases` News releases: restaurants and markets. *Moderated newsgroup*

1868 `clari.biz.industry.tourism` The tourism and hotel industry. *Moderated newsgroup*

1869 `clari.biz.industry.travel+leisure` The travel and leisure industries. *Moderated newsgroup*

1870 `clari.biz.industry.travel+leisure.cbd` CBD: travel, hotels. *Moderated newsgroup*

1871 `clari.biz.industry.travel+leisure.releases` News releases: travel, leisure industry. *Moderated newsgroup*

➤ **Hotels on the Net:** Information on hotels and special promotions in the Asia-Pacific region. (See entry 7836 for full listing.)

1872 **Le Chef College of Hospitality Careers:** Le Chef College of Hospitality Careers (Austin, Texas) is a two-year, degree-granting institution. This Web site is an interactive brochure where you may learn more about the school, follow along with their curriculum, ask their chefs culinary questions, discover foodways trivia, etc.
`http://sam.onr.com/chef/lechef.html`
INFO `72172.150@compuserve.com`

1873 `relcom.commerce.food` Food. *Newsgroup*

1874 **REST-IS:** For information-system professionals in the restaurant industry. *Mailing List*
± `rest-is-request@dirigiste.com` [subject = `subscribe`]
OWNER `aaron@dirigiste.com` (Aaron Herskowitz)
ARCHIVE `rest-is-request@dirigiste.com` [subject = `index archive help`]

1875 **REST-POS:** On restaurant point-of-sale systems. *Mailing List*
± `rest-pos-request@dirigiste.com`
OWNER `aaron@dirigiste.com` (Aaron Herskowitz)

➤ **TravelWeb:** A database of information on all sorts of accomodations from hotel and resort chains to bed and breakfasts. Allows you to search for information based on accomodation type, price ranges, and facilities available. (See entry 7852 for full listing.)

INDUSTRIES—INSURANCE

1876 `alt.business.insurance` All about the insurance industry. *Newsgroup*

1877 `bermuda.business.insurance` Information about Bermuda's insurance/re-insurance industry. *Newsgroup*

1878 `clari.biz.industry.insurance` The insurance industry. *Moderated newsgroup*

1879 `clari.biz.industry.insurance.releases` News releases: the insurance industry. *Moderated newsgroup*

1880 **LIFEINS-L:** On marketing life insurance. *Mailing List*
± `listserv@netcom.com` [body = `SUBSCRIBE lifeins-l`]
OWNER `wbristow@netcom.com` (Walt Bristow)

1881 **RAMBLINGS:** On actuarial science. *Mailing List*
`http://southernlife.com/`
± `majordomo@southernlife.com` [body = `subscribe ramblings`]
OWNER `davidb@southernlife.com` (David Blecher)
OWNER `dblecher@iafrica.com` (David Blecher)
OWNER `robertd@infosys.uct.ac.za` (Robert Dorrington)
FAQ `http://southernlife.com/actuary/rdresorc/rdpaper.htm`

➤ **RECMGMT:** For records and archival management professionals. (See entry 5709 for full listing.)

1882 **RISKnet:** Risk and insurance issues. *Mailing List, moderated*
`http://www.risknet.com/`
± `listproc@mcfeeley.cc.utexas.edu` [body = `SUBSCRIBE RISKNET first-name last-name`]
INFO `jim@risknet.com`

INFO `risknet_info@risknet.com`

ARCHIVE `http://www.kentlaw.edu/cgi-bin/ldn_news/-T+law.listserv.risknet`

Please Note: Subscription by approval only.

INDUSTRIES—MANUFACTURING

1883   `alt.building.manufacturing`   Building industry manufacturing. *Newsgroup*

1884   `alt.manufacturing.misc`   All about manufacturing. *Newsgroup*

➤   **Biomedical Market Newsletter:** A business, financial, marketing and regulatory newsletter on the medical manufacturing industry worldwide. (See entry 4901 for full listing.)

1885   `bit.listserv.quality`   TQM in manufacturing and service industries. *Moderated newsgroup*

1886   `clari.biz.industry.machinery`   Machine tools and general machinery. *Moderated newsgroup*

1887   `clari.biz.industry.machinery.cbd.components`   Bearings, cables, rope. *Moderated newsgroup*

1888   `clari.biz.industry.machinery.cbd.engines`   Engine accessories. *Moderated newsgroup*

1889   `clari.biz.industry.machinery.cbd.misc`   Miscellaneous machinery. *Moderated newsgroup*

1890   `clari.biz.industry.manufacturing`   Heavy industry. *Moderated newsgroup*

1891   `clari.biz.industry.manufacturing.releases`   News releases: manufacturing. *Moderated newsgroup*

1892   `clari.biz.industry.misc.cbd.misc_supplies`   Misc supplies and equipment. *Moderated newsgroup*

1893   **HEPDB:** For users of HEPDB, a database package designed to store and retrieve detector geometry, calibration information, production control, and perhaps also slow control. *Mailing List*

    ± `listserv@cernvm.cern.ch` [body = SUBSCRIBE HEPDB first-name last-name]

    INFO `hepdb-request@cernvm.cern.ch`

    ARCHIVE `listserv@cernvm.cern.ch` [body = INDEX HEPDB]

1894   **NewProd:** On new product development. *Mailing List*

    ± `majordomo@world.std.com` [body = SUBSCRIBE newprod]

    OWNER `vocalyst@world.std.com` (Bob Klein)

1895   `relcom.commerce.machinery`   Machinery, plant equipment. *Newsgroup*

1896   `sci.engr.manufacturing`   Manufacturing technology. *Newsgroup*

1897   **SmartCam:** Computer aided manufacturing software. *Mailing List*

    ± **OWNER** `charlie@tecnet.me.tufts.edu` (Charlie Rosenburg)

1898   **TOC-L:** On Eli Goldratt's Theory of Constraints for improving manufacturing processes. *Mailing List*

    ± `listserv@netcom.com` [body = SUBSCRIBE toc-l]

    OWNER `wbristow@netcom.com` (Walt Bristow)

INDUSTRIES—MINING

1899   `alt.building.mining`   Building-industry mining. *Newsgroup*

➤   **Chile Information Project (CHIP News):** News on economics, especially mining, and human rights and democratization in Chile. (See entry 7635 for full listing.)

1900   `clari.biz.industry.metals+mining`   Mining and metals processing. *Moderated newsgroup*

1901   `clari.biz.industry.metals+mining.cbd`   Ores, metals, and minerals. *Moderated newsgroup*

1902   `clari.biz.industry.metals+mining.releases`   News releases: mining, metals. *Moderated newsgroup*

1903   `clari.biz.industry.mining`   Mining for metals, minerals. *Moderated newsgroup*

1904   `relcom.commerce.metals`   Metals and metal products. *Newsgroup*

INDUSTRIES—PHARMACEUTICAL

1905 **Ciba Geigy AG (Ciba):** Home page for information and feedback to the biological and chemical company Ciba.
http://www.ciba.com/
INFO peter.warne@chbs.mhs.ciba.com

1906 `clari.tw.chemicals` Chemical firms and technology. *Moderated newsgroup*

1907 **Glaxo Wellcome:** The world's premier health-care company. Informative articles on disease and disease management issues. Free molecular modeling software. Online pharmacology guide. Health-care bookmarks. Contact details. News.
http://www.glaxowellcome.co.uk/
INFO enquiries@glaxowellcome.co.uk

INDUSTRIES—PRINTING & TYPESETTING

1908 **Digiteyes Multimedia TypeArt Library:** Original, type 1 and Truetype fonts on display in TypeArt foundry library (Mac, PC, traditional, grunge typefaces). Interactive catalog, typography quizzes, typesetting and font design tips, Digiteyes graphic art gallery.
http://www.typeart.com/
INFO lloydspr@typeart.com

➤ **fourcolor:** On color and color theory. (See entry 2480 for full listing.)

1909 **LetPress:** On letterpress printing (vintage printing presses). *Mailing List*
± listserv@unb.ca [body = SUBSCRIBE LETPRESS first-name last-name]
OWNER lithotek@unb.ca (Terry Oakes)

1910 **Litho-L:** On desktop publishing, printing, photocopying, and binding. *Mailing List*
± listserv@unb.ca [body = SUBSCRIBE LITHO-L first-name last-name]
INFO http://www.hil.unb.ca/UNB_G_Services/GSHomePage.html
OWNER lithotek@unb.ca (Terry Oakes)

1911 **LithoBid:** Global tendering system for printing. *Tendering System*
± listserv@unb.ca [body = SUBSCRIBE LITHOBID first-name last-name]
INFO http://www.hil.unb.ca/UNB_G_Services/lithohome.html
OWNER lithotek@unb.ca (Terry Oakes)
ARCHIVE listserv@unb.ca [body = INDEX LithoBid]

1912 **LithoQuoter:** Obtain competitive printing quotes quickly and easily. LithoQuoter is a free service that custom-matches your specs to printers that are suited to your job.
http://www.lithoquoter.com/
INFO balint@lithoquoter.com

1913 `misc.industry.pulp-and-paper` Technical topics in the pulp and paper industry. *Newsgroup*

INDUSTRIES—PRIVATE INVESTIGATION

1914 `alt.private.investigator` Digging up the dirt. *Newsgroup*

➤ **Find a Friend:** Resources to locate people; searches cover the entire United States. Results are e-mailed within 48 hours. (See entry 5783 for full listing.)

1915 **INFAQ Criminal History Research Page:** INFAQ, a criminal history research firm, offers criminal history checks to the general public through this Web site. Order online and get results through e-mail.
http://www.creativedirection.com/infaq/index.html
INFO infaq263@holli.com

1916 **InfoPro:** For information professionals and investigators. *Mailing List*
± **OWNER** jcook@netcom.com (James Cook)

1917 **The Investigative Resource Center:** Provided by Investigative Resources International, a professional investigation firm, this site offers pointers to many private investigators and legal and reference resources on the Web, including a good list of searchable databases helpful in locating people and unusual information.

http://www.factfind.com/factfind/linkpage.htm

INFO factfind@factfind.com

1918 **Metanoetics Inc. Home Page:** This private investigation firm's home page includes links to many interesting investigation resources on the Internet.

http://www.io.org/~gumshoe/

INFO gumshoe@io.org

1919 **Private Investigation Home Page:** A one-stop page for private investigators, investigative resources, products, and information related to private investigation around the globe. Includes lists of private investigators, how-to articles, law sites, private investigation products and services, an "Investigator's Toolkit," and pointers to other private investigation resources on the Internet.

http://www.pihome.com/

INFO lamont@pihome.com

1920 **Private-Eye:** The mailing list was created to be a place where private investigators and those interested in the business of private investigations can ask questions and find out what is going on in the world of private investigations. *Mailing List*

http://www.pimall.com/

± INFO private-eye-request@netcom.com [body = SUBSCRIBE   first-name last-name]

OWNER cibir@netcom.com

ARCHIVE ftp://ftp.netcom.com

INDUSTRIES—PUBLISHING

➤ **BookWire:** Book information galore. It includes information on publishers, bookstores, book events, and a "BookIndex" of book-related Internet resources. (See entry 99 for full listing.)

➤ **Digital BookWorld:** A Web site about books: includes information on new books, backlist books, authors, booksellers, and publishers. Also provides excerpts, reviews, and interviews. (See entry 100 for full listing.)

1921 alt.neo-tech   Books and ideas from Neo-Tech Publishing Company. *Newsgroup*

1922 bit.listserv.vpiej-l   Electronic publishing discussion list. *Newsgroup*

1923 biz.books.technical   Technical bookstore and publisher advertising and info. *Newsgroup*

1924 biz.oreilly.announce   New product announcements from O'Reilly and Associates. *Newsgroup*

➤ **Bookport:** Online editions of current books. Can be sampled, purchased, unlocked, and read online, or ordered from the publishers. (See entry 104 for full listing.)

➤ **CDR-L:** On the mastering of CDs—primarily hardware and software issues. (See entry 3784 for full listing.)

1925 clari.biz.industry.media   Publishing, journalism and other media. *Moderated newsgroup*

1926 **Cole's Newswire:** On the current state of the publishing systems supplier industry. *Newsletter*

http://colegroup.com/NW/

± macjordomo@colegroup.com [body = SUBSCRIBE NEWSWIRE first-name last-name]

INFO OWNER info@colegroup.com (David M. Cole)

ARCHIVE http://colegroup.com/NW/

Frequency: semimonthly

1927 **COPYEDITING-L:** For copy editors and other defenders of the English language who want to discuss anything related to editing. *Mailing List*

± listproc@cornell.edu [body = SUBSCRIBE COPYEDITING-L first-name last-name]

INFO copyediting-l-request

OWNER bgl1@cornell.edu (Beth Goelzer Lyons)

➤ **Magazine and Newsletter Editors' Resource List:** This no-graphics page has easy-to-follow links to sites regarding shipping, circulation, advertising, associations, going electronic, the Pulitzer Prize, and much more. (See entry 6093 for full listing.)

➤ **Open Book Systems (OBS):** An online publisher and bookstore in English, German, French, and Romanian. (See entry 119 for full listing.)

➤ **Pathfinder:** Web outlet of the Time Warner entertainment conglomerate. As well as shopping and news, this site contains content from and promotions for magazines, books, TV and cable, music, movies, and more. (See entry 6129 for full listing.)

1928 **Pehuen Publisher. Catalogue of books:** Pehuen Editores-Pehuen Publisher. Catalog of books about literature, poetry, art, education, essays, anthropology, politics, human rights, and plays. Chilean authors and classics. Mainly in Spanish.
http://www.geagroup.cl/pehuen/
INFO pehuen@geagroup.cl

1929 **Publishers' Catalogues Home Page :** A comprehensive list of publishers from around the entire world.
http://www.lights.com/publisher/
INFO scott@lights.com

1930 **PUBS-L:** For the staff of publications offices at educational and nonprofit institutions. *Mailing List*
± listserv@utkvm1.utk.edu [body = SUBSCRIBE PUBS-L first-name last-name]
INFO kelly@utkvx.bitnet
ARCHIVE listserv@utkvm1.utk.edu

1931 **Random House:** Promotional site for all books published by Random House, Inc. (including Knopf, Vintage, Ballantine, Crown, Del Rey, etc.). Site includes features on current books, a searchable catalog, sample chapters, contests, and ordering capability. Content changes weekly.
http://www.randomhouse.com/
INFO webmaster@www.randomhouse.com

➤ **rec.arts.books:** Books of all genres, and the publishing industry. *Newsgroup*

1932 **relcom.commerce.publishing** Books, publishing services. *Newsgroup*

1933 **SOAP-L:** On student opportunities for academic publishing. *Mailing List*
± listserv@uhccvm.its.hawaii.edu [body = SUBSCRIBE SOAP-L first-name last-name]
INFO soap-l-request@uhccvm.its.hawaii.edu
ARCHIVE listserv@uhccvm.its.hawaii.edu [body = INDEX SOAP-L]
Please Note: Subscription by approval only.

1934 **SPECPRESS:** On electronic books published by Spectrum Press. *Mailing List, moderated*
± OWNER 73774.2733@compuserve.com (Karen Olsen)
INFO EDITOR OWNER specpress@aol.com (Karen Olsen, Dan Agin, Odile Santiago)
ARCHIVE http://wl/iglou.com/hermit

1935 **Zanichelli Editore:** Zanichelli Editore is a leading Italian publisher in reference and school books, with a centennial history. Zanichelli's catalogue of reference and University books is now on line. Books can be bought at the electronic bookstore, there is a list of other scientific publishers on the net, and much more... (but you'll enjoy it better if you understand Italian).
http://www.doit.it/Zanichelli/
INFO maurizio@doit.it
INFO zanichelli@zanichelli.it

INDUSTRIES—REAL ESTATE

➤ **Building Industry Exchange (BIX):** BIX is a nonprofit clearinghouse and search index of educational, communication, and information resources for the building industry. (See entry 1825 for full listing.)

1936 **alt.building.realestate** Real estate and the building industry. *Newsgroup*

1937 `alt.real-estate-agents` Realty heads. *Newsgroup*

1938 `alt.realtor.relocation` Realtors helping with long moves. *Newsgroup*

➤ `alt.relocate`: Setting up a new home in a faraway place. *Newsgroup*

➤ **ArizonaWeb:** A web of information on and about Arizona. It includes real-estate information. (See entry 7891 for full listing.)

1939 `clari.biz.industry.real_est+const` Real estate and construction. *Moderated newsgroup*

1940 `clari.biz.industry.real_est+const.releases` News releases: real estate, construction. *Moderated newsgroup*

1941 `clari.biz.industry.real_estate` Housing and real estate. *Moderated newsgroup*

➤ **HOA-LIST:** For owners and residents in home owner associations (HOA). (See entry 6043 for full listing.)

1942 **Homes Internet Magazine:** Provides a broad variety of online real estate services including easy searching, color photos of homes, thousands of homes, an advanced mortgage calculator, search recall, and many other features.
http://www.homesmag.odc.com/
INFO bender@odc.com

1943 **IMOVEIS:** On property exchange: tourism, emigration, participatory communities. *Mailing List*
± esquina-das-listas@dcc.unicamp.br [body = inscreva imoveis first-name last-name]
OWNER adm3lcl@npd.ufsc.br (Luis Zeredo)
Language: Portugese & English

1944 `misc.invest.real-estate` Property investments. *Newsgroup*

1945 `realtynet.canada-intl` Canada and international real estate listings. *Newsgroup*

1946 `realtynet.commercial` Commercial real estate listings. *Newsgroup*

1947 `realtynet.east` Eastern U.S. real estate listings. *Newsgroup*

1948 `realtynet.general` General discussion about realtynet.*. *Newsgroup*

1949 `realtynet.government` Government property (VA, FHA, HUD) real estate listings. *Newsgroup*

1950 `realtynet.invest` Investment real estate listings. *Newsgroup*

1951 `realtynet.lending` Lending information real estate listings. *Newsgroup*

1952 `realtynet.mid` Midwestern U.S. real estate listings. *Newsgroup*

1953 `realtynet.qa` Questions & answers about Realtynet. *Newsgroup*

1954 `realtynet.residential` Residential real estate listings. *Newsgroup*

1955 `realtynet.south` Southern United States real estate listings. *Newsgroup*

1956 `realtynet.west` Western U.S. real estate listings. *Newsgroup*

1957 `relcom.commerce.estate` Real estate. *Newsgroup*

1958 **Residential-realestate:** On the buying and selling of residential real estate. *Mailing List*
± listserv@property.com [body = SUBSCRIBE RESIDENTIAL-REALESTATE first-name last-name]
OWNER ted.kraus@property.com (Ted Kraus)
ARCHIVE http://www.property.com/

INDUSTRIES—SECURITY

1959 `alt.locksmithing` You locked your keys in *where*? *Newsgroup*

1960 **BODYGUARD-101-L:** On an online e-course for professional bodyguards. *Mailing List, moderated*
± listserv@netcom.com [body = SUBSCRIBE bodyguard-101-l]
EDITOR cntrspy@best.com (Chris Hall)
OWNER cntrspy2@netcom.com (Frank Layton)

Please Note: Subscription by approval only.

1961 **BODYGUARD-L:** For professional bodyguards and the protective services industry. *Mailing List*
± `listserv@netcom.com` [body = `SUBSCRIBE bodyguard-l`]
EDITOR `cntrspy@best.com` (Chris Hall)
OWNER `cntrspy2@netcom.com` (Frank Layton)
Please Note: Subscription by approval only.

INDUSTRIES—TRANSPORTATION

1962 `alt.planning.transportation` Transportation planning issues and techniques. *Newsgroup*

1963 **Cargo-L:** On international cargo transportation and shipping. *Mailing List*
± `maiser@distart.ing.unibo.it` [body = `SUBSCRIBE CARGO-L first-name last-name`]
OWNER `markus_wiedemeier@intf.com` (Markus Wiedemeier)

1964 `clari.biz.industry.automotive` The car and truck industry. *Moderated newsgroup*

1965 `clari.biz.industry.transportation` Trains, buses, transit, shipping. *Moderated newsgroup*

1966 `clari.biz.industry.transportation.cbd` Shipping, marine and railway equipment. *Moderated newsgroup*

1967 `clari.biz.industry.transportation.releases` News releases: trains, buses, shipping. *Moderated newsgroup*

1968 `fj.rec.bus` Discussion about buses. *Newsgroup*

1969 `fj.soc.traffic` Socially oriented topics on traffic and transportation. *Newsgroup*

1970 **Marine-L:** On marine-related topics: education, navigation, ships, industry, meterology. *Mailing List*
± `listserver@cgc.ns.ca`
OWNER `jim@cgc.ns.ca` (Jim Calvesbert)

1971 `misc.transport.air-industry` Airlines, airports, commercial aircraft. *Moderated newsgroup*

1972 `misc.transport.marine` Maritime and inland waterways transportation. *Newsgroup*

1973 `misc.transport.misc` General transportation issues. *Newsgroup*

1974 `misc.transport.rail.americas` Railroads adrailways in North and South America. *Newsgroup*

1975 `misc.transport.rail.australia-nz` Railways in Australia and New Zealand. *Newsgroup*

1976 `misc.transport.rail.europe` Railroads and railways in all of Europe. *Newsgroup*

1977 `misc.transport.rail.misc` Miscellaneous rail issues and discussions. *Newsgroup*

1978 `misc.transport.road` Road and highway transportation. *Newsgroup*

1979 `misc.transport.trucking` Commercial trucking related issues. *Newsgroup*

1980 `misc.transport.urban-transit` Metropolitan public transportation systems. *Newsgroup*

1981 `ne.transportation` Transportation in New England (driving, MBTA, etc.). *Newsgroup*

1982 `relcom.commerce.transport` Vehicles and spare parts. *Newsgroup*

1983 **SHIPS:** On maritime transportation and the pattern of operation of oceangoing vessels. *Mailing List*
± `ships-request@access.digex.net`
OWNER `dannyb@access.digex.net` (Danny Boehr)

INDUSTRIES—VARIOUS

➤ **Business Sources on the Internet:** This site lists business sources available on the Internet. Resources listed include: Web and gopher servers, telnet services, mailing lists, lists and directories of commercial sites, company and financial information, country-specific business resources, government, statistical, economic, market and industry-specific resources, and a list of news sources. (See entry 1651 for full listing.)

1984 `alt.make.money.fast` And piss off thousands of people even faster. *Newsgroup*

1985 `alt.niteclub.commercial` Commercially owned nightclubs. *Newsgroup*

1986 `clari.biz.industry.automotive.cbd` Automotive, tractors, components. *Moderated newsgroup*

1987 `clari.biz.industry.household` Furniture, recreation equip, cleaning equip, etc. *Moderated newsgroup*

1988 `clari.biz.industry.household.cbd` Furniture, misc. items, food preparation equipment. *Moderated newsgroup*

1989 `clari.biz.industry.misc` Miscellaneous industries. *Moderated newsgroup*

1990 `clari.biz.industry.misc.cbd.equip_maint` Maintenance, repair, rebuilding. *Moderated newsgroup*

1991 `clari.biz.industry.misc.cbd.housekeeping` Utilities, housekeeping services. *Moderated newsgroup*

1992 `clari.biz.industry.misc.cbd.lab_supplies` Lab supplies and equipment. *Moderated newsgroup*

1993 `clari.biz.industry.misc.cbd.misc_services` Operation of gov't facilities. *Moderated newsgroup*

1994 `clari.biz.industry.misc.cbd.research` Research and development. *Moderated newsgroup*

1995 `clari.biz.industry.misc.cbd.studies` Special studies and analyses. *Moderated newsgroup*

1996 `clari.biz.industry.misc.releases` Press releases covering other industries. *Moderated newsgroup*

1997 `clari.biz.industry.retail` Retail stores and shops. *Moderated newsgroup*

1998 `clari.biz.industry.retail.releases` News releases about shops. *Moderated newsgroup*

1999 `clari.biz.industry.services` Consulting, brokerages, services. *Moderated newsgroup*

2000 `clari.biz.industry.utilities` Utilities. *Moderated newsgroup*

2001 `misc.business.consulting` The business of consulting. *Moderated newsgroup*

2002 `misc.industry.utilities.electric` The electric utility industry. *Newsgroup*

2003 **Trade Show Central:** A searchable database of international trade shows: 8,500+ events. Request full participation information online, link directly to all major events, and locate specialized trade-show service companies.
   `http://www.tscentral.com/`
   INFO `rice@convergent.com`

LABOR ORGANIZING

2004 **LaborNet:** A community of labor unions, activists, and organizations using computer networks for sharing information and collaboration with the intent of increasing the human rights and economic justice of workers.
   `http://www.labornet.org/labornet`
   INFO `outreach@labornet.org`
   INFO `labornet-info@labornet.apc.org` (infobot)

2005 `alt.society.labor-unions` Theory and practice of labor unions. *Newsgroup*

2006 `clari.news.labor` Unions, strikes. *Moderated newsgroup*

2007 `clari.news.labor.layoff` Layoffs in the news. *Moderated newsgroup*

2008 `clari.news.labor.misc` Labor and union news. *Moderated newsgroup*

2009 `clari.news.labor.strike` Strikes. *Moderated newsgroup*

➤ `clari.news.protests:` Protest movements and actions. *Moderated newsgroup*

➤ **COLLBARG:** On librarians and collective bargaining. (See entry 5715 for full listing.)

2010 **CPU: Working in the Computer Industry:** Focusing on work trends in the computer industry. CPU rejects the pro-management assumptions of most computer publications and focuses upon the employees themselves. *Newsletter*
   ± `listserv@cpsr.org` [body = SUBSCRIBE CPSR-CPU first-name last-name]
   INFO `stack@starnine.com` (Michael Stack)
   ARCHIVE `ftp://cpsr.org/cpsr/work`
   Frequency: monthly

2011 **GUILDNET-L:** For members of the news media and journalists to discuss working conditions. *Mailing List*

± `majordomo@acs.ryerson.ca` [body = `subscribe guildnet-l`]

EDITOR `dtudor@acs.ryerson.ca` (Dean Tudor)

OWNER `sysop@guildnet.org` (Colin Perkel)

2012 **LABOR-L:** On labor in the emerging global economy. *Mailing List*

± `listserv@vm1.yorku.ca` [body = `SUBSCRIBE LABOR-L` first-name last-name]

INFO `lanfran@yorku.ca` (Sam Lanfranco)

➤ **OSHA Computerized Information System (OCIS):** Information from the U.S. Department of Labor Occupational Safety & Health Administration. Includes data on OSHA programs and offices as well as texts of OSHA regulations and documents. (See entry 4986 for full listing.)

2013 **Processed World Wide Web:** Web site of *Processed World* magazine, the notorious "magazine with a bad attitude." Antiauthoritarian misfits go to work and and bite the hand that bores them.

`http://www.cyborganic.com/Hothouse/Perennials/pw/`

INFO `mleger@panix.com` (Mark Leger)

2014 **PUBLABOR:** On unionism in public-sector, or government, employment. *Mailing List*

± `listserver@relay.doit.wisc.edu` [body = `SUBSCRIBE PUBLABOR` first-name last-name]

OWNER `ktbuller@macc.wisc.edu` (Katie Buller)

ARCHIVE `gopher://garnet.berkeley.edu:1252/11/LABOR/E-MAIL`

Comments: Archived as part of the Economic Democracy Information Network (EDIN). Must be subscribed in order to post.

➤ **SAFETY:** On environmental health and safety: life safety issues (such as fire protection), chemical safety (waste disposal, laboratory safety, regulatory compliance), biological hazards, and radiation safety. (See entry 4854 for full listing.)

2015 **UNITED:** On the labor movement, national and international. *Mailing List*

± `united-request@cougar.com`

OWNER `len.wilson@cougar.com` (Len Wilson)

MANAGEMENT

2016 `alt.office.management` Office management issues. *Newsgroup*

2017 `alt.projectmng` Project management. *Newsgroup*

2018 `clari.biz.industry.misc.cbd.management` Admininstration, management support. *Moderated newsgroup*

2019 **Interactive Transactions of Operations Research and Managment Science:** The online journal of the Institute for Operations Research and Management Sciences at Oklahoma State University.

`http://orcs.bus.okstate.edu/itorms/`

INFO `sharda@okway.okstate.edu`

2020 **Management-Research:** On management research: methodology, training, networking, dissemination. *Mailing List*

± `mailbase@mailbase.ac.uk`

OWNER `mff@ukc.ac.uk` (Mike Fuller)

OWNER `m.f.fuller@ukc.ac.uk` (Mike Fuller)

ARCHIVES

`gopher://mailbase.ac.uk`

`http://www.mailbase.ac.uk/`

2021 `misc.entrepreneurs` Discussion on operating a business. *Newsgroup*

2022 `misc.entrepreneurs.moderated` Entrepreneur/business topics. *Moderated newsgroup*

2023 `misc.industry.quality` Quality standards and other issues. *Newsgroup*

2024 `misc.jobs.contract` Discussions about contract labor. *Newsgroup*

2025 **Quality Resources Online:** Links to regional, national, and international resources for quality professionals, including online American Society for Quality Control (ASQC) sections.

http://www.quality.org/qc

INFO help@quality.org

FAQ http://www.quality.org/qc/quality.org.notice.txt

MARKETING

2026 <u>**Marketing Lists on the Internet:**</u> A collection of pointers to marketing-related resources on the Internet.

http://www.bayne.com/wolfBayne/htmarcom/mktglist.html

ftp://usa.net/users/wolfBayne/

INFO kimmik@usa.net (Kim M. Bayne)

2027 <u>**MouseTracks:**</u> MouseTracks is a collection of marketing-related resources. The main sections include the Hall of Malls, ConferenceCalls, the MetaMarket, the New Medium, and NutsandBolts.

http://nsns.com/MouseTracks/

INFO chofack@nsns.com

➤ **The Advertising Law Internet Site:** This site points to numerous resources regarding advertising and marketing law. (See entry 1807 for full listing.)

2028 `alt.business.multi-level` Multilevel (network) marketing businesses. *Newsgroup*

2029 **AMODLMKT:** Applied modeling in marketing focusing on single-source UPC data use at panel, chain, market, and national levels of aggregation. *Mailing List*

http://www.umsl.edu/~sbmeade/amodlmkt.htm

± listserv@umslvma.umsl.edu [body = SUBSCRIBE AMODLMKT first-name last-name]

INFO sbmeade@umslvma.bitnet (Bill Meade, Ph.D.)

ARCHIVE listserv@umslvma.umsl.edu [body = INDEX AMODLMKT]

➤ **Biomedical Market Newsletter:** A business, financial, marketing and regulatory newsletter on the medical manufacturing industry worldwide. (See entry 4901 for full listing.)

➤ **dld:** Discount Long Distance Digest: marketing info on selling long distance telecom. (See entry 9625 for full listing.)

2030 **HTMARCOM:** On marketing communication as it relates to computers and other electronics. *Mailing List, moderated*

± **INFO** htmarcom-request@bayne.com

OWNER kimmik@bayne.com (Kim Miklofsky Bayne)

FAQ http://www.bayne.com/wolfBayne/htmarcom/htmlist.html

Please Note: Subscription by approval only.

➤ **Ideas DIGest ONLINE newsmagazine:** The small business guide to succeeding with innovation and the development of creative ideas for the market. (See entry 2067 for full listing.)

2031 **INET-MARKETING:** On marketing on the Internet. *Digest & Reflector, moderated*

± im-sub@popco.com [body = subscribe]

EDITOR OWNER glenn@popco.com (Glenn Fleishman)

ARCHIVE http://www.popco.com/hyper/inet-marketing/

➤ **The Internet Advertising Resource Guide:** Contains links to select sources of information about advertising and marketing on the Internet. (See entry 1811 for full listing.)

2032 **KAWASAKI:** The list for raging thunderlizards who want to change the world through great products and great marketing. *Mailing List*

± listserv@umslvma.umsl.edu [body = SUBSCRIBE KAWASAKI first-name last-name]

INFO sbmeade@umslvma.bitnet (Bill Meade, Ph.D.)

ARCHIVE listserv@umslvma.umsl.edu [body = INDEX KAWASAKI]

2033 **Market-L:** For discussions among marketing academics and practitioners. *Mailing List*

± `listproc@mailer.fsu.edu` [body = SUBSCRIBE MARKET-L first-name last-name]

INFO `chofack@cob.fsu.edu` (Charles Hofacker)

FAQ `http://nsns.com/MouseTracks/Market-L.FAQ.txt`

2034 MARKETNET-L: On marketing. *Mailing List, moderated*

± `majordomo@ax.apc.org` [body = SUBSCRIBE marketnet-l first-name last-name]

OWNER `uramar@ax.ibase.org.br` (Uramar Farias)

Language: Portugese, Spanish, English

2035 Perseus QualStar: QualStar is a periodic e-mail newsletter providing information about qualitative market research, including focus groups, customer satisfaction, and in-depth or face-to-face interviews. *Newsletter*

± INFO EDITOR `74774.157@compuserve.com` [body = subscribe qualstar] (Jeffrey Henning, Editor)

INFO OWNER `rnadler@mcimail.com` (Rich Nadler)

2036 SalesDoctors™: SalesDoctors magazine is written by sales professionals for sales professionals to help them sell more of any product or service, sell more efficiently, and keep their customers coming back for more.

`http://salesdoctors.com/`

INFO `info@salesdoctors.com`

2037 VALIDATA: On psychological measure development, testing, and validation. *Mailing List*

± `listserv@ua1vm.ua.edu` [body = SUBSCRIBE VALIDATA first-name last-name]

OWNER `lflynn@postoffice.cob.fsu.edu` (Leisa Reinecke Flynn)

NEWS

2038 `clari.apbl.biz.briefs` Hourly business news brief from the Associated Press. *Moderated newsgroup*

2039 `clari.apbl.biz.headlines` Headlines of top business stories. *Moderated newsgroup*

2040 `clari.apbl.reports.dollar_gold` Daily gold and dollar prices. *Moderated newsgroup*

2041 `clari.biz.briefs` Business news briefs. *Moderated newsgroup*

2042 `clari.biz.features` Business feature stories. *Moderated newsgroup*

2043 `clari.biz.front_page` Top five business stories each day. *Moderated newsgroup*

2044 `clari.biz.headlines` Two-line summaries of top business stories. *Moderated newsgroup*

2045 `clari.biz.mergers.releases` Press releases: mergers, acquisitions, spinoffs. *Moderated newsgroup*

2046 `clari.biz.misc` Other business news. *Moderated newsgroup*

2047 `clari.biz.review` Daily review of business news. *Moderated newsgroup*

2048 `clari.biz.top` Top business news. *Moderated newsgroup*

2049 `clari.biz.tradeshows.releases` Press releases covering trade shows. *Moderated newsgroup*

2050 `clari.biz.urgent` Breaking business news. *Moderated newsgroup*

2051 `clari.nb.business` Newsbytes: business and industry news. *Moderated newsgroup*

2052 `clari.tw.features` Features about technical industries and computers. *Moderated newsgroup*

➤ **Daily:** For Statistics Canada Daily data and publications. (See entry 7140 for full listing.)

➤ **INNOVATION:** Summary of trends, strategies, and innovations in business and technology. (See entry 9440 for full listing.)

➤ **M2 NewsWEB:** NewsWEB is an online service from M2 Communications, which provides permanent access to your company's news and background information to users of the Internet, wherever they are in the world and whenever they want it. (See entry 1812 for full listing.)

2053 NewsPage: A comprehensive source for daily business news. Access to news headlines and summaries is free. Some full-text articles are free to registered users; others require a small monthly subscription fee. The NewsPage Direct service provides personalized electronic newspapers to be sent to users' e-mail boxes daily.

`http://www.newspage.com/`

INFO `webmaster_newspage@individual.com`

FAQ `http://www.newspage.com/NEWSPAGE/help.html`

➤ **Quote.Com:** All sorts of financial market data including current quotes on stocks, options, commodity futures, mutual funds, and bonds; also, business news and market analysis. (See entry 1777 for full listing.)

➤ **Wall Street Journal Money and Investing Update:** Continually updated coverage of global markets and the top stories in business and finance worldwide. (See entry 1784 for full listing.)

NOT-FOR-PROFIT

2054 **The Contact Center Network:** This site provides a comprehensive directory to nonprofit organizations on the Internet, with links to over 4,000 sites arranged by issue and geography.

`http://www.contact.org/`

INFO `info@contact.org`

➤ **HandsNet:** HandsNet is a national, nonprofit network that promotes information sharing, cross-sector collaboration, and advocacy among individuals and organizations working on a broad range of public interest issues. The site includes action alerts, forums, and information on the various social programs that HandsNet is involved with. (See entry 9669 for full listing.)

2055 **Internet NonProfit Center:** This site includes a Nonprofit Locater that can search a database for information on almost any nonprofit in the U.S.; a library of publications and data about nonprofit organizations, the nonprofit sector, and how individual donors can evaluate nonprofits; a Parlor that includes a discussion area, a calandar of events, and nonprofit related news; and, of course, links to other nonprofit-related Internet sites.

`http://www.human.com/inc`

INFO `clandesm@panix.com` (Cliff Landesman)

2056 **Nonprofit Resources Catalogue:** A collection of resources of interest to nonprofit organizations. Covers: business and work, fundraising and giving, general nonprofit resources, general reference, health and human services, news sources, United States government, weather and disasters, and more.

`http://www.clark.net/pub/pwalker/home.html`

INFO `pwalker@clark.net`

➤ **Resources Nonprofit:** An extensive collection of Internet resource of interest to nonprofit organizations. As well as including listings on specific nonprofits and resources relating to specific social issues that nonprofits are often involved in, the site includes information on funding opportunities, nonprofit management issues, nonprofits and technology, philanthropy, volunteer activities, and business, corporate and government information. (See entry 9670 for full listing.)

2057 **CyberVPM:** CyberVPM is dedicated to the discussion of topics relevant to volunteer program management. Participation is free of charge and available to anyone who works with volunteers. *Mailing List*

`http://www.halcyon.com/penguin/svm.htm`

± `listserv@listserv.aol.com` [body = `SUBSCRIBE CyberVPM` first-name last-name or organization]

INFO OWNER `penguin@halcyon.com` (Nan Hawthorne)

Please Note: Subscription by approval only.

Comments: Limited to VPMs in Washington State and other AVA Region X states.

➤ **Impact ONLINE:** Impact Online promotes community involvement by offering information on nonprofits and on volunteer opportunities nationwide. Impact Online even offers "virtual volunteer" opportunities that can be done entirely online. The site also offers a complete online course for nonprofits interested in using technology for social change. (See entry 9671 for full listing.)

2058 **National Center for Nonprofit Boards:** Materials to help board members and senior staff of nonprofits work together to lead their organizations more effectively. Also includes information on management, fundraising, and other Internet resources for nonprofits.

`gopher://ncnb.org:7002`

INFO `ncnb@ncnb.org`

INFO `npboards@aol.com`

➤ **PUBS-L:** For the staff of publications offices at educational and nonprofit institutions. (See entry 1930 for full listing.)

2059   `soc.org.nonprofit`   Nonprofit organizations. *Newsgroup*

2060   **USNONPROFIT-L:** Nonprofit organizations and the folks they serve. *Mailing List, moderated*

     ± EDITOR OWNER `madeline.g@eworld.com` (Madeline Gonzalez)

     ± EDITOR OWNER `tan@pobox.com` (T. A. Newman)

     EDITOR `pbarber@eskimo.com` (Putnam Barber)

     Gated: `soc.org.nonprofit`

SMALL BUSINESES & ENTREPRENEURS

2061   <u>**Entrepreneurs on the Web**</u>: Information for entrepreneurs and small business owners.

     `http://www.eotw.com/eotw`

     INFO `eotw@eotw.com`

2062   `alt.business.home.pc`   For displaying PC home business plans and services. *Newsgroup*

➤   **BIDS4NYC:** On business improvement districts. (See entry 9755 for full listing.)

2063   **Big Dreams:** The focus of this newsletter is personal development and topics related to starting a small business. *Newsletter*

     `ftp://sumex-aim.stanford.edu/info-mac/per/bigd/`

     `http://www.wimsey.com/~duncans`

     ARCHIVES

     `ftp://sumex-aim.stanford.edu/info-mac/per/bigd/`

     `http://www.wimsey.com/~duncans`

     `http://www.nlc-bnc.ca/eppp-archive/bigdreams/`

     Frequency: monthly

2064   **BizOpList:** For announcements of new business opportunities & self-employment opportunities. *Distribution List, moderated*

     ± `bizbot@web-star.com` [body = SUBSCRIBE]

     INFO OWNER `syscon@web-star.com` (Howard Barton)

➤   **BookWeb:** All sorts of book information, brought to you by the American Booksellers Association. Includes book news, author tour information, a directory of bookstores, a monthly contest, information on how to open a book-store, and more. (See entry 105 for full listing.)

2065   **Electronic Money Tree:** Features articles written for, by, and about entrepreneurs. Home-based businesses and franchises are explored and discussed, as well as articles on taxes and investments. *Newsletter*

     OWNER `soos@soos.com`

     ARCHIVE `http://www.soos.com/$tree`

2066   **FAMBUS-L:** On family businesses: operations, taxes, estate planning. *Mailing List*

     ± `listserv@netcom.com` [body = SUBSCRIBE fambus-l]

     OWNER `wbristow@netcom.com` (Walt Bristow)

2067   **Ideas DIGest ONLINE newsmagazine:** The small business guide to succeeding with innovation and the development of creative ideas for the market. *E-Journal*

     `http://www.ideas.wis.net/`

     INFO `idig@wimsey.com` (Chris Webb)

     Frequency: 6 times per year

2068   **InfoLink's Ondernemersdisk/Business Disk Online:** A bimonthly Web magazine for Dutch and international small business owners. *Magazine*

     `http://iaehv.nl/users/kerstens/ildisk.htm`

     INFO OWNER `kerstens@iaehv.nl` (Robert Kerstens)

     Language: Dutch, English

     Frequency: bimonthly

➤ `misc.entrepreneurs.moderated`: Entrepreneur/business topics. *Moderated newsgroup*

2069 **National Computer Tectonics Online:** Computer magazine aimed at small business and home office users. *E-Journal*
http://www.awa.com/nct
INFO bmorris@usit.net (Bruce Morris)
Frequency: updated daily

2070 **NetMarque:** This site provides management guidance for executives, business owners, and entrepreneurs.
http://nmq.com/
INFO gumpcom@netmarquee.com

2071 **Network-News:** On networked computing and small business. *Newsletter*
± network-news@lists.primenet.com [body = *A brief dscription of your interest in small business along with your e-mail address.*]
OWNER gatlina@primenet.com (J. Alan Gatlin)
Please Note: Subscription by approval only.

2072 `pa.smallbusiness` Small-business discussions in Pennsylvania (no ads). *Newsgroup*

2073 **Small Business Administration:** All sorts of information from the U.S. government's Small Business Administration. Includes information on starting, financing, and expanding small businesses, as well as a shareware library of software helpful to running a business.
http://www.sbaonline.sba.gov/
ftp://www.sbaonline.sba.gov
gopher://www.sbaonline.sba.gov
INFO www@www.sbaonline.sba.gov

SOCIAL ISSUES

2074 `alt.business.accountability` Corporate accountability. *Newsgroup*

2075 `clari.biz.privatization` Privatizations and nationalizations. *Moderated newsgroup*

2076 **Institute for Business and Professional Ethics:** One of the largest resource sites relating to business and professional ethics, including an online journal, ethics discussions, and an ethics calendar.
http://www.depaul.edu/ethics
INFO lpincus@wppost.depaul.edu (Laura B. Pincus)

➤ **SRB:** On socially responsible business and investing. (See entry 1780 for full listing.)

COMPUTERS & THE INTERNET

2077 `comp.misc` General topics about computers not covered elsewhere. *Newsgroup*

2078 `kw.micro` Microcomputer discussion. *Newsgroup*

2079 `relcom.commerce.computers` Computer hardware. *Newsgroup*

2080 `relcom.commerce.software` Software. *Newsgroup*

2081 `tnn.hardware` Discussions about computer hardware. *Newsgroup*

2082 `tnn.software` Discussions about computer software. *Newsgroup*

ACORN

2083 `comp.binaries.acorn` Binary-only postings for Acorn machines. *Moderated newsgroup*

2084 `comp.sources.acorn` Source code-only postings for the Acorn. *Moderated newsgroup*

2085 `comp.sys.acorn.advocacy` Why Acorn computers and programs are better. *Newsgroup*

2086 `comp.sys.acorn.announce` Announcements for Acorn and ARM users. *Moderated newsgroup*

2087 `comp.sys.acorn.apps` Acorn software applications. *Newsgroup*

2088 `comp.sys.acorn.hardware` Acorn hardware. *Newsgroup*

2089 `comp.sys.acorn.misc` Acorn computing in general. *Newsgroup*

2090 `comp.sys.acorn.networking` Networking of Acorn computers. *Newsgroup*

2091 `comp.sys.acorn.programmer` Programming of Acorn computers. *Newsgroup*

➤ **PHOTODSK-L:** Discussion about the Acorn RISC-OS !Photodesk photo software. (See entry 2472 for full listing.)

AMIGA

2092 `alt.sources.amiga` Source code for the Amiga. *Newsgroup*

➤ `alt.sys.amiga.blitz:` The Blitz Basic programming language. *Newsgroup*

2093 `alt.sys.amiga.demos` Code and talk to show off the Amiga. *Newsgroup*

2094 `alt.sys.amiga.uucp` Amiga UUCP. *Newsgroup*

2095 **The AMOS Web Site:** Dedicated to the AMOS programming language.
http://dragon.res.cmu.edu/achurch/amos/
INFO achurch@cmu.edu

2096 `aus.computers.amiga` Discussions about Commodore Amiga computers. *Newsgroup*

2097 `bit.listserv.i-amiga` Info-Amiga list. *Newsgroup*

2098 `comp.binaries.amiga` Encoded public domain programs in binary. *Moderated newsgroup*

2099 `comp.sources.amiga` Source code-only postings for the Amiga. *Moderated newsgroup*

2100 `comp.sys.amiga.advocacy` Why an Amiga is better than XYZ. *Newsgroup*

2101 `comp.sys.amiga.announce` Announcements about the Amiga computers. *Moderated newsgroup*

2102 `comp.sys.amiga.applications` Miscellaneous applications. *Newsgroup*

2103 `comp.sys.amiga.audio` Music, MIDI, speech synthesis, other sounds. *Newsgroup*

2104 `comp.sys.amiga.cd32` Technical and computing talk for Commodore Amiga CD32. *Newsgroup*

2105 `comp.sys.amiga.datacomm` Methods of getting bytes in and out. *Newsgroup*

2106 `comp.sys.amiga.emulations` Various hardware and software emulators. *Newsgroup*

2107 `comp.sys.amiga.graphics` Charts, graphs, pictures, etc. *Newsgroup*

2108 `comp.sys.amiga.hardware` Amiga computer hardware, Q & A, reviews, etc. *Newsgroup*

2109 `comp.sys.amiga.introduction` Group for newcomers to Amiga's computers. *Newsgroup*

2110 `comp.sys.amiga.marketplace` Where to find it, prices, etc. *Newsgroup*

2111 `comp.sys.amiga.misc` Discussions not falling in another Amiga group. *Newsgroup*

➤ `comp.sys.amiga.multimedia`: Animations, video, and multimedia. *Newsgroup*

2112 `comp.sys.amiga.networking` Amiga networking software/hardware. *Newsgroup*

2113 `comp.sys.amiga.programmer` Developers and hobbyists discuss code. *Newsgroup*

2114 `comp.sys.amiga.reviews` Reviews of Amiga software, hardware. *Moderated newsgroup*

2115 `comp.sys.amiga.uucp` Amiga UUCP packages. *Newsgroup*

➤ `comp.unix.amiga`: Minix, SYSV4 and other *nix on an Amiga. *Newsgroup*

2116 **CSAA:** Announcements for Amiga users. Includes posts on product releases, updates, shows, and events, etc. *Mailing List, moderated*
    `http://seclab.cs.ucdavis.edu/~zerkle/announce/`
    INFO `zerkle@cs.ucdavis.edu` (Dan Zerkle)
    ARCHIVE `ftp://litamiga.epfl.ch`
    Gated: `Comp.sys.amiga.announce`

2117 **I-AMIGA:** All about the Amiga computer with a technical bent, including product releases and reviews; software development. *Mailing List*
    ± `listserv@ubvm.cc.buffalo.edu` [body = `SUBSCRIBE I-AMIGA` first-name last-name]
    INFO `owner-i-amiga@ubvm.cc.buffalo.edu`
    Gated: `bit.listserv.i-amiga`

2118 `okinawa.sys.amiga` Discussion about Amiga. *Newsgroup*

APPLE][

2119 `bit.listserv.apple2-l` Apple II list. *Newsgroup*

2120 `comp.binaries.apple2` Binary-only postings for the Apple II computer. *Newsgroup*

2121 `comp.emulators.apple2` Emulators of Apple II systems. *Newsgroup*

2122 `comp.sources.apple2` Source code and discussion for the Apple II. *Moderated newsgroup*

2123 `comp.sys.apple2` Discussion about Apple II micros. *Newsgroup*

2124 `comp.sys.apple2.comm` Apple II data communications. *Newsgroup*

2125 `comp.sys.apple2.gno` The Apple IIgs GNO multitasking environment. *Newsgroup*

2126 `comp.sys.apple2.marketplace` Buying, selling, and trading Apple II equipment. *Newsgroup*

2127 `comp.sys.apple2.programmer` Programming on the Apple II. *Newsgroup*

2128 `comp.sys.apple2.usergroups` All about Apple II user groups. *Newsgroup*

➤ **Minnie 386BSD Archive:** Archive of a BSD Unix for Intel x86 processor machines. Also contains some programs for Apple II computers, and some amateur radio files and software. (See entry 3935 for full listing.)

ARTIFICIAL INTELLIGENCE

2129 **Carnegie Mellon University Artificial Intelligence Repository:** Collection of nearly all materials of interest to AI researchers, educators, practitioners, and students.
    `http://www.cs.cmu.edu/Web/Groups/AI/html/air.html`
    `http://www.cs.cmu.edu/Web/Groups/AI/html/keys/keysform.html` ((for keyword searching))
    `ftp://ftp.cs.cmu.edu/user/ai`
    INFO `ai.repository@cs.cmu.edu`

➤ **Computer Vision Home Page:** The Computer Vision page points to the latest research groups and results in image processing, robotic vision, and automatic reconstruction of 3-D information from 2-D imagery. (See entry 2672 for full listing.)

2130 **Interactive Agent Page of Resources:** This page links to Web and FTP resources about interactive agents and animated characters. The topics are organized into four categories: avatars, bots, sims, and agents.
`http://www.petroglyph.com/characters.html`
INFO `powers@petroglyph.com`

2131 **AICS-L:** On architectures for intelligent control systems. *Mailing List*
± `listserv@ubvm.cc.buffalo.edu` [body = `SUBSCRIBE AICS-L` first-name last-name]
INFO `meystma@duvm.bitnet` (Michael Meystel)
ARCHIVE `ftp://impact.drexel.edu/pub/aics/archives`
Please Note: Subscription by approval only.

2132 `aus.ai` AI discussions. *Newsgroup*

2133 `aus.computers.ai` Artificial intelligence considered from Down Under. *Newsgroup*

➤ **Automated Reasoning Project (ARP):** Software, tools, and papers on automated reasoning and parallel and symbolic computing. (See entry 9163 for full listing.)

2134 `can.ai` Artificial intelligence in Canada. *Newsgroup*

2135 **CBL:** Computer-Based Learning Unit, The University of Leeds, United Kingdom.
`http://cbl.leeds.ac.uk/`
INFO `webmaster@cbl.leeds.ac.uk`

2136 `comp.ai` Artificial-intelligence discussions. *Newsgroup*

2137 `comp.ai.alife` Research about artificial life. *Newsgroup*

2138 `comp.ai.doc-analysis.misc` General document-understanding technologies. *Newsgroup*

2139 `comp.ai.doc-analysis.ocr` OCR research, algorithms, and software. *Newsgroup*

2140 `comp.ai.edu` Applications of artificial intelligence to education. *Newsgroup*

2141 `comp.ai.fuzzy` Fuzzy set theory, aka fuzzy logic. *Newsgroup*

2142 `comp.ai.games` Artificial intelligence in games and game playing. *Newsgroup*

2143 `comp.ai.genetic` Genetic algorithms in computing. *Newsgroup*

2144 `comp.ai.jair.announce` Announcements and abstracts of the *Journal of AI Research. Moderated newsgroup*

2145 `comp.ai.jair.papers` Papers published by the *Journal of AI Research. Moderated newsgroup*

2146 `comp.ai.nat-lang` Natural language processing by computers. *Newsgroup*

2147 `comp.ai.neural-nets` All aspects of neural networks. *Newsgroup*

2148 `comp.ai.nlang-know-rep` Natural language and knowledge representation. *Moderated newsgroup*

➤ `comp.ai.philosophy:` Philosophical aspects of artificial intelligence. *Newsgroup*

2149 `comp.ai.shells` Expert systems and other artificial-intelligence shells. *Newsgroup*

2150 `comp.ai.vision` Artificial-intelligence vision research. *Moderated newsgroup*

2151 `comp.cog-eng` Cognitive engineering. *Newsgroup*

2152 `comp.org.issnnet` The International Student Society for Neural Networks. *Newsgroup*

➤ `comp.speech:` Research and applications in speech science and technology. *Newsgroup*

2153 **Distributed Artificial Intelligence at HUJI:** Distributed artificial inteligence/multi-agent systems lab at the Hebrew University, Jerusalem, Israel.
`http://www.cs.huji.ac.il/labs/dai/`
INFO `clag@cs.huji.ac.il`
INFO `yish@cs.huji.ac.il`

2154 `fj.ai` Artificial-intelligence discussions. *Newsgroup*

➤ **FLN:** For scholarly discussion of figurative language—discussion is international and interdisciplinary (psychology, linguistics, AI, computational linguistics, literary studies). (See entry 5294 for full listing.)

2155 **Journal of Artificial Intelligence Research (JAIR):** The Journal of Artificial Intelligence Research (JAIR) is a refereed publication, covering all areas of artificial intelligence (AI). *E-Journal*

`ftp://p.gp.cs.cmu.edu/usr/jair/pub`

`gopher://p.gp.cs.cmu.edu`

`http://www.cs.washington.edu/research/jair/home.html`

± `jair@cs.cmu.edu` [subject = AUTORESPOND; body = HELP]

INFO `jair-ed@ptolemy.arc.nasa.gov` (Steven Minton)

ARCHIVES

`ftp://p.gp.cs.cmu.edu/usr/jair/pub`

`gopher://p.gp.cs.cmu.edu`

`http://www.cs.washington.edu/research/jair/home.html`

`jair@cs.cmu.edu` [subject = AUTORESPOND; body = HELP]

Gated: `comp.ai.jair.announce`

Frequency: irregular

➤ **Knowledge Discovery Mine:** This site provides information on data mining and knowledge discovery in databases. (See entry 2338 for full listing.)

2156 **Neuron:** On all aspects of neural networks. Topics include both artificial neural networks and biological systems. *Digest, moderated*

± **INFO** `neuron-request@psych.upenn.edu` (Peter Marvit)

EDITOR `marvit@cattell.psych.upenn.edu` (Peter Marvit)

ARCHIVES

`ftp://psych.upenn.edu`

`archive-server@psych.upenn.edu`

Gated: `comp.ai.neural-nets`

➤ **Robotics Internet Resources Page:** This page is a collection of robotics-related resources on the Internet. It includes pointers to Web pages, FTP sites, software, and robotics video demonstrations. (See entry 9572 for full listing.)

2157 **SCHOLAR:** On natural language processing. *Mailing List, moderated*

± `listserv@cunyvm` [body = SUBSCRIBE SCHOLAR first-name last-name]

INFO `scholar-request@cunyvm`

ARCHIVE `listserv@cunyvm` [body = INDEX SCHOLAR]

2158 **SIGART Electronic Information Service:** A public service to the AI community sponsored by ACM SIGART, the Special Interest Group on Artificial Intelligence.

`http://sigart.acm.org/`

INFO `www@sigart.acm.org`

2159 `triangle.neural-nets` Triangle area discussion of neural networks. *Newsgroup*

2160 `uk.ikbs` Discussion of Intelligent Knowledge Based Systems. *Newsgroup*

ATARI

2161 `comp.binaries.atari.st` Binary-only postings for the Atari ST. *Moderated newsgroup*

2162 `comp.sources.atari.st` Source code-only postings for the Atari ST. *Moderated newsgroup*

2163 `comp.sys.atari.8bit` Discussion about 8-bit Atari micros. *Newsgroup*

2164 `comp.sys.atari.advocacy` Attacking and defending Atari computers. *Newsgroup*

2165 `comp.sys.atari.announce` Atari-related hard/software announcements. *Moderated newsgroup*

2166 `comp.sys.atari.programmer` Programming on the Atari computers. *Newsgroup*

2167 `comp.sys.atari.st` Discussion about 16-bit Atari micros. *Newsgroup*

2168 `comp.sys.atari.st.tech` Technical discussions of Atari ST hard/software. *Newsgroup*

2169 `rec.games.video.atari` Discussion of Atari's video game systems. *Newsgroup*

BULLETIN BOARD SYSTEMS (BBSS)

2170 **The BBS Listings Homepage:** Listings of BBSs accessible from the Internet via telnet.
  `http://www.tiac.net/users/cody/bbs/bbslist.html`
  INFO bposner@gcomm.com

2171 **Select BBSs on the Internet:** A comprehensive listing of BBSs accessible from the Internet.
  `http://dkeep.com/sbi.htm`
  INFO cerebus@dkmail.dkeep.com

2172 `alt.bbs` Computer BBS systems and software. *Newsgroup*

2173 `alt.bbs.ads` Ads for various computer BBSs. *Newsgroup*

2174 `alt.bbs.allsysop` Sysop concerns of *all* networks and technologies. *Newsgroup*

2175 `alt.bbs.citadel` The Citadel BBS. *Newsgroup*

2176 `alt.bbs.doors` Bulletin board system add-on executables, or "doors". *Newsgroup*

2177 `alt.bbs.first-class` The First Class Mac GUI BBS. *Newsgroup*

2178 `alt.bbs.gigo-gateway` Garbage in, garbage out—`alt.*` in a nutshell. *Newsgroup*

2179 `alt.bbs.iniquity` Discussions about iNiQUiTY BBS Software. *Newsgroup*

2180 `alt.bbs.internet` BBSs that are hooked up to the Internet. *Newsgroup*

2181 `alt.bbs.lists` Postings of regional BBS listings. *Newsgroup*

2182 `alt.bbs.lists.d` Discussion and requests of regional BBS listings. *Newsgroup*

2183 `alt.bbs.majorbbs` The MajorBBS by Galacticomm, Inc. *Newsgroup*

2184 `alt.bbs.metal` The METAL telecommunications environment. *Newsgroup*

2185 `alt.bbs.pcboard` Technical support for the PCBoard BBS. *Newsgroup*

2186 `alt.bbs.pcbuucp` The commerical PCBoard gateway, PCB-UUCP. *Newsgroup*

2187 `alt.bbs.proboard` No description. *Newsgroup*

2188 `alt.bbs.ra` RemoteAccess discussion. *Newsgroup*

2189 `alt.bbs.renegade` The James Dean of BBSs. *Newsgroup*

2190 `alt.bbs.searchlight` Searchlight BBS system discussions. *Newsgroup*

2191 `alt.bbs.tribbs` Didn't Kirk have some trouble with tribbs? *Newsgroup*

2192 `alt.bbs.unixbbs` UnixBBS, from Nervous XTC. *Newsgroup*

2193 `alt.bbs.watergate` The WaterGate mail processor. *Newsgroup*

2194 `alt.bbs.wildcat` Wildcat! BBS from Mustang Software, Inc. *Newsgroup*

2195 `alt.bbs.wwiv` The WWIV bulletin board system. *Newsgroup*

2196 `alt.binaries.bbs.pcboard` Binaries for PCBoard systems. *Newsgroup*

➤ `clari.nb.online:` Newsbytes: online services, the Internet, BBSs. *Moderated newsgroup*

2197 `comp.bbs.majorbbs` Support and discussion of The Major BBS from Galacticomm. *Newsgroup*

2198 `comp.bbs.misc` All aspects of computer bulletin board systems. *Newsgroup*

2199 `comp.bbs.tbbs` The Bread Board System bulletin board software. *Newsgroup*

2200 `comp.bbs.waffle` The Waffle BBS and Usenet system on all platforms. *Newsgroup*

2201 `eug.bbs.excelsior` Discussion of Excelsior BBS software. *Newsgroup*

➤ `relcom.bbs.list:` Ex-USSR BBS file lists. *Newsgroup*

2202 `relcom.fido.su.hardw` FIDOnet, computer hardware. *Newsgroup*

2203 `relcom.fido.su.softw` FIDOnet, software in general. *Newsgroup*

2204 `sbay.waffle` Waffle BBS topics specific to the South Bay. *Newsgroup*

➤ `sdnet.waffle:` San Diego Waffle BBS discussions. *Newsgroup*

2205 **Traders' Connection BBS:** This BBS, accessible through the World Wide Web, provides e-mail, 1.5 million classified ads, over 80 multiplayer games, the Official Internet MUD (games) List, thousands of downloadable files, technical help, online publications, moderated special interest groups, Internet and Web services, personal Web pages, and more.
`http://www.trader.com/bbs`
`telnet://trader.com`
FAQ `http://www.trader.com/info`

2206 **WILDCAT-L:** On Wildcat! BBS software. *Mailing List*
OWNER `pete.nelson@terminal-one.com` (Pete Nelson)

CAD-CAM

2207 `alt.cad` Computer aided design. *Newsgroup*

2208 `alt.cad.autocad` CAD as practiced by customers of Autodesk. *Newsgroup*

2209 `alt.cad.cadkey` Cadkey, Datacad, and other Cadkey, Inc. products. *Newsgroup*

2210 `alt.sys.intergraph` Support for Intergraph machines. *Newsgroup*

2211 **artist-users:** Discussion group for users and potential users of the software tools from Cadence Design Systems. Not for graphic artists or AutoCad users. *Mailing List*
± INFO `artist-users-request@uicc.com`

2212 `comp.cad.autocad` AutoDesk's AutoCAD software. *Newsgroup*

2213 `comp.cad.cadence` Users of Cadence Design Systems products. *Newsgroup*

2214 `comp.cad.compass` Compass Design Automation EDA tools. *Newsgroup*

2215 `comp.cad.i-deas` SDRC I-DEAS Masters Series software. *Newsgroup*

2216 `comp.cad.microstation` MicroStation CAD software and related products. *Newsgroup*

2217 `comp.cad.pro-engineer` Parametric Technology's Pro/Engineer design package. *Newsgroup*

2218 `comp.cad.synthesis` Research and production in the field of logic synthesis. *Newsgroup*

➤ `comp.lsi.cad:` Electrical computer-aided design. *Newsgroup*

2219 `comp.sys.mentor` Mentor Graphics products and the Silicon Compiler System. *Newsgroup*

2220 `info.brl-cad` BRL's solid-modeling CAD system (`cad@arl.army.mil`). *Moderated newsgroup*

2221 `relcom.fido.ru.acad` FIDOnet, AutoCAD, problems and solutions. *Newsgroup*

2222 `sci.electronics.cad` Schematic drafting, printed circuit layout, simulation. *Newsgroup*

2223 **SIGDA Home Page:** This Web server provides access to online information services available from the ACM's Special Interest Group on Design Automation (SIGDA).
`http://sigda.acm.org/`
INFO `sigda@ee.pitt.edu`
MIRROR `http://www.acm.org/sigda`

2224 **SIGDA Newsletter:** Featuring articles, department reports, conferences, workshops, and symposia reports and programs, as well as announcements for upcoming design automation conferences, etc. *Newsletter*

```
http://info.acm.org/catalog/join.html
```
INFO sigda@ee.pitt.edu
ARCHIVE http://www.acm.org/sigda/newsletter/index.html
Frequency: biannual
Price: $15.00 for ACM members, $18.00 for nonmembers

CALCULATORS

2225 **alt.calculator.casio** Casio fx calculators. *Newsgroup*

2226 **alt.casio.calculator** Casio calculators. *Newsgroup*

2227 **bit.listserv.calc-ti** Texas Instruments graphics calulators. *Newsgroup*

2228 **bit.listserv.graph-ti** Discussion of the TI-8x series calculator. *Moderated newsgroup*

2229 **comp.sources.hp48** Programs for the HP48 and HP28 calculators. *Moderated newsgroup*

2230 **comp.sys.hp48** Hewlett-Packard's HP48 and HP28 calculators. *Newsgroup*

2231 **Hewlett-Packard Calculator Superiority:** A spirited reflection on the clear superiority of HP calculators over their competition. Touts RPN, HP's famous reliability, and the wide support enjoyed by HP users.
```
http://www.students.uiuc.edu/~ag-ho/hp.calc.html
```
INFO ag-ho@uiuc.edu

CASE

2232 **bit.listserv.authorware** Authorware professional authoring program. *Newsgroup*

2233 **comp.soft-sys.powerbuilder** Application development tools from PowerSoft. *Newsgroup*

2234 **comp.software-eng** Software engineering and related topics. *Newsgroup*

2235 **Computer Aided Engineering Center at UW-MADISON anonymous HP-UX FTP archive:** An archive for software that has been compiled and tested under HP-UX, maintained by the Computer Aided Engineering Center at the College of Engineering at the University of Wisconsin-Madison, Madison, Wisconsin.
```
http://hpux.cae.wisc.edu/
ftp://hpux.cae.wisc.edu
```
INFO ahmadz@engr.wisc.edu
FAQ http://hpux.cae.wisc.edu/pubdomain/FAQ_archive.html
MIRRORS
```
http://hpux.dsi.unimi.it/
http://hpux.ced.tudelft.nl/ARCHIVE/archive_intro.html
http://hpux.ee.ualberta.ca/
http://hpux.csc.liv.ac.uk/
http://hpux.ask.uni-karlsruhe.de/
http://hpux.cict.fr/
```

COMPANIES

COMPANIES—APPLE

2236 **clari.tw.computers.apple** Apple corporate and product news. *Moderated newsgroup*

2237 **clari.tw.computers.apple.releases** Releases: Apple Corp. and products. *Moderated newsgroup*

COMPANIES—DIGITAL EQUIPMENT CORPORATION

➤ **ALPHA-IDS:** OpenVMS AXP Internals programming. (See entry 4060 for full listing.)

2238 **bit.listserv.decnews** Digital Equipment Corporation news list. *Newsgroup*

2239 `biz.dec.decathena` DECathena discussions. *Newsgroup*

2240 `biz.dec.decnews` The DECNews newsletter. *Moderated newsgroup*

➤ `biz.dec.ip`: IP networking on DEC machines. *Newsgroup*

2241 `biz.digital.announce` Digital Equipment Corp. news and announcements. *Moderated newsgroup*

2242 `biz.digital.articles` Digital Equipment Corp. newsletter, catalog, and journal. *Moderated newsgroup*

2243 `cern.alpha` Discussion list on OpenVMS and OSF/1 Alpha machines. *Newsgroup*

2244 `comp.org.decus` Digital Equipment Computer Users Society newsgroup. *Newsgroup*

➤ `comp.os.vms`: DEC's VAX* line of computers and VMS. *Newsgroup*

2245 `comp.sys.dec` Discussions about DEC computer systems. *Newsgroup*

2246 `comp.sys.dec.micro` DEC micros (Rainbow, Professional 350/380). *Newsgroup*

➤ `comp.unix.ultrix`: Discussions about DEC's Ultrix. *Newsgroup*

➤ **DECMCC-L:** On DEC DECmcc (a network monitoring tool from DEC) and related software. (See entry 3233 for full listing.)

2247 **Digital Technical Journal:** The Digital Technical Journal is a refereed journal published quarterly by the Digital Equipment Corporation. *E-Journal*
`http://www.digital.com/info/DTJ/`
`ftp://ftp.digital.com/pub/Digital/info/DTJ`
INFO `blake@rdvax.enet.dec.com` (Jane Blake)
ARCHIVE `ftp://ftp.digital.com/pub/Digital/info/DTJ`
Gated: `biz.digital.articles`
Frequency: quarterly

2248 `kw.microvax` DEC Microvax users. *Newsgroup*

➤ **LANWORKS:** On Digital's PATHWORKS software. (See entry 3285 for full listing.)

2249 `triangle.decus` The Triangle DECUS newsletter and general DEC matters. *Newsgroup*

2250 `vmsnet.decus.journal` The DECUServe Journal. *Moderated newsgroup*

2251 `vmsnet.decus.lugs` Discussion of DECUS Local User Groups and related issues. *Newsgroup*

COMPANIES—HEWLETT PACKARD

2252 `comp.sys.hp.apps` Discussion of software and applications on all HP platforms. *Newsgroup*

2253 `comp.sys.hp.hardware` Discussion of Hewlett Packard system hardware. *Newsgroup*

2254 `comp.sys.hp.hpux` Issues pertaining to HP-UX and 9000 series computers. *Newsgroup*

2255 `comp.sys.hp.misc` Issues not covered in any other comp.sys.hp.* group. *Newsgroup*

2256 `comp.sys.hp.mpe` Issues pertaining to MPE and 3000 series computers. *Newsgroup*

➤ `comp.sys.hp48`: Hewlett-Packard's HP48 and HP28 calculators. *Newsgroup*

2257 `fj.sys.hp` Discussion on Hewlett Packard products. *Newsgroup*

2258 `han.sys.hp` Hewlett Packard computers, HP-UX. *Newsgroup*

2259 **HP3000-L:** For information exchange, discussion, questions, and answers dealing with the use and/or management of HP-3000 computers. *Mailing List*
± `listserv@utcvm.utc.edu` [body = SUBSCRIBE HP3000-L first-name last-name]
INFO `jeff@utcvm.utc.edu` (Jeff Kell)
ARCHIVE `listserv@utcvm.utc.edu` [body = INDEX HP3000-L]
Gated: `comp.sys.hp.mpe`

COMPANIES—MICROSOFT

2260 `alt.news.Microsoft` Gate's megacorp in the news. *Newsgroup*

COMPANIES—SILICON GRAPHICS, INC.

2261 `comp.sys.sgi.admin` System administration on Silicon Graphics's Irises. *Newsgroup*

2262 `comp.sys.sgi.announce` Announcements for the SGI community. *Moderated newsgroup*

2263 `comp.sys.sgi.apps` Applications which run on the Iris. *Newsgroup*

2264 `comp.sys.sgi.audio` Audio on SGI systems. *Newsgroup*

2265 `comp.sys.sgi.bugs` Bugs found in the IRIX operating system. *Newsgroup*

2266 `comp.sys.sgi.graphics` Graphics packages and issues on SGI machines. *Newsgroup*

2267 `comp.sys.sgi.hardware` Base systems and peripherals for Iris computers. *Newsgroup*

2268 `comp.sys.sgi.misc` General discussion about Silicon Graphics's machines. *Newsgroup*

2269 `fj.sys.sgi` Discussions about Silicon Graphics products. *Newsgroup*

2270 `tnn.sys.sgi` Discussions about SGI workstations. *Newsgroup*

COMPANIES—SUN MICROSYSTEMS

2271 `alt.russia.sun` Discussions about Sun hard- and software usage in the ex-USSR. *Newsgroup*

➤ `alt.solaris.x86`: Sun's Solaris on Intel x86 compatible computers. *Newsgroup*

2272 `alt.sys.sun` Technical discussion of Sun Microsystems products. *Newsgroup*

2273 `aus.computers.sun` Australian discussion of Sun computers. *Newsgroup*

2274 `aus.sun-works` Sun workstations. *Newsgroup*

2275 `cam.sug` Cambridge, United Kingdom, Sun user group information. *Newsgroup*

2276 `can.sun-stroke` Sun Microsystems users in Canada. *Newsgroup*

2277 `chile.comp.sun` News from Sun Microsystems Computer Corporation. *Newsgroup*

2278 `comp.sources.sun` Software for Sun workstations. *Moderated newsgroup*

2279 `comp.sys.sun.admin` Sun system administration issues and questions. *Newsgroup*

2280 `comp.sys.sun.announce` Sun announcements and Sunergy mailings. *Moderated newsgroup*

2281 `comp.sys.sun.apps` Software applications for Sun computer systems. *Newsgroup*

2282 `comp.sys.sun.hardware` Sun Microsystems hardware. *Newsgroup*

2283 `comp.sys.sun.misc` Miscellaneous discussions about Sun products. *Newsgroup*

2284 `comp.sys.sun.wanted` People looking for Sun products and support. *Newsgroup*

2285 `comp.unix.solaris` Discussions about the Solaris operating system. *Newsgroup*

➤ `comp.windows.news`: Sun Microsystems' NeWS window system. *Newsgroup*

2286 `fj.sys.sun` Discussion about Sun workstations. *Newsgroup*

2287 **FlashBack:** Press releases, product announcements, and technical articles for Sun users from organizations other than Sun Microsystems. *E-journal, moderated*

    `http://www.flashback.com/www/forms/subscribe-form.html`

    ± `http://www.flashback.com/www/forms/subscribe-form.html`

    ± `majordomo@flashback.com` [body = `subscribe flashback`]

    INFO EDITOR OWNER `johnj@flashback.com`

    ARCHIVE `http://www.flashback.com/www/forms/subscribe-form.html`

    Gated: `comp.sys.sun.com`

2288 `han.sys.sun` Sun workstation: SunOS, Solaris. *Newsgroup*

2289 `iij.sunflash` Flashnews from Sun Microsystems. *Moderated newsgroup*

2290 `okinawa.sys.sun` Discussion about Sun workstation. *Newsgroup*

2291 **Sun World Online:** For Sun/Unix users. *Magazine*
`http://www.sun.com/sunworldonline`
INFO `michael.mccarthy@sunworld.com` (Michael McCarthy, Editor-in-Chief/Publisher)
INFO `editors@sunworld.com` (Michael McCarthy, Editor-in-Chief/Publisher)
EDITOR `mark.cappel@sunworld.com` (Mark Cappel, Executive Editor)
Frequency: monthly, with frequent updates

2292 **sun-386i:** For owners and users of Sun Microsystems 386i "Roadrunner" computers. *Mailing List*
± INFO `sun-386i-request@itc.yorku.ca`

2293 **SunFlash:** Press releases, product announcements, and technical articles from Sun Microsystems, Inc., for Sun users. *E-journal, moderated*
`http://www.flashback.com/www/forms/subscribe-form.html`
± `http://www.flashback.com/www/forms/subscribe-form.html`
± `majordomo@flashback.com` [body = `subscribe sunflash`]
INFO EDITOR OWNER `johnj@flashback.com`
ARCHIVE `http://www.flashback.com/www/forms/subscribe-form.html`
Gated: `comp.sys.sun.com`

➤ **SunSITE:** This is the web interface to the massive SunSITE ftp archives, a weather server, information on Sun Microsystems, and "multimedia exhibits". The archives include government documents, software, educational materials, and much more. (See entry 3750 for full listing.)

2294 **SunSITE Sun Archives:** Information, patches, and fixes from and about Sun Computers.
`ftp://sunsite.unc.edu/pub/sun-info/`
INFO `ftpkeeper@sunsite.unc.edu`

2295 `uk.sun` Discussion of Sun computers. *Moderated newsgroup*

COMPANIES—VARIOUS

2296 `alt.aldus.misc` Aldus products not covered in another `alt.aldus` group. *Newsgroup*

2297 `alt.authorware` About Authorware, produced by Authorware. So subtle. *Newsgroup*

2298 `alt.destroy.microsoft` Do it, and do it *now! Newsgroup*

2299 `alt.fan.bill-gates` Fans of the original micro-softie. *Newsgroup*

2300 `bit.listserv.3com-l` 3Com Products discussion list. *Newsgroup*

2301 `bit.listserv.candle-l` Candle products discussion list. *Newsgroup*

2302 `biz.comp.mcs` MCSNet. *Moderated newsgroup*

2303 `biz.digex.announce` Announcements from Digex. *Moderated newsgroup*

2304 `biz.softquad.announce` SoftQuad Inc. news & announcements. *Newsgroup*

2305 `biz.univel.misc` Discussions and comments on Univel products. *Newsgroup*

2306 `comp.dcom.cell-relay` Forum for discussion of Cell Relay-based products. *Newsgroup*

2307 `comp.newprod` Announcements of new products of interest. *Moderated newsgroup*

2308 `comp.sys.intergraph` Intergraph hardware and software products. *Newsgroup*

2309 `comp.sys.oric` Oric computers (Oric1, Atmos, Telestrat, et cetera). *Newsgroup*

2310 `comp.sys.tahoe` CCI 6/32, Harris HCX/7, and Sperry 7000 computers. *Newsgroup*

2311 `comp.sys.unisys` Sperry, Burroughs, Convergent, and Unisys* systems. *Newsgroup*

2312 `comp.text.interleaf` Applications and use of Interleaf software. *Newsgroup*

2313 **Digital Press and Analysts News:** Electronic newsletter from Digital Equipment Corporation that contains product, service, alliance, and organizational announcements of interest to the Digital community. *Newsletter*

`http://www.digital.com/pub/Digital/info/html/unix-news/home.html`

± `pr-news@pa.dec.com`

INFO `pr-news-request@pa.dec.com` (Russ Jones)

ARCHIVE `ftp://ftp.digital.com/pub/Digital/info/pr-news`

Gated: `biz.digital.announce`

Frequency: irregular

2314 **The Information Alley:** A publication of Apple Computer, Inc., Support Information Services. The goal of The Information Alley is to help you get full use of your Apple computers, peripherals, and software. *Newsletter*

`ftp://ftp.info.apple.com/Apple.Support.Area/The.Information.Alley`

INFO EDITOR `alley@apple.com` (Janet Christian, Editor)

ARCHIVE `http://support.info.apple.com/info.alley/info.alley.html`

Frequency: biweekly

➤ **VTLS Inc.:** VTLS Inc. is an international library automation software and services company. (See entry 5735 for full listing.)

COMPUTING QUESTIONS

2315 `chile.revistas.microbyte` *Microbyte* magazine (questions and discussion). *Newsgroup*

2316 `comp.answers` Repository for periodic Usenet articles. *Moderated newsgroup*

2317 `fl.comp` General computers in Florida. *Newsgroup*

2318 `han.comp.questions` General question/answer about computer technology/science. *Newsgroup*

2319 `nz.comp` Computing and computers. *Newsgroup*

2320 `okinawa.comp.misc` General topics about computers not covered elsewhere. *Newsgroup*

2321 `pdx.computing` Computing information. *Newsgroup*

2322 `sdnet.computing` San Diego discussions of computing issues. *Newsgroup*

CONFERENCES & ORGANIZATIONS

2323 **ACM-L:** For members of the Association for Computer Machinery, a computer-science organization that includes computer engineers, MIS, and programmers. *Mailing List*

± `listserv@kentvm.kent.edu` [body = SUBSCRIBE ACM-L first-name last-name]

INFO OWNER `michael@kovacs.com`

ARCHIVE `listserv@kentvm.kent.edu`

Gated: `comp.org.acm`

2324 **Association for Computing Machinery (ACM):** Information on announcements, activities, services, promotions, affiliate organizations, awards, chapters, and conferences of the ACM.

`http://www.acm.org/`

`gopher://gopher.acm.org`

INFO `helpdesk@acm.org`

2325 `aus.aswec` Australian Software Engineering Conference. *Newsgroup*

➤ `aus.org.acs`: The Australian Computer Society. *Newsgroup*

➤ `aus.org.acs.books`: ACS book reviews. *Newsgroup*

2326 **Banks of the Boneyard:** The Journal of the Association for Computing Machinery (ACM) at the University of Illinois in Urbana-Champaign (student chapter newsletter). *E-Journal*

`http://www.acm.uiuc.edu/banks`

```
gopher://vixen.cso.uiuc.edu
```
INFO EDITOR boneyard@uiuc.edu

Frequency: monthly

2327 **comp.org.acm** Topics about the Association for Computing Machinery. *Newsgroup*

2328 **comp.org.isoc.interest** Discussion about the Internet Society. *Newsgroup*

2329 **comp.org.uniforum** UniForum Association activities. *Newsgroup*

2330 **comp.org.usenix** Usenix Association events and announcements. *Newsgroup*

2331 **comp.org.usenix.roomshare** Finding lodging during Usenix conferences. *Newsgroup*

➤ **Computer Events Directory:** Over 1,000 information-technology trade shows, conferences, and seminars worldwide. (See entry 5680 for full listing.)

2332 **info.ietf.isoc** Internet Society discussions (isoc-interest@relay.sgi.com). *Moderated newsgroup*

2333 **ne.org.neci.general** The New England Community Internet Project. *Newsgroup*

➤ **triangle.graphics**: North Carolina chapter of the National Computer Graphics Association. *Newsgroup*

DATABASES

2334 **bit.listserv.dasig** Database administration. *Newsgroup*

2335 **fj.comp.databases** Discussions about databases and data management. *Newsgroup*

2336 **iijnet.databases** Discussions about database systems and software. *Newsgroup*

2337 **KDD Nuggets:** News and information relevant to Knowledge Discovery in Databases (KDD), also known as Data(base) Mining—workshops, conferences, tools, reviews, and more. *Mailing List*

± kdd-request@gte.com [body = subscribe first-name last-name]

INFO gps@gte.com (Gregory Piatetsky-Shapiro)

ARCHIVES

```
http://info.gte.com/~kdd/
ftp://ftp.gte.com/pub/kdd/
```
Frequency: biweekly

2338 **Knowledge Discovery Mine:** This site provides information on data mining and knowledge discovery in databases.

```
http://info.gte.com/~kdd
```
INFO gps0%eureka@gte.com (Gregory Piatetsky-Shapiro)

INFO kdd@gte.com

➤ **LDBASE-L:** A discussion of listserv database search capability. (See entry 2855 for full listing.)

2339 **tnn.databases** Discussions about database systems and software. *Newsgroup*

DATABASES—APPLICATION & SYSTEMS

2340 **ACCESS-L:** For users of Microsoft Access database software.

± listserv@peach.ease.lsoft.com [body = SUB ACCESS-L first-name last-name]

OWNER nathan@lsoft.com (Nathan Brindle)

OWNER nathan@ubvm.cc.buffalo.edu (Nathan Brindle)

ARCHIVE listserv@peach.ease.lsoft.com [body = INDEX ACCESS-L]

2341 **MS-Access:** On the MS Access database program, including Access basic questions, reviews, rumors, etc. *Mailing List*

± **INFO** ms-access-request@eunet.co.at (Martin Hilger)

2342 **comp.databases.ms-access** MS Windows' relational database system, Access. *Newsgroup*

2343 **APPROACH:** For users and user support providers of the Lotus Approach relational database. *Mailing List*

± maiser@rmgate.pop.indiana.edu [body = SUBSCRIBE APPROACH]

INFO OWNER `jabrown@unix.infoserve.net` (John Brown)

INFO `maiser@rmgate.pop.indiana.edu` [body = SEND APPROACH.HI]

FAQ `maiser@rmgate.pop.indiana.edu` [body = AUML-FAQ.DOC]

Comments: Only MAISER commands should be sent to the admin address. All other inquiries should be sent to the list owner.

2344 **`bit.listserv.db2-l`** DB2 database discussion list. *Newsgroup*

2345 **`cern.oracle.cde`** Latest information about the Oracle CDE tools. *Newsgroup*

2346 **`comp.databases.ibm-db2`** Problem resolution with DB2 database products. *Newsgroup*

2347 **`comp.databases.informix`** Informix database management software discussions. *Newsgroup*

2348 **`comp.databases.ms-sqlserver`** Microsoft's SQL Server and related products. *Newsgroup*

2349 **`comp.databases.paradox`** Borland's database for DOS and MS Windows. *Newsgroup*

2350 **`comp.databases.progress`** The Progress 4GL and RDBMS. *Newsgroup*

2351 **`comp.databases.rdb`** The relational database engine RDB from DEC. *Newsgroup*

2352 **`comp.databases.xbase.fox`** Fox Software's xBase system and compatibles. *Newsgroup*

2353 **`comp.databases.xbase.misc`** Discussion of xBase (dBASE-like) products. *Newsgroup*

2354 **CSP-L:** For users of Cross System Product, an IBM mainframe 4GL application development and execution environment that allows embedding of SQL/DS, DB/2, VSAM databases. *Mailing List*

± INFO `suleyman.nazif.kutlu@ege.edu.tr` (Suleyman Nazif Kutlu)

2355 **DB4DOS-L:** On DataBoss for DOS. *Mailing List, moderated*

± `mail-server@brcnet.com` [body = SUBSCRIBE DB4DOS-L@BRCNET.COM]

OWNER `mail-manager@brcnet.com` (Craig Wells and Business Resource Center)

2356 **DB4WIN-L:** On DataBoss for Windows. *Mailing List, moderated*

± `mail-server@brcnet.com` [body = SUBSCRIBE DB4WIN-L@BRCNET.COM]

OWNER `mail-manager@brcnet.com` (Craig Wells and Business Resource Center)

2357 **FMPRO-L:** On Claris FileMaker Pro database software. *Mailing List*

OWNER `hades@coos.dartmouth.edu` (Brian V. Hughes)

2358 **`relcom.comp.dbms.foxpro`** FoxPro database development system. *Newsgroup*

2359 **Helix-L:** On Helix, the Macintosh relational database application. *Mailing List*

± `listserv@sjuvm.stjohn.edu` [body = SUBSCRIBE HELIX-L first-name last-name]

OWNER `holtzman@sjuvm.stjohns.edu` (Michael Holtzman)

OWNER `gibhenry@realpeople.com` (Gib Henry)

OWNER `pjyamamo@daisy.uwaterloo.ca` (Peter Yamamoto)

Gated: `bit.listserv.helix-l`

2360 **IMS-L:** On IBM's IMS database products. *Mailing List*

± `listserv@mizzou1.missouri.edu` [body = SUBSCRIBE IMS-L first-name last-name]

OWNER `ccflen@mizzou1.missouri.edu` (Len Rugen)

ARCHIVE `listserv@mizzou1.missouri.edu` [body = INDEX IMS-L]

2361 **`comp.databases.ingres`** Issues relating to INGRES products. *Newsgroup*

2362 **OBJECTPAL-L:** On ObjectPAL programming for Paradox for Windows database software. *Mailing List*

± `listproc@uhunix.uhcc.hawaii.edu` [body = SUBSCRIBE OBJECTPAL-L first-name last-name]

OWNER `halesci@uhunix.uhcc.hawaii.edu` (Philip A. Thomas)

2363 **RBase-L:** RBase database discussions. *Mailing List*

± `majordomo@netcom.com` [body = subscribe rbase-l e-mail-address]

OWNER `hwbass@netcom.com` (Harry Bass)

2364 `relcom.comp.clarion` CLARION database management system. *Newsgroup*

2365 `relcom.comp.dbms.clipper` Clipper database development system. *Newsgroup*

2366 `relcom.comp.dbms.vista` Db_Vista discussions.. *Newsgroup*

2367 `bit.databases.mssql-l` Microsoft SQL server. *Newsgroup*

2368 `comp.databases.gupta` Gupta SQLWindows client-server development. *Newsgroup*

2369 `comp.databases.oracle` The SQL database products of the Oracle Corporation. *Newsgroup*

2370 `comp.databases.sybase` Implementations of the SQL server. *Newsgroup*

2371 `relcom.comp.dbms.oracle` Oracle database system discussions. *Newsgroup*

2372 **CDS-ISIS:** For users of UNESCO's CDS/ISIS text retrieval program. *Mailing List, moderated*
± `listserv@hearn.nic.surfnet.nl` [body = `SUBSCRIBE CDS-ISIS` first-name last-name]
EDITOR `besemer@jka.bib.wau.nl` (Hugo Besemer)
OWNER `rta@health.pchrd.dost.gov.ph` (Reuel Avila)
ARCHIVE `listserv@hearn.nic.surfnet.nl` [body = `INDEX CDS-ISIS`]
Language: English, Spanish, French

2373 **Visual_dBASE:** On Borland's Visual dBASE software. *Newsletter*
± `listserv@borland.com` [body = `SUBSCRIBE VISUAL_DBASE` first-name last-name]
OWNER `chofmann@borland.com`
ARCHIVE `http://www.borland.com/`

DATABASES—THEORY & RESEARCH

2374 `comp.databases` Database and data management issues and theory. *Newsgroup*

2375 `comp.databases.object` Object-oriented paradigms in database systems. *Newsgroup*

2376 `comp.databases.olap` Analytical processing, multidimensional DBMS, EIS, DSS. *Newsgroup*

2377 `comp.databases.pick` Pick-like, post-relational, database systems. *Newsgroup*

2378 `comp.databases.theory` Discussing advances in database technology. *Newsgroup*

DESKTOP PUBLISHING

2379 `alt.aldus.pagemaker` Aldus Pagemaker advice. *Newsgroup*

2380 `alt.binaries.fonts` Give your word processor some style! *Newsgroup*

2381 `bit.listserv.pagemakr` PageMaker for desktop publishers. *Newsgroup*

2382 `comp.fonts` Typefonts—design, conversion, use, etc. *Newsgroup*

2383 `comp.text.desktop` Technology and techniques of desktop publishing. *Newsgroup*

2384 `comp.text.frame` Desktop publishing with FrameMaker. *Newsgroup*

➤ **Digiteyes Multimedia TypeArt Library:** Original, type 1 and Truetype fonts on display in TypeArt foundry library (Mac, PC, traditional, grunge typefaces). Interactive catalog, typography quizzes, typesetting and font design tips, Digiteyes graphic art gallery. (See entry 1908 for full listing.)

➤ **Litho-L:** On desktop publishing, printing, photocopying, and binding. (See entry 1910 for full listing.)

2385 **QUARKXPR:** On desktop publishing using QuarkXPress on the Macintosh. *Mailing List*
± `listserv@iubvm.ucs.indiana.edu` [body = `SUBSCRIBE QUARKXPR` first-name last-name]
INFO `quarkxpr-request@iubvm.ucs.indiana.edu`
ARCHIVE `listserv@iubvm.ucs.indiana.edu` [body = `INDEX QUARKXPR`]

➤ **UWO Engineering FTP site:** Archives mainted by the DA&MR Lab, Mechanical Engineering, University of Western Ontario, London, Ontario, Canada. Also includes archives of files related to the FrameMaker desktop publishing system. (See entry 9253 for full listing.)

E-MAIL

➤ **Accessing the Internet by E-Mail:** How to access Internet resources like FTP, gopher, Archie, Veronica, finger, Usenet, and WWW by e-mail. (See entry 2772 for full listing.)

2386 `bit.listserv.pmail` Pegasus mail discussions. *Newsgroup*

➤ `bit.listserv.x400-l:` X.400 protocol list. *Newsgroup*

2387 `bit.listserv.xmailer` Crosswell mailer. *Newsgroup*

2388 `comp.mail.elm` Discussion and fixes for the ELM mail system. *Newsgroup*

2389 `comp.mail.eudora.mac` Eudora e-mail software for Macintosh. *Newsgroup*

2390 `comp.mail.eudora.ms-windows` Eudora e-mail software for MS Windows. *Newsgroup*

2391 `comp.mail.headers` Gatewayed from the Internet header-people list. *Newsgroup*

2392 `comp.mail.maps` Various maps of the e-mail networks, including UUCP maps. *Moderated newsgroup*

2393 `comp.mail.mh` The UCI version of the Rand Message Handling System. *Newsgroup*

2394 `comp.mail.mime` Multipurpose Internet Mail Extensions of RFC 1341. *Newsgroup*

2395 `comp.mail.misc` General discussions about computer mail. *Newsgroup*

2396 `comp.mail.multi-media` Multimedia Mail. *Newsgroup*

2397 `comp.mail.mush` The Mail User's Shell (MUSH). *Newsgroup*

2398 `comp.mail.pine` The PINE mail user agent. *Newsgroup*

2399 `comp.mail.sendmail` Configuring and using the BSD Sendmail agent. *Newsgroup*

2400 `comp.mail.smail` Administering and using the Smail e-mail transport system. *Newsgroup*

2401 `comp.mail.uucp` Mail in the UUCP network environment. *Newsgroup*

2402 `comp.mail.zmail` The various Z-Mail products and their configurability. *Newsgroup*

2403 `comp.os.ms-windows.apps.winsock.mail` Winsock email applications. *Newsgroup*

➤ `comp.os.msdos.mail-news:` Administering mail and network news systems under MS-DOS. *Newsgroup*

➤ `comp.protocols.iso.x400:` X.400 mail protocol discussions. *Newsgroup*

➤ `comp.protocols.iso.x400.gateway:` X.400 mail gateway discussions. *Moderated newsgroup*

2404 `gnu.emacs.vm.bug` Bug reports on the EMACS VM mail package. *Newsgroup*

2405 `gnu.emacs.vm.info` Information about the EMACS VM mail package. *Newsgroup*

2406 **LMAIL-L:** The LMail give-and-take forum. *Mailing List*
± `listserv@searn.sunet.se` [body = `SUBSCRIBE LMAIL-L` first-name last-name]
INFO `lmail-l-request@searn.sunet.se`
ARCHIVE `listserv@searn.sunet.se` [body = `INDEX LMAIL-L`]

2407 **MAIL-ITA:** Open discussion list used by everyone who has information or problem reports on Italian e-mail systems. *Mailing List*
± `listserv@vm.cnuce.cnr.it` [body = `SUBSCRIBE MAIL-ITA` first-name last-name]
INFO `turso@mailserv.csata.it` (Giovanni Turso)
Language: English, Italian

➤ **POP:** The list is primarily for system administrators attempting to find, install, and run POP, IMAP, and similar protocol servers on their servers. (See entry 3261 for full listing.)

2408 **smail3-users:** For administrators of smail3.X-based mailers. Covers operational aspects, i.e., installation and administration. *Mailing List*
± INFO `smail3-users-request@cs.athabascau.ca`

2409 **smail3-wizards:** For developers of smail3.X. *Mailing List*
± INFO `smail3-wizards-request@cs.athabascau.ca`

2410 SSW-L: About Soft-Switch products. *Mailing List*
± listserv@list.nih.gov [body = SUBSCRIBE SSW-L first-name last-name]
INFO OWNER jdavis@pcc.ssw.dhhs.gov (James Davis)
ARCHIVE listserv@list.nih.gov [body = INDEX SSW-L]

2411 tnn.mail Discussions about mail software, standards, etc. *Newsgroup*

➤ **tnn.mail.uucp:** Discussion of UUCP network and its mail system. *Newsgroup*

2412 vmsnet.mail.misc Other electronic mail software. *Newsgroup*

2413 vmsnet.mail.mx MX e-mail system, gatewayed to MX mailing list. *Newsgroup*

2414 vmsnet.mail.pmdf PMDF e-mail system, gatewayed to ipmdf mailing list. *Newsgroup*

ELECTRONIC PUBLISHING

➤ **Bookport:** Online editions of current books. Can be sampled, purchased, unlocked, and read online, or ordered from the publishers. (See entry 104 for full listing.)

2415 comp.publish.electronic.developer Electronic publishing/developer tools. *Newsgroup*

2416 comp.publish.electronic.end-user Electronic publishing end-user tools. *Newsgroup*

2417 comp.publish.electronic.misc General electronic publishing issues. *Newsgroup*

2418 comp.publish.prepress Electronic prepress. *Newsgroup*

2419 Online Electronic Publishing Collection: Includes information on file formats, text readers and image viewers, audio and video players, multimedia and virtual reality publishing standards, and main languages. Also includes an index of electronic books and documents available online.
http://www.earthlink.net/~jlutgen/epublish.html
INFO jlutgen@earthlink.net

➤ **Open Book Systems (OBS):** An online publisher and bookstore in English, German, French, and Romanian. (See entry 119 for full listing.)

FREENETS & COMMUNITY NETWORKS

2420 akr.freenet Discussion about the Akron Regional Freenet. *Newsgroup*

2421 alt.freenet Free access to computer networks. *Newsgroup*

2422 The Center For Civic Networking: Included in this site is information on developing a sustainable information network, policy issues regarding electronic development, and information regarding municipalities and local governmental information networks. The Center for Civic Networking is a nonprofit organization whose goal is to help develop models of beneficial uses of the Internet for local, regional, and national organizations and governments.
http://civic.net:2401/
INFO webmaster@civicnet.org

2423 Community Networking Resources: This Web page is a collection of pointers to a variety of community networking resources, including Web sites of some existing community networks, papers on the subject, conference information, and more.
http://www.sils.umich.edu/Community/
INFO sils.cn@umich.edu

2424 Freenets and Community Networks: Freenet information, presented as a public service by Peter Scott at the University of Saskatchewan Libraries.
http://www.usask.ca/~scottp/free.html
INFO scottp@duke.usask.ca

➤ **ia.org.freenet:** Coordination discussions for Iowa Freenet activities. *Newsgroup*

2425 International Free-Net/Community Net Listing: This page is a listing of Freenets and community nets around the world.
http://www.uwec.edu/Info/Freenets/

INFO `latoga@acm.org`

➤   `niagara.freenet`:   Niagara regional Freenet. *Newsgroup*

2426   `pgh.freenet`   Three Rivers Freenet public access network. *Newsgroup*

➤   `sdnet.freenet`:   Freenet in San Diego, California. *Newsgroup*

2427   `wny.rochester.freenet`   Freenet in Rochester, New York. *Newsgroup*

GRAPHICS

2428   `alt.3d.misc`   Three-dimensional imaging. *Newsgroup*

2429   `alt.3d.sirds`   Especially for Single Image Random Dot Stereograms. *Newsgroup*

2430   `alt.alt`   ASCII stereograms. *Newsgroup*

2431   `alt.binaries.clip-art`   Distribution of DOS, Mac, and Unix clip art. *Newsgroup*

2432   `alt.binaries.pictures.12hr`   Pictures of clocks. *Newsgroup*

2433   `alt.binaries.pictures.animals`   Pictures of all types of animals. *Newsgroup*

2434   `alt.binaries.pictures.ascii`   Pictures composed of ASCII characters. *Newsgroup*

2435   `alt.binaries.pictures.boys`   GIFs, JPEGs, etc. of boys. *Newsgroup*

2436   `alt.binaries.pictures.children`   Pictures of children. *Newsgroup*

2437   `alt.binaries.pictures.d`   Discussions about picture postings. *Newsgroup*

2438   `alt.binaries.pictures.misc`   Have we saturated the network yet? *Newsgroup*

2439   `alt.binaries.pictures.utilities`   Posting of pictures-related utilities. *Newsgroup*

2440   `alt.graphics.pixutils`   Discussion of pixmap utilities. *Newsgroup*

2441   **CGE:** On visualization and computer graphics. *Mailing List*
    ± `listserv@vm.marist.edu` [body = SUBSCRIBE CGE first-name last-name]
    INFO `cge-request@vm.marist.edu`
    ARCHIVE `listserv@vm.marist.edu` [body = INDEX CGE]

2442   `comp.graphics.misc`   Computer graphics miscellany. *Newsgroup*

2443   `comp.graphics.visualization`   Info on scientific visualization. *Newsgroup*

➤   `comp.os.ms-windows.programmer.graphics`:   GDI, graphics, and printing. *Newsgroup*

2444   **MACCHAT:** For Mac*Chat: a Macintosh graphics newsletter. *Newsletter*
    `http://www.cts.com/browse/xxltony`
    ± `listserv@vm.temple.edu` [body = SUBSCRIBE MACCHAT first-name last-name]
    EDITOR `xxltony@crash.cts.com` (Tony Lindsey)
    OWNER `shrim@astro.ocis.temple.edu` (Sriram NCV)
    Gated: `comp.sys.mac.digest`

2445   `rec.arts.ascii`   ASCII art, information on archives, art, and artists. *Moderated newsgroup*

2446   **SD3D:** On 3-D imaging (all disciplines and platforms). *Mailing List*
    ± `listserv@bobcat.etsu.edu`
    ± `sd3d-request@sdsc.edu`
    INFO `brande@sdsc.edu` (Marc Brande)
    INFO `dekenj@sdsc.edu` (Joseph Deken)

2447   `triangle.graphics`   North Carolina chapter of the National Computer Graphics Association. *Newsgroup*

GRAPHICS—APPLICATION & SYSTEMS

2448   `alt.3d.studio`   For 3-D Studio users. *Newsgroup*

2449 `alt.aldus.freehand` Aldus Freehand graphics program. *Newsgroup*

2450 `alt.corel.graphics` The PClone package Corel Draw and related products. *Newsgroup*

2451 `alt.fractal-design.painter` Fractal Design's "Natural Media" painting. *Newsgroup*

2452 `alt.soft-sys.corel.draw` The Corel Draw graphics package. *Newsgroup*

2453 `aus.stats.s` Discussions of the S data analysis and graphics software. *Newsgroup*

2454 `comp.graphics.api.inventor` Object-oriented 3-D graphics in Inventor. *Newsgroup*

2455 `comp.graphics.api.opengl` The OpenGL 3-D application programming interface. *Newsgroup*

2456 `comp.graphics.api.pexlib` The PEXlib application programming interface. *Newsgroup*

2457 `comp.graphics.apps.alias` 3-D graphics software from Alias Research. *Newsgroup*

2458 `comp.graphics.apps.avs` The Application Visualization System. *Newsgroup*

2459 `comp.graphics.apps.data-explorer` IBM's Visualization Data Explorer (DX). *Newsgroup*

2460 `comp.graphics.apps.freehand` Questions, answers, tips and suggestions. *Newsgroup*

2461 `comp.graphics.apps.gnuplot` The gnuplot interactive function plotter. *Newsgroup*

2462 `comp.graphics.apps.iris-explorer` The IRIS Explorer, aka MVE. *Newsgroup*

2463 `comp.graphics.apps.lightwave` NewTek's Lightwave3D and related topics. *Newsgroup*

2464 `comp.graphics.apps.photoshop` Adobe Photoshop techniques and help. *Newsgroup*

2465 `comp.graphics.apps.softimage` Softimage applications and products. *Newsgroup*

2466 `comp.graphics.apps.wavefront` Wavefront software products, problems, etc. *Newsgroup*

2467 `comp.graphics.packages.3dstudio` Autodesk's 3D Studio software. *Newsgroup*

2468 `comp.graphics.rendering.renderman` RenderMan interface and shading language. *Newsgroup*

➤ `comp.sys.mentor:` Mentor Graphics products and the Silicon Compiler System. *Newsgroup*

➤ `comp.sys.sgi.graphics:` Graphics packages and issues on SGI machines. *Newsgroup*

2469 **CUSTOMERNEWS:** For Corel Customer News. *Newsletter*
± `customernews-sub@discuss.corelnet.com`
OWNER `dickman@corelnet.com` (Chris Dickman)
ARCHIVE `http://www.corelnet.com/`
Frequency: monthly

2470 **Discuss-Draw:** On CorelDRAW illustration software. *Mailing List*
± `discuss-draw-sub@discuss.corelnet.com`
OWNER `dickman@corelnet.com` (Chris Dickman)
ARCHIVE `http://www.corelnet.com/`

2471 **Infini-D:** On Infini-D, a 3-D and animation software package for Macintosh. *Mailing List*
± `listserv@uafsysb.uark.edu` [body = SUBSCRIBE INFINI-D first-name last-name]
OWNER `cblih@comp.uark.edu` (CB Lih)
ARCHIVE `listserv@uafsysb.uark.edu` [body = INDEX INFINI-D]

2472 **PHOTODSK-L:** Discussion about the Acorn RISC-OS !Photodesk photo software. *Mailing List*
± `maillist@quagmire.demon.co.uk` [subject = SUBSCRIBE; body = blank]
OWNER `kib@spacetec.demon.co.uk` (Keith Bailey)

2473 **UNIRAS:** For users of UNIRAS, device-independent computer graphics software package used for visualization of technical and scientific data. *Mailing List*
± `listserv@nic.surfnet.nl` [body = SUBSCRIBE UNIRAS first-name last-name]
INFO `vannes@ecn.nl` (Gerard van Nes, ECN, The Netherlands)
ARCHIVE `listserv@nic.surfnet.nl`

2474 XGKS: A level 2C implementation of GKS for the X-Windows system on Unix platforms. *Mailing List*
± majordomo@unidata.ucar.edu [body = subscribe xgks e-mail-address]
INFO xgks-request@unidata.ucar.edu (Steve Emmerson)
INFO xgks-approval@unidata.ucar.edu (human)
ARCHIVES
gopher://unidata.ucar.edu
http://www.unidata.ucar.edu/staff/steve/xgks

GRAPHICS—THEORY & RESEARCH

2475 comp.graphics.algorithms Algorithms used in producing computer graphics. *Newsgroup*

2476 comp.graphics.animation Technical aspects of computer animation. *Newsgroup*

2477 comp.graphics.api.misc Application programmer interface issue and methods. *Newsgroup*

2478 comp.graphics.rendering.misc Rendering comparisons, approaches, methods. *Newsgroup*

2479 comp.graphics.rendering.raytracing Ray-tracing software, tools, and methods. *Newsgroup*

2480 fourcolor: On color and color theory. *Mailing List*
± macjordomo@rdc.texel.com [body = subscribe fourcolor]
OWNER rc@rcdesignworks.com (Robert D. Caliendo)
OWNER rc@newton.texel.com (Robert D. Caliendo)
ARCHIVES
macjordomo@rdc.texel.com [body = index fourcolor]
ftp://ftp.texel.com/pub/rc/fourcolorlist/Digests/

2481 The Ray Tracing News: Discussion of research issues and software available for ray tracing and other rendering methods. *Newsletter*
http://wuarchive.wustl.edu/graphics/graphics/ray/RTNews/html/
ftp://ftp-graphics.stanford.edu/pub/Graphics/RTNews/html/index.html (WWW)
http://www.povray.org/rtn/index.html
± INFO erich@eye.com (Erich Haines)
ARCHIVES
ftp://princeton.edu/pub/Graphics/RTNews
ftp://wuarchive.wustl.edu/graphics/graphics/ray/RTNews
Gated: comp.graphics.raytracing
Frequency: irregular

HACKING & THE UNDERGROUND

2482 Materva's Hideout: Lots of programs for hackers, plus related e-texts. Barbed.
http://www.intersurf.com/~materva/files.html
INFO materva@intersurf.com

2483 Silicon Toad: Hundreds of links to resources on hacking, telephony, security and encryption. Very beautifully done.
http://www.rit.edu/~jmb8902/hacking.html
INFO jmb8902@rit.edu

2484 alt.2600 The magazine or the game system. You decide. *Newsgroup*

2485 alt.2600.moderated Moderated discussion on *2600* magazine. *Moderated newsgroup*

2486 alt.bonehead.kevin-mitnick Phone phreak phound. *Newsgroup*

2487 alt.comp.hardware.homebuilt Designing devious devices in the den. *Newsgroup*

2488 alt.comp.hardware.homedesigned Discussing home designed computer hardware. *Newsgroup*

2489 `alt.comp.hardware.pc-homebuilt` Building your PC from motherboards and cards. *Newsgroup*

2490 `alt.fan.kevin-mitnick` Hooked hacker. *Newsgroup*

2491 `alt.flame.phiber` Gripes about morons. *Newsgroup*

2492 `alt.hacker` For hackers and hacker wannabes. *Newsgroup.*

2493 `alt.hackers` Hackers news. *Moderated newsgroup*

2494 `alt.hackers.discuss` A self-moderated hackers discussion group. *Moderated newsgroup*

2495 `alt.hackers.groups` Discussion of various hacker groups. *Newsgroup*

2496 `alt.hackers.malicious` The really bad guys—don't take candy from them. *Newsgroup*

➤ `alt.hackintosh:` Clever programming on Apple's Macintosh. *Newsgroup*

2497 `alt.ph.uk` United Kingdom version of `alt.2600`. *Newsgroup*

2498 `alt.phreaking` Phreaking. *Newsgroup*

2499 **BLAST.famy:** Anarchy, reviews, rants, conspiracy theory, Gen-Xer diatribes, and Big Brother's technical specs. *E-Journal*
   `http://www.shmooze.net/pwcasual/ezines/blast`
   ± INFO `pwcasual@shmooze.net` (Mark Jeftovic)
   INFO `markjr@shmooze.net` (Mark Jeftovic)
   EDITOR `joe@shmooze.net` (Joe J. Deagnon)
   ARCHIVE `http://www.shmooze.net/pwcasual/ezines/blast`
   Frequency: a-PeriOdicAlLy (about once a month)

2500 **Chalisti:** Hackers' newsletter, in German. *Newsletter*
   ± OWNER `terra@nordwest.pop.de`
   ARCHIVE `ftp://ftp.nordwest.pop.de/pub/ccc/chalisti/`
   Language: German
   Frequency: every 8 weeks

➤ **Computer Underground Digest (CuD):** Discussion of legal, ethical, social, and other issues regarding computerized information and communications. Readers are encouraged to submit reasoned articles relating to computer culture and communication. (See entry 3719 for full listing.)

➤ `rec.games.frp.cyber:` Discussions of cyberpunk-related role-playing games. *Newsgroup*

2501 `relcom.fido.ru.hacker` FIDOnet, hackers and crackers (legal!). *Newsgroup*

2502 **SURFPUNK Technical Journal:** Dangerous multinational hacker zine originating near BARRNET in the fashionable western arm of the northern California matrix. Quantum Californians are spin surf or spin punk. Undetected, we are both, or neither. *E-Journal*
   ± `surfpunk-request@versant.com`
   INFO `strick@netcom.com` (Henry Strickland)
   ARCHIVES
   `ftp://ftp.yak.net/pub/surfpunk`
   `ftp://ftp.eff.org/pub/Publications/CuD/Surfpunk/`
   Frequency: irregular

➤ **Virus Source:** For resources and information on infecting and disinfecting: thorough and nonjudgmental. (See entry 4051 for full listing.)

HISTORY

2503 `alt.folklore.computers` Stories and anecdotes about computers (some true!). *Newsgroup*

2504 `comp.society.folklore` Computer folklore and culture, past and present. *Moderated newsgroup*

2505 **SHOTHC-L:** On the history of computing. *Mailing List* http://www.si.edu/ (Smithsonian Institute)

± listserv@sivm.si.edu [body = SUBSCRIBE SHOTHC-L first-name last-name]

INFO OWNER nasem001@sivm.bitnet (Paul Ceruzzi)

INFO OWNER irmss907@sivm.bitnet (Mignon Erixon-Stanford)

ARCHIVE listserv@sivm.si.edu [body = INDEX SHOTHC-L]

HYPERTEXT & HYPERMEDIA

➤ **WWW + HTML Developer's JumpStation:** The WWW + HTML Developer's JumpStation gives background on all aspects of HTML coding and WWW use. (See entry 3019 for full listing.)

2506 **ACROBAT:** On Adobe Acrobat document-viewing software. *Mailing List*

http://www.blueworld.com/lists/acrobat/

± acrobat-request@blueworld.com [body = SUBSCRIBE ACROBAT first-name last-name]

OWNER bill@blueworld.com (Bill Doerrfeld)

2507 **alt.hypertext** Discussion of hypertext—uses, transport, etc. *Newsgroup*

2508 **comp.infosystems.hyperg** The Hyper-G network hypermedia system and applications. *Newsgroup*

2509 **comp.sys.mac.hypercard** The Macintosh Hypercard: information and uses. *Newsgroup*

➤ **comp.text.frame:** Desktop publishing with FrameMaker. *Newsgroup*

2510 **HYPEREDU:** On using hypertext in education. *Mailing List, moderated*

± listserv@itocsivm.csi.it [body = SUBSCRIBE HYPEREDU first-name last-name]

OWNER eleonora.panto@csi.it (Eleonora Panto')

Language: English, some Italian & French

➤ **NWHQ:** Contemporary art and literature with a particular emphasis on hypertexted fiction. (See entry 573 for full listing.)

2511 **Phoenicia:** Collaborative WWW-based information management system (used to implement the CWIS at the University of Chicago).

http://www.bsd.uchicago.edu/

INFO m-lavenant@uchicago.edu

HYPERTEXT & HYPERMEDIA—HTML

2512 **"HTML & CGI Unleashed" Book Support Web:** "HTML & CGI Unleashed" covers the complete life cycle of Web development: planning, analysis, design, and HTML implementation and gateway programming using Perl, REXX, and C.

http://www.december.com/works/hcu.html

INFO john@december.com

➤ **comp.infosystems.www.authoring.html:** Writing HTML for the Web. *Newsgroup*

2513 **HTML Assistant Newsletter:** For users of HTML Assistant software. *Newsletter*

http://fox.nstn.ca/~harawitz/index.html

INFO sales@fox.nstn.ns.ca (Kieran Gillett)

EDITOR harawitz@fox.nstn.ns.ca (Howard Harawitz)

ARCHIVE gopher://ukoln.bath.ac.uk

Frequency: semi-irregular

2514 **HTML info/W3C:** HyperText Markup Language (HTML), working and background materials, from the World Wide Web Consortium.

http://www.w3.org/pub/WWW/MarkUp/

INFO connolly@w3.org

➤ **Web Training:** The University of Toronto Information Commons and High Performance and Research Computing Groups home page present information about HTTP, HTML, and networked multimedia training and technology. (See entry 2920 for full listing.)

IBM & COMPATIBLES

➤ `alt.comp.hardware.pc-homebuilt:` Building your PC from motherboards and cards. *Newsgroup*

2515 `alt.sys.pc-clone.acer` Acer computer systems. *Newsgroup*

2516 `alt.sys.pc-clone.dell` Dell computer systems. *Newsgroup*

2517 `alt.sys.pc-clone.gateway2000` A PC clone vendor. *Newsgroup*

2518 `alt.sys.pc-clone.micron` A PC clone vendor. *Newsgroup*

2519 `alt.sys.pc-clone.midwest-micro` A group discussing products from MidWest Micro. *Newsgroup*

2520 `alt.sys.pc-clone.zeos` Zeos computer systems. *Newsgroup*

2521 `aus.computers.ibm-pc` Discussions about the IBM PC and clones. *Newsgroup*

2522 `bit.listserv.ibm7171` Protocol converter list. *Newsgroup*

2523 `biz.marketplace.computers.pc-clone` PC-compatible hardware/software. *Newsgroup*

2524 `biz.zeos.announce` Zeos product announcements. *Moderated newsgroup*

2525 `biz.zeos.general` Zeos technical support and general information. *Newsgroup*

2526 `clari.nb.ibm` Newsbytes: IBM PC world coverage. *Moderated newsgroup*

2527 `clari.nb.pc` Newsbytes: hardware, software for PC products. *Moderated newsgroup*

2528 `clari.tw.computers.pc.hardware` Intel-based computer hardware. *Moderated newsgroup*

2529 `clari.tw.computers.pc.hardware.releases` News releases: Intel-based hardware. *Moderated newsgroup*

2530 `comp.arch.bus.vmebus` Hardware and software for VMEbus systems. *Newsgroup*

2531 `comp.binaries.ibm.pc` Binary-only postings for IBM PC/MS-DOS. *Moderated newsgroup*

2532 `comp.binaries.ibm.pc.d` Discussions about IBM-PC binary postings. *Newsgroup*

2533 `comp.binaries.ibm.pc.wanted` Requests for IBM PC and compatible programs. *Newsgroup*

➤ `comp.protocols.tcp-ip.ibmpc:` TCP/IP for IBM(-like) personal computers. *Newsgroup*

2534 `comp.sys.ibm.pc.demos` Demonstration programs which showcase programmer skill. *Newsgroup*

2535 `comp.sys.ibm.pc.digest` The IBM PC, PC-XT, and PC-AT. *Moderated newsgroup*

2536 `comp.sys.ibm.pc.games.action` Arcade-style games on PCs. *Newsgroup*

➤ `comp.sys.ibm.pc.games.marketplace:` PC clone games wanted and for sale. *Newsgroup*

2537 `comp.sys.ibm.pc.games.sports` Discussion of sports games for the IBM PC. *Newsgroup*

2538 `comp.sys.ibm.pc.hardware.cd-rom` CD-ROM drives and interfaces for the PC. *Newsgroup*

2539 `comp.sys.ibm.pc.hardware.chips` Processor, cache, memory chips, etc. *Newsgroup*

2540 `comp.sys.ibm.pc.hardware.comm` Modems and communication cards for the PC. *Newsgroup*

2541 `comp.sys.ibm.pc.hardware.misc` Miscellaneous PC hardware topics. *Newsgroup*

2542 `comp.sys.ibm.pc.hardware.networking` Network hardware and equipment for the PC. *Newsgroup*

2543 `comp.sys.ibm.pc.hardware.storage` Hard drives and other PC storage devices. *Newsgroup*

2544 `comp.sys.ibm.pc.hardware.systems` Whole IBM PC computer and clone systems. *Newsgroup*

2545 `comp.sys.ibm.pc.hardware.video` Video cards and monitors for the PC. *Newsgroup*

2546 `comp.sys.ibm.pc.misc` Discussion about IBM personal computers. *Newsgroup*

2547 `comp.sys.ibm.pc.rt` Topics related to IBM's RT computer. *Newsgroup*

2548   `comp.sys.ibm.pc.soundcard.advocacy`   Advocacy for a particular sound card. *Newsgroup*

2549   `comp.sys.ibm.pc.soundcard.misc`   Sound cards in general. *Newsgroup*

2550   `comp.sys.ibm.pc.soundcard.music`   Music and sound questions using sound cards. *Newsgroup*

2551   `comp.sys.ibm.pc.soundcard.tech`   Technical questions about PC sound cards. *Newsgroup*

2552   `comp.sys.ibm.ps2.hardware`   Microchannel hardware, any vendor. *Newsgroup*

➤   **CYBERNEWS:** For reviews of PC software, CD-ROMs, and hardware. (See entry 3341 for full listing.)

2553   `fj.sys.ibmpc`   Discussion about IBM personal computers and clones. *Newsgroup*

2554   `fj.sys.pc98`   Discussion about NEC PC-9800 and other computers. *Newsgroup*

2555   `han.sys.ibmpc`   IBM PC and compatibles, software, hardware, peripherals. *Newsgroup*

2556   `iijnet.sys.ibm-pc`   Discussions about IBM personal computers and clones. *Newsgroup*

2557   `okinawa.sys.ibmpc`   Discussion about IBM PC and its clones. *Newsgroup*

2558   `sanet.ibmpc`   Anything concerning ISA machines. *Newsgroup*

2559   **SOFTREVU:** On small-computer-systems software issues. *Mailing List*
     ± `listserv.aol.com`
     INFO `softrevu-request@listserv.aol.com` (SoftRevu Owner)
     OWNER `atropos@aol.net` (David B. O'Donnell)

2560   `tnn.sys.ibm-pc`   Discussions about IBM personal computers and clones. *Newsgroup*

2561   **towers:** On NCR tower computers. *Mailing List*
     ± **INFO** `bill@wlk.com` (Bill Kennedy)
     Gated: `comp.sys.ncr`

IBM & COMPATIBLES—DOS

2562   `alt.msdos.batch`   MS-DOS batch files. *Newsgroup*

2563   `alt.msdos.programmer`   For the serious MS-DOS programmer (no for-sale ads). *Newsgroup*

2564   `clari.nb.dos`   Newsbytes: DOS-specific news and products. *Moderated newsgroup*

➤   **COMMO:** On Commo, a DOS-based communications program. (See entry 3216 for full listing.)

2565   `comp.archives.msdos.announce`   Announcements about MS-DOS archives. *Moderated newsgroup*

2566   `comp.archives.msdos.d`   Discussion of materials available in MS-DOS archives. *Newsgroup*

2567   `comp.os.msdos.4dos`   The 4DOS command processor for MS-DOS. *Newsgroup*

2568   `comp.os.msdos.apps`   Discussion of applications that run under MS-DOS. *Newsgroup*

2569   `comp.os.msdos.desqview`   QuarterDeck's Desqview and related products. *Newsgroup*

2570   `comp.os.msdos.djgpp`   DOS GNU C/C++ applications and programming environment. *Newsgroup*

2571   `comp.os.msdos.mail-news`   Administering mail and network news systems under MS-DOS. *Newsgroup*

2572   `comp.os.msdos.misc`   Miscellaneous topics about MS-DOS machines. *Newsgroup*

2573   `comp.os.msdos.pcgeos`   GeoWorks PC/GEOS and PC/GEOS-based packages. *Newsgroup*

2574   `comp.os.msdos.programmer`   Programming MS-DOS machines. *Newsgroup*

2575   `comp.os.msdos.programmer.turbovision`   Borland's text application libraries. *Newsgroup*

➤   `comp.unix.dos-under-unix:`   MS-DOS running under Unix by whatever means. *Newsgroup*

2576   `fj.binaries.msdos`   Encoded MS-DOS programs in binary. *Moderated newsgroup*

2577   `fj.binaries.msdos.d`   Topics on software posted to `fj.binaries.msdos`. *Newsgroup*

2578   `fj.os.msdos`   Discussion about the MS-DOS operating system. *Newsgroup*

2579 **iijnet.os.msdos** Discussions about MS-DOS. *Newsgroup*

2580 **relcom.msdos** MS-DOS software. *Newsgroup*

2581 **tn.msdos** Discussion of DOS-related issues in Tennessee. *Newsgroup*

2582 **tnn.os.msdos** Discussions about MS-DOS. *Newsgroup*

IBM & COMPATIBLES—OS/2

2583 **alt.org.team-os2** For the discussion of topics relevant to Team OS/2. *Newsgroup*

2584 **aus.computers.os2** Aussie palaver on OS/2. *Newsgroup*

2585 **bit.listserv.os2-l** OS/2 discussion. *Newsgroup*

2586 **comp.binaries.os2** Binaries for use under the OS/2 ABI. *Moderated newsgroup*

2587 **comp.os.os2.advocacy** Supporting and flaming OS/2. *Newsgroup*

2588 **comp.os.os2.announce** Notable news and announcements related to OS/2. *Moderated newsgroup*

2589 **comp.os.os2.apps** Discussions of applications under OS/2. *Newsgroup*

2590 **comp.os.os2.beta** All aspects of beta releases of OS/2 systems software. *Newsgroup*

2591 **comp.os.os2.bugs** OS/2 system bug reports, fixes, and work-arounds. *Newsgroup*

2592 **comp.os.os2.comm** Modem/fax hardware/drivers/applications/utilities under OS/2. *Newsgroup*

2593 **comp.os.os2.games** Running games under OS/2. *Newsgroup*

2594 **comp.os.os2.mail-news** Mail and news applications/utilities (on- and offline) under OS/2. *Newsgroup*

2595 **comp.os.os2.marketplace** For sale/wanted; shopping; commercial ads; job postings. *Newsgroup*

2596 **comp.os.os2.misc** Miscellaneous topics about the OS/2 system. *Newsgroup*

2597 **comp.os.os2.multimedia** Multimedia on OS/2 systems. *Newsgroup*

2598 **comp.os.os2.networking.misc** Miscellaneous networking issues of OS/2. *Newsgroup*

2599 **comp.os.os2.networking.tcp-ip** TCP/IP under OS/2. *Newsgroup*

2600 **comp.os.os2.networking.www** World Wide Web (WWW) applications/utilities under OS/2. *Newsgroup*

2601 **comp.os.os2.programmer.misc** Programming OS/2 machines. *Newsgroup*

2602 **comp.os.os2.programmer.oop** Programming system objects (SOM, WPS, etc.). *Newsgroup*

2603 **comp.os.os2.programmer.porting** Porting software to OS/2 machines. *Newsgroup*

2604 **comp.os.os2.programmer.tools** Compilers, assemblers, interpreters under OS/2. *Newsgroup*

2605 **comp.os.os2.setup.misc** Installing/configuring OS/2; miscellaneous hardware/drivers. *Newsgroup*

2606 **comp.os.os2.setup.storage** Disk/tape/CD-ROM hardware/drivers under OS/2. *Newsgroup*

2607 **comp.os.os2.setup.video** Base video hardware/drivers under OS/2. *Newsgroup*

2608 **comp.os.os2.utilities** General purpose utilities (shells/backup/compression/etc.). *Newsgroup*

2609 **fj.os.os2** Discussion about the OS/2 operating system. *Newsgroup*

➤ **IBMTCP-L:** All about IBM TCP/IP software products for VM, MVS, OS/2, and for associated IBM TCP/IP hardware. (See entry 3303 for full listing.)

2610 **OS2PRO-L:** On OS/2 programming. *Mailing List*
   ± listserv@hearn.nic.surfnet.nl [body = SUBSCRIBE OS2PRO-L first-name last-name]
   OWNER turgut@vm3090.ege.edu.tr (Turgut Kalfaoglu)

2611 **relcom.comp.os.os2** FIDOnet area, OS/2 operating system. *Newsgroup*

2612 **relcom.comp.os.os2.comm** Communications and network under OS/2. *Newsgroup*

2613 **relcom.comp.os.os2.drv** Device drivers for OS/2. *Newsgroup*

2614 `relcom.comp.os.os2.faq.d` Discussions about FAQ on OS/2. *Newsgroup*

2615 `relcom.comp.os.os2.marginal` Related topics on OS/2. *Newsgroup*

2616 `relcom.comp.os.os2.prog` Programming under OS/2. *Newsgroup*

2617 `relcom.comp.os.os2.src` Sources related to OS/2. *Newsgroup*

2618 `relcom.comp.os.os2.wanted` Programs for OS/2 offered/wanted. *Newsgroup*

IBM & COMPATIBLES—SOFTWARE ARCHIVES

➤ <u>Games Domain:</u> A comprehensive games site; includes FAQs and pointers to games sites; covers all varieties of games. (See entry 6330 for full listing.)

➤ **Inter-Links Downloads:** Inter-Links listing of software archives, all of which can be accessed via the numerous links provided. (See entry 3748 for full listing.)

➤ **Medical Software Archive—State University of Campinas, Brazil:** One of the largest repositories of public-domain medical software for PCs, it includes a great variety of applications, including statistical packages, intensive-care utilities, medical and dental office management, medical education, artificial intelligence, health assessment and maintenance, etc. (See entry 5103 for full listing.)

➤ **SKY Online:** SKY Online is the premier source of astronomical news and information on the World Wide Web. It features excerpts from *Sky & Telescope* and *CCD Astronomy* magazines, along with a weekly news bulletin and celestial calendar, helpful tips for backyard skygazers, reviews of telescopes and accessories, downloadable BASIC programs to do astronomical calculations on your PC or Mac, and much more. (See entry 8939 for full listing.)

➤ **University of California, Irvine. Medical Education Software Archive.:** This site contains the medical education software collection based at the University of California, Irvine. (See entry 4837 for full listing.)

➤ **Washington University of St. Louis FTP Archive:** Huge software archive maintained by Washington University of St. Louis. (See entry 3752 for full listing.)

IBM & COMPATIBLES—WINDOWS

2619 `alt.flame.ms-windows` Power users *don't* "point 'n' click". *Newsgroup*

2620 `alt.os.windows95.crash.crash.crash` Early test runs have not impressed. *Newsgroup*

2621 `alt.windows.cde` The Common Desktop Environment. *Newsgroup*

2622 `clari.nb.windows` Newsbytes: Windows and Windows NT. *Newsgroup*

2623 `clari.tw.computers.pc.software.releases` Releases: Windows software. *Moderated newsgroup*

2624 `comp.binaries.ms-windows` Binary programs for Microsoft Windows. *Moderated newsgroup*

2625 `comp.emulators.ms-windows.wine` A free MS Windows emulator under X. *Newsgroup*

➤ `comp.infosystems.www.browsers.ms-windows`: Web browsers for MS Windows. *Newsgroup*

➤ `comp.infosystems.www.servers.ms-windows`: Web servers for MS Windows and NT. *Newsgroup*

➤ `comp.mail.eudora.ms-windows`: Eudora e-mail software for MS Windows. *Newsgroup*

2626 `comp.os.ms-windows.advocacy` Speculation and debate about Microsoft Windows. *Newsgroup*

2627 `comp.os.ms-windows.announce` Announcements relating to Windows. *Moderated newsgroup*

➤ `comp.os.ms-windows.apps.comm`: MS Windows communication applications. *Newsgroup*

➤ `comp.os.ms-windows.apps.financial`: MS Windows financial and tax software. *Newsgroup*

2628 `comp.os.ms-windows.apps.misc` MS Windows applications. *Newsgroup*

2629 `comp.os.ms-windows.apps.utilities` MS Windows utilities. *Newsgroup*

➤ `comp.os.ms-windows.apps.winsock.mail`: Winsock email applications. *Newsgroup*

➤ `comp.os.ms-windows.apps.winsock.misc`: Other Winsock applications. *Newsgroup*

➤ `comp.os.ms-windows.apps.winsock.news`: Winsock news applications. *Newsgroup*

➤ `comp.os.ms-windows.apps.word-proc`: MS Windows word-processing applications. *Newsgroup*

2630 `comp.os.ms-windows.misc` General discussions about Windows issues. *Newsgroup*

2631 `comp.os.ms-windows.networking.misc` Windows and other networks. *Newsgroup*

2632 `comp.os.ms-windows.networking.ras` Windows RAS networking. *Newsgroup*

➤ `comp.os.ms-windows.networking.tcp-ip`: Windows and TCP/IP networking. *Newsgroup*

2633 `comp.os.ms-windows.networking.windows` Windows' built-in networking. *Newsgroup*

2634 `comp.os.ms-windows.pre-release` Pre-release/beta versions of Windows. *Newsgroup*

2635 `comp.os.ms-windows.programmer.controls` Controls, dialogs, and VBXs. *Newsgroup*

2636 `comp.os.ms-windows.programmer.graphics` GDI, graphics, and printing. *Newsgroup*

2637 `comp.os.ms-windows.programmer.memory` Memory management issues. *Newsgroup*

2638 `comp.os.ms-windows.programmer.misc` Programming Microsoft Windows. *Newsgroup*

2639 `comp.os.ms-windows.programmer.multimedia` Multimedia programming. *Newsgroup*

2640 `comp.os.ms-windows.programmer.networks` Network programming. *Newsgroup*

2641 `comp.os.ms-windows.programmer.nt.kernel-mode` Windows NT driver development. *Newsgroup*

2642 `comp.os.ms-windows.programmer.ole` OLE2, COM, and DDE programming. *Newsgroup*

2643 `comp.os.ms-windows.programmer.tools.mfc` MFC-based development for Windows. *Newsgroup*

2644 `comp.os.ms-windows.programmer.tools.misc` Windows development tools. *Newsgroup*

2645 `comp.os.ms-windows.programmer.tools.owl` OWL-based development for Windows. *Newsgroup*

2646 `comp.os.ms-windows.programmer.tools.winsock` Winsock programming. *Newsgroup*

2647 `comp.os.ms-windows.programmer.vxd` Windows VxD and driver development. *Newsgroup*

2648 `comp.os.ms-windows.programmer.win32` 32-bit Windows programming interfaces. *Newsgroup*

2649 `comp.os.ms-windows.programmer.winhelp` WinHelp/Multimedia Viewer development. *Newsgroup*

2650 `comp.os.ms-windows.setup` Installing and configuring Microsoft Windows. *Newsgroup*

2651 `comp.os.ms-windows.win95.misc` Miscellaneous topics about Windows 95. *Newsgroup*

2652 `comp.os.ms-windows.win95.setup` Setup and configuration of Windows 95. *Newsgroup*

2653 `fj.os.ms-windows` Discussion relating to Microsoft Windows. *Newsgroup*

2654 `fj.windows.ms` About Microsoft Windows. *Newsgroup*

2655 `relcom.comp.os.windows` FIDOnet area, MS-Windows operating system. *Newsgroup*

2656 `relcom.comp.os.windows.nt` FIDOnet area, Windows NT operating system. *Newsgroup*

2657 `relcom.comp.os.windows.prog` FIDOnet area, programming under MS Windows. *Newsgroup*

2658 `tnn.window.windows` Discussions about Miscosoft Windows. *Newsgroup*

2659 `uk.comp.os.win95` U.K. focused group for discussing U.K. Windows 95-related topics. *Newsgroup*

2660 **WindoWatch:** On the various flavors of the Windows operating system. Also includes articles on the Internet, programming, and software/hardware. *Magazine*
`http://www.windowatch.com/`
`ftp://ftp.channel1.com/pub/WindoWatch/`
INFO EDITOR OWNER `lois.laulicht@channel1.com` (Publisher/Editor Lois B. Laulicht)
ARCHIVES
`ftp://ftp.channel1.com/pub/WindoWatch/`
`ftp://oak.oakland.edu/pub3/SimTal-win3/winwatch/`
Frequency: monthly

IBM & COMPATIBLES—WINDOWS NT

2661 `comp.os.ms-windows.nt.admin.misc` Windows NT system administration. *Newsgroup*

➤   `comp.os.ms-windows.nt.admin.networking`: Windows NT network administration. *Newsgroup*

2662 `comp.os.ms-windows.nt.advocacy` Windows NT advocacy arguments. *Newsgroup*

2663 `comp.os.ms-windows.nt.misc` General discussion about Windows NT. *Newsgroup*

2664 `comp.os.ms-windows.nt.pre-release` Unreleased and beta Windows NT versions. *Newsgroup*

2665 `comp.os.ms-windows.nt.setup.hardware` Windows NT hardware setup. *Newsgroup*

2666 `comp.os.ms-windows.nt.setup.misc` Windows NT software setup. *Newsgroup*

2667 `comp.os.ms-windows.nt.software.backoffice` Windows NT BackOffice. *Newsgroup*

2668 `comp.os.ms-windows.nt.software.compatibility` Windows NT software compatibility. *Newsgroup*

2669 `comp.os.ms-windows.nt.software.services` Windows NT system services software. *Newsgroup*

2670 `fj.os.windows-nt` Discussion about the Windows NT operating system. *Newsgroup*

2671 **NT-INFO:** Hungarians on Windows NT. *Mailing List*
± `listserv@huearn.sztaki.hu` [body = `SUBSCRIBE  NT-INFO` first-name last-name]
OWNER `frank@ilab.sztaki.hu` (From: Ferenc Jamrik)
OWNER `ica@huearn.sztaki.hu` (Ilona Toth)
Language: Hungarian & English

IMAGE PROCESSING

2672 **Computer Vision Home Page:** The Computer Vision page points to the latest research groups and results in image processing, robotic vision, and automatic reconstruction of 3-D information from 2-D imagery.
`http://www.cs.cmu.edu/~cil/txtvision.html` (text only web page)
`http://www.cs.cmu.edu/~cil/vision.html`
INFO `mwm@cmu.edu`

➤   **CGE:** On visualization and computer graphics. (See entry 2441 for full listing.)

➤   `comp.ai.doc-analysis.ocr`: OCR research, algorithms, and software. *Newsgroup*

➤   `comp.ai.vision`: Artificial-intelligence vision research. *Moderated newsgroup*

➤   `comp.graphics.apps.photoshop`: Adobe Photoshop techniques and help. *Newsgroup*

2673 `comp.soft-sys.khoros` The Khoros X11 visualization system. *Newsgroup*

2674 `fj.comp.image` Computer graphics, art, animation, image processing. *Newsgroup*

2675 **IRIS Explorer Center Information Server:** This WWW server provides information on the IRIS Explorer data visualization system.
`http://www.nag.co.uk/`
`http://www.nag.co.uk/Welcome_IEC.html`
INFO `webmaster@nag.co.uk`

2676 **Optoelectronic Computing Systems Laboratory at Colorado State University:** This site contains information on digital optical computing. It includes an archive of the lab's publications and technical reports on optical computing, plus GIFs from optical computing experiments.
`http://www.lance.colostate.edu/`
`ftp://guyot.lance.colostate.edu/pub`
INFO `irakliot@lance.colostate.edu`

➤   `rec.video.desktop`: Amateur, computer-based video editing and production. *Newsgroup*

2677 `sci.image.processing` Scientific image processing and analysis. *Newsgroup*

INTERNET

2678 NEW-LIST: For distributing announcements of new public mailing lists on the Internet. *Mailing List*
± listserv@vm1.nodak.edu [body = SUBSCRIBE NEW-LIST first-name last-name]
INFO hoag@plains.nodak.edu (Marty Hoag)
Gated: bit.listserv.NEW-LIST

2679 !PIXIN(*)COMPENDIUM!: A project to anthologize and promote the art of "transpixins" (digital Internet movies). *E-Journal*
http://www.rtvf.nwu.edu/compendium
INFO OWNER cwebbyoung@nwu.edu (C. Webb Young)
ARCHIVE http://www.rtvf.nwu.edu/compendium
Frequency: quarterly

2680 Advertising Blacklist: A compendium of advertisers who have misused Net access, compiled by Axel Boldt.
http://math-www.uni-paderborn.de/~axel/BL/blacklist.html
INFO axel@uni-paderborn.de
MIRROR http://www.cco.caltech.edu/~cbrown/BL/

2681 alt.answers As if anyone on alt has the answers. *Moderated newsgroup*

2682 alt.best.of.internet It was a time of sorrow, it was a time of joy. *Newsgroup*

➤ **alt.cyberspace:** Cyberspace and how it should work. *Newsgroup*

2683 alt.destroy.the.internet Demons in the wire. *Newsgroup*

2684 alt.internet.media-coverage The coverage of the Internet by the media. *Newsgroup*

2685 alt.internet.services Not available in the UUCP world, even via e-mail. *Newsgroup*

2686 ARIE-L: For users of Ariel, a document transmission system for the Internet developed by the Research Libraries Group.
± listserv@idbsu.idbsu.edu [body = SUBSCRIBE ARIE-L first-name last-name]
INFO alileste@idbsu.idbsu.edu (Dan Lester)
INFO dlester@bsu.idbsu.edu
ARCHIVE listserv@idbsu.idbsu.edu [body = INDEX ARIE-L]
Gated: bit.listserv.arie-l

2687 bit.listserv.help-net Help on Bitnet and the Internet. *Newsgroup*

2688 bit.listserv.lsoft-announce Listserv announcements. *Moderated newsgroup*

➤ **C-ARTS:** On arts resources on the Internet; associated with a database (C-ARTSdb). (See entry 1300 for full listing.)

➤ **Coalition for Networked Information (CNI):** A partnership of the Association of Research Libraries, CAUSE, and EDUCOM, the coalition's mission is to help realize the promise of high-performance networks and computers for the advancement of scholarship and the enrichment of intellectual productivity. (See entry 4497 for full listing.)

➤ **comp.infosystems:** Any discussion about information systems. *Newsgroup*

2689 comp.infosystems.harvest Harvest information discovery and access system. *Newsgroup*

2690 comp.infosystems.interpedia The Internet Encyclopedia. *Newsgroup*

2691 Glossary of Internet Terms: A glossary of terms used on and about the Internet.
http://www.matisse.net/files/glossary.html
INFO admin@matisse.net

➤ **HSPNET-L:** On the way computer wide area networks can be used for remote diagnosis and treatment, transfer of patient records, and supplementing rural health care. (See entry 5063 for full listing.)

2692 I/O Magazine: Technology, Internet, and computing journal (upgrade your head). *Magazine*
http://www.mother.com/iomag
INFO OWNER iomagazine@aol.com (Erin Smothers)

INFO OWNER iomag@mother.com

ARCHIVE http://www.mother.com/iomag

Frequency: monthly

➤   **INETBIB:** On integrating the Internet into German libraries. (See entry 5748 for full listing.)

2693   `info.big-internet`   Issues facing a huge Internet (`big-internet@munnari.oz.au`). *Moderated newsgroup*

2694   **Internet Citizen's Band (ICB):** ICB (Internet Citizen's Band) is an Internet teleconferencing program that uses a client-server model to allow users across the Internet to communicate with each other. This site provides information to help you get started with the ICB community.

http://icb.sjsu.edu/~kzin/icb.html

INFO kzin@isc.sjsu.edu

2695   **Internet Tools NIR:** A status report on networked information retrieval tools and groups, by Joint IETF/RARE/CNI Networked Information Retrieval Working Group.

ftp://mailbase.ac.uk/pub/lists/nir/files/nir.status.report

2696   **ISearch:** For participation in net search contests. *Distribution List, moderated*

http://www.cris.com/~is/isearch/

± http://www.cris.com/~is/isearch/maillist.shtml

± OWNER is@cris.com (Matt Alberts)

Frequency: twice monthly

2697   **IWatch:** For entertaining and useful sites, sources, and secrets of the net. *Distribution List, moderated*

± iwatch@pobox.com [subject = IRLNL]

OWNER cybernet@atlcom.net (Calvin Merrick)

ARCHIVE http://www.webcom.com/cybernet/iwatch.shtml

Comments: Price: $1.00/month

➤   **Nashville-Scout:** On Internet resources in Nashville, Tennessee. (See entry 8543 for full listing.)

2698   `news.announce.conferences`   Calls for papers and conference announcements. *Moderated newsgroup*

2699   `news.announce.important`   General announcements of interest to all. *Moderated newsgroup*

2700   **NIC-News:** For updates on Internet resources. *Newsletter*

± listproc@u.washington.edu [body = SUBSCRIBE NIC-NEWS first-name last-name]

OWNER erez@cac.washington.edu (Sheryl Erez)

ARCHIVE http://www.washington.edu/nic-news

Frequency: weekly

2701   **SunSITE Internet Talk Radio Archives:** Archives of the Internet Talk Radio shows.

ftp://sunsite.unc.edu/pub/talk-radio/

INFO ftpkeeper@sunsite.unc.edu

2702   **Texas Metronet, Inc.:** Internet for the individual. Includes extensive Perl archive, scripts, information, and distribution source. Internet services and information. Many other helpful sources and links. The entire archive is boolean WAIS indexed for easy searching and retrieval.

http://www.metronet.com/

gopher://gopher.metronet.com

INFO info@metronet.com

FAQ http://www.metronet.com/newinfo/faqs.html

2703   **University of Minnesota Gopher:** This is where it all started. The one, the original gopher server. Now doing double duty as the CWIS for the University of Minnesota and providing many other interesting services including weather for the USA and a database of recipes and movie reviews.

gopher://gopher.tc.umn.edu

INFO gopher@boombox.micro.umn.edu

FAQ gopher://mudhoney.micro.umn.edu/00/Gopher.FAQ

MIRROR `gopher://gopher.ebone.net` (canonical list of gophers)

2704 `us.config` Planning a USA national network news hierarchy. *Newsgroup*

INTERNET—ADMINISTRATION

2705 **ADVISE-L:** For advisers, consultants, and other user services staff at the various institutions on the net to exchange ideas and information. *Mailing List*

± `listserv@uga.cc.uga.edu` [body = `SUBSCRIBE ADVISE-L` first-name last-name]

± `listserv@vm1.nodak.edu` [body = `SUBSCRIBE ADVISE-L` first-name last-name]

± `listserv@ubvm.cc.buffalo.edu` [body = `SUBSCRIBE ADVISE-L` first-name last-name]

OWNER `lsvmaint@uga.cc.uga.edu` (Jean Snow)

OWNER `hoag@plains.nodak.edu` (Marty Hoag)

OWNER `harold@uga.cc.uga.edu` (Harold Pritchett)

OWNER `jesus.heras@rediris.es` (Jesus Heras)

ARCHIVES

`listserv@uga.cc.uga.edu`

`listserv@vm1.nodak.edu`

2706 `aus.net.directory.osi-ds` IETF OSI-DS WG mailing list. *Newsgroup*

2707 `aus.net.policy` Discussion of all aspects of Australian Internet policy. *Newsgroup*

2708 `backbone.general` Discussions of the Internet backbone. *Newsgroup*

2709 `bit.listserv.hdesk-l` Help desk operations. *Newsgroup*

2710 `bit.listserv.nodmgt-l` Node management. *Newsgroup*

2711 `chile.uucp` Information and discussions of the UUCP community in Chile. *Newsgroup*

2712 `ddn.mgt-bulletin` The DDN *Management Bulletin* from NIC.DDN.MIL. *Moderated newsgroup*

2713 **FTPADM-L:** For administrators of FTP archives. *Mailing List*

± `listserv@cesnet.cz` [body = `SUBSCRIBE FTPADM-L` first-name last-name]

INFO `il@cesnet.cz` (Ingrid Ledererova)

ARCHIVE `listserv@cesnet.cz`

2714 `info.rfc` Announcements of newly released RFCs (`rfc-request@nic.ddn.mil`). *Moderated newsgroup*

2715 **Internet Engineering Task Force (IETF):** A list of information about the Internet Engineering Task Force (IETF), its working groups, and technical work items.

`http://www.ietf.cnri.reston.va.us/home.html`

INFO `ietf-web@cnri.reston.va.us`

2716 **The Internet Society:** The site contians information on the Internet Society, its papers, and the conferences it sponsors.

`http://www.isoc.org/`

INFO `webmaster@isoc.org`

FAQ `http://info.isoc.org/whatis/what-is-isoc.html`

➤ **InterNIC:** The Internet Network Information Center; includes a Directory of Directories, White Pages, and Internet domain-name registration. (See entry 2741 for full listing.)

➤ `news.admin.censorship:` Censorship issues in news administration. *Newsgroup*

2717 `news.admin.net-abuse.announce` Information regarding network resource abuse. *Moderated newsgroup*

2718 `news.admin.net-abuse.misc` Network facility abuse, including spamming. *Newsgroup*

2719 `relcom.postmasters` For Relcom postmasters, official. *Moderated newsgroup*

2720 `relcom.postmasters.d` Discussion of postmaster's troubles and bright ideas. *Newsgroup*

➤ **RFC INFO:** Request For Comments (RFCs)—documents about various issues for discussion, covering a broad range of networking issues. This e-mail document lists where and how to get new RFCs. It details each location, and explains exactly how to use the source to obtain the RFC information. RFC INFO will send the actual documents via e-mail. (See entry 2913 for full listing.)

➤ **RFC Web:** Internet Request For Comments (RFC) in HTML, with cross-references among them as hyperlinks. (See entry 2914 for full listing.)

2721 **STD:** Internet standards, subseries of notes within the RFC series which document Internet standards.
   ftp://nic.merit.edu/documents/std/

INTERNET—CONSULTING

2722 **December Communications:** December Communications specializes in World Wide Web-based communication and consulting. It delivers presentations about the World Wide Web to groups of any size; publishes several net publications; and provides consulting in Web content development, publishing, and policy to organizations and individuals.
   http://www.december.com/
   INFO john@december.com

2723 **Finite Systems Consulting:** SC is a Toronto-based consultancy providing a broad range of Internet-related services to corporate- and public-sector clients throughout Canada and the northeastern USA.
   http://www.finite-systems.com/fsc/
   INFO fsc@finite-systems.com

2724 **Lone Wolf Web Design:** Lone Wolf Web Design is the premier provider of Web design and Internet consulting services. Located in beautiful Phoenix, Arizona, Lone Wolf supplies all the services your organization needs to establish a successful and enticing Internet presence, including market research, graphic design, Internet consulting, Web-site creation and maintenance, and more. If your organization is considering establishing an online presence, or would like to expand or improve its current site, don't miss the "Four Keys to a Successful Web Site."
   http://www.primenet.com/~shauna/lonewolf.html
   INFO shauna@primenet.com

➤ **Netcast Global Communications:** Internet broadcasting, consultation, and audio/video information provider. (See entry 6066 for full listing.)

2725 **Texas Internet Consulting and MIDS:** Texas Internet Consulting is a network consulting firm specializing in TCP/IP, Unix systems, and standards. MIDS (Matrix Information and Directory Services) publishes *Matrix News* and *Matrix Maps Quarterly*, and conducts Internet research.
   http://www.tic.com/
   ftp://ftp.tic.com
   gopher://gopher.tic.com
   INFO mids@mids.org
   INFO tic@tic.com

➤ **Who's Who Online:** Biographical and professional data about people of accomplishment who are part of the worldwide Internet community. Currently searchable by name, with geographic, nature of work, and language-capability searches to be added in 1996. (See entry 2769 for full listing.)

INTERNET—DIRECTORIES—GENERAL

➤ **All-in-One Search Page:** Collected search engines. (See entry 2754 for full listing.)

2726 **PEG, a Peripatetic, Eclectic Gopher:** A collection of pointers to all sorts of Internet resources. Especially strong are its virtual reference desk, Internet assistance, politics and government, medicine, and women's studies resource lists.
   gopher://peg.cwis.uci.edu:7000/00/gopher.welcome/peg/
   INFO cjboyer@uci.edu (Calvin J. Boyer)

➤ **All The Best Locations!:** URL submission service. Use this site (for a fee) to have your URL submitted to all the major Internet directories and catalogs. (See entry 2993 for full listing.)

2727 Alta Vista: Digital Equipment Corporation's Web and Usenet crawler. Use this site to search for keywords in documents on the Web or recent postings to Usenet.

`http://www.altavista.digital.com/`

INFO `suggestions.altavista@pa.dec.com`

2728 Awesome List: A list of useful resources, by John Makulowich.

`http://www.cais.com/makulow/awesome.html`

INFO `john@trainer.com`

MIRROR `http://www.trainer.com/pub/journalism/awesome.html`

2729 Clearinghouse for Subject-Oriented Internet Resource Guides: Topical guides which identify, describe, and evaluate Internet-based information resources.

`http://www.lib.umich.edu/chhome.html`

INFO `clearinghouse@argus-inc.com`

2730 The Creative Internet Home Page: A collection of fun and useful resources.

`http://www.cid.com/`

INFO `aure@galcit.caltech.edu`

2731 excite: This site sports a search engine for both the World Wide Web and Usenet, reviews of Web pages, and a real world news bulletin.

`http://www.excite.com/`

INFO `info@atext.com`

2732 The Free Internet Encyclopedia: This site is an encyclopedia made up of documents found on the Internet. Includes a "MacroReference" for large subject areas and a "MicroReference" for specific subjects.

`http://www.cs.uh.edu/~clifton/encyclopedia.html`

INFO `mfincann@hic.net`

INFO `clifton@cs.uh.edu`

FAQ `http://www.cs.uh.edu/~clifton/faq.html`

2733 FTP Sites Web: Perry Rover's listing of anonymous FTP sites throughout the world.

`http://www.info.net/Public/priInfo-toc.html`

`http://www.info.net/Public/ftp-list.html`

`ftp://rtfm.mit.edu/pub/usenet/news.answers/ftp-list/`

INFO `cherry@info.net`

FAQ `http://www.info.net/Public/help-toc.html`

MIRRORS

`http://www.banjo.com/Public/priInfo-toc.html`

`http://www.banjo.com/Public/ftp-list.html`

Comments: This list is very large and takes a long time to download; however, it is easy to use and eliminates the need to search multiple files. Many lynx clients cannot access this list as the older clients are limited to around 30 links per page.

2734 Galaxy: A service of EINet, a collection of information searchable via index or by topic trees.

`http://www.einet.net/galaxy.html`

INFO `galaxy@tradewave.com`

Comments: Tradewave Galaxy is copyright 1993, 1994, 1995 Tradewave Corporation. All Rights Reserved. Tradewave is a trademark of Tradewave, Corp.

2735 INFOMINE: Database of university-level Internet resources in most all academic disciplines.

`http://lib-www.ucr.edu/`

INFO `mmooney@ucrac1.ucr.edu` (Margaret Mooney) (Margaret Mooney)

INFO `smitch@ucrac1.ucr.edu` (Steve Mitchell) (Steve Mitchell)

Comments: This resource provides more access points (ways of getting at the information) than most other virtual libraries. It is also one of the most comprehensive virtual libraries maintaining a university-level focus.

2736 InfoSeek Guide: This guide combines a comprehensive database of WWW pages, postings from over 10,000 Usenet news groups, a browsable directory of the best resources on the Internet including FTP and gopher sites, and news and other features.

`http://guide.infoseek.com/`

INFO `comments-guide@infoseek.com`

2737 Infoseek Professional: This subscription-based service offers a wide range of fully searchable commercial data sources including wire services, computer and technical publications, health and medical databases, and corporate profiles.

`http://professional.infoseek.com/`

`http://www.infoseek.com/`

2738 InfoSlug: InfoSlug is an excellent all-purpose gopher information resource site put together by the UC Santa Cruz University Library.

`gopher://gopher.ucsc.edu`

`telnet://infosulg@infoslug.ucsc.edu`

INFO `slugadmin@gopher.ucsc.edu`

MIRROR `http://www.ucsc.edu/`

➤   **Inter-Links:** Internet resources, information, links, and search engines created by Rob Kabacoff at Nova Southeastern University. (See entry 2780 for full listing.)

2739 The Internet Directory Version 2.0: The contents of this book, online!

`http://www.randomhouse.com/tid`

INFO `tid@www.randomhouse.com`

2740 Internet Meta-Index: Internet Resources Meta-Index from the National Center for Supercomputing Applications (NCSA).

`http://www.ncsa.uiuc.edu/SDG/Software/Mosaic/MetaIndex.html`

INFO `mosaic@ncsa.uiuc.edu.`

2741 InterNIC: The Internet Network Information Center; includes a Directory of Directories, White Pages, and Internet domain-name registration.

`http://ds.internic.net/`

INFO `admin@ds.internic.net`

2742 Lycos™: A search engine that indexes over 90% of the World Wide Web.

`http://lycos.cs.cmu.edu/`

INFO `webmaster@lycos.com`

2743 McKinley Directory: A general online directory to the Internet with reviews and ratings for each site in the database.

`http://www.mckinley.com/`

INFO `feedback@mckinley.com`

2744 Netsurfer Digest: The net surfer's guide to cyberspace. Each week it brings you short, crisp newsbytes, notices, and site reviews providing informative and entertaining shapshots of the vast wired world. *Newsletter*

`ftp://ftp.netsurf.com/pub/nsd/`

`http://www.netsurf.com/nsd/`

± `nsdigest-request@netsurf.com` [body = subscribe `nsdigest-html` for HTML or subscribe `nsdigest-text` for ASCII]

± `http://www.netsurf.com/nsd/subscribe.html`

INFO `arthur@netsurf.com`

EDITOR `editor@netsurf.com` (Arthur Bebak)

OWNER `http://www.netsurf.com/`

ARCHIVES

`ftp://ftp.netsurf.com/pub/nsd/`

`http://www.netsurf.com/nsd/`

Frequency: twice weekly

2745 The Online World Monitor: A companion product to *The Online World* resources handbook. While the book describes the online world as it is, the newsletter tracks changes in online offerings on a global scale. *Newsletter*
http://login.eunet.no/~presno/bok/i.html
http://login.eunet.no/~presno/index.html
± listserv@vm1.nodak.edu [body = GET TOW MONITOR]
INFO opresno@extern.uio.no (Odd de Presno)
Frequency: bimonthly
Price: Norwegian kroner 175/year (around U.S.$25)

2746 Open Text Index: A search engine for the World Wide Web. You can search for exact phrases of any length, or switch to Power Search mode to search for combinations of words and phrases.
http://www.opentext.com:8080/
INFO marketing@opentext.com

2747 Spider's Web: A lists of links to lists, Web/net stuff, searchers, images, and references.
http://miso.wwa.com/~boba/spider.html
INFO boba@wwa.com

➤ **Submit It!:** A fast and centralized way to publicize a new Internet resources. (See entry 3013 for full listing.)

2748 UMBC Web: University of Maryland at Baltimore County; exceptional Internet-based resources by subject category.
http://www.umbc.edu/
INFO pauld@umbc.edu
MIRRORS
http://www.irc.umbc.edu/
http://lemur.acs.umbc.edu/
http://research.umbc.edu/
http://www.gl.umbc.edu/

➤ **University of Minnesota Gopher:** This is where it all started. The one, the original gopher server. Now doing double duty as the CWIS for the University of Minnesota and providing many other interesting services including weather for the USA and a database of recipes and movie reviews. (See entry 2703 for full listing.)

2749 WebCrawler: A World Wide Web search engine.
http://www.biotech.washington.edu/WebCrawler/
INFO bp@cs.washington.edu

2750 World Anonymous Ftp Sites: This is a list of all the known anonymous FTP sites in the world. As of November 1995 there are 2,588 entries in this listing. This list is usually updated monthly and is derived from Perry Rovers' ASCII distribution.
http://www.info.net/Public/ftp-list.html
INFO cherry@info.net

2751 WWW Virtual Library: WWW Virtual Library. A distributed subject catalog, arranged in a variety of ways, including by Library of Congress subject headings.
http://www.w3.org/hypertext/DataSources/bySubject/Overview.html
INFO vlib@mail.w3.org

2752 Yahoo!: A search engine and subject-oriented directory for resources on the World Wide Web.
http://www.yahoo.com/
INFO webmaster@yahoo.com
FAQ http://www.yahoo.com/docs/info/faq.html

2753 Yanoff List: Scott Yanoff's Special Internet Connections listing of resources by subject.
http://www.uwm.edu/Mirror/inet.services.html
INFO yanoff@alpha2.csd.uwm.edu

INTERNET—DIRECTORIES—SPECIALIZED

➤ **Aerospace Engineering: A Guide to Internet Resources:** List of Internet resources that contain information pertaining to aerospace engineering in general. (See entry 8944 for full listing.)

2754 All-in-One Search Page: Collected search engines.

http://www.albany.net/~wcross/all1srch.html

INFO wcross@mail.albany.net

➤ **Art Planet:** Art Planet is the Internet directory designed exclusively for fine-art sites. (See entry 453 for full listing.)

➤ **AskERIC Virtual Library:** ERIC is the Educational Resources Information Center (ERIC), a federally funded national information system that provides, through its sixteen subject-specific clearinghouses, associated adjunct clearinghouses, and support components, a variety of services and products on a broad range of education-related issues. (See entry 4477 for full listing.)

2755 BizWeb: A subject-oriented directory of companies on the Web.

http://www.bizweb.com/

INFO bob@bizweb.com

➤ **CISTI:** Canada Institute for Scientific and Technical Information—worldwide scientific, technical, and medical information. (See entry 9448 for full listing.)

➤ **Employment Opportunities and Job Resources on the Internet:** Includes resources for job listings and other job-related information on the Internet that can be accessed at no additional cost to the job hunter. Links to additional job-hunting guides and collected links are included. (See entry 1712 for full listing.)

➤ **Government Sources of Business and Economic Information on the Internet:** Includes agriculture, area codes, census, Congressional Directory, economic information, Edgar, EPA, FDA, GAO, health, labor, NIST, OSHA, patents, postal information, SEC, Social Security, state government resources, travel advisories, USDA, weather, the White House, and more. (See entry 5384 for full listing.)

2756 Hytelnet: A hypertext directory to Internet-accessible libraries, Freenets, BBSs, and other information sites.

http://library.usask.ca/hytelnet

INFO pscott@library.berkeley.edu

➤ **Interactive Agent Page of Resources:** This page links to Web and FTP resources about interactive agents and animated characters. The topics are organized into four categories: avatars, bots, sims, and agents. (See entry 2130 for full listing.)

➤ **Internet and E-mail Resources on Aging:** Includes commercial services, Freenets, online library catalogs, BBSs, mailing lists, e-journals, newsgroups, gopher sites, Web sites, and selected e-mail addresses. (See entry 9698 for full listing.)

➤ **Internet Resource Directory for Educators:** Online resources of value to teachers, trainers, and their students; includes Web pages, gophers, mailing lists, telnet sites, and FTP sites. Organized by education-related topic. (See entry 4479 for full listing.)

➤ **Internet Resources for Heritage Conservation, Historic Preservation, Archeology:** Resources for professionals in the fields of restoration architecture, historic preservation, and archaeology; and all others interested in identification, protection, and management of cultural resources. Maintained by the National Center for Preservation Technology and Training, National Park Service. (See entry 5133 for full listing.)

➤ **Journalism Directory:** A list of Internet resources that focus on journalism, compiled by John Makulowich. (See entry 6073 for full listing.)

➤ **Marketing Lists on the Internet:** A collection of pointers to marketing-related resources on the Internet. (See entry 2026 for full listing.)

➤ **The Middle East-North Africa Internet Resource Guide:** Internet resources dealing with the Middle East, which for this resource guide includes Mauritania, Pakistan, Somalia, and the Central Asian republics. (See entry 7525 for full listing.)

➤ **Net Connections for Communication Disorders and Sciences:** List of resources for professionals and students in the fields of speech-language pathology, audiology, and speech science, and persons with communication disabilities or differences and their support persons. (See entry 9871 for full listing.)

➤ **Not Just Cows:** Not Just Cows: a guide to Internet/Bitnet resources in agriculture and related sciences; includes libraries, gopher sites, BBSs, Web sites, WAIS databases, e-journals, and mail servers. (See entry 8904 for full listing.)

➤ **Philosophy Related Resources on the Internet:** Includes resources on ethics, religion, science, philosophy of science, and specific philosophers. Covers mailing lists, journals, and e-texts. (See entry 5315 for full listing.)

➤ **The Legal List (Law-Related Resources on the Internet and Elsewhere):** Lists numerous law-related government, educational, and corporate Internet resources. Copyright © 1995 Lawyers Cooperative Publishing. (See entry 5523 for full listing.)

➤ **The List™:** This site provides a huge list of Internet Service Providers. When shopping for an ISP make sure to check in here. (See entry 2807 for full listing.)

➤ **Zine.Net:** A guide to a vast assortment of independent, self-published zines: the goal is to generate sales for printed (hard-copy) zines. (See entry 1635 for full listing.)

➤ **The Canadian Internet Business Directory:** Search businesses and government and educational institutions in Canada by company, name, province, or type. (See entry 7126 for full listing.)

➤ **CMU Libraries CS, Robotics and Electrical Engineering Resources:** Pointers to Web resources in computer science, robotics and electrical engineering including reference tools, bibliographies, books, journals, patents, standards, technical reports, and more. (See entry 9166 for full listing.)

2757 **The December List:** A list summarizing Internet tools and computer-mediated communication forums; includes pointers to guides or information about each tool, by John December

```
http://www.rpi.edu/Internet/Guides/decemj/itools/top.html
ftp://ftp.rpi.edu/pub/communications/internet-tools.readme
```

2758 **Directory of Electronic Journals and Newsletters:** The new edition of the Directory of Electronic Journals, Newsletters, and Academic Discussion Lists is a compilation of entries for nearly 2,500 scholarly lists and 675 electronic journals, newsletters, and related titles.

```
gopher://arl.cni.org/11/scomm/edir
```
INFO ann@cni.org

2759 **Directory of Scholarly Electronic Conferences:** Descriptions of electronic conferences (e-conferences) on topics of interest to scholars.

```
http://www.austin.unimelb.edu.au:800/1s/acad
ftp://ksuvxa.kent.edu/library/acadlist.readme
gopher://info.monash.edu.au/11/Other/lists
```

2760 **Drakos List:** Subjective Electronic Information Repository, by Nikos Drakos.

```
http://cbl.leeds.ac.uk/nikos/doc/repository.html
```
INFO webmaster@cbl.leeds.ac.uk

2761 **Enns' Internet Training Resources:** Guides, lists, sites, and resources of interest and use to network newbies, collected by Neil Enns.

```
http://www.brandonu.ca/~ennsnr/Resources/
```

2762 **Gateway to the Internet:** Scholarly Internet resources geared toward a research university clientele, maintained by the University of Iowa Libraries' Information Arcade.

```
http://www.lib.uiowa.edu/gw/
```
INFO info-arcade@uiowa.edu (Paul Soderdahl)

➤ **GET A JOB!:** GET A JOB! shortens the searching process for you and offers one of the best collections of employment sites and resources available on the Web today. (See entry 1721 for full listing.)

➤ **Global Recycling Network:** GRN is the most comprehensive recycling information resource available on the Internet. Its goal is to offer a one-stop solution to the recycling information needs of business users, consultants, researchers, students, and consumers alike, while helping to develop the international trade of recyclable goods. (See entry 4628 for full listing.)

➤ **A Guide to Statistical Computing Resources on the Internet:** Listing of the most valuable and useful resources pertinent to statistical computing. It includes: resources dealing specifically with two of the most commonly used statistical packages, SAS and SPSS; information resources related to statistical computing in general, including such statistical packages as BMDP, S, and LISREL; and information resources on statistics in general. (See entry 9426 for full listing.)

2763 **HYTEL-L:** The Hytelnet updates distribution list. *Distribution List*

± listserv@library.berkeley.edu [body = SUBSCRIBE HYTEL-L first-name last-name]

INFO pscott@library.berkeley.edu

ARCHIVE http://library.usask.ca/hytelnet/

Gated: bit.listserv.hytel-l

2764 **Information Sources: the Internet and Computer Mediated Communication:** This list's purpose is to collect, organize, and present information describing the Internet and computer-mediated communication technologies, applications, culture, discussion forums, and bibliographies.

http://www.rpi.edu/Internet/Guides/decemj/internet-cmc.html

INFO john@december.com

➤ **Interactive games:** Zarf's List of Interactive Games on the Web. (See entry 6467 for full listing.)

2765 **Interest Groups List:** This is a searchable version of the List of Lists, a database of special-interest-group mailing lists available on the Internet.

http://catalog.com/vivian/interest-group-search.html

ftp://sri.com/netinfo/interest-groups.txt

mail-server@sri.com [body = send interest-groups] (infobot)

INFO vivian@catalog.com

➤ **The Internet Advertising Resource Guide:** Contains links to select sources of information about advertising and marketing on the Internet. (See entry 1811 for full listing.)

➤ **Internet-on-a-Disk:** Newsletter of public-domain and freely available electronic texts. (See entry 5676 for full listing.)

➤ **IOMA Business page:** A directory of business-related Internet resources listed alphabetically by topic from the Institute of Management and Administration (IOMA). (See entry 1694 for full listing.)

➤ **Magazine and Newsletter Editors' Resource List:** This no-graphics page has easy-to-follow links to sites regarding shipping, circulation, advertising, associations, going electronic, the Pulitzer Prize, and much more. (See entry 6093 for full listing.)

2766 **Network Research Navigator:** The Oak Ridge National Lab's Network Research Navigator, strong on technical aspects of networking.

http://www.epm.ornl.gov/networking.html

INFO batsell@msr.epm.ornl.gov

2767 **NOSC Page:** List of Internet-related sources, by Richard Bocker.

http://www.nosc.mil/planet_earth/info.html

INFO bocker@nosc.mil

➤ **On-line Resources for Earth Scientists (ORES):** Earth-science resources, including digital documents, news sources, software, data sets, and public online services. Subjects include the environment, forestry, geography, geology, geophysics, GIS, GPS, geodesy, mapping, paleontology, remote sensing, space, meteorology, wildlife, and jobs in earth sciences. (See entry 9333 for full listing.)

➤ **Point Communications Best of the Web:** A guide to Web resources, with ratings. (See entry 3037 for full listing.)

➤ **ShopDNet:** A list of virtual marketplaces, from Blake and Associates, Internet Marketing Consultants. (See entry 1711 for full listing.)

➤ **Subject Specific Resource List in Psychology:** Includes mailing lists, libraries and departments, software, newsgroups, e-journals, and virtual reality. (See entry 9543 for full listing.)

➤ **The Useless Pages:** "America's Funniest Home Hypermedia," a collection of strange, trivial, bizarre, unusual, and weird WWW pages, collected by Paul Phillips and Steve Berlin. (See entry 530 for full listing.)

2768 **WAIS sources:** A collection of WAIS sources, including searchable indexes and FAQs about WAIS.

gopher://liberty.uc.wlu.edu/11/internet/indexsearches/inetsearches

2769 **Who's Who Online:** Biographical and professional data about people of accomplishment who are part of the world-wide Internet community. Currently searchable by name, with geographic, nature of work, and language-capability searches to be added in 1996.

http://www.whoswho-online.com/

INFO goldspinners@whoswho-corporate.com

2770 **Whois Servers List:** A collection of whois servers to look up people.

gopher://sipb.mit.edu

INFO mhpower@mit.edu

➤   **The Zipper:** With this resource you can find your congressional representatives (both House and Senate) based on your zip code. (See entry 5470 for full listing.)

INTERNET—HOW-TO

2771 <u>Internet Web Text</u>: This is a hypertext guide to Internet resources, linking users to Internet resources: orientation, guides, reference materials, browsing and exploring tools, subject and word-oriented searching tools, and information about connecting with people.

http://www.rpi.edu/Internet/Guides/decemj/text.html

INFO john@december.com

2772 **Accessing the Internet by E-Mail:** How to access Internet resources like FTP, gopher, Archie, Veronica, finger, Usenet, and WWW by e-mail.

mail-server@rtfm.mit.edu [body = send
  usenet/news.answers/internet-services/access-via-email]

INFO bobrankin@mhv.net

➤   **excite:** This site sports a search engine for both the World Wide Web and Usenet, reviews of Web pages, and a real world news bulletin. (See entry 2731 for full listing.)

2773 **Explore the Internet Now! (tutorial):** Beginner's guide to the Internet.

http://www.clark.net/pub/lschank/home.html

INFO lschank@clark.net (Larry Schankman)

MIRROR http://www.mnsfld.edu/depts/lib/explore/explore.html

Comments: graphics included optionally, or download as a self-extracting, compressed file, from:
ftp://clark.net/pub/lschank/explore/explore.exe

2774 **Exploring the Internet:** Starter page with different methods for searching the Internet.

http://www.cen.uiuc.edu/exploring.html

INFO ejk@uiuc.edu

2775 **FAQ: How can I send a fax from the Internet?:** Answers the question "How can I send a fax from the Internet?", by Kevin Savetz.

http://www.northcoast.com/savetz/fax-faq.html

ftp://rtfm.mit.edu/pub/usenet/news.answers/internet-services/fax-faq

INFO savetz@northcoast.com

2776 **FYIs:** For Your Information sub-series of RFCs about topics which relate to the Internet.

http://www.ftp.com/techsup/fyi/fyi-index.html

ftp://nic.merit.edu/documents/fyi/

2777 **Gold in Networks!:** A description of gold nuggets in the network, by J. Martin.

ftp://nic.merit.edu/documents/fyi/fyi_10.txt

2778 **Hitchikers Guide:** Describes the Internet (circa September 1989), by Ed Krol.

ftp://nic.merit.edu/documents/rfc/rfc1118.txt

INFO e-krol@uiuc.edu

2779 **Hypermedia and the Internet :** Hypermedia and the Internet, compiled by David Green. This is a guide to the World Wide Web with numerous live links to sites containing FAQs, tutorials, and other resources.

`http://life.anu.edu.au/education/hypermedia.html`

2780 **Inter-Links:** Internet resources, information, links, and search engines created by Rob Kabacoff at Nova Southeastern University.

`http://www.nova.edu/Inter-Links/start.html`

INFO `kabacoff@alpha.acast.nova.edu`

2781 **Introducing the Internet:** Merit's directory of miscellaneous introductory Internet information.

`ftp://nic.merit.edu/introducing.the.internet/`

➤ **IRC FAQ:** Internet Relay Chat Frequently Asked Questions and answers. (See entry 2805 for full listing.)

➤ **Knowledge Discovery Mine:** This site provides information on data mining and knowledge discovery in databases. (See entry 2338 for full listing.)

2782 **Learning:** Books, tutorials, and hint sheets on the Internet.

`http://www.charm.net/learning.html`

INFO `admin@charm.net`

2783 **Newbies Anonymous: A Newcomer's Guide to the Internet:** A comprehensive guide to the Internet for the new user. Contains links to software, training, and tutorials, as well as a list of interesting, unusual, and just plain bizarre sites on the Web.

`http://www.geocities.com/TheTropics/1945/index1.htm`

INFO `mbowen@nando.net`

2784 `news.announce.newusers` Explanatory postings for new users. *Moderated newsgroup*

2785 `news.newusers.questions` Q & A for users new to Usenet. *Newsgroup*

2786 **The Online World:** This is the online hypertext version of the *Online World* handbook by Odd de Presno. It deals with practical aspects of using the rapidly growing global online information resource.

`http://login.eunet.no/~presno/index.html`

`listserv@vm1.nodak.edu` [body = GET TOW TOW]

INFO `opresno@extern.uio.no` (Odd de Presno)

2787 `relcom.newusers` Q & A of new Relcom users. *Newsgroup*

2788 **The Scout Toolkit:** The Scout Toolkit is a service of InterNIC Net Scout Services designed to collect, organize, and annotate a subset of the most effective network information tools for use by researchers, educators, and others interested in locating and using quality Internet resources.

`http://www.internic.net/scout/toolkit/`

INFO `scout@internic.net`

Comments: See Scout Report for further information about Internet resources and network tools.

2789 **Surfing the Internet:** A narrative of what the Internet has to offer, by Jean Armour Polly.

`ftp://nysernet.org/pub/resources/guides/surfing.2.0.3.txt`

INFO `http://www.well.com/user/polly/`

INFO `polly@well.com`

2790 **TERENA's Guide to Network Resource Tools:** Trans-European Research and Education Networking Association's Guide to Network Resources Tools in HTML.

`http://www.terena.nl/gnrt`

INFO `secretariat@terena.nl`

2791 **WWW/Internet:** A collection of links to manuals and demos.

`http://tecfa.unige.ch/info-www.html`

INFO `daniel.schneider@tecfa.unige.ch`

2792 **Zen and the Art of the Internet:** HTML version of the first edition of Brendan Kehoe's guide to the Internet.

`http://sundance.cso.uiuc.edu/Publications/Other/Zen/zen-1.0_toc.html`

`ftp://ftp.csn.org/pub/net/zen/`

INFO `brendan@zen.org`

INTERNET—INTERNET RELAY CHAT (IRC)

2793 `alt.irc` Internet Relay Chat material. *Newsgroup*

2794 `alt.irc.announce` Announcements about Internet Relay Chat (IRC). *Moderated newsgroup*

2795 `alt.irc.bots` Daemons on Internet Relay Chat. *Newsgroup*

2796 `alt.irc.games` Playing games on IRC. *Newsgroup*

2797 `alt.irc.hottub` Discussion of the IRC channel #hottub. *Newsgroup*

2798 `alt.irc.ircii` IRC, the sequel. *Newsgroup*

2799 `alt.irc.questions` How-to questions for IRC (International Relay Chat). *Newsgroup*

2800 `alt.irc.recovery` Withdrawing from IRC overdose. *Newsgroup*

2801 `alt.irc.undernet` The alternative IRC. *Newsgroup*

2802 `alt.irc.undernet.bards` Tales and poems from Undernet IRC's #Bards. *Moderated newsgroup*

2803 `alt.irc.undernet.chatzone` Discussion group for #chatzone on Undernet IRC. *Newsgroup*

2804 **Internet Relay Chat (IRC) Information:** Beginner's guide and pointers to other IRC sites.
http://www.brunel.ac.uk:8080/~cs93jtl/IRC.html
INFO cs93jtl@brunel.ac.uk
FAQS
http://www2.undernet.org:8080/~cs93jtl/irc_faq.txt
http://www2.undernet.org:8080/~cs93jtl/underfaq/
MIRRORS
http://www2.undernet.org:8080/~cs93jtl/IRC.html
http://b1000.brunel.ac.uk:4040/IRC.html

2805 **IRC FAQ:** Internet Relay Chat Frequently Asked Questions and answers.
http://www.kei.com/irc.html
INFO hrose@kei.com

2806 **MACIRC-L:** On Macintosh Internet Relay Chat (IRC) client design. *Mailing List*
± listserv@brownvm.brown.edu [body = SUBSCRIBE MACIRC-L first-name last-name]
INFO peter@brownvm.bitnet (Peter DiCamillo)
Please Note: Subscription by approval only.

INTERNET—INTERNET SERVICE PROVIDERS

➤ **FUNET NIC:** Network Information Center of the Finnish University and Research Network, FUNET. Includes FUNET information, pointers to all Finnish gophers and Web servers, WWW/gopher/FTP gateway to ftp.funet.fi archive, Finnish X.400 gateway address converter, and much more. (See entry 7613 for full listing.)

2807 **The List™:** This site provides a huge list of Internet Service Providers. When shopping for an ISP make sure to check in here.
http://thelist.com/
INFO thelist@iworld.com

2808 `alt.aol-sucks` Why some people hate AOL and its users. *Newsgroup*

2809 `alt.aol.rejects` Another forum for gripes about America Online. *Newsgroup*

2810 `alt.internet.access.wanted` "Oh. Okay, how about just an MX record for now?". *Newsgroup*

2811 `alt.online-service` Large commercial online services, and the Internet. *Newsgroup*

2812 `alt.online-service.america-online` Or should that be "America Offline"? *Newsgroup*

2813 `alt.online-service.compuserve` Discussions and questions about CompuServe. *Newsgroup*

2814 `alt.online-service.delphi` Run! It's the Delphoids! *Newsgroup*

2815 `alt.online-service.freenet` Public Freenet systems. *Newsgroup*

2816 `alt.online-service.genie` Discussions and questions about GEnie. *Newsgroup*

2817 `alt.online-service.gnn` For discussion of the GNN online service. *Newsgroup*

2818 `alt.online-service.imagination` Discussion of the Imagination Network. *Newsgroup*

2819 `alt.online-service.microsoft` MSN (Microsoft Network) online service. *Newsgroup*

2820 `alt.online-service.prodigy` The Sears Prodigy system. *Newsgroup*

2821 `alt.online-service.well` Talk about the Whole Earth 'Lectronic Link @well.com. *Newsgroup*

2822 `bermuda.ibl.announce` Announcements from Internet Bermuda Limited staff. *Newsgroup*

2823 `bermuda.ibl.general` Information about Internet Bermuda Limited. *Newsgroup*

2824 `bermuda.ibl.support` Technical issues relating to Internet Bermuda Limited. *Newsgroup*

2825 `bit.listserv.innopac` Innovative Interfaces Online Public Access. *Newsgroup*

2826 **CICNet:** Information on CICNet, a regional Internet access provider serving the Great Lakes and upper Midwest.
`http://www.cic.net/`
INFO `info@cic.net`
INFO `www@cic.net`

2827 `clari.nb.online` Newsbytes: online services, the Internet, BBSs. *Moderated newsgroup*

➤   **Czech Educational and Scientific NETwork (CESNET):** Information on CESNET and the Czech Republic. (See entry 7263 for full listing.)

2828 `demon.announce` Demon Internet announcements. *Moderated newsgroup*

2829 `demon.answers` FAQs relating to the Demon service. *Moderated newsgroup*

2830 `demon.archives.announce` News uploaded to `ftp.demon.co.uk`. *Moderated newsgroup*

2831 `demon.archives.d` Discussion of uploads. *Newsgroup*

2832 `demon.ip.developers` Developers of software for use with Demon. *Newsgroup*

2833 `demon.ip.winsock.dics` DICS PD software to access Demon Internet. *Newsgroup*

2834 `demon.news` Discussion/proposals for Demon groups. *Newsgroup*

2835 `demon.sales` Demon sales announcements. *Moderated newsgroup*

2836 `demon.sales.d` Discussion area for demon.sales. *Newsgroup*

2837 `demon.service` Complaints, praise, etc. at the level of service. *Newsgroup*

➤   `dfw.internet.providers`: Internet access providers in the Dallas/Fort Worth region. *Newsgroup*

2838 `dungeon.announce` DNS general service announcements. *Newsgroup*

2839 `dungeon.chatter` DNS user discussion area. *Newsgroup*

2840 `dungeon.forsale` DNS user for sale advertisements. *Newsgroup*

2841 `dungeon.support` DNS general support area. *Newsgroup*

➤   `houston.internet.providers`: For information and discussion on Internet access providers in the Houston area. *Newsgroup*

➤   `ny.nysernet`: Discussions about N.Y. State Educcation Research Network (NYSERnet). *Newsgroup*

2842 **Panix:** New York City Internet access provider Panix (Public Access Unix/Internet). The gopher server provides access to the archives of the Society for Electronic Access; various science-fiction resources (including the Del Rey Internet Newsletter, an events calendar, and information on the Lunacon convention); a directory to New York City information (including art, places, and organizations); archives of Ebikes, a NYC-area cycling mailing list; archive for the Voters Telecomm Watch; and the MIT Guide to Lock Picking.
`http://www.panix.com/`

```
gopher://gopher.panix.com
```
INFO `info-person@panix.com` (human)
INFO `info@panix.com` (infobot)

2843 `psi.stats`   PSINet network statistics. *Newsgroup*

➤ **REACCIUN:** Academic Network of National University Research Centers, Venezuela (Red Academica de Centros de Investigacion y Universidades Nacionales REACCIUN). Its mission is to empower and support research and cooperation between academic and research institutions in Venezuela. (See entry 7644 for full listing.)

➤ **SABINET:** Home page of the largest South African provider of online bibliographic material. (See entry 5742 for full listing.)

2844 **Superprism.net:** A site that provides many Internet services, including information, marketing, and networking.
```
http://www.superprism.net/doc/SERVICES/faq.html
http://www.superprism.net/
ftp://superprism.net
telnet://superprism.net
```
INFO `rwang@superprism.net`

➤ **SURFnet InfoServices:** SURFnet is the National Research Network Organisation of the Netherlands. The SURFnet WWW and gopher information servers contain documents and publications from SURFnet and affiliated organizations. InfoServices also maintains an FTP and mirror archive. The SURFnet server also provides access to all Dutch network resources accessible through NL-menu (Dutch National Entry Point) and subject access to Internet resources. The services are maintained by an editorial board staffed by the National Library of the Netherlands: the Koninklijke Bibliotheek. (See entry 7561 for full listing.)

➤ **Swiss Academic & Research Network:** This is a main site for Switzerland. It includes pointers to other Swiss resources, including libraries and educational institutions. It also includes an archive of well-indexed FAQs from all across the Internet that are searchable, and a directory of Swiss libraries. (See entry 7727 for full listing.)

INTERNET—LORE & HISTORY

2845 `alt.folklore.internet`   Internet myths and legends. *Newsgroup*

2846 `alt.internet.guru`   Recognizing the people responsible for Internet success. *Newsgroup*

➤ **Cool Site of the Day:** InfiNet's Cool Site of the Day brings browsers to interesting sites on the World Wide Web. (See entry 3036 for full listing.)

2847 **FREAKS:** On freaks on the Internet: snide discussion on twisted writing. *Mailing List*
± `listproc@echonyc.com` [body = SUBSCRIBE FREAKS first-name last-name]
OWNER `spingo@echonyc.com`

2848 **Internet History/ISOC:** Internet Society's collection of Internet history, including one as told by Vincent Cerf.
```
gopher://gopher.isoc.org/11/internet/history
```

2849 **Internet Hunt:** A game for learning about Internet resources.
```
http://www.hunt.org/
ftp://ftp.cic.net/pub/hunt
gopher://gopher.cic.net/11/hunt
```
INFO `webweavers@www.hunt.org`
MIRROR `ftp://ftp.cni.org/pub/net-guides/i-hunt/`

Comments: The hunt itself is not active anymore, however, the archives are well worth looking through to gain an understanding of how to search for things on the Internet.

2850 **The Internet Index:** An occasional collection of facts and statistics about the Internet and related activities. *Newsletter*
```
http://www.openmarket.com/info/internet-index/current
http://www.openmarket.com/info/internet-index/
```
± `internet-index-request@openmarket.com` [body = subscribe]

INFO treese@openmarket.com (Win Treese)

ARCHIVE http://www.openmarket.com/info/internet-index/

Frequency: irregular, but approximately monthly

➤ **The Internet Society:** The site contians information on the Internet Society, its papers, and the conferences it sponsors. (See entry 2716 for full listing.)

➤ **Nerdnosh:** For virtual storytelling: family fables, yarns, campfire tales. (See entry 470 for full listing.)

➤ **NET.SCANDAL:** A world repository of irritainment. (See entry 3729 for full listing.)

2851 **Netizen Anthology:** The Netizens and the Wonderful World of the Net—An Anthology, by Ronda and Michael Hauben.

http://www.columbia.edu/~hauben/project_book.html

INFO hauben@columbia.edu (Michael Hauben)

INFO ronda@panix.com (Ronda Hauben)

MIRRORS

http://studentweb.tulane.edu/~rwoods/netbook/contents/html

http://www.saitama-u.ac.jp/~hiro/netizen/netbook/

2852 **What is the Internet?:** by Krol and Hoffman.

ftp://nic.merit.edu/documents/fyi/fyi_20.txt

INFO e-krol@uiuc.edu

INTERNET—MAILING LISTS

2853 `comp.mail.list-admin.policy` Policy issues in running mailing lists. *Newsgroup*

2854 `comp.mail.list-admin.software` Software used in the running of mailing lists. *Newsgroup*

2855 **LDBASE-L:** A discussion of listserv database search capability. *Digest & Reflector*

± listserv@ukanvm.cc.ukans.edu [body = SUBSCRIBE LDBASE-L first-name last-name]

INFO OWNER pete-weiss@psu.edu (Pete Weiss)

ARCHIVE listserv@ukanvm.cc.ukans.edu [body = INDEX LDBASE-L]

2856 **LINKFAIL:** Bitnet link failure announcements. *Mailing List*

± listserv@bitnic.educom.edu [body = SUBSCRIBE LINKFAIL first-name last-name]

± listserv@hearn.nic.surfnet.nl [body = SUBSCRIBE LINKFAIL first-name last-name]

± listserv@vm.marist.edu [body = SUBSCRIBE LINKFAIL first-name last-name]

± listserv@uga.cc.uga.edu [body = SUBSCRIBE LINKFAIL first-name last-name]

± listserv@vm.gmd.de [body = SUBSCRIBE LINKFAIL first-name last-name]

INFO linkfail-request@uga.cc.uga.edu

ARCHIVES

listserv@bitnic.educom.edu [body = INDEX LINKFAIL]

listserv@uga.cc.uga.edu [body = INDEX LINKFAIL]

listserv@vm.gmd.de [body = INDEX LINKFAIL]

listserv@vm.marist.edu [body = INDEX LINKFAIL]

Gated: bit.listserv.linkfail

2857 **List-Managers:** On managing Internet mailing lists, including software, methods, mechanisms, techniques, and policies. *Mailing List*

± majordomo@greatcircle.com [body = subscribe list-managers or subscribe list-managers-digest]

INFO OWNER list-managers-owner@greatcircle.com

ARCHIVES

ftp://ftp.greatcircle.com/pub/list-managers/archive/

http://www.greatcircle.com/list-managers/

2858 LSTOWN-L: For owners, editors, and coordinators of listserv-based discussion and distribution lists. *Mailing List*

± `listserv@searn.sunet.se` [body = SUBSCRIBE LSTOWN-L first-name last-name]

INFO `lstown-l-request@searn.sunet.se`

ARCHIVE `listserv@searn.sunet.se` [body = INDEX LSTOWN-L]

2859 LSTSRV-L: Give-and-take forum on listserv software. *Mailing List*

± `listserv@uga.cc.uga.edu` [body = SUBSCRIBE LSTSRV-L first-name last-name]

INFO `lstsrv-l-request@uga.cc.uga.edu`

ARCHIVE `listserv@uga.cc.uga.edu` [body = INDEX LSTSRV-L]

Gated: `bit.listserv.lstsrv-1`

2860 LWGate: The LWGate is a freely available program that allows sites to make mailing list functionality available through an intuitive WWW interface.

`http://www.netspace.org/cgi-bin/lwgate`

INFO `dwb@netspace.org`

FAQ `http://www.netspace.org/users/dwb/lwgate/`

2861 MAILLIST-L: On the RiscOS application MailList, an e-mail list manager. *Mailing List*

± `listsurv@cray-3.xs4all.nl`

INFO OWNER `mhe@cray-3.xs4all.nl` (Maurice Hendrix)

Please Note: Subscription by approval only.

2862 Majordomo-Announce: This list is for announcements of new releases of the Majordomo mailing list manager. *Mailing List*

± `majordomo@greatcircle.com` [body = subscribe Majordomo-Announce]

INFO `majordomo-announce-request@greatcircle.com` (infobot)

ARCHIVE `ftp://greatcircle.com/pub/archives`

2863 Majordomo-Users: This list is for discussions (including bug reports, enhancement reports, and general usage tips) concerning the Majordomo mailing list manager. *Mailing List*

± `majordomo@greatcircle.com` [body = subscribe Majordomo-Users]

INFO `majordomo-users-request@greatcircle.com` (infobot)

ARCHIVE `ftp://ftp.greatcircle.com/pub/archive`

INTERNET—NET CITIZENSHIP & NETIQUETTE

➤ **ACTION:** On online activism: networking among activists, planning and strategy, sharing of experience and information, and coordination of efforts. From the Electronic Frontier Foundation. (See entry 5579 for full listing.)

2864 alt.newbie The altnet housewarming committee. *Newsgroup*

2865 alt.newbies Housewarming for a group. *Newsgroup*

2866 Netiquette: Netiquette: the Network Etiquette mailing list. *Mailing List*

± `netiquette-request@albion.com`

OWNER `seth@albion.com` (Seth Ross)

ARCHIVE `http://www.bookport.com/Albion/`

➤ **The Network Observer:** A free online newsletter about networks and democracy, with brief articles of practical advice, and commentary and pointers to useful net resources. (See entry 5611 for full listing.)

INTERNET—NEWS

2867 !Weird Online World!: A monthly news-and-views magazine about the online world. *E-Zine*

`http://www.dorsai.org/~tristan/MAG`

INFO `tristan@tnl.net` (Tristan Louis)

INFO `tristan@dorsai.org` (Tristan Louis)

ARCHIVE `http://www.dorsai.org/~tristan/MAG/back.html`

Frequency: monthly

2868 `alt.current-events.rimm-study` Debunking Marty Rimm's Rimm job of net.sex. *Newsgroup*

2869 `alt.internet.talk-radio` Carl Malamud's Internet Talk Radio program. *Newsgroup*

2870 `alt.net.scandal` Outrageous happenings on the net. *Newsgroup*

2871 `aus.net.announce` Announcements of resources available on the net. *Newsgroup*

➤ **The Australian Observer:** An Internet news magazine with an Australian focus. (See entry 7088 for full listing.)

2872 `bit.listserv.bitnews` News about Bitnet. *Moderated newsgroup*

2873 `clari.matrix_news` Monthly journal on the Internet. *Moderated newsgroup*

2874 `comp.infosystems.announce` Announcements of Internet information services. *Moderated newsgroup*

2875 `comp.internet.net-happenings` Announcements of network happenings. *Moderated newsgroup*

➤ **Computer Underground Digest (CuD):** Discussion of legal, ethical, social, and other issues regarding computerized information and communications. Readers are encouraged to submit reasoned articles relating to computer culture and communication. (See entry 3719 for full listing.)

2876 **cwd-l:** Brock Meeks' CyberWire Dispatch List. *Distribution List*
± `majordomo@cyberwerks.com` [body = `subscribe cwd-l`]
INFO EDITOR `brock@well.sf.ca.us` (Brock N. Meeks)
OWNER `verve@cyberwerks.com` (Eric S. Theise)
ARCHIVE `http://cyberwerks.com:70/1/cyberwire`

2877 **DGLINFO:** Computing and Internet news and tips. *Newsletter*
`http://www.dgl.com/`
± `dglinfo@softaid.net` [body = `SUBSCRIBE DGLINFO` e-mail-address]
ARCHIVE `http://www.dgl.com/`

➤ **EFFector Online:** For the Electronic Frontier Foundation (EFF). (See entry 9750 for full listing.)

➤ **HotWired:** Online sister of *Wired* magazine. Contains articles, discussion forums, and lots more for net hipsters and newbies alike. "Mainstream Culture for the 21st Century." (See entry 9826 for full listing.)

2878 **Internet Informer:** Encapsulating the Internet, blending it with our transforming world, and delivering it all in one package to your electronic mailbox as often as possible. *E-journal*
± `informer@cris.com`
INFO `stevenbaker@delphi.com` (Steven Baker)

2879 **Internet Talk Radio (ITR):** ITR is a news and information service about the Internet, distributed on the Internet. Internet Talk Radio is modeled on National Public Radio and has a goal of providing in-depth technical information to the Internet community.
`http://www.ncsa.uiuc.edu/radio/radio.html`
INFO `mosaic@ncsa.uiuc.edu`

2880 `misc.news.internet.announce` News bulletins from the Internet. *Moderated newsgroup*

2881 `misc.news.internet.discuss` Discussion of news bulletins from the net. *Newsgroup*

2882 **NetCetera:** On new Internet resources and tools and net-related news briefs. Net-related activities of NorthWestNet member organizations and clients are also highlighted. *Newsletter*
`gopher://gopher.nwnet.net/11/nwnet-info/netcetera`
`http://www.nwnet.net/`
± `netcetera-feedback@nwnet.net`
INFO `betsykc@nwnet.net` (Betsy King Chessler)
ARCHIVE `gopher://gopher.nwnet.net`
Frequency: weekly

2883 **NcWWW:** A magazine for and by Internet explorers. *E-Magazine*

```
http://newww.dartmouth.edu:8023/
```
INFO `newww-editors@mac.dartmouth.edu`

➤ **The Red Rock Eater News Service:** All the news that Phil Agre, media and communications professor at UCSD, thinks fit to print on the subject of how technology affects peoples' lives. (See entry 3732 for full listing.)

2884 **The Scout Report:** A weekly report of the best of newly announced Internet resources. *Distribution List*
```
http://rs.internic.net/scout_report-index.html
```
± `majordomo@lists.internic.net` [body = `subscribe scout-report`]

INFO `scout@internic.net`

➤ **Suck:** Suck is "an experiment in provocation, mordant deconstructionism, and buzz-saw journalism," or, to quote Brock Meeks, "a kind of de facto Web 'Ombudsmen' with Attitude." (See entry 654 for full listing.)

➤ **TidBITS:** A newsletter for users of Macintosh computers. (See entry 3096 for full listing.)

2885 **Tradewinds:** A monthly roundup of Internet coverage in trade and industry periodicals. *Newsletter*
```
gopher://gopher.harvard.edu:70/11/.vine/providers/baker_library/tradewinds
```
± INFO `kliss@hbs.harvard.edu` (Kenneth M. Liss)

ARCHIVE `gopher://gopher.harvard.edu:70/11/.vine/providers/baker_library/tradewinds`

Frequency: monthly

2886 **webNews:** Announcements of new Web sites, services, and software; a service of the Department of Computer and Information Sciences at the University of Alabama at Birmingham, Studies of Information Filtering Technology for Electronic Resources (SIFTER) Research Group.
```
http://twinbrook.cis.uab.edu:70/webNews.80
gopher://twinbrook.cis.uab.edu/7GO/webNews.70
```
INFO `samuell@cis.uab.edu`

2887 **What's New Too!:** What's New Too! posts over 700 new and unique announcements every day and you can search their database for interesting sites.
```
http://newtoo.manifest.com/search.html (Search URL)
http://newtoo.manifest.com/
```
INFO `manifest@manifest.com`

INTERNET—STANDARDS, PROTOCOLS & TOOLS

2888 **Internet Tools Summary:** The purpose of this document is to list tools available on the Internet that are used for network information retrieval (NIR) and computer-mediated communication (CMC). This is not meant to be a strict categorization or an exhaustive list, rather, a reference catalog.
```
http://www.rpi.edu/Internet/Guides/decemj/internet-tools.html
```
INFO `john@december.com`

2889 `alt.dcom.slip-emulators` Pseudo-SLIP/PPP with shell accounts. TIA, SLAP, etc. *Newsgroup*

2890 `alt.gopher` Discussion of the gopher information service. *Newsgroup*

2891 **ATMWWW-L:** On asynchronous transfer mode (ATM) technology and the World Wide Web. *Mailing List*
± `listserv@cmuvm.csv.cmich.edu` [body = `SUBSCRIBE ATMWWW-L` first-name last-name]

OWNER `daniel.ferrer@cmich.edu` (Daniel Ferrer)

2892 `aus.net.directory` For the discussion of the X.500 directory. *Newsgroup*

2893 `aus.net.directory.quipu` The Quipu implementation of the X.500 directory. *Newsgroup*

2894 **Beginner's Guide to URLs:** A Beginner's Guide to URLs (Uniform Resource Locators), by Marc Andreessen.
```
http://www.ncsa.uiuc.edu/demoweb/url-primer.html
```
INFO `mosaic@ncsa.uiuc.edu`

2895 `bit.listserv.tn3270-l` TN3270 protocol discussion list. *Newsgroup*

2896 `comp.infosystems.gopher` Discussion of the gopher information service. *Newsgroup*

2897 `comp.infosystems.wais` The Z39.50-based WAIS full-text search system. *Newsgroup*

➤ `comp.mail.mime`: Multipurpose Internet Mail Extensions of RFC 1341. *Newsgroup*

2898 `comp.protocols.ppp` Discussion of the Internet Point to Point Protocol. *Newsgroup*

➤ `comp.protocols.snmp`: The Simple Network Management Protocol. *Newsgroup*

➤ `comp.protocols.tcp-ip`: TCP and IP network protocols. *Newsgroup*

2899 `fj.net.infosystems.archie` Discussion about Archie. *Newsgroup*

2900 `fj.net.infosystems.dns` Discussion about DNS (Domain Name System). *Newsgroup*

2901 `fj.net.infosystems.ftp` Discussion about FTP (File Transfer Protocol). *Newsgroup*

2902 `fj.net.infosystems.gopher` Discussion about gopher. *Newsgroup*

2903 `fj.net.infosystems.misc` Discussion about information systems. *Newsgroup*

2904 `fj.net.infosystems.wais` Discussion about WAIS (Wide Area Information Servers). *Newsgroup*

2905 `fj.net.infosystems.wwfs` Discussion about WWFS (World Wide File Systems). *Newsgroup*

2906 `fj.net.ip` Internet protocol and routing. *Newsgroup*

➤ `fj.news.system.nntp`: Discussion about NNTP. *Newsgroup*

➤ **HTML info/W3C:** HyperText Markup Language (HTML), working and background materials, from the World Wide Web Consortium. (See entry 2514 for full listing.)

2907 `info.ietf` Internet Engineering Task Force (IETF) discussions (`ietf@venera.isi.edu`). *Moderated newsgroup*

➤ **Internet Engineering Task Force (IETF):** A list of information about the Internet Engineering Task Force (IETF), its working groups, and technical work items. (See entry 2715 for full listing.)

➤ **The Internet Society:** The site contians information on the Internet Society, its papers, and the conferences it sponsors. (See entry 2716 for full listing.)

➤ **Internet Talk Radio (ITR):** ITR is a news and information service about the Internet, distributed on the Internet. Internet Talk Radio is modeled on National Public Radio and has a goal of providing in-depth technical information to the Internet community. (See entry 2879 for full listing.)

2908 **MSP-L:** On RFC-1312 (Message Send Protocol 2), an experimental protocol that proposes a method to provide the ability to communicate one-on-one in "real time" under TCP/IP. *Mailing List*

   ± `listserv@albany.edu` [body = `SUBSCRIBE MSP-L` first-name last-name]

   INFO `bec@albany.edu` (Ben Chi)

2909 **MVSGOPHER:** For discussion the MVS implementation of the gopher client and server. *Mailing List*

   ± `listserver@lists.acs.ohio-state.edu` [body = `SUBSCRIBE MVSGOPHER` first-name last-name]

   INFO OWNER `seb@draper.com` (Stephen E. Bacher)

   OWNER `weaver@ohstmvsa.acs.ohio-state.edu` (Duane Weaver)

   POST `mvsgopher@lists.acs.ohio-state.edu`

➤ **NETNWS-L:** For operators and developers of various net news programs on non-Unix-to-Unix networks. (See entry 2974 for full listing.)

➤ `news.software.nntp`: The Network News Transfer Protocol (NNTP). *Newsgroup*

2910 **ntp:** Discussion of the Network Time Protocol. *Mailing List*

   `ftp://louie.udel.edu/pub/ntp`

   ± `ntp-request@ni.umd.edu`

   Gated: `comp.protocols.time.ntp`

2911 `comp.protocols.time.ntp` The Network Time Protocol. *Newsgroup*

➤ **POP:** The list is primarily for system administrators attempting to find, install, and run POP, IMAP, and similar protocol servers on their servers. (See entry 3261 for full listing.)

2912 **PPP:** Discussion between users of Morning Star PPP, and announcements from Morning Star Technologies about new versions, features, etc. *Mailing List* `http://www.morningstar.com/`

± INFO `ppp-users-request@morningstar.com`

FAQ `ftp://ftp.morningstar.com/pub/ppp/RELEASE-NOTES`

Comments: For announcments only, subscribe by sending e-mail to `ppp-announce-request@morningstar.com`

2913 **RFC INFO:** Request For Comments (RFCs)—documents about various issues for discussion, covering a broad range of networking issues. This e-mail document lists where and how to get new RFCs. It details each location, and explains exactly how to use the source to obtain the RFC information. RFC INFO will send the actual documents via e-mail.

`rfc-info@isi.edu` [body = `help: ways_to_get_rfcs`] (infobot)

INFO `rfc-manager@isi.edu`

2914 **RFC Web:** Internet Request For Comments (RFC) in HTML, with cross-references among them as hyperlinks.

`http://www.cis.ohio-state.edu/hypertext/information/rfc.html`

➤ **VRML Repository:** All about the Virtual Reality Modeling Language (VRML), including pointers to software archives, documentation, bibliographies, related mailing lists and newsgroups, job postings in the field, and more. (See entry 4042 for full listing.)

INTERNET—TRAINING

2915 `bit.listserv.nettrain` Network trainers list. *Moderated newsgroup*

2916 **IETF/TERENA:** Internet Engineering Task Force (IETF) Training Materials Catalogue.

`http://coolabah.itd.adelaide.edu.au/TrainMat/catalogue.html`

INFO `mrp@itd.adelaide.edu.au`

2917 **Let's Go Gopherin':** Jim Gerland and Dr. Richard Smith's course about gopher (via e-mail).

`http://wings.buffalo.edu/internet/info/gophern/`

`gopher://wings.buffalo.edu/11/internet/info/gophern`

INFO `gerland@acsu.buffalo.edu`

MIRROR `gopher://wealaka.okgeosurvey1.gov/11/K12/GOPHERN`

2918 **NETTRAIN:** For Internet/Bitnet network trainers. *Digest & Reflector, moderated*

± `listserv@ubvm.cc.buffalo.edu` [body = `SUBSCRIBE NETTRAIN` first-name last-name]

INFO OWNER `millesjg@sluvca.slu.edu` (Jim Milles)

ARCHIVE `listserv@ubvm.cc.buffalo.edu` [body = `INDEX NETTRAIN`]

Gated: `bit.listserv.nettrain`

2919 **TOURBUS:** A virtual tour of Internet hot spots. *Mailing List, moderated*

± `majordomo@colossus.net`

INFO `http://csbh.mhv.net/~bobrankin/tourbus`

OWNER `pcrispe1@ua1vm.ua.edu` (Patrick Crispen)

OWNER `bobrankin@mhv.net`

ARCHIVE `http://csbh.mhv.net/~bobrankin/tourbus`

FAQ `http://csbh.mhv.net/~bobrankin/tourbus`

Language: English, Spanish

2920 **Web Training:** The University of Toronto Information Commons and High Performance and Research Computing Groups home page present information about HTTP, HTML, and networked multimedia training and technology.

`http://www.hprc.utornto.ca/home.html`

INFO `webmaster@hprc.utoronto.ca`

INTERNET—USENET

2921 `alt.config` Alternative subnet discussions and connectivity. *Newsgroup*

2922 `alt.culture.usenet` A self-referential oxymoron. *Newsgroup*

2923 `alt.humor.best-of-usenet` What readers think is funniest in net news. *Moderated newsgroup*

2924 `alt.humor.best-of-usenet.d` Discussion of `alt.humor.best-of-usenet` posts. *Newsgroup*

2925 `alt.nocem.misc` Discussion about the NoCeM project, an effort to cancel spam postings on Usenet. *Newsgroup*

2926 `alt.nocem.test` Testing/development of the NoCeM project, an effort to cancel spam postings on Usenet. *Newsgroup*

2927 `alt.usenet.offline-reader` Getting your fix offline. *Newsgroup*

2928 `alt.winsock.trumpet` The Trumpet news reader. *Newsgroup*

➤ **Alta Vista:** Digital Equipment Corporation's Web and Usenet crawler. Use this site to search for keywords in documents on the Web or recent postings to Usenet. (See entry 2727 for full listing.)

2929 **An Introduction to Usenet News and the trn Newsreader:** This document by Jon Bell contains a brief description of the Usenet news system, a tutorial on the basic use of the trn news reader for reading and posting news articles, and a description of some intermediate-level features of trn (e.g., creating signatures, saving articles, and using kill files).

`ftp://cs1.presby.edu/pub/trn-intro/`

INFO `jtbell@presby.edu`

2930 **ANU-NEWS:** For discussion of the uses, bugs, and fixes for ANU-NEWS software, a Usenet news package for DEC's OpenVMS operating system. *Mailing List*

± `listserv@vm1.nodak.edu` [body = SUBSCRIBE ANU-NEWS first-name last-name]

INFO `sloane@kuhub.cc.ukans.edu`

ARCHIVE `listserv@vm1.nodak.edu`

Gated: `news.software.anu-news`

2931 `bit.general` Discussions relating to Bitnet/Usenet. *Newsgroup*

2932 `biz.pagesat` For discussion of the Pagesat Satellite Usenet Newsfeed. *Newsgroup*

2933 `ca.news` Usenet status and usage in California. *Newsgroup*

2934 `ca.usenet` Discussion of Usenet/news administration in California. *Newsgroup*

2935 `can.canet.d` An open forum for discussion of `can.*` net topics. *Moderated newsgroup*

2936 `can.canet.stats` Usenet statistics from major `can.*` net NNTP sites. *Newsgroup*

2937 `chi.news.stats` Chicago area Usenet statistics. *Newsgroup*

2938 `clari.net.admin` Announcements for news admins at ClariNet sites. *Moderated newsgroup*

2939 `clari.net.announce` Announcements for all ClariNet readers. *Moderated newsgroup*

2940 `clari.net.answers` Monthly postings for ClariNews readers. *Moderated newsgroup*

2941 `clari.net.info` Occasional announcements for readers. *Moderated newsgroup*

2942 `clari.net.newusers` Online info about ClariNet. *Moderated newsgroup*

2943 `clari.net.newusers.group_info.four-star` What each group is about. *Moderated newsgroup*

2944 `clari.net.talk` Discussion of ClariNet—*not* moderated. *Newsgroup*

2945 `clari.net.talk.admin` Discussion of adminstrative topics—*not* moderated. *Newsgroup*

2946 `comp.os.ms-windows.apps.winsock.news` Winsock news applications. *Newsgroup*

➤ `comp.os.msdos.mail-news`: Administering mail and network news systems under MS-DOS. *Newsgroup*

2947 **Deja News:** Searchable database of recent Usenet posts.

`http://dejanews.com/`

INFO `help@dejanews.com`

2948 `demon.ip.cppnews` For users of the Cppnews package. *Newsgroup*

➤ **excite:** This site sports a search engine for both the World Wide Web and Usenet, reviews of Web pages, and a real world news bulletin. (See entry 2731 for full listing.)

2949 `fj.news.group.misc` About newsgroups of all other kinds. *Newsgroup*

2950 `fj.news.group.net` About newsgroups for discussions of networks. *Newsgroup*

2951 `fj.news.group.rec` About newsgroups for discussions of recreations. *Newsgroup*

2952 `fj.news.group.sci` About newsgroups for discussions of sciences. *Newsgroup*

2953 `fj.news.group.soc` About newsgroups for discussions of social issues. *Newsgroup*

2954 `fj.news.lists` News-related statistics and lists. *Newsgroup*

2955 `fj.news.misc` Miscellaneous discussions of network news. *Newsgroup*

2956 `fj.news.policy` Discussions of fj newsgroup hierarchy itself. *Newsgroup*

2957 `fj.news.reader` General topics about network news reader software. *Newsgroup*

2958 `fj.news.reader.gn` Discussion about gn news reader. *Newsgroup*

2959 `fj.news.reader.gnus` Discussion about GNUS news reader. *Newsgroup*

2960 `fj.news.reader.mnews` Discussion about mnews. *Newsgroup*

2961 `fj.news.reader.rn` Discussion about rn family (rn, trn, . . .). *Newsgroup*

2962 `fj.news.reader.tin` Discussion about TIN. *Newsgroup*

2963 `fj.news.reader.winvn` Discussion about winvn. *Newsgroup*

2964 `fj.news.system` General topics about network news systems. *Newsgroup*

2965 `fj.news.system.b` Discussion about B news system. *Newsgroup*

2966 `fj.news.system.c` Discussion about C news system. *Newsgroup*

2967 `fj.news.system.dnas` Discussion about DNAS. *Newsgroup*

2968 `fj.news.system.inn` Discussion about INN news system. *Newsgroup*

2969 `fj.news.system.nntp` Discussion about NNTP. *Newsgroup*

2970 `fj.news.usage` Questions and discussions on how to work with the fj community. *Newsgroup*

2971 `gnu.emacs.gnews` News reading under GNU EMACS using Weemba's Gnews. *Newsgroup*

2972 `gnu.emacs.gnus` News reading under GNU EMACS using GNUS (in English). *Newsgroup*

2973 `info.admin` Administrative messages regarding `info.*` groups (`usenet@ux1.cso.uiuc.edu`). *Moderated newsgroup*

2974 **NETNWS-L:** For operators and developers of various net news programs on non-Unix-to-Unix networks. *Mailing List, moderated*
  ± `listserv@vm1.nodak.edu` [body = `SUBSCRIBE NETNWS-L` first-name last-name]
  INFO `hoag@plains.nodak.edu` (Marty Hoag)
  ARCHIVE `listserv@vm1.nodak.edu`
  Gated: `bit.listserv.netnws-l`

➤ `news.admin.censorship`: Censorship issues in news administration. *Newsgroup*

2975 `news.admin.hierarchies` Network news hierarchies. *Newsgroup*

2976 `news.admin.misc` General topics of network news administration. *Newsgroup*

2977 `news.admin.technical` Technical aspects of maintaining network news. *Moderated newsgroup*

2978 `news.announce.newgroups` Calls for new groups and announcements of same. *Moderated newsgroup*

➤ `news.answers`: Repository for periodic Usenet articles. *Moderated newsgroup*

2979 `news.groups` Discussions and lists of newsgroups. *Newsgroup*

2980 `news.groups.questions` Where can I find talk about topic X? *Newsgroup*

2981 `news.groups.reviews` What is going on in group or mailing list named X? *Moderated newsgroup*

2982 `news.lists` News-related statistics and lists. *Moderated newsgroup*

2983 `news.lists.ps-maps` Maps relating to Usenet traffic flow. *Moderated newsgroup*

2984 `news.misc` Discussions of Usenet itself. *Newsgroup*

2985 `news.software.anu-news` VMS B-news software from Australian National Univ. *Newsgroup*

2986 `news.software.b` Discussion about B-news-compatible software. *Newsgroup*

2987 `news.software.nn` Discussion about the nn news reader package. *Newsgroup*

2988 `news.software.nntp` The Network News Transfer Protocol (NNTP). *Newsgroup*

2989 `news.software.readers` Discussion of software used to read network news. *Newsgroup*

2990 **NNMVS-L:** MVS/TSO NNTP news reader (NNMVS) discussion. *Mailing List*
± `listserv@vma.cc.nd.edu` [body = `SUBSCRIBE NNMVS-L` first-name last-name]
INFO `seb@draper.com` (Stephen E. Bacher)

2991 **Ohio State University Math Department NNTPLINK archive:** Archive of nntplink software.
`ftp://math.ohio-state.edu`
INFO `postmaster@math.ohio-state.edu`

➤ **Open Text Index:** A search engine for the World Wide Web. You can search for exact phrases of any length, or switch to Power Search mode to search for combinations of words and phrases. (See entry 2746 for full listing.)

➤ `rec.answers`: Repository for periodic Usenet articles. *Moderated newsgroup*

➤ `talk.answers`: Repository for periodic Usenet articles. *Moderated newsgroup*

➤ **webNews:** Announcements of new Web sites, services, and software; a service of the Department of Computer and Information Sciences at the University of Alabama at Birmingham, Studies of Information Filtering Technology for Electronic Resources (SIFTER) Research Group. (See entry 2886 for full listing.)

INTERNET—WORLD WIDE WEB

2992 **"The World Wide Web Unleashed" Book Support Web:** This book is an overview and guide to the World Wide Web for a general audience; it covers how to get started with browsers, navigation techniques, a tour of applications, how to develop webs, server basics, and an exploration of future issues.
`http://www.december.com/works/wwwu.html`
INFO `john@december.com`

2993 **All The Best Locations!:** URL submission service. Use this site (for a fee) to have your URL submitted to all the major Internet directories and catalogs.
`http://netmar.com/~hamorder/url.html`
INFO `custom@sonic.net`

2994 `alt.culture.www` World Wide Web culture. *Newsgroup*

2995 `alt.fan.thespot` A discussion group for the Spot—the World Wide Web's hottest form of advertising. *Newsgroup*

2996 `alt.rec.spot` The Spot, the Cool Site of the Year on the Web. *Newsgroup*

2997 `alt.webgod` Discussion of the WebGod WWW server. *Newsgroup*

2998 **Archieplex:** A list of WWW Archie servers, both form-based and non-form-based, arranged by country.
`http://www.nexor.co.uk/archie.html`
INFO `webmaster@nexor.co.uk`

➤ **Beginner's Guide to URLs:** A Beginner's Guide to URLs (Uniform Resource Locators), by Marc Andreessen. (See entry 2894 for full listing.)

2999 `bit.listserv.www-vm` World Wide Web on VM platform list. *Newsgroup*

3000 `chinese.rec.magazines.multiworld` Discussion on WWW magazine *Multiworld*. *Newsgroup*

3001 `comp.infosystems.www.advocacy` Comments and arguments over the best and worst. *Newsgroup*

3002 `comp.infosystems.www.announce` World Wide Web announcements. *Moderated newsgroup*

3003 `comp.infosystems.www.misc` Miscellaneous World Wide Web discussion. *Newsgroup*

3004 `comp.infosystems.www.servers.mac` Web servers for the Macintosh platform. *Newsgroup*

3005 `comp.infosystems.www.servers.misc` Web servers for other platforms. *Newsgroup*

3006 `comp.infosystems.www.servers.ms-windows` Web servers for MS Windows and NT. *Newsgroup*

3007 `comp.infosystems.www.servers.unix` Web servers for Unix platforms. *Newsgroup*

➤ `comp.os.os2.networking.www`: World Wide Web (WWW) applications/utilities under OS/2. *Newsgroup*

3008 `demon.ip.www` World Wide Web-related discussion. *Newsgroup*

➤ **The EdWeb Project:** An online tutorial on education, technology, school reform, and the information highway; sponsored by the Corporation for Public Broadcasting. (See entry 4224 for full listing.)

3009 `fj.net.infosystems.www.servers` About WWW serving softwares. *Newsgroup*

3010 **General World Wide Web tools:** Internet Information Resources from the University of Texas, including catalogs and guides, search tools, publishing tools, browsers, and general employment resources on the Web.
`http://www.gslis.utexas.edu/internet/internet.html`
INFO `www@gslis.utexas.edu`

3011 `han.comp.www` World Wide Web server, clients, site information. *Newsgroup*

➤ **Hypermedia and the Internet :** Hypermedia and the Internet, compiled by David Green. This is a guide to the World Wide Web with numerous live links to sites containing FAQs, tutorials, and other resources. (See entry 2779 for full listing.)

➤ **Phoenicia:** Collaborative WWW-based information management system (used to implement the CWIS at the University of Chicago). (See entry 2511 for full listing.)

3012 `relcom.www.support` Computer support of WWW services, for professionals. *Newsgroup*

3013 **Submit It!:** A fast and centralized way to publicize a new Internet resources.
`http://www.submit-it.com/`
INFO `banister@uiuc.edu`
FAQ `http://www.submit-it.com/faq.html`

3014 `tnn.internet.www` World Wide Web topics and programs. *Newsgroup*

➤ **Tutorial gateway:** A filter for a CGI-compliant HTTP server that makes it slightly easier to develop tutorial-style questions for Web users. (See entry 3027 for full listing.)

➤ **Web Training:** The University of Toronto Information Commons and High Performance and Research Computing Groups home page present information about HTTP, HTML, and networked multimedia training and technology. (See entry 2920 for full listing.)

➤ **Web4Lib:** On World Wide Web (WWW) management and development for libraries. (See entry 5736 for full listing.)

➤ **webNews:** Announcements of new Web sites, services, and software; a service of the Department of Computer and Information Sciences at the University of Alabama at Birmingham, Studies of Information Filtering Technology for Electronic Resources (SIFTER) Research Group. (See entry 2886 for full listing.)

➤ **What's New Too!:** What's New Too! posts over 700 new and unique announcements every day and you can search their database for interesting sites. (See entry 2887 for full listing.)

3015 **WWW Servers:** A long list of registered WWW servers listed geographically by continent and country.
`http://www.w3.org/hypertext/DataSources/WWW/Servers.html`
INFO `www-admin@w3.org`

3016 **WWW talk:** Welcome to the World Wide Web! Tutorial slides by Mark Maimone, Carnegie Mellon Computer Science.
`http://www.cs.cmu.edu/~mwm/tutorial/`

INFO mwm@cmu.edu

➤ **WWW Virtual Library:** WWW Virtual Library. A distributed subject catalog, arranged in a variety of ways, including by Library of Congress subject headings. (See entry 2751 for full listing.)

➤ **WWWEDU:** On the potential of World Wide Web use in education. (See entry 4536 for full listing.)

3017 **Xerox Video:** An Overview of the Internet and World Wide Web, by Xerox Palo Alto Research Center.
http://pubweb.parc.xerox.com/hypertext/wwwvideo/wwwvideo.html
INFO putz@parc.xerox.com

INTERNET—WORLD WIDE WEB—AUTHORING

3018 **Web Weavers:** A collection of resources related to developing information on the World Wide Web, by Chris Beaumont.
http://www.nas.nasa.gov/NAS/WebWeavers/
INFO chris@ncafe.com (Chris Beaumont) (Chris Beaumont)
INFO cbeaumon@nas.nasa.gov

3019 **WWW + HTML Developer's JumpStation:** The WWW + HTML Developer's JumpStation gives background on all aspects of HTML coding and WWW use.
http://oneworld.wa.com/htmldev/devpage/dev-page.html
INFO singnet-www@singnet.com.sg

➤ **"HTML & CGI Unleashed" Book Support Web:** "HTML & CGI Unleashed" covers the complete life cycle of Web development: planning, analysis, design, and HTML implementation and gateway programming using Perl, REXX, and C. (See entry 2512 for full listing.)

3020 `comp.infosystems.www.authoring.cgi` Writing CGI scripts for the Web. *Newsgroup*

3021 `comp.infosystems.www.authoring.html` Writing HTML for the Web. *Newsgroup*

3022 `comp.infosystems.www.authoring.images` Using images, image maps on the Web. *Newsgroup*

3023 `comp.infosystems.www.authoring.misc` Miscellaneous Web authoring issues. *Newsgroup*

3024 `fj.net.infosystems.www.authoring` About WWW authoring techniques. *Newsgroup*

➤ **HTML Assistant Newsletter:** For users of HTML Assistant software. (See entry 2513 for full listing.)

➤ **HTML info/W3C:** HyperText Markup Language (HTML), working and background materials, from the World Wide Web Consortium. (See entry 2514 for full listing.)

3025 **International Directory of Women Web Designers:** The Web's only comprehensive international directory of Web design and related Internet consultancy firms that are owned and operated by women. Inside, you will find businesses that specialize in Web page design, server setup and maintenence, Internet training and consulting, and more. Companies have been broken down geographically to help you find a consultant or designer in your area. Links to company sites and contact information about the company are included.
http://www.primenet.com/~shauna/women.html
INFO shauna@primenet.com

➤ **Java™ Programming for the Internet:** All about the Java programming language, including tutorials, documentation, sample applets, downloadable SDKs, and liscensing information. (See entry 3563 for full listing.)

➤ **Scream Press:** For HTML tech talk and cool sites. (See entry 3039 for full listing.)

3026 **Sybase New Media:** Visitors to http://www.newmedia.sybase.com can exchange ideas about Web-site design and electronic commerce, learn about (and download) Sybase and Powersoft products, and see how leading developers are using Sybase products to conduct business on the Internet and create Web sites.
http://www.newmedia.sybase.com/
INFO newmedia-info@sybase.com

3027 **Tutorial gateway:** A filter for a CGI-compliant HTTP server that makes it slightly easier to develop tutorial-style questions for Web users.
http://www.civeng.carleton.ca/~nholtz/tut/doc/doc.html

INFO nholtz@ccs.carleton.ca

INTERNET—WORLD WIDE WEB—BROWSERS

3028 **alt.fan.mozilla** Discussions of Netscape's WWW browser Mozilla. *Newsgroup*

3029 **comp.infosystems.www.browsers.mac** Web browsers for the Macintosh platform. *Newsgroup*

3030 **comp.infosystems.www.browsers.misc** Web browsers for other platforms. *Newsgroup*

3031 **comp.infosystems.www.browsers.ms-windows** Web browsers for MS Windows. *Newsgroup*

3032 **comp.infosystems.www.browsers.x** Web browsers for the X-Windows system. *Newsgroup*

3033 **fj.net.infosystems.www.browsers** About WWW browsing softwares. *Newsgroup*

INTERNET—WORLD WIDE WEB—SURFING

3034 **BESTWEB:** On the best Web sites. *Mailing List*
± listserv@trearnpc.ege.edu.tr [body = SUBSCRIBE BESTWEB first-name last-name]
OWNER sysadm8@vm.ege.edu.tr (Veli Hazar)
OWNER turgut@vm.ege.edu.tr (Turgut Kalfaoglu)

3035 **Chaos Corner:** For things found wandering around the Internet—humorous and personal. *Newsletter*
± chaos-request@pelican.cit.cornell.edu
INFO drchaos@pelican.cit.cornell.edu (Bob Cowles)
ARCHIVES
ftp://pelican.cit.cornell.edu/pub
ftp://pelican.cit.cornell.edu
Frequency: irregular

3036 **Cool Site of the Day:** InfiNet's Cool Site of the Day brings browsers to interesting sites on the World Wide Web.
http://cool.infi.net/
INFO cool@infi.net

3037 **Point Communications Best of the Web:** A guide to Web resources, with ratings.
http://www.pointcom.com/
INFO chan@pointcom.com
FAQ http://www.pointcom.com/gifs/welcome/
MIRROR http://lycos-tmp2.psc.edu/

3038 **razorfish:** Web developer's site with some interesting WWW effects and journalistic content about the online world.
http://www.razorfish.com/
INFO info@razorfish.com

3039 **Scream Press:** For HTML tech talk and cool sites. *Magazine*
ARCHIVES
http://www.zoom.com/~whisper/ (WEBsurf America)
http://www.jsp.fi/~whisper/ (WEBsurf Europe)
ftp://ftp.etext.org/pub/Zines/Whisper/
Frequency: monthly

3040 **The Stick:** A monthly newsletter for Web surfers on the Internet's World Wide Web. *Newsletter*
http://www.vpm.com/tti/stick.html
INFO EDITOR OWNER rthayer@getnet.com (Rob Thayer, Editor)
Frequency: monthly

3041 Top Tens: From Internet Training and Consulting Services, resource lists that are picks of the net and Web in top-level resources, art, commerce, fun, Internet training, K-12 education, library resources, and Internet books and journals.

http://www.itcs.com/topten/

INFO webweaver@itcs.com

3042 URouLette: A way to pseudo-randomly choose a URL to visit.

http://www.uroulette.com:8000/

INFO uroulette@uroulette.com

Comments: A great way to cruise the Web.

INTERNET—WORLD WIDE WEB—TECHNICAL

➤   **LWGate:** The LWGate is a freely available program that allows sites to make mailing list functionality available through an intuitive WWW interface. (See entry 2860 for full listing.)

MACINTOSH

3043 `alt.hackintosh` Clever programming on Apple's Macintosh. *Newsgroup*

3044 `alt.sources.mac` Source code for Apple Macintosh computers. *Newsgroup*

3045 `alt.sys.mac.newuser-help` A forum for Macintosh users new to the Internet. *Newsgroup*

3046 `aus.computers.mac` Australian discussion of all things Macintosh. *Newsgroup*

3047 `aus.mac` The Apple Macintosh computer. *Newsgroup*

3048 `biz.marketplace.computers.mac` Macintosh hardware/software offered/wanted. *Newsgroup*

3049 `clari.nb.apple` Newsbytes: Apple/Macintosh news. *Moderated newsgroup*

3050 `comp.binaries.mac` Encoded Macintosh programs in binary. *Moderated newsgroup*

3051 `comp.emulators.mac.executor` ARDI's Mac emulator, Executor. *Newsgroup*

➤   `comp.infosystems.www.browsers.mac:` Web browsers for the Macintosh platform. *Newsgroup*

➤   `comp.infosystems.www.servers.mac:` Web servers for the Macintosh platform. *Newsgroup*

➤   `comp.lang.forth.mac:` The CSI MacForth programming environment. *Newsgroup*

➤   `comp.lang.lisp.mcl:` Discussing Apple's Macintosh Common LISP. *Newsgroup*

➤   `comp.mail.eudora.mac:` Eudora e-mail software for Macintosh. *Newsgroup*

➤   `comp.protocols.appletalk:` Appletalk hardware and software. *Newsgroup*

3052 `comp.soft-sys.middleware.opendoc` OpenDoc and its related technologies. *Newsgroup*

3053 `comp.sources.mac` Software for the Apple Macintosh. *Moderated newsgroup*

3054 `comp.sys.mac.advocacy` The Macintosh computer family compared to others. *Newsgroup*

3055 `comp.sys.mac.announce` Important notices for Macintosh users. *Moderated newsgroup*

3056 `comp.sys.mac.apps` Discussions of Macintosh applications. *Newsgroup*

3057 `comp.sys.mac.comm` Discussion of Macintosh communications. *Newsgroup*

3058 `comp.sys.mac.databases` Database systems for the Apple Macintosh databases. *Newsgroup*

3059 `comp.sys.mac.digest` Apple Macintosh: information and uses, but no programs. *Moderated newsgroup*

➤   `comp.sys.mac.games.action:` Action games for the Macintosh. *Newsgroup*

➤   `comp.sys.mac.games.adventure:` Adventure games for the Macintosh. *Newsgroup*

➤   `comp.sys.mac.games.announce:` Announcements for Macintosh gamers. *Moderated newsgroup*

➤   `comp.sys.mac.games.flight-sim:` Flight simulator game-play on the Macintosh. *Newsgroup*

➤   `comp.sys.mac.games.marketplace:` Macintosh games for sale and trade. *Newsgroup*

➤   `comp.sys.mac.games.misc:`   Macintosh games not covered in other groups. *Newsgroup*

➤   `comp.sys.mac.games.strategic:`   Strategy/planning games on the Macintosh. *Newsgroup*

3060   `comp.sys.mac.graphics`   Macintosh graphics: paint, draw, 3-D, CAD, animation. *Newsgroup*

3061   `comp.sys.mac.hardware.misc`   General Macintosh hardware topics not already covered. *Newsgroup*

3062   `comp.sys.mac.hardware.storage`   All forms of Macintosh storage hardware and media. *Newsgroup*

3063   `comp.sys.mac.hardware.video`   Video input and output hardware on the Macintosh. *Newsgroup*

3064   `comp.sys.mac.misc`   General discussions about the Apple Macintosh. *Newsgroup*

3065   `comp.sys.mac.oop.macapp3`   Version 3 of the MacApp object-oriented system. *Newsgroup*

3066   `comp.sys.mac.oop.misc`   Object-oriented programming issues on the Macintosh. *Newsgroup*

3067   `comp.sys.mac.oop.tcl`   Symantec's THINK Class Library for object programming. *Newsgroup*

3068   `comp.sys.mac.printing`   All about printing hardware and software on the Macintosh. *Newsgroup*

3069   `comp.sys.mac.programmer.codewarrior`   Macintosh programming using CodeWarrior. *Newsgroup*

3070   `comp.sys.mac.programmer.games`   Macintosh game programming. *Newsgroup*

3071   `comp.sys.mac.programmer.help`   Help with Macintosh programming. *Newsgroup*

3072   `comp.sys.mac.programmer.info`   Frequently requested information. *Moderated newsgroup*

3073   `comp.sys.mac.programmer.misc`   Other issues of Macintosh programming. *Newsgroup*

3074   `comp.sys.mac.programmer.tools`   Macintosh programming tools. *Newsgroup*

3075   **Comp.Sys.Mac.Programmers Digest:** A collection of the most interesting discussions from the Usenet newsgroup `comp.sys.mac.programmer` *Newsletter*
± `ftp://ftp.dartmouth.edu/pub/csmp-digest`
± `listserv@ens.fr` [body = SUBSCRIBE CSMP-DIGEST first-name last-name]
INFO `pottier@clipper.ens.fr` (Francois Pottier)
ARCHIVE `pottier@clipper.ens.fr` (Francois Pottier)
Gated: `comp.sys.mac.programme`
Frequency: irregular, roughly twice a week

3076   `comp.sys.mac.scitech`   Using the Macintosh in scientific and technological work. *Newsgroup*

3077   `comp.sys.mac.system`   Discussions of Macintosh system software. *Newsgroup*

3078   `comp.sys.mac.wanted`   Postings of "I want XYZ for my Mac". *Newsgroup*

➤   `comp.unix.aux:`   The version of Unix for Apple Macintosh computers. *Newsgroup*

3079   `demon.ip.support.mac`   Mac support issues. *Newsgroup*

3080   `dungeon.support.mac`   DNS Macintosh support area. *Newsgroup*

3081   `fj.binaries.mac`   Encoded Macintosh programs in binary. *Newsgroup*

3082   `fj.sys.mac`   Discussion about the Apple Macintosh and Lisa. *Newsgroup*

3083   `fj.sys.mac.programming`   Discussion about programming of Macintosh. *Newsgroup*

3084   `han.sys.mac`   Macintosh computer, Power Mac, MacOS. *Newsgroup*

➤   **Helix-L:** On Helix, the Macintosh relational database application. (See entry 2359 for full listing.)

➤   **Infini-D:** On Infini-D, a 3-D and animation software package for Macintosh. (See entry 2471 for full listing.)

3085   **Mac Media:** Macintosh-oriented variety magazine in DOCMaker format. *Magazine*
± INFO OWNER `taylorplus@aol.com` (Paul Taylor)
INFO OWNER `denisem@southwind.net` (Denise McNickle)
ARCHIVE `taylorplus@aol.com` (Paul Taylor)
Frequency: monthly

3086 Mac*Chat: Newsletter biased toward Macintosh computer users who are production-oriented professionals; no paid ads, unbiased reportage, questions and answers, shopping advice and more. *Newsletter*

ftp://info-mac/per/chat

± listserv@vm.temple.edu [body = SUBSCRIBE MACCHAT first-name last-name]

ARCHIVES

ftp://info-mac/per/chat

http://www.cts.com/browse/xxltony

Gated: comp.sys.mac.digests

Frequency: weekly

3087 MacAV-L: On Macintosh AV computers. *Mailing List*

± listserv@uafsysb.uark.edu [body = SUBSCRIBE MACAV-L first-name last-name]

OWNER cblih@comp.uark.edu (CB Lih)

ARCHIVES

http://www.csua.berkeley.edu/~jwang/AV/

listserv@uafsysb.uark.edu [body = INDEX MacAV-L]

FAQ http://www.csua.berkeley.edu/~jwang/AV/

➤   **MACCHAT:** For Mac*Chat: a Macintosh graphics newsletter. (See entry 2444 for full listing.)

3088 Macintosh Tips & Tricks: Macintosh Tips & Tricks is a news and productivity newsletter for Macintosh users.

http://www.intac.com/~gilesrd/mtt.html

INFO gilesrd@intac.com (Giles Road Press)

INFO http://www.intac.com/~gilesrd/

Comments: If you're interested in writing for Macintosh Tips & Tricks, write to the contact address. Put the word Guidelines in the message subject and writer's guidelines will be automatically forwarded back to you.

➤   **MACIRC-L:** On Macintosh Internet Relay Chat (IRC) client design. (See entry 2806 for full listing.)

3089 MacSense: The Macintosh E-Zine: Focusing on the mainstream Macintosh computer market, with in-depth product reviews. *Magazine*

http://tkb.colorado.edu/olm/zines.html

± mssubs@aol.com

INFO OWNER macsenseed.@eworld.com (Chris McVeigh)

Frequency: monthly

3090 misc.forsale.computers.mac-specific.cards.misc Macintosh expansion cards. *Newsgroup*

3091 misc.forsale.computers.mac-specific.cards.video Macintosh video cards. *Newsgroup*

3092 misc.forsale.computers.mac-specific.misc Other Macintosh equipment for sale. *Newsgroup*

3093 misc.forsale.computers.mac-specific.portables Portable Macintosh systems. *Newsgroup*

3094 misc.forsale.computers.mac-specific.systems Complete Macintosh systems for sale. *Newsgroup*

➤   **Monitor:** This program is a Macintosh application for downloading, storing, and graphing physiological data in real time. Requires System 7.0 or greater. (See entry 5107 for full listing.)

3095 okinawa.sys.mac Discussion about Macintosh. *Newsgroup*

➤   **think-c:** For users of the Think C and C++ compiler for the Macintosh. (See entry 3539 for full listing.)

3096 TidBITS: A newsletter for users of Macintosh computers. *Newsletter*

http://king.tidbits.com/

± listserv@ricevm1.rice.edu [body = SUBSCRIBE TIDBITS first-name last-name]

INFO info@tidbits.com

EDITOR OWNER ace@tidbits.com

ARCHIVE ftp://ftp.tidbits.com/pub/tidbits/issues/

Gated: comp.sys.mac.digest

3097 tnn.sys.mac Discussions about Macintosh computers. *Newsgroup*

➤ **The WP Mac News:** An electronic newsletter for users of WordPerfect for Macintosh. (See entry 3844 for full listing.)

MACINTOSH—SOFTWARE ARCHIVES

➤ <u>Games Domain</u>: A comprehensive games site; includes FAQs and pointers to games sites; covers all varieties of games. (See entry 6330 for full listing.)

3098 INFO-MAC: Questions and answers and details of new software posted to the info-mac archive (over 2GB of Mac software). *Digest, moderated*

`ftp://mirrors.aol.com/mirros/info-mac`

± `listserv@ricevm1.rice.edu` [body = SUBSCRIBE INFO-MAC first-name last-name]

INFO EDITOR OWNER `info-mac-request@sumex-aim.stanford.edu`

Gated: `comp.sys.mac.digest`

3099 Info-Mac: A massive repository of Macintosh software of all sorts. It is so popular that you can rarely get through to the main site itself, but one of the many mirrors is likely to be available. Remember to try and log on to the ones closest to you first.

`http://sumex-aim.stanford.edu/`

`ftp://sumex-aim.stanford.edu`

MIRRORS

`ftp://ftp.iij.ad.jp/pub/info-mac/` (Japan, IIJ)

`ftp://ftp.riken.go.jp/pub/info-mac/` (Japan, Riken)

`ftp://ftp.uni-stuttgart.de/pub/systems/mac/info-mac/` (Germany, Stuttgart)

`ftp://ftp.rrzn.uni-hannover.de/pub/info-mac/` (Germany, Hannover)

`ftp://info.nic.surfnet.nl/mirror-archive/software/info-mac/` (Netherlands, Surfnet)

`ftp://ftp.fenk.wau.nl/pub/mac/info-mac/` (Netherlands, WAU)

`ftp://ftp.pcvan.or.jp/pub/info-mac/` (Japan, pcvan)

`ftp://hwarang.postech.ac.kr/pub/mac/info-mac/` (Korea)

`ftp://ftp.edu.tw/Macintosh/info-mac/` (Taiwan, NCTU)

`ftp://ftp.center.osaka-u.ac.jp/info-mac/` (Japan, Osaka)

`ftp://ftp.univie.ac.at/mac/info-mac/` (Austria)

`ftp://ftp.ucs.ubc.ca/pub/mac/info-mac/` (Canada)

`ftp://ftp.francenet.fr/pub/miroirs/info-mac/` (Francenet)

`ftp://ftp.cs.tu-berlin.de/pub/mac/info-mac/` (Germany)

`ftp://ftp.funet.fi/pub/mac/info-mac/` (Finland)

`ftp://ftp.ibp.fr/pub/mac/info-mac/` (France, IBP)

`ftp://ftp.nus.sg/pub/mac/` (Singapore)

`ftp://ftp.info.au/micros/mac/info-mac/` (Australia)

`ftp://ftp.switch.ch/mirror/info-mac/` (Switzerland, SWITCH)

`ftp://ftp.dataplex.net/info-mac/` (USA, dataplex)

`ftp://ftp.orst.edu/pub/mirrors/sumex-aim.stanford.edu/mac/info-mac/` (USA, orst)

`ftp://ftp.pht.com/mirrors/info-mac/` (USA, Pacific HiTech)

`ftp://grind.isca.uiowa.edu/mac/infomac/` (USA, UIowa)

`ftp://mirrors.aol.com/pub/info-mac/` (USA, AOL)

`ftp://ftp.hawaii.edu/mirrors/info-mac/` (USA, Hawaii)

`ftp://wuarchive.wustl.edu/systems/mac/info-mac/` (USA, Wash Uni)

`ftp://hyperarchive.lcs.mit.edu/info-mac/` (USA, HyperArchive)

`ftp://ftp.sunet.se/pub/mac/info-mac/` (Sweden, sunet)

`ftp://src.doc.ic.ac.uk/packages/info-mac/` (UK)

`ftp://mirror.apple.com/mirrors/Info-Mac.Archive/` (USA, Apple)

```
ftp://uiarchive.cso.uiuc.edu/pub/systems/mac/info-mac (USA, UIUC)
ftp://ftp.uu.net/archive/systems/mac/info-mac/ (USA, UUNet, Virginia)
ftp://imftp.mgt.ncu.edu.tw/pub/mac/info-mac/ (Taiwan, NCU)
ftp://ftp.amug.org/pub/info-mac/ (USA, AMUG)
```

➤ **Inter-Links Downloads:** Inter-Links listing of software archives, all of which can be accessed via the numerous links provided. (See entry 3748 for full listing.)

➤ **SKY Online:** SKY Online is the premier source of astronomical news and information on the World Wide Web. It features excerpts from *Sky & Telescope* and *CCD Astronomy* magazines, along with a weekly news bulletin and celestial calendar, helpful tips for backyard skygazers, reviews of telescopes and accessories, downloadable BASIC programs to do astronomical calculations on your PC or Mac, and much more. (See entry 8939 for full listing.)

➤ **Washington University of St. Louis FTP Archive:** Huge software archive maintained by Washington University of St. Louis. (See entry 3752 for full listing.)

➤ **Wisconsin Primate Center Software Archive:** Wisconsin Regional Primate Research Center (University of Wisconsin-Madison). The archive's purpose is to provide a distribution point for software developed at WRPRC. (See entry 3753 for full listing.)

MAINFRAMES

3100 **alt.os.multics** 30 years old and going strong. *Newsgroup*

3101 **bit.listserv.c370-l** C/370 discussion list. *Newsgroup*

3102 **bit.listserv.ibm-main** IBM mainframe discussion list. *Newsgroup*

3103 **bit.listserv.opers-l** Mainframe operations discussion list. *Newsgroup*

3104 **bit.listserv.page-l** IBM 3812/3820 tips and problems discussion list. *Newsgroup*

3105 **CANDLE-L:** On Candle products, used for system-monitoring software for IBM mainframes. *Mailing List*
± listserv@ua1vm.ua.edu [body = SUBSCRIBE CANDLE-L first-name last-name]
INFO darren@ua1vm.ua.edu (Darren Evans-Young)
ARCHIVE listserv@ua1vm.ua.edu [body = INDEX CANDLE-L]

➤ **comp.protocols.ibm:** Networking with IBM mainframes. *Newsgroup*

3106 **comp.sys.cdc** Control Data Corporation computers (e.g., Cybers). *Newsgroup*

➤ **comp.unix.large:** Unix on mainframes and in large networks. *Newsgroup*

3107 **CPE:** On computer performance evaluation issues involved in the use of large-scale computing engines. *Mailing List*
± listserv@listserv.unc.edu [body = SUBSCRIBE CPE first-name last-name]
INFO OWNER lyman_ripperton@unc.edu (Lyman Ripperton)

3108 **DITTO-L:** For users of DITTO (Data Interfile Transfer, Testing, and Operations), an IBM product used to move data between various media. *Mailing List*
± listserv@vm.akh-wien.ac.at [body = SUBSCRIBE DITTO-L first-name last-name]
INFO OWNER christian.j.reichetzeder@awiimc12.imc.univie.ac.at (Christian Reichetzeder)
ARCHIVE listserv@vm.akh-wien.ac.at [body = INDEX DITTO-L]

3109 **IBM$KERM:** On IBM 370 Series Kermit development. *Mailing List*
± listserv@cuvmb.cc.columbia.edu [body = SUBSCRIBE IBM$KERM first-name last-name institution
 country]
INFO jchbn@cuvmb.cc.columbia.edu (John Chandler)
ARCHIVE listserv@cuvmb.cc.columbia.edu [body = INDEX IBM$KERM]

3110 **IBM-MAIN:** On IBM mainframes. *Digest & Reflector*
± listserv@ua1vm.ua.edu [body = SUBSCRIBE IBM-MAIN first-name last-name]
INFO darren@ua1vm.ua.edu (Darren Evans-Young)

ARCHIVE listserv@ua1vm.ua.edu [body = INDEX IBM-MAIN]
Gated: bit.listserv.ibm-main

3111 **OPERS-L:** On mainframe computer operations: careers, health concerns, tips, training. *Mailing List*
± listserv@vm1.cc.uakron.edu [body = SUBSCRIBE OPERS-L first-name last-name]
INFO olevert@akronvm.bitnet (Tom Evert)
ARCHIVE listserv@vm1.cc.uakron.edu [body = INDEX OPERS-L]
Gated: bit.listserv.opers-l

3112 **TSO-REXX:** On REXX as it pertains to its use in the IBM TSO environment.
INFO ts0007%ohstmvsa.bitnet@vm1.nodak.edu (Duane Weaver)
Gated: bit.listserv.tso-rexx

3113 **VECTOR-L:** For users of the IBM 3090 vector facility at any location. *Mailing List*
± listserv@listserv.unb.ca [body = SUBSCRIBE VECTOR-L first-name last-name]
INFO vector-l-request@listserv.unb.ca
ARCHIVE listserv@listserv.unb.ca [body = INDEX VECTOR-L]

3114 **YARDIMCI:** Discussions about IBM 3090 systems. *Mailing List*
INFO nur@trearn.bitnet (Nur Zincir)
Language: Turkish

MAINFRAMES—SOFTWARE ARCHIVES

➤ **Inter-Links Downloads:** Inter-Links listing of software archives, all of which can be accessed via the numerous links provided. (See entry 3748 for full listing.)

➤ **Washington University of St. Louis FTP Archive:** Huge software archive maintained by Washington University of St. Louis. (See entry 3752 for full listing.)

MICROPROCESSORS

3115 clari.nb.chips Newsbytes: microprocessors, microcontrollers, RAM. *Moderated newsgroup*

3116 comp.sys.arm The ARM processor architecture and support chips. *Newsgroup*

3117 comp.sys.ibm.as400.misc IBM AS/400 miscellaneous topics. *Newsgroup*

➤ comp.sys.ibm.pc.hardware.chips: Processor, cache, memory chips, etc. *Newsgroup*

3118 comp.sys.intel Discussions about Intel systems and parts. *Newsgroup*

3119 comp.sys.intel.ipsc310 Anything related to the Intel 310. *Newsgroup*

3120 comp.sys.m6809 Discussion about 6809s. *Newsgroup*

3121 comp.sys.m68k Discussion about 68ks. *Newsgroup*

3122 comp.sys.m68k.pc Discussion about 68k-based PCs. *Moderated newsgroup*

3123 comp.sys.m88k Discussion about 88k-based computers. *Newsgroup*

3124 comp.sys.mips Systems based on MIPS chips. *Newsgroup*

3125 comp.sys.nsc.32k National Semiconductor 32000 series chips. *Newsgroup*

3126 comp.sys.powerpc General PowerPC discussion. *Newsgroup*

3127 comp.sys.powerpc.advocacy Why the PowerPC is Good/Evil (delete one). *Newsgroup*

3128 comp.sys.powerpc.misc Miscellaneous questions about PowerPC processors. *Newsgroup*

3129 comp.sys.powerpc.tech Programming and architecture of PowerPC processors. *Newsgroup*

➤ **EDESIGN:** For professionals involved in the design and development of electronic circuitry. (See entry 9192 for full listing.)

3130 eunet.esprit.eurochip Esprit VLSI design—Eurochip. *Newsgroup*

3131 i860-users: For i860 chip users, primarily users of Stardent and OKI. *Mailing List*
± listproc@avs.com [body = SUBSCRIBE I860-USERS first-name last-name]
OWNER tasos@avs.com (Anastasios Kotsikonas)

3132 iijnet.mpu Discussions about Micro Processer Unit. *Newsgroup*

3133 iijnet.mpu.i486 Discussion of Intel 80486. *Newsgroup*

3134 iijnet.mpu.sparc Discussion of SPARC chips. *Newsgroup*

3135 POWER-L: For discussing the IBM RISC System/6000 family based on the Performance Optimization With Enhanced RISC (POWER) architecture. *Mailing List*
± listserv@vm1.nodak.edu [body = SUBSCRIBE POWER-L first-name last-name]
INFO OWNER hoag@plains.nodak.edu (Marty Hoag)
ARCHIVE listserv@vm1.nodak.edu [body = INDEX POWER-L]
Gated: bit.listserv.power-l

3136 tnn.mpu Discussions about microprocesser unit. *Newsgroup*

3137 tnn.mpu.i386 Discussions of Intel 80386. *Newsgroup*

3138 tnn.mpu.sparc Discussions of SPARC chip. *Newsgroup*

MIS

3139 CIS-L: On careers in information systems (IS). *Mailing List, moderated*
http://www.ubalt.edu/www/cis-l/home.html
± listserv@ube.ubalt.edu [body = SUBSCRIBE CIS-L first-name last-name]
± http://www.ubalt.edu/www/cis-l/cisfserv.html
OWNER earvaben@ube.ubalt.edu (Al Bento)
ARCHIVE listserv@ube.ubalt.edu [body = INDEX CIS-L]
Please Note: Subscription by approval only.

➤ **d.Comm:** An Internet-only magazine for network managers and other IT staff. The magazine covers all aspects of information technology from the PC on your desk to networking to communications. (See entry 9361 for full listing.)

➤ **IBSCG:** For members of International Business Schools Computing Association. (See entry 1700 for full listing.)

3140 INFOSYS: Electronic newsletter for information systems. *Newsletter*
http://www.rpi.edu/~okeefe/infosys/InfoSys/infosys.html
± listserv@american.edu [body = SUBSCRIBE INFOSYS first-name last-name]
EDITOR d.viehland@massey.ac.nz (Dennis W. Viehland)
OWNER gwelsh@american.edu (Greg Welsh)
POST infosys@american.edu

3141 misc.business.records-mgmt All aspects of professional records management. *Newsgroup*

MOBILE COMPUTING & PDAS

3142 biz.tadpole.sparcbook Discussions on the Sparcbook portable computers. *Newsgroup*

3143 clari.nb.pda Newsbytes: Personal Digital Assistants, handheld computers. *Moderated newsgroup*

➤ **clari.nb.pen:** Newsbytes: pen-based computing devices, software. *Moderated newsgroup*

3144 comp.binaries.newton Apple Newton binaries, sources, books, etc. *Moderated newsgroup*

3145 comp.binaries.psion Binaries for the range of Psion computers. *Moderated newsgroup*

3146 comp.os.magic-cap Everything about General Magic's Magic Cap OS. *Newsgroup*

3147 comp.sys.handhelds Handheld computers and programmable calculators. *Newsgroup*

3148 comp.sys.laptops Laptop (portable) computers. *Newsgroup*

3149 `comp.sys.mac.portables` Discussion particular to laptop Macintoshes. *Newsgroup*

3150 `comp.sys.newton.announce` Newton information posts. *Moderated newsgroup*

3151 `comp.sys.newton.misc` Miscellaneous discussion about Newton systems. *Newsgroup*

3152 `comp.sys.newton.programmer` Discussion of Newton software development. *Newsgroup*

3153 `comp.sys.palmtops` Super-powered calculators in the palm of your hand. *Newsgroup*

➤ `comp.sys.pen:` Interacting with computers through pen gestures. *Newsgroup*

3154 `comp.sys.psion` Discussion about PSION personal computers and organizers. *Newsgroup*

3155 `fj.binaries.x68000` Encoded free software for SHARP X68000. *Moderated newsgroup*

3156 `fj.sys.zaurus` Discussion on Zaurus palmtop computers. *Newsgroup*

3157 `misc.forsale.computers.pc-specific.portables` Portable PC systems. *Newsgroup*

3158 **NewtNews:** On the Apple Newton and related technologies. *Newsletter*
   `ftp://ftp.io.com/pub/usr/btorres/NewtNews`
   `ftp://newton.uiowa.edu/pub/newton/misc/Newton_News`
   `http://www.ridgecrest.ca.us/NewtNews/NN_top.html`
   ± `majordomo@tristero.io.com` [body = `subscribe newtnews`]
   INFO `newtnews@pobox.com`
   ARCHIVES
   `ftp://ftp.io.com/pub/usr/btorres/NewtNews`
   `ftp://newton.uiowa.edu/pub/newton/misc/Newton_News`
   Gated: `comp.sys.newton.misc`
   Frequency: weekly

3159 `tnn.sys.palmtops` Discussions about computers in the palm. *Newsgroup*

3160 `tnn.sys.zaurus` Discussions of Sharp ZAURUS. *Newsgroup*

3161 **ultralite-list:** For users or potential users of the original NEC UltraLite PC1701 and PC1702 computers. *Mailing List*
   ± `majordomo@best.com` [body = `subscribe ultralite-list` e-mail-address]
   INFO `owner-ultralite-list@lists.best.com` (Brian Smithson)
   ARCHIVE `http://www.grot.com/ultralite/`

3162 **zoomer-list:** On GEOS-based personal digital assistants (PDAs) such as the Zoomer, a personal digital assistant produced by Tandy, Casio, et al. *Mailing List*
   `http://www.grot.com/zoomer/`
   ± `majordomo@best.com` [body = `subscribe zoomer-list` e-mail-address]
   INFO `owner-zoomer-list@lists.best.com`
   OWNER `brian@grot.com` (Brian Smithson)
   ARCHIVE `http://www.grot.com/zoomer/zoomer-list/`

MODEMS

3163 `biz.comp.telebit` Support of the Telebit modems. *Newsgroup*

3164 `biz.comp.telebit.netblazer` The Telebit Netblazer. *Newsgroup*

3165 `comp.dcom.modems` Data communications hardware and software. *Newsgroup*

➤ `comp.sys.ibm.pc.hardware.comm:` Modems and communication cards for the PC. *Newsgroup*

3166 `fj.net.isdn` The Integrated Services Digital Network (ISDN). *Newsgroup*

3167 `fj.net.modems.fax` Fax-modem hardware, software, and protocols. *Newsgroup*

3168 `iijnet.dcom.modem` Discussion of modems. *Newsgroup*

3169 `misc.forsale.computers.modems` Modems for sale and wanted. *Newsgroup*

3170 `relcom.fido.ru.modem` Inter-network discussion on modems. *Newsgroup*

3171 `sanet.modems` Anything concerning modems and telecom hardware. *Newsgroup*

3172 `tnn.dcom.modems` Discussions about modems. *Newsgroup*

3173 `tnn.support.hucom.modem` Information for MICROCOM modems. *Newsgroup*

MUDS & MOOS

➤ **Games Domain:** A comprehensive games site; includes FAQs and pointers to games sites; covers all varieties of games. (See entry 6330 for full listing.)

3174 **MUD info:** Multiple User Dialogue/Dimension/Dungeon FAQs, lists, information, collections, servers, archives, and newsgroups, by Lydia Leong.

`http://www.cis.upenn.edu/~lwl/mudinfo.html`

3175 `alt.fan.furry.muck` FurryMUCK and other anthropomorphic MU*s. *Newsgroup*

3176 `alt.mud.island` The Island Multi-User Dungeon. *Newsgroup*

3177 `alt.mud.programming` Programming in text-based, virtual-reality environments. *Newsgroup*

3178 **Belior Rising MUSH:** Belior Rising is a small MUSH (Multiple User Shared Hallucination) based on Anne McCaffrey's Dragonriders of Pern series. It is a venue for those who love the world and for those who love to role-play.

`http://www.teleport.com/~voyager/br`
`telnet://brazil-nut.enmu.edu`
INFO `jbare@radix.net`

➤ **Internet Public Library:** An Internet-based library with reference, youth, teen, and librarian services sections. It also has a MOO and a reading room, a classroom, and an exhibit hall. (See entry 5741 for full listing.)

3179 **LambdaMOO:** One of the largest and most well-developed MOOs, LambdaMOO was created by Pavel Curtis (originator of MOOs themselves) at Xerox PARC.

`telnet://lambda.parc.xerox.com:8888`
INFO `lambda@parc.xerox.com`

➤ **Lysator Archives:** Archives of Lysator, an academic computer society at Linkoping University in Linkoping, Sweden. It includes the files of "Project Runeberg," a collection of free electronic texts in Scandinavian languages; MUD information; an extensive science-fiction archive; information about Sweden, Linkoping, and Linkoping University; and much more. (See entry 7617 for full listing.)

➤ **MediaMOO:** This MOO is run by researchers at the MIT Media Lab. It is a professional community for media researchers—a place for people interested in the future of media to network and collaborate. You must be doing some form of media research to become a member. (See entry 4039 for full listing.)

3180 **MOO Papers:** Pavel Curtis' collection of MU* papers.

`ftp://ftp.parc.xerox.com/pub/MOO/papers/`

3181 `rec.games.mud.admin` Administrative issues of multiuser dungeons. *Newsgroup*

3182 `rec.games.mud.announce` Informational articles about multiuser dungeons. *Moderated newsgroup*

3183 `rec.games.mud.diku` All about DikuMuds. *Newsgroup*

3184 `rec.games.mud.lp` Discussions of the LPMUD computer role-playing game. *Newsgroup*

3185 `rec.games.mud.misc` Various aspects of multiuser computer games. *Newsgroup*

3186 `rec.games.mud.tiny` Discussion about Tiny MUDs, like MUSH, MUSE, and MOO. *Newsgroup*

MULTIMEDIA

➤ **MEGA-MEDIA LINKS index @ OMNIBUS:EYE:** A searchable index of thousands of film/TV/radio/multimedia/new-media/cinema links subcategorized into over 60 helpful areas. (See entry 6055 for full listing.)

3187 `alt.binaries.multimedia` Sound, text, and graphics data rolled in one. *Newsgroup*

3188 `alt.binaries.multimedia.d` Discussion of digitized animation files. *Newsgroup*

3189 `alt.binaries.sounds.d` Sounding off. *Newsgroup*

3190 `alt.binaries.sounds.utilities` Sound utilities. *Newsgroup*

3191 `alt.cd-rom.reviews` Reviews of various published things available on CD-ROM. *Newsgroup*

➤ `alt.computer.workshop.live`: Interactive TV. *Newsgroup*

3192 `aus.computers.cdrom` CD-ROMs and associated computer topics. *Newsgroup*

➤ **Biomedical Multimedia Unit:** The home page of the Biomedical Multimedia Unit, School of Medicine, University of Melbourne. Contains information and resources relating to multimedia education in the medical sciences. (See entry 4827 for full listing.)

3193 **CD-ROM Online:** Reviews of new CD-ROM releases. *E-Zine*
± OWNER`cdrmag@nsimultimedia.com` [body = first-name last-name e-mail-address (Also include any topics that may interest you, and how you found out about the magazine.)]
INFO `http://www.li.net/~nsi/cdrom`
Frequency: monthly

➤ **CD-ROM Updater:** Information about new CD-ROM products, reviews, news, how to publish on CD-ROM, conferences, events. Limited to 100K per issue. (See entry 3783 for full listing.)

➤ **CDROM-L:** On uses of CD-ROM. (See entry 3785 for full listing.)

3194 `comp.ivideodisc` Interactive videodiscs—uses, potential, etc. *Newsgroup*

➤ `comp.mail.multi-media`: Multimedia Mail. *Newsgroup*

3195 `comp.multimedia` Interactive multimedia technologies of all kinds. *Newsgroup*

3196 `comp.music.midi` Computers as components in MIDI music systems. *Newsgroup*

3197 `comp.music.misc` Miscellaneous use of computers in music. *Newsgroup*

➤ `comp.os.ms-windows.programmer.multimedia`: Multimedia programming. *Newsgroup*

➤ `comp.publish.cdrom.hardware`: Hardware used in publishing with CD-ROMs. *Newsgroup*

3198 `comp.publish.cdrom.multimedia` Software for multimedia authoring and publishing. *Newsgroup*

3199 `comp.sys.amiga.multimedia` Animations, video, and multimedia. *Newsgroup*

3200 `iijnet.multimedia` Discussions about multimedia. *Newsgroup*

➤ **The Interactive Patient:** This teaching tool for physicians, residents, and medical students offers a case with a chief complaint to the user who then has to interact with the patient requesting additional history, performing a physical exam, and reviewing laboratory data and X-rays. (See entry 4832 for full listing.)

3201 **metacard-list:** On MetaCard, an application development system similar to HyperCard, for UNIX/X11/Motif environment. *Mailing List*
`http://www.grot.com/metacard/`
± `majordomo@best.com` [body = SUBSCRIBE METACARD-LIST e-mail-address]
OWNER `owner-metacard-list@lists.best.com` (Brian Smithson)
ARCHIVE `http://www.grot.com/metacard/`

➤ `misc.education.multimedia`: Multimedia for education. *Moderated newsgroup*

3202 **mkdist: Music Kit Distribution Mailing List:** On the Music Kit, an object-oriented software package for playing music and sound-related tasks under NeXTStep (available by FTP from `ccrma-ftp.stanford.edu`). *Mailing List*
`http://www-ccrma.stanford.edu/`
± INFO `mkdist-request@ccrma.stanford.edu`
± `listproc@ccrma.stanford.edu`
ARCHIVE `ftp://ccrma-ftp.stanford.edu`

➤ **Netcast Global Communications:** Internet broadcasting, consultation, and audio/video information provider. (See entry 6066 for full listing.)

➤ **Online Electronic Publishing Collection:** Includes information on file formats, text readers and image viewers, audio and video players, multimedia and virtual reality publishing standards, and main languages. Also includes an index of electronic books and documents available online. (See entry 2419 for full listing.)

➤ `rec.arts.int-fiction:` Discussions about interactive fiction. *Newsgroup*

3203 **The Sound Site Newsletter:** On PC sound and multimedia. Includes tips on sound configurations, where to get neat sound files, programming tips, sound programs, sound card release notes, and much more. *Newsletter*

`ftp://sound.usach.cl/pub/sound/newsletters`

`ftp://garbo.uwasa.fi/(pc.sound) soundXX.zip`

`ftp://oak.oakland.edu/(pub/sound)soundXX.zip`

INFO `davek@pixi.com` (Dave Komatsu)

INFO `davek@kestrok.com` (Dave Komatsu)

ARCHIVES

`ftp://sound.usach.cl/pub/sound/newsletters`

`ftp://garbo.uwasa.fi/(pc.sound) soundXX.zip`

`ftp://oak.oakland.edu/(pub/sound)soundXX.zip`

Frequency: quarterly

3204 **SunSITE multimedia Archives:** Software for manipulation of sound and video with computers, including a large collection of Chinese music.

`ftp://sunsite.unc.edu/pub/multimedia/`

INFO `ftpkeeper@sunsite.unc.edu`

3205 `tnn.multimedia.cdrom` Discussions about CD-ROM. *Newsgroup*

3206 `|T|E|L|E|C|I|N|E|:` The journal of new-media authoring in the digital domain. *Magazine*

`http://www.rtvf.nwu.edu/Omnibus/TelecineTOC.html`

INFO OWNER `cwebbyoung@nwu.edu` (C. Webb Young)

ARCHIVE `http://www.rtvf.nwu.edu/Omnibus/TelecineTOC.html`

Frequency: quarterly

NETWORKING

3207 `alt.comp.fsp` A file-transport protocol. *Newsgroup*

3208 `bit.listserv.arie-l` RLG Ariel Document Transmission group. *Newsgroup*

3209 `bit.listserv.edi-l` Electronic data interchange issues. *Newsgroup*

3210 `bit.listserv.x400-l` X.400 protocol list. *Newsgroup*

3211 **Carnegie Mellon University - Campus Networking Web Pages:** This is a Web site dedicated to campus networking issues at Carnegie Mellon University. It includes helpful hints about computer network design, resources at Carnegie Mellon University, and operating Windows 95, to name a few topics.

`http://www.net.cmu.edu/`

INFO `dc0m+www@andrew.cmu.edu`

3212 **Carnegie Mellon University Networking Archive:** This site is informally maintained by the Network Development (NetDev) staff at Carnegie-Mellon University in Pittsburgh, Pennsylvania, USA. The site's primary purpose is to distribute free networking software and related materials written by the NetDev group.

`http://www.net.cmu.edu/netdev`

`ftp://ftp.net.cmu.edu`

INFO `dc0m+@andrew.cmu.edu`

Comments: This is not a large general archive site for CMU, but rather a small casually-maintained site for the NetDev group (a small specific group of programmers). Everything is subject to change without notice including the site's very existence. Most files are in Unix tar format and should be transferred using binary representation.

➤ **CEARCH: Cisco Educational Archives:** Education archive; lists a variety of resources about school connectivity to the Internet as well as a catalog of educational resources organized by classroom and subject. (See entry 4493 for full listing.)

3213 **CILEA:** Italian network resources.
gopher://imicilea.cilea.it
INFO webmaster@cilea.it

3214 `clari.tw.computers.networking` Computer networking products. *Moderated newsgroup*

3215 `clari.tw.computers.networking.releases` News releases: computer networking. *Moderated newsgroup*

➤ **CNET-OP:** Information about CINECA (Italian research organization) and its networks (CINECAnet/GARR). (See entry 9450 for full listing.)

3216 **COMMO:** On Commo, a DOS-based communications program. *Mailing List*
± listserv@server.nlbbs.com [body = SUBSCRIBE COMMO first-name last-name]
OWNER cboldt@server.nlbbs.com

3217 `comp.client-server` Topics relating to client/server technology. *Newsgroup*

➤ `comp.dcom.telecom:` *Telecommunications Digest. Moderated newsgroup*

3218 `comp.networks.noctools.announce` Information and announcements about NOC tools. *Moderated newsgroup*

3219 `comp.networks.noctools.bugs` Bug reports and fixes for NOC tools. *Newsgroup*

3220 `comp.networks.noctools.d` Discussion about NOC tools. *Newsgroup*

3221 `comp.networks.noctools.submissions` New NOC tools submissions. *Newsgroup*

3222 `comp.networks.noctools.tools` Descriptions of available NOC tools. *Moderated newsgroup*

3223 `comp.networks.noctools.wanted` Requests for NOC tools/wanted software. *Newsgroup*

3224 `comp.org.fidonet` FidoNews digest, official news of FidoNet Association. *Moderated newsgroup*

3225 `comp.os.ms-windows.apps.comm` MS Windows communication applications. *Newsgroup*

➤ `comp.os.ms-windows.networking.misc:` Windows and other networks. *Newsgroup*

➤ `comp.os.ms-windows.networking.ras:` Windows RAS networking. *Newsgroup*

➤ `comp.os.ms-windows.networking.windows:` Windows' built-in networking. *Newsgroup*

➤ `comp.os.ms-windows.programmer.networks:` Network programming. *Newsgroup*

➤ `comp.os.os2.comm:` Modem/fax hardware/drivers/applications/utilities under OS/2. *Newsgroup*

➤ `comp.os.os2.networking.misc:` Miscellaneous networking issues of OS/2. *Newsgroup*

3226 `comp.protocols.ibm` Networking with IBM mainframes. *Newsgroup*

3227 `comp.protocols.iso.x400` X.400 mail protocol discussions. *Newsgroup*

3228 `comp.protocols.iso.x400.gateway` X.400 mail gateway discussions. *Moderated newsgroup*

3229 `comp.protocols.nfs` Discussion about the Network File System protocol. *Newsgroup*

3230 `comp.protocols.pcnet` Topics related to PCNET (a personal computer network). *Newsgroup*

3231 `comp.protocols.smb` SMB file sharing protocol and Samba SMB server/client. *Newsgroup*

3232 `comp.soft-sys.dce` The Distributed Computing Environment (DCE). *Newsgroup*

➤ **CYBERIA-L:** On the law and policy of computer networks. (See entry 5536 for full listing.)

➤ **DANTE IN PRINT:** Publication series containing all papers and articles published by or on behalf of DANTE (Delivery of Advanced Network Technology to Europe, Ltd.). It includes an overview of developments in DANTE services and other activities, all in the area of European research networking. (See entry 9549 for full listing.)

3233 **DECMCC-L:** On DEC DECmcc (a network monitoring tool from DEC) and related software. *Mailing List*
± listserv@american.edu [body = SUBSCRIBE DECMCC-L first-name last-name]

INFO sloane@kuhub.cc.ukans.edu

Gated: vmsnet.networks.management.decmcc

3234 **fj.net.misc** Discussions on networks in general. *Newsgroup*

3235 **fj.net.uucp** UUCP configuration and administration. *Newsgroup*

3236 **I-KERMIT:** Kermit software announcements. *Mailing List*
http://www.columbia.edu/kermit/
ftp://kermit.columbia.edu/kermit/
± listserv@cuvmb.cc.columbia.edu [body = SUBSCRIBE I$KERMIT first-name last-name]
± listserv@listserv.rediris.es [body = SUBSCRIBE I-KERMIT first-name last-name]
± listserv@vtvm1.cc.vt.edu [body = SUBSCRIBE I-KERMIT first-name last-name]
± listserv@uga.cc.uga.edu [body = SUBSCRIBE INFO-KERMIT first-name last-name]
INFO fdc@watsun.cc.columbia.edu (Frank da Cruz)
INFO cmg@watsun.cc.columbia.edu (Christine Gianone)
ARCHIVE ftp://kermit.columbia.edu/kermit/e/
FAQ ftp://kermit.columbia.edu/kermit/e/faq.txt
Gated: comp.protocols.kermit.misc
Comments: The unmoderated newsgroup comp.protocols.kermit.misc is the preferred, and more active, forum for discussion of Kermit software and protocol.

3237 **IBMDCE-L:** On DCE cells, especially with IBM components. *Mailing List*
± listserv@ucsbvm.ucsb.edu [body = SUBSCRIBE IBMDCE-L first-name last-name]
OWNER dwight@ucsbvm.ucsb.edu (Dwight McCann)

3238 **The Kermit Project at Columbia University:** Communications software for just about every type of computer and operating system on the planet.
http://www.columbia.edu/kermit/
ftp://kermit.columbia.edu/kermit/
kermit@kermit.columbia.edu
INFO kermit@columbia.edu (infobot)
INFO fdc@columbia.edu
Comments: Other Kermit resources include a newsgroup: comp.protocols.kermit.misc and Journal, "Kermit News" (http://www.columbia.edu/kermit/news.html)

3239 **comp.protocols.kermit.announce** Kermit announcements. *Moderated newsgroup*

3240 **comp.protocols.kermit.misc** Kermit protocol and software. *Newsgroup*

3241 **Matrix Maps Quarterly:** Maps of computer networks graphically showing features that are difficult to present with text or numbers alone. *E-Journal*
ftp://ftp.mids.org
gopher://gopher.mids.org
http://www.mids.org/
± mids-order@mids.org
INFO mids-help@mids.org (Eric McKinney)
ARCHIVE ftp://ftp.mids.org/matrix/maps/mmq
Frequency: quarterly
Price: $400, four issues, paper; $300, four issues, online

3242 **NETV-L:** On IBM's NETView. *Mailing List*
± listserv@vm.marist.edu [body = SUBSCRIBE NETV-L first-name last-name]
INFO netv-l-request@vm.marist.edu
ARCHIVE listserv@vm.marist.edu [body = INDEX NETV-L]

➤ **The Network Startup Resource Center:** This site contains information about: networking in the developing world, low-cost networking tools, general computer networking information, and networking tips and frequently asked questions. You can search for networking solutions and information by country. (See entry 9647 for full listing.)

3243 `relcom.fido.ru.networks` Inter-network discussion of global nets. *Newsgroup*

➤ `sanet.tech:` Networking in South Africa. *Moderated newsgroup*

3244 `tnn.dcom` Discussions about data communications. *Newsgroup*

3245 `tnn.mail.uucp` Discussion of UUCP network and its mail system. *Newsgroup*

3246 `vmsnet.networks.misc` General networking topics not covered elsewhere. *Newsgroup*

NETWORKING—ADMINISTRATION

3247 **BILLING:** For discussion of principles and techniques for reporting and billing for the use of computer resources. *Mailing List*
± `listserv@hearn.nic.surfnet.nl` [body = SUBSCRIBE BILLING first-name last-name]
INFO `vanhoboken@rc.tudelft.nl`
ARCHIVE `listserv@hearn.nic.surfnet.nl`
Gated: `bit.listserv.billing`

3248 `bit.listserv.snamgt-1` SNA Network Management discussion. *Newsgroup*

3249 `can.uucp` Canadian UUCP problems. *Newsgroup*

3250 `can.uucp.maps` Canadian UUCP maps are posted here. *Moderated newsgroup*

➤ **Carnegie Mellon University Networking Archive:** This site is informally maintained by the Network Development (NetDev) staff at Carnegie-Mellon University in Pittsburgh, Pennsylvania, USA. The site's primary purpose is to distribute free networking software and related materials written by the NetDev group. (See entry 3212 for full listing.)

➤ **CERT Coordination Center:** All about Internet and computer security. Includes advisories and bulletins on security events, technical tips for system administrators, and more. (See entry 3675 for full listing.)

3251 `comp.admin.policy` Discussions of site administration policies. *Newsgroup*

3252 `comp.dcom.net-management` Network management methods and applications. *Newsgroup*

3253 `comp.dcom.servers` Selecting and operating data communications servers. *Newsgroup*

3254 `comp.dcom.sys.cisco` Information on Cisco routers and bridges. *Newsgroup*

3255 `comp.dcom.sys.wellfleet` Wellfleet bridge and router systems hardware and software. *Newsgroup*

3256 `comp.os.ms-windows.nt.admin.networking` Windows NT network administration. *Newsgroup*

➤ `comp.os.msdos.mail-news:` Administering mail and network news systems under MS-DOS. *Newsgroup*

3257 `comp.protocols.snmp` The Simple Network Management Protocol. *Newsgroup*

➤ **d.Comm:** An Internet-only magazine for network managers and other IT staff. The magazine covers all aspects of information technology from the PC on your desk to networking to communications. (See entry 9361 for full listing.)

3258 **depot:** On the "depot" software-installation framework, a strategy for installing software packages that facilitates sharing across hardware platforms and corporate organizations. *Mailing List*
± `depot-request@merlin.cnri.reston.va.us`
OWNER `depot-owner@merlin.cnri.reston.va.us`

3259 **DRP-L:** On disaster recovery plans for computing services. *Mailing List*
± `listserv@vm.marist.edu` [body = SUBSCRIBE DRP-L first-name last-name]
INFO `drp-l-request@vm.marist.edu`
ARCHIVE `listserv@vm.marist.edu` [body = INDEX DRP-L]

➤ **LWUsers:** For users of LANWatch, a local area network analyzer for IBM compatibles. (See entry 3286 for full listing.)

3260 NIR-IT-L: For computer network managers in Italy. *Mailing List*

± `listserv@itocsivm.csi.it` [body = SUB NIR-IT-L first-name last-name]

OWNER `metitier@itocsivm.csi.it` (Fabio Metitieri)

Language: Italian

3261 POP: The list is primarily for system administrators attempting to find, install, and run POP, IMAP, and similar protocol servers on their servers. *Mailing List*

± `pop-request@jhunix.hcf.jhu.edu` [body = subscribe pop]

INFO `andy@jhunix.hcf.jhu.edu` (Andy S. Poling)

ARCHIVES

`ftp://jhunix.hcf.jhu.edu/mailing_lists/pop`

`gopher://jhunix.hcf.jhu.edu/11/mailing-lists/pop`

POST `pop@jhunix.hcf.jhu.edu`

3262 scruz.sysops For system operators in the Santa Cruz, California (USA) area. *Newsgroup*

3263 SNAMGT-L: On SNA network management. *Mailing List*

± `listserv@umrvmb.umr.edu` [body = SUBSCRIBE SNAMGT-L first-name last-name]

INFO `snamgt-l-request@umrvmb.umr.edu`

ARCHIVE `listserv@umrvmb.umr.edu` [body = INDEX SNAMGT-L]

➤ **SSW-L:** About Soft-Switch products. (See entry 2410 for full listing.)

3264 vmsnet.networks.management.misc Other network management solutions. *Newsgroup*

NETWORKING—GROUPWARE

3265 Groupware Yellow Pages: Pointers to groupware resources, groupware book reviews, and related groups and organizations.

`http://www.consensus.com/groupware/`

INFO `webmaster@consensus.com`

3266 comp.groupware Software and hardware for shared interactive environments. *Newsgroup*

3267 comp.groupware.groupwise Novell's Groupwise product (Wordperfect Office). *Newsgroup*

3268 comp.groupware.lotus-notes.admin Lotus Notes system administration. *Newsgroup*

3269 comp.groupware.lotus-notes.apps Application software for Lotus Notes. *Newsgroup*

3270 comp.groupware.lotus-notes.misc Lotus Notes-related discussions. *Newsgroup*

3271 comp.groupware.lotus-notes.programmer Programming for Lotus Notes. *Newsgroup*

3272 GSS-L: For group support systems researchers, covering research, products, facilitation, and conferences. *Mailing List*

`http://www.cba.uga.edu/groupware/groupware.html` (Groupware Central)

± `listserv@uga.cc.uga.edu` [body = SUBSCRIBE GSS-L first-name last-name]

INFO `adennis@uga.cc.uga.edu` (Alan Dennis)

OWNER `rwatson@uga.cc.uga.edu` (Richard Watson)

ARCHIVE `listserv@uga.cc.uga.edu` [body = INDEX GSS-L]

NETWORKING—LOCAL AREA NETWORKS

➤ **alt.winsock:** Windows Sockets. *Newsgroup*

➤ **alt.winsock.programming:** Programming Windows Sockets. *Newsgroup*

3273 bit.listserv.banyan-l Banyan Vines Network Software Discussions. *Newsgroup*

3274 CDLAN: On integrating CD-ROMs into LANs. *Mailing List*

± `maiser@zb.ub.uni-dortmund.de`

OWNER michael.schaarwaechter@ub.uni-dortmund.de (Michael Schaarwaechter)

ARCHIVE http://www.ub.uni-dortmund.de/Katalog/Sonst/EDV.html#LIS

FAQ http://www.ub.uni-dortmund.de/Katalog/Sonst/EDV.html#LIS

Language: German & English

3275 **CDROMLAN:** On using CD-ROMs on local area networks. *Mailing List*
± listserv@idbsu.idbsu.edu [body = SUBSCRIBE CDROMLAN first-name last-name]
INFO alileste@idbsu.idbsu.edu (Dan Lester)
INFO dlester@bsu.idbsu.edu
ARCHIVE listserv@idbsu.idbsu.edu [body = INDEX CDROMLAN]

3276 `clari.nb.network` Newsbytes: LANs and non-Internet networking. *Moderated newsgroup*

3277 `comp.dcom.lans.ethernet` Discussions of the Ethernet/IEEE 802.3 protocols. *Newsgroup*

3278 `comp.dcom.lans.fddi` Discussions of the FDDI protocol suite. *Newsgroup*

3279 `comp.dcom.lans.misc` Local area networks' hardware and software. *Newsgroup*

3280 `comp.dcom.lans.token-ring` Installing and using token ring networks. *Newsgroup*

3281 `comp.protocols.appletalk` Appletalk hardware and software. *Newsgroup*

3282 `fj.lan` Local area network hardware and software. *Newsgroup*

3283 `fj.net.fddi` The FDDI protocol suite. *Newsgroup*

3284 `fj.net.media.ethernet` The Ethernet/IEEE 802.3 protocols. *Newsgroup*

3285 **LANWORKS:** On Digital's PATHWORKS software. *Mailing List*
± listserv@ubvm.cc.buffalo.edu [body = SUBSCRIBE LANWORKS first-name last-name]
OWNER beckerja@sa.sunysysadmin.edu (Jim Becker)

3286 **LWUsers:** For users of LANWatch, a local area network analyzer for IBM compatibles. *Digest & Reflector*
± listserv@vm1.nodak.edu [body = SUBSCRIBE LWUSERS first-name last-name]
INFO OWNER hoag@plains.nodak.edu (Marty Hoag)
ARCHIVE listserv@vm1.nodak.edu [body = INDEX LWUsers]

3287 `relcom.lan` Inter-network discussion on local area networks. *Newsgroup*

3288 `relcom.lan.prog` FIDOnet, programming for networks. *Newsgroup*

3289 `relcom.lan.wanted` Programs for LAN wanted/offered. *Newsgroup*

➤ **WINSOCK-L:** On Windows Socket (Winsock) related and based applications; associated FTP site. (See entry 3324 for full listing.)

➤ **WinSock-L-Announce:** For announcements of uploads to the WinSock-L software archive (See entry 3325 for full listing.)

NETWORKING—NETWARE

3290 `bit.listserv.novell` Novell LAN interest group. *Newsgroup*

3291 `comp.os.netware.announce` Netware announcements. *Moderated newsgroup*

3292 `comp.os.netware.connectivity` Connectivity products (TCP/IP, SAA, NFS, MAC). *Newsgroup*

3293 `comp.os.netware.misc` General Netware topics. *Newsgroup*

3294 `comp.os.netware.security` Netware security issues. *Newsgroup*

3295 **NWP:** For NetWare programmers. *Mailing List*
± listproc@lists.pipex.com [body = SUBSCRIBE NWP first-name last-name]
INFO admin-nwp@lists.pipex.com
INFO listmaster@lists.pipex.com (technical problems)

NETWORKING—TCP/IP

3296 `biz.dec.ip` IP networking on DEC machines. *Newsgroup*

3297 `comp.dcom.lans.hyperchannel` Hyperchannel networks within an IP network. *Newsgroup*

3298 `comp.os.ms-windows.networking.tcp-ip` Windows and TCP/IP networking. *Newsgroup*

➤ `comp.os.os2.networking.tcp-ip`: TCP/IP under OS/2. *Newsgroup*

➤ `comp.protocols.ppp`: Discussion of the Internet Point to Point Protocol. *Newsgroup*

3299 `comp.protocols.tcp-ip` TCP and IP network protocols. *Newsgroup*

3300 `comp.protocols.tcp-ip.domains` Topics related to domain style names. *Newsgroup*

3301 `comp.protocols.tcp-ip.ibmpc` TCP/IP for IBM(-like) personal computers. *Newsgroup*

3302 `han.comp.internet` Technical aspects of Internet and TCP/IP protocols. *Newsgroup*

3303 **IBMTCP-L:** All about IBM TCP/IP software products for VM, MVS, OS/2, and for associated IBM TCP/IP hardware. *Mailing List*

± `listserv@pucc.princeton.edu` [body = SUBSCRIBE IBMTCP-L first-name last-name]

INFO `gettes@princeton.edu` (Michael Gettes)

ARCHIVE `listserv@pucc.princeton.edu` [body = INDEX IBMTCP-L]

Gated: `bit.listserv.ibmtcp-l`

3304 `relcom.tcpip` TCP/IP protocols and their implementation. *Newsgroup*

3305 **SNSTCP-L:** On Interlink SNS/TCP access products for MVS. *Mailing List*

INFO `snstcp-l-request@list.nih.gov` (Roger Fajman)

ARCHIVE `listserv@list.nih.gov`

3306 `trumpet.announce` Announcements of new releases of Trumpet programs. *Newsgroup*

3307 `trumpet.bugs` Reporting and discussion of bugs or "features". *Newsgroup*

3308 `trumpet.feedback` Feedback on Trumpet programs. *Newsgroup*

3309 `trumpet.questions` Questions and general discussion of Trumpet programs. *Newsgroup*

3310 `uk.jips` Discussion about JANET IP service matters. *Newsgroup*

3311 `vmsnet.networks.tcp-ip.cmu-tek` CMU-TEK TCP/IP package, gatewayed to `cmu-openvms-ip@drycas.club.cc.cmu.edu`. *Newsgroup*

3312 `vmsnet.networks.tcp-ip.misc` Other TCP/IP solutions for VMS. *Newsgroup*

3313 `vmsnet.networks.tcp-ip.multinet` TGV's Multinet TCP/IP, gatewayed to info-multinet. *Newsgroup*

3314 `vmsnet.networks.tcp-ip.tcpware` Discussion of Process Software's TCPWARE TCP/IP software. *Newsgroup*

3315 `vmsnet.networks.tcp-ip.ucx` DEC's VMS/Ultrix Connection (or TCP/IP services for VMS)product. *Newsgroup*

3316 `vmsnet.networks.tcp-ip.wintcp` The Wollongong Group's WIN-TCP TCP/IP software. *Newsgroup*

3317 **WINTCP-L:** On the Wollongong WIN/TCP (TCP/IP for VMS) software package. *Mailing List*

± `listserv@ubvm.cc.buffalo.edu` [body = SUBSCRIBE WINTCP-L first-name last-name]

INFO `wintcp-l-request@ubvm.cc.buffalo.edu`

Gated: `vmsnet.networks.tcp-ip.wintcp`

NETWORKING—WIDE AREA NETWORKS

➤ **ATMWWW-L:** On asynchronous transfer mode (ATM) technology and the World Wide Web. (See entry 2891 for full listing.)

3318 `comp.dcom.frame-relay` Technology and issues regarding frame relay networks. *Newsgroup*

➤ **HSPNET-L:** On the way computer wide area networks can be used for remote diagnosis and treatment, transfer of patient records, and supplementing rural health care. (See entry 5063 for full listing.)

3319 `tnn.dcom.routers` Discussions about routers. *Newsgroup*

NETWORKING—WINSOCK

3320 `alt.winsock` Windows Sockets. *Newsgroup*

3321 `alt.winsock.programming` Programming Windows Sockets. *Newsgroup*

➤ `alt.winsock.trumpet:` The Trumpet news reader. *Newsgroup*

3322 `alt.winsock.voice` Winsock voice communication. *Newsgroup*

➤ `comp.os.ms-windows.apps.winsock.mail:` Winsock email applications. *Newsgroup*

3323 `comp.os.ms-windows.apps.winsock.misc` Other Winsock applications. *Newsgroup*

➤ `comp.os.ms-windows.apps.winsock.news:` Winsock news applications. *Newsgroup*

3324 **WINSOCK-L:** On Windows Socket (Winsock) related and based applications; associated FTP site. *Mailing List*
± `list-admin@mama.indstate.edu`
OWNER `beast@papa.indstate.edu` (Issam Bandak)
ARCHIVE `ftp://papa.indstate.edu/winsock-l`

3325 **WinSock-L-Announce:** For announcements of uploads to the WinSock-L software archive *Distribution List, moderated*
± `list-admin@papa.indstate.edu`
OWNER `beast@papa.indstate.edu` (Issam Bandak)
OWNER `root@mama.indstate.edu` (Steve Baker)
ARCHIVES
`ftp://papa.indstate.edu/winsock-l/`
`http://papa.indstate.edu:8888/ftp/main.html`
Comments: Digest available

NEWS

3326 `alt.tcj` The Computer Journal. *Newsgroup*

➤ **cc:Browser:** A newsmagazine dedicated to converging technologies, published by Faulkner Information Services. (See entry 9435 for full listing.)

3327 `clari.nb.editorial` Newsbytes: editorials and commentaries. *Moderated newsgroup*

3328 `clari.nb.general` Newsbytes: general computer news. *Moderated newsgroup*

➤ `clari.nb.ibm:` Newsbytes: IBM PC world coverage. *Moderated newsgroup*

➤ `clari.nb.pc:` Newsbytes: hardware, software for PC products. *Moderated newsgroup*

3329 `clari.nb.review` Newsbytes: new product reviews. *Moderated newsgroup*

3330 `clari.nb.summary` Daily summary of newsbytes news. *Moderated newsgroup*

3331 `clari.nb.top` Newsbytes: top stories (cross-posted). *Moderated newsgroup*

3332 `clari.nb.trends` Newsbytes: new developments and trends. *Moderated newsgroup*

3333 `clari.tw.computers` Computer industry, applications, and developments. *Moderated newsgroup*

3334 `clari.tw.computers.cbd` Data processing and telecommunication. *Moderated newsgroup*

3335 `clari.tw.computers.industry_news` News of the computer industry. *Moderated newsgroup*

3336 `clari.tw.computers.misc` Miscellaneous computer news. *Moderated newsgroup*

➤ `clari.tw.computers.peripherals.releases:` Releases :computer peripherals. *Moderated newsgroup*

3337 `clari.tw.computers.releases` Releases: miscellaneous computer news. *Moderated newsgroup*

3338 `clari.tw.computers.retail.releases` News releases: the retail computer industry. *Moderated newsgroup*

3339 **Computer News:** Weekly news and articles related to computers. *Newsletter*
± `majordomo@libtech.com` [body = subscribe cn]
INFO `cnews@libtech.com` (Olcay Cirit)
ARCHIVE `cnews@libtech.com` (Olcay Cirit)
Frequency: weekly

3340 **The Computer Paper:** Web version of Canada's largest computer monthly. *E-Magazine*
`http://tcp.ca/`
± `subscriptions@mindlink.bc.ca`.
INFO `editorial@tcp.mindlink.bc.ca`
ARCHIVE `http://tcp.ca/BackIssues`
Frequency: monthly

➤ **Computer Underground Digest (CuD):** Discussion of legal, ethical, social, and other issues regarding computerized information and communications. Readers are encouraged to submit reasoned articles relating to computer culture and communication. (See entry 3719 for full listing.)

➤ **cwd-l:** Brock Meeks' CyberWire Dispatch List. (See entry 2876 for full listing.)

3341 **CYBERNEWS:** For reviews of PC software, CD-ROMs, and hardware. *Newsletter*
± `subscribe@supportu.com` [body = SUBSCRIBE CYBERNEWS where you heard of list]
INFO `http://www.crl.com/~supportu`
OWNER `patrick.grote@supportu.com` (Patrick Grote)
Frequency: monthly

3342 **Digital Media *Perspective:** Brief, concise version of in-depth reports and analysis in *Digital Media*, a paper newsletter covering high-tech industries with the digital technology itch. *Newsletter*
`http://www.sbexpos.com/`
± `perspective-request@digmedia.com` [subject = subscribe perspective; body = first-name last-name organization title]
INFO `info@digmedia.com` (Neil McManus, Editor)
ARCHIVES
`http://www.digmedia.com/perspective/`
`perspective-backissues@digmedia.com`
Frequency: twice monthly

3343 **Hi-Tech Bulletin:** A business computing/motor-sports Internet news publication by Doug Willoughby. *Newsletter*
INFO `dougw@pinc.com` (Doug Willoughby)
ARCHIVE `http://vvv.com/hi_tech/index.html`
Frequency: weekly

➤ **INNOVATION:** Summary of trends, strategies, and innovations in business and technology. (See entry 9440 for full listing.)

➤ **MeuPovo:** For informal computing news and chat from Brazil. (See entry 7643 for full listing.)

3344 **The Register:** News, analysis, comment, and humor on and around the subjects of semiconductors, operating software, and the computer industry in general. *Newsletter*
`http://www.hubcom.com/register`
± INFO `ac70@cityscape.co.uk` (John Lettice and Mike Magee)
Frequency: every two weeks

➤ **TidBITS:** A newsletter for users of Macintosh computers. (See entry 3096 for full listing.)

3345 **UCSMON:** The UCS MONITOR Computing News from Indiana University. *Distribution List, moderated*
`http://www.indiana.edu/~ucspubs/ucsmon/`
± `listserv@iubvm.ucs.indiana.edu` [body = SUBSCRIBE UCSMON first-name last-name]

EDITOR angie@indiana.edu (Angie Allen)
OWNER leftwich@indiana.edu (Brad Leftwich)
ARCHIVE listserv@iubvm.ucs.indiana.edu [body = INDEX UCSMON]

NEXT & NEXTSTEP

3346 **biz.next.newprod** New product announcements for NeXT. *Newsgroup*

3347 **comp.soft-sys.nextstep** The NeXTstep computing environment. *Newsgroup*

3348 **comp.sys.next.advocacy** The NeXT religion. *Newsgroup*

3349 **comp.sys.next.announce** Announcements related to the NeXT computer system. *Moderated newsgroup*

3350 **comp.sys.next.bugs** Discussion and solutions for known NeXT bugs. *Newsgroup*

3351 **comp.sys.next.hardware** Discussing the physical aspects of NeXT computers. *Newsgroup*

3352 **comp.sys.next.marketplace** NeXT hardware, software, and jobs. *Newsgroup*

3353 **comp.sys.next.misc** General discussion about the NeXT computer system. *Newsgroup*

3354 **comp.sys.next.programmer** NeXT-related programming issues. *Newsgroup*

3355 **comp.sys.next.software** Function, use, and availability of NeXT programs. *Newsgroup*

3356 **comp.sys.next.sysadmin** Discussions related to NeXT system administration. *Newsgroup*

3357 **fj.sys.next** NeXT workstation and related topics. *Newsgroup*

3358 **NeXT-icon:** For distribution of icons for NeXTStep and OpenStep operating systems. *Mailing List*
± INFO next-icon-request@gun.com (Timothy Reed)
ARCHIVE ftp://ftp.egr.uh.edu/pub/nextstep/graphics

3359 **Nextcomm:** On NeXTStep telecommunications. *Mailing List*
± INFO nextcomm-request@marble.com

3360 **okinawa.sys.next** Discussion about NeXT. *Newsgroup*

3361 **pgh.next-users** NeXT users in Pittsburgh. *Newsgroup*

3362 **sdnet.next** San Diego NeXT users group. *Newsgroup*

3363 **tnn.sys.next** Discussions about NeXT workstations. *Newsgroup*

OPERATING SYSTEMS

3364 **comp.os.misc** General OS-oriented discussion not carried elsewhere. *Newsgroup*

3365 **comp.os.research** Operating systems and related areas. *Moderated newsgroup*

3366 **fj.os.misc** Discussion about operating systems not covered elsewhere. *Newsgroup*

➤ **ieee.tcos:** The Technical Committee on Operating Systems. *Moderated newsgroup*

3367 **iijnet.os** Discussions about operating systems. *Newsgroup*

3368 **tnn.os** Discussions about operating systems. *Newsgroup*

3369 **tnn.os.research** Discussions about research for operating systems. *Newsgroup*

OPERATING SYSTEMS—VARIOUS

3370 **alt.comp.msx** Some sort of computer system. *Newsgroup*

3371 **alt.comp.tandem-users** Users of Tandem computers. *Newsgroup*

3372 **alt.sys.icl** International Computers Limited hardware and software. *Newsgroup*

3373 **alt.sys.pdp10** The trusty old PDP-10. *Newsgroup*

3374 **alt.sys.pdp11** The trusty old PDP-11. *Newsgroup*

3375 `alt.sys.pdp8` The trusty old PDP-8. *Newsgroup*

3376 `alt.sys.perq` PERQ graphics workstations. *Newsgroup*

3377 `clari.nb.pen` Newsbytes: pen-based computing devices, software. *Moderated newsgroup*

3378 `comp.binaries.cbm` For the transfer of 8-bit Commodore binaries. *Moderated newsgroup*

3379 `comp.binaries.geos` Binaries for the GEOS operating system. *Moderated newsgroup*

3380 `comp.emulators.announce` Emulator news, FAQs, announcements. *Moderated newsgroup*

3381 `comp.emulators.cbm` Emulators of C-64, C-128, PET, and VIC-20 systems. *Newsgroup*

3382 `comp.emulators.misc` Emulators of miscellaneous computer systems. *Newsgroup*

3383 `comp.os.aos` Topics related to Data General's AOS/VS. *Newsgroup*

3384 `comp.os.chorus` CHORUS microkernel issues, research and developments. *Newsgroup*

3385 `comp.os.coherent` Discussion and support of the Coherent operating system. *Newsgroup*

3386 `comp.os.cpm` Discussion about the CP/M operating system. *Newsgroup*

3387 `comp.os.cpm.amethyst` Discussion of Amethyst, CP/M-80 software package. *Newsgroup*

3388 `comp.os.geos` The GEOS operating system by GeoWorks for PC clones. *Newsgroup*

3389 `comp.os.lynx` Discussion of LynxOS and Lynx real-time systems. *Newsgroup*

➤   `comp.os.magic-cap:` Everything about General Magic's Magic Cap OS. *Newsgroup*

3390 `comp.os.minix` Discussion of Tanenbaum's MINIX system. *Newsgroup*

3391 `comp.os.os9` Discussions about the OS/9 operating system. *Newsgroup*

3392 `comp.os.parix` Forum for users of the parallel operating system PARIX. *Newsgroup*

3393 `comp.os.plan9` Plan 9 from Bell Labs. *Moderated newsgroup*

3394 `comp.os.qnx` Using and developing under the QNX operating system. *Newsgroup*

3395 `comp.os.rsts` Topics related to the PDP-11 RSTS/E operating system. *Newsgroup*

3396 `comp.os.v` The V distributed operating system from Stanford. *Newsgroup*

3397 `comp.os.vxworks` The VxWorks real-time operating system. *Newsgroup*

3398 `comp.os.xinu` The XINU operating system from Purdue (D. Comer). *Newsgroup*

3399 `comp.sys.3b1` Discussion and support of AT&T 7300/3B1/UnixPC. *Newsgroup*

3400 `comp.sys.alliant` Information and discussion about Alliant computers. *Newsgroup*

3401 `comp.sys.amstrad.8bit` Amstrad CPC/PcW/GX4000 software/hardware. *Moderated newsgroup*

3402 `comp.sys.apollo` Apollo computer systems. *Newsgroup*

3403 `comp.sys.att` Discussions about AT&T microcomputers. *Newsgroup*

3404 `comp.sys.cbm` Discussion about Commodore micros. *Newsgroup*

3405 `comp.sys.encore` Encore's MultiMax computers. *Newsgroup*

3406 `comp.sys.harris` Harris computer systems, especially real-time systems. *Newsgroup*

3407 `comp.sys.ibm.sys3x.misc` IBM System/34, System/36, System/38 diverse topics. *Newsgroup*

3408 `comp.sys.isis` The ISIS distributed system from Cornell. *Newsgroup*

3409 `comp.sys.misc` Discussion about computers of all kinds. *Newsgroup*

3410 `comp.sys.msx` The MSX home computer system. *Newsgroup*

3411 `comp.sys.ncr` Discussion about NCR computers. *Newsgroup*

3412 `comp.sys.northstar` Northstar microcomputer users. *Newsgroup*

3413 `comp.sys.pen` Interacting with computers through pen gestures. *Newsgroup*

3414 `comp.sys.prime` Prime computer products. *Newsgroup*

3415 `comp.sys.proteon` Proteon gateway products. *Newsgroup*

3416 `comp.sys.ridge` Ridge 32 computers and ROS. *Newsgroup*

3417 `comp.sys.sinclair` Sinclair computers, e.g., the ZX81, Spectrum, and QL. *Newsgroup*

3418 `comp.sys.stratus` Stratus products, including System/88, CPS-32, VOS, and FTX. *Newsgroup*

3419 `comp.sys.ti` Discussion about Texas Instruments. *Newsgroup*

3420 `comp.sys.ti.explorer` The Texas Instruments Explorer. *Newsgroup*

3421 `comp.sys.xerox` Xerox 1100 workstations and protocols. *Newsgroup*

3422 `comp.sys.zenith` Heath terminals and related Zenith products. *Newsgroup*

3423 `comp.sys.zenith.z100` The Zenith Z-100 (Heath H-100) family of computers. *Newsgroup*

3424 `comp.windows.garnet` The Garnet user interface development environment. *Newsgroup*

3425 `comp.windows.interviews` The InterViews object-oriented windowing system. *Newsgroup*

3426 `comp.windows.misc` Various issues about windowing systems. *Newsgroup*

3427 `comp.windows.suit` The SUIT user-interface toolkit. *Newsgroup*

3428 `eunet.works` Workstation (specifically European) topics. *Newsgroup*

3429 `fj.comp.dev.misc` Discussion on miscellaneous computer device. *Newsgroup*

3430 `fj.mail-lists.apollo` Apollo workstations mailing list. *Moderated newsgroup*

3431 `fj.sys.ews4800` Discussion about NEC EWS4800 workstation. *Newsgroup*

3432 `fj.sys.j3100` Discussion about TOSHIBA J3100-family computers. *Newsgroup*

3433 `fj.sys.luna` Discussion about OMRON LUNA workstations. *Newsgroup*

3434 `fj.sys.news` Discussion about Sony NEWS workstation. *Newsgroup*

3435 `fj.sys.x68000` Discussion about Sharp X68000 and other computers. *Newsgroup*

3436 `fj.windows.misc` Miscellaneous window systems. *Newsgroup*

3437 `iijnet.os.dosv` Discussions about DOS/V. *Newsgroup*

3438 **info-solbourne:** Discussions and information about Solbourne computers. *Mailing List*
± listserv@listserv.acsu.buffalo.edu [body = SUBSCRIBE INFO-SOLBOURNE first-name last-name]
INFO info-solbourne-request@listserv.acsu.buffalo.edu
ARCHIVE listserv@listserv.acsu.buffalo.edu [body = INDEX INFO-SOLBOURNE]

3439 `okinawa.os.misc` About operating systems not covered elsewhere. *Newsgroup*

3440 `okinawa.sys.misc` Various discussions about any computers. *Newsgroup*

3441 `relcom.commerce.software.demo` Demo versions of commercial software. *Newsgroup*

3442 `relcom.comp.binaries` Binary codes of freeware and shareware computer programs. *Newsgroup*

3443 `relcom.comp.binaries.d` Discussions of binary codes. *Newsgroup*

3444 `relcom.comp.demo` Demo versions of various software. *Moderated newsgroup*

3445 `relcom.comp.demo.d` Discussions on demo software. *Newsgroup*

3446 `tnn.os.dosv` Discussions about DOS/V. *Newsgroup*

3447 `tnn.sys.news` Discussion about Sony NEWS workstation. *Newsgroup*

3448 `vmsnet.pdp-11` PDP-11 hardware and software, gatewayed to info-pdp11. *Newsgroup*

OPTICAL CHARACTER & MARK RECOGNITION

3449　SCANTRON: On Scantron optical mark recognition (OMR) equipment, software, or scan forms. *Mailing List, moderated*

± `scantron@infi.net`
INFO `http://www.aladdin.co.uk/scantron/`
INFO `http://www.scantron.com/` (Scantron USA)
OWNER `tjesker@infi.net` (Tom Esker)

3450　SCRIB-L: For academic and industrial researchers and developers in the field of computerized handwriting recognition, including communication, graphs, pen-based interfaces, and forensic applications. *Mailing List*

± `listserv@hearn.nic.surfnet.nl` [body = `SUBSCRIBE SCRIB-L` first-name last-name]
INFO `hlt@espe1.la.asu.edu` (Hans-Leo Teulings)
INFO `schomaker@nici.kun.nl` (Lambert Schomaker)
ARCHIVES
`listserv@hearn.nic.surfnet.nl`
`http://www.nici.kun.nl/scrib-l.html`
`http://www.public.asu.edu/~teulings/scrib-l.html`

PERIPHERALS

3451 `alt.comp.periphs.mainboard.asus` ASUS motherboards. *Newsgroup*

3452 `alt.periphs.pcmcia` Credit card-size plug in peripherals (PCMCIA, JEDIA). *Newsgroup*

3453 `alt.sb.programmer` Programming the Sound Blaster PC sound card. *Newsgroup*

3454 `clari.tw.computers.peripherals.releases` Releases :computer peripherals. *Moderated newsgroup*

3455 `comp.dcom.cabling` Cabling selection, installation, and use. *Newsgroup*

3456 `comp.dcom.fax` Fax hardware, software, and protocols. *Newsgroup*

3457 `comp.laser-printers` Laser printers, hardware, and software. *Moderated newsgroup*

3458 `comp.periphs` Peripheral devices. *Newsgroup*

3459 `comp.periphs.printers` Information on printers. *Newsgroup*

➤　`comp.sys.ibm.pc.hardware.video:` Video cards and monitors for the PC. *Newsgroup*

3460 `comp.terminals` All sorts of terminals. *Newsgroup*

3461 `comp.terminals.bitgraph` The BB&N BitGraph Terminals. *Newsgroup*

3462 `comp.terminals.tty5620` AT&T Dot Mapped Display Terminals (5620 and BLIT). *Newsgroup*

3463 `fj.comp.dev.pcmcia` Discussion on PCMCIA card. *Newsgroup*

3464 `fj.comp.dev.scsi` Discussion on SCSI interfaces. *Newsgroup*

3465 `fj.comp.printers` Printers, hardware, and software. *Newsgroup*

3466 `fj.net.fax` Fax networks. *Newsgroup*

PROGRAMMING

➤　`alt.hackintosh:` Clever programming on Apple's Macintosh. *Newsgroup*

3467 `alt.lang.ca-realizer` The CA Realizer GUI programming environment. *Newsgroup*

➤　`alt.msdos.programmer:` For the serious MS-DOS programmer (no for-sale ads). *Newsgroup*

3468 `alt.sources` Alternative source code, unmoderated. Caveat emptor. *Newsgroup*

3469 `alt.sources.d` Discussion of posted sources. *Newsgroup*

3470 `alt.sources.index` Pointers to source code in `alt.sources.*`. *Moderated newsgroup*

➤　`alt.sources.mac:` Source code for Apple Macintosh computers. *Newsgroup*

3471 `alt.sources.wanted` Requests for source code. *Newsgroup*

➤ `alt.winsock.programming`: Programming Windows Sockets. *Newsgroup*

3472 `aus.lp` Logic programming. *Newsgroup*

➤ `comp.groupware.lotus-notes.programmer`: Programming for Lotus Notes. *Newsgroup*

➤ `comp.os.ms-windows.programmer.graphics`: GDI, graphics, and printing. *Newsgroup*

➤ `comp.os.ms-windows.programmer.misc`: Programming Microsoft Windows. *Newsgroup*

➤ `comp.os.ms-windows.programmer.multimedia`: Multimedia programming. *Newsgroup*

➤ `comp.os.ms-windows.programmer.networks`: Network programming. *Newsgroup*

➤ `comp.os.ms-windows.programmer.win32`: 32-bit Windows programming interfaces. *Newsgroup*

➤ `comp.os.msdos.programmer`: Programming MS-DOS machines. *Newsgroup*

➤ `comp.os.msdos.programmer.turbovision`: Borland's text application libraries. *Newsgroup*

➤ `comp.os.os2.programmer.misc`: Programming OS/2 machines. *Newsgroup*

➤ `comp.os.os2.programmer.porting`: Porting software to OS/2 machines. *Newsgroup*

➤ `comp.os.os2.programmer.tools`: Compilers, assemblers, interpreters under OS/2. *Newsgroup*

3473 `comp.programming` Programming issues that transcend languages and OSs. *Newsgroup*

3474 `comp.programming.contests` Announcements and results of programming contests. *Newsgroup*

3475 `comp.programming.literate` Knuth's "literate programming" method and tools. *Newsgroup*

3476 `comp.programming.threads` All issues about multithreaded programming. *Newsgroup*

3477 `comp.soft-sys.app-builder.appware` Novell's visual development environment. *Newsgroup*

3478 `comp.soft-sys.app-builder.uniface` Uniface client/server application development. *Newsgroup*

3479 `comp.software.config-mgmt` Configuration management, tools and procedures. *Newsgroup*

3480 `comp.software.international` Finding, using, and writing non-English software. *Newsgroup*

3481 `comp.software.testing` All aspects of testing computer systems. *Newsgroup*

3482 `comp.sources.3b1` Source code-only postings for the AT&T 3b1. *Moderated newsgroup*

➤ `comp.sources.acorn`: Source code-only postings for the Acorn. *Moderated newsgroup*

➤ `comp.sources.apple2`: Source code and discussion for the Apple II. *Moderated newsgroup*

3483 `comp.sources.bugs` Bug reports, fixes, discussion for posted sources. *Newsgroup*

3484 `comp.sources.d` For any discussion of source postings. *Newsgroup*

3485 `comp.sources.misc` Posting of software. *Moderated newsgroup*

3486 `comp.sources.reviewed` Source code evaluated by peer review. *Moderated newsgroup*

➤ `comp.sources.sun`: Software for Sun workstations. *Moderated newsgroup*

3487 `comp.sources.testers` Finding people to test software. *Newsgroup*

➤ `comp.sources.unix`: Postings of complete, Unix-oriented sources. *Moderated newsgroup*

3488 `comp.sources.wanted` Requests for software and fixes. *Newsgroup*

➤ `comp.sources.x`: Software for the X-Windows system. *Moderated newsgroup*

3489 `comp.specification.misc` Formal specification methods in general. *Newsgroup*

3490 `comp.specification.z` Discussion about the formal specification notation Z. *Newsgroup*

➤ `comp.sys.acorn.programmer`: Programming of Acorn computers. *Newsgroup*

➤ `comp.sys.amiga.programmer`: Developers and hobbyists discuss code. *Newsgroup*

➤ `comp.sys.apple2.programmer`: Programming on the Apple II. *Newsgroup*

➤   `comp.sys.atari.programmer`: Programming on the Atari computers. *Newsgroup*

➤   `comp.sys.ibm.pc.demos`: Demonstration programs which showcase programmer skill. *Newsgroup*

➤   `comp.sys.mac.programmer.codewarrior`: Macintosh programming using CodeWarrior. *Newsgroup*

➤   `comp.sys.mac.programmer.games`: Macintosh game programming. *Newsgroup*

➤   `comp.sys.mac.programmer.help`: Help with Macintosh programming. *Newsgroup*

➤   `comp.sys.mac.programmer.info`: Frequently requested information. *Moderated newsgroup*

➤   `comp.sys.mac.programmer.misc`: Other issues of Macintosh programming. *Newsgroup*

➤   `comp.sys.mac.programmer.tools`: Macintosh programming tools. *Newsgroup*

➤   **Comp.Sys.Mac.Programmers Digest:** A collection of the most interesting discussions from the Usenet newsgroup `comp.sys.mac.programmer` (See entry 3075 for full listing.)

➤   `comp.unix.programmer`: Q & A for people programming under Unix. *Newsgroup*

➤   `comp.unix.sco.programmer`: Programming in and for SCO environments. *Newsgroup*

➤   `comp.unix.shell`: Using and programming the Unix shell. *Newsgroup*

➤   `comp.windows.garnet`: The Garnet user interface development environment. *Newsgroup*

3491   **DDTs-Users:** Pure Software's DDTs defect/problem-tracking system. *Mailing List*
± `majordomo@bigbird.bu.edu` [body = `subscribe ddts-users`]
INFO `ddts-users-request@bigbird.bu.edu`
INFO OWNER `jbw@cs.bu.edu` (Joe Wells)

3492   `fj.net.programming` Network programming. *Newsgroup*

3493   `fj.sources` For the posting of software packages and documentation. *Newsgroup*

3494   `fj.sources.d` For any discussion of source postings. *Newsgroup*

3495   `gnu.ghostscript.bug` GNU Ghostscript interpreter bugs. *Moderated newsgroup*

3496   `gnu.misc.discuss` Serious discussion about GNU and freed software. *Newsgroup*

3497   `gnu.utils.bug` GNU utilities bugs (e.g., make, gawk, ls). *Moderated newsgroup*

➤   **JES3-L:** For programmers using JES3, IBM's job-entry subsystem 3 for MVS. (See entry 4064 for full listing.)

3498   **LEXX-L:** On the LEXX parsing editor. *Mailing List*
± `listserv@vma.cc.nd.edu` [body = `SUBSCRIBE LEXX-L` first-name last-name]
INFO `lexx-l-request@vma.cc.nd.edu`
ARCHIVE `listserv@vma.cc.nd.edu` [body = `INDEX LEXX-L`]

3499   `oau.sources` Distribution of source code in Orlando, Florida. *Newsgroup*

3500   `okinawa.sources` For the posting of software packages and documentation. *Newsgroup*

3501   `okinawa.sources.d` For any discussion of source postings. *Newsgroup*

➤   **OS2PRO-L:** On OS/2 programming. (See entry 2610 for full listing.)

3502   **POWERH-L:** For users of PowerHouse, a fourth-generation application development language published by Cognos. *Mailing List*
± `listserv@unb.ca` [body = `SUBSCRIBE POWERH-L` first-name last-name]
INFO OWNER `bourgeg@umoncton.ca` (Georges M. Bourgeois)
Gated: `bit.listserv.powerh-l`

3503   `relcom.comp.sources.misc` Software sources. *Newsgroup*

3504   `uk.sources` U.K.-wide group for sources/reposts/requests. *Newsgroup*

PROGRAMMING—LANGUAGES

3505   `alt.lang.design` Discussion for the design of computer languges. *Newsgroup*

3506   `comp.lang.functional` Discussion about functional languages. *Newsgroup*

3507   `comp.lang.sigplan` Information and announcements from ACM SIGPLAN. *Moderated newsgroup*

3508   `comp.lang.visual` General discussion of visual languages. *Moderated newsgroup*

3509   **SunSITE Computer Language Archives:** Compilers and interpreters for many computer languages.
    `ftp://sunsite.unc.edu/pub/languages/`
    INFO `ftpkeeper@sunsite.unc.edu`

PROGRAMMING—LANGUAGES—ADA

3510   `comp.lang.ada` Discussion about Ada. *Moderated newsgroup*

3511   `fj.lang.ada` Discussion about Ada. *Moderated newsgroup*

PROGRAMMING—LANGUAGES—APL

3512   **APLEDU-L:** On using the APL programming language in education. *Mailing List*
    ± `listserv@unb.ca` [body = SUBSCRIBE APLEDU-L first-name last-name]
    INFO `apledu-l-request@unb.ca`
    ARCHIVE `listserv@unb.ca` [body = INDEX APLEDU-L]

3513   `comp.lang.apl` Discussion about APL programming language. *Newsgroup*

PROGRAMMING—LANGUAGES—ASSEMBLY

3514   `alt.lang.asm` Assembly languages of various flavors. *Newsgroup*

3515   `bit.listserv.asm370` IBM 370 assembly programming discussions. *Newsgroup*

3516   `comp.lang.asm.x86` General 80x86 assembly language programming. *Newsgroup*

3517   `comp.lang.asm370` Programming in IBM System/370 assembly language. *Newsgroup*

PROGRAMMING—LANGUAGES—BASIC

3518   `alt.lang.basic` The Language That Would Not Die. *Newsgroup*

3519   `alt.sys.amiga.blitz` The Blitz Basic programming language. *Newsgroup*

3520   `comp.lang.basic.misc` Other dialects and aspects of BASIC. *Newsgroup*

3521   `comp.lang.basic.visual.3rdparty` Add-ins for Visual Basic. *Newsgroup*

3522   `comp.lang.basic.visual.announce` Official information on Visual Basic. *Moderated newsgroup*

3523   `comp.lang.basic.visual.database` Database aspects of Visual Basic. *Newsgroup*

3524   `comp.lang.basic.visual.misc` Visual Basic in general. *Newsgroup*

3525   `relcom.comp.lang.basic` FIDOnet area, BASIC programming language. *Newsgroup*

3526   **VB-ESP:** On Visual Basic. *Mailing List*
    ± `majordomo@ccc.uba.ar`
    OWNER `vb-adm@dia.edu.ar` (Alberto Daniel Teszkiewicz)
    Language: Spanish

PROGRAMMING—LANGUAGES—C

3527   **C370-L:** On C programming for 370-architecture machines.
    ± `listserv@cmuvm.csv.cmich.edu` [body = SUB C370-L first-name last-name]
    OWNER `34aaq77@cmuvm.csv.cmich.edu` (David Jelinek)
    Gated: `bit.listserv.c370-l`

3528   `comp.lang.c` Discussion about C programming language. *Newsgroup*

3529 **comp.lang.c.moderated** The C programming language. *Moderated newsgroup*

3530 **comp.std.c** Discussion about C language standards. *Newsgroup*

3531 **fj.lang.c** Discussion about C. *Newsgroup*

3532 **GCT:** On the Generic Coverage Tool (GCT), a freeware package that measures how thoroughly tests exercise C programs. *Mailing List, moderated*
± INFO gct-request@cs.uiuc.edu
OWNER marick@cs.uiuc.edu (Brian Marick)

3533 **gnu.gcc.announce** Announcements about the GNU C compiler. *Moderated newsgroup*

3534 **gnu.gcc.bug** GNU C compiler bug reports/suggested fixes. *Moderated newsgroup*

3535 **gnu.gcc.help** GNU C compiler (gcc) user queries and answers. *Newsgroup*

3536 **gnu.gdb.bug** Gcc/g++ DeBugger bugs and suggested fixes. *Moderated newsgroup*

3537 **relcom.fido.su.c-c++** FIDOnet, C & C++ language. *Newsgroup*

3538 **sanet.lang.c** C language conference. *Newsgroup*

3539 **think-c:** For users of the Think C and C++ compiler for the Macintosh. *Mailing List*
± listproc@rdatasys.com [body = SUBSCRIBE THINK-C first-name last-name]
INFO nagel@rdatasys.com (Mark Nagel)
ARCHIVE ftp://ftp.rdatasys.com/pub/think-c

PROGRAMMING—LANGUAGES—C++

3540 **comp.lang.c++** The object-oriented C++ programming language. *Newsgroup*

3541 **comp.lang.c++.leda** All aspects of the LEDA library. *Newsgroup*

3542 **comp.lang.c++.moderated** Technical discussion of the C++ programming language. *Moderated newsgroup*

3543 **comp.std.c++** Discussion about C++ language, library, standards. *Moderated newsgroup*

3544 **fj.lang.c++** Discussion about C++. *Newsgroup*

3545 **gnu.g++.announce** Announcements about the GNU C++ compiler. *Moderated newsgroup*

3546 **gnu.g++.bug** G++ bug reports and suggested fixes. *Moderated newsgroup*

3547 **gnu.g++.help** GNU C++ compiler (G++) user queries and answers. *Newsgroup*

3548 **gnu.g++.lib.bug** G++ library bug reports/suggested fixes. *Moderated newsgroup*

3549 **hepnet.lang.c++** The use of C++ for High Energy Physics work. *Newsgroup*

3550 **Quadralay C++ Archive:** The C++ archives at Quadralay are devoted to the C++ programming language. You'll find jumps to the Borland C++ Tech Support Page, C++ libraries, online books, and lots more.
http://www.quadralay.com/www/CCForum/CCForum.html
INFO greening@quadralay.com

3551 **TURBVIS :** For users of TurboVision, a free library that comes with Borland C++ and Borland Pascal programming languages. *Mailing List, moderated*
± listserv@vtvml.cc.vt.edu [body = SUBSCRIBE TURBVIS first-name last-name]
INFO daves@bev.net (Dave Sisson)
ARCHIVE listserv@vtvml.cc.vt.edu
Gated: comp.os.msdos.programmer.turbovision

PROGRAMMING—LANGUAGES—FORTH

3552 **comp.lang.forth** Discussion about Forth. *Newsgroup*

3553 **comp.lang.forth.mac** The CSI MacForth programming environment. *Newsgroup*

3554 **fj.lang.forth** Discussion about Forth. *Newsgroup*

3555 `relcom.comp.lang.forth` Inter-network, Forth programming language. *Newsgroup*

3556 `relcom.fido.su.forth` FIDOnet, Forth language. *Newsgroup*

PROGRAMMING—LANGUAGES—FORTRAN

3557 `bit.listserv.vfort-l` VS-FORTRAN discussion list. *Newsgroup*

3558 `comp.lang.fortran` Discussion about FORTRAN. *Newsgroup*

3559 `fj.lang.fortran` Discussion about FORTRAN programming language. *Newsgroup*

PROGRAMMING—LANGUAGES—JAVA

3560 **"Presenting Java" Book Support Web:** This support web for the book "Presenting Java" connects to Java demonstrations, example source code, an online Java bibliography, and online reference information about Java.
    `http://www.december.com/works/java.html`
    INFO `john@december.com`

3561 `alt.www.hotjava` Discussions of Sun Microsystems's Java language. *Newsgroup*

3562 `comp.lang.java` The Java programming language. *Newsgroup*

3563 **Java™ Programming for the Internet:** All about the Java programming language, including tutorials, documentation, sample applets, downloadable SDKs, and liscensing information.
    `http://java.sun.com/`
    INFO `webmaster@java.sun.com`

PROGRAMMING—LANGUAGES—LISP

➤ **Carnegie Mellon University Artificial Intelligence Repository:** Collection of nearly all materials of interest to AI researchers, educators, practitioners, and students. (See entry 2129 for full listing.)

3564 `comp.lang.clos` Common LISP Object System discussion. *Newsgroup*

3565 `comp.lang.lisp` Discussion about LISP language. *Newsgroup*

3566 `comp.lang.lisp.franz` The Franz LISP programming language. *Newsgroup*

3567 `comp.lang.lisp.mcl` Discussing Apple's Macintosh Common LISP. *Newsgroup*

3568 `comp.lang.lisp.x` The XLISP language system. *Newsgroup*

3569 `comp.lang.scheme` The Scheme programming language. *Newsgroup*

3570 `comp.lang.scheme.c` The Scheme language environment. *Newsgroup*

3571 `comp.org.lisp-users` Association of LISP Users related discussions. *Newsgroup*

3572 `comp.std.lisp` User group (ALU) supported standards. *Moderated newsgroup*

3573 `fj.lang.lisp` Discussion about LISP. *Newsgroup*

3574 `uk.comp.lang.lisp` Discussion of LISP, especially the draft standard. *Newsgroup*

3575 `uk.lisp` Discussion of LISP, especially the draft standard. *Newsgroup*

PROGRAMMING—LANGUAGES—PASCAL

3576 `comp.lang.pascal.ansi-iso` Pascal according to ANSI and ISO standards. *Newsgroup*

3577 `comp.lang.pascal.borland` Borland's Pascal. *Newsgroup*

3578 `comp.lang.pascal.delphi.components` Writing components in Borland Delphi. *Newsgroup*

3579 `comp.lang.pascal.delphi.databases` Database aspects of Borland Delphi. *Newsgroup*

3580 `comp.lang.pascal.delphi.misc` General issues with Borland Delphi. *Newsgroup*

3581 `comp.lang.pascal.mac` Macintosh-based Pascal. *Newsgroup*

3582   `comp.lang.pascal.misc` Pascal in general and ungrouped Pascals. *Newsgroup*

3583   `relcom.comp.lang.pascal` Using of Pascal programming language. *Newsgroup*

3584   `relcom.comp.lang.pascal.misc` Sources and materials, Pascal-kind languages. *Newsgroup*

➤   **TURBVIS** : For users of TurboVision, a free library that comes with Borland C++ and Borland Pascal programming languages. (See entry 3551 for full listing.)

PROGRAMMING—LANGUAGES—PERL

3585   `comp.lang.perl.announce` Announcements about Perl programming language. *Moderated newsgroup*

3586   `comp.lang.perl.misc` The Perl language in general. *Newsgroup*

➤   `comp.lang.perl.tk`: Using Tk (and X) from Perl. *Newsgroup*

3587   `fj.lang.perl` Discussion about Perl language. *Newsgroup*

➤   **Texas Metronet, Inc.:** Internet for the individual. Includes extensive Perl archive, scripts, information, and distribution source. Internet services and information. Many other helpful sources and links. The entire archive is boolean WAIS indexed for easy searching and retrieval. (See entry 2702 for full listing.)

PROGRAMMING—LANGUAGES—POSTSCRIPT

3588   `comp.lang.postscript` The PostScript page description language. *Newsgroup*

3589   `comp.sources.postscript` Source code for programs written in PostScript. *Moderated newsgroup*

3590   `fj.lang.postscript` PostScript language and related topics. *Newsgroup*

3591   `tnn.text.postscript` Discussions about PostScript. *Newsgroup*

PROGRAMMING—LANGUAGES—PROLOG

➤   <u>**Carnegie Mellon University Artificial Intelligence Repository**</u>: Collection of nearly all materials of interest to AI researchers, educators, practitioners, and students. (See entry 2129 for full listing.)

3592   `comp.lang.prolog` Discussion about Prolog programming language. *Newsgroup*

3593   `fj.lang.prolog` Discussion about Prolog. *Newsgroup*

3594   **PDC-L:** For users of PDC Prolog, a Prolog compiler that runs under DOS, Extended DOS, OS/2, Unix, and Xenix. Applications include gaming simulation, genetic pedigree analysis, and databases. *Mailing List*
    ± `listserv@hearn.nic.surfnet.nl` [body = SUBSCRIBE PDC-L first-name last-name]
    INFO `de_boer@eco.rug.nl` (Thomas de Boer)
    ARCHIVE `listserv@hearn.nic.surfnet.nl`

PROGRAMMING—LANGUAGES—TCL/TK

3595   `comp.lang.perl.tk` Using Tk (and X) from Perl. *Newsgroup*

3596   `comp.lang.tcl` The TCL programming language and related tools. *Newsgroup*

3597   `fj.lang.tcl` Discussion about Tcl/Tk. *Newsgroup*

3598   **XF-L:** On the XF software which is used to build X-Windows interfaces for Tcl/Tk based software. *Mailing List*
    ± `listserv@db0tui11.bitnet` [body = SUBSCRIBE XF-L first-name last-name]
    INFO `axel@avalanche.cs.tu-berlin.de` (Axel Mahler)
    INFO `sven@cimetrix.com` (Sven Delmas)
    ARCHIVE `listserv@db0tui11.bitnet`

PROGRAMMING—LANGUAGES—VARIOUS

3599   **ABC:** About the ABC programming language. *Mailing List*
    ± INFO `abc-list-request@cwi.nl` (Steven Pemberton)

ARCHIVES
http://www.cwi.nl/~steven/abc.html
ftp://ftp.cwi.nl/pub/abc/

3600 **alt.cobol** Relationship between programming and stone axes. *Newsgroup*

➤ **The AMOS Web Site:** Dedicated to the AMOS programming language. (See entry 2095 for full listing.)

3601 **bit.listserv.simula** The SIMULA language list. *Newsgroup*

3602 **comp.lang.awk** The AWK programming language. *Newsgroup*

3603 **comp.lang.clipper** Clipper and Visual Objects programming languages. *Newsgroup*

3604 **comp.lang.clu** The CLU programming language and related topics. *Newsgroup*

3605 **comp.lang.cobol** The COBOL language and software. *Newsgroup*

3606 **comp.lang.hermes** The Hermes language for distributed applications. *Newsgroup*

3607 **comp.lang.icon** Topics related to the ICON programming language. *Newsgroup*

3608 **comp.lang.idl** IDL (Interface Description Language) related topics. *Newsgroup*

3609 **comp.lang.idl-pvwave** IDL and PV-Wave language discussions. *Newsgroup*

3610 **comp.lang.logo** The Logo teaching and learning language. *Newsgroup*

3611 **comp.lang.misc** Different computer languages not specifically listed. *Newsgroup*

3612 **comp.lang.ml** ML languages including Standard ML, CAML, Lazy ML, etc. *Moderated newsgroup*

3613 **comp.lang.modula2** Discussion about Modula-2. *Newsgroup*

3614 **comp.lang.modula3** Discussion about the Modula-3 language. *Newsgroup*

3615 **comp.lang.mumps** The M (MUMPS) programming language and technology, in general. *Newsgroup*

3616 **comp.lang.oberon** The Oberon language and system. *Newsgroup*

3617 **comp.lang.pop** Pop11 and the Plug user group. *Newsgroup*

3618 **comp.lang.python** The Python computer language. *Newsgroup*

3619 **comp.lang.rexx** The REXX command language. *Newsgroup*

3620 **comp.lang.sather** The object-oriented computer language Sather. *Newsgroup*

3621 **comp.lang.verilog** Discussing Verilog and PLI. *Newsgroup*

3622 **comp.lang.vhdl** VHSIC Hardware Description Language, IEEE 1076/87. *Newsgroup*

3623 **comp.specification.larch** Larch family of formal specification languages. *Newsgroup*

3624 **comp.std.mumps** Discussions about MUMPS language/standards. *Moderated newsgroup*

3625 **fj.lang.awk** Discussion about Awk programming language. *Newsgroup*

3626 **fj.lang.cobol** Discussion on COBOL. *Newsgroup*

3627 **fj.lang.misc** Different computer languages not specifically listed. *Newsgroup*

3628 **gnu.smalltalk.bug** Bugs in GNU Smalltalk. *Moderated newsgroup*

3629 **REXXCOMP:** On the CMS REXX compiler. *Mailing List*
± listproc@list.cren.net [body = SUB REXXCOMP first-name last-name]
OWNER guardian@deaf-magazine.org (Nathan Prugh)
OWNER timothy.d.knox@x400gw.ameritech.com (Timothy D. Knox)
ARCHIVES
ftp://ftp.cren.net/archives/REXXCOMP
listproc@list.cren.net [body = INDEX REXXCOMP]
http://www.cren.net/
POST rexxcomp@list.cren.net

➤ **VRML Repository:** All about the Virtual Reality Modeling Language (VRML), including pointers to software archives, documentation, bibliographies, related mailing lists and newsgroups, job postings in the field, and more. (See entry 4042 for full listing.)

PROGRAMMING—OBJECT-ORIENTED

3630 **BETA:** For BETA users. BETA is a modern object-oriented programming language. *Mailing List*
  http://www.mjolner.dk/
  ± usergroup-request@mjolner.dk
  INFO info@mjolner.dk
  ARCHIVE ftp://ftp.daimi.aau.dk
  Gated: comp.lang.beta

3631 **cern.foot** CERN Forum for Object-Oriented Technology. *Newsgroup*

3632 **ch.si.choose** Addressing object-oriented programming issues. *Newsgroup*

➤ **comp.databases.object:** Object-oriented paradigms in database systems. *Newsgroup*

➤ **comp.graphics.api.inventor:** Object-oriented 3-D graphics in Inventor. *Newsgroup*

3633 **comp.lang.beta** The object-oriented programming language BETA. *Newsgroup*

➤ **comp.lang.c++:** The object-oriented C++ programming language. *Newsgroup*

➤ **comp.lang.c++.leda:** All aspects of the LEDA library. *Newsgroup*

➤ **comp.lang.clipper:** Clipper and Visual Objects programming languages. *Newsgroup*

➤ **comp.lang.clos:** Common LISP Object System discussion. *Newsgroup*

3634 **comp.lang.dylan** For discussion of the Dylan language. *Newsgroup*

3635 **comp.lang.eiffel** The object-oriented Eiffel programming language. *Newsgroup*

➤ **comp.lang.oberon:** The Oberon language and system. *Newsgroup*

3636 **comp.lang.objective-c** The Objective-C language and environment. *Newsgroup*

3637 **comp.lang.prograph** Prograph, a visual object-oriented dataflow language. *Newsgroup*

➤ **comp.lang.sather:** The object-oriented computer language Sather. *Newsgroup*

3638 **comp.lang.smalltalk** Discussion about Smalltalk 80. *Newsgroup*

3639 **comp.object** Object-oriented programming and languages. *Newsgroup*

3640 **comp.object.logic** Integrating object-oriented and logic programming. *Newsgroup*

➤ **comp.os.ms-windows.programmer.ole:** OLE2, COM, and DDE programming. *Newsgroup*

➤ **comp.os.os2.programmer.oop:** Programming system objects (SOM, WPS, etc.). *Newsgroup*

3641 **comp.sw.components** Software components and related technology. *Newsgroup*

➤ **comp.sys.mac.oop.macapp3:** Version 3 of the MacApp object-oriented system. *Newsgroup*

➤ **comp.sys.mac.oop.misc:** Object-oriented programming issues on the Macintosh. *Newsgroup*

➤ **comp.sys.mac.oop.tcl:** Symantec's THINK Class Library for object programming. *Newsgroup*

3642 **CS1OBJ-L:** On teaching object-oriented programming to first-year students. *Mailing List, moderated*
  ± listserv@psuvm.psu.edu [body = SUBSCRIBE CS1OBJ-L first-name last-name]
  INFO rhm1@psuvm.psu.edu (Rick Mercer)
  Comments: We welcome educators and software developers in the hope that we can help each other.

3643 **fj.comp.oops** Object-oriented programming, system, etc. *Newsgroup*

3644 **fj.lang.st80** Discussion about Smalltalk 80 programming language. *Newsgroup*

➤ **Java™ Programming for the Internet:** All about the Java programming language, including tutorials, documentation, sample applets, downloadable SDKs, and liscensing information. (See entry 3563 for full listing.)

3645 Python: On Python, an object-oriented, interpreted, extensible programming language. *Mailing List*
http://www.python.org/
± python-list-request@cwi.nl [body = e-mail-address] (Sjoerd Mullender)
ARCHIVE ftp://ftp.cwi.nl/pub/python
Gated: comp.lang.python

3646 Sci-Tools: Science Tools Group: on the development of a group of object-oriented, science-oriented software tools in the NeXTStep environment. *Mailing List*
± sci-tools-request@embl-heidelberg
INFO sci-tools-help@embl-heidelberg.de
ARCHIVES
http://www.nmr.embl-heidelberg.de:80/eduStep/SciTools/Documentation/Documentation.ht
ml
ftp://ftp.nmr.embl-heidelberg.de/pub/next/scitools/

SALES

3647 biz.marketplace.computers.discussion Discussion of computer merchandising. *Newsgroup*

➤ biz.marketplace.computers.mac: Macintosh hardware/software offered/wanted. *Newsgroup*

3648 biz.marketplace.computers.other Other computer hardware/software. *Newsgroup*

➤ biz.marketplace.computers.pc-clone: PC-compatible hardware/software. *Newsgroup*

3649 biz.marketplace.computers.workstation Computer workstation hardware/software. *Newsgroup*

3650 biz.marketplace.services.computers Computer services offered/wanted. *Newsgroup*

➤ comp.os.os2.marketplace: For sale/wanted; shopping; commercial ads; job postings. *Newsgroup*

➤ comp.sys.apple2.marketplace: Buying, selling, and trading Apple II equipment. *Newsgroup*

➤ comp.sys.next.marketplace: NeXT hardware, software, and jobs. *Newsgroup*

➤ comp.sys.sun.wanted: People looking for Sun products and support. *Newsgroup*

➤ comp.sys.tandy: Discussion about Tandy computers: new and old. *Newsgroup*

3651 misc.forsale.computers.mac-specific.software Macintosh software. *Newsgroup*

3652 misc.forsale.computers.memory Memory chips and modules for sale and wanted. *Newsgroup*

3653 misc.forsale.computers.monitors Monitors and displays for sale and wanted. *Newsgroup*

3654 misc.forsale.computers.net-hardware Networking hardware for sale and wanted. *Newsgroup*

3655 misc.forsale.computers.other.misc Miscellaneous other equipment. *Newsgroup*

3656 misc.forsale.computers.other.software Software for other systems. *Newsgroup*

3657 misc.forsale.computers.other.systems Complete other types of system. *Newsgroup*

3658 misc.forsale.computers.pc-specific.audio PC audio equipment for sale. *Newsgroup*

3659 misc.forsale.computers.pc-specific.cards.misc PC expansion cards. *Newsgroup*

3660 misc.forsale.computers.pc-specific.cards.video PC video cards. *Newsgroup*

3661 misc.forsale.computers.pc-specific.misc Other PC-specific equipment. *Newsgroup*

3662 misc.forsale.computers.pc-specific.motherboards PC motherboards. *Newsgroup*

3663 misc.forsale.computers.pc-specific.software PC software for sale. *Newsgroup*

3664 misc.forsale.computers.pc-specific.systems Complete PC systems for sale. *Newsgroup*

3665 misc.forsale.computers.printers Printers and plotters for sale and wanted. *Newsgroup*

3666 misc.forsale.computers.storage Disk, CD-ROM, and tape drives for sale and wanted. *Newsgroup*

3667 misc.forsale.computers.workstation Workstation-related computer items. *Newsgroup*

3668 **RCSnet Worldwide Internet Superstore:** An online computer store featuring over 20,000 items, specialists' advice, daily updated new releases, online technical support, and more.

`http://www.rcsnet.com/`

SECURITY & ENCRYPTION

➤ <u>Materva's Hideout:</u> Lots of programs for hackers, plus related e-texts. Barbed. (See entry 2482 for full listing.)

3669 `alt.fan.david-sternlight` David Sternlight, `sci.crypt` crusader. *Newsgroup*

3670 `alt.privacy.anon-server` Issues surrounding programs that aid anonymity. *Newsgroup*

3671 `alt.privacy.clipper` The U.S. administration's Clipper encryption plan. *Newsgroup*

3672 `alt.security` Security issues on computer systems. *Newsgroup*

3673 `alt.security.index` Pointers to good stuff in `alt.security`. *Moderated newsgroup*

3674 `alt.security.pgp` The Pretty Good Privacy package. *Newsgroup*

➤ `cern.security.unix`: Discussions about Unix security at CERN. *Newsgroup*

3675 **CERT Coordination Center:** All about Internet and computer security. Includes advisories and bulletins on security events, technical tips for system administrators, and more.

`ftp://info.cert.org/pub/`

INFO `cert@cert.org`

FAQS

`ftp://info.cert.org/pub/cert_faq`
`http://www.sei.cmu.edu/technology/cert.cc.html`

3676 **Chaos Digest (ChaosD):** Shares security information among computerists: computer security, frauds, hacking, phreaking, etc. *Newsletter*

± `linux-activists-request@niksula.hut.fi` [body = X-Mn.Admin: `join CHAOS_DIGEST`]

INFO `jeanbernard_condat@email.francenet.fr`

ARCHIVES

`ftp://kragar.eff.org/pub/cud/chaos`
`ftp://uglymouse.css.itd.umich.edu/pub/CuD/chaos`
`ftp://ftp.cic.net/e-serials/alphabetic/c/chaos-digest`
`ftp://halcyon.com/pub/mirror/cud/chaos`
`ftp://ftp.ee.mu.oz.au/pub/text/CuD/chaos`
`ftp://nic.funet.fi/pub/doc/cud/chaos`
`ftp://orchid.csv.warwick.ac.uk/pub/cud/chaos`

Language: French, English, or German

Frequency: weekly

➤ `comp.org.cpsr.talk`: Issues of computing and social responsibility. *Newsgroup*

➤ `comp.os.netware.security`: Netware security issues. *Newsgroup*

3677 `comp.protocols.kerberos` The Kerberos authentication server. *Newsgroup*

3678 `comp.security.announce` Announcements from the CERT about security. *Moderated newsgroup*

3679 `comp.security.firewalls` Anything pertaining to network firewall security. *Newsgroup*

3680 `comp.security.misc` Security issues of computers and networks. *Newsgroup*

3681 `comp.security.unix` Discussion of Unix security. *Newsgroup*

➤ `comp.society.privacy`: Effects of technology on privacy. *Moderated newsgroup*

3682 **Computer Security Resource Clearinghouse:** This site, sponsored by the National Institute of Standards and Technology, provides a wide range of information on computer security topics, including: general security risks, privacy, legal issues, viruses, assurance, policy, and training.

http://csrc.nist.gov/

INFO webmaster@csrc.nist.gov

3683 Cryptographic Software Archive: Various software and documentation related to cryptography and multiple precision arithmetic, including RIPEM. Some files are restricted and not accessible via anonymous FTP.

ftp://ripem.msu.edu

Comments: To apply for a non-anonymous FTP account to access these files, telnet to ripem.msu.edu, and login as ripem. An online application program will ask you a few simple questions. You must be a U.S. or Canadian citizen to be granted an account.

3684 demon.security Security/encryption-related issues. *Newsgroup*

3685 Firewall Product Overview: A long list of firewall products, both commercial and shareware, along with details on how to get them and brief descriptions of them.

http://www.waterw.com/~manowar/vendor.html

INFO cathyf@atvl.research.panasonic.com

MIRROR http://www.access.digex.net/~bdboyle/firewall.vendor.html

3686 firewalls: On Internet "firewall" security systems and related issues. *Mailing List*

± majordomo@greatcircle.com [body = subscribe firewalls]

INFO firewalls-request@greatcircle.com (infobot)

ARCHIVE ftp://ftp.greatcircle.com/pub/archive

3687 han.comp.security Computer and network security, protection, privacy issues. *Newsgroup*

3688 il.infosec Security, audit, and education issues of information-systems security. *Newsgroup*

3689 israel.infosec Security, audit, and education issues of information systems security. *Newsgroup*

➤ **National Institute of Standards & Technology (NIST):** Information about NIST programs, products, and activities. The site includes GAMS (Guide to Available Mathematical Software) and a computer security bulletin board. (See entry 5520 for full listing.)

3690 NIH Computer Security Information: This Web page is a good collection of computer security documents and related Web sites.

http://www.alw.nih.gov/Security

INFO jbk@alw.nih.gov

3691 Quadralay's Cryptography Archive: An archive of documents on all aspects of cryptography, including descriptions of many encryption schemes, pointers to available encryption software for various platforms, and information on current events in cryptography and related social issues.

http://www.quadralay.com/Crypto/crypto.html

INFO webmaster@quadralay.com

3692 relcom.comp.security Computer data security discussions. *Newsgroup*

3693 sci.crypt Different methods of data en/decryption. *Newsgroup*

3694 sci.crypt.research Cryptography, cryptanalysis, and related issues. *Moderated newsgroup*

3695 SEC-LABELLING: On security labeling of electronic documents, paper documents, and other objects. *Mailing List*

± listserver@daedalus.dra.hmg.gb

OWNER macdonald@hydra.dra.hmg.gb (Ruaridh Macdonald)

3696 talk.politics.crypto The relation between cryptography and government. *Newsgroup*

SIMULATION & MODELING

3697 alt.comp.fedem Discussion of FEDEM, a program for virtual prototyping. *Newsgroup*

3698 comp.simulation Simulation methods, problems, uses. *Moderated newsgroup*

3699 comp.soft-sys.ptolemy The Ptolemy simulation/code generation environment. *Newsgroup*

➤ **Emergency Management/Planning Newsletter:** The journal is used to discuss events and programs in the emergency management and planning community. (See entry 9891 for full listing.)

➤ `sci.electronics.cad`: Schematic drafting, printed circuit layout, simulation. *Newsgroup*

3700 **Spacesim:** An electronic newsletter for space-simulation enthusiasts. *Newsletter*
± http://chico.rice.edu/armadillo/Simulations/
INFO chris@tenet.edu (Chris Rowan)
ARCHIVE http://chico.rice.edu/armadillo/Simulations/
Frequency: monthly

SOCIAL ISSUES

➤ **ACTLab (Advanced Communication Technologies Laboratory):** Information on issues of human-computer interfaces, interaction, and agency. (See entry 9358 for full listing.)

3701 `alt.comp.acad-freedom.news` Academic freedom issues related to computers. *Moderated newsgroup*

3702 `alt.comp.acad-freedom.talk` Academic freedom issues related to computers. *Newsgroup*

➤ `alt.life.internet`: This may be the answer to "get a life" for some. *Newsgroup*

3703 `alt.politics.datahighway` Electronic interstate infrastructure. *Newsgroup*

➤ `bcs.activists`: Activist issues of the Boston Computer Society. *Newsgroup*

3704 `bit.listserv.ethics-l` Discussion of ethics in computing. *Newsgroup*

3705 `bit.listserv.pacs-l` Public-Access Computer System forum. *Moderated newsgroup*

3706 **C+Health:** About the health effects of computer use. *Mailing List, moderated*
± listserv@iubvm.ucs.indiana.edu [body = SUBSCRIBE C+HEALTH first-name last-name]
INFO sheehan@bronze.ucs.indiana.edu (Mark Sheehan)
ARCHIVE listserv@iubvm.ucs.indiana.edu
Gated: bit.listserv.c+health

3707 `clari.nb.law` Newsbytes: computer crime, legislation, privacy. *Moderated newsgroup*

3708 `clari.tw.issues` Technology and society; privacy, computer porn. *Moderated newsgroup*

➤ **Community Networking Resources:** This Web page is a collection of pointers to a variety of community networking resources, including Web sites of some existing community networks, papers on the subject, conference information, and more. (See entry 2423 for full listing.)

3709 `comp.home.misc` Media, technology, and information in domestic spaces. *Moderated newsgroup*

3710 `comp.human-factors` Issues related to human-computer interaction (HCI). *Newsgroup*

3711 `comp.org.cpsr.announce` Computer Professionals for Social Responsibility. *Moderated newsgroup*

3712 `comp.org.cpsr.talk` Issues of computing and social responsibility. *Newsgroup*

3713 `comp.org.eff.news` News from the Electronic Frontier Foundation. *Moderated newsgroup*

3714 `comp.org.eff.talk` Discussion of EFF goals, strategies, etc. *Newsgroup*

3715 `comp.risks` Risks to the public from computers and users. *Moderated newsgroup*

3716 `comp.society` The impact of technology on society. *Moderated newsgroup*

➤ `comp.society.development`: Computer technology in developing countries. *Newsgroup*

3717 `comp.society.privacy` Effects of technology on privacy. *Moderated newsgroup*

3718 **Computer Professionals for Social Responsibility (CPSR):** On the impact of technology on society, including political and social problems.
http://www.cpsr.org/dox/home.html
INFO cpsr@cpsr.org
FAQ http://www.cpsr.org/dox/cpsr/about-cpsr.html

Comments: CPSR welcomes everyone who uses or is concerned about the role of computer technology in our society.

➤ **Computer Security Resource Clearinghouse:** This site, sponsored by the National Institute of Standards and Technology, provides a wide range of information on computer security topics, including: general security risks, privacy, legal issues, viruses, assurance, policy, and training. (See entry 3682 for full listing.)

3719 **Computer Underground Digest (CuD):** Discussion of legal, ethical, social, and other issues regarding computerized information and communications. Readers are encouraged to submit reasoned articles relating to computer culture and communication. *Distribution List*

http://www.soci.niu.edu/~cudigest

± listproc@vmd.cso.uiuc.edu [body = SUB CUD first-name last-name]

INFO tk0jut2@mvs.cso.niu.edu (Jim Thomas and Gordon Meyer)

ARCHIVES

ftp://ftp.eff.org/pub/cud/

ftp://etext.archive.umich.edu/cud/

ftp://nic.funet.fi/pub/doc/cud/

Gated: comp.society.cu-digest

Frequency: weekly

➤ **Computer-Mediated Communication Magazine:** People, events, applications, and research related to computer-mediated communication (CMC). (See entry 5166 for full listing.)

3720 **COMSOC-L:** Discussion of the social impact of computers and computer-related technologies. *Digest & Reflector*

± listserv@american.edu [body = SUBSCRIBE COMSOC-L first-name last-name]

INFO comsoc-l-request@american.edu

➤ **CPU: Working in the Computer Industry:** Focusing on work trends in the computer industry. CPU rejects the pro-management assumptions of most computer publications and focuses upon the employees themselves. (See entry 2010 for full listing.)

3721 **CROSS-L:** On research in cross-cultural information systems. *Mailing List*

± INFO evaristo@du.edu (Roberto Evaristo)

➤ **cwd-l:** Brock Meeks' CyberWire Dispatch List. (See entry 2876 for full listing.)

➤ **CYBER-RIGHTS:** Campaign for cyber rights: "Don't let the grinch steal cyberspace!" (See entry 9748 for full listing.)

➤ **CYBERIA-L:** On the law and policy of computer networks. (See entry 5536 for full listing.)

➤ **Cyberpunk:** Texts for understanding technology and culture, from the English Server at CMU. (See entry 9819 for full listing.)

3722 **DIGIT-L:** For members of the Diffusion Interest Group in Information Systems. *Mailing List*

± listserv@cfrvm.cfr.usf.edu [body = SUBSCRIBE DIGIT-L first-name last-name]

OWNER mary@cfrvm.cfr.usf.edu (Mary Prescott)

Please Note: Subscription by approval only.

➤ **Electronic Frontier Foundation:** The Electronic Frontier Foundation is a 501(c)3 nonprofit organization "working in the public interest to protect privacy, free expression, and access to online resources and information." The site includes very important information on the interaction between our government and the Internet, as well as an extensive archive with documents on a wide range of topics, including activism, censorship, cryptography and computer security, net culture and cyber-anthropology, intellectual property, law, privacy, and more. It also archives various e-journals related to its mission. (See entry 9749 for full listing.)

➤ **EFFector Online:** For the Electronic Frontier Foundation (EFF). (See entry 9750 for full listing.)

3723 **EPIC Alert:** Online newsletter of the Electronic Privacy Information Center in Washington, D.C. Focuses on privacy and civil-liberties issues in the information age. *Newsletter*

http://www.epic.org/

± epic-news@epic.org [subject = subscribe]

INFO banisar@epic.org (David Banisar)

INFO POST alert@epic.org

ARCHIVE http://www.epic.org/alert/

Frequency: biweekly

➤ **From Now On: The Educational Technology Journal:** Devoted to issues of change and the introduction of new technologies to schools and the workplace. (See entry 4508 for full listing.)

➤ **futurework:** This list focuses on ways for communities worldwide to deal with economic globalization and technological change. (See entry 9761 for full listing.)

3724 **GNU's Bulletin:** The GNU's Bulletin is the semiannual newsletter of the Free Software Foundation, bringing you news about the GNU Project. *Newsletter*

± INFO info-gnu-request@prep.ai.mit.edu.

± INFO gnu@prep.ai.mit.edu

Gated: newsgroup gnu.announce

Frequency: semiannual

➤ **GovAccess:** On computer-assisted citizen participation in—and protection from—government. (See entry 5381 for full listing.)

➤ **GW-INFO:** On GW Micro products for computer access by the blind and learning disabled. (See entry 9866 for full listing.)

3725 **IFIP82-L:** On social and organizational factors implied by information technology and information systems. *Mailing List*

gopher://bingnet1.cc.binghamton.edu:70/11/funding/local/Ifipwg82

http://www.som.binghamton.edu/ifipwg82/

± listserv@bingvmb.cc.binghamton.edu [body = SUBSCRIBE IFIP82-L first-name last-name]

INFO rbask@bingsuns.cc.binghamton.edu (Richard L. Baskerville)

3726 **info-gnu:** Software development for social change: progress reports from the GNU Project and requests for help. Ask info-gnu-request@prep.ai.mit.edu for a list of other mailing lists and resources of all the GNU Project mailing lists and newsgroups. *Reflector & Resource, moderated*

± INFO info-gnu-request@prep.ai.mit.edu [body = HELP]

ARCHIVE ftp://prep.ai.mit.edu/pub/gnu/MailingListArchives/

FAQ ftp://prep.ai.mit.edu/pub/gnu/GNUinfo/MAILINGLISTS

Gated: gnu.announce

3727 **The League for Programming Freedom:** The League for Programming Freedom is a grassroots organization of professors, students, businessmen, programmers, and users dedicated to bringing back the freedom to write programs. Their aim is to reverse the recent changes that prevent programmers from doing their work by fighting software patents and "look and feel" interface copyrights.

http://www.lpf.org/

INFO lpf@lpf.org

3728 **misc.kids.computer** The use of computers by children. *Newsgroup*

➤ **MN-POLITICS:** On Minnesota politics, issues, and public policy. (See entry 8199 for full listing.)

3729 **NET.SCANDAL:** A world repository of irritainment. *Mailing List*

± net_scandal-request@io.org

INFO owner-net_scandal@io.org

OWNER evans@iguana.reptiles.org (Tom Evans)

➤ **Netiquette:** Netiquette: the Network Etiquette mailing list. (See entry 2866 for full listing.)

➤ **The Network Startup Resource Center:** This site contains information about: networking in the developing world, low-cost networking tools, general computer networking information, and networking tips and frequently asked questions. You can search for networking solutions and information by country. (See entry 9647 for full listing.)

3730 **pgh.cpsr** Computer Professionals for Social Responsibility, Pitt. *Newsgroup*

3731 **PRIVACY:** Discussion and analysis of issues relating to the general topic of privacy (both personal and collective) in the "information age." *Daily Digest, moderated*

http://www.vortex.com/
ftp://ftp.vortex.com
gopher://gopher.vortex.com
± privacy-request@vortex.com [body = SUBSCRIBE PRIVACY first-name last-name]
INFO OWNER POST privacy@vortex.com
ARCHIVES
http://www.vortex.com/
ftp://ftp.vortex.com
gopher://gopher.vortex.com
listserv@vortex.com [body = INDEX PRIVACY]
FAQ listserv@vortex.com [body = INFORMATION PRIVACY]

➤ **Processed World Wide Web:** Web site of *Processed World* magazine, the notorious "magazine with a bad attitude." Antiauthoritarian misfits go to work and and bite the hand that bores them. (See entry 2013 for full listing.)

3732 **The Red Rock Eater News Service:** All the news that Phil Agre, media and communications professor at UCSD, thinks fit to print on the subject of how technology affects peoples' lives. *Distribution List*

± rre-request@weber.ucsd.edu [body = SUBSCRIBE first-name last-name]
INFO rre-help@weber.ucsd.edu
OWNER pagre@weber.ucsd.edu (Phil Agre)
ARCHIVES
http://communication.ucsd.edu/pagre/archive_help.html
http://communication.ucsd.edu/pagre/archive_help.html

➤ **relcom.comp.law:** Political and legal aspects of computers. *Newsgroup*

3733 **RISKS:** On risks to the public in the use of computers and related systems—across all application areas, and including problems with security, reliability, safety, and human well-being. *Mailing List, moderated*

± risks-request@csl.sri.com [body = subscribe]
± listserv@ubvm.cc.buffalo.edu [body = SUBSCRIBE RISKS first-name last-name]
± listserv@uga.cc.uga.edu [body = SUBSCRIBE RISKS first-name last-name]
± listserv@vm.marist.edu [body = SUBSCRIBE RISKS first-name last-name]
INFO risks-request@csl.sri.com [body = info]
EDITOR OWNER neumann@csl.sri.com (Peter G. Neumann)
ARCHIVES
http://catless.ncl.ac.uk/Risks/
ftp://unix.sri.com/risks
listserv@uga.cc.uga.edu [body = INDEX RISKS]
listserv@vm.marist.edu [body = INDEX RISKS]
POST risks@csl.sri.com
Gated: comp.risks

3734 **sat.eff** Electronic Frontier Foundation in San Antonio, Texas. *Moderated newsgroup*

➤ **sci.philosophy.meta:** Discussions within the scope of "meta-philosophy". *Newsgroup*

➤ **The Villanova Information Law Chronicle:** The Villanova Information Law Chronicle is a hypertext publication that carries the latest in current events concerning information law, papers involving networking and the law, and essays discussing the future of the information infrastructure. (See entry 5546 for full listing.)

SOFTWARE & DOCUMENT ARCHIVES

➤ <u>Games Domain:</u> A comprehensive games site; includes FAQs and pointers to games sites; covers all varieties of games. (See entry 6330 for full listing.)

➤ **Netlib:** A collection of mathematical software, papers, and databases. (See entry 9373 for full listing.)

3735 `alt.binaries.misc` Random large files without a more appropriate group. *Newsgroup*

3736 `aus.archives` Announcements of available software. *Newsgroup*

3737 **Brown University Public Archive:** This archive is maintained by Computing and Information Services at Brown University in Providence, Rhode Island. Its main purpose is the distribution of software developed or modified at Brown University.

`ftp://ftp.brown.edu`

INFO `postmaster@brown.edu`

3738 `comp.archives` Descriptions of public access archives. *Moderated newsgroup*

3739 `comp.archives.admin` Issues relating to computer archive administration. *Newsgroup*

3740 `comp.doc` Archived public-domain documentation. *Moderated newsgroup*

3741 `comp.doc.techreports` Lists of technical reports/lists. *Moderated newsgroup*

➤ **EUnet Germany Information Service:** This is the information service of EUnet Germany, a network-services provider. It includes a large software archive and a German zip-code finder. (See entry 7310 for full listing.)

3742 `fj.archives.d` For any topics related to `fj.archives`. *Newsgroup*

3743 `fj.archives.documents` Repository for documents. *Newsgroup*

3744 `fj.archives.misc` Repository for miscellaneous data. *Newsgroup*

3745 `fj.binaries.misc` Encoded programs in binary not covered elsewhere. *Newsgroup*

3746 `fj.news.group.archives` About newsgroups for archives. *Newsgroup*

3747 **ICOT Free Software Newsletter:** Information about free software released by the Institute for New Generation Computer Technology. *Newsletter*

`http://www.icot.or.jp/ICOT/IFS/IFS-News/ifs-news.html`

± INFO `ifs@icot.or.jp` (Akira Aiba)

ARCHIVE `ftp://ftp.icot.or.jp/ifs/newsletter`

Language: English and Japanese

Frequency: irregular (about every two months)

3748 **Inter-Links Downloads:** Inter-Links listing of software archives, all of which can be accessed via the numerous links provided.

`http://www.nova.edu/Inter-Links/downloads.html`

INFO `kabacoff@alpha.acast.nova.edu`

3749 `misc.answers` Repository for periodic Usenet articles. *Moderated newsgroup*

➤ `news.answers`: Repository for periodic Usenet articles. *Moderated newsgroup*

➤ `rec.answers`: Repository for periodic Usenet articles. *Moderated newsgroup*

➤ **SKY Online:** SKY Online is the premier source of astronomical news and information on the World Wide Web. It features excerpts from *Sky & Telescope* and *CCD Astronomy* magazines, along with a weekly news bulletin and celestial calendar, helpful tips for backyard skygazers, reviews of telescopes and accessories, downloadable BASIC programs to do astronomical calculations on your PC or Mac, and much more. (See entry 8939 for full listing.)

3750 **SunSITE:** This is the web interface to the massive SunSITE ftp archives, a weather server, information on Sun Microsystems, and "multimedia exhibits". The archives include government documents, software, educational materials, and much more.

`http://sunsite.unc.edu/` (USA at University of North Carolina - Chapel Hill)

INFO `webmaster@sunsite.unc.edu`

MIRRORS

`http://sunsite.cnam.fr/index.html` (France at Conservatoire National des Arts-et-Metiers - Paris)

`http://sunsite.mff.cuni.cz/` (Czech Republic at Charles University - Prague)

http://sunsite.math.klte.hu/ (Hungary at Lajos Kossuth University- Debrecen)

http://sunsite.ust.hk/ (Hong Kong at University of Science and Tech. - Hong Kong)

http://sunsite.dcc.uchile.cl/ (Chile at Universidad de Chile - Santiago)

http://sunsite.doc.ic.ac.uk/ (Northern Europe at Imperial College - London)

http://sunsite.informatik.rwth-aachen.de/ (Central Europe at RWTH-Aachen - Germany)

http://ericir.sunsite.syr.edu/ (USA at AskERIC Syracuse University - Syracuse)

http://sunsite.wits.ac.za/ (Sun SITE South Africa at University of the Witwatersrand - Johannesburg)

http://sunsite.dsi.unimi.it/index.html (Italy at University of Milan - Milan)

http://sunsite.cs.msu.su/ (Russia at Moscow State University - Moscow)

http://sunsite.icm.edu.pl/ (Poland at Warsaw University - Warsaw)

http://sunsite.au.ac.th/ (Thailand at Assumption University - Bangkok)

http://sunsite.nus.sg/ (Singapore at National University of Singapore - Singapore)

http://sunsite.rediris.es/index.html (Spain at Consejo Superior de Investigaciones Cientificas, RedIRIS - Madrid)

http://sunsite.sut.ac.jp/ (Japan at Science University - Tokyo)

http://sunsite.huji.ac.il/sunsite.html (Israel at Hebrew University of Jerusalem - Jerusalem)

http://sunsite.snu.ac.kr/ (Korea at Seoul National University - Seoul)

http://sunsite.kth.se/ (Scandinavia at Kungliga Tekniska Hogskolan - Stockholm)

http://sunsite.unam.mx/ (Mexico at Universidad Nacional Autonoma de Mexico - Mexico)

3751 **SunSITE Document Archives:** A large selection of documents, books, speeches, papers, and tutorials on a wide variety of topics.

    ftp://sunsite.unc.edu/pub/docs/

    INFO ftpkeeper@sunsite.unc.edu

➤   **talk.answers:** Repository for periodic Usenet articles. *Moderated newsgroup*

3752 **Washington University of St. Louis FTP Archive:** Huge software archive maintained by Washington University of St. Louis.

    http://wuarchive.wustl.edu/

    ftp://wuarchive.wustl.edu

    INFO archives@wugate.wustl.edu.

    Comments: archives | e-text

3753 **Wisconsin Primate Center Software Archive:** Wisconsin Regional Primate Research Center (University of Wisconsin-Madison). The archive's purpose is to provide a distribution point for software developed at WRPRC.

    http://www.primate.wisc.edu/software/

    ftp://ftp.primate.wisc.edu/pub/

    INFO software@primate.wisc.edu

SOFTWARE PUBLISHING

3754 **alt.comp.shareware** "try before you buy" software marketing. *Newsgroup*

3755 **alt.comp.shareware.for-kids** "try before you buy" for children. *Newsgroup*

3756 **alt.fringeware** Riding the radical edge of the software wave. *Newsgroup*

➤   **CDR-L:** On the mastering of CDs—primarily hardware and software issues. (See entry 3784 for full listing.)

3757 **clari.tw.computers.pc.software** MS-DOS and Windows software. *Moderated newsgroup*

3758 **comp.publish.cdrom.hardware** Hardware used in publishing with CD-ROMs. *Newsgroup*

3759 **comp.publish.cdrom.software** Software used in publishing with CD-ROMs. *Newsgroup*

3760 **comp.software.licensing** Software licensing technology. *Newsgroup*

➤   **DDTs-Users:** Pure Software's DDTs defect/problem-tracking system. (See entry 3491 for full listing.)

3761 **Giles Road Press:** Giles Road Press is the publisher of *Macintosh Tips & Tricks*, *A BBS Caller's Guide to FirstClass*, and Macintosh shareware and freeware.

> http://www.intac.com/~gilesrd/
> INFO gilesrdprs@eworld.com (Maria Langer)

➤ **GNU's Bulletin:** The GNU's Bulletin is the semiannual newsletter of the Free Software Foundation, bringing you news about the GNU Project. (See entry 3724 for full listing.)

3762 **softpub:** Forum on entrepreneural software publishing, including (but not limited to) shareware. *Mailing List*

> ± INFO softpub-request@toolz.atl.ga.us
> EDITOR admin@toolz.atl.ga.us
> OWNER todd@toolz.atl.ga.us (Todd Merriman)

3763 **SOFTRACK:** On Softrack, a software licensing application. *Mailing List*

> ± listserver@le.ac.uk
> OWNER agl1@le.ac.uk (Alistair G. Lowe-Norris)
> ARCHIVE listserver@le.ac.uk

SPREADSHEETS

3764 **comp.apps.spreadsheets** Spreadsheets on various platforms. *Newsgroup*

STANDARDS

➤ **bit.listserv.x400-l:** X.400 protocol list. *Newsgroup*

3765 **CCNET-L:** On Chinese computing. *Mailing List*

> ± listserv@uga.cc.uga.edu [body = SUBSCRIBE CCNET-L first-name last-name]
> INFO jiang@ifcss.org (Yuan Jiang)
> ARCHIVES
> listserv@uga.cc.uga.edu
> ftp://ftp.ifcss.org/pub/china-studies/compute/ccnet-archive/

3766 **comp.benchmarks** Discussion of benchmarking techniques and results. *Newsgroup*

3767 **comp.protocols.iso** The ISO protocol stack. *Newsgroup*

3768 **comp.protocols.iso.dev-environ** The ISO development environment. *Newsgroup*

➤ **comp.protocols.iso.x400:** X.400 mail protocol discussions. *Newsgroup*

3769 **comp.protocols.misc** Various forms and types of protocol. *Newsgroup*

➤ **comp.protocols.nfs:** Discussion about the Network File System protocol. *Newsgroup*

➤ **comp.protocols.ppp:** Discussion of the Internet Point to Point Protocol. *Newsgroup*

➤ **comp.protocols.snmp:** The Simple Network Management Protocol. *Newsgroup*

➤ **comp.protocols.tcp-ip:** TCP and IP network protocols. *Newsgroup*

3770 **comp.std.announce** Announcements about standards activities. *Moderated newsgroup*

3771 **comp.std.internat** Discussion about international standards. *Newsgroup*

3772 **comp.std.misc** Discussion about various standards. *Newsgroup*

➤ **comp.std.mumps:** Discussions about MUMPS language/standards. *Moderated newsgroup*

3773 **comp.std.unix** Discussion for the P1003 committee on Unix. *Moderated newsgroup*

3774 **comp.std.wireless** Examining standards for wireless network technology. *Moderated newsgroup*

➤ **EDESIGN:** For professionals involved in the design and development of electronic circuitry. (See entry 9192 for full listing.)

➤ **comp.protocols.kermit.announce:** Kermit announcements. *Moderated newsgroup*

➤ `comp.protocols.kermit.misc:` Kermit protocol and software. *Newsgroup*

3775 NISO-L: For distribution of press releases and informational items from the National Information Standards Organization. *Mailing List*

± `listserv@nervm.nerdc.ufl.edu` [body = `SUBSCRIBE NISO-L` first-name last-name]

INFO `niso-l-request@nervm.nerdc.ufl.edu`

3776 PCI-SIG: On PCI (Peripheral Component Interconnect) bus, as defined by the PCI-SIG group. *Mailing List*

± `pci-sig-request@znyx.com` [subject = `subscribe`]

OWNER `alan@znyx.com` (Alan Deikman)

3777 Year2000: On the year 2000 computer date problem (01/01/00). *Mailing List*

± `listmanager@hookup.net`

OWNER `pdejager@hookup.net` (Peter de Jager)

ARCHIVE `http://www.year2000.com/`

3778 Z FORUM: On the formal specification notation Z. *Mailing List*

± INFO `zforum-request@comlab.ox.ac.uk`

INFO `j.p.bowen@reading.ac.uk`

ARCHIVES

`ftp://ftp.comlab.ox.ac.uk/pub/Zforum`

`http://www.comlab.ox.ac.uk/archive/z.html`

Gated: `comp.specification.z`

3779 Z3950IW: On implementation of Z39.50, a national standard protocol that defines rules for search and retrieval of information and using a client/server model. *Mailing List*

± `listserv@nervm.nerdc.ufl.edu` [body = `SUBSCRIBE Z3950IW` first-name last-name]

INFO `z3950iw-request@nervm.nerdc.ufl.edu`

ARCHIVE `listserv@nervm.nerdc.ufl.edu` [body = `INDEX Z3950IW`]

STORAGE TECHNOLOGY

3780 `alt.cd-rom` Discussions of optical storage media. *Newsgroup*

3781 `bit.listserv.cdromlan` CD-ROM on local area networks. *Newsgroup*

3782 `biz.stortek.forum` Storage Technology Corporation. *Newsgroup*

3783 CD-ROM Updater: Information about new CD-ROM products, reviews, news, how to publish on CD-ROM, conferences, events. Limited to 100K per issue. *Newsletter*

`http://www.scrg.cs.tcd.ie/scrg/u/aaron/cd-rom/issue.html`

INFO `aquigley@.tcd.ie` (A. Quigley)

ARCHIVES

`http://www.box.or.jp/pub/updater/archives`

`http://www.car-safe.or.jp/~klee/updater/archives`

➤ **CDLAN:** On integrating CD-ROMs into LANs. (See entry 3274 for full listing.)

3784 CDR-L: On the mastering of CDs—primarily hardware and software issues. *Mailing List*

± `listserv@tulsajc.tulsa.cc.ok.us` [body = `SUB CDR-L` first-name last-name]

OWNER `rmoss@tulsajc.tulsa.cc.ok.us` (Robert Moss)

ARCHIVE `listserv@tulsajc.tulsa.cc.ok.us` [body = `INDEX CDR-L`]

Comments: Not a discussion of commercially available CDs.

3785 CDROM-L: On uses of CD-ROM. *Mailing List*

± `listserv@listserv.ucop.edu` [body = `SUBSCRIBE CDROM-L` first-name last-name]

INFO `cdrom-l-request@listserv.ucop.edu`

Gated: `alt.cdrom`

Comments: Daily digest

➤ **CDROMLAN:** On using CD-ROMs on local area networks. (See entry 3275 for full listing.)

3786 `comp.arch.storage` Storage system issues, both hardware and software. *Newsgroup*

3787 `comp.periphs.scsi` Discussion of SCSI-based peripheral devices. *Newsgroup*

➤ `comp.sys.ibm.pc.hardware.storage`: Hard drives and other PC storage devices. *Newsgroup*

3788 `fj.comp.dev.cdrom` Discussion on CD-ROM device. *Newsgroup*

3789 `fj.comp.dev.disk` Discussion on magnetic/optical disk. *Newsgroup*

3790 `fj.comp.dev.tape` Discussion on tape devices. *Newsgroup*

➤ **MEMO-NET:** On library media and technology. (See entry 5729 for full listing.)

➤ `tnn.multimedia.cdrom`: Discussions about CD-ROM. *Newsgroup*

SUPERCOMPUTING & PARALLEL COMPUTING

➤ **German Climate Computer Center (DKRZ):** This is the German Climate Computing Center (Deutsches Klimarechenzentrum, DKRZ) providing resources and information in the area of climate research. This includes lists of climate data sets, weather maps, parallel computing information, and more. (See entry 4568 for full listing.)

3791 **Access Online:** National Center for Supercomputing Applications (NCSA) high-performance computing magazine. *E-Magazine*
http://www.ncsa.uiuc.edu/Pubs/access/accessDir.html
INFO orders@ncsa.uiuc.edu
Frequency: quarterly

3792 `aus.computers.parallel` Talking parallel computers Down Under. *Newsgroup*

3793 `cern.cernmpp` Parallel processing activity at CERN. *Newsgroup*

3794 `cern.vmtodc` VM to distributed computing issues. *Newsgroup*

3795 `clari.nb.supercomputer` Newsbytes: supercomputers, parallel processing. *Moderated newsgroup*

3796 `comp.parallel` Massively parallel hardware/software. *Moderated newsgroup*

3797 `comp.parallel.mpi` Message Passing Interface (MPI). *Newsgroup*

3798 `comp.parallel.pvm` The PVM system of multicomputer parallelization. *Newsgroup*

3799 `comp.sys.concurrent` The Concurrent/Masscomp line of computers. *Moderated newsgroup*

3800 `comp.sys.convex` Convex computer systems hardware and software. *Newsgroup*

3801 `comp.sys.sequent` Sequent systems (Balance and Symmetry). *Newsgroup*

3802 `comp.sys.super` Supercomputers. *Newsgroup*

3803 `comp.sys.transputer` The Transputer computer and OCCAM language. *Newsgroup*

➤ `comp.unix.cray`: Cray computers and their operating systems. *Newsgroup*

3804 `fj.comp.parallel` Discussion about parallel computing. *Newsgroup*

➤ **German National Research Center for Information Technology (GMD):** Home page of GMD, an institute that does research in many branches of information technology. (See entry 9365 for full listing.)

3805 `han.sys.cray` Cray supercomputer and Crayettes. *Newsgroup*

3806 **HPCwire:** High performance computing newsletter - featuring scientific and commercial applications, new products, industry announcements, conference listings and call for papers listings, and classified jobs section. *Newsletter*
http://www.tgc.com/hpcwire.html
± trial@hpcwire.tgc.com (infobot for trial subscription)
INFO brandie@tgc.com (Brandie Reum, Marketing Manager)

EDITOR editor@hpcwire.tgc.com (Dianna Husum, Alan Beck)

OWNER tabor@tgc.com (Thomas Tabor, Publisher)

Frequency: weekly

3807 Interface: Alabama Supercomputer Authority Journal: This quarterly publication is designed to inform users and interested organizations of recent developments at the Alabama Supercomputer Authority. *E-Journal*

http://www.asc.edu/

± INFO asajam01@asnmail.asc.edu (Ms. Josie McCrary)

EDITOR asnsav01@asnmail.asc.edu (Dr. Scott von Laven)

ARCHIVE http://www.asc.edu/

Frequency: quarterly

3808 Ohio Supercomputer Center (OSC): This document server includes information on the OSC (grant applications, calendar, publications, etc.) as well as information on the Columbus area and Ohio in general.

http://www.osc.edu/

gopher://gopher.osc.edu

INFO webmaster@osc.edu

3809 SCCE-L: On supercomputing in central Europe. *Mailing List*

± listserv@pltumk11.bitnet [body = SUBSCRIBE SCCE-L first-name last-name]

INFO andma@pltumk11.bitnet (Andrzej Marecki)

ARCHIVE listserv@pltumk11.bitnet

3810 SUPERIBM: For users of IBM equipment for high-performance scientific applications (supercomputing). *Mailing List*

± listserv@ukcc.uky.edu [body = SUBSCRIBE SUPERIBM first-name last-name]

INFO OWNER crovo@ukcc.uky.edu (Bob Crovo)

3811 Swiss Center for Scientific Computing (CSCS/SCSC) Info Server: This site provides information about Switzerland's national supercomputing center (CSCS/SCSC): its organization, its high-performance computing facilities and support services in the area of scientific computing, and so on.

http://pobox.cscs.ch/

gopher://pobox.cscs.ch

INFO mgay@cscs.ch

3812 uk.org.epsrc.hpc.discussion EPSRC High Performance Computing discussion. *Newsgroup*

3813 uk.org.epsrc.hpc.news EPSRC High Performance Computing news. *Moderated newsgroup*

3814 USA-HPCC Web: This server provides Internet users access to material about the National Coordination Office for Federal High Performance Computing and Communications (HPCC) Program.

http://www.hpcc.gov/

gopher://gopher.hpcc.gov

INFO wwwadmin@hpcc.gov

TANDY

3815 bit.listserv.coco Tandy Color Computer list. *Newsgroup*

3816 COCO: On the Tandy Color Computer. *Mailing List*

± listserv@pucc.princeton.edu [body = SUBSCRIBE COCO first-name last-name]

INFO steve@wuarchive.wustl.edu (Steve Wegert)

ARCHIVE listserv@pucc.princeton.edu

3817 comp.sys.tandy Discussion about Tandy computers: new and old. *Newsgroup*

TEXT PROCESSING

3818 alt.religion.emacs EMACS. *Newsgroup*

3819 **BIBSOFT:** About software for citations and bibliographies. *Mailing List*
± `listserv@indycms.iupui.edu` [body = `SUBSCRIBE BIBSOFT` first-name last-name]
INFO OWNER `sues@shamu.mtn.ncahec.org` (Sue Stigleman)
INFO OWNER `morganj@indyvax.iupui.edu`
ARCHIVE `listserv@indycms.iupui.edu` [body = `INDEX BIBSOFT`]

3820 `bit.listserv.endnote` Bibsoft Endnote discussions. *Newsgroup*

3821 `bit.listserv.wpcorp-l` WordPerfect Corporation products discussions. *Newsgroup*

3822 `bit.listserv.wpwin-l` WordPerfect for Windows. *Newsgroup*

3823 `bit.mailserv.word-mac` Word processing on the Macintosh. *Newsgroup*

3824 `bit.mailserv.word-pc` Word processing on the IBM PC list. *Newsgroup*

➤ **CCNET-L:** On Chinese computing. (See entry 3765 for full listing.)

3825 `comp.editors` Topics related to computerized text editing. *Newsgroup*

3826 `comp.emacs` EMACS editors of different flavors. *Newsgroup*

3827 `comp.os.ms-windows.apps.word-proc` MS Windows word-processing applications. *Newsgroup*

3828 `comp.text` Text processing issues and methods. *Newsgroup*

3829 `comp.text.pdf` Adobe Acrobat and Portable Document Format technology. *Newsgroup*

3830 `comp.text.sgml` ISO 8879 SGML, structured documents, markup languages. *Newsgroup*

➤ **E-HUG:** On all things relating to use of Hebrew, Yiddish, Judesmo, and Aramaic on computers. (See entry 5289 for full listing.)

3831 `fj.comp.text` Text processing issues and methods. *Newsgroup*

3832 `fj.editor.emacs` EMACS editors of different flavors. *Newsgroup*

3833 `fj.editor.misc` Talk about editors. *Newsgroup*

3834 `fj.editor.mule` Discussion about Mule. *Newsgroup*

3835 `gnu.emacs.announce` Announcements about GNU EMACS. *Moderated newsgroup*

3836 `gnu.emacs.bug` GNU EMACS bug reports and suggested fixes. *Moderated newsgroup*

3837 `gnu.emacs.help` User queries and answers. *Newsgroup*

3838 `gnu.emacs.sources` *only* (please!) C and LISP source code for GNU EMACS. *Newsgroup*

3839 `gnu.emacs.vms` VMS port of GNU EMACS. *Newsgroup*

3840 `gnu.epoch.misc` The Epoch X11 extensions to EMACS. *Newsgroup*

3841 `gnu.groff.bug` Bugs in the GNU roff program bugs. *Moderated newsgroup*

➤ **ITISALAT:** On Arabic computing. (See entry 7539 for full listing.)

3842 **PCARAB-L:** On the various tools used for applying Arabic letters to personal computers. *Weekly Digest*
± `listserv@sakfu00.bitnet` [body = `SUBSCRIBE PCARAB-L` first-name last-name]
INFO OWNER `nad@sakfu00.bitnet` (Mustafa AlGhazal)
INFO EDITOR OWNER `fachmn11@sakfu00.bitnet` (Dr. Hamed Nassar)
ARCHIVE `listserv@sakfu00.bitnet` [body = `INDEX PCARAB-L`]

3843 **PRO-CITE:** About personal bibliographic software. *Mailing List*
± `listserv@iubvm.ucs.indiana.edu` [body = `SUBSCRIBE PRO-CITE` first-name last-name]
INFO EDITOR OWNER `daym@indiana.edu` (Mark T. Day)
ARCHIVE `gopher://gopher.medlib.iupui.edu/11c%3a/temp`

➤ **TEXT21-L:** On technology and the written word. (See entry 5179 for full listing.)

➤ **Wisconsin Primate Center Software Archive:** Wisconsin Regional Primate Research Center (University of Wisconsin-Madison). The archive's purpose is to provide a distribution point for software developed at WRPRC. (See entry 3753 for full listing.)

3844 **The WP Mac News:** An electronic newsletter for users of WordPerfect for Macintosh. *Newsletter*

`http://www.novell.com/ServSupp/mac/macnews`

`ftp://ftp.wordperfect.com/pub/wpapps/mac/mac_news`

INFO `macmail@novell.com` (Daniel Midgley, Editor)

ARCHIVES

`http://www.novell.com/ServSupp/mac/macnews`

`ftp://ftp.wordperfect.com/pub/wpapps/mac/mac_news`

Frequency: monthly

3845 **WPWIN-L:** On WordPerfect for Windows. *Digest & Reflector*

± `listserv@ubvm.cc.buffalo.edu` [body = SUBSCRIBE WPWIN-L first-name last-name]

INFO `wpwin-l-request@ubvm.cc.buffalo.edu`

ARCHIVE `listserv@ubvm.cc.buffalo.edu` [body = INDEX WPWIN-L]

TEXT PROCESSING—TEX

3846 `aus.computers.tex` The TeX text processing language. *Newsgroup*

3847 `aus.tex` The TeX typesetting system. *Newsgroup*

3848 `bit.listserv.tex-l` The TeXnical topics list. *Newsgroup*

3849 `chile.text.tex` Discussion of LaTeX and TeX. *Newsgroup*

3850 `comp.text.tex` Discussion about the TeX and LaTeX systems and macros. *Newsgroup*

3851 `fj.comp.texhax` Discussion about TeXhax and delivery of mailing list. *Newsgroup*

3852 `ie.tex` TeX discussions in Ireland. *Newsgroup*

3853 **LATEX-L:** On the development of the successor to LaTeX version 2. *Mailing List*

± `listserv@urz.uni-heidelberg.de` [body = SUBSCRIBE LATEX-L first-name last-name]

INFO `schoepf@uni-mainz.de` (Rainer Schöpf)

3854 **LATEX-UG:** On the LaTeX typsetting system. *Mailing List*

± `listserv@saupm00.bitnet` [body = SUBSCRIBE LATEX-UG first-name last-name]

INFO `latex-ug-request@saupm00.bitnet`

3855 **RUSTEX-L:** About Russian TeX and Cyrillic text processing. *Mailing List*

± `listserv@ubvm.cc.buffalo.edu` [body = SUBSCRIBE RUSTEX-L first-name last-name]

INFO `dlv@dm.com` (Dr. Dimitri Vulis)

ARCHIVE `listserv@ubvm.cc.buffalo.edu`

3856 **TeX AND TUG NEWS:** A quarterly newsletter for and by the TeX community. (formerlyTeXhax Digest). *Newsletter*

INFO `tug@tug.org`

ARCHIVES

`ftp://ftp.shsu.edu/tex-archive/digests`

`ftp://ftp.dante.edu/tex-archive/digests`

`ftp://ftp.tex.ac.uk/tex-archive/digests`

Frequency: quarterly

TRAINING

➤ **IPCT-L:** Broad-ranging discussion on interpersonal computing and technology used in education. (See entry 4516 for full listing.)

➤ **NETTRAIN:** For Internet/Bitnet network trainers. (See entry 2918 for full listing.)

3857 Telos CBT (Computer Based Training) Development: Telos develops cost-effective, interactive CBT training courses for high-tech companies.
http://members.aol.com/telospilot/cbt/training.htm
INFO telospilot@aol.com

3858 Training Express Learning Guides: Instructor-led and self-study computer learning guides and multimedia training systems.
http://www.dgl.com/tebklist.html
INFO sales@dgl.com (Product Sales & Corporate Accounts)

3859 uk.comp.training Creating and presenting computer training courses. *Newsgroup*

TRANSACTION PROCESSING SYSTEMS

3860 CICS-L: On CICS, a transaction-oriented system from IBM. *Mailing List*
⊥ listserv@vm.ucs.ualberta.ca [body = SUBSCRIBE CICS-L first-name last-name]
± listserv@utarlvm1.uta.edu [body = SUBSCRIBE CICS-L first-name last-name]
INFO reichetz@awiimc12.bitnet (Christian Reichetzeder)
INFO christian.j.reichetzeder@awiimc12.imc.univie.ac.at (Christian Reichetzeder)
ARCHIVES
gopher://gopher.akh-wien.ac.at/1/list$nb/cics-l
listserv@vm.ucs.ualberta.ca [body = INDEX CICS-L]
listserv@utarlvm1.uta.edu [body = INDEX CICS-L]

3861 CICSTALK: On the CICS 6000 transaction-processing system. *Mailing List, moderated*
± listserv@imc.com [body = SUBSCRIBE CICSTALK first-name last-name]
OWNER lmorrow@imc.com (Lee Morrow)

3862 ENCTALK: On the Encina transaction processing system. *Mailing List, moderated*
± listserv@imc.com [body = SUBSCRIBE ENCTALK first-name last-name]
OWNER lmorrow@imc.com (Lee Morrow)

3863 TE-TALK: On the Top End transaction processing system. *Mailing List, moderated*
± listserv@imc.com [body = SUBSCRIBE TE-TALK first-name last-name]
OWNER lmorrow@imc.com (Lee Morrow)

3864 TUXTALK: On the TUXEDO transaction processing system. *Mailing List, moderated*
± listserv@imc.com [body = SUBSCRIBE TUXTALK first-name last-name]
OWNER lmorrow@imc.com (Lee Morrow)

UNIX

3865 alt.filesystems.afs The Andrew file system. *Newsgroup*

3866 alt.russia.unix-must-die Discussion about the future of un*x (Russian). *Newsgroup*

➤ **alt.sys.sun:** Technical discussion of Sun Microsystems products. *Newsgroup*

3867 alt.unix.wizards Like comp.unix.wizards, only unmoderated. *Newsgroup*

3868 aus.org.auug AUUG Inc.—Australian Unix User Group. *Newsgroup*

3869 bc.unix Talk about Unix in British Columbia. *Newsgroup*

3870 ca.unix Unix discussion/help. *Newsgroup*

3871 CACTUS Newsletter: Newsletter for members and sponsors of the Capital Area Central Texas Unix Society (CACTUS). *Newsletter*
± INFO newsletter@cactus.org
± INFO officers@cactus.org
ARCHIVE http://www.cactus.org/

Gated: `austin.general`
Frequency: monthly

3872 `cern.security.unix` Discussions about Unix security at CERN. *Newsgroup*

3873 `clari.nb.unix` Newsbytes: Unix news. *Moderated newsgroup*

3874 `clari.tw.computers.unix` News of Unix and similar operating systems. *Moderated newsgroup*

3875 `clari.tw.computers.unix.releases` Press releases covering Unix. *Moderated newsgroup*

➤ `comp.infosystems.www.servers.unix:` Web servers for Unix platforms. *Newsgroup*

➤ `comp.security.unix:` Discussion of Unix security. *Newsgroup*

3876 `comp.soft-sys.andrew` The Andrew system from CMU. *Newsgroup*

3877 `comp.sources.unix` Postings of complete, Unix-oriented sources. *Moderated newsgroup*

3878 `comp.sys.pyramid` Pyramid 90x computers. *Newsgroup*

➤ `comp.sys.sgi.admin:` System administration on Silicon Graphics's Irises. *Newsgroup*

➤ `comp.sys.sun.hardware:` Sun Microsystems hardware. *Newsgroup*

3879 `comp.unix.admin` Administering a Unix-based system. *Newsgroup*

3880 `comp.unix.advocacy` Arguments for and against Unix and Unix versions. *Newsgroup*

3881 `comp.unix.internals` Discussions on hacking Unix internals. *Newsgroup*

3882 `comp.unix.misc` Various topics that don't fit other groups. *Newsgroup*

3883 `comp.unix.programmer` Q & A for people programming under Unix. *Newsgroup*

3884 `comp.unix.questions` Unix neophytes group. *Newsgroup*

3885 `comp.unix.shell` Using and programming the Unix shell. *Newsgroup*

3886 `comp.unix.unixware.announce` Announcements related to UnixWare. *Moderated newsgroup*

3887 `comp.unix.unixware.misc` Products of Novell's Unix Systems Group. *Newsgroup*

3888 `comp.unix.user-friendly` Discussion of Unix user-friendliness. *Newsgroup*

3889 `comp.unix.wizards` For only true Unix wizards. *Moderated newsgroup*

3890 `demon.ip.support.unix` Unix support issues. *Newsgroup*

3891 `ed.unix-wizards` Unix discussions, Edinburgh systems. *Newsgroup*

3892 `fj.questions.unix` Questions especially about Unix. *Newsgroup*

3893 `fj.sys.rs6000` Discussion about IBM RS/6000 workstation and AIX. *Newsgroup*

3894 `fj.unix` Unix neophytes group. *Newsgroup*

➤ **FlashBack:** Press releases, product announcements, and technical articles for Sun users from organizations other than Sun Microsystems. (See entry 2287 for full listing.)

3895 `gnu.announce` Status and announcements from the Project. *Moderated newsgroup*

3896 `gnu.bash.bug` Bourne Again SHell bug reports and suggested fixes. *Moderated newsgroup*

3897 `hepnet.hepix` The use of Unix for High Energy Physics work. *Newsgroup*

3898 `ie.iuug` Irish Unix User Group (IUUG) business. *Newsgroup*

3899 `iijnet.os.unix` Discussions about Unix. *Newsgroup*

3900 `il.amix` Israeli Unix user's association. *Newsgroup*

3901 `info.bind` The Berkeley BIND server (`bind@arpa.berkeley.edu`). *Moderated newsgroup*

3902 `israel.amix` Israeli Unix (Open Systems) user's association. *Newsgroup*

3903 `okinawa.os.unix` Discussion about Unix. *Newsgroup*

3904 `sanet.unix.questions` Questions related to the Unix operating system. *Newsgroup*

3905 `sanet.unix.sources` Unix source code posted here. *Moderated newsgroup*

3906 `sanet.unix.talk` Talk about Unix. *Newsgroup*

➤   **Sun World Online:** For Sun/Unix users. (See entry 2291 for full listing.)

➤   **SunFlash:** Press releases, product announcements, and technical articles from Sun Microsystems, Inc., for Sun users. (See entry 2293 for full listing.)

3907 `tn.unix` Discussion of issues related to Unix in Tennessee. *Newsgroup*

3908 `tnn.forum.jus` Information about Japan Unix Society. *Newsgroup*

3909 `tnn.sys.sun` Discussions about Sun workstations and clones. *Newsgroup*

3910 **UKUUG Newsletter:** Newsletter of the United Kingdom Unix User Group. The group is independent of any manufacturer or supplier and encourages the use of Unix and open systems in the U.K. *Newsletter*
`http://web.dcs.bbk.ac.uk/ukuug/newsletter`
± `ukuug@uknet.ac.uk`
INFO `sue@dcs.bbk.ac.uk`
ARCHIVE `ftp://src.doc.ic.ac.uk`
Frequency: bimonthly

3911 **unictr-l:** On CA-Unicenter, a Unix systems automation package. *Mailing List*
± `listserve@byu.edu` (All platforms)
OWNER `sorrel@byu.edu` (Sorrel Jakins)

3912 **Unix Help:** Nova University's Unix help for new users.
`http://www.nova.edu/Inter-Links/UNIXhelp/TOP_.html`

3913 **Unix tutorials:** A collection of Unix, telnet, Archie, Usenet and FTP tutorials, from East Stroudsburg University.
`gopher://jake.esu.edu/11/Help/Tutorials`

3914 `wny.unix-wizards` Unix wizards in western New York. *Newsgroup*

UNIX—LINUX

3915 `alt.os.linux.caldera` The Caldera Network Desktop. *Newsgroup*

3916 `alt.uu.comp.os.linux.questions` Usenet University helps with Linux. *Newsgroup*

3917 `aus.computers.linux` Australian newsgroup about the Linux version of Unix. *Newsgroup*

3918 `comp.os.linux.advocacy` Benefits of Linux operating system compared to other operating systems. *Newsgroup*

3919 `comp.os.linux.announce` Announcements important to the Linux operating system community. *Moderated newsgroup*

3920 `comp.os.linux.answers` FAQs, how-tos, READMEs, etc. about Linux. *Moderated newsgroup*

3921 `comp.os.linux.development.apps` Writing Linux applications, porting to Linux. *Newsgroup*

3922 `comp.os.linux.development.system` Linux kernels, device drivers, modules. *Newsgroup*

3923 `comp.os.linux.hardware` Hardware compatibility with the Linux operating system. *Newsgroup*

3924 `comp.os.linux.misc` Linux-specific topics not covered by other groups. *Newsgroup*

3925 `comp.os.linux.networking` Networking and communications under Linux. *Newsgroup*

3926 `comp.os.linux.setup` Linux installation and system administration. *Newsgroup*

3927 `comp.os.linux.x` Linux X-Windows System servers, clients, libs, and fonts. *Newsgroup*

3928 `dc.org.linux-users` D.C.-area Linux users group announcements, etc. *Newsgroup*

3929 `fj.os.linux` Discussion on Linux. *Newsgroup*

3930 **han.sys.linux** Linux, free Unix for all. *Newsgroup*

3931 **Linux CD and Support Giveaway List:** A list of people around the world who are willing to give away one of their Linux CDs or help in installing/downloading Linux. Aimed at people new to Linux only. Recipient pays the postage.
http://emile.math.ucsb.edu:8000/giveaway.html
INFO boldt@math.ucsb.edu
Comments: Can also be gotten by sending e-mail to: boldt@math.ucsb.edu. Subject: send giveaway_list

3932 **okinawa.os.linux** Discussion about Linux. *Newsgroup*

3933 **tn.linux** Discussion of the Linux operating system in Tennessee. *Newsgroup*

UNIX—SOFTWARE ARCHIVES

3934 **Andrew User Interface System (AUIS):** Source and other information related to the Andrew User Interface System.
http://www.cs.cmu.edu/~AUIS
ftp://ftp.andrew.cmu.edu/pub/AUIS/
INFO info-andrew-request@andrew.cmu.edu
FAQ ftp://ftp.andrew.cmu.edu/pub/AUIS/FAQ
Comments: An Andrew release is included with each X Windows release. This is mirrored to all the FTP sites that mirror the X tape.

➤ **Astronomy and Earth Sciences Archive at Stanford:** Astronomy/earth science-oriented material for Unix users. Includes Earth topography data, the CIA World Map II vector outline database in a compressed binary Unix/C-readable format, software and data of interest for amateur astronomers, and information of general usefulness or interest for earth scientists. Also contains some generic utilities for Unix machines, including C source for a Morse code practice program for Unix machines. (See entry 9310 for full listing.)

➤ **Carnegie Mellon University Networking Archive:** This site is informally maintained by the Network Development (NetDev) staff at Carnegie-Mellon University in Pittsburgh, Pennsylvania, USA. The site's primary purpose is to distribute free networking software and related materials written by the NetDev group. (See entry 3212 for full listing.)

➤ **Inter-Links Downloads:** Inter-Links listing of software archives, all of which can be accessed via the numerous links provided. (See entry 3748 for full listing.)

3935 **Minnie 386BSD Archive:** Archive of a BSD Unix for Intel x86 processor machines. Also contains some programs for Apple II computers, and some amateur radio files and software.
ftp://minnie.cs.adfa.oz.au
INFO wkt@csadfa.cs.adfa.oz.au (Warren Toomey)

3936 **SunSITE Gnu Archives:** Unix software written by the Free Software Foundation.
ftp://sunsite.unc.edu/pub/gnu/
INFO ftpkeeper@sunsite.unc.edu

➤ **SunSITE X-Windows Archives:** Interesting packages that run under X-Windows. (See entry 4007 for full listing.)

➤ **Washington University of St. Louis FTP Archive:** Huge software archive maintained by Washington University of St. Louis. (See entry 3752 for full listing.)

➤ **Wisconsin Primate Center Software Archive:** Wisconsin Regional Primate Research Center (University of Wisconsin-Madison). The archive's purpose is to provide a distribution point for software developed at WRPRC. (See entry 3753 for full listing.)

UNIX—VARIETIES

3937 **alt.solaris.x86** Sun's Solaris on Intel x86 compatible computers. *Newsgroup*

3938 **comp.bugs.2bsd** Reports of Unix* version 2BSD related bugs. *Newsgroup*

3939 **comp.bugs.4bsd** Reports of Unix* version 4BSD related bugs. *Moderated newsgroup*

3940 **comp.bugs.4bsd.ucb-fixes** Bug reports/fixes for BSD Unix. *Moderated newsgroup*

3941   `comp.bugs.misc`   General Unix bug reports and fixes (including V7, UUCP). *Newsgroup*

3942   `comp.bugs.sys5`   Reports of USG (System III, V, etc.) bugs. *Newsgroup*

3943   `comp.os.mach`   The MACH OS from CMU and other places. *Newsgroup*

3944   `comp.unix.aix`   IBM's version of Unix. *Newsgroup*

3945   `comp.unix.amiga`   Minix, SYSV4 and other *nix on an Amiga. *Newsgroup*

3946   `comp.unix.aux`   The version of Unix for Apple Macintosh computers. *Newsgroup*

3947   `comp.unix.bsd.386bsd.announce`   Announcements pertaining to 386BSD. *Moderated newsgroup*

3948   `comp.unix.bsd.386bsd.misc`   386BSD operating system. *Newsgroup*

3949   `comp.unix.bsd.bsdi.announce`   Announcements pertaining to BSD. *Moderated newsgroup*

3950   `comp.unix.bsd.bsdi.misc`   BSD/OS operating system. *Newsgroup*

3951   `comp.unix.bsd.freebsd.announce`   Announcements pertaining to FreeBSD. *Moderated newsgroup*

3952   `comp.unix.bsd.freebsd.misc`   FreeBSD operating system. *Newsgroup*

3953   `comp.unix.bsd.misc`   BSD operating systems. *Newsgroup*

3954   `comp.unix.bsd.netbsd.announce`   Announcements pertaining to NetBSD. *Moderated newsgroup*

3955   `comp.unix.bsd.netbsd.misc`   NetBSD operating system. *Newsgroup*

3956   `comp.unix.cray`   Cray computers and their operating systems. *Newsgroup*

3957   `comp.unix.dos-under-unix`   MS-DOS running under Unix by whatever means. *Newsgroup*

3958   `comp.unix.large`   Unix on mainframes and in large networks. *Newsgroup*

3959   `comp.unix.machten`   The MachTen operating system and related issues. *Newsgroup*

3960   `comp.unix.osf.misc`   Various aspects of Open Software Foundation products. *Newsgroup*

3961   `comp.unix.osf.osf1`   The Open Software Foundation's OSF/1. *Newsgroup*

3962   `comp.unix.pc-clone.16bit`   Unix on 286 architectures. *Newsgroup*

3963   `comp.unix.pc-clone.32bit`   Unix on 386 and 486 architectures. *Newsgroup*

3964   `comp.unix.sco.announce`   SCO and related product announcements. *Moderated newsgroup*

3965   `comp.unix.sco.misc`   SCO Unix, systems, and environments. *Newsgroup*

3966   `comp.unix.sco.programmer`   Programming in and for SCO environments. *Newsgroup*

3967   `comp.unix.sys3`   System III Unix discussions. *Newsgroup*

3968   `comp.unix.sys5.misc`   Versions of System V which predate Release 3. *Newsgroup*

3969   `comp.unix.sys5.r3`   Discussing System V Release 3. *Newsgroup*

3970   `comp.unix.sys5.r4`   Discussing System V Release 4. *Newsgroup*

3971   `comp.unix.ultrix`   Discussions about DEC's Ultrix. *Newsgroup*

3972   `comp.unix.xenix.misc`   General discussions regarding Xenix (except SCO). *Newsgroup*

3973   `comp.unix.xenix.sco`   Xenix versions from the Santa Cruz Operation. *Newsgroup*

3974   `comp.windows.news`   Sun Microsystems' NeWS window system. *Newsgroup*

3975   `comp.windows.open-look`   Discussion about the Open Look GUI. *Newsgroup*

3976   `fj.os.386bsd`   Discussion on 386BSD. *Newsgroup*

3977   `fj.os.bsd.bsd-os`   Discussion about BSD/OS. *Newsgroup*

3978   `fj.os.bsd.freebsd`   Discussion about FreeBSD. *Newsgroup*

3979   `fj.os.bsd.misc`   Discussion about BSD operating systems not covered by other `fj.os.bsd.*` newsgroups. *Newsgroup*

3980   **fj.os.bsd.netbsd**   Discussion about NetBSD. *Newsgroup*

3981   **fj.os.minix**   Discussion about the MINIX operating system. *Newsgroup*

3982   **IAUG-L:**   Originally for members of the now defunct International AIX Users Group of AIX (IAUG). Now a general-purpose mailing list for AIX users. AIX is a Unix operating system forIBM computers. *Mailing List*
    ± listserv@psuvm.psu.edu [body = SUBSCRIBE   IAUG-L first-name last-name]
    INFO meo@pencom.com (Miles O'Neal)
    ARCHIVE listserv@psuvm.psu.edu

3983   **il.aix**   Israeli discussion of the AIX operating system. *Newsgroup*

3984   **info.mach**   The Mach operating system (info-mach@cs.cmu.edu). *Moderated newsgroup*

3985   **israel.lists.aix-il**   Israeli discussion of the AIX operating system. *Newsgroup*

3986   **scoann:**   Product, service, and business announcements of reasonable interest to the SCO community of developers, distributors, resellers, consultants, administrators, and end users. *Mailing List, moderated*
    ± INFO scoann-request@xenitec.on.ca [body = Add: scoann: e-mail-address]
    INFO edhew@xenitec.on.ca (Ed. A. Hew)
    ARCHIVE ftp://ftp.xenitec.on.ca/pub/news/
    Gated: comp.unix.sco.announce

3987   **scomsc:**   Questions, answers, comments and discussion about past, present, and future SCO and related third-party products and services, not more specifically covered by one of the other lists. , *moderated*
    INFO edhew@xenitec.on.ca (Ed. A. Hew)
    INFO scomsc-request@xenitec.on.ca
    ARCHIVE ftp://ftp.xenitec.on.ca/pub/news/
    Gated: comp.unix.sco.misc

3988   **scoprg:**   Questions, answers, comments, and discussion about past, present, and future SCO development system products and related software and issues. , *moderated*
    ± INFO scoprg-request@xenitec.on.ca [body = Add: scoprg: e-mail-address]
    INFO edhew@xenitec.on.ca (Ed. A. Hew)
    ARCHIVE ftp://ftp.xenitec.on.ca/pub/news/
    Gated: comp.unix.sco.programmer

3989   **tnn.os.44bsd**   Discussions about 4.4 BSD. *Newsgroup*

3990   **tnn.os.bsd-on-386**   Discussions on BSD systems on 386 machines. *Newsgroup*

3991   **tnn.os.bsd386.announce**   Important announcements about BSD 386 operating systems. *Moderated newsgroup*

3992   **tnn.os.bsd386.applications**   Applications on BSD 386. *Newsgroup*

3993   **tnn.os.bsd386.bugs**   BSD386 bug information. *Newsgroup*

3994   **tnn.os.bsd386.development**   Software, tools for developers on BSD386. *Newsgroup*

3995   **tnn.os.bsd386.japanese**   Japanese environment on BSD386. *Newsgroup*

UNIX—X-WINDOWS

3996   **alt.toolkits.xview**   The X-Windows XView toolkit. *Newsgroup*

3997   **comp.emacs.xemacs**   Bug reports, questions and answers about XEMACS. *Newsgroup*

➤   **comp.emulators.ms-windows.wine:**   A free MS Windows emulator under X. *Newsgroup*

➤   **comp.infosystems.www.browsers.x:**   Web browsers for the X-Windows system. *Newsgroup*

3998   **comp.sources.x**   Software for the X-Windows system. *Moderated newsgroup*

3999   **comp.windows.x**   Discussion about the X-Windows system. *Newsgroup*

4000   **comp.windows.x.apps**   Getting and using, not programming, applications for X. *Newsgroup*

4001 `comp.windows.x.i386unix` The XFree86 window system and others. *Newsgroup*

4002 `comp.windows.x.intrinsics` Discussion of the X toolkit. *Newsgroup*

4003 `comp.windows.x.motif` The Motif GUI for the X-Windows system. *Newsgroup*

4004 `ed.windows.x` X-Windows, Edinburgh systems. *Newsgroup*

4005 `fj.mail-lists.x-window` X-Windows mailing list from ARPA. *Moderated newsgroup*

4006 `fj.windows.x` About X-Windows systems. *Newsgroup*

4007 **SunSITE X-Windows Archives:** Interesting packages that run under X-Windows.
`ftp://sunsite.unc.edu/pub/X11/`
INFO `ftpkeeper@sunsite.unc.edu`

4008 **TeleUSErs:** Technical information, examples, tips, etc., for users of TeleUSE, a GUI application development software. *Mailing List*
± INFO `teleusers-request@alsys.com` (Kent Allen)
FAQ `http://www.jagunet.com/dalmatian/TeleUSE.html`
Gated: `comp.windows.ui-builders.teleuse`

4009 `tnn.os.bsd386.x-window` X-Windows on BSD386. *Newsgroup*

4010 `tnn.window.gui.motif` Discussions about graphical interface of Motif. *Newsgroup*

4011 `tnn.window.x` Discussions about X-Windows. *Newsgroup*

➤ **XF-L:** On the XF software which is used to build X-Windows interfaces for Tcl/Tk based software. (See entry 3598 for full listing.)

USER GROUPS

4012 `alt.amateur-comp` Discussion and input for *Amateur Computerist* newsletter. *Newsgroup*

4013 `alt.binaries.sounds.mods.d` Discussions of `alt.binaries.sounds.mods`. *Newsgroup*

4014 `av.mug` Antelope Valley Microcomputer Users' Group. *Newsgroup*

4015 `av.user` Users in the Antelope Valley. *Newsgroup*

4016 `az.swusrgrp` The Southwest User's Group. *Newsgroup*

4017 `bcs.activists` Activist issues of the Boston Computer Society. *Newsgroup*

4018 `bcs.announce` Announcements from the BCS. *Moderated newsgroup*

4019 `bcs.announce.d` Discussion of `bcs.announce`. *Newsgroup*

4020 `bcs.answers` Frequently Asked Questions about the Boston Computer Society. *Newsgroup*

4021 `bcs.misc` General discussion about the Boston Computer Society. *Newsgroup*

4022 `bcs.olsc` BCS Online Services Committee issues. *Newsgroup*

4023 `bcs.sig.mac` General discussion about BCS Macintosh user groups. *Newsgroup*

4024 `bcs.sig.misc` General discussion about BCS user groups. *Newsgroup*

4025 `bermuda.computer.society` The Computer Society of Bermuda. *Newsgroup*

4026 `can.usrgroup` Unix user group information in Canada. *Newsgroup*

4027 `ch.chuug` General topics of interest to the Swiss Unix Users Group. *Newsgroup*

4028 `comp.org.sug` Talk about/for the the Sun User's Group. *Newsgroup*

4029 `demon.ip.winsock` For users of Winsock. *Newsgroup*

4030 `il.novell` Novell interest group in Israel. *Newsgroup*

4031 `ne.org.bcs` The Boston Computer Society. *Newsgroup*

4032 `pnw.sys.sun` Sun users. *Newsgroup*

4033 `tnn.forum.nsug` Newsgroup for Nihon Sun User Group. *Moderated newsgroup*

4034 `tnn.forum.soft-sys.tippler` User's group for TIPPLER. *Newsgroup*

4035 `tnn.forum.splus` S-PLUS users group. *Newsgroup*

4036 `wny.rocslug` Sun User's Group in western New York. *Newsgroup*

VIRTUAL REALITY

4037 `alt.lang.vrml` Virtual Reality Modeling Language discussion. *Newsgroup*

4038 `alt.pub.dragons-inn` Fantasy virtual-reality pub similar to `alt.callahans`. *Newsgroup*

➤ `alt.uu.virtual-worlds.misc`: Studying virtual reality at Usenet University. *Newsgroup*

4039 **MediaMOO:** This MOO is run by researchers at the MIT Media Lab. It is a professional community for media researchers—a place for people interested in the future of media to network and collaborate. You must be doing some form of media research to become a member.
`telnet://mediamoo.media.mit.edu:8888`
INFO `mediamoo-registration@media.mit.edu`
FAQ `http://asb.www.media.mit.edu/people/asb/MediaMOO`

➤ **MOO Papers:** Pavel Curtis' collection of MU* papers. (See entry 3180 for full listing.)

4040 `sci.virtual-worlds` Virtual reality—technology and culture. *Moderated newsgroup*

➤ **VIRTED:** On using virtual reality in education. (See entry 4372 for full listing.)

4041 **VIRTPSY:** On social contracts and interactions, or pschology, within virtual reality (VR). *Mailing List*
± `listserv@sjuvm.stjohns.edu` [body = `SUBSCRIBE VIRTPSY` first-name last-name]
OWNER `plucas@vt.edu` (Perry Lucas)
OWNER `shrose@sjuvm.stjohns.edu` (Sheila Rosenberg)

4042 **VRML Repository:** All about the Virtual Reality Modeling Language (VRML), including pointers to software archives, documentation, bibliographies, related mailing lists and newsgroups, job postings in the field, and more.
`http://www.sdsc.edu/vrml`
INFO `nadeau@sdsc.edu` (David Nadeau)
INFO `moreland@sdsc.edu` (John Moreland)
INFO `ceubanks@sdsc.edu` (Charles Eubanks)
MIRROR `http://www.vislab.usyd.edu.au/vrml/` (University of Syndney, Australia)

VIRUSES

4043 **Open University Anti-Virus Information:** This site includes virus updates as well as documents on viruses in technology and pointers to other virus resources.
`http://www-tec.open.ac.uk/casg/avone.html`
INFO `d.phillips@open.ac.uk`

4044 `alt.comp.virus` An unmoderated forum for discussing viruses. *Newsgroup*

4045 `alt.comp.virus.source.code` The source code to various viruses. *Newsgroup*

4046 `comp.virus` Computer viruses and security. *Moderated newsgroup*

➤ **Computer Security Resource Clearinghouse:** This site, sponsored by the National Institute of Standards and Technology, provides a wide range of information on computer security topics, including: general security risks, privacy, legal issues, viruses, assurance, policy, and training. (See entry 3682 for full listing.)

4047 **ICARO:** On computer viruses: research, tests, warnings & reports. *Mailing List*
`http://www-iwi.unisg.ch/~sambucci/icaro/`
± `majordomo@dsi.unimi.it` [body = `subscribe icaro`]
OWNER `luca.sambucci@iwi.unisg.ch` (Luca Sambucci)
Please Note: Subscription by approval only.

4048 `relcom.comp.virus` Computer viruses. *Newsgroup*

4049 `relcom.fido.su.virus` FIDOnet, viruses and vaccines. *Newsgroup*

4050 Virus Bulletin: An international publication on computer virus detections, prevention, and removal. Includes comparative reviews of antivirus products.
> `http://www.virusbtn.com/`
> INFO `webmeister@virusbtn.com`

4051 Virus Source: For resources and information on infecting and disinfecting: thorough and nonjudgmental.
> `http://www.xcitement.com/virus/`
> INFO `reckless@xcitement.com`

VM/CMS & MVS

4052 `bit.listserv.9370-1` IBM 9370 and VM/IS specific topics list. *Newsgroup*

4053 `bit.listserv.sfs-1` VM Shared File System discussion list. *Newsgroup*

4054 `bit.listserv.vm-util` VM utilities discussion list. *Newsgroup*

➤   `bit.listserv.www-vm:` World Wide Web on VM platform list. *Newsgroup*

4055 `bit.listserv.xedit-1` VM system editor list. *Newsgroup*

4056 CMSPIP-L: For users of CMS Pipelines, part of IBM's VM/CMS operating system. *Mailing List*
> ± `listserv@vm.akh-wien.ac.at` [body = SUBSCRIBE CMSPIP-L first-name last-name]
> INFO `reichetz@awiimc12.bitnet` (Christian Reichetzeder)
> ARCHIVES
> `http://www.akh-wien.ac.at/pipeline.html`
> `gopher://gopher.akh-wien.ac.at/11/list$nb/cmspip-l`
> `ftp://vm.akh-wien.ac.at/cmspip-l`
> `listserv@vm.akh-wien.ac.at` [body = INDEX CMSPIP-L]

➤   **IBMTCP-L:** All about IBM TCP/IP software products for VM, MVS, OS/2, and for associated IBM TCP/IP hardware. (See entry 3303 for full listing.)

4057 JES2-L: Technical discussions on JES2, a component of the IBM MVS operating system. *Mailing List*
> ± `listserv@vm1.nodak.edu` [body = SUBSCRIBE JES2-L first-name last-name]
> ± `listserv@vtvm1.cc.vt.edu` [body = SUBSCRIBE JES2-L first-name last-name]
> INFO `p85025@barilvm.bitnet` (Doron Shikmoni)
> ARCHIVES
> `listserv@vtvm1.cc.vt.edu` [body = INDEX JES2-L]
> `listserv@vm1.nodak.edu` [body = INDEX JES2-L]

4058 MICS-L: For technical discussion about the MICS Information Control System. *Mailing List*
> ± `listserv@hearn.nic.surfnet.nl` [body = SUBSCRIBE MICS-L first-name last-name]
> INFO `rob.vanhoboken@rc.tudelft.nl`
> ARCHIVE `listserv@hearn.nic.surfnet.nl` [body = INDEX MICS-L]

4059 MVMUA-L: For members of the Metropolitan IBM VM Users Association. *Distribution List*
> ± `listserv@vm.marist.edu` [body = SUBSCRIBE MVMUA-L first-name last-name]
> OWNER `urmm@vm.marist.edu` (Martha McConachy)

➤   **MVSGOPHER:** For discussion the MVS implementation of the gopher client and server. (See entry 2909 for full listing.)

➤   **NNMVS-L:** MVS/TSO NNTP news reader (NNMVS) discussion. (See entry 2990 for full listing.)

➤   **SNSTCP-L:** On Interlink SNS/TCP access products for MVS. (See entry 3305 for full listing.)

VMS

4060 ALPHA-IDS: OpenVMS AXP Internals programming. *Mailing List*
OWNER goathunter@wkuvx1.wku.edu (Hunter Goatley)
OWNER goathunter@loki.com (Hunter Goatley)
ARCHIVE ftp://ftp.wku.edu/lists/alpha-ids/

4061 bit.listserv.vmslsv-1 VAX/VMS listserv discussion list. *Newsgroup*

➤ **cern.alpha:** Discussion list on OpenVMS and OSF/1 Alpha machines. *Newsgroup*

4062 comp.os.vms DEC's VAX* line of computers and VMS. *Newsgroup*

4063 HLPCMD-L: For discussing help commands for the VM/CMS computer operating system. *Mailing List*
± listserv@brownvm.brown.edu [body = SUBSCRIBE HLPCMD-L first-name last-name]
INFO cmsmaint@brownvm.brown.edu (Peter DiCamillo)

4064 JES3-L: For programmers using JES3, IBM's job-entry subsystem 3 for MVS. *Mailing List*
± listserv@uga.cc.uga.edu [body = SUBSCRIBE JES3-L first-name last-name]
INFO bsfinkel@anl.gov (Barry Finkel)
INFO harold@uga.cc.uga.edu (Harold Pritchett)

4065 relcom.comp.os.vms VMS operating system. *Newsgroup*

4066 VMS-L: The VMS give-and-take forum. *Mailing List*
± listserv@searn.sunet.se [body = SUBSCRIBE VMS-L first-name last-name]
INFO vms-l-request@searn.sunet.se
ARCHIVE listserv@searn.sunet.se [body = INDEX VMS-L]

4067 vmsnet.alpha Discussion about Alpha AXP architecture, systems, porting, etc. *Newsgroup*

4068 vmsnet.announce General announcements of interest to all. *Moderated newsgroup*

4069 vmsnet.announce.newusers Orientation information for new users. *Moderated newsgroup*

4070 vmsnet.employment Jobs sought/offered, workplace- and employment-related issues. *Moderated newsgroup*

4071 vmsnet.epsilon-cd DEC's free, unsupported OpenVMS AXP CD. *Newsgroup*

4072 vmsnet.groups Administration of the VMSnet newsgroups. *Newsgroup*

4073 vmsnet.infosystems.gopher Gopher software for VMS, gatewayed to VMSGopher-L. *Newsgroup*

4074 vmsnet.infosystems.misc Miscellaneous infosystem software for VMS (e.g. WAIS, WWW, etc.). *Newsgroup*

4075 vmsnet.internals VMS internals, MACRO-32, Bliss, etc., gatewayed to MACRO32 list. *Newsgroup*

4076 vmsnet.misc General VMS topics not covered elsewhere. *Newsgroup*

4077 vmsnet.networks.desktop.pathworks DEC Pathworks desktop integration software. *Newsgroup*

4078 vmsnet.networks.management.decmcc DECmcc and related software. *Newsgroup*

➤ **vmsnet.networks.management.misc:** Other network management solutions. *Newsgroup*

➤ **vmsnet.networks.misc:** General networking topics not covered elsewhere. *Newsgroup*

➤ **vmsnet.networks.tcp-ip.cmu-tek:** CMU-TEK TCP/IP package, gatewayed to cmu-openvms-ip@drycas.club.cc.cmu.edu. *Newsgroup*

➤ **vmsnet.networks.tcp-ip.misc:** Other TCP/IP solutions for VMS. *Newsgroup*

➤ **vmsnet.networks.tcp-ip.multinet:** TGV's Multinet TCP/IP, gatewayed to info-multinet. *Newsgroup*

➤ **vmsnet.networks.tcp-ip.tcpware:** Discussion of Process Software's TCPWARE TCP/IP software. *Newsgroup*

➤ **vmsnet.networks.tcp-ip.ucx:** DEC's VMS/Ultrix Connection (or TCP/IP services for VMS)product. *Newsgroup*

➤ **vmsnet.networks.tcp-ip.wintcp:** The Wollongong Group's WIN-TCP TCP/IP software. *Newsgroup*

4079 vmsnet.sources Source code postings *only*. *Moderated newsgroup*

4080 **vmsnet.sources.d** Discussion about or requests for sources. *Newsgroup*

4081 **vmsnet.sysmgt** VMS system management. *Newsgroup*

4082 **vmsnet.tpu** TPU language and applications, gatewayed to info-tpu. *Newsgroup*

4083 **vmsnet.uucp** DECUS uucp software, gatewayed to vmsnet mailing list. *Newsgroup*

4084 **vmsnet.vms-posix** Discussion about VMS POSIX. *Newsgroup*

EDUCATION

4085 `fj.education` About education in general. *Newsgroup*

4086 `misc.education` Discussion of the educational systems. *Newsgroup*

4087 `relcom.education` Education discussions, from preschool to higher. *Newsgroup*

ADMINISTRATION

4088 AAUA-L: For members of the American Association of University Administrators. *Mailing List*
± `listserv@ubvm.cc.buffalo.edu` [body = SUBSCRIBE AAUA-L first-name last-name]
INFO `neuner@canisius.bitnet` (Jerry Neuner)
ARCHIVE `listserv@ubvm.cc.buffalo.edu`
Gated: `bit.listserv.aaua-l`

4089 Academic Outreach Resources: A resource for academic administrators, scholars, and decision makers who are looking to serve the needs of an increasingly diverse population of learners and educational partners.
`http://www.outreach.umich.edu/`
INFO `aop-rt@umich.edu`

4090 ACUHOI-L: For college and university housing officers. *Mailing List*
± `listserv@psuvm.psu.edu` [body = SUBSCRIBE ACUHOI-L first-name last-name]
INFO `acuho@sru.bitnet` (Paula Olivero)

4091 ASC-L: On academic sexual correctness: privacy, consent, and institutional encroachment. *Mailing List, moderated*
± `request-asc-l@csulb.edu`
EDITOR `case@csulb.edu`
Please Note: Subscription by approval only.

4092 BPRREENG-L: On applying business process re-engineering (BPR) to universities. *Mailing List*
± `listserver@lists.acs.ohio-state.edu`
OWNER `minnis.3@osu.edu` (Mark Minnis)
OWNER `allen.31@osu.edu` (Dan Allen)

4093 `can.schoolnet.staff.development` Staff development. *Newsgroup*

4094 Canadian Journal of Educational Administration and Policy: Educational administration practice and policy. *E-journal*
± `listproc@cc.umanitoba.ca` [body = SUBSCRIBE CANJEDADPOL-L first-name last-name]
INFO EDITOR `riffel@bldgeduc.lan1.umanitoba.ca` (J.A. Riffel)
EDITOR `buchanan@bldgeduc.lan1.umanitoba.ca` (N. Buchanan)
ARCHIVE `gopher://gopher.cc.umanitoba.ca/Faculties and Departments/Faculty of Education/Electronic Journals in Education`

4095 CPARK-L: On campus parking administration. *Mailing List*
± `listserv@psuvm.psu.edu` [body = SUBSCRIBE CPARK-L first-name last-name]
INFO `pete-weiss@psu.edu` (Pete Weiss)
OWNER `wdh1@oas.psu.edu` (W. Douglas Holmes)

➤ **DIVERSITY-FORUM:** On human resource management of diversity in business, education & social work. (See entry 9892 for full listing.)

4096 EDAD-L: For discussions between departments of educational administration internationally. *Mailing List*
± `listserv@wvnvm.wvnet.edu` [body = SUBSCRIBE EDAD-L first-name last-name]
INFO `edad-l-request@wvnvm.wvnet.edu`

4097 The Electronic AIR: Newsletter for institutional researchers and college and university planners. Reports on news, publications, position openings, requests for help, etc. *Newsletter*
± `air@mailer.fsu.edu`

INFO EDITOR `nelson_l@salt.plu.edu` (Larry Nelson)
ARCHIVE `gopher://isaac.engr.washington.edu/11/pubs/air`
Frequency: biweekly

4098 **FACSER-L:** On facilities and services departments in universities. *Mailing List*
± `listserv@wvnvm.wvnet.edu` [body = SUBSCRIBE FACSER-L first-name last-name]
INFO `u42b5@wvnvm.wvnet.edu` (Kate Van Sant)

4099 **JANITORS:** College and university housekeeping information. *Digest & Reflector*
± `listserv@ukanvm.cc.ukans.edu` [body = SUBSCRIBE JANITORS first-name last-name]
INFO OWNER `pete-weiss@psu.edu` (Pete Weiss)
INFO OWNER `djackson@pps1-po.phyp.uiowa.edu` (Dave Jackson)
ARCHIVE `listserv@ukanvm.cc.ukans.edu` [body = INDEX JANITORS]

➤ **MEALTALK:** On child nutrition programs. (See entry 9732 for full listing.)

4100 **MTN:** On training by midwestern college and university physical-plant staffs. *Mailing List*
± `listserv@iubvm.ucs.indiana.edu` [body = SUBSCRIBE MTN first-name last-name]
INFO `mtn-request@iubvm.ucs.indiana.edu`
ARCHIVE `listserv@iubvm.ucs.indiana.edu` [body = INDEX MTN]

➤ **NASPA1-L:** Distribution on the National Association of Student Personnel Administrators REGION I and other related subjects. (See entry 4196 for full listing.)

4101 **PAYHR-L:** On payroll, benefits, and human resources in higher education. *Mailing List*
± `listserv@vm1.ucc.okstate.edu` [body = SUBSCRIBE PAYHR-L first-name last-name]
INFO `upsxxas@okway.okstate.edu`
ARCHIVE `listserv@vm1.ucc.okstate.edu`

4102 **PROSTAFF:** For discussion of matters of common concern to professional staff at universities, particularly employment issues. *Mailing List*
± `listserv@uwavm.u.washington.edu` [body = SUBSCRIBE PROSTAFF first-name last-name]
INFO `roseth@u.washington.edu`

4103 **school-management:** Education in schools, especially management and curriculum. *Mailing List*
± `mailbase@mailbase.ac.uk` [body = SUBSCRIBE SCHOOL-MANAGEMENT first-name last-name]
INFO OWNER `m.f.fuller@ukc.ac.uk` (Mike Fuller)

➤ **SCUP's Planning Pages:** Web resources relating to planning for the future of higher education, including indexes to past issues of the print scholarly journal, *Planning for Higher Education,* archives of SCUP E-Mail News, information about international and regional conferences and workshops . . . and links to other online resources of interest to planners. (See entry 4198 for full listing.)

➤ **SHS:** The Society for Human Sexuality mailing list. Intended for general discussion of human sexuality and as a way to distribute information about events put on by the Society for Human Sexuality (a sex-positive registered student organization at the University of Washington). (See entry 10120 for full listing.)

4104 **STU-DEV:** On campus problems, student affairs, and practical student development theory. *Mailing List*
± `listserv@cms.cc.wayne.edu` [body = SUBSCRIBE STU-DEV first-name last-name]
INFO `slingre@waynest1.bitnet` (Scot Lingrell)
ARCHIVE `listserv@cms.cc.wayne.edu`

4105 **UCEA-L:** For members of the University Council for Educational Administration, an institutional consortium dedicated to the improvement of administrator preparation. *Mailing List*
± `listserv@psuvm.psu.edu` [body = SUBSCRIBE UCEA-L first-name last-name]
INFO `ucea-l-request@psuvm.psu.edu`
ARCHIVE `listserv@psuvm.psu.edu` [body = INDEX UCEA-L]

ADULT EDUCATION

4106 CAUCE-L: For discussion of issues (broad, narrow, practical, theoretical, controversial, or mundane) related to university continuing education. *Mailing List*
± `listserv@max.cc.uregina.ca` [body = `SUBSCRIBE CAUCE-L` first-name last-name]
INFO `lhein@robinhood.engg.uregina.ca` (Dr. Larry Hein)
ARCHIVE `listserv@max.cc.uregina.ca`

4107 Journal of Extension: Adult education research, resources, successful applications, critical issues, and scholarly opinion. *E-Journal*
`gopher://joe.org/joe`
`http://joe.org/joe/`
± `alamanc@joe.org` [body = `SUBSCRIBE JOE`]
INFO `joe-ed@joe.org`
Please Note: Subscription by approval only.
Frequency: quarterly

4108 `misc.education.adult` Adult education and adult literacy practice/research. *Newsgroup*

➤ **National Center on Adult Literacy:** This server distributes the National Center on Adult Literacy's publications and points to Web and gopher resources relevant to researchers, policy makers, and practitioners in adult literacy. (See entry 4274 for full listing.)

➤ **The National Institute for Literacy:** Information on the institute and an extensive list of pointers to national, international, and statewide Internet adult literacy resources including family literacy, workplace literacy, learning disabilities, and English as a second language. (See entry 4275 for full listing.)

4109 New Horizons in Adult Education: Current research and ideas in adult education. *E-Journal*
`http://alpha.acast.nova.edu/education/aednet.html`
± `listproc@pulsar.acast.nova.edu` [body = `SUBSCRIBE aednet` first-name last-name]
INFO EDITOR `horizons@alpha.acast.nova.edu` (Nancy Gadbow, Editor)
Frequency: 2-3 times a year

➤ **`uk.education.16plus`:** All aspects of 16+, community, and adult education. *Newsgroup*

ALTERNATIVE

4110 `alt.education.alternative` School doesn't have to suck! *Newsgroup*

4111 ALTLEARN: On alternative approaches to learning. *Mailing List*
± `listserv@stjohns.edu` [body = `SUBSCRIBE ALTLEARN` first-name last-name]
INFO `drz@sjuvm.stjohns.edu` (Bob Zenhausern, Ph.D.)
ARCHIVE `listserv@stjohns.edu`

➤ **Bruderhof Homepage:** Information on the Bruderhof movement, its Plough Publishing House, schools, church community, an archive of *The Plough* (Bruderhof periodical), articles related to social issues like the death penalty and family problems, and more. (See entry 8694 for full listing.)

4112 Waldorf: On Waldorf schools and the educational philosophy of Rudolf Steiner. *Mailing List*
± `listserv@sjuvm.stjohns.edu` [body = `SUBSCRIBE WALDORF` first-name last-name]
OWNER `lefty@apple.com` (David "Lefty" Schlesinger)
ARCHIVE `listserv@sjuvm.stjohns.edu` [body = `INDEX Waldorf`]
FAQ `http://www.io.com/~lefty/Waldorf_FAQ.html`

ALUMNI ASSOCIATIONS

4113 `alt.alumni.bronx-science` Those crazy kids from Bronx Sci. *Newsgroup*

4114 `alt.elite.prepschools.alumni` Preppie alumni. *Newsgroup*

4115 `alt.itc.alumni` Alumni of ITC . *Newsgroup*

4116 `alt.prep.choate` Group for students and alumni of Choate-Rosemary Hall. *Newsgroup*

4117 `alt.prep.cranbrook.alumni` Cranbrook school alumni. *Newsgroup*

4118 `alt.prep.deerfield.academy` Deerfield Academy Students and Alumni. *Newsgroup*

4119 `alt.prep.groton.alumni` Groton alumni. *Newsgroup*

4120 `alt.prep.manhattan.trinity` Trinity Prep School Students and Alumni. *Newsgroup*

4121 `alt.prep.milton.academy` Milton Academy Students and Alumni. *Newsgroup*

4122 `alt.prep.phillips.andover` Phillips-Andover Academy students and alumni. *Newsgroup*

4123 `alt.prep.phillips.exeter.academy` Phillips-Exeter students and alumni. *Newsgroup*

4124 `alt.prep.st-pauls.school.alumni` St. Paul's School Alumni. *Newsgroup*

4125 **ALUMNET:** Newsletter for alumni of Trinity University, including campus and alumni news, campus newspaper headlines, messages from the alumni, job searches, and continuing education. *Digest & Reflector, moderated*

    ± `listserv@vm1.tucc.trinity.edu` [body = SUBSCRIBE ALUMNET first-name last-name]

    INFO `rblysone@trinity.edu` (Dr. Robert Blysone)

    INFO `scurry@trinity.edu` (Stephen Curry)

    Please Note: Subscription by approval only.

4126 **EC-ALUMNI:** For Earlham College alumni, present and former faculty & staff, & other friends of the College. *Mailing List*

    ± `listserv@hslc.org` [body = SUBSCRIBE EC-ALUMNI first-name last-name class]

    OWNER `simon@hslc.org` (Alan Simon)

4127 **Glenbrook Academy Class of 1995:** Phone, address, and electronic information for members of the class of 1995 of the Glenbrook Academy of International Studies.

    `http://www.students.uiuc.edu/~ag-ho/academy.html`

    INFO `ag-ho@uiuc.edu`

4128 **JTS-CAGSALUM:** Alumni of Albert List College of Jewish Studies & Graduate School of the Jewish Theological Seminary of America. *Mailing List*

    ± `listserv@jtsa.edu` [body = SUBSCRIBE JTS-CAGSALUM first-name last-name]

    OWNER `calevine@jtsa.edu` (Caren N. Levine)

    ARCHIVE `listserv@jtsa.edu` [body = INDEX JTS-CAGSALUM]

    Please Note: Subscription by approval only.

4129 **OXY-SF:** For alumni of Occidental College in the San Francisco, CA area; e-mail owner for lists for alumni living in other regions. *Mailing List*

    ± `listserv@netcom.com` [body = SUBSCRIBE oxy-sf]

    OWNER `helsinki@ix.netcom.com` (John Phillips)

4130 **OXY-XX:** Five lists for Occidental College alumni, faculty, students, and administrators: OXY-LA for Los Angeles, OXY-SD for San Diego, OXY-SEA for Seattle, OXY-NY for New York, OXY-SF for San Francisco *Mailing List*

    `http://www.oxy.edu/`

    ± `listserv@netcom.com` [body = SUBSCRIBE OXY-xx where xx is LA, SD, SEA or NY]

    OWNER `helsinki@ix.netcom.com` (John Phillips)

4131 **stuy-announce:** For Stuyvesant High School, New York alumni. *Mailing List, moderated*

    ± `majordomo@panix.com` [body = subscribe stuy-announce]

    OWNER `patlee@panix.com` (Patrick Lee)

    ARCHIVE `http://www.panix.com/~stuy`

COLLEGE ENTRANCE & STUDENT RECORDS

4132 **AMSSIS-L:** American Management System's Student Information System (AMSSIS), mainframe software for maintaining student information at colleges and universities. *Mailing List*

    ± `listserv@uafsysb.uark.edu` [body = SUBSCRIBE AMSSIS-L first-name last-name]

    INFO OWNER `allenf@uafsysa.uark.edu` (Allen Fields)

ARCHIVE `listserv@uafsysb.uark.edu` [body = INDEX AMSSIS-L]

4133 DARS-L: Degree Audit Reporting System, which tracks a college student's progress toward an academic degree. *Mailing List*

± `listserv@miamiu.acs.muohio.edu` [body = SUBSCRIBE DARS-L first-name last-name]

INFO `dars-l-request@miamiu.acs.muohio.edu`

ARCHIVE `listserv@miamiu.acs.muohio.edu` [body = INDEX DARS-L]

4134 ILSPEEDE: For discussion among a group of secondary and postsecondary school administrators who have developed an ANSI standard for electronic transmission of transcripts. *Mailing List*

± `listserv@postoffice.cso.uiuc.edu` [body = SUBSCRIBE ILSPEEDE first-name last-name]

INFO `ilspeede-request@postoffice.cso.uiuc.edu`

ARCHIVE `listserv@postoffice.cso.uiuc.edu` [body = INDEX ILSPEEDE]

4135 ISIS-L: For users of ISIS student-information software products, published by SCT. *Mailing List*

± `listserv@utdallas.edu` [body = SUBSCRIBE ISIS-L first-name last-name]

INFO `dholmes@utdallas.edu` (David Holmes)

ARCHIVE `listserv@utdallas.edu`

4136 PACE-L: For users of the PACE computer-assisted advisement and degree audit system. *Mailing List*

± `listproc@listproc.gsu.edu` [body = SUBSCRIBE PACE-L first-name last-name institution-name]

INFO `mark-elliott@gsu.edu` (Mark Elliott)

ARCHIVE `listproc@listproc.gsu.edu` [body = INDEX PACE-L]

➤   **RECMGMT:** For records and archival management professionals. (See entry 5709 for full listing.)

4137 Regist-L: For sharing of information, experiences, concerns, and advice about issues affecting records and registration professionals at colleges and universities. *Mailing List*

`http://cedar.evansville.edu/~pa5/regist.shtml`

± `listproc@listproc.gsu.edu` [body = SUB REGIST-L first-name last-name]

INFO OWNER `jlb@selu.edu` (Janet Busekist)

INFO OWNER `jgreene@gsu.edu` (Jim Greene)

INFO `syskec@panther.gsu.edu` (Keith Campbell)

INFO OWNER `aucoin@evansville.edu` (Paul Aucoin)

INFO `drichards@gsu.edu` (Dale Richards)

ARCHIVE `listproc@listproc.gsu.edu` [body = INDEX Regist-L]

4138 `soc.college.admissions` The university admissions process. *Newsgroup*

4139 SPEEDE-L: For members of the American Association of Collegiate Registrars and Admissions Officers (AACRAO). *Mailing List*

± `listserv@vtvm1.cc.vt.edu` [body = SUBSCRIBE SPEEDE-L first-name last-name]

INFO `creggerp@vtvm1.cc.vt.edu` (Trish Cregger)

ARCHIVE `listserv@vtvm1.cc.vt.edu`

4140 VACRAO: For members of the Virginia Associaton of Collegiate Registrars and Admissions Officers. *Mailing List*

± `listserv@wlu.edu` [body = SUBSCRIBE VACRAO first-name last-name]

OWNER `sdittman@wlu.edu` (Scott Dittman)

4141 Virginia Association of Collegiate Registrars and Admissions Officers (VACRAO): Listing of VACRAO member institutions with links to Web or gopher servers and other useful information useful to collegiate admissions and records professionals.

`http://www.wlu.edu/~registra/vacrao`

INFO `sdittman@wlu.edu` (Scott Dittman)

COMMUNITY COLLEGES

4142 Alamo Community College District CWIS: CWIS for Alamo Community Colleges in San Antonio, Texas.

```
gopher://accdvm.accd.edu
```
INFO sysworkl@accd.edu

4143 COMMCOLL: For faculty, staff, and administration at two-year institutions. *Mailing List*

± listserv@ukcc.uky.edu [body = SUBSCRIBE COMMCOLL first-name last-name]

INFO OWNER jccannek@ukcc.uky.edu (Anne Kearney)

OWNER larmbru@cello.gina.calstate.edu (Lynda Armbruster)

OWNER nvwildr@nv.cc.va.us (Robert W. Wildblood)

EARLY CHILDHOOD

➤ **CM:** An electronic viewing journal of Canadian materials for young people. Reviews and articles about Canadian books, videos, and materials for young people. (See entry 7139 for full listing.)

4144 ECEOL-L: Early Childhood Education On Line—idea and information exchange for early childhood educators. *Mailing List*

± listserv@maine.edu [body = SUBSCRIBE ECEOL-L first-name last-name]

INFO bonnieb@maine.bitnet (Bonnie Blagojevic)

ARCHIVE listserv@maine.edu

4145 ECPOLICY-L: On early childhood policy. *Mailing List*

± listserv@postoffice.cso.uiuc.edu [body = SUBSCRIBE ECPOLICY-L first-name last-name]

INFO cesarone@uiuc.edu

4146 ERIC Clearinghouse on Elementary and Early Childhood Education: Information and resources on the care, development, and education of children from birth through early adolescence.

```
http://ericps.ed.uiuc.edu/ericeece.html
```
INFO cesarone@uiuc.edu

➤ **ERIC/EECE Newsletter:** Newsletter of the ERIC Clearinghouse on Elementary and Early Childhood Education. One lead article and several short articles about educational programs and ideas, resources, news updates, Internet developments at ERIC/EECE, and announcements. (See entry 4226 for full listing.)

4147 ReadyWeb: All about school readiness. Includes government documents, bibliographies, and links to other Internet resources.

```
http://ericps.ed.uiuc.edu/readyweb/readyweb.html
```
INFO cesarone@uiuc.edu

ESL/EFL

4148 The ESL Virtual Catalog: A guide to Internet resources available to students and teachers of ESL and EFL (English as a second/foreign language).

```
http://www.pvp.com/esl.htm
```
INFO esl@pvp.com

4149 EFLWEB: An online magazine for those teaching and learning English as a foreign language.

```
http://www.u-net.com/eflweb/
```
INFO market@intecpub.demon.co.uk

4150 eslcc: For English as a second language (ESL) teachers at community colleges. *Mailing List*

± eslcc-request@hcc.hawaii.edu

OWNER garyjame@hcc.hawaii.edu (Gary James)

➤ **The National Institute for Literacy:** Information on the institute and an extensive list of pointers to national, international, and statewide Internet adult literacy resources including family literacy, workplace literacy, learning disabilities, and English as a second language. (See entry 4275 for full listing.)

4151 O-Hayo Sensei: The newsletter of English-teaching jobs in Japan. Includes current employment listings for all types of teaching positions in Japan: conversation schools, universities, high schools, etc. *Newsletter*

```
http://fuji.stanford.edu/japan_information/recruiting
```

± **EDITOR** ohayo@calon.com (Lynn Cullivan, Editor)

Frequency: about every two weeks (19 issues published in 1994)

➤ **SLART-L:** For scholarly discussion and exchange of information on second or foreign language education. (See entry 4264 for full listing.)

4152 **TESL-L:** On teaching English as a second/foreign language. *Mailing List, moderated*

± listserv@cunyvm.cuny.edu [body = SUBSCRIBE TESL-L first-name last-name]

OWNER abthc@cunyvm.cuny.edu (Anthea Tillyer)

ARCHIVE gopher://cunyvm.cuny.edu/subject specific gophers/Teaching English as a second/foreign language

Gated: bit.listserv.TESL-L

4153 **TESLK-12:** On teaching English as a second language to children. *Mailing List*

± listserv@cunyvm.cuny.edu [body = SUBSCRIBE TESLK-12 first-name last-name]

OWNER abthc@cunyvm.cuny.edu (Anthea Tillyer)

OWNER datcc@cunyvm.cuny.edu (David Tillyer)

FINANCIAL AID

4154 **FinAid: The Financial Aid Information Page:** A comprehensive resource for student financial aid information. It includes an online, searchable database of financial aid resources; loan calculators; pointers to other financial aid resources on the Web; and much more.

http://www.cs.cmu.edu/~finaid/finaid.html

INFO mkant@cs.cmu.edu (Mark Kantrowitz)

4155 **FINAID-L:** On student financial aid administration, including automation, federal regulations, professional judgment, and policies and procedures—not for applying for financial aid. *Digest & Reflector*

± listserv@psuvm.psu.edu [body = SUBSCRIBE FINAID-L first-name last-name]

INFO OWNER req1@psu.edu (Robert Quinn)

Comments: This list is *not: a medium through which to apply for financial aid* or to solicit for private business matters regardless of their relation to financial aid.

➤ **Loci:** An online magazine by and for college students. Includes entertainment information, games, chat forums, and more. Sponsored by Barnes & Noble booksellers. (See entry 650 for full listing.)

4156 **soc.college.financial-aid** Financial aid issues, college and beyond. *Newsgroup*

FOREIGN EXCHANGE & STUDIES ABROAD

4157 **alt.education.ib** The International Baccalaureate Diploma Program. *Newsgroup*

4158 **alt.students.exchange** Discussing specific interests of exchange students. *Newsgroup*

➤ **ASPIRE-L:** Helping students from Asian countries studying in the US to find jobs back home. (See entry 7050 for full listing.)

4159 **aus.students.overseas** Australian students abroad. *Newsgroup*

4160 **CANALA-L:** For links between Latin American and Canadian educators. *Mailing List*

± listproc@cunews.carleton.ca

INFO jhumphries@cbie.ca (Jenifer Humphries)

➤ **CHINA-NT:** Serves the community of overseas Chinese students and scholars by conducting in-depth discussions and debates of issues of their concerns and interests; also miscellaneous announcements and information circulation and service. (See entry 7243 for full listing.)

4161 **CNETIE:** On matters related to international education of concern to Canada. *Mailing List*

± majordomo@majordomo.srv.ualberta.ca [body = subscribe cnetie]

INFO OWNER barry.tonge@ualberta.ca (Barry Tonge)

ARCHIVES

```
http://admin1.intlcent.ualberta.ca/IC/InternetResources.html
majordomo@majordomo.srv.ualberta.ca
```

4162   **Council for International Exchange of Scholars:** Information on the Fulbright Senior Scholar Program, including international grant opportunities, listings of Fulbright Scholar participants and alumni, information on the United States Information Agency (the funding agency of the program), and more.

`http://www.cies.org/`

INFO `info@ciesnet.cies.org`

4163   **HOSPEX-L:** For discussion of the HOSPitality EXchange (homestays) program. *Mailing List*

`http://hospex.icm.edu.pl/hospex/`

± `listserv@plearn.edu.pl` [body = SUBSCRIBE HOSPEX-L first-name last-name]

INFO `hospex-owner@icm.edu.pl`

INFO `w.sylwestrzak@icm.edu.pl` (Wojtek Sylwestrzak)

ARCHIVE `listserv@plearn.edu.pl`

Please Note: Subscription by approval only.

Comments: Private to HospEx members

4164   **IB:** Forum for teachers, IB coordinators, and administrators involved with the International Baccalaureate Diploma Program. *Mailing List*

± `listserv@proteus.qc.ca` [body = subscribe IB first-name last-name]

INFO `hreha@vax2.concordia.ca` (Dr. Steve Hreha)

4165   **INTER-L:** For members of NAFSA: Association of International Educators. *Mailing List*

± `listserv@vtvm1.cc.vt.edu` [body = SUBSCRIBE INTER-L first-name last-name]

INFO `inter-l-request@vtvm1.cc.vt.edu`

OWNER `jgraham@lamar.colostate.edu` (James Graham)

FRATERNITIES & SORORITIES

4166   `alt.college.fraternities` College and university fraternities. *Newsgroup*

4167   `alt.college.fraternities.dlta-sigma-phi` Delta Sigma Phi. *Newsgroup*

4168   `alt.college.fraternities.sigma-alpha-epsilon` Sigma Alpha Epsilon. *Newsgroup*

4169   `alt.college.fraternities.sigma-pi` Sigma Pi: a fellowship of kindred minds. *Newsgroup*

4170   `alt.college.fraternities.zeta-psi` Zeta Psi fraternity topics. *Moderated newsgroup*

4171   `alt.college.sororities` College and university sororities. *Newsgroup*

4172   `alt.fraternity.sorority` Discussions of fraternity/sorority life and issues. *Newsgroup*

4173   **DELTACHI:** For the members of Delta Chi fraternity. *Mailing List*

± `listserv@vm.cc.latech.edu` [body = SUBSCRIBE DELTACHI first-name last-name]

INFO `deltachi-request@vm.cc.latech.edu`

ARCHIVE `listserv@vm.cc.latech.edu` [body = INDEX DELTACHI]

4174   `pitt.alpha.phi.omega` Information for members of Alpha Phi Omega, Pittsburgh. *Newsgroup*

4175   **SAM-L:** For members of Sigma Alpha Mu, a college fraternity. *Mailing List*

± `listserv@vm.temple.edu` [body = SUBSCRIBE SAM-L first-name last-name]

INFO `sam-l-request@vm.temple.edu`

Please Note: Subscription by approval only.

4176   **TKE-INFO:** Discussions relating to Tau Kappa Epsilon social fraternity. *Mailing List*

`http://www.tke.org/`

± `tke-info-request@tke.org`

INFO `tkeguys@tke.org`

Please Note: Subscription by approval only.

4177 ZBT: For the Zeta Beta Tau fraternity. *Mailing List, moderated*
± `majordomo@zbt.org`
INFO `majordomo-owner@zbt.org` (Technical questions)
OWNER `bill@nashville.net` (Bill Butler)

GIFTED EDUCATION

4178 ABILITY: On the academically, artistically, and athletically able. *Mailing List*
± `listserv@asuvm.inre.asu.edu` [body = SUBSCRIBE ABILITY first-name last-name]
INFO `ability-request@asuvm.inre.asu.edu`
Please Note: Subscription by approval only.

4179 `can.shad-valley` The Shad Valley Program for Gifted High School Students. *Newsgroup*

4180 GiftedNet-l: On educating gifted, or high ability, learners. *Mailing List*
± `listserver@listserv.cc.wm.edu`
OWNER `lnboyc@mail.wm.edu` (Linda Neal Boyce)

➤ **`k12.ed.tag`:** K-12 education for gifted and talented students. *Newsgroup*

➤ **`rec.org.mensa`:** Talking with members of the high-IQ society Mensa. *Newsgroup*

4181 TAGFAM: For mutual help and support for TAG families, and providing stimulating environments for talented and gifted children. *Mailing List*
± `listserv@sjuvm.stjohns.edu` [body = SUBSCRIBE TAGFAM first-name last-name]
OWNER `king@access.digex.net` (Valorie J. King)
OWNER `drz@sjuvm.stjohns.edu` (Dr. Robert Zenhausern)

GOVERNMENT & POLICY

4182 `bit.listserv.edpolyan` Education policy analysis forum. *Moderated newsgroup*

4183 Education Policy Analysis Archives: Publishes original research on education policy at all levels and in all nations. *E-Journal*
`http://www.asu.edu/asu-cwis/epaa/welcome.html`
`gopher://info.asu.edu/11/asu-cwis/epaa`
± `listserv@asu.edu.` [body = SUBSCRIBE EDPOLYAR first-name last-name]
INFO EDITOR `glass@asu.edu` (Gene V. Glass, Editor)
ARCHIVE `gopher://info.asu.edu/ASUCampus Wide Info`
Frequency: irregular (approx. 15 times a year)

4184 PUBPOL-L: For graduate students, faculty, and professionals of public policy. *Mailing List*
± `listserv@vm1.spcs.umn.edu` [body = SUBSCRIBE PUBPOL-L first-name last-name]
INFO `pubpol-l-request@vm1.spcs.umn.edu`
ARCHIVE `listserv@vm1.spcs.umn.edu` [body = INDEX PUBPOL-L]

GRANTS

➤ **Fedix:** Federal Information Exchange, Inc., access to a wide variety of government data. (See entry 5370 for full listing.)

➤ **Community of Science Web Server:** This site is designed to help scientists identify and locate researchers with interests and expertise similar to their own. It also contains a series of databases that provide information about research funded by the federal government. (See entry 9547 for full listing.)

➤ **Council for International Exchange of Scholars:** Information on the Fulbright Senior Scholar Program, including international grant opportunities, listings of Fulbright Scholar participants and alumni, information on the United States Information Agency (the funding agency of the program), and more. (See entry 4162 for full listing.)

➤ **National Science Foundation (NSF):** Information from the NSF, including programs, grants and funding guidelines, other NSF publications, and links to results of NSF-funded research. (See entry 9551 for full listing.)

➤ **NIHGDE-L:** Announcements of availability of NIH funds for biomedical and behavioral research and research training, and announcements of policy and administrative information. (See entry 5058 for full listing.)

➤ **Research Funding Agencies :** A list of WWW sites containing information of interest to researchers in all fields of science and technology that may be helpful in assisting faculty, students, and companies in identifying research funding opportunities. (See entry 9555 for full listing.)

➤ **Research Funding Opportunities and Administration (TRAM):** This site contains searchable research funding sources available from one location. The funding information is updated daily. TRAM also contains a set of grant application forms collected from various sources, as well as standard agreements for subcontracts, nondisclosures, licenses, and links to other servers related to research funding and administration. (See entry 9556 for full listing.)

➤ **USDA Cooperative State Research, Education, and Extension Service:** This site is set up to provide access to information from the USDA Extension Service, other USDA agencies, and other federal agencies as it relates to the Cooperative Extension System. (See entry 8922 for full listing.)

HIGHER EDUCATION

➤ **CAUSE:** CAUSE is the association for managing and using information resources in higher education. CAUSE is a source of information and professional development opportunities for those who plan for, implement, and manage information resources on campus. (See entry 4478 for full listing.)

4185 **ACADEME TODAY:** ACADEME TODAY is a service for subscribers to *The Chronicle of Higher Education*. It includes the full text of each week's newspaper, plus a concise briefing every weekday on higher-education issues, and additional features available only online.

http://www.chronicle.com/

http://chronicle.com/

telnet://chronicle.com

INFO editor@chronicle.com

Comments: ACADEME TODAY is available only to individual, paid subscribers to The Chronicle of Higher Education.

4186 **Academic Position Network:** Notices of available academic positions: faculty, staff, and administrative.

gopher://wcni.cis.umn.edu:1111

INFO apn@staff.tc.umn.edu

4187 **ACADV:** For the ACADV Network, on academic advising in higher education. *Mailing List, moderated*

± listserv@vm1.nodak.edu [body = SUBSCRIBE ACADV first-name last-name]

INFO 00hlcaldwell@bsuvc.bsu.edu (Harold L. Caldwell)

Please Note: Subscription by approval only.

Comments: Subscribers will be asked to indicate their employment in academic advising.

4188 **ADJUNCT:** On adjunct faculty topics. *Mailing List*

± listserv@vm1.nodak.edu [body = SUBSCRIBE ADJUNCT first-name last-name]

INFO http://www.sai.com/adjunct/

OWNER bing@umich.edu (John Cady)

➤ **Akademische Software Kooperation:** ASK-SISY: a database of higher-education software; ASK-SINA: searching all German FTP sites via WWW ASKnet: distributing commercial software at special retail prices to the higher-education community. (See entry 4481 for full listing.)

4189 **ASHE-L:** For communication concerning issues of higher education within the Association for the Study of Higher Education (ASHE). *Mailing List*

± listserv@american.edu [body = SUBSCRIBE ASHE-L first-name last-name]

INFO ashe-l-request@american.edu

Gated: bit.listserv.ashe-l

4190 **bit.listserv.ibm-hesc** IBM Higher Education Consortium. *Newsgroup*

➤ **BPRREENG-L:** On applying business process re-engineering (BPR) to universities. (See entry 4092 for full listing.)

➤ `clari.news.education.higher`: Colleges and Universities. *Newsgroup*

4191 **CYCOOP-L:** On cooperation between industry and universities. *Mailing List*
± `listserv@bruspvm.bitnet` [body = SUBSCRIBE CYCOOP-L first-name last-name]
INFO `plonski2@bruspvm.bitnet` (Guilherme Ary Plonski)
INFO `plonski2@usp.br` (Guilherme Ary Plonski)
Language: Portugese, Spanish, English

4192 **EE-HIGHER-ED:** On higher education in central and Eastern Europe, and in the NIS. *Mailing List*
± `listproc@cep.nonprofit.net` [body = SUBSCRIBE EE-HIGHER-ED first-name last-name]
OWNER `cep@minerva.cis.yale.edu` (Civic Education Project)

➤ **The Electronic AIR:** Newsletter for institutional researchers and college and university planners. Reports on news, publications, position openings, requests for help, etc. (See entry 4097 for full listing.)

4193 **HEP3-L:** A database of people in higher education, for networking and expertise searches. *Mailing List*
± `listserv@american.edu` [body = SUBSCRIBE HEP3-L first-name last-name]
OWNER `reimann@access.digex.net` (Carl Reimann)

4194 **HEPROC:** An array of 15 mailing lists and Web-based archives covering faculty development, assessment, institutional planning and development, strategic planning, quality, and other issues in higher education. *Mailing List, moderated*
`http://www.digimark.net/educ`
± `majordomo@world.std.com` [body = subscribe heproc-main-hall]
± `listserv@american.edu` [body = SUB HEPROC-L first-name last-name]
INFO `reimann@access.digex.net` (Carl Reimann)

➤ **IPCT-L:** Broad-ranging discussion on interpersonal computing and technology used in education. (See entry 4516 for full listing.)

➤ **MALACHI:** For the exchange of ideas and information about graduate courses among the universities in the Washington, D.C. metropolitan area. (See entry 8633 for full listing.)

4195 **MDPHD-L:** On dual-degree programs; for example, pursuing an M.D. along with a Ph.D. or a J.D. *Mailing List*
± `listserv@ubvm.cc.buffalo.edu` [body = SUBSCRIBE MDPHD-L first-name last-name year-in-program graduate-field]
INFO `mdphd-l-request@ubvm.cc.buffalo.edu`
OWNER `doc@uiuc.edu` (Jim Marco)
ARCHIVE `listserv@ubvm.cc.buffalo.edu` [body = INDEX MDPHD-L]
Gated: `bit.listserv.mdphd-l`

4196 **NASPA1-L:** Distribution on the National Association of Student Personnel Administrators REGION I and other related subjects. *Mailing List*
± `listserv@uconnvm.uconn.edu` [body = SUBSCRIBE NASPA1-L first-name last-name]
INFO `wtbyadm3@uconnvm.uconn.edu` (Stuart Brown)

➤ **PAYHR-L:** On payroll, benefits, and human resources in higher education. (See entry 4101 for full listing.)

➤ **PROSTAFF:** For discussion of matters of common concern to professional staff at universities, particularly employment issues. (See entry 4102 for full listing.)

➤ **PSYCGRAD:** Discussion forum for psychology graduate students. (See entry 9524 for full listing.)

➤ `sci.research.postdoc`: Anything about postdoctoral studies, including offers. *Newsgroup*

4197 **SCUP E-Mail News:** A service of the Society for College and University Planning (SCUP) providing timely and frequent exchange of information for those interested in planning for higher education. *Newsletter*
`http://www.umich.edu/!scup/`
± INFO `terry@scup.ra.itd.umich.edu` [body = SUBSCRIBE SCUP E-MAIL NEWS first-name last-name, title, institution/organization, address, telephone, fax, and e-mail address]

Frequency: monthly

4198 **SCUP's Planning Pages:** Web resources relating to planning for the future of higher education, including indexes to past issues of the print scholarly journal, *Planning for Higher Education,* archives of SCUP E-Mail News, information about international and regional conferences and workshops . . . and links to other online resources of interest to planners.

    http://www.umich.edu/~scup/

    INFO scup@umich.edu

Comments: The Society also has an electronic newsletter which is free to all who are interested in higher education planning. Send your name, title, organization, address, phone, fax, and email address to terry@scup.ra.itd.umich.edu.

➤ **SHS:** The Society for Human Sexuality mailing list. Intended for general discussion of human sexuality and as a way to distribute information about events put on by the Society for Human Sexuality (a sex-positive registered student organization at the University of Washington). (See entry 10120 for full listing.)

4199 **soc.college** College, college activities, campus life, etc. *Newsgroup*

4200 **soc.college.grad** General issues related to graduate schools. *Newsgroup*

4201 **soc.college.gradinfo** Information about graduate schools. *Newsgroup*

4202 **STLHE-L:** On teaching and learning in higher education. *Mailing List*

    ± listserv@unb.ca [body = SUBSCRIBE STLHE-L first-name last-name]

    INFO rgair@unb.ca (Reavley Gair)

    ARCHIVE listserv@unb.ca

Language: English, French

➤ **STUDIUM:** On the history of universities and higher education. (See entry 5269 for full listing.)

4203 **uk.education.16plus** All aspects of 16+, community, and adult education. *Newsgroup*

➤ **USDA Cooperative State Research, Education, and Extension Service:** This site is set up to provide access to information from the USDA Extension Service, other USDA agencies, and other federal agencies as it relates to the Cooperative Extension System. (See entry 8922 for full listing.)

4204 **WAKONS-L:** For discussion among individuals who have participated in the Wakonse Conference on improving teaching at the undergraduate level. *Mailing List*

    ± listserv@mizzou1.missouri.edu [body = SUBSCRIBE WAKONS-L first-name last-name]

    INFO wood@psysparc.psyc.missouri.edu (Phil Wood)

HOME SCHOOLING

4205 **Jon's Home-School Resource Page:** Extensive collection of home-schooling resources and information. Includes a lists of home-schooling mailing lists and newsgroups, pointers to FAQs on home-schooling topics, and a collection of many practical documents for to help home schoolers in their work.

    http://www.armory.com/~jon/hs/HomeSchool.html

    INFO jon@armory.com

    FAQ http://www.armory.com/~jon/hs/readme.html

4206 **alt.education.home-school.christian** Christian home schoolers. *Moderated newsgroup*

4207 **California Homeschool Network (CHN):** CHN exists to provide resources and information about home schooling; to protect the right of the family to educate its children at home in the manner it deems appropriate without regulation; and to foster community among home educators in California.

    http://www.comenius.org/chnpage.htm

    INFO janorsi@aol.com

4208 **Christian Homeschool Forum:** Home-schooling resources for Christians.

    http://www.gocin.com/homeschool/

    INFO 73612.2630@compuserve.com

4209 **Home Education Resources Center (HERC):** HERC is a jumping-off site for those interested in educational opportunities at home or on the net. Great links to Internet educational resources, home-school regulations and support groups listed by state, a suggested reading list, and a complete products catalog.

http://www.netsales.com/herc/

INFO pyandell@netsales.com

4210 **The Homespun Web of Home Educational Resources:** Home-schooling resources, including information on events, how-to, politics, home-schooling organizations, curriculum suppliers, other Internet resources, and a classified ads secton.

http://www.ictheweb.com/hs-web/index.html

INFO editor@ictheweb.com

4211 `misc.education.home-school.christian` Christian home-schooling. *Newsgroup*

4212 `misc.education.home-school.misc` Almost anything about home-schooling. *Newsgroup*

➤ `shamash.torch-d:` About religious Jewish home schooling. *Moderated newsgroup*

JOURNALS

4213 **ACADEME THIS WEEK:** ACADEME THIS WEEK offers a guide to the contents of *The Chronicle of Higher Education*. Also included are the job ads; calendar of events; deadlines for grants, papers, and fellowships; and selected Internet resources for academics. This online version is available every Tuesday at noon EST.

http://chronicle.merit.edu/

INFO editor@chronicle.merit.edu (Judith Axler Turner, Director)

4214 **Interpersonal Computing and Technology:** Promoting the electronic journal as a legitimate outlet for dissemination of scholarly studies suitable for credit toward promotion and tenure. *E-Journal*

± listserv@guvm.georgetown.edu [body = SUBSCRIBE IPCT-J]

INFO berge@umbc2.umbc.edu

ARCHIVE gopher://guvm.ccf.georgetown.edu

Frequency: quarterly

K-12

➤ **KIDLINK:** KIDLINK is a global networking project for youths 10-15. The KIDLINK list is for official news and information about the KIDLINK series of projects, which span many other lists and services. KIDLINK coordinates the worldwide dialog of thousands of youth 10-15 in scores of countries. Other KIDLINK lists are RESPONSE, KID-PROJ, KIDFORUM, the KIDCAFE family of lists, the KIDLEADER family of lists, KIDPLAN, and a family of project COORDination lists. (See entry 4480 for full listing.)

4215 **Bloomfield Hills Model High School:** Information on Bloomfield Hills Model High School.

http://www.bloomfield.k12.mi.us/

gopher://gopher.bloomfield.k12.mi.us

INFO maw@mhs-server.bloomfield.k12.mi.us

INFO gopher@mhs-server.bloomfield.k12.mi.us

4216 **BR_Cafe:** Book Review Cafe: place for kids to discuss what they're reading. *Mailing List, moderated*

± listproc@micronet.wcu.edu [body = SUBSCRIBE BR_CAFE first-name last-name]

EDITOR beam@micronet.wcu.edu (Bonnie Beam)

OWNER johnson@micronet.wcu.edu (Patti Johnson)

ARCHIVE http://micronet.wcu.edu/br_cafe.html

4217 **BR_Review:** For K-12 student-written book reviews. *Mailing List, moderated*

± listproc@micronet.wcu.edu [body = SUBSCRIBE BR_REVIEW first-name last-name]

EDITOR beam@micronet.wcu.edu (Bonnie Beam)

OWNER johnson@micronet.wcu.edu (Patti Johnson)

ARCHIVE http://micronet.wcu.edu/br_review.html

POST br_review@wcu.edu

➤ `can.schoolnet.arts.drama`: Drama studies in elementary/secondary schools. *Newsgroup*

➤ `can.schoolnet.arts.music`: Music studies in elementary/secondary schools. *Newsgroup*

➤ `can.schoolnet.biomed.jr`: SchoolNet biology and medicine for elementary students. *Newsgroup*

➤ `can.schoolnet.biomed.sr`: SchoolNet biology and medicine for high-school students. *Newsgroup*

➤ `can.schoolnet.chat.students.jr`: General talk by elementary school SchoolNet students. *Newsgroup*

➤ `can.schoolnet.chat.students.sr`: General talk by high-school SchoolNet students. *Newsgroup*

➤ `can.schoolnet.chat.teachers`: General talk by SchoolNet teachers. *Newsgroup*

➤ `can.schoolnet.chem.jr`: SchoolNet chemistry for elementary students. *Newsgroup*

➤ `can.schoolnet.chem.sr`: SchoolNet chemistry for high-school students. *Newsgroup*

➤ `can.schoolnet.comp.jr`: SchoolNet computer science for elementary students. *Newsgroup*

➤ `can.schoolnet.comp.sr`: SchoolNet computer science for high-school students. *Newsgroup*

➤ `can.schoolnet.earth.jr`: SchoolNet earth sciences for elementary students. *Newsgroup*

➤ `can.schoolnet.earth.sr`: SchoolNet earth sciences for high-school students. *Newsgroup*

➤ `can.schoolnet.elecsys.jr`: SchoolNet EE and systems eng. for elementary students. *Newsgroup*

➤ `can.schoolnet.elecsys.sr`: SchoolNet EE and systems eng. for high-school students. *Newsgroup*

➤ `can.schoolnet.eng.jr`: SchoolNet engineering for elementary students. *Newsgroup*

➤ `can.schoolnet.eng.sr`: SchoolNet engineering for high-school students. *Newsgroup*

➤ `can.schoolnet.english`: English elementary/secondary schools curriculum. *Newsgroup*

4218 `can.schoolnet.firefighters` Profession of firefighting and fire prevention. *Newsgroup*

➤ `can.schoolnet.history`: History studies in elementary/secondary schools. *Newsgroup*

➤ `can.schoolnet.jrjays`: Jr. Jays fan club for Toronto Blue Jays. *Newsgroup*

➤ `can.schoolnet.math.jr`: SchoolNet mathematics for elementary students. *Newsgroup*

➤ `can.schoolnet.math.sr`: SchoolNet mathematics for high-school students. *Newsgroup*

➤ `can.schoolnet.phys.jr`: SchoolNet physics for elementary school students. *Newsgroup*

➤ `can.schoolnet.phys.sr`: SchoolNet physics for high-school students. *Newsgroup*

➤ `can.schoolnet.physed`: Physical education in elementary/secondary schools. *Newsgroup*

4219 `can.schoolnet.problems` The group to gripe in about SchoolNet or find its FAQs. *Newsgroup*

4220 `can.schoolnet.projects.calls` SchoolNet CFPs, project announcements. *Newsgroup*

4221 `can.schoolnet.projects.discuss` SchoolNet project discussion. *Newsgroup*

➤ `can.schoolnet.school.improvement`: School improvement and enhancement. *Newsgroup*

➤ `can.schoolnet.socsci.jr`: SchoolNet social sciences for elementary students. *Newsgroup*

➤ `can.schoolnet.socsci.sr`: SchoolNet social sciences for high-school students. *Newsgroup*

➤ `can.schoolnet.space.jr`: SchoolNet space sciences for elementary students. *Newsgroup*

➤ `can.schoolnet.space.sr`: SchoolNet space sciences for high-school students. *Newsgroup*

➤ `can.schoolnet.staff.development`: Staff development. *Newsgroup*

➤ **CEARCH: Cisco Educational Archives:** Education archive; lists a variety of resources about school connectivity to the Internet as well as a catalog of educational resources organized by classroom and subject. (See entry 4493 for full listing.)

➤ `clari.news.education`: Primary and secondary education. *Moderated newsgroup*

➤ `clari.news.education.misc`: Primary and secondary education. *Moderated newsgroup*

4222 **Colorado K–12:** Support materials and networking for K-12 internet sites

```
http://k12.colostate.edu/
gopher://k12.colostate.edu
```
(Greg Redder)
INFO `redder@k12.colostate.edu` (Greg Redder)
INFO `mplitnik@k12.colostate.edu` (Matt Plitnik)

4223 **COM-WILD-L:** Communiques from the Wild: enhances children's appreciation of the natural world and makes science "come to life." *Distribution List, moderated*

± OWNER `claire@access.digex.net` (Claire Marie Van Holt)

Please Note: Subscription by approval only.

➤ **Cornell Theory Center Math and Science Gateway:** The Cornell Theory Center Math and Science Gateway provides links to resources in mathematics and science for educators and students in grades 9-12. (See entry 4300 for full listing.)

4224 **The EdWeb Project:** An online tutorial on education, technology, school reform, and the information highway; sponsored by the Corporation for Public Broadcasting.

```
http://k12.cnidr.org/
```
INFO `acarvin@k12.cnidr.org` (Andy Carvin)

4225 **ELED-L:** On elementary education. *Mailing List*

± `listserv@ksuvm.ksu.edu` [body = SUBSCRIBE ELED-L first-name last-name]
INFO `dzollman@ksuvm.bitnet`
ARCHIVE `listserv@ksuvm.ksu.edu`

➤ **ERIC Clearinghouse on Elementary and Early Childhood Education:** Information and resources on the care, development, and education of children from birth through early adolescence. (See entry 4146 for full listing.)

4226 **ERIC/EECE Newsletter:** Newsletter of the ERIC Clearinghouse on Elementary and Early Childhood Education. One lead article and several short articles about educational programs and ideas, resources, news updates, Internet developments at ERIC/EECE, and announcements. *Newsletter*

```
http://ericps.ed.uiuc.edu/eece/pubs/eece-nl.html
```
INFO `ericeece@ux1.cso.uiuc.edu`
EDITOR `cesarone@uiuc.edu`
ARCHIVE `gopher://ericps.ed.uiuc.edu`

Frequency: biannual

➤ **Global SchoolNet Foundation:** A nonprofit organization dedicated to the instructional applications of telecommunication. (See entry 4509 for full listing.)

4227 `k12.chat.teacher` Casual conversation for teachers of grades K-12. *Newsgroup*

4228 `k12.ed.art` Arts and crafts curricula in K-12 education. *Newsgroup*

4229 `k12.ed.business` Business education curricula in grades K-12. *Newsgroup*

4230 `k12.ed.comp.literacy` Teaching computer literacy in grades K-12. *Newsgroup*

➤ `k12.ed.health-pe:` Health and physical education curricula in grades K-12. *Newsgroup*

4231 `k12.ed.life-skills` Home economics, career education, and school counseling. *Newsgroup*

➤ `k12.ed.math:` Mathematics curriculum in K-12 education. *Newsgroup*

4232 `k12.ed.music` Music and performing arts curriculum in K-12 education. *Newsgroup*

➤ `k12.ed.science:` Science curriculum in K-12 education. *Newsgroup*

➤ `k12.ed.soc-studies:` Social studies and history curriculum in K-12 education. *Newsgroup*

➤ `k12.ed.special:` Educating students with handicaps and/or special needs. *Newsgroup*

4233 `k12.ed.tag` K-12 education for gifted and talented students. *Newsgroup*

➤ `k12.ed.tech:` Industrial arts and vocational education in grades K-12. *Newsgroup*

➤ `k12.lang.art:` The art of teaching language skills in grades K-12. *Newsgroup*

➤   `k12.lang.deutsch-eng`:   Bilingual German/English practice with native speakers. *Newsgroup*

➤   `k12.lang.esp-eng`:   Bilingual Spanish/English practice with native speakers. *Newsgroup*

➤   `k12.lang.francais`:   French practice with native speakers. *Newsgroup*

➤   `k12.lang.japanese`:   Bilingual Japanese/English with native speakers. *Newsgroup*

➤   `k12.lang.russian`:   Bilingual Russian/English practice with native speakers. *Newsgroup*

➤   `k12.library`:   Implementing information technologies in school libraries. *Newsgroup*

➤   `k12.sys.*`:   Hierarchy for current projects in K-12. *Newsgroup*

➤   `k12.sys.projects`:   Discussion of potential projects. *Newsgroup*

4234   **KIDLIT-L:** For educators, librarians, researchers, authors, and others interested in literature for children and youths, including teaching strategies, innovative course ideas, current research. *Mailing List, moderated*
± `listserv@bingvmb.cc.binghamton.edu` [body = SUBSCRIBE KIDLIT-L first-name last-name]
INFO `pstellin@bingvmb.bitnet` (Prue Stelling)
ARCHIVE `listserv@bingvmb.cc.binghamton.edu`

4235   **Kidopedia:** A child-authored Web-based encyclopedia. *Mailing List*
`http://rdz.stjohns.edu/kidopedia`
± `listserv@sjuvm.stjohns.edu` [body = SUBSCRIBE KIDOPEDIA first-name last-name]
INFO `kidopediainfo@computer.com`
OWNER `kevin@computer.com` (Kevin Sinclair)
Language: English and others

➤   **MathMagic-general-open:** For schools of education, professors, teachers, supervisors, and other interested parties to discuss math learning and the student exchanges observed in the K-12 MathMagic lists. (See entry 4311 for full listing.)

➤   **MEALTALK:** On child nutrition programs. (See entry 9732 for full listing.)

4236   `oh.k12`   Elementary education in Ohio. *Newsgroup*

4237   **Poudre School District World Wide Web Server:** This is the WWW server of the Poudre School District in Fort Collins, Colorado.
`http://www.psd.k12.co.us/`
INFO `larryb@psd.k12.co.us`

4238   `ri.k12.experiences`   K-12 oriented discussions about the Internet. *Newsgroup*

4239   `ri.k12.providers.funding`   Funding for Rhode Island K-12 networks. *Newsgroup*

4240   `ri.k12.providers.staff`   Staffing issues facing Rhode Island K-12 networks. *Newsgroup*

4241   `ri.k12.providers.tech`   Technical aspects facing Rhode Island K-12 networks. *Newsgroup*

➤   `ri.k12.socialstudies`:   Rhode Island K-12 social studies discussions. *Newsgroup*

➤   **Sierra Club Environmental Education:** For K-12 environmental education resources. (See entry 4604 for full listing.)

➤   **St. John's University:** This site serves as the university's CWIS, and hosts the SJU Electronic Rehabilitation Resource Center and the SJU Learning Styles Network. This site also contains some resources for K–12 teachers. (See entry 4450 for full listing.)

4242   **TALKBACK:** For children in Project Chatback. *Mailing List*
± `listserv@stjohns.edu` [body = SUBSCRIBE TALKBACK first-name last-name]
INFO `drz@sjuvm.stjohns.edu` (Bob Zenhausern, Ph.D.)

➤   **TESLK-12:** On teaching English as a second language to children. (See entry 4153 for full listing.)

LANGUAGES

4243   **AATG:** For the academic community, especially teaching professionals of German. *Mailing List*
± `listserv@indycms.iupui.edu` [body = SUBSCRIBE AATG first-name last-name]

INFO `reichelt@indyunix.iupui.edu` (Dr. Harry Reichelt)

OWNER `itae100@indycms.iupui.edu` (Dr. Harry Reichelt)

ARCHIVE `listserv@indycms.iupui.edu` [body = `INDEX AATG`]

Language: English & German

➤ `alt.usage.english`: English grammar, word usages, and related topics. *Newsgroup*

➤ `alt.usage.german`: Questions and answers about the German language. *Newsgroup*

➤ `alt.uu.lang.esperanto.misc`: Learning Esperanto at the Usenet University. *Newsgroup*

4244 APSA-L: For the American Portuguese Studies Association. *Digest & Reflector*

± `majordomo@beacon.bryant.edu`

OWNER `pmedeiro@research1.bryant.edu` (Paulo de Medeiros)

Language: English & Portuguese

Please Note: Subscription by approval only.

4245 BILINGUE-L: On developmental bilingual elementary education. *Mailing List*

± `listserv@reynolds.k12.or.us` [body = `SUBSCRIBE BILINGUE-L` first-name last-name]

EDITOR `lynn_thompson@reynolds.k12.or.us` (Lynn Thompson)

Language: English and Spanish

4246 `can.schoolnet.english` English elementary/secondary schools curriculum. *Newsgroup*

4247 A Course in Swedish Cursing: An extensive and systematic course in Swedish cursing with plenty of sound bites to assist learning the correct pronounciation and intonation.

`http://www.bart.nl/~sante/enginvek.html`

INFO `sante@bart.nl`

➤ **E-HUG:** On all things relating to use of Hebrew, Yiddish, Judesmo, and Aramaic on computers. (See entry 5289 for full listing.)

4248 ESPAN-L: For teachers of the Spanish language and literature. *Mailing List*

± `listserv@vm.tau.ac.il` [body = `SUBSCRIBE ESPAN-L` first-name last-name]

OWNER `rsitman@ccsg.tau.ac.il` (Rosalie Sitman)

Language: Spanish

➤ **esperanto:** On the neutral international language Esperanto. Often in Esperanto. (See entry 5290 for full listing.)

➤ `soc.culture.esperanto`: The neutral international language Esperanto. *Newsgroup*

➤ `alt.talk.esperanto`: Diskutoj per la internacia lingvo. *Newsgroup*

4249 FLTEACH: On teaching foreign languages. *Mailing List*

± `listserv@ubvm.cc.buffalo.edu` [body = `SUBSCRIBE FLTEACH` first-name last-name]

OWNER `ponterior@snycorva.cortland.edu` (Robert Ponterio)

OWNER `leloupj@snycorva.cortland.edu` (Jean W. LeLoup)

ARCHIVES

`http://www.cortland.edu/www_root/flteach/flteach.html`

`gopher://gopher.cortland.edu`

`listserv@ubvm.cc.buffalo.edu` [body = `INDEX FLTEACH`]

4250 Gakusei-L: A group of lists for discussion among students and native speakers of Japanese. *Mailing List*

± `listproc@hawaii.edu` [body = `SUBSCRIBE GAKUSEI-L` first-name last-name]

OWNER `kimotol@hawaii.edu` (Laura Kimoto)

ARCHIVE `listproc@hawaii.edu` [body = `get gakusei-l file.names`]

4251 International Language Development: International Language Development provides interactive language lessons in French, German, Japanese, Korean, Russian, and Spanish on the Internet.

`http://www.teleport.com/~sesame`

`http://www.ild.com/`

INFO info@ild.com

4252 **JTIT-L:** For Japanese teachers and instructional technology. *Mailing List*
± listserv@psuvm.psu.edu [body = SUBSCRIBE JTIT-L first-name last-name]
INFO OWNER tomita@vax001.kenyon.edu (HIDEO TOMITA)
INFO tomita@kenyon.edu (Hideo Tomita)
ARCHIVE listserv@psuvm.psu.edu

4253 **k12.lang.art** The art of teaching language skills in grades K-12. *Newsgroup*

4254 **k12.lang.deutsch-eng** Bilingual German/English practice with native speakers. *Newsgroup*

4255 **k12.lang.esp-eng** Bilingual Spanish/English practice with native speakers. *Newsgroup*

4256 **k12.lang.francais** French practice with native speakers. *Newsgroup*

4257 **k12.lang.japanese** Bilingual Japanese/English with native speakers. *Newsgroup*

4258 **k12.lang.russian** Bilingual Russian/English practice with native speakers. *Newsgroup*

4259 **KFLC-L:** On the annual Kentucky Foreign Language Conference. *Mailing List*
± listserv@ukcc.uky.edu [body = SUBSCRIBE KFLC-L first-name last-name]
OWNER engjlg@ukcc.uky.edu (John Greenway)

➤ **Kid's Window:** A multimedia resource for children to learn about Japanese language and culture. (See entry 9731 for full listing.)

4260 **LLTI:** For information on language learning and technology, including language-lab technology, computer-supported language learning, and interactive video and audio. *Mailing List, moderated*
http://elezar/LLTI/
± listserv@dartcms1.dartmouth.edu [body = SUBSCRIBE LLTI first-name last-name]
INFO otmar.k.e.foelsche@dartmouth.edu (Otmar Foelsche, Director, LRC)

4261 **misc.education.language.english** Teaching English to speakers of other languages. *Newsgroup*

➤ **NEDER-L:** An e-journal for the study of Dutch language and literature. (See entry 620 for full listing.)

4262 **NorWord:** To learn a Norwegian word or phrase a day. *Distribution List, moderated*
http://www.infoserve.net/netquest/nordic/norlitt.html
± listserv@gac.edu [body = SUBSCRIBE NORWORD first-name last-name]
INFO lctl@maroon.tc.umn.edu (Louis Janus)
INFO OWNER naarsvol@gac.edu (Nancy Aarsvold)
ARCHIVE gopher://spinner.gac.edu:70/77/pub/E-mail-archives/NorWord/.index/index

4263 **school.subjects.languages** English, Deutsch, Francais, etc. *Newsgroup*

➤ **sci.lang.japan:** The Japanese language, both spoken and written. *Newsgroup*

➤ **sci.lang.translation:** Problems and concerns of translators/interpreters. *Newsgroup*

➤ **scot.scots:** Scots language discussions. *Newsgroup*

4264 **SLART-L:** For scholarly discussion and exchange of information on second or foreign language education. *Mailing List*
± listserv@cunyvm.cuny.edu [body = SUBSCRIBE SLART-L first-name last-name]
INFO kgakb@cunyvm.cuny.edu (Kate Garretson)

➤ **soc.culture.catalan:** The Catalan language and the lands where it is spoken. *Newsgroup*

4265 **um.chinese** Newsgroup for students interested in Chinese. *Newsgroup*

4266 **WELSH-L:** On the Welsh, Breton, and Cornish languages. *Mailing List*
http://www.cs.brown.edu/fun/welsh/welsh.html
± listserv@irlearn.ucd.ie [body = SUBSCRIBE WELSH-L first-name last-name]
INFO OWNER briony@cstr.edinburgh.ac.uk (Briony Williams)

ARCHIVE `http://www.cs.brown.edu/fun/welsh/welsh.html`
Language: Welsh, Breton, Cornish, English, French

LITERACY

4267   `alt.education.email-project` The e-mail project for teaching English. *Newsgroup*

4268   `alt.literacy.adult` Adults, literacy, reading, writing. *Newsgroup*

4269   **BEE-net:** For beginning English teachers: coursework, experiences, writing, new ideas. *Mailing List*
± `listserv@titan.sfasu.edu` [body = SUBSCRIBE BEE-NET first-name last-name]
OWNER `gblalock@titan.sfasu.edu` (Glenn Blalock)
OWNER `philion@uic.edu` (Thomas Philion)
ARCHIVE `http://titan.sfasu.edu/~beenet`

4270   **CASLL:** On the learning and teaching of reading and writing, especially in Canada. *Mailing List*
± `listserv@unb.ca` [body = SUBSCRIBE CASLL first-name last-name]
INFO `hunt@academic.stu.stthomasu.ca` (Russ Hunt)
Please Note: Subscription by approval only.

4271   **ERIC Clearinghouse on Reading, English, and Communication:** This site provides a wide range of literacy-related educational materials, services, and coursework to parents, educators, students, and others interested in the language arts.
`http://www.indiana.edu/~eric_rec/`
INFO `sstroup@indiana.edu`

4272   **LEARNER:** For practice by adults learning to read and write. *Mailing List, moderated*
± `listserv@nysernet.org` [body = SUBSCRIBE LEARNER first-name last-name]
OWNER `mville3@nysernet.org` (Beverly Choltco-Devlin)

4273   **LITERACY:** On adult literacy: teaching, social issues, family literacy. *Mailing List, moderated*
± `listserv@nysernet.org` [body = SUBSCRIBE LITERACY first-name last-name]
OWNER `mville3@nysernet.org` (Beverly Choltco-Devlin)

4274   **National Center on Adult Literacy:** This server distributes the National Center on Adult Literacy's publications and points to Web and gopher resources relevant to researchers, policy makers, and practitioners in adult literacy.
`http://ncal.literacy.upenn.edu/`
`gopher://ncal.literacy.upenn.edu`
INFO `mailbox@literacy.upenn.edu`

4275   **The National Institute for Literacy:** Information on the institute and an extensive list of pointers to national, international, and statewide Internet adult literacy resources including family literacy, workplace literacy, learning disabilities, and English as a second language.
`http://novel.nifl.gov/`
INFO `webmaster@novel.nifl.gov`

MATH, SCIENCE & TECHNOLOGY EDUCATION

4276   <u>The Math Forum:</u> The Math Forum is home to Ask Dr. Math, MathMagic, the Internet Math Resource Collection, Problem of the Week/Project of the Month, public forums, the Geometry Forum, and many other projects coordinated in a virtual center for math education on the Internet. Your one-stop shop for math classroom resources on the World Wide Web.
`http://forum.swarthmore.edu/`
INFO `forum@forum.swarthmore.edu`
FAQ `http://forum.swarthmore.edu/about.forum.html`

4277   **AETS-L:** To promote leadership in, and support for those involved in, the professional development of teachers of science. *Mailing List*
`http://science.cc.uwf.edu/aets/aets.html`

± `listserv@uwf.cc.uwf.edu` [body = SUBSCRIBE AETS-L first-name last-name]
INFO `jpeters@uwf.bitnet` (Joe Peters)
Please Note: Subscription by approval only.

4278 **`alt.algebra.help`** Cheating on Homework 101. *Newsgroup*

4279 **`alt.math.undergrad`** Math help and discussion for non-math-major undergrads. *Newsgroup*

➤ **`alt.uu.math.misc:`** Learning math at the Usenet University. *Newsgroup*

4280 **`bit.listserv.tecmat-l`** Technology in secondary math. *Newsgroup*

4281 **`can.schoolnet.biomed.jr`** SchoolNet biology and medicine for elementary students. *Newsgroup*

4282 **`can.schoolnet.biomed.sr`** SchoolNet biology and medicine for high-school students. *Newsgroup*

4283 **`can.schoolnet.chem.jr`** SchoolNet chemistry for elementary students. *Newsgroup*

4284 **`can.schoolnet.chem.sr`** SchoolNet chemistry for high-school students. *Newsgroup*

4285 **`can.schoolnet.comp.jr`** SchoolNet computer science for elementary students. *Newsgroup*

4286 **`can.schoolnet.comp.sr`** SchoolNet computer science for high-school students. *Newsgroup*

4287 **`can.schoolnet.earth.jr`** SchoolNet earth sciences for elementary students. *Newsgroup*

4288 **`can.schoolnet.earth.sr`** SchoolNet earth sciences for high-school students. *Newsgroup*

4289 **`can.schoolnet.elecsys.jr`** SchoolNet EE and systems eng. for elementary students. *Newsgroup*

4290 **`can.schoolnet.elecsys.sr`** SchoolNet EE and systems eng. for high-school students. *Newsgroup*

4291 **`can.schoolnet.eng.jr`** SchoolNet engineering for elementary students. *Newsgroup*

4292 **`can.schoolnet.eng.sr`** SchoolNet engineering for high-school students. *Newsgroup*

4293 **`can.schoolnet.math.jr`** SchoolNet mathematics for elementary students. *Newsgroup*

4294 **`can.schoolnet.math.sr`** SchoolNet mathematics for high-school students. *Newsgroup*

4295 **`can.schoolnet.phys.jr`** SchoolNet physics for elementary school students. *Newsgroup*

4296 **`can.schoolnet.phys.sr`** SchoolNet physics for high-school students. *Newsgroup*

4297 **`can.schoolnet.space.jr`** SchoolNet space sciences for elementary students. *Newsgroup*

4298 **`can.schoolnet.space.sr`** SchoolNet space sciences for high-school students. *Newsgroup*

4299 **The Chance Project:** Database and information on a course for teaching probability and statistics.
`http://www.geom.umn.edu/locate/chance`
INFO `jlsnell@dartmouth.edu` (Laurie Snell) (Laurie Snell)

➤ **`comp.lang.logo:`** The Logo teaching and learning language. *Newsgroup*

4300 **Cornell Theory Center Math and Science Gateway:** The Cornell Theory Center Math and Science Gateway provides links to resources in mathematics and science for educators and students in grades 9-12.
`http://www.tc.cornell.edu/Edu/MathSciGateway/`
INFO `doc-comments@tc.cornell.edu`

➤ **Educational Space Simulations Project:** ESSP is all about Educational Space Simulations, an exciting way to teach mathematics and space science. (See entry 9587 for full listing.)

➤ **EE-Link:** EE-Link is funded by the U.S. EPA to provide access to environmental education resources on the Internet. Topics include classroom resources, organizations and projects, literature, funding, regional resources. (See entry 4603 for full listing.)

4301 **Exploratorium:** A collection of 650 interactive exhibits in the areas of science, art, and human perception.
`http://www.exploratorium.edu/`
INFO `ronh@exploratorium.edu`

4302 **Fitzroy:** A listing of undergraduate research experiences, which can serve as starting points or sources of advice for other undergrads looking for summer research opportunities.

```
http://firstmarket.com/fitzroy
```
INFO `maxwell@minerva.cis.yale.edu`

4303 `fj.education.math` Discussions on mathematics education. *Newsgroup*

4304 `geometry.college` Geometry at the College Level. *Newsgroup*

4305 `geometry.pre-college` Geometry for Secondary Education. *Newsgroup*

➤ **`geometry.puzzles`:** Recreational Geometry Problems. *Newsgroup*

➤ **GTRTI-L:** On research and teaching in global information technology. (See entry 9366 for full listing.)

➤ **HPSST-L:** On the history and philosophy of science and science teaching. (See entry 9351 for full listing.)

4306 IT Connections: Instructional Technology Connections from the School of Education at the University of Colorado at Denver; a resource index designed for students and practitioners of instructional technology. The resource links into the major domains of educational technology, providing an unusual focus on theory, philosophy, and research.
```
http://www.cudenver.edu/~mryder/itcon.html
gopher://ccnucd.cudenver.edu/h0/UCD/dept/edu/IT/ryder/itcon.html
```
INFO `mjryder@www.cudenver.edu`

4307 Journal of Statistics Education: Topics related to the teaching of statistics: experiments on pedagogical methods, case studies, anecdotal reports, review and opinion articles, and discussion of the impact of new technologies. *E-Journal*
```
http://www2.ncsu.edu/ncsu/pams/stat/info/jse/homepage.html
```
± `listserv@jse.stat.ncsu.edu` [body = SUBSCRIBE jse-announce]
INFO `arnold@stat.ncsu.edu` (Tim Arnold)
ARCHIVE `ftp://jse.stat.ncsu.edu/jse/v1n1/contents`
Frequency: three times a year

4308 Journal of Technology Education: Scholarly discussion on topics relating to technology education. Technology education is that school subject which teaches children *about* technology rather than just *with* technology (the latter being instructional technology). *E-Journal*
```
gopher://borg.lib.vt.edu/Ejournals/JTE
http://borg.lib.vt.edu/ejournals/JTE/jte.html
wais://jte.src
ftp://borg.lib.vt.edu/pub/JTE/
```
± `listserv@vtvm1.cc.vt.edu` [body = subscribe jte-l]
INFO EDITOR `msanders@vt.edu` (Dr. Mark Sanders, Edito)
ARCHIVES
```
gopher://borg.lib.vt.edu/Ejournals/JTE
http://borg.lib.vt.edu/ejournals/JTE/jte.html
wais://jte.src
ftp://borg.lib.vt.edu/pub/JTE/
listserv@vtvm1.cc.vt.edu [body = INDEX JTE-L]
```
Frequency: twice annually (fall and spring)

➤ **`k12.ed.comp.literacy`:** Teaching computer literacy in grades K-12. *Newsgroup*

4309 `k12.ed.math` Mathematics curriculum in K-12 education. *Newsgroup*

4310 `k12.ed.science` Science curriculum in K-12 education. *Newsgroup*

➤ **Mathematica World:** An online Mathematica user service. Mathematica World encourages users to develop their skill and expand their use of Mathematica. (See entry 9421 for full listing.)

4311 MathMagic-general-open: For schools of education, professors, teachers, supervisors, and other interested parties to discuss math learning and the student exchanges observed in the K-12 MathMagic lists. *Mailing List*
```
ftp://forum.swarthmore.edu/mathmagic
```

± `majordomo@forum.swarthmore.edu` [body = `subscribe mathmagic-general-open`]
INFO `alanh@laguna.epcc.edu` (Alan Hodson)
INFO `cshooper@tenet.edu` (Carol Hooper)
INFO `carol.hooper@f105.n381.z1.fidonet.org` (Carol Hooper)

➤ **MAW-LIST:** On Mathematics Awareness Week, April 21-27. The 1996 topic is "Mathematics and Decision Making." (See entry 9392 for full listing.)

4312 `misc.education.science` Issues related to science education. *Newsgroup*

4313 `mit.evat` Education Via Advanced Technologies at MIT. *Newsgroup*

4314 **NARST-L:** On improving the education of science teachers through research. *Mailing List*
`http://science.cc.uwf.edu/narst/narst.html`
± `listserv@uwf.cc.uwf.edu` [body = `SUBSCRIBE NARST-L first-name last-name`]
INFO `jpeters@uwf.cc.uwf.edu` (Joe Peters)
Please Note: Subscription by approval only.

4315 **NCTM-L:** On the National Council of Teachers of Mathematics (NCTM) standards. *Mailing List*
± `majordomo@forum.swarthmore.edu` [body = `subscribe nctm-l`]

➤ **NEXUS—National Network of Physics Societies:** This is the information service for physics students and societies connected to the Institute of Physics. It includes job information, events, Ph.D. and M.Sc. positions, society programs, and contact addresses and past copies of NEXUS News, the society's newsletter. (See entry 9472 for full listing.)

4316 `oh.acad-sci` OAS: science, engineering, technology, and education. *Newsgroup*

➤ **Physics Education News (PEN):** On physics and science education. From the education division of the American Institute of Physics (AIP). (See entry 9476 for full listing.)

4317 **SAIS-L:** On promoting science to students. *Mailing List*
± `listserv@unb.ca` [body = `SUBSCRIBE SAIS-L first-name last-name`]
INFO OWNER `sais@unb.ca` (Keith W. Wilson)
ARCHIVE `listserv@unb.ca` [body = `INDEX SAIS-L`]
Gated: `misc.education.science`

4318 `school.subjects.science` Physics, computer science, etc. *Newsgroup*

4319 `sci.stat.edu` Statistics education. *Newsgroup*

4320 **YESCAMP:** For organizers of YESCamps, which are summer camps intended to make math and science fun to learn for students in grades 5 to 8. *Mailing List*
± `listserv@listserv.unb.ca` [body = `SUBSCRIBE YESCAMP first-name last-name`]
INFO `yescamp-request@listserv.unb.ca`

MULTICULTURAL

4321 **Asia-Pacific EXchange (Electronic) Journal:** Promoting international, multicultural education on college campuses with special emphasis on Asia and the Pacific. *E-Journal*
`http://naio.kcc.hawaii.edu/`
`gopher://naio.kcc.hawaii.edu`
± `listserv@uhccvm.uhcc.hawaii.edu` [body = `SUBSCRIBE APEXJ-L first-name last-name`]
INFO `jamess@hawaii.edu` (Jim Shimabukuro, EdD)
ARCHIVES
`http://naio.kcc.hawaii.edu/`
`gopher://naio.kcc.hawaii.edu`
Frequency: twice a year (June and December)

4322 **EDEQUITY:** On education equity in multiculturalism contexts. *Mailing List, moderated*
± `majordomo@confer.edc.org` [body = `SUBSCRIBE edequity`]
OWNER `edequity-admin@confer.edc.org` (Gaea L. Honeycutt)

➤ **EE-Link:** EE-Link is funded by the U.S. EPA to provide access to environmental education resources on the Internet. Topics include classroom resources, organizations and projects, literature, funding, regional resources. (See entry 4603 for full listing.)

➤ **IECC:** International E-mail Classroom Connections (IECC) project for classroom (not individual pen pals) e-mail exchanges. (See entry 4341 for full listing.)

4323 **MULTC-ED:** For educators involved with multicultural curriculum development, teaching, or research. *Mailing List*

± `listserv@umdd.umd:edu` [body = SUBSCRIBE MULTC-ED first-name last-name]

OWNER `jlevy@gmu.edu` (Jack Levy)

OWNER `rh19@umail.umd.edu` (Ruth Heidelbach)

ARCHIVE `listserv@umdd.umd.edu` [body = INDEX MULTC-ED]

➤ **POS302-L:** Seminar-based college level discussion on race, ethnicity, and social inequality. (See entry 10064 for full listing.)

➤ **T-AMLIT:** On teaching a radically expanded literature of the United States. (See entry 621 for full listing.)

➤ **WORLD-L:** On non-Eurocentric world history. (See entry 5272 for full listing.)

NEWS

4324 `clari.news.education` Primary and secondary education. *Moderated newsgroup*

4325 `clari.news.education.higher` Colleges and Universities. *Newsgroup*

4326 `clari.news.education.misc` Primary and secondary education. *Moderated newsgroup*

4327 `clari.news.education.releases` Press releases covering education. *Moderated newsgroup*

ONLINE TEACHING & LEARNING

4328 `alt.education.distance` Learning from teachers who are far away. *Newsgroup*

4329 `alt.school.homework-help` Looking for assistance with schoolwork. *Newsgroup*

4330 `alt.uu.announce` Announcements of Usenet University. *Newsgroup*

4331 `alt.uu.future` Does Usenet University have a viable future? *Newsgroup*

4332 `alt.uu.lang.esperanto.misc` Learning Esperanto at the Usenet University. *Newsgroup*

4333 `alt.uu.math.misc` Learning math at the Usenet University. *Newsgroup*

4334 `alt.uu.virtual-worlds.misc` Studying virtual reality at Usenet University. *Newsgroup*

4335 **Best for ed:** This directory contains links to many of the most valuable gopher resources in the area of professional education.

`gopher://info.asu.edu/11/asu-cwis/education/other`

INFO `glass@asu.edu` (Gene V. Glass, Editor)

4336 **BR_Match:** For linking classrooms with each other, and to the authors of books that the classrooms are reading. *Mailing List*

`http://micronet.wcu.edu/projects/bookread`

± `listproc@micronet.wcu.edu` [body = SUBSCRIBE BR_MATCH first-name last-name]

EDITOR `beam@micronet.wcu.edu` (Bonnie Beam)

OWNER `johnson@micronet.wcu.edu` (Patti Johnson)

ARCHIVE `http://micronet.wcu.edu/br_match.html`

POST `br_match@wcu.edu`

4337 **CREAD:** This list is used to animate discussions on the uses of distance education in Latin America and the Caribbean. *Mailing List*

± `listserv@yorkvm1.bitnet` [body = SUBSCRIBE CREAD first-name last-name]

INFO `lanfran@yorku.ca` (Sam Lanfranco)

Language: English, Spanish, Portuguese

4338 **DeweyWeb:** Facilitates communication between students from all over the world.
`http://ics.soe.umich.edu/`
INFO `info@ics.soe.umich.edu`

4339 **EDRES-L:** On Internet educational resources: associated with a database (EDRES-DB). *Mailing List, moderated*
± `listserv@unb.ca` [body = `SUBSCRIBE EDRES-L first-name last-name`]
EDITOR OWNER `pkirby@cythera.unb.ca` (Patti Kirby)
OWNER `dsoucy@unb.ca` (Don Soucy)
OWNER `ryana@unb.ca` (Anne Ryan)

➤ **The EdWeb Project:** An online tutorial on education, technology, school reform, and the information highway; sponsored by the Corporation for Public Broadcasting. (See entry 4224 for full listing.)

➤ **Global SchoolNet Foundation:** A nonprofit organization dedicated to the instructional applications of telecommunication. (See entry 4509 for full listing.)

4340 **GLOSAS News:** Newsletter of the GLObal Systems Analysis and Simulation Association, which organizes periodic global multimedia telecommunications experiments and is dedicated to global electronic education. *Newsletter*
± `listserv@vm1.mcgill.ca` [body = `SUBSCRIBE GLOSAS`]
INFO EDITOR `wcsanton@ccs.carleton.ca` (Anton Ljutic, Publisher/Editor)
INFO `utsumi@columbia.edu` (Dr. Takeshi "Tak" Utsumi)
ARCHIVES
`gopher://mora.usr.dsi.unimi.it`
`ftp://chmaplaincollege.qc.ca/pub/glosas/global-education/newsletter`
Frequency: quarterly; about to increase in frequency (six times a year?)

➤ **Home Education Resources Center (HERC):** HERC is a jumping-off site for those interested in educational opportunities at home or on the net. Great links to Internet educational resources, home-school regulations and support groups listed by state, a suggested reading list, and a complete products catalog. (See entry 4209 for full listing.)

4341 **IECC:** International E-mail Classroom Connections (IECC) project for classroom (not individual pen pals) e-mail exchanges. *Mailing List*
± `iecc-request@stolaf.edu`
OWNER `cdr@stolaf.edu` (Craig D. Rice)
ARCHIVE `http://www.stolaf.edu/network/iecc/`   (IECC project home page)
Comments: Project includes four other mailing lists on specialized topics.

4342 **IECC-HE:** For intercultural higher education classroom e-mail exchanges: not interpersonal. *Mailing List, moderated*
± `iecc-he-request@stolaf.edu`
OWNER `cdr@stolaf.edu` (Craig D. Rice)
ARCHIVE `http://www.stolaf.edu/network/iecc/` (IECC project home page)
Language: Any

4343 **IL-EDU:** On using the Internet in the Israeli school system. *Mailing List*
± `majordomo@pluto.mscc.huji.ac.il`
OWNER `msgolan@pluto.mscc.huji.ac.il` (Danny Golan)

➤ **The Interactive Patient:** This teaching tool for physicians, residents, and medical students offers a case with a chief complaint to the user who then has to interact with the patient requesting additional history, performing a physical exam, and reviewing laboratory data and X-rays. (See entry 4832 for full listing.)

➤ **International Language Development:** International Language Development provides interactive language lessons in French, German, Japanese, Korean, Russian, and Spanish on the Internet. (See entry 4251 for full listing.)

➤ **JTIT-L:** For Japanese teachers and instructional technology. (See entry 4252 for full listing.)

4344 `k12.sys.*` Hierarchy for current projects in K-12. *Newsgroup*

4345 `k12.sys.projects` Discussion of potential projects. *Newsgroup*

4346 `school.teachers` Discussion and chat between teachers. *Newsgroup*

PEDAGOGY

➤ **ADJUNCT:** On adjunct faculty topics. (See entry 4188 for full listing.)

➤ **AETS-L:** To promote leadership in, and support for those involved in, the professional development of teachers of science. (See entry 4277 for full listing.)

4347 `alt.teachers.lesson-planning` Helping teachers plan their instruction. *Newsgroup*

4348 `can.schoolnet.chat.teachers` General talk by SchoolNet teachers. *Newsgroup*

4349 `can.schoolnet.school.improvement` School improvement and enhancement. *Newsgroup*

4350 **CORELINK:** On core curriculum: goals, methods, policies, politics. *Mailing List, moderated*
± `listproc@mercury.cair.du.edu`
OWNER `craschke@du.edu`

➤ **DEWEY-L:** Discussion of John Dewey's philosophy. (See entry 5327 for full listing.)

4351 **EARLI-AE:** On assessment and evaluation in education. *Mailing List*
± `listserv@nic.surfnet.nl` [body = SUBSCRIBE EARLI-AE first-name last-name]
OWNER `oicfdo@ouh.nl` (Dr. Filip J.R.C. Dochy)

4352 **Par-L:** On test making and scoring, especially ParSYSTEM test-making software. *Digest & Reflector*
± `majordomo@ccat.sas.upenn.edu` [body = subscribe par-l]
EDITOR `ngsapper@pcad-ml.actx.edu` (Neil Sapper)
OWNER `jod@ccat.sas.upenn.edu` (James J. O'Donnell)

4353 **Research & Reflection: A Journal of Educational Praxis:** A scholarly approach to education that combines theory and practice. *E-Journal*
± EDITOR `editor@gonzaga.edu`
INFO `strever@gonzaga.edu` (Jan Strever)
ARCHIVE `http://www.rosauer.gonzaga.edu/~rr/rr.html`
Frequency: semiannual

4354 **School of Education, University of Leeds:** School of Education, The University of Leeds, United Kingdom. This site includes teaching and research activities of the school.
`http://education.leeds.ac.uk/`
INFO `webmaster@education.leeds.ac.uk`

4355 `soc.college.teaching-asst` Issues affecting collegiate teaching assistants. *Newsgroup*

➤ **SUNY Cortland Education Department:** Education Department Information Server (EDIS) for the State University of New York College at Cortland. SUNY Cortland graduates the largest number of certified teachers in New York each year. The EDIS is a resource for students and potential students, in addition to educators worldwide. (See entry 4452 for full listing.)

4356 **T-ASSIST:** For university teaching assistants to share and discuss teaching and being a TA. *Mailing List*
± `listserv@unmvma.unm.edu` [body = SUBSCRIBE T-ASSIST first-name last-name]
INFO `jgruene@bootes.unm.edu`
INFO `rosati@access.digex.net` (Anthony V. Rosati)
OWNER `rosati@gusun.georgetown.edu` (Anthony V. Rosati)

PHYSICAL EDUCATION

4357 `can.schoolnet.physed` Physical education in elementary/secondary schools. *Newsgroup*

4358 `k12.ed.health-pe` Health and physical education curricula in grades K-12. *Newsgroup*

RESEARCH

➤ **AskERIC Virtual Library:** ERIC is the Educational Resources Information Center (ERIC), a federally funded national information system that provides, through its sixteen subject-specific clearinghouses, associated adjunct clearinghouses, and support components, a variety of services and products on a broad range of education-related issues. (See entry 4477 for full listing.)

4359 `alt.education.research` Studying about studying. *Newsgroup*

➤ **BIBSOFT:** About software for citations and bibliographies. (See entry 3819 for full listing.)

4360 BICOMPAL: For members of the Big Computer Pals. *Mailing List*

± `listserv@stjohns.edu` [body = SUBSCRIBE BICOMPAL first-name last-name]

INFO `drz@sjuvm.stjohns.edu` (Bob Zenhausern, Ph.D.)

➤ **BUZAN:** On virtual study skills and creativity—based on the work of Tony Buzan. (See entry 273 for full listing.)

4361 CANARIE: For associates of the Canada Network for Advancement of Research, Industry and Education (CANARIE). *Mailing List*

± `listserv@unb.ca` [body = SUBSCRIBE CANARIE first-name last-name]

INFO `canarie-request@unb.ca`

ARCHIVE `listserv@unb.ca` [body = INDEX CANARIE]

➤ **Center for Defense Information (CDI):** This site provides a variety of defense-related information, including an arms trade database, access to its paper publication *The Defense Monitor*, its TV program "America's Defense Monitor," a nifty "Military Spending Clock" that shows how fast your tax dollars are spent by the military, and pointers to other defense- and security-related resources on the Internet. (See entry 5492 for full listing.)

4362 CHATBACK: For the SJU Chatback planning group. *Mailing List*

± `listserv@stjohns.edu` [body = SUBSCRIBE CHATBACK first-name last-name]

INFO `drz@sjuvm.stjohns.edu` (Dr. Robert Zenhausern)

4363 CONSLT-L: For members of the International Mentoring Association. *Mailing List*

± `listserv@iubvm.ucs.indiana.edu` [body = SUBSCRIBE CONSLT-L first-name last-name]

INFO `brescia@indiana.edu` (Bill Brescia)

Please Note: Subscription by approval only.

4364 CSSE: For members of the Canadian Society for the Study of Education. *Mailing List*

± `majordomo@majordomo.srv.ualberta.ca` [body = SUBSCRIBE CSSE]

INFO `craig.montgomerie@ualberta.ca`

Please Note: Subscription by approval only.

Gated: `bit.listserv.csse`

4365 Edstyle: On learning styles theory and research. *Mailing List*

± `listserv@stjohns.edu` [body = SUBSCRIBE EDSTYLE first-name last-name]

INFO `drz@sjuvm.stjohns.edu` (Dr. Robert Zenhausern)

4366 Education Research & Perspectives: Academic journal covering all aspects of education. *E-Journal*

`ftp://decel.ecel.uwa.edu.au/gopher/data/archives/education/erp`

± **INFO** `cwhitehe@ecel.uwa.edu.au` (Assoc/Prof. Clive Whitehead, Editor)

Frequency: twice annually (June and December)

4367 The George Lucas Educational Foundation: The George Lucas Educational Foundation promotes innovative efforts to improve education using a variety of communications media and based on the conviction that education is the most significant investment this nation can make to improve its future.

`http://glef.org/`

`gopher://glef.org`

INFO `edutopia@glef.org`

4368 IFER-L: Institute for Educational Renewal. *Mailing List*

± `listserv@miamiu.acs.muohio.edu` [body = SUBSCRIBE IFER-L first-name last-name]

INFO `bedwards@miamiu.bitnet` (Barb Edwards)

➤ **PHILOSED:** For students and teachers discussing the philosophy of education, an unofficial service of the Philosophy of Education Society. (See entry 5339 for full listing.)

➤ **PRO-CITE:** About personal bibliographic software. (See entry 3843 for full listing.)

➤ **RAND:** Website of RAND, a nonprofit institution that helps improve public policy through research and analysis. The site includes RAND publications, a wide range of information on its projects, and initiatives. (See entry 9553 for full listing.)

4369 **RED-NET:** On research in education and didactics. *Mailing List*
± `listserv@icineca.cineca.it` [body = SUBSCRIBE RED-NET first-name last-name]
INFO `red-net-request@icineca.cineca.it`
ARCHIVE `listserv@icineca.cineca.it` [body = INDEX RED-NET]

➤ **Research & Reflection: A Journal of Educational Praxis:** A scholarly approach to education that combines theory and practice. (See entry 4353 for full listing.)

4370 **RPE-L:** On restructuring public education. *Mailing List*
± `listserv@uhccvm.uhcc.hawaii.edu` [body = SUB RPE-L first-name last-name]
OWNER `dwz2@columbia.edu` (David W. Zuckerman)
OWNER `daniel@hawaii.edu` (Daniel Blaine)
ARCHIVE `listserv@uhccvm.uhcc.hawaii.edu` [body = INDEX RPE-L]

4371 `sci.edu` The science of education. *Newsgroup*

➤ **Scout Report:** Weekly publication of InterNIC Information Services of resources and news primarily of interest to the research and education community. (See entry 4530 for full listing.)

4372 **VIRTED:** On using virtual reality in education. *Mailing List*
± `listserv@sjuvm.stjohns.edu` [body = SUBSCRIBE VIRTED first-name last-name]
OWNER `king@access.digex.com` (Valorie J. King)
OWNER `plucas@vt.edu` (Perry Lucas)
OWNER `drz@sjuvm.stjohns.edu` (Dr. Robert Zenhausern)

SOCIAL STUDIES

4373 `can.schoolnet.history` History studies in elementary/secondary schools. *Newsgroup*

4374 `can.schoolnet.socsci.jr` SchoolNet social sciences for elementary students. *Newsgroup*

4375 `can.schoolnet.socsci.sr` SchoolNet social sciences for high-school students. *Newsgroup*

4376 `k12.ed.soc-studies` Social studies and history curriculum in K-12 education. *Newsgroup*

4377 `ri.k12.socialstudies` Rhode Island K-12 social studies discussions. *Newsgroup*

SPECIAL EDUCATION

4378 **Special Education Resources:** A comprehensive list of resources relating to special education including information on learning disabilities, gifted children, behavioral and emotional disorders, mental retardation, health and physical impairments, autism and communication disorders, sensory impairments, and early childhood.
`http://www.webcom.com/pleasant/sarah/teach/sped.html`
INFO `z_blakesj@titan.sfasu.edu`

4379 `alt.education.disabled` Education for people with physical/mental disabilities. *Newsgroup*

4380 `alt.support.learning-disab` For individuals with learning disabilities. *Newsgroup*

4381 **AR:** For the Achiever Report, on mental and emotional problems that interfere with learning. *Newsletter*
± OWNER `moremind@aol.com`

4382 **Education of the Visually Impaired:** Description of curriculum issues related to education of blind and visually impaired students and links to related resources.
`http://www.webcom.com/pleasant/sarah/teach/blind-ed.html`
INFO `z_blakesj@titan.sfasu.edu`

4383 `k12.ed.special` Educating students with handicaps and/or special needs. *Newsgroup*

➤ **Lanugage Based Learning Disability:Remediation Research:** This site presents information related to remediation research efforts for language-based learning disability. Information related to dyslexia is also provided. Multiple forums and a live chat room are provided for parents, teachers, clinicians, and researchers. (See entry 9867 for full listing.)

4384 **Sarah's Special Needs Resource Page:** For educators and parents interested in the area of special education. It includes curriculum ideas and pointers to other special-ed and disabilities sites.

http://www.bushnet.qld.edu.au/~sarah/spec_ed/

INFO sarah.clutterbuck@bushnet.qld.edu.au

Comments: Contributions are welcome. The emphasis with this Web site is content and it is frequently updated. Ideas for thematic units are being developed.

4385 **Sepract:** On the field of special education, cutting across areas of specific disabilities. *Mailing List*

± majordomo@virginia.edu [body = subscribe sepract]

INFO johnl@virginia.edu (John Wills Lloyd)

4386 **spedtalk:** On the field of special education, cutting across areas of specific disabilities. *Mailing List*

± majordomo@virginia.edu [body = subscribe spedtalk]

INFO johnl@virginia.edu (John Wills Lloyd)

ARCHIVES

http://curry.edschool.virginia.edu/curry/cise/ose/archive/stdigs.html
majordomo@virginia.edu

STUDENT LIFE

➤ **Student & Budget Travel Guide:** A descriptive and critical guide to travel resources on the Internet, especially for those of use to student and budget travelers. (See entry 7818 for full listing.)

4387 **alt.college.food** Dining halls, cafeterias, mystery meat, and more. *Newsgroup*

4388 **alt.college.tunnels** Tunnelling beneath the campuses. *Newsgroup*

4389 **alt.college.us** Is that "us" as in "U.S.," or do you just mean y'all? *Newsgroup*

4390 **alt.education.higher.stu-affairs** Student affairs principles and practices. *Newsgroup*

4391 **alt.flame.roommate** Putting the pig on a spit. *Newsgroup*

4392 **alt.grad-student.tenured** Professional students. *Newsgroup*

4393 **alt.psychotic.roommates** Single white female seeks roommate. *Newsgroup*

4394 **alt.society.high-school** The vaguely alternative world of high school. *Newsgroup*

➤ **ASC-L:** On academic sexual correctness: privacy, consent, and institutional encroachment. (See entry 4091 for full listing.)

4395 **aus.students** Going to school in Australia. *Newsgroup*

4396 **bit.listserv.sganet** Student Government global mail network. *Newsgroup*

4397 **Black Graduate Student Association at Massachusetts Institute of Technology:** Support and social group for black graduate students at M.I.T.

http://www.mit.edu:8001/activities/bgsa/home.html

4398 **can.schoolnet.chat.students.jr** General talk by elementary school SchoolNet students. *Newsgroup*

4399 **can.schoolnet.chat.students.sr** General talk by high-school SchoolNet students. *Newsgroup*

4400 **can.university.grad** Graduate student issues in Canada. *Newsgroup*

4401 **Heproc-student-involvement:** On furthering student involvement in higher education. *Mailing List*

± majordomo@world.std.com [body = subscribe heproc-student-involvement]

OWNER reimann@access.digex.net (Carl Reimann)

➤ **Internet Herald:** A magazine of news, commentary, and a little something else by Generation X. (See entry 10175 for full listing.)

➤ **Loci:** An online magazine by and for college students. Includes entertainment information, games, chat forums, and more. Sponsored by Barnes & Noble booksellers. (See entry 650 for full listing.)

4402 **NACASC-L:** For the National Association for Campus Activities (NACA), South Central Region. *Mailing List*

± listserv@uafsysb.uark.edu

OWNER gfitch@comp.uark.edu (Gene Fitch)

4403 **SAO-L:** For student-affairs officers. *Mailing List*

± listserv@uhccvm.uhcc.hawaii.edu [body = SUBSCRIBE SAO-L first-name last-name]

INFO morton@uhunix.uhcc.hawaii.edu

Please Note: Subscription by approval only.

4404 `school.pupils` Discussion and chat between pupils. *Newsgroup*

➤ **SHS:** The Society for Human Sexuality mailing list. Intended for general discussion of human sexuality and as a way to distribute information about events put on by the Society for Human Sexuality (a sex-positive registered student organization at the University of Washington). (See entry 10120 for full listing.)

➤ `soc.college`: College, college activities, campus life, etc. *Newsgroup*

➤ **STU-DEV:** On campus problems, student affairs, and practical student development theory. (See entry 4104 for full listing.)

➤ **T@P Online:** College and young-person-oriented mega-site, including extreme sports, music, travel, film, and more (over 17 sections). (See entry 10179 for full listing.)

4405 **Texas A&M University Bonfire:** Each year, thousands of Texas A&M University students work together to build a massive bonfire—55 feet high with a circumference of 195 feet—that symbolizes their "burning desire" to beat the University of Texas in the annual football game. Coverage of the building process and burn is included.

http://terminator.tamu.edu/bonfire/

INFO bonfire@tamu.edu

4406 **wsl:** On college politics and the Washington Student Lobby. *Mailing List*

http://rowlf.cc.wwu.edu:8080/wsl/

± listproc@cc.wwu.edu [body = SUBSCRIBE WSL first-name last-name]

OWNER zachd@cc.wwu.edu (Zach Harmon)

FAQ http://rowlf.cc.wwu.edu:8080/wsl/faq.html

TELEVISION

➤ `alt.fan.bill-nye`: Bill Nye, the Science Guy (TV show). *Newsgroup*

➤ `alt.tv.beakmans-world`: Some sort of science and comedy show. *Newsgroup*

➤ `alt.tv.billnye`: The science guy. *Newsgroup*

➤ `alt.tv.sesame-street`: Sunny day. *Newsgroup*

UNIVERSITIES & COLLEGES

➤ <u>CS Departments</u>: Listing of Web and gopher servers of computer science (and related) departments at universities throughout the net. (See entry 9161 for full listing.)

➤ <u>Journalism/Comm schools</u>: A compilation of communications, journalism, and media sites in universities around the world by Ana Camargos, a graduate student at the University of Florida. (See entry 5162 for full listing.)

4407 **Academy of Sciences Slovakia CWIS:** CWIS of the Slovak Academy of Sciences, Bratislava, Slovakia.

http://www.savba.sk/

gopher://savba.savba.sk

INFO logos@savba.sk

INFO vystavil@savba.sk

4408 `alt.folklore.college` Collegiate humor. *Newsgroup*

4409 **American Universities:** A listing of American universities that grant bachelor or advanced degrees and have WWW home pages.
http://www.clas.ufl.edu/CLAS/american-universities.html
INFO mconlon@clas.ufl.edu

4410 **Bar-Ilan University CWIS:** Information about Bar-Ilan University—general information, faculties and departments, Jewish studies, libraries, and other services.
http://www.biu.ac.il/
gopher://vm.biu.ac.il
INFO webmaster@www.biu.ac.il

4411 **Bilkent University CWIS:** CWIS and other Bilkent University computer resources.
http://www.bilkent.edu.tr/
ftp://ftp.bilkent.edu.tr/pub/
gopher://gopher.bilkent.edu.tr
INFO akgul@bilkent.edu.tr (Mustafa Akgul)

4412 **Board of Governors of State Colleges and Universities, Illinois:** This service contains information from the Board of Governors Universities, the oldest multicampus public university system in Illinois.
http://www.ecnet.net/
gopher://gopher.ecn.bgu.edu
INFO xjjgude@bgu.edu
FAQ gopher://gopher.ecn.bgu.edu/11/helpdesk/helpdesk.faq

4413 **Boston University CWIS:** Campus Wide Information System for Boston University
http://web.bu.edu/
INFO webmaster@bu.edu

4414 **Bowling Green State University:** A mid-size residential university in northwest Ohio, BGSU offers programs through the doctoral degree to more than 17,000 students.
http://www.bgsu.edu/
gopher://gopher.bgsu.edu
INFO webmaster@bgnet.bgsu.edu

➤ **Brussels Free University - Vrije Universiteit Brussel (VUB) CWIS:** Campus wide information service for Brussels Free University. (See entry 7103 for full listing.)

4415 **The California State University:** Starting point for information on the California State University.
http://www.calstate.edu/
INFO webmaster@calstate.edu

➤ **Calvin College CWIS:** Information service for Calvin College and Calvin Theological Seminary. This site includes news and information about Calvin, a campus directory, campus library catalog, and an extensive set of pointers to Christian resources on the Internet. (See entry 8695 for full listing.)

4416 **Camosun College CWIS:** Campus Wide Information Service for Camosun College, Canada.
http://www.camosun.bc.ca/
gopher://gopher.camosun.bc.ca
INFO webmaster@camosun.bc.ca
Comments: Pictures of the college and its buildings are available at:
http://www.camosun.bc.ca/camviews.html

4417 **Case Western Reserve University CWIS:** Campus Wide Information Service for Case Western Reserve University.
http://www.cwru.edu/
INFO aurora@po.cwru.edu
FAQ http://www.cwru.edu/help/auroraFAQ.html

4418 **Catholic University of Eichstaett:** Campus wide information service for Catholic University of Eichstaett.
http://www.ku-eichstaett.de/

```
gopher://gopher.ku-eichstaett.de
INFO webmaster@ku-eichstaett.de
```

4419 Charles University: The network for the Charles University campus and the Prague metropolitan area.

```
http://www.cuni.cz/
gopher://gopher.cuni.cz
INFO webmaster@cuni.cz
INFO gopheradm@cuni.cz
```

4420 CUINFO (Cornell University CWIS): Campus Wide Information Service for Cornell University.

```
http://www.cornell.edu/CUinfo.html
INFO cuinfo-admin@cornell.edu
```

4421 Dartmouth College: This is the CWIS of Dartmouth College.

```
http://www.dartmouth.edu/
gopher://gopher.dartmouth.edu/
INFO http://www.dartmouth.edu/help/
```

➤ **Dresden University of Technology/ Department of Computer Science:** This is the information service of the Department of Computer Science, Dresden University of Technology, Germany. (See entry 9191 for full listing.)

4422 Georgia Southern University: This is the CWIS of Georgia Southern University, Statesboro, Georgia.

```
http://www.gasou.edu/
gopher://gopher.gasou.edu
INFO ken_williams@gasou.edu
```

4423 Gettysburg College Web: Home page for Gettysburg College. Access to college publications, department information, administrative information, and links to academic Web projects here and elsewhere.

```
http://www.gettysburg.edu/
INFO wilson@gettysburg.edu
```

4424 Heidelberg University Information Server: This is the CWIS of the University of Heidelberg, Germany. It consists of several WWW/gopher/WAIS servers; the main entrance is the central WWW/gopher server at the University Computing Center (URZ). It includes a database of a complete inventory of the Greek papyri of Egypt.

```
http://www.urz.uni-heidelberg.de/
gopher://gopher.urz.uni-heidelberg.de
wais://wais.urz.uni-heidelberg.de
INFO michael.hebgen@urz.uni-heidelberg.de
```

4425 HTWS Zittau/Görlitz: Campus Wide Information Service for HTWS Zittau/Görlitz; also includes local area tourism, and business information.

```
http://www.htw-zittau.de/
gopher://gopher.htw-zittau.de
INFO webmaster@www.htw-zittau.de
```

4426 Inside Illinois: Faculty/staff newsletter of the University of Illinois at Urbana-Champaign. *Newsletter*

```
http://www.uiuc.edu/
± gopher://gopher.uiuc.edu
INFO EDITOR m-payne@uiuc.edu (Mare Lehnherr Payne, Editor)
```

Frequency: first and third Thursdays of each month

➤ **Institute for Business and Professional Ethics:** One of the largest resource sites relating to business and professional ethics, including an online journal, ethics discussions, and an ethics calendar. (See entry 2076 for full listing.)

4427 ITESM - Campus Ciudad de Mexico: Information on the Institute of Technology and Higher Education of Monterrey, Mexico City campus (Instituto Tecnologico y de Estudios Superiores de Monterrey, Campus Ciudad de Mexico).

```
http://www.ccm.itesm.mx/
INFO ldelrinc@campus.ccm.itesm.mx
```

4428 IUPUI CWIS: This is the main CWIS of Indiana University–Purdue University, Indianapolis, Indiana.
http://www.iupui.edu/ithome/csc
gopher://gopher.iupui.edu
INFO helpdesk@indyunix.iupui.edu

4429 JHUNIVERSE: Johns Hopkins University on the Web: This is the CWIS of Johns Hopkins University. JHUniverse is a gateway to information resources at Johns Hopkins University, the nation's first true research university and now the leading U.S. university in research and development expenditures. The system also maintains links to information on JHU's sister institution, the Johns Hopkins Hospital and Health System.
http://www.jhu.edu/
INFO lee.watkins@jhu.edu

4430 JKU Info Service: This is the campus information service of the Johannes Kepler University of Linz, Austria.
http://www.uni-linz.ac.at/
gopher://gopher.edvz.uni-linz.ac.at
INFO netadmin@edvz.uni-linz.ac.at

4431 La Trobe University (Victoria, Australia): This is the CWIS of La Trobe University in Melbourne, Australia.
http://www.latrobe.edu.au/
INFO webmaster@latrobe.edu.au

4432 Lund University Electronic Library, Sweden: This Web site is managed by LUB NetLab, the development department of Lund University Library, as an electronic information service for Lund University, Lund, Sweden, and other users.
http://www.ub2.lu.se/
INFO traugott.koch@ub2.lu.se

➤ **MALACHI:** For the exchange of ideas and information about graduate courses among the universities in the Washington, D.C. metropolitan area. (See entry 8633 for full listing.)

4433 Massachusetts Institute of Technology: MIT is an independent, coeducational university located in Cambridge, Massachusetts. MIT's WWW pages provide information about MIT's schools, departments, and programs; educational resources; research at MIT; and library services. You'll also find admissions information, alumni services, publications, and more.
http://web.mit.edu/
INFO web-request@mit.edu

4434 Midland Crossroads Service Centre at Iowa State University: Midland Crossroads Service Centre is a facility for accessing computer resources at Iowa State University. Outbound connections are also provided to major Internet resources. Crossroads consists of twelve "buildings" on four "streets." Major facilities include: Video DMZ, Dining Car, Reading Nook, Gopher Grand Central, and an Internet Drive-In.
http://www.public.iastate.edu/~spires/crossroad.html
INFO jastruss@iastate.edu (Joe Struss)

4435 mit.* Massachusetts Institute of Technology newsgroups. *Newsgroup*

4436 mit.bboard MIT's bulletin board. *Newsgroup*

4437 Ohio Northern University CWIS: This is the CWIS of Ohio Northern University in Ada, Ohio.
http://www.onu.edu/
finger://ns2.onu.edu
ftp://ftp.onu.edu
gopher://gopher.onu.edu
INFO info@onu.edu
INFO r-beer@onu.edu

4438 Otterbein On-Line: Alumni, current students, and friends of Otterbein College in Westerville, Ohio can be e-mailed from this unofficial page.
http://falcon.cc.ukans.edu/~nsween/oc/bb-oc.html
http://pages.prodigy.com/OH/otterbein/oc.html

INFO nsween@falcon.cc.ukans.edu

4439 pitt.* Pittsburgh University newsgroups. *Newsgroup*

4440 Presbyterian College: This site offers a look at the people, campus, academic program, and extracurricular life of Presbyterian College in Clinton, South Carolina.

http://www.presby.edu/

INFO info@presby.edu

Comments: For futher information, call (800) 476-7272, or 1 (864) 833-2820, or send mail to the address below.

4441 Princeton University Information Service: The main Princeton University World Wide Web home page, with pointers to home pages of academic and administrative departments, as well as other regional home pages.

http://www.princeton.edu/

INFO www@princeton.edu

4442 Prompt: News tips and briefs for the North Carolina State University campus community. *Newsletter*

http://www2.ncsu.edu/ncsu/cc/pub/prompt/prompt_index.html

± listserv@listservncsu.edu [body = SUBSCRIBE PROMPT-L first-name last-name]

INFO sarah@ncsu.edu (Sarah Noell)

Frequency: as often as needed

4443 purdue.* Purdue University newsgroups. *Newsgroup*

4444 Queensland University of Technology, Brisbane: The QUT WWW pages and gopher provide people outside the university with information about QUT and direct the university's staff and students to outside Internet resources.

http://www.qut.edu.au/

INFO w.fisher@qut.edu.au

4445 RiceInfo: Campus Wide Information Service for Rice University.

http://riceinfo.rice.edu/

gopher://riceinfo.rice.edu:1170

INFO riceinfo@rice.edu

4446 Saint Louis University CWIS: This is the CWIS of Saint Louis University in St. Louis, Missouri.

gopher://gopher.slu.edu

INFO postmaster@sluvca.slu.edu

4447 San Diego State University, College of Sciences: This site provides various campus information and centralized access to other campus resources.

http://www.sdsu.edu/

INFO webmaster@sdsu.edu

➤ **Seneca Information Service:** This is the CWIS of Seneca College of Applied Arts and Technology, Toronto, Canada. (See entry 79 for full listing.)

4448 Skidmore College: This Web site and gopher offer campus information and access to diverse network resources at Skidmore College, an undergraduate liberal-arts college in upstate New York.

http://www.skidmore.edu/

gopher://gopher.skidmore.edu

INFO webmaster@skidmore.edu

4449 SpiGopher at Iowa State University: This is the Computation Center at Iowa State. The server itself is located on the ISUMVS system (WYLBUR) at Iowa State and primarily uses the SPIRES database facility. It includes a play concordance of eight fully indexed plays.

http://www.public.iastate.edu/~spires/crossroad.html

gopher://isumvs.iastate.edu

INFO jastruss@iastate.edu (Joe Struss)

4450 St. John's University: This site serves as the university's CWIS, and hosts the SJU Electronic Rehabilitation Resource Center and the SJU Learning Styles Network. This site also contains some resources for K–12 teachers.

```
http://www.stjohns.edu/
gopher://sjuvm.stjohns.edu
INFO holtzman@stjohns.edu
```

4451   **St. Olaf College WWW Server:** The campus wide information system for St. Olaf College in Northfield, Minnesota.

```
gopher://gopher.stolaf.edu
INFO gopher@stolaf.edu
```

4452   **SUNY Cortland Education Department:** Education Department Information Server (EDIS) for the State University of New York College at Cortland. SUNY Cortland graduates the largest number of certified teachers in New York each year. The EDIS is a resource for students and potential students, in addition to educators worldwide.

```
http://www.cortland.edu/~education/
INFO education@www.cortland.edu
```

4453   **Swarthmore College:** This is the CWIS for the Swarthmore College campus community. Swarthmore College is a small liberal-arts college in Swarthmore, Pennsylvania, a suburb of Philadelphia. Most of the college publications, such as the college catalog and student handbook, are online. College calendars, Swarthmore e-mail lookups, and almost anything pertaining to the college are there.

```
http://www.swarthmore.edu/
INFO tkrattel@swarthmore.edu (Tom Krattenmaker)
```

4454   **SyraCWIS: Syracuse University CWIS:** This is the CWIS of Syracuse University, Syracuse, New York.

```
http://www.syr.edu/
INFO webmaster@www.syr.edu
```

4455   **Tampere University of Technology (TUT), Finland:** Web server at Tampere University of Technology, Finland. Information about TUT in general, departments, research activities, education, services available on campus, contact addresses.

```
http://www.tut.fi/
INFO webmaster@cc.tut.fi
```

4456   **Texas A&M University World Wide Web:** This Texas A&M WWW site includes both a subject index and a keyword search to information offered by Web sites located throughout the College Station campus, the local community, and the entire Texas A&M system. Information regarding academics, research, events, employment, and campus sights are just a sampling of the topics included. It also includes information on the George Bush Presidential Library.

```
http://www.tamu.edu/
INFO www@tamu.edu
```

4457   **Trent University Information Service:** This is the CWIS for Trent University, Peterborough, Ontario, Canada. Includes distribution of faculty work/publications, notably D. Theall's work on James Joyce and Sarah Keefer's work on Old English.

```
http://www.trentu.ca/
ftp://ftp.trentu.ca
gopher://gopher.trentu.ca/2 (CS0)
gopher://gopher.trentu.ca
INFO webmaster@trentu.ca
```

4458   **trentu.***   Trent University newsgroups. *Newsgroup*

4459   **trentu.seminar**   Seminar announcements at Trent University. *Newsgroup*

4460   **U-Discover!:** CWIS for the University of Delaware.

```
http://www.udel.edu/
gopher://gopher.udel.edu
INFO www@udel.edu
```

4461   **UBWings:** This is the CWIS of the State University of New York at Buffalo.

```
http://wings.buffalo.edu/
INFO wings@acsu.buffalo.edu
```

4462 **UHINFO:** This is the CWIS for the University of Hawaii system, which includes UH Manoa, UH Hilo, UH West Oahu, Hawaii CC, Honolulu CC, Kapiolani CC, Kauai CC, Leeward CC, Maui CC, and Windward CC.

http://www.hawaii.edu/uhinfo.html

gopher://gopher.hawaii.edu

INFO webhead@www.hawaii.edu

FAQ http://www.hawaii.edu/uhinfo-faq/

4463 **UIC/ADN CWIS:** This is the CWIS of the University of Illinois at Chicago.

http://www.uic.edu/

INFO cthier@uic.edu

4464 **UNC-ECS (UNC System):** This server provides information services primarily to the 16 constituent institutions of the University of North Carolina.

http://www.ga.unc.edu/

INFO ltp@uncecs.edu (Lou Parker)

4465 **Universidad de Oviedo:** The WWW server of the University of Oviedo, Spain. You can get all information about the institution, studies, faculties, etc...

http://www.uniovi.es/

ftp://ftp.uniovi.es/

gopher://gopher.uniovi.es/

INFO wwwteam@dana.vicest.uniovi.es

INFO webmaster@dana.vicest.uniovi.es

MIRROR http://www3.uniovi.es/

4466 **University of California, Riverside:** This is the campus wide information service for University of California, Riverside.

http://www.ucr.edu/

INFO chuckm@marathon.ucr.edu (Chuck McDaniels)

4467 **University of Trento CWIS:** Campus Wide Information Service for University of Trento.

http://www.unitn.it/

INFO iori@science.unitn.it

➤ **UNK Department of Physics and Physical Science:** Web site of the department of Physics and Physical Science at the University of Nebraska at Kearney. (See entry 9493 for full listing.)

➤ **UNK Department of Sociology:** Web site of the department of sociology at the University of Nebraska at Kearney. (See entry 5367 for full listing.)

4468 **Victoria Univeristy of Wellington New Zealand:** This CWIS contains information about departments, staff, and courses offered at Victoria University of Wellington.

http://www.vuw.ac.nz/

INFO webmaster@vuw.ac.nz

➤ **Vienna University of Economics CWIS:** Campus wide information service for Vienna University of Economics. (See entry 5213 for full listing.)

➤ **Wyoming:** Everything you want to know about Wyoming, and some. It includes Who's Who in Wyoming on the Internet©, Wyoming E-mail Directory©, links to Wyoming schools and colleges, and government telephone directories. (See entry 8649 for full listing.)

UNIVERSITY NEWSPAPERS

4469 **Alligator Online:** The electronic version of the 32,000-copy college daily that serves the University of Florida community.

http://www.afn.org/~ifa/

INFO ifa@freenet.ufl.edu

4470 **The Bucknellian:** The weekly campus newspaper of Bucknell University. *Newsletter*

http://www.bucknell.edu/bucknellian
INFO bucknellian@bucknell.edu (Jeff Boulter)
ARCHIVE http://www.bucknell.edu/bucknellian
Frequency: weekly
Price: off-campus print subscriptions are $25/semester, $40/year

4471 **Campus Newspapers:** Campus Newspapers on the Internet, established by Jonathan Bell and maintained by Scott Kirkham.

http://beacon-www.asa.utk.edu/resources/papers.html
INFO online-editor@beacon.asa.utk.edu

4472 **North of Green:** Weekly (when classes are in session) newsletter for undergraduate students in the College of Engineering, University of Illinois at Urbana-Champaign. *Newsletter*

INFO birwin@ux1.cso.uiuc.edu (Bonnie J. Irwin)
ARCIIIVE http://www.cen.uiuc.edu/COE-Info/coe.top.html
Frequency: weekly, fall, and spring semesters

4473 **STUMEDIA:** On college and university level student journalism. *Mailing List*

± listserv@uabdpo.dpo.uab.edu [body = SUBSCRIBE STUMEDIA first-name last-name]
OWNER cba0027@uabdpo.dpo.uab.edu (Kenneth Pate)
OWNER sas1007@uabdpo.dpo.uab.edu (Steve Chappell)

4474 **The Thistle:** Student forum for the progressive and creative minds at MIT; debating undiscussed decision making at MIT and in the world and examining the alternative futures toward which we might work. *E-Journal*

INFO thistle@mit.edu (The Thistle Staff)
ARCHIVE http://www.mit.edu:8001/afs/athena/activity/t/thistle/www/thistle.html
Frequency: biweekly

4475 **University of Missouri, Columbia's Campus Computing:** Status of computing at University of Missouri: system changes, software updates and reviews, hours of computing operations, schedule of student computing sites, computing course offerings. *Newsletter*

http://www.missouri.edu/cc/news/
± INFO EDITOR ccmolly@mizzou1.missouri.edu (Molly Godsy, Editor)
ARCHIVE http://www.missouri.edu/cc/news/
Frequency: six times during the academic year

4476 **Virginia Tech Spectrum:** *Spectrum* is a faculty/staff tabloid published by the Office of University Relations, Virginia Polytechnic Institute and State University. *Newsletter*

gopher://borg.lib.vt.edu/11/spectrum
INFO gailmac@vt.edu (Gail McMillan)
INFO EDITOR spectrum@vtvm1.cc.vt.edu (John Ashby, Editor)
ARCHIVES
http://borg.lib.vt.edu/z-borg/www/ejournals/spectrum.html
gopher://borg.lib.vt.edu
Frequency: weekly during academic year

USING COMPUTERS & NETWORKS

4477 **AskERIC Virtual Library:** ERIC is the Educational Resources Information Center (ERIC), a federally funded national information system that provides, through its sixteen subject-specific clearinghouses, associated adjunct clearinghouses, and support components, a variety of services and products on a broad range of education-related issues.

http://ericir.syr.edu/
gopher://ericir.syr.edu
INFO askeric@ericir.syr.edu
FAQ gopher://ericir.syr.edu/11/FAQ

4478 **CAUSE:** CAUSE is the association for managing and using information resources in higher education. CAUSE is a source of information and professional development opportunities for those who plan for, implement, and manage information resources on campus.

```
http://cause-www.colorado.edu/
gopher://cause-gopher.colorado.edu/
```
INFO info@cause.colorado.edu

4479 **Internet Resource Directory for Educators:** Online resources of value to teachers, trainers, and their students; includes Web pages, gophers, mailing lists, telnet sites, and FTP sites. Organized by education-related topic.

```
http://www.tapr.org/~ird/index.html
```
INFO jbharris@tenet.edu (Judi Harris)

4480 **KIDLINK:** KIDLINK is a global networking project for youths 10-15. The KIDLINK list is for official news and information about the KIDLINK series of projects, which span many other lists and services. KIDLINK coordinates the worldwide dialog of thousands of youth 10-15 in scores of countries. Other KIDLINK lists are RESPONSE, KIDPROJ, KIDFORUM, the KIDCAFE family of lists, the KIDLEADER family of lists, KIDPLAN, and a family of project COORDination lists. *Mailing List, moderated*

```
http://www.kidlink.org/
```
± listserv@vm1.nodak.edu [body = SUBSCRIBE KIDLINK first-name last-name]

INFO kidlink-info@kidlink.org

INFO opresno@kidlink.org (Odd de Presno)

ARCHIVE listserv@vm1.nodak.edu [body = INDEX KIDLINK]

Language: English plus many others

4481 **Akademische Software Kooperation:** ASK-SISY: a database of higher-education software; ASK-SINA: searching all German FTP sites via WWW ASKnet: distributing commercial software at special retail prices to the higher-education community.

```
http://www.ask.uni-karlsruhe.de/
ftp://ftp.ask.uni-karlsruhe.de/
gopher://gopher.ask.uni-karlsruhe.de/
listproc@ask.uni-karlsruhe.de
telnet://askhp.ask.uni-karlsruhe.de
wais://askhp.ask.uni-karlsruhe.de/ASK-SISY-Software-Information.src
```
INFO boden@ask.uni-karlsruhe.de

INFO office@ask.uni-karlsruhe.de

Comments: A lot of information is only available in German!

4482 **APPL-L:** Computer applications in science and education. *Mailing List*

± listserv@vm.cc.uni.torun.pl [body = SUBSCRIBE APPL-L first-name last-name]

INFO appl-l-request@vm.cc.uni.torun.pl

ARCHIVE listserv@vm.cc.uni.torun.pl [body = INDEX APPL-L]

➤ **Association for Technology in Music Instruction:** For discussions of the use of technology in music instruction. (See entry 842 for full listing.)

➤ **aus.education.bio-newtech:** New technologies in biology teaching. *Newsgroup*

➤ **BIBSOFT:** About software for citations and bibliographies. (See entry 3819 for full listing.)

➤ **Biomedical Multimedia Unit:** The home page of the Biomedical Multimedia Unit, School of Medicine, University of Melbourne. Contains information and resources relating to multimedia education in the medical sciences. (See entry 4827 for full listing.)

4483 **bit.listserv.aect-l** Educational communication and technology. *Newsgroup*

4484 **bit.listserv.big-lan** Campus-size LAN discussion group. *Newsgroup*

4485 **bit.listserv.cw-email** Campus-wide e-mail discussion list. *Newsgroup*

4486 **bit.listserv.cwis-l** Campus-wide information systems. *Newsgroup*

4487 `bit.listserv.dectei-1` DECUS education software library discussions. *Newsgroup*

4488 `bit.listserv.edtech` EDTECH—educational technology. *Moderated newsgroup*

4489 `bit.listserv.edusig-1` EDUSIG discussions. *Newsgroup*

4490 `bit.listserv.mbu-1` Megabyte University—computers and writing. *Newsgroup*

4491 `bit.listserv.ucp-1` University Computing Project mailing list. *Newsgroup*

4492 **Buffer:** News journal of computing at the University of Denver. *Newsletter*
  INFO EDITOR `buffer@du.edu` (Rebecca Rowe)
  ARCHIVE `http://www.du.edu/~buffer/buffer.html`
  Frequency: monthly

4493 **CEARCH: Cisco Educational Archives:** Education archive; lists a variety of resources about school connectivity to the Internet as well as a catalog of educational resources organized by classroom and subject.
  `http://sunsite.unc.edu/cisco/edu-arch.html`
  INFO `cearch@sunsite.unc.edu`
  FAQ `http://sunsite.unc.edu/cisco/noc.html`
  MIRROR `http://sunsite.anu.edu.au/cisco/` (Australian National University)

4494 `clari.nb.education` Newsbytes: computers in education. *Moderated newsgroup*

4495 `clari.tw.computers.in_use` Using computers in industry, education. *Moderated newsgroup*

4496 **COAACAD:** For the SUNY Computer Officers Association Academic Subcommittee. *Mailing List*
  ± `listserv@ubvm.cc.buffalo.edu` [body = SUBSCRIBE COAACAD first-name last-name]
  INFO `gerland@ubvms.cc.buffalo.edu`
  INFO `http://www.acsu.buffalo.edu/~gerland` (Jim Gerland)
  OWNER `gerland@acsu.cc.buffalo.edu` (Jim Gerland)
  ARCHIVE `listserv@ubvm.cc.buffalo.edu`

4497 **Coalition for Networked Information (CNI):** A partnership of the Association of Research Libraries, CAUSE, and EDUCOM, the coalition's mission is to help realize the promise of high-performance networks and computers for the advancement of scholarship and the enrichment of intellectual productivity.
  `http://www.cni.org/CNI.homepage.html`
  INFO `info@cni.org`

➤ **Colorado K–12:** Support materials and networking for K-12 internet sites (See entry 4222 for full listing.)

4498 `comp.edu.composition` Writing instruction in computer-based classrooms. *Newsgroup*

4499 `comp.edu.languages.natural` Computer-assisted languages instruction issues. *Newsgroup*

4500 **CTI-TEXTUAL-STUDIES:** On using computers in textual studies: U.K. orientation. *Mailing List, moderated*
  ± `mailbase@mailbase.ac.uk`
  INFO `http://www.ox.ac.uk/depts/humanities/cti.html`
  INFO `cti-textual-studies-request@mailbase.ac.uk`
  OWNER `michael.popham@oucs.ox.ac.uk` (Mike Popham, Centre Manager)
  ARCHIVE `gopher://nisp.ncl.ac.uk/11/lists-other/cti/cti-textual-studies/archives`
  POST `cti-textual-studies@mailbase.ac.uk`

➤ **Czech Educational and Scientific NETwork (CESNET):** Information on CESNET and the Czech Republic. (See entry 7263 for full listing.)

4501 **DECTEI-L:** On Digital Equipment Corporation's Education Initiative program of discounts and services for educational institutions. *Mailing List*
  ± `listserv@ubvm.cc.buffalo.edu` [body = SUBSCRIBE DECTEI-L first-name last-name]
  INFO `wendt@wugate.wustl.edu` (Catherine Wendt-Bernal)
  ARCHIVES
  `http://passion.stanford.edu/`

listserv@ubvm.cc.buffalo.edu [body = INDEX DECTEI-L]

4502 DENet Information Server: This is the information service of the Danish national academic network, DENet. It is located at UNI-C, the Danish Computer Centre for Research and Education.

http://www.uni-c.dk/
http://www.denet.dk/
INFO steen.linden@uni-c.dk

4503 Educom Review: Articles, columns, and book reviews focused on information technology and higher education. *E-Journal*

gopher://educom.edu
INFO gehl@educom.edu (John Gehl)
ARCHIVES
gopher://educom.edu
http://www.educom.edu/
Frequency: bimonthly

➤ **Edupage:** Summary of information-technology news. (See entry 9363 for full listing.)

4504 EDUSIG-L: On education and the Digital Equipment Corporation. *Mailing List*

± listserv@ubvm.cc.buffalo.edu [body = SUBSCRIBE EDUSIG-L first-name last-name]
INFO gerland@ubvms.cc.buffalo.edu
ARCHIVE listserv@ubvm.cc.buffalo.edu

4505 EEC-L: On European training and technology. *Mailing List*

± listserv@american.edu [body = SUBSCRIBE EEC-L first-name last-name]
INFO dstruppa@gmu.edu (Daniele Struppa)
ARCHIVE listserv@american.edu

4506 ENGLISH: Discussions for departments of English faculty in the U.S. and Canada on using computers to teach literature and composition, and general discussions on literary studies. *Mailing List*

± listserv@utarlvm1.uta.edu [body = SUBSCRIBE ENGLISH first-name last-name]
INFO b399tary@utarlvm1.uta.edu (Tom Ryan)

4507 FACSUP-L: On university faculty efforts to use computers: support and objectives. *Mailing List*

± listserv@uconnvm.uconn.edu [body = SUBSCRIBE FACSUP-L first-name last-name]
OWNER tmills@uconnvm.uconn.edu (Ted Mills, Coordinator)
ARCHIVE listserv@uconnvm.uconn.edu [body INDEX FACSUP-L]

4508 From Now On: The Educational Technology Journal: Devoted to issues of change and the introduction of new technologies to schools and the workplace. *Newsletter*

http://www.pacificrim.net/~mckenzie/
± **INFO OWNER** mckenzie@pacificrim.net
ARCHIVE http://www.pacificrim.net/~mckenzie/
Frequency: monthly (ten per year)

4509 Global SchoolNet Foundation: A nonprofit organization dedicated to the instructional applications of telecommunication.

http://www.gsn.org/
INFO andresyv@cerf.net

4510 GLOSAS: On distance education and high technology. *Mailing List*

± listserv@vm1.mcgill.ca [body = SUBSCRIBE GLOSAS first-name last-name]
INFO anton@vax2.concordia.ca (Anton Ljutic)
Please Note: Subscription by approval only.

4511 **Harvard Computer Review Online:** The Harvard Computer Review (HCR) is the Harvard Computer Society's online magazine dedicated to reviewing trends in computing, focusing on their impact in a university environment (but especially Harvard). *Magazine*

http://hcs.harvard.edu/~hcr

± hcr-announce-request@hcs.harvard.edu [body = SUBSCRIBE]

INFO OWNER hcr@hcs.harvard.edu (Janet Rosenbaum)

INFO OWNER jerosenb@hcs.harvard.edu (Janet Rosenbaum)

OWNER info@hcs.harvard.edu (Harvard Computer Society)

ARCHIVE http://hcs.harvard.edu/~hcr

➤　**HYPEREDU:** On using hypertext in education. (See entry 2510 for full listing.)

4512 **ia.org.eee** Electronic Educational Exchange—technology for educators. *Newsgroup*

4513 **IAT Infobits:** Reviews and comments on a number of information technology and instruction technology sources of interest to educators. IAT Infobits is a service of the Institute for Academic Technology's Information Resources Group. *Newsletter*

± listserv@unc.edu [body = subscribe infobits first-name last-name]

INFO EDITOR OWNER carolyn_kotlas@unc.edu (Carolyn Kotlas)

ARCHIVES

http://www.iat.unc.edu/infobits/infobits.html

ftp://ftp.iat.unc.edu/pub/infobits

POST infobits@unc.edu

Frequency: monthly

4514 **IBM-HESC:** For discussion among the IBM Higher Education Software Consortium, which tries to enhance the academic process by making available IBM software and by sharing information on its effective use. *Mailing List*

± listserv@cc.pdx.edu [body = SUBSCRIBE IBM-HESC first-name last-name]

INFO willsr@pdx.edu (Ron Wills)

4515 **Institute for Academic Technology:** The University of North Carolina at Chapel Hill's Institute for Academic Technology (IAT) is dedicated to the proposition that information technology can be a valuable tool for improving the quality of student learning, increasing access to education, and containing the costs of instruction.

http://www.iat.unc.edu/

ftp://ftp.iat.unc.edu/pub/

INFO jon_pishney@unc.edu

4516 **IPCT-L:** Broad-ranging discussion on interpersonal computing and technology used in education. *Mailing List, moderated*

± listserv@listserv.georgetown.edu [body = SUBSCRIBE IPCT-L first-name last-name]

INFO berge@umbc2.umbc.edu

POST ipct-l@listserv.georgetown.edu

POST ipct-l@listserv@georgetown.edu

Gated: bit.listserv.ipct-l

4517 **JEI-L:** Technology in education. *Mailing List*

± listserv@umdd.umd.edu [body = SUBSCRIBE JEI-L first-name last-name]

INFO jei-l-request@umdd.umd.edu

ARCHIVE listserv@umdd.umd.edu [body = INDEX JEI-L]

➤　**JTIT-L:** For Japanese teachers and instructional technology. (See entry 4252 for full listing.)

4518 **k12.library** Implementing information technologies in school libraries. *Newsgroup*

4519 **MECCA (Memphis Educational Computer Connectivity Alliance):** An alliance of academic institutions in Memphis, Tennessee, with the purpose of enhancing Internet connectivity and programmed application of that connectivity for local schools to enhance educational infrastructure.

http://www.mecca.org/

INFO ltague@physio1.utmem.edu

➤ **MEMO-NET:** On library media and technology. (See entry 5729 for full listing.)

4520 `misc.education.multimedia` Multimedia for education. *Moderated newsgroup*

4521 `ne.nearnet.general` Discuss the New England Academic and Research Network (NEARnet). *Newsgroup*

4522 `ne.nearnet.tech` Technical operation and future of NEARnet. *Newsgroup*

➤ **NETTRAIN:** For Internet/Bitnet network trainers. (See entry 2918 for full listing.)

4523 **NFDL-L:** The Nordic Forum for Computer Aided Higher Education. *Mailing List*
± listserv@searn.sunet.se [body = SUBSCRIBE NFDL-L first-name last-name]
INFO nfdl-l-request@searn.sunet.se
ARCHIVE listserv@searn.sunet.se [body = INDEX NFDL-L]

➤ **PRO-CITE:** About personal bibliographic software. (See entry 3843 for full listing.)

4524 **The Public-Access Computer Systems Review:** Campus-wide information systems, CD-ROM LANs, document delivery systems, expert systems, hypermedia and multimedia systems, locally mounted databases, network-based information resources and tools, and more. *E-Journal*
gopher://info.lib.uh.edu/11/articles/e-journals/uhlibrary/pacsreview
gopher://info.lib.uh.edu
± listserv@uhupvm1.uh.edu [body = SUBSCRIBE PACS-P first-name last-name]
EDITOR cbailey@uh.edu (Charles W. Bailey, Jr., Editor-in-Chief)
ARCHIVES
gopher://info.lib.uh.edu
listserv@uhupvm1.uh.edu [body = INDEX PACS-P]
Frequency: irregular

4525 `relcom.relarn.general` Academic subnet RELARN: general issues. *Moderated newsgroup*

4526 **SCHOOL-L:** For address simplification of electronic mailing lists maintained by primary and post-primary schools. *Mailing List*
± listserv@irlearn.ucd.ie [body = SUBSCRIBE SCHOOL-L first-name last-name]
INFO pflynn@curia.ucc.ie (Peter Flynn)

4527 `school.general` General information about projects, news, etc. *Newsgroup*

4528 `school.project.esp` European School Project. *Newsgroup*

4529 `school.project.pluto` Project to Link Universities and Training Organizations. *Newsgroup*

4530 **Scout Report:** Weekly publication of InterNIC Information Services of resources and news primarily of interest to the research and education community. *Newsletter*
gopher://rs.internic.net
ftp://rs.internic.net/scout/
http://www.internic.net/scout
± listserv@lists.internic.net [body = SUBSCRIBE SCOUT first-name last-name]
INFO POST scout@internic.net
ARCHIVE http://www.internic.net/scout/report/archives
Frequency: weekly

4531 **SIGTEL-L:** On classroom use of telecommunications. *Mailing List, moderated*
http://isteonline.uoregon.edu/
± listproc@lists.acs.ohio-state.edu [body = SUBSCRIBE SIGTEL-L first-name last-name]
INFO kathyk@tenet.edu (Kathy Kothmann)
INFO lynd.7@osu.edu (Chuck Lynd)
FAQ http://isteonline.uoregon.edu/istehome/sig/sigtelfaq.html

4532 `tnn.edu+net.announce` Newsgroup for information exchange on education and network (announcements). *Moderated newsgroup*

4533 `tnn.edu+net.misc` Newsgroup for information exchange on education and network (miscellaneous). *Moderated newsgroup*

➤ **VETCAI-L:** On computer-assisted instruction in veterinary medicine. (See entry 9650 for full listing.)

4534 **VIDNET-L:** Specifically for the exchange of information between professionals who operate video networks at college campuses. *Mailing List*

± `listserv@uga.cc.uga.edu` [body = SUBSCRIBE VIDNET-L first-name last-name]

INFO OWNER `jstephen@uga.cc.uga.edu`

ARCHIVE `listserv@uga.cc.uga.edu` [body = INDEX VIDNET-L]

Please Note: Subscription by approval only.

4535 **WIOLE-L:** On writing intensive online learning environments. *Mailing List*

± `listserv@mizzou1.missouri.edu` [body = SUBSCRIBE WIOLE-L first-name last-name]

INFO `wiole-l-request@mizzou1.missouri.edu`

ARCHIVE `listserv@mizzou1.missouri.edu` [body = INDEX WIOLE-L]

4536 **WWWEDU:** On the potential of World Wide Web use in education. *Mailing List*

± `listproc@kudzu.cnidr.org` [body = SUBSCRIBE WWWEDU first-name last-name]

INFO `http://k12.cnidr.org/wwwedu.html`

OWNER `acarvin@k12.cnidr.org` (Andy Carvin)

ARCHIVE `http://k12.cnidr.org/wwwedu.html`

FAQ `http://k12.cnidr.org/wwwedu.html`

➤ `za.edu.comp:` The use of computers in education. *Newsgroup*

VOCATIONAL

4537 `bit.listserv.vocnet` Vocational education discussion group. *Newsgroup*

➤ **JobPlace:** On self-directed job-search training and placement: for trainers, educators, researchers. (See entry 1724 for full listing.)

4538 `k12.ed.tech` Industrial arts and vocational education in grades K-12. *Newsgroup*

➤ **Le Chef College of Hospitality Careers:** Le Chef College of Hospitality Careers (Austin, Texas) is a two-year, degree-granting institution. This Web site is an interactive brochure where you may learn more about the school, follow along with their curriculum, ask their chefs culinary questions, discover foodways trivia, etc. (See entry 1872 for full listing.)

4539 **STWNet:** On the school-to-work transition. *Mailing List*

± `majordomo@confer.edc.org`

EDITOR `cathyc@edc.org` (Cathy Corbitt)

EDITOR `stw-mod@confer.edc.org`

OWNER `joycem@edc.org` (Dr. Joyce Malyn-Smith)

OWNER `johnw@edc.org` (Dr. John Wong)

4540 **VOCNET:** On vocational education. *Mailing List, moderated*

± `listserv@cmsa.berkeley.edu` [body = SUB VOCNET first-name last-name]

INFO EDITOR OWNER `ccollins@uclink.berkeley.edu` (Carrie Collins)

OWNER `dcarlson@uclink.berkeley.edu` (David Carlson)

ARCHIVES

`listserv@cmsa.berkeley.edu` [body = INDEX VOCNET]

`gopher://ericir.syr.edu/11/Listservs/VOCNET`

POST `vocnet@cmsa.berkeley.edu`

Gated: `bit.listserv.vocnet`

WRITING

➤ **Poet Warrior Press Writer's Resource Center:** A guide to Internet resources for writers, including many areas such as fiction, journalism, screenwriting, and publishers. Includes several articles. (See entry 632 for full listing.)

4541 `alt.prose` Postings of original writings, fictional, and otherwise. *Newsgroup*

4542 `bit.listserv.wac-l` Writing Across the Curriculum. *Newsgroup*

4543 **childrens-voice:** For publishing K-8 children's writing. *Mailing List, moderated*
± `listproc@schoolnet.carleton.ca` [body = SUBSCRIBE CHILDRENS-VOICE first-name last-name]
INFO `http://schoolnet2.carleton.ca/english/arts/lit/c-voice/index.html`
OWNER `ar967@freenet.carleton.ca` (Michael McCarthy)
Language: English, French

➤ `christnet.writers`: Discussion group for Christian writers. *Newsgroup*

➤ `comp.edu.composition`: Writing instruction in computer-based classrooms. *Newsgroup*

4544 **CREWRT-L:** Creative writing in education for teachers and students. *Mailing List*
± `listserv@mizzou1.missouri.edu` [body = SUBSCRIBE CREWRT-L first-name last-name]
INFO OWNER `wleric@showme.missouri.edu` (Eric Crump)
ARCHIVE `listserv@mizzou1.missouri.edu`

4545 **EST-L:** On teaching English for scientific and technical writing. *Mailing List*
`http://www.wfi.fr/est/est.html` (mirror site)
± `listserv@asuvm.inre.asu.edu` [body = SUBSCRIBE EST-L first-name last-name]
OWNER `rbowers@cibnor.conacyt.mx` (Roy Bowers)
ARCHIVE `gopher://asuvm.inre.asu.edu:70/11/listserv/est-l`
FAQ `http://www.cibnor.conacyt.mx/est/est.html`

4546 **JAC Online: A Journal of Composition Theory:** A hypertextual version of *JAC: A Journal of Composition Theory*. *E-Journal*
`http://nosferatu.cas.usf.edu/JAC/index.html`
INFO EDITOR `taylor@chuma.cas.usf.edu` (Todd Taylor, Online Editor JAC)
Frequency: triannual

4547 `misc.writing` Discussion of writing in all of its forms. *Newsgroup*

4548 `misc.writing.screenplays` Aspects of writing and selling screenplays. *Newsgroup*

4549 **PURTOPOI:** On rhetoric, language, and professional writing. *Mailing List*
± `listserv@vm.cc.purdue.edu` [body = SUBSCRIBE PURTOPOI first-name last-name]
INFO `purtopoi-request@vm.cc.purdue.edu`
ARCHIVE `listserv@vm.cc.purdue.edu` [body = INDEX PURTOPOI]
Please Note: Subscription by approval only.

4550 `rec.arts.poems` For the posting of poems. *Newsgroup*

4551 `rec.arts.prose` Short works of prose fiction and follow-up discussion. *Newsgroup*

4552 **RhetNet:** A repository of net scholarship on rhetoric and writing. *E-Journal*
`http://www.missouri.edu/~rhetnet/`
`gopher://gopher.bgsu.edu`
± `listserv@mizzou1.missouri.edu` [body = SUBSCRIBE RHETNT-L first-name last-name]
INFO `wleric@showme.missouri.edu` (Eric Crump)
ARCHIVES
`http://www.missouri.edu/~rhetnet/`
`gopher://gopher.bgsu.edu`
Frequency: irregular

4553 **WAC-L:** Writing Across the Curriculum, an open forum for college-level faculty, administrators, and staff to exchange ideas about writing in the disciplines. *Mailing List*

  ± `listproc@postoffice.cso.uiuc.edu` [body = `SUBSCRIBE WAC-L` first-name last-name]

  INFO `s-gruber@ux1.cso.uiuc.edu` (Sibylle Gruber)

  INFO `hawisher@ux1.cso.uiuc.edu` (Gail E. Hawisher)

4554 **WordPlay-L:** On wordplay: metaphors, nuances, euphemism . . . *Digest*

  ± `mailserv@levels.unisa.edu.au`

  INFO `rollo.ross@unisa.edu.au` (Rollo Ross)

  OWNER `a.hariz@unisa.edu.au` (Ahsan Hariz)

  Frequency: twice per day.

ENVIRONMENT & NATURE

4555 **The EnviroLink Network:** This is the archive site of the EnviroLink Network and provides "the most comprehensive compilation of environmental information available online."

http://www.envirolink.org/
INFO admin@envirolink.org
INFO info@envirolink.org (infobot)

4556 **The Eco-Compass:** Featuring descriptions of and pointers to Internet resources of interest to professionals, academics, and citizen activists concerned with the environment. *Newsletter*

http://www.islandpress.com/
± majordomo@igc.apc.org [body = subscribe islandpress-l]
OWNER dowen@islandpress.com (Dylan Owen)
ARCHIVE http://www.islandpress.com/
Frequency: monthly

4557 **Electronic Green Journal:** International environmental topics: practical and scholarly articles, bibliographies, reviews, editorial comments, and announcements. *E-Journal*

http://www.lib.uidaho.edu:70/docs/egj.html
gopher://gopher.uidaho.edu/11/UI_gopher/library/egj
± majordomo@uidaho.edu [body = subscribe egj e-mail-address]
INFO POST majanko@uidaho.edu (Maria Jankowska)
ARCHIVE ftp://www.lib.uidaho.edu/pub/egj
Frequency: irregular

4558 **ONE-L:** On the mutual impact of organizations and the environment. *Mailing List*

± listserv@clvm.clarkson.edu [body = SUBSCRIBE ONE-L first-name last-name]
ARCHIVE listserv@clvm.clarkson.edu

ACTIVISM

➤ **alt.org.earth-first:** Discussion of the Earth First! society. *Newsgroup*

4559 **alt.save.the.earth** Environmentalist causes. *Newsgroup*

➤ **AUDUBON:** On the role of the National Audubon Society. (See entry 4678 for full listing.)

4560 **CIRCLE:** On the Sunbow 5 Walk for the Earth. *Mailing List*

http://www.sunbow5walk.org/sunbow5
± majordomo@sunbow5walk.org [body = SUBSCRIBE CIRCLE]
INFO info@sunbow5walk.org
OWNER phil@sunbow5walk.org (Philip Kratzer)
OWNER steven@sunbow5walk.org

➤ **GENTECH:** News for activists on biotechnology and genetic engineering. (See entry 9110 for full listing.)

➤ **The Grassroots World Government WWW Site:** This site's purpose is to organize and promote a grassroots movement toward a future world government. The site is not affiliated with any existing mainstream organization, but is rather a glass house for activism toward gobalism. (See entry 5586 for full listing.)

➤ **powderworks:** On the musical group Midnight Oil: socially and environmentally aware—and danceable. (See entry 1103 for full listing.)

BIODIVERSITY

4561 **BIN-REACH BIN21 Community Networking/Outreach Discussions:** BIN-REACH is a forum for discussing strategies and methods for extending the reach of biodiversity information to diverse communities of users and providers of biodiversity information, and seeks the opinions of these communities about the services and types of information they need. *Mailing List*

± `listserv@bdt.org.br` [body = `subscribe` `BIN-REACH` first-name last-name]

INFO OWNER `pdh@u.washington.edu` (Preston D. Hardison)

ARCHIVE `http://www.bdt.org.br:70/bin21/bin-reach.html`

4562 BIN-TECH BIN21 Technical Discussions: BIN-TECH has been organized for discussion of topics of hardware, software, and system administration related to the Biodiversity Information Network/Agenda 21 (`http://www.bdt.org.br/bin21/bin21.html`) and to the mission of the Technical Group of BIN21. *Mailing List*

± `listserv@bdt.org.br` [body = `subscribe` `BIN-TECH` first-name last-name]

INFO OWNER `hanusj@bcc.orst.edu` (Joe Hanus)

ARCHIVE `http://www.bdt.org.br:70/bin21/bin-tech.html`

4563 Biodiversity Information: The intention of the list is to discuss technical opportunities, administrative and economic issues, and practical limitations and scientific goals of the biodiversity information network. *Mailing List*

± `listserv@bdt.org.br` [body = `subscribe` `BIODIV-L` first-name last-name]

INFO EDITOR OWNER `dora@bdt.org.br` (Dora Ann Lange Canhos)

ARCHIVE `http://www.bdt.org.br:70/bin21/biodiv-l.html`

4564 Biodiversity Information Network: A network to support the Convention on Biological Diversity and the Agenda 21 that followed the Earth Summit at Rio, June 1992.

`http://www.bdt.org.br:70/bin21/`

INFO `bin21@bdt.org.br`

Comments: The BIN21 Secretariat is the Base de Dados Tropical (`http://www.bdt.org.br/`). The Secretariat was established as a focal point and clearing house to facilitate and coordinate the flow of information among those with an interest in biodiversity. As for today, there are 15 nodes worldwide.

4565 IRRO-L : Information Resource on the Release of Organisms into the enviroment *Mailing List*

± `listserv@bdt.org.br` [body = `subscribe` `IRRO-L` first-name last-name]

INFO OWNER `segal.mark@epamail.epa.gov` (Dr. Mark Segal)

ARCHIVE `http://www.bdt.org.br:70/cgi-bin/bdtnet/irro-l`

BUILT ENVIRONMENTS

4566 Built-environment: On the built environment: architecture, civil engineering, surveying. *Mailing List*

± `mailbase@mailbase.ac.uk` [body = `SUBSCRIBE` `BUILT-ENVIRONMENT` first-name last-name]

OWNER `c.kant@csu.napier.ac.uk` (Chris Kant)

OWNER `bu02@central.napier.ac.uk`

ARCHIVES

`http://www.napier.bs.ac.uk/www/construction.html`

`mailbase@mailbase.ac.uk`

Please Note: Subscription by approval only.

4567 Habitat2: On Habitat II: Second UN Conference on Human Settlements. *Mailing List*

`http://www.cedar.univie.ac.at/habitat/`

± `listproc@cedar.univie.ac.at` [body = `SUBSCRIBE` `HABITAT2` first-name last-name]

INFO OWNER `bernhard.lorenz@cedar.univie.ac.at` (Bernhard Lorenz)

ARCHIVE `ftp://ftp.cedar.univie.ac.at/pub/habitat/`

➤ **LArch-L:** On landscape architecture. (See entry 65 for full listing.)

➤ **Little Whale Cove at Depoe Bay, Oregon:** Little Whale Cove is a national award-winning development on the Oregon coast. Take a visual tour and see the low-density planning, extensive trail systems, whale-watching gazebos, and varied amenities. (See entry 8366 for full listing.)

CLIMATE

4568 **German Climate Computer Center (DKRZ):** This is the German Climate Computing Center (Deutsches Klimarechenzentrum, DKRZ) providing resources and information in the area of climate research. This includes lists of climate data sets, weather maps, parallel computing information, and more.

http://www.dkrz.de/

INFO www@dkrz.de

INFO henken@dkrz.de

MIRRORS

http://w3.gkss.de/images/mpeg/ (Webcopy GKSS)

http://www.avs.com/

http://www.seds.org/billa/tnp/

http://www.meteo.fr/tpsreel/images (Webcopy Meteo-France)

http://www.ecmwf.int/images/charts (Webcopy ECMWF)

http://www.met.fu-berlin.de/wetter/meteosat (Webcopy FU-Berlin)

4569 **bit.listserv.skywarn** Severe storm community warning discussions. *Newsgroup*

4570 **bit.listserv.wx-chase** Tornado chasers discussions. *Newsgroup*

4571 **bit.listserv.wx-talk** Weather issues discussions. *Newsgroup*

➤ **C14-L:** For technical discussion of radiocarbon and other radioisotope dating. (See entry 9313 for full listing.)

4572 **clari.apbl.weather** World weather reports. *Moderated newsgroup*

4573 **clari.apbl.weather.misc** Miscellaneous weather-related articles. *Moderated newsgroup*

4574 **clari.apbl.weather.storms** Major storms. *Moderated newsgroup*

4575 **clari.apbl.weather.usa** U.S. weather reports. *Moderated newsgroup*

4576 **clari.news.weather** Weather and temperature reports. *Moderated newsgroup*

4577 **clari.sfbay.weather** SF Bay and California weather reports. *Moderated newsgroup*

➤ **CNN Weather:** Current weather forecasts and news. Includes temperature maps and radar and satellite images for the entire world. (See entry 6141 for full listing.)

4578 **ECO Newsletter:** Newsletter published daily at UN climate meetings by the Climate Action Network—an international association of environmental organizations concerned with the implementation of the Climate Treaty. *Newsletter*

http://www.igc.apc.org/climate/Eco.html

ftp://ftp.igc.apc.org/pub/ECO

INFO larris@igc.apc.org (Lelani Arris, ASCII editions)

INFO relen@igc.apc.org (Richard Elen, WWW editions)

INFO medianatura@gn.apc.org (Chris Bligh, Paper editions)

INFO asieghart@gn.apc.org (Alister Sieghart, PageMaker editions)

ARCHIVES

http://www.igc.apc.org/climate/Eco.html

ftp://ftp.igc.apc.org/pub/ECO

larris@igc.apc.org (Lelani Arris, ASCII editions)

➤ **Fox Weather:** Web site of a private meteorological firm based in Oxnard, California, that specializes in satellite remote sensing and meteorological satellite interpretation, agricultural weather forecasting for California, Arizona, and western Mexico. This service is not free. (See entry 6142 for full listing.)

➤ **Marine-L:** On marine-related topics: education, navigation, ships, industry, meterology. (See entry 1970 for full listing.)

4579 **MET-JOBS:** For posts of employment opportunity announcements in meteorology, climatology, and other atmospheric sciences. *Mailing List*

± listproc@eskimo.com [body = SUBSCRIBE MET-JOBS first-name last-name]

OWNER ted.smith@mtnswest.com (Ted Smith)

ARCHIVE `ftp://ftp.eskimo.com/u/t/tcsmith/met-jobs`

4580 Meteorology Students: On latest research results in meteorology and current weather events, as well as student-related topics in meteorology such as scholarships, summer schools, conferences, and conditions of studying meteorology at a particular university, etc. *Mailing List*

`http://www.met.fu-berlin.de/deutsch/Student/met-stud.html`

± `listproc@grobi.met.fu-berlin.de` [body = SUBSCRIBE `met-stud` first-name last-name]

INFO `dennis@metw3.met.fu-berlin.de`

4581 National Center for Atmospheric Research: This site provides information about the research undertaken at the National Center for Atmospheric Research (NCAR). It includes pointers to all important atmospheric/oceanographic and meteorological resources.

`http://www.ucar.edu/`

`gopher://gopher.ucar.edu`

INFO `webmaster@ucar.edu`

INFO `gregmc@ucar.edu`

➤ **National Weather Service:** Weather forecasts, facsimile charts, climate information, snow cover data, weather data message standards, and related communication documents, and much more about the National Weather Service of the U.S. government. (See entry 6144 for full listing.)

➤ `ne.weather:` New England weather forecasts. *Newsgroup*

➤ **Organised Weather Links:** This site provides weather forecasts, data (temperature, rain, etc.), satellite images, surface information (fronts, etc.), radar images, weather warnings, and links to other weather-site home pages. (See entry 6147 for full listing.)

4582 `sci.geo.meteorology` Discussion of meteorology and related topics. *Newsgroup*

4583 U.S. Climate Action Network Hotline: The occasional newsletter of the U.S. Climate Action Network. It is intended to inform local activists and organizations about the threat of climate change and current efforts to avoid its effects. *Newsletter*

± INFO `uscan@igc.apc.org` (Jennifer Morgan, Coordinator)

± INFO `larris@igc.apc.org` (Lelani Arris, ASCII editions)

Frequency: irregular

4584 The Daily Planet™: Satellite images, weather maps, and lots of other weather information from the University of Illinois at Urbana-Champaign.

`http://www.atmos.uiuc.edu/`

INFO `web-masters@www.atmos.uiuc.edu`

4585 WXSAT-L: For distribution of NOAA status and prediction bulletins for the GOES and POES weather satellites, and discussions on weather satellites, direct readout ground stations, and related topics. *Mailing List*

± INFO `wxsat-request@ssg.com` (Richard B. Emerson)

CONSERVATION

➤ **Abbey's Web:** This site is devoted to the life and works of the environmental writer Edward Abbey. It includes a biography, a bibliography, quotes, reader contributions, a discussion group, links to related information, and more. (See entry 591 for full listing.)

➤ `alt.org.audubon:` Regarding the Audubon Society. *Newsgroup*

4586 `alt.org.earth-first` Discussion of the Earth First! society. *Newsgroup*

4587 `alt.org.sierra-club` Regarding the Sierra Club. *Newsgroup*

➤ `alt.pave.the.earth:` Damn the environmentalists, full speed ahead! *Newsgroup*

➤ `alt.save.the.earth:` Environmentalist causes. *Newsgroup*

➤ **Arctic Circle:** The purpose of Arctic Circle is to stimulate among viewers a greater interest in the peoples and environment of the Arctic and Subarctic region. This "electronic circle" has three interrelated themes: natural resources, history and culture, and social equity and environmental justice. New material is being added on a regular basis. (See entry 4630 for full listing.)

➤ `aus.environment.conservation`: Australian conservation issues. *Newsgroup*

4588 **Big Bend Audubon Society:** The Big Bend Audubon Society page provides local, state, regional, and national information on environmental issues. It also provides local information for bird-watchers and other interested people.
`http://rip.physics.unk.edu/audubon/bbas.html`
INFO `price@rip.physics.unk.edu`

➤ **Biodiversity Information Network:** A network to support the Convention on Biological Diversity and the Agenda 21 that followed the Earth Summit at Rio, June 1992. (See entry 4564 for full listing.)

4589 `clari.tw.environment.cbd` Natural resources and conservation services. *Moderated newsgroup*

4590 **CONSBIO:** Society for Conservation Biology list on conservation biology and biodiversity. *Mailing List*
± `listproc@u.washington.edu` [body = `subscribe consbio` first-name last-name]
INFO OWNER `pdh@u.washington.edu` (Preston D. Hardison)
ARCHIVES
`http://csf.colorado.edu/`
`gopher://csf.colorado.edu`

➤ **CONSGIS:** On biological conservation and geographical information systems. (See entry 9317 for full listing.)

4591 **CONSLINK:** On biological conservation. *Mailing List*
± `listserv@sivm.si.edu` [body = `SUBSCRIBE CONSLINK` first-name last-name]
INFO `nzpem001@sivm.si.edu` (Michael Stuwe)
ARCHIVE `listserv@sivm.si.edu`

➤ **CTURTLE:** On sea turtle biology and conservation. (See entry 4679 for full listing.)

➤ **env.seashepherd:** For the Sea Shepherd Conservation Society: international conservation law. (See entry 4643 for full listing.)

➤ **GEOSYN:** On the geosynthetics industry. (See entry 9257 for full listing.)

➤ **International Wildlife Education & Conservation:** IWEC offers lots of information on how to help wildlife conservation, education kits, adoption kits, project enrichment for captive animals, endangered species, animal-assisted therapy, a photo gallery, and more. (See entry 4681 for full listing.)

➤ **MOCAVES:** On exploring caves in the midwestern U.S. (See entry 6627 for full listing.)

4592 **NRLib-L:** For natural resources librarians and information specialists. *Mailing List*
± OWNER `annhed@cc.usu.edu` (Anne Hedrich)

4593 `sci.bio.conservation` Conservation biology research. *Moderated newsgroup*

4594 **U.S. Environmental Protection Agency:** Includes information about the EPA, its offices, laboratories' programs, initiatives, contracts, grants, rules, regulations, and legislations, as well as databases and pointers to other environmental resources on the net.
`http://www.epa.gov/`
INFO `internet_support@unixmail.rtpnc.epa.gov`

➤ **University of Florida School of Forest Resources and Conservation:** As well as providing information on the school itself (its academic programs, research, faculty, projects, etc.) this site includes a good collection of pointers to other Internet forestry resources. (See entry 4610 for full listing.)

DEEP ECOLOGY

➤ **Abbey's Web:** This site is devoted to the life and works of the environmental writer Edward Abbey. It includes a biography, a bibliography, quotes, reader contributions, a discussion group, links to related information, and more. (See entry 591 for full listing.)

➤ `alt.org.earth-first`: Discussion of the Earth First! society. *Newsgroup*

➤ **INDKNOW:** For indigenous knowledge systems, traditional ecological knowledge and development. (See entry 10071 for full listing.)

➤ **SNUFFIT-L:** The Church of Euthanasia. (See entry 528 for full listing.)

DISASTERS

4595 `alt.destroy.the.earth` Please leave the light on when you leave. *Newsgroup*

4596 `alt.disasters.earthquake` Did the "big one" shut down the net? *Newsgroup*

4597 `alt.disasters.misc` General discussion of disaster issues. *Newsgroup*

4598 `clari.news.disaster` Major problems, accidents, and natural disasters. *Moderated newsgroup*

4599 `clari.news.hot.japan_quake` News on the Kobe quake and related issues. *Moderated newsgroup*

➤　`clari.news.trouble.disaster`: Disasters. *Moderated newsgroup*

4600 **Disaster Research:** For creators and users of information regarding hazards and disasters. *Newsletter*
　　`http://adder.colorado.edu/~hazctr/Home.html`
　　± `listproc@lists.colorado.edu` [body = SUBSCRIBE HAZARDS first-name last-name]
　　INFO `hazctr@spot.colorado.edu` (David Butler)
　　ARCHIVES
　　`gopher://disaster.cprost.sfu.ca:5555`
　　`telnet://epix@disaster.cprost.sfu.ca`
　　Language: English and Spanish
　　Frequency: twice monthly

➤　**ENVSEC_D:** On environment, population, and security. (See entry 10108 for full listing.)

➤　`fj.misc.earthquake`: Information about earthquake. *Newsgroup*

4601 **Natural Hazards Center Home Page - Information on Hazards and Disasters:** The World Wide Web site of the Natural Hazards Research and Applications Information Center at the University of Colorado includes information about the Center, the Center's electronic newsletter, "Disaster Research"; numerous reports and papers summarizing recent disaster studies; lists of organizations, publications, conferences dealing with hazards and disasters; and much more.
　　`http://adder.colorado.edu/~hazctr/Home.html`
　　INFO `hazctr@spot.colorado.edu` (David Butler)

4602 `tnn.disasters.earthquake` About earthquake disasters. *Newsgroup*

EDUCATION

➤　**COM-WILD-L:** Communiques from the Wild: enhances children's appreciation of the natural world and makes science "come to life." (See entry 4223 for full listing.)

➤　**Communications for a Sustainable Future:** An interdisciplinary effort to facilitate more rapid change in social thought toward a viable future. This resource provides a collection of archives and mailing lists on sustainability. (See entry 5191 for full listing.)

➤　**EDUWLF-L:** For the College and University Wildlife Education Working Group. (See entry 4680 for full listing.)

4603 **EE-Link:** EE-Link is funded by the U.S. EPA to provide access to environmental education resources on the Internet. Topics include classroom resources, organizations and projects, literature, funding, regional resources.
　　`http://nceet.snre.umich.edu/`
　　`http://nceet.snre.umich.edu/EndSpp/Endangered.html`
　　INFO `eelink@nceet.snre.umich.edu`

➤　**Global_Ed:** From British Columbia Teachers for Peace and Global Education (PAGE): educators on peace, justice, freedom, and sustainability. For the exchange of information, ideas, and issues to further the development of global education. (See entry 10109 for full listing.)

➤　**Good Green Fun!-Children's Music and Forest Ecology:** Educational activities, ecology questions, Web links, sound samples, chords, and lyrics to this 1995 Parents' Choice Award-winning children's music recording. (See entry 221 for full listing.)

➤ **International Wildlife Education & Conservation:** IWEC offers lots of information on how to help wildlife conservation, education kits, adoption kits, project enrichment for captive animals, endangered species, animal-assisted therapy, a photo gallery, and more. (See entry 4681 for full listing.)

➤ **National Pollution Prevention Center for Higher Education (NPPC):** Educational materials for colleges and universities on pollution prevention, life cycle design and analysis, and industrial ecology. (See entry 4625 for full listing.)

4604 **Sierra Club Environmental Education:** For K-12 environmental education resources.
http://www.sierraclub.org/education/
INFO information@sierraclub.org

4605 **SNAP:** On developing and using school nature areas. *Mailing List*
± snap-request@stolaf.edu
INFO snapadm@stolaf.edu
OWNER vannorma@stolaf.edu (Karen Van Norman)

FORESTS

➤ **bionet.agroforestry:** Discussion of agroforestry. *Newsgroup*

4606 **Dendrome:** Forest tree genome research updates. *Newsletter*
http://s27w007.pswfs.gov/Newsletter/index.html
INFO dbn@s27w007.pswfs.gov (David B. Neale)

4607 **European Forest Institute:** This site provides information on the Institute and pointers to other forest and environmental resources on the Internet.
http://www.efi.joensuu.fi/
INFO efisec@efi.joensuu.fi

➤ **Good Green Fun!-Children's Music and Forest Ecology:** Educational activities, ecology questions, Web links, sound samples, chords, and lyrics to this 1995 Parents' Choice Award-winning children's music recording. (See entry 221 for full listing.)

➤ **in.forest-alliance:** Forestry Alliance in Indiana. *Newsgroup*

4608 **National Forest Listings by State:** A listing of all U.S. national forests with descriptions and access information. This resource is hosted by GORP (Great Outdoor Recreation Pages). It covers all national forests in the U.S., providing overall descriptions, plus detailed information on hiking, cross-country skiing, fishing, rafting, biking, wildlife viewing, and other activities.
http://www.gorp.com/gorp/resource/US_National_Forest/main.htm
INFO postmaster@www.gorp.com
Comments: skiing | cross-country

4609 **U.S. Departement of Agricultures Forest Service:** Gobs of information from the U.S. Departement of Agriculture's Forest Service. It includes access to Forest Service databases and software, as well as specific information on particular national forests, information on state and private forestry, conservation information, information on outdoor recreation, and more.
http://www.fs.fed.us/
INFO comments@www.fs.fed.us

4610 **University of Florida School of Forest Resources and Conservation:** As well as providing information on the school itself (its academic programs, research, faculty, projects, etc.) this site includes a good collection of pointers to other Internet forestry resources.
http://www.sfrc.ufl.edu/
INFO webmaster@www.sfrc.ufl.edu

GREEN BUSINESS & INDUSTRY

4611 **clari.biz.industry.agriculture** Agriculture, fishing, forestry. *Moderated newsgroup*

4612 **EIA:** On environmental impact assessment (EIA): economics, technology, legislation. *Mailing List, moderated*
± listproc@pan.cedar.univie.ac.at

EDITOR schanzeb@unep.no (Bernd Schanzenbacher)
OWNER dkahn@nywork2.undp.org (Douglas Kahn)
OWNER bernhard@cedar.univie.ac.at (Bernhard Lorenz)
ARCHIVES
http://pan.cedar.univie.ac.at/
gopher://pan.cedar.univie.ac.at

4613 **ENVBUS-L:** On environment and business in central and Eastern Europe. *Mailing List*
± listserv@rec.hu [body = SUBSCRIBE ENVBUS-L first-name last-name]
OWNER rossen@rec.hu (Rossen Roussev)

➤ **Global Recycling Network Newsletter:** Worldwide business news in the field of recycling: market insights, company news, resource prices, new regulatory issues, government programs, technical updates on new materials and industrial processes. (See entry 4629 for full listing.)

GREEN PARTIES

4614 `alt.politics.greens` Green Party politics and activities worldwide. *Newsgroup*

➤ **Electronic Green Journal:** International environmental topics: practical and scholarly articles, bibliographies, reviews, editorial comments, and announcements. (See entry 4557 for full listing.)

➤ **ENVSEC_D:** On environment, population, and security. (See entry 10108 for full listing.)

4615 **GROEN-LINKS:** For members and sympathizers of GroenLinks, a Dutch green party. *Mailing List*
± listserv@nic.surfnet.nl [body = SUBSCRIBE GROEN-LINKS first-name last-name]
OWNER camstra@ivip.frw.uva.nl (Ronald Camstra)
ARCHIVE listserv@nic.surfnet.nl [body = INDEX GROEN-LINKS]
Language: Dutch

INTERNATIONAL COOPERATION

➤ **International Security Network (IntSecNet):** A one-stop virtual library and information network for security and defense studies, peace and conflict research, and international relations. The International Security Network is a joint effort of diverse research institutions, financially supported by the Swiss government. (See entry 10110 for full listing.)

4616 **MEH2O-L:** On water in the Middle East, including limnology, oceanography, marine biotechnology, aquaculture, conservation, reclamation, ecology, geographic information systems, international shared-resource management, and policy issues. *Mailing List*
± listserv@taunivm.tau.ac.il [body = SUBSCRIBE MEH2O-L first-name last-name]
INFO chasan73@matrix.newpaltz.edu (Robert Chasan)
ARCHIVE listserv@taunivm.tau.ac.il

NEWS & EVENTS

4617 `clari.tw.environment` Environmental news, hazardous waste, forests. *Moderated newsgroup*

4618 `clari.tw.environment.releases` Environmental news. *Moderated newsgroup*

4619 **Environmental News Briefing:** ENN provides daily environmental news and information. *Newsletter*
http://www.enn.com/
INFO mgt@enn.com

4620 `talk.environment` Discussion the state of the environment and what to do. *Newsgroup*

PARKS

➤ `rec.outdoors.national-parks`: Activities and politics in national parks. *Newsgroup*

➤ **U.S. Departement of Agricultures Forest Service:** Gobs of information from the U.S. Departement of Agriculture's Forest Service. It includes access to Forest Service databases and software, as well as specific information on particular national forests, information on state and private forestry, conservation information, information on outdoor recreation, and more. (See entry 4609 for full listing.)

PEST CONTROL

4621 **BIOCONTROL-L Biological Control List:** This discussion list is directed to scientists, educators, students, legislators, extension specialists, and practicioners of biocontrol of pests around the world. *Mailing List*

± listserv@bdt.org.brb [body = subscribe BIOCONTROL-L first-name last-name]

INFO OWNER g.moraes@phx.ftpt.br (Gilberto de Moraes)

INFO lans@cnpda.embrapa.ansp.br (Luis Alexandre Nogueira de Sa)

ARCHIVE http://www.bdt.org.br:70/cgi-bin/bdtnet/biocontrol-l

Language: English, Portuguese, Spanish

➤ **Ciba Geigy AG (Ciba):** Home page for information and feedback to the biological and chemical company Ciba. (See entry 1905 for full listing.)

POLLUTION

➤ **Agency for Toxic Substances and Disease Registry (ATSDR):** The mission of the Agency for Toxic Substances and Disease Registry (ATSDR) is to prevent exposure and adverse human health effects and diminished quality of life associated with exposure to hazardous substances from waste sites, unplanned releases, and other sources of pollution present in the environment. (See entry 5035 for full listing.)

➤ **ATSDR Science Corner:** ATSDR Science Corner is a simple guide to search the World Wide Web for environmental health information. The primary focus is to find and share global information resources with the public on the linkage between human exposure to hazardous chemicals and adverse human health effects. (See entry 5038 for full listing.)

4622 **EPIC Pollution Prevention Information Clearinghouse:** The purpose of this site is to facilitate the exchange of U.S. Department of Energy Pollution Prevention Information between DOE sites, state and local governments, and private industries. The site contains many documents regarding pollution and hazardous wastes and how they must be dealt with.

http://epic.er.doe.gov/epic.htm

INFO susan.henson@mailgw.er.doe.gov

4623 **GT-ATMDC:** On the atmospheric dispersion of chemicals. *Mailing List*

http://dutw239.tudelft.nl/GRNSD/GT-ATMDC

± listserv@nic.surfnet.nl [body = SUBSCRIBE GT-ATMDC first-name last-name]

OWNER bouwmans@interduct.tudelft.nl

ARCHIVE http://dutw239.tudelft.nl/GRNSD/GT-ATMDC

4624 **The Industrial Pollution Projection System (IPPS):** The IPPS, created by the World Bank, is a modeling system that estimates industrial pollution parameters. The IPPS was developed to provide estimates on manufacturing sector pollution intensities even when there is no industrial emissions data available. Using the IPPS helps provide policy makers with the quantitative information they need to prioritize scarce pollution reduction resources and formulate sound regulatory options. The full text of the working paper on this project, as well as complete data sets, are available.

http://www.worldbank.org/html/research/ipps/home.html

INFO prdei@worldbank.org

4625 **National Pollution Prevention Center for Higher Education (NPPC):** Educational materials for colleges and universities on pollution prevention, life cycle design and analysis, and industrial ecology.

http://www.snre.umich.edu/nppc/

INFO nppc@umich.edu

➤ **U.S. Environmental Protection Agency:** Includes information about the EPA, its offices, laboratories' programs, initiatives, contracts, grants, rules, regulations, and legislations, as well as databases and pointers to other environmental resources on the net. (See entry 4594 for full listing.)

➤ **Wind Energy Weekly:** News of the wind energy industry worldwide—energy policy, wind energy technology, global climate change, sustainable development, and other issues relating to the future of this clean, renewable energy source. (See entry 9232 for full listing.)

POPULATION CONTROL

➤ `bionet.population-bio:` Technical discussions about population biology. *Newsgroup*

➤ **SNUFFIT-L:** The Church of Euthanasia. (See entry 528 for full listing.)

➤ **United Nations Development Programme Information System:** This site contains information related to the United Nations Development Program and other United Nations agencies. (See entry 5445 for full listing.)

RECYCLING & WASTE TREATMENT

➤ **Agency for Toxic Substances and Disease Registry (ATSDR):** The mission of the Agency for Toxic Substances and Disease Registry (ATSDR) is to prevent exposure and adverse human health effects and diminished quality of life associated with exposure to hazardous substances from waste sites, unplanned releases, and other sources of pollution present in the environment. (See entry 5035 for full listing.)

4626 `alt.building.recycle` Building-industry recycling. *Newsgroup*

➤ **ENVENG-L:** On environmental engineering. (See entry 9255 for full listing.)

➤ **EPIC Pollution Prevention Information Clearinghouse:** The purpose of this site is to facilitate the exchange of U.S. Department of Energy Pollution Prevention Information between DOE sites, state and local governments, and private industries. The site contains many documents regarding pollution and hazardous wastes and how they must be dealt with. (See entry 4622 for full listing.)

4627 **ET-LOKE:** Aquacultures for Wastewater Treatment. *Mailing List*
± `listserv@searn.sunet.se` [body = SUBSCRIBE ET-LOKE first-name last-name]
OWNER `foo@hq.unu.edu` (Mr. Eng-Leong Foo)
ARCHIVE `listserv@searn.sunet.se` [body = INDEX ET-LOKE]

➤ **GEOSYN:** On the geosynthetics industry. (See entry 9257 for full listing.)

4628 **Global Recycling Network:** GRN is the most comprehensive recycling information resource available on the Internet. Its goal is to offer a one-stop solution to the recycling information needs of business users, consultants, researchers, students, and consumers alike, while helping to develop the international trade of recyclable goods.
`http://grn.com/grn/`
`info@grn.com`
INFO `grn@grn.com` (Enrico Sala)

4629 **Global Recycling Network Newsletter:** Worldwide business news in the field of recycling: market insights, company news, resource prices, new regulatory issues, government programs, technical updates on new materials and industrial processes. *Newsletter*
`http://grn.com/grn/grn_news.htm`
± `subscribe@grn.com`
INFO `grn@grn.com` (Enrico Sala)
INFO `esala@grn.com` (Enrico Sala)
Frequency: monthly
Price: $180/year regular, $120/year nonprofit

➤ `kanto.misc.recycle:` About recycling. *Newsgroup*

➤ **U.S. Environmental Protection Agency:** Includes information about the EPA, its offices, laboratories' programs, initiatives, contracts, grants, rules, regulations, and legislations, as well as databases and pointers to other environmental resources on the net. (See entry 4594 for full listing.)

REGIONS & COUNTRIES

4630 **Arctic Circle:** The purpose of Arctic Circle is to stimulate among viewers a greater interest in the peoples and environment of the Arctic and Subarctic region. This "electronic circle" has three interrelated themes: natural resources, history and culture, and social equity and environmental justice. New material is being added on a regular basis.

```
http://www.lib.uconn.edu/ArcticCircle
```
INFO chance@spirit.lib.uconn.edu

4631 **The Arid Lands Newsletter:** On drylands environment and culture. Published by the Office of Arid Lands Studies at the University of Arizona. *Newsletter*
```
http://ag.arizona.edu/OALS/ALN/ALNHome.html
```
± INFO jbanc@ag.arizona.edu (John M. Bancroft, Editor)
ARCHIVE http://ag.arizona.edu/OALS/ALN/ALNHome.html
Frequency: semiannual

➤ **aus.environment.conservation:** Australian conservation issues. *Newsgroup*

➤ **aus.environment.misc:** Miscellaneous discussion on Australia's environment. *Newsgroup*

4632 **Australian Environmental Resources Information Network (ERIN):** Australian environmental information.
```
http://www.erin.gov.au/
gopher://gopher.erin.gov.au
```
INFO info@erin.gov.au

4633 **Central European Environmental Data Request Facility (CEDAR):** All about environmental resources and organizations in central and Eastern Europe, as well as many environmental online databases (INFOTERR, DANIS, HABITAT, etc.)
```
http://www.cedar.univie.ac.at/
ftp://ftp.cedar.univie.ac.at
gopher://gopher.cedar.univie.ac.at
```
INFO webmaster@cedar.univie.ac.at

4634 **chile.natura-l** Ecology and protection of environment in Chile and Latin America. *Newsgroup*

4635 **El Planeta Platica: Eco Travels in Latin America:** On ecotourism and conservation issues in Latin America, including environmental contact lists, bibliographies and an index of Spanish language schools. *Newsletter*
± INFO OWNER ron@versa.com (Ron Mader, Publisher)
± ronmader@aol.com
ARCHIVES
gopher://csf.colorado.edu/11/environment/orgs/El_Planeta_Platica
http://www.planeta.com/
Gated: soc.culture.latin-america
Frequency: quarterly

4636 **ENVIRONMENT-L:** On the environment, particularly in New York State. *Mailing List*
± listproc@cornell.edu [body = SUBSCRIBE ENVIRONMENT-L first-name last-name]
INFO OWNER cs10@cornell.edu (Chris Stuart)
ARCHIVES
```
http://www.cfe.cornell.edu/
listproc@cornell.edu
```

➤ **European Forest Institute:** This site provides information on the Institute and pointers to other forest and environmental resources on the Internet. (See entry 4607 for full listing.)

4637 **fj.soc.environment** Talks about natural environment and society. *Newsgroup*

➤ **pa.environment:** Information and discussion about Pennsylvania's environment. *Newsgroup*

4638 **Satellite Imagery of Southern Ontario and Africa:** Sample satellite imagery of Southern Ontario and Africa, with additional imagery from other countries being added.
```
http://www.geomatics.com/
```
INFO vivek_khindria@geomatics.com

➤   `scot.environment`:   Environmental issues in Scotland. *Newsgroup*

4639   **South Florida Environmental Reader:** SFER is a newsletter covering environmental topics concerning South Florida, which includes the areas south of Lake Okeechobee, including the Everglades and Florida Keys. *Newsletter*

`http://envirolink.org/florida/`

± `listserv@ucf1vm.cc.ucf.edu` [body = SUBSCRIBE SFER-L first-name last-name]

± `sfer-request@symbiosis.ahp.com`

INFO POST `sfer@symbiosis.ahp.com` (Andrew Mossberg)

EDITOR `aem@symbiosis.ahp.com`

ARCHIVES

`http://envirolink.org/florida/back.html`

`ftp://ftp.igc.apc.org/pub/SFER/`

Gated: `fl.general`

Frequency: irregular, approx. two issues per month

➤   **SUSDEV:** On sustainable development in Eastern Europe. (See entry 4660 for full listing.)

➤   **UNU.ISLANDS.FORUM:** Public forum on issues related to small islands: development, government, ecology. (See entry 4663 for full listing.)

RIVER, OCEAN & WATER

4640   <u>National Institutes for Water Resources (NIWR)</u>**:** Information on water resources and pointers to many water-related sites.

`http://wrri.ces.clemson.edu/`

INFO `scwrri@ces.clemson.edu`

➤   `alt.culture.virtual.oceania`:   Oceania project discussion and news. *Moderated newsgroup*

4641   `alt.great-lakes`   Discussions of the Great Lakes and adjacent places. *Newsgroup*

➤   `ca.water`:   Information on California water and Internet issues. *Newsgroup*

➤   **COASTGIS:** On coastal and deep-ocean applications of geographical information systems (GIS)—to further the work of the International Geographical Union Commission on Coastal Systems. (See entry 9315 for full listing.)

4642   **COASTNET:** On coastal management and resources. *Mailing List*

± `listserv@uriacc.uri.edu` [body = SUBSCRIBE COASTNET first-name last-name]

OWNER `aland@gsosun1.gso.uri.edu` (Alan Desbonnet)

➤   **CTURTLE:** On sea turtle biology and conservation. (See entry 4679 for full listing.)

➤   **DIATOM-L:** Devoted to research on the diatom algae. (See entry 9037 for full listing.)

4643   **env.seashepherd:** For the Sea Shepherd Conservation Society: international conservation law. *Mailing List, moderated*

`http://www.envirolink.org/orgs/seashep/`

± **INFO OWNER** `nvoth@estreet.com` (Nick Voth)

4644   **HUDSON-R:** On the Hudson River: ecology, transportation, planning, and development. *Mailing List*

± `majordomo@matrix.newpaltz.edu` [body = SUBSCRIBE HUDSON-R]

INFO `hrowner@matrix.newpaltz.edu`

OWNER `chasan73@matrix.newpaltz.edu` (Robert Chasan)

ARCHIVE `majordomo@matrix.newpaltz.edu`

POST `hudson-r@matrix.newpaltz.edu`

4645   **LAKES-L:** On lakes and watersheds: ecology, management, research. *Mailing List*

± `majordomo@badger.state.wi.us`

OWNER `lakebb@dnrmai.dnr.wisc.gov` (James Vennie)

4646   **MAR-FACIL:** On marine facilities, aquaculture, and aquaria. *Mailing List*

± mailserv@ac.dal.ca [body = SUBSCRIBE MAR-FACIL]

OWNER stratton@ac.dal.ca (John Stratton)

➤ **Marine-L:** On marine-related topics: education, navigation, ships, industry, meterology. (See entry 1970 for full listing.)

➤ **MEH2O-L:** On water in the Middle East, including limnology, oceanography, marine biotechnology, aquaculture, conservation, reclamation, ecology, geographic information systems, international shared-resource management, and policy issues. (See entry 4616 for full listing.)

➤ **misc.transport.marine:** Maritime and inland waterways transportation. *Newsgroup*

➤ **National Center for Atmospheric Research:** This site provides information about the research undertaken at the National Center for Atmospheric Research (NCAR). It includes pointers to all important atmospheric/oceanographic and meteorological resources. (See entry 4581 for full listing.)

➤ **rec.ponds:** Pond issues: plants, fish, design, maintenance. *Newsgroup*

4647 **sci.geo.oceanography** Oceanography, oceanology, and marine science. *Newsgroup*

4648 **sci.geo.rivers+lakes** Science of rivers and lakes. *Newsgroup*

➤ **Scripps Institution of Oceanography:** This site contains extensive information on the institute, including information on its programs, ships, databases, and the holdings of its library. (See entry 9446 for full listing.)

➤ **SEAGRASS_FORUM:** On seagrass biology and the ecology of seagrass ecosystems. (See entry 9046 for full listing.)

➤ **South Florida Environmental Reader:** SFER is a newsletter covering environmental topics concerning South Florida, which includes the areas south of Lake Okeechobee, including the Everglades and Florida Keys. (See entry 4639 for full listing.)

4649 **Tide and Current Predictor:** Tide level and current speed predictions for numerous U.S. and other sites.

http://tbone.biol.sc.edu/tide

INFO dean@tbone.biol.sc.edu

➤ **Trickle-L:** On trickle or drip irrigation. (See entry 8921 for full listing.)

4650 **U.S. Water News:** Keeps our readers up to date on national and international water news concerning supply, quality, policy, legislation, litigation, water rights, conservation, and climate. *Magazine*

http://www.mother.com/uswaternews/

INFO OWNER uswatrnews@aol.com (Thomas C. Bell)

EDITOR stevenuswn@aol.com (Steven D. Seibel)

ARCHIVE http://www.mother.com/uswaternews/

Frequency: monthly

➤ **Virginia Coast Reserve Information System (VCRIS):** This site includes weather and ecological data for Virginia coast sites. The site is operated by the Virginia Coast Reserve Long-Term Ecological Research Project (VCR/LTER). (See entry 9047 for full listing.)

➤ **Woods Hole Oceanographic Institution (WHOI):** This site contains information on the institution, its library and research laboratories, and pointers to other oceanographic resources on the Internet. (See entry 9447 for full listing.)

SUSTAINABLE DEVELOPMENT

4651 **alt.energy.renewable** Fueling ourselves without depleting everything. *Newsgroup*

4652 **alt.solar.photovoltaic** Generating voltage from the sun's energy. *Newsgroup*

➤ **Arctic Circle:** The purpose of Arctic Circle is to stimulate among viewers a greater interest in the peoples and environment of the Arctic and Subarctic region. This "electronic circle" has three interrelated themes: natural resources, history and culture, and social equity and environmental justice. New material is being added on a regular basis. (See entry 4630 for full listing.)

4653 **CAMASE-L:** On agro-ecological computer models. *Newsletter*

OWNER plentinger@ab.dlo.nl

4654 CARLU: On contemporary agriculture and rural land use. *Mailing List*

± `listserv@ukcc.uky.edu` [body = SUBSCRIBE CARLU first-name last-name]

OWNER `thgros00@ukcc.uky.edu` (Ted Grossardt)

ARCHIVE `listserv@ukcc.uky.edu` [body = INDEX CARLU]

➤ **Communications for a Sustainable Future:** An interdisciplinary effort to facilitate more rapid change in social thought toward a viable future. This resource provides a collection of archives and mailing lists on sustainability. (See entry 5191 for full listing.)

➤ **CONSBIO:** Society for Conservation Biology list on conservation biology and biodiversity. (See entry 4590 for full listing.)

4655 Conscious Choice: Conscious Choice, The Journal of Ecology and Natural Living, is a bimonthly midwestern magazine that reports on environmental issues and natural alternatives in health care, food, and nutrition. *Magazine*

`http://www.consciouschoice.com/`

INFO `info@consciouschoice.com` (Ross Thompson)

ARCHIVE `http://www.consciouschoice.com/`

Comments: Frequency: bi-monthly (6/yr)

➤ **EARTHSAVE:** On personal food choices and the ecology of the planet. (See entry 5836 for full listing.)

4656 ECOCT-A: On sustainable urban development. *Distribution List*

± `listserv@searn.sunet.se`

OWNER `eng-leong.foo@mtc.ki.se` (Eng-Leong Foo)

4657 ET-IUFRO: On Ecotech '94 workshop on wood energy in the tropics. *Mailing List, moderated*

± `listserv@searn.sunet.se`

OWNER `eng-leong.foo@mtc.ki.se` (Eng-Leong Foo)

➤ **futurework:** This list focuses on ways for communities worldwide to deal with economic globalization and technological change. (See entry 9761 for full listing.)

➤ **Global_Ed:** From British Columbia Teachers for Peace and Global Education (PAGE): educators on peace, justice, freedom, and sustainability. For the exchange of information, ideas, and issues to further the development of global education. (See entry 10109 for full listing.)

4658 GRNSD-XX: For the Global Research Network on Sustainable Development, a worldwide, independent forum of researchers who aim to increase the effectiveness and efficiency of the global sustainable development research process. *Mailing List*

`http://infolabwww.kub.nl:2080/grnsd/`

± `listserv@hearn.nic.surfnet.nl` [body = SUBSCRIBE GRNSD-*XX* first-name last-name (where *XX* is MF for the member forum or SD for the information systems development group)]

INFO `grnsd@kub.nl` (Aldo de Moor)

ARCHIVE `listserv@hearn.nic.surfnet.nl` [body = INDEX GRNSD-XX]

➤ **INDKNOW:** For indigenous knowledge systems, traditional ecological knowledge and development. (See entry 10071 for full listing.)

➤ **MEH2O-L:** On water in the Middle East, including limnology, oceanography, marine biotechnology, aquaculture, conservation, reclamation, ecology, geographic information systems, international shared-resource management, and policy issues. (See entry 4616 for full listing.)

➤ **National Pollution Prevention Center for Higher Education (NPPC):** Educational materials for colleges and universities on pollution prevention, life cycle design and analysis, and industrial ecology. (See entry 4625 for full listing.)

➤ **North Carolina Cooperative Extension Gopher:** This is the NC Cooperative Extension WWW server located at North Carolina State University, Raleigh, North Carolina. (See entry 8918 for full listing.)

4659 NRSOCSCI: For discussing relationships between people and natural resources, including conflict resolution, sustainable development, eco-tourism, and ecological economics. *Mailing List*

± `listproc@u.washington.edu` [body = SUBSCRIBE NRSOCSCI first-name last-name]

INFO `rimu@selway.umt.edu`

ARCHIVE `listproc@u.washington.edu`

➤ **OneWorld Online:** This site has an extensive amount of information on global issues. The site is indexed and includes documents on global justice, conflict, aid, trade, education, health, human rights, population, and sustainable human development, as well as daily news summaries. It also hosts information for numerous international development and relief organizations. (See entry 10052 for full listing.)

4660 **SUSDEV:** On sustainable development in Eastern Europe. *Mailing List*
± almanac@parti.inforum.org
EDITOR aponce@iif.kfki.hu (Ana Maria Ponce)
OWNER nagy_arpad.inbox@parti.inforum.org (Prof. Nagy Arpad)

4661 **Tenure:** On access rights to land and other natural resources. *Mailing List*
± listserver@relay.doit.wisc.edu
OWNER sadlshoe@macc.wisc.edu (Steven G. Smith)
OWNER owner-tenure@relay.doit.wisc.edu (Steven G. Smith)
POST tenure@relay.doit.wisc.edu

➤ **United Nations Development Programme Information System:** This site contains information related to the United Nations Development Program and other United Nations agencies. (See entry 5445 for full listing.)

4662 **UNU.ISLANDS.AN:** Small Islands Network: sustainable development in the Pacific Island States. *Mailing List, moderated*
± listproc@caren.net [body = SUBSCRIBE UNU.ISLANDS.AN first-name last-name (organization)]
INFO paoletto@hq.unu.edu (Mr. Glen Paoletto, Network Coordinator)
OWNER foo@hq.unu.edu (Mr. Eng-Leong Foo)

4663 **UNU.ISLANDS.FORUM:** Public forum on issues related to small islands: development, government, ecology. *Mailing List*
± listproc@caren.net [body = SUBSCRIBE UNU.ISLANDS.FORUM first-name last-name]
OWNER foo@hq.unu.edu (Mr. Eng-Leong Foo)
OWNER paoletto@hq.unu.edu (Mr. Glen Paoletto, Network Coordinator)

4664 **UNU.LISTS:** For United Nations University lists on ecology and sustainable technology. *Distribution List, moderated*
± listproc@caren.net
OWNER foo@hq.unu.edu (Mr. Eng-Leong Foo)

4665 **UNU.ZERI.IBS:** On integrated biosystems. *Mailing List, moderated*
± listproc@caren.net [body = SUBSCRIBE UNU.ZERI.IBS first-name last-name]
OWNER foo@hq.unu.edu (Mr. Eng-Leong Foo)

➤ **Wind Energy Weekly:** News of the wind energy industry worldwide—energy policy, wind energy technology, global climate change, sustainable development, and other issues relating to the future of this clean, renewable energy source. (See entry 9232 for full listing.)

TRANSPORTATION & MASS TRANSIT

4666 **EV:** On the state of the art and future directions for electric vehicles. *Mailing List*
± listserv@sjsuvm1.sjsu.edu [body = SUBSCRIBE EV first-name last-name]
INFO ev-request@sjsuvm1.sjsu.edu
INFO mbahlke@mcd.intel.com
OWNER kd6gwn@amsat.org (Clyde R. Visser)
OWNER cvisser@cyberg8t.com
ARCHIVE listserv@sjsuvm1.sjsu.edu [body = INDEX EV]

➤ **Mark Dewell's Railway Preservation Pages:** A guide to all preserved railways, locomotives, societies, and museums in the U.K. The guide includes full timetables and details of special events on the railways featured. An online database of preserved railway locomotives is also available. (See entry 6644 for full listing.)

➤ **misc.transport.urban-transit:** Metropolitan public transportation systems. *Newsgroup*

4667 **PedNet:** For pedestrian activists and advocates: pleasures of the sidewalk. *Mailing List*

```
ftp://ftp.europa.com/outgoing/pednet
```
± pednet-request@europa.com [\outgoing\pednet]
OWNER pjudd@europa.com (Pam Judd)
OWNER ellenv@hevanet.com (Ellen Vanderslice)
OWNER peterson@europa.com (Robin Peterson)
OWNER http://edgewood.portland.or.us/WALK/pednet

➤ **rec.bicycles.soc:** Societal issues of bicycling. *Newsgroup*

WILDLIFE

4668 **alt.animals.dolphins** Flipper, Darwin, and all their friends. *Newsgroup*

4669 **alt.animals.felines.lions** Royalty of the beasts. *Newsgroup*

4670 **alt.animals.foxes** Foxes. *Newsgroup*

4671 **alt.animals.lampreys** Large suctorial mouths are cool. *Newsgroup*

4672 **alt.animals.raccoons** Discussion of raccoons and raccoon-related topics. *Newsgroup*

4673 **alt.fan.lemurs** Little critters with *big* eyes. *Newsgroup*

4674 **alt.lemmings** Rodents with a death wish. *Newsgroup*

4675 **alt.org.audubon** Regarding the Audubon Society. *Newsgroup*

4676 **alt.skunks** Le pew. *Newsgroup*

4677 **alt.wolves** Discussing wolves and wolf-mix dogs. *Newsgroup*

4678 **AUDUBON:** On the role of the National Audubon Society. *Mailing List*
± autoshare@rip.physics.unk.edu [body = SUBSCRIBE AUDUBON first-name last-name]
OWNER price@rip.physics.unk.edu
OWNER price@platte.unk.edu (Robert I. Price)
ARCHIVE autoshare@rip.physics.unk.edu [body = INDEX AUDUBON]

➤ **COM-WILD-L:** Communiques from the Wild: enhances children's appreciation of the natural world and makes science "come to life." (See entry 4223 for full listing.)

➤ **CONSBIO:** Society for Conservation Biology list on conservation biology and biodiversity. (See entry 4590 for full listing.)

4679 **CTURTLE:** On sea turtle biology and conservation. *Mailing List*
± listserv@nervm.nerdc.ufl.edu [body = SUBSCRIBE CTURTLE first-name last-name]
INFO bolten@monarch.zoo.ufl.edu
Language: English, Spanish, French

4680 **EDUWLF-L:** For the College and University Wildlife Education Working Group. *Mailing List*
± listserv@uriacc.uri.edu [body = SUBSCRIBE EDUWLF-L first-name last-name]
OWNER wallam@uriacc.uri.edu (Mark C. Wallace)

➤ **EE-Link:** EE-Link is funded by the U.S. EPA to provide access to environmental education resources on the Internet. Topics include classroom resources, organizations and projects, literature, funding, regional resources. (See entry 4603 for full listing.)

4681 **International Wildlife Education & Conservation:** IWEC offers lots of information on how to help wildlife conservation, education kits, adoption kits, project enrichment for captive animals, endangered species, animal-assisted therapy, a photo gallery, and more.
```
http://earthlink.net/~iwec
```
INFO iwec@earthlink.net

➤ **On-line Resources for Earth Scientists (ORES):** Earth-science resources, including digital documents, news sources, software, data sets, and public online services. Subjects include the environment, forestry, geography, geology, geophysics, GIS, GPS, geodesy, mapping, paleontology, remote sensing, space, meteorology, wildlife, and jobs in earth sciences. (See entry 9333 for full listing.)

4682 `rec.animals.wildlife` Wildlife-related discussions/information. *Newsgroup*

4683 `rec.birds` Hobbyists interested in bird-watching. *Newsgroup*

4684 **The Rookery:** A plethora of penguin links and resources. Your one-stop penguin shop! For the true penguin fan or those just interested in learning more about one of nature's most intriquing animals.

`http://www.webcom.com/jimallen/penguin.html`

INFO `stuntlips@aol.com`

4685 **U.S. Fish and Wildlife Service:** On habitat protection, waterfowl management, and endangered species recovery. The U.S. Fish and Wildlife Service strives to conserve this nation's fish and wildlife resources and ensure their continued existence for future generations of Americans.

`http://www.fws.gov/`

INFO `alan_fisher@mail.fws.gov`

4686 **URBWLF-L:** For the interchange of ideas and experiences among researchers, managers, planners, and educators concerned with wildlife habitats, urban ecosystems, and the quality of life in urban areas. *Mailing List*

± `listserv@uriacc.uri.edu` [body = SUBSCRIBE URBWLF-L first-name last-name]

INFO `urbwlf-l-request@uriacc.uri.edu`

OWNER `wallam@uriacc.uri.edu` (Mark C. Wallace)

HEALTH & MEDICINE

4687 <u>Cyberspace Hospital</u>: A collection of Internet medical resources organized into a virtual hospital.
```
http://www.ch.nus.sg/
```
INFO `coflunkc@nus.sg`

4688 <u>Health Economics: Places to Go</u>: A list of sites on the Internet related to the economics of health care. It includes sections on pharmacoeconomics, public health, and managed care.
```
http://www.uni-bayreuth.de/departments/vwliv/hec.html
```
INFO `ansgar.hebborn@uni-bayreuth.de`

4689 <u>HyperDOC</u>: Multimedia access to National Library of Medicine projects, programs, and data.
```
http://www.nlm.nih.gov/
ftp://nlmpubs.nlm.nih.gov
gopher://gopher.nlm.nih.gov
```
INFO `admin@gopher.nlm.nih.gov`
INFO `ftpadmin@nlmpubs.nlm.nih.gov`
INFO `publicinfo@occshost.nlm.nih.gov`

4690 <u>MedWeb: Biomedical Internet Resources</u>: Begun in April 1994, MedWeb has evolved into a catalog of over 7,000 sites, databases, documents, and electronic journals divided into 80 categories.
```
http://www.cc.emory.edu/WHSCL/medweb.html
```
INFO `libsf@web.cc.emory.edu`

4691 <u>PaperChase®</u>: This site allows you to search many health databases simultaneously. The databases include MEDLINE, CANCERLIT, AIDSLINE, CINAHL, and the Health Planning and Administration (HEALTH) database.
```
http://enterprise.bih.harvard.edu/paperchase
telnet://pch:signup@pch.bih.harvard.edu
```
INFO `pch@bih.harvard.edu`
FAQ `http://enterprise.bih.harvard.edu/paperchase/faq.html`
MIRROR `telnet://pch:signup@pch2.bih.harvard.edu`

➤   <u>PEG, a Peripatetic, Eclectic Gopher</u>: A collection of pointers to all sorts of Internet resources. Especially strong are its virtual reference desk, Internet assistance, politics and government, medicine, and women's studies resource lists. (See entry 2726 for full listing.)

4692 <u>HMatrix-L</u>: On online health resources. The intent of this list is to share and document the location, access directions, and quality of information found online. *Mailing List*
± `listserv@www.kumc.edu` [body = SUBSCRIBE HMATRIX-L first-name last-name]
OWNER `lhancock@kumc.edu` (Lee Hancock)

4693 <u>Med Help</u>: This site has thousands of articles on various medical and health topics all written in nontechnical terminology.
```
http://medhlp.netusa.net/index.htm
telnet://medhlp.netusa.net
```
INFO `staff@medhlp.netusa.net`
FAQ `http://medhlp.netusa.net/general/faq.txt`

4694 <u>Medical Meeting Place</u>: Ths site lists upcoming meetings in the field of medicine, with descriptions and online forms to request meeting brochures.
```
http://www.opennet.com/medical
```
INFO `depp@packet.net`

4695 <u>MEDSTUFF</u>: Commercial medical information service provided by physicians and allied health professionals who have joined together to offer to the general public the information gleaned through many years of practice and experience at all levels in the profession of medicine.
```
http://www.opennet.com/medstuff/expert.html
```

INFO webmaster@opennet.com

4696 **sci.med** Medicine and its related products and regulations. *Newsgroup*

ADDICTION

4697 <u>**Web of Addiction**</u>: For accurate information about alcohol and other drug addictions.
http://www.well.com/user/woa/
INFO razer@ix.netcom.com
INFO ahomer@mail.coin.missouri.edu

4698 **ADDICT-L:** On addictions other than alcohol and drug addiction.
± listserv@kentvm.kent.edu [body = SUBSCRIBE ADDICT-L first-name last-name]
INFO OWNER ddelmoni@kentvm.bitnet
ARCHIVE listserv@kentvm.kent.edu [body = INDEX ADDICT-L]

4699 **alt.recovery** For people in recovery programs (e.g., AA, ACA, GA). *Newsgroup*

4700 **alt.recovery.aa** Recovery and Alcoholics Anonymous. *Newsgroup*

4701 **alt.recovery.addiction.sexual** Recovering sex addicts. *Newsgroup*

4702 **alt.recovery.codependency** Mutually destructive relationships. *Newsgroup*

4703 **alt.recovery.compulsive-eat** Food is an addictive drug. *Newsgroup*

4704 **alt.recovery.na** Recovery and Narcotics Anonymous. *Newsgroup*

4705 **alt.recovery.sexual-addiction** Getting over being addicted to sex. *Newsgroup*

4706 **alt.support.stop-smoking** Getting over the nicotine addiction. *Newsgroup*

4707 **clari.news.alcohol** Drunk driving, alcoholism. *Moderated newsgroup*

➤   **NHCTEN:** On how health-care reforms may affect mental health and substance-abuse treatment. (See entry 5001 for full listing.)

4708 **NOSMOKE:** Support list for people trying to quit smoking or help others quit smoking. *Mailing List*
± maiser@earth.execnet.com [body = SUBSCRIBE NOSMOKE e-mail-address]
OWNER angel2@ptd.net

4709 **SEXADD-L:** On sexual addiction: clinical and research focus—*not a recovery group. Mailing List*
± listserv@kentvm.kent.edu [body = SUBSCRIBE SEXADD-L first-name last-name]
OWNER ddelmoni@kentvm.kent.edu (David Delmonico)
ARCHIVE listserv@kentvm.kent.edu [body = INDEX SEXADD-L]

➤   **shamash.jacs:** Jews in recovery from alcoholism and drugs. *Moderated newsgroup*

4710 **SMARTREC:** For Self-Management and Recovery Training: mutual help for abstaining. *Mailing List*
± listserv@sjuvm.stjohns.edu [body = SUBSCRIBE SMARTREC first-name last-name]
INFO sharia@aol.com
OWNER jschale@american.edu (Jeffrey A. Schaler, Ph.D.)
OWNER tompar@world.std.com (Ann Parmenter, L.I.C.S.W.)
ARCHIVE listserv@sjuvm.stjohns.edu [body = INDEX SMARTREC]

ADVOCACY

➤   **ADVOCACY:** On the rights of people with disabilities. (See entry 9852 for full listing.)

➤   **AECUDEP-L:** On universal design in education, practice, or advocacy. (See entry 9853 for full listing.)

➤   **DeathNET:** This site is an archive specializing in all aspects of death and dying. DeathNET houses a number of self-contained Web sites such as: The Living Will Center (about living wills, advance directives, and patients' rights), The Garden of Remembrance (online obituaries), Life's End (shopping center for "end of life" needs), and DeathTALK (for discussions on death and dying). (See entry 9840 for full listing.)

➤ **MADNESS:** MADNESS is an electronic action and information discussion list for people who experience mood swings, fright, voices, and visions. (See entry 4950 for full listing.)

4711 **Support Coalition & Dendron News:** Dendron News is the voice of Support Coalition, a nonprofit alliance of 30 grass-roots advocacy, human rights, and support groups. "Breaking the silence about psychiatric oppression!" "Heal Normally, Naturally!" These are some of the slogans from a little-known, diverse 25-year-old social change movement: The psychiatric surivors liberation movement, sometimes known as "mad lib." Stop forced drugs and forced electroshock!

  `http://www.efn.org/~dendron`
  INFO `dendron@efn.org`

ALTERNATIVE MEDICINE

4712 `alt.aromatherapy` The effects of scents. *Newsgroup*

4713 `alt.backrubs` Lower . . . to the right . . . aaaah! *Newsgroup*

4714 `alt.folklore.herbs` Discussion of all aspects of herbs and their uses. *Newsgroup*

4715 `alt.healing.reiki` The healing system called reiki. *Newsgroup*

4716 `alt.health.ayurveda` Really old medicine from India. *Newsgroup*

4717 `alt.health.oxygen-therapy` Discussion of oxygen and ozone therapy. *Newsgroup*

4718 `alt.med.vision.improve` Improving vision. *Newsgroup*

4719 **The Alternative Medicine Hompage:** A jumpstation for sources of information on unconventional, unorthodox, unproven, or alternative, complementary, innovative, integrative therapies.

  `http://www.pitt.edu/~cbw/altm.html`
  INFO `cbw@med.pitt.edu` (Charles B. Wessel, M.L.S.)

➤ **Conscious Choice:** Conscious Choice, The Journal of Ecology and Natural Living, is a bimonthly midwestern magazine that reports on environmental issues and natural alternatives in health care, food, and nutrition. (See entry 4655 for full listing.)

4720 **Health & Longevity:** A monthly newsletter dealing with natural healing through naturopathy, herbology, nutrition, and homeopathy. *Newsletter*

  `http://www.sims.net/naturopath/`
  INFO `naturopath@sc.net` (D. Pearce)
  ARCHIVE `ftp://ftp.sims.net`
  Frequency: monthly

➤ **High Times:** On hemp, marijuana, and psychedelic drugs such as LSD and Ecstasy. Industrial uses of hemp (paper, cloth, food, oil) are extensively covered. (See entry 9905 for full listing.)

4721 **Homeopathic Internet Resources List:** Sites and data on the Internet about homeopathy.

  `ftp://antenna.apc.org/pub/homeo/resource.lst`
  INFO `evgalen@gn.apc.org` (E van Galen)

4722 **HOMEOWEB:** Links to homeopathy Web sites and other Internet sites on complementary medicine.

  `http://antenna.nl/homeoweb/`
  INFO `evgalen@gn.apc.org` (E van Galen)

4723 **Jarrett's Journal:** An electronic journal of newsbytes, book reviews, and features relating to disabilities/disabled, health, medical, alternative therapies, and nutrition. *Newsletter*

  ± `listserv@sjuvm.stjohns.edu` [body = SUBSCRIBE J-JRNL first-name last-name]
  INFO OWNER `anndell@rdz.stjohns.edu` (Ann Dellarocco)
  ARCHIVE `gopher://sjuvm.stjohns.edu`
  Gated:
  Frequency: monthly

4724 **The Medical Reporter:** For health-care consumers; emphasizes preventive medicine, primary care, patient advocacy, education, and support. *Magazine*

http://www.dash.com/netro/nwx/tmr/tmr.html

INFO EDITOR jcooper@medreport.com (Joel R. Cooper, Editor-in-Chief)

INFO adverts@dash.com (Angel W. Prouty, Advertising)

Gated:

Frequency: monthly

4725 `misc.health.alternative` Alternative, complementary, and holistic health care. *Newsgroup*

4726 **PAIN-L:** On the many ramifications of pain: political, ecological, and *all* other. *Mailing List*

± listserv@sjuvm.stjohns.edu [body = SUBSCRIBE PAIN-L first-name last-name]

OWNER odin@gate.net (Hank Roth)

4727 **Shuffle Brain:** A growing anthology of serious but nontechnical works on the mind/body question. *E-journal*

http://ezinfo.ucs.indiana.edu/~pietsch/

INFO OWNER pietsch@indiana.edu (Paul Pietsch, Ph.D)

ARCHIVE http://www.indiana.edu/~pietsch/home.html

Frequency: irregular

➤ **Transcultural-Psychology:** On the delivery of mental health services to diverse cultures. (See entry 5026 for full listing.)

ANESTHESIOLOGY

4728 **Anesthesia Virtual Library:** All sorts of information on anesthesia and anesthesiology. Includes links to many anesthesiology departments worldwide.

http://gasnet.med.yale.edu/index.html

INFO ruskin@gasnet.med.yale.edu (Keith J. Ruskin, MD)

4729 **GASNet Anesthesiology Home Page:** GASNet contains information that is helpful to anyone with a professional interest in anesthesiology. Services include a distributed, hypermedia textbook of anesthesiology, the only online journal of anesthesiology, a clip-art library, and more.

http://gasnet.med.yale.edu/

gopher://gasnet.med.yale.edu

INFO ruskin@gasnet.med.yale.edu (Keith J. Ruskin, MD)

4730 **SUNY HSC Syracuse Anesthesiology Home page:** Anesthesiology department of the State University of New York at Syracuse. The site contains information about the residency program in anesthesiology, clickable image map of anesthesia resources on the World Wide Web, information about CME programs, and a clinical case discussion forum is under development.

http://eja.anes.hscsyr.edu/anes/home.html

INFO sopchaka@vax.cs.hscsyr.edu

CANCER

4731 <u>Breast Cancer Information Clearinghouse</u>: Information on breast cancer and pointers to other breast cancer resources on the Internet maintained by the New York State Education and Research Network. Includes access to mailing lists.

http://nysernet.org/bcic/

INFO kennett@nysernet.org

4732 <u>Doctor's Guide to Breast Cancer Information & Resources</u>: Lots of information on breast cancer and pointers to other breast cancer resources on the Internet.

http://www.pslgroup.com/BREASTCANCER.HTM

INFO webmaster@pslgroup.com

4733 <u>Quick Information About Cancer for Patients and Their Families</u>: This excellent document is a well-organized hypertext starting point for information on all aspects of breast cancer. It covers the range of issues cancer patients and their families ask about just after a diagnosis, including: possible causes, types of cancer, treatment possibilites, where to go for treatment and for support, and more.

`http://asa.ugl.lib.umich.edu/chdocs/cancer/CANCERGUIDE.HTML`

INFO `srhinton@umich.edu`

INFO `jgourdji@umich.edu`

4734 alt.support.cancer Emotional aid for people with cancer. *Newsgroup*

4735 alt.support.cancer.prostate Helping men with prostate cancer. *Newsgroup*

4736 HEM-ONC: On hematologic malignancies, incl. leukemia, lymphoma, and myeloma *Mailing List*

± `listserv@sjuvm.stjohns.edu` [body = SUB HEM-ONC first-name last-name]

INFO `hem-onc-request@sjuvm.stjohns.edu`

OWNER `lackritz@mo.net` (Barbara Lackritz)

OWNER `kevin@computer.com` (Kevin Sinclair)

ARCHIVE `listserv@sjuvm.stjohns.edu` [body = INDEX HEM-ONC]

4737 National Cancer Center, Tokyo, Japan: Information service for the National Cancer Center in Tokyo, Japan.

`gopher://gopher.ncc.go.jp`

INFO `gopher-admin@ncc.go.jp`

4738 One Woman's Reconstruction: A description of one woman's experience with breast reconstruction after a mastectomy due to breast cancer.

`http://www1.mhv.net/~delaney/owr.htm`

INFO `delaney@mhv.net`

4739 Ovarian: On ovarian cancer and other ovarian disorders: for patients, family, friends, researchers, and physicians. *Mailing List*

± `listserv@sjuvm.stjohns.edu` [body = SUBSCRIBE OVARIAN first-name last-name]

OWNER `kevin@computer.com` (Kevin Sinclair)

ARCHIVE `listserv@sjuvm.stjohns.edu` [body = INDEX OVARIAN]

➤   **PROSTATE:** On the prostate: prostatitis, BPH, prostate cancer. For clinicians & support networks. (See entry 4811 for full listing.)

4740 sci.med.diseases.cancer Diagnosis, treatment, and prevention of cancer. *Newsgroup*

4741 sci.med.prostate.cancer Prostate cancer. *Newsgroup*

4742 Yorkshire Cancer Registry: Yorkshire Cancer Registry, United Kingdom.

`http://www.yco.leeds.ac.uk/`

INFO `c.l.bennett@cbl.leeds.ac.uk`

CHRONIC FATIGUE SYNDROME

4743 alt.health.cfids-action Chronic fatigue syndrome action group. *Moderated newsgroup*

4744 alt.med.cfs Chronic fatigue syndrome discussions. *Moderated newsgroup*

4745 bit.listserv.cfs.newsletter Chronic Fatigue Syndrome Newsletter. *Moderated newsgroup*

4746 CATHAR-M: For Cartharsis, a newsmagazine of personal health, intellect, and creativity for the chronic fatigue syndrome community. *E-Zine*

± `listserv@sjuvm.stjohns.edu` [body = SUBSCRIBE CATHAR-M first-name last-name]

INFO `cathar-m-request@sjuvm.stjohns.edu`

ARCHIVE `listserv@sjuvm.stjohns.edu` [body = INDEX CATHAR-M]

Gated: `alt.med.cfs.zine`

4747 CFS-FILE: Chronic fatigue syndrome medical files—a database of medical files on CFS and related illnesses. *Mailing List*

± `listserv@sjuvm.stjohns.edu` [body = SUBSCRIBE CFS-FILE first-name last-name]

INFO `cfs-file-request@sjuvm.stjohns.edu` (Molly Holzschlag)

4748   **CFS-L:** Chronic fatigue syndrome general discussion. *Mailing List, moderated*

± `listserv@list.nih.gov` [body = SUBSCRIBE CFS-L first-name last-name]

INFO `cfs-l-request@list.nih.gov` (Roger Burns)

FAQS

`listserv@list.nih.gov` [body = GET CFS FAQ (for answers to frequently asked questions about CFS)]

`listserv@list.nih.gov` [body = GET CFS INDEX (for a complete list of basic CFS documents on-line)]

`listserv@list.nih.gov` [body = GET CFS LISTS (for a description of CFS-oriented mailing lists)]

`listserv@list.nih.gov` [body = GET CFS NET-HELP (for a detailed info about CFS resources on the Internet)]

Gated: `alt.med.cfs`

4749   **CFS-WIRE:** For news wire-style exchange of news articles and information among chronic fatigue syndrome/CFIDS/ME support groups. *Mailing List*

± `listserv@sjuvm.stjohns.edu` [body = SUBSCRIBE CFS-WIRE first-name last-name]

INFO `cfs-wire-request@sjuvm.stjohns.edu`

ARCHIVE `listserv@sjuvm.stjohns.edu` [body = INDEX CFS-WIRE]

Gated: `alt.med.cfs.wire`

4750   **Chronic Fatigue Syndrome Electronic Newsletter (CFS-NEWS):** Newsletter about chronic fatigue syndrome with an emphasis on news of recent medical research. *Newsletter*

`http://metro.turnpike.net/C/cfs-news/cfs-news.html`

± `listserv@list.nih.gov` [body = SUBSCRIBE CFS-NEWS first-name last-name]

INFO EDITOR `cfs-news@list.nih.gov` (Roger Burns)

ARCHIVES

`ftp://list.nig.gov/cfs-news`

`listserv@list.nih.gov` [body = INDEX CFS-NEWS]

Gated: `bit.listserv.cfs.newsletter`

Frequency: between one and four issues each month

➤   **immune:** A support group for people with immune-system breakdowns (and their symptoms) such as chronic fatigue syndrome, lupus, candida, hypoglycemia, multiple allergies, chemical sensitivities, etc. No diagnosis turned away. Friends and family, medical and disability professionals, etc., are also welcome. (See entry 4805 for full listing.)

DENTISTRY

4751   **ADA Online:** The American Dental Association's Web site, offering dental news, practice and professional resources, descriptions of products and services, and consumer information for dentists, dental team members, and consumers worldwide.

`http://www.ada.org/`

INFO `wwwedit@www.ada.org`

4752   `alt.braces`   Discussion group for wearers of orthodontic devices. *Newsgroup*

4753   **DBLIST:** On computers and infomatics issues related to dentistry. *Mailing List*

± `listproc@list.ab.umd.edu` [body = SUBSCRIBE DBLIST first-name last-name]

INFO `jlz4@columbia.edu`

4754   **DENTALIB:** On libraries at dental schools: information, ideas, questions & concerns *Mailing List, moderated*

± `listproc@usc.edu` [body = SUBSCRIBE DENTALIB first-name last-name]

INFO OWNER `fmason@hsc.usc.edu` (Frank Mason)

ARCHIVE `listproc@usc.edu`

4755   **Dentistry Online:** Journal for all members of the dental team, with an information section for the lay readership (including advice on dentistry in general). *E-Journal* `http://www.cityscape.co.uk/users/ad88/dent.htm`

INFO OWNER `dn47@cityscape.co.uk` (Dr. Robert J. Glenning, BSc BDS DGDPRCS MIMgt)

ARCHIVE `http://www.cityscape.co.uk/users/ad88/dent.htm`

Frequency: regular updates

4756   `sci.med.dentistry`   Dentally related topics; all about teeth. *Newsgroup*

DIABETES

4757   `alt.support.diabetes.kids`   Support for kids with diabetes and their families. *Newsgroup*

4758   **DIABETES-NEWS:** On diabetes: health and care. *Newsletter*

± `listserv@netcom.com` [body = `SUBSCRIBE diabetes-news`]

Frequency: weekly

4759   **DIABETIC-MAX:** Planning projects for computer-mediated communication among diabetic children and adolescents. *Mailing List*

`http://www.franken.de/users/daneel/C.Renner/diabetic.welcome.file.html`

± `majordomo@rachael.franken.de` [body = `subscribe diabetic-max e-mail-address`]

OWNER `c.renner@daneel.franken.de` (Dr. Christian Renner)

Language: English & German

4760   `misc.health.diabetes`   Discussion of diabetes management in day-to-day life. *Newsgroup*

DISEASES & CONDITIONS

4761   **Allergy:** On human allergies: self-care and prevention. *Mailing List*

`http://www.io.com/~kinnaman/allergy.html`

± `listserv@tamvm1.tamu.edu` [body = `SUBSCRIBE ALLERGY first-name last-name`]

OWNER `kinnaman@immune.com` (Ballew Kinnaman)

ARCHIVES

`listserv@tamvm1.tamu.edu` [body = `INDEX ALLERGY`]

`http://tamvm1.tamu.edu/~allergy/`

4762   `alt.med.allergy`   Helping people with allergies. *Newsgroup*

4763   `alt.support.herpes`   Discussing herpes. *Newsgroup*

4764   `alt.herpes`   People suffering with herpes. *Newsgroup*

➤   `alt.personals.herpes`:   Contacting people with herpes. *Newsgroup*

4765   `alt.med.fibromyalgia`   Fibromyalgia fibrositis list. *Newsgroup*

4766   `alt.skincare.acne`   Skincare - acne. *Newsgroup*

4767   `alt.support.asthma`   Dealing with labored breathing. *Newsgroup*

4768   `alt.support.ataxia`   Ataxia support group. *Newsgroup*

4769   `alt.support.attn-deficit`   Attention deficit disorder. *Newsgroup*

4770   `alt.support.cerebral-palsy`   Cerebral palsy support. *Newsgroup*

4771   `alt.support.crohns-colitis`   Support for sufferers of ulcerative colitis. *Newsgroup*

4772   `alt.support.dystonia`   The cyberspace support group for dystonia. *Newsgroup*

4773   `alt.support.epilepsy`   Epilepsy support. *Newsgroup*

4774   `alt.support.headaches.migraine`   Discussion of migraine and headache ailments. *Newsgroup*

4775   `alt.support.hemophilia`   Hemophilia support group. *Newsgroup*

4776   `alt.support.inter-cystitis`   The urinary tract disease, interstitial cystitis. *Newsgroup*

4777   `alt.support.kidney-failure`   Helping people deal with kidney problems. *Newsgroup*

4778 `alt.support.marfan` Marfan syndrome support group. *Newsgroup*

4779 `alt.support.mult-sclerosis` Living with multiple sclerosis. *Newsgroup*

4780 `alt.support.osteogenesis.imperfecta` Discussing brittle bone disease. *Newsgroup*

4781 `alt.support.ostomy` For those recovering from -ostomy procedures. *Newsgroup*

4782 `alt.support.post-polio` Post-polio syndrome discussion area. *Newsgroup*

4783 `alt.support.sinusitis` Inflammation of the sinuses. *Newsgroup*

4784 `alt.support.skin-diseases` Psoriasis and other common skin afflictions. *Newsgroup*

4785 `alt.support.skin-diseases.psoriasis` Discussing the skin disease psoriasis. *Newsgroup*

4786 `alt.support.sleep-disorder` For all types of sleep disorders. *Newsgroup*

4787 `alt.support.tinnitus` Coping with ringing ears and other head noises. *Newsgroup*

4788 `alt.support.tourette` Support for folks with Tourette's Syndrome. *Newsgroup*

4789 **Alzheimer Web:** Resources for researchers in the field of Alzheimer's disease and for the people who have an interest in research developments.
   `http://werple.mira.net.au/~dhs/ad.html`
   INFO `david_small@muwayf.unimelb.edu.au`

4790 `bionet.neuroscience.amyloid` Alzheimer's disease and related disorders. *Newsgroup*

4791 `alt.support.arthritis` Helping people with stiff joints. *Newsgroup*

4792 `misc.health.arthritis` Arthritis and related disorders. *Newsgroup*

4793 **BIFIDA-L:** On spina bifida: support and information. *Mailing List*
   ± `listserv@mercury.dsu.edu`
   OWNER `aman1@columbia.dsu.edu` (Loren Aman)

4794 `alt.support.spina-bifida` Support for people dealing with spina bifida. *Newsgroup*

4795 `bit.listserv.tbi-support` Traumatic brain injury support list. *Moderated newsgroup*

4796 `bit.listserv.transplant` Transplant recipients list. *Newsgroup*

4797 **bmt-talk:** For support and information on bone marrow transplants. *Mailing List*
   ± `bmt-talk-request@ai.mit.edu`
   INFO `laurel@ai.mit.edu` (Laurel Simmons)
   ARCHIVE `http://www.ai.mit.edu/people/laurel/Bmt-talk/bmt-talk.html`

4798 **CEL-KIDS:** On children with gluten and wheat intolerance, and related conditions. *Mailing List, moderated*
   ± `listserv@sjuvm.stjohns.edu` [body = SUBSCRIBE CEL-KIDS first-name last-name]
   INFO `michael.jones@digital.net` (Michael Jones)
   EDITOR `kathryn.jones@stonebow.otago.ac.nz` (Kathryn Jones)
   OWNER `maxwell@lamg.com` (William S. Elkus)
   OWNER `lylesj@cadcam.atg.gmeds.com` (Jim Lyles)
   Comments: An extensive set of files containing celiac-related information can be retrieved; send a message containing INDEX CEL-KIDS and INDEX CELIAC to `LISTSERV@SJUVM.STJOHNS.EDU` for a list and description of these files.

4799 **CELIAC:** This list for those interested in celiac disease (*coeliac sprue*), dermatitis herpetiformis, gluten intolerance, wheat allergy, and coincident intolerances such as casein or lactose intolerance. *Mailing List*
   ± `listserv@sjuvm.stjohns.edu` [body = SUBSCRIBE CELIAC first-name last-name]
   OWNER `bill_elkus@jefco.com` (Bill Elkus)
   ARCHIVE `listserv@sjuvm.stjohns.edu` [body = INDEX CELIAC]

4800 **CYSTIC-L:** Discussion and support group for cystic fibrosis. *Mailing List*
   ± `listserv@yalevm.cis.yale.edu` [body = SUBSCRIBE CYSTIC-L first-name last-name]

INFO antony.dugdale@yale.edu (Anthony Dugdale)

FAQ listserv@yalevm.cis.yale.edu [body = GET CYSTIC-L PACKAGE]

4801 **Dysphagia:** A mail list that caters to medical professionals dealing with patients who have swallowing disorders. Research and instrumentation issues related to swallowing and its disorders are also discussed on this mail list. *Mailing List, moderated*

± majordomo@cyberport.com [body = subscribe dysphagia]

INFO OWNER ppalmer@cyberport.com (Phyllis M. Palmer)

INFO OWNER kevin@cyberport.com (Kevin M. Rosenberg, M.D.)

4802 **Dysphagia Resource Center:** A collection of resources on the Internet related to swallowing and its disorders.

http://www.dysphagia.com/

INFO ppalmer@dysphagia.com

➤ **Fragilex:** On Fragile X Syndrome Single-Gene Disorder, the most common cause of inherited mental retardation. (See entry 9882 for full listing.)

4803 **HEPV-L:** Support and information for people with chronic hepatitis and caregivers. *Mailing List*

± listserv@sjuvm.stjohns.edu [body = SUBSCRIBE HEPV-L first-name last-name]

OWNER gthorpe@infinet.com (Geff Thorpe)

4804 `sci.med.diseases.hepatitis` Hepatitis diseases. *Newsgroup*

4805 **immune:** A support group for people with immune-system breakdowns (and their symptoms) such as chronic fatigue syndrome, lupus, candida, hypoglycemia, multiple allergies, chemical sensitivities, etc. No diagnosis turned away. Friends and family, medical and disability professionals, etc., are also welcome. *Mailing List*

http://weber.ucsd.edu/~cnorman/immune.html

± INFO immune-request@weber.ucsd.edu

ARCHIVE ftp://weber.ucsd.edu/pub/immune

4806 `misc.health.infertility` Treatment and support of infertility. *Newsgroup*

4807 `alt.infertility` Discussion of infertility causes and treatments. *Newsgroup*

4808 **LEISH-L Leishmaniasis Network:** The intention of this list is to encourage discussion and contact among those interested in leishmaniasis and to help identify important topic areas within the field. *Mailing List*

± listserv@bdt.org.br [body = subscribe LEISH-L first-name last-name]

INFO OWNER j.shaw@phoenix.bdt.org.br (Jeffrey Jon Shaw)

ARCHIVE http://www.bdt.org.br:70/cgi-bin/bdtnet/leish-1

➤ **National Institutes of Allergy and Infectious Disease (NIAID):** This site provides information on HIV/AIDS, as well as on other infectious diseases, allergic and immunologic diseases, asthma, transplantation, and more. It also includes information about the organization like job vacancies, an organizational chart, its press releases, fact sheets, publication order forms, and a calendar of events. (See entry 4894 for full listing.)

4809 **OMERACT:** On Outcome MEasures in Rheumatoid Arthritis Clinical Trials. *Mailing List*

± listserv@nic.surfnet.nl [body = SUBSCRIBE OMERACT first-name last-name]

OWNER boers@intmed.rulimburg.nl (Dr. Maarten Boers)

ARCHIVE listserv@nic.surfnet.nl [body = INDEX OMERACT]

4810 **PARKINSN:** Parkinson's disease information exchange network. *Mailing List*

± listserv@vm.utcc.utoronto.ca

OWNER patterso@fhs.csu.mcmaster.ca (Barbara Patterson)

➤ **PharmInfoNet:** Pharmaceutical Information Network (PharmInfoNet™) includes a drug database, hundreds of drug-related articles, highlights from major medical meetings, disease information centers for patients, an online PharmMall for advertisers, links to pharmaceutical resources on the net, a gallery of pharmacy and pharmaceutical-related art and photographs, and more. (See entry 4994 for full listing.)

4811 **PROSTATE:** On the prostate: prostatitis, BPH, prostate cancer. For clinicians & support networks. *Mailing List*

± listserv@sjuvm.stjohns.edu [body = SUBSCRIBE PROSTATE first-name last-name]

INFO prostate-request@sjuvm.stjohns.edu

OWNER kevin@computer.com (Kevin Sinclair)
OWNER eprice@awod.com (Ed Price)

4812 `alt.support.prostate.prostatitis` For individuals with prostatitis. *Newsgroup*

4813 `sci.med.prostate.prostatitis` Prostatitis. *Newsgroup*

4814 `sci.med.prostate.bph` Benign prostatic hypertrophy. *Newsgroup*

4815 RPLIST: Support for people with retinal degenerations, including retinitis pigmentosa and macular degeneration. *Mailing List*
± `listserv@sjuvm.stjohns.edu` [body = SUBSCRIBE RPLIST first-name last-name]
OWNER `rplist-request@lri.fr` (Nicolas Graner)
OWNER `myers@ab.wvnet.edu` (Roger Myers)

4816 Stroke-L: For exchange of ideas and information on strokes (cerebrovascular disease) among professionals, stroke survivors, and their supporters. *Mailing List*
± `listserv@ukcc.uky.edu` [body = SUBSCRIBE STROKE-L first-name last-name]
INFO `stroke-l-request@ukcc.uky.edu`
ARCHIVE `listserv@ukcc.uky.edu` [body = INDEX STROKE-L]

4817 VITILIGO: On vitiligo, a skin disease affecting pigmentation patterns. *Mailing List*
± `listserv@sjuvm.stjohns.edu` [body = SUBSCRIBE VITILIGO first-name last-name]
OWNER `efricker@aol.com` (Eric Fricker)
ARCHIVE `listserv@sjuvm.stjohns.edu` [body = INDEX VITILIGO]

4818 WITSENDO: For women who suffer from endometriosis, emphasizing coping with the disease and its treatment, and sharing information on current treatments, research, and educational literature. *Mailing List*
± `listserv@listserv.dartmouth.edu` [body = SUBSCRIBE WITSENDO first-name last-name]
INFO OWNER `davida@bunter.dartmouth.edu` (David Avery)
EDITOR OWNER `jbullock@sednet.mcd.on.ca` (John Bullock)
EDITOR OWNER `thompson@cu48.crl.aecl.ca` (Martin Thompson)
EDITOR OWNER `ivykline@netq.com` (Ivy Kline)
ARCHIVE `listserv@listserv.dartmouth.edu`

4819 `alt.support.endometriosis` Endometriosis support group. *Newsgroup*

4820 YEAST-L: On yeast-related medical problems: overgrowth, allergies, treatment. *Mailing List*
± `listserv@psuhmc.hmc.psu.edu` [body = SUBSCRIBE YEAST-L first-name last-name]
OWNER `jbayliss@psuhmc.hmc.psu.edu` (Judy Bayliss)
ARCHIVE `listserv@psuhmc.hmc.psu.edu` [body = INDEX YEAST-L]

DOCTORS

4821 Doctor's Guide to the Internet: A guide to information on the Internet designed especially for healthcare professionals.
`http://www.pslgroup.com/docguide.htm`
INFO `webmaster@pslgroup.com`

4822 Resources For Primary Care Physicians: Resources for primary-care physicians.
`http://www.coolware.com/health/pcp/pcphome.html`
INFO `jcooper@medreport.com` (Joel R. Cooper, Editor-in-Chief)

4823 ARTS-MD: On physicians who are also performing artists. *Mailing List, moderated*
± `mailserv@ncal.kaiperm.org` [body = SUBSCRIBE ARTS-MD]
OWNER `ssfnhs@ncal.kaiperm.org` (Neal Shorstein, MD)
OWNER `estragon@aol.com` (Neal Shorstein, MD)

4824 Medscape: A free, interactive, multi-specialty journal and medical education resource for clinicians.

```
http://www.medscape.com/
```
INFO seitz@scp.com

4825 **Physician Finder Online:** Visit this site to find physicians or dentists by name, specialty, city, or state. Or use their keyword search to find, for example, all physicians or dentists that speak Spanish, carry Blue Cross™ insurance, or practice knee surgery.

```
http://msa2.medsearch.com/pfo/
```
INFO office@medsearch.com

4826 **Physicians Guide to the Internet:** A site for doctors to enhance physician personal and professional well-being. Articles on physician lifestyle and links to clinical, educational, and other medical sites; listings of medical meetings; job opportunities; and more.

```
http://physiciansguide.com/pgi
```
INFO golanty@ccnet.com

EDUCATION

4827 **Biomedical Multimedia Unit:** The home page of the Biomedical Multimedia Unit, School of Medicine, University of Melbourne. Contains information and resources relating to multimedia education in the medical sciences.

```
http://www.medfac.unimelb.edu.au/BMU/
```
INFO darren_williams@muwayf.unimelb.edu.au

4828 **bit.listserv.medforum** Medical students discussions. *Moderated newsgroup*

➤ **can.schoolnet.biomed.jr:** SchoolNet biology and medicine for elementary students. *Newsgroup*

➤ **can.schoolnet.biomed.sr:** SchoolNet biology and medicine for high-school students. *Newsgroup*

4829 **COCAMED:** Computers in Canadian medical education. *Mailing List*

± listserv@utoronto.bitnet [body = SUBSCRIBE COCAMED first-name last-name]

INFO grace.paterson@dal.ca (Grace Paterson)

ARCHIVES

```
http://www.mcms.dal.ca/dme/micocamd.html
listserv@utoronto.bitnet [body = INDEX COCAMED]
```

4830 **Cochlear Fluids Research Laboratory:** All about your inner ear. Includes a pictorial guide, and information on inner-ear research programs.

```
http://lab9924.wustl.edu/
```
INFO salt_a@kids.wustl.edu

4831 **Interactive Medical Student Lounge:** A place for medical school students to browse medical resources on the Internet.

```
http://falcon.cc.ukans.edu/~nsween
```
INFO nsween@falcon.cc.ukans.edu

4832 **The Interactive Patient:** This teaching tool for physicians, residents, and medical students offers a case with a chief complaint to the user who then has to interact with the patient requesting additional history, performing a physical exam, and reviewing laboratory data and X-rays.

```
http://musom.marshall.edu/medicus.htm
```
INFO khayes@musom02.mu.wvnet.edu

INFO clehmann@musom02.mu.wvnet.edu

➤ **International Union of Pharmacology:** The purpose of this site is to provide a comprehensive database and repository of software available for teaching pharmacology together with reviews, demonstrations, pricing, and availability to promote effective pharmacology education. In addition, the site also provides access to the latest newsletters, meetings, and positions available in pharmacology. (See entry 4993 for full listing.)

➤ **JHUNIVERSE: Johns Hopkins University on the Web:** This is the CWIS of Johns Hopkins University. JHUniverse is a gateway to information resources at Johns Hopkins University, the nation's first true research university and now the leading U.S. university in research and development expenditures. The system also maintains links to information on JHU's sister institution, the Johns Hopkins Hospital and Health System. (See entry 4429 for full listing.)

4833 Mashall University School of Medicine, West Virginia: Information on the medical school and its primary-care based curricula as well on its Internet projects, which include the Interactive Patient, Rural Net, and vital health and population statistics for West Virginia.

`http://musom.mu.wvnet.edu/0u:/root.htm|/`

INFO `blucas@musom02.mu.wvnet.edu`

INFO `khayes@musom02.mu.wvnet.edu`

➤ **Mayo Clinic:** News, information for patients and medical professionals, and more from the Mayo clinic. (See entry 5055 for full listing.)

4834 `misc.education.medical` Issues related to medical education. *Newsgroup*

➤ **ParentsPlace.com:** Resource for parents. Includes discussion groups, articles on parenting, and a shopping mall. (See entry 9935 for full listing.)

4835 Royal Postgraduate Medical WWW: This facility is provided by the Centre for Computing Services, Royal Postgraduate Medical School, Hammersmith Hospital, London, England, and provides an information retrieval system for the RPMS, MRC and Hammersmith Hospitals NHS Trust.

`http://www.rpms.ac.uk/`

INFO `www@rpms.ac.uk`

➤ **SHS:** The Society for Human Sexuality mailing list. Intended for general discussion of human sexuality and as a way to distribute information about events put on by the Society for Human Sexuality (a sex-positive registered student organization at the University of Washington). (See entry 10120 for full listing.)

4836 SMCDCME: On continuing medical education. *Mailing List*

INFO `rbollin@cms.cc.wayne.edu` (Robert Bollinger)

ARCHIVE `listserv@cms.cc.wayne.edu`

4837 University of California, Irvine. Medical Education Software Archive.: This site contains the medical education software collection based at the University of California, Irvine.

`http://orion.oac.uci.edu/~sclancy/med-ed.html`

`ftp://ftp.uci.edu/med-ed/msdos or med-ed/mac`

INFO `slclancy@uci.edu` (Steve Clancy)

Comments: To receive notice of updates, send the message SUBSCRIBE UCI-FTP-UPDATE to `listserv@stat.com`

➤ **The Virtual Hospital™:** A continuously updated digital health sciences library from the Department of Radiology, University of Iowa College of Medicine. (See entry 4909 for full listing.)

EMERGENCY SERVICES, EMERGENCY MEDICINE & CRITICAL CARE

4838 Critical Care Medicine: Various medical manuscripts, journal club, case discussions from CCM-L, and links to other sites.

`http://www.pitt.edu/~crippen/index.html`

INFO `crippen+@pitt.edu` (David W. Crippen, MD)

4839 CSAR: On using computers and related technology for search-and-rescue operations. *Digest, moderated*

± `csarreq@hpasdd.mayfield.hp.com`

OWNER `paul@hpasdd.mayfield.hp.com` (Paul Lufkin)

ARCHIVE `ftp://hairball.ecst.csuchico.edu/pub/ems/sar/csar_digest`

4840 Emergency Services WWW Site List: This is a list of known dire/rescue/EMS/emergency services sites that can be found on the net.

`http://gilligan.uafadm.alaska.edu/www-911.htm`

INFO `fndjt2@yukon.uafadm.alaska.edu`

4841 EMS-EDU-L: On the education of prehospital care practitioners: paramedics, EMT, CPR. *Mailing List*

± `listserv@informatics.sunysb.edu`

OWNER `pwerfel@epo.som.sunysb.edu` (Paul A. Werfel, EMT-P)

4842 EMSNY-L: On emergency medical services for providers in the state of New York. *Mailing List, moderated*
± `listserv@health.state.ny.us` [body = `SUB EMSNY-L` first-name last-name]
INFO `jdl02@health.state.ny.us` (John Lewis)
ARCHIVE `listserv@health.state.ny.us` [body = `INDEX EMSNY-L`]

4843 HAZMATMED: On emergency medical response to exposure to hazardous materials. *Mailing List*
± `listserv@mediccom.norden1.com`
EDITOR `churton.budd@mediccom.norden1.com` (Churton Budd, RN, EMTP)
OWNER `hlevi@ix.netcom.com` (Howard Levitin, MD, FACEP)

4844 `misc.emerg-services` Forum for paramedics and other first responders. *Newsgroup*

4845 NCEMSF: For the National Collegiate Emergency Medical Services Foundation. *Mailing List*
± `listproc@hubcap.clemson.edu`
INFO `http://www.ncemsf.org/`
OWNER `ssavett@clemson.edu` (Scott C. Savett, EMT)
ARCHIVE `http://www.ncemsf.org/`

4846 Trauma WWW Home Page: Material on trauma, injury prevention, and treatment.
`http://rmstewart.uthscsa.edu/`
INFO `stewartr@uthscsa.edu` (Ronald M. Stewart, MD)

EMF HEALTH ISSUES

4847 `bionet.emf-bio` Interactions of EM fields with biological systems. *Newsgroup*

EMPLOYMENT OPPORTUNITIES

4848 APS-Academic Physician and Scientist gopher server: A job bank of positions in academic medicine.
`gopher://acad-phy-sci.com`
INFO `info@acad-phy-sci.com`

4849 MEDSearch America: This site is for employers seeking employees and vice versa in all fields of the health profession.
`http://www.medsearch.com/`
`gopher://gopher.medsearch.com:9001/1`
INFO `office@medsearch.com`

➤   **Physicians Guide to the Internet:** A site for doctors to enhance physician personal and professional well-being. Articles on physician lifestyle and links to clinical, educational, and other medical sites; listings of medical meetings; job opportunities; and more. (See entry 4826 for full listing.)

ENDOCRINOLOGY & METABOLISM

4850 STRUCT-IEM: On organizing the discussion of inborn errors of metabolism: no laymen please. *Mailing List*
± `majordomo@rachael.franken.de` [body = `subscribe struct-iem`]
OWNER `c.renner@daneel.franken.de` (Dr. Christian Renner)
ARCHIVE `http://www.franken.de/users/daneel/C.Renner/index.html`

4851 METAB-L: For professionals on inborn errors of metabolism. *Mailing List*
`http://www.franken.de/users/daneel/C.Renner/index.html`
± `majordomo@rachael.franken.de` [body = `SUBSCRIBE metab-l` e-mail-address]
OWNER `c.renner@daneel.franken.de` (Dr. Christian Renner)
Please Note: Subscription by approval only.
Comments: *Physicians, biochemists, and scientists working in the field of inborn errors of metabolism only.*

ENVIRONMENTAL HEALTH

4852 **Environmental Health Briefing:** On U.K./European environmental health legislation. *Newsletter*
± INFO `postmaster@ehas.demon.co.uk` (David Denton)
ARCHIVE `http://www.bdt.org.br:70/bioline/bin/ehas.cgi`
Frequency: weekly
Price: $945 annually

➤ **OSHA Computerized Information System (OCIS):** Information from the U.S. Department of Labor Occupational Safety & Health Administration. Includes data on OSHA programs and offices as well as texts of OSHA regulations and documents. (See entry 4986 for full listing.)

4853 **Rachel's Environment & Health Weekly:** All aspects of environmental health, especially as it affects human health. Translates mainstream science and medical journal articles into something people can understand and use to protect their local environments. *Newsletter*
`ftp://ftp.std.com/periodicals/rachel`
`gopher://gopher.std.com`
± INFO `erf@igc.apc.org` (Peter Montague)
± `rachel-weekly-request@world.std.com` [body = SUBSCRIBE]
Frequency: weekly

4854 **SAFETY:** On environmental health and safety: life safety issues (such as fire protection), chemical safety (waste disposal, laboratory safety, regulatory compliance), biological hazards, and radiation safety. *Mailing List*
`http://quasar.tach.net/web/vtisiri`
`gopher://quasar.tach.net`
± `listserv@uvmvm.uvm.edu` [body = SUBSCRIBE SAFETY first-name last-name]
INFO `rstuart@moose.uvm.edu` (Ralph Stuart)
ARCHIVES
`http://quasar.tach.net/web/vtisiri`
`gopher://quasar.tach.net`
`listserv@uvmvm.uvm.edu` [body = INDEX SAFETY]

EPIDEMIOLOGY

4855 `bionet.biology.vectors` Research and control of arthropods that transmit disease. *Newsgroup*

4856 **Centers for Disease Control and Prevention (CDC):** Information on diseases, disease prevention, and health in general from the U.S. government Centers for Disease Control and Prevention.
`http://www.cdc.gov/`
INFO `netinfo@cdc1.cdc.gov`

4857 **Ebola Links:** A pageful of links to Web pages on the ebola virus and its recent outbreaks.
`http://icgroup.net/~brussel/personal/ebola.html`
INFO `brussel@icgroup.net`
MIRROR `http://www.av.qnet.com/~brettr/personal/ebola.html`

4858 **EGRET-L:** For users of EGRET, a statistical software package for biostatisticians and epidemiologists. *Mailing List, moderated*
± `listserv@listserv.dartmouth.edu` [body = SUB EGRET-L first-name last-name]
INFO OWNER `stephen.baker@ummed.edu`
ARCHIVE `listserv@listserv.dartmouth.edu` [body = INDEX EGRET-L]

4859 **Emerging Infectious Diseases (EID):** Information on emerging infectious diseases addressing factors underlying disease emergence, summaries of disease syndromes, and laboratory and epidemiologic reports of international scope. *E-Journal*
`http://www.cdc.gov/ncidod/EID/eid.htm`
INFO `eideditor@cidod1.em.cdc.gov` (National Center for Infectious Diseases)
Frequency: four times a year

➤ **IMMNET-L:** On medical immunization-tracking systems. (See entry 5041 for full listing.)

➤ **International Antiviral News:** Reviews, articles, and abstracts concerning antiviral agents. (See entry 5054 for full listing.)

4860 **Morbidity and Mortality Weekly Report (MMWR):** This site provides the Centers for Disease Control and Prevention's Morbidity and Mortality Weekly Report and its serial publications for download in Adobe™ Acrobat™ format. International and supranational public health bulletins are also available at this site.

```
http://www.cdc.gov/epo/mmwr/mmwr.html
ftp://ftp.cdc.gov
```

INFO mmwr-questions@list.cdc.gov

Comments: Users can subscribe to a list server to receive either a table of contents and instructions how to receive each document or the full .pdf (Adobe™ Acrobat™ portable document format) as an e-mail attachment. To subscribe, send an e-mail message to lists@list.cdc.gov. The body content of the e-mail should read: subscribe mmwr-toc for the table of contents and subscribe mmwr-pdf for the full pdf document. Upon subscription, users will receive instructions about additional e-mail commands, such as commands for retrieving documents, sending messages to the system orperator, canceling a subscription, or sending an e-mail change of address.

➤ **National Institutes of Allergy and Infectious Disease (NIAID):** This site provides information on HIV/AIDS, as well as on other infectious diseases, allergic and immunologic diseases, asthma, transplantation, and more. It also includes information about the organization like job vacancies, an organizational chart, its press releases, fact sheets, publication order forms, and a calendar of events. (See entry 4894 for full listing.)

4861 **NUTEPI:** On nutritional epidemiology. *Mailing List*

± listserv@db0tui11.bitnet [body = SUBSCRIBE NUTEPI first-name last-name]

INFO mensink@db0tui11.bitnet (Gert Mensink)

ARCHIVE listserv@db0tui11.bitnet

➤ **The World Health Organization:** This site provides information on epidemiology, world health statistics, international travel vaccination requirements, and more. (See entry 5043 for full listing.)

FIRST AID

4862 **First Aid Online:** Handy first-aid instructions for minor medical conditions (with the obligatory disclaimer!).

```
http://www.symnet.net/Users/afoster/safety/
```

INFO cicely@vivid.net

FITNESS

4863 **alt.yoga** All forms and aspects of yoga. *Newsgroup*

4864 **ATHTRN-L:** The discussion list for athletic trainers. *Mailing List*

± listserv@iubvm.ucs.indiana.edu [body = SUBSCRIBE ATHTRN-L first-name last-name]

INFO athtrn-l-request@iubvm.ucs.indiana.edu

EDITOR OWNER pminger@scifac.indstate.edu (Chris Ingersoll)

EDITOR OWNER ray@hope.cit.hope.edu (Rich Ray)

4865 **Balance: Health and Fitness:** A monthly health and fitness magazine covering diet and nutrition, personal training, exercise and lifestyle. A new issue on the first of each month. *Magazine*

```
http://www.hyperlink.com/balance/
```

± http://www.hyperlink.com/balance/

INFO balance@hyperlink.com (Howard Jardine)

Frequency: monthly

4866 **FIT-L:** On exercise, diet, and wellness. *Mailing List*

± listserv@etsuadmn.etsu.edu [body = SUBSCRIBE FIT-L first-name last-name]

INFO fit-l-request@etsuadmn.etsu.edu

ARCHIVE listserv@etsuadmn.etsu.edu [body = INDEX FIT-L]

4867 **FITNESS:** On fitness. *Mailing List*

± listserv@indycms.iupui.edu [body = SUBSCRIBE FITNESS first-name last-name]

INFO betjones@indycms.iupui.edu (Betty Jones)

ARCHIVE listserv@indycms.iupui.edu

➤ **Health in Perspective:** News and research on the relationship between health, nutrition, and lifestyle. (See entry 4981 for full listing.)

➤ **The Michael Scott Fitness Centerfolds:** This site features fitness models from the Michael Scott Agency. (See entry 6799 for full listing.)

4868 misc.fitness.aerobic All forms of aerobic activity. *Newsgroup*

4869 misc.fitness.misc All other general fitness topics. *Newsgroup*

➤ misc.fitness.weights: Bodybuilding, weight lifting, resistance. *Newsgroup*

➤ **SPORTPSY:** On exercise and sport psychology. (See entry 6699 for full listing.)

4870 **weights:** On all aspects of using weights in exercise. *Mailing List*

± INFO weights-request@fa.disney.com (Michael Sullivan)

➤ **WISHPERD:** On women in sports, health, physical education, recreation, and dance. (See entry 7023 for full listing.)

GENERAL HEALTH

4871 **AMIA Family Practice/Primary Care Working Group Newsletter:** The newsletter of the Family Practice/Primary Care Working Group of the American Medical Informatics Association. *Newsletter*

http://www.med.ufl.edu/medinfo/docs/pcnews.html

INFO OWNER rrathe@ufl.edu (Richard Rathe, MD)

ARCHIVE http://www.med.ufl.edu/medinfo/docs/pcnews.html

Frequency: irregular (3-4 issues per year)

4872 fj.life.health Discussion about health. *Newsgroup*

4873 **International Health News:** Understandable abstracts from medical and scientific journals on health. Focusing on diet, supplements, exercise, lifestyle, drug side effects, warnings about medical procedures, and more. *Newsletter*

http://vvv.com/healthnews/

INFO health@pinc.com (Hans R. Larsen MSc ChE)

Frequency: monthly

Price: U.S.$15 ($20 Canadian) per year

4874 **Primary Care Internet Guide:** A guide to primary health care on the net, with an emphasis on Norway.

http://www.uib.no/isf/guide/guide.htm

INFO hogne.sandvik@isf.uib.no

4875 tnn.medical Discussions in medical issues. *Newsgroup*

GERIATRICS & AGING

➤ <u>Internet and E-mail Resources on Aging</u>: Includes commercial services, Freenets, online library catalogs, BBSs, mailing lists, e-journals, newsgroups, gopher sites, Web sites, and selected e-mail addresses. (See entry 9698 for full listing.)

➤ **Alzheimer Web:** Resources for researchers in the field of Alzheimer's disease and for the people who have an interest in research developments. (See entry 4789 for full listing.)

➤ bionet.neuroscience.amyloid: Alzheimer's disease and related disorders. *Newsgroup*

➤ bionet.molbio.ageing: Discussions of cellular and organismal aging. *Newsgroup*

➤ **GERIATRIC-NEUROPSYCHIATRY:** On neurobehavioral disorders in middle-aged and elderly adults. (See entry 4948 for full listing.)

4876 **GERINET:** On geriatric health care. *Mailing List*

± `listserv@ubvm.cc.buffalo.edu` [body = SUBSCRIBE GERINET first-name last-name]
INFO `phil@wubios.wustl.edu` (Phil Miller)
ARCHIVE `listserv@ubvm.cc.buffalo.edu`

➤ **PARKINSN:** Parkinson's disease information exchange network. (See entry 4810 for full listing.)

HEALTH ADMINISTRATION

4877 **CPRI-L:** On computerized patient records (CPRs). *Mailing List*
`http://www.cpri.org/`
± `listserv@kumchttp.mc.ukans.edu` [body = subscribe cpri-l first-name last-name]
EDITOR `dv02@academia.swt.edu` (Deanie French)
OWNER `lhancock@kumc.edu` (Lee Hancock)
Comments: Unix list processor software and not LISTSERV.

4878 **HBS International, Inc.:** Specialists in integrated health-care outcomes assessment and analysis software tools in the areas of cost, resource use, functional status, patient satisfaction, and clinical outcomes.
`http://hbsi.com/`
INFO `info@hbsi.com`

4879 **HOMEHLTH:** For home health-care managers: agencies, hospices, suppliers. *Mailing List*
± `listserv@usa.net` [body = SUBSCRIBE HOMEHLTH first-name last-name]
OWNER `philk@ucg.com` (Phil Kemelor)

4880 **MHCARE-L:** On managed health care and clinical process management. *Mailing List*
± `listserv@mizzou1.missouri.edu` [body = SUBSCRIBE MHCARE-L first-name last-name]
INFO `medinfab@mizzou1.bitnet` (Andrew Balas)
ARCHIVE `listserv@mizzou1.missouri.edu`

4881 **NRCH:** On health-care information systems: for managers and clinicians. *Mailing List*
± `majordomo@usa.net` [body = subscribe nrch]
OWNER `philk@ucg.com` (Phil Kemelor)

HEALTH CARE

4882 `clari.biz.industry.health` The health care business. *Moderated newsgroup*
4883 `clari.biz.industry.health.care` Health-care business, hospitals, doctors. *Moderated newsgroup*
4884 `clari.biz.industry.health.care.releases` News releases: hospitals, doctors. *Moderated newsgroup*
4885 `clari.biz.industry.health.cbd` Medical, dental and veterinary supplies. *Moderated newsgroup*
4886 `clari.tw.health` Disease, medicine, health care, sick celebrities. *Moderated newsgroup*

➤ **New York Academy of Medicine and Health Information:** Information on and from the academy, including its publications, a calendar of events and exhibitions, its HIV/AIDS information and outreach project and its fellowships, and its medical history library. (See entry 4899 for full listing.)

4887 `relcom.commerce.medicine` Medical services, equipment, drugs. *Newsgroup*

HIV & AIDS

4888 **AIDS Information Newsletter:** Electronic journal primarily for health-care professionals. *Newsletter*
± `majordomo@wubios.wustl.edu` [body = subscribe aids]
INFO `hivinfo@itsa.ucsf.edu` (Michael Howe)
ARCHIVES
`gopher://gopher.niaid.nih.gov/11/aids/vaain`
`http://www.cmpharm.ucsf.edu/~troyer/safesex/vanews/`
Gated: `sci.med.aids`

Frequency: biweekly

4889 AIDSBKRV: For reviews of materials on AIDS, safer sex, and sexually transmitted diseases (STDs). *Mailing List*

http://www.grd.org/grd/aids/abrj

http://www.uic.edu/depts/lib/aidsbkrv/

± INFO EDITOR OWNER hrm@uic.edu (H. Robert Malinowsky)

4890 bionet.molbio.hiv Discussions about the molecular biology of HIV. *Newsgroup*

4891 clari.tw.health.aids AIDS stories, research, political issues. *Moderated newsgroup*

➤ **HICNet Medical News: Health Information by Computer:** Health newsletter featuring: FDA bulletins, AIDS daily news summary, Centers for Disease Control MMWR, conference announcements, medical software reviews, and more. (See entry 4968 for full listing.)

4892 HIV: An electronic media information review: Electronic media review of information on HIV. Targeted at Australian health-care workers without ready access to the Net. *Newsletter*

http://florey.biosci.uq.edu.au/hiv/HIV_EMIR.html

± hiv@florey.biosci.uq.oz.au [subject = subscribe hiv_emir]

INFO hiv@florey.biosci.uq.oz.au

INFO zimitat@florey.biosci.uq.edu.au

ARCHIVE hiv_emir@florey.biosci.uq.oz.au (Craig Zimitat)

Frequency: fortnightly

➤ **International Antiviral News:** Reviews, articles, and abstracts concerning antiviral agents. (See entry 5054 for full listing.)

4893 misc.health.aids AIDS issues and support. *Newsgroup*

4894 National Institutes of Allergy and Infectious Disease (NIAID): This site provides information on HIV/AIDS, as well as on other infectious diseases, allergic and immunologic diseases, asthma, transplantation, and more. It also includes information about the organization like job vacancies, an organizational chart, its press releases, fact sheets, publication order forms, and a calendar of events.

http://www.niaid.nih.gov/

INFO ocpostoffice@flash.niaid.nih.gov

4895 NEUROPSYCH-HIV-AIDS: On psychological, neuropsychiatric, and neurocognitive dysfunction in people who have HIV/AIDS. *Mailing List*

± OWNER eliot@netcom.com (Eliot Aronstern)

Please Note: Subscription by approval only.

Comments: For medical, research and mental health professionals.

➤ **New York Academy of Medicine and Health Information:** Information on and from the academy, including its publications, a calendar of events and exhibitions, its HIV/AIDS information and outreach project and its fellowships, and its medical history library. (See entry 4899 for full listing.)

➤ **Planet Q:** Interactive multimedia services for, by, and/or about the queer community: gay, lesbian, bisexual, transgendered, and HIV+ people and their supporters. (See entry 9972 for full listing.)

4896 sci.med.aids AIDS: treatment, pathology/biology of HIV, prevention. *Moderated newsgroup*

4897 aids: Mostly about medical issues of AIDS, with some discussion of political and social issues. *Mailing List*

± listserv@vm.usc.edu [body = SUBSCRIBE AIDS first-name last-name]

± majordomo@wubios.wustl.edu [body = subscribe aids]

INFO aids-request@cs.ucla.edu (Daniel R. Greening)

INFO aids-request@wubios.wustl.edu

Gated: sci.med.aids

➤ **sci.med.immunology:** Medical/scientific aspects of immune illness. *Newsgroup*

HOSPITALS & MEDICAL CENTERS

4898 <u>Hospital Web:</u> An index to all hospitals and medical centers on the World Wide Web.

http://neuro-www.mgh.harvard.edu/hospitalweb.html

INFO lester@helix.mgh.harvard.edu (John Lester)

➤ **Mayo Clinic:** News, information for patients and medical professionals, and more from the Mayo clinic. (See entry 5055 for full listing.)

INSTITUTES

➤ **National Institutes of Health (NIH):** This site provides health and biomedical information useful to the NIH intramural research community in Bethesda, Maryland, and biomedical researchers around the world. (See entry 5057 for full listing.)

4899 **New York Academy of Medicine and Health Information:** Information on and from the academy, including its publications, a calendar of events and exhibitions, its HIV/AIDS information and outreach project and its fellowships, and its medical history library.

http://www.nyam.org/

gopher://gopher.nyam.org

INFO admin@nyam.org

4900 **The Salk Institute for Biological Studies:** A private, nonprofit research organization in La Jolla, California. Scientists there do fundamental research in biology and its relation to health, studying such problems as the organization and operation of the brain, the control of gene activity, and the molecular origins of disease.

http://www.salk.edu/

INFO anita_weld@qm.salk.edu (Anita Weld)

INFO webmaster@salk.edu

Comments: Public information requests should be addressed to: Anita Weld, Director of Public Relations

E-mail: anita_weld@qm.salk.edu

Tel.: (619) 453-4100, ext. 1225

Fax: (619) 453-3015

JOURNALS & PUBLICATIONS

➤ **AJN Network:** This service includes forums, databases, access to Internet resources relevant to nursing, online journal clubs, educational software. Its primary audience is nurses. AJN Online includes the American Journal of Nursing and the American Journal of Maternal Child Nursing online along with the AJN Guide and Multimedia Catalog. (See entry 4969 for full listing.)

4901 **Biomedical Market Newsletter:** A business, financial, marketing and regulatory newsletter on the medical manufacturing industry worldwide.

http://www.biomedical-market-news.com/bmn

INFO disaacs@iwy.com

4902 **British Medical Journal:** Contents, editiorials, classifieds, and more from the *Journal*.

http://www.bmj.com/bmj/

INFO bmj@bmj.com

➤ **Frontiers in Bioscience: A Journal and Virtual Library:** A forum for scientific communication in any discipline in biology and medicine including biochemistry, microbiology, parasitology, virology, immunology, biotechnology, and bioinformatics. (See entry 9007 for full listing.)

4903 **Medicine Online:** First electronic journal of medicine available on the World Wide Web. *E-Journal*

http://www.cityscape.co.uk/users/ad88/med.htm

INFO OWNER ad88@cityscape.co.uk (Dr. Ben Green, Editor)

ARCHIVE http://www.cityscape.co.uk/users/ad88/med.htm

Frequency: monthly

➤ **St. Francis Journal of Medicine:** Published quarterly by the St. Francis Medical Center in Pittsburgh; editorial balance includes clinical investigations, a clinicopathological conference, and review articles. (See entry 5062 for full listing.)

LIBRARIES & INFORMATION SERVICES

➤ **CISTI:** Canada Institute for Scientific and Technical Information—worldwide scientific, technical, and medical information. (See entry 9448 for full listing.)

➤ **Cyberspace Hospital:** A collection of Internet medical resources organized into a virtual hospital. (See entry 4687 for full listing.)

➤ **HyperDOC:** Multimedia access to National Library of Medicine projects, programs, and data. (See entry 4689 for full listing.)

➤ **PaperChase®:** This site allows you to search many health databases simultaneously. The databases include MEDLINE, CANCERLIT, AIDSLINE, CINAHL, and the Health Planning and Administration (HEALTH) database. (See entry 4691 for full listing.)

4904 **Biomedical Library Acquisitions Bulletin (BLAB):** News and opinion contributed by readers concerning biomedical library acquisitions and collection development; emphasis on notices of new publications and issues in biomedical library management. *Newsletter*

± **INFO EDITOR** dmorse@hsc.usc.edu (David H. Morse)

ARCHIVE http://www.ghsl.nwu.edu/BLAB/BLAB_home.html

Frequency: irregular, basically monthly

Publication of the Medical Library Association Collection Development Section

4905 **bit.listserv.medlib-l** Medical libraries discussion list. *Newsgroup*

➤ **Custom Medical Stock Photos Online:** This site is maintained by the Chicago, Illinois, company that offers access to more than 250,000 medical and scientific images. (See entry 1239 for full listing.)

4906 **GFULMED:** On using the Grateful Med medical database search software. *Mailing List*

± listserv@vm1.nodak.edu [body = SUBSCRIBE GFULMED first-name last-name]

OWNER kevin@computer.com (Kevin Sinclair)

ARCHIVE listserv@vm1.nodak.edu [body = INDEX GFULMED]

➤ **Med Help:** This site has thousands of articles on various medical and health topics all written in nontechnical terminology. (See entry 4693 for full listing.)

4907 **MEDIBIB-L:** On medical libraries in Germany, Austria, and Switzerland. *Mailing List*

± **INFO** medibib-l-request@uni-muenster.de

OWNER obsto@uni-muenster.de (Oliver Obst)

ARCHIVE http://medweb.uni-muenster.de/zbm/archiv.html

Language: German

➤ **MMATRIX-L:** For the official American Medical Informatics Association Internet Working Group. (See entry 5106 for full listing.)

➤ **Morbidity and Mortality Weekly Report (MMWR):** This site provides the Centers for Disease Control and Prevention's Morbidity and Mortality Weekly Report and its serial publications for download in Adobe™ Acrobat™ format. International and supranational public health bulletins are also available at this site. (See entry 4860 for full listing.)

4908 **Multimedia Medical Reference Library:** A collection of Internet resources in all areas of medicine including medical software, a listing of medical schools and curricula, pointers to medical journals, online hospitals, and more.

http://www.tiac.net/users/jtward/index.html

INFO jtward@tiac.net (Jonathan Tward)

4909 **The Virtual Hospital™:** A continuously updated digital health sciences library from the Department of Radiology, University of Iowa College of Medicine.

http://vh.radiology.uiowa.edu/

INFO librarian@vh.radiology.uiowa.edu

FAQ `http://vh.radiology.uiowa.edu/Help/VHfaqs.html`

MIRROR `http://www2.osaka-med.ac.jp/Iowa/VirtualHospital.html`

LYME DISEASE

4910 **LymeNet Newsletter:** A publication providing readers with medical, scientific, and political information on Lyme disease. *Newsletter*

`http://www.lymenet.org/`

± `listserv@lehigh.edu` [body = INDEX LYMENET-L]

INFO `a229@lehigh.edu` (Marc Gabriel)

ARCHIVES

`ftp://ftp.lehigh.edu/pub/listserv/lymenet-l/Newsletters`

`http://www.lehigh.edu/lists/lymenet-l`

POST `lymenet-l@lehigh.edu`

Gated: `sci.med.diseases.lyme`

Frequency: twice per month

4911 `sci.med.diseases.lyme`   Lyme disease: patient support, research, and information. *Newsgroup*

MEDICAL HUMANITIES & HISTORY

4912 **anes-hist:** On the history of anesthesia, pain management & critical care medicine. *Mailing List*

± `listproc@gasnet.med.yale.edu` [body = SUBSCRIBE ANES-HIST first-name last-name]

OWNER `ruskin@gasnet.med.yale.edu` (Keith J. Ruskin, MD)

OWNER `meds002@uabdpo.dpo.uab.edu` (A. J. Wright)

4913 **CADUCEUS-L:** On the history of health sciences. *Mailing List, moderated*

± `mailserv@beach.utmb.edu` [body = SUBSCRIBE CADUCEUS-L]

INFO `ibowman@beach.utmb.edu` (Inci Bowman)

ARCHIVE `mailserv@beach.utmb.edu` [body = INDEX]

4914 **New York University School of Medicine Medical Humanities Pages:** Database of literature and medicine, medical humanities directory and syllabi, archives of the lit-med discussion group messages, and pointers to related resources.

`http://mchip00.med.nyu.edu/lit-med/medhum.html`

`gopher://mchip00.med.nyu.edu`

INFO `aullf01@popmail.med.nyu.edu`

MEDICAL IMAGING

4915 `alt.image.medical`   Medical image exchange discussions. *Newsgroup*

4916 **Austin & Repatriation Medical Centre:** Positron emission tomography images and pointers to other medical sites.

`http://www.austin.unimelb.edu.au/`

`gopher://gopher.austin.unimelb.edu.au`

INFO `www@austin.unimelb.edu.au`

4917 `comp.protocols.dicom` Digital imaging and communications in medicine. *Newsgroup*

4918 **nucmed:** A discussion of nuclear medicine and related issues. Of particular concern is the Interfile format for nuclear medicine digital images. *Mailing List*

`http://www.largnet.uwo.ca/`

± INFO `nucmed-request@largnet.uwo.ca`

± INFO `postmaster@largnet.uwo.ca`

ARCHIVE `ftp://ftp.largnet.uwo.ca`

4919 `sci.techniques.mag-resonance` Magnetic resonance imaging and spectroscopy. *Newsgroup*

MEN'S HEALTH

➤ **The Men's Issues Page:** On the full range of men's concerns: health, parenting, justice, self-awareness, and growth. (See entry 10056 for full listing.)

MENTAL ILLNESS & HEALTH

4920 **Internet Mental Health Resources:** Links on every aspect of mental health.
   `http://freenet.msp.mn.us/ip/health/stockley/mental_health.html` (Search engine for resources not at site)
   `http://freenet.msp.mn.us/ip/stockley/mental_health.html`
   INFO `stock022@maroon.tc.umn.edu` (Herb Stockley)

➤ **AAGT:** On Gestalt therapy: philosophy, theory, practice, and research. (See entry 5029 for full listing.)

4921 `alt.anger` Seething rage. *Newsgroup*

4922 `alt.angst` Anxiety in the modern world. *Newsgroup*

4923 `alt.clearing.technology` Traumatic incident reduction and clearing. *Newsgroup*

4924 `alt.psychology.help` An alt.support group away from home. *Newsgroup*

➤ `alt.psychology.nlp:` Neuro-linguistic programming. *Newsgroup*

➤ `alt.recovery:` For people in recovery programs (e.g., AA, ACA, GA). *Newsgroup*

➤ `alt.recovery.codependency:` Mutually destructive relationships. *Newsgroup*

➤ `alt.recovery.compulsive-eat:` Food is an addictive drug. *Newsgroup*

➤ `alt.sexual.abuse.recovery:` Helping others deal with traumatic experiences. *Newsgroup*

4925 `alt.society.mental-health` Keeping your marbles in the modern world. *Newsgroup*

4926 `alt.support` Dealing with emotional situations and experiences. *Newsgroup*

4927 `alt.support.abuse-partners` People with people who were abused. *Newsgroup*

4928 `alt.support.anxiety-panic` Support for people who have panic attacks. *Newsgroup*

4929 `alt.support.depression` Depression and mood disorders. *Newsgroup*

4930 `alt.support.depression.manic` Extremely serious depression problems. *Newsgroup*

4931 `alt.support.depression.seasonal` Depression that comes and goes. *Newsgroup*

4932 `alt.support.dissociation` For persons with dissociative disorders. *Newsgroup*

4933 `alt.support.ex-cult` Recovering from cult experiences. *Newsgroup*

4934 `alt.support.grief` Support group for the grieving. *Newsgroup*

4935 `alt.support.loneliness` It's not easy being green. *Newsgroup*

4936 `alt.support.ocd` For overcoming obsessive-compulsive disorder. *Newsgroup*

4937 `alt.support.personality` Group for those with personality disorders. *Newsgroup*

4938 `alt.support.schizophrenia` Mutual support for schizophrenics. *Newsgroup*

4939 `alt.support.shyness` Um, er (blush), well, maybe I will post, after all. *Newsgroup*

4940 `alt.support.social-phobia` For sufferers of phobias of the social sort. *Newsgroup*

4941 `alt.support.survivors.prozac` Survivors of Prozac and all other SSRIs. *Newsgroup*

➤ **Alzheimer Web:** Resources for researchers in the field of Alzheimer's disease and for the people who have an interest in research developments. (See entry 4789 for full listing.)

➤ **Applied and Interactive Theater guide:** Information on and links to psychodrama, drama therapy, sociodrama, playback theater, Boal centers and practitioners, community-issues groups, and training and development specialists. Maintained by Joel Plotkin. (See entry 1614 for full listing.)

4942 artthxlst: For art therapy students and professors. *Mailing List*
± OWNER angelque@aol.com (Angelique Zeringue)

4943 `bit.listserv.autism` Autism list. *Newsgroup*

4944 Clinical-Psychophysiology: For clinical pschophysiology: biofeedback, stress, physical health. *Mailing List*
± listserv@netcom.com [body = SUBSCRIBE clinical-psychophysiology]
OWNER biosee@freud.tau.ac.il (Dr. Arnon Rolnick)

4945 DEPRESS: On depression: its experience and its treatment. *Mailing List*
± listserv@soundprint.org [body = SUBSCRIBE DEPRESS]
OWNER beth@soundprint.org (Beth Lewand)
ARCHIVE gopher://soundprint.org

4946 Depression: On mood disorders in clinical and research settings. *Mailing List*
± mailbase@mailbase.ac.uk [body = JOIN DEPRESSION first-name last-name]
OWNER depression-request@mailbase.ac.uk
Comments: Part of InterPsych

4947 EVALTEN: On evaluation methodology and statistics in mental health. *Mailing List*
± listserv@sjuvm.stjohns.edu [body = SUBSCRIBE EVALTEN first-name last-name]
OWNER shea@hsri.org (Sharon Shea)
POST evalten@sjuvm.stjohns.edu

4948 GERIATRIC-NEUROPSYCHIATRY: On neurobehavioral disorders in middle-aged and elderly adults. *Mailing List*
± listserv@netcom.com [body = SUBSCRIBE geriatric-neuropsychiatry]
OWNER mikeusman@aol.com (Mike Usman)

4949 The GlobalPsych Institute: GlobalPsych is a loose confederation of cooperating individuals and organizations that promotes debate and investigation of issues in health, behavior, cognition, and education, from a broad, multidisciplinary perspective.
http://www.shef.ac.uk/uni/projects/gpp/index.html
INFO i.pitchford@interpsych.telme.com
MIRROR http://rdz.stjohns.edu/gp/index.html (U.S.A.)

➤ **Helplessness:** On helplessness and explanatory style: research on animals and humans, biological substratum, depression, anxiety, prevention, CAVE, politics, children, personal control, health, battering, bereavement, PTSD, sex differences, pessimism, work, and heritability. (See entry 5013 for full listing.)

➤ **Kathy's Resources on Parenting, Domestic Violence, Abuse, Trauma & Dissociation:** Friendly and exhaustive index to resources that foster interpersonal respect and nonviolence. (See entry 9932 for full listing.)

4950 MADNESS: MADNESS is an electronic action and information discussion list for people who experience mood swings, fright, voices, and visions. *Mailing List*
http://www.io.org/madness
± listserv@sjuvm.stjohns.edu [body = SUBSCRIBE first-name last-name]
INFO sylviac@netcom.com (Sylvia Caras)
FAQ listserv@sjuvm.stjohns.edu [body = INDEX MADNESS]
Comments: MADNESS generates at least 40 messages a day.

➤ **`misc.health.therapy.occupational`:** All areas of occupational therapy. *Newsgroup*

➤ **NHCTEN:** On how health-care reforms may affect mental health and substance-abuse treatment. (See entry 5001 for full listing.)

4951 Oblomov: For the promotion of psychological research on procrastination. *Mailing List*
± listproc@rug.nl [body = SUBSCRIBE OBLOMOV first-name last-name]
OWNER schouwen@bureau.rug.nl (Henri C. Schouwenburg)
ARCHIVE listproc@rug.nl

4952 OCD-L: On obsessive compulsive disorder. *Mailing List*

± `listserv@vm.marist.edu` [body = SUBSCRIBE OCD-L first-name last-name]
OWNER `jzid@maristb.marist.edu` (Chris Vertullo)
ARCHIVE `listserv@vm.marist.edu` [body = INDEX OCD-L]

4953 **OUTCMTEN:** On assessing outcomes of interventions with mental health systems. *Mailing List*
± `listserv@sjuvm.stjohns.edu` [body = SUBSCRIBE OUTCMTEN first-name last-name]
OWNER `shea@hsri.org` (Sharon Shea)

➤ **PARKINSN:** Parkinson's disease information exchange network. (See entry 4810 for full listing.)

4954 **SCHIZ-L:** Academically oriented list for schizophrenia research. *Mailing List, moderated*
± `listproc@list.ab.umd.edu` [body = SUBSCRIBE SCHIZ-L first-name last-name]
OWNER `sdaviss@umabnet.ab.umd.edu` (Steven R. Daviss, M.D.)
POST `schiz-l@list.ab.umd.edu`
FAQ `listproc@list.ab.umd.edu` [body = SUBSCRIBE SCHIZ-L first-name last-name]
Please Note: Subscription by approval only.

4955 **SCHIZOPH:** Exchanging information on schizophrenia among various support networks. *Mailing List*
± `listserv@vm.utcc.utoronto.ca`
OWNER `cglover@oise.on.ca` (Chris Glover)
OWNER `carlson@tis.llnl.gov` (John Carlson)

4956 `soc.support.depression.crisis` Personal crisis situations. *Newsgroup*

4957 `soc.support.depression.family` Coping with depressed people. *Newsgroup*

4958 `soc.support.depression.manic` Bipolar/manic-depression. *Newsgroup*

4959 `soc.support.depression.misc` Depression and mood disorders. *Newsgroup*

4960 `soc.support.depression.seasonal` Seasonal affective disorder. *Newsgroup*

4961 `soc.support.depression.treatment` Treatments of depression. *Newsgroup*

4962 **TCAN:** For the Texas Counseling Association Network. *Mailing List*
± `listserv@etsuadmn.etsu.edu` [body = SUBSCRIBE TCAN first-name last-name]
OWNER `ronald@merlin.etsu.edu` (Ron Crawford)

➤ **Traumatic-Stress:** On the investigation, assessment, and treatment of the immediate and long-term psychosocial, biophysiological, and existential consequences of highly stressful (traumatic) events. Of special interest are efforts to identify a cure of PTSD (Post-traumatic Stress Disorder). (See entry 5027 for full listing.)

4963 **Turning-Point:** This mailing list is intended to be a forum for Christian-oriented discussion of mental health topics and the role that God plays in mental health. Subscriptions are managed via the WWW. *Mailing List*
± `pleasant@webcom.com` [body = SUBSCRIBE TURNING-POINT]
± `http://www.webcom.com/pleasant/turnpoint.html`
INFO OWNER `pleasant@webcom.com`

➤ **YES-LIST:** On youth in entertainment and sports: problems with fame. (See entry 10181 for full listing.)

NEWS

4964 **Biomedicine and Health in the News:** Quick access to the biomedical, scientific, and health journal literature referenced in newspaper articles appearing in *The New York Times*.
`http://cortex.uchc.edu/~libweb/libpg1.html`
`gopher://inform.uchc.edu/11gopher_root%3A%5B_data04._data0401%5D`
INFO `richetelle@nso.uchc.edu`

4965 `bit.listserv.mednews` *Health Info-Com Network* newsletter. *Moderated newsgroup*

4966 `clari.tw.health.misc` General health topics. *Moderated newsgroup*

4967 **CLINALRT:** For clinical alerts from the National Institutes of Health—intended for medical professionals. *Distribution List, moderated*

± listproc@list.ab.umd.edu [body = SUBSCRIBE CLINALRT first-name last-name]

OWNER gfreibur@hsl1.ab.umd.edu (Gary Freiburger)

ARCHIVE listproc@list.ab.umd.edu

Frequency: approx. twice yearly

4968 **HICNet Medical News: Health Information by Computer:** Health newsletter featuring: FDA bulletins, AIDS daily news summary, Centers for Disease Control MMWR, conference announcements, medical software reviews, and more. *Newsletter*

± listserv@asuvm.inre.asu.edu [body = SUBSCRIBE MEDNEWS first-name last-name]

± INFO david@stat.com (David Dodell)

± hicn-notify-request@stat.com

ARCHIVES

david@stat.com (David Dodell)

ftp://vm1.nodak.edu/hicnews/

Frequency: weekly

NURSING

➤ <u>Midwifery Internet Resources:</u> Contains information about and instructions for accessing Internet resources for midwives. (See entry 5113 for full listing.)

4969 **AJN Network:** This service includes forums, databases, access to Internet resources relevant to nursing, online journal clubs, educational software. Its primary audience is nurses. AJN Online includes the American Journal of Nursing and the American Journal of Maternal Child Nursing online along with the AJN Guide and Multimedia Catalog.

http://www.ajn.net/

INFO marizzolo@ajn.org (Mary Anne Rizzollo, Project Director)

INFO karen.dubois@ajn.org (Karen DuBois, Project Coordinator)

4970 **alt.npractitioners** Nurse practitioners. *Newsgroup*

4971 **bit.listserv.snurse-1** International nursing student group. *Newsgroup*

4972 **GLOBALRN:** On nursing, culture, and health: trans- and cross-cultural issues. *Mailing List*

± listserv@itssrv1.ucsf.edu [body = SUBSCRIBE GLOBALRN first-name last-name]

OWNER chuckp@itsa.ucsf.edu (Chuck Pitkofsky, MS, RN)

➤ **HOMEHLTH:** For home health-care managers: agencies, hospices, suppliers. (See entry 4879 for full listing.)

4973 **ivtherapy-1:** For dissemination of information by and for IV therapy nurses. *Mailing List*

± listserv@netcom.com [body = SUBSCRIBE ivtherapy-1]

OWNER sarahk@netcom.com (Sarah Kuykendall)

ARCHIVE ftp://ohsu.edu/pub/IVtherapy

4974 **NURSENET:** On nursing: education, adminstration, practice, research. *Mailing List*

± listserv@vm.utcc.utoronto.ca

INFO jnorris@oise.on.ca (Judy Norris)

4975 **NurseRes:** On nursing research. *Mailing List, moderated*

± listserv@kentvm.kent.edu [body = SUB NURSERES first-name last-name]

EDITOR lthede@kentvm.kent.edu (Linda Thede)

4976 **RN-TRAVEL:** For traveling RNs. *Mailing List*

± listproc@online.nonprofit.net [body = SUBSCRIBE RN-TRAVEL first-name last-name]

INFO growrnx2@aol.com (Linda Owen)

OWNER owenc@gcnet.com (Chris Owen)

4977 **SCHLRN-L:** For school nurses. *Mailing List*

± listserv@ubvm.cc.buffalo.edu [body = SUBSCRIBE SCHLRN-L first-name last-name]

OWNER bergren@acsu.buffalo.edu (Martha Dewey Bergen)

4978 **sci.med.nursing** Nursing questions and discussion. *Newsgroup*

NUTRITION

4979 **alt.support.food-allergies** Discussion group for people with food allergies. *Newsgroup*

➤ **CEL-KIDS:** On children with gluten and wheat intolerance, and related conditions. (See entry 4798 for full listing.)

4980 **Center for Food Safety & Applied Nutrition:** The Center for Food Safety & Applied Nutrition maintains a public Web server with consumer information on food safety, nutrition information, FDA food and nutrition press releases, and cosmetics information.

http://vm.cfsan.fda.gov/list.html

INFO lrd@vm.cfsan.fda.gov

4981 **Health in Perspective:** News and research on the relationship between health, nutrition, and lifestyle. *Newsletter*

http://www.perspective.com/health

± sample@perspective.com

± hip-order@perspective.com

INFO info@perspective.com

INFO EDITOR ari@perspective.com (Ari Kornfeld, Editor)

Frequency: monthly

Price: U.S.$15/ 12 issues (one year); Can.$20/12 issues

4982 **IFIC Foundation:** The IFIC Foundation provides sound, scientific information on food safety and nutrition.

http://ificinfo.health.org/

INFO carbog@ific.health.org

INFO foodinfo@ific.health.org

4983 **International Food Information Council (IFIC) Foundation:** Information available on this site includes scientific research, informational materials, graphics, and other information on a broad range of food issues.

http://ificinfo.health.org/

INFO foodinfo@ific.health.org

➤ **MEALTALK:** On child nutrition programs. (See entry 9732 for full listing.)

➤ **NUTEPI:** On nutritional epidemiology. (See entry 4861 for full listing.)

4984 **sci.med.nutrition** Physiological impacts of diet. *Newsgroup*

OCCUPATIONAL SAFETY & HEALTH

➤ **C+Health:** About the health effects of computer use. (See entry 3706 for full listing.)

4985 **Occ-Env-Med-L:** On occupational and environmental medicine. *Mailing List*

± majordomo@list.mc.duke.edu [body = subscribe occ-env-med-l]

INFO OWNER green011@mc.duke.edu (Gary Greenberg, MD)

ARCHIVES

http://dmi-www.mc.duke.edu/cfm/occ&env/index.html

gopher://gopher.mc.duke.edu/

FAQS

http://dmi-www.mc.duke.edu/cfm/occ&env/index.html

gopher://gopher.mc.duke.edu/

4986 **OSHA Computerized Information System (OCIS):** Information from the U.S. Department of Labor Occupational Safety & Health Administration. Includes data on OSHA programs and offices as well as texts of OSHA regulations and documents.

http://www.osha-slc.gov/

INFO webmaster@osha-slc.gov

4987   `sci.med.occupational`   Repetitive Strain Injuries (RSI) and job injury issues. *Newsgroup*

4988   `tnn.living.health`   Discussions about healthy living for workers. *Newsgroup*

PARAPROFESSIONALS

4989   `sci.med.transcription`   Information for and about medical transcriptionists. *Newsgroup*

PHARMACOLOGY & PHARMACEUTICALS

4990   `alt.fan.asprin`   I'm fond of buffered analgesics. Robert Lynn Asprin too. *Newsgroup*

➤   **Ciba Geigy AG (Ciba):** Home page for information and feedback to the biological and chemical company Ciba. (See entry 1905 for full listing.)

4991   `clari.biz.industry.health.pharma`   Pharmaceutical industry. *Moderated newsgroup*

4992   `clari.biz.industry.health.pharma.releases`   News releases: drugs, equipment. *Moderated newsgroup*

➤   **Glaxo Wellcome:** The world's premier health-care company. Informative articles on disease and disease management issues. Free molecular modeling software. Online pharmacology guide. Health-care bookmarks. Contact details. News. (See entry 1907 for full listing.)

4993   **International Union of Pharmacology:** The purpose of this site is to provide a comprehensive database and repository of software available for teaching pharmacology together with reviews, demonstrations, pricing, and availability to promote effective pharmacology education. In addition, the site also provides access to the latest newsletters, meetings, and positions available in pharmacology.

     `http://iuphar.pharmacology.unimelb.edu.au/`

     INFO `darren_williams@muwayf.unimelb.edu.au`

4994   **PharmInfoNet:** Pharmaceutical Information Network (PharmInfoNet™) includes a drug database, hundreds of drug-related articles, highlights from major medical meetings, disease information centers for patients, an online PharmMall for advertisers, links to pharmaceutical resources on the net, a gallery of pharmacy and pharmaceutical-related art and photographs, and more.

     `http://pharminfo.com/`

     INFO `webmaster@pharminfo.com`

4995   **Physicians GenRx:** This site is a complete drug-compendium resource of all U.S. FDA-approved pharmaceuticals. Search by name (generic or brand) or category. Customized report generation, a drug interactions function, and extensive prescribing information highlight this most functional professional medical resource.

     `http://www.genrx.com/`

     INFO `genrx-developers@icsi.net`

     MIRROR `http://www.icsi.net/GenRx`

➤   **Psycho-Pharm:** For the professional discussion of all aspects of clinical psychopharmacology. (See entry 5023 for full listing.)

4996   `sci.med.pharmacy`   The teaching and practice of pharmacy. *Newsgroup*

POLICY

4997   **BC-HEALTH-REFORM:** On health reform in British Columbia, Canada. *Mailing List*

     ± `majordomo@mars.ark.com`

     OWNER `rbell@mars.ark.com` (Bob Ell)

     OWNER `rbell@bcsc02.gov.bc.ca` (Bob Ell)

     ARCHIVE `http://mars.ark.com/~rbell/hlthrfrm.html`

4998   **CANCHID:** For the Canadian Network on Health in International Development. *Mailing List*

     ± `listserv@vm1.yorku.ca` [body = SUBSCRIBE CANCHID first-name last-name]

     INFO `lanfran@yorku.ca` (Sam Lanfranco)

     Language: English, French, Spanish, Portuguese

4999   **HEALTHPLAN:** Official White House announcements on health reform. *Distribution List, moderated*

± OWNER sfreedkin@igc.apc.org (Steve Freedkin)

Comments: Occasionally, a congressional newsletter advocating single-payer health reform is sent to the list. Rarely, other related items that do not originate from the White House are sent.

5000 **HealthRe:** On health-care reform. *Mailing List*

± listserv@ukcc.uky.edu [body = SUBSCRIBE HEALTHRE first-name last-name]

INFO healthre-request@ukcc.uky.edu

ARCHIVE listserv@ukcc.uky.edu [body = INDEX HEALTHRE]

5001 **NHCTEN:** On how health-care reforms may affect mental health and substance-abuse treatment. *Mailing List*

± listserv@sjuvm.stjohns.edu [body = SUBSCRIBE NHCTEN first-name last-name]

INFO shea@hsri.org (Sharon Shea)

➤ **NISHEALTH:** For information on conferences on public health administration in the former Soviet Union (NIS). (See entry 7599 for full listing.)

➤ **The Robert Wood Johnson Foundation:** Information about The Robert Wood Johnson Foundation—the nation's largest private philanthropy devoted to health care. (See entry 5059 for full listing.)

5002 **talk.politics.medicine** The politics and ethics involved with health care. *Newsgroup*

PSYCHIATRY & CLINICAL PSYCHOLOGY

5003 **alt.psychology.nlp** Neuro-linguistic programming. *Newsgroup*

5004 **American Academy of Child and Adolescent Psychiatry:** Home page for the American Academy of Child and Adolescent Psychiatry.

http://www.psych.med.umich.edu/web/aacap/

INFO mhuang@umich.edu

➤ **APASD-L:** On research and funding opportunities for psychologists. (See entry 9511 for full listing.)

5005 **ASSESS-P:** On psychological assessment and psychometrics. *Mailing List*

± listserv@sjuvm.stjohns.edu [body = SUBSCRIBE ASSESS-P first-name last-name]

OWNER ddilalla@siu.edu (David L. DiLalla, Ph.D.)

5006 **Attachment:** On Bowlby-Ainsworth's theory of attachment. From theoretical and philosophical issues, to clinical or applied issues. *Mailing List, moderated*

± mailbase@mailbase.ac.uk [body = JOIN ATTACHMENT first-name last-name]

OWNER attachment-request@mailbase.ac.uk

Comments: Part of InterPsych group of lists

5007 **BEHAV-AN:** On behavior analysis: research and clinical issues. *Mailing List*

± listserv@vm1.nodak.edu [body = SUBSCRIBE BEHAV-AN first-name last-name]

INFO http://rs1.cc.und.nodak.edu/misc/jBAT/

OWNER plaud@badlands.nodak.edu

5008 **Child-Psychiatry:** On child and adolescent psychiatry: treatment issues, psychopharmacology, inpatient/outpatient care plans, emergency child/adolescent psychiatry, et cetera. *Mailing List*

± mailbase@mailbase.ac.uk [body = JOIN CHILD-PSYCHIATRY first-name last-name]

OWNER child-psychiatry-request@mailbase.ac.uk

Comments: Part of InterPsych group of lists

5009 **Clinical-Psychologists:** On clinical psychology: cases, research and treatment, professional concerns. *Mailing List*

± listserv@vm1.nodak.edu [body = SUBSCRIBE CLINICAL-PSYCHOLOGISTS first-name last-name]

INFO http://rs1.cc.und.nodak.edu/misc/jBAT/

OWNER plaud@badlands.nodak.edu

ARCHIVE http://rs1.cc.und.nodak.edu/misc/jBAT/

POST clinical-psychologists@vm1.nodak.edu

POST clinipsy@vm1.nodak.edu

5010 **Clinical-Psychology:** For the exchange of ideas on matters relevant to clinical psychology, and particularly to the practice of clinical psychology. *Mailing List*
± mailbase@mailbase.ac.uk [body = JOIN CLINICAL-PSYCHOLOGY first-name last-name]
OWNER clinical-psychology-request@mailbase.ac.uk
Comments: Part of InterPsych group of lists

➤ **Depression:** On mood disorders in clinical and research settings. (See entry 4946 for full listing.)

5011 **DIV12:** Official APA Division of Clinical Psychology list. *Mailing List, moderated*
± listserv@vm1.nodak.edu [body = SUBSCRIBE DIV12 first-name last-name]
INFO http://rs1.cc.und.nodak.edu/misc/jBAT/
OWNER plaud@badlands.nodak.edu
Please Note: Subscription by approval only.

5012 **Forensic-psychiatry:** For scholarly discussion of forensic psychiatry. *Mailing List*
± listserv@netcom.com [body = SUBSCRIBE forensic-psychiatry]
OWNER psyharry@mizzou1.missouri.edu (Bruce Harry, M.D.)
OWNER 3004rs@west.net (Ronald Shlensky, M.D., J.D.)
OWNER forensic-psych@netcom.com
Please Note: Subscription by approval only.

5013 **Helplessness:** On helplessness and explanatory style: research on animals and humans, biological substratum, depression, anxiety, prevention, CAVE, politics, children, personal control, health, battering, bereavement, PTSD, sex differences, pessimism, work, and heritability. *Mailing List*
± mailbase@mailbase.ac.uk [body = JOIN HELPLESSNESS first-name last-name]
OWNER helplessness-request@mailbase.ac.uk
Comments: Part of InterPsych group of lists

5014 **HYPNOSIS:** On hypnosis, suggestion, and suggestibility: for researchers and clinicians. *Mailing List*
± listserv@netcom.com [body = SUBSCRIBE hypnosis]
INFO irvingk@uconnvm.uconn.edu
Please Note: Subscription by approval only.
Comments: Membership is limited to academics, health care professionals (e.g., M.D.'s, Ph.D.'s), and qualified students.

5015 **InterPsych:** A collection of several lists on different aspects of psychiatry. *Mailing Lists*
± mailbase@mailbase.ac.uk
INFO i.pitchford@sheffield.ac.uk
ARCHIVE http://www.psych.med.umich.edu/web/intpsych/

5016 **Journal of Behavior Analysis and Therapy (jBAT):** The Journal of Behavior Analysis and Therapy (jBAT) is a peer-reviewed journal of basic behavior analysis, applied behavior analysis, and behavior theory and therapy. *E-Journal*
http://rs1.cc.und.nodak.edu/misc/jBAT/
INFO OWNER plaud@badlands.nodak.edu
INFO OWNER plaud@plains.nodak.edu (Joseph J. Plaud, Ph.D.)
ARCHIVE http://rs1.cc.und.nodak.edu/misc/jBAT/
Frequency: quarterly

➤ **MADNESS:** MADNESS is an electronic action and information discussion list for people who experience mood swings, fright, voices, and visions. (See entry 4950 for full listing.)

➤ **NEUROPSYCH-HIV-AIDS:** On psychological, neuropsychiatric, and neurocognitive dysfunction in people who have HIV/AIDS. (See entry 4895 for full listing.)

5017 **NUVUPSY:** Points of view critical of the "therapeutic state" and institutional psychiatry. *Mailing List*
± listserv@sjuvm.stjohns.edu [body = SUBSCRIBE NUVUPSY first-name last-name]
OWNER jschale@american.edu (Jeffrey A. Schaler, Ph.D.)

ARCHIVE `listserv@sjuvm.stjohns.edu` [body = `INDEX NUVUPSY`]

➤ **OUTCMTEN:** On assessing outcomes of interventions with mental health systems. (See entry 4953 for full listing.)

5018 Psy-Language: On language and psychopathology. *Mailing List*
± `mailbase@mailbase.ac.uk` [body = `JOIN PSY-LANGUAGE` first-name last-name]
OWNER `psy-language-request@mailbase.ac.uk`
Comments: Part of InterPsych group of lists

5019 Psychiatry: This forum will act as a bridge between those taking a biomedical approach to psychiatry and those taking a psychodynamic approach. *Mailing List*
± `mailbase@mailbase.ac.uk`
OWNER `psychiatry-request@mailbase.ac.uk`
Comments: Part of InterPsych group of lists

5020 Psychiatry On-line: Psychiatry and allied subjects: covering diagnoses, research, management, psychotherapy, pharmacology, neurosciences, service issues, and more. *E-Journal*
`http://www.cityscape.co.uk/users/ad88/psych.htm`
INFO EDITOR `ad88@cityscape.co.uk` (Dr. Ben Green, Editor)
OWNER `http://www.cityscape.co.uk/users/ad88/pme.htm`
ARCHIVE `ad88@cityscape.co.uk` (Dr. Ben Green, Editor)
Frequency: monthly

5021 Psychiatry-Assessment: On research and clinical issues related to use of psychological tests (including traditional clinical instruments and normal personality measures) in psychiatry and clinical psychology. *Mailing List*
± `mailbase@mailbase.ac.uk` [body = `JOIN PSYCHIATRY-ASSESSMENT` first-name last-name]
OWNER `psychiatry-assessment-request@mailbase.ac.uk`
Comments: Part of InterPsych group of lists

5022 Psychiatry-Resources: For the compilation of a resource guide to enable clinicians and academics in the areas of psychiatry and abnormal psychology to gain maximum benefit from the facilities available over the Internet. *Mailing List*
± `mailbase@mailbase.ac.uk` [body = `JOIN PSYCHIATRY-RESOURCES` first-name last-name]
OWNER `psychiatry-resources-request@mailbase.ac.uk`
Comments: Part of InterPsych group of lists

5023 Psycho-Pharm: For the professional discussion of all aspects of clinical psychopharmacology. *Mailing List*
± `listserv@netcom.com` [body = `subscribe psycho-pharm` e-mail address]
Comments: Part of InterPsych group of lists

5024 sci.med.psychobiology Dialogue and news in psychiatry and psychobiology. *Newsgroup*

5025 SCR-L: On cognitive rehabilitation. *Mailing List*
± `listserv@mizzou1.missouri.edu` [body = `SUBSCRIBE SCR-L` first-name last-name]
INFO `jsilsby@mail.coin.missouri.edu`
ARCHIVE `listserv@mizzou1.missouri.edu` [body = `INDEX SCR-L`]
Comments: Main contributors tend to be professionals and students of cogntive rehabilitation.

➤ **Support Coalition & Dendron News:** Dendron News is the voice of Support Coalition, a nonprofit alliance of 30 grass-roots advocacy, human rights, and support groups. "Breaking the silence about psychiatric oppression!" "Heal Normally, Naturally!" These are some of the slogans from a little-known, diverse 25-year-old social change movement: The psychiatric surivors liberation movement, sometimes known as "mad lib." Stop forced drugs and forced electroshock! (See entry 4711 for full listing.)

5026 Transcultural-Psychology: On the delivery of mental health services to diverse cultures. *Mailing List*
± `mailbase@mailbase.ac.uk` [body = `JOIN TRANSCULTURAL-PSYCHOLOGY` first-name last-name]
OWNER `transcultural-psychology-request`
Comments: Part of InterPsych group of lists.

5027   **Traumatic-Stress:** On the investigation, assessment, and treatment of the immediate and long-term psychosocial, biophysiological, and existential consequences of highly stressful (traumatic) events. Of special interest are efforts to identify a cure of PTSD (Post-traumatic Stress Disorder). *Mailing List*

± `mailbase@mailbase.ac.uk` [body = JOIN TRAUMATIC-STRESS first-name last-name]

OWNER `traumatic-stress-request@mailbase.ac.uk`

Comments: Part of InterPsych group of lists

5028   **University of Michigan Department of Psychiatry:** Home page for the University of Michigan Hospital's Department of Psychiatry.

`http://www.psych.med.umich.edu/web/UMpsych/`

INFO `mhuang@umich.edu`

PSYCHOTHERAPY

5029   **AAGT:** On Gestalt therapy: philosophy, theory, practice, and research. *Mailing List*

± `majordomo@indy.net` [body = SUBSCRIBE AAGT e-mail-address]

OWNER `btohara@aol.com` (Brian T. O'Hara)

5030   **The American Psychoanalytic Association:** Home page of the American Psychoanalytic Association, a professional organization of psychoanalysts throughout the United States.

`http://apsa.org/`

INFO `webmaster@apsa.org`

➤   **EMPATHY:** For teachers of interpersonal communication courses. (See entry 5173 for full listing.)

5031   **FreudNet: The A.A. Brill Library :** Information on Sigmund Freud from the A. A. Brill Library.

`http://plaza.interport.net/nypsan/`

INFO `mvu@pipeline.com`

5032   **group-psychotherapy:** On group psychotherapy and group work. *Digest & Reflector*

`http://freud.tau.ac.il/~haimw/group2.html`

± `majordomo@freud.apa.org` [body = SUBSCRIBE GROUP-PSYCHOTHERAPY or SUBSCRIBE GROUP-PSYCHOTHERAPY-DIGEST]

INFO `http://freud.tau.ac.il/~haimw/group2.html`

OWNER `haimw@freud.tau.ac.il` (Haim Weinberg)

Please Note: Subscription by approval only.

➤   **The Magic of Differences:** Home page of Judith Sherven, Ph.D., and James Sniechowski, Ph.D., who in their own words "can help you turn the challenges of intimacy into the deepest intimacy of your life." (See entry 6008 for full listing.)

5033   **PsyNetUSA:** A network of psychologists discussing issues of practice. Part of a 50-state network of individual mailing lists. *Mailing List, moderated*

± `listserv@sjuvm.stjohns.edu` [body = SUBSCRIBE PSYNETUSA first-name last-name]

EDITOR OWNER `jmroraback@aol.com` (John M. Roraback, Ph.D.)

Please Note: Subscription by approval only.

Comments: Limited to licensed psychologists and academic research psychologists studying or teaching psychological practice-related issues.

PUBLIC HEALTH & SAFETY

5034   **A Primer on Health Risk Communication Principles and Practices:** The Primer covers issues and guiding principles for communicating health risk, accompanied by specific suggestions for presenting information to the public and for interacting effectively with the media.

`http://atsdr1.atsdr.cdc.gov:8080/HEC/primer.html`

INFO `txt2@atsod3.em.cdc.gov`

5035   **Agency for Toxic Substances and Disease Registry (ATSDR):** The mission of the Agency for Toxic Substances and Disease Registry (ATSDR) is to prevent exposure and adverse human health effects and diminished quality of life associated with exposure to hazardous substances from waste sites, unplanned releases, and other sources of pollution present in the environment.

`http://atsdr1.atsdr.cdc.gov:8080/`

5036 `alt.support.non-smokers` Discussing issues relating to secondhand smoke. *Newsgroup*

5037 `alt.support.non-smokers.moderated` The dangers of secondhand smoke. *Moderated newsgroup*

5038 **ATSDR Science Corner:** ATSDR Science Corner is a simple guide to search the World Wide Web for environmental health information. The primary focus is to find and share global information resources with the public on the linkage between human exposure to hazardous chemicals and adverse human health effects.

`http://atsdr1.atsdr.cdc.gov:8080/cx.html`

INFO `chx1@atsoaa1.em.cdc.gov` (Dr. Charlie Xintaras)

➤ **Centers for Disease Control and Prevention (CDC):** Information on diseases, disease prevention, and health in general from the U.S. government Centers for Disease Control and Prevention. (See entry 4856 for full listing.)

5039 `clari.news.smoking` Smoking and tobacco issues. *Moderated newsgroup*

5040 **FOODLINK:** For food safety specialists. *Mailing List*

± `listproc@listproc.wsu.edu` [body = SUBSCRIBE FOODLINK first-name last-name]

OWNER `wright@wsu.edu` (Tony Wright)

5041 **IMMNET-L:** On medical immunization-tracking systems. *Mailing List, moderated*

± `listserv@listserv.dartmouth.edu` [body = SUB IMMNET-L first-name last-name]

INFO OWNER `jlevin@umnhcs.labmed.umn.edu` (James E. Levin, MD, PhD)

➤ **Morbidity and Mortality Weekly Report (MMWR):** This site provides the Centers for Disease Control and Prevention's Morbidity and Mortality Weekly Report and its serial publications for download in Adobe™ Acrobat™ format. International and supranational public health bulletins are also available at this site. (See entry 4860 for full listing.)

➤ **SAFETY:** On environmental health and safety: life safety issues (such as fire protection), chemical safety (waste disposal, laboratory safety, regulatory compliance), biological hazards, and radiation safety. (See entry 4854 for full listing.)

5042 **Utposten:** Norwegian journal for general practice and public health.

`http://www.uib.no/isf/utposten/utposten.htm`

INFO `hogne.sandvik@isf.uib.no`

5043 **The World Health Organization:** This site provides information on epidemiology, world health statistics, international travel vaccination requirements, and more.

`http://www.who.ch/Welcome.html`

INFO `inf@who.ch`

RADIOLOGY

5044 **medphys:** On the physics of the diagnostic and therapeutic use of radiation in medicine. *Mailing List*

± `listserv@cms.cc.wayne.edu` [body = SUBSCRIBE MEDPHYS first-name last-name]

INFO `medphys-request@radonc.duke.edu` (Raj K. Mitra)

➤ **nucmed:** A discussion of nuclear medicine and related issues. Of particular concern is the Interfile format for nuclear medicine digital images. (See entry 4918 for full listing.)

5045 **Radiology Update:** For referring physicians to let them know about specific events planned by the Department of Radiology at Brigham and Women's Hospital and to present articles to aid physicians in being educated consumers for imaging procedures. *Newsletter*

INFO `gmammone@dsg.harvard.edu` (GL Mammone)

EDITOR `sedwards@ulna.bwh.harvard.edu` (Sally Edwards)

ARCHIVES

`http://www.med.harvard.edu/BWHRad/HomeDocs/BWHPublications.html`

`http://www.med.harvard.edu/BWHRad/newsworthy.html#Pubs`

http://www.med.harvard.edu/BWHRad/
Frequency: 6 times per year

5046 `sci.med.radiology` All aspects of radiology. *Newsgroup*

REPETITIVE STRESS INJURY

5047 `misc.health.injuries.rsi.misc` All about repetitive strain injuries. *Newsgroup*

5048 `misc.health.injuries.rsi.moderated` Experts answer questions about RSI. *Moderated newsgroup*

5049 **Patient's Guide to Carpel Tunnel Syndrome:** All about carpal tunnel syndrome, a common problem that affects the hand and wrist.
http://www.cyberport.net/mmg/cts/ctsintro.html
INFO mmg@cyberport.net
FAQ http://www.cyberport.net/mmg/cts/ctsfaq.txt

5050 **RSI-UK:** U.K.-specific discussion on repetitive strain injuries. *Mailing List*
http://www.demon.co.uk/
± listserver@tictac.demon.co.uk
OWNER ellen@tictac.demon.co.uk (Ellen Mizzell)

➤ `sci.med.occupational`: Repetitive Strain Injuries (RSI) and job injury issues. *Newsgroup*

RESEARCH

➤ `bionet.biology.cardiovascular`: Scientists engaged in cardiovascular research. *Newsgroup*

5051 `bionet.prof-society.afcr` American Federation for Clinical Research. *Moderated newsgroup*

➤ **Extracorporeal Technology (Perfusion) Pages:** A forum for communication and an internationally accessible point of dissemination for information of interest to members of the perfusion community. (See entry 5099 for full listing.)

➤ **PPM-L:** On extracorporeal technology, esp. for perfusionists. (See entry 5100 for full listing.)

5052 `fj.sci.medical` Topics related to medical science. *Newsgroup*

➤ **Frontiers in Bioscience: A Journal and Virtual Library:** A forum for scientific communication in any discipline in biology and medicine including biochemistry, microbiology, parasitology, virology, immunology, biotechnology, and bioinformatics. (See entry 9007 for full listing.)

5053 **IARPE-L:** On radiation protection. *Mailing List*
± listserv@slacvm.slac.stanford.edu [body = SUBSCRIBE IARPE-L first-name last-name]
INFO OWNER vylet@slac.stanford.edu (Vashek Vylet)
ARCHIVE ftp://ehssun1.lbl.gov/IARPE/

5054 **International Antiviral News:** Reviews, articles, and abstracts concerning antiviral agents. *E-Journal*
http://www.meditech.co.uk/iavn.html
± **INFO OWNER** elinor@meditech.co.uk (Elinor Thompson)
EDITOR hjf10@cam.ac.uk (Dr Hugh J Field)
ARCHIVE http://www.meditech.co.uk/iavn.html
Frequency: 10 per year

➤ **Lanuage Based Learning Disability:Remediation Research:** This site presents information related to remediation research efforts for language-based learning disability. Information related to dyslexia is also provided. Multiple forums and a live chat room are provided for parents, teachers, clinicians, and researchers. (See entry 9867 for full listing.)

5055 **Mayo Clinic:** News, information for patients and medical professionals, and more from the Mayo clinic.
http://www.mayo.edu/
INFO pishotta@mayo.edu
FAQ http://www.mayo.edu/general/q_a.html

➤ **Medicine Online:** First electronic journal of medicine available on the World Wide Web. (See entry 4903 for full listing.)

5056 **MEDLAB-L:** For medical laboratory professionals. *Mailing List*

± `listserv@ubvm.cc.buffalo.edu` [body = `SUBSCRIBE MEDLAB-L` first-name last-name]

OWNER `pletendr@gpu.srv.ualberta.ca` (Pat Letendre)

5057 **National Institutes of Health (NIH):** This site provides health and biomedical information useful to the NIH intramural research community in Bethesda, Maryland, and biomedical researchers around the world.

`http://www.nih.gov/`

`gopher://gopher.nih.gov`

INFO `nihinfo@od31tm1.od.nih.gov`

5058 **NIHGDE-L:** Announcements of availability of NIH funds for biomedical and behavioral research and research training, and announcements of policy and administrative information. *Distribution List, moderated*

`gopher://gopher.nih.gov/11/res/nih-guide`

± `listserv@list.nih.gov` [body = `SUBSCRIBE NIHGDE-L` (or `NIHTOC-L` for table of contents only) first-name last-name]

INFO `brocketm@odrockm1.od.nih.gov` (Myra Brockett)

ARCHIVE `listserv@list.nih.gov` [body = `INDEX NIHGDE-L` (or `NIHTOC-L` for table of contents archive)]

➤ **RAND:** Website of RAND, a nonprofit institution that helps improve public policy through research and analysis. The site includes RAND publications, a wide range of information on its projects, and initiatives. (See entry 9553 for full listing.)

5059 **The Robert Wood Johnson Foundation:** Information about The Robert Wood Johnson Foundation—the nation's largest private philanthropy devoted to health care.

`http://www.rwjf.org/`

`gopher://gopher.rwjf.org:4500`

INFO `publications@rwjf.org`

5060 `sci.med.laboratory` All aspects of laboratory medicine and management. *Newsgroup*

5061 `sci.med.physics` Issues of physics in medical testing/care. *Newsgroup*

5062 **St. Francis Journal of Medicine:** Published quarterly by the St. Francis Medical Center in Pittsburgh; editorial balance includes clinical investigations, a clinicopathological conference, and review articles. *E-journal*

`http://www.pitt.edu/~leff2/journal/journal.html`

INFO EDITOR `leff+@pitt.edu` (Louis E. Leff, M.D., Internet Editor)

Frequency: quarterly

➤ **The Virtual Hospital™:** A continuously updated digital health sciences library from the Department of Radiology, University of Iowa College of Medicine. (See entry 4909 for full listing.)

RURAL AREAS

➤ `bit.org.peace-corps`: Peace Corps. *Newsgroup*

5063 **HSPNET-L:** On the way computer wide area networks can be used for remote diagnosis and treatment, transfer of patient records, and supplementing rural health care. *Mailing List*

± `listserv@health.state.ny.us` [body = `SUBSCRIBE HSPNET-L` first-name last-name]

INFO `dfp10@health.state.ny.us` (Donald F. Parsons, M.D.)

ARCHIVE `listserv@health.state.ny.us` [body = `INDEX HSPNET-L`]

Gated: `sci.med.telemedicine`

➤ **Mashall University School of Medicine, West Virginia:** Information on the medical school and its primary-care based curricula as well on its Internet projects, which include the Interactive Patient, Rural Net, and vital health and population statistics for West Virginia. (See entry 4833 for full listing.)

5064 **Rural-Care:** Support for rural and bush health-care workers: techniques, telemedicine, isolation. *Mailing List*

`http://www.shef.ac.uk/uni/projects/gpp/rural.html`

± listserv@netcom.com [body = SUBSCRIBE rural-care]

OWNER afbhs@vms.acad2.alaska.edu (B. Hudnall Stamm, Ph.D.)

5065 RuralNet-L: On rural healthcare: delivery, improvement, technology, education & research *Mailing List*

± listserv@musom01.mu.wvnet.edu [body = SUBSCRIBE RURALNET-L first-name last-name]

INFO EDITOR mccarthy@marshall.edu (Mike McCarthy)

ARCHIVE http://ruralnet.mu.wvnet.edu/ (RuralNet WWW Server)

SELF-HELP

➤ <u>**Internet Mental Health Resources:**</u> Links on every aspect of mental health. (See entry 4920 for full listing.)

5066 alt.self-improve Self-improvement in less than 14 characters. *Newsgroup*

5067 alt.skincare Epidermal grooming on-line. *Newsgroup*

5068 alt.support.breast-implant Discussion of breast implants. *Newsgroup*

➤ **The Magic of Differences:** Home page of Judith Sherven, Ph.D., and James Sniechowski, Ph.D., who in their own words "can help you turn the challenges of intimacy into the deepest intimacy of your life." (See entry 6008 for full listing.)

5069 Psychology in Daily Life Page: From the public-affairs office of the American Psychological Association—several Web brochures on mental health and psychological issues.

http://www.apa.org/pubinfo/pubinfo.html

INFO public.affairs@apa.org

➤ **SELF-HELP-RESEARCH:** Academic discussion of self-help research. (See entry 9542 for full listing.)

5070 SLFHLP-L: Discussion group for self-help researchers. *Mailing List*

± postoffice.cso.uiuc.edu [body = SUBSCRIBE SLFHLP-L first-name last-name]

OWNER slfhlp-l-request@vmd.cso.uiuc.edu

SPECIALTIES

5071 ACCRI-L: On Internet resources about anesthesiology and critical care. *Mailing List*

± listserv@uabdpo.dpo.uab.edu [body = SUBSCRIBE ACCRI-L first-name last-name]

OWNER meds002@uabdpo.dpo.uab.edu (A. J. Wright)

5072 ADTA: A discussion list related to matters of concern to dance/movement therapy. *Mailing List*

± listproc@list.ab.umd.edu [body = SUBSCRIBE ADTA first-name last-name]

INFO OWNER hchaikli@ssw02.ab.umd.edu

INFO jblumenf@ssw02.ab.umd.edu

5073 Australasian Anaesthesia Web Pages: Information on Macintosh-to-medical-device-connecting cables, Australian snake and spider bites and their management, anesthesia meeting list, and pointers to other Australian WWW sites.

http://www.usyd.edu.au/su/anaes/anaes.html

INFO clt@extro.ucc.su.oz.au (Dr. Chris Thompson)

5074 bit.med.resp-care.world Respiratory Care World. *Newsgroup*

➤ **CDMAJOR:** On communication disorders, primarily for students and faculty in speech-language pathology, audiology, speech science, or hearing-science programs. (See entry 9873 for full listing.)

5075 DERM-L: On dermatology. *Mailing List, moderated*

± listserv@yalevm.cis.yale.edu [body = subscribe derm-l first-name last-name]

OWNER rlangdon@biomed.med.yale.edu (Robert Langdon)

Please Note: Subscription by approval only.

➤ **Extracorporeal Technology (Perfusion) Pages:** A forum for communication and an internationally accessible point of dissemination for information of interest to members of the perfusion community. (See entry 5099 for full listing.)

➤ **PPM-L:** On extracorporeal technology, esp. for perfusionists. (See entry 5100 for full listing.)

5076 **FAMILY-L:** On academic issues in family medicine. *Mailing List*
OWNER `clgjerde@facstaff.wisc.edu` (Craig Gjerde)
OWNER `fprmaxc@ukcc.uky.edu` (MAX A. CROCKER)
OWNER `jsrowe@u.washington.edu` (Jennifer Rowe)
ARCHIVE `listserv@mizzou1.missouri.edu`
Please Note: Subscription by approval only.

5077 **FlightMed:** For air medical professionals: flight nurses & paramedics, pilots, physicians. *Mailing List*
± `listserv@rotor.com` [body = SUBSCRIBE FLIGHTMED first-name last-name]
INFO `aland@imt.net` (Alan Dobrowolski)
OWNER `david.lutes@rotor.com` (David Lutes)

5078 `misc.health.therapy.occupational` All areas of occupational therapy. *Newsgroup*

5079 **Neuromuscular Physiology:** Home page of the Neuromuscular Physiology Lab at the University of California.
`http://www-neuromus.ucsd.edu/MusIntro/Jump.html`
`http://www-neuromus.ucsd.edu/`
INFO `webmaster@www-neuromus.ucsd.edu`

5080 **OANDP-L:** On orthotics and prosthetics. *Mailing List, moderated*
± `listserv@nervm.nerdc.ufl.edu` [body = SUBSCRIBE OANDP-L first-name last-name]
OWNER `prusape.rehab@shands.ufl.edu` (Paul E. Prusakowski, CO)

5081 **OPHTHAL:** For ophthalmologists. *Mailing List, moderated*
± `listserv@ubvm.cc.buffalo.edu` [body = SUBSCRIBE OPHTHAL first-name last-name]
EDITOR OWNER `oopraym@ubvms.cc.buffalo.edu` (Ray Magauran)
ARCHIVE `listserv@ubvm.cc.buffalo.edu` [body = INDEX OPHTHAL]
Please Note: Subscription by approval only.

5082 **OTOHNS:** On otolaryngology. *Mailing List*
`http://www.bcm.tmc.edu/oto/`
± OWNER `ronaldk@bcm.tmc.edu` (Ron Kuppersmith, M.D.)
Please Note: Subscription by approval only.

5083 **PEDINFO: A Pediatrics WebServer:** A Web site dedicated to the dissemination of online information for pediatricians and others interested in child health.
`http://www.lhl.uab.edu/pedinfo`
INFO `spooner@aol.com` (Andy Spooner, M.D)

5084 **RC_WORLD:** For health professionals to discuss respiratory therapy. *Mailing List, moderated*
± `listserv@indycms.iupui.edu` [body = SUBSCRIBE RC_WORLD first-name last-name]
EDITOR OWNER `72624.1202@compuserve.com` (John A. Hannigan, MBA, RRT)
ARCHIVES
`listserv@indycms.iupui.edu` [body = INDEX RC_WORLD]
`listserv@indycms.iupui.edu` [body = INDEX RC_WORLD]
POST `rc_world@indycms.iupui.edu`
Gated: `bit.med.resp-care.world`
Comments: Mailing list is for users without access to Usenet.

5085 `sci.med.cardiology` All aspects of cardiovascular diseases. *Newsgroup*

5086 `sci.med.immunology` Medical/scientific aspects of immune illness. *Newsgroup*

5087 `sci.med.orthopedics` Orthopedic surgery, related issues, and management. *Moderated newsgroup*

5088 `sci.med.pathology` Pathology and laboratory medicine. *Newsgroup*

5089 `bit.med.mxdiag-l` Molecular pathology and diagnostics. *Newsgroup*

5090 `sci.med.vision` Human vision, visual correction, and visual science. *Newsgroup*

5091 **SURGINET:** On general surgery: ideas, knowledge, information. *Mailing List*
± `listserv@utoronto.bitnet` [body = SUBSCRIBE SURGINET first-name last-name]
OWNER `tgilas@hookup.net` (Tom Gilas MD, FRCSC, FACS)
Please Note: Subscription by approval only.

5092 **TRNSPLNT:** For organ transplant recipients and anyone else interested in transplantation. *Mailing List*
± `listserv@wuvmd.wustl.edu` [body = SUBSCRIBE TRNSPLNT first-name last-name]
INFO OWNER `sysflasar@wugcrc.wustl.edu` (Dan Flasar)
INFO `sysflasar@gcrc1.wustl.edu` (Dan Flasar)
OWNER `mike.holloway@stjude.org.edu`
ARCHIVE `listserv@wuvmd.wustl.edu` [body = INDEX TRNSPLNT]

TECHNOLOGY

5093 `alt.med.equipment` Discussion of medical equipment. *Newsgroup*

5094 **American Medical Informatics Association (AMIA):** All about the American Medical Informatics Association.
`http://www.amia.org/`
INFO `webmaster@amia2.amia.org`

5095 **Australian Biomedical And Medical Device Page:** This site offers newsletters from the Society for Medical and Biological Engineering and I. E. Australia, lists of Australian hospitals, a list of Australian medical device companies, and so forth.
`http://www.zeta.org.au/~hpbridel`
INFO `hpbridel@zeta.org.au` (Hilary Bridel)

5096 `bionet.diagnostics.prenatal` Research in prenatal diagnostics. *Newsgroup*

5097 **The Center for Biomedical Informatics:** Research and education center of the State University of Campinas, Brazil (home page). Portuguese and English.
`http://brasil.emb.nw.dc.us/NIB/welcome.htm` (U.S.A)
INFO `sabbatin@cesar.unicamp.br` (Renato M.E. Sabbatini)
MIRROR `http://www.unicamp.br/NIB/welcome.htm`

5098 `clari.nb.health` Newsbytes: computers in medicine. *Moderated newsgroup*

5099 **Extracorporeal Technology (Perfusion) Pages:** A forum for communication and an internationally accessible point of dissemination for information of interest to members of the perfusion community.
`http://eja.anes.hscsyr.edu/perf/ect.html`
INFO `searlesb@vax.cs.hscsyr.edu` (Bruce Searles)

5100 **PPM-L:** On extracorporeal technology, esp. for perfusionists. *Mailing List*
`http://eja.anes.hscsyr.edu/perf/ect.html`
± `listserv@ubvm.cc.buffalo.edu` [body = SUB PPM-L first-name last-name]
INFO OWNER `searlesb@vax.cs.hscsyr.edu` (Bruce Searles)
ARCHIVE `http://eja.anes.hscsyr.edu/perf/mailing_list/PPM-L/PPM-L_page`

5101 **IBEGROUP:** On biomedical engineering, especially electrophysiological recording equipment. *Mailing List*
± OWNER `vdbergen@acadvm1.uottawa.ca` (Herman van den Bergen)
± OWNER `vdbergen@aix1.uottawa.ca` (Herman van den Bergen)
Please Note: Subscription by approval only.

5102 **International Medical Informatics Association Home Page:** Contains information on IMIA publications, working groups, meetings, etc.
`http://www.eur.nl/FGG/MI/imia/home.html`
INFO `imia@mi.fgg.eur.nl`

5103 **Medical Software Archive—State University of Campinas, Brazil:** One of the largest repositories of public-domain medical software for PCs, it includes a great variety of applications, including statistical packages, intensive-care utilities, medical and dental office management, medical education, artificial intelligence, health assessment and maintenance, etc.

`http://brasil.emb.nw.dc.us/NIB` (U.S.A)

`ftp://ftp.unicamp.br/pub/medicine`

INFO `sabbatini@turing.unicamp.br` (Renato M.E. Sabbatini)

MIRRORS

`ftp://sunsite.unc.edu/pub/academic/medicine/brazil`

`ftp://qmec.herston.uq.oz.au/QMECServer/Pub/Brazil`

Comments: All files are stored in ZIP format. Some include the source.

5104 **MEDITECH-L:** On Meditech's medical information software. *Mailing List*

± `majordomo@nic.iii.net`

OWNER `jml@iii.net` (Joseph Lapolito)

OWNER `lapolito@umassmed.ummed.edu` (Joseph Lapolito)

5105 **MEDNETS:** On the role of global computer networks in the clinical, research, and administrative areas of medicine. *Digest & Reflector*

± `listserv@vm1.nodak.edu` [body = SUBSCRIBE MEDNETS first-name last-name]

INFO OWNER `hoag@plains.nodak.edu` (Marty Hoag)

ARCHIVE `listserv@vm1.nodak.edu` [body = INDEX MEDNETS]

5106 **MMATRIX-L:** For the official American Medical Informatics Association Internet Working Group. *Mailing List*

± `listserv@www.kumc.edu` [body = SUBSCRIBE MMATRIX-L first-name last-name]

OWNER `lhancock@kumc.edu` (Lee Hancock)

5107 **Monitor:** This program is a Macintosh application for downloading, storing, and graphing physiological data in real time. Requires System 7.0 or greater.

`http://www.usyd.edu.au/su/anaes/Monitor.html`

`ftp://ftp.su.oz.au/anaes/Monitor`

INFO `jderrick@cuhk.hk` (James Derrick)

➤ **NRCH:** On health-care information systems: for managers and clinicians. (See entry 4881 for full listing.)

5108 **Proceedings of the 1995 Southeastern Medical Informatics Conference:** Proceedings of a conference held June 10, 1995, at the University of Florida. It includes 24 abstracts of scientific paper and poster presentations.

`http://www.med.ufl.edu/medinfo/smic95/smic95.html`

INFO `rrathe@ufl.edu` (Richard Rathe, MD)

5109 `sci.engr.biomed` Discussing the field of biomedical engineering. *Newsgroup*

5110 `sci.med.informatics` Computer applications in medical care. *Newsgroup*

5111 `sci.med.telemedicine` Hospital/physician networks. No diagnosis questions. *Newsgroup*

5112 **Telemedicine Information Exchange (TIE):** Searchable databases of telemedicine information including: citations and abstracts of telemedicine-related articles from legal, business, medical, and technical sources; details of active telemedicine programs; upcoming meetings in the field; and sources of funding.

`http://tie.telemed.org/`

INFO `library@telemed.org` (information issues)

INFO `tieadmin@telemed.org` (technical issues)

Comments: The TIE welcomes submissions of any new information on telemedicine, including meetings, programs, and publications. Submissions can be made using the online form available on the TIE WWW site, or by emailing them to `library@telemed.org`

➤ **University of California, Irvine. Medical Education Software Archive.:** This site contains the medical education software collection based at the University of California, Irvine. (See entry 4837 for full listing.)

WOMEN'S HEALTH

5113 Midwifery Internet Resources: Contains information about and instructions for accessing Internet resources for mid-wives.

> `http://www.csv.warwick.ac.uk:8000/midwifery-resources.html`
> **INFO** `cudma@csv.warwick.ac.uk` (Denis Anthony)

5114 `alt.support.menopause` Helping women through menopause. *Newsgroup*

5115 e-jog: Electronic Journal of OB/GYN: articles, case reports, clinical trials, reviews. *E-journal, moderated*

> ± `listserv@bcm.tmc.edu` [body = SUBSCRIBE E-JOG first-name last-name]
> **OWNER POST** `gklein@bcm.tmc.edu` (Geffrey H. Klein, MD)

➤ **FeMiNa:** According to maintainers, this is the only searchable database for woman- and girl-oriented sites on the Web. Very good women's health coverage. (See entry 10156 for full listing.)

5116 OB-GYN-L: A list for the obstetrician and gynecologist. *Mailing List*

> `http://www.bcm.tmc.edu/obgyn/obgyn-ce/ob-gyn.html`
> ± `listserv@bcm.tmc.edu` [body = SUBSCRIBE OB-GYN-L first-name last-name]
> **OWNER** `gklein@bcm.tmc.edu` (Geffrey H. Klein, MD)

➤ **Ovarian:** On ovarian cancer and other ovarian disorders: for patients, family, friends, researchers, and physicians. (See entry 4739 for full listing.)

5117 PRENAT-L: For data and information on perinatal outcomes, and access to—and outcomes of—prenatal care. *Mailing List*

> ± `listserv@health.state.ny.us` [body = SUBSCRIBE PRENAT-L first-name last-name]
> **INFO** `cmb04@health.state.ny.us` (Colene Byrne)

5118 WH-NEWS: A newsletter about women's health. *Newsletter*

> `http://www.son.washington.edu/`
> ± `listserv@uwavm.u.washington.edu` [body = SUBSCRIBE WH-NEWS first-name last-name]
> **INFO** `khayward@u.washington.edu` (Kendra Hayward)
> **ARCHIVE** `listserv@uwavm.u.washington.edu` [body = INDEX WH-NEWS]

5119 Women's Health Weekly: Newsweekly on women's health. Includes complete articles database.

> `http://www.newsfile.com/1w.htm`
> **INFO** `whw@yourhealthnet.com`

5120 WomenSpace: An area for young women and girls full of fun, uninhibiting information about health, relationships, sexuality, and a host of other information of special interest to young women and girls.

> `http://www.womenspace.com/`
> **INFO** `adormond@aol.com`

HUMANITIES & SOCIAL SCIENCES

➤ **SunSITE Academic Archives:** Software, documents, files, and more in most academic disciplines. (See entry 8895 for full listing.)

5121 `humanities.answers` Repository for periodic Usenet articles. *Moderated newsgroup*

5122 `humanities.misc` General topics in the arts and humanities. *Newsgroup*

5123 **ICPSR Bulletin:** Announcements of new data releases and updates to the holdings of the Inter-university Consortium for Political and Social Research, which offers access to the world's largest repository of computer-readable social science data for research and instruction. *Newsletter*

   EDITOR `netmail@icpsr.umich.edu` (Mary B. Vardigan)

   ARCHIVE `gopher://gopher.icpsr.umich.edu`

   Frequency: quarterly

5124 `school.subjects.humanities` Politics, religion, history, geography, etc. *Newsgroup*

ANTHROPOLOGY

5125 `alt.memetics` The evolution of ideas in societies. *Newsgroup*

5126 **ANTHRO-L:** On general anthropology. *Digest & Reflector*

   ± `listserv@ubvm.cc.buffalo.edu` [body = SUBSCRIBE ANTHRO-L first-name last-name]

   INFO `psmiller@acsu.buffalo.edu` (Patrick S. M. Miller, List Manager)

   INFO OWNER `antowner@ubvm.cc.buffalo.edu` (owners of Anthro-L)

➤ **Eastern European Jewish History (EEJH):** Forum for discussion of historical, archaeological, linguistic, cultural, genealogical, and genetic evidence on the Jewish people of eastern Europe from Greco-Roman times to the present. (See entry 5245 for full listing.)

5127 **galist:** On generative anthropology.

   ± `maiser@humnet.ucla.edu` [body = SUBSCRIBE GALIST]

5128 **Anthropoetics:** Publishes articles (and book reviews) relevant to generative anthropology and the theory of mimetic desire, on theoretical or literary-cultural subject matter. *E-Journal*

   `gopher://www.humnet.ucla.edu`

   `http://www.humnet.ucla.edu/Electronic Journals`

   ± `http://www.humnet.ucla.edu/Electronic Journals`

   INFO OWNER `anthro@humnet.ucla.edu` (Eric Gans)

   ARCHIVES

   `http://www.humnet.ucla.edu/Electronic Journals`

   `http://www.humnet.ucla.edu/humnet/anthropoetics/views/`

   Frequency: three issues per year (fall, winter, spring)

➤ **INDKNOW:** For indigenous knowledge systems, traditional ecological knowledge and development. (See entry 10071 for full listing.)

➤ **PURTOPOI:** On rhetoric, language, and professional writing. (See entry 4549 for full listing.)

5129 **QUALRS-L:** On qualitative research for the human sciences. *Mailing List*

   ± `listserv@uga.cc.uga.edu` [body = SUBSCRIBE QUALRS-L first-name last-name]

   INFO `jude@uga.cc.uga.edu` (Judith Preissle)

   ARCHIVE `listserv@uga.cc.uga.edu` [body = INDEX QUALRS-L]

   Gated: `bit.listserv.qualrs-l`

5130 `sci.anthropology` All aspects of studying humankind. *Newsgroup*

5131 `sci.anthropology.paleo` Evolution of man and other primates. *Newsgroup*

5132 **Theoretical Anthropology:** Reflects the diversity of the science and the scholars. Topics from all subdisciplines — social, visual, religious, aesthetic, of material culture, etc.—and related sciences are welcomed. *E-Journal*

INFO `theoretical.anthropology@univie.ac.at` (Thomas Fillitz and Ralph Fichtner)
ARCHIVE `http://www.univie.ac.at/voelkerkunde/theoretical-anthropology/`

➤ **XCULT-L:** For discussing intercultural communication. Topics range from nondominant cultures in the U.S. to corporate cultures to the use of nonverbal methods in international communication. (See entry 5180 for full listing.)

ARCHEOLOGY

5133 <u>**Internet Resources for Heritage Conservation, Historic Preservation, Archeology:**</u> Resources for professionals in the fields of restoration architecture, historic preservation, and archaeology; and all others interested in identification, protection, and management of cultural resources. Maintained by the National Center for Preservation Technology and Training, National Park Service.
`http://www.cr.nps.gov/ncptt/irg/`
`gopher://gopher.ncptt.nps.gov`
INFO `mcarroll@alpha.nsula.edu` (Mary S. Carroll)

5134 **ARCH-ARCTIC:** On arctic archaeology. *Mailing List*
± `maiser@natmus.min.dk`
OWNER `dok-lwh@palais.natmus.min.dk` (Lars Wilfred Hansen)
ARCHIVE `maiser@natmus.min.dk`

➤ **C14-L:** For technical discussion of radiocarbon and other radioisotope dating. (See entry 9313 for full listing.)

➤ `sci.anthropology.paleo`: Evolution of man and other primates. *Newsgroup*

5135 `sci.archaeology` Studying antiquities of the world. *Newsgroup*

5136 `sci.archaeology.mesoamerican` The field of meso-American archaeology. *Newsgroup*

AREAS & CULTURES

AREAS & CULTURES—AFRICAN-AMERICAN STUDIES

5137 **ABSLST-L:** For members of the Association of Black Sociologists and other interested scholars. *Mailing List*
± `listserv@cmuvm.csv.cmich.edu` [body = SUBSCRIBE ABSLST-L first-name last-name]
INFO `3zasib3@cmuvm.bitnet` (Robert G. Newby)
EDITOR `hildie@bucknell.edu`
Please Note: Subscription by approval only.

5138 **AFAM-L:** On African-American research. *Mailing List*
± `listserv@mizzou1.missouri.edu` [body = SUBSCRIBE AFAM-L first-name last-name]
INFO `elspaula@mizzou1.bitnet` (Paula Roper)
ARCHIVE `listserv@mizzou1.missouri.edu`

➤ **EDEQUITY:** On education equity in multiculturalism contexts. (See entry 4322 for full listing.)

5139 **Isis Pages:** Isis is a Web site devoted to the art and culture of women of African descent.
`http://www.netdiva.com/isisplus.html`

➤ **ONE:** A chronicle of progressive Black politics and culture that will fuse a diverse body of thought into one cohesive agenda: freedom of expression. (See entry 9697 for full listing.)

➤ **POS302-L:** Seminar-based college level discussion on race, ethnicity, and social inequality. (See entry 10064 for full listing.)

5140 `soc.culture.african.american` Discussions about African-American issues. *Newsgroup*

AREAS & CULTURES—AMERICAN STUDIES

5141 `alt.culture.us.1960s` Discussion of 1960s culture (US and world). *Newsgroup*

5142 `alt.culture.us.1970s` At least pick a *good* decade to be stuck in the past. *Newsgroup*

5143 `alt.culture.us.1980s` The Me Decade. *Newsgroup*

5144 **SIXTIES-L:** For interdisciplinary discussion of the cultures and politics of the 1960s in the U.S. and internationally. *Mailing List, moderated*
`http://jefferson.village.virginia.edu/sixties/home.html`
± `listproc@jefferson.village.virginia.edu` [body = subscribe `sixties-l` first-name last-name]
OWNER `kalital@minerva.cis.yale.edu` (Kali Tal)
ARCHIVE `gopher://jefferson.village.virginia.edu`

AREAS & CULTURES—ASIAN AMERICAN STUDIES

➤ **EDEQUITY:** On education equity in multiculturalism contexts. (See entry 4322 for full listing.)

➤ **POS302-L:** Seminar-based college level discussion on race, ethnicity, and social inequality. (See entry 10064 for full listing.)

AREAS & CULTURES—ASIAN STUDIES

5145 **Asian Studies Newsletter:** The newsletter is issued five times a year and includes notices of fellowships, grants, and conferences, as well as a job-placement registry and information from the Secretariat. *Newsletter*
`http://www.easc.indiana.edu/~aas`
± `postmaster@aasianst.org`
INFO OWNER `jalewis@indiana.edu` (Jason Lewis)
ARCHIVE `jalewis@indiana.edu` (Jason Lewis)
Frequency: five times a year

5146 **CHINA:** Chinese studies list. *Mailing List, moderated*
± `listserv@pucc.princeton.edu` [body = SUBSCRIBE CHINA first-name last-name]
INFO `q4356@pucc.bitnet` (Tom Nimick and David Wright)
ARCHIVE `listserv@pucc.princeton.edu`
Comments: Subscription requests will be sent to list owners for approval. Owners require that all participants agree to abide by list guidelines.

5147 **CJKLIB-L:** For members of the European Association of Sinological Librarians (EASL) and anyone interested in the subject of librarianship of print materials in the languages of Chinese, Japanese, and Korean. *Mailing List*
`http://sun.sino.uni-heidelberg.de/sin/easl/easl.html`
± `listserv@vm.urz.uni-heidelberg.de` [body = SUBSCRIBE CJKLIB-L first-name last-name]
INFO `g42@vm.urz.uni-heidelberg.de` (Thomas Hahn)
ARCHIVE `gopher://gopher.urz.uni-heidelberg.de/11/subject/hd/fak8/sin/cjklib-l`

➤ **ID-Line:** An idea exchange for Chinese communication scholars. (See entry 5175 for full listing.)

5148 `soc.culture.asian.american` Issues and discussion about Asian-Americans. *Newsgroup*

5149 `tnn.culture.asia` Newsgroup for the whole culture of Asia. *Newsgroup*

5150 `tnn.forum.asia-economy-p` Asian economy and politics information exchange. *Newsgroup*

AREAS & CULTURES—EUROPEAN STUDIES

5151 **Central European Regional Research Organization (CERRO):** Information about the economic restructuring of central Europe.
`gopher://gopher.wu-wien.ac.at/11/.cerro.ind/`
INFO `gunther.maier@wu-wien.ac.at`

➤ **Eastern European Jewish History (EEJH):** Forum for discussion of historical, archaeological, linguistic, cultural, genealogical, and genetic evidence on the Jewish people of eastern Europe from Greco-Roman times to the present. (See entry 5245 for full listing.)

AREAS & CULTURES—LATIN AMERICAN STUDIES

5152 **CANALC:** Canadian Association for Latin American and Caribbean Studies. *Mailing List*

± listserv@vm1.yorku.ca [body = SUBSCRIBE CANALC first-name last-name]

INFO lanfran@yorku.ca (Sam Lanfranco)

Language: English, Spanish, Portuguese

➤ **EDEQUITY:** On education equity in multiculturalism contexts. (See entry 4322 for full listing.)

5153 `soc.culture.latin-america` Topics about Latin America. *Newsgroup*

5154 **University of Texas—Latin American Network Information Center:** The objective is to provide Latin American users with access to academic databases and information services worldwide, and to provide Latin Americanists around the world with access to the information on and from Latin America.

http://lanic.utexas.edu/

gopher://lanic.utexas.edu

INFO info@lanic.utexas.edu

AREAS & CULTURES—MIDDLE EAST STUDIES

5155 **ABZU: A Guide to Ancient Near East Studies:** Abzu is an experimental guide to the rapidly increasing and widely distributed data relevant to the study and public presentation of the Ancient Near East via the Internet.

http://www-oi.uchicago.edu/OI/DEPT/RA/ABZU/ABZU.HTML

INFO cejo@midway.uchicago.edu (Charles E. Jones, Editor)

AREAS & CULTURES—RUSSIAN & EAST EUROPEAN STUDIES

5156 **Slavic Review:** American quarterly of Russian, Eurasian, and east European studies. *E-Journal*

± gopher://ccat.sas.upenn.edulynx

± http://ccat.sas.upenn.edu/slavrev/slavrev.html

INFO slavrev@sas.upenn.edu (Richard Frost)

OWNER aaass@hcs.harvard.edu (American Assn. for the Advancement of Slavic Studies)

Frequency: quarterly

CLASSICS

➤ `alt.etext:` Texts made available for electronic redistribution. *Newsgroup*

➤ **ANCIEN-L:** On the history of the ancient Mediterranean. (See entry 5234 for full listing.)

➤ **Bryn Mawr Reviews:** Umbrella list for the Bryn Mawr Medieval Review, and the Bryn Mawr Classical Review both of which are about scholarly literature in the humanities, including: conference announcements, news bulletins, commentary, reviews, and dialogue. (See entry 5275 for full listing.)

5157 **Canadian Classical Bulletin/Bulletin canadien des etudes:** Canadian Classical Bulletin/Bulletin canadien des études anciennes newsletter. *Newsletter*

http://137.122.12.15/Docs/Societies/ClassAC/Classic.Assoc.html

gopher://tornade.ere.umontreal.ca:7071

INFO kkinzl@trentu.ca (Professor Konrad H. Kinzl)

Language: English and French

Frequency: monthly or bimonthly

5158 **CLASSICS:** On all aspects of classical Greek and Latin scholarship. *Mailing List*

± listproc@u.washington.edu [body = SUBSCRIBE CLASSICS first-name last-name]

INFO lwright@cac.washington.edu (Linda Wright)

ARCHIVE http://weber.u.washington.edu/~lwright/classics.html

5159 **Classics Ireland:** Journal of Classical Association of Ireland, publishing articles on classics, ancient history, and archaeology. *E-Journal*

http://www.ucd.ie/~classics/ClassicsIreland.html

INFO andrew.erskine@ucd.ie (Andrew Erskine)

EDITOR urbain@macollamh.ucd.ie (Theresa Urbainczyk)

ARCHIVE http://www.ucd.ie/~classics/ClassicsIreland.html

Frequency: yearly

➤ **LATIN-L:** For Latin and NeoLatin discussions. (See entry 5296 for full listing.)

5160 `sci.classics` Studying classical history, languages, art, and more. *Newsgroup*

5161 **TLG:** The Thesaurus Linguae Graecae information server offers information about the TLG.

http://www.tlg.uci.edu/~tlg

gopher://tlg.cwis.uci.edu:7011/11/

INFO tlg@uci.edu

COMMUNICATIONS

5162 <u>Journalism/Comm schools:</u> A compilation of communications, journalism, and media sites in universities around the world by Ana Camargos, a graduate student at the University of Florida.

http://www.jou.ufl.edu/commres/jouwww.htm

INFO anacamargos@ufcc.ufl.edu

➤ **ACTLab (Advanced Communication Technologies Laboratory):** Information on issues of human-computer interfaces, interaction, and agency. (See entry 9358 for full listing.)

➤ `alt.memetics`: The evolution of ideas in societies. *Newsgroup*

5163 `alt.speech.debate` High school and collegiate debate and forensics. *Newsgroup*

5164 `alt.speech.misc` Various speech and forensics topics. *Newsgroup*

➤ **ARCO:** On art and literature, psychology and communication. (See entry 278 for full listing.)

5165 **COMLIB-L:** On communication libraries and librarians. *Mailing List*

± listserv@ukcc.uky.edu [body = SUB COMLIB-L first-name last-name]

EDITOR rjones@ukcc.uky.edu (Reinette F. Jones)

5166 **Computer-Mediated Communication Magazine:** People, events, applications, and research related to computer-mediated communication (CMC). *E-Journal*

http://www.december.com/cmc/mag/current/toc.html

INFO john@december.com

ARCHIVE http://www.december.com/cmc/mag/index.html

Frequency: monthly

5167 **CONTEMPORANEA:** On communication and contemporary culture. *Mailing List*

± listproc@ufba.br [body = SUBSCRIBE CONTEMPORANEA first-name last-name]

OWNER palacios@ufba.br (Marcos Silva Palacios)

OWNER wilsonsg@ufba.br (Wilson da Silva Gomes)

Language: Portugese, English & Others

5168 **Critical Mass:** On mass communication and cultural change. *E-Journal*

http://fas.sfu.ca/comm/c-mass/c-mass.html

INFO OWNER murrayb@sfu.ca (Pam Murray)

INFO OWNER cmass-info@sfu.ca

ARCHIVE http://fas.sfu.ca/comm/c-mass/c-mass.html

Frequency: monthly

5169 **CRTNET:** A magazine about communication research and theory. *Mailing List, moderated*

± listserv@psuvm.psu.edu [body = SUBSCRIBE CRTNET first-name last-name]

INFO t3b@psuvm.psu.edu (Tom Benson)

ARCHIVE listserv@psuvm.psu.edu [body = INDEX CRTNET]

5170 CRTNet (Communication Research and Theory Network): All topics related to human communications. *Newsletter*
± `listserv@psuvm.bitnet` [body = SUBSCRIBE CRTNET first-name last-name]
INFO `t3b@psuvm.psu.edu` (Tom Benson)
ARCHIVE `listserv@psuvm.bitnet` [body = INDEX CRTNET]
Frequency: irregular

5171 EJournal: Electronic networks and "texts"; theory and practice; social, psychological, economic, artistic implications and more. Peer-reviewed. *E-Journal*
± `listserv@albany.edu` [body = SUBSCRIBE EJRNL first-name last-name]
INFO EDITOR `ejournal@albany.edu` (Ted Jennings, Editor)
ARCHIVES
`ftp://hanover.edu/` gopher, University at Albany Library
`listserv@albany.edu` [body = INDEX EJRNL]
Frequency: irregular

5172 Electronic Journal of Communication: Bilingual English/French academic journal devoted to the study of communication theory, research, practice, and policy. *E-Journal*
± `comserve@vm.its.rpi.edu` [body = JOIN EJCREC]
INFO `support@vm.its.rpi.edu` (Timothy Stephen or Teresa Harrison)
INFO `harrison@vm.its.rpi.edu` (Teresa M. Harrison)
ARCHIVES
`comserve@vm.its.rpi.edu` [body = SEND EJCREC DIRECTRY]
`gopher://gopher.cic.net`
Language: French & English
Frequency: four issues per volume, one volume a year

5173 EMPATHY: For teachers of interpersonal communication courses. *Mailing List, moderated*
± `listserv@uga.cc.uga.edu` [body = SUBSCRIBE EMPATHY first-name last-name]
OWNER `edwards@uga.cc.uga.edu` (Bill Edwards)
ARCHIVE `listserv@uga.cc.uga.edu` [body = INDEX EMPATHY]

5174 H-RHETOR: On the history of rhetoric, writing, and communication; part of H-NET. *Mailing List, moderated*
± `listserv@uicvm.uic.edu` [body = SUBSCRIBE H-RHETOR first-name last-name affiliation]
EDITOR `gary_hatch@byu.edu` (Gary L. Hatch)
EDITOR `lvavra@uic.edu` (Linda Vavra)

5175 ID-Line: An idea exchange for Chinese communication scholars. *Mailing List*
± `listserv@uriacc.uri.edu` [body = SUBSCRIBE ID-LINE first-name last-name]
INFO `cqm101@uriacc.bitnet` (Guo-Ming Chen)

➤ **Information Sources: the Internet and Computer Mediated Communication:** This list's purpose is to collect, organize, and present information describing the Internet and computer-mediated communication technologies, applications, culture, discussion forums, and bibliographies. (See entry 2764 for full listing.)

➤ **McLuhan-List:** To revitalize and update the work of the late media guru (Marchall McLuhan). (See entry 6094 for full listing.)

➤ **MEME:** On cyberspace and its social impact from a historical point of view. (See entry 9829 for full listing.)

5176 NETCOMTALK: An interactive journal about the College of Communication at Boston University, featuring faculty and student articles as well as student photography (also includes new multimedia lab feature). *E-Journal*
`http://web.bu.edu/COM/communication.html`
INFO `wlord@bu.edu` (Professor William Lord)
ARCHIVE `http://web.bu.edu/COM/communication.html`
Frequency: updated daily

5177 **Newsline:** Newsletter that describes additions to or changes in Comserve, the electronic information and discussion service for communication faculty and students. *Newsletter*

± comserve@vm.its.rpi.edu [body = SUBSCRIBE NEWSLINE]

INFO support@vm.its.rpi.edu (Timothy Stephen or Teresa Harrison)

ARCHIVE comserve@vm.its.rpi.edu [body = SEND NEWS DIRECTRY]

Frequency: irregular

➤ **The Red Rock Eater News Service:** All the news that Phil Agre, media and communications professor at UCSD, thinks fit to print on the subject of how technology affects peoples' lives. (See entry 3732 for full listing.)

➤ **RELIGCOM:** On religious communication and communication in religious contexts. (See entry 8866 for full listing.)

5178 **The Satellite TV Page:** The Satellite TV (and radio) page puts together a collection of various Web sites focusing on satellites. Included are a collection of satellite TV images, the Satellite Journal International Archives, FAQ sites, a collection of network and cable TV home pages, as well as other miscellaneous satellite-related links.

http://itre.ncsu.edu/misc/sat.html

INFO jay@itre.ncsu.edu

➤ **SPEED:** SPEED: An Electronic Journal of Technology, Media, and Society provides a forum for the critical investigation of technology, media, and society. (See entry 6097 for full listing.)

5179 **TEXT21-L:** On technology and the written word. *Mailing List*

http://las.alfred.edu/

± listserv@bigvax.alfred.edu [text21]

OWNER text21@bigvax.alfred.edu (Text21)

5180 **XCULT-L:** For discussing intercultural communication. Topics range from nondominant cultures in the U.S. to corporate cultures to the use of nonverbal methods in international communication. *Mailing List*

± listserv@psuvm.psu.edu [body = SUBSCRIBE XCULT-L first-name last-name]

INFO xcult-l-request@psuvm.psu.edu

ARCHIVE listserv@psuvm.psu.edu [body = INDEX XCULT-L]

CULTURAL STUDIES

5181 **CONTENT:** On content analysis of text and images: theory and practice. *Mailing List*

± listproc@listproc.gsu.edu [body = SUBSCRIBE CONTENT first-name last-name]

OWNER evans@gsu.edu (Bill Evans)

➤ **CTHEORY / Canadian Journal of Political and Social Theory:** An international review focusing on theory, technology, and culture from a critical perspective. (See entry 5359 for full listing.)

5182 **Cultural Interaction:** On the interdisciplinary study of encounters between cultures. *E-Journal*

http://www.gold.ac.uk/history/ci/ci.htm

INFO d.keown@gold.ac.uk (Damien Keown)

INFO davdean@ccs.carleton.ca (David Dean)

Frequency: No "issues" as such: articles published individually

5183 **DE PROVERBIO:** An electronic journal of international proverb studies. *E-Journal*

http://info.utas.edu.au/docs/flonta/

± INFO EDITOR deproverbio.editor@modlang.utas.edu.au (Teodor Flonta)

Language: English, Romance Languages

Frequency: twice a year

5184 **Depth Probe:** Depth Probe presents perspectives and historical influences of the 1990s American experience via reviews, dreams, and commentary. *E-Journal*

http://www.neo.com/Depthprobe/zine/index/home.html

± INFO alan@sirius.com (Alan Eyzaguirre)

ARCHIVE http://www.neo.com/Depthprobe/zine/index/home.html

Frequency: weekly

5185 **DERRIDA:** On Jacques Derrida and deconstruction. *Mailing List*

`http://www.cas.usf.edu/journal/index.html`

± `listserv@cfrvm.bitnet` [body = SUBSCRIBE DERRIDA first-name last-name]

INFO `erben@moyi.cas.usf.edu` (David Erben)

Please Note: Subscription by approval only.

5186 **Postmodern Culture:** Ranges from analytical essays and reviews to video scripts and other new literary forms, opening discussion of postmodernism to a wide audience. The Web version includes video clips, sound clips, and still images. *E-Journal*

`http://jefferson.village.virginia.edu/pmc/contents.all.html`

`ftp://ftp.ncsu.edu/pub/ncsu/pmc`

`gopher://jefferson.village.virginia.edu/pub/pubs/pmc`

± `listserv@listserv.ncsu.edu` [body = SUBSCRIBE PMC-LIST first-name last-name]

INFO POST `pmc@jefferson.village.virginia.edu`

ARCHIVES

`ftp://ftp.ncsu.edu/pub/ncsu/pmc`

`gopher://jefferson.village.virginia.edu/pub/pubs/pmc`

Frequency: three times per year (September, January, May)

➤ **SIXTIES-L:** For interdisciplinary discussion of the cultures and politics of the 1960s in the U.S. and internationally. (See entry 5144 for full listing.)

➤ **VICTORIA:** For sharing of ideas and information about all aspects of 19th-century British culture and society. (See entry 5270 for full listing.)

ECONOMICS

➤ **Business Sources on the Internet:** This site lists business sources available on the Internet. Resources listed include: Web and gopher servers, telnet services, mailing lists, lists and directories of commercial sites, company and financial information, country-specific business resources, government, statistical, economic, market and industry-specific resources, and a list of news sources. (See entry 1651 for full listing.)

➤ **Health Economics: Places to Go:** A list of sites on the Internet related to the economics of health care. It includes sections on pharmacoeconomics, public health, and managed care. (See entry 4688 for full listing.)

➤ **Antitrust Policy:** An online resource linking economic research, policy, and legal cases. The site includes a public discussion area, information on current antitrust actions, and other related information including price-fixing, mergers, and vertical restraints. (See entry 5529 for full listing.)

➤ **CED-NET:** Discussion on the trends, opportunities, and changes in community economic development. The list's goal is to focus on what communities can do for themselves in terms of programs and funds, among other things. (See entry 9757 for full listing.)

➤ **Central European Regional Research Organization (CERRO):** Information about the economic restructuring of central Europe. (See entry 5151 for full listing.)

5187 `clari.apbl.reports.economy` General economic reports. *Newsgroup*

5188 `clari.biz.economy` Economic news and indicators. *Moderated newsgroup*

5189 `clari.biz.economy.usa` News of the U.S. economy. *Moderated newsgroup*

5190 `clari.biz.economy.world` Economy stories for non-U.S. countries. *Moderated newsgroup*

5191 **Communications for a Sustainable Future:** An interdisciplinary effort to facilitate more rapid change in social thought toward a viable future. This resource provides a collection of archives and mailing lists on sustainability.

`http://csf.colorado.edu/`

INFO `roper@csf.colorado.edu`

5192 `comp.soft-sys.shazam` The SHAZAM econometrics computer program. *Newsgroup*

5193 Computational Economics Gopher: Papers, publications, and databases, and conferences in computational economics.
`gopher://gopher.sara.nl/Computational Economics`
INFO `amman@sara.nl`

5194 Economic-Growth: For researchers working in the field of economic growth. *Mailing List, moderated*
± `majordomo@ufsia.ac.be` [body = `SUBSCRIBE ECONOMIC-GROWTH`]
OWNER `dse.vanhoudt.p@alpha.ufsia.ac.be` (Patrick VANHOUDT)

5195 EE-ECON: On general economic issues in central and Eastern Europe, and in the NIS. *Mailing List*
± `listproc@cep.nonprofit.net` [body = `SUBSCRIBE EE-ECON` first-name last-name]
OWNER `cep@minerva.cis.yale.edu` (Civic Education Project)

5196 EH-NEWS: For economic history-related material of general interest. *Mailing List, moderated*
`http://cs.muohio.edu/`
± `lists@cs.muohio.edu` [body = `SUBSCRIBE` first-name last-name institution]
INFO `help@cs.muohio.edu`
EDITOR `swilliamson@cs.muohio.edu` (Samuel H. Williamson, Miami University)
Comments: Sponsored by the Cliometric Society

5197 EH.DISC: On teaching and research in economic history. *Mailing List, moderated*
`http://cs.muohio.edu/`
± `lists@cs.muohio.edu` [body = `SUBSCRIBE EH.DISC` first-name last-name]
INFO `csociety@cs.muohio.edu`
ARCHIVE `http://cs.muohio.edu/Archives`
Please Note: Subscription by approval only.

5198 EH.EASTBLOC: On the economic history of the Eastern Bloc countries. *Mailing List, moderated*
`http://cs.muohio.edu/`
± `lists@cs.muohio.edu` [body = `SUBSCRIBE EH.EASTBLOC` first-name last-name institution]
INFO `help@cs.muohio.edu`
EDITOR `steiner@rummelplatz.uni-mannheim.de` (Andre Steiner)
Comments: Sponsored by the Cliometric Society

5199 EH.MACRO: On macroeconomic history: business cycles, long-run growth and productivity, and interaction between goods and financial markets. *Mailing List, moderated*
`http://cs.muohio.edu/`
± `lists@cs.muohio.edu` [body = `SUBSCRIBE EH.MACRO` first-name last-name institution]
± `business`
INFO `help@cs.muohio.edu`
EDITOR `bdelong@cs.muohio.edu` (J. Bradford DeLong)
EDITOR `ljohnston@cs.muohio.edu`
Comments: Sponsored by the Cliometric Society

5200 EH.RES: For requests for information and brief responses directly related to research in the subject of economic history. *Mailing List*
`http://cs.muohio.edu/`
± `lists@cs.muohio.edu` [body = `SUBSCRIBE EH.RES` first-name last-name]
EDITOR `jrosenbloom@cs.muohio.edu` (Joshua Rosenbloom)
Comments: Sponsored by the Cleometric Society

5201 ekonomika: On the Czech economy. *Mailing List*
± `listserv@vse.cz` [body = `SUBSCRIBE EKONOMIKA` first-name last-name]
OWNER `xmedh02@manes.vse.cz` (Hynek Med)
Language: Czech

5202   `fj.sci.economics` Discussion on economics. *Newsgroup*

➤   `fj.soc.economy`:   Topics about economy and economic policies. *Newsgroup*

5203   **GLOBAL.CHANGE:** For discussion among economic historians and others engaged in the study of major, long-run structural changes in economic and social organization. *Mailing List, moderated*

     `http://cs.muohio.edu/`

     ± `lists@cs.muohio.edu` [body = SUBSCRIBE GLOBAL.CHANGE first-name last-name institution]

     INFO `help@cs.muohio.edu`

     EDITOR `kharley@cs.muohio.edu` (C. Knick Harley)

     EDITOR `korourke@cs.muohio.edu` (Kevin J. O'Rourke)

     EDITOR `ataylor@cs.muohio.edu` (Alan M. Taylor)

     Comments: Sponsored by the Cliometric Society

5204   **H-Business:** On business history. *Mailing List, moderated*

     ± `lists@cs.muohio.edu` [body = SUBSCRIBE H-BUSINESS first-name last-name institution]

     INFO `help@cs.muohio.edu`

     EDITOR `jatack@cs.muohio.edu` (Jeremy Atack)

     EDITOR `akerr@cs.muohio.edu` (Austin Kerr)

     ARCHIVE `http://cs.muohio.edu/`

     Comments: Jointly sponsored by the Cliometric Society, the Business History Conference, and H-Net

➤   **Industry Canada:** This site was created to promote jobs and growth in Canada in a world characterized by global integration and the growth of knowledge-based economies. (See entry 7144 for full listing.)

➤   **International Trade Law Project (ITLP):** Network resources for legal research and education in the field of international trade law. (See entry 5567 for full listing.)

5205   **Internet Economics Collection:** The economics of the Internet, information goods, intellectual property, and related issues.

     `http://www.sims.berkeley.edu/resources/infoecon/`

     INFO `infoecon@sims.berkeley.edu`

5206   **Journal of Financial Abstracts:** Abstracts of major working and accepted papers in financial economics, organized into five categories: corporate finance, real estate, derivatives, banking and economics, and capital markets. *E-Journal*

     `http://www.crimson.com/fen`

     ± `sandy_barnes@journal.com`

     INFO `paul_hopper@socsci.com`

     INFO `michael_jensen@socsci.com`

     Frequency: daily

     Price: varying fees

➤   **Journal of World-Systems Research:** Research articles and theoretical discussions relevant to the study of the modern world-system and earlier regional intersocietal networks. (See entry 5282 for full listing.)

5207   **OMRI Economic Digest:** Coverage of economic developments in the former Soviet Union and east-central and southeastern Europe. *Newsletter*

     INFO `econ@omri.cz`

     Frequency: weekly

➤   **People's Tribune:** Devoted to the proposition that an economic system that can't or won't feed, clothe, and house its people ought to be changed. (See entry 5666 for full listing.)

5208   **QUANHIST.RECURRENT:** On comparative approaches to history and economic history. *Mailing List, moderated*

     ± `lists@cs.muohio.edu` [body = SUBSCRIBE QUANHIST.RECURRENT first-name last-name institution]

     INFO `help@cs.muohio.edu`

     EDITOR `fgalassi@cs.muohio.edu` (Francesco Galassi)

     EDITOR `broehner@cs.muohio.edu` (Bertrand Roehner)

ARCHIVE `http://cs.muohio.edu/`

Comments: Sponsored by the Cliometric Society

5209 **RIP-POL-ECON:** On international political economy: understanding and facilitating social change. *Mailing List*

± `mailbase@mailbase.ac.uk` [body = `join RIP-POL-ECON` first-name last-name]

INFO `ripe@sussex.ac.uk` (Angus Cameron)

ARCHIVE `gopher://mailbase.ac.uk/11/lists-p-t/rip-pol-econ`

5210 `sci.econ` The science of economics. *Newsgroup*

5211 `sci.econ.research` Research in all fields of economics. *Moderated newsgroup*

➤ **Studies in Nonlinear Dynamics and Econometrics:** The SNDE is formed in recognition that advances in statistics and dynamical systems theory may increase our understanding of economic and financial markets. The journal seeks both theoretical and applied papers. (See entry 1782 for full listing.)

5212 **Turku School of Economics:** Information service of the Turku School of Economics and Business Administration, Turku, Finland.

`http://www.tukkk.fi/`

INFO `webmaster@tukkk.fi`

5213 **Vienna University of Economics CWIS:** Campus wide information service for Vienna University of Economics.

`http://www.wu-wien.ac.at/`

INFO `webmaster@wu-wien.ac.at`

ETHNOMUSICOLOGY

5214 **ETHMUS-L:** EthnoFORUM, a global ethnomusicology forum. *Mailing List, moderated*

`http://www.inform.umd.edu:8080/EdRes/ReadingRoom/Newsletters/EthnoMusicology`

± `listserv@umdd.umd.edu` [body = `SUBSCRIBE ETHMUS-L` first-name last-name]

INFO `signell@umdd.bitnet` (Dr. Karl Signell)

Please Note: Subscription by approval only.

Comments: Subscription is limited to networkers with a professional interest in ethnomusicology: professors, graduate students, researchers, and librarians.

5215 **Ethnomusicology Online:** Scholarly and general audience resources on music of the world. Includes peer-reviewed articles and reviews, general articles, links to ethnomusicology resources, and examples of Web-assisted teaching.

`http://www.wiu.edu/efhm`

`http://umbc.edu/eol`

INFO `signell@umbc.edu` (Karl Signell)

5216 **Ethnomusicology Online (EOL):** Multimedia ethnomusicology Web site with journal for scholars, resources for general public. *E-journal & Web site*

`http://umbc.edu/eol`

GENDER STUDIES

5217 `alt.fan.camille-paglia` Amy Fisher would understand. *Newsgroup*

➤ **ASC-L:** On academic sexual correctness: privacy, consent, and institutional encroachment. (See entry 4091 for full listing.)

➤ **EDEQUITY:** On education equity in multiculturalism contexts. (See entry 4322 for full listing.)

➤ **Isis Pages:** Isis is a Web site devoted to the art and culture of women of African descent. (See entry 5139 for full listing.)

5218 **MEDGAY-L:** On gay-lesbian medieval studies—official list of the Society for the Study of Homosexuality in the Middle Ages. *Mailing List*

± `listserv@ksuvm.ksu.edu` [body = `SUBSCRIBE MEDGAY-L` first-name last-name]

INFO `rclark@ksuvm.bitnet` (Robert Clark)

ARCHIVE `listserv@ksuvm.ksu.edu`

➤ **Paglia-L:** On the writings and ideas of Dr. Camille Paglia. (See entry 10161 for full listing.)

➤ **WIG-L:** On the feminist study of German literature. (See entry 622 for full listing.)

5219 **WMST-L:** For scholarly discussion of women's-studies teaching, research, and program administration. *Mailing List*

INFO `korenman@umbc2.umbc.edu` (Joan Korenman)

ARCHIVES

`listserv@umdd.umd.edu`

`http://inform.umd.edu:86/Educational_Resources/AcademicResourcesByTopic/WomensStudie`
`s/`

GENEALOGY

5220 **ANCANACH:** For the members of the Clan Henderson Society of U.S./Canada, a Scottish heritage and geneology organization. *Mailing List, moderated*

± `listserv@uabdpo.dpo.uab.edu` [body = SUBSCRIBE ANCANACH first-name last-name]

INFO `0004241803@mcimail.com` (Henry N. McCarl)

INFO `edancan@aol.com` (Russell Henderson)

OWNER `busf038@uabdpo.dpo.uab.edu` (Henry N. McCarl)

ARCHIVE `listserv@uabdpo.dpo.uab.edu`

Please Note: Subscription by approval only.

5221 **Everton's Genealogical Helper:** On genealogy in the online world. *Not* an online edition of our print magazine, *Everton's Genealogical Helper,* but a separate publication. *Newsletter*

`http://www.everton.com/`

± INFO `ghonline@everton.com` (Jay Hall)

Frequency: twice monthly

5222 **GEDCOM-L:** For discussion of the enhancement of GEnealogical Data COMmunication. *Mailing List*

± `listserv@vm1.nodak.edu` [body = SUBSCRIBE GEDCOM-L first-name last-name]

OWNER `cmanis@csf.com` (Cliff Manis)

ARCHIVE `listserv@vm1.nodak.edu` [body = INDEX GEDCOM-L]

➤ **GER-RUS:** On Germans from Russia. (See entry 7311 for full listing.)

5223 **LINES-L:** For discussing enhancements to LifeLines Genealogical Database and Report Generator, an experimental genealogical software for Unix. *Mailing List*

± `listserv@vm1.nodak.edu` [body = SUBSCRIBE LINES-L first-name last-name]

INFO OWNER `cmanis@csoftec.csf.com` (Cliff Manis)

ARCHIVE `listserv@vm1.nodak.edu` [body = INDEX LINES-L]

Gated: `bit.listserv.lines-l`

5224 **ROOTS-L:** On genealogical matters. *Mailing List*

± `listserv@mail.eworld.com` [body = SUBSCRIBE ROOTS-L first-name last-name]

OWNER `alf.christophersen@basalmed.uio.no` (Alf Christophersen)

OWNER `karen@rand.org` (Karen Isaacson)

OWNER `cchase@cecasun.utc.edu` (Dan Chase)

OWNER `jdcoates@cintech.com` (John Coates)

OWNER `chance@eskimo.com` (Vicki Lindsay)

OWNER `cmains@progcons.com` (Cliff Manis)

OWNER `salter@interramp.com` (John Salter)

5225 `soc.genealogy.african` Genealogy of Africa and the African Diaspora. *Newsgroup*

5226 `soc.genealogy.australia+nz` Australia, New Zealand, and their territories. *Newsgroup*

HISTORY

➤ **The Conspiracy Page:** Well-rounded guide to net resources on conspiracy and secret histories. (See entry 9765 for full listing.)

5227 **AERA-F:** For exchange of information among scholars and researchers studying educational history and historiography. *Mailing List, moderated*

± `listserv@asuvm.inre.asu.edu` [body = SUBSCRIBE AERA-F first-name last-name]

INFO `dsoucy@unb.ca` (Don Soucy)

INFO `glass@asu.edu` (Gene V. Glass, Editor)

5228 `alt.history.what-if` What would the net have been like without this group? *Newsgroup*

5229 `alt.revisionism` "It *can't* be that way 'cause here's the *facts*". *Newsgroup*

5230 `alt.war` Not just collateral damage. *Newsgroup*

5231 `alt.war.civil.usa` Discussion of the U.S. Civil War (1861-1865). *Newsgroup*

5232 `alt.war.korea` Open discussions on topics dealing with the Korean War. *Newsgroup*

5233 `alt.war.vietnam` Discussion of all aspects of the Vietnam War. *Newsgroup*

5234 **ANCIEN-L:** On the history of the ancient Mediterranean. *Mailing List*

± `listserv@ulkyvm.louisville.edu` [body = SUBSCRIBE ANCIEN-L first-name last-name]

INFO `jacock01@ulkyvm.bitnet` (Jim Cocks)

ARCHIVE `listserv@ulkyvm.louisville.edu` [body = INDEX ANCIEN-L]

5235 **ANSAX-L:** Scholarly discussions on topics in Anglo-Saxon studies (7th to 11th centuries). *Mailing List*

± `listserv@wvnvm.wvnet.edu` [body = SUBSCRIBE ANSAX-L first-name last-name]

OWNER `u47c2@wvnvm.bitnet`

OWNER `schipper@morgan.ucs.mun.ca` (William Schipper)

Please Note: Subscription by approval only.

5236 **ARCANA:** On occultism: history, literature, language, spells.

`http://remus.rutgers.edu/~woj/arcana/`

± `listserv@brownvm.brown.edu` [body = SUB ARCANA first-name last-name]

OWNER `arcana-request@brownvm.brown.edu` (Jae Walker)

Please Note: Subscription by approval only.

Comments: Prospective members must fill out a "profile form" before being added to the list.

➤ **ARIL-L:** Members of the Association for Religion and Intellectual Life, publisher of Cross Currents. (See entry 8775 for full listing.)

5237 **AZTLAN:** On pre-Columbian history—part of The History Network. *Mailing List*

± `listserv@ulkyvm.louisville.edu` [body = SUBSCRIBE AZTLAN first-name last-name]

OWNER `jacock01@ulkyvm.louisville.edu` (James A. Cocks)

ARCHIVE `listserv@ulkyvm.louisville.edu` [body = INDEX AZTLAN]

5238 **BiblioNumis-L:** On the literature of numismatics (study of coins). *Mailing List, moderated*

± `majordomo@netcom.com` [body = subscribe biblionumis-l]

OWNER `hwbass@netcom.com` (Harry Bass)

5239 `bit.listserv.history` History list. *Newsgroup*

5240 **C18-L:** For interdisciplinary discussion of the 18th century. *Mailing List*

± `listserv@psuvm.psu.edu` [body = SUBSCRIBE C18-L first-name last-name]

INFO `bcj@psuvm.psu.edu`

ARCHIVE `listserv@psuvm.psu.edu`

Language: English, French

➤ **CADUCEUS-L:** On the history of health sciences. (See entry 4913 for full listing.)

5241 `clari.apbl.today_history` Today in History feature. *Moderated newsgroup*

5242 `clari.living.history` News and human interest about history. *Newsgroup*

5243 `clari.living.history.today` Today in History feature. *Moderated newsgroup*

➤ **CW-REENACTORS:** Discussions of American Civil War reenacting. (See entry 6584 for full listing.)

5244 **DATABASES:** On the design and management of historical databases. *Mailing List, moderated*
    `http://cs.muohio.edu/`
    ± `lists@cs.muohio.edu` [body = SUBSCRIBE DATABASES first-name last-name institution]
    INFO `help@cs.muohio.edu`
    EDITOR `mgregson@cs.muohio.edu` (Mary Eschelbach Gregson)
    EDITOR `dschaefer@cs.muohio.edu` (Don Schaefer)
    Comments: Sponsored by the Cliometric Society

➤ **The DuPont Building, Burlington, Vermont:** Joanna Oltman's historic preservation project traces the history of the classic DuPont Building on the waterfront in Burlington, Vermont. (See entry 62 for full listing.)

5245 **Eastern European Jewish History (EEJH):** Forum for discussion of historical, archaeological, linguistic, cultural, genealogical, and genetic evidence on the Jewish people of eastern Europe from Greco-Roman times to the present. *Mailing List*
    ± `majordomo@ort.org` [body = SUBSCRIBE EEJH]
    INFO OWNER `kbrook@acad.bryant.edu` (Kevin Brook)
    Comments: Operated at ORT of London, United Kingdom, with the help of Mike Shain, Carolyn Shafran, and June Mares. Opened December 3, 1995. New subscribers always welcome!

5246 **ECCHST-L:** On ecclesiastical history: history of the church, Christianity, and theology. *Mailing List, moderated*
    ± `listserv@bgu.edu` [body = SUBSCRIBE ECCHST-L first-name last-name]
    OWNER `ugsingle@uxa.ecn.bgu.edu` (Gregory H. Singleton)

➤ **EH-NEWS:** For economic history-related material of general interest. (See entry 5196 for full listing.)

➤ **EH.EASTBLOC:** On the economic history of the Eastern Bloc countries. (See entry 5198 for full listing.)

➤ **EH.MACRO:** On macroeconomic history: business cycles, long-run growth and productivity, and interaction between goods and financial markets. (See entry 5199 for full listing.)

➤ **Electronic Journal of Australian and New Zealand History:** Historical documents and new work on Australian and New Zealand history. (See entry 7090 for full listing.)

➤ **GLOBAL.CHANGE:** For discussion among economic historians and others engaged in the study of major, long-run structural changes in economic and social organization. (See entry 5203 for full listing.)

5247 **H-AmRel:** On the influence of history on American religion. *Mailing List*
    ± `listserv@msu.edu` [body = SUBSCRIBE H-AMREL first-name last-name]
    EDITOR `ugsingle@uxa.ecn.bgu.edu` (Gregory H. Singleton)
    Please Note: Subscription by approval only.
    Comments: Part of H-Net

5248 **H-AMSTDY:** Research and professional news for American studies, part of The History Network (H-Net). *Mailing List, moderated*
    ± `listserv@uicvm.uic.edu` [body = SUBSCRIBE H-AMSTDY first-name last-name school/affiliation]
    OWNER `finlay_j@spcvxa.spc.edu` (Jeff Finlay)

➤ **H-Business:** On business history. (See entry 5204 for full listing.)

5249 **H-RURAL:** On the history of agriculture and rural areas. *Mailing List, moderated*
    ± `listserv@msu.edu` [body = SUBSCRIBE H-RURAL first-name last-name]
    INFO `joberly@uwec.edu`
    ARCHIVE `http://www.uwec.edu/Academic/History/rurweb.html`

5250 HISTORY: Scholarly dicussion of history; topics include history as a science, computers and historians, cultural development, cultural differences, and philosophy. *Digest & Reflector*

± `listserv@ukanvm.cc.ukans.edu` [body = SUBSCRIBE HISTORY first-name last-name]

ARCHIVE `listserv@ukanvm.cc.ukans.edu` [body = INDEX HISTORY]

Frequency: weekly

5251 HTECH-L: On the history of technology. *Mailing List*

± `listserv@sivm.si.edu` [body = SUBSCRIBE HTECH-L first-name last-name]

INFO `mah0h06@sivm.si.edu` (Steven Lubar)

ARCHIVE `listserv@sivm.si.edu`

➤ **Journal of Political Ecology:** Promoting interdisciplinary dialogue and research on the interface between political economy and ecology. (See entry 5279 for full listing.)

➤ **The Ladies Pavilion, Central Park, New York City:** Joanna Oltman's historic preservation project traces the history of one of Central Park's architectural gems, the Ladies' Pavilion. (See entry 64 for full listing.)

5252 LT-ANTIQ: On the "late antiquity" period. *Mailing List*

± `listserv@univscvm.csd.scarolina.edu` [body = SUBSCRIBE LT-ANTIQ first-name last-name]

OWNER `n330009@univscvm.csd.scarolina.edu` (Ralph W. Mathisen)

5253 MARHST-L: On maritime history and maritime museums. *Mailing List*

± `listserv@qucdn.queensu.ca` [body = SUBSCRIBE MARHST-L first-name last-name]

EDITOR OWNER `walter.lewis@sheridanc.on.ca` (Walter Lewis)

EDITOR OWNER `mmuseum@qucdn.queensu.ca` (Maurice D. Smith)

OWNER `jsummers@inforamp.net` (John Summers)

➤ **MEDGAY-L:** On gay-lesbian medieval studies—official list of the Society for the Study of Homosexuality in the Middle Ages. (See entry 5218 for full listing.)

➤ **MEDSCI-L:** On medieval and Renaissance science. (See entry 9352 for full listing.)

5254 NYHIST-L: On New York State history. *Mailing List, moderated*

± `listproc@unix10.nysed.gov` [body = SUBSCRIBE NYHIST-L first-name last-name]

INFO OWNER `bevans@mail.nysed.gov` (William Evans)

ARCHIVE `listproc@unix10.nysed.gov`

5255 Overland-Trails: On the emigrant & supply trails of the mid-19th century American West. *Mailing List*

± `listserv@bobcat.etsu.edu` [body = SUBSCRIBE OVERLAND-TRAILS first-name last-name]

EDITOR `wier@bobcat.etsu.edu` (Bob Wier)

EDITOR `jansen@plains.uwyo.edu` (Lesley Wischmann)

➤ `pgh.org.sca`: Pgh chapter, Society for Creative Anachronism (SCA). *Newsgroup*

5256 Pirradazish: Bulletin of Achaemenian Studies: Gathers information, primarily bibliographical, related to the study of the Achaemenian empire, as well as material on the periods immediately preceding and following it. *Newsletter*

± `ftp://oi.uchicago.edu/pub/research/achaemenid/`

INFO EDITOR `cejo@midway.uchicago.edu` (Charles E. Jones, Editor)

ARCHIVE `ftp://oi.uchicago.edu/pub/research/achaemenid/`

Frequency: semiannual

➤ **QUANHIST.RECURRENT:** On comparative approaches to history and economic history. (See entry 5208 for full listing.)

➤ `rec.arts.books.hist-fiction`: Historical fictions (novels) in general. *Newsgroup*

5257 `rec.heraldry` Discussion of coats of arms. *Newsgroup*

5258 RENAIS-L: On early modern history—the Renaissance. *Digest & Reflector*

± `listserv@ulkyvm.louisville.edu` [body = SUBSCRIBE RENAIS-L first-name last-name]

INFO `jacock01@ulkyvm.louisville.edu` (James A. Cocks)

ARCHIVE `listserv@ulkyvm.louisville.edu` [body = INDEX RENAIS-L]
Frequency: daily

5259 **SHAKER:** About the United Society of Believers (Shakers). *Mailing List*
± `listserv@ukcc.uky.edu` [body = SUBSCRIBE SHAKER first-name last-name]
INFO OWNER `rhorer@ukcc.uky.edu` (Marc Rhorer)
ARCHIVE `listserv@ukcc.uky.edu`

5260 **SHARP-L:** For scholars in all disciplines interested in furthering the study of the history of the printed word. *Mailing List*
`http://www.indiana.edu/~sharp`
± `listserv@iubvm.ucs.indiana.edu` [body = SUBSCRIBE SHARP-L first-name last-name]
INFO `pleary@indiana.edu` (Patrick Leary)
ARCHIVE `listserv@iubvm.ucs.indiana.edu` [body = INDEX SHARP-L]
FAQ `http://www.indiana.edu/~sharp/sharp-l.html`

➤ **SHOTHC-L:** On the history of computing. (See entry 2505 for full listing.)

➤ **SIXTIES-L:** For interdisciplinary discussion of the cultures and politics of the 1960s in the U.S. and internationally. (See entry 5144 for full listing.)

5261 `soc.culture.jewish.holocaust` The Shoah. *Moderated newsgroup*

5262 `soc.history` Discussions of things historical. *Newsgroup*

5263 `soc.history.living` Living history and reenactment, issues and information. *Newsgroup*

5264 `soc.history.medieval` The historic period of the Middle Ages. *Newsgroup*

5265 `soc.history.moderated` All aspects of history. *Moderated newsgroup*

5266 `soc.history.war.us-civil-war` Aspects of the U.S. Civil War. *Moderated newsgroup*

5267 `soc.history.war.vietnam` The Vietnam War. *Moderated newsgroup*

5268 `soc.history.war.world-war-ii` History and events of World War Two. *Moderated newsgroup*

➤ `soc.history.what-if`: Alternate history. *Newsgroup*

5269 **STUDIUM:** On the history of universities and higher education. *Mailing List, moderated*
± OWNER `marc.nelissen@bib.kuleuven.ac.be` (Marc Nelissen)
Please Note: Subscription by approval only.

5270 **VICTORIA:** For sharing of ideas and information about all aspects of 19th-century British culture and society. *Digest & Reflector*
`http://www.indiana.edu/~victoria`
± `listserv@iubvm.ucs.indiana.edu` [body = SUBSCRIBE VICTORIA first-name last-name]
INFO `pleary@indiana.edu` (Patrick Leary)
ARCHIVE `listserv@iubvm.ucs.indiana.edu` [body = INDEX VICTORIA]

5271 **Wey South: The WWW page of the Wey & Arun Canal Trust:** This is the Web page of the Wey & Arun Canal Trust. It describes the work of the trust and its conservation work on this canal, which is in southern England.
`http://sable.ox.ac.uk/~sjoh0014/weysouth.html`
INFO `dan.evans@sjc.ox.ac.uk`

5272 **WORLD-L:** On non-Eurocentric world history. *Mailing List*
`http://neal.ctstateu.edu/history/world_history/world_history.html` (World History Archives)
± `listserv@ubvm.cc.buffalo.edu` [body = SUBSCRIBE WORLD-L first-name last-name]
INFO `brownh@ccsua.ctstateu.edu` (Haines Brown)
ARCHIVE `http://neal.ctstateu.edu/history/world_history/archives/archives.html` (World History Archives)

INSTITUTES

5273 IATH Research Reports: Research reports of the annual fellows of the Institute for Advanced Technology in the Humanities. *E-Journal*

http://jefferson.village.virginia.edu/reports.html

INFO OWNER iath@virginia.edu (John Unsworth)

ARCHIVE http://jefferson.village.virginia.edu/reports.html

Frequency: annual

INTERDISCIPLINARY STUDIES

➤ **Arctic Circle:** The purpose of Arctic Circle is to stimulate among viewers a greater interest in the peoples and environment of the Arctic and Subarctic region. This "electronic circle" has three interrelated themes: natural resources, history and culture, and social equity and environmental justice. New material is being added on a regular basis. (See entry 4630 for full listing.)

5274 bit.listserv.sos-data Social science data list. *Newsgroup*

5275 Bryn Mawr Reviews: Umbrella list for the Bryn Mawr Medieval Review, and the Bryn Mawr Classical Review both of which are about scholarly literature in the humanities, including: conference announcements, news bulletins, commentary, reviews, and dialogue. *E-Journal*

gopher://gopher.lib.virginia.edu (medieval studies)

± listserv@cc.brynmawr.ed [body = SUBSCRIBE BMMR-L (for the Medieval Review) or BMCR-L (for the Classical Review) or BMR-L (for both) followed by first-name last-name]

INFO jod@ccat.sas.upenn.edu (James J. O'Donnell)

INFO bmcr@cc.brynmawr.edu (James J. O'Donnnell)

ARCHIVES

gopher://gopher.lib.virginia.edu/11/alpha/bmcr (medieval studies)

ftp://gopher.lib.virginia.edu/pub/alpha/bmcr (medieval studies)

Frequency: irregular (approx. 200 times a year)

5276 CEP-ANNOUNCE: On the Civic Education Project: strengthening democracy in central and Eastern Europe and the NIS through the revitalization of the social sciences in universities and institutes of higher education. *Mailing List, moderated*

http://cep.nonprofit.net/

± listproc@listproc.nonprofit.net [body = SUBSCRIBE CEP-ANNOUNCE first-name last-name]

INFO cep@minerva.cis.yale.edu (Civic Education Project)

FAQ http://cep.nonprofit.net/

5277 Deep South: An interdisciplinary journal run by the graduate students of the English department at the University of Otago in Dunedin, New Zealand. *E-Journal*

http://elwing.otago.ac.nz:889/dsouth/home-page.html

± majordomo@stonebow.otago.ac.nz [body = subscribe deep-south]

INFO dsouth@elwing.otago.ac.nz (Deep South)

➤ **Eastern European Jewish History (EEJH):** Forum for discussion of historical, archaeological, linguistic, cultural, genealogical, and genetic evidence on the Jewish people of eastern Europe from Greco-Roman times to the present. (See entry 5245 for full listing.)

5278 INTERDIS: On interdisciplinary studies. *Mailing List*

± listserv@miamiu.acs.muohio.edu [body = SUBSCRIBE INTERDIS first-name last-name]

INFO crwolfe@miavx1.muohio.edu

ARCHIVE http://miavx1.muohio.edu/~wcpcwis/ais.html

➤ **Interpersonal Computing and Technology:** Promoting the electronic journal as a legitimate outlet for dissemination of scholarly studies suitable for credit toward promotion and tenure. (See entry 4214 for full listing.)

5279 Journal of Political Ecology: Promoting interdisciplinary dialogue and research on the interface between political economy and ecology. *E-Journal*

ftp://miles.library.arizona.edu/pub/peso

```
gopher://www.library.arizona.edu/11/ej/PE
http://www.library.arizona.edu/ej/jpe/jpeweb.html
telnet://sabio.arizona.edu
```
[At the Sabio menu, select `Other databases;Electronic journals`]

INFO `jgreenber@ccit.arizona.edu` (Dr. James B. Greenberg)

INFO `tpark@ccit.arizona.edu` (Dr. Thomas K. Park)

Frequency: annual, with articles published incrementally at irregular intervals during the year.

➤ **Journal of World-Systems Research:** Research articles and theoretical discussions relevant to the study of the modern world-system and earlier regional intersocietal networks. (See entry 5282 for full listing.)

➤ **SIXTIES-L:** For interdisciplinary discussion of the cultures and politics of the 1960s in the U.S. and internationally. (See entry 5144 for full listing.)

5280 **Surfaces:** An interdisciplinary, refereed, electronic journal in the humanities and social sciences and an open international forum oriented toward the reorganization of knowledge in the humanities. *E-Journal*

```
gopher://ftp.umontreal.ca:7070/Surfaces
http://132.204.10.24/~boudreaj
ftp://ftp.umontreal.ca/Surfaces
```
INFO EDITOR `guedon@ere.umontreal.ca`

EDITOR `cochrant@ere.umontreal.ca`

ARCHIVES

```
gopher://ftp.umontreal.ca:7070/Surfaces
ftp://ftp.umontreal.ca/Surfaces
```
Language: English, French, German, others

Frequency: irregular

5281 **Trincoll Journal:** The Trincoll Journal is a liberal-arts multimedia magazine created by students from Trinity College. It is the Internet's first worldwide magazine and was the first to go multimedia. *E-Journal*

```
http://www.trincoll.edu/tj/trincolljournal.html
```
INFO `journal@trincoll.edu`

INFO `frank.sikernitsky@trincoll.edu` (Frank Sikernitsky)

Frequency: weekly

➤ **Undercurrent:** Intellectual analysis of the currents beneath current events. (See entry 6136 for full listing.)

➤ **VICTORIA:** For sharing of ideas and information about all aspects of 19th-century British culture and society. (See entry 5270 for full listing.)

INTERNATIONAL STUDIES

5282 **Journal of World-Systems Research:** Research articles and theoretical discussions relevant to the study of the modern world-system and earlier regional intersocietal networks. *E-Journal*

```
http://csf.colorado.edu/wsystems/jwsr.html
gopher://csf.colorado.edu/wsystems/journals
```
± `listproc@csf.colorado.edu` [body = `subscribe wsn`]

INFO `chriscd@jhu.edu` (Chris Chase-Dunn)

Frequency: semiannually

5283 **KONFER-L:** For schedules and related data of international conferences, seminars, and workshops all around the world. *Mailing List*

INFO `turgut@trearn.bitnet` (Turgut Kalfaoglu)

INFO `aytac@triyte.bitnet` (Dr. Sitki Aytac)

LINGUISTICS & HUMAN LANGUAGES

5284 **ADS-L:** For members of the American Dialect Society. *Mailing List*

```
http://www.msstate.edu/Archives/ADS/
```
(Europe/USA)

± `listserv@uga.cc.uga.edu` [body = SUBSCRIBE ADS-L first-name last-name]
INFO `maynor@ra.msstate.edu` (Natalie Maynor)

5285 `alt.fan.noam-chomsky`   Noam Chomsky's writings and opinions. *Newsgroup*

➤ `alt.japanese.text:`   Postings in Japanese; Japanese-language software. *Newsgroup*

➤ `alt.language.urdu.poetry:`   Poetry in the Indic Urdu language. *Newsgroup*

➤ `alt.memetics:`   The evolution of ideas in societies. *Newsgroup*

5286 `alt.usage.english`   English grammar, word usages, and related topics. *Newsgroup*

5287 `alt.usage.german`   Questions and answers about the German language. *Newsgroup*

➤ `bit.listserv.albanian:`   Albanian discussion list. *Moderated newsgroup*

5288 `bit.listserv.words-1`   English-language discussion group. *Newsgroup*

➤ **CSLI Calendar of Public Events:** Weekly announcements of CSLI-affiliated events (Center for the Study of Language and Information, Stanford University). (See entry 9157 for full listing.)

➤ **DE PROVERBIO:** An electronic journal of international proverb studies. (See entry 5183 for full listing.)

5289 **E-HUG:** On all things relating to use of Hebrew, Yiddish, Judesmo, and Aramaic on computers. *Newsletter*
± `listserv@dartcms1.dartmouth.edu` [body = SUBSCRIBE E-HUG first-name last-name]
INFO OWNER `david@dartcms1.bitnet` (David Avery)
INFO `ari@ivritype.com` (Ari Davidow, Oakland, CA, US)
ARCHIVE `listserv@dartcms1.dartmouth.edu` [body = INDEX E-HUG]

5290 **esperanto:** On the neutral international language Esperanto. Often in Esperanto. *Mailing List*
± INFO `esperanto-1-request@netcom.com` (Mike Urban)
FAQ `http://wwwtios.cs.utwente.nl/esperanto/faq.html`
Gated: `soc.culture.esperanto`

5291 `soc.culture.esperanto`   The neutral international language Esperanto. *Newsgroup*

5292 `alt.talk.esperanto`   Diskutoj per la internacia lingvo. *Newsgroup*

5293 `fj.sci.lang`   Natural languages, communication, etc. *Newsgroup*

5294 **FLN:** For scholarly discussion of figurative language—discussion is international and interdisciplinary (psychology, linguistics, AI, computational linguistics, literary studies). *Mailing List*
± `listserv@icineca.cineca.it` [body = SUBSCRIBE FLN first-name last-name]
INFO `fln-request@icineca.cineca.it`
ARCHIVE `listserv@icineca.cineca.it` [body = INDEX FLN]

5295 `humanities.language.sanskrit`   The Sanskrit language and related topics. *Newsgroup*

5296 **LATIN-L:** For Latin and NeoLatin discussions. *Mailing List*
± `listserv@psuvm.psu.edu` [body = SUBSCRIBE LATIN-L first-name last-name]
INFO `latin-1-request@psuvm.psu.edu`
ARCHIVE `listserv@psuvm.psu.edu` [body = INDEX LATIN-L]

5297 **LINGUA:** About linguistics at the University of Arizona. *Mailing List*
± `listserv@listserv.arizona.edu` [body = SUBSCRIBE LINGUA first-name last-name]
INFO `langendt@arizona.edu` (Terry Langendoen)
ARCHIVE `listserv@listserv.arizona.edu` [body = INDEX LINGUA]
Please Note: Subscription by approval only.

5298 **Model Languages:** On the hobby of model (made up) languages. *Newsletter*
± INFO `74774.157@compuserve.com` (Jeffrey Henning, Editor)
Comments: Frequency: monthly

➤ **NAT-LANG:** On the languages of aboriginal peoples. (See entry 10073 for full listing.)

5299 **Nordic Linguistic Bulletin:** On Nordic linguistics. *Newsletter*
http://www.hd.uib.no/
± nlb@hd.uib.no
INFO anne.lindebjerg@hd.uib.no (Anne Lindebjerg)
EDITOR arne.svindland@fa.uib.no
OWNER helge.dyvik@foli.uib.no (Nordic Association of Linguists (NAL))
ARCHIVES
ftp://nora.hd.uib.nopub/nlb
gopher://nora.hd.uib.no/Nordic Linguistic Bulletin
Language: English and Norwegian
Frequency: monthly

5300 `sci.lang` Natural languages, communication, etc. *Newsgroup*

5301 `sci.lang.japan` The Japanese language, both spoken and written. *Newsgroup*

5302 `sci.lang.translation` Problems and concerns of translators/interpreters. *Newsgroup*

5303 `scot.scots` Scots language discussions. *Newsgroup*

5304 `sdnet.crl` News from the UCSD Center for Research in Language. *Newsgroup*

5305 **SEELANGS:** On Slavic and eastern European languages and literatures. *Mailing List*
± listserv@cunyvm.cuny.edu [body = SUBSCRIBE SEELANGS first-name last-name]
INFO seelangs-request@cunyvm.cuny.edu (Alex Rudd & Roger Whittake)

5306 **Sign Linguistics Resource Index:** An index of resources of interest to people researching sign languages
http://www.vuw.ac.nz/~nzsldict/
INFO dave.moskovitz@vuw.ac.nz

5307 **SLLING-L:** For the discussion of sign language linguistics. *Mailing List*
http://www.vuw.ac.nz/~nzsldict/slling-l/
± listserv@yalevm.ycc.yale.edu [body = SUBSCRIBE SLLING-L first-name last-name]
INFO adam.schembri@pgrad.arts.su.edu.au (Adam Schembri)
ARCHIVE listserv@yalevm.ycc.yale.edu

5308 `soc.culture.catalan` The Catalan language and the lands where it is spoken. *Newsgroup*

5309 `tnn.lang` Discussions about languages. *Newsgroup*

ORGANIZATIONAL STUDIES

5310 **AMINT-L:** For worldwide links among scholars and practitioners of management. *Mailing List*
± listserv@psuvm.psu.edu [body = SUBSCRIBE AMINT-L first-name last-name]
INFO amint-l-request@psuvm.psu.edu

➤   **BPRREENG-L:** On applying business process re-engineering (BPR) to universities. (See entry 4092 for full listing.)

5311 **CARDEVNET:** Career Development Network discussion list. *Mailing List*
± cardevnet-request@world.std.com
OWNER js@world.std.com (Jerry Sturman)

5312 **ISO9000:** For discussion of standards for ISO 9000, a quality management system for businesses or organizations. *Mailing List*
± listserv@vm1.nodak.edu [body = SUBSCRIBE ISO9000 first-name last-name]
INFO iso9000-request@vm1.nodak.edu
ARCHIVE listserv@vm1.nodak.edu [body = INDEX ISO9000]
Gated: bit.listserv.ISO9000

5313 **OIC:** On organizational issues and research: papers, professional meetings, information. *Mailing List, moderated* `http://haas.berkeley.edu/~seidel/ad.html`

± `listproc@ursus.jun.alaska.edu` [body = SUBSCRIBE OIC first-name last-name]

OWNER `mdseidel@cmsa.berkeley.edu` (Marc-David Seidel)

➤ **ONE-L:** On the mutual impact of organizations and the environment. (See entry 4558 for full listing.)

➤ **ORCS-L:** On the interface between operations research and computer science. (See entry 9201 for full listing.)

5314 **ORGMGT-L:** On organization and management studies. *Mailing List, moderated*

± OWNER `hees@siswo.uva.nl` (Bert van Hees)

Please Note: Subscription by approval only.

PHILOSOPHY

5315 **Philosophy Related Resources on the Internet:** Includes resources on ethics, religion, science, philosophy of science, and specific philosophers. Covers mailing lists, journals, and e-texts.

`http://www.liv.ac.uk/~srlclark/list.html`

`ftp://una.hh.lib.umich.edu/inetdirsstacks/philosophy:morville`

INFO `srlclark@liverpool.ac.uk` (Stephen Clark)

INFO `morville@umich.edu` (Peter Morville)

5316 **Sean's One-Stop Philosophy Shop:** A collection of philosophy resources across the Internet.

`http://www.rpi.edu/~cearls/phil.html`

INFO `cearls@rpi.edu` (Sean Cearley)

5317 **ThinkNet:** A cluster of almost one hundred lists on various topics in philosophy, including aesthetics, classical philosophy, mysticism, modern philosophy, and systems theory. Part of DialogNet. *Distribution List*

± `listserv@think.net` [body = SUBSCRIBE listname first-name last-name]

INFO `dialogue@think.net`

INFO `thinknet@netcom.com`

INFO `news@think.net`

INFO `census@think.net` (For number of subscribers to each list, send a blank message)

OWNER `palmer@netcom.com` (Jim Palmer)

OWNER `palmer@think.net`

Frequency: irregular

5318 **alfrednorth:** On the philosophy of Alfred North Whitehead. *Mailing List*

± `majordomo@world.std.com` [body = subscribe alfrednorth]

OWNER `eweinmann@delphi.com` (Edmund Weinmann)

5319 `alt.individualism` Philosophies where individual rights are paramount. *Newsgroup*

5320 `alt.paranet.metaphysics` Philosphophy, ontology, cosmology, and cosmetology. *Newsgroup*

5321 `alt.philosophy.debate` Back to basics. *Newsgroup*

5322 `alt.philosophy.jarf` The Jarf philosphy/metaphysics/religion/culture. *Newsgroup*

5323 `alt.philosophy.objectivism` A product of the Ayn Rand corporation. *Newsgroup*

5324 `alt.philosophy.taoism` All aspects of Taoism. *Newsgroup*

5325 **ANALYTIC:** On analytic philosophy, spanning work from Frege to Quine to Dummett. Topics of interest include mind, language, and metaphysics. *Digest & Reflector, moderated*

± `analytic-request@lt.org`

OWNER `rv@lt.org` (Rodrigo Vanegas)

ARCHIVE `http://lt.org/analytic/`

FAQ `http://lt.org/analytic/`

➤ **ARIL-L:** Members of the Association for Religion and Intellectual Life, publisher of Cross Currents. (See entry 8775 for full listing.)

➤ **Automated Reasoning Project (ARP):** Software, tools, and papers on automated reasoning and parallel and symbolic computing. (See entry 9163 for full listing.)

➤ **Belief-L:** On personal beliefs: politics, ethics, morality, and interpersonal banter. (See entry 8861 for full listing.)

➤ `christnet.philosophy`: Philosophy in Christianity. *Newsgroup*

5326 `comp.ai.philosophy` Philosophical aspects of artificial intelligence. *Newsgroup*

5327 **DEWEY-L:** Discussion of John Dewey's philosophy. *Mailing List*
± `listserv@postoffice.cso.uiuc.edu` [body = SUBSCRIBE DEWEY-L first-name last-name]
OWNER `tlekan@uiuc.edu` (Todd Lekan)

5328 **Electronic Journal of Analytic Philosophy:** Analytical philosophy including, but not limited to: philosophical logic, metaphysics, epistemology, the philosophies of language, science, and mind, and the history of analytic philosophy. *E-Journal*
± EDITOR `ejap@phil.indiana.edu` (Tim Maletic, EJAP Technical Editor)
ARCHIVES
`ftp://phil.indiana.edu/ejap`
`gopher://phil.indiana.edu`
`http://www.phil.indiana.edu/ejap/`
Frequency: irregular

➤ **Extropians:** Spin-off of *Extropy* magazine—advanced technology, self-transformation, futurist philosophy, life extension, voluntarism. (See entry 9823 for full listing.)

5329 `fj.sci.philosophy` Discussion about philosophy. *Newsgroup*

5330 **FOP-L:** On philosophical fiction and philosophy that uses fiction as a mode of inquiry. *Mailing List*
± `listserv@vm.cc.purdue.edu` [body = SUBSCRIBE FOP-L first-name last-name]
INFO OWNER `sondheim@panix.com` (Alan Sondheim)
OWNER `cubbison@sage.cc.purdue.edu` (Laurie Cubbison)
OWNER `tbone@wwa.com` (T-Bone Prone)
ARCHIVE `listserv@vm.cc.purdue.edu` [body = INDEX FOP-L FOP-L]

5331 **HEGEL-L:** On the thought and influence of the philosopher G. W. F. Hegel. *Mailing List*
± `listserv@bucknell.edu` [body = SUBSCRIBE HEGEL-L first-name last-name]
OWNER `fwilson@bucknell.edu` (Frank Wilson)
ARCHIVE `listserv@bucknell.edu` [body = INDEX HEGEL-L]
Please Note: Subscription by approval only.

5332 **HOPOS-L:** On the history of the philosophy of science. *Mailing List*
± `listserv@ukcc.uky.edu` [body = SUBSCRIBE HOPOS-L first-name last-name]
INFO `einphil@ukcc.uky.edu` (Don Howard)
INFO OWNER `crovo@ukcc.uky.edu` (Bob Crovo)
ARCHIVE `listserv@ukcc.uky.edu` [body = INDEX HOPOS-L]

5333 **International Kierkegaard Newsletter:** Annual scholarly paper containing information about the latest books, articles, etc. on Soeren Kierkegaard; also about Kierkegaard libraries, societies, conferences, etc. *Newsletter*
`gopher://info.utas.edu.au/11/Publications/Kierkegaard`
`ftp://info.utas.edu.au`
`gopher://info.utas.edu.au/Publications/Kierkegaard`
INFO `julia.watkin@human.utas.edu.au` (Julia Watkin)
ARCHIVE `http://www.utas.edu.au/docs/humsoc/humanities/`
Comments: Regularly updated

➤ **La Revue Intemporelle - The timeless magazine:** Publishing since 1988, once a year, a free magazine treating fundamental themes such as human dignity, the planet Earth, consciousness, love and the creation of a planetary federation. (See entry 10139 for full listing.)

5334   **MEANING:** On the meaning of life and other weighty contemplations. *Mailing List*
± `listserv@asuvm.inre.asu.edu` [body = SUBSCRIBE MEANING first-name last-name]
INFO `shah@asu.edu` (Shah)
ARCHIVE `listserv@asuvm.inre.asu.edu` [body = INDEX MEANING]

5335   **Metaphysical Review:** Metaphysical Review is dedicated to essays on the foundations and conceptual bases of physics. *E-Journal*
`http://einstein.unh.edu:1905/MetaphysicalReview/MetaphysicalReview.html`
± **EDITOR** `metaphysical.review@unh.edu` (Timothy Paul Smith, editor)
± `http://einstein.unh.edu:1905/MetaphysicalReview/Metaphysical_subscribe.html`
ARCHIVE `http://einstein.unh.edu:1905/MetaphysicalReview/Metaphysical_Back.html`
Frequency: monthly

5336   **NIETZSCH:** For scholarly discussion of the philosophy of Friedrich Nietzsche. *Mailing List, moderated*
± `listserv@dartmouth.edu` [body = SUBSCRIBE NIETZSCH first-name last-name]
OWNER `malcolm.b.brown@dartmouth.edu` (Malcolm Brown)

5337   **Nonserv:** Discussions on the philosophy of Max Stirner and other insurrective spirits. *Mailing List*
`http://pierce.ee.washington.edu/~davisd/egoist/`
`http://www.math.uio.no/~solan/Stirner/stirner.html`
± **INFO** `nonserv-request@math.uio.no`
OWNER `solan@math.uio.no` (Svein Olav Nyberg)
Comments: Is twinned with Non Serviam, an infrequent newsletter for more elaborate articles.

5338   **Omega-Point-Theory:** On Omega Point Theory in Frank J. Tipler's book, *The Physics of Immortality*. *Mailing List*
± `majordomo@world.std.com` [body = subscribe omega-point-theory]
OWNER `eweinmann@delphi.com` (Edmund Weinmann)
ARCHIVE `majordomo@world.std.com`

➤   **PDG:** On game theory, especially Prisoner's Dilemma-type problems. (See entry 9396 for full listing.)

5339   **PHILOSED:** For students and teachers discussing the philosophy of education, an unofficial service of the Philosophy of Education Society. *Mailing List*
± `maiser@sued.syr.edu`
INFO `tfgreen@mailbox.syr.edu` (Thomas F. Green)

5340   **PHILOSOP:** For scholarly discussion of philosophy, and for sharing information relevant to the discipline. *Mailing List*
± `majordomo@majordomo.srv.ualberta.ca` [body = SUBSCRIBE PHILOSOP]
INFO `istvan.berkeley@ualberta.ca` (Istvan Berkeley)
EDITOR OWNER `istvan@gpu.srv.ualberta.ca` (Istvan Berkeley)

5341   **POLANYI:** On the thought of Michael Polanyi: "post-critical" thought. *Mailing List*
± `majordomo@sbu.edu` [body = subscribe polanyi]
OWNER `apczynski@sbu.edu` (John Apczynski)

➤   **POPPER:** Discussions on philosophy of science and Sir Karl R. Popper's views on rationalism and humanitarianism. (See entry 9577 for full listing.)

➤   **POSTCOLONIAL:** On culture affected by the imperial process: loss, agency, and recovery; on the political and cultural situation of the so-called "Third World." (See entry 280 for full listing.)

➤   **Postmodern Jewish Philosophy Network:** Dedicated both to a philosophic review of the variety of postmodern Jewish discourses and to postmodern reflections on the variety of Jewish philosophies and Jewish philosophic theologies. (See entry 8817 for full listing.)

➤   **Principia Cybernetica Mailing List:** PCP is a computer-supported collaborative attempt to develop an integrated evolutionary-systemic philosophy or worldview focusing on the clear formulation of principles of the cybernetic approach. (See entry 9212 for full listing.)

➤ **PSYCOLOQUY:** Brief reports of new ideas and findings in all areas of psychology and its related fields (biobehavioral, cognitive, neural, social, etc.). (See entry 9527 for full listing.)

➤ **PURTOPOI:** On rhetoric, language, and professional writing. (See entry 4549 for full listing.)

5342 `relcom.sci.philosophy` Philosophic discussions and related projects. *Newsgroup*

5343 **RUSSELL-L:** On Bertrand Russell (1872-1970), British philosopher, essayist, and peace activist. *Mailing List*
± `listproc@mcmaster.ca`
OWNER `blackwk@mcmaster.ca`
ARCHIVE `http://www.mcmaster.ca/russdocs/russell.htm`

5344 `sci.philosophy.meta` Discussions within the scope of "meta-philosophy". *Newsgroup*

5345 `sci.philosophy.tech` Technical philosophy: math, science, logic, etc. *Newsgroup*

➤ **Shuffle Brain:** A growing anthology of serious but nontechnical works on the mind/body question. (See entry 4727 for full listing.)

5346 **SOPHIA:** On ancient philosophy (from Hesiod to Iamblichus, Spain to Palestine). *Mailing List*
`http://www.liv.ac.uk/~srlclark/philos.html`
± `listserv@liverpool.ac.uk` [body = SUBSCRIBE SOPHIA first-name last-name]
INFO `larvor@liverpool.ac.uk` (Brendan Larvor)
OWNER `srlclark@liverpool.ac.uk` (Stephen Clark)
ARCHIVE `gopher://gopher.liv.ac.uk/hh/lists/sophia`

5347 **SORITES:** Electronic quarterly of analytical philosophy. Dedicated to the promotion of analytical standards of clarity and rigor in philosophical debates. *E-Journal*
`ftp://olmo.csic.es/pub/sorites/Sorites.html`
± INFO `sorites@olmo.csic.es` (Prof. Lorenzo Penya)
INFO OWNER `laurentius@pinar1.csic.es`
INFO `aliz@ull.es`
ARCHIVES
`http://www.sc.ehu.es/revistas/revistas.html`
`gopher://scdx01.sc.ehu.es:70/11/09%7c%20SORITES/`
`ftp://olmo.csic.es/pub/sorites`
FAQ `ftp://olmo.csic.es/pub/sorites/SORITES.faq`
Frequency: quarterly

5348 **STEINER:** On the philosophy of Rudolf Steiner, visionary social and technical theorist. *Mailing List*
± `listserv@sjuvm.stjohns.edu` [body = SUBSCRIBE STEINER first-name last-name]
OWNER `lefty@apple.com` (David "Lefty" Schlesinger)
ARCHIVE `listserv@sjuvm.stjohns.edu` [body = INDEX STEINER]
FAQ `http://www.io.com/~lefty/Human_Future.html`

5349 **Tabula Rasa:** Philosophical journal, run by advanced students and assistants of philosophy at the University of Jena, Germany; widespread topics. *E-Journal*
`http://www.uni-jena.de/~xnx/tabula_rasa.html`
INFO OWNER `xnx@rz.uni-jena.de` (Frank Staeudner)
ARCHIVE `http://www.uni-jena.de/~xnx/tabula_rasa.html`
Language: German, English
Frequency: irregular (four to five issues per year)

5350 `talk.philosophy.humanism` Humanism in the modern world. *Newsgroup*

5351 `talk.philosophy.misc` Philosophical musings on all topics. *Newsgroup*

PHILOSOPHY—AYN RAND

5352 **AYN-RAND:** For scholarly discussion of Ayn Rand's objectivist philosophy. *Mailing List*
± listserv@iubvm.ucs.indiana.edu [body = SUBSCRIBE AYN-RAND first-name last-name]
INFO ayn-rand-request@iubvm.ucs.indiana.edu
ARCHIVE listserv@iubvm.ucs.indiana.edu [body = INDEX AYN-RAND]

PHILOSOPHY—ETHICS

5353 **The Ethical Spectacle:** The charter of the Ethical Spectacle is to discuss, and promote discussion of, practical, applied ethics; to identify hypocrisy; and especially to spotlight double standards wherever found in our society. *Newsletter*
http://www.tagsys.com/Spectacle/
OWNER jblumen@interramp.com (Jonathan Blumen)

➤ **Institute for Business and Professional Ethics:** One of the largest resource sites relating to business and professional ethics, including an online journal, ethics discussions, and an ethics calendar. (See entry 2076 for full listing.)

5354 **Online Journal of Ethics:** The Online Journal of Ethics explores both theoretical and applied ethical issues involved in the practice of business and the professions. *E-Journal*
http://condor.depaul.edu/ethics/ethg1.html
INFO OWNER lpincus@wppost.depaul.edu (Laura B. Pincus)
ARCHIVE http://condor.depaul.edu/ethics/ethg1.html
Frequency: ongoing

PHILOSOPHY—LOGIC

5355 **Bulletin of the Interest Group of Pure and Applied Logics:** The Bulletin is the official publication of the International Interest Group in Pure and Applied Logics (IGPL), which is sponsored by The European Foundation for Logic, Language, and Information (FoLLI). *E-Journal*
http://www.mpi-sb.mpg.de/igpl/Bulletin/
INFO OWNER ohlbach@mpi-sb.mpg.de (Dr. Hans Juergen Ohlbach)
ARCHIVE ftp://ftp.mpi-sb.mpg.de/pub/igpl/Bulletin
Frequency: irregular

5356 **LOGIC-L:** On the teaching and study of elementary logic. *Mailing List*
± listserv@bucknell.edu [body = SUBSCRIBE LOGIC-L first-name last-name]
OWNER fwilson@bucknell.edu (Frank Wilson)
OWNER chappen@bucknell.edu (Ted Chappen)
POST logic-l@bucknell.edu

5357 **sci.logic** Logic—math, philosophy, and computational aspects. *Newsgroup*

5358 **SILFS-L:** Italian Society of Logic and Philosophy of Sciences. *Mailing List*
± listserv@vm.cineca.it [body = SUBSCRIBE SILFS-L first-name last-name]
OWNER mc3430@mclink.it (Gino Roncaglia)
ARCHIVE listserv@vm.cineca.it [body = INDEX SILFS-L]
Language: Italian & English

POLITICAL SCIENCE

5359 **CTHEORY / Canadian Journal of Political and Social Theory:** An international review focusing on theory, technology, and culture from a critical perspective. *E-Journal*
± ctheory-request@concordia.ca
ARCHIVES
http://www.freedonia.com/ctheory/
http://english-www.hss.cmu.edu/ctheory/
Frequency: weekly reviews; articles, interviews, and event-scenes monthly

➤ **Journal of Political Ecology:** Promoting interdisciplinary dialogue and research on the interface between political economy and ecology. (See entry 5279 for full listing.)

➤ **PDG:** On game theory, especially Prisoner's Dilemma-type problems. (See entry 9396 for full listing.)

5360 **POSCIM:** Forum for those researching, teaching, or studying the subject as well as the practice of politics. *Mailing List*

± INFO ups500@ibm.rhrz.uni-bonn.de

± INFO markus@unik.no (Markus Schlegel)

Please Note: Subscription by approval only.

➤ **SIXTIES-L:** For interdisciplinary discussion of the cultures and politics of the 1960s in the U.S. and internationally. (See entry 5144 for full listing.)

5361 **talk.politics.theory** Theory of politics and political systems. *Newsgroup*

SOCIOLOGY

➤ **ABSLST-L:** For members of the Association of Black Sociologists and other interested scholars. (See entry 5137 for full listing.)

5362 **alt.sci.sociology** People are really interesting when you watch them. *Newsgroup*

5363 **ELIAS-I:** For social scientists using the ideas of Norbert Elias in their research. *Mailing List*

± listserv@nic.surfnet.nl [body = SUBSCRIBE ELIAS-I first-name last-name]

OWNER verrips@siswo.uva.nl (Kitty Verrips)

➤ **FAMLYSCI:** For the Family Science Network: marriage, therapy, sociology, and behavioral-science aspects of family medicine. (See entry 9925 for full listing.)

➤ **Paglia-L:** On the writings and ideas of Dr. Camille Paglia. (See entry 10161 for full listing.)

5364 **QNTEVA-L:** On the theory and design of quantitative methods to evaluate social, educational, psychological, and other forms of programs and policies. *Mailing List*

± listserv@psuvm.psu.edu [body = SUBSCRIBE QNTEVA-L first-name last-name]

INFO qnteva-l-request@psuvm.psu.edu

ARCHIVE listserv@psuvm.psu.edu [body = INDEX QNTEVA-L]

5365 **SASPAC-L:** For users of the SAS software package to access census and other public data files. *Mailing List*

ftp://oseda.missouri.edu

± listserv@umslvma.umsl.edu [body = SUBSCRIBE SASPAC-L first-name last-name]

INFO c1921@umslvma.bitnet

ARCHIVES

http://www.oseda.missouri.edu/uic

listserv@umslvma.umsl.edu [body = INDEX SASPAC-L]

5366 **SEMNET:** Structural Equation Modeling Special Interest Group (SEMSIG), a multidisciplinary special interest group organized to support the application of structural equation modeling with latent variables across the social and behavioral sciences. *Mailing List*

± listserv@ua1vm.ua.edu [body = SUBSCRIBE SEMNET first-name last-name]

INFO cferguso@alston.cba.ua.edu (Carl Ferguson)

ARCHIVE listserv@ua1vm.ua.edu

➤ **SOCIOBIO:** On the evolution of social behavior. (See entry 9022 for full listing.)

5367 **UNK Department of Sociology:** Web site of the department of sociology at the University of Nebraska at Kearney.

http://rip.physics.unk.edu/soc/unksoc.html

INFO price@rip.physics.unk.edu

URBAN STUDIES

5368 **alt.planning.urban** Urban development. *Newsgroup*

LAW, GOVERNMENT & POLITICS

GOVERNMENT

5369 <u>The Federal Web Locator:</u> The Federal Web Locator is a service provided by the Villanova Center for Information Law and Policy and is a one-stop shopping point for federal government information on the World Wide Web. The site covers the executive, judicial, and legislative branches of the federal government, as well as the executive agencies (departments), the independent establishments and government corporations, and the nongovernment federally related sites.

> http://www.law.vill.edu/Fed-Agency/fedwebloc.html (U.S.)
>
> INFO kmortens@mail.law.vill.edu (Kenneth P. Mortensen)

5370 <u>Fedix:</u> Federal Information Exchange, Inc., access to a wide variety of government data.

> http://web.fie.com/
>
> INFO webmaster@fedix.fie.com

5371 <u>Fedworld web:</u> A gateway to U.S. government information operated by the Department of Commerce's National Technical Information Service (NTIS).

> http://www.fedworld.gov/
>
> telnet://fedworld.gov
>
> INFO webmaster@fedworld.gov

5372 <u>Government Information Locator Service (GILS):</u> A service to help the public locate and access public information resources throughout the U.S. federal government.

> http://www.usgs.gov/gils
>
> ftp://ftp.cni.org/pub/gils/
>
> INFO echristi@usgs.gov

➤ <u>PEG, a Peripatetic, Eclectic Gopher:</u> A collection of pointers to all sorts of Internet resources. Especially strong are its virtual reference desk, Internet assistance, politics and government, medicine, and women's studies resource lists. (See entry 2726 for full listing.)

5373 `alt.government.abuse` About governmental abuses of its power. *Newsgroup*

5374 `can.gov.general` For general discussion of Canadian government issues. *Newsgroup*

5375 `clari.nb.govt` Newsbytes: legal and government computer news. *Moderated newsgroup*

5376 `clari.news.usa.gov.misc` Miscellaneous U.S. domestic policy. *Moderated newsgroup*

5377 `clari.news.usa.gov.personalities` Personalities and private lives. *Moderated newsgroup*

GOVERNMENT—AGENCIES

➤ <u>The Federal Web Locator:</u> The Federal Web Locator is a service provided by the Villanova Center for Information Law and Policy and is a one-stop shopping point for federal government information on the World Wide Web. The site covers the executive, judicial, and legislative branches of the federal government, as well as the executive agencies (departments), the independent establishments and government corporations, and the nongovernment federally related sites. (See entry 5369 for full listing.)

➤ <u>Government Sources of Business and Economic Information on the Internet:</u> Includes agriculture, area codes, census, Congressional Directory, economic information, Edgar, EPA, FDA, GAO, health, labor, NIST, OSHA, patents, postal information, SEC, Social Security, state government resources, travel advisories, USDA, weather, the White House, and more. (See entry 5384 for full listing.)

➤ <u>Agency for Toxic Substances and Disease Registry (ATSDR):</u> The mission of the Agency for Toxic Substances and Disease Registry (ATSDR) is to prevent exposure and adverse human health effects and diminished quality of life associated with exposure to hazardous substances from waste sites, unplanned releases, and other sources of pollution present in the environment. (See entry 5035 for full listing.)

➤ <u>AJAX Military and Intelligence Agencies Access:</u> This site is an extensive collection of pointers to the Web sites of U.S. and international government military, intelligence, and security agencies. (See entry 5480 for full listing.)

➤ **alt.politics.org.cia:** The United States Central Intelligence Agency. *Newsgroup*

➤ **alt.politics.org.nsa:** The ultrasecret security arm of the US government. *Newsgroup*

➤ **Centers for Disease Control and Prevention (CDC):** Information on diseases, disease prevention, and health in general from the U.S. government Centers for Disease Control and Prevention. (See entry 4856 for full listing.)

➤ **HUD USER:** HUD USER is the primary source for federal government reports and information on housing policy and programs, building technology, economic development, urban planning, and other housing-related topics. (See entry 6044 for full listing.)

➤ **The NASA Home Page:** Information about the National Aeronautics and Space Administration. Includes NASA news, and information on space sciene, aeronautics, the Mission to Planet Earth, human space flight, all of NASA's centers, space technology, and a gallery of photos, sounds and movies. (See entry 9591 for full listing.)

➤ **National Institute of Standards & Technology (NIST):** Information about NIST programs, products, and activities. The site includes GAMS (Guide to Available Mathematical Software) and a computer security bulletin board. (See entry 5520 for full listing.)

➤ **National Institutes of Health (NIH):** This site provides health and biomedical information useful to the NIH intramural research community in Bethesda, Maryland, and biomedical researchers around the world. (See entry 5057 for full listing.)

➤ **National Science Foundation (NSF):** Information from the NSF, including programs, grants and funding guidelines, other NSF publications, and links to results of NSF-funded research. (See entry 9551 for full listing.)

➤ **North Carolina Cooperative Extension Gopher:** This is the NC Cooperative Extension WWW server located at North Carolina State University, Raleigh, North Carolina. (See entry 8918 for full listing.)

➤ **OSHA Computerized Information System (OCIS):** Information from the U.S. Department of Labor Occupational Safety & Health Administration. Includes data on OSHA programs and offices as well as texts of OSHA regulations and documents. (See entry 4986 for full listing.)

➤ **U.S. Agency for International Development:** This site provides access to information on USAID programs, as well as to some interesting databases including a famine early warning system, and more. USAID is an independent federal government agency that conducts foreign assistance and humanitarian aid to advance the political and economic interests of the United States. (See entry 10054 for full listing.)

➤ **U.S. Environmental Protection Agency:** Includes information about the EPA, its offices, laboratories' programs, initiatives, contracts, grants, rules, regulations, and legislations, as well as databases and pointers to other environmental resources on the net. (See entry 4594 for full listing.)

➤ **U.S. Immigration and Naturalization Service:** An official U.S. government site, the INS Web page (and gopher) includes the following: general information on the INS, a table of immigration to the U.S. in 1994, INS press releases, regulations from the CFR, and the full text of the Immigration and Nationality Act. (See entry 10043 for full listing.)

➤ **U.S. Office of Scientific and Technical Information (OSTI):** The Office of Scientific and Technical Information (OSTI) manages the Department of Energy's (DOE) program for the collection, processing, and availability of scientific and technical information (STI) generated and acquired by the Department of Energy. (See entry 9231 for full listing.)

5378 **U.S. Patents and Trademarks:** The home page of the U.S. Patents and Trademarks office includes intellectual property and the national information infrastructure issues.

http://www.uspto.gov/
INFO www@uspto.gov

5379 **U.S. Postal Service:** Includes a ZIP code database, postage rates, a stamp center, consumer fraud protection information, and information on consumer and business products and services, including Postal Business Center lookup, forms, and publications. There is even a history of the Postal Service and other organizational information.

http://www.usps.gov/
INFO jwilli17@email.usps.gov

➤ **USDA Cooperative State Research, Education, and Extension Service:** This site is set up to provide access to information from the USDA Extension Service, other USDA agencies, and other federal agencies as it relates to the Cooperative Extension System. (See entry 8922 for full listing.)

GOVERNMENT—ASSET SALES

5380 GOVSALES: For government asset sales and auctions; part of Al Gore's FinanceNet. *Mailing List, moderated*

± `listproc@financenet.gov` [body = SUBSCRIBE GOVSALES]

OWNER `preston.rich@nsf.gov` (B. Preston Rich)

ARCHIVE `http://www.financenet.gov/sales.htm`

GOVERNMENT—CITIZENSHIP

➤ **The Center For Civic Networking:** Included in this site is information on developing a sustainable information network, policy issues regarding electronic development, and information regarding municipalities and local governmental information networks. The Center for Civic Networking is a nonprofit organization whose goal is to help develop models of beneficial uses of the Internet for local, regional, and national organizations and governments. (See entry 2422 for full listing.)

➤ `clari.news.immigration`:   Refugees, immigration, migration. *Moderated newsgroup*

5381 GovAccess: On computer-assisted citizen participation in—and protection from—government. *Mailing List, moderated*

± `majordomo@well.com` [body = SUBSCRIBE GOVACCESS e-mail-address]

INFO `majordomo@well.com` [body = info GovAccess]

OWNER `jwarren@well.com` (Jim Warren)

ARCHIVE `http://www.cpsr.org/cpsr/states/california/govaccess`

➤ `misc.immigration.usa`:   USA immigration issues. *Newsgroup*

➤ **RIGHTS-L:** For persons interested in the ongoing effort to create a bill of rights and responsibilities for electronic citizens. (See entry 5612 for full listing.)

5382 U.S. Flag: Dedicated to the flag of the United States of America: history, culture, ideals, symbolism, protocol—intelligent patriotism.

`http://www.elk-grove.k12.il.us/usflag/`

INFO `duanes@elk-grove.k12.il.us`

GOVERNMENT—DOCUMENTS

5383 Federal Government: This guide was compiled primarily for librarians who provide reference assistance for United States government documents and contains Internet sites that provide information from or about the federal government. This information is compiled by Maggie Parhamovich, Internet specialist.

`http://www.nevada.edu/library/GOVT/index.html#contents`

`gopher://una.hh.lib.umich.edu/00/inetdirsstacks/usfedgov%3aparhamovich`

INFO `magoo@nevada.edu`

➤ **The Federal Web Locator:** The Federal Web Locator is a service provided by the Villanova Center for Information Law and Policy and is a one-stop shopping point for federal government information on the World Wide Web. The site covers the executive, judicial, and legislative branches of the federal government, as well as the executive agencies (departments), the independent establishments and government corporations, and the nongovernment federally related sites. (See entry 5369 for full listing.)

➤ **Fedix:** Federal Information Exchange, Inc., access to a wide variety of government data. (See entry 5370 for full listing.)

5384 Government Sources of Business and Economic Information on the Internet: Includes agriculture, area codes, census, Congressional Directory, economic information, Edgar, EPA, FDA, GAO, health, labor, NIST, OSHA, patents, postal information, SEC, Social Security, state government resources, travel advisories, USDA, weather, the White House, and more.

`ftp://una.hh.lib.umich.edu/inetdirsstacks/govdocs:tsangaustin`

INFO `kimbayer@sils.umich.edu`

INFO `tmurphy@sils.umich.edu` (Terese Austin)

5385 `bit.listserv.govdoc-l` Discussion of government-document issues. *Newsgroup*

5386 Code of Federal Regulations on the Internet: Counterpoint's CFR files are derived from the official typesetting tapes created by the United States Government Printing Office. These files contain all the text, tables, and charts from the original GPO files. *Newsletter*

http://www.counterpoint.com/

INFO hal@counterpoint.com (Hal P. Kingsley)

ARCHIVE hal@counterpoint.com (Hal P. Kingsley)

Frequency: daily

Available by paid subscription only

5387 Counterpoint Publishing's Federal Register: The full text of the Federal Register, a subscription-based service.

http://www.counterpoint.com/

INFO info@counterpoint.com

5388 Electronic Public Information Newsletter: On federal information dissemination policy and practices. *Newsletter*

± INFO epin@access.digex.net (James McDonough)

ARCHIVE epin@access.digex.net (James McDonough)

Frequency: monthly

5389 Federal Register on the Internet: Electronic equivalent of the *Federal Register* for use on personal computers or networks; identical text, tables, and charts as found in the paperbound version. *Newsletter*

http://www.counterpoint.com/

± majordomo@counterpoint.com

INFO hal@counterpoint.com (Hal P. Kingsley)

Frequency: daily

Price: starts at $375.00 per year

➤ **GovAccess:** On computer-assisted citizen participation in—and protection from—government. (See entry 5381 for full listing.)

5390 GOVDOC-L: On dissemination of government information and government information policy. Includes federal, state, and international, with particular emphasis on U.S. federal. *Mailing List, moderated*

± listserv@psuvm.psu.edu [body = SUBSCRIBE GOVDOC-L first-name last-name]

± listserv@vm.ucs.ualberta.ca [body = SUBSCRIBE GOVDOC-L first-name last-name]

INFO raeann@uiuc.edu (Raeann Dossett)

INFO dkovacs@kentvm.kent.edu (Diane Kovacs)

ARCHIVE listserv@psuvm.psu.edu [body = INDEX GOVDOC-L]

5391 Government Documents at Yale: Information on the Government Documents Center of the Yale University Libraries. The site has an excellent series of pages that help you locate government information on the Web. The site also provides listings of the databases, collections, and CD-ROMs available at the center itself.

http://www.library.yale.edu/govdocs/gdchome.html

INFO govdoc@yalevm.cis.yale.edu

5392 GPO Access on the Web: WAIS searches of selected volumes of Congressional Bills, the Congressional Record Index, the Congressional Record, the Federal Register, the General Accounting Office's "blue book" reports, the History of Bills, the Public Laws, the Unified Agenda, the United States Code, the Congressional Directory, the Economic Indicators, and the House and Senate Calendars.

http://thorplus.lib.purdue.edu/gpo/

INFO cary@thorplus.lib.purdue.edu (Cary Kerr)

5393 GPO Gate: Access to a wide variety of government documents from the Government Printing Office (GPO). Documents available include: Congressional Bills, Congressional Directory, Congressional Documents, Congressional Record, Congressional Reports, Economic Indicators, Federal Register, GAO Reports, GILS Records, Government Manual, History of Bills, House Calendars, Privacy Act Issuances, Public Laws, Senate Calendars, Unified Agenda, and the United States Code.

http://ssdc.ucsd.edu/gpo/

INFO gpogate@sassy.ucsd.edu

5394 Taurus: On Project Taurus: pay-per-use access to documents on government contracting. *Mailing List*

`gopher://gopher.counterpoint.com`

± `majordomo@counterpoint.com` [body = `subscribe taurus`]

INFO `info@counterpoint.com`

EDITOR `hal@counterpoint.com` (Hal P. Kingsley)

ARCHIVE `http://www.counterpoint.com/`

5395 U.S. Government Printing Office Home Page: Information on the GPO and access to a host of the documents published through GPO.

`http://www.access.gpo.gov/`

INFO `wwwadmin@www.access.gpo.gov`

FAQ `http://www.access.gpo.gov/na001.html`

GOVERNMENT—EMBASSIES

5396 Embassy of Israel - Washington, D.C.: The official WWW site of the embassy of Israel to Washington, D.C.

`http://www.israelemb.org/`

INFO `dcisrael@ix.netcom.com`

GOVERNMENT—EXECUTIVE BRANCH

➤ **The Federal Web Locator:** The Federal Web Locator is a service provided by the Villanova Center for Information Law and Policy and is a one-stop shopping point for federal government information on the World Wide Web. The site covers the executive, judicial, and legislative branches of the federal government, as well as the executive agencies (departments), the independent establishments and government corporations, and the nongovernment federally related sites. (See entry 5369 for full listing.)

➤ **Government Sources of Business and Economic Information on the Internet:** Includes agriculture, area codes, census, Congressional Directory, economic information, Edgar, EPA, FDA, GAO, health, labor, NIST, OSHA, patents, postal information, SEC, Social Security, state government resources, travel advisories, USDA, weather, the White House, and more. (See entry 5384 for full listing.)

5397 `alt.current-events.clinton.whitewater` The Clinton Whitewater scandal. *Newsgroup*

5398 `alt.dear.whitehouse` When Hints from Heloise aren't enough. *Newsgroup*

5399 `alt.fan.dan-quayle` For discussion of a past U.S. vice president. *Newsgroup*

5400 `alt.fan.g-gordon-liddy` Crime does pay, or we wouldn't have so much of it. *Newsgroup*

5401 `alt.fan.richard-nixon` Even people who are not crooks die. *Newsgroup*

5402 `alt.fan.ronald-reagan` Jellybeans and all. *Newsgroup*

5403 `alt.impeach.clinton` Some think he performs as though he is impeared. *Newsgroup*

5404 `alt.politics.bush` The politics of shrubbery. *Newsgroup*

5405 `alt.politics.clinton` President Bill Clinton. *Newsgroup*

5406 `alt.president.clinton` Will the CIA undermine his efforts? *Newsgroup*

5407 `clari.news.usa.gov.white_house` Presidential news. *Moderated newsgroup*

5408 `clari.usa.gov.white_house` White House news. *Moderated newsgroup*

5409 CLINTON: Discussion of the presidency of Bill Clinton. *Mailing List*

± `listserv@vm.marist.edu` [body = `SUBSCRIBE CLINTON` first-name last-name]

INFO OWNER `urls@vm.marist.edu` (Lee Sakkas)

ARCHIVE `listserv@vm.marist.edu` [body = `INDEX CLINTON`]

5410 U.S. National Performance Review: The home page for the National Performance Review, where you can obtain highlights of recent NPR developments, NPR reports and news, the NPR library, and links to other related World Wide Web servers.

`http://www.npr.gov/`

INFO netresults@npr.gsa.gov

5411 U.S. White House: U.S. White House.

http://www.whitehouse.gov/

INFO feedback@www.whitehouse.gov

➤ **United States Trade Representatives Homepage:** Home page for the United States Trade Representative. Providing information related to the office and activities of the USTR. (See entry 1801 for full listing.)

GOVERNMENT—FEDERAL EMPLOYEES

5412 EMPLOY: Forum to assist federal employees and others in the sharing of job opportunities and ideas on gaining employment. The primary emphasis is on DoD jobs and employment-related issues. *Mailing List*

± listserv@odcsper-nt1.hqusareur.army.mil [body = SUBSCRIBE EMPLOY first-name last-name]

OWNER bstring@odcsper-nt.hqusareur.army.mil (Bob Stringfield)

ARCHIVE http://odcsper-nt.hqusareur.army.mil/

Please Note: Subscription by approval only.

GOVERNMENT—FINANCE, BUDGET & TAXATION

➤ **Government Sources of Business and Economic Information on the Internet:** Includes agriculture, area codes, census, Congressional Directory, economic information, Edgar, EPA, FDA, GAO, health, labor, NIST, OSHA, patents, postal information, SEC, Social Security, state government resources, travel advisories, USDA, weather, the White House, and more. (See entry 5384 for full listing.)

5413 AGA: List for members of the Association of Government Accountants. *Digest & Reflector, moderated*

http://www.financenet.gov/

± listproc@financenet.gov [body = SUBSCRIBE AGA first-name last-name]

OWNER preston.rich@nsf.gov (B. Preston Rich)

ARCHIVE listproc@financenet.gov [body = HELP]

5414 alt.irs.class-action Discussing a class-action suit against the U.S.'s IRS. *Newsgroup*

5415 asset-liab-mgt: List for government financial asset and liability management. *Distribution List, moderated*

http://www.financenet.gov/

± listproc@financenet.gov [body = SUBSCRIBE ASSET-LIAB-MGT first-name last-name]

OWNER preston.rich@nsf.gov (B. Preston Rich)

ARCHIVE listproc@financenet.gov [body = HELP]

5416 budget-net: List for government budgeteers. *Digest & Reflector, moderated*

http://www.financenet.gov/

± listproc@financenet.gov [body = SUBSCRIBE BUDGET-NET first-name last-name]

OWNER preston.rich@nsf.gov (B. Preston Rich)

ARCHIVE listproc@financenet.gov [body = HELP]

5417 Calendar: For Public Financial Managers: part of Al Gore's FinanceNet. *Mailing List*

± listproc@financenet.gov [body = SUBSCRIBE CALENDAR first-name last-name]

OWNER support@financenet.gov

5418 can.taxes Discussion of how to pay or not pay taxes in Canada. *Newsgroup*

➤ **City of Grande Prairie, Alberta, Canada:** Information on strategic and business planning in a municipal setting. (See entry 5513 for full listing.)

5419 clari.news.usa.gov.financial Fiscal and financial U.S. policy. *Moderated newsgroup*

5420 clari.world.gov.budgets National budgets, deficits, loans, and debt. *Moderated newsgroup*

5421 corporate-welfare: On eliminating special-interest handouts: "corporate welfare." *Distribution List*

± listproc@essential.org [body = SUBSCRIBE CORPORATE-WELFARE first-name last-name]

OWNER jshields@essential.org (Janice Shields)

5422 Daybook: For the General Accounting Office (GAO)'s Daybook: reports and testimony. *Distribution List*
± `majordomo@www.gao.gov` [body = SUBSCRIBE DAYBOOK]
INFO `info@www.gao.gov`
OWNER `documents@gao.gov`

5423 fin-audits: List for government financial audits. *Distribution List, moderated*
`http://www.financenet.gov/`
± `listproc@financenet.gov` [body = SUBSCRIBE FIN-AUDITS first-name last-name]
OWNER `preston.rich@nsf.gov` (B. Preston Rich)
ARCHIVE `listproc@financenet.gov` [body = HELP]

5424 fin-jobs: List for government jobs in financial management. *Distribution List, moderated*
`http://www.financenet.gov/news.htm`
± `listproc@financenet.gov` [body = SUBSCRIBE FIN-JOBS first-name last-name]
OWNER `preston.rich@nsf.gov` (B. Preston Rich)
ARCHIVE `listproc@financenet.gov` [body = HELP]
Gated: `news.financenet.gov`

5425 fin-reporting: List for government financial statements and reporting. *Distribution List, moderated*
`http://www.financenet.gov/`
± `listproc@financenet.gov` [body = SUBSCRIBE FIN-REPORTING first-name last-name]
OWNER `preston.rich@nsf.gov` (B. Preston Rich)
ARCHIVE `listproc@financenet.gov` [body = HELP]

5426 fin-systems: List for issues in government financial systems. *Distribution List, moderated*
`http://www.financenet.gov/`
± `listproc@financenet.gov` [body = SUBSCRIBE FIN-SYSTEMS first-name last-name]
OWNER `preston.rich@nsf.gov` (B. Preston Rich)
ARCHIVE `listproc@financenet.gov` [body = HELP]

5427 GFOA: List for members of the Government Finance Officers Association. *Digest & Reflector, moderated*
`http://www.financenet.gov/`
± `listproc@financenet.gov` [body = SUBSCRIBE GFOA first-name last-name]
OWNER `preston.rich@nsf.gov` (B. Preston Rich)
ARCHIVE `listproc@financenet.gov` [body = HELP]

➤ **Industry Canada:** This site was created to promote jobs and growth in Canada in a world characterized by global integration and the growth of knowledge-based economies. (See entry 7144 for full listing.)

5428 `misc.taxes` Tax laws and advice. *Newsgroup*

➤ **MuniNet:** List for municipal government administrators. (See entry 5475 for full listing.)

5429 procurement: List for government procurement, acquisition, and electronic commerce. *Distribution List, moderated*
`http://www.financenet.gov/`
± `listproc@financenet.gov` [body = SUBSCRIBE PROCUREMENT first-name last-name]
OWNER `preston.rich@nsf.gov` (B. Preston Rich)
ARCHIVE `listproc@financenet.gov` [body = HELP]

5430 TAX THE RICH: A campaign to promote taxation of the rich.
`http://www.webcom.com/ttr/home.html`
INFO `ttr@webcom.com`

5431 U.S. Internal Revenue Service: Tax information galore. Download tax forms, get tax help, give feedback to your favorite government agency, and more!
`http://www.irs.ustreas.gov/`
`ftp://ftp.fedworld.gov/pub/`

INFO `helpdesk@fedworld.gov`

5432 The Villanova Tax Law Compendium: An online publication that consists of papers done by faculty, practitioners, and students concerning tax law. It contains timely and informative pieces on tax law in a hypertext format to simplify the research for the tax practitioner.

`http://www.law.vill.edu/vill.tax.l.compen/`

`gopher://gopher.law.vill.edu/11/.tax/`

INFO `vcilp@mail.law.vill.edu`

GOVERNMENT—FIREFIGHTING

5433 Firefighter: Sergeant Tom Wright's firefighters home page, with many links to fire departments and much more.

`http://www.mich.com/~kimsey`

INFO `kimsey@mich.com`

5434 `bit.listserv.fire-1` Firefighting discussions. *Moderated newsgroup*

5435 `clari.sfbay.fire` Stories from fire departments of the SF Bay Area. *Moderated newsgroup*

GOVERNMENT—FOREIGN POLICY

5436 `clari.news.usa.gov.foreign_policy` U.S. foreign policy. *Moderated newsgroup*

5437 `clari.usa.gov.policy.foreign.mideast` U.S. government foreign policy in the Middle East. *Moderated newsgroup*

5438 `clari.usa.gov.policy.foreign.misc` U.S. government foreign policy. *Moderated newsgroup*

5439 `clari.world.gov.intl_relations` Relations between governments. *Moderated newsgroup*

➤ **RAND:** Website of RAND, a nonprofit institution that helps improve public policy through research and analysis. The site includes RAND publications, a wide range of information on its projects, and initiatives. (See entry 9553 for full listing.)

GOVERNMENT—INTERNATIONAL ORGANIZATIONS

➤ **`alt.politics.org.un`:** Politics at the "United" Nations. *Newsgroup*

5440 `clari.world.organizations` The UN and other organizations. *Moderated newsgroup*

5441 `clari.world.organizations.misc` News of international organizations. *Moderated newsgroup*

5442 `clari.world.organizations.un` News of the United Nations. *Moderated newsgroup*

5443 `clari.world.organizations.un.conferences` UN summits and conferences. *Moderated newsgroup*

➤ **ICGEBnet:** This is the information server of the International Center for Genetic Engineering and Biotechnology, Trieste, Italy. It carries molecular biology and biotechnology-related information. This site also contains information on safety aspects of biotechnology and of genetically modified organisms. (See entry 9113 for full listing.)

➤ **International Security Network (IntSecNet):** A one-stop virtual library and information network for security and defense studies, peace and conflict research, and international relations. The International Security Network is a joint effort of diverse research institutions, financially supported by the Swiss government. (See entry 10110 for full listing.)

5444 NATODATA: Public data from the North Atlantic Treaty Organization (NATO). *Distribution List, moderated*

`gopher://gopher.nato.int:70/1`

`http://www.nato.int/`

± `listserv@cc1.kuleuven.ac.be` [body = SUBSCRIBE NATODATA first-name last-name]

INFO `natodoc@hq.nato.int`

OWNER `scheurweghs@hq.nato.int` (Chris Scheurweghs)

Language: English/French

Comments: Sub-distribution lists are available.

5445 United Nations Development Programme Information System: This site contains information related to the United Nations Development Program and other United Nations agencies.

http://www.undp.org/
gopher://gopher.undp.org
INFO webmaster@undp.org

5446 The World Bank: This site contains information about the World Bank, its press releases, country and project Information, regional information, publications, and research studies.

http://www.worldbank.org/
INFO comments@www.worldbank.org
FAQ http://www.worldbank.org/html/faq/TOC.html

➤ **The World Health Organization:** This site provides information on epidemiology, world health statistics, international travel vaccination requirements, and more. (See entry 5043 for full listing.)

GOVERNMENT—JUDICIAL BRANCH

5447 The Federal Court Locator: The Federal Court Locator is a service provided by the Villanova Center for Information Law and Policy and is intended to be the home page for the federal court system on the Internet. This page provides links to information concerning the federal judiciary, including slip opinions, that can be viewed or downloaded by the net citizen. If you learn of a federal court site on the Internet, please mail us so that we can add it to this page and continue to improve the access to our courts.

http://www.law.vill.edu/Fed-Ct/fedcourt.html
INFO kmortens@mail.law.vill.edu (Kenneth P. Mortensen)

➤ **The Federal Web Locator:** The Federal Web Locator is a service provided by the Villanova Center for Information Law and Policy and is a one-stop shopping point for federal government information on the World Wide Web. The site covers the executive, judicial, and legislative branches of the federal government, as well as the executive agencies (departments), the independent establishments and government corporations, and the nongovernment federally related sites. (See entry 5369 for full listing.)

➤ **Antitrust Policy:** An online resource linking economic research, policy, and legal cases. The site includes a public discussion area, information on current antitrust actions, and other related information including price-fixing, mergers, and vertical restraints. (See entry 5529 for full listing.)

5448 clari.news.usa.law.supreme The U.S. Supreme Court. *Moderated newsgroup*

5449 clari.usa.law.supreme The U.S. Supreme Court. *Moderated newsgroup*

5450 courts.usa.federal.supreme U.S. Supreme Court. *Moderated newsgroup*

5451 courts.usa.state.ohio.appls-8th Ohio Court of Appeals, Eighth District. *Moderated newsgroup*

5452 courts.usa.state.ohio.supreme Ohio Supreme Court. *Moderated newsgroup*

5453 law.court.federal Discussion group for placing federal court materials on the Internet. *Newsgroup*

5454 Supreme Court Decisions: Access to the decisions of the U.S. Supreme Court since 1990; indexed by topic and keyword. This site is sponsored by the Legal Information Institute at Cornell University.

http://www.law.cornell.edu/supct/
INFO lii@lii.law.cornell.edu

➤ **U.S. Securites & Exchange Commission (SEC):** Access to the EDGAR database and other information from the SEC. (See entry 1783 for full listing.)

GOVERNMENT—LAW ENFORCEMENT

5455 alt.binaries.pictures.cops Pictures of police officers. *Newsgroup*

5456 alt.law-enforcement No, Ossifer, there's nothing illegal going on in alt. *Newsgroup*

5457 alt.politics.org.fbi The United States Federal Bureau of Investigation. *Newsgroup*

5458 alt.prisons Can I get an alt.* feed in the slammer? *Newsgroup*

5459 CJUST-L: Criminal justice discussion list. *Mailing List, moderated*

± listserv@cunyvm.cuny.edu [body = SUBSCRIBE CJUST-L first-name last-name]
INFO cjust-l-request@cunyvm.cuny.edu (Alex Rudd)

5460 **clari.news.law_enforce** Police officers, prisons, law enforcement. *Moderated newsgroup*

➤ **clari.sfbay.police:** Stories from the police departments of the SF Bay Area. *Moderated newsgroup*

5461 **POLICE-L:** On policing—restricted to sworn police officers. *Mailing List*
± listserv@cunyvm.cuny.edu [body = SUBSCRIBE POLICE-L first-name last-name]
INFO police-l-request@cunyvm.cuny.edu
Please Note: Subscription by approval only.
Comments: All subscription requests will be subject to employment status verification.

GOVERNMENT—LEGISLATIVE BRANCH

➤ **The Federal Web Locator:** The Federal Web Locator is a service provided by the Villanova Center for Information Law and Policy and is a one-stop shopping point for federal government information on the World Wide Web. The site covers the executive, judicial, and legislative branches of the federal government, as well as the executive agencies (departments), the independent establishments and government corporations, and the nongovernment federally related sites. (See entry 5369 for full listing.)

➤ **Library of Congress:** Information from the Library of Congress, including access to other Library of Congress Internet services that are available via gopher (LC MARVEL), file transfer protocol (FTP), and telnet (LOCIS). The library's home page provides access to electronic exhibits and events, digitized collections, government information, and other World Wide Web resources. (See entry 5737 for full listing.)

5462 **alt.politics.usa.congress** Discussions relating to U.S. House and Senate. *Newsgroup*

➤ **alt.politics.usa.constitution:** U.S. constitutional politics. *Newsgroup*

5463 **CONG-REFORM:** For the Congressional Accountability Project: briefings on congressional reform. *Mailing List*
± listserver@essential.org
EDITOR OWNER gary@essential.org (Gary Ruskin)

➤ **Daybook:** For the General Accounting Office (GAO)'s Daybook: reports and testimony. (See entry 5422 for full listing.)

5464 **Office of Senator Bob Kerrey:** This is the home page of Senator Bob Kerrey of Nebraska
ftp://ftp.senate.gov/member/ne/kerrey/general/kerrey.html
INFO webmaster@kerrey.senate.gov

5465 **Office of U.S. Senator Jeff Bingaman:** The home page of U.S. Senator Jeff Bingaman, Democrat-New Mexico
http://www.senate.gov/~bingaman
ftp://ftp.senate.gov/member/nm/bingaman
gopher://gopher.senate.gov/member/nm/bingaman
INFO webcomments@bingaman.senate.gov

5466 **U.S. General Accounting Office (GAO):** Website of the investigative arm of Congress. The GAO is charged with examining matters relating to the receipt and disbursement of public funds. It performs audits and evaluations of government programs and activities.
http://www.gao.gov/
INFO webmaster@www.gao.gov
FAQ http://www.gao.gov/faq/faq.htm

5467 **U.S. Senate:** U.S. Senate online information services.
http://www.senate.gov/
gopher://gopher.senate.gov
INFO webmaster@scc.senate.gov
FAQ http://www.senate.gov/other/faq.html

5468 **U.S. Thomas:** U.S. legislative information.

```
http://thomas.loc.gov/
```
INFO thomas@loc.gov

5469 US House: U.S. House of Representatives online information services.
```
http://www.house.gov/
gopher://gopher.house.gov
```
INFO househlp@hr.house.gov

5470 The Zipper: With this resource you can find your congressional representatives (both House and Senate) based on your zip code.
```
http://www.stardot.com/zipper/
```
INFO info@stardot.com

GOVERNMENT—MANAGEMENT

➤ **asset-liab-mgt:** List for government financial asset and liability management. (See entry 5415 for full listing.)

➤ **fin-audits:** List for government financial audits. (See entry 5423 for full listing.)

5471 fin-policy: List for government financial administrative policy. *Distribution List, moderated*
```
http://www.financenet.gov/
```
± listproc@financenet.gov [body = SUBSCRIBE FIN-POLICY first-name last-name]
OWNER preston.rich@nsf.gov (B. Preston Rich)
ARCHIVE listproc@financenet.gov [body = HELP]

➤ **fin-reporting:** List for government financial statements and reporting. (See entry 5425 for full listing.)

➤ **fin-systems:** List for issues in government financial systems. (See entry 5426 for full listing.)

5472 fin-training: List for government financial management training. *Distribution List, moderated*
```
http://www.financenet.gov/
```
± listproc@financenet.gov [body = SUBSCRIBE FIN-TRAINING first-name last-name]
OWNER preston.rich@nsf.gov (B. Preston Rich)
ARCHIVE listproc@financenet.gov [body = HELP]

5473 GOVMANAG: On management and leadership in government. *Mailing List*
± listserv@list.nih.gov [body = SUBSCRIBE GOVMANAG first-name last-name]
OWNER smg@vm.cfsan.fda.gov (Steven Gendel)

5474 int-controls: List for internal controls issues in government. *Distribution List, moderated*
```
http://www.financenet.gov/
```
± listproc@financenet.gov [body = SUBSCRIBE INT-CONTROLS first-name last-name]
OWNER preston.rich@nsf.gov (B. Preston Rich)
ARCHIVE listproc@financenet.gov [body = HELP]

5475 MuniNet: List for municipal government administrators. *Digest & Reflector, moderated*
```
http://www.financenet.gov/
```
± listproc@financenet.gov [body = SUBSCRIBE MuniNet first-name last-name]
OWNER preston.rich@nsf.gov (B. Preston Rich)
ARCHIVE listproc@financenet.gov [body = HELP]

5476 payroll: List for government payroll. *Digest & Reflector, moderated*
```
http://www.financenet.gov/
```
± listproc@financenet.gov [body = SUBSCRIBE PAYROLL first-name last-name]
OWNER preston.rich@nsf.gov (B. Preston Rich)
ARCHIVE listproc@financenet.gov [body = HELP]

5477 perf-measures: List for performance measurement in government. *Distribution List, moderated*
```
http://www.financenet.gov/
```

± listproc@financenet.gov [body = SUBSCRIBE PERF-MEASURES first-name last-name]
OWNER preston.rich@nsf.gov (B. Preston Rich)
ARCHIVE listproc@financenet.gov [body = HELP]

➤ **soc.veterans:** Social issues relating to military veterans. *Newsgroup*

5478 **state-county:** List for state and local government administrators. *Digest & Reflector, moderated*
http://www.financenet.gov/
± listproc@financenet.gov [body = SUBSCRIBE STATE-COUNTY first-name last-name]
OWNER preston.rich@nsf.gov (B. Preston Rich)
ARCHIVE listproc@financenet.gov [body = HELP]

5479 **travel:** List for government travel administration. *Distribution List, moderated*
http://www.financenet.gov/
± listproc@financenet.gov [body = SUBSCRIBE TRAVEL first-name last-name]
OWNER preston.rich@nsf.gov (B. Preston Rich)
ARCHIVE listproc@financenet.gov [body = HELP]

➤ **U.S. National Performance Review:** The home page for the National Performance Review, where you can obtain highlights of recent NPR developments, NPR reports and news, the NPR library, and links to other related World Wide Web servers. (See entry 5410 for full listing.)

GOVERNMENT—MILITARY

5480 **AJAX Military and Intelligence Agencies Access:** This site is an extensive collection of pointers to the Web sites of U.S. and international government military, intelligence, and security agencies.
http://www.users.interport.net/~sagal/ajax.html
INFO sagal@interport.net

5481 **alt.culture.military-brats** We learned to walk in Army bootees. *Newsgroup*

5482 **alt.desert-storm** Continuing proof that alt groups never die. *Newsgroup*

5483 **alt.folklore.military** Military-oriented urban legends and folklore. *Newsgroup*

5484 **alt.military.aas** The Air Force's cadet honor society, Arnold Air. *Newsgroup*

5485 **alt.military.afrotc** Air Force ROTC discussions. *Newsgroup*

5486 **alt.military.cadet** Preparing for the coming apocalypse. *Newsgroup*

5487 **alt.military.police** Discussions of military police matters. *Newsgroup*

5488 **alt.politics.org.cia** The United States Central Intelligence Agency. *Newsgroup*

5489 **alt.politics.org.nsa** The ultrasecret security arm of the US government. *Newsgroup*

➤ **alt.war:** Not just collateral damage. *Newsgroup*

➤ **BosNews:** News about Bosnia and Herzegovina, including news from the international press. (See entry 7805 for full listing.)

5490 **can.community.military** Issues about military-community life. *Newsgroup*

5491 **can.military-brats** Current and former dependents of the Canadian military. *Newsgroup*

5492 **Center for Defense Information (CDI):** This site provides a variety of defense-related information, including an arms trade database, access to its paper publication *The Defense Monitor*, its TV program "America's Defense Monitor," a nifty "Military Spending Clock" that shows how fast your tax dollars are spent by the military, and pointers to other defense- and security-related resources on the Internet.
http://www.cdi.org/
INFO info@cdi.org

5493 **clari.news.usa.military** News of the U.S. military. *Moderated newsgroup*

5494 **clari.tw.defense** Defense industry issues. *Moderated newsgroup*

5495 `clari.tw.defense.cbd` Weapons, ammunition, nuclear ordnance. *Moderated newsgroup*

5496 `clari.usa.military` News of the U.S. military. *Moderated newsgroup*

5497 `clari.world.military` News of militaries from around the world. *Moderated newsgroup*

➤ **Department of Defense (DoD) Information Analysis Center (IAC) Hub Page:** The purpose of this site is to provide access to information produced by and about the DoD IACs that may be appropriate to the requirements of sponsoring technical communities. (See entry 9362 for full listing.)

➤ **DISARM-L:** On disarmament, including military and political strategy; technology; sociology; peace activism; conventional, chemical, and biological weapons; superpower intervention and exploitation of the Third World; economic disruption; and nonaggression. (See entry 10107 for full listing.)

➤ **International Security Network (IntSecNet):** A one-stop virtual library and information network for security and defense studies, peace and conflict research, and international relations. The International Security Network is a joint effort of diverse research institutions, financially supported by the Swiss government. (See entry 10110 for full listing.)

5498 **ISN:** Data from the International Relations and Security Network (ISN), previously the Academic Defence and Security Network (DEFSEC-NET). *Distribution List, moderated*
`gopher://gopher.nato.int:70/1`
`http://www.fsk.ethz.ch/FSK/`
`http://www.nato.int/`
± `listserv@cc1.kuleuven.ac.be` [body = SUBSCRIBE ISN first-name last-name]
INFO `scheurwe@hq.nato.int` (Chris Scheurweghs)
EDITOR `koeppel@sipo.reok.ethz.ch` (Thomas Koeppel)
Language: English/French

➤ **NATODATA:** Public data from the North Atlantic Treaty Organization (NATO). (See entry 5444 for full listing.)

5499 **NATOPRES:** Press releases from the North Atlantic Treaty Organization (NATO). *Distribution List, moderated*
`gopher://gopher.nato.int:70/1`
`http://www.nato.int/`
± `listserv@cc1.kuleuven.ac.be` [body = SUBSCRIBE NATOPRES first-name last-name]
INFO `natodoc@hq.nato.int`
OWNER `scheurweghs@hq.nato.int` (Chris Scheurweghs)
Language: English/French

5500 **Navy News Service (NAVNEWS):** United States Department of Navy news about fleet operations, exercises, personnel, policies, budget actions, and more. *Newsletter*
`gopher://marvel.loc.gov`
`http://www.navy.mil/navpalib/news/navnews/.www/navnews.html`
`http://www.navy.mil/navpalib/news/navnews/.www/navnews.html`
`ftp://ftp.navy.mil/navpalib/news/navnews`
INFO `waterman@media.mediacen.navy.mil` (LT Dave Waterman)
INFO `navnews-request@ncts.navy.mil`
EDITOR `navnews@opnav-emh.navy.mil` (JO1 Laurie Butler)
ARCHIVES
`gopher://marvel.loc.gov`
`http://www.navy.mil/navpalib/news/navnews/.www/navnews.html`
`ftp://ftp.navy.mil/navpalib/news/navnews`
Frequency: weekly

5501 `sci.military.moderated` Military technology. *Moderated newsgroup*

5502 `sci.military.naval` Navies of the world, past, present and future. *Newsgroup*

5503 `soc.history.war.misc` History and events of wars in general. *Newsgroup*

5504 **soc.politics.arms-d** Arms discussion digest. *Moderated newsgroup*

5505 **soc.veterans** Social issues relating to military veterans. *Newsgroup*

5506 **SUBOPS:** For submarine operators, past and present: just us bubbleheads. *Mailing List*
± majordomo@c2.org
OWNER hroller@metronet.com
Please Note: Subscription by approval only.

5507 **VWAR-L:** For communication among veterans, scholars, and students of the Vietnam War—the networking component of the Vietnam Veterans Oral History and Folklore Project. *Digest & Reflector*
± listserv@ubvm.cc.buffalo.edu [body = SUBSCRIBE VWAR-L first-name last-name]
INFO vwar-l-request@ubvm.cc.buffalo.edu
ARCHIVE listserv@ubvm.cc.buffalo.edu [body = INDEX VWAR-L]

GOVERNMENT—NEWS

5508 **C-SPAN:** Cable-Satellite Public Affairs Network's Web and gopher sites to information about C-SPAN, job opportunities, reports, articles, press releases, historic documents and speeches, and more.
http://www.c-span.org/
gopher://c-span.org
INFO viewer@c-span.org

5509 **can.gov.announce** Announcements from the Canadian government. *Moderated newsgroup*

5510 **clari.usa.gov.policy.social** U.S. government social policy. *Moderated newsgroup*

5511 **clari.usa.gov.releases** U.S. government press releases. *Moderated newsgroup*

➤ **The Washington Weekly:** Political newsmagazine offering conservative opinion, unbiased news reporting, and extensive information on bills, speeches, and transcripts. (See entry 5608 for full listing.)

GOVERNMENT—REFORM & REENGINEERING

➤ **alt.politics.equality:** An oxymoron. *Newsgroup*

5512 **alt.politics.reform** Political reform. *Newsgroup*

➤ **BPRREENG-L:** On applying business process re-engineering (BPR) to universities. (See entry 4092 for full listing.)

5513 **City of Grande Prairie, Alberta, Canada:** Information on strategic and business planning in a municipal setting.
http://www.ccinet.ab.ca/city-of-gp/homepage.html
INFO cmeek@city.grande-prairie.ab.ca (Chet Meek)

5514 **clari.news.corruption** Corruption in government. *Moderated newsgroup*

➤ **CONG-REFORM:** For the Congressional Accountability Project: briefings on congressional reform. (See entry 5463 for full listing.)

➤ **corporate-welfare:** On eliminating special-interest handouts: "corporate welfare." (See entry 5421 for full listing.)

➤ **fin-audits:** List for government financial audits. (See entry 5423 for full listing.)

➤ **perf-measures:** List for performance measurement in government. (See entry 5477 for full listing.)

➤ **U.S. National Performance Review:** The home page for the National Performance Review, where you can obtain highlights of recent NPR developments, NPR reports and news, the NPR library, and links to other related World Wide Web servers. (See entry 5410 for full listing.)

GOVERNMENT—STATE & LOCAL

➤ **Government Sources of Business and Economic Information on the Internet:** Includes agriculture, area codes, census, Congressional Directory, economic information, Edgar, EPA, FDA, GAO, health, labor, NIST, OSHA, patents, postal information, SEC, Social Security, state government resources, travel advisories, USDA, weather, the White House, and more. (See entry 5384 for full listing.)

5515 `clari.news.usa.gov.state+local` State and local governments. *Moderated newsgroup*

5516 `clari.usa.gov.state+local` State and local governments. *Moderated newsgroup*

➤ **state-county:** List for state and local government administrators. (See entry 5478 for full listing.)

GOVERNMENT—TECHNOLOGY POLICY

➤ **City of Grande Prairie, Alberta, Canada:** Information on strategic and business planning in a municipal setting. (See entry 5513 for full listing.)

➤ **CMEP-LIST:** Public Citizen's action alerts on energy policy. (See entry 9225 for full listing.)

➤ `comp.org.cpsr.talk:` Issues of computing and social responsibility. *Newsgroup*

5517 **Digital Information Infrastructure Guide (DIIG):** A resource to facilitate the development of the National Information Infrastructure (NII).
`http://farnsworth.mit.edu/diig.html`
INFO `diig@farnsworth.mit.edu`

➤ **Economic Democracy Information Network (EDIN):** A project dedicated to expanding the voice of community organizations on the information superhighway. (See entry 9646 for full listing.)

5518 **GII:** Agenda for Cooperation, by Al Gore and Ron Brown.
`http://ntiaunix1.ntia.doc.gov:70/0/papers/documents/giiagend.html`

➤ **Internet Economics Collection:** The economics of the Internet, information goods, intellectual property, and related issues. (See entry 5205 for full listing.)

5519 **IP Policy OnRamp:** A service by the General Services Administration (GSA), Office of Information Technology (IT) Policy and Leadership, USA; information about information technology policy.
`http://www.itpolicy.gsa.gov/`
INFO `it.policy@gsa.gov`

5520 **National Institute of Standards & Technology (NIST):** Information about NIST programs, products, and activities. The site includes GAMS (Guide to Available Mathematical Software) and a computer security bulletin board.
`http://www.boulder.nist.gov/`
`http://www.nist.gov/`
`gopher://gopher-server.nist.gov`
INFO `webmaster@nist.gov`

5521 **NII Scan:** Compilation of NII (National Information Infrastructure) policies worldwide. Distibuted from Singapore. *Newsletter*
`http://www.ncb.gov.sg/nii/scan.html`
± `http://www.ncb.gov.sg/nii`
INFO `cheemeng@ncb.gov.sg` (Mr Chee-Meng Loh, Deputy Director, NII Division)
INFO `eileen@ncb.gov.sg` (Eileen Lim)
OWNER `http://www.ncb.gov.sg/`
ARCHIVE `http://www.ncb.gov.sg/nii`
Frequency: monthly

➤ **RAND:** Website of RAND, a nonprofit institution that helps improve public policy through research and analysis. The site includes RAND publications, a wide range of information on its projects, and initiatives. (See entry 9553 for full listing.)

➤ **TELECOMREG:** On telecommunication regulation. (See entry 9638 for full listing.)

➤ **TELXCH-L:** On telecomunications in the state of New York and national telecommunications and policy issues related to digital infrastructure. (See entry 9640 for full listing.)

➤ **USA-HPCC Web:** This server provides Internet users access to material about the National Coordination Office for Federal High Performance Computing and Communications (HPCC) Program. (See entry 3814 for full listing.)

LAW

5522   <u>**Cornel Law School:**</u> Web site of the Law School at Cornel University. As well as hosting a database of all recent Supreme Court decisions, this site hosts a number of other useful law resources.

http://www.law.cornell.edu/

INFO majeroni@law.mail.cornell.edu

➤   <u>**Legal ResearchNet:**</u> This site provides links to all kinds of law resources on the Internet. (See entry 5570 for full listing.)

5523   <u>**The Legal List (Law-Related Resources on the Internet and Elsewhere):**</u> Lists numerous law-related government, educational, and corporate Internet resources. Copyright © 1995 Lawyers Cooperative Publishing.

http://www.lcp.com/

ftp://ftp.lcp.com/pub/LegalList/legallist.txt

gopher://gopher.lcp.com

listserv@lcp.com [body = subscribe legal-list first-name last-name]

INFO lgregory@lcp.com (Lisa K. Gregory)

MIRROR ftp://una.hh.lib.umich.edu/inetdirsstacks/law:heels

5524   clari.news.usa.law Legal news and U.S. lawsuits. *Moderated newsgroup*

5525   **Court TV Law Center:** This site offers basic legal guidance on everything from family law to small-business issues. There are seminars, games, discussion forums, and an "Ask the Laywers" section where you can submit legal questions via e-mail.

http://www.courttv.com/

INFO comment@courttv.com

5526   misc.legal Legalities and the ethics of law. *Newsgroup*

5527   misc.legal.moderated All aspects of law. *Moderated newsgroup*

5528   **ReligionLaw:** On religion and the law; technical orientation. *Mailing List*

± listserv@grizzly.ucla.edu [body = SUBSCRIBE RELIGIONLAW first-name last-name]

OWNER volokh@law.ucla.edu (Eugene Volokh)

LAW—ANTITRUST

5529   **Antitrust Policy:** An online resource linking economic research, policy, and legal cases. The site includes a public discussion area, information on current antitrust actions, and other related information including price-fixing, mergers, and vertical restraints.

http://www.vanderbilt.edu/Owen/froeb/antitrust/antitrust.html

INFO luke.froeb@macpost.vanderbilt.edu

5530   law.school.antitrust Electronic study group for antitrust. *Newsgroup*

LAW—BUSINESS & COMMERCIAL

5531   **ADLAW:** For changes, updates, and additions to Advertising Law Internet Site. *Mailing List, moderated*

± advertising-law-request@webcom.com

OWNER lewrose@arentfox.com (Lewis Rose)

ARCHIVE http://www.webcom.com/~lewrose/home.html

FAQ http://www.webcom.com/~lewrose/home.html

➤   **Antitrust Policy:** An online resource linking economic research, policy, and legal cases. The site includes a public discussion area, information on current antitrust actions, and other related information including price-fixing, mergers, and vertical restraints. (See entry 5529 for full listing.)

5532   **The Bankruptcy Lawfinder:** This site includes listings on case law, statutes and regulations, bankruptcy-related federal government locations, and bankruptcy-related legal resources on the Internet.

http://www.tiac.net/users/agin/blawfind.html

INFO agin@tiac.net

5533 **The Securities Law Home Page:** This Web site is designed to provide information to the Internet community regarding the law as it relates to the United States financial markets, and those who participate in those markets—stockbrokers and investors.

http://www.seclaw.com/

INFO astarita@seclaw.com

LAW—COMPUTER & TECHNOLOGY

5534 `comp.patents` Discussing patents of computer technology. *Moderated newsgroup*

5535 **Computer Law Observer:** On current legal issues relating to computers and technology (for nonlawyers). Includes information on software, hardware, and online systems and communications. *Newsletter*

± OWNER wgalkin@earthlink.net (William S. Galkin)

Frequency: Weekly

➤ **Computer Security Resource Clearinghouse:** This site, sponsored by the National Institute of Standards and Technology, provides a wide range of information on computer security topics, including: general security risks, privacy, legal issues, viruses, assurance, policy, and training. (See entry 3682 for full listing.)

➤ **Computer Underground Digest (CuD):** Discussion of legal, ethical, social, and other issues regarding computerized information and communications. Readers are encouraged to submit reasoned articles relating to computer culture and communication. (See entry 3719 for full listing.)

➤ **CYBER-RIGHTS:** Campaign for cyber rights: "Don't let the grinch steal cyberspace!" (See entry 9748 for full listing.)

5536 **CYBERIA-L:** On the law and policy of computer networks. *Mailing List*

± listserv@listserv.cc.wm.edu [body = SUBSCRIBE CYBERLAW first-name last-name]

INFO thardy@mail.wm.edu (Trotter Hardy)

5537 **Harvard Journal of Law & Technology:** Subscription information and table of contents of the *Journal*.

http://studorg.law.harvard.edu/jolt/

INFO jolt@law.harvard.edu

5538 **Information Law Alert:** A newsletter on technology, telecommunications, and intellectual property. *Newsletter*

± INFO voorhees@interport.net (Mark Voorhees)

ARCHIVE voorhees@interport.net (Mark Voorhees)

Frequency: twenty times a year

Price: $275 a year for twenty issues

5539 **Legal Bytes:** Newsletter of current legal issues on computers and communications. *Newsletter*

http://www.eff.org/pub/Publications/E-Journals/Legal_Bytes/

http://www.iyp.com/usa/tx/austin/lawfirms/gdf/lbytes.htm

± legal-bytes-request@io.com [body = subscribe legal-bytes]

INFO pkennedy@io.com (Pete Kennedy)

ARCHIVE gopher://gopher.eff.org/11/Publications/E-Journals/Legal_Bytes

Frequency: quarterly

5540 `misc.legal.computing` Discussing the legal climate of the computing world. *Newsgroup*

5541 **Net-Lawyers:** On using the Internet in the practice of law. *Digest & Reflector, moderated*

± listproc@lawlib.wuacc.edu [body = SUBSCRIBE NET-LAWYERS first-name last-name]

OWNER lewrose@arentfox.com (Lewis Rose)

ARCHIVE http://lawlib.wuacc.edu/archives.html Net-lawyers

5542 **NetWatchers Cyberzine:** A monthly cyberzine covering developments in the law of cyberspace and the online world. *Newsletter*

http://www.ionet.net/~mdyer/netwatch.html

± INFO OWNER mdyer@ionet.net (Marshall Dyer)

ARCHIVE mdyer@ionet.net (Marshall Dyer)

Frequency: monthly

5543 `relcom.comp.law` Political and legal aspects of computers. *Newsgroup*

5544 **Richmond Journal of Law & Technology:** Student law journal published at the University of Richmond School of Law, and dedicated to the publication of timely articles on the evolving field of law and technology. *E-Journal*

`http://www.urich.edu/~jolt`

INFO EDITOR OWNER `jlt@uofrlaw.urich.edu` (Richard P. Klau, Editor in Chief.)

EDITOR `klaurich@uofrlaw.urich.edu` (Rick Klau)

Frequency: twice a year

➤ **SEA: the society for electronic access.:** A New York City-based organization that promotes civil liberties and access in cyberspace. (See entry 9751 for full listing.)

5545 **StudentLawTech:** For law students interested in issues related to law and technology. *Mailing List*

`http://www.infi.net/~rklau/studentlawtech/`

± `listserv@listserv.law.cornell.edu` [body = SUBSCRIBE STUDENTLAWTECH first-name last-name]

OWNER `owner-studentlawtech@listserv.law.cornell.edu`

OWNER `heels@justice.eliot.me.us` (Erik Heels)

OWNER `klaurich@uofrlaw.urich.edu` (Rick Klau)

ARCHIVE `http://www.kentlaw.edu/cgi-bin/ldn_news/-T+law.listserv.studentlawtech`

FAQ `http://www.infi.net/~rklau/studentlawtech/faq.html`

5546 **The Villanova Information Law Chronicle:** The Villanova Information Law Chronicle is a hypertext publication that carries the latest in current events concerning information law, papers involving networking and the law, and essays discussing the future of the information infrastructure.

`http://www.law.vill.edu/vill.info.l.chron/`

`ftp://ftp.law.vill.edu/pub/law/chron/`

`gopher://gopher.law.vill.edu/11/.chron/`

INFO `vcilp@mail.law.vill.edu`

LAW—CONSTITUTIONAL

5547 `alt.politics.usa.constitution` U.S. constitutional politics. *Newsgroup*

LAW—COUNTRIES

5548 `can.legal` Canadian law and legal matters. *Newsgroup*

5549 **EE-LAW:** On general legal issues in central and Eastern Europe, and in the NIS. *Mailing List*

± `listproc@cep.nonprofit.net` [body = SUBSCRIBE EE-LAW first-name last-name]

OWNER `cep@minerva.cis.yale.edu` (Civic Education Project)

5550 `fj.soc.law` Topics on law and rights. *Newsgroup*

5551 **IRISHLAW:** On Irish law (Ireland and Northern Ireland). *Mailing List*

`http://web.rtc-tallaght.ie/staff/academic/law/irlaw.html`

± `listserv@irlearn.ucd.ie` [body = SUBSCRIBE IRISHLAW first-name last-name]

INFO `darius.whelan@rtc-tallaght.ie` (Darius Whelan)

ARCHIVE `listserv@irlearn.ucd.ie` [body = INDEX IRISHLAW]

FAQ `http://web.rtc-tallaght.ie/staff/academic/law/faq.htm`

Please Note: Subscription by approval only.

5552 **lawsoc-l:** On the study of law and society in the Canadian context. *Mailing List*

± `listproc@cc.umanitoba.ca`

OWNER `rsmandy@cc.umanitoba.ca`

5553 `relcom.jusinf` Information on laws by "Justicinform". *Moderated newsgroup*

5554 `uk.legal` U.K. legal issues. *Newsgroup*

LAW—CRIMINAL

5555 `alt.fan.marcia-clark` No one would know her, but she prosecuted O. J. Simpson. *Newsgroup*

5556 **CRIMPROF:** On the substantive and pedagogical issues in teaching criminal law and procedure. *Mailing List*
± `listserv@chicagokent.kentlaw.edu` [body = SUBSCRIBE CRIMPROF first-name last-name title institution]
OWNER `ssowle@kentlaw.edu` (Prof. Stephen D. Sowle)
Please Note: Subscription by approval only.

➤ **Forensic-psychiatry:** For scholarly discussion of forensic psychiatry. (See entry 5012 for full listing.)

➤ **Journal of Criminal Justice and Popular Culture:** Reviews of movies with a criminal-justice theme, and refereed papers on criminal justice and popular culture. (See entry 704 for full listing.)

LAW—EDUCATION

➤ **Cornel Law School:** Web site of the Law School at Cornel University. As well as hosting a database of all recent Supreme Court decisions, this site hosts a number of other useful law resources. (See entry 5522 for full listing.)

5557 `bit.listserv.lawsch-l` Law school discussion list. *Newsgroup*

5558 `bit.listserv.lawsch.internships` Law school internships. *Newsgroup*

5559 **EdLaw:** On law and education. *Mailing List*
± `listserv@ukcc.uky.edu` [body = SUBSCRIBE EDLAW first-name last-name]
INFO `nordin@ukcc.uky.edu` (Virginia Davis-Nordin)
INFO OWNER `crovo@ukcc.uky.edu` (Bob Crovo)
ARCHIVE `listserv@ukcc.uky.edu`

5560 **PRELAW-L:** For pre-law advisors: advising prelaw students and running a pre-law program. *Mailing List*
± `prelaw-l-request@vax1.elon.edu`
OWNER `batchelo@vax1.elon.edu` (Dr. Nim Batchelor)

LAW—INSTITUTES

➤ **RAND:** Website of RAND, a nonprofit institution that helps improve public policy through research and analysis. The site includes RAND publications, a wide range of information on its projects, and initiatives. (See entry 9553 for full listing.)

LAW—INTELLECTUAL PROPERTY & PATENTS

➤ **The Advertising Law Internet Site:** This site points to numerous resources regarding advertising and marketing law. (See entry 1807 for full listing.)

➤ **Computer Law Observer:** On current legal issues relating to computers and technology (for nonlawyers). Includes information on software, hardware, and online systems and communications. (See entry 5535 for full listing.)

➤ **Electronic Frontier Foundation:** The Electronic Frontier Foundation is a 501(c)3 nonprofit organization "working in the public interest to protect privacy, free expression, and access to online resources and information." The site includes very important information on the interaction between our government and the Internet, as well as an extensive archive with documents on a wide range of topics, including activism, censorship, cryptography and computer security, net culture and cyber-anthropology, intellectual property, law, privacy, and more. It also archives various e-journals related to its mission. (See entry 9749 for full listing.)

5561 `fj.soc.copyright` Discussion about copyright. *Newsgroup*

➤ **GNU's Bulletin:** The GNU's Bulletin is the semiannual newsletter of the Free Software Foundation, bringing you news about the GNU Project. (See entry 3724 for full listing.)

➤   **info-gnu:** Software development for social change: progress reports from the GNU Project and requests for help. Ask `info-gnu-request@prep.ai.mit.edu` for a list of other mailing lists and resources of all the GNU Project mailing lists and newsgroups. (See entry 3726 for full listing.)

5562   **The Internet Patent Search System:** This site is Source Translation & Optimization's (STO) Internet Patent Search System, a way for people around the world to perform patent searches and access information on the patenting process.

   `http://sunsite.unc.edu/patents/intropat.html`

   INFO `patents@world.std.com`

5563   `misc.int-property` Discussion of intellectual property rights. *Newsgroup*

5564   **Patent Resources Institute, Inc.:** Thousands of engineers, physical scientists, and biotechnologists rapidly learned and lucratively practice patent law without being lawyers. Patent Resources Institute taught them. Find out how.

   `http://www.infor.com/pri`

   INFO `rbh@infor.com`

5565   **Texas Intellectual Property Law Journal:** Searchable abstracts of articles published in recent issues of the *Journal*, the full text of which is currently available online via the WESTLAW® and LEXIS® legal research services.

   `http://www.law.utexas.edu/journals/tiplj/tiplj.html`

   INFO `tiplj@tarlton.law.utexas.edu`

➤   **U.S. Patents and Trademarks:** The home page of the U.S. Patents and Trademarks office includes intellectual property and the national information infrastructure issues. (See entry 5378 for full listing.)

LAW—INTERNATIONAL

5566   `clari.world.law` Non-U.S. laws and lawsuits. *Moderated newsgroup*

5567   **International Trade Law Project (ITLP):** Network resources for legal research and education in the field of international trade law.

   `http://ra.irv.uit.no/trade_law/itlp.html`

   INFO `ralph@irv.uit.no` (Ralph Amissah)

   INFO `ananse@irv.uit.no`

   MIRROR `http://ananse.irv.uit.no/trade_law/nav/trade.html`

LAW—JOURNALS

5568   **E Law: Murdoch Electronic Journal of Law:** Law-related current events, scholarly works, peer-reviewed papers, and law resources on the net. *E-Journal*

   `ftp://infolib.murdoch.edu.au/pub/subj/law/jnl/elaw`

   `gopher://infolib.murdoch.edu.au`

   ± `majordomo@cleo.murdoch.edu.au` [body = subscribe elaw-j]

   INFO `zariski@csuvax1.murdoch.edu.au` (Archie Zariski)

   ARCHIVES

   `ftp://infolib.murdoch.edu.au/pub/subj/law/jnl/elaw`

   `gopher://infolib.murdoch.edu.au`

   Frequency: quarterly

➤   **Harvard Journal of Law & Technology:** Subscription information and table of contents of the *Journal*. (See entry 5537 for full listing.)

➤   **Texas Intellectual Property Law Journal:** Searchable abstracts of articles published in recent issues of the *Journal*, the full text of which is currently available online via the WESTLAW® and LEXIS® legal research services. (See entry 5565 for full listing.)

5569   **Web Journal of Current Legal Issues:** Legal issues in judicial decisions, law reform, legislation, legal research, policy-related socio-legal research, legal information, information technology, and practice. *E-journal*

   `http://www.ncl.ac.uk/~nlawwww/`

   INFO EDITOR `mike.allen@newcastle.ac.uk` (Michael J. Allen, Editor)

Frequency: bimonthly

LAW—LEGAL RESEARCH

5570 **Legal ResearchNet:** This site provides links to all kinds of law resources on the Internet.
http://law.fsu.edu/lawtech/lawserch.html
Comments: In addition to providing nationwide resources, there is also an emphasis on legal resources in Florida.

LAW—LIBRARIES

5571 **HALL-L:** For law librarians in the Houston, Texas area. *Mailing List*
± majordomo@albertus.lawlib.uh.ed
INFO http://www.law.uh.edu/hall/
OWNER guajardo@uh.edu (Richard R. Guajardo)
ARCHIVE http://www.law.uh.edu/hall/

5572 **NOCALL:** Northern California Association of Law Libraries (NOCALL) and the Southern California Association of Law Libraries (SCALL) Internet buddies program was formed to encourage use of the Internet and provide training assistance to their members through guides to using the Internet and directories to legal topics.
http://lawlib.wuacc.edu/nocall/buddies/home.html
INFO loftus@netcom.com
MIRROR ftp://ftp.netcom.com/pub/lo/loftus/nocall/buddies/home.html

5573 **NOCALL-LIST:** For Northern California Association of Law Libraries (NOCALL). *Mailing List*
± listserv@netcom.com [body = SUBSCRIBE nocall-list]
OWNER loftus@netcom.com

5574 **SWALL-L:** For the Southwestern Association of Law Libraries. *Mailing List*
± mailserv@post-office.uh.edu
OWNER guajardo@uh.edu (Richard R. Guajardo)
ARCHIVE http://www.law.uh.edu/swall/

LAW—PERSONAL INJURY & NEGLIGENCE

➤ **civil-justice:** On measures aimed at restricting victims' rights and weakening liability laws. (See entry 9776 for full listing.)

➤ **MEDSTUFF:** Commercial medical information service provided by physicians and allied health professionals who have joined together to offer to the general public the information gleaned through many years of practice and experience at all levels in the profession of medicine. (See entry 4695 for full listing.)

LAW—PROFESSIONAL GROUPS

5575 **bit.listserv.ada-law** ADA law discussions. *Newsgroup*

5576 **PARALEGAL-L:** On the legal assistant/paralegal profession. *Mailing List*
http://lawlib.wuacc.edu/paralegal/paralegal.html
± listserv@lawlib.wuacc.edu [body = SUBSCRIBE PARALEGAL-L first-name last-name]
OWNER ander994@acc.wuacc.edu (Katherine Anderson)

➤ **RECMGMT:** For records and archival management professionals. (See entry 5709 for full listing.)

POLITICS

5577 **Janyne's Political Site Hotlist:** This site lists, and links to, sites that cover budgetary and political issues of interest.
http://www.geocities.com/TheTropics/2063/poli-hot.html
INFO jmkizer@nando.net

5578 **The Jefferson Project:** A guide to political resources on the Internet.

```
http://www.stardot.com/jefferson/
```
INFO jefferson@stardot.com

➤ **PEG, a Peripatetic, Eclectic Gopher:** A collection of pointers to all sorts of Internet resources. Especially strong are its virtual reference desk, Internet assistance, politics and government, medicine, and women's studies resource lists. (See entry 2726 for full listing.)

POLITICS—ACTIVISM

➤ **HandsNet:** HandsNet is a national, nonprofit network that promotes information sharing, cross-sector collaboration, and advocacy among individuals and organizations working on a broad range of public interest issues. The site includes action alerts, forums, and information on the various social programs that HandsNet is involved with. (See entry 9669 for full listing.)

➤ **LaborNet:** A community of labor unions, activists, and organizations using computer networks for sharing information and collaboration with the intent of increasing the human rights and economic justice of workers. (See entry 2004 for full listing.)

5579 **ACTION:** On online activism: networking among activists, planning and strategy, sharing of experience and information, and coordination of efforts. From the Electronic Frontier Foundation. *Mailing List*

± listserv@eff.org [body = SUBSCRIBE ACTION first-name last-name]

5580 **ACTIV-L:** Information for activists involved in peace, empowerment, human rights, and justice. *Mailing List, moderated*

± listserv@mizzou1.missouri.edu [body = SUBSCRIBE ACTIV-L first-name last-name]

INFO mathrich@mizzou1.missouri.edu

ARCHIVE listserv@mizzou1.missouri.edu

Gated: misc.activism.progressive

5581 alt.activism Activities for activists. *Newsgroup*

5582 alt.activism.d A place to discuss issues in alt.activism. *Newsgroup*

➤ alt.org.food-not-bombs: The Food Not Bombs homeless aid organization. *Newsgroup*

5583 alt.politics.equality An oxymoron. *Newsgroup*

5584 bit.listserv.quaker-p Discussion group for Quakers and like-minded people on peace and social action issues. *Moderated newsgroup*

➤ **CAVEAT-L:** To stop interpersonal violence: discussion, information, activism. (See entry 10103 for full listing.)

5585 clari.news.protests Protest movements and actions. *Moderated newsgroup*

➤ **Electronic Frontier Foundation:** The Electronic Frontier Foundation is a 501(c)3 nonprofit organization "working in the public interest to protect privacy, free expression, and access to online resources and information." The site includes very important information on the interaction between our government and the Internet, as well as an extensive archive with documents on a wide range of topics, including activism, censorship, cryptography and computer security, net culture and cyber-anthropology, intellectual property, law, privacy, and more. It also archives various e-journals related to its mission. (See entry 9749 for full listing.)

➤ eug.local.activists: Paul Harrison's local activism list gateway. *Newsgroup*

➤ **The Fourth World Documentation Project:** An electronic library containing over 400 primary texts on political struggles waged by indigenous peoples worldwide for sovereignty, self-determination, and human rights. (See entry 10070 for full listing.)

➤ **futurework:** This list focuses on ways for communities worldwide to deal with economic globalization and technological change. (See entry 9761 for full listing.)

5586 **The Grassroots World Government WWW Site:** This site's purpose is to organize and promote a grassroots movement toward a future world government. The site is not affiliated with any existing mainstream organization, but is rather a glass house for activism toward gobalism.

```
http://www.webcom.com/worldgov
```
INFO crop@ix.netcom.com

5587 Homelands: About national and regional autonomy and independence movements in America and around the world.

http://www.wavefront.com/~Contra_M/homelands/

INFO contra_mundum@wavefront.com

➤ **Human Rights Gopher:** Host of a variety of human-rights organizations. (See entry 10028 for full listing.)

➤ **Hyperreal Drugs Archive:** Includes information on recreational drugs, including subjective reports from users and research into safety issues, as well as items related to drug policy. (See entry 9906 for full listing.)

5588 In Motion Magazine: A U.S. publication that promotes grassroots organizing and discusses art for social change. Includes two special columns, one on affirmative action, the other called "Rural America," which is coedited by the Missouri Rural Crisis Center.

http://www.inmotionmagazine.com/

http://www.cts.com/browse/publish/index3.html

INFO publish@cts.com

➤ **The League for Programming Freedom:** The League for Programming Freedom is a grassroots organization of professors, students, businessmen, programmers, and users dedicated to bringing back the freedom to write programs. Their aim is to reverse the recent changes that prevent programmers from doing their work by fighting software patents and "look and feel" interface copyrights. (See entry 3727 for full listing.)

➤ **Loci:** An online magazine by and for college students. Includes entertainment information, games, chat forums, and more. Sponsored by Barnes & Noble booksellers. (See entry 650 for full listing.)

➤ **McSpotlight:** An online library of detailed, accurate, up-to-date information about the McDonald's Corporation, its business practices, and its effects on the world. Everything you could ever need to know about the "McLibel Trial" and worldwide opposition and resistance to the company (and others like them) can be found on this Web site. Possibly the most comprehensive and damning collection of material on a multinational corporation ever assembled. (See entry 9782 for full listing.)

5589 misc.activism.militia Citizens bearing arms for the common defense. *Moderated newsgroup*

5590 misc.activism.progressive Information for progressive activists. *Moderated newsgroup*

➤ **The Network Observer:** A free online newsletter about networks and democracy, with brief articles of practical advice, and commentary and pointers to useful net resources. (See entry 5611 for full listing.)

5591 PARtalk-L: On participatory action and socially transformative research. *Mailing List, moderated*

± listproc@cornell.edu [body = SUBSCRIBE PARTALK-L first-name last-name]

INFO parnet@cornell.edu [/PARnet]

INFO http://munex.arme.cornell.edu/

ARCHIVE http://munex.arme.cornell.edu/

➤ **QUAKER-P:** On Quaker concerns related to peace and social-justice issues. (See entry 8765 for full listing.)

➤ **reg.easttimor:** E-mail distribution of postings from the Alliance for Progressive Communications (APC) conference on East Timor and Indonesia. Includes reports from a wide range of advocacy and support groups, as well as reports and translations from the international press, and official documents and statements from the UN, national governments, and other sources. (See entry 7698 for full listing.)

➤ **TAX THE RICH:** A campaign to promote taxation of the rich. (See entry 5430 for full listing.)

➤ **Ultimate Pro-Life Resource List:** The Ultimate Pro-Life Resource List is the most comprehensive listing of right-to-life information on the Internet. (See entry 9683 for full listing.)

➤ **Voters Telecomm Watch (VTW):** A volunteer organization, concentrating on legislation as it relates to telecommunications and civil liberties. (See entry 9752 for full listing.)

POLITICS—ANARCHY

5592 alt.anarchism Anarchists of the world, unite! *Newsgroup*

➤ **alt.fan.noam-chomsky:** Noam Chomsky's writings and opinions. *Newsgroup*

5593 alt.society.anarchy Societies without rulers. *Newsgroup*

➤ **FringeWare:** Fringe culture dispersed through design and undesign, community, humor, the marketplace, the net. (See entry 9824 for full listing.)

➤ **Processed World Wide Web:** Web site of *Processed World* magazine, the notorious "magazine with a bad attitude." Antiauthoritarian misfits go to work and and bite the hand that bores them. (See entry 2013 for full listing.)

5594 **TAO:** As "freedom and independent consciousness face the threat of cyber-design and virtual reality," this site provides a wise and impassioned response.

http://www.lglobal.com/TAO/

INFO tao@lglobal.com

POLITICS—CENSORSHIP

5595 `alt.censorship` Discussion about restricting speech/press. *Newsgroup*

5596 `alt.defeat.s314` The dreaded Exon censorship bill. *Newsgroup*

5597 `alt.fan.karla-homolka` Why are there so few hot, exhibitionist S & M women? *Newsgroup*

5598 `clari.news.censorship` Censorship, government control of media. *Moderated newsgroup*

5599 `clari.news.issues.censorship` Censorship, government control of media. *Moderated newsgroup*

➤ **Electronic Frontier Foundation:** The Electronic Frontier Foundation is a 501(c)3 nonprofit organization "working in the public interest to protect privacy, free expression, and access to online resources and information." The site includes very important information on the interaction between our government and the Internet, as well as an extensive archive with documents on a wide range of topics, including activism, censorship, cryptography and computer security, net culture and cyber-anthropology, intellectual property, law, privacy, and more. It also archives various e-journals related to its mission. (See entry 9749 for full listing.)

5600 `news.admin.censorship` Censorship issues in news administration. *Newsgroup*

➤ **SEA: the society for electronic access.:** A New York City-based organization that promotes civil liberties and access in cyberspace. (See entry 9751 for full listing.)

POLITICS—CONSERVATIVE

5601 `alt.fan.newt-gingrich` Conservatives return with a vengeance. *Newsgroup*

5602 `alt.fan.rush-limbaugh` Derogation of others for fun and profit. *Newsgroup*

5603 `alt.fan.rush-limbaugh.tv-show` Rush's television program. *Newsgroup*

5604 `alt.flame.rush-limbaugh` The opposition's version of `alt.fan.rush-limbaugh`. *Newsgroup*

5605 `alt.rush-limbaugh` Fans of the conservative activist radio announcer. *Newsgroup*

5606 `alt.society.conservatism` Social, cultural, and political conservatism. *Newsgroup*

➤ **AYN-RAND:** For scholarly discussion of Ayn Rand's objectivist philosophy. (See entry 5352 for full listing.)

➤ **C-LIB:** For conservative librarians. (See entry 5699 for full listing.)

5607 **C-News:** For news and information on conservative politics: "*not a discussion list.*" *Distribution List, moderated*

http://world.std.com/~icrn

± majordomo@world.std.com [body = subscribe c-news]

INFO icrn@world.std.com (Internet Conservative Resource Network)

➤ **The Jolly Roger:** A monthly journal of conservative thought which publishes contemporary literature written in the context of the Western canon. (See entry 616 for full listing.)

5608 **The Washington Weekly:** Political newsmagazine offering conservative opinion, unbiased news reporting, and extensive information on bills, speeches, and transcripts. *Newsletter*

http://www.federal.com/

EDITOR info@dolphin.gulf.net (Marvin Lee, Editor)

ARCHIVE http://www.federal.com/backindex.html

Frequency: weekly

POLITICS—DEMOCRATIC PARTY

5609 `alt.politics.democrats.d` U.S. Democratic Party. *Newsgroup*

5610 **The Principle:** The official publication of the Brown College Democrats (Brown University, Providence, R.I.). *Newsletter*
`http://www.brown.edu/Students/Brown_College_Democrats/activity.html`
± `democrats@brown.edu`
INFO OWNER `jeffrey_mai@brown.edu` (Jeffrey Mai)
INFO OWNER `katharine_mayerson@brown.edu` (Katharine Mayerson)
ARCHIVE `http://www.brown.edu/Students/Brown_College_Democrats/activity.html`
Frequency: biannually

POLITICS—E-DEMOCRACY

➤ **ACTION:** On online activism: networking among activists, planning and strategy, sharing of experience and information, and coordination of efforts. From the Electronic Frontier Foundation. (See entry 5579 for full listing.)

➤ **The Center For Civic Networking:** Included in this site is information on developing a sustainable information network, policy issues regarding electronic development, and information regarding municipalities and local governmental information networks. The Center for Civic Networking is a nonprofit organization whose goal is to help develop models of beneficial uses of the Internet for local, regional, and national organizations and governments. (See entry 2422 for full listing.)

➤ **GOVDOC-L:** On dissemination of government information and government information policy. Includes federal, state, and international, with particular emphasis on U.S. federal. (See entry 5390 for full listing.)

➤ **MN-POLITICS:** On Minnesota politics, issues, and public policy. (See entry 8199 for full listing.)

5611 **The Network Observer:** A free online newsletter about networks and democracy, with brief articles of practical advice, and commentary and pointers to useful net resources. *Newsletter*
`http://communication.ucsd.edu/pagre/tno.html`
± `rre-request@weber.ucsd.edu` [subject = help]
INFO `pagre@ucsd.edu` (Phil Agre)
ARCHIVES
`http://communication.ucsd.edu/pagre/tno.html`
`rre-request@weber.ucsd.edu`
Frequency: monthly through 1994, irregular afterward

5612 **RIGHTS-L:** For persons interested in the ongoing effort to create a bill of rights and responsibilities for electronic citizens. *Mailing List*
± `listserv@american.edu` [body = SUBSCRIBE RIGHTS-L first-name last-name]
INFO `frank@american.edu` (Frank Connolly)
ARCHIVE `listserv@american.edu`

POLITICS—ELECTIONS

5613 `alt.politics.elections` All about the process of electing leaders. *Newsgroup*

5614 `clari.news.usa.gov.politics` Party politics and electioneering. *Moderated newsgroup*

5615 `uk.politics.electoral` Discussion of elections and electoral systems in the U.K. *Newsgroup*

POLITICS—FORUMS

5616 `alt.usenet.manifestoes` Mission statements, purposes on the net. *Moderated newsgroup*

➤ **Bad Subjects: Political Education for Everyday Life:** Political implications of everyday life. Rethinking American progressive and leftist politics. (See entry 5621 for full listing.)

➤ **Belief-L:** On personal beliefs: politics, ethics, morality, and interpersonal banter. (See entry 8861 for full listing.)

5617 `bit.listserv.politics` Forum for discussion of politics. *Moderated newsgroup*

➤ **MN-POLITICS:** On Minnesota politics, issues, and public policy. (See entry 8199 for full listing.)

➤ **ne.politics:** Discussion of New England political issues. *Newsgroup*

5618 **POLITICS:** For serious discussion of political issues. *Mailing List*
 `http://drycas.club.cc.cmu.edu/~swede/politics.html`
 ± `listserv@villvm.bitnet` [body = SUBSCRIBE POLITICS first-name last-name]
 INFO OWNER `saboe@ucis.vill.edu` (Linda Saboe)
 OWNER `swede@drycas.club.cc.cmu.edu` (Gary W Olson)
 ARCHIVE `listserv@villvm.bitnet` [body = INDEX POLITICS]
 FAQ `http://drycas.club.cc.cmu.edu/~swede/faq.html`
 Gated: `bit.listserv.politics`

5619 `soc.politics` Political problems, systems, solutions. *Moderated newsgroup*

5620 `talk.politics.misc` Political discussions and ravings of all kinds. *Newsgroup*

POLITICS—LIBERAL & PROGRESSIVE

5621 **Bad Subjects: Political Education for Everyday Life:** Political implications of everyday life. Rethinking American progressive and leftist politics. *E-Journal*
 ± `bad@english-www.hss.cmu.edu` [body = SUBSCRIBE BAD first-name last-name]
 INFO `annaleen@garnet.berkeley.edu` (Annalee Newitz)
 INFO `jillians@violet.berkeley.edu` (Jillian Sandell)
 ARCHIVES
 `gopher://uclink.berkeley.edu:52673`
 `ftp://english.hss.cmu.edu/English.Server/Journals/Bad/`
 `http://english-www.hss.cmu.edu/BS/html`
 POST `bad@uclink.berkeley.edu`
 Frequency: six to eight times a year

➤ **PNEWS-L:** For progressive news and views—the Left perspective. (See entry 5670 for full listing.)

POLITICS—LIBERTARIAN

➤ **alt.philosophy.objectivism:** A product of the Ayn Rand corporation. *Newsgroup*

5622 `alt.politics.libertarian` The libertarian ideology. *Newsgroup*

5623 `alt.society.sovereign` Independence in society. *Newsgroup*

5624 **ca-liberty:** Announcement of California libertarian meetings, events, activities, etc. *Mailing List*
 ± `ca-liberty-request@shell.portal.com`
 INFO `ca-liberty-approval@shell.portal.com`

5625 **CEI:** From the Competitive Enterprise Institute: free-market approach with limited government. *Mailing List*
 ± `cei@digex.com` (attn: Deborah Toy)

➤ **Extropians:** Spin-off of *Extropy* magazine—advanced technology, self-transformation, futurist philosophy, life extension, voluntarism. (See entry 9823 for full listing.)

5626 **Libernet:** For dissemination of libertarian-related information. *Distribution List*
 ± `libernet-request@dartmouth.edu` [body = subscribe libernet-batch-list or subscribe libernet-reflected-list]
 INFO `owner-libernet@dartmouth.edu` (human)
 ARCHIVE `ftp://coos.dartmouth.edu/pub/Libernet`

5627 `talk.politics.libertarian` Libertarianism politics and political philosophy. *Newsgroup*

5628 **VILA:** For Vancouver Island Libertarian Association: Canadian libertarians. *Mailing List*

http://www.spinnaker.com/VILA/
± majordomo@spinnaker.com [body = subscribe vila]
OWNER waynec@spinnaker.com (Wayne Chapeskie)

5629 **Xchange:** Culture from a libertarian viewpoint. *Mailing List, moderated*
± listproc@gmu.edu [body = SUBSCRIBE XCHANGE first-name last-name]
INFO tburns@osf1.gmu.edu (T. David Burns)
EDITOR exchange@mcs.com (Daniel R. McCloskey)
ARCHIVE http://www.c2.org/~tburns/xchn.html

POLITICS—PARTIES & GROUPS

5630 alt.politics.org.misc Political organizations. *Newsgroup*

5631 alt.politics.perot Discussion of the noncandidate. *Newsgroup*

➤ clari.news.usa.gov.politics: Party politics and electioneering. *Moderated newsgroup*

5632 pdaxs.issues.democrats Democratic Party and their stands on issues. *Newsgroup*

POLITICS—POLITICAL OPINION

5633 alt.bosnia.action.now Aruging about more involvement in Bosnia. *Newsgroup*

5634 alt.politics.correct A Neil Bush fan club. *Newsgroup*

5635 alt.politics.economics War = poverty, and other discussions. *Newsgroup*

5636 alt.politics.sex Not a good idea to mix them, sez Marilyn and Profumo. *Newsgroup*

5637 clari.feature.mike_royko Chicago opinion columnist Mike Royko. *Moderated newsgroup*

5638 **Cornell Political Forum:** Undergraduate political journal from the students of Cornell University.
http://cpf.slife.cornell.edu/
INFO cu_forum@cornell.edu (Cornell Political Forum)
ARCHIVE http://cpf.slife.cornell.edu/
Frequency: twice per semester

➤ **U.S. News Online:** Daily news plus in-depth analysis from the award-winning writers and editors at *U.S. News & World Report*. Includes interactive games on current events, a searchable database, an e-mail directory to Congress, sound bites, and more. (See entry 6135 for full listing.)

POLITICS—REGIONS & COUNTRIES

5639 alt.politics.british Politics and a real queen, too. *Newsgroup*

5640 alt.politics.ec The European economic community. *Newsgroup*

5641 alt.politics.europe.misc The general political situation in Europe. *Newsgroup*

5642 alt.politics.italy Political happenings in Italy. *Newsgroup*

5643 alt.politics.korea A forum for Korean politics. *Moderated newsgroup*

5644 alt.politics.org.un Politics at the "United" Nations. *Newsgroup*

➤ alt.politics.usa.constitution: U.S. constitutional politics. *Newsgroup*

5645 alt.politics.usa.misc Miscellaneous U.S. politics. *Newsgroup*

➤ be.politics: Belgian politics. *Newsgroup*

5646 bermuda.politics Politics in Bermuda. *Newsgroup*

5647 can.politics Canadian politics. *Newsgroup*

➤ **CenAsia:** On all political, economic, and military issues involving the central Asian republics of the former Soviet Union. (See entry 7592 for full listing.)

5648 `chinese.talk.politics` Political talks in Chinese. *Newsgroup*

5649 `clari.world.gov.politics` World politics. *Moderated newsgroup*

5650 `eunet.politics` (European) political discussions (and flames!). *Newsgroup*

➤ **NDPZOO-L:** Discussion of New Democratic Party reform in Canada. (See entry 7145 for full listing.)

5651 `qc.politique` Politics of Quebec. *Newsgroup*

5652 `relcom.politics` Political discussions. *Newsgroup*

5653 `sanet.talk.politics` Talk about politics. *Newsgroup*

5654 `talk.politics.soviet` Discussion of Soviet politics, domestic, and foreign. *Newsgroup*

5655 `talk.politics.tibet` The politics of Tibet and the Tibetan people. *Newsgroup*

5656 `uk.politics` U.K. political discussion. *Newsgroup*

POLITICS—REPUBLICAN PARTY

5657 `alt.politics.usa.newt-gingrich` Discussion of House Speaker Gingrich. *Newsgroup*

5658 `alt.politics.usa.republican` Discussions of the U.S. Republican Party. *Newsgroup*

5659 `pdaxs.issues.republicans` Republican Party and their stands on issues. *Newsgroup*

5660 **REPUBLIC:** For information about Republican happenings and a forum for discussion. *Mailing List*
± `majordomo@ulc199.residence.gatech.edu` [body = `subscribe republic`]
INFO `vaps2km@prism.gatech.edu` (Kenneth Merry)
INFO `gt7640c@prism.gatech.edu` (John Trainor)
ARCHIVE `majordomo@ulc199.residence.gatech.edu`

POLITICS—REVOLUTION

5661 `alt.politics.radical-left` Who remains after the radicals left? *Newsgroup*

5662 `alt.revolution.american.second` Jeffersonian dreams. *Newsgroup*

5663 `alt.revolution.counter` Discussions of counterrevolutionary issues. *Newsgroup*

5664 `alt.society.resistance` Ohm's law applied to social science. *Newsgroup*

5665 `alt.society.revolution` Espousing Jeffersonian ideals. *Newsgroup*

➤ **The Fourth World Documentation Project:** An electronic library containing over 400 primary texts on political struggles waged by indigenous peoples worldwide for sovereignty, self-determination, and human rights. (See entry 10070 for full listing.)

➤ **Homelands:** About national and regional autonomy and independence movements in America and around the world. (See entry 5587 for full listing.)

5666 **People's Tribune:** Devoted to the proposition that an economic system that can't or won't feed, clothe, and house its people ought to be changed. *Newsletter*
`http://www.mcs.com/~jdav/league.html`
± `pt.dist-request@noc.org`
INFO `jdav@igc.org`
INFO `pt@noc.org`
ARCHIVES
`gopher://gopher.cic.net`
`ftp://etext.archive.umich.edu/pub/politics/Peoples.Tribune`
Frequency: weekly

POLITICS—SOCIALIST

5667 `alt.politics.socialism.mao` Maoist thought in theory and practice. *Newsgroup*

5668 `alt.politics.socialism.trotsky` Trotskyite socialism discussions. *Newsgroup*

5669 **MIM Notes:** Maoist Internationalist Movement Notes; speaking to and from the viewpoint of the world's oppressed majority. We are a revolutionary communist vanguard opposing imperialism and patriarchy. *Newsletter*

± **INFO** `mim@nyxfer.blythe.org` (MIM Distributors)

ARCHIVE `mim@nyxfer.blythe.org` (MIM Distributors)

Gated: `alt.politics.radical-left`

Frequency: monthly

Price: $12/year

5670 **PNEWS-L:** For progressive news and views—the Left perspective. *Mailing List*

± `listserv@sjuvm.stjohns.edu` [body = SUBSCRIBE PNEWS-L first-name last-name]

OWNER `odin@gate.net` (Hank Roth)

POLITICS—WHITE NATIONALISM

5671 `alt.politics.nationalism.white` About white supremacy. *Newsgroup*

5672 `alt.politics.white-power` People who believe in white supremacy. *Newsgroup*

5673 **Stormfront:** A collection of resources on white nationalism.

`http://www.stormfront.org/stormfront/`

INFO `dblack@jbx.com`

FAQ `http://www2.stormfront.org/wn-faq.html`

MIRROR `http://www2.stormfront.org/`

LIBRARIES & INFORMATION SERVICES

E-TEXTS

5674   `alt.etext` Texts made available for electronic redistribution. *Newsgroup*

➤   **Bookport:** Online editions of current books. Can be sampled, purchased, unlocked, and read online, or ordered from the publishers. (See entry 104 for full listing.)

➤   `comp.internet.library`: Discussing electronic libraries. *Moderated newsgroup*

➤   **DIGLIB - Digital Libraries Research Discussion List:** For librarians, information scientists, and other information professionals to discuss the constellation of issues and technologies pertaining to the creation of digital libraries. (See entry 5740 for full listing.)

➤   **The Fourth World Documentation Project:** An electronic library containing over 400 primary texts on political struggles waged by indigenous peoples worldwide for sovereignty, self-determination, and human rights. (See entry 10070 for full listing.)

5675   **GUTNBERG:** On Project Gutenberg, an effort to create large numbers of publically accessible texts on-line. *Mailing List, moderated*

     http://jg.cso.uiuc.edu/pg_home.html

     ± listserv@vmd.cso.uiuc.edu [body = SUBSCRIBE GUTNBERG first-name last-name]

     INFO hart@vmd.cso.uiuc.edu (Michael Hart)

     ARCHIVE listserv@vmd.cso.uiuc.edu [body = INDEX GUTNBERG]

     Gated: bit.listserv.gutnberg

5676   **Internet-on-a-Disk:** Newsletter of public-domain and freely available electronic texts. *Newsletter*

     http://www.tiac.net/users/samizdat

     Frequency: monthly (with time off over the summer)

➤   **MEK-L:** Issues related to the Hungarian Electronic Library project. (See entry 5754 for full listing.)

5677   **The On-line Books Page:** The On-line Books Page provides an index to hundreds of online books, as well as a guide for common repositories of online books and other documents.

     http://www.cs.cmu.edu/Web/books.html

     INFO spok+books@cs.cmu.edu

➤   **Online Electronic Publishing Collection:** Includes information on file formats, text readers and image viewers, audio and video players, multimedia and virtual reality publishing standards, and main languages. Also includes an index of electronic books and documents available online. (See entry 2419 for full listing.)

5678   **The Oxford Text Archive:** This archive maintained by Oxford University Computing Services, Oxford University, Oxford, U.K., exists to serve the interests of the academic community by providing archival and dissemination facilities for electronic texts.

     http://info.ox.ac.uk/~archive

     INFO archive@sable.ox.ac.uk

5679   **Project Runeberg:** Project Runeberg publishes free electronic editions of classic Nordic literature and art over the Internet since 1992.

     http://www.lysator.liu.se/runeberg/

     INFO runeberg@lysator.liu.se

➤   **SunSITE Document Archives:** A large selection of documents, books, speeches, papers, and tutorials on a wide variety of topics. (See entry 3751 for full listing.)

EVENT CALENDARS

5680   **Computer Events Directory:** Over 1,000 information-technology trade shows, conferences, and seminars worldwide.

     http://www.kweb.com/

     INFO info@astrology.net

INFO kelli@astrology.net

➤ **The Concert Connection:** A concert tour information interactive resource. The site includes tour and news updates on over 600 bands and 5,000 venues worldwide. Updated weekly. (See entry 755 for full listing.)

5681 **Internet Conference Calendar:** Listings of upcoming conferences, workshops, expos, courses, seminars, and other events of all kinds. Have you got an event to publicize? You can publicize it here using the submission form. The calendar can be browsed by geography or type of event. A list of other conference lists is also included.

http://www.calendar.com/conferences/

INFO skip@calendar.com

➤ **Musi-Cal:** A calendar that provides access to worldwide live music information: concerts, festivals, gigs, and other musical events. (See entry 765 for full listing.)

➤ **Trade Show Central:** A searchable database of international trade shows: 8,500+ events. Request full participation information online, link directly to all major events, and locate specialized trade-show service companies. (See entry 2003 for full listing.)

FAQS

➤ <u>Games Domain</u>: A comprehensive games site; includes FAQs and pointers to games sites; covers all varieties of games. (See entry 6330 for full listing.)

➤ <u>MUD info</u>: Multiple User Dialogue/Dimension/Dungeon FAQs, lists, information, collections, servers, archives, and newsgroups, by Lydia Leong. (See entry 3174 for full listing.)

➤ `alt.games.video.sony-playstation.faqs`: Up to date Playstation FAQs. *Newsgroup*

➤ **Amateur Radio:** The world of Internet amateur (ham) radio. (See entry 6155 for full listing.)

➤ `chinese.newsgroups.answers`: FAQs, etc. of `chinese.*`. *Moderated newsgroup*

➤ `comp.emulators.announce`: Emulator news, FAQs, announcements. *Moderated newsgroup*

➤ `comp.os.linux.answers`: FAQs, how-tos, READMEs, etc. about Linux. *Moderated newsgroup*

➤ `demon.answers`: FAQs relating to the Demon service. *Moderated newsgroup*

➤ **Drakos List:** Subjective Electronic Information Repository, by Nikos Drakos. (See entry 2760 for full listing.)

➤ **EFLWEB:** An online magazine for those teaching and learning English as a foreign language. (See entry 4149 for full listing.)

➤ **FAQ: How can I send a fax from the Internet?:** Answers the question "How can I send a fax from the Internet?", by Kevin Savetz. (See entry 2775 for full listing.)

➤ `fj.archives.answers`: Repository for FAQ (Frequently Asked Questions). *Newsgroup*

➤ `han.answers`: FAQ and periodic articles of `han.*` newsgroups. *Moderated newsgroup*

➤ `humanities.answers`: Repository for periodic Usenet articles. *Moderated newsgroup*

➤ **IRC FAQ:** Internet Relay Chat Frequently Asked Questions and answers. (See entry 2805 for full listing.)

5682 `news.answers` Repository for periodic Usenet articles. *Moderated newsgroup*

5683 `rec.answers` Repository for periodic Usenet articles. *Moderated newsgroup*

➤ `rec.arts.disney.announce`: FAQs, lists, information, announcements. *Moderated newsgroup*

➤ **The rec.food.drink.beer FAQ:** This is the general FAQ for the Usenet newsgroup `rec.food.drink.beer` (See entry 5888 for full listing.)

➤ `rec.games.computer.doom.announce`: Info/FAQs/reviews about DOOM. *Moderated newsgroup*

➤ `rec.pets.dogs.info`: General information and FAQs posted here. *Moderated newsgroup*

➤ `rec.skiing.announce`: FAQ, competition results, automated snow reports. *Moderated newsgroup*

➤ `sci.answers`: Repository for periodic Usenet articles. *Moderated newsgroup*

➤ `soc.answers`: Repository for periodic Usenet articles. *Moderated newsgroup*

➤ **Swiss Academic & Research Network:** This is a main site for Switzerland. It includes pointers to other Swiss resources, including libraries and educational institutions. It also includes an archive of well-indexed FAQs from all across the Internet that are searchable, and a directory of Swiss libraries. (See entry 7727 for full listing.)

5684 `talk.answers` Repository for periodic Usenet articles. *Moderated newsgroup*

➤ `uk.net.news.announce`: For RFDs, CFVs, FAQs, etc. within the `uk.*` hierarchy. *Moderated newsgroup*

LIBRARIES

5685 `bit.listserv.axslib-l` Library access for people with disabilities. *Newsgroup*

5686 `soc.libraries.talk` Discussing all aspects of libraries. *Newsgroup*

LIBRARIES—INDEXING & CATALOGING

5687 **AUTOCAT:** On library cataloging and authorities, or that part of library cataloging that relates to the establishment of headings (names, subjects, and uniform titles) used in catalogs. *Mailing List*

± `listserv@ubvm.cc.buffalo.edu` [body = SUBSCRIBE AUTOCAT first-name last-name]
INFO `ulcjh@ubvm.cc.buffalo.edu`
INFO `winship@tenet.edu`
ARCHIVE `listserv@ubvm.cc.buffalo.edu` [body = INDEX AUTOCAT]
Gated: `bit.listserv.autocat`

5688 **INDEX-L:** On indexing, including the intellectual, philosophical, and technical aspects of index preparation. *Mailing List*

± `listserv@bingvmb.cc.binghamton.edu` [body = SUBSCRIBE INDEX-L first-name last-name]
OWNER `skuster@bingvmb.cc.binghamton.edu` (Charlotte Skuster)
ARCHIVE `listserv@bingvmb.cc.binghamton.edu` [body = INDEX INDEX-L]

5689 **LC Cataloging Newsline:** Statements from the Library of Congress relevant to cataloging and of potential interest to the library community, such as policy decisions, technological developments, publications, reports, and more. *Newsletter*

`http://lcweb.loc.gov/catdir/catdir.html`
`gopher://marvel.loc.gov/11/services/cataloging/lccn`
± `listproc@loc.gov` [body = SUBSCRIBE LCCN first-name last-name]
INFO `rhia@loc.gov` (Robert M. Hiatt)
ARCHIVE `listproc@loc.gov` [body = INDEX LCCN]
Frequency: irregular, but at least quarterly

➤ **USMARC-L:** On the USMARC formats (Machine-Readable Cataloging) and other related topics. (See entry 5733 for full listing.)

➤ **USNPLIST:** On the United States Newspaper Program (USNP): storing and cataloging newspapers. (See entry 5713 for full listing.)

LIBRARIES—LIBRARY & INFORMATION SCIENCE

5690 **Acquisitions Librarians Electronic Network (ACQNET):** A newsletter/bulletin board for library professionals in acquisitions, serials management, collection development, and administration. *Newsletter*

`http://www.library.vanderbilt.edu/law/acqs/acqs.html`
± `listserv@appstate.edu` [body = SUBSCRIBE ACQNET first-name last-name]
EDITOR `cookei@conrad.appstate.edu` (Eleanor Cook)

5691 **ALA-PLAN:** On program planning for conferences of the American Library Association (ALA). *Mailing List, moderated*

± `listserv@sun.cc.westga.edu` [body = SUBSCRIBE ALA-PLAN first-name last-name]
EDITOR OWNER `cgoodson@westga.edu` (Carol Goodson)

5692 ALCTS Network News (AN2): Timely and comprehensive coverage of items of concern to librarians in collection management, acquisitions, cataloging, serials, preservation, and the reproduction of library materials. *Newsletter*

http://www.ala.org/

± listserv@ala.org [body = SUBSCRIBE AN2 first-name last-name]

INFO alcts@ala.org

ARCHIVE listserv@ala.org [body = INDEX AN2]

Frequency: irregular

5693 The ALISE Home Page: The Association for Library and Information Science Education (ALISE) is an association devoted to the advancement of knowledge and learning in the interdisciplinary field of information studies.

http://www.sils.umich.edu/ALISE/

INFO elenhart@sils.umich.edu

5694 alt.info-science This is really about library science. *Newsgroup*

5695 Archives & Archivists: On archives and archivists. *Mailing List*

± listserv@miamiu.muohio.edu [body = SUBSCRIBE ARCHIVES first-name last-name]

INFO http://miavx1.muohio.edu/~ArchivesList/

OWNER harlanjb@muohio.edu (John B Harlan)

ARCHIVE listserv@miamiu.muohio.edu [body = INDEX ARCHIVES]

5696 ASIS-L: For members of the American Society for Information Science. *Mailing List*

± listserv@vmd.cso.uiuc.edu [body = SUBSCRIBE ASIS-L first-name last-name]

INFO mbl@uiuc.edu (Merri Beth Lavagnino)

OWNER mbl@ux1.cso.uiuc.edu (Merri Beth Lavagnino)

OWNER dlords@alexandria.lib.utah.edu (Debbie Lords)

OWNER dcarlson@uclink.berkeley.edu (David Carlson)

OWNER jennifer.bates@dlep1.itg.ti.com (Jennifer Bates)

OWNER brush@lis.pitt.edu (Cassandra Brush)

Gated: bit.listserv.asis-l

5697 bit.listserv.libres Library and information science research. *Moderated newsgroup*

5698 bit.listserv.lis-l Library and information science students. *Newsgroup*

5699 C-LIB: For conservative librarians. *Mailing List, moderated*

± listserv@utarlvm1.uta.edu [body = SUBSCRIBE C-LIB first-name last-name]

OWNER anderson@library.uta.edu (Noel Anderson)

5700 CIRCPLUS: On library circulation issues. *Mailing List*

± listserv@idbsu.idbsu.edu [body = SUBSCRIBE CIRCPLUS first-name last-name]

INFO alileste@idbsu.idbsu.edu (Dan Lester)

INFO dlester@bsu.idbsu.edu

ARCHIVE listserv@idbsu.idbsu.edu [body = INDEX CIRCPLUS]

Gated: bit.listserv.circplus

5701 International Federation of Library Associations and Institutions (IFLA): The International Federation of Library Associations and Institutions (IFLA) is a worldwide organization created to provide librarians around the world with a forum for exchanging ideas, promoting international cooperation, research, and development in all fields of library activity.

http://www.nlc-bnc.ca/ifla/

INFO ifla@nlc-bnc.ca (Coordinator, UDT Core Programme)

Comments: IFLA Headquarters P.O.B. 95312 2509 CH The Hague The Hague, Netherlands

Telephone: 31-70-314-0884 Fax: 31-70-383-4827

5702 IFLA-L: Mailing list of the International Federation of Libraries Associations (IFLA). For information on activities of the IFLA and for discussion about general topics of interest to librarianship. *Mailing List, moderated*

http://www.nlc-bnc.ca/ifla/services/iflalist.htm

± listserv@infoserv.nlc-bnc.ca [body = SUBSCRIBE IFLA-L first-name last-name]

INFO EDITOR OWNER ifla@nlc-bnc.ca (Coordinator, UDT Core Programme)

ARCHIVE http://www.nlc-bnc.ca/ifla/services/iflalist.htm

5703   The Katherine Sharp Review: Student scholarship and research within the interdisciplinary scope of library and information science. *E-journal*

INFO sharp-review@alexia.lis.uiuc.edu (Kevin Ward)

ARCHIVE http://edfu.lis.uiuc.edu/review

5704   LIBJOBS: For the submission of employment opportunities for librarians and information professionals. *Mailing List, moderated*

http://www.nlc-bnc.ca/ifla/services/iflalist.htm

± listserv@infoserv.nlc-bnc.ca [body = SUBSCRIBE LIBJOBS first-name last-name]

INFO EDITOR OWNER ifla@nlc-bnc.ca (Coordinator, UDT Core Programme)

ARCHIVE http://www.nlc-bnc.ca/ifla/services/iflalist.htm

Comments: Please do not submit resumes to the list as they will not be forwarded. Posters should be attentive to including the complete contact information in the body of the message. Headers may be removed by the moderators.

5705   LIBREF-L: On library reference issues. *Mailing List, moderated*

± listserv@kentvm.kent.edu [body = SUBSCRIBE LIBREF-L first-name last-name]

INFO librefed@kentvm.bitnet

ARCHIVE listserv@kentvm.kent.edu

Gated: bit.listserv.libref-l

5706   LIS-JOBLIST: Library job list for Atlantic Canada. *Mailing List, moderated*

± mailserv@ac.dal.ca [body = SUBSCRIBE LIS-JOBLIST]

EDITOR bpholmes@ac.dal.ca (Boyd Holmes)

5707   LISA-L: For student assistants who work in academic or public libraries. *Mailing List, moderated*

± listserv@ulkyvm.louisville.edu [body = SUBSCRIBE LISA-L first-name last-name]

OWNER rmalle01@ulkyvm.louisville.edu (Robert Allen)

ARCHIVE listserv@ulkyvm.louisville.edu [body = INDEX LISA-L]

5708   Newsletter on Serials Pricing Issues: Concerning the pricing of library serials. Contributions list titles considered overpriced, publishers' actions to reduce prices, meeting announcements, meeting reports, and more. *Newsletter*

http://sunsite.unc.edu/reference/prices/prices.html

http://sunsite.unc.edu/reference/prices/prices.html

± listserv@unc.edu [body = SUBSCRIBE PRICES first-name last-name]

INFO tuttle@gibbs.oit.unc.edu (Marcia Tuttle)

ARCHIVES

http://sunsite.unc.edu/reference/prices/prices.html

gopher://sunsite.unc.edu/UNC Internet Library/Electronic Journals

listserv@unc.edu [body = INDEX PRICES]

Frequency: irregular

5709   RECMGMT: For records and archival management professionals. *Mailing List*

± listserv@listserv.syr.edu [body = SUBSCRIBE RECMGMT first-name last-name]

INFO mph@hbll1.byu.edu (Maralyn Harmston)

ARCHIVE listserv@listserv.syr.edu [body = INDEX RECMGMT]

5710   relcom.sci.libraries Discussion of libraries and related information. *Moderated newsgroup*

➤   **The Scout Toolkit:** The Scout Toolkit is a service of InterNIC Net Scout Services designed to collect, organize, and annotate a subset of the most effective network information tools for use by researchers, educators, and others interested in locating and using quality Internet resources. (See entry 2788 for full listing.)

5711 SERIALST: On management of serial publications in libraries: cataloging, acquisitions collection management, budgets and pricing issues, binding, preservation, microfilm, union list activities, news, announcements, and job postings. *Digest & Reflector, moderated*

± listserv@uvmvm.uvm.edu [body = SUBSCRIBE SERIALST first-name last-name]

INFO bmaclenn@uvmvm.bitnet (Birdie MacLennan)

ARCHIVE listserv@uvmvm.uvm.edu

5712 SILS-L: On the SUNY at Buffalo School of Information and Library Studies. *Mailing List*

OWNER yerkey@acsu.buffalo.edu (Neil Yerkey)

OWNER schnell.9@osu.edu (Eric Schnell)

ARCHIVE listserv@ubvm.cc.buffalo.edu

5713 USNPLIST: On the United States Newspaper Program (USNP): storing and cataloging newspapers. *Mailing List*

± listserver@leo.vsla.edu [body = Subscribe USNPLIST first-name last-name]

INFO OWNER tmccarty@leo.vsla.edu (Trudy McCarty)

LIBRARIES—LIBRARY ADMINISTRATION

5714 Associates: Issues concerning library support staff. *E-Journal*

± listserv@ukanvm.cc.ukans.edu [body = SUBSCRIBE ASSOCIATES first-name last-name]

INFO associat@ukanvm.cc.ukans.edu (Kendall Simmons)

ARCHIVES
http://rodent.lib.rochester.edu/ssp/
listserv@ukanvm.cc.ukans.edu [body = INDEX ASSOCIATES]

Frequency: three times a year (March, July, November)

5715 COLLBARG: On librarians and collective bargaining. *Mailing List, moderated*

± listserv@cms.cc.wayne.edu [body = SUBSCRIBE COLLBARG first-name last-name]

OWNER wkane@cms.cc.wayne.edu (William P. Kane)

5716 Leads from LAMA: Timely and comprehensive coverage of items of concern to librarians in general library administration and management, including buildings & equipment, personnel, fundraising, public relations, and statistics. *Newsletter*

± listserv@ala.org [body = SUBSCRIBE LAMA first-name last-name]

INFO karen.mueller@ala.org (Karen Muller)

Frequency: irregular

5717 LIBADMIN: On library administration and management. *Mailing List*

± listproc@list.ab.umd.edu [body = SUBSCRIBE LIBADMIN first-name last-name]

INFO pbluh@umabnet.ab.umd.edu (Pamela Bluh)

➤ **LIBPLN-L:** On university library planning. (See entry 5765 for full listing.)

LIBRARIES—LIBRARY TECHNOLOGY

5718 ADAPT-L: On library adaptive technology. *Mailing List*

± listserv@american.edu [body = SUBSCRIBE ADAPT-L first-name last-name]

INFO clewis@american.edu (Chris Lewis)

ARCHIVE listserv@american.edu [body = INDEX ADAPT-L]

5719 ADVANC-L: For users of Geac Advance, a library computer system. *Mailing List*

± listserv@idbsu.idbsu.edu [body = SUBSCRIBE ADVANC-L first-name last-name]

INFO alileste@idbsu.idbsu.edu (Dan Lester)

ARCHIVE listserv@idbsu.idbsu.edu

Gated: bit.listserv.advanc-l

5720 ATLAS-L: For users of ATLAS, a library automation system published by Data Research Associates. *Mailing List*

± `listserv@tcubvm.bitnet` [body = SUBSCRIBE ATLAS-L first-name last-name]
INFO `j.mayne@tcu.edu` (Jim Mayne)
ARCHIVE `listserv@tcubvm.bitnet` [body = INDEX ATLAS-L]

5721 BCK2SKOL: For Internet training for librarians and other information professionals. *Distribution List*
`http://web.csd.sc.edu/bck2skol/bck2skol.html`
± `listserv@univscvm.csd.sc.edu` [body = SUBSCRIBE BCK2SKOL first-name last-name]
INFO `tobias@sc.edu` (Tobias Brasier)
OWNER `1700007@univscvm.csd.sc.edu` (Ellen Chamberlain)
ARCHIVE `ftp://univscvm.csd.sc.edu/bck2skl.191`

5722 BI-L: Bibliographic Instruction discussion group—on educating library users to be self-sufficient in using new-technology resources at libraries. *Mailing List, moderated*
± `listserv@bingvmb.cc.binghamton.edu` [body = SUBSCRIBE BI-L first-name last-name]
INFO `mraish@bingvmb.cc.binghamton.edu` (Martin Raish)
ARCHIVE `listserv@bingvmb.cc.binghamton.edu` [body = INDEX BI-L]

5723 bit.listserv.imagelib Image Databases in Libraries List. *Newsgroup*

5724 CARL-L: About the CARL system. *Mailing List*
± `listserv@uhccvm.its.hawaii.edu` [body = SUBSCRIBE CARL-L first-name last-name]
INFO `carl-l-request@uhccvm.its.hawaii.edu`
ARCHIVE `listserv@uhccvm.its.hawaii.edu` [body = INDEX CARL-L]

5725 Current Cites: Over 30 journals in librarianship and computer technology are scanned for selected articles on electronic publishing, multimedia and hypermedia, computer networks and networking, and optical-disc technology. *Newsletter*
`http://sunsite.berkeley.edu/CurrentCites`
± `listproc@library.berkeley.edu` [body = SUBSCRIBE cites first-name last-name]
INFO EDITOR `trinne@library.berkeley.edu` (Teri Andrews Rinne, Editor)
ARCHIVES
`ftp://ftp.lib.berkeley.edu/pub/Current.Cites`
`ftp://ftp.cni.org/current.cites`
Frequency: monthly

➤ **DLA Bulletin:** News and articles about the University of California's online union catalog (known as the MELVYL® catalog) and University-wide efforts in library automation and networking. (See entry 5761 for full listing.)

5726 DOBLIB: On DOBIS/LIBIS library software. *Mailing List*
± `listserv@cc1.kuleuven.ac.be` [body = SUBSCRIBE DOBLIB first-name last-name]
OWNER `koen.jacobs@libis.kuleuven.ac.be` (Koen Jacobs)

5727 EUREKA-L: On Eureka, Research Libraries Group's patron-oriented search software. *Mailing List*
± `listproc@lyra.stanford.edu` [body = SUBSCRIBE EUREKA-L first-name last-name]
OWNER `br.wcc@rlg.stanford.edu` (Walt Crawford)

➤ **GFULMED:** On using the Grateful Med medical database search software. (See entry 4906 for full listing.)

➤ **Knowledge Discovery Mine:** This site provides information on data mining and knowledge discovery in databases. (See entry 2338 for full listing.)

5728 MEDIALIB: On audiovisual/media services in libraries. Supported by the University of South Florida, St. Petersburg. *Mailing List*
± `listserv@cfrvm.cfr.usf.edu` [body = SUBSCRIBE MEDIALIB first-name last-name]
OWNER `notaro@bayflash.stpt.usf.edu` (Jerry Notaro)

5729 MEMO-NET: On library media and technology. *Mailing List*
`http://www.lme.mankato.msus.edu/other/memo.html`
± `listserv@vax1.mankato.msus.edu` [body = SUBSCRIBE MEMO-NET first-name last-name]

EDITOR OWNER `descy@vax1.mankato.msus.edu` (Don E. Descy, Ph.D.)

➤ **NETTRAIN:** For Internet/Bitnet network trainers. (See entry 2918 for full listing.)

5730 **SLA-TECH:** On technical services in small and special libraries and information centers of any sort. *Mailing List*

± `listserv@ukcc.uky.edu` [body = SUBSCRIBE SLA-TECH first-name last-name]

INFO `lmesner@ukcc.uky.edu` (Lillian Mesner)

INFO `techlib3@lexmark.com` (Debbie Hatfield)

5731 **SLSCk...the Newsletter:** From SUNY on university-wide library automation program using multiLIS software and the SUNYNet network: current software problems and work-arounds, tips and techniques, program updates. *Newsletter*

`gopher://slscva.ca.sunycentral.edu`

± `schumaje@slscva.ca.sunycentral.edu` (John Schumacher)

INFO `schumaje@slscva.ca.sunycentral.edu` (John Schumacher)

ARCHIVE `gopher://slscva.ca.sunycentral.edu`

Frequency: biweekly

5732 **Updata CD-ROM Catalog:** A comprehensive catalog of CD-ROMs covering topics from art, adventure games, anatomy, and astronomy to education, medical reference, statistics, and zoology, and more. Updata provides service to libraries, schools, government agencies, businesses, and medical facilities. They do not to sell to consumers and dealers.

`http://www.updata.com/`

INFO `cdrom@updata.com`

5733 **USMARC-L:** On the USMARC formats (Machine-Readable Cataloging) and other related topics. *Mailing List, moderated*

`http://lcweb.loc.gov/marc`

± `listproc@loc.gov` [body = SUBSCRIBE USMARC-L first-name last-name]

INFO `rgue@loc.gov` (Rebecca Guenther)

ARCHIVES

`gopher://marvel.loc.gov/11/services/usmarc`

`listproc@loc.gov`

5734 **VTLS Express:** From VTLS Inc., a library automation and information system vendor. *Newsletter*

INFO `gulbenkiang@vtls.com` (Gail Gulbenkian)

ARCHIVES

`telnet://bubl@bubl.bath.ac.uk`

`gopher://bubl.bath.ac.uk:7070`

`http://www.bubl.bath.ac.uk/BUBL/home.html`

`http://www.vtls.com/`

Frequency: irregular

5735 **VTLS Inc.:** VTLS Inc. is an international library automation software and services company.

`http://www.vtls.com/`

INFO `gulbenkiang@vtls.com` (Gail Gulbenkian)

5736 **Web4Lib:** On World Wide Web (WWW) management and development for libraries. *Mailing List*

`http://sunsite.berkeley.edu/Web4Lib/`

± `listserv@library.berkeley.edu` [body = SUBSCRIBE WEB4LIB first-name last-name]

INFO `rtennant@library.berkeley.edu` (Roy Tennant, Head)

LIBRARIES—ONLINE LIBRARIES

➤ **Hytelnet:** A hypertext directory to Internet-accessible libraries, Freenets, BBSs, and other information sites. (See entry 2756 for full listing.)

5737 **Library of Congress:** Information from the Library of Congress, including access to other Library of Congress Internet services that are available via gopher (LC MARVEL), file transfer protocol (FTP), and telnet (LOCIS). The library's home page provides access to electronic exhibits and events, digitized collections, government information, and other World Wide Web resources.

http://www.loc.gov/

ftp://ftp.loc.gov

gopher://marvel.loc.gov (for information about research at the Library of Congress)

telnet://locis.loc.gov (for the Librarie's online catalog)

INFO lcweb@loc.gov

5738 `comp.internet.library` Discussing electronic libraries. *Moderated newsgroup*

5739 **DIGLIB:** On the issues and techologies of digital libraries. *Mailing List, moderated*

± listserv@infoserv.nlc-bnc.ca [body = SUBSCRIBE DIGLIB first-name last-name]

OWNER ifla@nlc-bnc.ca (Coordinator, UDT Core Programme)

ARCHIVE http://www.nlc-bnc.ca/cgi-bin/ifla-lwgate/DIGLIB/

5740 **DIGLIB - Digital Libraries Research Discussion List:** For librarians, information scientists, and other information professionals to discuss the constellation of issues and technologies pertaining to the creation of digital libraries. *Mailing List, moderated*

http://www.nlc-bnc.ca/ifla/services/iflalist.htm

± listserv@infoserv.nlc-bnc.ca [body = SUBSCRIBE DIGLIB first-name last-name]

INFO EDITOR OWNER ifla@nlc-bnc.ca (Coordinator, UDT Core Programme)

ARCHIVE http://www.nlc-bnc.ca/ifla/services/iflalist.htm

➤ **Electronic Library Information Service at ANU (ELISA):** This is an information delivery service of the Library of the Australian National University. (See entry 5762 for full listing.)

5741 **Internet Public Library:** An Internet-based library with reference, youth, teen, and librarian services sections. It also has a MOO and a reading room, a classroom, and an exhibit hall.

http://ipl.org/

INFO ipl@umich.edu

FAQ http://ipl.org/about/iplfaq.html

5742 **SABINET:** Home page of the largest South African provider of online bibliographic material.

http://www.sabinet.co.za/

INFO sabinet@info1.sabinet.co.za

➤ **WWW Virtual Library:** WWW Virtual Library. A distributed subject catalog, arranged in a variety of ways, including by Library of Congress subject headings. (See entry 2751 for full listing.)

LIBRARIES—REGIONAL LIBRARIES

➤ **Hytelnet:** A hypertext directory to Internet-accessible libraries, Freenets, BBSs, and other information sites. (See entry 2756 for full listing.)

5743 **AACRL:** For members of the Alabama Association of College and Research Libraries. *Mailing List*

± listserv@uabdpo.dpo.uab.edu [body = SUBSCRIBE AACRL first-name last-name]

OWNER slb2009@uabdpo.dpo.uab.edu (Craig W. Beard)

OWNER slb2006@uabdpo.dpo.uab.edu (J. Fred Olive)

ARCHIVE listserv@uabdpo.dpo.uab.edu [body = INDEX AACRL]

5744 **AIB-CUR:** On libraries in Italy. *Mailing List*

± listserv@icineca.cineca.it [body = SUBSCRIBE AIB-CUR first-name last-name]

INFO aib-cur-request@icineca.cineca.it

ARCHIVE listserv@icineca.cineca.it [body = INDEX AIB-CUR]

5745 **ALACRO-L:** For those involved in the leadership of state and regional library associations. *Mailing List*

INFO u59936@uicvm.bitnet

5746 DALNET: On the Detroit area library network, primarily concerned with the NOTIS installation. *Mailing List*
± listserv@cms.cc.wayne.edu [body = SUBSCRIBE DALNET first-name last-name]
INFO dalnet-request@cms.cc.wayne.edu
ARCHIVE listserv@cms.cc.wayne.edu [body = INDEX DALNET]

5747 FLADOCS: For southeastern U.S. document librarians. *Mailing List*
± listserv@nervm.nerdc.ufl.edu [body = SUBSCRIBE FLADOCS first-name last-name]
INFO fladocs-request@nervm.nerdc.ufl.edu

5748 INETBIB: On integrating the Internet into German libraries. *Mailing List*
± maiser@ub.uni-dortmund.de
OWNER michael.schaarwaechter@zb.ub.uni-dortmund.de (Michael Schaarwaechter)
ARCHIVE http://www.ub.uni-dortmund.de/
Language: German, English

5749 KATALIST: Information sources (CD-ROM, Internet, etc.) for Hungarian librarians. *Mailing List*
± listserv@huearn.sztaki.hu [body = SUBSCRIBE KATALIST first-name last-name]
INFO kondrot@gold.uni-miskolc.hu (Drotos Laszlo)
ARCHIVES
listserv@huearn.sztaki.hu
gopher://huearn.sztaki.hu/11/listak/lsvarch/KATALIST
POST katalist@huearn.sztaki.hu
Language: English and Hungarian
Gated: hun.lists.katalist

5750 LIB-L: On German libraries. *Mailing List*
± maiser@ub.uni-dortmund.de
OWNER michael.schaarwaechter@zb.ub.uni-dortmund.de (Michael Schaarwaechter)
ARCHIVE http://www.ub.uni-dortmund.de/
Language: German

5751 LIBIDAHO: On libraries in the state of Idaho. *Mailing List*
± listserv@idbsu.idbsu.edu [body = SUBSCRIBE LIBIDAHO first-name last-name]
OWNER alileste@idbsu.idbsu.edu (Dan Lester)

5752 LoanStar: On resource sharing, document delivery, and interlibrary loans in Texas. *Mailing List, moderated*
± listserv@twu.edu [body = subscribe LoanStar first-name last-name]
EDITOR OWNER s_natale@twu.edu (Joe Natale)
POST loanstar@twu.edu

5753 MARYLIB: For Maryland area librarians, support staff, and information specialists. *Mailing List*
± listproc@list.ab.umd.edu [body = SUBSCRIBE MARYLIB first-name last-name]
OWNER dfishman@umabnet.ab.umd.edu (Diane Fishman)

5754 MEK-L: Issues related to the Hungarian Electronic Library project. *Mailing List*
gopher://gopher.mek.iif.hu
± listserv@huearn.sztaki.hu [body = SUBSCRIBE MEK-L first-name last-name]
INFO OWNER kondrot@gold.uni-miskolc.hu (Drotos Laszlo)
OWNER moldovan@pernix.bke.hu (Istvan Moldovan)
ARCHIVES
gopher://huearn.sztaki.hu/11/listak/lsvarch/MEK-L
listserv@huearn.sztaki.hu [body = INDEX MEK-L]
Language: Hungarian and English

5755 MELIBS-L: On library service in the state of Maine. *Mailing List*

± listserv@maine.maine.edu [body = SUBSCRIBE MELIBS-L first-name last-name]

OWNER kbeiser@maine.maine.edu (Karl Beiser)

5756 National Library News/Nouvelles de la Bibliotheque nationale: Newsletter of the National Library of Canada. *Newsletter*

INFO publications@nlc-bnc.ca

EDITOR willadean.leo@nlc-bnc.ca (Willadean Leo (English))

EDITOR jean-marie.briere@nlc-bnc.ca (Jean-Marie Briere (French))

OWNER http://www.nlc-bnc.ca/

ARCHIVES

gopher://gopher.nlc-bnc.ca/
http://www.nlc-bnc.ca/publications/nl-news/elnews.htm
http://www.nlc-bnc.ca/publications/nl-news/flnews.htm

Language: English and French

Frequency: ten times a year

5757 NYSLAA-L: For the New York State Library Assistants' Association. *Mailing List*

± listproc@cornell.edu [body = SUBSCRIBE NYSLAA-L first-name last-name]

OWNER wcj1@cornell.edu (Bill Jenkins)

➤   **SABINET:** Home page of the largest South African provider of online bibliographic material. (See entry 5742 for full listing.)

5758 SEALib: On libraries in southeast Asia. *Mailing List*

± OWNER sealib_s@merlion.iseas.ac.sg

5759 triangle.libsci Notes of interest to libraries in North Carolina. *Newsgroup*

LIBRARIES—SCHOOL & UNIVERSITY LIBRARIES

5760 ALF-L: For exploring the working conditions of academic librarians. *Mailing List*

± listserv@yorku.ca [body = SUBSCRIBE ALF-L first-name last-name]

INFO tkodar@yorku.ca (Tiit Ko~dar)

Language: English and French

5761 DLA Bulletin: News and articles about the University of California's online union catalog (known as the MELVYL® catalog) and University-wide efforts in library automation and networking. *Newsletter*

± ftp://dla.ucop.edu/pub/dlabulletin

± gopher://scilibx.ucsc.edu

INFO EDITOR mj.moore@ucop.edu (Mary Jean Moore, Editor)

Frequency: irregular, two to three times a year

5762 Electronic Library Information Service at ANU (ELISA): This is an information delivery service of the Library of the Australian National University.

http://elisa.anu.edu.au/elisa.html
gopher://elisa.anu.edu.au

INFO infodesk@info.anu.edu.au

5763 The GrimFacts: A quarterly newsletter about the Southern Connecticut State University Library, the Connecticut State University Library System, and other swell stuff. *Newsletter*

± INFO hoyer@scsud.ctstateu.edu (Edward Hoyer, Jr.)

ARCHIVES

hoyer@scsud.ctstateu.edu (Edward Hoyer, Jr.)
http://www.bubl.bath.ac.uk/BUBL/Library.html

Frequency: quarterly

5764 **Information Arcade Bulletin:** Newsletter of the Information Arcade in the Main Library at the University of Iowa. Includes short articles, illustrations, and announcements about the resources, services, and activities of the Information Arcade. *Newsletter*

INFO `info-arcade@uiowa.edu` (Paul Soderdahl)

ARCHIVE `http://www.lib.uiowa.edu/arcade/newsletters/`

Frequency: two or three per year

➤ `k12.library:` Implementing information technologies in school libraries. *Newsgroup*

5765 **LIBPLN-L:** On university library planning. *Mailing List*

± `listserv@ukanvm.cc.ukans.edu` [body = SUBSCRIBE LIBPLN-L first-name last-name]

INFO `sp05@ukanvm.cc.ukans.edu` (John Miller)

INFO `mreed@ukanvm.cc.ukans.edu` (Marianne Reed)

INFO `cnoble@ukanvm.cc.ukans.edu` (Cherrie Noble)

ARCHIVE `listserv@ukanvm.cc.ukans.edu` [body = INDEX LIBPLN-L]

Please Note: Subscription by approval only.

5766 **MC Journal: The Journal of Academic Media Librarianship:** Academic audiovisual librarianship including cataloging, reference, collection development, equipment, and administration. *E-Journal*

`gopher://wings.buffalo.edu/hh/libraries/publications/mcjrnl`

± `listserv@ubvm.cc.buffalo.edu` [body = SUBSCRIBE MCJRNL first-name last-name]

INFO `widz@acsu.buffalo.edu` (Lori Widzinski)

ARCHIVES

`ftp://ubvm.cc.buffalo.edu/MCJRNL`

`gopher://wings.buffalo.edu`

`http://wings.buffalo.edu/publications/mcjrnl/`

Frequency: irregular

5767 **OFFCAMP:** On off-campus library services. *Mailing List*

± `listserv@cms.cc.wayne.edu` [body = SUBSCRIBE OFFCAMP first-name last-name]

INFO `offcamp-request@cms.cc.wayne.edu`

5768 **University of Iowa Libraries-Wide Information System (LWIS):** The University of Iowa Libraries-Wide Information System (LWIS) contains local information about the university libraries and access to online services, including their gateway to the Internet.

`http://www.lib.uiowa.edu/`

INFO `info-arcade@uiowa.edu` (Paul Soderdahl)

LIBRARIES—SPECIALTY LIBRARIES

5769 **ATLANTIS:** For members of the American Theological Library Association and others. Emphasis is on librarianship, not theological discussion. *Mailing List*

± `listserv@harvarda.harvard.edu` [body = SUBSCRIBE ATLANTIS first-name last-name]

INFO `cwillard@div.harvard.edu`

➤ **Biomedical Library Acquisitions Bulletin (BLAB):** News and opinion contributed by readers concerning biomedical library acquisitions and collection development; emphasis on notices of new publications and issues in biomedical library management. (See entry 4904 for full listing.)

5770 `bit.listserv.buslib-l` Business libraries list. *Newsgroup*

➤ `bit.listserv.medlib-l:` Medical libraries discussion list. *Newsgroup*

5771 `bit.listserv.mla-l` Music Library Association. *Newsgroup*

5772 **EXLIBRIS:** On rare book and manuscript librarianship. *Mailing List*

± `listproc@library.berkeley.edu` [body = SUBSCRIBE EXLIBRIS first-name last-name]

INFO `ewilkie@ix.netcom.com` (Everett C. Wilkie, Jr.)

5773 FEDREF-L: For reference librarians in the federal government. *Mailing List, moderated*
± `listproc@loc.gov` [body = SUBSCRIBE FEDREF-L first-name last-name]
EDITOR OWNER `sker@loc.gov` (Steven Kerchoff)

➤ **HALL-L:** For law librarians in the Houston, Texas area. (See entry 5571 for full listing.)

5774 INT-LAW: On foreign, comparative, and international law librarianship. *Mailing List*
± `listserv@vm1.spcs.umn.edu` [body = SUBSCRIBE INT-LAW first-name last-name]
INFO `m-rush@vm1.spcs.umn.edu` (Milagros Rush)
ARCHIVE `listserv@vm1.spcs.umn.edu`

5775 IWETEL: On Spanish-language libraries and information services. *Mailing List*
± `iwetel-request@sarenet.es` [body = Subscribe IWETEL first-name last-name]
INFO `phipola@ugr.es` [subject = Information on IWETEL] (Pedro Hipola)
ARCHIVE `gopher://ganeko.sarenet.es`
Language: Spanish

➤ **MEDIBIB-L:** On medical libraries in Germany, Austria, and Switzerland. (See entry 4907 for full listing.)

➤ **NOCALL:** Northern California Association of Law Libraries (NOCALL) and the Southern California Association of Law Libraries (SCALL) Internet buddies program was formed to encourage use of the Internet and provide training assistance to their members through guides to using the Internet and directories to legal topics. (See entry 5572 for full listing.)

➤ **NOCALL-LIST:** For Northern California Association of Law Libraries (NOCALL). (See entry 5573 for full listing.)

5776 NYSO-L: For members of the New York State/Ontario chapter of the Music Library Association. *Mailing List*
± `listserv@ubvm.cc.buffalo.edu` [body = SUBSCRIBE NYSO-L first-name last-name]
INFO `mmlrick@ubvm.bitnet` (Rick McRae)
ARCHIVE `listserv@ubvm.cc.buffalo.edu`

➤ **STS-L:** On science and technology libraries. (See entry 9369 for full listing.)

➤ **STS Signal:** Newsletter of the Science and Technology Section (STS) of the Association of College and Research Libraries. Distributed through the STS-L electronic discussion group. (See entry 9370 for full listing.)

➤ **SWALL-L:** For the Southwestern Association of Law Libraries. (See entry 5574 for full listing.)

PHONE NUMBERS

➤ **Reference Resources via the World Wide Web:** A variety of reference resources via the World Wide Web, including airline toll-free numbers, U.S. area codes, city/zip code lookup, congressional information, and subway information. The site is maintained by Larry Dusold of the FDA. (See entry 5779 for full listing.)

➤ **Wyoming:** Everything you want to know about Wyoming, and some. It includes Who's Who in Wyoming on the Internet©, Wyoming E-mail Directory©, links to Wyoming schools and colleges, and government telephone directories. (See entry 8649 for full listing.)

POSTAL INFORMATION

5777 `alt.snail-mail` Mail sent on paper. Some people still do that. *Newsgroup*

5778 National Address Server: Know an address but not the ZIP code? Use this database at this site to find it. It even corrects your address, and you get a PostScript file with your address, ready for printing on an envelope.
`http://www.cedar.buffalo.edu/adserv.html`
INFO `srihari@cedar.buffalo.edu` (Sargur N. Srihari)

➤ **Reference Resources via the World Wide Web:** A variety of reference resources via the World Wide Web, including airline toll-free numbers, U.S. area codes, city/zip code lookup, congressional information, and subway information. The site is maintained by Larry Dusold of the FDA. (See entry 5779 for full listing.)

➤ **U.S. Postal Service:** Includes a ZIP code database, postage rates, a stamp center, consumer fraud protection information, and information on consumer and business products and services, including Postal Business Center lookup, forms, and publications. There is even a history of the Postal Service and other organizational information. (See entry 5379 for full listing.)

REFERENCE

➤ **PEG, a Peripatetic, Eclectic Gopher:** A collection of pointers to all sorts of Internet resources. Especially strong are its virtual reference desk, Internet assistance, politics and government, medicine, and women's studies resource lists. (See entry 2726 for full listing.)

➤ **Directory of Electronic Journals and Newsletters:** The new edition of the Directory of Electronic Journals, Newsletters, and Academic Discussion Lists is a compilation of entries for nearly 2,500 scholarly lists and 675 electronic journals, newsletters, and related titles. (See entry 2758 for full listing.)

➤ **The Free Internet Encyclopedia:** This site is an encyclopedia made up of documents found on the Internet. Includes a "MacroReference" for large subject areas and a "MicroReference" for specific subjects. (See entry 2732 for full listing.)

➤ **Government Documents at Yale:** Information on the Government Documents Center of the Yale University Libraries. The site has an excellent series of pages that help you locate government information on the Web. The site also provides listings of the databases, collections, and CD-ROMs available at the center itself. (See entry 5391 for full listing.)

➤ **INFOMINE:** Database of university-level Internet resources in most all academic disciplines. (See entry 2735 for full listing.)

➤ **Infoseek Professional:** This subscription-based service offers a wide range of fully searchable commercial data sources including wire services, computer and technical publications, health and medical databases, and corporate profiles. (See entry 2737 for full listing.)

5779 **Reference Resources via the World Wide Web:** A variety of reference resources via the World Wide Web, including airline toll-free numbers, U.S. area codes, city/zip code lookup, congressional information, and subway information. The site is maintained by Larry Dusold of the FDA.

http://vm.cfsan.fda.gov/referenc.html

INFO lrd@vm.cfsan.fda.gov

5780 **STUMPERS-L:** Where to turn when all other library reference searches fail: for people who are, in essence, stumped. *Mailing List, moderated*

INFO roslibrefrc@crf.cuis.edu

ARCHIVE gopher://crf.cuis.edu

5781 **UNCAT: The Catalog of UNCATaloged Titles™:** Titles from businesses, nonprofit groups, and self-publishers covering art, education, finance, health, history, products, relationships, self-development, travel, and "other."

http://www.sapphire.com/UNCAT/

INFO uncat@sapphire.com

5782 **UnCover:** Index to periodicals, document delivery service, and current awareness service.

http://www.carl.org/uncover/unchome.html

INFO uncover@carl.org

SEARCH SERVICES & WHITE PAGES

5783 **Find a Friend:** Resources to locate people; searches cover the entire United States. Results are e-mailed within 48 hours.

http://www.ais.net/findafriend

INFO ctdmsrb@mailhost.ais.net (Rick Botthof) (Rick Botthof)

5784 **LookUP!:** Searching for e-mail addresses based on a database. LookUP! also provides home pages to its members.

http://www.lookup.com/

INFO lookup@netsmart.com

FAQ http://www.lookup.com/faq.html

➤ **Whois Servers List:** A collection of whois servers to look up people. (See entry 2770 for full listing.)

TRAINING

➤   **BI-L:** Bibliographic Instruction discussion group—on educating library users to be self-sufficient in using new-technology resources at libraries. (See entry 5722 for full listing.)

LIVING

5785 `alt.party` Parties, celebration, and general debauchery. *Newsgroup*

5786 `clari.living` Fashion, leisure, lifestyle. *Moderated newsgroup*

5787 `clari.living.goodnews` Stories of success and survival. *Moderated newsgroup*

5788 `fj.living` Discussions about various things in daily life. *Newsgroup*

➤ **Loci:** An online magazine by and for college students. Includes entertainment information, games, chat forums, and more. Sponsored by Barnes & Noble booksellers. (See entry 650 for full listing.)

5789 `misc.rural` Devoted to issues concerning rural living. *Newsgroup*

CLOTHING & FASHION

5790 `alt.binaries.fashion.magazines` Binaries related to fashion magazines. *Newsgroup*

5791 `alt.binaries.pictures.supermodels.kate-moss` Kate Moss pictures. *Newsgroup*

5792 `alt.clothing.lingerie` The special secrets under wraps. *Newsgroup*

5793 `alt.clothing.sneakers` Sports, casual, collection, or just one pair. *Newsgroup*

5794 `alt.fan.elite` Maker of supermodels. *Newsgroup*

5795 `alt.fan.kate-moss` Sandwich, please. *Newsgroup*

5796 `alt.fashion` All facets of the fashion industry discussed. *Newsgroup*

5797 `alt.pantyhose` Stockings are sexier. *Newsgroup*

5798 `alt.sewing` A group that is knot as it seams. *Newsgroup*

5799 `alt.society.underwear` What's the big deal, anyway? *Newsgroup*

5800 **CaliforniaMart Tour:** CaliforniaMart Tour, a fashion Web site designed for the wholesale apparel industry, provides a directory of fashion resources, products' images, runway news, and special fashion events.
`http://californiamart.com/`
INFO `michelle@bienlogic.com`

5801 `clari.living.fashion` Fashion, clothing. *Moderated newsgroup*

5802 **Fabulous, Yet Friendly, Fashion Tips:** A tongue-in-cheek look at fashion on the World Wide Web. Resource lists are updated regularly, and new "fashion features" are added occasionally.
`http://www.sils.umich.edu/~sooty/fashion.html`
INFO `sooty@sils.umich.edu`

5803 **Fashion Internet:** Fashion Internet is the first online fashion magazine created exclusively for the net. Fashion Internet is filled with hip editorial and innovative advertising created by the top designers, writers, and photographers in the industry.
`http://www.finy.com/`
INFO `editor@finy.com`

5804 **The Fashion Page:** Fashion industry news.
`http://www.charm.net/~jakec/`
INFO `lms@genesis.nred.ma.us`

5805 **h-costume:** Re-creation of historical clothing: techniques, accuracy, supply sources. *Mailing List*
± INFO `h-costume-request@andrew.cmu.edu`
ARCHIVE `majordomo@lunch.engr.sgi.com`

➤ **High Times:** On hemp, marijuana, and psychedelic drugs such as LSD and Ecstasy. Industrial uses of hemp (paper, cloth, food, oil) are extensively covered. (See entry 9905 for full listing.)

➤ **InterQuilt:** On quilting. (See entry 1267 for full listing.)

➤ `rec.crafts.textiles.sewing:` Sewing: clothes, furnishings, costumes, etc. *Newsgroup*

5806 **St. Michael's Virtual Showroom:** A New York City gothic Renaissance shop specializing in custom leather work, clothing, jewelry, makeup and accessories.
`http://members.aol.com/stmichemp/`
INFO `stmichemp@aol.com`

➤ **Total New York:** A cutting-edge spin on New York City trends, art, film, politics, music, and fashion. Total New York includes the most complete online database for New York City restaurants, bars and clubs, retail, sports, city information, etc. (See entry 8322 for full listing.)

5807 **vintage:** On vintage clothing and costume jewelry. *Mailing List*
± `listserv@brownvm.brown.edu` [body = SUBSCRIBE VINTAGE first-name last-name]
OWNER `smh@cs.brown.edu` (Suzanne Hader)
ARCHIVE `http://www.cs.brown.edu/people/smh/vintage/vintage.html`

ETIQUETTE

5808 `clari.living.columns.miss_manners` Etiquette advice from Miss Manners. *Moderated newsgroup*

FOOD

5809 `alt.cereal` Breakfast cereals and their (m)ilk. *Newsgroup*

5810 `alt.cheese` This is cheezy. *Newsgroup*

5811 `alt.chips.salt-n-vinegar` People fond of salt-and-vinegar potato chips. *Newsgroup*

5812 `alt.crackers` Snack food in little bits or big bytes. *Newsgroup*

5813 `alt.food.chocolate` Aphrodisiac confections. *Newsgroup*

5814 `alt.food.cocacola` An American classic. Buy our nostalgic art. *Newsgroup*

5815 `alt.food.dennys` Breakfast, all day and all night. *Newsgroup*

5816 `alt.food.fast-food` Fast food restaurants. *Newsgroup*

5817 `alt.food.fat-free` Very low-fat foods; not necessarily about weight loss. *Newsgroup*

5818 `alt.food.grits` Ground hominy, germless. *Newsgroup*

5819 `alt.food.ice-cream` I scream, you scream, we all scream for ice cream. *Newsgroup*

5820 `alt.food.low-fat` Low-fat diets, food, and cooking. *Newsgroup*

5821 `alt.food.mcdonalds` Carl Sagan's favorite burger place. *Newsgroup*

5822 `alt.food.pancakes` Fun with flapjacks. *Newsgroup*

5823 `alt.food.pez` Legendary tiny brick-shaped candy pellets in toy dispensers. *Newsgroup*

5824 `alt.food.professionals` Fruit of the Loom. *Newsgroup*

5825 `alt.food.red-lobster` For the seafood lover in you. *Newsgroup*

5826 `alt.food.sushi` The ancient art of preparing raw fish. *Newsgroup*

5827 `alt.food.taco-bell` Make a run for the border. *Newsgroup*

5828 `alt.food.waffle-house` Not just for breakfast anymore. *Newsgroup*

5829 `alt.gourmand` Recipes and cooking information. *Moderated newsgroup*

5830 `alt.ketchup` Whack whack . . . shake . . . whack . . . damn, all over my tie. *Newsgroup*

5831 `alt.mcdonalds` Can I get fries with that? *Newsgroup*

5832 `alt.spam` What is that stuff that doth jiggle in the breeze? *Newsgroup*

5833 `alt.spam.tin` Spam must be contained. *Newsgroup*

➤ **ChipNet:** ChipNet topics include computer chat, sports, cooking and travel, video games, general interests, opinions, advice, humor, and more. (See entry 645 for full listing.)

5834 **CHOCO:** The Chocolate Archives: for recipes that contain chocolate. *Distribution List, moderated*
± `majordomo@apk.net` [body = `subscribe choco`]
OWNER `mkidd@apk.net` (Monee Kidd)
ARCHIVE `http://www.qrc.com/~sholubek/choco/recipes.htm`
FAQ `http://www.qrc.com/~sholubek/choco/recipes.htm`
Frequency: monthly

5835 `clari.living.entertainment` Entertainment news. *Moderated newsgroup*

5836 **EARTHSAVE:** On personal food choices and the ecology of the planet. *Mailing List*
± `listserv@sjuvm.stjohns.edu` [body = `SUBSCRIBE EARTHSAVE` first-name last-name]
OWNER `efricker@aol.com` (Eric Fricker)
OWNER `eric1@lmsc.lockheed.com` (Eric Fricker)
ARCHIVE `listserv@sjuvm.stjohns.edu` [body = `INDEX EARTHSAVE`]

5837 **Epicurious:** A net food magazine "for people who eat," brought to you by the people at Conde Nast who do *Bon Appetit* and *Gourmet* magazines. It includes recipes, articles, contests, and more.
`http://www.epicurious.com/epicurious/home.html`
INFO `ghorwood@epicurious.com`
Comments: query: original text was "Conde Nast's Bon who do Appetit"; I changed it to "Conde Nast who do *Bon Appetit*", but I don't in fact know that that is the correct magazine name.

5838 `fj.rec.food` Food, wine, spirits, cooking, cookbooks, and recipes. *Newsgroup*

5839 **Food on the 'Net:** A collection of food pages around the net.
`http://www.geocities.com/TheTropics/2063/hob-food.html`
INFO `jmkizer@nando.net`

5840 **FOODWINE:** On the academic study of food and its accompaniments. *Digest & Reflector*
± `listserv@cmuvm.csv.cmich.edu` [body = `SUBSCRIBE FOODWINE` first-name last-name]
INFO OWNER `32hyfev@cmuvm.csv.cmich.edu` (Musa Knickerbocker)
INFO `3zlufur@cmuvm.bitnet` (Elliott Parker)
ARCHIVE `listserv@cmuvm.csv.cmich.edu` [body = `INDEX FOODWINE`]

5841 `han.rec.food` All about things to eat or drink. *Newsgroup*

➤ **International Food Information Council (IFIC) Foundation:** Information available on this site includes scientific research, informational materials, graphics, and other information on a broad range of food issues. (See entry 4983 for full listing.)

➤ **International Teletimes:** General-interest culture magazine with varying monthly themes such as education, history, and travel. Regular columns include "Cuisine," "Keepers of the Light" (photography), and "The Wine Enthusiast." (See entry 649 for full listing.)

5842 **The Internet Epicurian:** An Internet food magazine. Includes articles, recipes, and more.
`http://www.epicurean.com/`
INFO `chef@epicurean.com`

➤ `kanto.rec.food`: About food. *Newsgroup*

➤ **MEALTALK:** On child nutrition programs. (See entry 9732 for full listing.)

5843 `rec.food.chocolate` Chocolate. *Newsgroup*

5844 `rec.food.cooking` Food, cooking, cookbooks, and recipes. *Newsgroup*

5845 `rec.food.historic` The history of food-making arts. *Newsgroup*

5846 `rec.food.preserving` Preserving foodstuffs, herbs, and medicinals. *Newsgroup*

5847 `rec.food.recipes` Recipes for interesting food and drink. *Moderated newsgroup*

5848   `rec.food.restaurants`   Discussion of dining out. *Newsgroup*

5849   `rec.food.sourdough`   Making and baking with sourdough. *Newsgroup*

5850   `rec.food.veg`   Vegetarian. *Newsgroup*

5851   `rec.food.veg.cooking`   Vegetarian recipes, cooking, nutrition. *Moderated newsgroup*

5852   `relcom.commerce.food.sweets`   Sweeties, sugar. *Newsgroup*

5853   **Richards Restaurant Ranking:** Gourmet restaurant ranking. Information about, and links to, some of the world's best restaurants.
`http://www.lagerling.se/rest.html`

5854   `tnn.foods.recipes`   Special and interesting original recipies. *Newsgroup*

5855   **Wayne's Chili Page:** Includes recipes, tips, news, and pointers to other network resources.
`http://www.tpoint.net/~wallen/chili.html`
INFO `wallen@tpoint.net`

FOOD—DRINKS

5856   `alc.alc.bier.pils`   Discussion about Pils beer. *Newsgroup*

5857   `alc.alc.c2h5oh`   General discussion on ethanol. *Newsgroup*

5858   `alt.alcohol`   Don't drink and drive on the info . . . no, I can't say it. *Newsgroup*

5859   `alt.bacchus`   Disciples of the god of wine. *Newsgroup*

5860   `alt.beer`   Good for what ales ya. *Newsgroup*

5861   `alt.beer.like-molson-eh`   A beer that Canadians can be like, uh, proud of, eh? *Newsgroup*

5862   `alt.coffee`   Another group worshiping caffeine. *Newsgroup*

5863   `alt.drinks.jolt`   Super buzz. *Newsgroup*

5864   `alt.drinks.kool-aid`   Beverage break on the information superhighway. *Newsgroup*

5865   `alt.drinks.snapple`   Made from the best stuff on Earth. *Newsgroup*

5866   `alt.drugs.caffeine`   All about the world's most-used stimulant drug. *Newsgroup*

5867   `alt.fan.dr-pepper`   Dr. Pepper—love him or hate him. *Newsgroup*

5868   `alt.fan.ok-soda`   It's not that good, it's just okay. *Newsgroup*

5869   `alt.food.coffee`   Black gold of another sort. Colombian tea. *Newsgroup*

5870   `alt.food.wine`   All about wine, for oeneophiles. *Newsgroup*

5871   `alt.hangover`   Pass the aspirin and a barrel of coffee. *Newsgroup*

5872   `alt.tequilla`   It becomes hard to spell when you drink too much. *Newsgroup*

5873   `alt.zima`   A clear malt beverage, better with lime. *Newsgroup*

➤   **The Atlanta Beer Guide:** A guide to finding good beer in and around Atlanta, Georgia. (See entry 8084 for full listing.)

5874   **The Beer Classifieds:** A place for providers of beer-related products and services to announce their wares.
`http://www.beerinfo.com/~jlock/beerads0.html`
INFO `editor@beerinfo.com`

5875   **The Beer Periodicals List:** A comprehensive list of beer-related magazines, newspapers, and club letters.
`http://www.beerinfo.com/~jlock/beermag0.html`
`ftp://ftp.stanford.edu/pub/clubs/homebrew/beer/rfdb/beer-mags`
INFO `editor@beerinfo.com`

5876   **BOP:** On "brew on premise" commercial breweries that let the customer brew the beer. *Mailing List, moderated*
± `tcel-list-server@tcel.com`

OWNER gobrew@tcel.com (Kersten Kloss)

ARCHIVES

http://www.tcel.com/~gobrew

http://www.cask.com/

http://www.tcel.com/~gobrew

5877 **BrewStarter:** This collection of pages is an attempt to aid the fermentation start-up process by gathering and organizing contact information in the various subject areas.

http://www.beerinfo.com/~jlock/brewstr0.html

INFO editor@beerinfo.com

➤ **clari.living.entertainment:** Entertainment news. *Moderated newsgroup*

5878 **fj.rec.drink** Topics about various drinks. *Newsgroup*

5879 **fj.rec.drink.liquor** Topics about alcoholic beverages. *Newsgroup*

5880 **fj.rec.wine** Topics about wine. *Newsgroup*

5881 **Homebrew:** On the amateur production of beer and other fermented (but not distilled) beverages. *Digest & Reflector*

± homebrew-request@hpfcmgw.fc.hp.com

OWNER homebrew-owner@hpfcmgw.fc.hp.com

ARCHIVE ftp://sierra.stanford.edu

5882 **BEER-L:** On homebrewing—a redistribution of Homebrew. *Digest, moderated*

± listserv@ua1vm.ua.edu [body = SUBSCRIBE BEER-L first-name last-name]

INFO darren@ua1vm.ua.edu (Darren Evans-Young)

Frequency: ?

➤ **International Teletimes:** General-interest culture magazine with varying monthly themes such as education, history, and travel. Regular columns include "Cuisine," "Keepers of the Light" (photography), and "The Wine Enthusiast." (See entry 649 for full listing.)

5883 **OZWINE:** On the wines of Australia and New Zealand. *Mailing List*

± maiser@koala.cs.cowan.edu.au

± INFO http://www.cowan.edu.au/~kstott/ozwine.html

OWNER gprewett@fin.ad.cowan.edu.au (Gerry Prewett)

5884 **rec.crafts.brewing** The art of making beers and meads. *Newsgroup*

5885 **rec.crafts.winemaking** The tasteful art of making wine. *Newsgroup*

5886 **rec.food.drink** Wines and spirits. *Newsgroup*

5887 **rec.food.drink.beer** All things beer. *Newsgroup*

5888 **The rec.food.drink.beer FAQ:** This is the general FAQ for the Usenet newsgroup rec.food.drink.beer

http://www.beerinfo.com/~jlock/rfdbeer0.html

ftp://ftp.stanford.edu/pub/clubs/homebrew/beer/rfdb/rfd-beer.faq

INFO editor@beerinfo.com

5889 **rec.food.drink.coffee** The making and drinking of coffee. *Newsgroup*

5890 **rec.food.drink.tea** Tea as beverage and culture. *Newsgroup*

5891 **relcom.commerce.food.drinks** Spirits and soft drinks. *Newsgroup*

5892 **tnn.foods.liquor** Topics and information about liquor. *Newsgroup*

5893 **WWW Virtual Library's Beer and Brewing Index:** This section of the Virtual Library is devoted to the subject of beer and brewing around the world.

http://www.beerinfo.com/~jlock/wwwbeer0.html

INFO editor@beerinfo.com

GARDENING

5894 `alt.binaries.pictures.gardens` Images of plots of ground where flowers, fruits, herbs, and vegetables are cultivated. *Newsgroup*

5895 `alt.bonsai` Little trees and battle screams. *Newsgroup*

5896 `alt.chinese.fengshui` The aesthete of location, Chinese style. *Newsgroup*

➤ `alt.folklore.herbs`: Discussion of all aspects of herbs and their uses. *Newsgroup*

5897 `alt.home.repair` Bob Vila would love this group. *Newsgroup*

➤ `aus.gardens`: Gardens and gardening in Australia. *Newsgroup*

5898 **BONSAI:** On Bonsai, the art of growing and shaping trees in shallow pots to represent full-size trees. *Mailing List*
± `listserv@cms.cc.wayne.edu` [body = SUBSCRIBE BONSAI first-name last-name]
INFO `dan@pass.wayne.edu` (Daniel Cwiertniewicz)
ARCHIVE `listserv@cms.cc.wayne.edu` [body = INDEX BONSAI]
POST `bonsai@cms.cc.wayne.edu`
FAQ `www.pass.wayne.edu/~dan/bonsai.html`
Gated: `rec.arts.bonsai`

➤ **Books That Work:** Web site of The Home Improvement Software Company. This site includes demonstrations of the company's home improvement and gardening software, related reference materials, and a directory of other home improvement and gardening resources on the Internet. (See entry 6040 for full listing.)

5899 **GARDENS:** On gardens and gardening. *Mailing List*
± `listserv@ukcc.uky.edu` [body = SUBSCRIBE GARDENS first-name last-name]
INFO OWNER `crovo@ukcc.uky.edu` (Bob Crovo)
ARCHIVE `listserv@ukcc.uky.edu`

5900 **HORT-L:** On environmentally sound horticultural practices by Virginia Cooperative Extension Service agents. A service of the Virginia Tech Horticulture Department's programs in consumer horticulture. *Newsletter*
`gopher://gopher.ext.vt.edu`
± `listserv@vtvm1.cc.vt.edu` [body = SUBSCRIBE HORT-L first-name last-name]
INFO `xnet@vtvm1.bitnet` (Extension Information Systems)
INFO `pdrelf` (Diane Relf)
Frequency: monthly

5901 **HORTPGM:** For the Virgina Tech horticulture department's programs in consumer horticulture. *Mailing List*
± `listserv@vtvm1.cc.vt.edu` [body = SUBSCRIBE HORTPGM first-name last-name]
INFO `pdrelf@vt.edu` (Diane Relf)
ARCHIVE `gopher://gopher.ext.vt.edu`

➤ **MaxLife-L:** Towards a positive, healthy lifestyle without consumerism. (See entry 9781 for full listing.)

5902 **MGARDEN:** On the Master Gardening program and all aspects of gardening. *Mailing List*
± `listproc@listproc.wsu.edu` [body = SUBSCRIBE MGARDEN first-name last-name]
OWNER `wright@wsu.edu` (Tony Wright)

5903 `misc.consumers.house` Discussion about owning and maintaining a house. *Newsgroup*

➤ **North Carolina Cooperative Extension Gopher:** This is the NC Cooperative Extension WWW server located at North Carolina State University, Raleigh, North Carolina. (See entry 8918 for full listing.)

➤ **Orchid Weblopedia:** The Orchid Weblopedia is a wonderful resource for both professional and nonprofessional orchid enthusiasts. It includes a great bulletin board to create a dialogue with respected individuals in the field of orchids. (See entry 9038 for full listing.)

5904 **PPC-L:** For the People-Plant Council, to report research and programs in the use of horticulture to enhance life quality. *Distribution List*
`gopher://gopher.ext.vt.edu`

± `listserv@vtvm1.cc.vt.edu` [body = SUBSCRIBE PPC-L first-name last-name]
INFO `xnet@vtvm1.bitnet` (Extension Information Systems)
INFO `pdrelf@vt.edu` (Diane Relf)

5905 `rec.arts.bonsai` Dwarfish trees and shrubbery. *Newsgroup*

5906 `rec.gardens` Gardening, methods and results. *Newsgroup*

5907 `rec.gardens.orchids` Growing, hybridizing, and general care of orchids. *Newsgroup*

5908 `rec.gardens.roses` Gardening information related to roses. *Newsgroup*

5909 `rec.ponds` Pond issues: plants, fish, design, maintenance. *Newsgroup*

5910 `relcom.commerce.household` All for house—furniture, freezers, ovens, etc. *Newsgroup*

5911 `tnn.bonsai` Information on bonsai. *Newsgroup*

5912 `triangle.gardens` Gardens and gardening. *Newsgroup*

➤ **Trickle-L:** On trickle or drip irrigation. (See entry 8921 for full listing.)

➤ `uk.rec.gardening`: To discuss gardening topics of interest in the U.K. *Newsgroup*

GENERAL CHAT & GOSSIP

5913 **Emporium:** Two hundred links to chat lines from all over the world.
`http://www.webcom.com/fi/empo.html`
INFO `goghi@mbox.vol.it`

5914 `alt.anonymous.messages` An anonymous message-pool newgroup, whatever that is. *Newsgroup*

➤ `alt.bitterness`: No matter what it's for, you know how it'll turn out. *Newsgroup*

5915 `alt.callahans` Callahan's Bar for puns and fellowship. *Newsgroup*

5916 `alt.coffee.clutch` A family-channel chitchat, like a klatch. *Newsgroup*

5917 `alt.cynicism` Bitter on the outside, idealistic on the inside! *Newsgroup*

5918 `alt.good.news` A place for some news that's good news. *Newsgroup*

5919 `alt.life.sucks` Another whingy `alt` group. *Newsgroup*

5920 `alt.peeves` Discussion of peeves and related pets. *Newsgroup*

5921 `alt.personals.fetish` Romance for object-oriented people. *Newsgroup*

5922 `alt.pub.cafe-bob` Coffeehouse of the Usenet subplot. *Newsgroup*

5923 `alt.pub.coffeehouse.amethyst` Realistic place to meet and chat with friends. *Newsgroup*

5924 `alt.revenge` Two wrongs trying to make a right. *Newsgroup*

5925 `alt.selfpity` Because we need it! *Newsgroup*

5926 `alt.timewasters` A pretty good summary of making the list of `alt` groups. *Newsgroup*

5927 `alt.whine` Why me? *Newsgroup*

5928 `chile.irc` For IRC users from Chile. *Newsgroup*

5929 **Juice's Psychodellic Lollipop Syte:** This "psychodellic syte" will provide hot information on soccer, pizza dough and other recipes, dog care, great places to download PC game demos, and a chance to meet the love of your life!
`http://www.infinet.com/~dejesus`
INFO `dejesus@infinet.com`

5930 `misc.misc` Various discussions not fitting in any other group (believe it or not). *Newsgroup*

5931 `relcom.talk` Unfettered talk. *Newsgroup*

5932 `talk.rumors` For the posting of rumors. *Newsgroup*

5933 **World Wide Wibble Message Board:** A fun free-for-all page for anyone to post a message onto, about anything.

```
http://www.jellinek.com/wwwboard/
```
INFO wibble@jellinek.com

Comments: A pointless but nevertheless mildly interesting site.

GETTING TOGETHER

GETTING TOGETHER—CLUBS & SOCIAL ORGANIZATIONS

5934 **alt.freemasonry** Someone will build my basement for free? Cool. *Newsgroup*

5935 **alt.masonic.demolay** Demonstrating how to build a basement. *Newsgroup*

5936 **alt.masonic.members** Freemasons. *Newsgroup*

5937 **alt.org.toastmasters** Public speaking and Toastmasters International. *Newsgroup*

➤ **An Internet Scouting Web:** Information on local, regional, and national Boy Scouts of America. Includes Cub Scouts, Boy Scouts, Explorer posts, Girl Scouts, and international scouting. 1997 National Scout Jamboree home page with Who's Who on the Trail to the 1997 National Scout Jamboree©. (See entry 6619 for full listing.)

5938 **bit.listserv.freemasonry** Freemasonry discussion list. *Moderated newsgroup*

5939 **CKI-L:** For members of Circle-K(iwanis), a student service organization. *Mailing List*
± listserv@tamvm1.tamu.edu [body = SUBSCRIBE CKI-L first-name last-name]
OWNER fhd@tamvm1.tamu.edu (H. Alan Montgomery)

5940 **Job's Daughters:** Job's Daughters in Casper and Wyoming, with links to worldwide International Order of Job's Daughters.
```
http://w3.trib.com/~dont/jobs.html
```
INFO dont@trib.com

5941 **KIWANIS:** For discussion of issues relating to running a chapter of Kiwanis International. *Distribution List*
± listserv@tamvm1.tamu.edu [body = SUBSCRIBE KIWANIS first-name last-name]
OWNER fhd@tamvm1.tamu.edu (H. Alan Montgomery)

5942 **PHIKAP-L:** For members of Phi Kappa Theta, a national social fraternity. *Mailing List*
± listserv@psuvm.psu.edu [body = SUBSCRIBE PHIKAP-L first-name last-name]
INFO phikap-l-request@psuvm.psu.edu
Please Note: Subscription by approval only.

5943 **rec.org.mensa** Talking with members of the high-IQ society Mensa. *Newsgroup*

5944 **soc.org.service-clubs.misc** General information on all service topics. *Newsgroup*

GETTING TOGETHER—FRIENDSHIP

➤ **Marriage Resources:** This page provides information about marriage, codependency, and friendships. (See entry 6026 for full listing.)

5945 **"I Just Want To Be Friends":** "Joelogon's Foolproof Guide to Making Any Woman Your Platonic Friend."
```
http://www.phantom.com/~joelogon/platonic.html
```
INFO joelogon@phantom.com

5946 **alt.love** Love and loving people, discussions, poems. *Newsgroup*

5947 **alt.soulmates** Richard Bach and his Herculean odds. *Newsgroup*

5948 **Pen Pal Connection:** A place to find pen pals. Register your name, or browse the list of registered people.
```
http://www.start.com/start/ppmenu.html
```
INFO idea@hlc.net

5949 **Penpal Connection!:** Free pen-pal service for the gay community.
```
http://www.chanton.com/penpals.html
```

INFO penpals@chanton.com

5950 `relcom.penpals` To find friends, colleagues, etc. *Newsgroup*

5951 `soc.penpals` In search of net.friendships. *Newsgroup*

5952 `triangle.personals.friendship` Friendship personals. *Newsgroup*

GETTING TOGETHER—PERSONALS

5953 `alt.binaries.pictures.personal` People publishing photos of themselves. *Newsgroup*

5954 `alt.personals.herpes` Contacting people with herpes. *Newsgroup*

5955 `alt.herpes.personals` People with herpes looking for companionship. *Newsgroup*

5956 `alt.personals` Do you really want to meet someone this way? *Newsgroup*

5957 `alt.personals.ads` Geek seeks dweeb. Object: low-level interfacing. *Newsgroup*

5958 `alt.personals.aliens` Looking for out-of-this-world love. *Newsgroup*

5959 `alt.personals.bi` Personals by or seeking bisexuals. *Newsgroup*

5960 `alt.personals.big-folks` Romance for large people. *Newsgroup*

5961 `alt.personals.bondage` Are you tied up this evening? *Newsgroup*

5962 `alt.personals.fat` Romance for fat people. *Newsgroup*

5963 `alt.personals.intercultural` Sometimes the twain can meet. *Newsgroup*

5964 `alt.personals.intergen` Where the old meet the young. *Newsgroup*

5965 `alt.personals.jewish` Advertising for romance with Jewish people. *Newsgroup*

5966 `alt.personals.misc` Dweeb seeks geek. Object: low-level interfacing. *Newsgroup*

5967 `alt.personals.motss` Romance for gay people. *Newsgroup*

5968 `alt.personals.poly` Hi, there, do you multiprocess? *Newsgroup*

5969 `alt.personals.spanking` Oedipus gives this group a thumbs-up. *Newsgroup*

5970 `alt.personals.spanking.punishment` In search of bad butt burn. *Newsgroup*

5971 `alt.personals.tall` Romance for tall people. *Newsgroup*

5972 `alt.personals.teen` Teen personal ads and e-mail-me ads. *Newsgroup*

5973 `alt.personals.transgendered` People seeking TV/TS friends. *Newsgroup*

5974 `alt.romance.mature-adult` Discussions and personals for mature adults. *Newsgroup*

5975 `aus.personals` Australian personals. *Newsgroup*

5976 `av.personals` Meeting people in the Antelope Valley. *Newsgroup*

5977 `ba.personals` Personal ads of Bay Area interest. *Newsgroup*

5978 **Bureau One Personals:** Bureau One Personals—over 5,000 current personal ads from around the U.S., organized by area code.
   http://www.cupidnet.com/bureau1
   INFO cupid@cupidnet.com

5979 `chi.personals` Chicago, Illinois (USA) personals. *Newsgroup*

5980 **Computerized Matchmaking Online!:** The title says it all!
   http://www.calweb.com/~swifty/match.html
   INFO swifty@calweb.com

➤ **Cupid's Net:** The largest network of "romantic eligibles" services on the World Wide Web. (See entry 6012 for full listing.)

5981 **Cupid's Women of the World:** Women from around the world looking to date and marry American men.

```
http://www.cupidnet.com/womenwld
```
INFO `cupid@cupidnet.com`

5982 **houston.personals** How to meet someone in Houston, Texas. *Newsgroup*

5983 **la.personals** Meeting people in Los Angeles, California. *Newsgroup*

5984 **niagara.personals** Meeting people in the Niagara region. *Newsgroup*

5985 **nv.personals** Personal ads—any nature. *Newsgroup*

5986 **nyc.personals** Personals ads for New York City and environs. *Newsgroup*

5987 **pnw.personals** Personals listings for the Pacific Northwest region. *Newsgroup*

5988 **sat.personals** Personal ads in San Antonio, Texas. *Newsgroup*

5989 **sdnet.personals** San Diego area (only!) personals. *Newsgroup*

5990 **triangle.personals** Personal ads. *Newsgroup*

5991 **triangle.personals.bi** Personal ads for the bisexual crowd. *Newsgroup*

5992 **triangle.personals.m-seeking-m** Personals for men seeking men. *Newsgroup*

5993 **triangle.personals.m-seeking-w** Personals for men seeking women. *Newsgroup*

5994 **triangle.personals.motss** Personal ads for the same-sex crowd. *Newsgroup*

5995 **triangle.personals.variations** Alternative and miscellaneous personals. *Newsgroup*

5996 **triangle.personals.w-seeking-m** Personals for women seeking men. *Newsgroup*

5997 **triangle.personals.w-seeking-w** Personals for women seeking women. *Newsgroup*

5998 **vegas.personals** Personal ads—any nature. *Newsgroup*

5999 **webpersonals.com:** This semimoderated, free service is intended for people who want to meet others for romance, companionship, or other activities.
```
http://www.webpersonals.com/
```
INFO `love@webpersonals.com`
FAQ `http://www.webpersonals.com/date/help/`

GETTING TOGETHER—RELATIONSHIPS

6000 **alt.binaries.pictures.girlfriend** Pictures of girlfriends. *Newsgroup*

6001 **alt.romance** Discussion about the romantic side of love. *Newsgroup*

6002 **alt.romance.chat** Chitchat about romance, often silly. *Newsgroup*

6003 **alt.romance.teen** Talk about teen love and infatuations. *Newsgroup*

6004 **alt.romance.unhappy** `alt.angst` on the run. *Newsgroup*

6005 **alt.support.divorce** Discussion of marital breakups. *Newsgroup*

➤ **clari.news.childrn+family:** Children and families, adoption, marriage. *Moderated newsgroup*

6006 **Couples-L:** On heterosexual couplehood: communication, love, sex, romance, relationship. *Mailing List, moderated*
± `listproc@cornell.edu` [body = SUB COUPLES-L first-name last-name]
INFO `couples-owners-l@cornell.edu`
OWNER `cgl1@cornell.edu` (Chuck Goelzer Lyons)
OWNER `gil@nh.destek.net` (Gil Emery Jr.)
FAQ `http://goelzer.cornell.edu/Couples-L`

6007 **Halia:** A web page about hugging!
```
http://www.uta.fi/~ms54336/halia.htm
```
INFO `marko.salonen@uta.fi`

6008 **The Magic of Differences:** Home page of Judith Sherven, Ph.D., and James Sniechowski, Ph.D., who in their own words "can help you turn the challenges of intimacy into the deepest intimacy of your life."

http://www3.imall.com/Magic_Of_Differences/

INFO jimjude@ix.netcom.com

6009 `soc.couples` Discussions for couples (cf. `soc.singles`). *Newsgroup*

6010 `soc.couples.intercultural` Intercultural and interracial relationships. *Newsgroup*

➤ **WME-L:** On the Worldwide Marriage Encounter workshops: sacrament of matrimony and holy orders. (See entry 8734 for full listing.)

GETTING TOGETHER—SINGLES

6011 **American Singles:** Free nonprofit profile dating service.

http://www.as.org/

6012 **Cupid's Net:** The largest network of "romantic eligibles" services on the World Wide Web.

http://www.cupidnet.com/

INFO cupid@cupidnet.com

6013 **FSI-L:** For Fun Singles International regarding group social activities. *Mailing List, moderated*

± dlistmgr@info-net.com [body = SUBSCRIBE FSI-L e-mail-address phone-number last-name.first-name.middle-initials]

INFO OWNER donna.meadows@info-net.com (Donna Meadows)

Comments: Confidential information of DListMgr users will not be distributed to anyone other than the sponsor of the e-mail list.

6014 `houston.singles` Discussions of singles activities in Houston, Texas. *Newsgroup*

6015 `ne.singles` New England "singles" issues, events, and personal ads. *Newsgroup*

6016 `nv.singles` Talk for singles. *Newsgroup*

6017 `nyc.singles` Discussions of being single in the New York City area. *Newsgroup*

➤ `ont.singles:` Singles in Ontario, Canada. *Newsgroup*

➤ `ott.singles:` Ottawa singles group. *Newsgroup*

6018 `pgh.singles` Pittsburgh singles network. *Newsgroup*

6019 `phl.singles` Single people and their activities in Philadelphia. *Newsgroup*

➤ `sdnet.singles:` San Diego singles scene. *Newsgroup*

6020 `soc.singles` Newsgroup for single people, their activities, etc. *Newsgroup*

6021 `triangle.singles` Meeting other single individuals in central North Carolina. *Newsgroup*

6022 `uk.singles` Personal ads, or discussions. *Newsgroup*

6023 `vegas.singles` Talk for singles. *Newsgroup*

GETTING TOGETHER—WEDDINGS, MARRIAGE & DOMESTIC PARTNERSHIP

6024 **Commercial wedding-related WWW pages:** An extensive list of Web sites that offer wedding-related commercial services.

http://www.wam.umd.edu/~sek/wedcommerce.html

INFO sek@wam.umd.edu (Sonja Kueppers)

6025 **Domestic Partnerships and Same Sex Marriages:** Pointers to net-wide information on domestic partnerships and same-sex marriages.

http://www.cs.cmu.edu/afs/cs.cmu.edu/user/scotts/domestic-partners/mainpage.html

INFO corwin+@cmu.edu

6026 **Marriage Resources:** This page provides information about marriage, codependency, and friendships.

```
http://www.webcom.com/pleasant/sarah/marriage/marriage.html
```
INFO z_pleasantkt@titan.sfasu.edu

6027 `alt.wedding` Use `soc.couples.wedding` instead. *Newsgroup*

6028 **Bisexual Spouse Support Mailing List (SSML):** The Spouse Support Mailing List (SSML) is an Internet mailing list in both standard and digest formats for monogamous, straight spouses and their bisexual partners who are trying to make their marriages survive and thrive. Membership is moderated and confidential. *Mailing List, moderated*

± majordomo@texsys.com [body = subscribe spouse-support or subscribe spouse-support-digest]

INFO OWNER owner-spouse-support@texsys.com (Spouse Support Mailing List Owner)

FAQ http://www.qrd.org/qrd/electronic/email/spouse-support

6029 **Married Man Home Page:** This page was created by Ritchie White and Dan Starks, who created it out of their realization that they both have wives. It is is meant as encouragement to those men who are or will be married someday. The site also includes links to other marriage-related Web sites.

```
http://www.ldl.net/~dstarks/index.html
```
INFO dstarks@ldl.net

INFO ritchiew@aol.com

6030 **Partners Task Force for Gay & Lesbian Couples:** This site provides extensive information on issues of concern to same-sex couples, including legal marriage and sources of support.

```
http://www.eskimo.com/~demian/partners.html
```
INFO demian@eskimo.com

6031 `soc.couples.wedding` Wedding planning. *Newsgroup*

6032 **soc.couples.wedding WWW page:** Compendium of wedding-planning information. This is the WWW site for the `soc.couples.wedding` Usenet newsgroup.

```
http://www.wam.umd.edu/~sck/wedding.html
```
INFO sek@wam.umd.edu (Sonja Kueppers)

6033 **Weddings Online:** Interactive wedding planning help and brochures on service vendors in 27 different categories nationwide.

```
http://weddings-online.com/
```
INFO wol@weddings-online.com

HOUSING & HOMES

➤ **Accurate New Home Builder Web Guide:** This Web site lists new home builder pages that contain valuable information. Items such as location maps, floor plans, photos, and renderings are important to new home buyers. (See entry 1827 for full listing.)

6034 `alt.binaries.pictures.furniture` Images of furniture. *Newsgroup*

6035 `alt.construction` The construction industry. See also `alt.pave.the.earth`. *Newsgroup*

6036 `alt.housing.nontrad` Communes, co-housing, and alternative living arrangements. *Newsgroup*

6037 `alt.how-to` Do-it-yourself (DIY) topics. *Newsgroup*

6038 `alt.hvac` Heating, venting, and air conditioning. *Newsgroup*

6039 `alt.relocate` Setting up a new home in a faraway place. *Newsgroup*

6040 **Books That Work:** Web site of The Home Improvement Software Company. This site includes demonstrations of the company's home improvement and gardening software, related reference materials, and a directory of other home improvement and gardening resources on the Internet.

```
http://www.btw.com/
```
INFO webmaster@btw.com

➤ **Build.com:** This site is an online resource and directory for building and home improvement products and information. (See entry 1842 for full listing.)

6041   **CHIMNEYS-L:** On professional chimney and stove maintenance. *Mailing List*

http://www.olympic.net/chimneys/list-pge.html
http://chatservice.com/
± listserv@peach.ease.lsoft.com [body = SUBSCRIBE CHIMNEYS-L first-name last-name]
INFO OWNER chimneys@olympic.net (David C. McKnew)
INFO OWNER chimneys@aol.com (David C. McKnew)

Comments: Charge: $12/year

6042   **Don Vandervort's HomeSource:** Home-improvement authority Don Vandervort offers advice and information to home owners. Included are excerpts from his book, *Home Magazine's How Your House Works* (Ballantine Books), monthly home-maintenance tips, home-improvement articles, an "Ask the Expert" feature, and links to other home-improvement sites.

http://www.earthlink.net/~donvander/
INFO donvander@earthlink.net

Comments: From the author of Home Magazine's How Your House Works, (Ballantine Books).

6043   **HOA-LIST:** For owners and residents in home owner associations (HOA). *Mailing List*

± hoa-list-request@netcom.com
OWNER owner-hoa-list@netcom.com (John Raphael)
ARCHIVE ftp://ftp.netcom.com/pub/jr/jraphael/hoa.html

6044   **HUD USER:** HUD USER is the primary source for federal government reports and information on housing policy and programs, building technology, economic development, urban planning, and other housing-related topics.

http://www.huduser.org/
gopher://huduser.org:73
INFO huduser@aspensys.com

➤   **nj.market.housing:** For sale/rent/wanted: housing, land, roommates. *Newsgroup*

➤   **nyc.market.housing:** Housing in the New York City area. *Newsgroup*

6045   **Possum-Lodge:** Discussion about the [New] Red Green Show. Quotes from the shows and duct tape are likely to be discussed. *Mailing List*

± majordomo@austin.brandonu.ca [body = subscribe possum-lodge]
INFO OWNER ennsnr@brandonu.ca (Neil Enns)
ARCHIVE http://www.brandonu.ca/~ennsnr/RedGreen/

➤   **sdnet.housing:** San Diego places to live wanted/available. *Newsgroup*

6046   **uk.d-i-y** Do it yourself. *Newsgroup*

PERSONAL FINANCE

➤   **clari.living.goodnews:** Stories of success and survival. *Moderated newsgroup*

6047   **Credit Help:** A credit handbook to help get you out of debt.

http://www.webcom.com/credit/welcome.html

6048   **ESTPLAN-L:** On estate planning: professional character. *Mailing List*

± listserv@netcom.com [body = SUBSCRIBE estplan-l]
OWNER wbristow@netcom.com (Walt Bristow)

6049   **fj.life.money** Discussions on handling money. *Newsgroup*

6050   **FRUGAL-L:** On frugal living. *Mailing List, moderated*

± majordomo@best.com [body = subscribe frugal-l]
OWNER frugal@best.com (Linda Henneman)

➤   **MaxLife-L:** Towards a positive, healthy lifestyle without consumerism. (See entry 9781 for full listing.)

6051   **misc.consumers.frugal-living** Practicing a frugal lifestyle. *Newsgroup*

6052 **Money Issues:** Canada's first regular financial-planning magazine, available simultaneously in print and in electronic form. *E-Magazine*

http://www.cyberplex.com/CyberPlex/MoneyIssues.html

INFO waysmag@hookup.net (Kirk Kelly)

6053 **TaxDigest:** A tax newsletter. *Newsletter*

http://www.unf.edu/students/jmayer/taxdig.html

± OWNER taxdigest@aol.com (Gary Hoskins)

6054 **The Underground:** Information on how to obtain a new credit file and identity.

http://www.usa.net/underground

INFO execgrp@usa.net

MEDIA & NEWS

6055 **MEGA-MEDIA LINKS index @ OMNIBUS:EYE:** A searchable index of thousands of film/TV/radio/multimedia/new-media/cinema links subcategorized into over 60 helpful areas.

http://www.rtvf.nwu.edu/links

INFO cwebbyoung@nwu.edu (C. Webb Young)

6056 **Newslink:** Newslink is a comprehensive online news resource providing direct links to more than 2.300 online newspapers, magazines, broadcast stations and networks, news services, and other Web sites of journalistic interest.

http://www.newslink.org/

INFO info@newslink.org

6057 **Touch Today:** For nifty table of sources for online news.

http://www.clickit.com/touch/news/news.htm

INFO arosenfield@clickit.com

6058 `alt.news-media` Don't believe the hype. *Newsgroup*

6059 `clari.biz.industry.media.releases` Press releases covering the media. *Moderated newsgroup*

6060 `clari.living.human_interest` General human-interest stories. *Moderated newsgroup*

6061 `fj.soc.media` Discussions on the social aspects of media for communication including broadcasting, publishing, etc. *Newsgroup*

➤ **Hawaii Hypermedia, Inc.:** Hawaii Hypermedia is the publisher/host of many of Hawaii's online publications, including Surf News Network Hawaii, Brew Hawaii, PC Currents, PennySaver, and more. (See entry 648 for full listing.)

➤ `uk.media:` Discussion of media in the U.K. *Newsgroup*

BROADCASTING

6062 **ALLIANCE-MA:** Mailing list for the mid-Atlantic region of the Alliance for Community Media. *Mailing List*

± listproc@access.org [body = SUBSCRIBE ALLIANCE-MA first-name last-name]

INFO EDITOR OWNER list-mgr@access.org (Ron Fitzherbert)

➤ **Arlington Community Television's Homepage:** Home page for Channel 33—Arlington, Virginia's community access cable station. This home page offers information about ACT and access in general, contact information, and examples of the type of progams produced through the facilities. (See entry 1487 for full listing.)

6063 `clari.biz.industry.broadcasting` The television and radio industry. *Moderated newsgroup*

6064 **Data Broadcasting News (DBN):** Data Broadcasting News (including VSAT Today) is a bimonthly newsletter that covers the worldwide market for data transmissions and point-to-point/multipoint communications by satellite, cable, and radio-based systems.

http://www.m2.com/

INFO di@m2.com

6065 **NBS-AEP:** For members of National Broadcasting Society-Alpha Epsilon Rho, an organization for bridging school and careers in broadcasting. *Mailing List*

± listserv@cunyvm.cuny.edu [body = SUBSCRIBE NBS-AEP first-name last-name]

INFO regbc@cunyvm.bitnet (Reg Gamar)

ARCHIVE listserv@cunyvm.cuny.edu

6066 **Netcast Global Communications:** Internet broadcasting, consultation, and audio/video information provider.

http://www.world-wide.com/Netcast/

INFO farpoint@world-wide.com

6067 **PBS Online®:** This site provides listings of PBS's programs, such as science and nature, documentaries, history, biography, how-to, and instructional television. Also included on this site is information about your local PBS station, the PBS store, learning services, and an online news service.

```
http://www.pbs.org/
INFO www@pbs.org
```

➤ **RADIO-L:** On developing digital audio broadcasting (DAB) standards. (See entry 9636 for full listing.)

6068 **Service Communications:** A bimonthly newsletter that covers developments and news in the mobile and fixed communications and IT sectors for the police, fire, ambulance, military, and emergency service/utilities sector.
```
http://www.m2.com/
INFO sc-edit@m2.com
```

6069 **TV-film-video:** Vortex Technology's collection of materials relating to television, film, and video, including "Professor Neon's TV & Movie Mania" and other topic areas.
```
http://www.vortex.com/ProfNeon
gopher://vortex.com/11/tv-film-video
INFO www@vortex.com
```

6070 **TVFA-Talk:** On voluntarily and dramatically reducing the amount of TV Americans watch. *Mailing List*
± listproc@essential.org [body = SUBSCRIBE TVFA-TALK first-name last-name]
EDITOR OWNER mburke@essential.org (Monte Burke)

6071 **United States Public Broadcasting Service (PBS):** PBS Online™ provides listings of their programs, in categories such as science and nature, documentaries, history, biography, how-to, and instructional television. Also included on this site is information about your local PBS station, the PBS store, learning services, and an online news service.
```
http://www.pbs.org/
INFO www@pbs.org
```

6072 **PBS PREVIEWS:** This weekly online resource highlights upcoming happenings on PBS Online™ (http://www.pbs.org), the Public Broadcasting Service home page. Also included are highlights of weekly PBS broadcast features. *Newsletter*
± www@pbs.org [body = sub web-update]
± http://www.pbs.org/insidePBS/wnsignup.html
INFO OWNER www@pbs.org

JOURNALISM & MEDIA CRITICISM

6073 **Journalism Directory:** A list of Internet resources that focus on journalism, compiled by John Makulowich.
```
http://www.cais.com/makulow/vlj.html
john@trainer.com
```

➤ **Journalism/Comm schools:** A compilation of communications, journalism, and media sites in universities around the world by Ana Camargos, a graduate student at the University of Florida. (See entry 5162 for full listing.)

6074 **Louisiana Tech Journalism Web Server:** Includes links to journalism job sites, online college and high school publications and various other journalism-related sources.
```
http://eb.journ.latech.edu/
INFO blick@vm.cc.latech.edu
```

➤ **Poet Warrior Press Writer's Resource Center:** A guide to Internet resources for writers, including many areas such as fiction, journalism, screenwriting, and publishers. Includes several articles. (See entry 632 for full listing.)

6075 **SFSU Journalism Online:** San Francisco State University's journalism department Web site. Contains original content and pointers to other journalism-related resources.
```
http://www.journalism.sfsu.edu/
INFO gbarker@sfsu.edu
```

6076 `alc.stat` News-related statistics and lists. *Moderated newsgroup*

6077 `alt.journalism` Shoptalk by journalists and journalism students. *Newsgroup*

6078 `alt.journalism.criticism` I write, therefore I'm biased. *Newsgroup*

6079 `alt.journalism.freelance` Clearinghouse for freelance writers. *Newsgroup*

6080 **alt.journalism.gay-press** News from a gay viewpoint. *Newsgroup*

6081 **alt.journalism.gonzo** Hunter S. Thompson's approach to reporting. *Newsgroup*

6082 **alt.journalism.moderated** The profession of journalism. *Moderated newsgroup*

6083 **alt.journalism.music** Reporting on topics of music. *Newsgroup*

6084 **alt.journalism.newspapers** Writing in the newspaper industry. *Newsgroup*

6085 **alt.journalism.photo** The work of photojournalists. *Newsgroup*

6086 **alt.journalism.print** For newspaper, magazine, and online reporters. *Newsgroup*

6087 **alt.journalism.students** People studying to be journalists. *Newsgroup*

6088 **alt.politics.media** How the mass media is involved in shaping politics. *Newsgroup*

➤ **alt.tv.news-shows:** Tabloid journalism on the television. *Newsgroup*

6089 **bit.listserv.nppa-1** National Press Photographers Association. *Moderated newsgroup*

6090 **CANCAR-L:** On computer-assisted reporting related to Canadian issues. *Mailing List*
± majordomo@acs.ryerson.ca [body = subscribe cancar-1]
OWNER dtudor@acs.ryerson.ca (Dean Tudor)

➤ **clari.biz.industry.media:** Publishing, journalism and other media. *Moderated newsgroup*

6091 **clari.biz.industry.print_media** Newspapers, publishers, magazines. *Moderated newsgroup*

6092 **Fat City News:** The world's lone repository of outlandish and gonzo journalism.
http://www.dnaco.net/~exposure/FCN/
INFO exposure@dnaco.net

➤ **GlasNews:** Newsletter for communications professionals in the former Soviet Union and in America. (See entry 7597 for full listing.)

➤ **GUILDNET-L:** For members of the news media and journalists to discuss working conditions. (See entry 2011 for full listing.)

6093 **Magazine and Newsletter Editors' Resource List:** This no-graphics page has easy-to-follow links to sites regarding shipping, circulation, advertising, associations, going electronic, the Pulitzer Prize, and much more.
http://www.tfs.net/personal/tgoff/erlist.html
INFO tedgoff@aol.com

6094 **McLuhan-List:** To revitalize and update the work of the late media guru (Marchall McLuhan). *Mailing List, moderated*
± majordomo@astral.magic.ca
OWNER mclr@inforamp.net (Robert Appel)

6095 **NPPA-L:** For the National News Photographers Association: multi-discipline visual communication. *Mailing List*
http://sunsite.unc.edu/nppa
± listserv@cmuvm.csv.cmich.edu [body = SUBSCRIBE NPPA-L first-name last-name]
OWNER 3zlufur@cmuvm.csv.cmich.edu (Elliott Parker)
ARCHIVE listserv@cmuvm.csv.cmich.edu [body = INDEX NPPA-L]
Gated: bit.listserv.nppa-1

6096 **ProfNet:** A global collaborative of 2,200 public information officers linked by the Internet to provide journalists and authors convenient access to expert sources. About 250 posts per week. Also a newsletter on employment opportunities and ProfNet and Internet news. *Distribution List, moderated*
± **INFO** profnet@vyne.com (Dan Forbush)
ARCHIVE http://www.vyne.com/profnet/
Frequency: monthly
Price: Resource is free to journalists; available by subscription to public information officers

➤ **SNDPRINT:** On the public radio documentary series *Soundprint*. (See entry 1289 for full listing.)

6097 **SPEED:** SPEED: An Electronic Journal of Technology, Media, and Society provides a forum for the critical investigation of technology, media, and society. *E-Journal*

± _speed_@alishaw.ucsb.edu

INFO nideffer@alishaw.ucsb.edu (Robert Nideffer)

ARCHIVES

gopher://alishaw.ucsb.edu

ftp://alishaw.ucsb.edu/pub/_SPEED_

Frequency: triannually

➤ **UnCover:** Index to periodicals, document delivery service, and current awareness service. (See entry 5782 for full listing.)

➤ **Zapatistas in Cyberspace:** For net sources of information and news on Chiapas and the Zapatistas. (See entry 7523 for full listing.)

NEW MEDIA & MEDIA RESEARCH

6098 `biz.clarinet`   Announcements about ClariNet. *Newsgroup*

6099 `biz.clarinet.sample`   Samples of ClariNet newsgroups for the outside world. *Newsgroup*

➤ **CANCAR-L:** On computer-assisted reporting related to Canadian issues. (See entry 6090 for full listing.)

6100 `clari.feature.experimental`   New trial and experimental features. *Newsgroup*

6101 `clari.tw.new_media`   Online services, multimedia, the Internet. *Moderated newsgroup*

6102 `clari.tw.new_media.online.releases`   News releases: online services, products. *Moderated newsgroup*

6103 `clari.tw.new_media.releases`   News releases: new media, multimedia. *Moderated newsgroup*

6104 **Devmedia:** On the democratization of media and communication: radio, TV, video. *Mailing List*

± listserv@uoguelph.ca [body = SUBSCRIBE DEVMEDIA first-name last-name]

OWNER drichard@res.uoguelph.ca (Don Richardson)

➤ **FringeWare:** Fringe culture dispersed through design and undesign, community, humor, the marketplace, the net. (See entry 9824 for full listing.)

➤ **MediaMOO:** This MOO is run by researchers at the MIT Media Lab. It is a professional community for media researchers—a place for people interested in the future of media to network and collaborate. You must be doing some form of media research to become a member. (See entry 4039 for full listing.)

➤ **Netcast Global Communications:** Internet broadcasting, consultation, and audio/video information provider. (See entry 6066 for full listing.)

6105 `relcom.comp.newmedia`   Global networks as a new mass media. *Newsgroup*

➤ **Sybase New Media:** Visitors to http://www.newmedia.sybase.com can exchange ideas about Web-site design and electronic commerce, learn about (and download) Sybase and Powersoft products, and see how leading developers are using Sybase products to conduct business on the Internet and create Web sites. (See entry 3026 for full listing.)

ONLINE GENERAL NEWS

6106 **Daily News:** This page lists those sites on the Internet that provide significant news on a daily basis.

http://www.helsinki.fi/~lsaarine/news.html

gopher://gopher.nstn.ca/11/Cybrary/News/news

INFO samsam@vm1.yorku.ca (Sam Sternberg)

6107 **Boston.Com:** Mega-Web site for New England featuring the Boston Globe Online.

http://www.boston.com/

INFO desisto@globe.com

➤ **C-SPAN:** Cable-Satellite Public Affairs Network's Web and gopher sites to information about C-SPAN, job opportunities, reports, articles, press releases, historic documents and speeches, and more. (See entry 5508 for full listing.)

6108 `clari.apbl.briefs` Hourly news brief from the Associated Press. *Moderated newsgroup*

6109 `clari.apbl.review` Daily review of the news. *Moderated newsgroup*

6110 `clari.net.talk.news` Discussion of events in the news—*not* moderated. *Newsgroup*

6111 `clari.news.briefs` Regular news summaries. *Moderated newsgroup*

6112 `clari.news.features` Unclassified feature stories. *Moderated newsgroup*

6113 `clari.news.flash` Ultra-important once-a-year news flashes. *Moderated newsgroup*

6114 `clari.news.front_page` The top five news stories of the day. *Moderated newsgroup*

6115 `clari.news.obituaries` Obituaries and notable deaths. *Moderated newsgroup*

6116 `clari.news.photos` Photos from the general news. *Moderated newsgroup*

6117 `clari.news.review` Daily news review. *Moderated newsgroup*

6118 `clari.news.top` Top U.S. news stories. *Moderated newsgroup*

6119 `clari.news.trouble` Less major accidents, problems, and mishaps. *Moderated newsgroup*

6120 `clari.news.trouble.accidents` Accidents and mishaps. *Moderated newsgroup*

6121 `clari.news.urgent` Major breaking stories of the day. *Moderated newsgroup*

6122 `clari.world.briefs` Brief of world events. *Moderated newsgroup*

6123 `clari.world.top` Top news from around the world. *Moderated newsgroup*

6124 **CNN Interactive:** Text, video clips, and sound files from breaking stories around the world.
`http://cnn.com/`
INFO `cnn.feedback@cnn.com`

6125 **CURRENT-L:** For discussing current events: news, politics, anything else. *Mailing List*
± `majordomo@world.std.com` [body = `subscribe current-l`]
OWNER `czguris@ix.netcom.com` (Christopher Zguris)

➤ **excite:** This site sports a search engine for both the World Wide Web and Usenet, reviews of Web pages, and a real world news bulletin. (See entry 2731 for full listing.)

➤ **Glow:** A New York-based, general-interest multimedia publication with a focus on culture and the human side of world events. (See entry 647 for full listing.)

➤ **The Hollywood Reporter:** The Hollywood Reporter Web site provides an exclusive look at the next day's headlines and news briefs prior to press time, highlighting breaking film, television, music, and other entertainment industry news. (See entry 301 for full listing.)

6126 `misc.headlines` Current interest: drug testing, terrorism, etc. *Newsgroup*

6127 `misc.news.east-europe.rferl` Radio Free Europe/Radio Liberty daily report. *Moderated newsgroup*

6128 **Mobile Press Register:** Alabama's oldest newspaper.
`http://www.mobol.com/`
INFO `di@dibbs.net`

➤ **NewsPage:** A comprehensive source for daily business news. Access to news headlines and summaries is free. Some full-text articles are free to registered users; others require a small monthly subscription fee. The NewsPage Direct service provides personalized electronic newspapers to be sent to users' e-mail boxes daily. (See entry 2053 for full listing.)

➤ **OneWorld Online:** This site has an extensive amount of information on global issues. The site is indexed and includes documents on global justice, conflict, aid, trade, education, health, human rights, population, and sustainable human development, as well as daily news summaries. It also hosts information for numerous international development and relief organizations. (See entry 10052 for full listing.)

6129 **Pathfinder:** Web outlet of the Time Warner entertainment conglomerate. As well as shopping and news, this site contains content from and promotions for magazines, books, TV and cable, music, movies, and more.
`http://www.pathfinder.com/`

INFO `pathfinder-webmaster@pathfinder.com`

6130 San Francisco Chronicle: Best front-page format on the Web, plus good food coverage and the beloved Herb Caen.
`http://www.sfgate.com/chronicle/index.shtml`
INFO `chronfeedback@sfgate.com`

6131 San Jose Mercury News: Mercury Center is the source for news, information, and communication for the Silicon Valley Community.
`http://www.sjmercury.com/`
INFO `feedback@sjmercury.com`
FAQ `http://www.sjmercury.com/help/index.htm`
Comments: Subscription fee

6132 Time: Online version of *Time* magazine: great photography and past-issue index.
`http://pathfinder.com/@@*wq@GSJIkwMAQDKe/time/daily/time/1995/latest.html`
`Letters@time.com`
INFO `time-webmaster@pathfinder.com`
INFO `letters@time.com`

6133 TimesFax: For the Adobe Acrobat version of *The New York Times*, plus a good index to other news sources. Clean, clear design.
`http://nytimesfax.com/`
INFO `webmaster@nytimesfax.com`

6134 `tnn.current-events` Information of current events. *Newsgroup*

6135 U.S. News Online: Daily news plus in-depth analysis from the award-winning writers and editors at *U.S. News & World Report*. Includes interactive games on current events, a searchable database, an e-mail directory to Congress, sound bites, and more.
`http://www.usnews.com/`
INFO `webmaster@usnews.com`

6136 Undercurrent: Intellectual analysis of the currents beneath current events. *E-Journal*
`http://darkwing.uoregon.edu/~heroux/home.html`
± `mailserv@oregon.uoregon.edu` [body = SUBSCRIBE UNDERCURRENT e-mail-address]
ARCHIVE `http://darkwing.uoregon.edu/~heroux/home.html`
Frequency: 3 times/year

6137 USA Today: Familiar emphasis on good graphics and succinct coverage.
`http://www.usatoday.com/`
`http://www.usatoday.com/feedback/comment1.htm`

6138 The VNewsPaper: For "real news on virtual paper": news plus a good index to other online news sources.
`http://aristotle.isu.edu/VNewspaper2.html`
INFO `justin@aristotle.isu.edu`

6139 WHNT 19 News: From Huntsville, Alabama: a prototype TV news presence on the Web.
`http://www.whnt19.com/`
INFO `cjahelka@whnt19.com` [Craig Jahelka]
INFO `jamey@traveller.com` [Jamey Tucker]
INFO `bbowers@traveller.com` [Barton Bowers]

WEATHER

➤ `bc.weather:` British Columbia Environment Canada forecasts. *Newsgroup*

6140 Cape Town Weather Watch: Great link for southern African weather; satellite images; short, medium, and long-term forecasts; radar images; climate information; educational pages; model forecasts; real-time weather (e.g., temperatures, pressure in South African cities); upper-air data plots; and more.

```
http://os2.iafrica.com/weather/index.html
```
INFO stormchaser@comet.net

6141 CNN Weather: Current weather forecasts and news. Includes temperature maps and radar and satellite images for the entire world.
```
http://www.cnn.com/WEATHER
```
INFO cnn.feedback@cnn.com

6142 Fox Weather: Web site of a private meteorological firm based in Oxnard, California, that specializes in satellite remote sensing and meteorological satellite interpretation, agricultural weather forecasting for California, Arizona, and western Mexico. This service is not free.
```
http://www.foxweather.com/
```
INFO weather@foxweather.com

6143 houston.weather Houston weather forcasts. *Moderated newsgroup*

6144 National Weather Service: Weather forecasts, facsimile charts, climate information, snow cover data, weather data message standards, and related communication documents, and much more about the National Weather Service of the U.S. government.
```
http://www.nws.noaa.gov/
```
INFO webmaster@smtpgate.ssmc.noaa.gov

6145 NBC News INTELLICAST: Worldwide weather forecasts, satellite images, and skiing conditions.
```
http://www.intellicast.com/
```
INFO info@intellicast.com
FAQ http://www.intellicast.com/help/

6146 ncar.weather USA weather bulletins from NCAR. *Newsgroup*

6147 Organised Weather Links: This site provides weather forecasts, data (temperature, rain, etc.), satellite images, surface information (fronts, etc.), radar images, weather warnings, and links to other weather-site home pages.
```
http://www.comet.net/weather/
```
INFO storm@comet.net

6148 ott.weather Weather forecasts for the Ottawa area. *Moderated newsgroup*

6149 pdx.weather Portland, Oregon weather forecasts. *Newsgroup*

6150 phl.weather Weather forecasts for the Philadelphia area. *Newsgroup*

6151 Weather Scape: Live color radar, satellite images, weather maps, enhanced and organized with a 3-D navigation system. Links to city information.
```
http://www.onworld.com/WS/
```
INFO submit@onworld.com

➤ **The Daily Planet™:** Satellite images, weather maps, and lots of other weather information from the University of Illinois at Urbana-Champaign. (See entry 4584 for full listing.)

RECREATION & SPORTS

6152 `rec.misc` General topics about recreational/participant sports. *Newsgroup*

AMATEUR, SHORTWAVE & PIRATE RADIO

6153 `alt.radio.digital` Digital radio signals. *Newsgroup*

6154 `alt.radio.pirate` Hide the gear, here come the magic station wagons. *Newsgroup*

6155 **Amateur Radio:** The world of Internet amateur (ham) radio.
`http://www.acs.ncsu.edu/HamRadio/`
INFO `lou_williams@ncsu.edu`

6156 `aus.radio` Amateur radio. *Newsgroup*

6157 `aus.radio.amateur.digital` Digital techniques (packet, etc.) in amateur radio. *Newsgroup*

6158 `aus.radio.amateur.misc` Amateur radio. *Newsgroup*

6159 `aus.radio.amateur.wicen` Wireless Institute Civil Emergency Network. *Newsgroup*

6160 `aus.radio.amsat` Amateur radio satellites. *Newsgroup*

6161 **draker8:** For users of the Drake R8 family of shortwave-radio receivers. *Mailing List*
± INFO `draker8-request@terra.pwd.hp.com` (Mik Butler, moderator)

6162 `fj.rec.ham` Topics about ham radio. *Newsgroup*

➤ **Minnie 386BSD Archive:** Archive of a BSD Unix for Intel x86 processor machines. Also contains some programs for Apple II computers, and some amateur radio files and software. (See entry 3935 for full listing.)

➤ **Radio Resistor's Bulletin:** A conduit for the voices, ideas, and concerns of those who care passionately about the state of noncommercial radio, including community radio, public radio, college radio, pirate radio, and shortwave. (See entry 1283 for full listing.)

6163 `rec.radio.amateur.antenna` Antennas: theory, techniques, and construction. *Newsgroup*

6164 `rec.radio.amateur.digital.misc` Packet radio and other digital radio modes. *Newsgroup*

6165 `rec.radio.amateur.equipment` All about production amateur radio hardware. *Newsgroup*

6166 `rec.radio.amateur.homebrew` Amateur radio construction and experimentation. *Newsgroup*

6167 `rec.radio.amateur.misc` Amateur radio practices, contests, events, rules, etc. *Newsgroup*

6168 `rec.radio.amateur.policy` Radio use and regulation policy. *Newsgroup*

6169 `rec.radio.amateur.space` Amateur radio transmissions through space. *Newsgroup*

6170 `rec.radio.cb` Citizen-band radio. *Newsgroup*

6171 `rec.radio.scanner` "utility" broadcasting traffic above 30 MHz. *Newsgroup*

6172 `rec.radio.shortwave` Shortwave radio enthusiasts. *Newsgroup*

6173 `relcom.radio` Radio electronics, noncommercial. *Newsgroup*

6174 `relcom.radio.diagrams` Diagrams and pictures for articles in `relcom.radio`. *Newsgroup*

6175 `sbay.hams` South Bay amateur radio-related news and events. *Newsgroup*

6176 **TAPR-TNC:** On Tucson Amateur Packet Radio (TAPR). *Mailing List*
`http://www.tapr.org/~n2wx/`
± `listproc@tapr.org` [body = SUBSCRIBE TAPR-TNC first-name last-name]
INFO `n2wx@tapr.org` (Howard Goldstein)
OWNER `hg@n2wx.ampr.org` (Howard Goldstein)
FAQ `http://www.tapr.org/tapr/html/virtlib.html`

6177 `tnn.radio.amateur` Discussions about radio technologies for amateurs. *Newsgroup*

6178 `triangle.radio` Triangle area ham radio dialogue. *Newsgroup*

6179 `uk.radio.amateur` Amateur radio and related matters. *Newsgroup*

ANIMALS, INSECTS & PETS

6180 `alt.animals.badgers` Wombat love. *Newsgroup*

6181 `alt.animals.bears` Who's gonna win the Super Bowl? Da Bears! *Newsgroup*

6182 `alt.animals.felines` Cats of all types. *Newsgroup*

6183 `alt.aquaria` The aquarium and related as a hobby. *Newsgroup*

6184 `alt.aquaria.killies` Killifish, members of family cyprinodontidae. *Newsgroup*

6185 `alt.pets.chia` Makes a wonderful male pattern baldness coverup, too. *Newsgroup*

6186 `alt.pets.ferrets` Ferrets and the people who love them. *Newsgroup*

6187 `alt.pets.hamsters` Make that wheel go round. *Newsgroup*

6188 `alt.pets.rabbits` Coneys abound. See also alt.fan.john-palmer. *Newsgroup*

6189 `alt.sport.falconry` Hunting with birds of prey. *Newsgroup*

6190 `alt.wolf.hybrid` Discussing wolf hybrids. *Newsgroup*

6191 `alt.wolves.hybrid` Wolf-dogs and other crosses. *Newsgroup*

➤ `aus.pets:` Discussions of pets in Australia. *Newsgroup*

6192 **CHIHUA-L:** On Chihuahuas. *Mailing List*
± `listserv@plearn.edu.pl` [body = SUBSCRIBE CHIHUA-L first-name last-name]
OWNER `fjack01@emory.edu` (Frank Jackson)

6193 `clari.living.animals` Human-interest stories about animals. *Moderated newsgroup*

6194 **Dog Sites for Sore Eyes:** A selective catalog of canine-related links.
`http://www.tiac.net/users/smcgrath/dogsites.html`
INFO `smcgrath@staff.ichange.com`

6195 **DOM_BIRD:** On domesticated birds: owners, breeders & farmers. *Mailing List*
± `listserv@plearn.edu.pl` [body = SUBSCRIBE DOM_BIRD first-name last-name]
OWNER `katsmith@vt.edu` (Kathryn A. Smith)

6196 **EXOTIC-L:** On exotic pet birds: care, feeding, research, joys. *Mailing List*
± `listserv@plearn.edu.pl` [body = SUBSCRIBE EXOTIC-L first-name last-name]
OWNER `katsmith@vt.edu` (Kathryn A. Smith)
ARCHIVE `http://www.upatsix.com/upatsix/faq/`
POST `exotic-l@plearn.edu.pl`

6197 **ferrets:** All about domestic pet ferrets (*Mustela putorius furo*). Topics include suitability as pets, health information, funny ferret stories, etc. *Daily Digest, moderated*
± INFO `ferret-request@cunyvm.cuny.edu` [To subscribe include your name and mention that you'd like to be added to the FML. Any questions about the FML may also be sent to this above address.] (Bill Gruber)
ARCHIVE `listserv@cunyvm.cuny.edu` [body = INDEX ferret]
FAQ `http://www.optics.rochester.edu:8080/users/pgreene/`

6198 `fj.rec.pets` Talk about pets. *Newsgroup*

6199 `fj.rec.pets.aqua` Discussion about aquatic pets. *Newsgroup*

6200 **In-Fur-Nation:** Electronic version of In-Fur-Nation, the news and information resource for anthropomorphic animal fandom (furry fandom), including the ConFurence Progress Report. *Newsletter*
`http://www.confurence.com/`
± `list@confurence.com`

INFO sylys@netcom.com
Gated: alt.fan.furry
Frequency: quarterly, on average

6201 **Janyne's Dog Page:** This site offers information about dogs and links to many other dog-related Web sites.
http://www.geocities.com/TheTropics/2063/hob-dog.html
INFO jmkizer@nando.net

6202 **KENNEL-L:** On managing dog kennels: professional. *Mailing List, moderated*
± listserv@peach.ease.lsoft.com [body = SUBSCRIBE KENNEL-L first-name last-name]
INFO sturk@earthlink.net (Steven Turk)
OWNER sturkajo@aol.com (Steven Turk)
Please Note: Subscription by approval only.

6203 **PetBunny:** On pet rabbits. *Mailing List*
± listserv@ukcc.uky.edu [body = SUBSCRIBE PETBUNNY first-name last-name]
OWNER crovo@ukcc.uky.edu (Bob Crovo)
ARCHIVE listserv@ukcc.uky.edu [body = INDEX PetBunny]

6204 `rec.aquaria` Keeping fish and aquaria as a hobby. *Newsgroup*

6205 `rec.pets` Pets, pet care, and household animals in general. *Newsgroup*

6206 `rec.pets.birds` The culture and care of indoor birds. *Newsgroup*

6207 `rec.pets.cats` Discussion about domestic cats. *Newsgroup*

6208 `rec.pets.dogs.activities` Dog events: showing, obedience, agility, etc. *Newsgroup*

6209 `rec.pets.dogs.behavior` Behaviors and problems: housetraining, chewing, etc. *Newsgroup*

6210 `rec.pets.dogs.breeds` Breed specific—breed traits, finding breeders, etc. *Newsgroup*

6211 `rec.pets.dogs.health` Info about health problems and how to care for dogs. *Newsgroup*

6212 `rec.pets.dogs.info` General information and FAQs posted here. *Moderated newsgroup*

6213 `rec.pets.dogs.misc` All other topics, chat, humor, etc. *Newsgroup*

6214 `rec.pets.dogs.rescue` Information about breed rescue, placing and adopting. *Newsgroup*

6215 `rec.pets.herp` Reptiles, amphibians, and other exotic vivarium pets. *Newsgroup*

➤ **The Rookery:** A plethora of penguin links and resources. Your one-stop penguin shop! For the true penguin fan or those just interested in learning more about one of nature's most intriquing animals. (See entry 4684 for full listing.)

AUTOMOBILES

6216 `alt.auto.mercedes` Discussing Mercedes-Benz cars. *Newsgroup*

6217 `alt.autos.camaro.firebird` A couple of American sports cars. *Newsgroup*

6218 `alt.autos.ferrari` Discussion of Ferrari automobiles. *Newsgroup*

6219 `alt.autos.macho-trucks` For macho-truck enthusiasts. Big block or bust. *Newsgroup*

6220 `alt.autos.sport.rally` Discussion of sport rally auto racing. *Newsgroup*

6221 `alt.binaries.pictures.vehicles` Images of vehicles. *Newsgroup*

6222 `alt.hotrod` High-speed automobiles. *Moderated newsgroup*

6223 `alt.rv` Rotten varmints or recreational vehicles, you decide. *Newsgroup*

6224 `aus.cars` Australian newsgroup for automobile aficionados. *Newsgroup*

6225 **british-cars:** Discussion of owning, repairing, racing, cursing, and loving British cars, predominantly sports cars; some Land Rover and sedan stuff. *Digest & Reflector*

± **INFO** `british-cars-request@autox.team.net`

6226 `clari.sports.motor` Racing, motor sports. *Moderated newsgroup*

6227 **VETTE-L:** On Corvettes, including shows around the country, service information, and more. *Mailing List*
± `listserv@emuvm1.cc.emory.edu` [body = SUBSCRIBE VETTE-L first-name last-name]
INFO `osdtm@emuvm1.bitnet`
ARCHIVE `listserv@emuvm1.cc.emory.edu`

➤ **EV:** On the state of the art and future directions for electric vehicles. (See entry 4666 for full listing.)

6228 `fj.rec.autos` Automobiles, automotive products, and laws. *Newsgroup*

6229 `fj.rec.autos.sports` About auto sports. *Newsgroup*

6230 `fj.rec.autos.wagon` Discussion about station wagons. *Newsgroup*

6231 `alt.cars.Ford-Probe` "PROBE ME"—actual Viriginia woman's license plate. *Newsgroup*

6232 `rec.autos.makers.ford.mustang` Ford Mustangs in all their flavors. *Newsgroup*

➤ **Hi-Tech Bulletin:** A business computing/motor-sports Internet news publication by Doug Willoughby. (See entry 3343 for full listing.)

6233 **HONDA-L:** On Honda and Acura automobiles, including information and advice on purchases, and on repair or parts. *Mailing List*
± `listserv@brownvm.brown.edu` [body = SUBSCRIBE HONDA-L first-name last-name]
INFO `honda-l-request@brownvm.brown.edu`
ARCHIVE `listserv@brownvm.brown.edu` [body = INDEX HONDA-L]

6234 **miata:** For owners and fans of Mazda Miata cars. *Mailing List*
`http://miata.net/`
± `listserv@jhunix.hcf.jhu.edu` [body = SUBSCRIBE MIATA first-name last-name]
INFO `list_admin@miata.net`
ARCHIVES
`ftp://jhunix.hcf.jhu.edu/mailing_lists/miata`
`gopher://jhunix.hcf.jhu.edu/Academic Computing/JHUNIX Archive/mailing-lists/miata`

6235 **mazda-list:** Technical correspondance and discussion of Mazda-designed vehicles. *Mailing List*
± **INFO** `mazda-list-request@ms.uky.edu`
OWNER `abbott@ms.uky.edu`
ARCHIVES
`ftp://ftp.ms.uky.edu/pub/mailing.lists/mazda-list`
`http://www.ms.uky.edu/mazda-list.html`

6236 `rec.audio.car` Discussions of automobile audio systems. *Newsgroup*

6237 `rec.autos.4x4` The on- and off-road four-wheel-drive vehicle. *Newsgroup*

6238 `tnn.rec.4wd` User's group for 4-wheel-drive automobile enthusiasts. *Newsgroup*

6239 `rec.autos.antique` Discussing all aspects of automobiles over 25 years old. *Newsgroup*

6240 `rec.autos.driving` Driving automobiles. *Newsgroup*

6241 `rec.autos.makers.chrysler` Dodge, Plymouth, Jeep, Eagle, etc. information/talk. *Newsgroup*

6242 `rec.autos.makers.saturn` All about Saturn cars, fans, and company. *Newsgroup*

6243 `rec.autos.marketplace` Buy/sell/trade automobiles, parts, tools, accessories. *Newsgroup*

6244 `rec.autos.misc` Miscellaneous discussion about automobiles. *Newsgroup*

6245 `rec.autos.rod-n-custom` High-performance automobiles. *Newsgroup*

6246 `rec.autos.simulators` Discussion of automotive simulators. *Newsgroup*

6247 `rec.autos.sport.f1` Formula 1 motor racing. *Newsgroup*

6248 `rec.autos.sport.indy` Indy Car motor racing. *Newsgroup*

6249 `rec.autos.sport.info` Auto racing news, results, announcements. *Moderated newsgroup*

6250 `rec.autos.sport.misc` Organized, legal auto competitions. *Newsgroup*

6251 `rec.autos.sport.nascar` NASCAR and other professional stock car racing. *Newsgroup*

6252 `rec.autos.sport.rally` Any type of interest in any form of rally motorsport. *Newsgroup*

6253 `rec.autos.sport.tech` Technical aspects and technology of auto racing. *Newsgroup*

6254 `rec.autos.tech` Technical aspects of automobiles, et al. *Newsgroup*

6255 `rec.autos.vw` Issues pertaining to Volkswagen products. *Newsgroup*

6256 `relcom.wheels` Anything concerning auto/motor transport and sport. *Newsgroup*

6257 `rec.autos.makers.vw.aircooled` Bug, Bus, Ghia, Squareback, Thing, etc. *Newsgroup*

6258 `rec.autos.makers.vw.watercooled` Golf, Jetta, Corrado, Vanagon, new models, etc. *Newsgroup*

AVIATION

6259 **AIRCRAFT:** On fixed-wing and rotary-wing aircraft, modern, classic, and antique, including listings of air shows and similar events. *Mailing List*
± `listserv@iubvm.ucs.indiana.edu` [body = SUBSCRIBE AIRCRAFT first-name last-name]
INFO `fragakis@indiana.edu` (Stelios Fragakis)
INFO `sheehan@indiana.edu` (Mark C. Sheehan)
ARCHIVE `listserv@iubvm.ucs.indiana.edu`

6260 `aus.aviation` Planes, gliders, flying, etc. *Newsgroup*

➤   **AV-ROTOR:** On civil helicopters: their uses, and related legislation and regulations. (See entry 1817 for full listing.)

6261 **Aviation Trader:** On aviation. *Newsletter*
`http://www.direct.ca/flying/`
± INFO EDITOR OWNER `avtrade@direct.ca` (Gordon Staples, Editor)

6262 **balloon:** For balloonists of any sort: hot air or gas, commercial or sport. *Mailing List*
± INFO `balloon-request@lut.ac.uk` (Dave Temple)

6263 `can.aviation.rgs` Air Cadet Gliding Program, news and views in Canada. *Newsgroup*

6264 `fj.rec.aerospace` About aviation. Airplanes, air sports, etc. *Newsgroup*

6265 **hang-gliding:** Topics covering all aspects of hang gliding and para-gliding. *Mailing List*
± `hang-gliding-request@lists.utah.edu`
INFO `hang-gliding-request@lists.utah.edu`
ARCHIVE `gopher://gopher.utah.edu:70/11/Off%20Campus%20Information/Recreation/hang-gliding`
FAQ `gopher://gopher.utah.edu:70/11/Off%20Campus%20Information/Recreation/hang-gliding`

6266 **Kitfox:** On owning, building, or flying Kitfox airplanes. *Mailing List*
`http://dunkin.princeton.edu/.kitfox/`
`ftp://dunkin.princeton.edu/.kitfox/`
± `listproc@lists.colorado.edu`
OWNER `jim.simmons@uchsc.edu` (Jim Simmons)

6267 **The Ornithopter Home Page:** Photos, designs, history, and more on ornithopters.
`http://www.bucknell.edu/~chronstr/orn.html`
INFO `chronstr@coral.bucknell.edu`

6268 `rec.aviation.announce` Events of interest to the aviation community. *Moderated newsgroup*

6269 `rec.aviation.answers` Frequently asked questions about aviation. *Moderated newsgroup*

6270 `rec.aviation.hang-gliding` Hang gliding, paragliding, foot-launched flight. *Newsgroup*

6271 `rec.aviation.homebuilt` Selecting, designing, building, and restoring aircraft. *Newsgroup*

6272 `rec.aviation.ifr` Flying under Instrument Flight Rules. *Newsgroup*

6273 `rec.aviation.marketplace` Aviation classifieds. *Newsgroup*

6274 `rec.aviation.military` Military aircraft of the past, present, and future. *Newsgroup*

6275 `rec.aviation.misc` Miscellaneous topics in aviation. *Newsgroup*

6276 `rec.aviation.owning` Information on owning airplanes. *Newsgroup*

6277 `rec.aviation.piloting` General discussion for aviators. *Newsgroup*

6278 `rec.aviation.products` Reviews and discussion of products useful to pilots. *Newsgroup*

6279 `rec.aviation.questions` Aviation questions and answers. *Moderated newsgroup*

6280 `rec.aviation.rotorcraft` Helicopters and other rotary wing aircraft. *Newsgroup*

6281 `rec.aviation.simulators` Flight simulation on all levels. *Newsgroup*

6282 `rec.aviation.soaring` All aspects of sailplanes and hang gliders. *Newsgroup*

6283 `rec.aviation.stories` Anecdotes of flight experiences. *Moderated newsgroup*

6284 `rec.aviation.student` Learning to fly. *Newsgroup*

6285 `rec.aviation.ultralight` Light aircraft in general, all topics. *Newsgroup*

6286 `rec.travel.air` Airline travel around the world. *Newsgroup*

6287 **ultralight-flight:** On ultralight airplanes: joys and responsibilities of flying. *Mailing List*
    ± `ultralight-flight-request@inslab.uky.edu`
    INFO `ultralight-flight-request@inslab.uky.edu`
    OWNER `hempy@inslab.uky.edu` (David Hempy)
    ARCHIVE `ftp://ftp.mscf.uky.edu/pub/mailing.lists/ultralight-flight`

COLLECTING

➤ `alt.collecting.8-track-tapes:` Fans of the endless-loop cartridge. *Newsgroup*

➤ `alt.collecting.autographs:` *wow!* You got Pete Rose's? What about Kibo's? *Newsgroup*

6288 `alt.collecting.pens-pencils` Pen and pencil collecting. *Newsgroup*

➤ `alt.collecting.teddy-bears:` Collecting stuffed toy bears. *Newsgroup*

6289 **Collection Connection:** A resource and forum for collectors of all types. *Newsletter*
    `http://www.trader.com/users/5010/5491/`
    ± `eagle@trader.com` [subject = SUBSCRIBE COLLECT; body = SUBSCRIBE COLLECT e-mail-address]
      (William E. Miller)
    INFO OWNER `eagle@trader.com` (William E. Miller)
    ARCHIVE `ftp://ftp.trader.com/users/5010/5491/`

➤ **Czechkrystal, Ltd.:** Importers of fine hand-blown, hand-engraved crystal from the Czech Republic, and gifts from around the world for the discriminating shopper. (See entry 7264 for full listing.)

6290 **POSTCARD:** For discussing and exchanging picture postcards. *Mailing List*
    `http://cyclops.idbsu.edu/`
    ± `listserv@idbsu.idbsu.edu` [body = SUBSCRIBE POSTCARD first-name last-name]
    OWNER `dlester@bsu.idbsu.edu`
    ARCHIVE `listserv@idbsu.idbsu.edu` [body = INDEX POSTCARD]
    Gated: `bit.listserv.postcard`

6291 `rec.antiques` Discussing antiques and vintage items. *Newsgroup*

6292 `rec.antiques.marketplace` Buying/selling/trading antiques. *Newsgroup*

6293 `rec.antiques.radio+phono` Audio devices and materials of yesteryear. *Newsgroup*

6294 `rec.arts.disney.merchandise` Toys, videos, music, books, art, collectibles. *Newsgroup*

6295 `rec.collecting` Discussion among collectors of many things. *Newsgroup*

6296 `rec.collecting.cards.discuss` Discussion of sports and non-sports cards. *Newsgroup*

6297 `rec.collecting.cards.non-sports` Non-sports cards. *Newsgroup*

6298 `rec.collecting.coins` Coin, currency, medal, etc. collecting forum. *Newsgroup*

6299 `rec.collecting.phonecards` Information and marketplace group for phone cards. *Newsgroup*

6300 `rec.collecting.postal-history` Study of the movement of the mails worldwide. *Newsgroup*

➤   `rec.collecting.sport.hockey`: Hockey memorabilia (cards, photos, etc.). *Newsgroup*

➤   `rec.collecting.sport.misc`: Sports memorabilia not in any other group. *Newsgroup*

6301 `rec.collecting.stamps` Discussion of all things related to philately. *Newsgroup*

6302 `rec.collecting.villages` Collectible houses, cottages, villages, and accessories. *Newsgroup*

6303 **rockhounds:** For gem and mineral collectors. *Mailing List*
± INFO `rockhounds-request@infodyn.com` (Tom Corson)

➤   **teddy-bears:** Teddy bear collecting & making. (See entry 7019 for full listing.)

CYCLING

6304 `aus.bicycle` Push bikes. *Newsgroup*

6305 `ba.bicycles` Bicycling issues specific to the San Francisco Bay Area. *Newsgroup*

6306 `bc.cycling` Discussion regarding bicycling in British Columbia, Canada. *Newsgroup*

6307 `dc.biking` Bicycles and biking in the Washington, D.C. metro area. *Newsgroup*

6308 `fj.rec.bicycles` Topics on bicycles. *Newsgroup*

➤   **GORP (Great Outdoor Recreation Pages):** This site contains a wealth of information on what to do and where to go in the great outdoors. It includes information on national parks, forests, wilderness areas, wildlife refuges, and monuments, as well as data on types of outdoor recreation (hiking, biking, climbing, etc.) and sources for outdoor recreation products and services. (See entry 6626 for full listing.)

➤   **National Forest Listings by State:** A listing of all U.S. national forests with descriptions and access information. This resource is hosted by GORP (Great Outdoor Recreation Pages). It covers all national forests in the U.S., providing overall descriptions, plus detailed information on hiking, cross-country skiing, fishing, rafting, biking, wildlife viewing, and other activities. (See entry 4608 for full listing.)

6309 `ont.bicycle` Bicycling in Ontario, Canada. *Newsgroup*

6310 `phl.bicycles` Bicycles, bike trails, recreation, and transportation. *Newsgroup*

6311 `rec.bicycles.marketplace` Buying, selling, and reviewing items for cycling. *Newsgroup*

6312 `rec.bicycles.misc` General discussion of bicycling. *Newsgroup*

6313 `rec.bicycles.off-road` All aspects of off-road bicycling. *Newsgroup*

6314 `rec.bicycles.racing` Bicycle racing techniques, rules, and results. *Newsgroup*

6315 `rec.bicycles.rides` Discussions of tours and training or commuting routes. *Newsgroup*

6316 `rec.bicycles.soc` Societal issues of bicycling. *Newsgroup*

6317 `rec.bicycles.tech` Cycling product design, construction, maintenance, etc. *Newsgroup*

6318 `rec.sport.unicycling` All sorts of fun on one wheel. *Newsgroup*

6319 `uk.rec.cycling` Discussion of U.K. cycling issues. *Newsgroup*

GAMBLING

6320 `alt.lotto.players` Gambling with the state as bookmaker. *Newsgroup*

6321 `alt.sweepstakes` Discussing sweepstakes. *Newsgroup*

6322 **Green Felt Casino Cyberspace Guide:** Winners Publishing presents the most current links to nationwide casino sites, room deals in Las Vegas/Reno/Tahoe/Atlantic City, scores/lines/picks, daily Lotto numbers, Vegas entertainment schedule, Vegas links galore, weekly "Deal Me In" columns, gambling FAQs, and some of the very best gambling locations, updated daily, on the information highway.
`http://www.winner.com/winner/`
INFO `winners@winner.com`

6323 **PCLotto:** Lotto predictor. Up-to-date Lotto databases online. Approximately 90 Lotto systems, including all U.S. and Canada. Also provides Bet Slip Printing for most lotto systems in the world.
`ftp://ftp.islandnet.com/PCLotto`
INFO `klestil@islandnet.com` (AL Klestil)

6324 `rec.gambling.craps` Analysis of and strategy for the dice game craps. *Newsgroup*

6325 `rec.gambling.lottery` Strategy and news of lotteries and sweepstakes. *Newsgroup*

6326 `rec.gambling.misc` All other gambling topics including travel. *Newsgroup*

6327 `rec.gambling.other-games` Gambling games not covered elsewhere. *Newsgroup*

6328 `rec.gambling.racing` Wagering on animal races. *Newsgroup*

6329 `rec.gambling.sports` Wagering on human sporting events. *Newsgroup*

GAMES

6330 **Games Domain:** A comprehensive games site; includes FAQs and pointers to games sites; covers all varieties of games.
`http://www.gamesdomain.co.uk/`
INFO `djh@gamesdom.demon.co.uk`
FAQ `http://www.gamesdomain.co.uk/gdfaq/gdfaq.html`
MIRRORS
`http://gamesdomain.co.za/` (South Africa)
`http://gamesdomain.com/` (USA)
Comments: Although the site is only maintained by one person, the information is supplied by thousands of gamers all around the world.

6331 `alt.games.cosmic-wimpout` A dice game popular in the computer crowd. *Newsgroup*

6332 `aus.games` Discussions of games. *Newsgroup*

➤ `clari.living.leisure:` Leisure, the outdoors, games. *Moderated newsgroup*

6333 `fj.rec.games` Discussion about games. *Newsgroup*

6334 `iijnet.games` Topics and discussions about games. *Newsgroup*

6335 `okinawa.rec.games` Discussion about games. *Newsgroup*

6336 `pdaxs.games.misc` Everything else except head games (see counseling). *Newsgroup*

6337 `pdx.games` Talk about games. *Newsgroup*

6338 `rec.games.abstract` Perfect information, pure strategy games. *Newsgroup*

6339 `rec.games.design` Discussion of game design related issues. *Newsgroup*

6340 `rec.games.misc` Games and computer games. *Newsgroup*

6341 `tnn.games` Topics and discussions about games. *Newsgroup*

6342 `triangle.gamers` Gaming buffs in central North Carolina. *Newsgroup*

6343   **uk.games.misc**   Various topics on gaming in the U.K. *Newsgroup*

GAMES—BOARD

6344   **alt.chess.bdg**   The Blackmar-Diemer Gambit. *Newsgroup*

6345   **alt.chess.ics**   The Internet Chess Server valkyries.andrew.cmu.edu. *Newsgroup*

6346   **CHESS-L:** On chess, including tournaments, chess problems, and interesting games. *Mailing List*
± listserv@nic.surfnet.nl [body = SUBSCRIBE CHESS-L first-name last-name]
INFO OWNER maximus@iaehv.nl (Frank Maximus)
OWNER info@surfnet.nl
ARCHIVE listserv@nic.surfnet.nl [body = INDEX CHESS-L]

6347   **chessnews:** About chess played both by and against computers and humans. *Digest & Reflector*
± INFO chessnews-request@tssi.com
Gated: rec.games.chess

6348   **OGRE:** On GEV and the world of OGRE, Steve Jackson's tactical combat board game. *Mailing List*
± majordomo@pentagon.io.com [body = subscribe ogre-l]
OWNER kerry@io.com (Kerry Harrison)

6349   **pdaxs.games.board**   Not bored, board. Like checkers, Chinese checkers. *Newsgroup*

6350   **pdaxs.games.chess**   Okay, I'm Fischer and you can be Spassky. *Newsgroup*

6351   **rec.games.backgammon**   Discussion of the game of backgammon. *Newsgroup*

6352   **rec.games.board**   Discussion and hints on board games. *Newsgroup*

6353   **rec.games.board.ce**   The Cosmic Encounter board game. *Newsgroup*

6354   **rec.games.board.marketplace**   Trading and selling of board games. *Newsgroup*

6355   **rec.games.chess**   Chess and computer chess. *Newsgroup*

6356   **rec.games.chess.analysis**   Analysis of openings/middle games/endgames. *Newsgroup*

6357   **rec.games.chess.misc**   Forum for news/discussion related to chess. *Newsgroup*

6358   **rec.games.chess.play-by-email**   Reports/discussions regarding e-mail chess. *Newsgroup*

6359   **rec.games.chess.politics**   News of national/international chess organizations. *Newsgroup*

6360   **rec.games.chinese-chess**   Discussion of the game of Chinese chess, Xiangqi. *Newsgroup*

6361   **rec.games.go**   Discussion about Go. *Newsgroup*

6362   **SHOGI-L:** On the strategic Japanese board game *shogi. Mailing List*
± listserv@technion.technion.ac.il [body = SUBSCRIBE SHOGI-L first-name last-name]
INFO stoutepf@chemsci5.dmpc.com
INFO kenney@embl-heidelberg.de
INFO mutz@fmi.uni-passau.de
INFO ccslist@technion.technion.ac.il
ARCHIVES
listserv@technion.technion.ac.il [body = INDEX SHOGI-L]
http://www.fwi.uva.nl/~bobd/shogi-list/
FAQS
http://www.halcyon.com/stouten/shogi.html
http://www.ed.ac.uk/~rjhare/shogi/intro.html

6363   **uk.games.board**   All about board games in the U.K. *Newsgroup*

GAMES—CARD

6364 `alt.games.jyhad` Another trading card game, like Magic: the Gathering. *Newsgroup*

6365 `aus.games.bridge` Australasian bridge players. *Newsgroup*

6366 **ba-poker-list:** On poker in the San Franciso Bay Area (broadly defined). Topics include upcoming events, unusual games, strategies, comparisons of various venues, and player "networking." *Mailing List*
± `majordomo@lists.best.com` [body = `subscribe ba-poker-list`]
INFO OWNER `owner-ba-poker@lists.best.com` (Martin Veneroso)

6367 `pdaxs.games.bridge` Who's the dummy now? *Newsgroup*

6368 **Poker World Magazine:** A magazine about poker.
`http://unix.mclv.net/poker`
INFO `poker@unix.mclv.net`

6369 `rec.gambling.blackjack` Analysis of and strategy for blackjack, aka 21. *Newsgroup*

6370 `rec.gambling.poker` Analysis and strategy of live poker games. *Newsgroup*

6371 `rec.games.bridge` Hobbyists interested in bridge. *Newsgroup*

6372 `rec.games.playing-cards` Recreational (non-gambling) card playing. *Newsgroup*

6373 `rec.games.trading-cards.announce` Important news about trading-card games. *Moderated newsgroup*

6374 `rec.games.trading-cards.jyhad` Jyhad trading card game discussions. *Newsgroup*

6375 `rec.games.trading-cards.magic.misc` General Magic: The Gathering postings. *Newsgroup*

6376 `rec.games.trading-cards.magic.rules` "Magic: the Gathering" rules Q & A. *Newsgroup*

6377 `rec.games.trading-cards.magic.strategy` Magic: The Gathering strategy. *Newsgroup*

6378 `rec.games.trading-cards.marketplace` Sales, auctions, trades of game cards. *Newsgroup*

6379 `rec.games.trading-cards.marketplace.magic.auctions` Auctions of Magic cards. *Newsgroup*

6380 `rec.games.trading-cards.marketplace.magic.sales` Selling Magic cards. *Newsgroup*

6381 `rec.games.trading-cards.marketplace.magic.trades` Trading Magic cards. *Newsgroup*

6382 `rec.games.trading-cards.marketplace.misc` Trading trading-card stuff. *Newsgroup*

6383 `rec.games.trading-cards.misc` Other trading-card game discussions. *Newsgroup*

6384 `uk.games.trading-card` Trading-card games (Magic, etc.) in the U.K. *Newsgroup*

GAMES—COMPUTER & VIDEO

6385 `alt.atari-jaguar.discussion` Atari Jaguar discussion. *Newsgroup*

6386 `alt.atari.2600` The Atari 2600 game system, not *2600* magazine. *Newsgroup*

6387 `alt.binaries.descent` The Decline and Fall of the `alt.binaries` Empire. *Newsgroup*

6388 `alt.binaries.doom` Binaries for or of the DOOM PC game. *Newsgroup*

6389 `alt.binaries.games` Terabytes of copyright violations. *Newsgroup*

6390 `alt.binaries.games.discussion` Discussing binaries from alt.binaries.games. *Newsgroup*

6391 `alt.binaries.games.vga-planets` Conquer the universe via uudecode. *Newsgroup*

6392 `alt.binaries.mac.games` Games for the Macintosh. *Newsgroup*

6393 `alt.fan.sonic-hedgehog` Sega's spinning blue hero. *Newsgroup*

6394 `alt.games.air-warrior` The Air Warrior combat computer game. *Newsgroup*

6395 `alt.games.apogee` A real high point in any gamer's day. *Newsgroup*

6396 `alt.games.command-n-conq` Computer game Command and Conquer. *Newsgroup*

6397 `alt.games.dark-forces` Discussion of Star Wars-related game. *Newsgroup*

6398 `alt.games.descent` Computer adventure game in 3D. *Newsgroup*

6399 `alt.games.doom` A really popular PC game. *Newsgroup*

6400 `alt.games.doom.announce` Announcements about the PC game DOOM. *Moderated newsgroup*

6401 `alt.games.doom.ii` Ladies and gentlemen, we are in hell. On Earth! *Newsgroup*

6402 `alt.games.doom.newplayers` Helping people new to a really popular PC game. *Newsgroup*

6403 `alt.games.dune-ii.virgin-games` Virgin Games computer game Dune II. *Newsgroup*

6404 `alt.games.final-fantasy` The Final Fantasy game. *Newsgroup*

6405 `alt.games.killer-instinct` Serial psychos give it two thumbs up. *Newsgroup*

6406 `alt.games.lynx` The Atari Lynx. *Newsgroup*

6407 `alt.games.marathon` Discussion of the Macintosh sf game Marathon. *Newsgroup*

6408 `alt.games.mechwarrior2` Activision's Second Battletech Simulator. *Newsgroup*

6409 `alt.games.mk` Struggling in Mortal Kombat! *Newsgroup*

6410 `alt.games.mk.mk3` Mortal Kombat III. *Newsgroup*

6411 `alt.games.mtrek` Multi-Trek, a multiuser Star Trek-like game. *Newsgroup*

6412 `alt.games.netrek.paradise` Discussion of the Paradise version of Netrek. *Newsgroup*

6413 `alt.games.playmaker-football` Playmaker Football discussion area. *Newsgroup*

6414 `alt.games.sf2` The video game Street Fighter 2. *Newsgroup*

6415 `alt.games.ultima.dragons` Hints for Ultima games. *Newsgroup*

6416 `alt.games.vampire.the.masquerade` A World of Dark game. *Newsgroup*

6417 `alt.games.vga-planets` Discussion of Tim Wisseman's VGA Planets. *Newsgroup*

6418 `alt.games.video.classic` Video games from before the mid-1980s. *Newsgroup*

6419 `alt.games.video.import.japanese` Video games imported from Japan. *Newsgroup*

6420 `alt.games.video.sony-playstation` Sony's Playstation. *Newsgroup*

6421 `alt.games.video.sony-playstation.faqs` Up to date Playstation FAQs. *Newsgroup*

6422 `alt.games.wing-commander` Shoot 'em up from the air. *Newsgroup*

6423 `alt.games.xpilot` Discussion on all aspects of the X11 game Xpilot. *Newsgroup*

6424 `alt.games.xtrek` The networked game Xtrek. *Newsgroup*

6425 `alt.mechwarrior2` Use `alt.games.mechwarrior2` instead. *Newsgroup*

6426 `alt.sega.genesis` Another addiction. *Newsgroup*

6427 `alt.sega.nhl` For players of Sega's National Hockey League game. *Newsgroup*

6428 `alt.video.games.reviews` Reviews of video games. *Newsgroup*

6429 `bit.listserv.games-l` Computer games list. *Newsgroup*

6430 **Brett Russell's Descent Levels:** Original descent levels and more from Brett Russell.
   http://mail.icgroup.net/~brussel
   INFO brussel@icgroup.net
   MIRROR http://icgroup.net/~brussel

6431 `ccc.battletech` Discussions of BattleTech, Virtual World, et al. *Newsgroup*

➤ **ChipNet:** ChipNet topics include computer chat, sports, cooking and travel, video games, general interests, opinions, advice, humor, and more. (See entry 645 for full listing.)

6432 `clari.tw.computers.entertainment.releases` Releases: computer entertainment. *Moderated newsgroup*

➤ `comp.os.os2.games`: Running games under OS/2. *Newsgroup*

6433 `comp.sources.games` Postings of recreational software. *Moderated newsgroup*

6434 `comp.sources.games.bugs` Bug reports and fixes for posted game software. *Newsgroup*

6435 `comp.sys.acorn.games` Discussion of games for Acorn machines. *Newsgroup*

6436 `comp.sys.amiga.games` Discussion of games for the Commodore Amiga. *Newsgroup*

➤ `comp.sys.ibm.pc.games.action:` Arcade-style games on PCs. *Newsgroup*

6437 `comp.sys.ibm.pc.games.adventure` Adventure (non-RPG) games on PCs. *Newsgroup*

6438 `comp.sys.ibm.pc.games.announce` Announcements for all PC gamers. *Moderated newsgroup*

6439 `comp.sys.ibm.pc.games.flight-sim` Flight simulators on PCs. *Newsgroup*

6440 `comp.sys.ibm.pc.games.marketplace` PC clone games wanted and for sale. *Newsgroup*

6441 `comp.sys.ibm.pc.games.misc` Games not covered by other PC groups. *Newsgroup*

6442 `comp.sys.ibm.pc.games.rpg` Role-playing games on the PC. *Newsgroup*

➤ `comp.sys.ibm.pc.games.sports:` Discussion of sports games for the IBM PC. *Newsgroup*

6443 `comp.sys.ibm.pc.games.strategic` Strategy/planning games on PCs. *Newsgroup*

6444 `comp.sys.ibm.pc.soundcard.games` Questions about using sound cards with games. *Newsgroup*

6445 `comp.sys.mac.games.action` Action games for the Macintosh. *Newsgroup*

6446 `comp.sys.mac.games.adventure` Adventure games for the Macintosh. *Newsgroup*

6447 `comp.sys.mac.games.announce` Announcements for Macintosh gamers. *Moderated newsgroup*

6448 `comp.sys.mac.games.flight-sim` Flight simulator game-play on the Macintosh. *Newsgroup*

6449 `comp.sys.mac.games.marketplace` Macintosh games for sale and trade. *Newsgroup*

6450 `comp.sys.mac.games.misc` Macintosh games not covered in other groups. *Newsgroup*

6451 `comp.sys.mac.games.strategic` Strategy/planning games on the Macintosh. *Newsgroup*

6452 **Computer Gaming World:** Web version of Computer Gaming World. Containing three of the top articles from the latest print edition of *Computer Gaming World* plus original reviews, links to FTP sites, and more. *Magazine*
   INFO OWNER `gjones@zd.com` (George Jones)
   ARCHIVE `http://www.zdnet.com/~gaming`
   Frequency: updates weekly

6453 **crossfire:** On the development of the multiplayer graphical arcade game for X-Windows environments. *Mailing List*
   ± `crossfire-request@ifi.uio.no`
   INFO `owner-crossfire@ifi.uio.no` (Frank Tore Johansen)
   ARCHIVE `ftp://ftp.ifi.uio.no/pub/crossfire/archive/`

6454 **dungeon.chatter.doom** Dungeon net sys DOOM/DOOM II/HERETIC discussions. *Newsgroup*

6455 **FBPRO:** Discussions of Dynamix Front Page Sport's Football Pro game: Internet leagues, teams, players, and strategy. *Mailing List*
   ± OWNER `jvancl@3do.com`

6456 `fj.rec.games.video.arcade` Discussion about video game in arcades. *Newsgroup*

6457 `fj.rec.games.video.arcade.kakutou` Discussion about fighting game in arcades. *Newsgroup*

6458 `fj.rec.games.video.home` Discussion about video game for console. *Newsgroup*

6459 `fj.rec.games.video.home.playstation` Topics about PlayStation. *Newsgroup*

6460 `fj.rec.games.video.home.saturn` Topics about Saturn. *Newsgroup*

6461 `fj.rec.games.video.pc` Discussion about video game for personal computer. *Newsgroup*

6462 **GALCIV-L:** On the Galactic Civilization for OS/2 simulation game. *Mailing List*

± `listserv@trearnpc.ege.edu.tr` [body = SUBSCRIBE GALCIV-L first-name last-name]
OWNER `turgut@vm3090.ege.edu.tr` (Turgut Kalfaoglu)

6463 **Game Zero Magazine:** World Wide Web-based, video-games-related magazine. *E-Magazine*
`http://www.gamezero.com/team-0`
INFO `team-0@gamezero.com`
EDITOR `gmezero@gz.bomb.com` (Bryan Carter, Co-Editor)
ARCHIVES
`http://www.gamezero.com/team-0`
`ftp://tethys1.tethys.net/gamezero`
Frequency: frequent to biweekly

6464 **GAMES-L:** On computer games—all platforms. *Mailing List*
± `listserv@brownvm.brown.edu` [body = SUBSCRIBE GAMES-L first-name last-name]
INFO `games-l-request@brownvm.brown.cdu` (David W. Baker)
Gated: `bit.listserv.games-l`

6465 `gnu.chess` Announcements about the GNU Chess program. *Newsgroup*

6466 `han.rec.games` Computer games, electronic amusement. *Newsgroup*

6467 **Interactive games:** Zarf's List of Interactive Games on the Web.
`http://www.cs.cmu.edu/afs/andrew/org/kgb/www/zarf/games.html`
INFO `erkyrath@cmu.edu`

6468 **PBEM: Play by E-mail:** A fanzine for free computer-moderated, play-by-electronic-mail war games. *E-Journal*
`ftp://ftp.funet.fi/pub/doc/games/play-by-mail/magazines/pbem`
INFO `gl8f@virginia.edu` (Greg Lindahl)
ARCHIVES
`http://fermi.clas.virginia.edu/~gl8f/pbem_magazine.html`
`ftp://ftp.pbm.com/pub/pbm/magazines/pbem`
Gated: `rec.games.pbm`
Frequency: irregular (6-9 times a year)

6469 `rec.games.bolo` The networked strategy war game Bolo. *Newsgroup*

6470 `rec.games.chess.computer` Reports on game servers, databases, software. *Newsgroup*

6471 `rec.games.computer.doom.announce` Info/FAQs/reviews about DOOM. *Moderated newsgroup*

6472 `rec.games.computer.doom.editing` Editing and hacking DOOM-related files. *Newsgroup*

6473 `rec.games.computer.doom.help` DOOM help service (new players welcome). *Newsgroup*

6474 `rec.games.computer.doom.misc` Talking about DOOM and id Softwar. *Newsgroup*

6475 `rec.games.computer.doom.playing` Playing DOOM and user-created levels. *Newsgroup*

6476 `rec.games.computer.puzzle` Puzzle-solving computer game. *Newsgroup*

6477 `rec.games.computer.xpilot` About the X11 game XPilot. *Newsgroup*

6478 `rec.games.corewar` The Core War computer challenge. *Newsgroup*

6479 `rec.games.empire` Discussion and hints about Empire. *Newsgroup*

6480 `rec.games.netrek` Discussion of the X window system game Netrek (XtrekII). *Newsgroup*

6481 `rec.games.programmer` Discussion of adventure-game programming. *Newsgroup*

6482 `rec.games.roguelike.angband` The computer game Angband. *Newsgroup*

6483 `rec.games.roguelike.announce` Major information about Rogue-styled games. *Moderated newsgroup*

6484 `rec.games.roguelike.misc` Rogue-style dungeon games without other groups. *Newsgroup*

6485 `rec.games.roguelike.moria` The computer game Moria. *Newsgroup*

6486 `rec.games.roguelike.nethack` The computer game Nethack. *Newsgroup*

6487 `rec.games.roguelike.rogue` The computer game Rogue. *Newsgroup*

6488 `rec.games.vectrex` The Vectrex game system. *Newsgroup*

6489 `rec.games.video.3do` Discussion of 3DO video game systems. *Newsgroup*

6490 `rec.games.video.advocacy` Debate on merits of various video game systems. *Newsgroup*

6491 `rec.games.video.arcade` Discussions about coin-operated video games. *Newsgroup*

6492 `rec.games.video.arcade.collecting` Collecting, converting, repairing, etc. *Newsgroup*

6493 `rec.games.video.cd-i` CD-i topics with emphasis on games. *Newsgroup*

6494 `rec.games.video.cd32` Gaming talk, information, and help for the Amiga CD32. *Newsgroup*

6495 `rec.games.video.classic` Older home video entertainment systems. *Newsgroup*

6496 `rec.games.video.marketplace` Home video game stuff for sale or trade. *Newsgroup*

6497 `rec.games.video.misc` General discussion about home video games. *Newsgroup*

6498 `rec.games.video.nintendo` All Nintendo video game systems and software. *Newsgroup*

6499 `rec.games.video.sega` All Sega video game systems and software. *Newsgroup*

6500 `rec.games.video.sony` Sony game hardware and software. *Newsgroup*

6501 `rec.games.xtank.play` Strategy and tactics for the distributed game Xtank. *Newsgroup*

6502 `rec.games.xtank.programmer` Coding the Xtank game and its robots. *Newsgroup*

6503 `relcom.games` Discussion of computer, deck and other games. *Newsgroup*

6504 `vmsnet.sources.games` Recreational software postings. *Newsgroup*

6505 **XYZZYnews: The Magazine for Interactive Fiction:** For fellow gamers who are crazy about computer adventure games, especially text-based adventures that compel players to face intellectual challenges or a series of logic puzzles in order to complete a storyline. *E-Zine*
  `http://www.interport.net/~eileen/design/xyzzynews.html`
  `ftp://ftp.gmd.de/if-archive/magazines/XYZZYnews/`
  INFO `eileen@interport.net` (Eileen Mullin)
  INFO `xyzzynews@aol.com`
  Frequency: bimonthly

GAMES—ROLE-PLAYING

6506 **ADND-L:** For players of the Advanced Dungeons and Dragons role-playing game. *Mailing List*
  ± `listserv@utarlvm1.uta.edu` [body = SUBSCRIBE ADND-L first-name last-name]
  INFO `bsamek@uta.edu` (Brad Samek)

6507 `alt.cardgame.spellfire` TSR's SpellFire game. *Newsgroup*

6508 `alt.flame.mud` To all the MUDs I've loved before. *Newsgroup*

6509 `alt.games.dust` Hints and discussion of Dust: A Tale of the Wired West. *Newsgroup*

6510 `alt.games.final-fantasy.rpg` Storytelling in the Final Fantasy universe. *Newsgroup*

6511 `alt.games.frp.2300ad` 2300 A.D. *Newsgroup*

6512 `alt.games.frp.dnd-util` Computer utilities for Dungeons and Dragons. *Newsgroup*

6513 `alt.games.frp.nurpg` Stories for the NuRPG. Let your imagination go wild. *Newsgroup*

6514 `alt.games.frp.tekumel` Empire of the Petal Throne fantasy role-playing game by M. A. R. Barker. *Newsgroup*

6515 `alt.games.illuminati` It's just a game, isn't it? Fnord. *Newsgroup*

6516 `alt.games.wc3` A sequel to the infamous Water Closet games. *Newsgroup*

6517 `alt.games.whitewolf` Discussion of WhiteWolf's line of gothic/horror RPGs. *Newsgroup*

6518 `alt.games.whitewolf.rage` Rage, White Wolf's trading-card game. *Newsgroup*

6519 `aus.games.roleplay` Discussions of role-playing games. *Newsgroup*

6520 **Chaosium Digest:** On Chaosium's role-playing games, including Call of Cthulhu, Elric!, Elfquest, Pendragon, and many others. *Digest*
± `appel@erzo.org` (Shannon Appel)
ARCHIVE `ftp://ftp.csua.berkeley.edu/pub/chaosium/archives`
Frequency: weekly

6521 **The Diplomatic Pouch:** The Diplomatic Pouch is a World Wide Web-based online magazine for the players of Avalon Hill's game of Diplomacy and its many variants. *E-Zine*
`http://www.csn.net/~mhand/DipPouch/`
EDITOR `mhand@csn.net` (Manus Hand)
ARCHIVE `http://www.csn.net/~mhand/DipPouch/`
Frequency: five times a year on a regular schedule

6522 **Who-RPG-L:** Discussion of role-playing in the universe of Dr. Who. *Mailing List*
± `listproc@lists.pipex.com` [body = SUBSCRIBE WHO-RPG-L first-name last-name]
INFO `http://www.tardis.ac.uk/`
OWNER `type40@tardis.ed.ac.uk` (Ian McDonald)
OWNER `mcdonald@biochem.ucl.ac.uk` (Ian McDonald)
ARCHIVES
`ftp://ftp.tardis.ed.ac.uk`
`http://www.lists.pipex.com/cgi-bin/listproc/digests?list=who-rpg-l`

6523 **GMAST-L:** For general discussion on role-playing games. *Mailing List*
± `listserv@utcvm.utc.edu` [body = SUBSCRIBE GMAST-L first-name last-name]
INFO `jeff@utcvm.utc.edu` (Jeff Kell)
ARCHIVE `listserv@utcvm.utc.edu`

➤   **Interactive games:** Zarf's List of Interactive Games on the Web. (See entry 6467 for full listing.)

6524 `rec.games.diplomacy` The conquest game Diplomacy. *Newsgroup*

6525 `rec.games.frp.advocacy` Flames and rebuttals about various role-playing systems. *Newsgroup*

6526 `rec.games.frp.announce` Announcements of happenings in the role-playing world. *Moderated newsgroup*

6527 `rec.games.frp.archives` Archivable fantasy stories and other projects. *Moderated newsgroup*

6528 `rec.games.frp.cyber` Discussions of cyberpunk-related role-playing games. *Newsgroup*

6529 `rec.games.frp.dnd` Fantasy role-playing with TSR's Dungeons and Dragons. *Newsgroup*

6530 `rec.games.frp.gurps` The GURPS role-playing games. *Newsgroup*

6531 `rec.games.frp.live-action` Live-action role-playing games. *Newsgroup*

6532 `rec.games.frp.marketplace` Role-playing-game materials wanted and for sale. *Newsgroup*

6533 `rec.games.frp.misc` General discussions of role-playing games. *Newsgroup*

6534 `rec.games.frp.storyteller` World of Darkness and StoryTeller games. *Newsgroup*

6535 `rec.games.frp.super-heroes` Superhero role-playing games. *Newsgroup*

6536 **ShadowRN:** Discussion of the role-playing game Shadowrun, published by FASA. *Mailing List*
`http://www.cybernothing.org/jdfalk/shadowrun/`
± `majordomo@listproc.itribe.net` [body = subscribe shadowrn]
INFO OWNER `owner-shadowrn@listproc.itribe.net` (ShadowRN Listowner)

6537 Star Fleet Battles: On the Star Fleet Battles role-playing game. *Mailing List, moderated*
± INFO hcobb@slip.net
ARCHIVE ftp://ftp.cdrom.com/pub/misc/sfb
FAQ ftp://ftp.cdrom.com/pub/misc/sfb/FAQ.txt
Please Note: Subscription by approval only.
Comments: If you don't like it, go run your own. (I've got at least one "competitor" so far, looking for more.)

6538 SW-RPG: On the Star Wars role playing game. *Mailing List*
± mailserv@drycas.club.cc.cmu.edu
INFO http://drycas.club.cc.cmu.edu/~jae/sw/sw-list.html
OWNER jae@drycas.club.cc.cmu.edu (Jae Walker)
ARCHIVE http://drycas.club.cc.cmu.edu/~jae/sw/sw-list.html

6539 tnn.games.rpg Table talk role-playing games. *Newsgroup*

6540 visionary-l: From Visionary Publishing: relating storytelling, role-playing, myths, and games. *Mailing List*
http://www.io.com/~mjg
± majordomo@io.com [body = subscribe visionary-l]
OWNER mjg@io.com (Mitchell J. Gross)

GAMES—SIMULATION

6541 alt.binaries.warcraft Warcraft pics, levels, configurations. *Newsgroup*

6542 alt.games.warcraft The craft of war. *Newsgroup*

➤   **alt.sport.basketball.pro.fantasy:** Rotisserie league basketball. *Newsgroup*

➤   **alt.sports.hockey.fantasy:** Rotisserie league ice hockey. *Newsgroup*

6543 CONSIM-L: On conflict-simulation games. *Mailing List*
± listserv@listserv.uni-c.dk [body = SUB CONSIM-L first-name last-name]
INFO OWNER erik.lawaetz@uni-c.dk (Erik Lawaetz)
INFO OWNER hgerber@gpu.srv.ualberta.ca (Hjalmar Gerber)

6544 ISAGA-L: For members of the International Simulation and Gaming Association. *Mailing List*
± listserv@uhccvm.its.hawaii.edu [body = SUBSCRIBE ISAGA-L first-name last-name]
INFO isaga-l-request@uhccvm.its.hawaii.edu
ARCHIVE listserv@uhccvm.its.hawaii.edu [body = INDEX ISAGA-L]

GAMES—VARIOUS

6545 alt.games.mornington.cresent You can't get there from here. *Newsgroup*

6546 alt.games.quake Natural disasters as sport. *Newsgroup*

6547 alt.games.tiddlywinks Flip the discs—fun for hours on end! *Newsgroup*

6548 alt.sport.foosball Table soccer and dizzy little men. *Newsgroup*

6549 alt.sport.pool Knock your balls into your pockets for fun. *Newsgroup*

6550 BEATCALC: For mental math exercises. *Distribution List*
± beatcalc@aol.com
OWNER blclay@aol.com (B. Lee Clay)

6551 fj.rec.games.arcade.pinball Topics about pinball. *Newsgroup*

6552 fj.rec.games.mahjong Topics about mah-jongg. *Newsgroup*

6553 fj.rec.games.pachinko Discussion about pachinko game. *Newsgroup*

6554 rec.games.int-fiction All aspects of interactive fiction games. *Newsgroup*

6555 `rec.games.mecha` Giant robot games. *Newsgroup*

6556 `rec.games.miniatures.historical` Historical and modern tabletop war-gaming. *Newsgroup*

6557 `rec.games.miniatures.misc` Miniatures and various tabletop war games. *Newsgroup*

6558 `rec.games.miniatures.warhammer` War-gaming in the Warhammer Universe. *Newsgroup*

6559 `rec.games.pbm` Discussion about Play by Mail games. *Newsgroup*

6560 `rec.games.pinball` Discussing pinball-related issues. *Newsgroup*

6561 `rec.games.trivia` Discussion about trivia. *Newsgroup*

6562 `rec.puzzles` Puzzles, problems, and quizzes. *Newsgroup*

6563 `rec.puzzles.crosswords` Making and playing gridded word puzzles. *Newsgroup*

6564 `rec.sport.billiard` Billiard sports, including pool, snooker, carom games. *Newsgroup*

6565 **Strat-O-Matic:** On Strat-O-Matic board and computer games; especially sports oriented. *Mailing List*
± `majordomo@indiana.edu` [body = `subscribe strat-bb` (for SOM baseball) or `subscribe strat-misc` (for all other SOM games)]
INFO `rscott@mail.coin.missouri.edu` (Richard Scott)

GUNS & SHOOTING

➤ **Handguns & Accessories for Women & Southpaws:** Handguns as a self-defense tool. Solid information and arguments. (See entry 10007 for full listing.)

6566 `info.firearms` Nonpolitical firearms discussions (`firearms@ns1.rutgers.edu`). *Moderated newsgroup*

➤ `tx.guns:` Texans talk about firearms. *Newsgroup*

GYMNASTICS

6567 **gymn:** For the discussion of all aspects of gymnastics. *Mailing List*
± `listserv@psuvm.psu.edu` [body = SUBSCRIBE GYMN first-name last-name]
INFO `gymn-l-request@psuvm.psu.edu`

HORSES

6568 `alt.sport.horse-racing` Run for the roses: breeding, betting on, and racing horses. *Newsgroup*

6569 `alt.sport.horse-racing.systems` Horse-race handicapping systems and strategies. *Newsgroup*

6570 **Caballo-L:** A mailing list for Peruvian Paso horse breeders and owners. *Mailing List*
`http://www.islandnet.com/~creator/caballo.html`
± `caballo-l-request@islandnet.com` [subject = SUBSCRIBE]
INFO `caballo-l-request@islandnet.com`
OWNER `creator@islandnet.com` (Matt Elrod)
POST `caballo-l@islandnet.com`

6571 `clari.sports.horse_racing` Coverage of horse racing. *Moderated newsgroup*

6572 **derby:** About horse racing, mostly thoroughbred handicapping, but other racing-related topics welcome. *Mailing List*
± INFO `derby-request@ekrl.com`
OWNER `stevem@inslab.uky.edu`
ARCHIVE `ftp://ftp.inslab.uky.edu/pub/Derby/List/Digests`

6573 `fj.rec.sports.keiba` About horse racing. *Newsgroup*

6574 `rec.equestrian` Discussion of things equestrian. *Newsgroup*

HUNTING & FISHING

6575 `fj.rec.fishing` Topics about fishing. *Newsgroup*

➤ **GORP (Great Outdoor Recreation Pages):** This site contains a wealth of information on what to do and where to go in the great outdoors. It includes information on national parks, forests, wilderness areas, wildlife refuges, and monuments, as well as data on types of outdoor recreation (hiking, biking, climbing, etc.) and sources for outdoor recreation products and services. (See entry 6626 for full listing.)

6576 **HUNTING:** This list is a reflection of the moderated Usenet group `rec.hunting` for those folks that prefer to read this group via mail instead of a newsreader. *Digest & Reflector, moderated*

　　`http://tamvm1.tamu.edu/~hunting/`

　　± `listserv@tamu.edu` [body = `subscribe HUNTING` first-name last-name]

　　INFO `huntmod@tamvm1.tamu.edu` (Chris Barnes)

　　Gated: `rec.hunting`

➤ **National Forest Listings by State:** A listing of all U.S. national forests with descriptions and access information. This resource is hosted by GORP (Great Outdoor Recreation Pages). It covers all national forests in the U.S., providing overall descriptions, plus detailed information on hiking, cross-country skiing, fishing, rafting, biking, wildlife viewing, and other activities. (See entry 4608 for full listing.)

6577 `rec.hunting` Discussions about hunting. *Moderated newsgroup*

6578 `rec.hunting.dogs` Hunting topics specifically related to using dogs. *Moderated newsgroup*

6579 `rec.outdoors.fishing` All aspects of sport and commercial fishing. *Newsgroup*

6580 `rec.outdoors.fishing.fly` Fly fishing in general. *Newsgroup*

6581 `rec.outdoors.fishing.saltwater` Saltwater fishing, methods, gear, Q & A. *Newsgroup*

➤ **U.S. Fish and Wildlife Service:** On habitat protection, waterfowl management, and endangered species recovery. The U.S. Fish and Wildlife Service strives to conserve this nation's fish and wildlife resources and ensure their continued existence for future generations of Americans. (See entry 4685 for full listing.)

LIVING HISTORY

6582 `alt.history.living` A forum for discussing the hobby of living history. *Newsgroup*

6583 `austin.org.sca` The Society for Creative Anachronism in Austin, Texas. *Newsgroup*

6584 **CW-REENACTORS:** Discussions of American Civil War reenacting. *Digest & Reflector*

　　± `majordomo@world.std.com` [body = `subscribe cw-reenactors`]

　　OWNER `ata@world.std.com` (Alan Aronson)

　　Frequency: daily

6585 `pgh.org.sca` Pgh chapter, Society for Creative Anachronism (SCA). *Newsgroup*

➤ `rec.heraldry`: Discussion of coats of arms. *Newsgroup*

6586 `rec.org.sca` Society for Creative Anachronism. *Newsgroup*

6587 **SCA:** On the Society for Creative Anachronism (SCA), a worldwide medieval and Renaissance living-history organization. *Mailing List*

　　± INFO `sca-request@mc.lcs.mit.edu`

6588 **sca-west:** On topics of interest to the Society for Creative Anachronism members in the West (including Northern and Central California, Northern Nevada, Alaska, Australia, and Japan). *Mailing List*

　　`http://www.ecst.csuchico.edu/~rodmur/sca/`

　　± `listproc@ecst.csuchico.edu` [body = `SUBSCRIBE SCA-WEST` first-name last-name]

　　INFO `sca-west-owner@ecst.csuchico.edu`

6589 **SCAHRLDS:** From the Society for Creative Anachronism—on medieval and Renaissance heralds, coats of arms, ceremony, and diplomacy. *Mailing List*

　　± `listserv@listserv.aol.com` [body = `SUBSCRIBE SCAHRLDS` first-name last-name]

　　INFO `vnend@aol.net`

MARTIAL ARTS

6590 AIKIDO-L: On aikido, a Japanese martial art. *Mailing List*
± listserv@psuvm.psu.edu [body = SUBSCRIBE AIKIDO-L first-name last-name]
INFO jdc128@psu.edu (John Corro)

6591 alt.zen+budo Zen in combination with budo and other martial arts. *Newsgroup*

6592 KARATE: On traditional Japanese/Okinawan karate. *Mailing List*
± listproc@ukanaix.cc.ukans.edu [body = SUBSCRIBE KARATE first-name last-name]
INFO dojo@ukanaix.cc.ukans.edu (Howard S. High)
INFO jkrk@tyrell.net
Please Note: Subscription by approval only.
Comments: Potential subscribers must fill out an application questionaire

6593 rec.martial-arts Discussion of the various martial arts forms. *Newsgroup*

MOTORCYCLES & MOTORSPORTS

6594 alt.autos.karting Racing go-karts. *Newsgroup*

6595 alt.scooter Motor scooters, like Vespas, Lambrettas, etc. *Newsgroup*

6596 alt.scooter.classic Classic motor scooters, like Vespas, Lambrettas, etc. *Newsgroup*

6597 alt.snowmobiles For bikers who don't like two wheels in snow and ice. *Newsgroup*

6598 aus.motorcycles Discussion of motorcycles and motorcycling. *Newsgroup*

6599 ba.motorcycles Bay Area motorcycle issues. *Newsgroup*

6600 fj.rec.motorcycles Topics on motorcycles. *Newsgroup*

6601 ky.motorcycles Motorcycling in Kentucky. *Newsgroup*

6602 ne.motorcycles The Northeast branch of the Denizens of Doom. *Newsgroup*

6603 nyc.motorcycles Motorcycling and motorcyclists in the New York City area. *Newsgroup*

6604 ott.motorcycles Motorcycles and motorcyling in Ottawa, Canada. *Newsgroup*

6605 rec.motorcycles Motorcycles and related products and laws. *Newsgroup*

6606 rec.motorcycles.dirt Riding motorcycles and ATVs off-road. *Newsgroup*

6607 rec.motorcycles.harley All aspects of Harley-Davidson motorcycles. *Newsgroup*

6608 rec.motorcycles.racing Discussion of all aspects of racing motorcycles. *Newsgroup*

6609 tnn.rec.motorcycles User's group for motorcycles. *Newsgroup*

6610 tnn.rec.motorsport User's group for motor sports. *Newsgroup*

6611 Two-Strokes: On two-stroke motorcycle technology, maintenance, and riding. (Mostly about street and road racing, with some dirt bike discussion.) *Mailing List*
http://www.scruznet.com/~ab/2strokes/
± INFO OWNER 2strokes-request@microunity.com
ARCHIVE http://www.scruznet.com/~ab/2strokes/

6612 tx.motorcycles Biker Texans. *Newsgroup*

➤ **uk.rec.motorsport.misc:** U.K. motor sports, primarily from those involved. *Newsgroup*

NATURISTS

➤ **alt.binaries.pictures.nudism:** Images featuring nudists. *Newsgroup*

6613 alt.cult.nudism Crackpots in the nudist movement. *Newsgroup*

6614 Naturist-Action: Naturist action alerts; no discussion. *Mailing List, moderated*

± listserv@netcom.com [body = SUBSCRIBE naturist-action]

OWNER bhami@netcom.com (Bruce Hamilton)

6615 **rec.nude** Hobbyists interested in naturist/nudist activities. *Newsgroup*

OUTDOORS

6616 **alt.caving** Spelunking. *Newsgroup*

6617 **alt.culture.beaches** Surf's up! *Newsgroup*

6618 **alt.org.h-h-harriers** Running and drinking with the Hash House Harriers. *Newsgroup*

6619 **An Internet Scouting Web:** Information on local, regional, and national Boy Scouts of America. Includes Cub Scouts, Boy Scouts, Explorer posts, Girl Scouts, and international scouting. 1997 National Scout Jamboree home page with Who's Who on the Trail to the 1997 National Scout Jamboree©.

http://w3.trib.com/~dont/scouting/scouting.html

INFO dont@trib.com

INFO http://w3.trib.com/~dont/

➤ **aus.sport.scuba:** Scuba diving and related aquatic activities. *Newsgroup*

➤ **Big Bend Audubon Society:** The Big Bend Audubon Society page provides local, state, regional, and national information on environmental issues. It also provides local information for bird-watchers and other interested people. (See entry 4588 for full listing.)

6620 **bit.listserv.scuba-l** Scuba diving Discussion List. *Newsgroup*

6621 **can.scout-guide** About Canadian Boy Scouts and other scouting groups. *Newsgroup*

6622 **clari.living.leisure** Leisure, the outdoors, games. *Moderated newsgroup*

6623 **Dive Destinations & Dive Travel:** Online magazine for scuba and snorkel dive travel and the online trade magazine for the seller of dive vacations. *Magazine*

http://www.empg.com/

INFO dive@netpoint.net

ARCHIVE dive@netpoint.net

Frequency: bimonthly

6624 **Expedition News:** A monthly review of world-class expeditions, research projects, and adventures. This new forum on the outdoors covers projects that stimulate, motivate, and educate. *Newsletter*

INFO blumassoc@aol.com

INFO 76226.773@compuserv.com

ARCHIVE http://microship.ucsd.edu/Expedition_News

Frequency: monthly

Price: $36 per year for 12 issues.

6625 **fj.rec.outdoor** Discussion about outdoor sports/life. *Newsgroup*

6626 **GORP (Great Outdoor Recreation Pages):** This site contains a wealth of information on what to do and where to go in the great outdoors. It includes information on national parks, forests, wilderness areas, wildlife refuges, and monuments, as well as data on types of outdoor recreation (hiking, biking, climbing, etc.) and sources for outdoor recreation products and services.

http://www.gorp.com/

INFO postmaster@www.gorp.com

6627 **MOCAVES:** On exploring caves in the midwestern U.S. *Mailing List*

± listserv@umslvma.umsl.edu [body = SUBSCRIBE MOCAVES first-name last-name]

INFO sjalaws@umslvma.bitnet

ARCHIVE listserv@umslvma.umsl.edu

Comments: For conservation reasons, exact location of caves will not be discussed.

➤ **National Forest Listings by State:** A listing of all U.S. national forests with descriptions and access information. This resource is hosted by GORP (Great Outdoor Recreation Pages). It covers all national forests in the U.S., providing overall descriptions, plus detailed information on hiking, cross-country skiing, fishing, rafting, biking, wildlife viewing, and other activities. (See entry 4608 for full listing.)

6628 **OUTDOOR-L:** On the outdoors. *Mailing List*
± listserv@ulkyvm.louisville.edu [body = SUBSCRIBE OUTDOR-L first-name last-name]
INFO jacock01@ulkyvm.louisville.edu (James A. Cocks)

6629 **phl.outdoors** Outdoor recreation—camping, hiking, parks. *Newsgroup*

6630 **rec.backcountry** Activities in the great outdoors. *Newsgroup*

6631 **rec.climbing** Climbing techniques, competition announcements, etc. *Newsgroup*

6632 **rec.outdoors.camping** General camping, any camping you could do by auto. *Newsgroup*

6633 **rec.outdoors.marketplace** All business related to the outdoors. *Newsgroup*

6634 **rec.outdoors.national-parks** Activities and politics in national parks. *Newsgroup*

6635 **rec.outdoors.rv-travel** Discussions related to recreational vehicles. *Newsgroup*

6636 **rec.scuba** Hobbyists interested in scuba diving. *Newsgroup*

6637 **rec.scuba.equipment** Scuba equipment, purchase, pros/cons, use. *Newsgroup*

6638 **rec.scuba.locations** Scuba travel, location questions. *Newsgroup*

6639 **rec.sport.snowmobiles** Snowmobiling and related issues. *Newsgroup*

➤ **scot.birds:** Scottish birdwatching discussion. *Newsgroup*

➤ **uk.rec.climbing:** Rock climbing, ice climbing, and mountaineering. *Newsgroup*

➤ **uk.rec.scouting:** Discussion of scouting and guiding in the U.K. *Newsgroup*

➤ **uk.rec.walking:** To exchange information on walking, hiking, or rambling in the U.K. *Newsgroup*

RAILROADS

6640 **alt.binaries.pictures.rail** Forum for ferroequinologist photos. *Newsgroup*

6641 **aus.rail.models** Model railways. *Newsgroup*

6642 **bit.listserv.railroad** Railroad List. *Newsgroup*

6643 **fj.rec.rail** Discussion about railways and railroads. *Newsgroup*

6644 **Mark Dewell's Railway Preservation Pages:** A guide to all preserved railways, locomotives, societies, and museums in the U.K. The guide includes full timetables and details of special events on the railways featured. An online database of preserved railway locomotives is also available.
http://www.uel.ac.uk/pers/1278/Rly-Pres
INFO m.dewell@uel.ac.uk (Mark Dewell)

➤ **uk.railway:** Trains. *Newsgroup*

SAILING & BOATING

6645 **alt.sailing.asa** The American Sailing Association. *Newsgroup*

6646 **alt.sport.jet-ski** Discussion of personal watercraft. *Newsgroup*

6647 **cern.ycc** CERN's sailing club. *Newsgroup*

6648 **fj.rec.marine** Marine recreation. Diving, swimming, yachting, etc. *Newsgroup*

6649 **HYDROLETTER:** On unlimited hydroplane boat racing. *Mailing List*
± OWNER mcfoofoo@ix.netcom.com (J Michael Kenyon)
ARCHIVE http://www-leland.stanford.edu/~lglitch/hydro/index.html

6650 **NYCKayaker:** For paddlers and small boaters in New York City and environs. *Mailing List*

± majordomo@world.std.com [body = subscribe nyckayaker]
OWNER clandesm@panix.com (Cliff Landesman)

6651 rec.boats Hobbyists interested in boating. *Newsgroup*

6652 rec.boats.building Boat building, design, restoration, and repair. *Newsgroup*

6653 rec.boats.cruising Cruising in boats. *Newsgroup*

6654 rec.boats.marketplace Boating products for sale and wanted. *Moderated newsgroup*

6655 rec.boats.paddle Talk about any boats with oars, paddles, etc. *Newsgroup*

6656 rec.boats.racing Boat racing. *Newsgroup*

6657 rec.boats.racing.power Speed-based competition of all motorized watercraft. *Newsgroup*

6658 rec.sport.rowing Crew for competition or fitness. *Newsgroup*

6659 rec.windsurfing Riding the waves as a hobby. *Newsgroup*

6660 TALLSHIP: On traditional sailing vessels. *Mailing List*
± listserv@vccscent.bitnet [body = SUBSCRIBE TALLSHIP first-name last-name]
OWNER cbromley@nv.cc.va.us (Cap Bromley)

6661 WaveLength: Kayaks, canoes, and the ecologically sensitive paddling environment. *Mailing List*
± wavelength-request@lists.intelenet.net [body = subscribe wavelength]
OWNER hstiff@bbs.sd68.nanaimo.bc.ca (Howard Stiff)
FAQ hstiff@bbs.sd68.nanaimo.bc.ca (Howard Stiff)

SKIING

6662 fj.rec.sports.ski About skiing. *Newsgroup*

➤ **GORP (Great Outdoor Recreation Pages):** This site contains a wealth of information on what to do and where to go in the great outdoors. It includes information on national parks, forests, wilderness areas, wildlife refuges, and monuments, as well as data on types of outdoor recreation (hiking, biking, climbing, etc.) and sources for outdoor recreation products and services. (See entry 6626 for full listing.)

➤ **National Forest Listings by State:** A listing of all U.S. national forests with descriptions and access information. This resource is hosted by GORP (Great Outdoor Recreation Pages). It covers all national forests in the U.S., providing overall descriptions, plus detailed information on hiking, cross-country skiing, fishing, rafting, biking, wildlife viewing, and other activities. (See entry 4608 for full listing.)

6663 rec.skiing.alpine Downhill skiing technique, equipment, etc. *Newsgroup*

6664 rec.skiing.announce FAQ, competition results, automated snow reports. *Moderated newsgroup*

6665 rec.skiing.backcountry Backcountry skiing. *Newsgroup*

6666 rec.skiing.marketplace Items for sale/wanted. *Newsgroup*

6667 rec.skiing.nordic Cross-country skiing technique, equipment, etc. *Newsgroup*

6668 rec.skiing.resorts.europe Skiing in Europe. *Newsgroup*

6669 rec.skiing.resorts.misc Skiing in other than Europe and North America. *Newsgroup*

6670 rec.skiing.resorts.north-america Skiing in North America. *Newsgroup*

6671 rec.skiing.snowboard Snowboarding technique, equipment, etc. *Newsgroup*

6672 SKI-L: The Skiing Discussion List: all about skiing (except waterskiing). *Mailing List*
± listproc@list.cren.net [body = SUBSCRIBE SKI-L first-name last-name]
INFO ctanski@quest.arc.nasa.gov (Chris Tanski)
POST ski-l@list.cren.net

SPORTS

6673 **AEK-L:** On the AEK Greek Team—worldwide fans' list. *Mailing List*
± listserv@afrodite.cti.gr [body = SUB AEK-L first-name last-name]
OWNER p.kappos@afrodite.cti.gr (Panayotis Kappos)
ARCHIVE http://www.cti.gr/People/Kappos/Sports/AEK.html
Language: Greek

6674 **alt.binaries.pictures.sports** Binary sports images. *Newsgroup*

6675 **alt.sport.officiating** Being a referee. *Newsgroup*

➤ **atl.olympics:** The Olympics in Atlanta, Georgia. *Newsgroup*

6676 **aus.snow** Winter sports in Australia. *Newsgroup*

6677 **ba.sports** Discussion of sports in the Bay Area. *Newsgroup*

➤ **bermuda.sports:** Newsgroup related to sports in Bermuda. *Newsgroup*

6678 **clari.sports.briefs** General sports scoreboard. *Moderated newsgroup*

6679 **clari.sports.features** Sports feature stories. *Moderated newsgroup*

6680 **clari.sports.local.southwest.misc** News of other southwest athletics. *Moderated newsgroup*

6681 **clari.sports.misc** Other sports, plus general sports news. *Moderated newsgroup*

6682 **clari.sports.olympic** The Olympic Games. *Moderated newsgroup*

6683 **clari.sports.others** Other sports news. *Moderated newsgroup*

➤ **clari.sports.photos:** Sports photographs. *Moderated newsgroup*

6684 **clari.sports.schedules** Upcoming sports schedules. *Moderated newsgroup*

6685 **clari.sports.top** Top sports news. *Moderated newsgroup*

➤ **The Cleveland Sports Mailing List:** On anything related to the Cleveland, Ohio, sports scene. (See entry 8343 for full listing.)

➤ **DISPORT:** On sports and athletics for disabled people, especially amputees. (See entry 9862 for full listing.)

6686 **hawaii.sports** Hawai'i local sports discussions. *Newsgroup*

6687 **houston.sports** Sports discussions in Houston, Texas. *Newsgroup*

6688 **iijnet.sports** Topics about sports. *Newsgroup*

6689 **okinawa.sports.misc** Talk about sports. *Newsgroup*

6690 **pdx.sports** Sports in Portland, Oregon. *Newsgroup*

6691 **phl.sports** Sporting events and discussions. *Newsgroup*

6692 **rec.collecting.sport.misc** Sports memorabilia not in any other group. *Newsgroup*

6693 **rec.sport.misc** Spectator sports. *Newsgroup*

6694 **rec.sport.olympics** All aspects of the Olympic Games. *Newsgroup*

6695 **sbay.sports** South Bay sports. *Newsgroup*

6696 **sdnet.sports** San Diego teams and sporting events. *Newsgroup*

6697 **SPORTMGT:** On sport management. *Mailing List*
± listserv@unb.ca [body = SUBSCRIBE SPORTMGT first-name last-name]
INFO haggerty@jupiter.sun.csd.unb.ca (Terry R. Haggerty)

6698 **SPORTPC:** On the use of computers in sports. *Mailing List*
± listserv@unb.ca [body = SUBSCRIBE SPORTPC first-name last-name]
INFO haggerty@unb.ca (Terry R. Haggerty)

6699 **SPORTPSY:** On exercise and sport psychology. *Mailing List*
± listserv@vm.temple.edu [body = SUBSCRIBE SPORTPSY first-name last-name]

INFO v5289e@vm.temple.edu (Michael Sachs)
ARCHIVE listserv@vm.temple.edu [body = INDEX SPORTPSY]
Gated: bit.listserv.sportpsy

6700 **SPORTSCIENCE:** On the science of sport and exercise performance. *Mailing List*
± listproc@stonebow.otago.ac.nz [body = SUB SPORTSCIENCE first-name last-name]
EDITOR OWNER will.hopkins@stonebow.otago.ac.nz (Will Hopkins, PhD)

6701 **tnn.sports** Topics about sports. *Newsgroup*

6702 **Top of the Key:** Weekly sports magazine. *Newsletter*
± INFO OWNER kweitz@aol.com [subject = subscribe; body = e-mail-address] (Keith Weitz)
± kweitz@aol.com [subject = subscribe; body = e-mail-address] (Keith Weitz)
INFO OWNER kweitz@aol.com (Keith Weitz)
ARCHIVE kweitz@aol.com (Keith Weitz)
Frequency: weekly

6703 **triangle.sports** Discussion of sports in the Raleigh-Durham-Chapel-Hill area. *Newsgroup*

SPORTS—BASEBALL

6704 **alt.fan.robert-jordan** Baseball's most popular minor leaguer. *Newsgroup*

6705 **alt.sports.baseball.atlanta-braves** Atlanta Braves major league baseball. *Newsgroup*

6706 **alt.sports.baseball.balt-orioles** Baltimore Orioles major league baseball. *Newsgroup*

6707 **alt.sports.baseball.bos-redsox** Boston Red Sox major league baseball. *Newsgroup*

6708 **alt.sports.baseball.calif-angels** California Angels major league baseball. *Newsgroup*

6709 **alt.sports.baseball.chi-whitesox** Chicago White Sox major league baseball. *Newsgroup*

6710 **alt.sports.baseball.chicago-cubs** Chicago Cubs major league baseball. *Newsgroup*

6711 **alt.sports.baseball.cinci-reds** Cincinnati Reds major league baseball. *Newsgroup*

6712 **alt.sports.baseball.cleve-indians** Cleveland Indians major league baseball. *Newsgroup*

6713 **alt.sports.baseball.col-rockies** Colorado Rockies major league baseball. *Newsgroup*

6714 **alt.sports.baseball.detroit-tigers** Detroit Tigers major league baseball. *Newsgroup*

6715 **alt.sports.baseball.fla-marlins** Florida Marlins major league baseball. *Newsgroup*

6716 **alt.sports.baseball.houston-astros** Houston Astros major league baseball. *Newsgroup*

6717 **alt.sports.baseball.kc-royals** Kansas City Royals major league baseball. *Newsgroup*

6718 **alt.sports.baseball.la-dodgers** Los Angeles Dodgers major league baseball. *Newsgroup*

6719 **alt.sports.baseball.minor-leagues** Minor league baseball talk. *Newsgroup*

6720 **alt.sports.baseball.mke-brewers** Milwaukee Brewers major league baseball. *Newsgroup*

6721 **alt.sports.baseball.mn-twins** Minnesota Twins major league baseball. *Newsgroup*

6722 **alt.sports.baseball.montreal-expos** Montreal Expos major league baseball. *Newsgroup*

6723 **alt.sports.baseball.ny-mets** New York Mets major league baseball. *Newsgroup*

6724 **alt.sports.baseball.ny-yankees** New York Yankees major league baseball. *Newsgroup*

6725 **alt.sports.baseball.oakland-as** Oakland As major league baseball. *Newsgroup*

6726 **alt.sports.baseball.phila-phillies** Philadelphia Phillies major league baseball. *Newsgroup*

6727 **alt.sports.baseball.pitt-pirates** Pittsburgh Pirates major league baseball. *Newsgroup*

6728 **alt.sports.baseball.sd-padres** San Diego Padres major league baseball talk. *Newsgroup*

6729 **alt.sports.baseball.sea-mariners** Seattle Mariners major league baseball. *Newsgroup*

6730   `alt.sports.baseball.sf-giants`   San Francisco Giants major league baseball. *Newsgroup*

6731   `alt.sports.baseball.stl-cardinals`   St. Louis Cardinals major league baseball. *Newsgroup*

6732   `alt.sports.baseball.texas-rangers`   Texas Rangers major league baseball. *Newsgroup*

6733   `alt.sports.baseball.tor-bluejays`   Toronto Blue Jays major league baseball. *Newsgroup*

6734   **Baseball Manager's Dream League:** A new and exciting rotisserie-style fantasy baseball league. Compete against other baseball minds for great monthly and year-end cash prizes. The Web site offers a overview of the league as well as a copy of the rule book and an easy on-site entry form.
`http://www.wp.com/FANTASYBASEBALL`
INFO `jasonm@ix.netcom.com`

6735   `can.schoolnet.jrjays`   Jr. Jays fan club for Toronto Blue Jays. *Newsgroup*

6736   `clari.sports.baseball`   Baseball scores, stories, stats. *Moderated newsgroup*

6737   `clari.sports.baseball.games`   Baseball games and box scores. *Moderated newsgroup*

6738   `clari.sports.baseball.major`   News of major-league baseball. *Moderated newsgroup*

6739   `clari.sports.baseball.major.al.games`   AL previews, recaps, box scores. *Moderated newsgroup*

6740   `clari.sports.baseball.major.al.stats`   AL stats and standings. *Moderated newsgroup*

6741   `clari.sports.baseball.major.nl.games`   NL previews, recaps, box scores. *Moderated newsgroup*

6742   `clari.sports.baseball.major.nl.stats`   NL stats and standings. *Moderated newsgroup*

6743   `clari.sports.baseball.minor`   Minor-league baseball. *Moderated newsgroup*

6744   `fj.rec.sports.baseball`   Discussion about baseball. *Newsgroup*

6745   `pdaxs.sports.baseball`   America's pastime in the Rose City. *Newsgroup*

6746   `rec.collecting.sport.baseball`   Baseball memorabilia (cards, photos, etc.). *Newsgroup*

6747   `rec.sport.baseball`   Discussion about baseball. *Newsgroup*

6748   `rec.sport.baseball.analysis`   Analysis and discussion of baseball. *Moderated newsgroup*

6749   `rec.sport.baseball.college`   Baseball on the collegiate level. *Newsgroup*

6750   `rec.sport.baseball.data`   Raw baseball data (stats, birthdays, schedules). *Newsgroup*

6751   `rec.sport.baseball.fantasy`   Rotisserie (fantasy) baseball play. *Newsgroup*

SPORTS—BASKETBALL

6752   `alt.sport.basketball.pro.fantasy`   Rotisserie league basketball. *Newsgroup*

6753   `alt.sports.basketball.ivy.penn`   U. of Pennsylvania (*not* Penn State!) basketball. *Newsgroup*

6754   `alt.sports.basketball.nba.atlanta-hawks`   Atlanta Hawks NBA basketball. *Newsgroup*

6755   `alt.sports.basketball.nba.boston-celtics`   Boston Celtics NBA basketball. *Newsgroup*

6756   `alt.sports.basketball.nba.char-hornets`   Charlotte Hornets NBA basketball. *Newsgroup*

6757   `alt.sports.basketball.nba.chicago-bulls`   Chicago Bulls NBA basketball. *Newsgroup*

6758   `alt.sports.basketball.nba.dallas-mavs`   Dallas Mavericks NBA basketball. *Newsgroup*

6759   `alt.sports.basketball.nba.denver-nuggets`   Denver Nuggets NBA basketball. *Newsgroup*

6760   `alt.sports.basketball.nba.det-pistons`   Detroit Pistons NBA basketball. *Newsgroup*

6761   `alt.sports.basketball.nba.gs-warriors`   Golden State Warriors NBA basketball. *Newsgroup*

6762   `alt.sports.basketball.nba.hou-rockets`   Houston Rockets NBA basketball. *Newsgroup*

6763   `alt.sports.basketball.nba.ind-pacers`   Indiana Pacers NBA basketball. *Newsgroup*

6764   `alt.sports.basketball.nba.la-lakers`   Los Angeles Lakers NBA basketball. *Newsgroup*

6765　`alt.sports.basketball.nba.miami-heat`　Miami Heat NBA basketball. *Newsgroup*

6766　`alt.sports.basketball.nba.mil-bucks`　Milwaukee Bucks NBA basketball. *Newsgroup*

6767　`alt.sports.basketball.nba.mn-wolves`　Minnesota Timberwolves NBA basketball. *Newsgroup*

6768　`alt.sports.basketball.nba.nj-nets`　New Jersey Nets NBA basketball. *Newsgroup*

6769　`alt.sports.basketball.nba.orlando-magic`　Orlando Magic NBA basketball. *Newsgroup*

6770　`alt.sports.basketball.nba.phila-76ers`　Philadelphia 76ers NBA basketball. *Newsgroup*

6771　`alt.sports.basketball.nba.phx-suns`　Phoenix Suns NBA basketball. *Newsgroup*

6772　`alt.sports.basketball.nba.sa-spurs`　San Antonio Spurs NBA basketball. *Newsgroup*

6773　`alt.sports.basketball.nba.sac-kings`　Sacramento Kings NBA basketball. *Newsgroup*

6774　`alt.sports.basketball.nba.seattle-sonics`　Seattle SuperSonics NBA basketball. *Newsgroup*

6775　`alt.sports.basketball.nba.utah-jazz`　Utah Jazz NBA basketball. *Newsgroup*

6776　`alt.sports.basketball.nba.wash-bullets`　Washington Bullets NBA basketball. *Newsgroup*

6777　`alt.sports.basketball.pro.ny-knicks`　New York Knicks NBA basketball. *Newsgroup*

6778　**CELTICS:** On the NBA's Boston Celtics basketball team. *Mailing List*
± `majordomo@hillel.com`
OWNER `hillel@hillel.com` (Hillel N. Cooperman)
Please Note: Subscription by approval only.

6779　`clari.sports.basketball`　Basketball coverage. *Moderated newsgroup*

6780　`clari.sports.basketball.college`　College basketball coverage. *Moderated newsgroup*

6781　`clari.sports.basketball.college.men`　News of men's college basketball. *Moderated newsgroup*

6782　`clari.sports.basketball.college.men.games`　Previews, recaps, box scores. *Moderated newsgroup*

6783　`clari.sports.basketball.college.men.stats`　Stats, standings, summaries. *Moderated newsgroup*

6784　`clari.sports.basketball.college.women`　Women's college basketball. *Moderated newsgroup*

6785　`clari.sports.basketball.minor`　News of minor league basketball. *Moderated newsgroup*

6786　`clari.sports.basketball.nba`　News of NBA basketball. *Moderated newsgroup*

6787　`clari.sports.basketball.nba.games`　NBA basketball games. *Moderated newsgroup*

6788　`clari.sports.basketball.nba.stats`　NBA stats and standings. *Moderated newsgroup*

6789　`fj.rec.sports.basketball`　About basketball. *Newsgroup*

6790　`pdaxs.sports.basketball`　Blazers, Pilots, and other hoops. *Newsgroup*

6791　`rec.collecting.sport.basketball`　Basketball memorabilia (cards, photos, etc.). *Newsgroup*

6792　`rec.sport.basketball.college`　Hoops on the collegiate level. *Newsgroup*

6793　`rec.sport.basketball.europe`　A European basketball forum. *Newsgroup*

6794　`rec.sport.basketball.misc`　Discussion about basketball. *Newsgroup*

6795　`rec.sport.basketball.pro`　Talk of professional basketball. *Newsgroup*

6796　`rec.sport.basketball.women`　Women's basketball at all levels. *Newsgroup*

6797　**UCONN-BBALL:** On the University of Connecticut Huskies men's and women's basketball teams. *Mailing List*
± `uconn-bball-request@toto.com`
INFO OWNER `misha@toto.com` (Brett M. Rabideau)

6798　**WBBALL-L:** On women's basketball. *Mailing List*
± OWNER `dq894@cleveland.freenet.edu` (Rob Polinsky)

SPORTS—BODYBUILDING

6799   **The Michael Scott Fitness Centerfolds:** This site features fitness models from the Michael Scott Agency.
http://www.xcitement.com/msa
INFO rwalton@xcitement.com

6800   `misc.fitness.weights` Bodybuilding, weight lifting, resistance. *Newsgroup*

SPORTS—FOOTBALL

6801   `alt.college.college-bowl` Discussions of the College Bowl competition. *Newsgroup*

6802   `alt.flame.football.notre-dame` Flames directed toward Notre Dame football. *Newsgroup*

6803   `alt.sports.football.arena` Arena football (U.S. style, not soccer). *Newsgroup*

6804   `alt.sports.football.college.fsu-seminoles` Florida U. Seminoles football. *Newsgroup*

6805   `alt.sports.football.mn-vikings` Minnesota Vikings NFL football talk. *Newsgroup*

6806   `alt.sports.football.oak-raiders` Oakland Raiders NFL football. *Newsgroup*

6807   `alt.sports.football.pro.atl-falcons` Atlanta Falcons NFL football. *Newsgroup*

6808   `alt.sports.football.pro.buffalo-bills` Buffalo Bills NFL football. *Newsgroup*

6809   `alt.sports.football.pro.car-panthers` Carolina Panthers NFL football. *Newsgroup*

6810   `alt.sports.football.pro.chicago-bears` Chicago Bears NFL football. *Newsgroup*

6811   `alt.sports.football.pro.cinci-bengals` Cincinnati Bengals NFL football. *Newsgroup*

6812   `alt.sports.football.pro.cleve-browns` Cleveland Browns NFL football talk. *Newsgroup*

6813   `alt.sports.football.pro.dallas-cowboys` Dallas Cowboys NFL football. *Newsgroup*

6814   `alt.sports.football.pro.denver-broncos` Denver Broncos NFL football. *Newsgroup*

6815   `alt.sports.football.pro.detroit-lions` Detroit Lions NFL football. *Newsgroup*

6816   `alt.sports.football.pro.gb-packers` Green Bay Packers NFL football. *Newsgroup*

6817   `alt.sports.football.pro.houston-oilers` Houston Oilers NFL football. *Newsgroup*

6818   `alt.sports.football.pro.indy-colts` Indianapolis Colts NFL football. *Newsgroup*

6819   `alt.sports.football.pro.jville-jaguars` Jacksonville Jaguars NFL football. *Newsgroup*

6820   `alt.sports.football.pro.kc-chiefs` Kansas City Chiefs NFL football. *Newsgroup*

6821   `alt.sports.football.pro.la-raiders` Los Angeles Raiders NFL football. *Newsgroup*

6822   `alt.sports.football.pro.la-rams` Los Angeles Rams NFL football. *Newsgroup*

6823   `alt.sports.football.pro.miami-dolphins` Miami Dolphins NFL football. *Newsgroup*

6824   `alt.sports.football.pro.ne-patriots` New England Patriots NFL football. *Newsgroup*

6825   `alt.sports.football.pro.no-saints` New Orleans Saints NFL football. *Newsgroup*

6826   `alt.sports.football.pro.ny-giants` New York Giants NFL football. *Newsgroup*

6827   `alt.sports.football.pro.ny-jets` New York Jets NFL football. *Newsgroup*

6828   `alt.sports.football.pro.oak-raiders` Oakland Raiders. *Newsgroup*

6829   `alt.sports.football.pro.phila-eagles` Philadelphia Eagles NFL football. *Newsgroup*

6830   `alt.sports.football.pro.phoe-cardinals` Phoenix Cardinals NFL football. *Newsgroup*

6831   `alt.sports.football.pro.pitt-steelers` Pittsburgh Steelers NFL football. *Newsgroup*

6832   `alt.sports.football.pro.sd-chargers` San Diego Chargers NFL football. *Newsgroup*

6833   `alt.sports.football.pro.sea-seahawks` Seattle Seahawks NFL football. *Newsgroup*

6834   `alt.sports.football.pro.sf-49ers` San Francisco 49ers NFL football. *Newsgroup*

6835 `alt.sports.football.pro.stl-rams` St. Louis Rams NFL football. *Newsgroup*

6836 `alt.sports.football.pro.tampabay-bucs` Tampa Bay Buccaneers NFL football. *Newsgroup*

6837 `alt.sports.football.pro.wash-redskins` Washington Redskins NFL football. *Newsgroup*

6838 `aus.sport.aussie-rules` Australian rules football. *Newsgroup*

6839 **The Beaver Believer Mailing List:** A place where fans of the Oregon State Beavers football team can gather and discuss the team. *Mailing List*
   `http://www.cat.pdx.edu/~caseyh/beaver/index.html`
   ± `majordomo@ee.pdx.edu` [body = `subscribe gobeavs` first-name last-name]
   INFO OWNER `caseyh@ee.pdx.edu`
   INFO `hopkins@mtjeff.com` (Scott Hopkins)

6840 `clari.sports.football` Pro football coverage. *Moderated newsgroup*

6841 `clari.sports.football.cfl` Coverage of the Canadian Football League. *Moderated newsgroup*

6842 `clari.sports.football.college` College football coverage. *Moderated newsgroup*

6843 `clari.sports.football.college.games` Football previews, recaps, box scores. *Moderated newsgroup*

6844 `clari.sports.football.college.stats` Football stats, standings, summaries. *Moderated newsgroup*

6845 `clari.sports.football.games` Coverage of individual pro games. *Moderated newsgroup*

6846 `clari.sports.football.nfl` Coverage of the National Football League. *Moderated newsgroup*

6847 `clari.sports.football.nfl.games` NFL football games. *Moderated newsgroup*

6848 `clari.sports.football.nfl.stats` NFL stats and standings. *Moderated newsgroup*

6849 `dc.redskins` The Washington Redskins pro football team. *Newsgroup*

➤ **FBPRO:** Discussions of Dynamix Front Page Sport's Football Pro game: Internet leagues, teams, players, and strategy. (See entry 6455 for full listing.)

6850 **NFL-List:** A general NFL football discussion list. *Mailing List*
   ± OWNER `rscott@mail.coin.missouri.edu` (Richard Scott)

6851 `pdaxs.sports.football` NFL, semi-pro, and high school. *Newsgroup*

6852 `rec.collecting.sport.football` Football memorabilia (cards, photos, etc.). *Newsgroup*

6853 `rec.sport.football.australian` Discussion of Australian (rules) football. *Newsgroup*

6854 `rec.sport.football.canadian` All about Canadian rules football. *Newsgroup*

6855 `rec.sport.football.college` U.S.-style college football. *Newsgroup*

6856 `rec.sport.football.fantasy` Rotisserie (fantasy) football play. *Newsgroup*

6857 `rec.sport.football.misc` Discussion about American-style football. *Newsgroup*

6858 `rec.sport.football.pro` U.S.-style professional football. *Newsgroup*

SPORTS—GOLF

6859 `clari.sports.golf` Golf coverage. *Moderated newsgroup*

6860 `fj.rec.sports.golf` About golf. *Newsgroup*

6861 **GOLF-L:** On golf. *Mailing List*
   ± `listserv@ubvm.cc.buffalo.edu` [body = `SUBSCRIBE GOLF-L` first-name last-name]
   INFO `ctanski@quest.arc.nasa.gov` (Chris Tanski)
   Gated: `rec.sport.golf`

6862 `pdaxs.sports.golf` Speak softly and carry a big stick. *Newsgroup*

6863 `rec.sport.golf` Discussion about all aspects of golfing. *Newsgroup*

SPORTS—HOCKEY

6864 `alt.sport.street-hockey` Discussions of street hockey. *Newsgroup*

6865 `alt.sports.hockey.echl` EC Hockey League. *Newsgroup*

6866 `alt.sports.hockey.fantasy` Rotisserie league ice hockey. *Newsgroup*

6867 `alt.sports.hockey.ihl` International Hockey League. *Newsgroup*

6868 `alt.sports.hockey.nhl.ana-mighty-ducks` Discussion of the Mighty Ducks. *Newsgroup*

6869 `alt.sports.hockey.nhl.boston-bruins` Boston Bruins NHL hockey. *Newsgroup*

6870 `alt.sports.hockey.nhl.buffalo-sabres` Buffalo Sabres NHL hockey. *Newsgroup*

6871 `alt.sports.hockey.nhl.chi-blackhawks` Chicago Black Hawks NHL hockey. *Newsgroup*

6872 `alt.sports.hockey.nhl.clgry-flames` Calgary Flames NHL hockey. *Newsgroup*

6873 `alt.sports.hockey.nhl.dallas-stars` Dallas Stars NHL hockey. *Newsgroup*

6874 `alt.sports.hockey.nhl.det-redwings` Detroit Redwings NHL hockey. *Newsgroup*

6875 `alt.sports.hockey.nhl.edm-oilers` Edmonton Oilers NHL hockey. *Newsgroup*

6876 `alt.sports.hockey.nhl.hford-whalers` Hartford Whalers NHL hockey. *Newsgroup*

6877 `alt.sports.hockey.nhl.la-kings` Los Angeles Kings NHL hockey. *Newsgroup*

6878 `alt.sports.hockey.nhl.mtl-canadiens` Montreal Canadiens NHL hockey. *Newsgroup*

6879 `alt.sports.hockey.nhl.nj-devils` New Jersey Devils NHL hockey. *Newsgroup*

6880 `alt.sports.hockey.nhl.ny-islanders` New York Islanders NHL hockey. *Newsgroup*

6881 `alt.sports.hockey.nhl.ny-rangers` New York Rangers NHL hockey. *Newsgroup*

6882 `alt.sports.hockey.nhl.ott-senators` Ottawa Senators Hockey fan group. *Newsgroup*

6883 `alt.sports.hockey.nhl.phila-flyers` Philadelphia Flyers NHL hockey. *Newsgroup*

6884 `alt.sports.hockey.nhl.pit-penguins` Pittsburgh Penguins NHL hockey. *Newsgroup*

6885 `alt.sports.hockey.nhl.que-nordiques` Quebec Nordiques NHL hockey. *Newsgroup*

6886 `alt.sports.hockey.nhl.sj-sharks` San Jose Sharks NHL hockey. *Newsgroup*

6887 `alt.sports.hockey.nhl.stl-blues` Saint Louis Blues NHL hockey. *Newsgroup*

6888 `alt.sports.hockey.nhl.tor-mapleleafs` Toronto Maple Leafs NHL hockey. *Newsgroup*

6889 `alt.sports.hockey.nhl.vanc-canucks` Vancouver Canucks NHL hockey. *Newsgroup*

6890 `alt.sports.hockey.nhl.wash-capitals` Washington Captials NHL hockey. *Newsgroup*

6891 `alt.sports.hockey.nhl.winnipeg-jets` Winnipeg Jets NHL hockey. *Newsgroup*

6892 `alt.sports.hockey.rhi` Some hockey league, maybe. *Newsgroup*

6893 `alt.sports.hockey.whl` Some hockey league, maybe. *Newsgroup*

6894 **BROOMS-L:** On broomball, a sport similar to ice hockey. *Mailing List*
   `http://www.ozemail.com.au/~kshapley/index.html`
   ± `listserv@trearnpc.ege.edu.tr` [body = SUB BROOMS-L first-name last-name]
   OWNER `100250.612@compuserve.com` (Kim Shapley)
   ARCHIVE `100250.612@compuserve.com` (Kim Shapley)
   POST `brooms-l@trearnpc.ege.edu.tr`

6895 `clari.sports.hockey` NHL coverage. *Moderated newsgroup*

6896 `clari.sports.hockey.ahl` Coverage of the American Hockey League. *Moderated newsgroup*

6897 `clari.sports.hockey.ihl` Coverage of the International Hockey League. *Moderated newsgroup*

6898 `clari.sports.hockey.nhl` Coverage of the National Hockey League. *Moderated newsgroup*

6899 `clari.sports.hockey.nhl.games` NHL previews, recaps, box scores. *Moderated newsgroup*

6900 `clari.sports.hockey.nhl.stats` NHL stats, standings, summaries. *Moderated newsgroup*

6901 **HOCKEY-L:** On collegiate ice hockey, including scores, team information, schedules, etc. *Mailing List*
± `listserv@maine.edu` [body = SUBSCRIBE HOCKEY-L first-name last-name]
INFO `pkester@csci.csc.com` (Peter Kester)
INFO `wts@maine.maine.edu` (Wayne Smith)
INFO `machnik@max.tiac.net` (Mike Machnik)

6902 **Ian Clark's Goaltending Schools:** The purpose of this page is to highlight the programs and services of Ian Clark's Goaltending Schools, as well as to provide free information on hockey goaltending.
`http://www.islandnet.com/~icgschol/index.html`
INFO `icgschol@islandnet.com`

6903 **ISLES-LIST:** On the New York Islanders hockey team. *Mailing List*
± `listserv@netcom.com` [body = SUBSCRIBE isles-list]
OWNER `dstrauss@netcom.com` (David Strauss)
ARCHIVES
`http://www.eskimo.com/~dstrauss/isles.html`
`ftp://ftp.eskimo.com/u/d/dstrauss/isles/`
`listserv@netcom.com`

6904 **Junior A Hockey:** Complete statistics and scores on the Central Wyoming Outlaws and the American Frontier Hockey League, with links to other hockey resources worldwide.
`http://w3.trib.com/~dont/hockey/hockey.html`
INFO `dont@trib.com`
INFO `http://w3.trib.com/~dont/`

6905 **OLYMPUCK:** On Olympic ice hockey: players, coaches, teams, and the games. *Digest & Reflector*
`gopher://maine.maine.edu/11/MISCINFO/LSTSERV/OLYMPUCK`
± `listserv@maine.edu` [body = SUBSCRIBE OLYMPUCK first-name last-name]
INFO `slavin@gauss.umemat.maine.edu` (Charlie Slavin)
ARCHIVE `listserv@maine.edu`

6906 `rec.collecting.sport.hockey` Hockey memorabilia (cards, photos, etc.). *Newsgroup*

6907 `rec.sport.hockey` Discussion about ice hockey. *Newsgroup*

6908 `rec.sport.hockey.field` Discussion of the sport of field hockey. *Newsgroup*

6909 **uk-hockey:** About ice hockey as played in and by Great Britain: news, gossip, league tables, match reports, and results. *Mailing List*
± INFO `uk-hockey-request@cee.hw.ac.uk` (Steve Salvini)

SPORTS—NEWS

6910 `clari.sports.review` Daily review of sports. *Moderated newsgroup*

SPORTS—RACQUET SPORTS

6911 `alt.sport.racquetball` All aspects of indoor racquetball and related sports. *Newsgroup*

6912 `alt.sport.squash` With the proper technique, vegetables can go very fast. *Newsgroup*

6913 `alt.sports.badminton` Discussion about badminton. *Newsgroup*

6914 `clari.sports.tennis` Tennis news and scores. *Moderated newsgroup*

6915 `rec.sport.squash` Forum for all apects of squash. *Newsgroup*

6916 `rec.sport.table-tennis` Things related to table tennis (aka Ping Pong). *Newsgroup*

SPORTS—RUGBY

6917 `aus.sport.rugby-league` Rugby league football. *Newsgroup*

6918 `fj.rec.sports.rugby` About rugby. *Newsgroup*

6919 `rec.sport.rugby` Discussion about the game of rugby. *Newsgroup*

6920 `rec.sport.rugby.league` Everything related to playing/supporting Rugby League. *Newsgroup*

6921 `rec.sport.rugby.union` Everything related to playing/supporting Rugby Union. *Newsgroup*

SPORTS—SKATING

6922 `alt.fan.oksana.bayul` Another figure-skater fan group. *Newsgroup*

6923 `alt.skate-board` Discussion of all apsects of skateboarding. *Newsgroup*

6924 `rec.sport.skating.ice.figure` Figure/artistic skating. *Newsgroup*

6925 `rec.sport.skating.ice.recreational` Recreational ice skating. *Newsgroup*

6926 `rec.sport.skating.inline` In-line skating, aka Rollerblading. *Newsgroup*

6927 `rec.sport.skating.misc` Miscellaneous skating topics. *Newsgroup*

6928 `rec.sport.skating.racing` Racing and speed skating. *Newsgroup*

6929 `rec.sport.skating.roller` Conventional (quad) roller-skating. *Newsgroup*

SPORTS—SOCCER

6930 `alt.sports.soccer.european` Football, European style. *Newsgroup*

6931 `alt.sports.soccer.european.uk` Football, British style. *Newsgroup*

6932 `clari.sports.soccer` Coverage of soccer. *Moderated newsgroup*

6933 `fj.rec.sports.soccer` About soccer (Association football). *Newsgroup*

6934 `rec.sport.soccer` Discussion about soccer (Association Football). *Newsgroup*

6935 `rec.sport.table-soccer` Table soccer of all types: foosball and subbuteo. *Newsgroup*

6936 **SOCCER-L:** For discussion of soccer-related issues and news—lots of scores are posted from subscribers world-wide. *Digest & Reflector*
± `listserv@ukcc.uky.edu` [body = SUBSCRIBE SOCCER-L first-name last-name]
INFO `systrent@ukcc.uky.edu` (Trent Fraebel)
INFO `crovo@ukcc.uky.edu` (Bob Crovo)

6937 **SOCREF-L:** For soccer referees: distribution of game mechanics, rule interpretations, and other important stuff. *Mailing List*
± `listserv@uriacc.uri.edu` [body = SUBSCRIBE SOCREF-L first-name last-name]
OWNER `opus@uriacc.uri.edu` (Mark Oliver)
ARCHIVE `listserv@uriacc.uri.edu` [body = INDEX SOCREF-L]

6938 `tnn.soccer.j-league` Information and discussion about J-league. *Newsgroup*

6939 `tnn.soccer.j-league.antlers` Information and disccusion about Kashima-Antlers. *Newsgroup*

6940 `tnn.soccer.j-league.grampus-eight` Information and discussion about Grampus-Eight. *Newsgroup*

6941 `tnn.soccer.j-league.marinos` Information and disccusion about Yokohama-Marinos. *Newsgroup*

SPORTS—SWIMMING

➤ `fj.rec.marine:` Marine recreation. Diving, swimming, yachting, etc. *Newsgroup*

6942 `rec.sport.swimming` Training for and competing in swimming events. *Newsgroup*

6943 `rec.sport.water-polo` Discussion of water polo. *Newsgroup*

6944 **Synchro-S:** On synchronized swimming. *Mailing List*
± `majordomo@unixg.ubc.ca` [body = subscribe synchro-s]
OWNER `camcastl@unixg.ubc.ca` [body = subscribe synchro-s] (Cara Camcastle)

SPORTS—TENNIS

6945 **ATP Tour Weekly Electronic Newsletter:** Newsletter of the ATP Tour, the official governing body for men's professional tennis. *Newsletter*
`http://atptour.com/`
INFO `rvach@jax.jaxnet.com` (Rick Vach)
ARCHIVE `rvach@jax.jaxnet.com` (Rick Vach)
Frequency: weekly

6946 `rec.sport.tennis` Things related to the sport of tennis. *Newsgroup*

SPORTS—UNIVERSITY

6947 `alt.sports.college.acc` The Atlantic Coast conference. *Newsgroup*

6948 `alt.sports.college.big-east` Discussions of college sports in the Big East. *Newsgroup*

6949 `alt.sports.college.big10` The Big 10 college athletic conference. *Newsgroup*

6950 `alt.sports.college.big10.purdue` Purdue University sports. *Newsgroup*

6951 `alt.sports.college.conference-usa` The Conference USA college athletic conference. *Newsgroup*

6952 `alt.sports.college.ivy-league` Ivy League athletics. *Newsgroup*

6953 `alt.sports.college.michigan` Sports at Michigan colleges. *Newsgroup*

6954 `alt.sports.college.notre-dame` Notre Dame sports. *Newsgroup*

6955 `alt.sports.college.ohio-state` OSU sports plus a whole lot more. *Newsgroup*

6956 `alt.sports.college.pac-10` Discussions of college sports in the Pac 10. *Newsgroup*

6957 `alt.sports.college.syracuse` Sports at Syracuse University. *Newsgroup*

6958 `alt.sports.college.utexas` University of Texas at Austin athletics. *Newsgroup*

➤ `alt.sports.football.college.fsu-seminoles:` Florida U. Seminoles football. *Newsgroup*

➤ `clari.sports.basketball.college:` College basketball coverage. *Moderated newsgroup*

➤ `clari.sports.basketball.college.men:` News of men's college basketball. *Moderated newsgroup*

➤ `clari.sports.basketball.college.men.games:` Previews, recaps, box scores. *Moderated newsgroup*

➤ `clari.sports.basketball.college.men.stats:` Stats, standings, summaries. *Moderated newsgroup*

➤ `clari.sports.basketball.college.women:` Women's college basketball. *Moderated newsgroup*

➤ `clari.sports.football.college:` College football coverage. *Moderated newsgroup*

➤ `clari.sports.football.college.games:` Football previews, recaps, box scores. *Moderated newsgroup*

➤ `clari.sports.football.college.stats:` Football stats, standings, summaries. *Moderated newsgroup*

6959 **nwu-sports:** On Northwestern University sports, also known as "da cats." *Mailing List*
± INFO `nwu-sports-request@tssi.com`
INFO `nolan@tssi.com`

➤ `rec.sport.baseball.college:` Baseball on the collegiate level. *Newsgroup*

➤ `rec.sport.basketball.college:` Hoops on the collegiate level. *Newsgroup*

➤ `rec.sport.football.college:` U.S.-style college football. *Newsgroup*

6960 **VANDAL:** On the University of Idaho Vandal teams. *Mailing List*
± `majordomo@uidaho.edu` [body = SUBSCRIBE VANDAL]

OWNER pcorless@claven.idbsu.edu (Phil Corless)

SPORTS—VARIOUS

6961 `alt.boomerang` The angular throwing club, not the Eddie Murphy flick. *Newsgroup*

6962 `alt.culture.bullfight` To understand and appreciate the bullfight. *Newsgroup*

6963 `alt.sport.bowling` In the gutter again. *Newsgroup*

6964 `clari.sports.bowling` Bowling coverage. *Moderated newsgroup*

6965 `alt.sport.bungee` Like `alt.suicide` with rubber bands. *Newsgroup*

6966 `alt.sport.darts` Look what you've done to the wall! *Newsgroup*

6967 `alt.sport.korfball` Discussion of the sport of Korfball. *Newsgroup*

6968 `alt.sport.lacrosse` The game of lacrosse. *Newsgroup*

6969 `alt.sport.lasertag` Indoor splatball with infrared lasers. *Newsgroup*

6970 **gutsfrisbee-l:** On the sport of Guts Frisbee. *Mailing List*
± majordomo@mtu.edu
EDITOR dkwalika@mtu.edu (Dennis Walikainen (Wally))
ARCHIVE http://www.sas.it.mtu.edu/~dkwalika/frisbee/

6971 `rec.kites` Talk about kites and kiting. *Newsgroup*

6972 `rec.running` Running for enjoyment, sport, exercise, etc. *Newsgroup*

6973 `rec.skydiving` Hobbyists interested in skydiving. *Newsgroup*

6974 `rec.sport.archery` All aspects of archery for archers of any skill level. *Newsgroup*

6975 `alt.archery` Robin Hood had the right idea. *Newsgroup*

6976 `rec.sport.cricket` Discussion about the sport of cricket. *Newsgroup*

6977 `rec.sport.cricket.info` News, scores, and information related to cricket. *Moderated newsgroup*

6978 `rec.sport.disc` Discussion of flying-disc based sports. *Newsgroup*

6979 `rec.sport.fencing` All aspects of swordplay. *Newsgroup*

6980 `rec.sport.orienteering` All matters related to the sport of orienteering. *Newsgroup*

6981 `rec.sport.paintball` Discussing all aspects of the survival game paintball. *Newsgroup*

6982 `alt.sport.paintball` Splat, you're it. *Newsgroup*

6983 `rec.sport.triathlon` Discussing all aspects of multi-event sports. *Newsgroup*

6984 `rec.sport.waterski` Waterskiing and other boat-towed activities. *Newsgroup*

6985 `tnn.sports.triathlon` User's group for triathletes and duathletes. *Newsgroup*

6986 **ULTRA:** On ultrarunning (longer than a marathon, or shorter specialty races). *Mailing List*
± listserv@listserv.dartmouth.edu [body = SUBSCRIBE ULTRA first-name last-name]
OWNER an241@cleveland.freenet.edu (Joe Jurczyk)
OWNER zuckerj@howland.isu.edu (Joel Zucker)

SPORTS—VOLLEYBALL

6987 `fj.rec.sports.volleyball` About volleyball. *Newsgroup*

6988 `rec.sport.volleyball` Discussion about volleyball. *Newsgroup*

SURFING

➤　`alt.culture.beaches:` Surf's up! *Newsgroup*

6989 `alt.surfing` Riding the ocean waves. *Newsgroup*

6990 `alt.surfing.bodyboard` Bodyboard surfing. *Newsgroup*

6991 **Surf News Network Hawaii:** Hawaii's authoratative surfing Web site from Surf News Network Hawaii. Find the latest surf condition updates from Sunset Beach to Diamond Head. Check out Hawaii's most beautiful women in bikinis through the lens of the Surf News Babe Cam.

`http://hypermedia.net/`
`http://surf-news.com/`
INFO `surfer@hypermedia.net`
Comments: Surf News Network Hawaii is published and hosted by Hawaii Hypernedia, Inc.

TOBACCO

6992 `alt.butts` Cigarettes, guns, logs, casks, you name it. *Newsgroup*

6993 `alt.smokers` Puffing on tobacco. *Newsgroup*

6994 `alt.smokers.cigars` From stogies to Cubans. *Newsgroup*

6995 `alt.smokers.pipes` Briars, meerschaums, and calabashes. *Newsgroup*

6996 `clari.news.issues.smoking` Smoking and tobacco issues. *Moderated newsgroup*

6997 `fj.rec.smoking` Smoking as a hobby and/or recreation. *Newsgroup*

6998 `fj.soc.smoking` About smoking issues and manners. *Newsgroup*

6999 **Pipes Digest:** For all those who enjoy smoking, collecting, or sharing information on pipes, tobacco, and related topics. *Digest, moderated*

± INFO `pipes-request@paul.rutgers.edu` (Steve Masticola)

ARCHIVES
`ftp://ftp.netcom.com/pub/br/brookfld/pipes_digest`
`http://www.pointcom.com/`

7000 `relcom.commerce.tobacco` Cigarettes and tobacco. *Newsgroup*

TOYS & MODELS

7001 **The Complete RC Websites Index:** This is the most extensive, best-organized listing of Web sites related to radio control models. Use it to conveniently access all other sites on this and related topics.

`http://www.bucknell.edu/~chronstr/rc.html`
INFO `chronstr@bucknell.edu`

7002 `alt.collecting.teddy-bears` Collecting stuffed toy bears. *Newsgroup*

➤ `alt.culture.electric-midget`: The "culture" of little robots. *Newsgroup*

➤ `alt.fan.robotech`: Discussing all things relating to Robotech. *Newsgroup*

7003 `alt.toys.hi-tech` Optimus Prime is my hero. *Newsgroup*

7004 `alt.toys.transformers` From robots to vehicles and back again. *Newsgroup*

7005 `fj.rec.models` About models. *Newsgroup*

7006 `rec.collecting.dolls` Doll and bear collecting and crafting. *Newsgroup*

7007 `rec.crafts.dollhouses` Collecting and making of dollhouse miniatures. *Newsgroup*

7008 `rec.models.railroad` Model railroads of all scales. *Newsgroup*

7009 `rec.models.rc` Radio-controlled models for hobbyists. *Newsgroup*

7010 `rec.models.rc.air` Radio-controlled air models. *Newsgroup*

7011 `rec.models.rc.land` Radio-controlled land models. *Newsgroup*

7012 `rec.models.rc.misc` Radio-controlled miscellaneous items. *Newsgroup*

7013　**rec.models.rc.water** Radio-controlled water models. *Newsgroup*

7014　**rec.models.rockets** Model rockets for hobbyists. *Newsgroup*

7015　**rec.models.scale** Construction of models. *Newsgroup*

7016　**rec.toys.cars** Toy car collecting. *Newsgroup*

7017　**rec.toys.lego** Discussion of Lego, Duplo (and compatible) toys. *Newsgroup*

7018　**rec.toys.misc** Discussion of toys that lack a specific newsgroup. *Newsgroup*

7019　**teddy-bears:** Teddy bear collecting & making. *Mailing List*
± teddy-bears-request@rhein.de
OWNER owner-teddy-bears@rhein.de (Nadia Verleger & Andreas Oesterhelt)

VARIOUS

➤　**alt.party:** Parties, celebration, and general debauchery. *Newsgroup*

7020　**rec.knives** Anything that goes cut or has an edge. *Newsgroup*

7021　**rec.pyrotechnics** Fireworks, rocketry, safety, and other topics. *Newsgroup*

WOMEN'S SPORTS

7022　**WWW Women's Sports Page:** A comprehensive collection of links to women's sports pages around the net, compiled by Amy Lewis.
http://www.gslis.utexas.edu/~lewisa/womsprt.html
INFO lewisa@gslis.utexas.edu (Amy Lewis) (Amy Lewis)

➤　**clari.sports.basketball.college.women:** Women's college basketball. *Moderated newsgroup*

➤　**rec.sport.basketball.women:** Women's basketball at all levels. *Newsgroup*

➤　**WBBALL-L:** On women's basketball. (See entry 6798 for full listing.)

7023　**WISHPERD:** On women in sports, health, physical education, recreation, and dance. *Mailing List*
± listserv@sjsuvm1.sjsu.edu [body = SUBSCRIBE WISHPERD first-name last-name]
OWNER christen@sjsuvm1.sjsu.edu (Carol Christensen)

WRESTLING & BOXING

7024　**alt.sport.wrestling.amateur** Traditional Greco-Roman rasslin'. *Newsgroup*

7025　**clari.sports.boxing** Boxing coverage. *Moderated newsgroup*

7026　**fj.rec.sports.prowrestling** About pro wrestling. *Newsgroup*

7027　**rec.sport.boxing** Boxing in all its pugilistic facets and forms. *Newsgroup*

7028　**rec.sport.pro-wrestling** Discussion about professional wrestling. *Newsgroup*

7029　**rec.sport.pro-wrestling.fantasy** Rotisserie league professional wrestling. *Newsgroup*

REGIONS, CULTURES & TRAVEL

7030 `soc.answers` Repository for periodic Usenet articles. *Moderated newsgroup*

REGIONS & CULTURES

7031 `alt.suburbs` Living on the skirt of the city. *Newsgroup*

7032 `soc.culture.misc` Group for discussion about other cultures. *Newsgroup*

REGIONS & CULTURES—AFGHANISTAN

7033 `soc.culture.afghanistan` Discussion of the Afghan society. *Newsgroup*

REGIONS & CULTURES—AFRICA

7034 `clari.world.africa.eastern` News of eastern Africa. *Moderated newsgroup*

7035 `clari.world.africa.northwestern` News of northwestern Africa. *Moderated newsgroup*

7036 `clari.world.africa.southern` News of southern Africa. *Moderated newsgroup*

7037 `clari.world.africa.western` News of western Africa. *Moderated newsgroup*

7038 `rec.travel.africa` Travel on the African continent. *Newsgroup*

7039 `soc.culture.kenya` Kenyan peoples, politics, culture, and affairs. *Newsgroup*

7040 `soc.culture.malagasy` Madagascar and the Malagasy culture. *Newsgroup*

7041 `soc.culture.zimbabwe` Culture and other issues pertaining to Zimbabwe. *Newsgroup*

7042 **Sudan-L:** On Sudan. *Mailing List*
± `listserv@emuvm1.cc.emory.edu` [body = SUBSCRIBE SUDAN-L first-name last-name]
OWNER `younis@rmy.emory.edu` (Dr. Abdelmoneim I. Younis)

REGIONS & CULTURES—AFRICA—SUB-SAHARA

7043 `bit.tech.africana` Information technology and Africa. *Newsgroup*

7044 `clari.world.africa` Translated reports from Africa. *Moderated newsgroup*

7045 `soc.culture.african` Discussions about Africa and things African. *Newsgroup*

7046 `soc.culture.nigeria` Nigerian affairs, society, cultures, and peoples. *Newsgroup*

7047 `soc.culture.sierra-leone` The culture of Sierra Leone. *Newsgroup*

7048 `soc.culture.somalia` Somalian affairs, society, and culture. *Newsgroup*

REGIONS & CULTURES—ARCTIC & ANTARCTIC

➤ **Arctic Circle:** The purpose of Arctic Circle is to stimulate among viewers a greater interest in the peoples and environment of the Arctic and Subarctic region. This "electronic circle" has three interrelated themes: natural resources, history and culture, and social equity and environmental justice. New material is being added on a regular basis. (See entry 4630 for full listing.)

7049 **Australian Antarctic Division:** Information on Antarctica from the Australian government's Australian Antarctic Division of the Department of the Environment, Sport and Territories. Includes weather reports.
`http://www.antdiv.gov.au/`
INFO `info@antdiv.gov.au`

REGIONS & CULTURES—ASIA

7050 **ASPIRE-L:** Helping students from Asian countries studying in the US to find jobs back home. *Mailing List, moderated*

```
http://www-iub.indiana.edu/~intlcent/aspire/aspire.html
```
± listserv@iubvm.ucs.indiana.edu [body = SUBSCRIBE ASPIRE-L first-name last-name]
INFO aspirel@ucs.indiana.edu (Chun-Perng Cheah)
ARCHIVE listserv@iubvm.ucs.indiana.edu [body = INDEX ASPIRE-L]

➤ **CenAsia:** On all political, economic, and military issues involving the central Asian republics of the former Soviet Union. (See entry 7592 for full listing.)

➤ **clari.biz.stocks.report.asia:** Asian stock market reports. *Moderated newsgroup*

7051 **clari.world.asia.south** News of South Asia (Pakistan, Bangladesh, etc.). *Newsgroup*

➤ **Hotels on the Net:** Information on hotels and special promotions in the Asia-Pacific region. (See entry 7836 for full listing.)

7052 **soc.culture.mongolian** Everything related to Mongols and Mongolia. *Newsgroup*

7053 **soc.culture.nepal** Discussion of people and things in and from Nepal. *Newsgroup*

REGIONS & CULTURES—AUSTRALIA

7054 **AAA Australia Announce Archive:** G'day net surfers. This is virtually Australia, thanks to links to some of the top sites on the island, interestingly organized into dozens of categories. From today's TV listings for Sydney and Perth, to the plight (and photos) of the koala, this is an all-too-easy way to spend an hour. Personals ads, too!
```
http://www.com.au/aaa
```
INFO radio@mpx.com.au

7055 **aus.ads.commercial** Advertising from commercial enterprises. *Newsgroup*

7056 **aus.ads.forsale** Private for-sale ads. *Newsgroup*

7057 **aus.ads.forsale.computers** Private for-sale ads for computers. *Newsgroup*

7058 **aus.ads.jobs** Jobs available and wanted. *Newsgroup*

7059 **aus.ads.wanted** Private wanted ads. *Newsgroup*

➤ **aus.bicycle:** Push bikes. *Newsgroup*

7060 **aus.books** Australian discussion of books. *Newsgroup*

7061 **aus.bushwalking** Bushwalking in Australia. *Newsgroup*

➤ **aus.cars:** Australian newsgroup for automobile aficionados. *Newsgroup*

7062 **aus.cdrom** CD-ROM-related topics of Australian interest. *Newsgroup*

7063 **aus.computers** Miscellaneous computer types. *Newsgroup*

7064 **aus.conserve** Information and discussion of conservation issues. *Newsgroup*

7065 **aus.education** Helping educators in Australia. *Newsgroup*

7066 **aus.environment.conservation** Australian conservation issues. *Newsgroup*

7067 **aus.environment.misc** Miscellaneous discussion on Australia's environment. *Newsgroup*

7068 **aus.films** Movies, cinema, TV. *Newsgroup*

7069 **aus.flame** Abusive noise, posted by morons. *Newsgroup*

7070 **aus.flame.usa** Reasoned criticism of the United States of America. *Newsgroup*

7071 **aus.gardens** Gardens and gardening in Australia. *Newsgroup*

7072 **aus.general** General information, announcements, etc. *Newsgroup*

7073 **aus.legal** Legal issues in Australasia. *Newsgroup*

➤ **aus.mathematics:** Mathematics research in Australasia. *Newsgroup*

7074 **aus.net.access** Internet access. *Newsgroup*

7075 **aus.org.acs** The Australian Computer Society. *Newsgroup*

7076 `aus.org.acs.books` ACS book reviews. *Newsgroup*

7077 `aus.org.waia` Discussion forum for the Western Australia Internet Association. *Newsgroup*

7078 `aus.pets` Discussions of pets in Australia. *Newsgroup*

7079 `aus.politics` Politics, debates, rational (?) arguments. *Newsgroup*

7080 `aus.radio.broadcast` Australian broadcast radio. *Newsgroup*

➤ `aus.sex:` Australian discussion of matters sexual. *Newsgroup*

➤ `aus.snow:` Winter sports in Australia. *Newsgroup*

7081 `aus.sport` Generic discussions of sport. *Newsgroup*

7082 `aus.sport.motor` Motor sports. *Newsgroup*

7083 `aus.sport.scuba` Scuba diving and related aquatic activities. *Newsgroup*

7084 `aus.talk.ltuae` Life, the universe, and everything. *Newsgroup*

7085 `aus.theatre` The theater. *Newsgroup*

7086 `aus.tv` Television. *Newsgroup*

7087 **Australian Back Packers Information:** All sorts of information on backpacking and traveling in Australia.
`http://www.com.au/aaa/Back_Pack.html`
INFO `radio@mpx.com.au`

➤ **Australian Biomedical And Medical Device Page:** This site offers newsletters from the Society for Medical and Biological Engineering and I. E. Australia, lists of Australian hospitals, a list of Australian medical device companies, and so forth. (See entry 5095 for full listing.)

7088 **The Australian Observer:** An Internet news magazine with an Australian focus. *E-Journal*
`http://www.observer.com.au/observer/`
± INFO `observer@observer.com.au`

7089 `clari.world.oceania.australia` News of Australia. *Moderated newsgroup*

7090 **Electronic Journal of Australian and New Zealand History:** Historical documents and new work on Australian and New Zealand history. *E-Journal, moderated*
ARCHIVE `gopher://marlin.jcu.edu.au/JCU Academic Departments/History`
Frequency: irregular

7091 **Internet Australasia:** Print and Web-based magazine dealing with all aspects of the Internet in Australia, New Zealand, and Asia. *Magazine*
`http://www.interaus.net/magazine`
INFO EDITOR `ed@interaus.net` (Sarah Kent, Editor)
Frequency: monthly

➤ **La Trobe University (Victoria, Australia):** This is the CWIS of La Trobe University in Melbourne, Australia. (See entry 4431 for full listing.)

➤ `misc.transport.rail.australia-nz:` Railways in Australia and New Zealand. *Newsgroup*

➤ **Queensland University of Technology, Brisbane:** The QUT WWW pages and gopher provide people outside the university with information about QUT and direct the university's staff and students to outside Internet resources. (See entry 4444 for full listing.)

7092 `rec.travel.australia+nz` Travel information for Australia and New Zealand. *Newsgroup*

7093 `soc.culture.australian` Australian culture and society. *Newsgroup*

REGIONS & CULTURES—BELGIUM

7094 `be.announce` Important announcements. *Moderated newsgroup*

7095 `be.commercial` Commercial postings for Belgium. *Newsgroup*

7096 `be.comp` Computers in Belgium. *Newsgroup*

7097 `be.forsale` Noncommercial sales announcements in Belgium. *Newsgroup*

7098 `be.jobs` The job marketplace in Belgium. *Newsgroup*

7099 `be.misc` Miscellaneous topics relevant to Belgium. *Newsgroup*

7100 `be.politics` Belgian politics. *Newsgroup*

7101 `be.science` About science and scientific research in Belgium. *Newsgroup*

7102 `be.tv` About television programs in Belgium. *Newsgroup*

7103 **Brussels Free University - Vrije Universiteit Brussel (VUB) CWIS:** Campus wide information service for Brussels Free University.
`http://www.vub.ac.be/`
INFO `webmaster@vub.ac.be`

7104 `soc.culture.belgium` Belgian society, culture(s) and people. *Newsgroup*

➤ `soc.culture.netherlands`: People from the Netherlands and Belgium. *Newsgroup*

REGIONS & CULTURES—CANADA

➤ `ab.politics`: Discussion of politics in Alberta, Canada. *Newsgroup*

7105 `alt.canadian.beaver` More from "Things that make you go 'Eh?'". *Newsgroup*

➤ `alt.fan.karla-homolka`: Why are there so few hot, exhibitionist S & M women? *Newsgroup*

➤ `alt.music.canada`: Oh, Canada, eh? *Newsgroup*

7106 `alt.radio.networks.cbc` Radio programming by the Canadian Broadcasting Corp. *Newsgroup*

7107 `alt.travel.canada` All about traveling to Canada. *Newsgroup*

➤ `bionet.prof-society.cfbs`: Canadian Federation of Biological Societies. *Newsgroup*

➤ `bionet.prof-society.csm`: Canadian Society of Microbiologists. *Moderated newsgroup*

➤ **Bolen Books:** Bolen Books is an independent bookstore whose Web site offers online ordering and pages of interesting forthcoming new titles and new arrivals. (See entry 116 for full listing.)

7108 `ca.seminars` Seminars in Canada. *Newsgroup*

➤ **Camosun College CWIS:** Campus Wide Information Service for Camosun College, Canada. (See entry 4416 for full listing.)

7109 `can.com.ad-agencies` Ad agency discussions in Canada. *Newsgroup*

7110 `can.community.asian` Discussions by/about/within the Asian-Canadian community. *Newsgroup*

➤ `can.community.military`: Issues about military-community life. *Newsgroup*

7111 `can.english` About the English-speaking population (in English). *Newsgroup*

7112 `can.francais` About the Francophone population (in French). *Newsgroup*

7113 `can.general` Items of general interest to Canadians. *Newsgroup*

➤ `can.gov.announce`: Announcements from the Canadian government. *Moderated newsgroup*

7114 `can.infobahn` For discussion of the Internet and related topics in Canada. *Newsgroup*

7115 `can.infohighway` For discussion of the Internet and related issues in Canda. *Newsgroup*

7116 `can.jobs` Jobs in Canada. *Newsgroup*

➤ `can.legal`: Canadian law and legal matters. *Newsgroup*

7117 `can.med.misc` Medical issues in Canada. *Newsgroup*

➤ `can.military-brats`: Current and former dependents of the Canadian military. *Newsgroup*

7118 `can.newprod` New products/services of interest to Canadian readers. *Newsgroup*

7119 `can.org.cata` Canadian Advanced Technology Association (high-tech forum). *Newsgroup*

7120 `can.org.cips` Canadian Information Processing Society. *Newsgroup*

7121 `can.org.misc` Miscellaneous Canadian organizations. *Newsgroup*

➤ `can.politics:` Canadian politics. *Newsgroup*

7122 `can.rsc.discussion.professeurs` General teacher discussions in French. *Newsgroup*

➤ `can.schoolnet.arts.music:` Music studies in elementary/secondary schools. *Newsgroup*

➤ `can.schoolnet.biomed.jr:` SchoolNet biology and medicine for elementary students. *Newsgroup*

➤ `can.schoolnet.biomed.sr:` SchoolNet biology and medicine for high-school students. *Newsgroup*

➤ `can.schoolnet.chat.students.jr:` General talk by elementary school SchoolNet students. *Newsgroup*

➤ `can.schoolnet.chat.students.sr:` General talk by high-school SchoolNet students. *Newsgroup*

➤ `can.schoolnet.chat.teachers:` General talk by SchoolNet teachers. *Newsgroup*

➤ `can.schoolnet.chem.jr:` SchoolNet chemistry for elementary students. *Newsgroup*

➤ `can.schoolnet.chem.sr:` SchoolNet chemistry for high-school students. *Newsgroup*

➤ `can.schoolnet.comp.jr:` SchoolNet computer science for elementary students. *Newsgroup*

➤ `can.schoolnet.comp.sr:` SchoolNet computer science for high-school students. *Newsgroup*

➤ `can.schoolnet.earth.jr:` SchoolNet earth sciences for elementary students. *Newsgroup*

➤ `can.schoolnet.earth.sr:` SchoolNet earth sciences for high-school students. *Newsgroup*

➤ `can.schoolnet.elecsys.jr:` SchoolNet EE and systems eng. for elementary students. *Newsgroup*

➤ `can.schoolnet.elecsys.sr:` SchoolNet EE and systems eng. for high-school students. *Newsgroup*

➤ `can.schoolnet.eng.jr:` SchoolNet engineering for elementary students. *Newsgroup*

➤ `can.schoolnet.eng.sr:` SchoolNet engineering for high-school students. *Newsgroup*

➤ `can.schoolnet.english:` English elementary/secondary schools curriculum. *Newsgroup*

➤ `can.schoolnet.firefighters:` Profession of firefighting and fire prevention. *Newsgroup*

➤ `can.schoolnet.history:` History studies in elementary/secondary schools. *Newsgroup*

➤ `can.schoolnet.jrjays:` Jr. Jays fan club for Toronto Blue Jays. *Newsgroup*

➤ `can.schoolnet.math.jr:` SchoolNet mathematics for elementary students. *Newsgroup*

➤ `can.schoolnet.math.sr:` SchoolNet mathematics for high-school students. *Newsgroup*

➤ `can.schoolnet.phys.jr:` SchoolNet physics for elementary school students. *Newsgroup*

➤ `can.schoolnet.phys.sr:` SchoolNet physics for high-school students. *Newsgroup*

➤ `can.schoolnet.physed:` Physical education in elementary/secondary schools. *Newsgroup*

➤ `can.schoolnet.problems:` The group to gripe in about SchoolNet or find its FAQs. *Newsgroup*

➤ `can.schoolnet.projects.calls:` SchoolNet CFPs, project announcements. *Newsgroup*

➤ `can.schoolnet.projects.discuss:` SchoolNet project discussion. *Newsgroup*

➤ `can.schoolnet.school.improvement:` School improvement and enhancement. *Newsgroup*

➤ `can.schoolnet.socsci.jr:` SchoolNet social sciences for elementary students. *Newsgroup*

➤ `can.schoolnet.socsci.sr:` SchoolNet social sciences for high-school students. *Newsgroup*

➤ `can.schoolnet.space.jr:` SchoolNet space sciences for elementary students. *Newsgroup*

➤ `can.schoolnet.space.sr:` SchoolNet space sciences for high-school students. *Newsgroup*

➤ `can.schoolnet.staff.development:` Staff development. *Newsgroup*

➤ `can.scout-guide:` About Canadian Boy Scouts and other scouting groups. *Newsgroup*

➤ **can.sun-stroke:** Sun Microsystems users in Canada. *Newsgroup*

7123 **can.talk.bilingualism** Flames about Canadian English or French, depending. *Newsgroup*

➤ **can.talk.guns:** Flames about Canadian gun owners, nonowners, and laws. *Newsgroup*

7124 **can.talk.smoking** Flames about/from Canadian smokers. *Newsgroup*

➤ **can.taxes:** Discussion of how to pay or not pay taxes in Canada. *Newsgroup*

➤ **can.vlsi:** Canadian group for discussion of Very Large Scale Integration (integrated circuit fabrication). *Newsgroup*

7125 **Canada-L:** For discussion of political, social, cultural, and economic issues in Canada. *Mailing List*
    ± listserv@vm1.mcgill.ca [body = SUBSCRIBE CANADA-L first-name last-name]
    OWNER adsa@musica.mcgill.ca (Anastassia Khouri)
    ARCHIVE listserv@vm1.mcgill.ca [body = INDEX CANADA-L]
    Language: French & English

7126 **The Canadian Internet Business Directory:** Search businesses and government and educational institutions in Canada by company, name, province, or type.
    http://www.cibd.com/
    INFO house@9to5.com

➤ **Canadian Journal of Educational Administration and Policy:** Educational administration practice and policy. (See entry 4094 for full listing.)

➤ **CANARIE:** For associates of the Canada Network for Advancement of Research, Industry and Education (CANARIE). (See entry 4361 for full listing.)

➤ **CANCAR-L:** On computer-assisted reporting related to Canadian issues. (See entry 6090 for full listing.)

➤ **CANCHID:** For the Canadian Network on Health in International Development. (See entry 4998 for full listing.)

➤ **City of Grande Prairie, Alberta, Canada:** Information on strategic and business planning in a municipal setting. (See entry 5513 for full listing.)

7127 **clari.sports.local.canada.atlantic_provs** News of Atlantic Province athletics. *Moderated newsgroup*

7128 **clari.sports.local.canada.brit_columbia** News of British Columbia athletics. *Moderated newsgroup*

7129 **clari.sports.local.canada.ontario.misc** News of Ontario athletics. *Moderated newsgroup*

7130 **clari.sports.local.canada.ontario.toronto** News of Toronto athletics. *Moderated newsgroup*

7131 **clari.sports.local.canada.prairie_provs** News of Prairie Province athletics. *Moderated newsgroup*

7132 **clari.sports.local.canada.quebec** News of Quebec athletics. *Moderated newsgroup*

7133 **clari.world.americas.canada** General Canadian news. *Moderated newsgroup*

7134 **clari.world.americas.canada.biz** Canadian business news. *Moderated newsgroup*

7135 **clari.world.americas.canada.briefs** News briefs from Canada. *Moderated newsgroup*

7136 **clari.world.americas.canada.business** Canadian business news. *Moderated newsgroup*

7137 **clari.world.americas.canada.general** General Canadian news. *Moderated newsgroup*

7138 **clari.world.americas.canada.review** Daily review of Canadian news. *Moderated newsgroup*

7139 **CM:** An electronic viewing journal of Canadian materials for young people. Reviews and articles about Canadian books, videos, and materials for young people. *E-Journal*
    http://www.mbnet.mb.ca/cm
    ± INFO camera@mbnet.mb.ca (Peter Tittenberger)
    Frequency: weekly

➤ **CNET:** On community network building in remote and rural Canadian communities. (See entry 9758 for full listing.)

➤ **COCAMED:** Computers in Canadian medical education. (See entry 4829 for full listing.)

➤ **CSEA-L:** On visual-arts education in Canada. (See entry 77 for full listing.)

➤ **CSSE:** For members of the Canadian Society for the Study of Education. (See entry 4364 for full listing.)

7140 **Daily:** For Statistics Canada Daily data and publications. *Distribution List, moderated*
gopher://gopher.statcan.ca
http://www.statcan.ca/
ftp://ftp.statcan.ca
± listproc@statcan.ca [body = SUBSCRIBE DAILY first-name last-name]
INFO godfrey@statcan.ca
OWNER thoemic@statcan.ca (Michael Thoen)
Language: English, French

7141 **Error 404:** Online magazine with a Canadian focus. Relates to WWW activities, and business on the net. *E-Zine*
http://www.cban.com/error404/
± majordomo@cban.com [body = index error4041]
INFO OWNER asj@cban.com (Andrew Stanley-Jones)
ARCHIVES
http://www.cban.com/error404/
ftp://ftp.cban.com/pub/error404/
Frequency: bimonthly

7142 **Global Monitor:** Canada's first online computer magazine. *E-Magazine*
http://www.monitor.ca/monitor/
INFO info@monitor.ca
OWNER http://www.monitor.ca/
OWNER office@monitor.ca
ARCHIVE http://www.monitor.ca/monitor/backissues.html
Frequency: monthly

7143 **Government Information in Canada/Information:** Quarterly electronic journal for discussion and study of Canadian federal, provincial/territorial, and local government information. *E-Journal*
http://www.usask.ca/library/gic
INFO EDITOR hubbertz@sklib.usask.ca (Andrew Hubbertz - Editor/Redacteur en chef)
Language: English and French
Frequency: quarterly

➤ **House of Speculative Fiction:** Ottowa-based bookseller of science-fiction and fantasy books. (See entry 118 for full listing.)

7144 **Industry Canada:** This site was created to promote jobs and growth in Canada in a world characterized by global integration and the growth of knowledge-based economies.
http://info.ic.gc.ca/ic-data/
INFO cmb@info.ic.gc.ca

➤ **kw.networks:** Connectivity and networking within the Kitchener-Waterloo, Canada community. *Newsgroup*

➤ **lawsoc-l:** On the study of law and society in the Canadian context. (See entry 5552 for full listing.)

➤ **misc.immigration.canada:** Canada immigration issues. *Newsgroup*

7145 **NDPZOO-L:** Discussion of New Democratic Party reform in Canada. *Mailing List*
± mailserv@odie.ccs.yorku.ca [body = SUBSCRIBE NDPZOO-L first-name last-name]
OWNER samuela@husc.harvard.edu (Alexandra Samuel)
OWNER robcott@islandnet.com (Rob Cottingham)

➤ **The Official Online Guide to Canada's West Coast Music Industry:** The most comprehensive guide to Vancouver and British Columbia's music industry. Free listings for businesses and musicians. Also includes classified ads. (See entry 767 for full listing.)

7146 **pei.crafts** Crafts in the Prince Edward Island (Canada) area. *Newsgroup*

7147 **soc.culture.canada** Discussions of Canada and its people. *Newsgroup*

➤ **VILA:** For Vancouver Island Libertarian Association: Canadian libertarians. (See entry 5628 for full listing.)

7148 **wpg.politics** Discussion of political matters in Winnipeg. *Newsgroup*

REGIONS & CULTURES—CANADA—ALBERTA

7149 **ab.general** Items of general interest in Alberta, Canada. *Newsgroup*

7150 **ab.jobs** Jobs in Alberta, Canada. *Newsgroup*

7151 **ab.politics** Discussion of politics in Alberta, Canada. *Newsgroup*

7152 **ed.*** Newsgroups from Edinburgh, Scotland. *Newsgroup*

7153 **edm.forsale** Edmonton, Alberta, Canada, for sale. *Newsgroup*

7154 **edm.general** Items of general interest in Edmonton, Alberta, Canada. *Newsgroup*

7155 **edm.news.stats** Network news statistics in Edmonton. *Newsgroup*

7156 **edm.usrgrp** Unix Users Group in Edmonton, Alberta, Canada. *Newsgroup*

REGIONS & CULTURES—CANADA—BRITISH COLUMBIA

7157 **bc.bcnet** The British Columbian network. *Newsgroup*

➤ **bc.cycling:** Discussion regarding bicycling in British Columbia, Canada. *Newsgroup*

7158 **bc.general** Items of general interest in British Columbia. *Newsgroup*

7159 **bc.jobs** The job market in British Columbia, Canada. *Newsgroup*

7160 **bc.news.stats** Network news statistics in British Columbia. *Newsgroup*

7161 **bc.politics** Political discussion relating to British Columbia. *Newsgroup*

7162 **bc.weather** British Columbia Environment Canada forecasts. *Newsgroup*

REGIONS & CULTURES—CANADA—NEW BRUNSWICK

7163 **nb.biz** Commercial postings for New Brunswick, Canada. *Newsgroup*

7164 **nb.forsale** Personal items for sale in New Brunswick, Canada. *Newsgroup*

7165 **nb.francais** Discussions in French for New Brunswick, Canada. *Newsgroup*

7166 **nb.general** General discussions on any topic of interest to New Brunswickers. *Newsgroup*

7167 **nb.jobs** Jobs offered or sought in New Brunswick, Canada. *Newsgroup*

REGIONS & CULTURES—CANADA—NOVA SCOTIA

7168 **ns.announce** Announcements for Nova Scotia. *Moderated newsgroup*

7169 **ns.general** Items of general interest to folks in Nova Scotia. *Newsgroup*

REGIONS & CULTURES—CANADA—ONTARIO

7170 **kw.bb.sale** Things for sale in the Kitchener-Waterloo, Canada, area. *Newsgroup*

7171 **kw.birthdays** Happy birthday. *Newsgroup*

7172 **kw.cpsr** Kitchener-Waterloo branch of Computer Professionals for Social Responsibility. *Newsgroup*

7173 **kw.eats** Restaurant reviews. *Newsgroup*

7174 **kw.forsale** Things for sale. *Newsgroup*

7175 **kw.fun** Fun stuff in the Kitchener-Waterloo, Canada, area. *Newsgroup*

7176 `kw.general` General information in Kitchener-Waterloo, Canada. *Newsgroup*

7177 `kw.housing` Rooms for rent in Kitchener-Waterloo, Canada. *Newsgroup*

7178 `kw.jobs` Job postings for Kitchener-Waterloo, Canada. *Newsgroup*

➤ `kw.movies:` Film reviews. *Newsgroup*

7179 `kw.networks` Connectivity and networking within the Kitchener-Waterloo, Canada community. *Newsgroup*

7180 `kw.news` Usenet in Kitchener-Waterloo, Canada. *Newsgroup*

7181 `kw.news.stats` Usenet statistics in Kitchener-Waterloo, Canada. *Newsgroup*

➤ `kw.theatre:` Theater reviews, etc. *Newsgroup*

7182 `ont.archives` Archives in Ontario, Canada. *Newsgroup*

➤ `ont.bicycle:` Bicycling in Ontario, Canada. *Newsgroup*

7183 `ont.conditions` Current highway conditions for winter driving. *Newsgroup*

7184 `ont.events` Ontario, Canada happenings. *Newsgroup*

7185 `ont.forsale` Items for sale/wanted in Ontario, Canada. *Newsgroup*

7186 `ont.general` Items of general interest in Ontario, Canada. *Newsgroup*

7187 `ont.jobs` Jobs in Ontario, Canada. *Newsgroup*

7188 `ont.micro` Microcomputer-related postings in Ontario, Canada. *Newsgroup*

7189 `ont.singles` Singles in Ontario, Canada. *Newsgroup*

7190 `ont.uucp` UUCP-related postings in Ontario, Canada. *Newsgroup*

7191 `ott.events` Seminars and the like at Ottawa sites. *Newsgroup*

7192 `ott.forsale.computing` Computers and related equipment for sale/wanted in Ottawa. *Newsgroup*

7193 `ott.forsale.other` Otherwise unclassified items for sale/wanted in Ottawa. *Newsgroup*

7194 `ott.general` General news local to Ottawa sites. *Newsgroup*

7195 `ott.housing` Places to live wanted, for sale or for rent. *Newsgroup*

7196 `ott.jobs` Employment in Ottawa, Canada. *Newsgroup*

➤ `ott.motorcycles:` Motorcycles and motorcyling in Ottawa, Canada. *Newsgroup*

7197 `ott.news` Network news operations in Ottawa, Canada. *Newsgroup*

7198 `ott.rides` Rides wanted/offered to or from Ottawa. *Newsgroup*

7199 `ott.singles` Ottawa singles group. *Newsgroup*

7200 `ott.vietnamese` Vietnamese interest group. *Newsgroup*

➤ `ott.weather:` Weather forecasts for the Ottawa area. *Moderated newsgroup*

➤ **Seneca Information Service:** This is the CWIS of Seneca College of Applied Arts and Technology, Toronto, Canada. (See entry 79 for full listing.)

7201 `tor.eats` Where to eat and not to eat in the Toronto area. *Newsgroup*

7202 `tor.events` Events in and around Toronto, Canada. *Newsgroup*

7203 `tor.forsale` Items for sale/wanted in Toronto, Canada. *Newsgroup*

7204 `tor.general` Items of general interest in Toronto, Canada. *Newsgroup*

7205 `tor.housing` Housing in and around Toronto, Canada. *Newsgroup*

7206 `tor.jobs` Jobs in Toronto, Canada. *Newsgroup*

7207 `tor.news` Usenet in Toronto, Canada. *Newsgroup*

7208 `tor.news.stats` Usenet statistics in Toronto, Canada. *Newsgroup*

➤ **Trent University Information Service:** This is the CWIS for Trent University, Peterborough, Ontario, Canada. Includes distribution of faculty work/publications, notably D. Theall's work on James Joyce and Sarah Keefer's work on Old English. (See entry 4457 for full listing.)

REGIONS & CULTURES—CANADA—QUEBEC & MONTREAL

7209 `mtl.freenet.org` Montreal Freenet/LiberTel, discussions nontechniques. *Newsgroup*

7210 `mtl.general` General stuff in Montreal, Canada. *Newsgroup*

7211 `mtl.vendre-forsale` Petites annonces a Montreal. *Newsgroup*

7212 `qc.general` General interest items about Quebec, Canada. *Newsgroup*

7213 `qc.jobs` Jobs in Quebec. *Newsgroup*

➤ `qc.politique`: Politics of Quebec. *Newsgroup*

7214 `soc.culture.quebec` Quebec, Canada society and culture. *Newsgroup*

REGIONS & CULTURES—CARIBBEAN

7215 `alt.current-events.antigua` Current events on the island of Antigua. *Newsgroup*

7216 `alt.current-events.haiti` News about Haiti. *Newsgroup*

7217 `bermuda.for.sale` A discussion of items for sale in Bermuda. *Newsgroup*

7218 `bermuda.forsale` Items for sale or looking to buy in Bermuda. *Newsgroup*

7219 `bermuda.general` General information and questions about Bermuda. *Newsgroup*

➤ `bermuda.ibl.announce`: Announcements from Internet Bermuda Limited staff. *Newsgroup*

➤ `bermuda.ibl.general`: Information about Internet Bermuda Limited. *Newsgroup*

➤ `bermuda.ibl.support`: Technical issues relating to Internet Bermuda Limited. *Newsgroup*

7220 `bermuda.jobs.offered` Jobs available in Bermuda. *Newsgroup*

➤ `bermuda.politics`: Politics in Bermuda. *Newsgroup*

7221 `bermuda.sports` Newsgroup related to sports in Bermuda. *Newsgroup*

7222 `clari.world.americas.caribbean` News of the Caribbean island nations. *Moderated newsgroup*

➤ **CREAD:** This list is used to animate discussions on the uses of distance education in Latin America and the Caribbean. (See entry 4337 for full listing.)

7223 **Cruz Bay Villas, St. John, U.S. Virgin Islands:** Information on accommodations on St. John, U.S. Virgin Islands—very private/quiet 1-bedroom, 1-bath villas. 10-minute walk into Cruz Bay and minutes from the national park.
`http://www.crl.com/~koyn/CBV.html`
INFO koyn@crl.com

7224 **CUBA-L:** On contemporary Cuba. *Distribution List, moderated*
± listserv@unmvma.unm.edu [body = SUBSCRIBE CUBA-L first-name last-name]
INFO nvaldes@unm.edu (Nelson P Valdes)
Language: English, Spanish
Comments: $60/year individual; $80/year institution

7225 **LASPAU-L:** For announcements of conferences and seeking help with research projects in or about Latin America and the Caribbean. *Mailing List*
± listserv@harvarda.harvard.edu [body = SUBSCRIBE LASPAU-L first-name last-name]
INFO laspau-l-request@harvarda.harvard.edu
ARCHIVE listserv@harvarda.harvard.edu [body = INDEX LASPAU-L]

7226 `rec.travel.caribbean` Travel to the islands of the Caribbean, sans pirates. *Newsgroup*

7227 **SDOMINGO:** On the culture and society of the Dominican Republic. *Mailing List*

± `listserv@enlace.bitnet` [body = SUBSCRIBE SDOMINGO first-name last-name]
INFO `fmoncion@pucmm.edu.do` (Flavio Moncion)

7228 `soc.culture.caribbean` Life in the Caribbean. *Newsgroup*

7229 `soc.culture.cuba` Cuban culture, society, and politics. *Newsgroup*

7230 `soc.culture.dominican-rep` The life and people of the Dominican Republic. *Newsgroup*

7231 `soc.culture.haiti` Haitian specific development and cultural issues. *Newsgroup*

7232 `soc.culture.puerto-rico` Puerto Rican culture, society, and politics. *Newsgroup*

REGIONS & CULTURES—CELTIC

7233 **Celtic Heritage Online:** On Celtic culture, history, literature, and music.
`http://fox.nstn.ca/~celtic/index.html`
INFO `celtic@fox.nstn.ns.ca`

7234 **CELTIC-L:** On Celtic culture. *Mailing List*
± `listserv@irlearn.ucd.ie` [body = SUBSCRIBE CELTIC-L first-name last-name]
INFO `smaccona@ccvax.ucd.ie` (Seamus Mac Conaonaigh)
ARCHIVE `listserv@irlearn.ucd.ie` [body = INDEX CELTIC-L]
Language: Mostly English; some Celtic languages with English translation

➤ **folkdj-l:** For folk/bluegrass/Celtic DJs. (See entry 872 for full listing.)

➤ `rec.music.celtic`: Traditional and modern music with a Celtic flavor. *Newsgroup*

7235 `soc.culture.celtic` Irish, Scottish, Breton, Cornish, Manx, and Welsh. *Newsgroup*

REGIONS & CULTURES—CENTRAL AMERICA

7236 **CENTAM-L:** For interchange of academically oriented ideas regarding Central America. *Mailing List*
± `listserv@ubvm.cc.buffalo.edu` [body = SUBSCRIBE CENTAM-L first-name last-name]
OWNER `dsoto@indiana.edu` (Daniel Soto)
OWNER `angelo.calderon@adm.monash.edu.au` (Angel Calderon)
Gated: `bit.listserv.centam-l`

7237 `soc.culture.costa-rica` Topics about Costa Rica. *Newsgroup*

7238 `soc.culture.el-salvador` Topics about El Salvador, Central America. *Newsgroup*

➤ `soc.culture.latin-america`: Topics about Latin America. *Newsgroup*

REGIONS & CULTURES—CHINA

➤ **ACMR-L:** For members of the Association for Chinese Music Research. (See entry 1184 for full listing.)

7239 `alt.chinese.computing` Discussion group for Chinese computing. *Newsgroup*

7240 `alt.chinese.text` Postings in Chinese; Chinese-language software. *Newsgroup*

7241 `alt.chinese.text.big5` Posting in Chinese (BIG 5). *Newsgroup*

7242 `aus.culture.china` `soc.culture.china` redistributed. *Newsgroup*

➤ **CCNET-L:** On Chinese computing. (See entry 3765 for full listing.)

➤ **china-link:** Weekly newsletter of import/export business with China. (See entry 1794 for full listing.)

7243 **CHINA-NT:** Serves the community of overseas Chinese students and scholars by conducting in-depth discussions and debates of issues of their concerns and interests; also miscellaneous announcements and information circulation and service. *Mailing List*
± `listserv@uga.cc.uga.edu` [body = SUBSCRIBE CHINA-NT first-name last-name]
INFO `nxliu@well.com` (Newton X. Liu")

EDITOR `ccf-editor@ifcss.org`

➤ **Chinese Community Information Center (CCIC):** The CCIC site is the Chinese Community Information Center set up by IFCSS (Independent Federation of Chinese Students and Scholars in the U.S.) to serve its community and its friends. Includes news, information for Chinese expatriates, information on Chinese & computers, and more. (See entry 9705 for full listing.)

7244 **Chinese Computing Network:** On software and hardware technologies relating to the use of Chinese on computers. *Newsletter*

± `listserv@uga.uga.edu` [body = SUB CCNET-L first-name last-name]

INFO `jiang@ifcss.org` (Yuan Jiang)

INFO `yjj@ctr.columbia.edu` (Yuan Jiang)

ARCHIVES

`ftp://ftp.ifcss.org/china-studies/compute/ccnet-archive`

`http://ftp.ifcss.org/`

Gated: `alt.chinese.software`

Frequency: irregular

7245 `chinese.comp.software` Discussion of Chinese software and Chinese computing. *Newsgroup*

7246 `chinese.newsgroups.announce` Important announcements of `chinese.*` hierarchy. *Moderated newsgroup*

7247 `chinese.newsgroups.answers` FAQs, etc. of `chinese.*`. *Moderated newsgroup*

7248 `chinese.newsgroups.newusers` Postings by new users. *Newsgroup*

7249 `chinese.rec.misc` Miscellaneous recreational discussion. *Newsgroup*

7250 `chinese.rec.sports` Sports activities and comments, etc. *Newsgroup*

7251 `chinese.talk.misc` Miscellaneous talks in Chinese. *Newsgroup*

➤ `chinese.talk.politics:` Political talks in Chinese. *Newsgroup*

7252 `clari.world.asia.china` News of China. *Moderated newsgroup*

7253 `clari.world.asia.china.biz` Chinese business news. *Moderated newsgroup*

7254 `clari.world.asia.hong_kong` News of Hong Kong. *Moderated newsgroup*

7255 `clari.world.asia.taiwan` News of the Republic of China (Taiwan). *Moderated newsgroup*

➤ **CPGIS-L:** On Chinese geographic information systems. (See entry 9318 for full listing.)

7256 `fj.soc.culture.chinese` Chinese or China-related culture and related topics. *Newsgroup*

➤ **ID-Line:** An idea exchange for Chinese communication scholars. (See entry 5175 for full listing.)

7257 **LYTX:** LYTX (Lian/ Yi\ Tong- Xun\ ) contains riginally written, unpublished Chinese articles on literature, poems, science and technology, topics of general interest, and things related to CSSP (Chinese students, scholars, and professionals). *E-Journal*

± `listproc@uwalpha.uwinnipeg.ca` [body = SUBSCRIBE LYTX-BIG5 first-name last-name]

INFO `lytx-cm@uwalpha.uwinnipeg.ca` [Editorial Board List] (Editorial Board List)

ARCHIVES

`ftp://cnd.org/pub/fcssc/lytx`

`ftp://ifcss.org/org/lytx`

`ftp://uwalpha.uwinnipeg.ca/pub/fcssc/lytx`

`ftp://ftp.met.kth.se/pub/LYTX`

`http://www.ifcss.org/www/pub/org/lytx/`

`http://uwalpha.uwinnipeg.ca/`

`http://tappet.ime.nrc.ca:8001/`

`gopher://sunrise.cc.mcgill.ca`

Language: Chinese

Frequency: monthly

7258 `pgh.org.uccp` The University Chinese Club of Pittsburgh. *Newsgroup*

7259 `soc.culture.china` About China and Chinese culture. *Newsgroup*

➤ `soc.culture.hongkong`: Discussions pertaining to Hong Kong. *Newsgroup*

➤ `soc.culture.hongkong.entertainment`: Entertainment in Hong Kong. *Newsgroup*

7260 `soc.culture.taiwan` Discussion about things Taiwanese. *Newsgroup*

7261 `talk.politics.china` Discussion of political issues related to China. *Newsgroup*

➤ `um.chinese`: Newsgroup for students interested in Chinese. *Newsgroup*

7262 **USTC85-L:** For discussion among past and current students at the University of Science and Technology in China. *Mailing List*

± `listserv@ricevm1.rice.edu` [body = SUBSCRIBE USTC85-L first-name last-name]

INFO `jun@aurora.rice.edu`

ARCHIVE `http://math.wisc.edu/~cliu/ustc/`

REGIONS & CULTURES—CZECH REPUBLIC

7263 **Czech Educational and Scientific NETwork (CESNET):** Information on CESNET and the Czech Republic.

`http://www.cesnet.cz/`

`gopher://gopher.cesnet.cz`

INFO `gopheradm@gopher.cesnet.cz`

INFO `wwwadm@www.cesnet.cz`

MIRRORS

`gopheradm@gopher.cesnet.cz`

`http://www2.cesnet.cz/`

`gopher://gopher2.cesnet.cz`

7264 **Czechkrystal, Ltd.:** Importers of fine hand-blown, hand-engraved crystal from the Czech Republic, and gifts from around the world for the discriminating shopper.

`http://www.czechkrystal.com/`

INFO `white@czechkrystal.com`

7265 **EUnet Czechia:** This is the information service of EUnet Czechia, the network service provider in the Czech Republic. This site also contains information about top-level domain `.cz`

`http://info.eunet.cz/`

`http://infox.eunet.cz/`

`http://www.eunet.cz/`

INFO `info@eunet.cz`

7266 **Internet CZ - EUnet Czech Republic:** WWW server that offers commercial, business, and finance information not only about the Czech Republic but also about central Europe, including the Prague stock exchange, exchange rates, statistical information, databases of Czech commercial subjects involved in the Czech Coupon Privatization, municipal information, bus and train timetables, Czech firms' advertisements, news and journals, and so on. Other important databases and resources are in progress.

`http://info.eunet.cz/`

INFO `info@eunet.cz`

MIRROR `http://infox.eunet.cz/`

7267 `soc.culture.czecho-slovak` Bohemian, Slovak, Moravian, and Silesian life. *Newsgroup*

REGIONS & CULTURES—EUROPE

➤ **AccomoDATA:** A resource with listings of hotels, bed and breakfasts, cottage rentals, and boat rentals in England, Wales, Scotland, Ireland, and France, plus the rest of Europe. You can make direct bookings from this site. (See entry 7820 for full listing.)

➤ **alt.politics.ec:** The European economic community. *Newsgroup*

➤ **alt.politics.europe.misc:** The general political situation in Europe. *Newsgroup*

➤ **alt.satellite.tv.europe:** All about European satellite TV. *Newsgroup*

7268 **bit.listserv.albanian** Albanian discussion list. *Moderated newsgroup*

7269 **bit.listserv.mideur-1** Middle Europe discussion list. *Newsgroup*

7270 **cern.badmarket** Bad quality of services, goods, etc. in the region. *Newsgroup*

➤ **clari.biz.stocks.report.europe.western:** Western European stock markets reports. *Moderated newsgroup*

7271 **clari.world.europe.alpine** Austria, Switzerland, Liechtenstein. *Moderated newsgroup*

7272 **clari.world.europe.benelux** Belgium, the Netherlands, Luxembourg. *Moderated newsgroup*

7273 **clari.world.europe.union** News about the European Union. *Moderated newsgroup*

➤ **DANTE IN PRINT:** Publication series containing all papers and articles published by or on behalf of DANTE (Delivery of Advanced Network Technology to Europe, Ltd.). It includes an overview of developments in DANTE services and other activities, all in the area of European research networking. (See entry 9549 for full listing.)

➤ **EEC-L:** On European training and technology. (See entry 4505 for full listing.)

➤ **eunet.aviation:** European aviation rules, means and methods. *Newsgroup*

7274 **eunet.misc** Miscellaneous discussions (replaces eunet.general/followup). *Newsgroup*

7275 **eunet.newprod** Announcements of new products of European interest. *Newsgroup*

7276 **eunet.news** Group for news topics, limited to EUnet. *Newsgroup*

7277 **eunet.news.group** Discussion on and proposals for new EUnet newsgroups. *Newsgroup*

➤ **eunet.politics:** (European) political discussions (and flames!). *Newsgroup*

7278 **eunet.sources** EUnet-wide (only!) group for posting sources. *Newsgroup*

➤ **Europe by Eurail:** "The Internet resource for traveling Europe by train." Plan your Eurail or BritRail vacation with ease. Rail-pass descriptions, trip planning tools, ticket and schedule database, and an online conference for asking travel questions and sharing experiences. (See entry 7830 for full listing.)

➤ **European Forest Institute:** This site provides information on the Institute and pointers to other forest and environmental resources on the Internet. (See entry 4607 for full listing.)

7279 **Information Market EUROPE:** I*M (Info Market)—WWW server from the EC (DGXIII) for supporting the European electronic information market.

http://www.echo.lu/

INFO webmaster@echo.lu

FAQS

http://www.echo.lu/echo/faqs/ted-faq.html
http://www.echo.lu/echo/faqs/echo-faq.html

➤ **JKU Info Service:** This is the campus information service of the Johannes Kepler University of Linz, Austria. (See entry 4430 for full listing.)

➤ **misc.transport.rail.europe:** Railroads and railways in all of Europe. *Newsgroup*

➤ **Novice-MZT (News from MZT):** News from the Ministry for Science and Technology of the Republic of Slovenia. (See entry 9441 for full listing.)

7280 **Organisation for Security and Co-operation in Europe (OSCE):** The Swiss presidency of the OSCE in 1996 provides a Web server with materials on the OSCE. Materials include basic texts, press communiques, reports on missions, and speeches of the Swiss foreign minister, as well as links to the foreign ministries of all OSCE states.

http://www.fsk.ethz.ch/osce/

INFO postmaster@sipo.reok.ethz.ch

7281 **rec.travel.europe** Travel in European travel. *Newsgroup*

7282 `soc.culture.albanian` Albania and Albanians around the world. *Newsgroup*

7283 `soc.culture.austria` Austria and its people. *Newsgroup*

7284 `soc.culture.europe` Discussing all aspects of all-European society. *Newsgroup*

7285 `talk.politics.european-union` The EU and political integration in Europe. *Newsgroup*

➤ **Vienna University of Economics CWIS:** Campus wide information service for Vienna University of Economics. (See entry 5213 for full listing.)

➤ **WELSH-L:** On the Welsh, Breton, and Cornish languages. (See entry 4266 for full listing.)

REGIONS & CULTURES—EUROPE—BALTICS

7286 **BALT-L:** On the Baltic republics. *Mailing List, moderated*
`http://www.ibs.ee/news/balt-l/`
± `listserv@listserv.rl.ac.uk` [body = SUBSCRIBE BALT-L first-name last-name]
± `listserv@ubvm.cc.buffalo.edu` [body = SUBSCRIBE BALT-L first-name last-name]
INFO EDITOR OWNER `a.e.b.bevan@open.ac.uk` (Edis Bevan)
INFO `jmyhg@uottawa.bitnet` (Jean-Michel Thizy)
Gated: `bit.listserv.balt-l`

➤ **NORDBALT:** About networking among Nordic and Baltic countries. (See entry 7618 for full listing.)

➤ **Scandinavian Indie:** The place for independent music coming from any Scandinavian country, plus the Baltic countries. (See entry 1206 for full listing.)

7287 `soc.culture.baltics` People of the Baltic states. *Newsgroup*

7288 `soc.culture.estonia` Estonian culture, language, news, politics. *Moderated newsgroup*

REGIONS & CULTURES—EUROPE—CENTRAL & EASTERN

➤ **HuDir — Hungarian Internet Directory:** HuDir is the largest and most complete hierarchical listing of all Hungarian Internet resources in the world, featuring approximately 3,000 URLs, and growing daily. (See entry 7319 for full listing.)

➤ **Academy of Sciences Slovakia CWIS:** CWIS of the Slovak Academy of Sciences, Bratislava, Slovakia. (See entry 4407 for full listing.)

➤ `alt.beograd:` City and people of Beograd (Belgrade, former Yugoslavia). *Newsgroup*

7289 `alt.news.macedonia` News concerning Macedonia in the Balkan region. *Newsgroup*

7290 `bit.listserv.e-europe` Eastern Europe business network. *Moderated newsgroup*

7291 `bit.listserv.euearn-l` Eastern Europe list. *Newsgroup*

7292 `bit.listserv.slovak-l` Slovak discussion list. *Newsgroup*

7293 **Carolina:** Student newsletter from the Czech Republic, "published" in the context of a reporting-and-editing workshop for journalism students. *Newsletter*
± `listserv@earn.cvut.cz` [body = Subscribe CAR-CS (for Czech version) or CAR-ENG (for English version) first-name last-name]
INFO `carolina@cuni.cz` (Ludmila Truneckova or Jan Jirak)
ARCHIVE `gopher.cuni.cz`
Language: English and Czech
Frequency: weekly during term-time; biweekly during vacations

➤ **Central European Environmental Data Request Facility (CEDAR):** All about environmental resources and organizations in central and Eastern Europe, as well as many environmental online databases (INFOTERR, DANIS, HABITAT, etc.) (See entry 4633 for full listing.)

➤ **CEP-ANNOUNCE:** On the Civic Education Project: strengthening democracy in central and Eastern Europe and the NIS through the revitalization of the social sciences in universities and institutes of higher education. (See entry 5276 for full listing.)

7294 **CERRO-L:** On research of the central Europe region. *Mailing List*
± listserv@aearn.aco.net [body = SUBSCRIBE CERRO-L first-name last-name]
INFO cerro-l-request@aearn.aco.net
ARCHIVE listserv@aearn.aco.net [body = INDEX CERRO-L]
Gated: wu.mail.cerro-l

7295 **CET-ONLINE:** Central Europe Today News Service: politics, business, daily life. *Distribution List*
± cet-online-request@eunet.cz
INFO cet-info@eunet.cz
OWNER hewes@traveller.cz (Cameron M. Hewes)
ARCHIVE cet-online-request@eunet.cz

➤ **clari.biz.stocks.report.europe.eastern:** Eastern European stock reports. *Moderated newsgroup*

7296 **clari.world.europe.central** Poland, Czech Republic, Slovakia, Hungary. *Moderated newsgroup*

7297 **clari.world.europe.eastern** Translated reports from eastern Europe. *Moderated newsgroup*

7298 **E-List:** News and discussion on Estonia. *Mailing List, moderated*
± INFO jaak.vilo@cs.helsinki.fi (Jaak Vilo)
ARCHIVE http://muhu.cs.helsinki.fi/
Language: Estonian & English
Please Note: Subscription by approval only.

➤ **Eastern European Jewish History (EEJH):** Forum for discussion of historical, archaeological, linguistic, cultural, genealogical, and genetic evidence on the Jewish people of eastern Europe from Greco-Roman times to the present. (See entry 5245 for full listing.)

➤ **EE-ECON:** On general economic issues in central and Eastern Europe, and in the NIS. (See entry 5195 for full listing.)

➤ **EE-HIGHER-ED:** On higher education in central and Eastern Europe, and in the NIS. (See entry 4192 for full listing.)

➤ **EE-JOBS:** On employment opportunities in Eastern and central Europe, and in the NIS. (See entry 7596 for full listing.)

➤ **EE-WOMEN:** On women's issues in central and Eastern Europe, and in the NIS. (See entry 10155 for full listing.)

➤ **eeurope-business:** For doing business in eastern Europe. (See entry 1796 for full listing.)

➤ **ekonomika:** On the Czech economy. (See entry 5201 for full listing.)

➤ **EUEARN-L:** On eastern European telecommunications. (See entry 9628 for full listing.)

➤ **EUnet Czechia:** This is the information service of EUnet Czechia, the network service provider in the Czech Republic. This site also contains information about top-level domain .cz (See entry 7265 for full listing.)

➤ **The Khazaria Info Center:** These pages explore the history of the Khazar Jewish empire in southern Russia (650–1016). Many links to other important Jewish, historical, eastern European, and miscellaneous sites are also provided. (See entry 8811 for full listing.)

7299 **Mailing Lists:** Information on mailing lists from southern Slavic countries. *Mailing List*
http://www.krpan.arnes.si/krpan
± INFO mailing-lists@krpan.arnes.si

➤ **MEK-L:** Issues related to the Hungarian Electronic Library project. (See entry 5754 for full listing.)

7300 **MIDEUR-L:** About middle Europe. *Mailing List*
± listserv@ubvm.cc.buffalo.edu [body = SUBSCRIBE MIDEUR-L first-name last-name]
INFO mideur-l-request@ubvm.cc.buffalo.edu
ARCHIVE listserv@ubvm.cc.buffalo.edu [body = INDEX MIDEUR-L]

Gated: `bit.listserv.mideur-l`

➤ **NT-INFO:** Hungarians on Windows NT. (See entry 2671 for full listing.)

➤ **OMRI Economic Digest:** Coverage of economic developments in the former Soviet Union and east-central and southeastern Europe. (See entry 5207 for full listing.)

7301 **romanians:** Discussions, news, and information in the Romanian language. *Mailing List*

± `listproc@sep.stanford.edu` [body = SUBSCRIBE ROMANIANS first-name last-name]

INFO `mihai@sep.stanford.edu` (Mihai Popovici)

ARCHIVE `listproc@sep.stanford.edu` [body = get romanians *yymmdd* where *yy* is the year *mm* is month and *dd* is the day]

Language: Romanian, English

➤ **SEELANGS:** On Slavic and eastern European languages and literatures. (See entry 5305 for full listing.)

7302 `soc.culture.bulgaria` Discussing Bulgarian society. *Newsgroup*

7303 `soc.culture.romanian` Discussion of Romanian and Moldavian people. *Newsgroup*

➤ **SUSDEV:** On sustainable development in Eastern Europe. (See entry 4660 for full listing.)

REGIONS & CULTURES—FRANCE

7304 `clari.world.europe.france` News of France and Monaco. *Moderated newsgroup*

7305 `clari.world.europe.france.biz` French business news. *Moderated newsgroup*

➤ **Cybersphere:** French magazine on cyberculture: corporate philosophical bent. (See entry 9820 for full listing.)

7306 `soc.culture.french` French culture, history, and related discussions. *Newsgroup*

REGIONS & CULTURES—GERMANY

➤ **German Climate Computer Center (DKRZ):** This is the German Climate Computing Center (Deutsches Klimarechenzentrum, DKRZ) providing resources and information in the area of climate research. This includes lists of climate data sets, weather maps, parallel computing information, and more. (See entry 4568 for full listing.)

7307 **9NOV89-L:** On the fall of the Berlin Wall. *Mailing List*

± `listserv@listserv.gmd.de` [body = SUBSCRIBE 9NOV89-L first-name last-name]

INFO `9nov89-l-request@listserv.gmd.de`

ARCHIVE `listserv@listserv.gmd.de` [body = INDEX 9NOV89-L]

Gated: `bit.listserv.9nov89-l`

➤ **AATG:** For the academic community, especially teaching professionals of German. (See entry 4243 for full listing.)

➤ **Akademische Software Kooperation:** ASK-SISY: a database of higher-education software; ASK-SINA: searching all German FTP sites via WWW ASKnet: distributing commercial software at special retail prices to the higher-education community. (See entry 4481 for full listing.)

➤ `alt.usage.german:` Questions and answers about the German language. *Newsgroup*

7308 `clari.world.europe.germany` News of Germany. *Moderated newsgroup*

7309 `clari.world.europe.germany.biz` German business news. *Moderated newsgroup*

➤ **Dresden University of Technology/ Department of Computer Science:** This is the information service of the Department of Computer Science, Dresden University of Technology, Germany. (See entry 9191 for full listing.)

7310 **EUnet Germany Information Service:** This is the information service of EUnet Germany, a network-services provider. It includes a large software archive and a German zip-code finder.

`http://www.germany.eu.net/`

INFO `webmaster@germany.eu.net`

MIRROR `http://surf.germany.eu.net/`

7311 **GER-RUS:** On Germans from Russia. *Mailing List*

± listserv@vm1.nodak.edu [body = SUBSCRIBE GER-RUS first-name last-name]
INFO mmmiller@badlands.nodak.edu (Michael Miller)
ARCHIVE listserv@vm1.nodak.edu
Gated: bit.listserv.GER-RUS

➤ **German National Research Center for Information Technology (GMD):** Home page of GMD, an institute that does research in many branches of information technology. (See entry 9365 for full listing.)

➤ **Heidelberg University Information Server:** This is the CWIS of the University of Heidelberg, Germany. It consists of several WWW/gopher/WAIS servers; the main entrance is the central WWW/gopher server at the University Computing Center (URZ). It includes a database of a complete inventory of the Greek papyri of Egypt. (See entry 4424 for full listing.)

➤ **HTWS Zittau/Görlitz:** Campus Wide Information Service for HTWS Zittau/Görlitz; also includes local area tourism, and business information. (See entry 4425 for full listing.)

➤ **INETBIB:** On integrating the Internet into German libraries. (See entry 5748 for full listing.)

7312 `soc.culture.german` Discussions about German culture and history. *Newsgroup*

REGIONS & CULTURES—GREECE

➤ **AEK-L:** On the AEK Greek Team—worldwide fans' list. (See entry 6673 for full listing.)

7313 `bit.listserv.hellas` The Hellenic discussion list. *Moderated newsgroup*

7314 `clari.world.europe.greece` News of Greece. *Moderated newsgroup*

7315 **HELLAS:** To exchange news and information of Greece and Greeks at home and abroad. *Mailing List*
http://velox.stanford.edu/hellas
± listserv@uga.cc.uga.edu [body = SUBSCRIBE HELLAS first-name last-name]
INFO sliolis@utcvm.utc.edu (Spiros Liolis)
INFO george@pop.psu.edu (Nikos George)
INFO eh9174a@american.edu (Eleftherios Hazapis)
ARCHIVE ftp://ftp.american.edu/pub/listlogs/hellas
Language: Greek
Gated: Bit.Listserv.Hellas

7316 **MGSA-L:** For scholars of modern Greek culture, society and literature—of special interest to graduate students in Modern Greek studies. *Mailing List*
± listserv@cmsa.berkeley.edu [body = SUBSCRIBE MGSA-L first-name last-name]
INFO moore@qal.berkeley.edu

7317 `soc.culture.greek` Group about Greeks. *Newsgroup*

7318 **Thrace:** For Turkish-minority members of West Thracia (a province of Greece). *Mailing List*
± listserv@vm3090.ege.edu.tr [body = SUBSCRIBE THRACE first-name last-name]
INFO http://umbc9.umbc.edu/~kosmas/thrace_list.html
OWNER 924610ts@udcf.gla.ac.uk (Nihat Tsolak)
ARCHIVE listserv@vm3090.ege.edu.tr [body = INDEX Thrace]
Language: English, Turkish

REGIONS & CULTURES—HUNGARY

7319 **HuDir — Hungarian Internet Directory:** HuDir is the largest and most complete hierarchical listing of all Hungarian Internet resources in the world, featuring approximately 3,000 URLs, and growing daily.
http://www.hungary.com/hudir/
INFO hudir@hungary.com

7320 `bit.listserv.hungary` Hungarian discussion list. *Newsgroup*

7321 Hungarian Information Service (HIX): This is the largest Hungarian information system on the Internet, publishing more than 200 pages daily to 10,000 people in more than 45 countries. Includes daily news from Hungary and a Hungarian-English online dictionary.

```
http://hix.mit.edu/
gopher://hix.mit.edu/11/
```
INFO hollosi@hix.com

INFO help@hix.com

FAQ http://hix.mit.edu/hungarian-faq/

MIRROR gopher://hix.elte.hu/11/

7322 HUNGARY-REPORT: For weekly news of Hungary. *Newsletter*

± hungary-report-request@hungary.yak.net [body = SUBSCRIBE]

INFO info.hrep@isys.hu (infobot)

EDITOR OWNER bruner@ind.eunet.hu (Rick E. Bruner)

EDITOR jbrown@isys.hu (Jennifer Brown)

EDITOR fenyo@isys.hu (Krisztina Fenyo)

OWNER steve@isys.hu (Steven Carlson)

ARCHIVES
```
http://www.isys.hu/hrep/
ftp://ftp.isys.hu/pub/hrep/
```

7323 Hungary.Network — The GateWWWay to Hungary: Hungary.Network is the premier Internet presence provider in Hungary, providing corporate presence, publishing, and directory services on the Internet.

```
http://www.hungary.com/
info@hungary.com
help@hungary.com
market@hungary.com
```
INFO webmaster@hungary.com

7324 HuWho — Hungarian Who's Who Online: A growing list of Hungarian people and their home pages online.

```
http://www.hungary.com/huwho/
```
INFO huwho@hungary.com

➤ **KATALIST:** Information sources (CD-ROM, Internet, etc.) for Hungarian librarians. (See entry 5749 for full listing.)

7325 soc.culture.magyar The Hungarian people and their culture. *Newsgroup*

REGIONS & CULTURES—IBERIA

7326 alt.culture.astur Information about Asturies. *Newsgroup*

7327 bit.listserv.basque-l Basque culture list. *Moderated newsgroup*

7328 bit.listserv.catala Catalan discussion list. *Newsgroup*

7329 clari.world.europe.iberia Spain, Portugal, and Andorra. *Moderated newsgroup*

➤ **COMEDIA:** On Spanish Golden Age theater. (See entry 1619 for full listing.)

➤ **RedIRIS, CSIC, Spain:** RedIRIS is the Spanish Academic and Research Network (See entry 9554 for full listing.)

➤ soc.culture.catalan: The Catalan language and the lands where it is spoken. *Newsgroup*

7330 soc.culture.portuguese Discussion of the people of Portugal. *Newsgroup*

7331 soc.culture.spain Spain and the Spanish. *Newsgroup*

➤ **Universidad de Oviedo:** The WWW server of the University of Oviedo, Spain. You can get all information about the institution, studies, faculties, etc... (See entry 4465 for full listing.)

REGIONS & CULTURES—INDIA

7332 `alt.culture.karnataka` Culture and language of the Indian state of Karnataka. *Newsgroup*

7333 `alt.culture.us.asian-indian` Asian Indians in the U.S. and Canada. *Newsgroup*

7334 `alt.india.progressive` Progressive politics in the Indian subcontinent. *Moderated newsgroup*

7335 `clari.world.asia.india` News of India. *Moderated newsgroup*

➤ **darpan:** A literary magazine devoted to reflections on India, published by students at the University of Illinois at Urbana-Champaign. (See entry 614 for full listing.)

7336 **INDIA-D:** For discussion on the affairs of the Indian subcontinent. *Mailing List*
± `listserv@indnet.bgsu.edu` [body = SUBSCRIBE INDIA-D first-name last-name]
INFO `india-d-request@indnet.bgsu.edu`
ARCHIVE `listserv@indnet.bgsu.edu` [body = INDEX INDIA-D]

7337 **INDIA-L:** For news on the Indian subcontinent. *Mailing List*
± `listserv@indnet.bgsu.edu` [body = SUBSCRIBE INDIA-L first-name last-name]
INFO `india-l-request@indnet.bgsu.edu`
ARCHIVE `listserv@indnet.bgsu.edu` [body = INDEX INDIA-L]

7338 **INDIANS:** For Asian Indians in the central New York region, especially cultural activities. *Mailing List*
± `listserv@listserv.syr.edu` [body = SUBSCRIBE INDIANS first-name last-name]
INFO `skpandey@mailbox.syr.edu` (Sanjay K. Pandey)
INFO `dalia@cat.syr.edu` (Apurva F. Dalia)

7339 `misc.news.southasia` News from Bangladesh, India, Nepal, etc. *Moderated newsgroup*

7340 `rec.arts.movies.local.indian` Indian movies and the Indian film industry. *Newsgroup*

7341 `soc.culture.bengali` Socio-cultural identity of worldwide Bengali population. *Newsgroup*

7342 `soc.culture.indian` Group for discussion about India and things Indian. *Newsgroup*

7343 `soc.culture.indian.delhi` Information related to Delhi, capital of India. *Newsgroup*

7344 `soc.culture.indian.gujarati` Gujarati cultural group. *Newsgroup*

7345 `soc.culture.indian.info` Info group for soc.culture.indian, etc. *Moderated newsgroup*

7346 `soc.culture.indian.kerala` Culture of the people of Keralite origin. *Newsgroup*

7347 `soc.culture.indian.marathi` Discussion related to Marathi culture. *Newsgroup*

7348 `soc.culture.indian.telugu` The culture of the Telugu people of India. *Newsgroup*

7349 `soc.culture.punjab` Punjab and Punjabi culture. *Newsgroup*

7350 **Telugu Page :** About the Telugu region of India, its language, and its culture.
`http://www.engr.csulb.edu/~somanchi/index.html`
INFO `somanchi@engr.csulb.edu`

REGIONS & CULTURES—IRELAND

7351 `clari.world.europe.british_isles.ireland` News of Ireland. *Moderated newsgroup*

7352 `clari.world.europe.british_isles.uk.n-ireland` News of Northern Ireland. *Moderated newsgroup*

7353 `clari.world.europe.ireland` News of the Republic of Ireland. *Moderated newsgroup*

➤ **Classics Ireland:** Journal of Classical Association of Ireland, publishing articles on classics, ancient history, and archaeology. (See entry 5159 for full listing.)

7354 `ie.announce` Important announcements in Ireland. *Newsgroup*

7355 `ie.events` Events announcements in Ireland. *Newsgroup*

7356 `ie.followup` Follow-ups to articles in `ie.general`. *Newsgroup*

7357 `ie.general` General discussions for Ireland. *Newsgroup*

➤   `ie.jobs`: Job offerings in Ireland. *Newsgroup*

7358 `ie.net` News about the network in Ireland. *Newsgroup*

7359 `ie.news` News about network news in Ireland. *Newsgroup*

7360 `ie.news.group` New newsgroups discussion for `ie.*`. *Newsgroup*

➤   `ie.tex`: TeX discussions in Ireland. *Newsgroup*

➤   **IRISHLAW:** On Irish law (Ireland and Northern Ireland). (See entry 5551 for full listing.)

7361 **IRL-POL:** On current Irish politics. *Mailing List*
± `listserv@irlearn.ucd.ie` [body = SUBSCRIBE IRL-POL first-name last-name]
INFO `fin@educom.ie`
OWNER `fin@irlearn.ucd.ie`
ARCHIVE `listserv@irlearn.ucd.ie` [body = INDEX IRL-POL]
POST `irl-pol@irlearn.ucd.ie`

➤   **IRTRAD-L:** On Irish traditional music. (See entry 874 for full listing.)

➤   **MATHDEP:** For notices on mathematical science seminars in Ireland, and mathematics with some Irish connection. (See entry 9391 for full listing.)

➤   **ModBrits:** On modern British and Irish literature from 1895 to 1955. (See entry 618 for full listing.)

7362 `soc.culture.irish` Ireland and Irish culture. *Newsgroup*

REGIONS & CULTURES—ISRAEL

➤   **A - Z of Jewish & Israel Related Resources:** Large collection of Internet resources related to Jewish and Israeli issues. (See entry 8800 for full listing.)

➤   **A-Z-ANNOUNCE:** For announcements of new Jewish and Israel Web resources. (See entry 8801 for full listing.)

7363 **CJI:** Listings of computer jobs in Israel. *Newsletter*
± `listproc@jer1.co.il` [body = subscribe cji first-name last-name]
OWNER `jrichman@jr.co.il` (Jacob Richman)
OWNER `jrichman@jer1.co.il` (Jacob Richman)
ARCHIVE `listproc@jer1.co.il` [body = index cji]
Frequency: bi-weekly

7364 `clari.world.mideast.israel` News of Israel and occupied lands. *Moderated newsgroup*

➤   **Embassy of Israel - Washington, D.C.:** The official WWW site of the embassy of Israel to Washington, D.C. (See entry 5396 for full listing.)

7365 **IIRS:** For information retrieval specialists in Israel. *Mailing List*
± `listserv@taunivm.tau.ac.il` [body = SUBSCRIBE IIRS first-name last-name]
INFO `rafarber@weizmann.bitnet` (Miriam Farber)
ARCHIVE `listserv@taunivm.tau.ac.il`

7366 **IL-ADS:** Israel bulletin board for single-party, noncommercial advertisements, such as selling a personal car or computer, or providing piano lessons. *Mailing List*
± `listserv@vm.tau.ac.il` [body = SUBSCRIBE IL-ADS first-name last-name]
INFO `il-ads-request@vm.tau.ac.il`
Gated: `il.ads`

7367 `il.ads` Israel bulletin board for advertisements. *Newsgroup*

7368 `il.board` Israel bulletin board service. *Newsgroup*

➤   `il.cs.board`: Israeli computer science. *Newsgroup*

7369 `il.irc` Internet Relay Chat in Israel. *Newsgroup*

7370 **il.israeline** News summary from Israeli consulate, New York. *Moderated newsgroup*

7371 **il.jobs.misc** Employment, workplaces, careers in Israel. *Newsgroup*

7372 **il.jobs.resumes** Resumes and "situation wanted" ads for jobs in Israel. *Newsgroup*

7373 **il.net.failures** Israeli system and network failure annoucements. *Newsgroup*

7374 **il.news.admin** Israeli news administration. *Newsgroup*

➤ **il.novell:** Novell interest group in Israel. *Newsgroup*

7375 **il.talk** Israel general discussion forum. *Newsgroup*

7376 **israel.ads.personals** Ads of the personal kind. *Newsgroup*

7377 **israel.cs.board** Israel Computer Science Board. *Moderated newsgroup*

7378 **israel.irc** Internet Relay Chat, Israel. *Newsgroup*

7379 **israel.israeline** News summary from Israeli consulate, New York. *Moderated newsgroup*

7380 **israel.jobs.misc** Employment, workplaces, careers in Israel. *Newsgroup*

7381 **israel.jobs.offered** Announcements of positions available in Israel. *Newsgroup*

7382 **israel.jobs.resumes** Resumes and "situation wanted" ads for jobs in Israel. *Newsgroup*

7383 **israel.lists.il-ads** Israel bulletin board for advertisements. *Newsgroup*

7384 **israel.lists.il-board** Israel bulletin board service. *Newsgroup*

7385 **israel.lists.il-fail** Israeli system and network failure annoucements. *Newsgroup*

7386 **israel.lists.il-talk** Israel general discussion forum. *Newsgroup*

7387 **israel.news.admin** Israeli news administration and configuration. *Newsgroup*

7388 **israel.sport.football** Issues related to the game of football (soccer) in Israel. *Newsgroup*

7389 **israel.test** For testing on the israel.* hierarchy. *Newsgroup*

7390 **soc.culture.israel** Israel and Israelis. *Newsgroup*

7391 **Talknow:** Talking between Israeli and Palestinian K-12 students: peace, and no adults. *Mailing List, moderated*
± listproc@csf.colorado.edu
EDITOR mkragen@access.digex.net (Marshall Kragen)
EDITOR cabdullh@freenet.columbus.oh.us (Cheryl Abdullah)
EDITOR tshawish@cais.cais.com (Tony Shawish)
EDITOR fischela@elwha.evergreen.edu (Anne Fischel)
OWNER talknow@csf.colorado.edu

7392 **The World Wide Web server for Israel:** Directory to Internet resources in Israel.
http://www.ac.il/
INFO www@www.ac.il

REGIONS & CULTURES—ITALY

➤ **AIB-CUR:** On libraries in Italy. (See entry 5744 for full listing.)

➤ **alt.politics.italy:** Political happenings in Italy. *Newsgroup*

➤ **CILEA:** Italian network resources. (See entry 3213 for full listing.)

7393 **clari.world.europe.italy** News of Italy and San Marino. *Moderated newsgroup*

➤ **CNET-OP:** Information about CINECA (Italian research organization) and its networks (CINECAnet/GARR). (See entry 9450 for full listing.)

➤ **Darklava:** Darklava: The marvelous world of the fantastic is news from editors of science-fiction, fantasy, and horror books recent and upcoming in Italy. (See entry 1319 for full listing.)

7394 GARR-OP: For the network operation center of GARR. *Mailing List*
± listserv@vm.cineca.it [body = SUBSCRIBE GARR-OP first-name last-name]
INFO g.neri@cineca.it (Gabriele Neri)
Language: Italian
Please Note: Subscription by approval only.

➤ **ICGEBnet:** This is the information server of the International Center for Genetic Engineering and Biotechnology, Trieste, Italy. It carries molecular biology and biotechnology-related information. This site also contains information on safety aspects of biotechnology and of genetically modified organisms. (See entry 9113 for full listing.)

7395 La Piazza: ItNet: For links on Italian culture and technology.
http://www.it.net/whatsnew.html (What's New in Italy)
http://www.it.net/interest.html (ITnet News)
http://lapiazza.it.net/
INFO webmaster@it.net
INFO maurizio@it.net

➤ **MAIL-ITA:** Open discussion list used by everyone who has information or problem reports on Italian e-mail systems. (See entry 2407 for full listing.)

➤ **NIR-IT-L:** For computer network managers in Italy. (See entry 3260 for full listing.)

7396 soc.culture.italian The Italian people and their culture. *Newsgroup*

7397 What's new in Italy: Here you can find the latest novelties available on Italian WWW servers.
http://www.it.net/whatsnwe.html
INFO maurizio@it.net

REGIONS & CULTURES—JAPAN

7398 The X-Guide to Japan Information: Key information sources on Japan currently available over the Internet.
http://fuji.stanford.edu/XGUIDE/
INFO jguide@fuji.stanford.edu

7399 alt.japanese.text Postings in Japanese; Japanese-language software. *Newsgroup*

7400 bit.listserv.japan Japanese business and economics network. *Moderated newsgroup*

7401 clari.world.asia.japan News of Japan. *Moderated newsgroup*

7402 clari.world.asia.japan.biz Japanese business news. *Moderated newsgroup*

7403 comp.research.japan The nature of research in Japan. *Moderated newsgroup*

7404 fj.announce *important* and timely announcements of interest to all. *Newsgroup*

7405 fj.archives.answers Repository for FAQ (Frequently Asked Questions). *Newsgroup*

➤ **fj.editor.mule:** Discussion about Mule. *Newsgroup*

➤ **fj.engr.arch:** Topics about architecture. *Newsgroup*

7406 fj.fleamarket.* Japanese for-sale groups. *Newsgroup*

➤ **fj.jokes:** Jokes and humor. *Newsgroup*

➤ **fj.jokes.d:** Discussion about jokes. *Newsgroup*

7407 fj.kanakan.misc Discussion about kana-kanji henkan. *Newsgroup*

7408 fj.kanakan.wnn Discussion about Wnn kana-kanji henkan system. *Newsgroup*

7409 fj.life.in-japan Topics on life of foreigners in Japan. *Newsgroup*

➤ **fj.life.money:** Discussions on handling money. *Newsgroup*

➤ **fj.living:** Discussions about various things in daily life. *Newsgroup*

7410 fj.misc.earthquake Information about earthquake. *Newsgroup*

7411   `fj.net.infosystems.announce` Announcements of information systems. *Newsgroup*

➤   `fj.net.media.ethernet`: The Ethernet/IEEE 802.3 protocols. *Newsgroup*

7412   `fj.net.providers` Discussion on network service providers. *Newsgroup*

7413   `fj.news.net-abuse` Charter is here! *Newsgroup*

7414   `fj.org.ipsj` Topics about Information Processing Society of Japan. *Newsgroup*

7415   `fj.personal-ads.friends` Requests for friends. *Newsgroup*

7416   `fj.personal-ads.misc` Nonprofit personal advertisements. *Newsgroup*

7417   `fj.personal-ads.penpals` Requests for pen pals. *Newsgroup*

➤   `fj.rec.fishing`: Topics about fishing. *Newsgroup*

7418   `fj.rec.idol` General topics about idols. *Newsgroup*

➤   `fj.rec.movies`: Reviews and discussions of movies. *Newsgroup*

➤   `fj.rec.sf`: Discussion about science fiction. *Newsgroup*

➤   `fj.rec.smoking`: Smoking as a hobby and/or recreation. *Newsgroup*

7419   `fj.rec.travel.japan` Traveling in Japan. *Newsgroup*

➤   `fj.sci.human-factors`: Discussion about human factors and ergonomics. *Newsgroup*

➤   `fj.soc.copyright`: Discussion about copyright. *Newsgroup*

7420   `fj.soc.culture` Group about Japanese culture. *Newsgroup*

7421   `fj.soc.economy` Topics about economy and economic policies. *Newsgroup*

➤   `fj.soc.environment`: Talks about natural environment and society. *Newsgroup*

➤   `fj.soc.law`: Topics on law and rights. *Newsgroup*

➤   `fj.soc.media`: Discussions on the social aspects of media for communication including broadcasting, publishing, etc. *Newsgroup*

➤   `fj.soc.smoking`: About smoking issues and manners. *Newsgroup*

7422   `fj.soc.war-and-peace` Discussion about war and peace. *Newsgroup*

➤   `fj.sources`: For the posting of software packages and documentation. *Newsgroup*

7423   `fj.wanted` Requests for things that are needed. *Newsgroup*

7424   `iijnet.dcom.carrier` Discussions about carriers in Japan. *Newsgroup*

7425   `iijnet.real-estate` Information of real estate in important areas in Japan. *Newsgroup*

7426   `il.jobs.offered` Announcements of positions available in Israel. *Newsgroup*

7427   **ISSHO:** For the Issho Kikaku (Project Together): internationalization of Japanese culture. *Mailing List, moderated*
`http://www.ishiilab.dnj.ynu.ac.jp/~Alberto/issho/`
± `listproc@ishiilab.dnj.ynu.ac.jp` [body = SUBSCRIBE ISSHO first-name last-name]
OWNER `alberto@ishiilab.dnj.ynu.ac.jp` (Alberto Tomita,Jr.)
ARCHIVE `ftp://ftp.ishiilab.dnj.ynu.ac.jp/pub/issho/`
FAQ `ftp://ftp.ishiilab.dnj.ynu.ac.jp/pub/issho/`

7428   **Japan from the View of a Frog - an Art Journey:** Explore a less known—and humorous—side of Japan through a journey of the world of Japanese arts and crafts.
`http://www.japancrafts.com/cafe`
INFO `hanske@pobox.com`
MIRROR `http://www.webcom.com/cafe`
Comments: Presented by Internet Cafe (Tokyo) Japan - a cross culture marketing company.

7429   **Japan Window:** A U.S.-Japan collaboration for Internet-based Japan information.

```
http://jw.nttam.com/
http://jw.stanford.edu/
INFO jw@fuji.stanford.edu
```

➤ **JTIT-L:** For Japanese teachers and instructional technology. (See entry 4252 for full listing.)

7430 `kanto.meetings.enkai` About enkai. *Newsgroup*

7431 `kanto.misc.recycle` About recycling. *Newsgroup*

7432 `kanto.news.followup` Follow-ups to articles in `kanto.news.general`. *Newsgroup*

7433 `kanto.news.general` Announcements for Kanto newsgroups. *Newsgroup*

7434 `kanto.news.group` About Kanto newsgroups. *Newsgroup*

7435 `kanto.rec.food` About food. *Newsgroup*

7436 `kanto.rec.misc` About hobbies not covered elsewhere. *Newsgroup*

7437 `kanto.town.akihabara` About Akihabara. *Newsgroup*

7438 `kanto.town.misc` About towns not covered elsewhere. *Newsgroup*

➤ **Kid's Window:** A multimedia resource for children to learn about Japanese language and culture. (See entry 9731 for full listing.)

➤ **National Cancer Center, Tokyo, Japan:** Information service for the National Cancer Center in Tokyo, Japan. (See entry 4737 for full listing.)

7439 `okinawa.*` Newsgroups for Okinawa, Japan. *Newsgroup*

7440 `okinawa.books` Talk about books and bookstores. *Newsgroup*

7441 `okinawa.chat` Chat (we Okinawan say it *"yuntaku"*). *Newsgroup*

➤ `okinawa.comp.misc:` General topics about computers not covered elsewhere. *Newsgroup*

7442 `okinawa.events` Entertainments, meetings, and other events. *Newsgroup*

7443 `okinawa.food.misc` Talk about foods. *Newsgroup*

7444 `okinawa.general` Topics concerned with all members who read `okinawa.*`. *Newsgroup*

7445 `okinawa.life.misc` Talk about restaurants, shortcuts, sell and buy. *Newsgroup*

7446 `okinawa.mail-lists.nirai-kanai` Gateway for Nirai-Kanai mailing list. *Newsgroup*

7447 `okinawa.misc` DIscussions that match no other groups. *Newsgroup*

7448 `okinawa.networks` Talk about networks. *Newsgroup*

7449 `okinawa.networks.bbs` Talk about BBSs in Okinawa. *Newsgroup*

7450 `okinawa.networks.isdn` Talk about ISDNs in Okinawa. *Newsgroup*

7451 `okinawa.networks.uucp` Talk about UUCPs in Okinawa. *Newsgroup*

7452 `okinawa.news.groups` Discussions and lists of newsgroups of `okinawa.*`. *Newsgroup*

7453 `okinawa.news.usage` How to use the newsgroup `okinawa.*`. *Newsgroup*

7454 `okinawa.recycle` For sale, requests for need and give. *Newsgroup*

➤ `sci.lang.japan:` The Japanese language, both spoken and written. *Newsgroup*

➤ `sci.lang.translation:` Problems and concerns of translators/interpreters. *Newsgroup*

7455 `soc.culture.japan` Everything Japanese, except the Japanese language. *Newsgroup*

7456 **Social Science Japan:** From the Institute of Social Science, University of Tokyo—provides information in English on key people, important literature, and recent developments in four fields of social science research on Japan: economics, political science, law, and sociology. *Newsletter*

```
http://www.iss.u-tokyo.ac.jp/center/SSJ.html
INFO ssjinfo@iss.u-tokyo.ac.jp
```

Frequency: twice a year

7457 `tnn.culture.kansai` Discussion on Kansai culture. *Newsgroup*

7458 `tnn.examination` Information on qualifying examinations, etc. *Newsgroup*

7459 `tnn.foods.kansai` Information about foods and restaurants in Kansai area. *Newsgroup*

7460 `tnn.foods.tokyo` Information about foods and restaurants in Tokyo. *Newsgroup*

7461 `tnn.forsale` Short, tasteful postings about items for sale. *Newsgroup*

7462 `tnn.forum.global-brain` Information from Japan Computer Access (JCA). *Moderated newsgroup*

7463 `tnn.forum.hello-tokyo` Tokyo Internet forum "Hello! TOKYO". *Moderated newsgroup*

7464 `tnn.forum.ventures` Venture and new-business newsgroup. *Moderated newsgroup*

7465 `tnn.general` General interest to readers in tnn. *Newsgroup*

7466 `tnn.horoscope` Weekly fortune-telling. *Moderated newsgroup*

7467 `tnn.internauts` Announcement, requests, etc. about people on the Internet. *Newsgroup*

7468 `tnn.interv-e` InterVnet in English. *Newsgroup*

7469 `tnn.interv.info` Information on InterVnet. *Moderated newsgroup*

7470 `tnn.interv.linktech` Technical discussion on linking BBS to InterVnet. *Newsgroup*

7471 `tnn.interv.misc` Miscellaneous discussion on InterVnet. *Newsgroup*

7472 `tnn.interv.volunteers.wanted` Volunteers to be wanted. *Newsgroup*

7473 `tnn.interv.volunteers.wanted.quake` Earthquake-related volunteers to be wanted. *Newsgroup*

7474 `tnn.jobs` Professional positions offered. *Newsgroup*

7475 `tnn.living` Topics and discussions about various things in daily life. *Newsgroup*

7476 `tnn.living.child-care` Discussions about child care for workers. *Newsgroup*

7477 `tnn.netnews` Discussions about net news software, systems, etc. *Newsgroup*

7478 `tnn.netnews.stats` News-related statistics and lists. *Moderated newsgroup*

7479 `tnn.newsgroups` Discussions and lists of newsgroups. *Newsgroup*

7480 `tnn.newsite` Posting new site announcements. *Newsgroup*

7481 `tnn.questions` Questions about miscellaneous subjects. *Newsgroup*

7482 `tnn.real-estate` Information of real estate in important area in Japan. *Newsgroup*

7483 `tnn.wanted` Requests for things that are needed. *Newsgroup*

REGIONS & CULTURES—KOREA

➤ `alt.politics.korea`: A forum for Korean politics. *Moderated newsgroup*

7484 `clari.world.asia.koreas` News of North and South Korea. *Moderated newsgroup*

7485 `han.announce` Announcement to all Korean Usenet subscribers. *Newsgroup*

7486 `han.answers` FAQ and periodic articles of `han.*` newsgroups. *Moderated newsgroup*

7487 `han.comp.hangul` How Korean Hangul can be used in computers. *Newsgroup*

➤ `han.comp.questions`: General question/answer about computer technology/science. *Newsgroup*

7488 `han.misc.forsale` Things for sale, wanted to buy. *Newsgroup*

7489 `han.net.misc` News for other networks and BBSs in Korea. *Newsgroup*

7490 `han.net.services` Internet services in Korea, Q/A and discussion. *Newsgroup*

7491 `han.news.admin` Usenet administration, distribution, new group discussion. *Newsgroup*

7492 `han.news.stats` Statistics and reports on Korean news servers. *Newsgroup*

7493 `han.news.users` Usenet users, new user question/discussion. *Newsgroup*

7494 `mex.politica` Mexican politics. *Newsgroup*

7495 `soc.culture.korean` Discussions about Korea and things Korean. *Newsgroup*

REGIONS & CULTURES—MEXICO

7496 `alt.mexico` The people of Central America's largest nation. *Newsgroup*

7497 `clari.world.americas.mexico` News of Mexico. *Moderated newsgroup*

7498 **Coyuntura:** Mexican political, social, and economic analysis. From the Instituto de Estudios de la Revolucion Democratica. *Magazine*
http://csgrs6k2.uwaterloo.ca/coyuntur/home.html
± INFO OWNER cynthia@mail.internet.com.mx (Cynthia Litchi)
ARCHIVE cynthia@mail.internet.com.mx (Cynthia Litchi)
Language: Spanish
Frequency: monthly

➤ **ITESM - Campus Ciudad de Mexico:** Information on the Institute of Technology and Higher Education of Monterrey, Mexico City campus (Instituto Tecnologico y de Estudios Superiores de Monterrey, Campus Ciudad de Mexico). (See entry 4427 for full listing.)

7499 `mex.artes` Mexican arts, music, etc. *Newsgroup*

7500 `mex.artes.musica` Mexican music. *Newsgroup*

7501 `mex.ciencia` Science and technology-related topics. *Newsgroup*

7502 `mex.comp` Computer-related issues. *Newsgroup*

7503 `mex.deportes` Sports. *Newsgroup*

7504 `mex.edu` Issues about education. *Newsgroup*

7505 `mex.empresarial` Entrepreneurs and private sector. *Newsgroup*

7506 `mex.general` Messages of a general nature. *Newsgroup*

7507 `mex.general.anuncios` All types of announcements. *Newsgroup*

7508 `mex.indigena` Topics about indigenous people. *Newsgroup*

7509 `mex.joven` Mexican newsgroup on youth issues. *Newsgroup*

7510 `mex.noticias` News and only news. *Moderated newsgroup*

7511 `mex.noticias.disc` Discussion about the news reported in `mex.noticias`. *Newsgroup*

7512 `mex.productividad` Productivity issues on all walks of life. *Newsgroup*

7513 `mex.rec` Recreation and entertainment. *Newsgroup*

7514 `mex.rec.chistes` Jokes and humor. *Newsgroup*

7515 `mex.red` Discussions about the net and new groups in Mexico. *Newsgroup*

7516 `mex.tradiciones` Mexican traditions and folklore. *Newsgroup*

7517 `mex.tradiciones.cocina` Mexican cooking. *Newsgroup*

7518 `mex.turismo` Tourism-related information. *Newsgroup*

7519 **Mexico City:** Web guide to Mexico City.
http://www.ccm.itesm.mx/~lrincon/mexico/ciudad.html
INFO ldelrinc@campus.ccm.itesm.mx

7520 **Mexico Information Page:** Thoughtful list of links on Mexican culture, politics, sports, and education.
http://gaia.ecs.csus.edu/~arellano/index.html

INFO `arellanolr@csus.edu`

7521 **soc.culture.mexican** Discussion of Mexico's society. *Newsgroup*

7522 **soc.culture.mexican.american** Mexican-American/Chicano culture and issues. *Newsgroup*

7523 **Zapatistas in Cyberspace:** For net sources of information and news on Chiapas and the Zapatistas.
`http://www.eco.utexas.edu/Homepages/Faculty/Cleaver/chiapas95.html`
INFO `hmcleave@mundo.eco.utexas.edu`

REGIONS & CULTURES—MIDDLE EAST & NORTH AFRICA

7524 <u>Arab Countries WWW Site</u>: Links to sites covering all countries in the Arab world.
`http://www.liii.com/~hajeri/arab.html`
INFO `hajeri@liii.com`

7525 <u>The Middle East-North Africa Internet Resource Guide</u>: Internet resources dealing with the Middle East, which for this resource guide includes Mauritania, Pakistan, Somalia, and the Central Asian republics.
`http://www.lib.umich.edu/chhome.html`
`http://http2.sils.umich.edu/~lou/chhome.html`
`ftp://una.hh.lib.umich.edu/inetdirsstacks/mideastnafrica:roberts`
`gopher://una.hh.lib.umich.edu/11/inetdirs`
INFO `joseph.roberts@m.cc.utah.edu` (Joseph W. Roberts)

7526 **alt.culture.saudi** The life and times of the people of Saudi Arabia. *Newsgroup*

7527 **alt.malta** The Mediterranean Maltese Islands. *Newsgroup*

➤ **Arab Trade:** A group of companies helping businesses worldwide increase their business in the Arabian Gulf and the Middle East by finding agents, partners, and distributors for their products. (See entry 1790 for full listing.)

7528 **AWAIR (Arab World & Islamic Resources):** Educational materials created to expand awareness and appreciation for Arabic and Islamic culture.
`http://www.telegraphave.com/gui/awairproductinfo.html`
INFO `gui@dnai.com`

7529 **clari.world.mideast** News from the Middle East. *Moderated newsgroup*

7530 **clari.world.mideast.arabia** News of the Arabian Peninsula. *Moderated newsgroup*

7531 **clari.world.mideast.egypt** News of Egypt. *Moderated newsgroup*

7532 **clari.world.mideast.iran** News of Iran. *Moderated newsgroup*

7533 **clari.world.mideast.iraq** News of Iraq. *Moderated newsgroup*

7534 **clari.world.mideast.kuwait** News of Kuwait. *Moderated newsgroup*

7535 **clari.world.mideast.misc** News of other Middle Eastern countries. *Moderated newsgroup*

7536 **clari.world.mideast.palestine** News of the West Bank and Gaza. *Moderated newsgroup*

7537 **clari.world.mideast.turkey** News of Turkey. *Moderated newsgroup*

7538 **Iranian Cultural and Information Center:** Materials related to Iran and to Persian culture.
`http://tehran.stanford.edu/`
`ftp://tehran.stanford.edu`
INFO `webmaster@tehran.stanford.edu` (Farhad Shakeri)

➤ **Isfahan Online:** Architectural guide and "walking tour" of the city of Isfahan, Iran. (See entry 8792 for full listing.)

7539 **ITISALAT:** On Arabic computing. *Mailing List*
± `listserv@guvm.ccf.georgetown.edu` [body = SUBSCRIBE ITISALAT first-name last-name]
INFO `itisalat-request@listserv.georgetown.edu`
INFO OWNER `roochnik@ios.com` (Paul Roochnik)
ARCHIVE `listserv@guvm.ccf.georgetown.edu` [body = INDEX ITISALAT]

7540 Kuwait Information Page: A site providing pages of information about Kuwait useful to travelers and researchers.
http://www.cs.cmu.edu/~anwar/kuwait.html
http://www.kuwait.org/
INFO anwar+@cs.cmu.edu

7541 Kuwait-list: A mailing list for Kuwaitis and longtime residents of Kuwait on the Internet. *Mailing List*
± kuwait-list-request@cs.cmu.edu [body = SUBSCRIBE KUWAIT-LIST e-mail-address]
INFO anwar+kulist@cs.cmu.edu (Anwar M. Ghuloum)
Language: English,Arabic

➤ **The Occupation of Kuwait: Legacy of Pain:** A site documenting in words, pictures, and video the human-rights violations and environmental tragedy suffered by Kuwaitis during Iraq's occupation of Kuwait. (See entry 10029 for full listing.)

7542 soc.culture.algeria From A to Z about Algeria. *Newsgroup*

7543 soc.culture.arabic Technological and cultural issues, *not* politics. *Newsgroup*

7544 soc.culture.assyrian Assyrian culture, history, language, current diaspora. *Newsgroup*

7545 soc.culture.berber The Berber language, history, and culture. *Newsgroup*

7546 soc.culture.egyptian Egypt, and its society, culture, heritage, etc. *Newsgroup*

7547 soc.culture.iranian Discussions about Iran and things Iranian/Persian. *Newsgroup*

7548 soc.culture.iraq Iraq, its society, culture, and heritage. *Newsgroup*

7549 soc.culture.jordan All topics concerning the Hashemite Kingdom of Jordan. *Newsgroup*

7550 soc.culture.kuwait Kuwaiti culture, society, and history. *Newsgroup*

7551 soc.culture.lebanon Discussion about things Lebanese. *Newsgroup*

7552 soc.culture.liberia The culture of Liberia. *Newsgroup*

7553 soc.culture.maghreb North African society and culture. *Newsgroup*

7554 soc.culture.palestine Palestinian people, culture, and politics. *Newsgroup*

7555 soc.culture.syria Syrian cultural matters and affairs. *Newsgroup*

7556 talk.politics.mideast Discussion and debate over Middle Eastern events. *Newsgroup*

7557 TSC-L: Distribution of information on the Tunisian Scientific Consortium (TSC). *Distribution List*
http://www.rennes.enst-bretagne.fr/~hamdi/TSC.html
± tsc-bd@me.umn.edu
INFO jomaa@utkux4.utcc.utk.edu
Language: English, French and transliterated Arabic
Please Note: Subscription by approval only.

REGIONS & CULTURES—NETHERLANDS

7558 The Dutch Home Pages: The most interesting and useful links related to the Netherlands.
http://www.eeb.ele.tue.nl/dhp/index.html
INFO dhp@eeb.ele.tue.nl

➤ **InfoLink's Ondernemersdisk/Business Disk Online:** A bimonthly Web magazine for Dutch and international small business owners. (See entry 2068 for full listing.)

➤ **NEDER-L:** An e-journal for the study of Dutch language and literature. (See entry 620 for full listing.)

7559 soc.culture.netherlands People from the Netherlands and Belgium. *Newsgroup*

7560 STUNET-L: A place for Dutch students (or those who feel akin) to freely discuss just about any subject. *Mailing List*
± listserv@nic.surfnet.nl [body = SUBSCRIBE STUNET-L first-name last-name]
INFO owner-stunet-l@nic.surfnet.nl

ARCHIVE `listserv@nic.surfnet.nl` [body = INDEX STUNET-L]

Language: Dutch, English

7561 SURFnet InfoServices: SURFnet is the National Research Network Organisation of the Netherlands. The SURFnet WWW and gopher information servers contain documents and publications from SURFnet and affiliated organizations. InfoServices also maintains an FTP and mirror archive. The SURFnet server also provides access to all Dutch network resources accessible through NL-menu (Dutch National Entry Point) and subject access to Internet resources. The services are maintained by an editorial board staffed by the National Library of the Netherlands: the Koninklijke Bibliotheek.

`http://www.nic.surfnet.nl/infoserv.eng/` (English)

`http://www.nic.surfnet.nl/nlmenu/nlmenu.html` (NL-menu, Dutch)

`http://www.nic.surfnet.nl/nlmenu.eng/nlmenu.html` (NL-menu, English)

`http://www.nic.surfnet.nl/` (Dutch)

`ftp://ftp.nic.surfnet.nl`

`gopher://gopher.nic.surfnet.nl`

INFO `infoservices@surfnet.nl`

MIRROR `ftp://ftp.nic.surfnet.nl/mirror-archive/`

REGIONS & CULTURES—NEW ZEALAND

7562 `clari.world.oceania.new_zealand` News of New Zealand. *Moderated newsgroup*

➤ **Deep South:** An interdisciplinary journal run by the graduate students of the English department at the University of Otago in Dunedin, New Zealand. (See entry 5277 for full listing.)

➤ **Electronic Journal of Australian and New Zealand History:** Historical documents and new work on Australian and New Zealand history. (See entry 7090 for full listing.)

➤ **Internet Australasia:** Print and Web-based magazine dealing with all aspects of the Internet in Australia, New Zealand, and Asia. (See entry 7091 for full listing.)

➤ `misc.transport.rail.australia-nz`: Railways in Australia and New Zealand. *Newsgroup*

7563 `nz.archives` Announcements of available software. *Newsgroup*

7564 `nz.arts` Discussion on the arts. *Newsgroup*

7565 `nz.biz.misc` Moderated group for commercial postings. *Moderated newsgroup*

7566 `nz.biz.misc.discuss` Discussions arising from postings in `nz.biz.misc`. *Newsgroup*

➤ `nz.comp`: Computing and computers. *Newsgroup*

7567 `nz.general` General information, announcements, etc. *Newsgroup*

7568 `nz.net.announce` Status of local and international networks. *Moderated newsgroup*

7569 `nz.netstatus` Status of local and international net links. *Newsgroup*

7570 `nz.org.isocnz` The Internet Society of New Zealand. *Newsgroup*

7571 `nz.org.net-society` Discussions relating to the Net Society of New Zealand. *Newsgroup*

7572 `nz.politics` Politics in New Zealand. *Newsgroup*

7573 `nz.rec` Recreation. *Newsgroup*

7574 `nz.soc` Social issues. *Newsgroup*

7575 `nz.soc.green` Environmental issues. *Newsgroup*

7576 `nz.wanted` Requests for sources, information. *Newsgroup*

7577 `soc.culture.new-zealand` Discussion of topics related to New Zealand. *Newsgroup*

➤ **Victoria Univeristy of Wellington New Zealand:** This CWIS contains information about departments, staff, and courses offered at Victoria University of Wellington. (See entry 4468 for full listing.)

REGIONS & CULTURES—OCEANIA

7578 `alt.culture.french-polynesia` The culture and tourism of French Polynesia. *Newsgroup*

➤ `alt.culture.virtual.oceania:` Oceania project discussion and news. *Moderated newsgroup*

7579 `clari.world.oceania` News of Oceania. *Moderated newsgroup*

7580 **Michael Ogden's WWW Things:** Links to resources in, on, or about the Pacific Islands, including the countries and territories of Melanesia, Micronesia, and Polynesia.
`http://www2.hawaii.edu/usr-cgi/ssis/~ogden/ogden-pacintro.html`
`http://www2.hawaii.edu/usr-cgi/ssis/~ogden/ogden-newpacific.html`
INFO `ogden@hawaii.edu`

7581 `soc.culture.pacific-island` Culture of the Pacific islands (except Hawaii). *Newsgroup*

➤ **UNU.ISLANDS.FORUM:** Public forum on issues related to small islands: development, government, ecology. (See entry 4663 for full listing.)

REGIONS & CULTURES—PAKISTAN

7582 `bit.listserv.pakistan` Pakistan news service. *Moderated newsgroup*

7583 `bit.listserv.pns-1` Pakistan news service discussions. *Moderated newsgroup*

7584 **Pakistan News Service:** News relating to Pakistan. All subjects from art to politics to sports, etc. *Newsletter*
± `listserv@asuvm.inre.asu.edu` [body = SUBSCRIBE PAKISTAN first-name last-name]
INFO OWNER `pakeditr@asuvm.inre.asu.edu` (Nauman Mysorewala)
OWNER `mughal@alumni.caltech.edu` (Asim Mughal)
OWNER `irfan@cisco.com` (Syed Irfan Ashraf)
ARCHIVE `listserv@asuvm.inre.asu.edu` [body = INDEX Pakistan News Service]
POST `pakistan@asuvm.inre.asu.edu`
Gated: `bit.listserv.pakistan`

7585 `soc.culture.pakistan` Topics of discussion about Pakistan. *Newsgroup*

REGIONS & CULTURES—POLAND

7586 `soc.culture.polish` Polish culture, Polish past, and Polish politics. *Newsgroup*

7587 **Spojrzenia:** Magazine covering chiefly, but not exclusively, various aspects of Polish culture, history, and politics. *E-Magazine*
± `spojrz@k-vector.chem.washington.edu`
± `spojrz@info.unicaen.fr`
INFO `krzystek@k-vector.chem.washington.edu` (Jurek Krzystek)
ARCHIVES
`ftp://k-vector.chem.washington.edu/pub`
`http://k-vector.chem.washington.edu/begin_spo.html`
`http://k-vector.chem.washington.edu/~spojrz`
Language: Polish
Frequency: biweekly

➤ **Warsaw University Physics Department:** Information on the physics department, local tourism, and other Polish resources. (See entry 9494 for full listing.)

REGIONS & CULTURES—RUSSIA & FORMER SOVIET REPUBLICS

7588 **A & G Information Services:** Business news and information about Russia and St. Petersburg. *Newsletter*
± INFO `ag@panix.com` (Elena Artemova)
INFO `spbeac@sovam.com`

Frequency: one to two times weekly
Price: "not free"

7589 `alt.culture.tuva` Topics related to the Republic of Tuva, South Siberia. *Newsgroup*

7590 `alt.current-events.russia` Current happenings in Russia. *Newsgroup*

7591 `alt.current-events.ukraine` Current and fast-paced Ukrainian events. *Newsgroup*

➤ `alt.russia.sun:` Discussions about Sun hard- and software usage in the ex-USSR. *Newsgroup*

7592 **CenAsia:** On all political, economic, and military issues involving the central Asian republics of the former Soviet Union. *Mailing List*

± `listserv@vm1.mcgill.ca` [body = SUBSCRIBE CENASIA first-name last-name]

INFO `czgk@musica.mcgill.ca` (Keith Martin)

➤ **CEP-ANNOUNCE:** On the Civic Education Project: strengthening democracy in central and Eastern Europe and the NIS through the revitalization of the social sciences in universities and institutes of higher education. (See entry 5276 for full listing.)

7593 **CivilSoc:** On civil society resources for former Soviet Union. *Mailing List, moderated*

± `listproc@solar.rtd.utk.edu`

INFO OWNER `ccsi@u.washington.edu` (Center for Civil Society International)

INFO `http://solar.rtd.utk.edu/~ccsi/ccsihome.html`

ARCHIVE `http://solar.rtd.utk.edu/~ccsi/ccsihome.html`

7594 `clari.world.asia.central` Ex-Soviet republics in Central Asia. *Moderated newsgroup*

7595 `clari.world.europe.russia` News of Russia. *Moderated newsgroup*

➤ **EE-ECON:** On general economic issues in central and Eastern Europe, and in the NIS. (See entry 5195 for full listing.)

➤ **EE-HIGHER-ED:** On higher education in central and Eastern Europe, and in the NIS. (See entry 4192 for full listing.)

7596 **EE-JOBS:** On employment opportunities in Eastern and central Europe, and in the NIS. *Mailing List, moderated*

± `listproc@cep.nonprofit.net` [body = SUBSCRIBE EE-JOBS first-name last-name]

OWNER `cep@minerva.cis.yale.edu` (Civic Education Project)

POST `ee-jobs@cep.nonprofit.net`

➤ **EE-WOMEN:** On women's issues in central and Eastern Europe, and in the NIS. (See entry 10155 for full listing.)

➤ **eeurope-business:** For doing business in eastern Europe. (See entry 1796 for full listing.)

➤ **EH.EASTBLOC:** On the economic history of the Eastern Bloc countries. (See entry 5198 for full listing.)

7597 **GlasNews:** Newsletter for communications professionals in the former Soviet Union and in America. *Newsletter*

`http://solar.rtd.utk.edu/~aboyle/glasnews/master.html`

`ftp://ftp.eskimo.com/GlasNews`

`http://solar.rtd.utk.edu/~aboyle/glasnews/master.html`

± `majordomo@eskimo.com` [body = SUBSCRIBE GLASNEWS]

INFO OWNER `glasnews@eskimo.com` (Alan Boyle)

INFO OWNER `73420.753@compuserve.com` (David Endicott)

ARCHIVES

`ftp://ftp.eskimo.com/GlasNews`

`http://solar.rtd.utk.edu/~aboyle/glasnews/master.html`

Frequency: quarterly

7598 **Info-Russ:** Info-search and communication in Russian-speaking (or having related interests) community of (mostly) emigrants from the former USSR. *Mailing List, moderated*

`http://psi.ece.jhu.edu/~kaplan/IRUSS/inforuss.html`

± INFO `info-russ-request@smarty.ece.jhu.edu` (Alexander Kaplan)

Language: English, Russian

Please Note: Subscription by approval only.

➤ **The Khazaria Info Center:** These pages explore the history of the Khazar Jewish empire in southern Russia (650-1016). Many links to other important Jewish, historical, eastern European, and miscellaneous sites are also provided. (See entry 8811 for full listing.)

7599 **NISHEALTH:** For information on conferences on public health administration in the former Soviet Union (NIS). *Distribution List*
  INFO OWNER nphhi@igc.apc.org (Mark Storey and Mark Doctoroff)
  Comments: Other: On Glasnet, so they're unable to set up automatic mail service. E-mail contacts for more information.

➤ **OMRI Economic Digest:** Coverage of economic developments in the former Soviet Union and east-central and southeastern Europe. (See entry 5207 for full listing.)

7600 **Open Media Reseach Institute Daily Digest:** Daily compilation of news, information, and analysis on east-central and southeastern Europe, and the former Soviet Union. *Newsletter*
  http://www.omri.cz/Index.html
  ± listserv@ubvm.cc.buffalo.edu [body = SUBSCRIBE OMRI-L first-name last-name]
  INFO omripub@omri.cz (Jiri Pehe)
  ARCHIVES
  omripub@omri.cz (Jiri Pehe)
  http://www.omri.cz/Publications/Digests/DigestIndex.html
  Frequency: daily (Monday-Friday)

7601 relcom.bbs BBS news. *Newsgroup*

7602 relcom.bbs.list Ex-USSR BBS file lists. *Newsgroup*

7603 relcom.commerce.computers.ctrlsystems Control systems and data gathering systems. *Newsgroup*

7604 relcom.commerce.infoserv Information services. *Newsgroup*

7605 relcom.commerce.talk Discussions about commercial groups. *Newsgroup*

➤ relcom.jusinf: Information on laws by "Justicinform". *Moderated newsgroup*

7606 relcom.netnews Information about new network capabilities and services. *Newsgroup*

7607 relcom.netnews.big General *big* articles. *Newsgroup*

➤ relcom.politics: Political discussions. *Newsgroup*

➤ relcom.relarn.science: Scientific publications and discussions. *Moderated newsgroup*

➤ relcom.religion: Discussions on religions and related topics. *Newsgroup*

7608 soc.culture.rep-of-georgia The Caucasian Republic of Georgia and Georgians. *Newsgroup*

7609 soc.culture.russian All things Russian in the broadest sense. *Newsgroup*

7610 soc.culture.soviet Topics relating to Russian or Soviet culture. *Newsgroup*

7611 soc.culture.ukrainian The lives and times of the Ukrainian people. *Newsgroup*

➤ talk.politics.soviet: Discussion of Soviet politics, domestic, and foreign. *Newsgroup*

7612 **UKRAINA:** An academic list on the study of Ukraine. *Mailing List, moderated*
  ± listserv@ukanaix.cc.ukans.edu [body = SUBSCRIBE UKRAINA first-name last-name]
  OWNER cossack@ukanaix.cc.ukans.edu (Howard High)
  Please Note: Subscription by approval only.

REGIONS & CULTURES—SCANDINAVIA

7613 **FUNET NIC:** Network Information Center of the Finnish University and Research Network, FUNET. Includes FUNET information, pointers to all Finnish gophers and Web servers, WWW/gopher/FTP gateway to ftp.funet.fi archive, Finnish X.400 gateway address converter, and much more.

```
http://www.funet.fi/
ftp://ftp.funet.fi
gopher://gopher.funet.fi
```

7614 clari.world.europe.northern Scandinavia, Finland, Iceland. *Moderated newsgroup*

➤ **A Course in Swedish Cursing:** An extensive and systematic course in Swedish cursing with plenty of sound bites to assist learning the correct pronounciation and intonation. (See entry 4247 for full listing.)

➤ **DENet Information Server:** This is the information service of the Danish national academic network, DENet. It is located at UNI-C, the Danish Computer Centre for Research and Education. (See entry 4502 for full listing.)

➤ **FINLANDIA:** On Finnish classical music: composers, performances, recordings. (See entry 811 for full listing.)

7615 Jyvaskyla University: CWIS for Jyvaskyla University, Finland.

```
http://www.jyu.fi/
gopher://gopher.jyu.fi
INFO webmaster@jyu.fi
```

7616 kulturCHOCK!: A Swedish-American journal of being neither here nor there. Information and commentary for the Swede living in the U.S. and the American living in Sweden. *E-Zine*

```
http://www.webcom.com/eha/kchock.html
± http://www.webcom.com/eha/kchock.html
± kulturchock-request@webcom.com [body = SUBSCRIBE <e-mail address>]
INFO OWNER eha@winternet.com (David Curle)
ARCHIVE http://www.webcom.com/eha/kchock.html
```
Language: English, Swedish

➤ **Lund University Electronic Library, Sweden:** This Web site is managed by LUB NetLab, the development department of Lund University Library, as an electronic information service for Lund University, Lund, Sweden, and other users. (See entry 4432 for full listing.)

7617 Lysator Archives: Archives of Lysator, an academic computer society at Linkoping University in Linkoping, Sweden. It includes the files of "Project Runeberg," a collection of free electronic texts in Scandinavian languages; MUD information; an extensive science-fiction archive; information about Sweden, Linkoping, and Linkoping University; and much more.

```
http://www.lysator.liu.se/
gopher://gopher.lysator.liu.se
INFO www@lysator.liu.se
```

7618 NORDBALT: About networking among Nordic and Baltic countries. *Mailing List*

```
± listserv@searn.sunet.se [body = SUBSCRIBE NORDBALT first-name last-name]
INFO nordbalt-request@searn.sunet.se
ARCHIVE listserv@searn.sunet.se [body = INDEX NORDBALT]
```

7619 NORWEAVE: Social network for Norwegians and friends of Norway. *Mailing List*

```
± listserv@nki.no [body = SUBSCRIBE NORWEAVE first-name last-name]
INFO morten@nki.no (Morten Flate Paulsen)
```

➤ **Primary Care Internet Guide:** A guide to primary health care on the net, with an emphasis on Norway. (See entry 4874 for full listing.)

➤ **Project Runeberg:** Project Runeberg publishes free electronic editions of classic Nordic literature and art over the Internet since 1992. (See entry 5679 for full listing.)

➤ **Scandinavian Indie:** The place for independent music coming from any Scandinavian country, plus the Baltic countries. (See entry 1206 for full listing.)

7620 soc.culture.nordic Discussion about culture up north. *Newsgroup*

7621 Swede-L: For anybody having *any* sort of interest in things Swedish. *Mailing List*

```
± listproc@u.washington.edu
```

OWNER anderss@u.washington.edu (Mike Andersson)

7622 Swedish Information Service: A one-stop guide to the country of Sweden, provided by the Swedish Information Service in New York.

http://www.webcom.com/sis

INFO swedinfo@ix.netcom.com

➤ **Tampere University of Technology (TUT), Finland:** Web server at Tampere University of Technology, Finland. Information about TUT in general, departments, research activities, education, services available on campus, contact addresses. (See entry 4455 for full listing.)

➤ **Turku School of Economics:** Information service of the Turku School of Economics and Business Administration, Turku, Finland. (See entry 5212 for full listing.)

➤ **Utposten:** Norwegian journal for general practice and public health. (See entry 5042 for full listing.)

REGIONS & CULTURES—SOUTH & CENTRAL AMERICA

➤ **alt.tv.xuxa:** That Connie Dobbs clone, her TV show, and her double Xs. *Newsgroup*

7623 argentina: On Argentine and Latin American social/political issues. *Mailing List*

± INFO argentina-requests@journal.math.indiana.edu [body = first-name-last-name , e-mail-address, phone number, address, and topics of interest] (Elena Fraboschi/Jorge Gatica)

7624 CHILE-L: For discussion on Chile. *Mailing List*

± listserv@utarlvm1.uta.edu [body = SUBSCRIBE CHILE-L first-name last-name]

INFO chile-1-request@utarlvm1.uta.edu

ARCHIVE listserv@utarlvm1.uta.edu [body = INDEX CHILE-L]

7625 chile.anuncios Any type of announcement. *Newsgroup*

7626 chile.chilenet National Academic Network (Red Academica Nacional) and Bitnet. *Newsgroup*

➤ **chile.cine:** Chileans discuss movies. *Newsgroup*

7627 chile.compraventas Buy and sell. *Newsgroup*

7628 chile.futbol Grupo sobre Jurbol en chile y entre chilenos. *Newsgroup*

7629 chile.grupos Chilean newsgroup creation. *Newsgroup*

7630 chile.grupos.anuncios Anuncios relativos a la jerarquia chile. *Moderated newsgroup*

7631 chile.scout Movimiento de Guias y Boy Scouts. *Newsgroup*

7632 chile.soft-1 Software for microcomputers. *Newsgroup*

7633 chile.trabajos Job offers. *Newsgroup*

7634 chile.varios Miscellaneous. *Newsgroup*

7635 Chile Information Project (CHIP News): News on economics, especially mining, and human rights and democratization in Chile. *E-Journal*

http://www.chip.cl/

INFO anderson@chip.mic.cl (Steve Anderson)

ARCHIVE http://www.chip.cl/

Frequency: daily

7636 clari.world.americas.argentina News of Argentina. *Moderated newsgroup*

7637 clari.world.americas.brazil News of Brazil. *Moderated newsgroup*

7638 clari.world.americas.central News of Central America. *Moderated newsgroup*

7639 clari.world.americas.peru News of Peru. *Moderated newsgroup*

7640 clari.world.americas.south News of South America. *Moderated newsgroup*

7641 clari.world.americas.south.misc News of South America. *Moderated newsgroup*

7642 **COLEXT:** For Columbians who live outside Columbia. *Mailing List*
± `listserv@cdcnet.uniandes.edu.co` [body = SUBSCRIBE COLEXT]
INFO `jfarjona@andescol.bitnet`
Language: Spanish
Gated: `colombia.listas.colext`

➤ **CONICIT—VENEZUELA:** This site, sponsored by CONICIT (Consejo Nacional de Investigaciones Cientificas y Tecnologicas), the National Council of Science and Technology Rresearch in Venezuela, provides news and events in science and technology in Venezuela. (See entry 9548 for full listing.)

➤ **CREAD:** This list is used to animate discussions on the uses of distance education in Latin America and the Caribbean. (See entry 4337 for full listing.)

7643 **MeuPovo:** For informal computing news and chat from Brazil. *Mailing List, moderated*
`http://lci.ufrj.br/mpovo/meupovo.htm`
± `listserv@lci.ufrj.br` [body = SUB MEUPOVO]
INFO EDITOR OWNER `dariomor@lci.ufrj.br` (Dario Mor)
FAQ `listserv@lci.ufrj.br` [body = SUB MEUPOVO]
Language: Portugese

7644 **REACCIUN:** Academic Network of National University Research Centers, Venezuela (Red Academica de Centros de Investigacion y Universidades Nacionales REACCIUN). Its mission is to empower and support research and cooperation between academic and research institutions in Venezuela.
`http://www.reac.net.ve/`
`ftp://www.reac.net.ve`
`gopher://www.reac.net.ve`
INFO `jrivas@conicit.ve`
INFO `avivas@conicit.ve`

7645 `rec.travel.latin-america` Travel in Caribbean, Central, and South America. *Newsgroup*

7646 `soc.culture.argentina` All about life in Argentina. *Newsgroup*

7647 `soc.culture.bolivia` Bolivian people and culture. *Newsgroup*

7648 `soc.culture.brazil` Talking about the people and country of Brazil. *Newsgroup*

7649 `soc.culture.chile` All about Chile and its people. *Newsgroup*

7650 `soc.culture.colombia` Colombian talk, social, politics, science. *Newsgroup*

7651 `soc.culture.ecuador` The culture and people of Ecuador. *Newsgroup*

➤ `soc.culture.latin-america:` Topics about Latin America. *Newsgroup*

7652 `soc.culture.peru` All about the people of Peru. *Newsgroup*

7653 `soc.culture.uruguay` Discussions of Uruguay for those at home and abroad. *Newsgroup*

7654 `soc.culture.venezuela` Discussion of topics related to Venezuela. *Newsgroup*

7655 **Venezuela's Web Server:** This is the place where one can get a lot of information and news about Venezuela.
`http://venezuela.mit.edu/`
INFO `hb@mit.edu`

REGIONS & CULTURES—SOUTH AFRICA

➤ **Cape Town Weather Watch:** Great link for southern African weather; satellite images; short, medium, and long-term forecasts; radar images; climate information; educational pages; model forecasts; real-time weather (e.g., temperatures, pressure in South African cities); upper-air data plots; and more. (See entry 6140 for full listing.)

7656 `clari.world.africa.south_africa` News from South Africa. *Moderated newsgroup*

➤ **RAMBLINGS:** On actuarial science. (See entry 1881 for full listing.)

7657 `relcom.rec.tourism` Hiking, sport tourism discussions. *Newsgroup*

➤ **SABINET:** Home page of the largest South African provider of online bibliographic material. (See entry 5742 for full listing.)

7658 `sanet.announce` Announcements about Sanet. *Moderated newsgroup*

7659 `sanet.flame` Sanet's version of `alt.flame`. *Newsgroup*

7660 `sanet.newsletters` UniForum and other newsletters. *Moderated newsgroup*

7661 `sanet.newsletters.d` Discussion about the newsletters in `sanet.newsletters`. *Newsgroup*

➤ `sanet.talk.politics:` Talk about politics. *Newsgroup*

➤ `sanet.talk.religion:` Talk about religion. *Newsgroup*

7662 `sanet.tech` Networking in South Africa. *Moderated newsgroup*

7663 `sanet.uniforum` Discussion about UniForum-SA. *Newsgroup*

7664 `soc.culture.south-africa` South African society, culture, and politics. *Newsgroup*

7665 `soc.culture.south-africa.afrikaans` The Afrikaans and speakers. *Newsgroup*

7666 `za.ads.jobs` Looking for a job? Offering a job? *Newsgroup*

7667 `za.ads.lifts` Want a lift from Jo'burg to Cape Town via Durbs? *Newsgroup*

7668 `za.ads.misc` For sale/to swap/wanted to buy. *Newsgroup*

7669 `za.archives` Who's got what, where, and how. *Newsgroup*

7670 `za.culture.xhosa` Ingxoxo ngolwini, amasiko nezithete zakwaXhosa. *Newsgroup*

7671 `za.edu.comp` The use of computers in education. *Newsgroup*

7672 `za.environment` Environmental issues. *Newsgroup*

7673 `za.events` Conferences, events, and happenings nationally. *Newsgroup*

7674 `za.flame` A cool imitation of the real thing. *Newsgroup*

7675 `za.frd.announce` General announcements from the Foundation for Research Development. *Moderated newsgroup*

7676 `za.humour` Those wacky South Africans. *Newsgroup*

7677 `za.info-policy` Telecommunications and information policy in Southern Africa. *Newsgroup*

7678 `za.misc` General chat, comments, announcements, etc. *Newsgroup*

7679 `za.net.maps` Local UUCP maps. *Moderated newsgroup*

7680 `za.net.misc` Miscellaneous ramblings on networking in ZA. *Newsgroup*

7681 `za.net.stats` Statistics on network usage, automated postings, etc. *Newsgroup*

7682 `za.net.uninet` Announcements and feedback from the Uninet-ZA office. *Newsgroup*

7683 `za.org.cssa` Computer Society of South Africa. *Newsgroup*

7684 `za.politics` Regional politics. *Newsgroup*

7685 `za.schools` Issues affecting primary and secondary education. *Newsgroup*

7686 `za.sport` Finer points of jukskei or the Comrades. *Newsgroup*

7687 `za.unix.misc` General discussion, questions, and chat about Unix in ZA. *Newsgroup*

REGIONS & CULTURES—SOUTHEAST ASIA

7688 `alt.comp.malaysia` Computers in Malaysia. *Newsgroup*

7689 `alt.sci.tech.indonesian` Science and technology in Indonesia. *Newsgroup*

7690 `alt.talk.korean` A lighthearted place for discussions concerning Koreans. *Newsgroup*

7691 **BERITA-L:** For news on Malaysia, Singapore, Southeast Asia, and Islam. *Mailing List*

± listserv@vmd.cso.uiuc.edu [body = SUBSCRIBE BERITA-L first-name last-name]

INFO http://www.uiuc.edu/ph/www/chai/

OWNER chai@uiuc.edu (Ian Chai)

ARCHIVES

listserv@vmd.cso.uiuc.edu [body = INDEX BERITA-L]

http://st-www.cs.uiuc.edu/users/chai/malaysia.html

FAQ http://st-www.cs.uiuc.edu/users/chai/bhow

Language: English, Malay

Gated: bit.listserv.berita

7692 **bit.listserv.berita** News about Malaysia and Singapore. *Moderated newsgroup*

➤ **bit.listserv.pakistan:** Pakistan news service. *Moderated newsgroup*

➤ **bit.listserv.pns-l:** Pakistan news service discussions. *Moderated newsgroup*

7693 **bit.listserv.seasia-l** Southeast Asia discussion list. *Newsgroup*

7694 **clari.world.asia.indochina.misc** Thailand, Laos, Cambodia, Myanmar. *Moderated newsgroup*

7695 **clari.world.asia.philippines** News of the Philippines. *Moderated newsgroup*

7696 **clari.world.asia.southeast** News of Southeast Asia. *Moderated newsgroup*

7697 **clari.world.asia.vietnam** News of Vietnam. *Moderated newsgroup*

➤ **East Timor Action Network News:** Regular newsletter of the East Timor Action Network—United States consiting of current news, reports, and calls to action regarding human rights and self-determination for East Timor. (See entry 10026 for full listing.)

➤ **misc.news.southasia:** News from Bangladesh, India, Nepal, etc. *Moderated newsgroup*

7698 **reg.easttimor:** E-mail distribution of postings from the Alliance for Progressive Communications (APC) conference on East Timor and Indonesia. Includes reports from a wide range of advocacy and support groups, as well as reports and translations from the international press, and official documents and statements from the UN, national governments, and other sources. *Mailing List*

http://iconz.co.nz/~calliope/Nettalk.html

gopher://gopher.igc.apc.org/11/peace/timor.gopher

± fbp@igc.apc.org [body = please subscibe me to Reg.easttimor]

INFO OWNER fbp@igc.apc.org

INFO OWNER cscheiner@igc.apc.org (Charles Scheiner)

INFO timor-info@igc.apc.org

OWNER tapol@igc.apc.org

ARCHIVES

http://amadeus.inesc.pt/~jota/Timor/

almanac@gn.apc.org

Comments: An abridged, read-only version of reg.easttimor, with an average of two daily postings, is on APC as the conference tapol.etimor. This is also available as e-mail; send a note to maggie@gn.apc.org to receive it.

7699 **SEASIA-L:** About Southeast Asia, including current events. *Daily Digest*

± listserv@msu.edu [body = SUBSCRIBE SEASIA-L first-name last-name]

INFO OWNER 3zlufur@cmuvm.csv.cmich.edu (Elliott Parker)

ARCHIVE listserv@msu.edu [body = INDEX SEASIA-L]

Gated: bit.listserv.seasia-l

7700 **SIFlash:** A biweekly news journal on current affairs from the Singapore International Foundation. *Newsletter*

INFO siflash@technet.sg

ARCHIVE gopher://spore.island.city.state

Frequency: biweekly

7701 **Singapore-ITI:** Information Technology Institute (ITI), the applied R & D arm of the National Computer Board (NCB) of Singapore.
`http://www.iti.gov.sg/`

7702 `soc.culture.asean` Countries of the Association of Southeast Asian Nations. *Newsgroup*

7703 `soc.culture.bangladesh` Issues and discussion about Bangladesh. *Newsgroup*

7704 `soc.culture.burma` Politics, culture, news, discussion about Burma. *Newsgroup*

7705 `soc.culture.cambodia` Cambodia and its people. *Newsgroup*

7706 `soc.culture.filipino` Group about the Filipino culture. *Newsgroup*

7707 `soc.culture.indonesia` All about the Indonesian nation. *Newsgroup*

7708 `soc.culture.laos` Cultural and social aspects of Laos. *Newsgroup*

7709 `soc.culture.malaysia` All about Malaysian society. *Newsgroup*

7710 `soc.culture.singapore` The past, present, and future of Singapore. *Newsgroup*

7711 `soc.culture.sri-lanka` Things and people from Sri Lanka. *Newsgroup*

7712 `soc.culture.tamil` Tamil language, history, and Tamil culture. *Newsgroup*

7713 `soc.culture.thai` Thai people and their culture. *Newsgroup*

7714 `soc.culture.vietnamese` Issues and discussions of Vietnamese culture. *Newsgroup*

➤   `talk.politics.tibet:` The politics of Tibet and the Tibetan people. *Newsgroup*

REGIONS & CULTURES—SOUTHWEST ASIA

➤   `soc.culture.iranian:` Discussions about Iran and things Iranian/Persian. *Newsgroup*

➤   `soc.culture.iraq:` Iraq, its society, culture, and heritage. *Newsgroup*

7715 `soc.culture.kurdish` People from Kurdistan and Kurds around the world. *Newsgroup*

REGIONS & CULTURES—SWITZERLAND

7716 `ch.general` Miscellaneous items of interest to Swiss newsgroups reader. *Newsgroup*

7717 `ch.network` Discussion and announcements of network-related issues. *Newsgroup*

7718 `ch.philo.agenda` Current affairs/events/etc. of philosophical nature. *Newsgroup*

7719 `ch.si.general` Miscellaneous items of interest to Swiss Informatiker Gesellschaft. *Newsgroup*

➤   **Organisation for Security and Co-operation in Europe (OSCE):** The Swiss presidency of the OSCE in 1996 provides a Web server with materials on the OSCE. Materials include basic texts, press communiques, reports on missions, and speeches of the Swiss foreign minister, as well as links to the foreign ministries of all OSCE states. (See entry 7280 for full listing.)

7720 `soc.culture.swiss` Swiss culture. *Newsgroup*

7721 `srg.drs1` Swiss Radio DRS1, program information. *Newsgroup*

7722 `srg.drs2` Swiss Radio DRS2, program information. *Newsgroup*

7723 `srg.drs3` Swiss Radio DRS3, program information. *Newsgroup*

7724 `srg.info` Swiss Broadcasting Corp. (SRG) related info. *Newsgroup*

7725 `srg.programme` Swiss Radio DRS, combined program information. *Newsgroup*

7726 `srg.tvdrs` Swiss TV-related information; sources: ELSA and SRG. *Newsgroup*

7727 **Swiss Academic & Research Network:** This is a main site for Switzerland. It includes pointers to other Swiss resources, including libraries and educational institutions. It also includes an archive of well-indexed FAQs from all across the Internet that are searchable, and a directory of Swiss libraries.
`http://www.switch.ch/`

```
gopher://gopher.switch.ch
```
INFO `switchinfo@switch.ch`
INFO `webmaster@www.switch.ch`

Comments: The file server has an acceptable-use statement you get in the banner of the FTP login session or via `http://www.switch.ch/switch/info/ftp.html`

REGIONS & CULTURES—TURKEY

➤ **Bilkent University CWIS:** CWIS and other Bilkent University computer resources. (See entry 4411 for full listing.)

7728   `soc.culture.turkish`   Discussion about things Turkish. *Newsgroup*

➤ **Thrace:** For Turkish-minority members of West Thracia (a province of Greece). (See entry 7318 for full listing.)

7729   **TSA-L:** For the Turkish Studies Association. *Mailing List*
   ± `listserv@msu.edu` [body = SUBSCRIBE   TSA-L first-name last-name]
   INFO `alan@ah2.cal.msu.edu` (Alan Fisher)
   ARCHIVE `listserv@msu.edu`

➤ **WOMEN:** On women's issues in Turkey and in other developing countries. (See entry 10166 for full listing.)

REGIONS & CULTURES—UK

➤ **AccomoDATA:** A resource with listings of hotels, bed and breakfasts, cottage rentals, and boat rentals in England, Wales, Scotland, Ireland, and France, plus the rest of Europe. You can make direct bookings from this site. (See entry 7820 for full listing.)

7730   `alt.fan.british-accent`   "oooh, he just sounds soooo cool! (Giggle)". *Newsgroup*

7731   `alt.floors.uk`   Apparently Great Britain has some unique flooring. *Newsgroup*

➤ `alt.politics.british`:   Politics and a real queen, too. *Newsgroup*

7732   `alt.radio.uk`   Radio in the United Kingdom. *Newsgroup*

7733   `alt.radio.uk.talk-radio`   Talk radio (call-in) programs in the British Isles. *Newsgroup*

7734   `alt.scottish.clans`   Discussions about Scottish clans. *Newsgroup*

➤ **ANCANACH:** For the members of the Clan Henderson Society of U.S./Canada, a Scottish heritage and geneology organization. (See entry 5220 for full listing.)

7735   `cam.misc`   Yo! Cambridge, United Kingdom. *Newsgroup*

➤ `cam.sug`:   Cambridge, United Kingdom, Sun user group information. *Newsgroup*

7736   `clari.world.europe.british_isles.uk`   News of the U.K. *Moderated newsgroup*

7737   `clari.world.europe.british_isles.uk.biz`   Business news of the U.K. *Moderated newsgroup*

7738   `clari.world.europe.uk`   News of the United Kingdom. *Moderated newsgroup*

➤ **GOODIES-L:** On the British television comedy show *The Goodies*. (See entry 244 for full listing.)

➤ **Liverpool University, Computer Science, United Kingdom:** This is the Computer Service departmental Web server at the University of Liverpool, United Kingdom. It includes HP-UX information and information on Mereyside and U.K. National Lotteries. (See entry 9199 for full listing.)

7739   `lon.misc`   Miscellaneous news from London, England. *Newsgroup*

➤ **ModBrits:** On modern British and Irish literature from 1895 to 1955. (See entry 618 for full listing.)

➤ **School of Education, University of Leeds:** School of Education, The University of Leeds, United Kingdom. This site includes teaching and research activities of the school. (See entry 4354 for full listing.)

7740   `scot.announce`   Scotland/North England-wide: general announcements. *Newsgroup*

7741   `scot.bairns`   Scottish newsgroup for or about children. *Newsgroup*

7742   `scot.birds`   Scottish birdwatching discussion. *Newsgroup*

7743 **scot.environment** Environmental issues in Scotland. *Newsgroup*

7744 **scot.followup** Follow-ups to scot.general articles. *Newsgroup*

7745 **scot.general** Scotland/North England-wide: general articles. *Newsgroup*

➤ **scot.scots:** Scots language discussions. *Newsgroup*

7746 **soc.culture.british** Issues about Britain and those of British descent. *Newsgroup*

7747 **soc.culture.hongkong** Discussions pertaining to Hong Kong. *Newsgroup*

7748 **soc.culture.hongkong.entertainment** Entertainment in Hong Kong. *Newsgroup*

7749 **soc.culture.scottish** Anything regarding Scotland or things Scots. *Newsgroup*

7750 **soc.culture.welsh** The people, language, and history of Wales. *Newsgroup*

➤ **UK Theatre Web:** A guide to professional and amateur theatre in the U.K. Covers opera, plays, musicals, dance, theatre news, and more. This site is the only online theatre guide to cover the whole of the U.K. (See entry 1632 for full listing.)

➤ **uk-hockey:** About ice hockey as played in and by Great Britain: news, gossip, league tables, match reports, and results. (See entry 6909 for full listing.)

7751 **uk.adverts.computer** Advertisements in the U.K. for computer-related items. *Newsgroup*

7752 **uk.adverts.other** Adverts in the U.K. for items not covered by other groups. *Newsgroup*

7753 **uk.announce** General announcements of UK interest. *Newsgroup*

7754 **uk.announce.d** Discussion of articles in **uk.announce**. *Newsgroup*

7755 **uk.announce.events** Forthcoming events within the U.K. *Moderated newsgroup*

7756 **uk.announce.events.d** Discussion of articles in **uk.announce.events**. *Newsgroup*

7757 **uk.answers** Repository for periodic UK specific USENET articles. *Newsgroup*

7758 **uk.bcs.announce** Announcements relating to the British Computer Society. *Newsgroup*

7759 **uk.bcs.misc** Discussion of topics relevant to the British Computer Society. *Newsgroup*

7760 **uk.comp.misc** Miscellaneous UK-related computing issues. *Newsgroup*

7761 **uk.consultants** Discussion in all areas relevant to U.K. consultants. *Newsgroup*

➤ **uk.d-i-y:** Do it yourself. *Newsgroup*

➤ **uk.education.16plus:** All aspects of 16+, community, and adult education. *Newsgroup*

7762 **uk.education.misc** For discussion about U.K. education issues. *Newsgroup*

7763 **uk.education.teachers** For discussion by/about teachers. *Newsgroup*

7764 **uk.environment** U.K. environmental matters. *Newsgroup*

7765 **uk.events** Forthcoming events (conferences, etc.). No discussions. *Newsgroup*

➤ **uk.finance:** U.K. financial issues. *Newsgroup*

7766 **uk.food+drink.misc** Food and drink in all forms within the U.K. *Newsgroup*

7767 **uk.food+drink.restaurants** Independent guide to U.K. restaurants. *Newsgroup*

7768 **uk.forsale** Advertisements. *Newsgroup*

➤ **uk.games.misc:** Various topics on gaming in the U.K. *Newsgroup*

7769 **uk.gov.local** Local government in the United Kingdom. *Newsgroup*

7770 **uk.jobs.contract** This group is for placement of advertisements for contractors. *Newsgroup*

7771 **uk.jobs.d** Discussions about situations vacant and wanted. *Newsgroup*

7772 **uk.jobs.offered** Situations vacant. No discussions. *Newsgroup*

7773 **uk.jobs.wanted** Situations wanted. No discussions. *Newsgroup*

7774 `uk.media` Discussion of media in the U.K. *Newsgroup*

7775 `uk.media.films` To discuss films among all inhabitants of the U.K. *Newsgroup*

7776 `uk.media.tv.brookside` The Channel 4 TV program *Brookside*. *Newsgroup*

7777 `uk.misc` General interest to everyone on U.K. net. *Newsgroup*

7778 `uk.net.maps` U.K. net maps. *Newsgroup*

7779 `uk.net.news` U.K. net news. *Newsgroup*

7780 `uk.net.news.announce` For RFDs, CFVs, FAQs, etc. within the `uk.*` hierarchy. *Moderated newsgroup*

7781 `uk.org.bcs.announce` Announcements relating to the British Computer Society. *Moderated newsgroup*

7782 `uk.org.bcs.misc` Discussion of topics relevant to the British Computer Society. *Newsgroup*

7783 `uk.org.community` U.K. CommUnity matters. *Newsgroup*

7784 `uk.org.community.committee` U.K. CommUnity committee matters. *Moderated newsgroup*

➤ `uk.org.epsrc.hpc.discussion:` EPSRC High Performance Computing discussion. *Newsgroup*

7785 `uk.org.women-in-comp` Discussion of Women in Computing. *Newsgroup*

➤ `uk.people.deaf:` Discussion group for the deaf in the UK. *Newsgroup*

7786 `uk.people.disability` Discussion of disability-related topics in the U.K. *Newsgroup*

➤ `uk.politics:` U.K. political discussion. *Newsgroup*

7787 `uk.railway` Trains. *Newsgroup*

7788 `uk.rec.climbing` Rock climbing, ice climbing, and mountaineering. *Newsgroup*

7789 `uk.rec.crafts` Newsgroup for craft-related topics in the U.K. . *Newsgroup*

➤ `uk.rec.cycling:` Discussion of U.K. cycling issues. *Newsgroup*

7790 `uk.rec.gardening` To discuss gardening topics of interest in the U.K. *Newsgroup*

7791 `uk.rec.motorsport.misc` U.K. motor sports, primarily from those involved. *Newsgroup*

7792 `uk.rec.scouting` Discussion of scouting and guiding in the U.K. *Newsgroup*

7793 `uk.rec.walking` To exchange information on walking, hiking, or rambling in the U.K. *Newsgroup*

7794 `uk.rec.waterways` For discussing British waterways. *Newsgroup*

7795 `uk.rec.youth-hostel` Discussion of youth hostels and hosteling. *Newsgroup*

➤ `uk.religion.interfaith:` Discussion of interfaith and ecumenical religious issues in the UK. *Newsgroup*

➤ `uk.religion.jewish:` Judaism in the United Kingdom. *Newsgroup*

➤ `uk.religion.misc:` Religion in the UK. *Newsgroup*

➤ `uk.religion.other-faiths:` Other faiths without a specific U.K. newsgroup. *Newsgroup*

➤ `uk.singles:` Personal ads, or discussions. *Newsgroup*

➤ `uk.sources:` U.K.-wide group for sources/reposts/requests. *Newsgroup*

7796 `uk.transport` Transport-related U.K. issues. *Newsgroup*

7797 `uk.transport.ride-sharing` Sharing rides in cars around the U.K. *Newsgroup*

➤ `uk.wic:` Discussion of women in computing. *Newsgroup*

7798 **United Kingdom Government Information Service (CCTA):** This site provides information from 115 organizations and 60 government departments and agencies, including ministerial speeches, press notices, and statistical data.
`http://www.open.gov.uk/`
INFO `info@ccta.gov.uk`

➤ **VICTORIA:** For sharing of ideas and information about all aspects of 19th-century British culture and society. (See entry 5270 for full listing.)

➤ **Wey South: The WWW page of the Wey & Arun Canal Trust:** This is the Web page of the Wey & Arun Canal Trust. It describes the work of the trust and its conservation work on this canal, which is in southern England. (See entry 5271 for full listing.)

➤ `uk.media.tv.sf.x-files`: A group for all you U.K. *X Files*. *Newsgroup*

➤ **Yorkshire Cancer Registry:** Yorkshire Cancer Registry, United Kingdom. (See entry 4742 for full listing.)

REGIONS & CULTURES—YUGOSLAV PENINSULA

7799 `alt.beograd` City and people of Beograd (Belgrade, former Yugoslavia). *Newsgroup*

7800 `alt.current-events.bosnia` The strife of Bosnia-Herzegovina. *Newsgroup*

7801 `alt.news.fyrom` News on the Former Yugoslav Republic Of Macedonia. *Newsgroup*

7802 `bit.listserv.bosnet` Bosnia news. *Moderated newsgroup*

7803 `bit.listserv.croatia` Croatian news. *Moderated newsgroup*

7804 `bit.listserv.hrvatska` Croatian news. *Moderated newsgroup*

7805 **BosNews:** News about Bosnia and Herzegovina, including news from the international press. *Distribution List, moderated*

  ± `listproc@doc.ic.ac.uk` [body = `SUBSCRIBE BOSNEWS` first-name last-name] (Comprehensive list of Bosnia/Herzogovenia Internet resources.)

  INFO `listproc@doc.ic.ac.uk` [body = `INFORMATION BOSNEWS`] (Comprehensive list of Bosnia/Herzogovenia Internet resources.)

  INFO `zelb@dwe.csiro.au` (Zeljko Bodulovic)

  INFO `dzevat@ee.mcgill.ca` (Dzevat Omeragic)

  ARCHIVE `ftp://triples.math.mcgill.ca/pub/bosnia/BOSNET`

7806 `clari.world.europe.balkans` Former Yugoslavia, Romania, Bulgaria. *Moderated newsgroup*

7807 **Cro-News:** News coming from Croatia. *Mailing List*

  ± `listserv@well.ox.ac.uk` [body = `SUBSCRIBE CRO-NEWS` first-name last-name]

  INFO EDITOR OWNER `nino@well.ox.ac.uk` (Nino Margetic)

  ARCHIVE `listserv@well.ox.ac.uk` [body = `INDEX CRO-NEWS`]

  Language: English, Croatian

7808 `misc.news.bosnia` News, articles, reports, and information on Bosnia. *Moderated newsgroup*

7809 **RokPress:** News from Slovenia. *Mailing List, moderated*

  `http://maveric0.uwaterloo.ca/RP/`

  ± **INFO POST** `rokpress@krpan.arnes.si`

  Language: Slovene

7810 **SCCro-Digest:** Mailing list for people without access to the Usenet newsgroup `soc.culture.croatia` *Mailing List*

  ± `listserv@well.ox.ac.uk` [body = `SUBSCRIBE SCCRO-DIGEST` first-name last-name]

  INFO EDITOR OWNER `nino@well.ox.ac.uk` (Nino Margetic)

  ARCHIVE `listserv@well.ox.ac.uk` [body = `INDEX SCCRO-DIGEST`]

  Language: English, Croation

  Gated: `soc.culture.croatia`

7811 **SLOVAK-L:** Discussion of Slovak issues. *Mailing List*

  ± `listserv@ubvm.cc.buffalo.edu` [body = `SUBSCRIBE SLOVAK-L` first-name last-name]

  INFO EDITOR OWNER `gfrajkor@ccs.carleton.ca` (George Frajkor)

  Language: English and Slovak and other Slavic languages

  Gated: `bit.listserv.slovak-l`

7812 **SLOVAK-WORLD:** For contacting Slovaks and friends all around the world. *Mailing List*

`http://www.fris.sk/Slovak-World`
± `listproc@fris.sk` [body = SUBSCRIBE SLOVAK-WORLD first-name last-name]
OWNER `pobis@fris.sk` (Ivan Pobis)
OWNER `gecovic@fris.sk` (Miroslav Gecovic)
Language: English, Slovak

7813 **Slovakia Online:** Multimedia magazine about the society and culture of Slovakia.
`http://www.savba.sk/logos/list-e.html`
INFO `logos@savba.sk`

7814 `soc.culture.bosna-herzgvna` The independent state of Bosnia and Herzegovina. *Newsgroup*

7815 `soc.culture.croatia` The lives of people of Croatia. *Newsgroup*

7816 `soc.culture.slovenia` Slovenia and Slovenian people. *Newsgroup*

7817 `soc.culture.yugoslavia` Discussions of Yugoslavia and its people. *Newsgroup*

TRAVEL

7818 **Student & Budget Travel Guide:** A descriptive and critical guide to travel resources on the Internet, especially for those of use to student and budget travelers.
`http://www.lib.umich.edu/chdocs/travel/travel-guide.html`
INFO `travel-guide@umich.edu`
INFO `tfalk@umich.edu` (Tanya Falk)
FAQ `tfalk@umich.edu` (Tanya Falk)

7819 **Aarons's Catalog Listings:** A large directory to motels and hotels all over the United States.
`http://www.prairieweb.com/aarons/`
INFO `aarons@prairieweb.com`

7820 **AccomoDATA:** A resource with listings of hotels, bed and breakfasts, cottage rentals, and boat rentals in England, Wales, Scotland, Ireland, and France, plus the rest of Europe. You can make direct bookings from this site.
`http://www.accomodata.co.uk/`
INFO `tech@accomodata.co.uk`
MIRROR `http://www.cityscape.co.uk/users/eb19/`

7821 `alt.travel.rides` Usenet ride-sharing board. *Newsgroup*

7822 `alt.travel.road-trip` Ever go to Montreal for pizza—from Albany? *Newsgroup*

7823 `alt.visa.us` Discussion/information on visas pertaining to U.S. *Newsgroup*

7824 `bermuda.tourism` Information about the Bermuda tourism scene. *Newsgroup*

7825 `bit.listserv.travel-l` Tourism discussions list. *Newsgroup*

7826 **City.Net:** Guide to communities around the world; a virtual tourist's heaven.
`http://www.city.net/`
INFO `altis@city.net`

7827 **Conde Nast Traveler Online:** More than one thousand pages of sophisticated travel information and fine photography. *Magazine*
`http://www.cntraveler.com/`
INFO EDITOR OWNER `asugar@cntraveler.com` (Aaron Sugarman, Editor)
INFO `feedback@condenet.com`
EDITOR `traveler@condenet.com` (Aaron Sugarman)
Frequency: irregular

7828 **The Connected Traveler:** A multimedia magazine of travel, culture, and humor featuring stories, sound, and pictures from around the world. *E-Journal*
`http://www.travelmedia.com/world/connected/`

INFO `travelmdia@aol.com` (Russell Johnson)

7829 The Cyber Maze: An online compilation of the *PPSA Magazine*. Topics include: real-life stories and road trips, humor, photos and art, editorials and commentary on social issues and current events. *E-Zine*

`http://www.ppsa.com/ppsa/`

INFO `jjohnson@ppsa.com` (John Johnson)

Frequency: updated weekly

➤ **DRIVE-INS:** On drive-in movie theaters and classic indoor bijous. (See entry 700 for full listing.)

7830 Europe by Eurail: "The Internet resource for traveling Europe by train." Plan your Eurail or BritRail vacation with ease. Rail-pass descriptions, trip planning tools, ticket and schedule database, and an online conference for asking travel questions and sharing experiences.

`http://www.eurail.com/`

`info@eurail.com`

INFO `cmartin@eurail.com`

➤ **Expedition News:** A monthly review of world-class expeditions, research projects, and adventures. This new forum on the outdoors covers projects that stimulate, motivate, and educate. (See entry 6624 for full listing.)

7831 Farm, Ranch & Country Vacations in America: Promotional Web site for the book *Farm, Ranch & Country Vacation in America*, a guide that includes names, numbers, locations, rates, and detailed descriptions of vacation sites in the West, the East, and mid-America.

`http://www.netzone.com/~advguide`

INFO `advguide@netzone.com` (Maria G. Flores-Beck)

7832 `fj.rec.travel` Traveling all over the world. *Newsgroup*

7833 `fj.rec.travel.air` Topics on air travel. *Newsgroup*

7834 `fj.rec.travel.world` Traveling all over the world. *Newsgroup*

7835 HOSPEX: The HOSPitality EXchange (homestays) database. *Distribution List, moderated*

`http://hospex.icm.edu.pl/`

± INFO `hospex-owner@icm.edu.pl`

INFO `w.sylwestrzak@icm.edu.pl` (Wojtek Sylwestrzak)

Please Note: Subscription by approval only.

Comments: E-mail `hospex-owner@icm.edu.pl` for information on membership.

7836 Hotels on the Net: Information on hotels and special promotions in the Asia-Pacific region.

`http://www.hotelasia.com.hk/`

INFO `info@hotelasia.com.hk`

7837 `iijnet.travel` Topics and discussions about traveling. *Newsgroup*

➤ **IMOVEIS:** On property exchange: tourism, emigration, participatory communities. (See entry 1943 for full listing.)

➤ **International Teletimes:** General-interest culture magazine with varying monthly themes such as education, history, and travel. Regular columns include "Cuisine," "Keepers of the Light" (photography), and "The Wine Enthusiast." (See entry 649 for full listing.)

➤ **Loci:** An online magazine by and for college students. Includes entertainment information, games, chat forums, and more. Sponsored by Barnes & Noble booksellers. (See entry 650 for full listing.)

7838 `okinawa.rec.travel` Discussion about traveling. *Newsgroup*

7839 `rec.travel.asia` Travel in Asia. *Newsgroup*

7840 `rec.travel.cruises` Travel by cruise ships. *Newsgroup*

7841 `rec.travel.marketplace` Tickets and accomodations wanted and for sale. *Newsgroup*

7842 `rec.travel.misc` Everything and anything about travel. *Newsgroup*

7843 `rec.travel.usa-canada` Travel in the United States and Canada. *Newsgroup*

7844 `relcom.commerce.tour` Tourism, leisure and entertainment opportunities. *Newsgroup*

➤   **RN-TRAVEL:** For traveling RNs. (See entry 4976 for full listing.)

7845   **ROADSIDE:** On roadside attractions: alligator ranches, coffeepot-shaped restaurants, and the like. *Mailing List*
     http://www.brettnews.com/~brettnews
     ± listproc@echonyc.com [body = SUBSCRIBE ROADSIDE first-name last-name]
     OWNER brett@echonyc.com (Brett Leveridge)

7846   **Shoestring Travel:** Providing the shoestring traveler with information on itineraries, hotels, B & Bs, hostels, transportation, and other items pertaining to saving money while traveling. *E-Zine*
     ARCHIVE http://uptown.turnpike.net/eadler/index.html
     Frequency: at least twice a month

7847   **tnn.travel** Topics and discussions about traveling. *Newsgroup*

7848   **tnn.travel.globe** "Wanderes", student's travel information square. *Moderated newsgroup*

7849   **tnn.travel.report** Report of your travel reports. *Newsgroup*

7850   **TravelGram:** An up-to-the-minute bulletin on the latest worldwide airfare discounts, car rental offers, hotel specials, and resort packages, plus villas and condos for rent. *Newsletter*
     ± INFO travel@mailback.com [body = send contents *carriage return* end]
     ARCHIVE http://www.csn.net/~johnhart/travgram.html

7851   **Travel-L:** Discussion of travel experiences. *Mailing List*
     ± listserv@listserv.net [body = Subscribe TRAVEL-L first-name last-name]
     ± listserv@vm.ege.edu.tr [body = Subscribe TRAVEL-L first-name last-name]
     INFO travel-l-request@listserv.net
     OWNER jschaefer@grog.ric.edu (James A. Schaefer)
     POST travel-l@trearn.bitnet
     Gated: bit.listserv.travel-L

7852   **TravelWeb:** A database of information on all sorts of accomodations from hotel and resort chains to bed and breakfasts. Allows you to search for information based on accomodation type, price ranges, and facilities available.
     http://www.travelweb.com/
     INFO travelweb@thisco.com

➤   **uk.rec.youth-hostel:** Discussion of youth hostels and hosteling. *Newsgroup*

7853   **Web Travel Review:** The finest in travel literature, profusely illustrated, free on the Web. Over 2,000 photographs and 600 pages of text. Winner of Best of the Web '94. *Magazine*
     http://webtravel.org/webtravel/
     INFO OWNER philg@mit.edu (Philip Greenspun)
     ARCHIVE http://webtravel.org/webtravel/
     Frequency: continuous

7854   **The Webfoot's Travel Guide:** Personable list of links on traveling in Germany, Austria, British Virgin Islands, France, Italy, Spain, Vatican City, and Hawaii.
     http://www.webfoot.com/travel/guides/guides.top.html
     INFO ducky@webfoot.com

US

➤   **alt.culture.us.1970s:** At least pick a *good* decade to be stuck in the past. *Newsgroup*

➤   **alt.culture.us.1980s:** The Me Decade. *Newsgroup*

7855   **alt.current-events.usa** What's new in the United States. *Newsgroup*

➤   **alt.politics.usa.constitution:** U.S. constitutional politics. *Newsgroup*

➤   **alt.politics.usa.misc:** Miscellaneous U.S. politics. *Newsgroup*

7856 Country Connect: Small-town USA listings. This site is dedicated to small towns and the people, events, and markets that make them up. You will find information on country living and the pleasures of small community living.

`http://country.ccrtc.com/jja/jja.html`

`http://country.ccrtc.com/cchome/cchome.html`

INFO `greg@country.ccrtc.com`

Comments: This site is new and will continue to grow rapidly. Small towns around the world are encouraged to participate in Country Connect.

➤ **Overland-Trails:** On the emigrant & supply trails of the mid-19th century American West. (See entry 5255 for full listing.)

7857 soc.culture.usa The culture of the United States of America. *Newsgroup*

US— REGIONS—MIDWEST

7858 clari.sports.local.midwest.misc Other Midwest athletics. *Moderated newsgroup*

US— REGIONS—NORTHEAST

7859 alt.new-england The USA's northeastern region. *Newsgroup*

➤ **Boston.Com:** Mega-Web site for New England featuring the Boston Globe Online. (See entry 6107 for full listing.)

7860 capdist.general General topic postings for the New York capital district. *Newsgroup*

7861 capdist.misc Miscellaneous discussion topics in the capdist. *Newsgroup*

7862 clari.sports.local.new_england.misc Other athletics in New England. *Moderated newsgroup*

7863 ne.food New England food and restaurant reviews. *Newsgroup*

➤ **ne.forsale:** Short postings on items for sale in New England. *Newsgroup*

7864 ne.general General interest discussions pertinent to New England. *Newsgroup*

7865 ne.general.selected General discussion for the Northeast (USA). *Moderated newsgroup*

7866 ne.housing Short postings on housing wanted or available in New England. *Newsgroup*

7867 ne.jobs New England job listings. *Newsgroup*

7868 ne.jobs.contract Postings of contract openings in New England. *Newsgroup*

➤ **ne.motorcycles:** The Northeast branch of the Denizens of Doom. *Newsgroup*

➤ **ne.motss:** Issues pertaining to homosexuality in New England. *Newsgroup*

➤ **ne.nearnet.general:** Discuss the New England Academic and Research Network (NEARnet). *Newsgroup*

7869 ne.politics Discussion of New England political issues. *Newsgroup*

7870 ne.seminars New England upcoming talks, seminars, etc. *Newsgroup*

7871 ne.wanted New England want ads. *Newsgroup*

7872 ne.weather New England weather forecasts. *Newsgroup*

US— REGIONS—PACIFIC NORTHWEST

➤ <u>Writers' Resources</u>: Interesting list of useful links for writers. Special focus on science fiction and the Pacific Northwest. (See entry 633 for full listing.)

7873 clari.sports.local.northwest.misc Athletics in the Pacific Northwest. *Moderated newsgroup*

➤ **NetCetera:** On new Internet resources and tools and net-related news briefs. Net-related activities of NorthWestNet member organizations and clients are also highlighted. (See entry 2882 for full listing.)

7874 pnw.education Education issues in the Pacific Northwest. *Newsgroup*

7875 pnw.forsale Things for sale. *Newsgroup*

7876 pnw.general General information. *Newsgroup*

7877   `pnw.motss`   Issues about homosexuality in the Pacific Northwest. *Newsgroup*

7878   `pnw.news`   General news issues. *Newsgroup*

➤   `pnw.personals`:   Personals listings for the Pacific Northwest region. *Newsgroup*

US— REGIONS—SOUTHEAST

7879   `alt.appalachian`   Appalachian region awareness, events, and culture. *Newsgroup*

7880   `alt.thought.southern`   Pass the barbeque sandwiches and take the Southern view of things for a while. *Newsgroup*

7881   `bit.listserv.sthcult`   Southern cultures discussions. *Newsgroup*

7882   `clari.sports.local.south`   Athletics in other areas of the South. *Moderated newsgroup*

US— REGIONS—SOUTHWEST

7883   `alt.culture.us.southwest`   Basking in the sun of the U.S.'s lower left. *Newsgroup*

US—ALABAMA

➤   **AACRL:** For members of the Alabama Association of College and Research Libraries. (See entry 5743 for full listing.)

7884   `clari.local.alabama`   News of Alabama. *Moderated newsgroup*

7885   `hsv.forsale`   Items for sale in Huntsville, Alabama. *Newsgroup*

7886   `hsv.general`   Items of general interest in Huntsville, Alabama. *Newsgroup*

7887   `hsv.jobs`   Huntsville, Alabama job postings. *Newsgroup*

➤   **Mobile Press Register:** Alabama's oldest newspaper. (See entry 6128 for full listing.)

➤   **North Alabama Country Dance Newsletter:** This newsletter includes a schedule of opportunities for participatory dance, especially contra, Appalachian squares, and traditional round dances, within reasonable driving distance of Huntsville, Alabama. (See entry 286 for full listing.)

➤   **WHNT 19 News:** From Huntsville, Alabama: a prototype TV news presence on the Web. (See entry 6139 for full listing.)

US—ALASKA

7888   `ak.admin`   Alaskan network news administration. *Newsgroup*

➤   `ak.bushnet.thing`:   Alaskan Public Access Networking. *Newsgroup*

7889   `alt.culture.alaska`   Is this where the ice weasels come from? *Newsgroup*

7890   `clari.local.alaska`   News of Alaska. *Moderated newsgroup*

US—ARIZONA

7891   **ArizonaWeb:** A web of information on and about Arizona. It includes real-estate information.
`http://www.arizonaweb.com/`
INFO `realtor@primenet.com`

7892   `az.forsale`   Buy and sell in Arizona. *Newsgroup*

7893   `az.general`   Items of general interest in Arizona. *Newsgroup*

7894   `az.internet`   Discussions of Internet topics local to Arizona. *Newsgroup*

7895   `az.jobs`   Available jobs in Arizona. *Newsgroup*

7896   `az.politics`   Discussion of Arizona politics. *Newsgroup*

➤   `az.swusrgrp`:   The Southwest User's Group. *Newsgroup*

7897 `az.teens` Arizona teen discussions. *Newsgroup*

7898 `az.wanted` Looking for stuff in Arizona. *Newsgroup*

7899 `clari.local.arizona` News of Arizona. *Moderated newsgroup*

7900 `clari.sports.local.southwest.arizona` News of Arizona athletics. *Moderated newsgroup*

US—ARKANSAS

7901 `clari.local.arkansas` News of Arkansas. *Newsgroup*

US—CALIFORNIA

7902 `alt.california` The state and the state of mind. *Newsgroup*

7903 **The Big Bear Source:** The Big Bear Source is a full information service for the Big Bear, California, area, including travel and recreation resources and news for the Big Bear Lake area.
http://www.sddt.com/~bigbear
INFO bbsource@earthlink.net

7904 `ca.driving` California freeways and back roads. *Newsgroup*

7905 `ca.earthquakes` What's shakin' in California. *Newsgroup*

7906 `ca.environment` Environmental concerns in California. *Newsgroup*

7907 `ca.environment.earthquakes` Same as `ca.earthquakes`. *Newsgroup*

7908 `ca.forsale` Things for sale in California. *Newsgroup*

7909 `ca.general` Of general interest to readers in California only. *Newsgroup*

7910 `ca.govt-bulletins` Public information from California government agencies. *Moderated newsgroup*

7911 `ca.news.group` Existing or proposed newsgroups for `ca` distribution. *Newsgroup*

7912 `ca.politics` Political topics of interest to California readers only. *Newsgroup*

7913 `ca.wanted` For sale/wanted postings throughout California. *Newsgroup*

7914 `ca.water` Information on California water and Internet issues. *Newsgroup*

➤ **California Homeschool Network (CHN):** CHN exists to provide resources and information about home schooling; to protect the right of the family to educate its children at home in the manner it deems appropriate without regulation; and to foster community among home educators in California. (See entry 4207 for full listing.)

7915 `clari.local.california` News of California. *Moderated newsgroup*

7916 `clari.local.california.gov` California state government news. *Moderated newsgroup*

7917 `clari.local.california.lottery` California state lottery news. *Moderated newsgroup*

7918 `clari.local.california.northern` News of northern California. *Moderated newsgroup*

7919 `clari.local.california.southern.misc` News of southern California. *Moderated newsgroup*

7920 `clari.sports.local.southwest.california` News of other California athletics. *Moderated newsgroup*

➤ **Hallucinet:** Southern California's "koolest, neato-est, freakiest zine/site/good karma meeting place." Site for Lethal Records, Cleopatra Records, Retail Slut, and several zines including Caffeine, Underscope, Asylum, and more. (See entry 1646 for full listing.)

➤ **Midsummer Mozart Festival:** The Midsummer Mozart Festival gives concerts of the works of Wolfgang Amadeus Mozart and his contemporaries. These concerts take place in the San Francisco Bay Area in the summer. A 41-piece orchestra is conducted by maestro George Cleve. (See entry 816 for full listing.)

7921 **Virtually California:** The place to find and explore online resources in California. Plan your vacation, search for fine dining, and shop online for "Californian" items in the Virtually California Plaza.
http://www.virtually.com/
INFO dgs@virtually.com

US—CALIFORNIA—ANTELOPE VALLEY

7922 **av.computer** Computers in the Antelope Valley. *Newsgroup*

7923 **av.dining** Dining in the Antelope Valley. *Newsgroup*

7924 **av.forsale** Things for sale in the Antelope Valley. *Newsgroup*

7925 **av.general** Items of general interest in the Antelope Valley. *Newsgroup*

7926 **av.jobs** Employment in the Antelope Valley, Rosamond, and Edwards AFB. *Newsgroup*

➤   **av.mug:** Antelope Valley Microcomputer Users' Group. *Newsgroup*

7927 **av.news** Usenet in the Antelope Valley. *Newsgroup*

➤   **av.personals:** Meeting people in the Antelope Valley. *Newsgroup*

7928 **av.seminars** Seminars in the Antelope Valley. *Newsgroup*

➤   **av.user:** Users in the Antelope Valley. *Newsgroup*

7929 **av.wanted** Things wanted in the Antelope Valley. *Newsgroup*

US—CALIFORNIA—LOS ANGELES

7930 **clari.local.california.los_angeles** News of Los Angeles. *Moderated newsgroup*

7931 **clari.local.los_angeles** News of Los Angeles, California. *Moderated newsgroup*

7932 **clari.sports.local.southwest.california.los_angeles** Los Angeles sports. *Moderated newsgroup*

7933 **la.eats** Dining in Los Angeles, California. *Newsgroup*

7934 **la.forsale** Things for sale in Los Angeles, California. *Newsgroup*

7935 **la.general** Items of general interest in Los Angeles, California. *Newsgroup*

7936 **la.jobs** Employment in Los Angeles, Ventura, and Orange County. *Newsgroup*

7937 **la.news** Usenet in Los Angeles, CA. *Newsgroup*

➤   **la.personals:** Meeting people in Los Angeles, California. *Newsgroup*

7938 **la.seminars** Seminars in Los Angeles, California. *Newsgroup*

7939 **la.transportation** Anything related to transportation in Los Angeles. *Newsgroup*

7940 **la.wanted** Things wanted in Los Angeles, California. *Newsgroup*

US—CALIFORNIA—ORANGE COUNTY

7941 **oc.eats** Dining out around Orange County, California. *Newsgroup*

7942 **oc.forsale** Items for sale in Orange County, California. *Newsgroup*

7943 **oc.general** Items of general interest in Orange County, California. *Newsgroup*

7944 **oc.slug** Sun Local Users' Group in Orange County, California. *Newsgroup*

7945 **oc.wanted** Items wanted in Orange County, California. *Newsgroup*

➤   **University of California, Riverside:** This is the campus wide information service for University of California, Riverside. (See entry 4466 for full listing.)

US—CALIFORNIA—SACRAMENTO REGION

7946 **sac.general** General talk group. *Newsgroup*

7947 **sac.swap** Sacramento for-sale group. *Newsgroup*

7948 **yolo.general** General discussion about Yolo County, California. *Newsgroup*

7949 **yolo.life** Life in Yolo County, California. *Newsgroup*

7950 **yolo.news** General interest news about Yolo County, California. *Newsgroup*

7951 **yolo.news.admin** News administration for the Yolo County, California hierarchy. *Newsgroup*

US—CALIFORNIA—SAN DIEGO

7952 **The San Diego Source:** The San Diego Source is a full information service for the San Diego area, including finance, business, real estate news, and arts and leisure activities.
      http://www.sddt.com/
      INFO webmaster@sddt.com

➤ **San Diego State University, College of Sciences:** This site provides various campus information and centralized access to other campus resources. (See entry 4447 for full listing.)

7953 **sdnet.books** Book reviews and discussion in the San Diego area. *Newsgroup*

7954 **sdnet.cerfnet** San Diego city/county CERFNet news. *Newsgroup*

➤ **sdnet.computing:** San Diego discussions of computing issues. *Newsgroup*

➤ **sdnet.crl:** News from the UCSD Center for Research in Language. *Newsgroup*

7955 **sdnet.eats** San Diego restaurant news and reviews. *Newsgroup*

7956 **sdnet.events** San Diego announcements about events around town. *Newsgroup*

7957 **sdnet.forsale** San Diego stuff for sale (see also sdnet.wanted). *Newsgroup*

7958 **sdnet.freenet** Freenet in San Diego, California. *Newsgroup*

7959 **sdnet.general** San Diego items of general interest. *Newsgroup*

7960 **sdnet.hemp** San Diego hemp legalization discussions. *Newsgroup*

7961 **sdnet.housing** San Diego places to live wanted/available. *Newsgroup*

7962 **sdnet.jobs** San Diego jobs wanted/offered in town only. *Newsgroup*

7963 **sdnet.jobs.discuss** Discussion related to jobs in greater San Diego area. *Newsgroup*

7964 **sdnet.jobs.offered** Jobs offered in the greater San Diego area. *Newsgroup*

7965 **sdnet.jobs.services** Job placement services for the greater San Diego area. *Newsgroup*

7966 **sdnet.jobs.wanted** Jobs wanted for the greater San Diego area. *Newsgroup*

7967 **sdnet.lit** San Diego literary discusions. *Newsgroup*

7968 **sdnet.misc** San Diego discussions that don't have their own group. *Newsgroup*

7969 **sdnet.motss** San Diego gay, bi, lesbians, and friends. *Newsgroup*

7970 **sdnet.movies** San Diego movie reviews and comments. *Newsgroup*

7971 **sdnet.music** San Diego concert/performance reviews and comments. *Newsgroup*

➤ **sdnet.next:** San Diego NeXT users group. *Newsgroup*

➤ **sdnet.personals:** San Diego area (only!) personals. *Newsgroup*

7972 **sdnet.politics** San Diego city and county politics. *Newsgroup*

7973 **sdnet.rideshare** San Diego rides wanted/offered. *Newsgroup*

7974 **sdnet.seminars** San Diego talks, lectures, seminars, announcments. *Newsgroup*

7975 **sdnet.singles** San Diego singles scene. *Newsgroup*

➤ **sdnet.sports:** San Diego teams and sporting events. *Newsgroup*

7976 **sdnet.theatre** San Diego plays and performance reviews and comments. *Newsgroup*

7977 **sdnet.tv** San Diego local TV features and criticism. *Newsgroup*

7978 **sdnet.waffle** San Diego Waffle BBS discussions. *Newsgroup*

7979 `sdnet.wanted` San Diego items wanted (see also `sdnet.forsale`). *Newsgroup*

7980 `sdnet.weather` Late night and early morning clouds, clearing mid-morning. *Newsgroup*

7981 `sdnet.writing` Writers and publishers in San Diego. *Newsgroup*

US—CALIFORNIA—SAN FRANCISCO BAY AREA

7982 `ba.announce` Announcements of general interest to all readers. *Moderated newsgroup*

➤   `ba.bicycles`: Bicycling issues specific to the San Francisco Bay Area. *Newsgroup*

7983 `ba.broadcast` Bay Area TV/radio issues. *Newsgroup*

➤   `ba.consumers`: Bay Area (USA) group for consumer topics. *Newsgroup*

7984 `ba.dance` Discussion about local dance events. *Newsgroup*

7985 `ba.food` Bay Area restaurants and eating places. *Newsgroup*

7986 `ba.general` Announcements of general interest to all readers. *Newsgroup*

7987 `ba.helping-hand` Requests for assistance for the needy. *Moderated newsgroup*

7988 `ba.internet` Discussions about Bay Area Internet connectivity. *Newsgroup*

➤   `ba.jobs.contract`: Listings of Bay Area (USA) contract job opportunites. *Newsgroup*

7989 `ba.jobs.misc` Discussions about the job market in the Bay Area. *Newsgroup*

7990 `ba.jobs.offered` Job postings in the Bay Area. *Newsgroup*

7991 `ba.jobs.resumes` Resume postings for Bay Area jobs. *Newsgroup*

7992 `ba.market.computers` For sale/wanted: computers and software. *Newsgroup*

7993 `ba.market.housing` For sale/rent/wanted: housing, land, roommates. *Newsgroup*

7994 `ba.market.misc` For sale/wanted: miscellaneous. *Newsgroup*

7995 `ba.market.vehicles` For sale/wanted: autos, cycles, trucks, etc. *Newsgroup*

➤   `ba.motorcycles`: Bay Area motorcycle issues. *Newsgroup*

➤   `ba.motss`: Newsgroup for Bay Area MOTSSers. *Newsgroup*

7996 `ba.mountain-folk` Living in the hills and mountains around the Bay Area. *Newsgroup*

7997 `ba.music` Musical events in the Bay Area. *Newsgroup*

7998 `ba.news.group` Meta-discussions about newsgroups in `ba.*` distribution. *Newsgroup*

➤   `ba.personals`: Personal ads of Bay Area interest. *Newsgroup*

7999 `ba.politics` Political topics of interest to Bay Area readers. *Newsgroup*

8000 `ba.seminars` Announcements of Bay Area seminars. *Newsgroup*

8001 `ba.singles` Local newsgroup for single people. *Newsgroup*

➤   `ba.sports`: Discussion of sports in the Bay Area. *Newsgroup*

8002 `ba.transportation` Discussion of Bay Area transit/commute/driving issues. *Newsgroup*

8003 `ba.weather` National Weather Service updates. *Newsgroup*

8004 `clari.local.california.sfbay.biz` San Francisco Bay Area business news. *Moderated newsgroup*

8005 `clari.local.california.sfbay.briefs` San Francisco Bay Area daily brief. *Moderated newsgroup*

8006 `clari.local.california.sfbay.crime` San Francisco Bay Area crime news. *Moderated newsgroup*

8007 `clari.local.california.sfbay.fire` San Francisco Bay Area fire news. *Moderated newsgroup*

8008 `clari.local.california.sfbay.gov` Bay Area local government news. *Moderated newsgroup*

8009 `clari.local.california.sfbay.law` San Francisco Bay Area laws and lawsuits. *Moderated newsgroup*

8010 `clari.local.california.sfbay.living` Entertainment, human interest. *Moderated newsgroup*

8011 `clari.local.california.sfbay.transport` Bay Area transit and road news. *Moderated newsgroup*

8012 `clari.local.california.sfbay.transport.conditions` Road and transit status. *Moderated newsgroup*

8013 `clari.local.california.sfbay.trouble` San Francisco Bay Area accident reports. *Moderated newsgroup*

8014 `clari.local.california.sfbay.weather` Bay Area weather. *Moderated newsgroup*

8015 `clari.local.sfbay` News of San Francisco Bay Area. *Moderated newsgroup*

8016 `clari.sfbay.briefs` Twice-daily news roundups for SF Bay Area. *Moderated newsgroup*

8017 `clari.sfbay.entertain` Reviews and entertainment news for SF Bay Area. *Moderated newsgroup*

➤ `clari.sfbay.fire:` Stories from fire departments of the SF Bay Area. *Moderated newsgroup*

8018 `clari.sfbay.general` Main stories for SF Bay Area. *Moderated newsgroup*

8019 `clari.sfbay.misc` Shorter general items for SF Bay Area. *Moderated newsgroup*

8020 `clari.sfbay.police` Stories from the police departments of the SF Bay Area. *Moderated newsgroup*

8021 `clari.sfbay.roads` Reports from Caltrans and the CHP. *Moderated newsgroup*

8022 `clari.sfbay.short` Very short items for SF Bay Area. *Moderated newsgroup*

➤ `clari.sfbay.weather:` SF Bay and California weather reports. *Moderated newsgroup*

8023 `clari.sports.local.southwest.california.sfbay` Bay Area sports. *Moderated newsgroup*

8024 **The LP Lover's Guide to San Francisco:** For descriptions and ratings of the best used record stores throughout the San Francisco Bay Area, visit The LP Lover's Guide to San Francisco.
`http://www.webcom.com/bg63/`
INFO `bg63@ix.netcom.com`

8025 `nbn.housing` Houses for rent, sale, or wanted in the North Bay. *Newsgroup*

8026 `nbn.market` Want to buy, want to sell in the North Bay. *Newsgroup*

8027 `nbn.misc` News and events in the North Bay. *Newsgroup*

8028 `nbn.novato` News and discussion of Novato, California. *Newsgroup*

8029 `nbn.westmarin` News and discussion of West Marin County, California. *Newsgroup*

8030 **pacifica-l:** On the city of Pacifica, California. *Mailing List*
± `listserv@netcom.com` [body = SUBSCRIBE pacifica-l]
OWNER `bruce@hallman.org` (Bruce Hallman)

8031 `sbay.forsale` Items for sale (noncommercial) in the South Bay. *Newsgroup*

8032 `sbay.general` Miscellaneous topics specific to the South Bay. *Newsgroup*

➤ `sbay.hams:` South Bay amateur radio-related news and events. *Newsgroup*

8033 `sbay.news.config` South Bay connectivity and maps. *Newsgroup*

8034 `sbay.news.group` South Bay newsgroup meta-discussion. *Newsgroup*

8035 `sbay.news.stats` South Bay automated statistics and site information. *Newsgroup*

➤ `sbay.sports:` South Bay sports. *Newsgroup*

8036 `sbay.test` Testing area for South Bay sites. *Newsgroup*

➤ `sbay.waffle:` Waffle BBS topics specific to the South Bay. *Newsgroup*

US—CALIFORNIA—SILICON VALLEY & SANTA CRUZ

8037 **Palo Alto Weekly:** Covering the San Francisco Peninsula communities of Palo Alto, Menlo Park, Stanford, Portola Valley, Los Altos Hills, and East Palo Alto. Online version contains entire editorial content plus classified advertising.

http://www.service.com/paw/home.html
INFO OWNER paweekly@netcom.com (Bill Johnson, Publisher)
ARCHIVE http://www.service.com/paw/home.html
Frequency: twice weekly (Wednesdays and Fridays)

8038 `scruz.events` Happenings in and around the Santa Cruz, California region. *Newsgroup*

8039 `scruz.general` General discussions from Santa Cruz, California. *Newsgroup*

8040 `scruz.market` Buy and sell in the Santa Cruz, California region. *Newsgroup*

8041 `scruz.poetry` Poetry and poets in the Santa Cruz, California (USA) area. *Newsgroup*

8042 `scruz.politics` Politics in the Santa Cruz, California (USA) area. *Newsgroup*

➤ `scruz.sysops`: For system operators in the Santa Cruz, California (USA) area. *Newsgroup*

US—COLORADO

8043 `alt.forsale.grandjunction` Items for sale in Grand Junction, Colorado. *Newsgroup*

8044 `boulder.general` Items of general interest to Boulder, Colorado. *Newsgroup*

8045 `clari.local.colorado` News of Colorado. *Newsgroup*

8046 `clari.sports.local.southwest.colorado` Colorado athletics. *Moderated newsgroup*

8047 `co.fort-collins.ads` Fort Collins for-sale postings. *Newsgroup*

8048 `co.fort-collins.general` General discussion for Fort Collins, Colorado. *Newsgroup*

8049 `co.general` Items of general interest to Colorado. *Newsgroup*

8050 `co.jobs` Employment in Colorado. *Newsgroup*

8051 `co.media.rmn` Editorials and letters from the *Rocky Mountain News. Newsgroup*

8052 `co.politics` Discussion of political issues related to Colorado. *Newsgroup*

8053 `co.politics.amend2.discuss` Discussion regarding Colorado's Amendment 2. *Newsgroup*

8054 `co.politics.amend2.info` Information on Colorado's Amendment 2. *Moderated newsgroup*

US—CONNECTICUT

8055 `clari.local.connecticut` News of Connecticut. *Newsgroup*

8056 `clari.sports.local.new_england.connecticut` Connecticut athletics. *Moderated newsgroup*

8057 **Housatonic Valley Tourism:** These pages, updated regularly, provide calendars of events, historic site information and local recreation and sports information on the Housatonic Valley area in western Connecticut. Also includes information on the life and music of Charles Ives, the Danbury area's most famous composer.
http://acad.bryant.edu/~kbrook/housaval.html
INFO kbrook@acad.bryant.edu (Kevin Brook)

➤ `ne.forsale`: Short postings on items for sale in New England. *Newsgroup*

US—DELAWARE

8058 `clari.local.delaware` News of Delaware. *Newsgroup*

➤ **U-Discover!:** CWIS for the University of Delaware. (See entry 4460 for full listing.)

US—FLORIDA

➤ **Alligator Online:** The electronic version of the 32,000-copy college daily that serves the University of Florida community. (See entry 4469 for full listing.)

8059 `clari.local.florida` News of Florida. *Moderated newsgroup*

8060 `clari.sports.local.south.florida.miami` News of Miami athletics. *Moderated newsgroup*

8061 `clari.sports.local.south.florida.misc` News of other Florida athletics. *Moderated newsgroup*

8062 `clari.sports.local.south.florida.tampa_bay` News of Tampa Bay athletics. *Moderated newsgroup*

8063 **Community Blood Centers of South Florida:** Community Blood Centers of South Florida is a nonprofit, all-voluntary blood collection agency, providing over 100,000 pints of blood and blood products to hospital and kidney dialysis patients each year.
`http://www.bocanet.com/cbc`
INFO `webmaster2@bocanet.com`

8064 `fl.announce` Important announcements for everyone in Florida. *Newsgroup*

8065 `fl.attractions` Florida attractions and entertainment. *Newsgroup*

➤ `fl.comp:` General computers in Florida. *Newsgroup*

8066 `fl.comp.rep` Technical computer repair or modifications in Florida. *Newsgroup*

8067 `fl.forsale` Items for sale in Florida. *Newsgroup*

8068 `fl.general` General topics in Florida. *Newsgroup*

8069 `fl.jobs` The Florida job market. *Newsgroup*

8070 `fl.mail` Mail systems, routers, paths in Florida. *Newsgroup*

8071 `fl.news` News problems and features in Florida. *Newsgroup*

8072 `fl.politics` Politics in Florida. *Newsgroup*

8073 `fl.travel` Travel within Florida. *Newsgroup*

8074 `fl.yumyum` Reviews and advice on restaurants in Florida. *Newsgroup*

8075 `oau.biz` Commercial postings in Orlando, Florida. *Newsgroup*

8076 `oau.forsale` Items for sale in Orlando, Florida. *Newsgroup*

8077 `oau.news` Orlando, Florida news. *Newsgroup*

➤ **South Florida Environmental Reader:** SFER is a newsletter covering environmental topics concerning South Florida, which includes the areas south of Lake Okeechobee, including the Everglades and Florida Keys. (See entry 4639 for full listing.)

➤ **Youth Activity Center of Boca Raton, Florida:** The Youth Activity Center in Boca Raton, Florida, is a nonsectarian corporation established to provide an alternative positive social environment for youth and their parents. YAC differs from other youth centers because it gives youth and parents a safe place to play, learn, and socialize. (See entry 10182 for full listing.)

US—GEORGIA

8078 `atl.arno` Atlanta Regional Network Organization (ARNO). *Newsgroup*

8079 `atl.general` Items of general interest in Atlanta, Georgia. *Newsgroup*

8080 `atl.jobs` Jobs in Atlanta, Georgia. *Newsgroup*

8081 `atl.olympics` The Olympics in Atlanta, Georgia. *Newsgroup*

8082 `atl.resumes` Resumes in Atlanta, Georgia. *Newsgroup*

8083 `atl.singles` Discussion area for greater-Atlanta singles. *Newsgroup*

8084 **The Atlanta Beer Guide:** A guide to finding good beer in and around Atlanta, Georgia.
`http://www.beerinfo.com/~jlock/atlbeer0.html`
`ftp://ftp.stanford.edu/pub/clubs/homebrew/beer/rfdb/beer-atlanta`
INFO `editor@beerinfo.com`

8085 `ats.homenet.misc` SLIP/homenet for platforms not in rest of ats.homenet.*. *Newsgroup*

8086 `clari.local.georgia` News of Georgia. *Moderated newsgroup*

8087 `clari.sports.local.south.georgia` News of Georgia athletics. *Moderated newsgroup*

➤   **Georgia Southern University:** This is the CWIS of Georgia Southern University, Statesboro, Georgia. (See entry 4422 for full listing.)

US—HAWAII

8088   `alt.culture.hawaii`   Ua Mau Ke Ea O Ka 'Aina I Ka Pono. *Newsgroup*

8089   `alt.radio.free`   Discussing Radio Free Hawaii radio station. *Newsgroup*

8090   `clari.local.hawaii`   News of Hawaii. *Newsgroup*

8091   `hawaii.ads.forsale`   For-sale ads from private individuals in Hawai'i. *Newsgroup*

8092   `hawaii.ads.misc`   Other Hawai'i-specific ads. *Moderated newsgroup*

8093   `hawaii.ads.wanted`   Wanted-to-buy ads from individuals in Hawai'i. *Newsgroup*

8094   `hawaii.announce`   Only announcements (events, happenings) in Hawai'i. *Newsgroup*

8095   `hawaii.inet-providers`   Discussion of Hawai'i's Internet providers. *Newsgroup*

8096   `hawaii.military`   Talk about the military's role in Hawai'i. *Newsgroup*

8097   `hawaii.misc`   General talk about Hawai'i. *Newsgroup*

8098   `hawaii.politics`   Talk about Hawai'i politics. *Newsgroup*

➤   `hawaii.sports:`   Hawai'i local sports discussions. *Newsgroup*

8099   **PC Currents:** Pacific Cyber Currents (PC Currents) is a Hawaiian home-grown e-magazine dedicated to serving Hawaii and the Pacific with Internet- and computer-related news and information. *E-Magazine*

     `http://hypermedia.net/webdir`

     `http://hypermedia.net/`

     INFO `info@hypermedia.net`

     OWNER `sean@hypermedia.net`

     ARCHIVE `http://pc-currents.com/`

➤   **Surf News Network Hawaii:** Hawaii's authoratative surfing Web site from Surf News Network Hawaii. Find the latest surf condition updates from Sunset Beach to Diamond Head. Check out Hawaii's most beautiful women in bikinis through the lens of the Surf News Babe Cam. (See entry 6991 for full listing.)

➤   **UHINFO:** This is the CWIS for the University of Hawaii system, which includes UH Manoa, UH Hilo, UH West Oahu, Hawaii CC, Honolulu CC, Kapiolani CC, Kauai CC, Leeward CC, Maui CC, and Windward CC. (See entry 4462 for full listing.)

US—IDAHO

8100   `clari.local.idaho`   News of Idaho. *Newsgroup*

➤   **LIBIDAHO:** On libraries in the state of Idaho. (See entry 5751 for full listing.)

US—ILLINOIS

8101   `chi.eats`   Group for discussion of Chicagoland restaurants. *Newsgroup*

8102   `chi.forsale`   Chicago area for-sale notices. *Newsgroup*

8103   `chi.general`   General discussions, Chicago area, not for sale/wanted. *Newsgroup*

8104   `chi.internet`   Discussion of net offerings in Chicagoland. *Newsgroup*

8105   `chi.jobs`   Jobs in the Chicago area. *Newsgroup*

8106   `chi.mail`   Discussion of Chicago area e-mail issues. *Newsgroup*

8107   `chi.media`   Discussions on Chicago-area radio, television, and print media. *Newsgroup*

8108   `chi.places`   Group for announcements of Chicago area events. *Newsgroup*

8109   `chi.politics`   Political issues at all levels in and around Chicago. *Newsgroup*

8110 `chi.wanted` Chicago area wanted notices. *Newsgroup*

8111 `chi.weather` Chicago area weather. *Newsgroup*

8112 Chicago Moving Image Scene: The online resource and directory for Chicagoland producers of film, video, and multimedia. Free professional listings.
`http://www.rtvf.nwu.edu/chicago`
INFO `cwebbyoung@nwu.edu` (C. Webb Young)

8113 `clari.apbl.reports.commodity` Chicago Board of Trade report. *Moderated newsgroup*

8114 `clari.local.chicago` News of Chicago. *Moderated newsgroup*

8115 `clari.local.illinois` News of Illinois. *Moderated newsgroup*

8116 `clari.local.illinois.chicago` News of the Chicago area. *Moderated newsgroup*

8117 `clari.local.illinois.misc` News of Illinois. *Moderated newsgroup*

8118 `clari.sports.local.midwest.illinois` News of Illinois athletics. *Moderated newsgroup*

8119 `evv.config` Discussion regarding configuration of the evv hierarchy. *Newsgroup*

8120 `evv.riverboat` Riverboat gambling in Evansville, Illinois. *Newsgroup*

8121 `evv.sport.aces` Aces basketball and other U of E sports. *Newsgroup*

8122 `evv.toyota` The Tri-State's Toyota factory. *Newsgroup*

➤ **UIC/ADN CWIS:** This is the CWIS of the University of Illinois at Chicago. (See entry 4463 for full listing.)

US—INDIANA

8123 `clari.local.indiana` News of Indiana. *Moderated newsgroup*

8124 `clari.sports.local.midwest.indiana` News of Indiana athletics. *Moderated newsgroup*

8125 `in.forest-alliance` Forestry Alliance in Indiana. *Newsgroup*

8126 `in.jobs` Employment opportunities in Indiana. *Newsgroup*

➤ **IUPUI CWIS:** This is the main CWIS of Indiana University–Purdue University, Indianapolis, Indiana. (See entry 4428 for full listing.)

8127 OISNEWS: News for Indiana University international students and scholars. *Mailing List*
± `listserv@iubvm.ucs.indiana.edu` [body = SUBSCRIBE OISNEWS first-name last-name]
INFO `oisnews-request@iubvm.ucs.indiana.edu`
ARCHIVE `listserv@iubvm.ucs.indiana.edu` [body = INDEX OISNEWS]

US—IOWA

8128 `clari.local.iowa` News of Iowa. *Moderated newsgroup*

8129 `ia.answers` Repository for periodic Usenet articles. *Newsgroup*

8130 `ia.comp.infosystems.misc` General topics about Iowa-based information systems. *Newsgroup*

8131 `ia.dot.road-work` Iowa Dept of Transportation—road construction reports. *Newsgroup*

8132 `ia.gov.house` Iowa government—Iowa House of Representatives. *Newsgroup*

8133 `ia.gov.senate` Iowa government—Iowa Senate. *Newsgroup*

8134 `ia.org.freenet` Coordination discussions for Iowa Freenet activities. *Newsgroup*

8135 `ia.talk.misc` Varied discussions concerning Iowa issues. *Newsgroup*

8136 `ia.weather` Weather forecasts for the state of Iowa. *Newsgroup*

US—KANSAS

8137 `clari.local.kansas` News of Kansas. *Newsgroup*

8138   **InfoZine:** Kansas City's Digital Publishing Company. *Magazine*
http://www.fileshop.com/infozine/
± infozine@fileshop.com [body = subscribe]
INFO OWNER infozine@fileshop.com (Richard Greene)
ARCHIVE ftp://infozine.fileshop.com/pub/infozine
Frequency: monthly

8139   **Kansas Sights:** You aren't in *Kansas* anymore? With Internet access, you are never more than a "click" away from visiting Kansas Sights.
http://falcon.cc.ukans.edu/~nsween/europa.html
INFO nsween@falcon.cc.ukans.edu

8140   **kc.chat**   Kansas City-related discussions. *Newsgroup*

8141   **kc.forsale**   Goods and services for sale in the Kansas City area. *Newsgroup*

8142   **kc.general**   General information about Kansas City. *Newsgroup*

8143   **kc.wanted**   Goods and services wanted in the Kansas City area. *Newsgroup*

8144   **ks.admin**   Administration in Kansas. *Newsgroup*

8145   **ks.misc**   Miscellaneous postings in Kansas. *Newsgroup*

US—KENTUCKY

8146   **clari.local.kentucky**   News of Kentucky. *Newsgroup*

8147   **KENTUCKY:** For discussion of civic affairs and politics in Kentucky. *Mailing List*
± listserv@ukcc.uky.edu [body = SUBSCRIBE KENTUCKY first-name last-name]
INFO kentucky-request@ukcc.uky.edu
ARCHIVE listserv@ukcc.uky.edu [body = INDEX KENTUCKY]

8148   **ky.weather**   Weather in Kentucky. *Moderated newsgroup*

8149   **ky.weather.d**   Everybody talks about it but no one does anything. *Newsgroup*

US—LOUISIANA

8150   **alt.culture.cajun**   Cajun culture, history, genealogy, events. *Newsgroup*

8151   **clari.local.louisiana**   News of Louisiana. *Moderated newsgroup*

8152   **lou.general**   Items of general interest in Louisiana. *Newsgroup*

8153   **lou.lft.forsale**   For-sale and want-to-buy postings for the Lafayette area. *Newsgroup*

8154   **lou.lft.general**   Lafayette topics of general interest. *Newsgroup*

8155   **lou.lft.jobs**   Job postings for the Lafayette area. *Newsgroup*

8156   **lou.lft.PASA**   The Performing Arts Society of Acadiana. *Newsgroup*

8157   **New-Orleans:** On the city of New Orleans, Louisiana. *Mailing List*
± mail-server@mintir.new-orleans.la.us [body = subscribe New-Orleans]
INFO OWNER elendil@yatcom.com (Edward J. Branley)
FAQ http://www.yatcom.com/~noml
Gated: neworleans.info
Comments: Daily and Weekly digests available.

8158   **neworleans.general**   News and information of general interest in the New Orleans area. *Newsgroup*

8159   **neworleans.info**   New Orleans' history, culture, people, food, etc. *Moderated newsgroup*

US—MAINE

8160 `clari.local.maine` News of Maine. *Newsgroup*

8161 `me.communities.biddeford` Biddeford, Maine issues. *Newsgroup*

8162 `me.communities.can` MaineCAN (Community Access Network) Freenet effort. *Newsgroup*

8163 `me.communities.portland` Portland, Maine issues. *Newsgroup*

8164 `me.communities.yarmouth` Yarmouth, Maine issues. *Newsgroup*

8165 `me.config` Discussion of me.* newsgroup additions and deletions. *Newsgroup*

8166 `me.forsale` Items offered or wanted for sale in Maine. *Newsgroup*

8167 `me.general` Maine-related posts that do not fall in another group. *Newsgroup*

8168 `me.internet` Discussion of the Internet in Maine. *Newsgroup*

8169 `me.jobs` Jobs wanted/offered in Maine. *Newsgroup*

8170 `me.politics` Discussion of Maine politics. *Newsgroup*

➤ **MELIBS-L:** On library service in the state of Maine. (See entry 5755 for full listing.)

➤ `ne.forsale`: Short postings on items for sale in New England. *Newsgroup*

US—MARYLAND

8171 `balt.general` General discussions in the Baltimore area. *Newsgroup*

8172 `balt.jobs` Jobs available or sought in the Baltimore, Maryland (USA) area. *Newsgroup*

8173 `clari.local.maryland` News of Maryland. *Moderated newsgroup*

8174 `clari.sports.local.south.maryland` News of Maryland athletics. *Moderated newsgroup*

➤ **JHUNIVERSE: Johns Hopkins University on the Web:** This is the CWIS of Johns Hopkins University. JHUniverse is a gateway to information resources at Johns Hopkins University, the nation's first true research university and now the leading U.S. university in research and development expenditures. The system also maintains links to information on JHU's sister institution, the Johns Hopkins Hospital and Health System. (See entry 4429 for full listing.)

➤ **MARYLIB:** For Maryland area librarians, support staff, and information specialists. (See entry 5753 for full listing.)

8175 `md.annapolis` Maryland's state capitol area. *Newsgroup*

8176 `md.announcements` General announcements about Maryland or local areas. *Moderated newsgroup*

8177 `md.config` Issues involving Maryland's md.* hierarchy. *Newsgroup*

8178 `md.eastern-shore` Maryland's Eastern Shore area miscellaneous items. *Newsgroup*

8179 `md.forsale` Items/services for sale in Maryland. *Newsgroup*

8180 `md.general` Maryland in general. *Newsgroup*

8181 `md.jobs` Maryland jobs offered/jobs wanted. *Newsgroup*

8182 `md.mont` Maryland's Montgomery County miscellaneous items. *Newsgroup*

8183 `md.personals` Personal ads for Maryland. *Newsgroup*

8184 `md.pg` Maryland's Prince George's County miscellaneous items. *Newsgroup*

8185 `md.pg.tricentennial` Maryland's Prince George's 300th Birthday Party. *Newsgroup*

8186 `md.politics` Annapolis' care and feeding of Baltimore City. *Newsgroup*

➤ **MDSW:** A discussion list on topics of social-work interest for people in Maryland and surrounding areas. (See entry 10123 for full listing.)

US—MASSACHUSETTS

8187 `clari.local.massachusetts` News of Massachusetts. *Moderated newsgroup*

8188 `clari.sports.local.new_england.massachusetts` Massachusetts athletics. *Moderated newsgroup*

➤ **Massachusetts Institute of Technology:** MIT is an independent, coeducational university located in Cambridge, Massachusetts. MIT's WWW pages provide information about MIT's schools, departments, and programs; educational resources; research at MIT; and library services. You'll also find admissions information, alumni services, publications, and more. (See entry 4433 for full listing.)

8189 `sudbury.misc` News, politics, and current affairs in Sudbury, Massachusetts, USA. *Newsgroup*

➤ **WordsWorth Books:** WordsWorth Books is a large independent bookstore with a complete search-and-order Web site. (See entry 121 for full listing.)

US—MICHIGAN

8190 `clari.local.michigan` News of Michican. *Moderated newsgroup*

8191 `clari.sports.local.midwest.michigan` News of Michigan athletics. *Moderated newsgroup*

8192 `mi.jobs` Jobs offered and sought in Michigan. *Newsgroup*

8193 `mi.map` Usenet maps in Michigan. *Moderated newsgroup*

8194 `mi.misc` Catch-all for Michigan. *Newsgroup*

8195 `mi.news` Usenet news and mail discussions. *Newsgroup*

8196 `mi.wanted` Jobs and products, wanted and offered. *Newsgroup*

US—MINNESOTA

8197 `clari.local.minnesota` News of Minnesota. *Moderated newsgroup*

8198 `clari.sports.local.midwest.minnesota` News of Minnesota athletics. *Moderated newsgroup*

➤ **Fox Studio Limited:** A full-service commercial photography studio in Minneapolis, MN. (See entry 1241 for full listing.)

➤ **Minnesota Extension Service:** The official electronic information service for the Minnesota Extension Service, St. Paul campus of the University of Minnesota. (See entry 8917 for full listing.)

8199 **MN-POLITICS:** On Minnesota politics, issues, and public policy. *Mailing List*
`http://freenet.msp.mn.us/govt/e-democracy/`
± `majordomo@mr.net` [body = `subscribe mn-politics`]
INFO OWNER `masouder@alex.stkate.edu` (Mick Souder)

8200 `mn.archive` Archive sites in Minnesota. *Newsgroup*

8201 `mn.arts` Discussions and announcements of the Minnesota art community. *Newsgroup*

8202 `mn.forsale` Bric-a-bracs and knicknacks for purchase in Minneapolis and environs. *Newsgroup*

8203 `mn.general` Items of general interest to Minnesota. *Newsgroup*

8204 `mn.map` Minnesota UUCP map postings. *Moderated newsgroup*

8205 `mn.net` Computer networking in Minnesota. *Newsgroup*

8206 `mn.politics` Minnesota politics. *Newsgroup*

8207 `mn.traffic` Minnesota Usenet traffic statistics. *Newsgroup*

8208 `mn.uum` For discussion of Unix Users of Minnesota related topics. *Newsgroup*

US—MISSISSIPPI

8209 `clari.local.mississippi` News of Mississippi. *Newsgroup*

US—MISSOURI

8210 `clari.local.missouri` News of Missouri. *Moderated newsgroup*

8211 `clari.sports.local.midwest.missouri` News of Missouri athletics. *Moderated newsgroup*

➤   **InfoZine:** Kansas City's Digital Publishing Company. (See entry 8138 for full listing.)

➤   `kc.chat:`   Kansas City-related discussions. *Newsgroup*

8212   `kc.jobs`   Jobs offered/wanted in the Kansas City metro area. *Newsgroup*

8213   **MMNUG-L:** For mid-Missouri network users. *Mailing List*
± `listserv@mizzou1.missouri.edu` [body = SUBSCRIBE MMNUG-L first-name last-name]
INFO `mmnug-l-request@mizzou1.missouri.edu`
ARCHIVE `listserv@mizzou1.missouri.edu` [body = INDEX MMNUG-L]

8214   `stl.config`   Discussion of changes for the `stl.*` (St. Louis) hierarchy. *Newsgroup*

8215   `stl.dining`   Eating out around St. Louis, Missouri. *Newsgroup*

8216   `stl.forsale`   Stuff wanted and for sale in St Louis, Missouri. *Newsgroup*

8217   `stl.general`   General interest items for St. Louis sites. *Newsgroup*

8218   `stl.jobs`   St. Louis job information. *Newsgroup*

8219   `stl.jobs.offered`   Employment offerings in St. Louis, Missouri. *Moderated newsgroup*

8220   `stl.jobs.resumes`   Resumes of those seeking employment in St. Louis. *Moderated newsgroup*

8221   `stl.news`   St. Louis Usenet information. *Newsgroup*

8222   `stl.rec`   St. Louis recreational information. *Newsgroup*

US—MONTANA

8223   `clari.local.montana`   News of Montana. *Newsgroup*

US—NEBRASKA

8224   `clari.local.nebraska`   News of Nebraska. *Moderated newsgroup*

8225   `nebr.biz`   Nebraska business. *Newsgroup*

8226   `nebr.edu`   Nebraska education. *Newsgroup*

8227   `nebr.flame`   Flaming regarding Nebraska people and issues. *Newsgroup*

8228   `nebr.gov`   Nebraska government. *Newsgroup*

8229   `nebr.humor`   Good life humor. *Newsgroup*

8230   `nebr.jobs`   Discussions and postings concerning jobs in Nebraska. *Newsgroup*

8231   `nebr.marketplace`   Things in Nebraska to buy, sell, etc. *Newsgroup*

8232   `nebr.misc`   Discussions and postings about anything in Nebraska. *Newsgroup*

8233   `nebr.news.announce`   Announcements about nebr news hierarchy. *Newsgroup*

8234   `nebr.news.general`   General discussions about the nebr news hierarchy. *Newsgroup*

8235   `nebr.news.test`   For testing news software and distribution in `nebr.*`. *Newsgroup*

8236   `nebr.rec`   Recreation in Nebraska. *Newsgroup*

8237   `nebr.sports.misc`   Sports in Nebraska. *Newsgroup*

8238   `nebr.sports.unl`   University of Nebraska-Lincoln Husker sports. *Newsgroup*

➤   **UNK Department of Physics and Physical Science:** Web site of the department of Physics and Physical Science at the University of Nebraska at Kearney. (See entry 9493 for full listing.)

➤   **UNK Department of Sociology:** Web site of the department of sociology at the University of Nebraska at Kearney. (See entry 5367 for full listing.)

US—NEVADA

8239   `alt.vacation.las-vegas`   Everything you always wanted to know about Vegas. *Newsgroup*

8240   `clari.local.nevada`   News of Nevada. *Newsgroup*

8241   `nv.forsale`   For sale/want ads (no commercials, please!). *Newsgroup*

8242   `nv.general`   General discussion. *Newsgroup*

8243   `nv.jobs`   Jobs offered and wanted in Nevada. *Newsgroup*

8244   `nv.motss`   MOTSS community talk. *Newsgroup*

8245   `vegas.food`   Anything about food in Las Vegas. *Newsgroup*

8246   `vegas.for-sale`   For sale/want ads (no commercials, please!). *Newsgroup*

8247   `vegas.general`   General discussion. *Newsgroup*

8248   `vegas.jobs`   Jobs offered and wanted in Las Vegas. *Newsgroup*

➤   `vegas.motss:`   MOTSS community talk. *Newsgroup*

US—NEW HAMPSHIRE

8249   `clari.local.new_hampshire`   News of New Hampshire. *Moderated newsgroup*

➤   `ne.forsale:`   Short postings on items for sale in New England. *Newsgroup*

8250   `nh.general`   General discussion newsgroup for New Hampshire (USA). *Newsgroup*

US—NEW JERSEY

8251   `clari.local.new_jersey`   News of New Jersey. *Moderated newsgroup*

8252   `clari.sports.local.mid-atlantic.new_jersey`   News of New Jersey athletics. *Moderated newsgroup*

8253   `nj.events`   Events in New Jersey. *Newsgroup*

8254   `nj.forsale`   Items for sale in New Jersey. *Newsgroup*

8255   `nj.general`   Items of general interest in New Jersey. *Newsgroup*

8256   `nj.jobs`   Employment in the New Jersey area. *Newsgroup*

8257   `nj.market.autos`   For sale/wanted: autos, cycles, trucks, etc. *Newsgroup*

8258   `nj.market.computers`   For sale/wanted: computers and software. *Newsgroup*

8259   `nj.market.housing`   For sale/rent/wanted: housing, land, roommates. *Newsgroup*

8260   `nj.market.misc`   For sale/wanted: miscellaneous. *Newsgroup*

8261   `nj.misc`   `nj` topics that don't fall into other categories. *Newsgroup*

8262   `nj.politics`   Political topics of interest to New Jersey readers. *Newsgroup*

8263   `nj.wanted`   New Jersey want ads. *Newsgroup*

8264   `nj.weather`   Weather in New Jersey. *Newsgroup*

➤   **Princeton University Information Service:** The main Princeton University World Wide Web home page, with pointers to home pages of academic and administrative departments, as well as other regional home pages. (See entry 4441 for full listing.)

US—NEW MEXICO

8265   `clari.local.new_mexico`   News of New Mexico. *Moderated newsgroup*

8266   `nm.forsale`   Advertisements by New Mexico businesses and residents. *Newsgroup*

8267   `nm.general`   Yes, New Mexico is a state. *Newsgroup*

8268   `nm.jobs`   New Mexico job and resume postings. *Newsgroup*

8269   `taos.general`   Topics of general interest in Taos, New Mexico. *Newsgroup*

US—NEW YORK

8270 `alt.culture.ny-upstate` New York State above Westchester. *Newsgroup*

8271 `capdist.seminars` Conferences and seminars in the local area. *Newsgroup*

8272 `clari.local.new_york` News of New York. *Moderated newsgroup*

8273 `clari.local.new_york.misc` News of New York State. *Moderated newsgroup*

8274 `clari.sports.local.mid-atlantic.new_york` News of New York State athletics. *Moderated newsgroup*

8275 `clari.sports.local.mid-atlantic.new_york.nyc` New York City athletics. *Moderated newsgroup*

➤ **ENVIRONMENT-L:** On the environment, particularly in New York State. (See entry 4636 for full listing.)

8276 `ithaca.jobs` Jobs offered/jobs wanted in Ithaca area. *Newsgroup*

8277 `ithaca.marketplace` Buying and selling in the Ithaca area. *Newsgroup*

8278 `ithaca.personals` Meeting people in and around Ithaca. *Newsgroup*

8279 `li.events` Events on Long Island, NY (USA). *Newsgroup*

8280 `li.forsale` Things for sale in the Long Island, NY (USA) area. *Newsgroup*

8281 `li.jobs` Employment in the Long Island, New York region. *Newsgroup*

8282 `li.misc` Topical to Long Island. *Newsgroup*

8283 `li.politics` Discussion of Long Island, NY politics. *Newsgroup*

8284 `li.wanted` Long Island's most-wanted list (classifieds). *Newsgroup*

8285 `niagara.announce` Announcements of general interest in Niagara. *Newsgroup*

8286 `niagara.arts` Theater, music, etc. in the Niagara region. *Newsgroup*

8287 `niagara.falls` The seventh natural wonder of the world. *Newsgroup*

8288 `niagara.falls.cam` Live images of Niagara Falls on the Web. *Newsgroup*

8289 `niagara.forsale` Buying and selling in the Niagara region. *Newsgroup*

8290 `niagara.freenet` Niagara regional Freenet. *Newsgroup*

8291 `niagara.general` General discussion for the Niagara region. *Newsgroup*

8292 `niagara.jobs` Jobs in the Niagara region. *Newsgroup*

8293 `niagara.police` Mmm . . . Niagara, donut capital of the world . . . *Newsgroup*

8294 `niagara.wine` Wine and wineries in the Niagara Region. *Newsgroup*

8295 `ny.forsale` Things for sale in New York. *Newsgroup*

8296 `ny.general` Items of general interest in New York. *Newsgroup*

8297 `ny.nysernet` Discussions about N.Y. State Educaction Research Network (NYSERnet). *Newsgroup*

8298 `ny.politics` Politics in New York. *Newsgroup*

8299 `ny.seminars` Seminars in New York. *Newsgroup*

8300 `ny.wanted` New York want ads. *Newsgroup*

➤ **NYHIST-L:** On New York State history. (See entry 5254 for full listing.)

➤ **Skidmore College:** This Web site and gopher offer campus information and access to diverse network resources at Skidmore College, an undergraduate liberal-arts college in upstate New York. (See entry 4448 for full listing.)

➤ **TELXCH-L:** On telecomunications in the state of New York and national telecommunications and policy issues related to digital infrastructure. (See entry 9640 for full listing.)

➤ **UBWings:** This is the CWIS of the State University of New York at Buffalo. (See entry 4461 for full listing.)

8301 `wny.events` Events in western New York. *Newsgroup*

8302 **wny.general** General stuff in western New York. *Newsgroup*

8303 **wny.news** News items in western New York. *Newsgroup*

8304 **wny.seminar** Seminars in western New York. *Newsgroup*

➤ **wny.unix-wizards:** Unix wizards in western New York. *Newsgroup*

8305 **wny.wanted** Wanted ads in western New York. *Newsgroup*

8306 **wny.wbfo** NPR Buffalo news. *Newsgroup*

8307 **wny.yumyum** Gourmet news in western New York. *Newsgroup*

US—NEW YORK—NEW YORK CITY

8308 **clari.local.new_york.nyc** News of greater New York City. *Moderated newsgroup*

8309 **clari.local.nyc** News of New York City, New York. *Moderated newsgroup*

8310 **The East Harlem/El Barrio Community Info Web Pages:** Information related to the politics, elected officials, and institutions of the East Harlem community.
http://www.east-harlem.com/campaign/
INFO campaign@webcom.com

➤ **The Ladies Pavilion, Central Park, New York City:** Joanna Oltman's historic preservation project traces the history of one of Central Park's architectural gems, the Ladies' Pavilion. (See entry 64 for full listing.)

8311 **nyc.announce** Announcements in New York City. *Newsgroup*

8312 **nyc.food** Eating out around the New York City area. *Newsgroup*

8313 **nyc.general** Items of general interest in New York City. *Newsgroup*

8314 **nyc.jobs.contract** Postings for contract and consulting work in New York City area. *Newsgroup*

8315 **nyc.jobs.misc** General discussion of New York City job market. *Newsgroup*

8316 **nyc.jobs.offered** Job postings for New York City area. *Newsgroup*

8317 **nyc.jobs.wanted** Individuals seeking jobs in New York City area. *Newsgroup*

8318 **nyc.market.housing** Housing in the New York City area. *Newsgroup*

➤ **nyc.motorcycles:** Motorcycling and motorcyclists in the New York City area. *Newsgroup*

➤ **nyc.personals:** Personals ads for New York City and environs. *Newsgroup*

8319 **nyc.politics** Political discussions about New York City and its environs. *Newsgroup*

8320 **nyc.seminars** Announcements of seminars in the New York City area. *Newsgroup*

➤ **nyc.singles:** Discussions of being single in the New York City area. *Newsgroup*

8321 **nyc.transit** Discussions about transportation in New York City and its environs. *Newsgroup*

➤ **NYCKayaker:** For paddlers and small boaters in New York City and environs. (See entry 6650 for full listing.)

8322 **Total New York:** A cutting-edge spin on New York City trends, art, film, politics, music, and fashion. Total New York includes the most complete online database for New York City restaurants, bars and clubs, retail, sports, city information, etc.
http://totalny.com/
INFO feedback@totalny.com
INFO janicegj@totalny.com

US—NORTH CAROLINA

8323 **clari.local.north_carolina** News of North Carolina. *Moderated newsgroup*

8324 **clari.sports.local.south.north_carolina** News of North Carolina athletics. *Moderated newsgroup*

8325 **nc.charlotte.entertainment** All the fun places to be in Charlotte, North Carolina. *Newsgroup*

8326 **nc.charlotte.sports** Past and upcoming sports events in Charlotte, North Carolina. *Newsgroup*

8327 **nc.general** Items of general interest in North Carolina. *Newsgroup*

8328 **triangle.arts** Miscellaneous arts discussion. *Newsgroup*

8329 **triangle.dining** Restaurants and dining in central North Carolina. *Newsgroup*

8330 **triangle.forsale** North Carolina want ads. *Newsgroup*

8331 **triangle.freenet** Starting a Freenet in the Triangle area. *Newsgroup*

8332 **triangle.general** General discussion in North Carolina. *Newsgroup*

8333 **triangle.jobs** Jobs offered and wanted in North Carolina. *Newsgroup*

➤ **triangle.movies:** Movies discussions in North Carolina. *Newsgroup*

8334 **triangle.politics** Politics affecting the Triangle area of North Carolina. *Newsgroup*

8335 **triangle.singles.announce** Events for singles in North Carolina. *Moderated newsgroup*

8336 **triangle.systems** North Carolina system admin notices. *Newsgroup*

8337 **triangle.talks** Seminars and conferences notices in North Carolina. *Newsgroup*

8338 **triangle.wanted** Things you want to buy or trade for. *Newsgroup*

➤ **UNC-ECS (UNC System):** This server provides information services primarily to the 16 constituent institutions of the University of North Carolina. (See entry 4464 for full listing.)

US—NORTH DAKOTA

8339 **clari.local.north_dakota** News of North Dakota. *Moderated newsgroup*

US—OHIO

➤ **akr.freenet:** Discussion about the Akron Regional Freenet. *Newsgroup*

8340 **Butler County (Ohio) Pioneers:** Add your own or contact others who had ancestors living in Butler County, Ohio, in the early 1800s. Genealogy site.
http://falcon.cc.ukans.edu/gen/butler-co.html
INFO nsween@falcon.cc.ukans.edu

8341 **clari.local.ohio** News of Ohio. *Moderated newsgroup*

8342 **clari.sports.local.midwest.ohio** News of Ohio athletics. *Moderated newsgroup*

8343 **The Cleveland Sports Mailing List:** On anything related to the Cleveland, Ohio, sports scene. *Mailing List*
ftp://ftp.apk.net/pub/users/richard/cle_sports.html (Cleveland Sports web page)
± INFO sports-request@wariat.org
Gated: cle.sports

8344 **cmh.forsale** Columbus buy, sell, trade. *Newsgroup*

8345 **cmh.general** Columbus general news. *Newsgroup*

8346 **cmh.groups** Meta-discussions about newsgroups in cmh.* distribution. *Newsgroup*

8347 **cmh.jobs** Columbus job postings. *Newsgroup*

8348 **cmh.network** Columbus network connections, computing, etc. *Newsgroup*

➤ **courts.usa.state.ohio.appls-8th:** Ohio Court of Appeals, Eighth District. *Moderated newsgroup*

➤ **courts.usa.state.ohio.supreme:** Ohio Supreme Court. *Moderated newsgroup*

➤ **oh-motss:** The Ohio Members Of The Same Sex mailing list is for open discussion of lesbian, gay, and bisexual issues in and affecting Ohio. (See entry 9970 for full listing.)

8349 **oh.biz** Business advertisements in Ohio. *Newsgroup*

8350 **oh.chem** Chemistry in Ohio. *Newsgroup*

8351 `oh.forsale` For-sale and wanted items in Ohio. Ohio *only*, please. *Newsgroup*

8352 `oh.general` Items of general interest in Ohio, USA. *Newsgroup*

8353 `oh.jobs` Jobs available and wanted in Ohio. *Newsgroup*

8354 `oh.news` Usenet in Ohio. *Newsgroup*

8355 `oh.newsadmin` Usenet news flow and groups in Ohio. *Newsgroup*

8356 `oh.osc.software` Ohio Supercomputing Center. *Newsgroup*

➤ **Ohio Supercomputer Center (OSC):** This document server includes information on the OSC (grant applications, calendar, publications, etc.) as well as information on the Columbus area and Ohio in general. (See entry 3808 for full listing.)

US—OKLAHOMA

➤ `alt.current-events.amfb-explosion`: Terrorism in America's heartland. *Newsgroup*

8357 `clari.local.oklahoma` News of Oklahoma. *Newsgroup*

8358 `ok.admin` `ok.*` hierarchy administration. *Newsgroup*

8359 `ok.announce` Announcements of general interest for Oklahomans. *Newsgroup*

8360 `ok.general` Items of general interest in Oklahoma, USA. *Newsgroup*

8361 `ok.marketplace` For sale/wanted in Oklahoma. *Newsgroup*

8362 `ok.test` Usenet testing in Oklahoma. *Newsgroup*

8363 `ok.tulsa.general` Topics of general interest in Tulsa, Oklahoma. *Newsgroup*

US—OREGON

8364 `alt.culture.oregon` Discussion about the state of Oregon. *Newsgroup*

➤ **The Beaver Believer Mailing List:** A place where fans of the Oregon State Beavers football team can gather and discuss the team. (See entry 6839 for full listing.)

8365 `clari.local.oregon` News of Oregon. *Moderated newsgroup*

8366 **Little Whale Cove at Depoe Bay, Oregon:** Little Whale Cove is a national award-winning development on the Oregon coast. Take a visual tour and see the low-density planning, extensive trail systems, whale-watching gazebos, and varied amenities.
`http://www.whalecove.com/`
INFO `kristih@whalecove.com`

8367 `or.forsale` Oregon want ads. *Newsgroup*

8368 `or.general` Items of general interest in Oregon. *Newsgroup*

8369 `or.politics` Discussion of Oregon political issues and events. *Newsgroup*

➤ `pdx.computing`: Computing information. *Newsgroup*

US—OREGON—EUGENE

8370 `eug.access.video` Public access video in Eugene/Springfield, Oregon. *Newsgroup*

➤ `eug.bbs.excelsior`: Discussion of Excelsior BBS software. *Newsgroup*

8371 `eug.forsale` Stuff for sale in/near Eugene/Springfield, Oregon. *Newsgroup*

8372 `eug.hungryhead` Books/events at Hungry Head Bookstore. *Newsgroup*

8373 `eug.local.activists` Paul Harrison's local activism list gateway. *Newsgroup*

8374 `eug.local.connectivity.politics` Eugene/Springfield (Oregon) net politics. *Newsgroup*

8375 `eug.nwmusic.news` Pacific Northwest music discussion/news. *Newsgroup*

8376 `eug.register.guard` Discussion re: Eugene Oregon's *Register-Guard* newspaper. *Newsgroup*

US—OREGON—PORTLAND

8377 `pdaxs.ads.appliances` Appliances for sale and stores that sell them. *Newsgroup*

8378 `pdaxs.ads.audio_video` Audio and video equipment. *Newsgroup*

8379 `pdaxs.ads.boats` Boats, yachts, and dinghies for sale. *Newsgroup*

8380 `pdaxs.ads.books` Books for sale or wanted and stores that sell them. *Newsgroup*

8381 `pdaxs.ads.cars` Cars for sale or wanted. *Newsgroup*

8382 `pdaxs.ads.cars.audio` Car stereo and security systems. *Newsgroup*

8383 `pdaxs.ads.cars.misc` Car stuff that doesn't fit elsewhere. *Newsgroup*

8384 `pdaxs.ads.cars.rv` Recreational vehicles for sale or rent. *Newsgroup*

8385 `pdaxs.ads.cars.service` People who work on cars. *Newsgroup*

8386 `pdaxs.ads.clothing` Clothing for sale. *Newsgroup*

8387 `pdaxs.ads.computers` Computers, software, and accessories for sale. *Newsgroup*

8388 `pdaxs.ads.food` Cook's equipment, groceries, cooperatives, etc. *Newsgroup*

8389 `pdaxs.ads.furniture` Places to sit and stores that sell it. *Newsgroup*

8390 `pdaxs.ads.homes.n` Homes for sale in north Portland. *Newsgroup*

8391 `pdaxs.ads.homes.ne` Homes for sale in northeast Portland, Oregon. *Newsgroup*

8392 `pdaxs.ads.homes.nw` Homes for sale in northwest Portland. *Newsgroup*

8393 `pdaxs.ads.homes.se` Homes for sale in southeast Portland. *Newsgroup*

8394 `pdaxs.ads.homes.sw` Homes for sale in southwest Portland. *Newsgroup*

8395 `pdaxs.ads.hotels` Hotels, motels, inns, and bed-and-breakfasts. *Newsgroup*

8396 `pdaxs.ads.jewelry` Flaunt it if you've got it. *Newsgroup*

8397 `pdaxs.ads.lostrfound` Items or animals lost or found. *Newsgroup*

8398 `pdaxs.ads.misc` What the heck is it? Sell it here. *Newsgroup*

8399 `pdaxs.ads.movies` Theaters, posters, sneak previews. *Newsgroup*

8400 `pdaxs.ads.music` Music stores, places to hear music, instruments. *Newsgroup*

8401 `pdaxs.ads.notices` We have to tell you that. *Newsgroup*

8402 `pdaxs.ads.office` Office space for rent or for lease. *Newsgroup*

8403 `pdaxs.ads.printing` Desktop publishing, printing, binding. *Newsgroup*

8404 `pdaxs.ads.real_estate` Real estate that doesn't fit somewhere else. *Newsgroup*

8405 `pdaxs.ads.restaurants` Good places to eat and what you can eat there. *Newsgroup*

8406 `pdaxs.ads.sales` Garage sales, auctions, liquidation sales, etc. *Newsgroup*

8407 `pdaxs.ads.sports` Sporting goods and activities. *Newsgroup*

8408 `pdaxs.ads.tickets` Concert tickets, plane tickets, traffic tickets. Oops. *Newsgroup*

8409 `pdaxs.ads.tools` Tools for cutting wood, bending metal, drilling holes. *Newsgroup*

8410 `pdaxs.ads.wanted` Have a framistan you're not using? I want it. *Newsgroup*

8411 `pdaxs.arts.auditions` Tryouts for plays, dance companies, movies, bands. *Newsgroup*

8412 `pdaxs.arts.museums` What's that hanging on the wall? *Newsgroup*

8413 `pdaxs.arts.music` Talk about local musicians and food stamps. *Newsgroup*

8414 `pdaxs.arts.print` Books, newspapers, magazines in Portland. *Newsgroup*

8415 `pdaxs.arts.radio` Why isn't there a decent station in town? *Newsgroup*

8416 `pdaxs.arts.tv` Cable, local shows, Kathy Smith's hair color. *Newsgroup*

8417 `pdaxs.calendar.art` Exhibits, showings, and other art events. *Newsgroup*

8418 `pdaxs.calendar.computers` Computer-related events of interest. *Newsgroup*

8419 `pdaxs.calendar.misc` Other stuff. *Newsgroup*

8420 `pdaxs.calendar.music` Who's playing where and when. *Newsgroup*

8421 `pdaxs.calendar.volunteers` We need people to show up for. *Newsgroup*

➤ `pdaxs.games.board`: Not bored, board. Like checkers, Chinese checkers. *Newsgroup*

➤ `pdaxs.games.bridge`: Who's the dummy now? *Newsgroup*

➤ `pdaxs.games.chess`: Okay, I'm Fischer and you can be Spassky. *Newsgroup*

➤ `pdaxs.games.misc`: Everything else except head games (see counseling). *Newsgroup*

➤ `pdaxs.issues.democrats`: Democratic Party and their stands on issues. *Newsgroup*

8422 `pdaxs.issues.education` Educational issues—college, high school, etc. *Newsgroup*

8423 `pdaxs.issues.portland` What's really wrong with this town is. *Newsgroup*

➤ `pdaxs.issues.republicans`: Republican Party and their stands on issues. *Newsgroup*

8424 `pdaxs.jobs.clerical` File clerks, administrative assistants. *Newsgroup*

8425 `pdaxs.jobs.computers` Computer sales, support, programming. *Newsgroup*

8426 `pdaxs.jobs.construction` We can rebuild it. Or build it. *Newsgroup*

8427 `pdaxs.jobs.delivery` Delivery jobs of all sorts. *Newsgroup*

8428 `pdaxs.jobs.domestic` Help with the home. *Newsgroup*

8429 `pdaxs.jobs.engineering` That's a software problem. *Newsgroup*

8430 `pdaxs.jobs.management` Management positions or trainee positions. *Newsgroup*

8431 `pdaxs.jobs.misc` What you'll do is hard to describe. *Newsgroup*

8432 `pdaxs.jobs.restaurants` Waitpersons, cooks, bartenders, buspersons. *Newsgroup*

8433 `pdaxs.jobs.retail` Clothing, hardware, bookstores, electronics. *Newsgroup*

8434 `pdaxs.jobs.sales` The second-oldest profession. The first, really. *Newsgroup*

8435 `pdaxs.jobs.secretary` Secretarial jobs. *Newsgroup*

8436 `pdaxs.jobs.temporary` Temporary work of all kinds. *Newsgroup*

8437 `pdaxs.jobs.volunteers` We need people to help us do. *Newsgroup*

8438 `pdaxs.jobs.wanted` Will work for food. And a car. *Newsgroup*

➤ `pdaxs.religion.christian`: Christian religion and activities. *Newsgroup*

➤ `pdaxs.religion.jewish`: Jewish religion and activities. *Newsgroup*

➤ `pdaxs.religion.misc`: Who'd we leave out? *Newsgroup*

➤ `pdaxs.religion.moslem`: Muslim religion and activities. *Newsgroup*

8439 `pdaxs.religion.newage` New Age religions and activities. *Newsgroup*

8440 `pdaxs.schools.acting` Is that a smile on your face or are you crying? *Newsgroup*

8441 `pdaxs.schools.cooking` If you make it, you have to eat it. *Newsgroup*

8442 `pdaxs.schools.dance` Up on those toes! Now do the funky chicken. *Newsgroup*

8443 `pdaxs.schools.fitness` Ve vill pump you up! *Newsgroup*

8444　`pdaxs.schools.kids` Languages, camps, and private schools. *Newsgroup*

8445　`pdaxs.schools.martial` Karate, tae kwon do, ben wa, kung fu. *Newsgroup*

8446　`pdaxs.schools.misc` What we teach is hard to describe. *Newsgroup*

8447　`pdaxs.schools.music` Musical lessons. *Newsgroup*

8448　`pdaxs.schools.sports` How to play golf, tennis, etc. *Newsgroup*

8449　`pdaxs.services.accounting` Accounting, bookkeeping, tax advice. *Newsgroup*

8450　`pdaxs.services.appliance` Get that toaster fixed. *Newsgroup*

8451　`pdaxs.services.carpentry` Tired of hitting your thumb with the hammer? *Newsgroup*

8452　`pdaxs.services.cleaning` Is it that time of year again? *Newsgroup*

8453　`pdaxs.services.computers` Get yours fixed or learn how to use it. *Newsgroup*

8454　`pdaxs.services.consulting` We empty wallets quickly and efficiently. *Newsgroup*

8455　`pdaxs.services.counseling` Why are you the way you are? *Newsgroup*

8456　`pdaxs.services.electrical` Things that go bzzzztt in the night. *Newsgroup*

8457　`pdaxs.services.financial` Got some money? *Newsgroup*

8458　`pdaxs.services.fitness` Personal trainers and other hardbodies. *Newsgroup*

8459　`pdaxs.services.gardening` Watering, pruning, nurturing. *Newsgroup*

8460　`pdaxs.services.graphics` Pictures and images to order. *Newsgroup*

8461　`pdaxs.services.insurance` Fire, auto, life, etc. *Newsgroup*

8462　`pdaxs.services.int_design` Designs on your interior. *Newsgroup*

8463　`pdaxs.services.landscaping` Your lawn needs some help. *Newsgroup*

8464　`pdaxs.services.legal` Incorporation, bankruptcy, divorce, etc. *Newsgroup*

8465　`pdaxs.services.massage` Feeling a little stiff? *Newsgroup*

8466　`pdaxs.services.misc` What we do is hard to describe. *Newsgroup*

8467　`pdaxs.services.moving` Tired of the same place? *Newsgroup*

8468　`pdaxs.services.music` Learn to play the tuba! *Newsgroup*

8469　`pdaxs.services.painting` Tired of a blue house? *Newsgroup*

8470　`pdaxs.services.pets` Why is Rover green? *Newsgroup*

8471　`pdaxs.services.photo` Photographers and videotapers. *Newsgroup*

8472　`pdaxs.services.plumbing` Why is the furniture floating past me? *Newsgroup*

8473　`pdaxs.services.roofing` Raindrops keep falling on my head. *Newsgroup*

8474　`pdaxs.services.security` Security systems for sale. *Newsgroup*

8475　`pdaxs.services.storage` Can't bear to throw it away? *Newsgroup*

8476　`pdaxs.services.wordproc` Papers and novels done dirt cheap. *Newsgroup*

➤　`pdaxs.sports.baseball:` America's pastime in the Rose City. *Newsgroup*

➤　`pdaxs.sports.basketball:` Blazers, Pilots, and other hoops. *Newsgroup*

➤　`pdaxs.sports.football:` NFL, semi-pro, and high school. *Newsgroup*

➤　`pdaxs.sports.golf:` Speak softly and carry a big stick. *Newsgroup*

8477　`pdx.arts` Portland Oregon local arts topics. *Newsgroup*

8478　`pdx.forsale` Stuff for sale. *Newsgroup*

8479　`pdx.soc` Social events in Portland, Oregon. *Newsgroup*

➤　`pdx.sports`:　Sports in Portland, Oregon. *Newsgroup*

➤　`pdx.telecom`:　Issues regarding telecommunications. *Newsgroup*

➤　`pdx.weather`:　Portland, Oregon weather forecasts. *Newsgroup*

US—PENNSYLVANIA

8480　`clari.local.pennsylvania`　News of Pennsylvania. *Moderated newsgroup*

8481　`clari.sports.local.mid-atlantic.pennsylvania`　News of Pennsyvania athletics. *Moderated newsgroup*

8482　`pa.admin`　Net administration and UUCP connectivity in Pennsylvania. *Newsgroup*

8483　`pa.environment`　Information and discussion about Pennsylvania's environment. *Newsgroup*

8484　`pa.forsale`　Items for sale in Pennsylvania. *Newsgroup*

8485　`pa.general`　Items of general interest in Pennsylvania. *Newsgroup*

8486　`pa.hbg.forsale`　Items for sale in the Harrisburg, Pennsylvania area. *Newsgroup*

8487　`pa.hbg.general`　Items of general interest in Harrisburg, Pennsylvania area. *Newsgroup*

8488　`pa.hbg.wanted`　Items wanted in the Harrisburg, Pennsylvania area. *Newsgroup*

8489　`pa.jobs.offered`　Employment available in Pennsylvania. *Newsgroup*

8490　`pa.jobs.wanted`　Employment wanted in Pennsylvania. *Newsgroup*

8491　`pa.lv.forsale`　Items for sale in the Lehigh Valley, Pennsylvania area. *Newsgroup*

8492　`pa.lv.general`　Items of general interest in Lehigh Valley, Pennsylvania area. *Newsgroup*

8493　`pa.lv.wanted`　Items wanted in the Lehigh Valley, Pennsylvania area. *Newsgroup*

8494　`pa.motss`　Gay, lesbian, and bisexual people and issues in Pennsylvania. *Newsgroup*

8495　`pa.ne.announce`　Announcements (not discussion) in the northeast Pennsylvania area. *Newsgroup*

8496　`pa.ne.forsale`　Items for sale in the Northeast Pennsylvania area. *Newsgroup*

8497　`pa.ne.general`　Items of general interest in the Scranton/Wilkes-Barre area. *Newsgroup*

8498　`pa.ne.politics`　Political discussions about the northeast Pennsylvania area. *Newsgroup*

8499　`pa.ne.wanted`　Items wanted in the northeast Pennsylvania area. *Newsgroup*

8500　`pa.politics`　Politicians and campaign issues in Pennsylvania. *Newsgroup*

8501　`pa.rdg.forsale`　Items for sale in the Reading, Pennsylvania area. *Newsgroup*

8502　`pa.rdg.general`　Items of general interest in the Reading, Pennsylvania area. *Newsgroup*

8503　`pa.rdg.wanted`　Items wanted in the Reading, Pennsylvania area. *Newsgroup*

➤　`pa.smallbusiness`:　Small-business discussions in Pennsylvania (no ads). *Newsgroup*

8504　`pa.wanted`　Items wanted in Pennsylvania. *Newsgroup*

➤　`pgh.org.sca`:　Pgh chapter, Society for Creative Anachronism (SCA). *Newsgroup*

➤　`pgh.org.uccp`:　The University Chinese Club of Pittsburgh. *Newsgroup*

US—PENNSYLVANIA—PHILADELPHIA

8505　`clari.sports.local.mid-atlantic.pennsylvania.philadelphia`　Philadelphia sports. *Moderated newsgroup*

8506　`phl.announce`　Announcements of general interest in Philadelphia. *Newsgroup*

➤　`phl.bicycles`:　Bicycles, bike trails, recreation, and transportation. *Newsgroup*

➤　`phl.dance`:　Dance events, reviews, and discussions. *Newsgroup*

8507　`phl.food`　Restaurant information and reviews. *Newsgroup*

8508 `phl.forsale` Items for sale in Philadelphia. *Newsgroup*

8509 `phl.housing` Houses/apartments/roomates available/wanted in Philadelphia. *Newsgroup*

8510 `phl.jobs.offered` Employment available in Philadelphia. *Newsgroup*

8511 `phl.jobs.wanted` Employment wanted in Philadelphia. *Newsgroup*

8512 `phl.media` Newspapers, radio, and TV in Philadelphia. *Newsgroup*

➤ `phl.misc`: Miscellaneous postings. *Newsgroup*

8513 `phl.music` Musical events, reviews, and discussions. *Newsgroup*

➤ `phl.outdoors`: Outdoor recreation—camping, hiking, parks. *Newsgroup*

8514 `phl.scanner` Scanning the airwaves in Philadelphia. *Newsgroup*

➤ `phl.sports`: Sporting events and discussions. *Newsgroup*

8515 `phl.theatre` Theater events, reviews, and discussions. *Newsgroup*

8516 `phl.transportation` Getting around in the Philadelphia region. *Newsgroup*

8517 `phl.wanted` Items wanted in Philadelphia. *Newsgroup*

➤ `phl.weather`: Weather forecasts for the Philadelphia area. *Newsgroup*

US—PENNSYLVANIA—PITTSBURGH

8518 `pgh.apartments` Rental housing in the greater Pittsburgh area. *Newsgroup*

8519 `pgh.food` Food in Pittsburgh, Pennsylvania. *Newsgroup*

8520 `pgh.forsale` Items for sale in greater Pittsburgh area. *Newsgroup*

➤ `pgh.freenet`: Three Rivers Freenet public access network. *Newsgroup*

8521 `pgh.general` Items of general interest in Pittsburgh. *Newsgroup*

8522 `pgh.jobs.offered` Employment available in the greater Pittsburgh area. *Newsgroup*

8523 `pgh.jobs.wanted` Employment desired in the greater Pittsburgh area. *Newsgroup*

8524 `pgh.motss` Lesbian, gay, and bisexual issues in Pittsburg. *Newsgroup*

8525 `pgh.opinion` Where to post them if you got them. *Newsgroup*

US—RHODE ISLAND

8526 `alt.rhode_island` A little state with apparently worldwide interest. *Newsgroup*

8527 `clari.local.rhode_island` News of Rhode Island. *Moderated newsgroup*

8528 **Providence Business News:** Weekly business newspaper covering Rhode Island and southeast Massachusetts. *Newsletter*
http://pbn.com/
INFO EDITOR editor@pbn.com (Roger Bergenheim)
INFO circulation@pbn.com
INFO publisher@pbn.com (Roger Bergenheim)
Frequency: weekly

8529 `ri.admin` Rhode Island hierarchy administrative discussions. *Newsgroup*

8530 `ri.general` General discussion in Rhode Island, USA. *Newsgroup*

8531 `ri.politics` Politics in the state of Rhode Island. *Newsgroup*

➤ **Robinson Green Beretta Corporation:** RGB is the largest architectural, engineering, and interior design firm in Rhode Island. (See entry 66 for full listing.)

US—SOUTH CAROLINA

8532 `clari.local.south_carolina` News of South Carolina. *Newsgroup*

➤ **Presbyterian College:** This site offers a look at the people, campus, academic program, and extracurricular life of Presbyterian College in Clinton, South Carolina. (See entry 4440 for full listing.)

➤ **University of South Carolina Department of Mathematics:** A multi-topic information service hosted at the University of South Carolina's Department of Mathematics in Columbia, South Carolina. It includes information on wavelet-related mathematical materials and archives of *Wavelet Digest*. (See entry 9404 for full listing.)

US—SOUTH DAKOTA

8533 `clari.local.south_dakota` News of South Dakota. *Newsgroup*

US—TENNESSEE

8534 `clari.local.tennessee` News of Tennessee. *Newsgroup*

➤ **MECCA (Memphis Educational Computer Connectivity Alliance):** An alliance of academic institutions in Memphis, Tennessee, with the purpose of enhancing Internet connectivity and programmed application of that connectivity for local schools to enhance educational infrastructure. (See entry 4519 for full listing.)

8535 `memphis.dining` Restaurants and other eating establishments in Memphis, Tennessee. *Newsgroup*

8536 `memphis.employment` Jobs needed or offered in the Memphis area. *Newsgroup*

8537 `memphis.events` Special events—Mid-South Fair, Memphis in May, etc. *Newsgroup*

8538 `memphis.for-sale` Postings of items which are for sale in the area. *Newsgroup*

8539 `memphis.general` Discussion about miscellaneous Memphis-related issues. *Newsgroup*

8540 `memphis.networking` Discussion of computer networking and connectivity. *Newsgroup*

8541 `memphis.newsgroups` Issues dealing with the Memphis newsgroup hierarchy. *Newsgroup*

8542 `memphis.wanted` Postings for items which someone would like to find or buy. *Newsgroup*

8543 **Nashville-Scout:** On Internet resources in Nashville, Tennessee. *Newsletter*
± majordomo@listserv.nashville.net
INFO majordomo-owner@listserv.nashville.net
OWNER bill@nashville.net (Bill Butler)
ARCHIVE http://www.nashville.net/local/

8544 `nashville.general` General discussion for Nashvillites. *Newsgroup*

8545 `tn.flame` Flames in Tennessee. *Newsgroup*

8546 `tn.general` Items of general interest in Tennessee. *Newsgroup*

8547 `tn.talk` Talk in Tennessee. *Newsgroup*

➤ `tn.unix`: Discussion of issues related to Unix in Tennessee. *Newsgroup*

8548 `tnn.arts` Topics about arts, museums, etc. *Newsgroup*

US—TEXAS

➤ **Alamo Community College District CWIS:** CWIS for Alamo Community Colleges in San Antonio, Texas. (See entry 4142 for full listing.)

8549 **Armadillo's World Wide Web Server:** Instructional resources and information about Texas.
http://riceinfo.rice.edu/armadillo/
gopher://riceinfo.rice.edu:1170
INFO armadillo@rice.edu

8550 **Austin City Limits:** Home of everything that's cool in Austin, Texas.
http://www.quadralay.com/Austin/austin.html
INFO greening@quadralay.com

➤ **Austin Symphony Home Page:** The Austin Symphony Orchestra's Web site posts all recent press releases and the season schedule. (See entry 808 for full listing.)

8551 `clari.local.texas` News of Texas. *Moderated newsgroup*

➤ **LoanStar:** On resource sharing, document delivery, and interlibrary loans in Texas. (See entry 5752 for full listing.)

➤ **Texas A&M University Bonfire:** Each year, thousands of Texas A&M University students work together to build a massive bonfire—55 feet high with a circumference of 195 feet—that symbolizes their "burning desire" to beat the University of Texas in the annual football game. Coverage of the building process and burn is included. (See entry 4405 for full listing.)

➤ **Texas A&M University World Wide Web:** This Texas A&M WWW site includes both a subject index and a keyword search to information offered by Web sites located throughout the College Station campus, the local community, and the entire Texas A&M system. Information regarding academics, research, events, employment, and campus sights are just a sampling of the topics included. It also includes information on the George Bush Presidential Library. (See entry 4456 for full listing.)

➤ **Texas Metronet, Inc.:** Internet for the individual. Includes extensive Perl archive, scripts, information, and distribution source. Internet services and information. Many other helpful sources and links. The entire archive is boolean WAIS indexed for easy searching and retrieval. (See entry 2702 for full listing.)

8552 `tx.flame` Texas flames. *Newsgroup*

8553 `tx.forsale` Stuff for sale in Texas. *Newsgroup*

8554 `tx.general` Items of general interest in Texas. *Newsgroup*

8555 `tx.guns` Texans talk about firearms. *Newsgroup*

8556 `tx.jobs` Jobs in Texas. *Newsgroup*

➤ `tx.motorcycles`: Biker Texans. *Newsgroup*

8557 `tx.politics` Politics in Texas. *Newsgroup*

8558 `tx.usenet.stats` `tx.*` hierarchy Usenet statistics. *Newsgroup*

8559 `tx.wanted` Texas want ads. *Newsgroup*

8560 **TXDXN-L:** For news and discussion of availability and dissemination of Texas state government information to the public, requests concerning specific publications, reference questions, guides, and bibliographies. *Mailing List, moderated*

± `listserv@uhupvm1.uh.edu` [body = SUBSCRIBE TXDXN-L first-name last-name]

INFO `mbcmw@uh.edu` (Marek B. Waterstone)

OWNER `guajardo@uh.edu` (Richard R. Guajardo)

ARCHIVE `listserv@uhupvm1.uh.edu`

POST `txdxn-l@uhupvm1.uh.edu`

FAQ `http://www.lawlib.uh.edu/txdxn/`

Comments: One need not be a subscriber to post information for distribution to the list; however, commercial solicitations or advertisements are not distributed. TXDXN-L has basically an educational purpose, and we welcome, indeed encourage, questions and comments which focus on government information.

US—TEXAS—AUSTIN

8561 `austin.announce` Announcement newsgroup for the Austin, Texas (USA) area. *Moderated newsgroup*

8562 `austin.autos` Care and (mis)use of automobiles in Austin, Texas. *Newsgroup*

8563 `austin.eff` The Electronic Frontier Foundation in Austin, Texas. *Moderated newsgroup*

8564 `austin.flame` Flamefesting followup for Austin, Texas. *Newsgroup*

8565 `austin.food` Eating, cooking, and culinary delights in Austin, Texas. *Newsgroup*

8566 `austin.forsale` Items for sale in Austin, Texas. *Newsgroup*

8567 `austin.general` Items of general interest in Austin, Texas. *Newsgroup*

8568 `austin.internet` Discussion of Internet issues and connectivity in Austin. *Newsgroup*

8569 `austin.jobs` Jobs available, wanted, and discussion in Austin, Texas. *Newsgroup*

8570 `austin.music` Music around Austin, Texas. *Newsgroup*

➤ `austin.org.sca:` The Society for Creative Anachronism in Austin, Texas. *Newsgroup*

8571 `austin.politics` Political issues in Austin, Texas. *Newsgroup*

8572 `austin.talk` Talk in Austin, Texas. *Newsgroup*

US—TEXAS—DALLAS

8573 `dfw.eats` Dining in Dallas/Fort Worth. *Newsgroup*

8574 `dfw.flame` Flaming in Dallas/Fort Worth. *Newsgroup*

8575 `dfw.forsale` Items for sale in Dallas/Fort Worth. *Newsgroup*

8576 `dfw.general` Items of general interest in Dallas/Fort Worth. *Newsgroup*

8577 `dfw.internet.providers` Internet access providers in the Dallas/Fort Worth region. *Newsgroup*

8578 `dfw.jobs` Employment in the Dallas/Fort Worth region. *Newsgroup*

8579 `dfw.personals` Personals ads in the Dallas/Fort Worth area. *Newsgroup*

8580 `dfw.politics` Political discussion in and about the Dallas/Fort Worth region. *Newsgroup*

8581 `dfw.singles` Single folks in the Dallas/Fort Worth region. *Newsgroup*

US—TEXAS—HOUSTON

8582 `houston.eats` Dining in Houston, Texas. *Newsgroup*

8583 `houston.efh.talk` Electronic Frontiers of Houston discussions. *Newsgroup*

8584 `houston.forsale` Items for sale in Houston, Texas. *Newsgroup*

8585 `houston.general` Items of general interest in Houston, Texas. *Newsgroup*

8586 `houston.internet.providers` For information and discussion on Internet access providers in the Houston area. *Newsgroup*

8587 `houston.jobs.offered` Jobs available in Houston, Texas. *Newsgroup*

8588 `houston.jobs.wanted` People wanting jobs in Houston, Texas. *Newsgroup*

8589 `houston.music` Musical happenings and discussions in Houston, Texas. *Newsgroup*

➤ `houston.personals:` How to meet someone in Houston, Texas. *Newsgroup*

8590 `houston.politics` Politics in Houston, Texas. *Newsgroup*

➤ `houston.singles:` Discussions of singles activities in Houston, Texas. *Newsgroup*

➤ `houston.sports:` Sports discussions in Houston, Texas. *Newsgroup*

8591 `houston.usenet.stats` Usenet statistics in Houston, Texas. *Newsgroup*

8592 `houston.wanted` Things wanted in Houston, Texas. *Newsgroup*

➤ `houston.weather:` Houston weather forcasts. *Moderated newsgroup*

US—TEXAS—SAN ANTONIO

8593 `sat.announce` San Antonio area announcements. *Moderated newsgroup*

8594 `sat.food` Food, recipies, and culinary delights in San Antonio, Texas. *Newsgroup*

8595 `sat.forsale` For sale group in San Antonio, Texas area. *Newsgroup*

8596 `sat.general` General items of interest around San Antonio, Texas. *Newsgroup*

8597 `sat.jobs` Job announcements and discussions in San Antonio, Texas. *Newsgroup*

8598 `sat.music` Music around San Antonio, Texas. *Newsgroup*

➤ `sat.personals:` Personal ads in San Antonio, Texas. *Newsgroup*

US—UTAH

8599 `clari.local.utah` News of Utah. *Moderated newsgroup*

8600 `clari.sports.local.southwest.utah` News of Utah athletics. *Moderated newsgroup*

US—VERMONT

8601 `clari.local.vermont` News of Vermont. *Newsgroup*

➤ **The DuPont Building, Burlington, Vermont:** Joanna Oltman's historic preservation project traces the history of the classic DuPont Building on the waterfront in Burlington, Vermont. (See entry 62 for full listing.)

➤ `ne.forsale:` Short postings on items for sale in New England. *Newsgroup*

US—VIRGINIA

➤ **Arlington Community Television's Homepage:** Home page for Channel 33—Arlington, Virginia's community access cable station. This home page offers information about ACT and access in general, contact information, and examples of the type of progams produced through the facilities. (See entry 1487 for full listing.)

8602 `clari.local.virginia+dc` News of Virginia and Washington, D.C. *Moderated newsgroup*

8603 `va.general` For folks in Virginia. *Newsgroup*

➤ **Virginia Coast Reserve Information System (VCRIS):** This site includes weather and ecological data for Virginia coast sites. The site is operated by the Virginia Coast Reserve Long-Term Ecological Research Project (VCR/LTER). (See entry 9047 for full listing.)

US—WASHINGTON

8604 `clari.local.washington` News of Washington State. *Moderated newsgroup*

8605 `clari.sports.local.northwest.washington` News of Washington athletics. *Moderated newsgroup*

➤ **CyberVPM:** CyberVPM is dedicated to the discussion of topics relevant to volunteer program management. Participation is free of charge and available to anyone who works with volunteers. (See entry 2057 for full listing.)

8606 `seattle.eats` Food in the Seattle,Washington area. *Newsgroup*

8607 `seattle.forsale.computers` Computer-related items in Seattle. *Newsgroup*

8608 `seattle.forsale.housing` Housing-related items in Seattle. *Newsgroup*

8609 `seattle.forsale.misc` Various for sale/wanted items in Seattle. *Newsgroup*

8610 `seattle.forsale.transportation` Transportation related items in Seattle. *Newsgroup*

8611 `seattle.general` Items of general interest in Seattle, Washington. *Newsgroup*

8612 `seattle.jobs.offered` Employment offered in Seattle, Washington. *Newsgroup*

8613 `seattle.jobs.wanted` Employment sought in Seattle, Washington. *Newsgroup*

8614 `seattle.politics` Discussion of politics in Seattle, Washington, USA. *Newsgroup*

8615 `tacoma.events` Happenings around Tacoma/Pierce County, Washington. *Newsgroup*

8616 `tacoma.general` General discussions for Tacoma/Pierce County Washington. *Newsgroup*

8617 `tacoma.politics` Political discussions for Tacoma/Pierce County, Washington. *Newsgroup*

➤ **Village Books:** A community-based bookstore located in Bellingham, Washington. This site includes event listings, author comments about the store, and links to other interesting book-related sites. (See entry 120 for full listing.)

➤ **WACCNET-L:** For accountants in the state of Washington. (See entry 1662 for full listing.)

8618 `wash.assistive-tech` Forum about AT issues, products, and services in Washington. *Newsgroup*

8619 `wash.general` Discussion of general matters in Washington State, USA. *Newsgroup*

8620 `yakima.general` Items of general interest in Yakima, Washington. *Newsgroup*

US—WASHINGTON, D.C.

➤ `clari.local.virginia+dc:` News of Virginia and Washington, D.C. *Moderated newsgroup*

8621 `clari.sports.local.south.washington_dc` Washington, D.C. athletics. *Moderated newsgroup*

➤ `dc.biking:` Bicycles and biking in the Washington, D.C. metro area. *Newsgroup*

8622 `dc.dining` Dining in the Washington, D.C. area. *Newsgroup*

8623 `dc.driving` Highway travel around Washington, D.C. *Newsgroup*

8624 `dc.forsale.computers` Computer equipment and computer peripherals. *Newsgroup*

8625 `dc.forsale.misc` Items wanted and for sale in the Washington, D.C. area. *Newsgroup*

8626 `dc.general` Items of general interest to the Washington, D.C. area. *Newsgroup*

8627 `dc.housing` Housing in the Washington, D.C. area. *Newsgroup*

8628 `dc.jobs` Job offerings and jobs wanted around Washington, D.C. *Newsgroup*

8629 `dc.media` Newspapers, radio, and TV in the D.C. area. *Newsgroup*

8630 `dc.music` Music-related issues in the D.C. area. *Newsgroup*

➤ `dc.org.linux-users:` D.C.-area Linux users group announcements, etc. *Newsgroup*

8631 `dc.politics` Discussion group for D.C.-area local politics. *Newsgroup*

8632 `dc.romance` Romance for couples and singles in the USA's capital area. *Newsgroup*

➤ `dc.smithsonian:` Smithsonian Institute-related events in the Washington, D.C. area. *Newsgroup*

8633 **MALACHI:** For the exchange of ideas and information about graduate courses among the universities in the Washington, D.C. metropolitan area. *Mailing List*
± `listserv@umdd.umd.edu` [body = SUBSCRIBE MALACHI first-name last-name]
INFO `kent_norman@umail.umd.edu` (Kent Norman)
ARCHIVE `listserv@umdd.umd.edu` [body = INDEX MALACHI]

US—WEST VIRGINIA

8634 `clari.local.west_virginia` News of West Virginia. *Moderated newsgroup*

US—WISCONSIN

8635 `clari.local.wisconsin` News of Wisconsin. *Moderated newsgroup*

8636 `clari.sports.local.midwest.wisconsin` News of Wisconsin athletics. *Moderated newsgroup*

8637 `milw.general` Items of general interest in Milwaukee. *Newsgroup*

8638 `milw.jobs` Jobs available and wanted in the Milwaukee area. *Newsgroup*

8639 `wi.forsale` Items for sale in Wisconsin. *Newsgroup*

8640 `wi.general` Items of general interest in Wisconsin. *Newsgroup*

8641 `wi.transit` Open forum on transportation issues in Wisconsin. *Newsgroup*

8642 `wyo.recreation` Discussions of Wyoming's recreational activities and issues. *Newsgroup*

US—WYOMING

8643 `clari.local.wyoming` News of Wyoming. *Moderated newsgroup*

➤ **Job's Daughters:** Job's Daughters in Casper and Wyoming, with links to worldwide International Order of Job's Daughters. (See entry 5940 for full listing.)

➤ **Junior A Hockey:** Complete statistics and scores on the Central Wyoming Outlaws and the American Frontier Hockey League, with links to other hockey resources worldwide. (See entry 6904 for full listing.)

8644 `wyo.education` Discussions concerning education in Wyoming. *Newsgroup*

8645 `wyo.energy` Discussion of energy-related topics in Wyoming. *Newsgroup*

8646 `wyo.general` General issues related to Wyoming. *Newsgroup*

8647 `wyo.internet` General discussions of the Internet in Wyoming. *Newsgroup*

8648 `wyo.jobs` Group to advertise and discuss jobs and job-related issues. *Newsgroup*

8649 **Wyoming:** Everything you want to know about Wyoming, and some. It includes Who's Who in Wyoming on the Internet©, Wyoming E-mail Directory©, links to Wyoming schools and colleges, and government telephone directories.

`http://w3.trib.com/~dont/Wyoming.html`

INFO `dont@trib.com`

INFO `http://w3.trib.com/~dont/`

RELIGION & SPIRITUALITY

8650 `alt.recovery.religion` The twelve steps from the Ten Commandments. *Newsgroup*

8651 Areopagus: Shedding light on fringe ideas and groups on the religious and spiritual spectrum. We tend to look at experience-based articles and stories (as well as short fiction and poetry). *E-Zine*
`http://www.catalog.com/lionsden/areo/index.html`
INFO EDITOR `craigm@iclnet93.iclnet.org` (Craig Martin, Editor)
EDITOR `aconnoll@is.dal.ca` (Andrew Connolly, Assistant Editor)
Frequency: highly irregular

8652 `aus.religion` Discussions of, or related to, religions. *Newsgroup*

➤ `clari.living.goodnews:` Stories of success and survival. *Moderated newsgroup*

8653 `clari.news.religion` Religion, religious leaders, televangelists. *Moderated newsgroup*

8654 `fj.life.religion` Discussion on religion. *Newsgroup*

8655 `relcom.religion` Discussions on religions and related topics. *Newsgroup*

8656 `sanet.talk.religion` Talk about religion. *Newsgroup*

ATHEISM

8657 `alt.atheism` Godless heathens. *Newsgroup*

8658 `alt.atheism.moderated` Focused godless heathens. *Moderated newsgroup*

8659 `alt.atheism.satire` Atheism-related humor and satire . *Newsgroup*

8660 `alt.blasphemy` Irreverence on the net? Who would have thought. *Newsgroup*

8661 `soc.atheism` Living as an atheist and atheism in society. *Moderated newsgroup*

8662 `talk.atheism` Debate about the validity and nature of atheism. *Newsgroup*

BUDDHISM

8663 `alt.buddha.short.fat.guy` Religion. And not religion. Both. Neither. *Newsgroup*

8664 `alt.philosophy.zen` Meditating on how the `alt.*` namespace works. *Newsgroup*

8665 `alt.religion.buddhism.nichiren` Nichiren believers unite. *Newsgroup*

8666 `alt.religion.buddhism.tibetan` The teachings of Buddha as studied in Tibet. *Newsgroup*

8667 `alt.zen` It is. *Newsgroup*

8668 BUDDHA-L: On Buddhist studies: history, culture, and politics. *Mailing List, moderated*
± `listserv@ulkyvm.louisville.edu` [body = SUBSCRIBE BUDDHA-L first-name last-name]
INFO OWNER `cxev@musica.mcgill.ca` (Richard Hayes)
INFO OWNER `jacock01@ulkyvm.louisville.edu` (James A. Cocks)

8669 BUDDHIST: On all aspects of Buddhism. *Mailing List*
± `listserv@vm1.mcgill.ca` [body = SUBSCRIBE BUDDHIST first-name last-name]
OWNER `pbb@fw.gs.com` (Paul Bellan-Boyer)
ARCHIVE `listserv@vm1.mcgill.ca` [body = INDEX BUDDHIST]

8670 Still Point: From the Dharma Rain Zen Center. *Newsletter*
`http://www.teleport.com/~ldotm/STILLPOINT.html`
± `ldotm@teleport.com` (Ken Lawson, Linda McNeeley)
INFO `g.carlson1@genie.geis.com`

8671 `talk.religion.buddhism` All aspects of Buddhism as religion and philosophy. *Newsgroup*

8672 `tnn.religion.buddhism.shinshu` Exchange of ideas on Shinshu Buddhism. *Newsgroup*

8673 `uk.religion.buddhist` Buddhism in the United Kingdom. *Newsgroup*

CHRISTIANITY

8674 **ICLNet:** Large collection of Christian resources, and information.
http://www.iclnet.org/
INFO webmaster@www.iclnet.org

8675 **Not Just Bibles:** Guide to Christian resources on the Internet.
http://www.iclnet.org/pub/resources/christian-resources.html
INFO njb@iclnet.org

➤ `alt.books.cs-lewis`: Narnia and other C. S. Lewis tales. *Newsgroup*

8676 `alt.brother-jed` The born-again minister touring U.S. campuses. *Newsgroup*

8677 `alt.christnet` Gathering place for Christian ministers and users. *Newsgroup*

8678 `alt.christnet.bible` Bible discussion and research. *Newsgroup*

8679 `alt.christnet.christianlife` How to live what Christians believe. *Newsgroup*

8680 `alt.christnet.ethics` Ethics in the Christian value system. *Newsgroup*

8681 `alt.christnet.evangelical` Some aspects of evangelism. *Newsgroup*

8682 `alt.christnet.philosophy` Philosophical implications of Christianity. *Newsgroup*

8683 `alt.christnet.prayer` Prayer in the lives of Christians. *Newsgroup*

8684 `alt.christnet.second-coming.real-soon-now` It could happen. *Newsgroup*

➤ `alt.christnet.theology`: The distinctives of God of Christian theology. *Newsgroup*

➤ `alt.education.home-school.christian`: Christian home schoolers. *Moderated newsgroup*

8685 `alt.fan.jesus-christ` Israel in 4 B.C. had no mass communication. *Newsgroup*

8686 `alt.org.promisekeepers` The Christian organization PromiseKeepers. *Newsgroup*

8687 `alt.religion.christian` Unmoderated forum for discussing Christianity. *Newsgroup*

8688 `alt.religion.christian.last-days` In anticipation of Christ's second coming. *Newsgroup*

8689 `alt.religion.gnostic` History and philosophies of the Gnostic sects. *Newsgroup*

8690 `alt.religion.mormon` Mormon religion. *Newsgroup*

8691 **apologia-l:** Biblical Christians exploring orthodox apologetics. *Mailing List, moderated*
http://diakonos.hum.utah.edu/philosophy/religion/apologia/
± majordomo@netcom.com [body = SUBSCRIBE apologia-l]
OWNER apologia-l-owner@netcom.com
ARCHIVE ftp://ftp.netcom.com/pub/th/think/apologetics/
Please Note: Subscription by approval only.

➤ **ARIL-L:** Members of the Association for Religion and Intellectual Life, publisher of Cross Currents. (See entry 8775 for full listing.)

8692 `aus.religion.christian` Christianity and issues relevant to Christianity. *Newsgroup*

8693 `bit.listserv.christia` Practical Christian life. *Moderated newsgroup*

8694 **Bruderhof Homepage:** Information on the Bruderhof movement, its Plough Publishing House, schools, church community, an archive of *The Plough* (Bruderhof periodical), articles related to social issues like the death penalty and family problems, and more.
http://www.esslink.com/~brud/bruderhof.html
INFO webmaster@bruderhof.org

8695 Calvin College CWIS: Information service for Calvin College and Calvin Theological Seminary. This site includes news and information about Calvin, a campus directory, campus library catalog, and an extensive set of pointers to Christian resources on the Internet.

http://www.calvin.edu/

INFO webmaster@calvin.edu

8696 CELL-CHURCH: Cell-based churches discussion group *Mailing List, moderated*

ftp://bible.acu.edu

http://www-sal.cs.uiuc.edu/~jreid/cell-church/

± listserv@bible.acu.edu [body = SUBSCRIBE CELL-CHURCH first-name last-name]

OWNER kennyk@singnet.com.sg (Kenny Kon)

OWNER dolan@bible.acu.edu (Kenny Kon)

OWNER jreid@uiuc.edu (Jon Reid)

ARCHIVE cell-church-archives@bible.acu.edu [body = help]

POST cell-church@bible.acu.edu

FAQ cell-church-archives@bible.acu.edu [body = SENDME FAQ]

Please Note: Subscription by approval only.

8697 Center-L: On "centering prayer," a Christian contemplative practice. *Mailing List*

http://www.io.com/~lefty/COHome.html

± center-l-request@netcom.com

OWNER lefty@apple.com (David "Lefty" Schlesinger)

8698 CHR-EXP: For a Christian explanation of the Scriptures to Jews. *Mailing List*

± listserv@nic.surfnet.nl [body = SUBSCRIBE CHR-EXP first-name last-name]

EDITOR OWNER t.benschop@pobox.ruu.nl (Teus Benschop)

8699 CHRISTIA: For discussing practical Christian living—wide range of denominations, experiences, and scholarly backgrounds. *Mailing List*

± listserv@asuvm.inre.asu.edu [body = SUBSCRIBE CHRISTIA first-name last-name]

INFO drake@asu.edu (Mark Drake)

ARCHIVE listserv@asuvm.inre.asu.edu

POST christia@asuvm.inre.asu.edu

Gated: bit.listserv.christia

8700 Christian Bookstore: The Christian Bookstore of Fort Lauderdale, Florida, is a complete source for church supplies, clergy apparel, robes, Christian books, gospel music, Bibles, and religious goods.

http://www.christianbookstore.com/

christbkst@aol.com

INFO webmaster@bocanet.com

MIRROR http://www.bocanet.com/cbs

8701 Christian Growth: Intended to help Christians grow. Includes personal testimonies, encouraging articles, and book reviews. *Newsletter*

http://www.olsen.ch/~dansmith/cgn.html

INFO bible@olsen.ch (Laura and Dan Smith)

Frequency: monthly

➤   **Christian Homeschool Forum:** Home-schooling resources for Christians. (See entry 4208 for full listing.)

8702 Christian Software News: On Christian and church-related software. *Distribution List*

± serious@mindspring.com (Jerry Lovett)

OWNER serious@mindspring.com (Jerry Lovett)

ARCHIVE http://www.viper.net/clients/serious/csn.htm

8703 ChristLit: On Christianity and literature. *Mailing List, moderated*

± `listserv@bethel.edu` [body = `SUBSCRIBE CHRISTLIT` first-name last-name]
OWNER `d-ritchie@bethel.edu` (Daniel E. Ritchie)

8704 **`christnet.admin`** Christnet-Usenet administrative group. *Newsgroup*

➤ **`christnet.bible`**: Bible research and talk. *Newsgroup*

8705 **`christnet.christianlife`** Applied Christianity. *Newsgroup*

8706 **`christnet.christnews`** Your news on the Christian scene. *Newsgroup*

8707 **`christnet.ethics`** Christian scripture and ethics. *Newsgroup*

8708 **`christnet.evangelical`** The good news of the gospel. *Newsgroup*

8709 **`christnet.general`** General address—public e-mail. *Newsgroup*

8710 **`christnet.ladies`** Christian ladies. *Newsgroup*

8711 **`christnet.philosophy`** Philosophy in Christianity. *Newsgroup*

8712 **`christnet.poetry`** Christian poetry. *Newsgroup*

8713 **`christnet.prayer`** Prayer and counsel. *Newsgroup*

8714 **`christnet.religion`** Discussion of religious ideas. *Moderated newsgroup*

8715 **`christnet.theology`** Christian theology. *Newsgroup*

8716 **`christnet.writers`** Discussion group for Christian writers. *Newsgroup*

8717 **CHURCHPLANTERS:** On Christian "Church Planters." *Mailing List*
± `churchplanters-request@bible.acu.edu`
EDITOR `bollow@pobox.com` (Norbert Bollow)

8718 **CONYERS:** On recent apparitions of Jesus Christ to Nancy Fowler in Conyers, Georgia. *Mailing List*
± `listserv@ubvm.cc.buffalo.edu` [body = `SUBSCRIBE CONYERS` first-name last-name]
OWNER `drzymala@ubvm.cc.buffalo.edu` (Jim Drzymala)
POST `conyers@ubvm.cc.buffalo.edu`

8719 **Cross Way Publications:** Publishers of poetic works focusing on Christianity. *Magazine*
`http://www.pennet.net/resident/hoffman/crossway.html`
± INFO EDITOR OWNER `crosspub@pennet.net` (Jerry Hoffman, Editor)
ARCHIVE `crosspub@pennet.net` (Jerry Hoffman, Editor)
Frequency: monthly

8720 **CURSILLO:** On the Catholic, Episcopal and Methodist Cursillo Movement. *Mailing List*
± `majordomo@list.us.net` [body = `subscribe cursillo` *carriage-return* end]
OWNER `sward@us.net` (Scotty Ward)

8721 **DIFTX-L:** For expansive, counter-fundamentalist discussion of "different" Christianity. *Mailing List*
± `listserv@yalevm.cis.yale.edu` [body = `SUB DIFTX-L` first-name last-name]
OWNER `antdug1@minerva.cis.yale.edu` (Antony Dugdale)

8722 **ECOTHEOL:** On environmental issues from a theological or ethical perspective. *Mailing List*
± `mailbase@mailbase.ac.uk` [body = `SUBSCRIBE ECOTHEOL` first-name last-name]
INFO OWNER `i.j.tilsed@exeter.ac.uk` (Ian Tilsed)
ARCHIVE `mailbase@mailbase.ac.uk` [body = `INDEX ECOTHEOL`]

➤ **Feminist-Theology:** On Jewish and Christian feminist theology. (See entry 8781 for full listing.)

8723 **IFC:** On resources for Christians on the net. *Distribution List, moderated*
± `ifc-request@gospelcom.net` [body = `subscribe` e-mail-address]
INFO OWNER `schu@calvin.edu` (Quentin Schultze)
ARCHIVE `http://www.gospelcom.net/ifc/newsletter.html`
Frequency: biweekly

8724 **JOHNLITR:** For scholarly, insightful discussion of the Gospel of John. *Mailing List*
± listserv@univscvm.csd.scarolina.edu [body = SUBSCRIBE JOHNLITR first-name last-name]

8725 **The Lighthouse:** A monthly Christian music (all genres) magazine featuring an upcoming album list, album reviews, artist interviews, industry press releases, brief reviews of all new products, and an indie section. Rated top 5% Web site. *E-Journal*
http://tlem.netcentral.net/
INFO lighthouse@netcentral.net
Frequency: monthly

➤ **MERELEWIS:** On the life, works, and influence of C. S. Lewis. (See entry 602 for full listing.)

➤ **misc.education.home-school.christian:** Christian home-schooling. *Newsgroup*

8726 **pdaxs.religion.christian** Christian religion and activities. *Newsgroup*

8727 **PRCL-L:** On using the Revised Common Lectionary: welcomes many Christian traditions. *Mailing List*
± listserv@ulkyvm.louisville.edu [body = SUBSCRIBE PRCL-L first-name last-name]
OWNER jimadams@cris.com (Rev. James W. Adams)

➤ **rec.music.christian:** Christian music, both contemporary and traditional. *Newsgroup*

8728 **SCICHR-L:** On Christianity and science. *Mailing List, moderated*
± INFO EDITOR OWNER s-schim@uiuc.edu (Steven H. Schimmrich)
ARCHIVE http://hercules.geology.uiuc.edu/~schimmri/christianity/scichr.html
Please Note: Subscription by approval only.

8729 **Scripture Studies:** A journal dedicated to the study and exposition of the Bible. *E-Journal*
http://www.kaiwan.com/~ssper/sstdys.html
± INFO OWNER ssper@aol.com (Scott Sperling)
ARCHIVES
http://www.kaiwan.com/~ssper/sstdys.html
ftp://sanar.kaiwan.com/user/ssper/
Frequency: monthly

8730 **soc.religion.christian** Christianity and related topics. *Moderated newsgroup*

8731 **soc.religion.christian.bible-study** Examining the Holy Bible. *Moderated newsgroup*

8732 **sportsflash:** On Christians in sports. *Distribution List*
http://www.gospelcom.net/gf/sf
± sportsflash-request@gospelcom.net
OWNER andy@gospelcom.net (Andy Padjen)
Frequency: weekly

➤ **Turning-Point:** This mailing list is intended to be a forum for Christian-oriented discussion of mental health topics and the role that God plays in mental health. Subscriptions are managed via the WWW. (See entry 4963 for full listing.)

8733 **uk.religion.christian** Christianity in the United Kingdom. *Newsgroup*

8734 **WME-L:** On the Worldwide Marriage Encounter workshops: sacrament of matrimony and holy orders. *Mailing List*
± listserv@american.edu [body = SUBSCRIBE WME-L first-name last-name]
OWNER jvogel@dgs.dgsys.com (John Vogel)

8735 **Youth Ministry Forum:** On ministry to teenagers. *Mailing List*
http://gospelcom.net/ys/
± youthministry-l-request@gospelcom.net
INFO ys@gospelcom.net
OWNER mikea@gospelcom.net (Mike Atkinson)

CHRISTIANITY—ANGLICAN/EPISCOPALIAN

8736 ANGLICAN: On matters pertaining to the Episcopal Church and members of the Anglican Communion. *Mailing List*
± listserv@american.edu [body = SUBSCRIBE ANGLICAN first-name last-name]
INFO cms@dragon.com (Cindy Smith)
INFO cts@dragon.com (Charles Smith)
ARCHIVE listserv@american.edu [body = INDEX ANGLICAN]
POST anglican@american.edu

8737 Anglicans Online: A large online resource center for the Anglican and Episcopal community.
http://infomatch.com/~haibeck/anglican.html
INFO tod@anglican.ca

8738 CANANG-L: On Canadian Anglican issues. *Mailing List*
± listserv@pdomain.uwindsor.ca [body = SUB CANANG-L first-name last-name]
OWNER bobgc@uwindsor.ca (Prof. Bob Chandler, MSW)
ARCHIVE listserv@pdomain.uwindsor.ca [body = INDEX CANANG-L]

8739 EPISCOPAL: By members of the Episcopal Diocese of Washington, DC. *Mailing List*
± majordomo@list.us.net [body = subscribe episcopal *carriage-return* end]
OWNER sward@us.net (Scotty Ward)

CHRISTIANITY—CATHOLIC

8740 alt.recovery.catholicism Getting over a Roman Catholic upbringing. *Newsgroup*

8741 AMERCATH: On the history of American Catholicism. *Mailing List*
± listserv@ukcc.uky.edu [body = SUBSCRIBE AMERCATH first-name last-name]
INFO OWNER jccannek@ukcc.uky.edu (Anne Kearney)
Please Note: Subscription by approval only.

8742 APAR-L: On apparitions approved by the Catholic Church. *Mailing List, moderated*
± listserv@ubvm.cc.buffalo.edu [body = SUBSCRIBE APAR-L first-name last-name]
INFO http://www.frontier.net/~mbd/apparitions.html
OWNER drzymala@ubvm.cc.buffalo.edu (Jim Drzymala)
ARCHIVE http://www.frontier.net/~mbd/apparitions.html
Gated: bit.listserv.apar-l

8743 bit.listserv.catholic Free Catholic List. *Newsgroup*

8744 CATHOLIC: On matters pertaining to the Catholic churches (Anglican, Roman, Orthodox). *Mailing List*
± listserv@american.edu [body = SUBSCRIBE CATHOLIC first-name last-name]
INFO cms@dragon.com (Cindy Smith)
INFO cts@dragon.com (Charles Smith)
ARCHIVES
ftp://listserv.american.edu/pub/catholic
listserv@american.edu [body = INDEX CATHOLIC]
Gated: bit.listserv.catholic

8745 Catholic Doctrine: On orthodox Catholic theology. *Mailing List*
± INFO catholic-request@sarto.gaithersburg.md.us
Comments: The catholic-request e-mail address is the moderator, not a program. Just describe what you want when you use the address.

Catholic University of Eichstaett: Campus wide information service for Catholic University of Eichstaett. (See entry 4418 for full listing.)

8746 OLDCTH-L: On the independent Catholic movement and the Old Catholic Communion. *Mailing List, moderated*

```
http://www.maths.tcd.ie/~thomas/oldcath.html
```
± majordomo@biddeford.com [body = subscribe oldcth-l]
OWNER jgilhous@biddeford.com (Fr. John-Mark Gilhousen)

➤   **St. John's University:** This site serves as the university's CWIS, and hosts the SJU Electronic Rehabilitation Resource Center and the SJU Learning Styles Network. This site also contains some resources for K–12 teachers. (See entry 4450 for full listing.)

8747   **tnn.religion.catholic** Discussion and information about Catholic or Catholicism. *Newsgroup*

CHRISTIANITY—ORTHODOX

8748   **Copt-Net Newsletter:** On the faith, teachings, and traditions of the Coptic Orthodox Church, and the history and culture of the Copts. Associated with Copt-Net Digest, a daily available only to members of the Coptic Church. *Newsletter*
```
http://cs-www.bu.edu/faculty/best/pub/cn/Menu.html
ftp://pharos.bu.edu
```
± INFO cn-request@cs.bu.edu (Azer Bestavros)
INFO best@cs.bu.edu (Azer Bestavros)
ARCHIVE ftp://pharos.bu.edu/CN/newsletters
FAQ ftp://pharos.bu.edu/CN/COPT-NET.charter
Frequency: three or four times a year.

8749   **EOCHR-L:** On Eastern Orthodox Christianity. *Mailing List*
± listserv@qucdn.queensu.ca [body = SUBSCRIBE EOCHR-L first-name last-name]
INFO vukomano@qucdn.queensu.ca (Dragic Vukomanovic)
Please Note: Subscription by approval only.

CHRISTIANITY—PROTESTANT

8750   **alt.religion.christian.anabaptist.brethren** Anabaptist religion. *Newsgroup*

8751   **alt.religion.christian.boston-church** The International Church of Christ. *Newsgroup*

8752   **Antithesis:** A review of Reformed Presbyterian thought and practice.
```
http://www.wavefront.com/~Contra_M/antithesis/
```
INFO contramundum@wavefront.com (T.E. Wilder)

8753   **BAPTIST:** Open Baptist discussion. *Mailing List*
± listserv@ukcc.uky.edu [body = SUBSCRIBE BAPTIST first-name last-name]
INFO baptist-request@ukcc.uky.edu
ARCHIVE listserv@ukcc.uky.edu [body = INDEX BAPTIST]

8754   **DOCDISC:** Disciples of Christ Discussion Group. *Mailing List*
± majordomo@ux1.cso.uiuc.edu
INFO docdisc-owner@ux1.cso.uiuc.edu
OWNER mcmillan@alexia.lis.uiuc.edu (Jim McMillan)

8755   **LTHRN-L:** On Lutheranism: liturgy, worship, theology, history, social issues. *Mailing List*
± listproc2@bgu.edu
OWNER pbb@fw.gs.com (Paul Bellan-Boyer)

8756   **Presbyterian Church in America:** Unofficial home page for the Presbyterian Church in America (PCA), with addresses of denominational offices and links to home pages of individual congregations and to online articles relevant to the PCA.
```
http://www.wavefront.com/~Contra_M/pca/
```
INFO contramundum@wavefront.com (T.E. Wilder)

8757 Presbyterian College Gopher Server: This is the gopher server of Presbyterian College. It includes a collection of religious documents (Bible, Koran, etc.) on which full-text searches can be performed.

`gopher://cs1.presby.edu`

INFO `gopher-admin@presby.edu`

8758 REFORMED: On Calvinism. *Mailing List*

± `listserv@listserv.syr.edu` [body = SUBSCRIBE REFORMED first-name last-name]

OWNER `clstampe@mailbox.syr.edu` (Chris Stamper)

8759 SDAnet: Discussion about Seventh-Day Adventists for members and those who are interested. *Digest & Reflector, moderated*

`http://www.sdanet.org/`

`gopher://gopher.sdanet.org`

± `listserv@sdanet.org` [body = subscribe sdanet]

INFO `listserv@sdanet.org` [body = info sdanet]

INFO `sdanet-request@sdanet.org`

EDITOR OWNER `timm@sdanet.org` (Steve Timm)

POST `sdanet@sdanet.org`

Comments: Contact list owner for information about other Seventh Day Adventist Internet resources (SDAnews & SDAtalk).

➤ **SHAKER:** About the United Society of Believers (Shakers). (See entry 5259 for full listing.)

8760 STONE-CAMPBELL: On the Stone-Campbell movement and the Churches of Christ. *Mailing List, moderated*

± `listserv@bible.acu.edu` [body = SUBSCRIBE STONE-CAMPBELL]

INFO `kennyk@singnet.com.sg` (Kenny Kon)

ARCHIVES

`stone-campbell-archives@bible.acu.edu` [body = help]

`ftp://bible.acu.edu/stone-campbell`

8761 UM-LIST: For United Methodists. *Mailing List*

± `listserv@ulkyvm.louisville.edu` [body = SUBSCRIBE UM-LIST first-name last-name]

OWNER `dmullens@holli.com` (David Mullens)

8762 WTD: A scholarly forum for critical discussion of religious and theological issues from a Wesleyan/holiness perspective. *Mailing List, moderated*

± INFO EDITOR OWNER `tphillip@sun.cis.smu.edu` (Tom Phillips)

OWNER `bfraser@umich.edu` (Bob Fraser)

OWNER `gllyons@exodus.nnc.edu` (George Lyons)

OWNER `bmalas@i2020.net` (Bill Malas)

Please Note: Subscription by approval only.

Comments: Subscribers must have a Ph.D. or be enrolled in a Ph.D. program.

CHRISTIANITY—QUAKER

8763 QUAKER-K: Discussion group for Quaker children ages 5 to 12. *Digest & Reflector, moderated*

± `listserv@postoffice.cso.uiuc.edu` [body = SUBSCRIBE QUAKER-K first-name last-name]

INFO `quaker-k-request@postoffice.cso.uiuc.edu`

ARCHIVE `listserv@postoffice.cso.uiuc.edu` [body = GET QUAKER-K LOG*yymm* where *yy* is the year and *mm* is month]

Please Note: Subscription by approval only.

8764 QUAKER-L: For general discussions of Quakers and Quakerism. *Digest & Reflector, moderated*

`http://www.quaker.org/quaker-l`

± `listserv@postoffice.cso.uiuc.edu` [body = SUBSCRIBE QUAKER-L first-name last-name]

INFO `quaker-l-request@postoffice.cso.uiuc.edu`
INFO `b-dienes@uiuc.edu` (Bruce Dienes)
ARCHIVE `ftp://postoffice.cso.uiuc.edu/quaker-l`
FAQ `listserv@postoffice.cso.uiuc.edu` [body = `info quaker-l`]

8765 **QUAKER-P:** On Quaker concerns related to peace and social-justice issues. *Digest & Reflector*
`http://www.quaker.org/quaker-p`
± `listserv@postoffice.cso.uiuc` [body = SUBSCRIBE QUAKER-P first-name last-name]
INFO `quaker-p-request@postoffice.cso.uiuc.edu`
INFO `b-dienes@uiuc.edu` (Bruce Dienes)
ARCHIVE `ftp://postoffice.cso.uiuc.edu/quaker-p`
FAQ `listserv@postoffice.cso.uiuc.edu` [body = INFO QUAKER-P]
Gated: `bit.listserv.quaker-p`

8766 **The Religious Society of Friends:** Information on the society, known also as Quakers. Includes lists of Quaker organizations, meetings, places of worship, history, and more.
`http://www.quaker.org/`
INFO `nelson@quaker.org`

8767 **`soc.religion.quaker`** The Religious Society of Friends. *Newsgroup*

DIVINATION, ASTROLOGY & TAROT

8768 **`alt.astrology`** Twinkle, twinkle, little planet. *Newsgroup*

8769 **`alt.astrology.asian`** The stars as they appear over Asia. *Newsgroup*

8770 **`alt.prophecies.nostradamus`** Mystic verse. *Newsgroup*

8771 **`alt.tarot`** Your destiny is in the cards. *Newsgroup*

8772 **Astrology.Net:** Astrology readings direct to your personal computer. Gain new insights into your personal life, relationships, and career opportunities.
`http://astrology.net/`
INFO `chartmaster@astrology.net`

8773 **oracle-a:** On astrology. *Mailing List, moderated*
`http://idirect.com/oracle`
± `oracle-a-request@idirect.com`
INFO OWNER `nitefall@idirect.com` (Brandi Jasmine)

8774 **`tnn.astro`** Discussions about astrology. *Newsgroup*

ECUMENICAL

8775 **ARIL-L:** Members of the Association for Religion and Intellectual Life, publisher of Cross Currents. *Mailing List*
± `listserv@ucsbvm.ucsb.edu` [body = SUB ARIL-L first-name last-name]
EDITOR `aril-l-request@ucsbvm.ucsb.edu`

8776 **BRIDGE-L:** "The Bridge Across Consciousness" on the epistemology of religion and spiritual foundations for a pluralistic society—being used to develop an international database on ecumenical and universal religion. *Mailing List*
± `listserv@ucsbvm.ucsb.edu` [body = SUBSCRIBE BRIDGE-L first-name last-name]
INFO `origin@rain.org` (Bruce Schuman)
ARCHIVE `http://www.rain.org/~origin`

8777 **MINISTRY:** On ministry: community involvement, professional concerns, keeping faith. *Mailing List*
± `listserv@ls.csbsju.edu` [body = SUBSCRIBE MINISTRY (title) first-name last-name]
INFO `jmuggli@tiny.computing.csbsju.edu` (John Muggli)

OWNER kudut@ritz.mordor.com (Kenneth Udut)

8778 `soc.religion.unitarian-univ` Unitarian-Universalism and non-creedal religions. *Moderated newsgroup*

8779 `uk.religion.interfaith` Discussion of interfaith and ecumenical religious issues in the UK. *Newsgroup*

FEMINIST PERSPECTIVES

➤ `christnet.ladies`: Christian ladies. *Newsgroup*

8780 **COE:** Circles of Exchange: 10 years' mail exchange on women's spirituality goes cyber. *Mailing List*
± listserv@listserv.aol.com [body = SUBSCRIBE COE first-name last-name]
INFO OWNER klong@phoenix.net [body = SUBSCRIBE COE] (Kimberly Long)
Please Note: Subscription by approval only.
Comments: Participation restricted to women.

8781 **Feminist-Theology:** On Jewish and Christian feminist theology. *Mailing List*
± mailbase@mailbase.ac.uk [body = SUBSCRIBE FEMINIST-THEOLOGY first-name last-name]
OWNER natalie.knodel@durham.ac.uk
ARCHIVE mailbase@mailbase.ac.uk [body = INDEX FEMINIST-THEOLOGY]

8782 **FEMREL-L:** Women, religion, and feminist theology. *Mailing List*
± listserv@listserv.aol.com [body = SUBSCRIBE FEMREL-L first-name last-name]
INFO femrel-l-request@listserv.aol.com
ARCHIVE listserv@listserv.aol.com [body = INDEX FEMREL-L]

➤ **Wicca and Women's Spirituality:** Intelligent and concise discussion of modern Wicca, along with thoughtful links. (See entry 8857 for full listing.)

HINDUISM

8783 `alt.hindu` The Hindu religion. *Moderated newsgroup*

8784 **The Hindu Universe:** Comprehensive guide to Hinduism: scriptures, images, festivals, organizations, net resources.
http://rbhatnagar.csm.uc.edu:8080/hindu_universe.html
INFO editor@rbhatnagar.csm.uc.edu

8785 `soc.religion.hindu` Discussion about the Hindu dharma, philosophy, culture. *Moderated newsgroup*

8786 `soc.religion.vaishnava` All aspects of Vishnu and Vaishnavism. *Moderated newsgroup*

8787 `uk.religion.hindu` Hinduism in the United Kingdom. *Newsgroup*

ISLAM

8788 `alt.islam.sufism` Discussions of the mystical dimensions of Islam. *Newsgroup*

8789 `alt.religion.islam` Discussion of Islamic faith and `soc.religion.islam`. *Newsgroup*

8790 `alt.sufi` "Come, come, whoever you are, this caravan is not of despair . . .". *Newsgroup*

8791 `bit.listserv.muslims` Islamic information and news network. *Moderated newsgroup*

8792 **Isfahan Online:** Architectural guide and "walking tour" of the city of Isfahan, Iran.
http://www.anglia.ac.uk/~trochford/isfahan.html
INFO trochford@bridge.anglia.ac.uk

8793 **ISLAM-L:** On the history of Islam. *Mailing List*
± listserv@ulkyvm.louisville.edu [body = SUBSCRIBE ISLAM-L first-name last-name]
INFO OWNER jacock01@ulkyvm.louisville.edu (James A. Cocks)
ARCHIVE listserv@ulkyvm.louisville.edu [body = INDEX ISLAM-L]

8794 **MUSLIMS:** Academic and nonpolitical education on issues relating to Islam and Muslims, including news, conferences, Muslim student groups, discussion of books by and about Muslims. *Mailing List, moderated*

± `listserv@asuvm.inre.asu.edu` [body = SUBSCRIBE MUSLIMS first-name last-name]
INFO `mughal@alumni.caltech.edu` (Asim Mughal)
Gated: `bit.listserv.muslims`

➤ **NAHIA-L:** For North American historians of Islamic art. (See entry 70 for full listing.)

8795 **OICISNET:** Network project to support the developmental activities of Organization of Islamic Conference (OIC) member countries and their institutions. *Mailing List*
± `listserv@sairti00.bitnet` [body = SUBSCRIBE OICISNET first-name last-name]
INFO `amin@sairti00.bitnet` (Amin Abdullah Said)
Please Note: Subscription by approval only.

8796 `pdaxs.religion.moslem` Muslim religion and activities. *Newsgroup*

8797 `soc.religion.islam` Discussions of the Islamic faith. *Moderated newsgroup*

8798 `uk.religion.islam` Islam in the U.K. *Newsgroup*

8799 **USC Muslim Students Association Islamic Server:** This site contains a wealth of information on Islam. It covers the fundamentals of Islam, Islam and society (including economics, history, politics, human rights, and the role of women in Islam), what is *not* Islam, stories of new Muslims, Islam and other religions, and information on the Muslim community.
`http://www.usc.edu/dept/MSA/`
INFO `msa@usc.edu`

JUDAISM

8800 **A - Z of Jewish & Israel Related Resources:** Large collection of Internet resources related to Jewish and Israeli issues.
`http://www.ort.org/anjy/a-z/`
INFO `matthew@ort.org` (Matthew Album)

➤ `alt.music.jewish`: Music from the Jewish heritage. *Newsgroup*

➤ **ARIL-L:** Members of the Association for Religion and Intellectual Life, publisher of Cross Currents. (See entry 8775 for full listing.)

8801 **A-Z-ANNOUNCE:** For announcements of new Jewish and Israel Web resources. *Distribution List, moderated*
± `majordomo@ort.org` [body = SUBSCRIBE a-z-announce]
INFO `http://www.ort.org/anjy/resource/a-znew.htm`
OWNER `matthew@ort.org` (Matthew Album)

➤ **Bar-Ilan University CWIS:** Information about Bar-Ilan University—general information, faculties and departments, Jewish studies, libraries, and other services. (See entry 4410 for full listing.)

8802 **A Byte Of Torah (and) A MegaByte Of Torah:** A Byte Of Torah is a weekly newsletter on the Torah portion of the week. A MegaByte Of Torah is a monthly newsletter that explores various Jewish topics usually related to the current Jewish month. *Newsletter*
`ftp://israel.nysernet.org/~ftp/israel/judaica/tanach/commentaries/bytetorah`
`gopher://israel.nysernet.org/Jews and Judaism/Tanach and Commentaries/A Byte Of`
  `Torah`
± `listserv@israel.nysernet.org` [body = SUB BYTETORAH first-name last-name]
INFO `bytetorah@israel.nysernet.org` (Zev S. Itzkowitz)
ARCHIVES
`gopher://israel.nysernet.org/Jews and Judaism/Tanach and Commentaries/A Byte Of`
  `Torah`
`ftp://israel.nysernet.org/g/~ftp/israel/tanach/commentary/bytetorah/`
Frequency: weekly and monthly

➤ **CHR-EXP:** For a Christian explanation of the Scriptures to Jews. (See entry 8698 for full listing.)

8803 **CJ-L:** On the beliefs and practices of Conservative Judaism. *Mailing List*

± `listserv@cnsibm.albany.edu` [body = SUBSCRIBE CJ-L first-name last-name]

INFO `mark@csc.albany.edu` (Mark Steinberger)

ARCHIVE `http://shamash.org/lists/cj-l`

8804 `clari.news.jews` Jewish news. *Moderated newsgroup*

8805 **Divrei:** These are lists providing weekly commentaries and discussion on the Torah: shabbatshalom, Top, Enayim, Oxford and Bytetorah. *Distribution List*

± `listserv@israel.nysernet.org` [body = SUBSCRIBE *listname* first-name last-name]

OWNER `ness@aecom.yu.edu` (Seth Ness)

➤ **E-HUG:** On all things relating to use of Hebrew, Yiddish, Judesmo, and Aramaic on computers. (See entry 5289 for full listing.)

➤ **Eastern European Jewish History (EEJH):** Forum for discussion of historical, archaeological, linguistic, cultural, genealogical, and genetic evidence on the Jewish people of eastern Europe from Greco-Roman times to the present. (See entry 5245 for full listing.)

8806 **EMUNIM:** On the Jewish campus network in Michigan. Serves the Jewish students and college faculty primarily in the American Midwest. Open to all. *Mailing List*

INFO `loomer@pilot.msu.edu` (Marc Loomer)

ARCHIVE `listserv@msu.edu`

➤ **Feminist-Theology:** On Jewish and Christian feminist theology. (See entry 8781 for full listing.)

8807 `il.ioudaios` First-century Judaism discussion forum. *Newsgroup*

8808 `israel.lists.ioudaios-l` First-century Judaism discussion forum. *Newsgroup*

8809 **JewishGT:** For members of the Jewish community at Georgia Tech and other interested Jews. *Mailing List*

± `listproc@list.gatech.edu` [body = SUBSCRIBE JEWISHGT first-name last-name]

INFO `gt5549d@prism.gatech.edu` (Aviva Starkman)

Please Note: Subscription by approval only.

8810 **JMIL-Link:** On Jews in the military. *Mailing List*

± `listserv@jtsa.edu` [body = SUB JMIL-LINK first-name last-name]

OWNER `elson@v22c.npt.nuwc.navy.mil` (Lieutenant Commander Erving Elson)

ARCHIVE `listserv@jtsa.edu` [body = INDEX JMIL-LINK]

Please Note: Subscription by approval only.

Comments: Limited to Jewish personnel in the U.S. military.

➤ **JTS-CAGSALUM:** Alumni of Albert List College of Jewish Studies & Graduate School of the Jewish Theological Seminary of America. (See entry 4128 for full listing.)

8811 **The Khazaria Info Center:** These pages explore the history of the Khazar Jewish empire in southern Russia (650-1016). Many links to other important Jewish, historical, eastern European, and miscellaneous sites are also provided.

`http://acad.bryant.edu/~kbrook/khazaria.html`

INFO `kbrook@acad.bryant.edu` (Kevin Brook)

8812 **Liberal-Judaism:** On liberal Judaism (Reform, Reconstructionist, Secular Humanistic, etc.) and liberal Jewish issues, practices, opinions, and beliefs. *Digest, moderated*

`ftp://shamash.nysernet.org/israel/lists/mail.liberal-judaism`

8813 **MASORTI:** On the Masorti (Conservative) Movement in Israel. *Distribution List*

± `listserv@jtsa.edu` [body = SUBSCRIBE MASORTI first-name last-name]

8814 **MOCHIN:** Mind, Matter, and Mashiach: on world transformation and ultimate reality in the context of Jewish metaphysical thought. Based on the book *Project Mind* by T. Kun. *Mailing List, moderated*

`http://www.webscope.com/project_mind/project_mind.html`

± `listproc@shamash.nysernet.org` [body = SUBSCRIBE MOCHIN first-name last-name]

INFO EDITOR OWNER `marshlu@vms.huji.ac.il` (David S. Devor)

OWNER jshepher@loyalistc.on.ca (Jan Shepherd)

8815 `pdaxs.religion.jewish` Jewish religion and activities. *Newsgroup*

8816 **PJD-L:** For Jewish events and activities in Philadelphia, Pennsylvania. *Mailing List*
± listserv@vm.temple.edu [body = SUBSCRIBE PJD-L first-name last-name]
OWNER rajter@ccc.medcolpa.edu (Jean-Jacques Rajter)

8817 **Postmodern Jewish Philosophy Network:** Dedicated both to a philosophic review of the variety of postmodern Jewish discourses and to postmodern reflections on the variety of Jewish philosophies and Jewish philosophic theologies. *Newsletter*
http://www.drew.edu/~pmjp
± daseidenberg@jtsa.edu (David Seidenberg)
EDITOR pochs@drew.edu
ARCHIVE http://www.drew.edu/~pmjp
Frequency: quarterly

8818 `shamash.daf-hashavua` Weekly sedra United Synagogue London. *Moderated newsgroup*

8819 `shamash.jacs` Jews in recovery from alcoholism and drugs. *Moderated newsgroup*

8820 `shamash.mlj` Liberal Judaism mailing list. *Moderated newsgroup*

8821 `shamash.torch-d` About religious Jewish home schooling. *Moderated newsgroup*

8822 `soc.culture.jewish` Jewish culture and religion (cf. `talk.politics.mideast`). *Newsgroup*

➤ `soc.culture.jewish.holocaust`: The Shoah. *Moderated newsgroup*

8823 `soc.culture.jewish.parenting` Issues about raising Jewish children. *Moderated newsgroup*

8824 **tikkun-on-line:** For discussion on the contents of *Tikkun* magazine: "progressive politics of meaning." *Mailing List, moderated*
± listproc@shamash.nysernet.org [body = SUBSCRIBE TIKKUN-ON-LINE first-name last-name]
INFO mrand@dorsai.org (Michael Rand)
ARCHIVE listproc@shamash.nysernet.org [body = INDEX tikkun-on-line]
Gated:

➤ **Trek-cochavim:** On Star Trek from a Jewish perspective. (See entry 1384 for full listing.)

8825 `uk.religion.jewish` Judaism in the United Kingdom. *Newsgroup*

8826 **WOMENRAB:** A discussion group for women rabbis, cantors, women rabbinical and cantorial students. *Mailing List*
± listserv@jtsa.edu [body = SUBSCRIBE WOMENRAB first-name last-name]
EDITOR plutzera@ujafedny.org (Ann Plutzer)

LIBRARIES

➤ **ATLANTIS:** For members of the American Theological Library Association and others. Emphasis is on librarianship, not theological discussion. (See entry 5769 for full listing.)

MAGICK

➤ `alt.folklore.herbs`: Discussion of all aspects of herbs and their uses. *Newsgroup*

8827 `alt.magick` For discussion about supernatural arts. *Newsgroup*

8828 `alt.magick.chaos` Do not meddle in the affairs of wizards. *Newsgroup*

8829 `alt.magick.ethics` Discussion of the ethics/morals of magickal work. *Newsgroup*

8830 `alt.magick.folk` Discussion of folk magick traditions. *Newsgroup*

8831 `alt.magick.moderated` Serious discussion of magickal practices. *Moderated newsgroup*

8832 `alt.magick.sex` Pursuing spirituality through sexuality and vice versa. *Newsgroup*

8833 **alt.magick.tantra** Discussing tantric yoga and other esoteric practices. *Newsgroup*

➤ **alt.magick.tyagi:** Magick as revealed by Mordred Nagasiva. *Newsgroup*

➤ **alt.necronomicon:** Big time death wish. *Newsgroup*

➤ **ARCANA:** On occultism: history, literature, language, spells. (See entry 5236 for full listing.)

➤ **Coven Pride:** Semi-literary map of the Coptic, neo-Goth city of Coven Pride. It's all about love, labor, and traversing one's days over a landscape of pain. It lets in unsolicited submissions and keeps out only academes and homophobes. (See entry 1639 for full listing.)

➤ **Mariposa's Wings:** The take-off point for the gay-pagan Internet. (See entry 9966 for full listing.)

➤ **MOCHIN:** Mind, Matter, and Mashiach: on world transformation and ultimate reality in the context of Jewish metaphysical thought. Based on the book *Project Mind* by T. Kun. (See entry 8814 for full listing.)

8834 **relcom.arts.magick** Discussing magick and related subjects. *Newsgroup*

8835 **relcom.fido.su.magic** FIDOnet, magic and occult sciences. *Newsgroup*

NEW AGE

8836 **alt.divination** Divination techniques (e.g., I Ching, tarot, runes). *Newsgroup*

8837 **alt.dreams** What do they mean? *Newsgroup*

8838 **alt.dreams.castaneda** The dreaming techniques of Carlos Castaneda. *Newsgroup*

➤ **alt.dreams.lucid:** What do they *really* mean? *Newsgroup*

8839 **alt.religion.angels** Belief in angels. *Newsgroup*

8840 **CELESTINE-L:** On the book *The Celestine Prophecy* by James Redfield: synchronicity, baby! *Mailing List*
± INFO listserv@newciv.org [body = SUBSCRIBE CELESTINE-L]
OWNER idnic@tenet.edu (Cindi Leigh Creaton)
FAQ listserv@newciv.org [body = SUBSCRIBE CELESTINE-L]

8841 **KOF:** For Keepers of the Flame, an unaffiliated spiritual path involving an accelerated form of spoken prayers called dynamic decrees. *Mailing List*
± majordomo@usa.net [body = SUBSCRIBE kof first-name last-name]
± owner-kof@usa.net
OWNER karanjit@siyan.com (Karanjit Siyan)
Please Note: Subscription by approval only.

➤ **MOCHIN:** Mind, Matter, and Mashiach: on world transformation and ultimate reality in the context of Jewish metaphysical thought. Based on the book *Project Mind* by T. Kun. (See entry 8814 for full listing.)

8842 **The New Sun Newspaper:** Reflecting the positive aspects of life. Featuring award-winning writers, insightful and humorous articles, classic short stories, poems, and celebrity interviews. All around coverage of hope. *E-Journal*
http://shebute.com/NewSun/Today/
EDITOR newsun@pipeline.com (Ms. Lese Dunton, Editor & Publisher)

8843 **oracle-n:** On the New Age: all manner of spiritual and mystical topics are encouraged. *Mailing List, moderated*
http://idirect.com/oracle
± oracle-n-request@idirect.com
OWNER nitefall@idirect.com (Brandi Jasmine)

8844 **Partners:** Spiritual - Divine Partnership. *Mailing List*
± majordomo@god-mind.com [body = subscribe partners]
INFO info@god-mind.com (infobot)
OWNER teamup@smartnet.net (Jean K. Foster)

8845 **talk.religion.newage** Esoteric and minority religions and philosophies. *Newsgroup*

8846 **TECHSPIRIT-L:** On "technospirituality": the use and effect of new technology on spirituality. *Mailing List*

```
http://weber.u.washington.edu/~jpearce/techspirit.html
```
± listproc@u.washington.edu [body = SUBSCRIBE TECHSPIRIT-L first-name last-name]
INFO jpearce@u.washington.edu (John B. Pearce)

8847 The Weaver: Current developments in human consciousness and ancient spiritual wisdom. It covers mythology, astrology, deities, eastern traditions, psychology, psychotherapy, holistic health, and New Age. *Magazine*
```
http://hyperlink.com/weaver
```
INFO EDITOR weaver@hyperlink.com (Alex Campbell, Editor)
ARCHIVE http://hyperlink.com/weaver
Frequency: monthly

PAGAN & EARTH-CENTERED

8848 alt.pagan Discussions about paganism and religion. *Newsgroup*

8849 alt.pagan.magick Pagan magick and ritual discussion. *Newsgroup*

8850 alt.religion.all-worlds Grokking the Church of All Worlds from Heinlein's book. *Newsgroup*

8851 alt.religion.druid Druids and their ideas, practices, and beliefs. *Newsgroup*

8852 alt.religion.wicca Give me that real old-time religion. *Newsgroup*

➤ **Mariposa's Wings:** The take-off point for the gay-pagan Internet. (See entry 9966 for full listing.)

8853 The Neopagan Archives: Large and thorough archive. Part of the Lysator religious archive.
```
http://www.lysator.liu.se/religion/neopagan/index.html
```
INFO ceci@lysator.liu.se

8854 pagan: The Pagan Digest: on the religions, philosophy, etc. of paganism. *Digest*
± uther+pagan-request@drycas.club.cc.cmu.edu
OWNER uther@drycas.club.cc.cmu.edu (Stacey Greenstein)

8855 Rowan Fairgrove's Page: Well-rounded list of links from a modern pagan. Eclectic.
```
http://www.crc.ricoh.com/~rowanf/TRINE/trine.html
```
(Witches Trine)
```
http://www.crc.ricoh.com/~rowanf/IFP/presidio.html
```
(Interfaith Center at the Presidio)
```
http://www.crc.ricoh.com/~rowanf/CTS/cts.html
```
(Celebrating the Spirit: Toward a Global Ethic)
```
http://www.crc.ricoh.com/~rowanf/BAPA/bapa.html
```
(Bay Area Pagan Assemblies)
```
http://www.crc.ricoh.com/people/rowanf/rowanf.html
```
```
http://www.crc.ricoh.com/~rowanf/COG/cog.html
```
(NCLC Covenant of the Goddess)
INFO rowanf@conjure.com

➤ **SNUFFIT-L:** The Church of Euthanasia. (See entry 528 for full listing.)

8856 tx.religion.pagan Discussion about Paganism in Texas. *Newsgroup*

8857 Wicca and Women's Spirituality: Intelligent and concise discussion of modern Wicca, along with thoughtful links.
```
http://www.io.com/~cortese/spirituality/wicca.html
```
INFO cortese@netcom.com

PHILOSOPHY

8858 LISTENING-L: On the teachings of Jiddu Krishnamurti. *Mailing List*
± listserv@zrz.tu-berlin.de [body = SUBSCRIBE LISTENING-L first-name last-name]
OWNER lutzeb@cs.tu-berlin.de (Dirk Lutzebaeck)

➤ **Omega-Point-Theory:** On Omega Point Theory in Frank J. Tipler's book, *The Physics of Immortality*. (See entry 5338 for full listing.)

THEOLOGY & RELIGIOUS STUDIES

8859 Electric Mystics Guide: Directory of materials on Religious Studies, by Michael Strangelove.

`ftp://panda1.uottawa.ca/pub/religion/`

8860 `alt.christnet.theology` The distinctives of God of Christian theology. *Newsgroup*

8861 **Belief-L:** On personal beliefs: politics, ethics, morality, and interpersonal banter. *digest & reflector*
± `listserv@listserv.aol.com` [body = SUBSCRIBE BELIEF-L first-name last-name]
INFO `http://www.cais.com/atropos/elf-bile/belief-l.html`
OWNER `atropos@aol.net` (David B. O'Donnell)
ARCHIVE `listserv@listserv.aol.com` [body = INDEX Belief-L]
POST `belief-l@listserv.aol.com`
FAQ `http://www.cais.com/atropos/elf-bile/belief-l-faq.html`
Gated: `aol.lists.belief-l`

8862 `christnet.bible` Bible research and talk. *Newsgroup*

➤   `christnet.theology:` Christian theology. *Newsgroup*

8863 **Contra Mundum:** Quarterly review of culture, politics, and theology. *E-Journal*
`http://www.wavefront.com/~contra_m/cm/cm.html`
INFO OWNER `contramundum@wavefront.com` (T.E. Wilder)
ARCHIVE `http://www.wavefront.com/~contra_m/cm/cm.html`
Frequency: quarterly

➤   **ECCHST-L:** On ecclesiastical history: history of the church, Christianity, and theology. (See entry 5246 for full listing.)

➤   **International Kierkegaard Newsletter:** Annual scholarly paper containing information about the latest books, articles, etc. on Soeren Kierkegaard; also about Kierkegaard libraries, societies, conferences, etc. (See entry 5333 for full listing.)

➤   **JOHNLITR:** For scholarly, insightful discussion of the Gospel of John. (See entry 8724 for full listing.)

8864 **LARELS-L:** Religions in Los Angeles and southern California. *Mailing List*
± `listserv@ucsbvm.ucsb.edu` [body = SUB LARELS-L first-name last-name]
INFO EDITOR `larels-l-request@ucsbvm.ucsb.edu`
Please Note: Subscription by approval only.

8865 **REHU-L:** For religious humor—a spinoff of ECCHST-L (Ecclesiastical History). *Mailing List*
± `listserv@bgu.edu` [body = SUBSCRIBE REHU-L first-name last-name]
OWNER `ugsingle@uxa.ecn.bgu.edu` (Gregory H. Singleton)

8866 **RELIGCOM:** On religious communication and communication in religious contexts. *Mailing List*
± `listserv@ukcc.uky.edu` [body = SUBSCRIBE RELIGCOM first-name last-name]
INFO `religcom-request@ukcc.uky.edu`
ARCHIVE `listserv@ukcc.uky.edu` [body = INDEX RELIGCOM]

➤   **ReligionLaw:** On religion and the law; technical orientation. (See entry 5528 for full listing.)

8867 **SSREL-L:** For scholarly discussion of issues relevant to scientific study of religion. *Mailing List*
± `listserv@utkvm1.utk.edu` [body = SUBSCRIBE SSREL-L first-name last-name]
INFO `dploch@utk.edu` (Donald R. Ploch)
ARCHIVE `listserv@utkvm1.utk.edu`

8868 `talk.origins` Evolution versus creationism (sometimes hot!). *Newsgroup*

8869 `talk.religion.misc` Religious, ethical, and moral implications. *Newsgroup*

8870 `uk.religion.misc` Religion in the UK. *Newsgroup*

8871 **Union Seminary Quarterly Review:** A journal of theology and religion published by Union Theological Seminary/Columbia University in the city of New York. *E-Journal*
`http://www.cc.columbia.edu/~pm47/`

± **INFO OWNER** pm47@columbia.edu (Patrick Minges)
Frequency: biannual

VARIOUS

8872 `alt.consciousness.4th-way` The Fourth Way, Gurdjieff, Ouspensky. *Newsgroup*

8873 `alt.consciousness.mysticism` The quest for ultimate reality. *Newsgroup*

8874 `alt.meditation` General discussion of meditation. *Newsgroup*

8875 `alt.meditation.quanyin` The Quan Yin method of meditation. *Newsgroup*

8876 `alt.meditation.shabda` Spiritual freedom through inner sound and light. *Newsgroup*

8877 `alt.meditation.transcendental` Contemplation of states beyond the teeth. *Newsgroup*

8878 `alt.messianic` Messianic traditions. *Newsgroup*

➤ `alt.philosophy.taoism:` All aspects of Taoism. *Newsgroup*

8879 `alt.religion.course-miracle` A Course in Miracles (ACIM). *Newsgroup*

8880 `alt.religion.eckankar` Eckankar, the religion of the Light and Sound of God. *Newsgroup*

8881 `alt.religion.scientology` L. Ron Hubbard's Church of Scientology. *Newsgroup*

8882 `alt.religion.universal-life` Universal Life Church. *Newsgroup*

8883 `alt.religion.urantia-book` Discussions about the Urantia Book. *Newsgroup*

8884 `alt.religion.vaisnava` Discussion of the Vaisnava spiritual tradition. *Newsgroup*

8885 `alt.religion.zoroastrianism` Zoraster/Zarathustra's religion, Mazdaism. *Newsgroup*

8886 `alt.satanism` Not such a bad dude once you get to know him. *Newsgroup*

➤ `alt.yoga:` All forms and aspects of yoga. *Newsgroup*

8887 `bit.listserv.uus-l` Unitarian-Universalist list. *Newsgroup*

8888 `pdaxs.religion.misc` Who'd we leave out? *Newsgroup*

8889 `soc.religion.bahai` Discussion of the Baha'i faith. *Moderated newsgroup*

8890 `soc.religion.eastern` Discussions of Eastern religions. *Moderated newsgroup*

8891 `soc.religion.gnosis` Gnosis, marifat, jnana, and direct sacred experience. *Moderated newsgroup*

8892 `soc.religion.shamanism` Discussion of the full range of shamanic experience. *Moderated newsgroup*

8893 `soc.religion.sikhism` Sikh religion and Sikhs all over the world. *Moderated newsgroup*

8894 `uk.religion.other-faiths` Other faiths without a specific U.K. newsgroup. *Newsgroup*

SCIENCE & TECHNOLOGY

8895　**SunSITE Academic Archives:** Software, documents, files, and more in most academic disciplines.
　　　`ftp://sunsite.unc.edu/pub/academic/`
　　　INFO `ftpkeeper@sunsite.unc.edu`

8896　`clari.tw.science`　General science stories. *Moderated newsgroup*

8897　**NATOSCI:** For data from NATO Scientific Affairs Division on scientific, especially environmental, projects. *Distribution List, moderated*
　　　`http://www.nato.int/`
　　　± `listserv@cc1.kuleuven.ac.be` [body = SUBSCRIBE NATOSCI first-name last-name]
　　　INFO EDITOR `natodoc@hq.nato.int`
　　　OWNER `scheurweghs@hq.nato.int` (Chris Scheurweghs)
　　　ARCHIVE `gopher://gopher.nato.int:70/1`
　　　Language: English/French

8898　`relcom.relarn.science`　Scientific publications and discussions. *Moderated newsgroup*

8899　`sci.answers`　Repository for periodic Usenet articles. *Moderated newsgroup*

8900　`sci.misc`　Short-lived discussions on subjects in the sciences. *Newsgroup*

8901　**Science Articles Archive at Berkeley Lab:** Archive of more than 300 science articles covering a range of scientific disciplines. The information online is written so that it is understandable for those who want to know but don't speak the language.
　　　`http://www.lbl.gov/Science-Articles/Archive-dir.html`
　　　INFO `jbkahn@lbl.gov` (Jeff Kahn, LBL Public Information)

8902　**Thesis :** A science and technology magazine covering traditional fields like medical research and information technology, plus new developments in computer imaging, the Internet, and science in finance. *Magazine*
　　　`http://www.hyperlink.com/thesis/`
　　　INFO EDITOR OWNER `thesis@hyperlink.com` (Clive Davidson, Editor)
　　　Frequency: bimonthly

8903　**YSN:** The Young Scientists' Network: activism on employment issues for scientists just beginning their careers. *Mailing List*
　　　INFO `ysnadm@crow-t-robot.stanford.edu`
　　　ARCHIVE `http://snorri.chem.washington.edu/ysarchive`

AGRICULTURE

8904　**Not Just Cows:** Not Just Cows: a guide to Internet/Bitnet resources in agriculture and related sciences; includes libraries, gopher sites, BBSs, Web sites, WAIS databases, e-journals, and mail servers.
　　　`http://www.snymor.edu/~drewwe/njc/`
　　　`ftp://info.monash.edu.au/pub/library/guides/agriculture.txt`
　　　`gopher://info.monash.edu.au/00/Other/sources/agriculture.txt`
　　　INFO `drewwe@snymorva.cs.snymor.edu` (Wilfred Drew)
　　　MIRRORS
　　　`http://asa.ugl.lib.umich.edu/chdocs/agriculture.html`
　　　`http://www.bib.wau.nl/agralin/drew/guide.html` (Netherlands)
　　　`gopher://una.hh.lib.umich.edu/00/inetdirsstacks/agri:drew` (U.S.A.)
　　　`http://www.monash.edu.au/library/guides/agriculture.html`
　　　`http://www.lib.lsu.edu/sci/njc.html`
　　　`http://www.bubl.bath.ac.uk/BUBL/Cows.html` (United Kingdom)

8905　**AGENG-L:** On agricultural engineering and intelligent control. *Mailing List*

± `listserv@gwdg.de` [body = SUBSCRIBE AGENG-L first-name last-name]
INFO `jbeilag@gwdg.de` (Johannes grosse Beilage)

8906 AGINFO: Information on agriculture and its teaching, research, and extension.
`gopher://bluehen.ags.udel.edu`
INFO `betsy@bluehen.ags.udel.edu` (Betsy Mackenzie)

8907 Agricultural Genome Information Server : WWW, Gopher, FTP, and WAISmail access to genome databases.
`http://probe.nalusda.gov/`
`ftp://probe.nalusda.gov/pub`
`gopher://probe.nalusda.gov`
`waismail@probe.nalusda.gov` [body = help]
INFO `help@probe.nalusda.gov`
INFO `feedback@probe.nalusda.gov`

8908 `alt.agriculture.fruit` Fruit production. *Newsgroup*

8909 `alt.chinchilla` The nature of chinchilla farming in America today. *Newsgroup*

➤   **`alt.hemp`:** It's about knot-tying with rope. Knot! *Newsgroup*

8910 `alt.sustainable.agriculture` Such as the Mekong delta before Agent Orange. *Newsgroup*

8911 APIS: Apicultural Information and Issues, Florida Cooperative Extension Beekeeping Newsletter *Newsletter*
`http://gnv.ifas.ufl.edu/~entweb/apis/apis.htm`
± INFO `mts@gnv.ifas.ufl.edu` (Dr. Malcolm T. Sanford)
ARCHIVES
`http://gnv.ifas.ufl.edu/~entweb/apis/apis.htm`
`gopher://gnv.ifas.ufl.edu/11gopher_root3%3a%5bdatabase%5d`
Frequency: monthly

8912 The Bean Bag: Legume systematics. Featuring six columns: "From the Editors," "News," "Latin American Legume Report," "Nodulation and Nitrogen Fixation," "Gleanings," and "Recent Legume LIterature." *Newsletter*
`http://muse.bio.cornell.edu/`
`http://www.rbgkew.org.uk:80/herbarium/legumes`
`gopher://muse.bio.cornell.edu`
± INFO `jkirkbride@asrr.arsusda.gov` [body = name,address, telephone numbers, and e-mail address] (for some hard-copy back issues)
ARCHIVE `ftp://muse.bio.cornell.edu/pub/newsletters/beanbag/`
Language: English, Spanish, Portuguese
Frequency: May and November of each year

8913 BEEF-L: For beef specialists. *Mailing List*
± `listproc@listproc.wsu.edu` [body = SUBSCRIBE BEEF-L first-name last-name]
INFO `pace@coopext.cahe.wsu.edu` (Guy L. Pace)
OWNER `wright@wsu.edu` (Tony Wright)
OWNER `pace@coopext.cahe.wsu.edu` (Guy L. Pace)

8914 `bionet.agroforestry` Discussion of agroforestry. *Newsgroup*

➤   **`bit.org.peace-corps`:** Peace Corps. *Newsgroup*

➤   **BROM-L Bromeliad Taxonomists:** This list was created to share and discuss information and experiences of bromeliad taxonomists and growers. (See entry 9033 for full listing.)

➤   **CARLU:** On contemporary agriculture and rural land use. (See entry 4654 for full listing.)

8915 `clari.biz.industry.agriculture.releases` News releases: ag, fishing, forestry. *Moderated newsgroup*

➤   **EARTHSAVE:** On personal food choices and the ecology of the planet. (See entry 5836 for full listing.)

8916 GOATS: On goat management: nonthreatening—no question too basic. *Mailing List*
± listproc@listproc.wsu.edu [body = SUBSCRIBE GOATS first-name last-name]
INFO EDITOR OWNER garyf@coopext.cahe.wsu.ed

➤ **GrainGenes, A Plant Genome Database for Small Grains and Sugarcane:** This is the online version of the USDA Plant Genome Research Program's genome database for wheat, barley, oats, and related species. (See entry 9111 for full listing.)

➤ **H-RURAL:** On the history of agriculture and rural areas. (See entry 5249 for full listing.)

➤ **HORTPGM:** For the Virgina Tech horticulture department's programs in consumer horticulture. (See entry 5901 for full listing.)

➤ **Maize Genome Database:** Database of the corn genome. (See entry 9114 for full listing.)

8917 Minnesota Extension Service: The official electronic information service for the Minnesota Extension Service, St. Paul campus of the University of Minnesota.
http://www.mes.umn.edu:80/
INFO dmadison@mes.umn.edu

8918 North Carolina Cooperative Extension Gopher: This is the NC Cooperative Extension WWW server located at North Carolina State University, Raleigh, North Carolina.
http://www.ces.ncsu.edu/
INFO webmaster@www.ces.ncsu.edu

8919 sci.agriculture Farming, agriculture, and related topics. *Newsgroup*

8920 sci.agriculture.beekeeping Beekeeping, bee culture, and hive products. *Newsgroup*

8921 Trickle-L: On trickle or drip irrigation. *Mailing List*
± listserv@unl.edu [body = SUBSCRIBE TRICKLE-L first-name last-name]
OWNER rmead@asrr.arsusda.gov (Richard Mead)
ARCHIVE http://asset.arsusda.gov/wmrl/wmrl.html
Comments: International group of scientists, engineers and home gardeners

➤ **UNU.ZERI.IBS:** On integrated biosystems. (See entry 4665 for full listing.)

8922 USDA Cooperative State Research, Education, and Extension Service: This site is set up to provide access to information from the USDA Extension Service, other USDA agencies, and other federal agencies as it relates to the Cooperative Extension System.
http://www.reeusda.gov/
gopher://esusda.gov
INFO gopher-admin@esusda.gov
INFO webmaster@reeusda.gov
Comments: EA: in long-desc field I deleted the "1890" between "17" and "historically"; it made no sense.

ASTRONOMY

8923 adass.archiving Astronomical data archiving systems and software. *Newsgroup*

8924 adass.fits.oirfits Data formats and keywords for optical/infrared data. *Newsgroup*

8925 alt.binaries.pictures.astro Very black pictures. *Newsgroup*

8926 alt.sci.planetary Studies in planetary science. *Newsgroup*

8927 alt.telescopes.meade.lx200 Discussion of Meade's LX200 telescope. *Newsgroup*

➤ **Astronomy and Earth Sciences Archive at Stanford:** Astronomy/earth science-oriented material for Unix users. Includes Earth topography data, the CIA World Map II vector outline database in a compressed binary Unix/C-readable format, software and data of interest for amateur astronomers, and information of general usefulness or interest for earth scientists. Also contains some generic utilities for Unix machines, including C source for a Morse code practice program for Unix machines. (See entry 9310 for full listing.)

8928   **Be Star Newsletter:** On early-type stars and especially hot, near-main-sequence stars. The goal is to foster communication among researchers interested in the field of stellar astronomy. *Newsletter*
http://chara.gsu.edu/BeNews/intro.html
± EDITOR gies@chara.gsu.edu (Technical Editor)
INFO peters@hyades.dnet.nasa.gov (Geraldine J. Peters, Editor-in-Chief)
Frequency: twice yearly

8929   **EUVE Observatory Newsletter:** On NASA's Extreme Ultraviolet Explorer satellite (EUVE). *Newsletter*
http://www.cea.berkeley.edu/
± majordomo@cea.berkeley.edu [body = subscribe euvenews]
INFO EDITOR bretts@cea.berkeley.edu (Brett A. Stroozas)
INFO ceanews@cea.berkeley.edu
OWNER http://www.cea.berkeley.edu/
ARCHIVE http://www.cea.berkeley.edu/
POST euvenews@cea.berkeley.edu
Frequency: monthly (with additional news "flashes" as events warrant)

8930   `fj.sci.astro` Discussion about stars, planets, and comets. *Newsgroup*

8931   `han.sci.astro` Stars and planets, astronomy and space. *Newsgroup*

➤   **Physics and Astronomy Department, University of Oklahoma:** This site provides information on the Department of Physics and Astronomy at the University of Oklahoma. (See entry 9475 for full listing.)

8932   `relcom.fido.su.astronomy` FIDOnet, problems of astronomy, without astrology. *Newsgroup*

8933   `sci.astro` Astronomy discussions and information. *Newsgroup*

8934   `sci.astro.amateur` Amateur astronomy equipment, techniques, information, etc. *Newsgroup*

8935   `sci.astro.fits` Issues related to the Flexible Image Transport System. *Newsgroup*

8936   `sci.astro.hubble` Processing Hubble Space Telescope data. *Moderated newsgroup*

8937   `sci.astro.planetarium` Discussion of planetariums. *Newsgroup*

8938   `sci.astro.research` Forum in astronomy/astrophysics research. *Moderated newsgroup*

8939   **SKY Online:** SKY Online is the premier source of astronomical news and information on the World Wide Web. It features excerpts from *Sky & Telescope* and *CCD Astronomy* magazines, along with a weekly news bulletin and celestial calendar, helpful tips for backyard skygazers, reviews of telescopes and accessories, downloadable BASIC programs to do astronomical calculations on your PC or Mac, and much more.
http://www.skypub.com/
INFO webmaster@skypub.com

8940   `uk.org.starlink.hardware` Hardware for data acquisition/reduction. *Newsgroup*

8941   `uk.org.starlink.misc` Open forum (discussion related to astronomy). *Newsgroup*

8942   `uk.org.starlink.research` Discussion on aspects of astronomical research. *Newsgroup*

8943   `uk.org.starlink.software` Software for data acquisition/reduction. *Newsgroup*

AVIATION & AERONAUTICS

8944   **Aerospace Engineering: A Guide to Internet Resources:** List of Internet resources that contain information pertaining to aerospace engineering in general.
ftp://una.hh.lib.umich.edu/inetdirsstacks/aerospace:potsiedalq
gopher://una.hh.lib.umich.edu/1/inetdirs/Clearinghouse of Subject-Oriented Internet Resource Guides (UMich)/Aerospace Engineering
INFO dalquist@nmc.edu (Dave Dalquist)
INFO dalquist@login1.sils.umich.edu (Dave Dalquist)
INFO potluck@cris.com

INFO potsie@umich.edu (Christopher A. Poterala)

➤ **AIRCRAFT:** On fixed-wing and rotary-wing aircraft, modern, classic, and antique, including listings of air shows and similar events. (See entry 6259 for full listing.)

➤ **FlightMed:** For air medical professionals: flight nurses & paramedics, pilots, physicians. (See entry 5077 for full listing.)

➤ **The NASA Home Page:** Information about the National Aeronautics and Space Administration. Includes NASA news, and information on space sciene, aeronautics, the Mission to Planet Earth, human space flight, all of NASA's centers, space technology, and a gallery of photos, sounds and movies. (See entry 9591 for full listing.)

8945 `sci.aeronautics` The science of aeronautics and related technology. *Moderated newsgroup*

8946 `sci.aeronautics.airliners` Airliner technology. *Moderated newsgroup*

8947 `sci.aeronautics.simulation` Aerospace simulation technology. *Moderated newsgroup*

8948 **Shuttle Elements:** On getting Keplerian Elements out as quickly as possible during Space Shuttle flights. *Mailing List, moderated*

± shuttle-elts-request@ucsd.edu

INFO http://www.cts.com/browse/garym/elements

ARCHIVE ftp://ftp.cts.com/pub/garym/elements/last-shuttle-elset

BIOLOGY

8949 **The Life Page:** Large collection of biological, ecological, geographical, cultural heritage, and complex-systems information and services.

http://life.csu.edu.au/

INFO www-manager@life.csu.edu.au

INFO dgreen@csu.edu.au

➤ **MedWeb: Biomedical Internet Resources:** Begun in April 1994, MedWeb has evolved into a catalog of over 7,000 sites, databases, documents, and electronic journals divided into 80 categories. (See entry 4690 for full listing.)

8950 **APStracts:** Online publication of abstracts of current research manuscripts accepted for publication in the journals of The American Physiological Society. *Newsletter*

http://www.uth.tmc.edu/apstracts

gopher://gopher.uth.tmc.edu:3300

INFO aps_server@oac.hsc.uth.tmc.edu (Jacqueline McKee, Marketing Manager)

INFO mckee@aps.faseb.org (Jacqueline McKee)

ARCHIVE gopher://gopher.uth.tmc.edu:3300/11/publications/apstracts (Abstracts)

Frequency: weekly

8951 `aus.education.bio-newtech` New technologies in biology teaching. *Newsgroup*

8952 **Base de Dados Tropical:** Databases and other resources on tropical and Brazilian biological information.

http://www.bdt.org.br:70/

ftp://ftp.bdt.org.br

INFO manager@bdt.org.br

8953 **Bioinformatics at the Weizmann Institute of Science:** Data and software related to bioinformatics and molecular biology.

http://bioinformatics.weizmann.ac.il/

ftp://bioinformatics.weizmann.ac.il/pub/

gopher://bioinformatics.weizmann.ac.il

INFO lsprilus@weizmann.weizmann.ac.il (Jaime Prilusky) (Jaime Prilusky)

8954 **Bioline Publications:** Bioline Publications is an electronic publishing service for bioscientists. In collaboration with scientific publishers, newsletter editors, and authors of reports, it makes scientific material available more easily and more cheaply.

http://www.bdt.org.br:70/bioline/

INFO bio@biostrat.demon.co.uk (Bioline Publications)

Comments: The service is provided by Bioline Publications in association with http://www.bdt.org.br/, Base de Dados Tropical (BDT), Brazil.

8955 **Biomch-L:** On biomechanics and human/animal movement science. *Mailing List*
http://dragon.acadiau.ca/~pbaudin/biomch.html
± listserv@nic.surfnet.nl [body = SUBSCRIBE BIOMCH-L first-name last-name]
INFO bogert@acs.ucalgary.ca (Ton van den Bogert)
ARCHIVES
listserv@nic.surfnet.nl [body = INFO DATABASE]
gopher://hearn.nic.surfnet.nl/11/1.%20LISTSERVs%20public%20archives%20on%20HEARN.nic
.SURFnet.NL/BIOMCH-L

8956 **bionet.announce** Announcements of widespread interest to biologists. *Moderated newsgroup*

8957 **bionet.audiology** Topics in audiology and hearing science. *Newsgroup*

8958 **bionet.biology.cardiovascular** Scientists engaged in cardiovascular research. *Newsgroup*

8959 **bionet.biology.computational** Computer and mathematical applications. *Moderated newsgroup*

8960 **bionet.biology.symbiosis** Research in symbiosis. *Newsgroup*

8961 **bionet.biology.tropical** Discussions about tropical biology. *Newsgroup*

8962 **bionet.biophysics** The science and profession of biophysics. *Newsgroup*

8963 **bionet.celegans** The model organism Caenorhabditis elegans. *Newsgroup*

8964 **bionet.cellbiol** Discussions about cell biology. *Newsgroup*

8965 **bionet.cellbiol.cytonet** The cytoskeleton, plasma membrane and cell wall. *Newsgroup*

8966 **bionet.cellbiol.insulin** Biology and chemistry of insulin and related receptors. *Moderated newsgroup*

8967 **bionet.diagnostics** Problems and techniques in all fields of diagnostics. *Newsgroup*

➤　**bionet.ecology.physiology:** Research & education in physiological ecology. *Moderated newsgroup*

➤　**bionet.emf-bio:** Interactions of EM fields with biological systems. *Newsgroup*

8968 **bionet.general** General bioscience discussion. *Newsgroup*

8969 **bionet.glycosci** Carbohydrate and glycoconjugate molecules. *Newsgroup*

8970 **bionet.immunology** Discussions about research in immunology. *Newsgroup*

8971 **bionet.info-theory** Discussions about biological information theory. *Newsgroup*

8972 **bionet.jobs.offered** Job openings in the biological sciences. *Moderated newsgroup*

8973 **bionet.jobs.wanted** Requests for employment in the biological sciences. *Newsgroup*

8974 **bionet.journals.contents** Contents of biology journal publications. *Moderated newsgroup*

8975 **bionet.journals.letters.biotechniques** Discussion of the journal Biotechniques. *Newsgroup*

8976 **bionet.journals.letters.tibs** Letters to editor of *Trends in Biochemical Science*. *Moderated newsgroup*

8977 **bionet.journals.note** Advice on dealing with journals in biology. *Newsgroup*

8978 **bionet.microbiology** The science and profession of microbiology. *Newsgroup*

8979 **bionet.neuroscience** Research issues in the neurosciences. *Newsgroup*

8980 **bionet.organisms.pseudomonas** Research on the genus Pseudomonas. *Newsgroup*

8981 **bionet.organisms.schistosoma** Discussions about Schistosoma research. *Newsgroup*

8982 **bionet.parasitology** Research discussions in parasitology. *Newsgroup*

8983 **bionet.population-bio** Technical discussions about population biology. *Newsgroup*

8984 **bionet.prof-society.ascb** The American Society for Cell Biology. *Moderated newsgroup*

8985 **bionet.prof-society.biophysics** Biophysical Society official announcements. *Moderated newsgroup*

8986 **bionet.prof-society.cfbs** Canadian Federation of Biological Societies. *Newsgroup*

8987 **bionet.prof-society.csm** Canadian Society of Microbiologists. *Moderated newsgroup*

8988 **bionet.prof-society.faseb** Fed of American Societies for Experimental Biology. *Newsgroup*

8989 **bionet.prof-society.navbo** North American Vascular Biology Organization. *Newsgroup*

8990 **bionet.protista** Discussion on ciliates and other protists. *Newsgroup*

8991 **bionet.sci-resources** Information about funding agencies, etc. *Moderated newsgroup*

8992 **bionet.software** Information about software for biology. *Newsgroup*

8993 **bionet.software.sources** Software source relating to biology. *Moderated newsgroup*

8994 **bionet.software.www** Information about WWW sources of interest to biologists. *Moderated newsgroup*

8995 **bionet.toxicology** Research in toxicology. *Newsgroup*

8996 **bionet.users.addresses** Who's who in biology. *Newsgroup*

8997 **bionet.virology** Discussions about research in virology. *Newsgroup*

8998 **bionet.women-in-bio** Discussions about women in biology. *Newsgroup*

8999 **BIOPI-L:** For secondary and post-secondary biology teachers. *Mailing List*
± `listserv@ksuvm.ksu.edu` [body = SUBSCRIBE BIOPI-L first-name last-name]
INFO `tmanney@ksuvm.bitnet`
ARCHIVE `listserv@ksuvm.ksu.edu` [body = INDEX BIOPI-L]
Please Note: Subscription by approval only.
Comments: Open to biology teachers only.

9000 **biosym:** For users of Biosym Technologies software. *Mailing List*
± **INFO** `dibug-request@comp.bioz.unibas.ch` (Reinhard Doelz)
ARCHIVES
`ftp://bioftp.unibas.ch`
`gopher://biox.unibas.ch`

9001 **bit.sci.purposive-behavior** Control system group network. *Newsgroup*

➤   **CAOS/CAMM Center:** Netherlands national facility for computer-aided chemistry and bioinformatics. (See entry 9131 for full listing.)

9002 **CBR-L:** On Craniofacial Biology Research: the growth and development of the human head. *Mailing List*
± `majordomo@po.cwru.edu` [body = SUBSCRIBE cbr-l]
OWNER `dean@lucifer.cwru.edu` (David Dean)

➤   **CONSBIO:** Society for Conservation Biology list on conservation biology and biodiversity. (See entry 4590 for full listing.)

➤   **CONSGIS:** On biological conservation and geographical information systems. (See entry 9317 for full listing.)

9003 **CRUST-L:** On all aspects of the biology of the crustacea, including systematics, physiology, ecology, etc. *Mailing List*
`http://www.vims.edu/~jeff/crust-l.html`
± `majordomo@vims.edu` [body = subscribe crust-l e-mail-address]
INFO `jeff@vims.edu` (Dr. Jeffrey Shields)
ARCHIVE `http://www.nmnh.si.edu/crustsoc`

9004 **cryonics:** On cryonics: way low temperature biology. *Mailing List*
± **INFO** `kqb@whscad1.att.com` (Kevin Q. Brown)
± `majordomo@cryonet.org`
OWNER `kqb@cryonet.org` (Kevin Q. Brown)
Gated: `sci.cryonics`

9005 **FISICOMP-L:** On comparative physiology. *Mailing List*
gopher://cpd.furg.br
± listserv@if.usp.br [body = SUBSCRIBE FISICOMP-L]
OWNER dcfeucly@cpd.furg.br (Euclydes A. Santos Filho)

➤ **Fitzroy:** A listing of undergraduate research experiences, which can serve as starting points or sources of advice for other undergrads looking for summer research opportunities. (See entry 4302 for full listing.)

9006 **fj.sci.bio** Discussion on biology. *Newsgroup*

9007 **Frontiers in Bioscience: A Journal and Virtual Library:** A forum for scientific communication in any discipline in biology and medicine including biochemistry, microbiology, parasitology, virology, immunology, biotechnology, and bioinformatics.
http://bioscience.com/
INFO tabibzadeh@moffitt.usf.edu
MIRROR http://bioinformatics.weizmann.ac.il/bioscience

9008 **IUBIO Archive for Biology:** This site is an archive of biology data and software. The archive includes items to browse, search, and fetch molecular data, software, and biology news and documents, as well as links to remote information sources in biology and elsewhere.
http://iubio.bio.indiana.edu/
http://flybase.bio.indiana.edu:82/
ftp://iubio.bio.indiana.edu
gopher://flybase.bio.indiana.edu:72
gopher://iubio.bio.indiana.edu
INFO archive@bio.indiana.edu
FAQ ftp://iubio.bio.indiana.edu/Readme
MIRRORS
ftp://bioinformatics.weizmann.ac.il/pub/software/ (partial FTP mirror)
ftp://ftp.funet.fi/pub/sci/molbio/iubiomolbio/ (partial FTP mirror)
gopher://www.embl-ebi.ac.uk:7071 (Flybase Gopher mirror)
http://www.embl-ebi.ac.uk:7081/ (Flybase WWW mirror)
ftp://ftp.ddbj.nig.ac.jp/pub/mirror/IUBIO/ (partial FTP mirror)
ftp://ftp.gdbnet.ad.jp/ftpsync/ftp.bio.indiana.edu/

➤ **LEISH-L Leishmaniasis Network:** The intention of this list is to encourage discussion and contact among those interested in leishmaniasis and to help identify important topic areas within the field. (See entry 4808 for full listing.)

9009 **MARINE_PATHOL:** MARINE_PATHOL is a mailing list for scientists and laypeople interested in all aspects of the pathology of marine organisms. *Mailing List*
± majordomo@vims.edu [body = subscribe marine_pathol e-mail-address]
± http://www.vims.edu/~jeff/pathol.html
INFO OWNER jeff@vims.edu (Dr. Jeffrey Shields)
ARCHIVE http://www.vims.edu/~jeff/pathol.html

9010 **Microbial Strain Data Network (MSDN):** MSDN provides communication and information services to scientists worldwide, principally within the microbiology and biotechnology communities.
http://www.bdt.org.br:70/msdn/
INFO msdn@sheffield.ac.uk

9011 **MORPHMET:** On biological morphometrics, the study of size and shape of organisms. *Mailing List*
± listserv@cunyvm.cuny.edu [body = SUBSCRIBE MORPHMET first-name last-name]
INFO marcus@amnh.org (Leslie Marcus)
INFO lamqc@cunyvm.cuny.edu (Leslie Marcus)

9012 **MOTORDEV:** About human motor skill development. *Mailing List*
± listserv@umdd.umd.edu [body = SUBSCRIBE MOTORDEV first-name last-name]

INFO `motordev-request@umdd.umd.edu`

ARCHIVE `listserv@umdd.umd.edu` [body = INDEX MOTORDEV]

➤ **Neuron:** On all aspects of neural networks. Topics include both artificial neural networks and biological systems. (See entry 2156 for full listing.)

➤ **The Salk Institute for Biological Studies:** A private, nonprofit research organization in La Jolla, California. Scientists there do fundamental research in biology and its relation to health, studying such problems as the organization and operation of the brain, the control of gene activity, and the molecular origins of disease. (See entry 4900 for full listing.)

9013 `sci.bio` Biology and related sciences. *Newsgroup*

9014 `sci.bio.evolution` Discussions of evolutionary biology. *Moderated newsgroup*

9015 `sci.bio.food-science` Topics related to food science and technology. *Newsgroup*

9016 `sci.bio.microbiology` Protists, fungi, algae, other microscopic organisms. *Newsgroup*

9017 `sci.bio.misc` Biology and related sciences. *Newsgroup*

9018 `sci.bio.systematics` Systematics, taxonomy, and the tree of life. *Newsgroup*

9019 `sci.cryonics` Theory and practice of biostasis, suspended animation. *Newsgroup*

9020 `sci.life-extension` Slowing, stopping, or reversing the aging process. *Newsgroup*

9021 **Society for Mathematical Biology Digest:** From the Society for Mathematical Biology. Containing items of current interest submitted by readers, including scientific queries, announcements of publications, meetings and job opportunities, news items, etc. *Newsletter*

`gopher://gopher.nih.gov/11/res/SMBdigest`

`http://www.iam.ubc.ca/spider/spiros/smb/index.html`

± `listserv@fconvx.ncifcrf.gov` [body = subscribe smbnet first-name last-name]

INFO `ray@helix.nih.gov` (Raymond Mejia)

ARCHIVE `ftp://fconvx.ncifcrf.gov/smb/digest`

Frequency: monthly or more often as deemed necessary

9022 **SOCIOBIO:** On the evolution of social behavior. *Mailing List*

± `listserv@sjuvm.stjohns.edu` [body = SUBSCRIBE SOCIOBIO first-name last-name]

OWNER `garelli@attach.edu.ar` (Juan C. Garelli)

9023 `tnn.bio` Discussions about biology. *Newsgroup*

➤ **UNU.ZERI.IBS:** On integrated biosystems. (See entry 4665 for full listing.)

9024 **Virology on the Net:** A comprehensive collection of virology resources available on the Internet. Includes notations as to the intended audience of the resources (scientific, educational, etc.) and a rating of exceptional resources.

`http://www.mmb.lu.se/virology.html`

INFO `jonas.blomberg@alinks.se`

BIOLOGY—BOTANY

➤ **The Bean Bag:** Legume systematics. Featuring six columns: "From the Editors," "News," "Latin American Legume Report," "Nodulation and Nitrogen Fixation," "Gleanings," and "Recent Legume LIterature." (See entry 8912 for full listing.)

9025 **BEN: Botanical Electronic News:** BEN deals with botany and plant ecology of British Columbia and the Pacific Northwest. *E-Journal*

± INFO `aceska@freenet.victoria.bc.ca` (Dr. Adolf Ceska)

ARCHIVE `gopher://freenet.victoria.bc.ca/11/environment/Botany/ben`

Gated: `bionet.plants`

Frequency: irregular, biweekly

9026 `bionet.biology.grasses` The biology of grasses: cereal, forage, turf, etc. *Newsgroup*

9027 `bionet.biology.n2-fixation` Research issues on biological nitrogen fixation. *Newsgroup*

9028 `bionet.chlamydomonas` Discussions about the green alga Chlamydomonas. *Newsgroup*

9029 `bionet.mycology` Discussions about filamentous fungi. *Newsgroup*

9030 `bionet.photosynthesis` Discussions about research on photosynthesis. *Newsgroup*

9031 `bionet.plants` Discussion about all aspects of plant biology. *Newsgroup*

9032 `bionet.plants.education` Education issues in plant biology. *Newsgroup*

9033 **BROM-L Bromeliad Taxonomists:** This list was created to share and discuss information and experiences of bromeliad taxonomists and growers. *Mailing List*
± `listserv@bdt.org.br` [body = `subscribe BROM-L` first-name last-name]
INFO EDITOR OWNER `cavdberg@carpa.ciagri.usp.br` (Cassio van den Berg)
ARCHIVE `http://www.bdt.org.br:70/structure/brom-l.html`

9034 **CELLWALL:** On plant and fungal cell wall research. *Mailing List*
± `listserv@vm1.nodak.edu` [body = `SUBSCRIBE CELLWALL` first-name last-name]
OWNER `alwhite@plains.nodak.edu` (Alan White)

9035 **CYAN-TOX:** For exchange of information about cyanobacterial toxins, toxic cyanobacteria (blue-green algae), and related topics. *Mailing List*
± `listserv@odysseus.bio.auth.gr` [body = `SUBSCRIBE CYAN-TOX` first-name last-name]
INFO `lanaras@odysseus.bio.auth.gr` (Tom Lanaras)
POST `cyan-tox@odysseus.bio.auth.gr`

➤ **Dendrome:** Forest tree genome research updates. (See entry 4606 for full listing.)

9036 **The Diatom Home Page:** A central resource for scientists and amateurs interested in the diatom algae (Bacillariophyceae).
`http://www.indiana.edu/~diatom/diatom.html`
INFO `sweets@ucs.indiana.edu` (P. Roger Sweets)

9037 **DIATOM-L:** Devoted to research on the diatom algae. *Mailing List*
`http://www.indiana.edu/~diatom/diatom.html`
± `listserv@iubvm.ucs.indiana.edu` [body = `SUBSCRIBE DIATOM-L` first-name last-name]
INFO `sweets@ucs.indiana.edu` (P. Roger Sweets)

9038 **Orchid Weblopedia:** The Orchid Weblopedia is a wonderful resource for both professional and nonprofessional orchid enthusiasts. It includes a great bulletin board to create a dialogue with respected individuals in the field of orchids.
`http://conbio.bio.uci.edu/orchid/`
INFO `jferran@uci.edu`

9039 `sci.bio.botany` The scientific study of plants. *Newsgroup*

9040 `sci.bio.phytopathology` All aspects of plant diseases and pests. *Moderated newsgroup*

➤ **SEAGRASS_FORUM:** On seagrass biology and the ecology of seagrass ecosystems. (See entry 9046 for full listing.)

BIOLOGY—ECOLOGY

➤ **BEN: Botanical Electronic News:** BEN deals with botany and plant ecology of British Columbia and the Pacific Northwest. (See entry 9025 for full listing.)

9041 `bionet.ecology.physiology` Research & education in physiological ecology. *Moderated newsgroup*

➤ **Communications for a Sustainable Future:** An interdisciplinary effort to facilitate more rapid change in social thought toward a viable future. This resource provides a collection of archives and mailing lists on sustainability. (See entry 5191 for full listing.)

➤ **CONSBIO:** Society for Conservation Biology list on conservation biology and biodiversity. (See entry 4590 for full listing.)

➤ **CONSGIS:** On biological conservation and geographical information systems. (See entry 9317 for full listing.)

9042 **ECOVIS-L:** On trends in ecology of vision—for scientists working within biology, ecology, and visual science. *Mailing List*

± listserv@yalevm.ycc.yale.edu [body = SUBSCRIBE ECOVIS-L first-name last-name]

INFO palacios-adrian@yale.edu (Adrian Palacios)

ARCHIVE http://pantheon.cis.yale.edu/~palacios/ecovis.html

Please Note: Subscription by approval only.

➤ **INDKNOW:** For indigenous knowledge systems, traditional ecological knowledge and development. (See entry 10071 for full listing.)

➤ **Journal of Political Ecology:** Promoting interdisciplinary dialogue and research on the interface between political economy and ecology. (See entry 5279 for full listing.)

➤ **La Revue Intemporelle - The timeless magazine:** Publishing since 1988, once a year, a free magazine treating fundamental themes such as human dignity, the planet Earth, consciousness, love and the creation of a planetary federation. (See entry 10139 for full listing.)

➤ **MEH2O-L:** On water in the Middle East, including limnology, oceanography, marine biotechnology, aquaculture, conservation, reclamation, ecology, geographic information systems, international shared-resource management, and policy issues. (See entry 4616 for full listing.)

9043 `relcom.ecology` Ecological discussions. *Newsgroup*

9044 `sci.bio.ecology` Ecological research. *Newsgroup*

9045 `sci.environment` Discussions about the environment and ecology. *Newsgroup*

9046 **SEAGRASS_FORUM:** On seagrass biology and the ecology of seagrass ecosystems. *Mailing List*

± majordomo@essun1.murdoch.edu.au [body = subscribe seagrass_forum]

OWNER keulen@murdoch.edu.au (Mike van Keulen)

ARCHIVE majordomo@essun1.murdoch.edu.au [body = index seagrass_forum]

9047 **Virginia Coast Reserve Information System (VCRIS):** This site includes weather and ecological data for Virginia coast sites. The site is operated by the Virginia Coast Reserve Long-Term Ecological Research Project (VCR/LTER).

http://atlantic.evsc.virginia.edu/

INFO jporter@lternet.edu

BIOLOGY—ENTOMOLOGY

➤ **APIS:** Apicultural Information and Issues, Florida Cooperative Extension Beekeeping Newsletter (See entry 8911 for full listing.)

9048 **BEE-L:** On the biology of bees, including sociobiology, behavior, ecology, adaptation/evolution, genetics, taxonomy, physiology, pollination, and flower nectar and pollen production of bees. *Mailing List*

± listserv@cnsibm.albany.edu [body = SUBSCRIBE BEE-L first-name last-name]

INFO erik@acspr1.acs.brockport.edu (Erik Seielstad)

9049 **LEPS-L:** On Lepidoptera (moths and butterflies). *Mailing List*

± listserv@yalevm.ycc.yale.edu [body = SUBSCRIBE LEPS-L first-name last-name]

INFO lawrence.gall@yale.edu (Larry Gall)

ARCHIVES

gopher://gopher.peabody.yale.edu (under Entomology)

listserv@yalevm.ycc.yale.edu [body = INDEX LEPS-L]

Gated: sci.bio.entomology.lepidoptera

9050 `sci.bio.entomology.lepidoptera` Lepidoptera: butterflies and moths. *Newsgroup*

9051 `sci.bio.entomology.misc` General insect study and related issues. *Newsgroup*

9052 **SOCINSCT:** For university-level discussion of the biology of social insects (bees, wasps, ants, and termites). *Mailing List*

± listserv@cnsibm.albany.edu [body = SUBSCRIBE SOCINSCT first-name last-name]
INFO erik@acspr1.acs.brockport.edu (Erik Seielstad)
INFO bec@albany.edu (Ben Chi)

9053 UD Insect Database: Database of photos and descriptions of many insects.
http://bluehen.ags.udel.edu/insects/descriptions/entohome.html
INFO betsy@bluehen.ags.udel.edu (Betsy Mackenzie) (Betsy Mackenzie)

BIOLOGY—MOLECULAR

9054 aus.mbio Molecular biology, molecular. *Newsgroup*

9055 bionet.metabolic-reg Kinetics and thermodynamics at the cellular level. *Newsgroup*

9056 bionet.molbio.ageing Discussions of cellular and organismal aging. *Newsgroup*

9057 bionet.molbio.bio-matrix Computer applications to biological databases. *Newsgroup*

➤ **bionet.molbio.hiv:** Discussions about the molecular biology of HIV. *Newsgroup*

9058 bionet.molbio.methds-reagnts Requests for information and lab reagents. *Newsgroup*

9059 bionet.molbio.proteins Research on proteins and protein databases. *Newsgroup*

9060 bionet.molbio.proteins.7tms_r Research on G-protein coupled receptors. *Newsgroup*

9061 bionet.molbio.proteins.fluorescent Fluorescent proteins and bioluminescence. *Newsgroup*

9062 bionet.molbio.yeast The molecular biology and genetics of yeast. *Newsgroup*

9063 bionet.molec-model The physical and chemical aspects of molecular modeling. *Newsgroup*

9064 bionet.molecules.peptides Chemical and biological aspects of peptides. *Newsgroup*

9065 bionet.molecules.repertoires Generation and use of libraries of molecules. *Newsgroup*

9066 bionet.software.x-plor X-PLOR for 3D macromolecular structure determination. *Newsgroup*

9067 bionet.structural-nmr Exploring the structure of macromolecules using NMR. *Newsgroup*

9068 bionet.xtallography Discussions about protein crystallography. *Newsgroup*

➤ **CELLWALL:** On plant and fungal cell wall research. (See entry 9034 for full listing.)

9069 European Molecular Biology Laboratory (EMBL): A large collection of online services, databases, software, and other information for molecular biology in Europe.
http://www.embl-heidelberg.de/
ftp://ftp.embl-heidelberg.de
gopher://gopher.embl-heidelberg.de
INFO webmaster@embl-heidelberg.de

9070 Journal of Biological Chemistry: Full text of the Journal of Biological Chemistry Online since April 1995. The online version includes links to Medline and PDF files for printing, and is jointly published by the ASBMB and the HighWire Press.
http://www-jbc.stanford.edu/jbc/
INFO jbc-feedback@forsythe.stanford.edu

9071 Molecular Biology Computational Resource at Baylor College of Medicine: Information for biological and biomedical research.
http://mbcr.bcm.tmc.edu/
gopher://mbcr.bcm.tmc.edu
INFO www@mbcr.bcm.tmc.edu
INFO mbcrhelp@mbcr.bcm.tmc.edu

➤ **Molecular Evolution & Organelle Genomics Site:** This site contains information from a variety of organelle and evolutionary biology research efforts in Canada. It includes: Organelle Genome Megasequencing Program (OGMP), Organelle Genome Database (GOBASE), Fungal Mitochondrial Genome Project (FMGP), Protist Image Database

(PID), MegaGopher, and the Gopher Hole on Organelle Research/Molecular Evolution. (See entry 9116 for full listing.)

➤ **National Institutes of Health (NIH):** This site provides health and biomedical information useful to the NIH intramural research community in Bethesda, Maryland, and biomedical researchers around the world. (See entry 5057 for full listing.)

BIOLOGY—ZOOLOGY

9072 **arachnology:** On the study of arachnids. *Mailing List*
http://sesoserv.ufsia.ac.be/Arachnology/Arachnology.html
± majordomo@ufsia.ac.be [body = subscribe arachnology]
OWNER dse.vanuytven.h@alpha.ufsia.ac.be (Herman Vanuytven)

9073 `bionet.drosophila`   Discussions about the biology of fruit flies. *Newsgroup*

➤ `bionet.molbio.molluscs:`   Discussions about research on mollusc DNA. *Newsgroup*

9074 `bionet.organisms.urodeles`   Research scientists using urodele amphibians. *Newsgroup*

9075 `bionet.organisms.zebrafish`   Research using the model organism zebra fish. *Newsgroup*

9076 **CAMEL-L:** On the field of camel researches and studies. It is launched by the Camel Research Center at King Faisal University, Saudi Arabia. *Mailing List*
± listserv@sakfu00.bitnet [body = SUBSCRIBE CAMEL-L first-name last-name]
INFO devmtg12@sakfu00.bitnet (Mustafa Alghazal)
INFO OWNER nad@sakfu00.bitnet (Mustafa AlGhazal)
ARCHIVE listserv@sakfu00.bitnet [body = INDEX CAMEL-L]

9077 **CHAETOZONE:** An e-mail newsletter for researchers on polychaete annelid worms. *Newsletter*
http://www.actrix.gen.nz/users/chaeto/index.html
gopher://muse.bio.cornell.edu/11/newsletters/chaetozone
± INFO gread@actrix.gen.nz (Dr. Geoffrey B. Read)
Frequency: two-monthly

9078 **CICHLID-L:** On the perciform fish family Cichlidae: primarily an academic forum. *Mailing List*
± listserv@nrm.se
INFO OWNER cichlid-l-request@nrm.se
ARCHIVE http://www.nrm.se/cgi-bin/lwgate/CICHLID-L/archives/

➤ **CTURTLE:** On sea turtle biology and conservation. (See entry 4679 for full listing.)

9079 **ETHOLOGY:** On animal behavior and behavioral ecology.   *Mailing List*
± listserv@searn.sunet.se [body = SUBSCRIBE ETHOLOGY first-name last-name]
INFO jarmo.saarikko@helsinki.fi
ARCHIVES
gopher://searn.sunet.se:70/11/ETHOLOGY
listserv@searn.sunet.se [body = INDEX ETHOLOGY]
Gated: sci.bio.ethology

9080 `sci.aquaria`   Only scientifically oriented postings about aquaria. *Newsgroup*

9081 `sci.bio.ethology`   Animal behavior and behavioral ecology. *Newsgroup*

9082 `sci.bio.fisheries`   All aspects of fisheries science and fish biology. *Newsgroup*

9083 `sci.bio.herp`   Biology of amphibians and reptiles. *Newsgroup*

BIOTECHNOLOGY & GENETICS

➤ **Agricultural Genome Information Server :** WWW, Gopher, FTP, and WAISmail access to genome databases. (See entry 8907 for full listing.)

9084 **alt.bio.hackers** Individualist uses of biotechnology. *Newsgroup*

➤ **Bioline Publications:** Bioline Publications is an electronic publishing service for bioscientists. In collaboration with scientific publishers, newsletter editors, and authors of reports, it makes scientific material available more easily and more cheaply. (See entry 8954 for full listing.)

9085 **BIOLINE-L:** The Bioline Publications List informs interested users of new developments in this electronic publications service and provides regular updates on new material added to the Bioline (http://www.bdt.org.br/bioline/) database. *Mailing List, moderated*

±   listserv@bdt.org.br [body = subscribe BIOLINE-L first-name last-name]

INFO bio@biostrat.demon.co.uk (Bioline Publications)

ARCHIVE http://www.bdt.org.br:70/lists/bioline-l.cgi

9086 **bionet.genome.arabidopsis** Information about the Arabidopsis project. *Newsgroup*

9087 **bionet.genome.chromosomes** Mapping and sequencing of eucaryote chromosomes. *Newsgroup*

9088 **bionet.molbio.embldatabank** Information about the EMBL nucleic acid database. *Newsgroup*

9089 **bionet.molbio.evolution** How genes and proteins have evolved. *Newsgroup*

9090 **bionet.molbio.gdb** Messages to and from the GDB database staff. *Newsgroup*

9091 **bionet.molbio.genbank** Information about the GenBank nucleic acid database. *Newsgroup*

9092 **bionet.molbio.genbank.updates** Hot off the presses! *Moderated newsgroup*

9093 **bionet.molbio.gene-linkage** Discussions about genetic linkage analysis. *Newsgroup*

9094 **bionet.molbio.genome-program** Discussion of Human Genome Project issues. *Newsgroup*

9095 **bionet.molbio.molluscs** Discussions about research on mollusc DNA. *Newsgroup*

9096 **bionet.molbio.rapd** Research on Randomly Amplified Polymorphic DNA. *Newsgroup*

9097 **bionet.molbio.recombination** Research on the recombination of DNA or RNA. *Newsgroup*

9098 **bionet.software.acedb** Discussions by users of genome DBs using ACEDB. *Newsgroup*

9099 **bionet.software.gcg** Discussions about using the ACEDB software. *Newsgroup*

9100 **bionet.software.srs** Sequence Retrieval System (SRS) software. *Newsgroup*

9101 **bionet.software.staden** Using the Staden molecular sequence analysis software. *Newsgroup*

9102 **BIOTECH:** For open discussion of all issues related to biotechnology. *Mailing List, moderated*

±   listserv@umdd.umd.edu [body = SUBSCRIBE BIOTECH first-name last-name]

INFO dan@umdd.bitnet (Dan Jacobs)

ARCHIVE listserv@umdd.umd.edu

9103 **BioTech:** This site is a hybrid biology/chemistry educational resource and research tool that includes a biotechnology resource database and a biotechnology dictionary.

http://biotech.chem.indiana.edu/

INFO feedback@biotech.chem.indiana.edu

9104 **BIZ-BIOTECH:** On business and biotech: an opportunities forum. *Digest & Reflector, moderated*

±   listserv@netcom.com [body = SUBSCRIBE biz-biotech]

OWNER grunwald@netcom.com (Stefan Gruenwald)

➤ **CAOS/CAMM Center:** Netherlands national facility for computer-aided chemistry and bioinformatics. (See entry 9131 for full listing.)

9105 **clari.tw.biotechnology** Biotechnology news. *Moderated newsgroup*

➤ **Dendrome:** Forest tree genome research updates. (See entry 4606 for full listing.)

➤ **European Molecular Biology Laboratory (EMBL):** A large collection of online services, databases, software, and other information for molecular biology in Europe. (See entry 9069 for full listing.)

9106 **GenBank:** The NIH genetic sequence database, a collection of all known DNA sequences.

```
http://www.ncbi.nlm.nih.gov/
ftp://ncbi.nlm.nih.gov
```
INFO info@ncbi.nlm.nih.gov

9107 GENE-COMBIS: A peer-reviewed electronic journal devoted to computing problems in the field of molecular biology including gene and genome mapping and protein sequencing. *E-Journal*

```
http://www.elsevier.com/locate/genecombis
http://www.elsevier.nl/locate/genecombis
```
± genecombis-e@elsevier.nl (Subscription Office)

INFO OWNER j.clark@elsevier.nl (Jonathan Clark, Marketing Manager)

EDITOR ma11@gen.cam.ac.uk (Michael Ashburner)

EDITOR genecombis-m@elsevier.nl (Editorial Office)

ARCHIVES

```
http://www.elsevier.com/locate/genecombis
http://www.elsevier.nl/locate/genecombis
```
Frequency: Articles added as soon as accepted (weekly)

GENE-COMBIS is available only to those scientists working at locations whose library subscribes to the journal *Gene*.

9108 Genethon-Human Research Genome Center: This site provides access to public data from CEPH and Genethon research projects.

```
http://www.genethon.fr/
ftp://ftp.genethon.fr
gopher://gopher.genethon.fr
```
INFO info-ftp@genethon.fr

9109 GENTALK: Primarily for high school and college level investigation of genetics and biotechnology. *Mailing List, moderated*

± listproc@usa.net [body = SUBSCRIBE GENTALK first-name last-name]

EDITOR OWNER lundberg@kadets.d20.co.edu (Doug Lundberg)

9110 GENTECH: News for activists on biotechnology and genetic engineering. *Mailing List*

± gentech-request@tribe.ping.de

OWNER w.reis@tribe.ping.de (Werner Reisberger, Germany)

9111 GrainGenes, A Plant Genome Database for Small Grains and Sugarcane: This is the online version of the USDA Plant Genome Research Program's genome database for wheat, barley, oats, and related species.

```
http://wheat.pw.usda.gov/
gopher://greengenes.cit.cornell.edu
```
INFO matthews@greengenes.cit.cornell.edu

MIRROR gopher://probe.nalusda.gov:7000/11/genome.database/graingenes

9112 GSA: For genetic stock administrators. *Mailing List*

± listserv@iubvm.ucs.indiana.edu [body = SUBSCRIBE GSA first-name last-name]

INFO matthewk@fly.bio.indiana.edu (Kathy Matthews)

9113 ICGEBnet: This is the information server of the International Center for Genetic Engineering and Biotechnology, Trieste, Italy. It carries molecular biology and biotechnology-related information. This site also contains information on safety aspects of biotechnology and of genetically modified organisms.

```
http://www.icgeb.trieste.it/
gopher://icgeb.trieste.it
```
INFO pongor@icgeb.trieste.it

9114 Maize Genome Database: Database of the corn genome.

```
http://www.agron.missouri.edu/
```
INFO db_request@teosinte.agron.missouri.edu

FAQ http://www.agron.missouri.edu/more_info.html

9115 MegaGopher—DNA Sequencing and Organellar Genome Research: The MegaGopher supports the information requirements for the MegaSequencing project, centered at the University of Montreal, Canada.

gopher://megasun.bch.umontreal.ca

INFO langf@bch.umontreal.ca

9116 Molecular Evolution & Organelle Genomics Site: This site contains information from a variety of organelle and evolutionary biology research efforts in Canada. It includes: Organelle Genome Megasequencing Program (OGMP), Organelle Genome Database (GOBASE), Fungal Mitochondrial Genome Project (FMGP), Protist Image Database (PID), MegaGopher, and the Gopher Hole on Organelle Research/Molecular Evolution.

http://megasun.bch.umontreal.ca/

INFO langf@bch.umontreal.ca

➤ **National Institutes of Health (NIH):** This site provides health and biomedical information useful to the NIH intramural research community in Bethesda, Maryland, and biomedical researchers around the world. (See entry 5057 for full listing.)

➤ **Neuron:** On all aspects of neural networks. Topics include both artificial neural networks and biological systems. (See entry 2156 for full listing.)

9117 Ribosomal Database Project: This is the Ribosomal Database Project server at the University of Illinois at Urbana-Champaign, Urbana, Illinois. It offers microbiologists unique access to a database of rRNA sequence data, alignments, phylogenetic trees, associated sequence manipulation programs, and a variety of other software.

http://rdpwww.life.uiuc.edu/

ftp://rdp.life.uiuc.edu

gopher://rdpgopher.life.uiuc.edu

INFO server@rdp.life.uiuc.edu [body = HELP COMPLETE]

INFO mrmike@geta.life.uiuc.edu

9118 sci.bio.technology Any topic relating to biotechnology. *Newsgroup*

9119 Spanish EMBnet Node Gopher Server: This gopher holds data of interest to biologists working in sequence analysis.

gopher://gopher.cnb.uam.es

INFO jrvalverde@samba.cnb.uam.es

9120 Stanford Genome Information: Genome databases and centers at Stanford University.

http://genome-www.stanford.edu/

ftp://genome-ftp.stanford.edu

gopher://genome-gopher.stanford.edu

INFO arab-curator@genome.stanford.edu (General AtDB Project Contact Address)

INFO yeast-curator@genome.stanford.edu (General SGD Project Contact Address)

➤ **UNU.ZERI.IBS:** On integrated biosystems. (See entry 4665 for full listing.)

9121 Webcutter: WebCutter provides free, custom restriction maps of DNA sequences. It features automated sequence search-and-entry from NCBI's GenBank, as well as monthly enzyme database updates from NEBiolabs. Resources for teachers are also included.

http://firstmarket.com/cutter

INFO maxwell@minerva.cis.yale.edu

CHAOS & COMPLEX SYSTEMS

9122 Nonlinearity and Complexity Home Page: A compendium of resources on complex systems, chaos, fractals, and other related fields.

http://www.cc.duth.gr/~mboudour/nonlin.html

INFO mboudour@duth.gr

9123 bit.listserv.frac-l Fractal discussion list. *Newsgroup*

➤ **Cellular-Automata:** On cellular automata and lattice gases, including theory, applications, and available software packages. (See entry 9381 for full listing.)

9124 Chaos Introduction: A good description of chaos theory for beginners. Includes a bibliography and covers the topics of bifurcation and periodicity, strange attractors, and fractal geometry.
http://www.students.uiuc.edu/~ag-ho/chaos/chaos.html
INFO ag-ho@students.uiuc.edu
MIRROR http://www.cen.uiuc.edu/~ag-ho/chaos/chaos.html

9125 The Chaos Network: This Web site contains a brief introduction to chaos and complex systems theory, pointers to other chaos and complex systems resources on the net, and information on The Chaos Network, which is an international association of people applying the discoveries from the science of chaos and complex systems to social systems.
http://www.prairienet.org/business/ptech/
INFO chaos@tmn.com

9126 Fractal Explorer: A nifty Web interface to viewing many different kinds of fractals (including Mandelbrot, Julia, Lyapunov, Magnet, and more).
http://www.vis.colostate.edu/~user1209/fractals/index.html
INFO kettler@cs.colostate.edu

9127 Nonlinear Science e-Print Archive: A searchable archive of articles in the field of nonlinear systems.
http://xyz.lanl.gov/
INFO www-admin@xxx.lanl.gov
FAQ http://xxx.lanl.gov/help

9128 sci.fractals Objects of nonintegral dimension and other chaos. *Newsgroup*

9129 sci.nonlinear Chaotic systems and other nonlinear scientific study. *Newsgroup*

CHEMISTRY

9130 alt.drugs.chemistry Discussion of drug chemistry and synthesis. *Newsgroup*

➤ **BioTech:** This site is a hybrid biology/chemistry educational resource and research tool that includes a biotechnology resource database and a biotechnology dictionary. (See entry 9103 for full listing.)

➤ **C14-L:** For technical discussion of radiocarbon and other radioisotope dating. (See entry 9313 for full listing.)

9131 CAOS/CAMM Center: Netherlands national facility for computer-aided chemistry and bioinformatics.
http://www.caos.kun.nl/
ftp://ftp.caos.kun.nl
gopher://gopher.caos.kun.nl
INFO jackl@caos.kun.nl

9132 CHEMCORD: For coordinators of general chemistry courses for colleges and universities. *Mailing List*
± listserv@umdd.umd.edu [body = SUBSCRIBE CHEMCORD first-name last-name]
INFO wharwood@deans.umd.edu (Bill Harwood)
ARCHIVE listserv@umdd.umd.edu

9133 CHEME-L: On the role of chemical engineering in the world economy, including research trends, public and federal support, and education. *Mailing List*
http://www.louisville.edu/~r0mira01/cheme-l
± listserv@ulkyvm.louisville.edu [body = SUBSCRIBE CHEME-L first-name last-name]
INFO r0mira01@ulkyvm.louisville.edu (Raul Miranda)

9134 CHEMED-L: On chemistry education at all grade levels. *Mailing List*
± listserv@uwf.cc.uwf.edu [body = SUBSCRIBE CHEMED-L first-name last-name]
INFO whalpern@uwf.bitnet (Bill Halpern)
ARCHIVE listserv@uwf.cc.uwf.edu

9135 CHEMIC-L: On chemistry in Israel. *Mailing List*
± listserv@vm.tau.ac.il [body = SUBSCRIBE CHEMIC-L first-name last-name]
INFO chemic-l-request@vm.tau.ac.il

9136 CHEMLAB-L: On chemistry laboratories: academic and industrial, experiments, apparatus, lab waste disposal, and safety. *Mailing List*
± listserv@beaver.bemidji.msus.edu [body = SUBSCRIBE CHEMLAB-L first-name last-name]
INFO gmchem@vax1.bemidji.msus.edu (Dr. Gerald Morine)

9137 CHMINF-L: On chemical information sources. *Mailing List*
± listserv@iubvm.ucs.indiana.edu [body = SUBSCRIBE CHMINF-L first-name last-name]
INFO wiggins@indiana.edu (Gary Wiggins)
ARCHIVES
listserv@iubvm.ucs.indiana.edu
http://atlas.chemistry.uakron.edu:8080/cdept.docs/CHMINF/hmail.html (Hypermail)
POST chminf-l@iubvm.indiana.edu

➤ **Ciba Geigy AG (Ciba):** Home page for information and feedback to the biological and chemical company Ciba. (See entry 1905 for full listing.)

9138 CZE-ITP: Discussion on problems of capillary electrophoretic methods. *Mailing List*
± listserv@csbrmu11.bitnet [body = SUBSCRIBE CZE-ITP first-name last-name]
INFO vdolnik@csbrmu11.bitnet
ARCHIVE listserv@csbrmu11.bitnet

9139 fj.sci.chem Discussion on chemistry. *Newsgroup*

➤ **GT-ATMDC:** On the atmospheric dispersion of chemicals. (See entry 4623 for full listing.)

9140 HIRIS-L: On high-resolution infrared spectroscopy, including utility programs for handling high-resolution spectra. *Mailing List, moderated*
± listserv@vm.cineca.it [body = SUBSCRIBE HIRIS-L first-name last-name]
INFO g1wudd32@vm.cineca.it (Alberto Gambi)

9141 IACIS: The International Association of Colloid and Interface Scientists (IACIS) is a voluntary, nonprofit organization of individuals who are actively interested in promoting the field of colloid and interface science.
http://www.fenk.wau.nl/iacis
INFO iacis@fenk.wau.nl

9142 ICS-L: On the International Chemometrics Society. *Mailing List*
± listserv@umdd.umd.edu [body = SUBSCRIBE ICS-L first-name last-name]
INFO thomas_c_ohaver@umail.umd.edu (Tom O'Haver)
ARCHIVE listserv@umdd.umd.edu

9143 iijnet.chem Discussions about chemistry. *Newsgroup*

9144 INFOCHIM: On computing in chemistry in Italy. *Mailing List*
± listserv@vm.cineca.it [body = SUBSCRIBE INFOCHIM first-name last-name]
INFO g1wudd32@vm.cineca.it (Alberto Gambi)
Language: Italian
Please Note: Subscription by approval only.

9145 ISISFORUM-L: Forum for users of MDL's ISIS software. *Mailing List*
http://www.mdli.com/
± mailserv@mdli.com [body = SUBSCRIBE ISISFORUM-L first-name last-name]
EDITOR 74222.2372@compuserve.com (John Vinson, PhD)
OWNER osman@mdli.com (Osman F. Guner, PhD)

➤ **Journal of Biological Chemistry:** Full text of the Journal of Biological Chemistry Online since April 1995. The online version includes links to Medline and PDF files for printing, and is jointly published by the ASBMB and the HighWire Press. (See entry 9070 for full listing.)

➤ `oh.chem:` Chemistry in Ohio. *Newsgroup*

9146 `relcom.commerce.chemical` Chemical production. *Newsgroup*

9147 `sci.chem` Chemistry and related sciences. *Newsgroup*

9148 `sci.chem.analytical` Analytical chemistry. *Newsgroup*

9149 `sci.chem.coatings` Paints and coatings practitioners. *Newsgroup*

9150 `sci.chem.electrochem` The field of electrochemistry. *Newsgroup*

9151 `sci.chem.electrochem.battery` Analyzing all aspects of all types of batteries. *Newsgroup*

9152 `sci.chem.labware` Chemical laboratory equipment. *Newsgroup*

9153 `sci.chem.organomet` Organometallic chemistry. *Newsgroup*

9154 `tnn.chem` Discussions in chemistry area. *Newsgroup*

COGNITIVE SCIENCE

9155 `ch.si.sgaico` Topics of the Swiss Group of AI and Cognitive Science. *Newsgroup*

9156 **COLORCAT:** On color categorization. *Mailing List*
± `listserv@brownvm.brown.edu` [body = SUBSCRIBE COLORCAT first-name last-name]
OWNER `dlmiller@brownvm.brown.edu` (David Miller)
ARCHIVE `listserv@brownvm.brown.edu` [body = INDEX COLORCAT]

9157 **CSLI Calendar of Public Events:** Weekly announcements of CSLI-affiliated events (Center for the Study of Language and Information, Stanford University). *Newsletter*
± `friends-request@csli.stanford.edu`
INFO `csli-request@csli.stanford.edu` (Tom Burke)
ARCHIVES
`gopher://csli-gopher.stanford.edu/11/CSLI/`
`http://www-csli.stanford.edu/csli/`
Frequency: weekly (during the academic year)

9158 **The Observer:** Newsletter on Humberto Maturana's and Francisco Varela's theories of autopoiesis and "enactive cognitive science," and their linkages to systems theory, cognitive science, phenomenology, artificial life, etc. *Newsletter*
± INFO `rwhitaker@falcon.al.wpafb.af.mil` (Randall Whitaker)
± INFO `rwhit@informatik.umu.se` (permanent relay to Whitaker)

9159 `pgh.org.cnbc` Notices for the Center for the Neural Basis of Cognition. *Newsgroup*

➤ **PSYCHE-D:** Discussions on the electronic journal PSYCHE. (See entry 9525 for full listing.)

➤ **PSYCOLOQUY:** Brief reports of new ideas and findings in all areas of psychology and its related fields (biobehavioral, cognitive, neural, social, etc.). (See entry 9527 for full listing.)

9160 `sci.cognitive` Perception, memory, judgement, and reasoning. *Newsgroup*

➤ **SCR-L:** On cognitive rehabilitation. (See entry 5025 for full listing.)

COMPUTER SCIENCE

➤ <u>**Carnegie Mellon University Artificial Intelligence Repository:**</u> Collection of nearly all materials of interest to AI researchers, educators, practitioners, and students. (See entry 2129 for full listing.)

9161 <u>**CS Departments:**</u> Listing of Web and gopher servers of computer science (and related) departments at universities throughout the net.
`http://www.cs.cmu.edu/~anwar/CS-departments.html`

INFO `anwar+@cs.cmu.edu`

➤ **Netlib:** A collection of mathematical software, papers, and databases. (See entry 9373 for full listing.)

9162 **Online journals:** Collection of resources for online journals, concentrating on those relevant to computer scientists.
`http://www.library.cmu.edu/bySubject/CS+ECE/lib/journals.html`
INFO `missy@cs.cmu.edu`

9163 **Automated Reasoning Project (ARP):** Software, tools, and papers on automated reasoning and parallel and symbolic computing.
`http://arp.anu.edu.au/`
INFO `greg.restall@anu.edu.au`

9164 **Carnegie Mellon University Software Engineering Institute:** The Software Engineering Institute (SEI) is a federally funded research and development center sponsored by the U.S. Department of Defense and operated by Carnegie Mellon University.
`http://www.sei.cmu.edu/`
`ftp://ftp.sei.cmu.edu`
INFO `customer-relations@sei.cmu.edu`

➤ **CBL:** Computer-Based Learning Unit, The University of Leeds, United Kingdom. (See entry 2135 for full listing.)

➤ **Cellular-Automata:** On cellular automata and lattice gases, including theory, applications, and available software packages. (See entry 9381 for full listing.)

9165 **`chile.sccc`** Sociedad Chilena de Ciencia de la Computacion (Chilean CS). *Newsgroup*

9166 **CMU Libraries CS, Robotics and Electrical Engineering Resources:** Pointers to Web resources in computer science, robotics and electrical engineering including reference tools, bibliographies, books, journals, patents, standards, technical reports, and more.
`http://www.library.cmu.edu/bySubject/CS+ECE/`
INFO `missy@cs.cmu.edu`
Comments: This list is maintained by the libraries at Carnegie Mellon University.

9167 **`comp.arch`** Computer architecture. *Newsgroup*

9168 **`comp.arch.arithmetic`** Implementing arithmetic on computers/digital systems. *Newsgroup*

9169 **`comp.arch.embedded`** Embedded computer systems topics. *Newsgroup*

9170 **`comp.arch.fpga`** Field Programmable Gate Array-based computing systems. *Newsgroup*

9171 **`comp.compilers`** Compiler construction, theory, etc. *Moderated newsgroup*

9172 **`comp.compilers.tools.pccts`** Construction of compilers and tools with PCCTS. *Newsgroup*

9173 **`comp.compression`** Data compression algorithms and theory. *Newsgroup*

9174 **`comp.compression.research`** Discussions about data compression research. *Moderated newsgroup*

9175 **`comp.constraints`** Constraint processing and related topics. *Newsgroup*

9176 **`comp.dsp`** Digital Signal Processing using computers. *Newsgroup*

9177 **`comp.edu`** Computer science education. *Newsgroup*

➤ **`comp.programming`:** Programming issues that transcend languages and OSs. *Newsgroup*

9178 **`comp.realtime`** Issues related to real-time computing. *Newsgroup*

9179 **`comp.society.futures`** Events in technology affecting future computing. *Newsgroup*

➤ **`comp.software-eng`:** Software engineering and related topics. *Newsgroup*

9180 **`comp.speech`** Research and applications in speech science and technology. *Newsgroup*

9181 **`comp.theory`** Theoretical computer science. *Newsgroup*

9182 **`comp.theory.cell-automata`** Discussion of all aspects of cellular automata. *Newsgroup*

9183 **`comp.theory.dynamic-sys`** Ergodic theory and dynamical systems theory. *Newsgroup*

9184 `comp.theory.info-retrieval` Information retrieval topics. *Moderated newsgroup*

9185 `comp.theory.self-org-sys` Topics related to self-organization. *Newsgroup*

9186 Computists' Communique: A career-oriented newsletter serving professionals in artificial intelligence, information science, and computer science. Available to members of Computists International, a networking group for computer and information scientists. This newsletter is not free; for more information send e-mail to the contact address. *Newsletter*

± INFO `laws@ai.sri.com` (Dr. Kenneth I. Laws)

Please Note: Subscription by approval only.

Frequency: weekly

Price: varies with subscription type

➤ **CONTENT:** On content analysis of text and images: theory and practice. (See entry 5181 for full listing.)

9187 Cornell Theory Center: The Cornell Theory Center provides the advanced supercomputing resources to promote research in a broad spectrum of scientific and engineering fields. In this site you can find descriptions of research and work accomplished by CTC faculty and staff.

`http://www.tc.cornell.edu/`

INFO `cal@tc.cornell.edu`

9188 Crossroads, The ACM Student Magazine: Crossroads is a magazine produced by and for student members of the ACM (Association of Computing Machinery). Crossroads features four themed issues a year.

`http://www.acm.org/crossroads/`

INFO `saracarl@rice.edu`

➤ **CS1OBJ-L:** On teaching object-oriented programming to first-year students. (See entry 3642 for full listing.)

9189 CYBSYS-L: For interdisciplinary discussion of systems science, cybernetics, and related fields. *Mailing List*

± `listserv@bingvmb.cc.binghamton.edu` [body = SUBSCRIBE CYBSYS-L first-name last-name]

INFO `cybsys-l-request@bingvmb.cc.binghamton.edu`

9190 dataflow-list: On dataflow, its implementation as a model of computation, and related topics. *Mailing List*

`http://odyssey.ucc.ie/www/user-dirs/oregan/dataflow.html`

± `dataflow-request@boole.ucc.ie`

OWNER `owner-dataflow@boole.ucc.ie` (Dataflow Moderator)

OWNER `oregan@boole.ucc.ie` (John O'Regan)

ARCHIVE `http://odyssey.ucc.ie/www/user-dirs/oregan/archive/index.html`

➤ **DMANET:** On the mathematical analysis of discrete structures and the design of discrete algorithms and their applications in operations research, computer science, and engineering. (See entry 9383 for full listing.)

9191 Dresden University of Technology/ Department of Computer Science: This is the information service of the Department of Computer Science, Dresden University of Technology, Germany.

`http://www.inf.tu-dresden.de/`

`gopher://gopher.inf.tu-dresden.de`

INFO `gopher@gopher.inf.tu-dresden.de`

9192 EDESIGN: For professionals involved in the design and development of electronic circuitry. *Mailing List*

± `listserv@acadvm1.uottawa.ca` [body = SUBSCRIBE EDESIGN first-name last-name]

OWNER `vdbergen@acadvm1.uottawa.ca` (Herman van den Bergen)

9193 `fj.comp.arch` Computer architecture. *Newsgroup*

9194 `fj.comp.dsp` Discussion about digital signal processing. *Newsgroup*

9195 `fj.comp.speech` Academic discussions and technical interchanges on speech processing. *Newsgroup*

9196 `fj.comp.theory` Theoretical aspects of computer science. *Newsgroup*

9197 GRAFOS-L: On the mathematical and computational aspects of graphs. *Mailing List*

± `listserv@ufrj.bitnet` [body = SUBSCRIBE GRAFOS-L first-name last-name]

INFO cerioli@ufrj.bitnet (Marcia Cerioli)

Language: Portugese

Please Note: Subscription by approval only.

9198 `il.cs.board` Israeli computer science. *Newsgroup*

➤ **Impulsiv:** A German e-journal on math, physics, and computer science. Entertaining. (See entry 9390 for full listing.)

➤ **INFOSYS:** Electronic newsletter for information systems. (See entry 3140 for full listing.)

➤ **Knowledge Discovery Mine:** This site provides information on data mining and knowledge discovery in databases. (See entry 2338 for full listing.)

9199 **Liverpool University, Computer Science, United Kingdom:** This is the Computer Service departmental Web server at the University of Liverpool, United Kingdom. It includes HP-UX information and information on Mereyside and U.K. National Lotteries.

http://www.csc.liv.ac.uk/

INFO webmaster@csc.liv.ac.uk

9200 **MICRO-EL:** On microelectronics research in Israel. *Mailing List*

± listserv@vm.tau.ac.il [body = SUBSCRIBE MICRO-EL first-name last-name]

INFO micro-el-request@vm.tau.ac.il

➤ **MOO Papers:** Pavel Curtis' collection of MU* papers. (See entry 3180 for full listing.)

9201 **ORCS-L:** On the interface between operations research and computer science. *Mailing List*

http://orcs.bus.okstate.edu/orcs-l

± listserv@vm1.ucc.okstate.edu [body = SUBSCRIBE ORCS-L first-name last-name]

INFO OWNER sharda@okstate.edu (Ramesh Sharda)

9202 **PetriNets:** On PetriNets, a graphical language for modeling concurrent systems. *Mailing List, moderated*

± petrinets-request@daimi.aau.dk

EDITOR schristensen@daimi.aau.dk (Soren Christensen)

EDITOR khm@daimi.aau.dk (Kjeld H. Mortensen)

ARCHIVE http://www.daimi.aau.dk/~petrinet/

FAQ http://www.daimi.aau.dk/~petrinet/

9203 **Purdue CS Information Service:** This is the information service for the Purdue University Department of Computer Sciences, West Lafayette, Indiana.

http://www.cs.purdue.edu/

gopher://gopher.cs.purdue.edu

INFO webmaster@cs.purdue.edu

9204 **RPI CS Lab:** This site provides access to information, software, and technical reports from the Rensselaer Polytechnic Institute Computer Science Department.

http://www.cs.rpi.edu/

INFO www@cs.rpi.edu

9205 `sci.data.formats` Modeling, storage, and retrieval of scientific data. *Newsgroup*

➤ **SIGART Electronic Information Service:** A public service to the AI community sponsored by ACM SIGART, the Special Interest Group on Artificial Intelligence. (See entry 2158 for full listing.)

9206 **Sonoma State University Computer Science Department:** This is the WWW server for the computer science department at Sonoma State University, Rohnert Park, California. Includes information for computer-science majors at Sonoma State, and Project Censored (a media research project on censorship) "Top Ten Censored Stories" lists.

http://cs.sonoma.edu/

INFO webmaster@zippy.sonoma.edu

9207 **THEORYNT:** On computer-science theory. *Mailing List*

± listserv@vm1.nodak.edu [body = SUBSCRIBE THEORYNT first-name last-name]

INFO u32799@uicvm.cc.uic.edu (Uri Peled)

ARCHIVE listserv@vm1.nodak.edu [body = INDEX THEORYNT]

➤ **Thesis** : A science and technology magazine covering traditional fields like medical research and information technology, plus new developments in computer imaging, the Internet, and science in finance. (See entry 8902 for full listing.)

9208 **tnn.sys.realtime** Discussions about real-time systems. *Newsgroup*

9209 **UVa Computer Science Museum:** This page contains a growing collection of historical computers and computer-related artifacts.

http://www.cs.virginia.edu/brochure/museum.html

INFO robins@cs.virginia.edu

CYBERNETICS & SYSTEMS THEORY

➤ **Cellular-Automata:** On cellular automata and lattice gases, including theory, applications, and available software packages. (See entry 9381 for full listing.)

➤ **comp.theory.dynamic-sys:** Ergodic theory and dynamical systems theory. *Newsgroup*

9210 **dynsys:** The dynamical systems mailing list. On ergodic theory and dynamical systems. *Mailing List*

± listserv@unc.edu [body = SUBSCRIBE DYNSYS]

INFO karl_petersen@unc.edu

9211 **E-letter on Systems, Control, and Signal Processing:** Developments in the area of systems, control, and signal processing: book and conference announcements, future issues' contents tables, address changes, and other timely news. *Newsletter*

± **INFO** eletter-request@win.tue.nl (Dr. Anton A. Stoorvogel or Dr. S. Weiland)

ARCHIVES

gopher://gopher.utdallas.edu/11/research/scad ftp

ftp://ftp.utdallas.edu/11/research/scad ftp

Frequency: monthly

➤ **MCRIT-L:** On multi-criteria analysis, a discipline that helps to formulate decisions in the face of (sometimes) conflicting criteria. (See entry 9393 for full listing.)

➤ **The Observer:** Newsletter on Humberto Maturana's and Francisco Varela's theories of autopoiesis and "enactive cognitive science," and their linkages to systems theory, cognitive science, phenomenology, artificial life, etc. (See entry 9158 for full listing.)

9212 **Principia Cybernetica Mailing List:** PCP is a computer-supported collaborative attempt to develop an integrated evolutionary-systemic philosophy or worldview focusing on the clear formulation of principles of the cybernetic approach. *Mailing List*

http://pespmc1.vub.ac.be/

± **INFO** pcp@vnet3.vub.ac.be (Dr. Francis Heylighen, Editor)

INFO cjoslyn@bingsuns.cc.binghamton.edu (Cliff Joslyn)

ARCHIVE ftp.vub.ac.be [pub/projects/Principia_Cybernetica/]

Frequency: irregular

9213 **Principia Cybernetica Web:** This is the WWW server of the Principia Cybernetica Project (PCP). The Project's aim is the computer-supported collaborative development of an evolutionary-systemic philosophy. Put more simply, PCP tries to tackle age-old philosophical questions with the help of the most recent cybernetic theories and technologies.

http://pespmc1.vub.ac.be/

INFO pcp@vnet3.vub.ac.be (Dr. Francis Heylighen, Editor)

9214 **sci.systems** The theory and application of systems science. *Newsgroup*

➤ **Studies in Nonlinear Dynamics and Econometrics:** The SNDE is formed in recognition that advances in statistics and dynamical systems theory may increase our understanding of economic and financial markets. The journal seeks both theoretical and applied papers. (See entry 1782 for full listing.)

DEVELOPING NATIONS

9215 AFRIK-IT: On the African information technology/"Telematics" industry. *Mailing List*
± `listserv@irlearn.ucd.ie` [body = SUBSCRIBE AFRIK-IT first-name last-name]
OWNER `cdzidonu@stats.tcd.ie` (Clement Dzidonu)

9216 comp.society.development Computer technology in developing countries. *Newsgroup*

9217 DEVEL-L: On technology transfer in international development. *Mailing List*
± `listserv@american.edu` [body = SUBSCRIBE DEVEL-L first-name last-name]
INFO `devel-l-request@american.edu`
Gated: `bit.listserv.devel-l`

9218 DNN-L: The Volunteers in Technical Assistance's DevelopNet. *Mailing List*
± `listserv@american.edu` [body = SUBSCRIBE DNN-L first-name last-name]
INFO `dnn-l-request@american.edu`

9219 ENEWS: an International Newsletter on Energy Efficiency: Informs people in developing countries of ongoing projects, analyzes energy issues, disseminates funding information; special emphasis on energy-efficient and renewable technologies. *Newsletter*
`http://www.fem.unicamp.br/enews.html`
± `listserv@fem.unicamp.br` [body = SUBSCRIBE X-ENEWS]
INFO EDITOR `enews@fem.unicamp.br` (Gilberto Jannuzzi)
ARCHIVES
`ftp://cesar.unicamp.br/pub1/gopher-data/Bibliotecas/E-News` (Electronic Library)
`gopher://cesar.unicamp.br`
Frequency: twice a year

➤ **EUEARN-L:** On eastern European telecommunications. (See entry 9628 for full listing.)

➤ **The Network Startup Resource Center:** This site contains information about: networking in the developing world, low-cost networking tools, general computer networking information, and networking tips and frequently asked questions. You can search for networking solutions and information by country. (See entry 9647 for full listing.)

ENERGY

9220 AESP-Net: From the Association of Energy Services Professionals: discussion of current topics in the energy services and demand-side management field. *Mailing List*
± `majordomo@aesp.org`
INFO `http://www.aesp.org/AESP`
OWNER `harrym@aesp.org` (Harry Misuriello)

➤ **alt.energy.renewable:** Fueling ourselves without depleting everything. *Newsgroup*

➤ **alt.solar.photovoltaic:** Generating voltage from the sun's energy. *Newsgroup*

9221 alt.solar.thermal Sun. Heat. An obvious connection to most. *Newsgroup*

➤ **ATP-EMTP:** For users of the Alternative Transients program, electromagnetic transients software used in the electrical power industry. (See entry 9261 for full listing.)

9222 clari.biz.industry.energy Oil, gas, coal, alternatives. *Moderated newsgroup*

9223 clari.biz.industry.energy.releases News releases: oil, gas, coal, alternatives. *Moderated newsgroup*

9224 clari.tw.nuclear Nuclear power and waste. *Moderated newsgroup*

9225 CMEP-LIST: Public Citizen's action alerts on energy policy. *Distribution List, moderated*
± `listproc@essential.org` [body = SUBSCRIBE CMEP-LIST first-name last-name organizational-affiliation home-state]
INFO `cmep@citizen.org`
ARCHIVE `http://www.essential.org/CMEP`

Please Note: Subscription by approval only.

9226 **Energy Research Clearing House:** The Energy Research Clearing House (ERCH) is an oil and gas industry consortium promoting cooperative research in exploration and production.

`http://www.main.com/~ERCH`

INFO `roger@erch.harc.edu`

➤ **ENEWS: an International Newsletter on Energy Efficiency:** Informs people in developing countries of ongoing projects, analyzes energy issues, disseminates funding information; special emphasis on energy-efficient and renewable technologies. (See entry 9219 for full listing.)

9227 **NUC-OPS:** For operators of nuclear power plants. *Mailing List*

± `listproc@pge.com` [body = SUBSCRIBE NUC-OPS first-name last-name]

OWNER `gpb2@pge.com`

Please Note: Subscription by approval only.

➤ **Oak Ridge Laboratory Review:** The latest and greatest research and development activities at the Oak Ridge National Laboratory. (See entry 9552 for full listing.)

9228 `relcom.commerce.energy` Gas, coal, oil, fuel, generators, etc. *Newsgroup*

9229 `sci.energy` Discussions about energy, science, and technology. *Newsgroup*

9230 `sci.energy.hydrogen` All about hydrogen as an alternative fuel. *Newsgroup*

9231 **U.S. Office of Scientific and Technical Information (OSTI):** The Office of Scientific and Technical Information (OSTI) manages the Department of Energy's (DOE) program for the collection, processing, and availability of scientific and technical information (STI) generated and acquired by the Department of Energy.

`http://www.osti.gov/`

INFO `webmaster@zeus.osti.gov`

9232 **Wind Energy Weekly:** News of the wind energy industry worldwide—energy policy, wind energy technology, global climate change, sustainable development, and other issues relating to the future of this clean, renewable energy source. *Newsletter*

± INFO `tomgray@econet.org`

ARCHIVES

`http://solstice.crest.org/`

`http://www.igc.apc.org/awea/`

Frequency: weekly

ENGINEERING

➤ **Aerospace Engineering: A Guide to Internet Resources:** List of Internet resources that contain information pertaining to aerospace engineering in general. (See entry 8944 for full listing.)

9233 **ACES-L:** For members of the Atlantic Congress of Engineering Students (ACES)—topics relating to engineering students in the Atlantic region of Canada. *Mailing List*

± `listserv@unb.ca` [body = SUBSCRIBE ACES-L first-name last-name]

INFO `aces-l-request@unb.ca`

9234 `alt.engr.explosives` *boom!* *Newsgroup*

9235 `alt.horology` A group for the science of clocks and watches. *Newsgroup*

➤ **AutomationNET:** A forum for anyone who makes automation products, integrates automation systems, needs automated systems, or for anyone who just wants to learn more about the automation industry. (See entry 9566 for full listing.)

9236 **SEBSEL:** For international networking of black engineers and scientists (no discussion, information only). *Distribution List*

± `listserv@listserv.arizona.edu` [body = SUBSCRIBE SEBSEL first-name last-name]

INFO `geobro@delphi.com` (George Brooks)

ARCHIVES

```
http://listserv.arizona.edu/listserv.html
listserv@listserv.arizona.edu [body = INDEX SEBSEL]
```
FAQ emart@enet.net

9237 **BTO:** For international networking of black engineers and scientists (discussion network). *Mailing List*
± listserv@listserv.arizona.edu [body = SUBSCRIBE BTO first-name last-name]
INFO geobro@delphi.com (George Brooks)
ARCHIVE http://listserv.arizona.edu/listserv.html

➤ **CMU Libraries CS, Robotics and Electrical Engineering Resources:** Pointers to Web resources in computer science, robotics and electrical engineering including reference tools, bibliographies, books, journals, patents, standards, technical reports, and more. (See entry 9166 for full listing.)

9238 `fj.engr.misc` General topics about engineering. *Newsgroup*

9239 `fj.sci.human-factors` Discussion about human factors and ergonomics. *Newsgroup*

➤ **IACIS:** The International Association of Colloid and Interface Scientists (IACIS) is a voluntary, nonprofit organization of individuals who are actively interested in promoting the field of colloid and interface science. (See entry 9141 for full listing.)

9240 **Journal of Fluids Engineering:** Disseminating high-quality scientific information of interest to the fluids-engineering community. *E-Journal*
```
http://scholar.lib.vt.edu/ejournals/JFE/jfe.html
ftp://borg.lib.vt.edu/pub/JFE
```
INFO gailmac@vt.edu (Gail McMillan)
INFO EDITOR telionis@vtvm1.cc.vt.edu (Dr. Demetri Telionis)
ARCHIVES
```
http://scholar.lib.vt.edu/ejournals/JFE/jfe.html
ftp://borg.lib.vt.edu/pub/JFE
```
Frequency: irregular

9241 **PACES-L:** For Publications Association of Canadian Engineering Students (PACES), an organization for editors of student engineering publications in Canada. *Mailing List*
± listserv@unb.ca [body = SUBSCRIBE PACES-L first-name last-name]
INFO paces-l-request@unb.ca

9242 `sci.engr` Technical discussions about engineering tasks. *Newsgroup*

9243 `sci.engr.chem` All aspects of chemical engineering. *Newsgroup*

9244 `sci.engr.heat-vent-ac` Heating, ventilating, air conditioning, and refrigeration. *Newsgroup*

9245 `sci.engr.lighting` Light, vision, and color in architecture, media, etc. *Newsgroup*

9246 `sci.engr.marine.hydrodynamics` Marine hydrodynamics. *Newsgroup*

9247 `sci.engr.safety` All aspects of the safety of engineered systems. *Newsgroup*

9248 `sci.mech.fluids` All aspects of fluid mechanics. *Newsgroup*

9249 `sci.op-research` Research, teaching, and application of operations research. *Newsgroup*

9250 **STAADUG-L:** For users of STAAD-III, a program widely used by civil and structural engineers. *Mailing List*
± listserv@mecheng.asme.org [body = subscribe staadug-l]
OWNER gfitch@ibm.net (Graham Fitch)
OWNER fs3!pixley@fwecleb.attmail.com (Ray Pixley)

9251 **TDR-L:** On time domain reflectometry. *Mailing List*
± listserv@listserv.acns.nwu.edu [body = SUBSCRIBE TDR-L first-name last-name]
INFO r-mchenry@nwu.edu (Renee McHenry)
INFO c-dowding@nwu.edu (Chuck Dowding)

9252 University of Tennessee, College of Engineering: Engineering School information and pointers to other engineering information.

INFO wholmes@utk.edu (Winston Holmes)

INFO gopher://www.engr.utk.edu

9253 UWO Engineering FTP site: Archives mainted by the DA&MR Lab, Mechanical Engineering, University of Western Ontario, London, Ontario, Canada. Also includes archives of files related to the FrameMaker desktop publishing system.

ftp://ftp.engrg.uwo.ca

INFO ftp-owner@engrg.uwo.ca

ENGINEERING—CIVIL & ENVIRONMENTAL

➤ **Building Industry Exchange (BIX):** BIX is a nonprofit clearinghouse and search index of educational, communication, and information resources for the building industry. (See entry 1825 for full listing.)

➤ **BuildNet:** This site provides links, resources, and opportunities for all the members of the construction industry, including architects, contractors, and engineers. (See entry 1826 for full listing.)

➤ **Built-environment:** On the built environment: architecture, civil engineering, surveying. (See entry 4566 for full listing.)

9254 CIVIL-L: On civil engineering research and education. *Mailing List*

± listserv@unb.ca [body = SUBSCRIBE CIVIL-L first-name last-name]

INFO eldo@unb.ca (Eldo Hildebrand)

ARCHIVE listserv@unb.ca

9255 ENVENG-L: On environmental engineering. *Mailing List*

± listproc@pan.cedar.univie.ac.at [body = SUBSCRIBE ENVENG-L first-name last-name]

OWNER haascn@dunx1.ocs.drexel.edu (Charles N. Haas)

ARCHIVE http://www.cedar.univie.ac.at/arch/

9256 fj.engr.civil Topics about civil engineering. *Newsgroup*

9257 GEOSYN: On the geosynthetics industry. *Mailing List*

± majordomo@csn.org [body = subscribe geosyn]

OWNER gwlpi@lpitech.com (Glenn Lippman)

➤ **SAFETY:** On environmental health and safety: life safety issues (such as fire protection), chemical safety (waste disposal, laboratory safety, regulatory compliance), biological hazards, and radiation safety. (See entry 4854 for full listing.)

9258 sci.engr.civil Topics related to civil engineering. *Newsgroup*

9259 Softek Home Page: 2-D and 3-D civil structural engineering demo software.

http://web.idirect.com/~softek

ftp://ftp.idirect.com/com/softek

INFO eric_pullerits@msn.com

ENGINEERING—ELECTRICAL & COMPUTER

➤ **AICS-L:** On architectures for intelligent control systems. (See entry 2131 for full listing.)

➤ **alt.comp.hardware.homebuilt:** Designing devious devices in the den. *Newsgroup*

➤ **alt.comp.hardware.homedesigned:** Discussing home designed computer hardware. *Newsgroup*

➤ **alt.comp.hardware.pc-homebuilt:** Building your PC from motherboards and cards. *Newsgroup*

9260 alt.engineering.electrical Discussing electrical engineering. *Newsgroup*

➤ **alt.radio.digital:** Digital radio signals. *Newsgroup*

9261 ATP-EMTP: For users of the Alternative Transients program, electromagnetic transients software used in the electrical power industry. *Mailing List*

```
ftp://ftp.ee.mtu.edu/pub/atp
ftp://ftp.rrzn.uni-hannover.de/pub/special/atp
http://www.ee.mtu.edu/atp
```
± `listserv@vm1.nodak.edu` [body = `SUBSCRIBE ATP-EMTP` first-name last-name affiliation country-of-residence]
INFO `bamork@mtu.edu` (Bruce Mork)
ARCHIVE `listserv@vm1.nodak.edu` [body = `INDEX ATP-EMTP`]
Gated: `bit.listserv.ATP-EMTP`

9262   **aus.electronics**   Discussion of electronics. *Newsgroup*

9263   **Caltech Physics of Computation Laboratory Archive:** Primarily analog VLSI stuff, maintained by Carver Mead's laboratory at Caltech. It includes: Caltech VLSI design tools (analog, wol, until, view), analog VLSI scanners, archive of addresses, events and papers about analog VLSI.
```
http://www.pcmp.caltech.edu/
ftp://ftp.pcmp.caltech.edu/pub/
```
INFO `root@hobiecat.pcmp.caltech.edu`

9264   **can.vlsi**   Canadian group for discussion of Very Large Scale Integration (integrated circuit fabrication). *Newsgroup*

➤   **co.ocs:**   Discussion on optoelectronic computing at CU and CSU. *Newsgroup*

9265   **comp.lsi**   Large-scale integrated circuits. *Newsgroup*

9266   **comp.lsi.cad**   Electrical computer-aided design. *Newsgroup*

9267   **comp.lsi.testing**   Testing of electronic circuits. *Newsgroup*

9268   **comp.org.ieee**   Issues and announcements about the IEEE and its members. *Newsgroup*

9269   **ELTMAG-L:** Discussions on applied electromagnetism in Brazil. *Mailing List*
± `listproc@cpdee.ufmg.br` [body = `SUBSCRIBE ELTMAG-L` first-name last-name]
INFO `renato@cpdee.ufmg.br` (Renato Cardoso Mesquita)
Language: Portugese

9270   **fj.engr.control**   Topics about control system engineering. *Newsgroup*

9271   **fj.engr.elec**   Electrical and electronic engineering. *Newsgroup*

9272   **fj.org.ieee**   About Institute of Electrical and Electronics Engineers. *Newsgroup*

9273   **ieee.***   Newsgroups for members of the Institute of Electrical and Electronics Engineers. *Newsgroup*

9274   **ieee.eab.general**   Educational activities—general discussion. *Newsgroup*

9275   **ieee.pub.announce**   Publishing activities—announcements. *Newsgroup*

9276   **ieee.pub.general**   Publishing activities—general discussion. *Newsgroup*

9277   **ieee.rab.announce**   Regional Activities Board—announcements. *Newsgroup*

9278   **ieee.rab.general**   Regional Activities Board—general discussion. *Newsgroup*

9279   **ieee.region1**   Region 1 announcements. *Newsgroup*

9280   **ieee.stds.announce**   Standards Department—announcements. *Newsgroup*

9281   **ieee.stds.general**   Standards Department—general discussion. *Newsgroup*

9282   **ieee.tab.announce**   Technical Activities Board—announcements. *Newsgroup*

9283   **ieee.tab.general**   Technical Activities Board—general discussion. *Newsgroup*

9284   **ieee.tcos**   The Technical Committee on Operating Systems. *Moderated newsgroup*

9285   **mit.eecs.discuss**   Electrical engineering and computer science at MIT. *Newsgroup*

➤   **OPT-PROC:** On holography and optical computing. (See entry 9497 for full listing.)

➤ **OPTICS-L:** News on optics, electro-optics, and lasers in Israel. (See entry 9498 for full listing.)

➤ **Optoelectronic Computing Systems Laboratory at Colorado State University:** This site contains information on digital optical computing. It includes an archive of the lab's publications and technical reports on optical computing, plus GIFs from optical computing experiments. (See entry 2676 for full listing.)

➤ **RADIO-L:** On developing digital audio broadcasting (DAB) standards. (See entry 9636 for full listing.)

9286 `sci.electronics` Circuits, theory, electrons, and discussions. *Newsgroup*

9287 `sci.electronics.basics` Elementary questions about electronics. *Newsgroup*

9288 `sci.electronics.components` Integrated circuits, resistors, capacitors. *Newsgroup*

9289 `sci.electronics.design` Electronic circuit design. *Newsgroup*

9290 `sci.electronics.equipment` Test, lab, & industrial electronic products. *Newsgroup*

9291 `sci.electronics.misc` General discussions of the field of electronics. *Newsgroup*

9292 `sci.electronics.repair` Fixing electronic equipment. *Newsgroup*

9293 `sci.engr.control` The engineering of control systems. *Newsgroup*

9294 `sci.engr.semiconductors` Semiconductor devices, processes, materials, physics. *Newsgroup*

9295 `tnn.sys.arch` Discussions about computer architecture. *Newsgroup*

ENGINEERING—MECHANICAL & MATERIALS

9296 `fj.engr.materials` Topics about materials engineering. *Newsgroup*

9297 `fj.engr.mech` Topics about mechanical engineering. *Newsgroup*

9298 **Materials-L:** On teaching and research in materials science and engineering. *Mailing List*
± `listproc@liverpool.ac.uk` [body = SUBSCRIBE MATERIALS-L first-name last-name]
OWNER `materials-l-request@liverpool.ac.uk`

9299 **MECH-L:** On mechanical engineering. *Mailing List*
± `listserv@utarlvm1.uta.edu` [body = SUBSCRIBE MECH-L first-name last-name]
INFO `nomura@uta.edu` (S. Nomura)
ARCHIVE `listserv@utarlvm1.uta.edu` [body = INDEX MECH-L]

9300 `sci.engr.mech` The field of mechanical engineering. *Newsgroup*

9301 `sci.engr.metallurgy` Metallurgical engineering. *Newsgroup*

9302 `sci.materials` All aspects of materials engineering. *Newsgroup*

9303 `sci.materials.ceramics` Ceramic science. *Newsgroup*

9304 `sci.polymers` All aspects of polymer science. *Newsgroup*

ETHICS & SOCIETY

➤ `sci.philosophy.meta`: Discussions within the scope of "meta-philosophy". *Newsgroup*

GEOSCIENCE

➤ **The Life Page:** Large collection of biological, ecological, geographical, cultural heritage, and complex-systems information and services. (See entry 8949 for full listing.)

9305 **ACDGIS-L:** On Geographical Information Systems (GIS) and related technologies with focus on middle Europe. *Mailing List*
± `listserv@vm.akh-wien.ac.at` [body = SUBSCRIBE ACDGIS-L first-name last-name]
INFO `zoltan@wigeo.wu-wien.ac.at` (Zoltan Daroczi)

9306 `alt.aapg.announce` Announcements from the American Association of Petroleum Geologists. *Newsgroup*

9307 `alt.aapg.general` Discussion for the American Association of Petroleum Geologists. *Newsgroup*

9308 `alt.folklore.gemstones` Stories about minerals. *Newsgroup*

9309 `alt.mining.recreational` Digging rock as a hobby. *Newsgroup*

9310 **Astronomy and Earth Sciences Archive at Stanford:** Astronomy/earth science-oriented material for Unix users. Includes Earth topography data, the CIA World Map II vector outline database in a compressed binary Unix/C-readable format, software and data of interest for amateur astronomers, and information of general usefulness or interest for earth scientists. Also contains some generic utilities for Unix machines, including C source for a Morse code practice program for Unix machines.

     `ftp://sepftp.stanford.edu/pub`
     INFO `mihai@sep.stanford.edu` (Mihai Popovici)
     INFO `joe@sep.stanford.edu`

9311 `bit.listserv.uigis-l` User Interface for Geographical Info Systems. *Newsgroup*

9312 **Byrd Polar Research Center:** Information on the Arctic and Antarctic regions, including images and remote sensing data.

     `http://www-bprc.mps.ohio-state.edu/`
     INFO `timdavis+@osu.edu` (Tim Davis)

9313 **C14-L:** For technical discussion of radiocarbon and other radioisotope dating. *Mailing List*

     ± `listserv@listserv.arizona.edu` [body = SUBSCRIBE C14-L first-name last-name]
     OWNER `dsew@packrat.aml.arizona.edu` [body = SUBSCRIBE C14-L first-name last-name] (David Sewell)
     ARCHIVES
     `http://packrat.aml.arizona.edu/`
     `listserv@listserv.arizona.edu` [body = INDEX C14-L]

➤   `ca.environment.earthquakes:` Same as `ca.earthquakes`. *Newsgroup*

9314 **CLIMLIST:** For distribution of information to professionals in the field of climatology. *Digest & Reflector, moderated*

     ± INFO EDITOR OWNER `john.arnfield@osu.edu` (John Arnfield)
     ARCHIVE `listserv@psuvm.psu.edu` [body = SUBSCRIBE CLIMLIST first-name last-name]
     Please Note: Subscription by approval only.

9315 **COASTGIS:** On coastal and deep-ocean applications of geographical information systems (GIS)—to further the work of the International Geographical Union Commission on Coastal Systems. *Mailing List*

     ± INFO `stgg8004@iruccvax.ucc.ie` (Darius Bartlett)

9316 `comp.infosystems.gis` All aspects of Geographic Information Systems. *Newsgroup*

9317 **CONSGIS:** On biological conservation and geographical information systems. *Mailing List*

     ± `listserv@uriacc.uri.edu` [body = SUBSCRIBE CONSGIS first-name last-name]
     INFO `pete@edcserv.edc.uri.edu`
     ARCHIVE `listserv@uriacc.uri.edu`

9318 **CPGIS-L:** On Chinese geographic information systems. *Mailing List*

     ± `listserv@ubvm.cc.buffalo.edu` [body = SUBSCRIBE CPGIS-L first-name last-name]
     INFO `v096trqh@ubvms.bitnet` (Jieyuan Song)
     ARCHIVE `listserv@ubvm.cc.buffalo.edu`

9319 `fj.sci.geo` Discussion on earth and planetary sciences. *Newsgroup*

9320 **GEOGED:** On geography education. *Mailing List*

     ± `listserv@ukcc.uky.edu` [body = SUBSCRIBE GEOGED first-name last-name]
     INFO `jstayl0@ukcc.uky.edu` (Jon Taylor)

9321 **GEOGFEM:** On feminism in geography. *Mailing List*

     ± `listserv@ukcc.uky.edu` [body = SUBSCRIBE GEOGFEM first-name last-name]
     INFO OWNER `orfroe01@ukcc.uky.edu` (Oliver Froehling)

9322 **GeoGopher, UT El Paso, Department of Geological Sciences:** Gateway to earth science resources available on the Internet, hosted by the UTEP Department of Geological Sciences.

`gopher://geo.utep.edu`
INFO `montana@utep.edu`

9323 **GEOGRAPH:** For academic discussions concerning geographical matters. *Mailing List*
± `listserv@searn.sunet.se` [body = SUBSCRIBE GEOGRAPH first-name last-name]
INFO OWNER `mervi.pyyhtia@helsinki.fi` (Mervi Pyyhtia)
INFO `pellervo.kokkonen@helsinki.fi` (Pellervo Kokkonen)
ARCHIVE `listserv@searn.sunet.se` [body = INDEX GEOGRAPH]
Gated: `bit.listserv.geograph`

9324 **GEONET-L:** For geoscience librarians and information specialists, including problem reference questions, shared resources, and developments in publishing books, journals, and maps. *Mailing List*
`http://library.berkeley.edu/GIS`
± `listserv@iubvm.indiana.edu` [body = SUBSCRIBE GEONET-L first-name last-name]
INFO `heiser@indiana.edu` (Lois Heiser)

9325 **GEOPOL:** On political geography: conferences, books, data sets, jobs. *Mailing List*
± `listserv@ukcc.uky.edu` [body = SUBSCRIBE GEOPOL first-name last-name]
EDITOR `brunn@ukcc.uky.edu` (Stan Brunn)
OWNER `orfroe01@ukcc.uky.edu` (Oliver Froehling)

9326 **GEOSCI-JOBS:** For job postings in the geosciences. *Mailing List, moderated*
± `listproc@eskimo.com` [body = SUBSCRIBE GEOSCI-JOBS first-name last-name]
OWNER `ted.smith@mtnswest.com` (Ted Smith)
ARCHIVE `ftp://ftp.eskimo.com/u/t/tcsmith/geosci-jobs`

9327 **GLRC:** For researchers on scholarly or scientific topics related to the Great Lakes region of the U.S. *Mailing List, moderated*
± `listserv@suvm.acs.syr.edu` [body = SUBSCRIBE GLRC first-name last-name]
INFO `jpmanno@mailbox.syr.edu` (Jack Manno)
Please Note: Subscription by approval only.

9328 `han.sci.earth` Our planet, earth, geoscience and meteorology. *Newsgroup*

9329 **HimNet:** For geologists and/or geographers working in the Himalayas. *Mailing List, moderated*
`http://www.lehigh.edu/~inees/himnet/himnet.html`
OWNER `daspencer@erdw.ethz.ch` (Dr. David A. Spencer)
ARCHIVE `ftp://dharma.geo.lehigh.edu/Pub`

9330 **MAPS-L:** On maps, air photos, and GIS. For map librarians, cartographers, geographers, and people interested in maps and mapping information. *Mailing List, moderated*
± `listserv@uga.cc.uga.edu` [body = SUBSCRIBE MAPS-L first-name last-name]
INFO `jsutherl@uga.bitnet`
ARCHIVE `listserv@uga.cc.uga.edu` [body = INDEX MAPS-L]

9331 **MWTOPSEM:** For announcements of meetings of the Midwest Topology Seminar. *Mailing List*
± `listserv@vma.cc.nd.edu` [body = SUBSCRIBE MWTOPSEM first-name last-name]
INFO `taylor@laotse.helios.nd.edu` (Laurence Taylor)
ARCHIVE `listserv@vma.cc.nd.edu`

9332 **The New South Polar Times:** The New South Polar Times is a newsletter written by one of the staff at the Admundsen-Scott South Pole Station, South Pole, Antarctica. *Newsletter*
`http://139.132.40.31/NSPT/NSPThomePage.html`
± `listserv@vm1.spcs.umn.edu` [body = SUBSCRIBE NSPT-SP first-name last-name]
ARCHIVE `http://139.132.40.31/NSPT/NSPThomePage.html`

9333 **On-line Resources for Earth Scientists (ORES):** Earth-science resources, including digital documents, news sources, software, data sets, and public online services. Subjects include the environment, forestry, geography, geology, geophysics, GIS, GPS, geodesy, mapping, paleontology, remote sensing, space, meteorology, wildlife, and jobs in earth sciences.

```
http://www.gisnet.com/gis/
ftp://ftp.csn.org/COGS/ores.txt
ftp://una.hh.lib.umich.edu/inetdirsstacks/earthsci:thoen
gopher://una.hh.lib.umich.edu/inetdirs/
```

INFO bthoen@gisnet.com (Bill Thoen)

9334 **QUAKE-L:** On earthquakes. *Digest & Reflector*

± listserv@vm1.nodak.edu [body = SUBSCRIBE QUAKE-L first-name last-name]

INFO OWNER hoag@plains.nodak.edu (Marty Hoag)

ARCHIVE listserv@vm1.nodak.edu

9335 `relcom.comp.gis` Geographical information systems. *Newsgroup*

➤ **rockhounds:** For gem and mineral collectors. (See entry 6303 for full listing.)

9336 **Samizdat Press:** Samizdat Press is devoted to the free distribution of books and lecture notes via the Internet. The current focus of the press is geophysics, but it will be expanding.

```
http://www.cwp.mines.edu/
http://landau.mines.edu/~samizdat
```

INFO jscales@mines.edu

INFO samizdat@landau.mines.edu

➤ **Satellite Imagery of Southern Ontario and Africa:** Sample satellite imagery of Southern Ontario and Africa, with additional imagery from other countries being added. (See entry 4638 for full listing.)

9337 `sci.engr.geomechanics` Geomechanics issues and related topics. *Newsgroup*

9338 `sci.engr.surveying` Measurement and mapping of the earth surface. *Newsgroup*

9339 `sci.geo.earthquakes` For discussion of earthquakes and related matters. *Newsgroup*

9340 `sci.geo.eos` NASA's Earth Observation System (EOS). *Newsgroup*

9341 `sci.geo.fluids` Discussion of geophysical fluid dynamics. *Newsgroup*

9342 `sci.geo.geology` Discussion of solid earth sciences. *Newsgroup*

9343 `sci.geo.hydrology` Surface and groundwater hydrology. *Newsgroup*

9344 `sci.geo.petroleum` All aspects of petroleum and the petroleum industry. *Newsgroup*

9345 `sci.geo.satellite-nav` Satellite navigation systems, especially GPS. *Newsgroup*

9346 **teprints:** Topology Eprints: reprints of abstracts of recent results in topology. *Distribution List, moderated*

```
http://www.math.ufl.edu/~teprints/teprints.html
```

± **INFO** teprints@math.ufl.edu

Please Note: Subscription by approval only.

9347 **USGS National Marine and Coastal Geology Program:** This site provides scientific data and mapping information, primarily of marine geology and geophysics, for the geological, geophysical, and oceanographic reseach community. It includes a form where you can ask a geologist any earth-science questions you might have.

```
http://marine.usgs.gov/
```

INFO jrobb@nobska.er.usgs.gov (James Robb)

MIRROR http://bramble.er.usgs.gov/

9348 **VOLCANO:** On volcanology, the study of volcanoes. Also includes daily, weekly, and monthly updates about volcanic eruptions provided by the Smithsonian Institution's Global Volcanism Network, and by a variety of volcano observatories around the world. *Mailing List, moderated*

± listserv@asuvm.inre.asu.edu [body = SUBSCRIBE VOLCANO first-name last-name]

INFO jon.fink@asu.edu (Jon Fink)

Please Note: Subscription by approval only.

HISTORY OF SCIENCE

➤ <u>University of California Museum of Paleontology:</u> Online exhibits and collections databases from the University of California Museum of Paleontology, the fourth largest paleontological museum in the United States. Also includes information on geology, phylogeny, or evolutionary biology and the history of science. (See entry 9451 for full listing.)

➤ **AIP History of Physics Newsletter:** Reports activities of the Center and its Niels Bohr Library, and other information on work in the history of physics and allied sciences. (See entry 9454 for full listing.)

9349 `alt.folklore.science` The folklore of science, not the science of folklore. *Newsgroup*

9350 **The Galileo Project:** A hypertext guide to the life and work of Galileo Galilei.
`http://www.rice.edu/Galileo`
INFO `galileo@rice.edu`

➤ **HOPOS-L:** On the history of the philosophy of science. (See entry 5332 for full listing.)

9351 **HPSST-L:** On the history and philosophy of science and science teaching. *Mailing List*
± `listserv@qucdn.queensu.ca` [body = SUBSCRIBE HPSST-L first-name last-name]
INFO `hillss@qucdn.bitnet` (Skip Hills)
INFO `farquhad@qucdn.bitnet` (Doug Farquhar)
ARCHIVE `listserv@qucdn.queensu.ca`

➤ **HTECH-L:** On the history of technology. (See entry 5251 for full listing.)

9352 **MEDSCI-L:** On medieval and Renaissance science. *Mailing List*
± `listserv@brownvm.brown.edu` [body = SUBSCRIBE MEDSCI-L first-name last-name]
INFO `st001424@brownvm.bitnet`
INFO OWNER `brandon@gauss.math.brown.edu` (Joshua Brandon)
ARCHIVE `listserv@brownvm.brown.edu`

9353 `soc.history.science` History of science and related areas. *Newsgroup*

HUMOR

9354 **HotAIR - home page of The Annals of Improbable Research (AIR):** The excitingly graphical and trendoid home page of the Annals of Improbable Research (AIR).
`http://www.improb.com/`
INFO `air@improb.com`
INFO `ringo@leland.stanford.edu`
Comments: AIR also produces and distributes mini-AIR, a monthly e-mail suppliment to AIR.

9355 **Science Jokes:** Poking fun at mathematics, chemistry, biology, and more.
`http://www.princeton.edu/~pemayer/ScienceJokes.html`
INFO `mayer@wagner.princeton.edu`

INDUSTRIAL DESIGN

9356 **COLORING:** On the coloring of paints, plastics, fabrics, inks, ceramics, and other material. *Mailing List, moderated*
OWNER `wmdawes@infi.net` (William Dawes)
ARCHIVE `http://www.infi.net/~wmdawes/coloring/index.html`

9357 **IDFORUM:** On industrial/product design and design education. *Mailing List*
± `listserv@yorku.ca` [body = SUBSCRIBE IDFORUM first-name last-name]
INFO `gl250267@venus.yorku.ca` (Maurice Barnwell)

➤ **NDDESIGN:** For graphic and industrial design educators. (See entry 294 for full listing.)

INFORMATION TECHNOLOGY

➤   <u>**CAUSE:**</u> CAUSE is the association for managing and using information resources in higher education. CAUSE is a source of information and professional development opportunities for those who plan for, implement, and manage information resources on campus. (See entry 4478 for full listing.)

9358   **ACTLab (Advanced Communication Technologies Laboratory):** Information on issues of human-computer interfaces, interaction, and agency.

     `http://www.actlab.utexas.edu/`
     `ftp://ftp.actlab.utexas.edu`
     `gopher://gopher.actlab.utexas.edu`
     INFO `support@actlab.utexas.edu`
     INFO `captain@actlab.utexas.edu`
     INFO `gopher@actlab.utexas.edu`
     INFO `webmaster@actlab.utexas.edu`

9359   `comp.infosystems`   Any discussion about information systems. *Newsgroup*

9360   `comp.infosystems.kiosks`   Informational and transactional kiosks. *Moderated newsgroup*

9361   **d.Comm:** An Internet-only magazine for network managers and other IT staff. The magazine covers all aspects of information technology from the PC on your desk to networking to communications. *Magazine*

     `http://www.d-comm.com/`
     EDITOR `eddieh@d-comm.com` (Eddie Hold)

9362   **Department of Defense (DoD) Information Analysis Center (IAC) Hub Page:** The purpose of this site is to provide access to information produced by and about the DoD IACs that may be appropriate to the requirements of sponsoring technical communities.

     `http://www.dtic.mil/iac/`
     INFO `iac@dtic.mil`

➤   **DIGLIB:** On the issues and techologies of digital libraries. (See entry 5739 for full listing.)

9363   **Edupage:** Summary of information-technology news. *Newsletter*

     ± `listproc@educom.edu` [body = SUBSCRIBE EDUPAGE first-name last-name]
     INFO EDITOR `comments@educom.edu` (John Gehl, Editor)
     ARCHIVES
     `gopher://educom.edu`
     `http://educom.edu/`
     Frequency: three times a week

     Translations available in Bulgarian, Estonian, French, German, Hungarian, Italian, Portuguese, Spanish, and Vietnamese

9364   **ENET-L:** For educators and researchers interested in information technology. *Mailing List*

     ± `listserv@uhccvm.uhcc.hawaii.edu`
     OWNER `daniel@uhunix.uhcc.hawaii.edu` (Daniel Blaine)

9365   **German National Research Center for Information Technology (GMD):** Home page of GMD, an institute that does research in many branches of information technology.

     `gopher://gopher.gmd.de`
     INFO `web-editors@gmd.de`

9366   **GTRTI-L:** On research and teaching in global information technology. *Mailing List*

     ± `listserv@gsuvml.gsu.edu` [body = SUBSCRIBE GTRTI-L first-name last-name]
     INFO `strouble@acad.udallas.edu` (Dennis Strouble)
     ARCHIVE `listserv@gsuvml.gsu.edu`

➤   **IFIP82-L:** On social and organizational factors implied by information technology and information systems. (See entry 3725 for full listing.)

9367   **INFOMART Magazine:** Discusses hot topics for the information systems industry such as client/server, multimedia, ATM, and networking. *E-journal*

```
http://www.infomartusa.com/
```
INFO `benesh@onramp.net` (Bruce Benesh)
Frequency: quarterly

9368 **IR-LIST Digest:** Information retrieval theory and technology—contains queries, meeting/publication announcements, job listings, conference proceedings, bibliographies, dissertation abstracts, and more. *Digest, moderated*
```
http://www.dcs.gla.ac.uk/scripts/global/wais/ir_list_form
```
INFO EDITOR `ncg@dla.ucop.edu` (Nancy Gusack)
ARCHIVE `ftp://dla.ucop.edu/pub/IRL/`
Frequency: weekly

LIBRARY

9369 **STS-L:** On science and technology libraries. *Mailing List, moderated*
± `listserv@utkvm1.utk.edu` [body = SUBSCRIBE STS-L first-name last-name]

9370 **STS Signal:** Newsletter of the Science and Technology Section (STS) of the Association of College and Research Libraries. Distributed through the STS-L electronic discussion group. *Newsletter*
± `listserv@utkvm1.utk.edu` [body = SUBSCRIBE STS-L first-name last-name]
INFO `gsbaker@utk.edu` (Gayle Baker)
Frequency: twice a year (May, November)

MATHEMATICS

9371 **Centre for Experimental and Constructive Mathematics (CECM):** Collection of Internet resources and tools for mathematics and computers.
```
http://www.cecm.sfu.ca/
gopher://gopher.cecm.sfu.ca
```
INFO `www@cecm.sfu.ca`
INFO `cecm@cecm.sfu.ca`
FAQ `http://www.cecm.sfu.ca/cecm_info/`

➤ **The Math Forum:** The Math Forum is home to Ask Dr. Math, MathMagic, the Internet Math Resource Collection, Problem of the Week/Project of the Month, public forums, the Geometry Forum, and many other projects coordinated in a virtual center for math education on the Internet. Your one-stop shop for math classroom resources on the World Wide Web. (See entry 4276 for full listing.)

9372 **Mathematics Information Servers:** A comprehensive list of mathematics resources on the Internet.
```
http://www.math.psu.edu/MathLists/Contents.html
```
INFO `webmaster@math.psu.edu`
MIRRORS
```
http://dan-emir.euromath.dk/OtherMath.html
```
(Denmark)
```
http://www.emis.de/
```
(Germany)

9373 **Netlib:** A collection of mathematical software, papers, and databases.
```
http://www.netlib.org/
ftp://ftp.netlib.org
gopher://gopher.netlib.org
netlib@netlib.org [body = send index]
```
INFO `netlib_maintainers@netlib.org`
FAQ `http://www.netlib.org/netlib/netlib_faq.html`
MIRRORS
```
http://www.hensa.ac.uk/ftp/mirrors/netlib/master/
```
(England)
```
http://www.netlib.no/
```
(Norway)
```
ftp://draci.cs.uow.edu.au/netlib/
```
(Australia)

`http://elib.zib-berlin.de/netlib/master/readme.html` (Germany)
`http://netlib.att.com/` (New Jersey)
`http://www.netlib.org/` (Tennessee)

9374 Acta Mathematica Universatis Comenianae: This journal is an electronic version of *Acta Mathematica Universitatis Comenianae*. It contains scientific research papers in pure and applied mathematics and related topics. *E-Journal*

`gopher://center.fmph.uniba.sk`

`ftp://ftp.fmph.uniba.sk/amuc/_html/`

`http://www.uniba.sk/amuc/_amuc.html`

± `http://www.uniba.sk/amuc/_sub.html`

INFO OWNER `amuc@fmph.uniba.sk`

EDITOR `siran@cvt.stuba.sk`

ARCHIVES

`ftp://ftp.fmph.uniba.sk/amuc/_html/`
`http://www.uniba.sk/amuc/_amuc.html`

Frequency: semiannual

9375 `alt.math.iams` Internet Amateur Mathematics Society. *Moderated newsgroup*

9376 AMATH-IL: Notices of seminars and other information pertinent to applied mathematics at Tel Aviv University. *Mailing List*

± `listserv@taunivm.tau.ac.il` [body = SUBSCRIBE AMATH-IL first-name last-name]

INFO `turkel@math.tau.ac.il` (Eli Turkel)

9377 Archivum Mathematicum: This is the electronic version of Archivum Mathematicum (Brno).

`http://www.emis.de/journals/AM/index.html`

`ftp://ftp.emis.de/journals/AM/`

INFO `janyska@math.muni.cz` (Josef Janyska)

Comments: Archivum Mathematicum is part of the Electronic Library of the European Mathematical Society. Mirror servers exist in several countries—please look at the EMIS home page (`http://www.emis.de/`) for the actual list.

9378 AT-NET: On approximation theory (mathematics), a monthly bulletin. *Mailing List, moderated*

± `listproc@gauss.technion.ac.il` [body = SUBSCRIBE AT-NET first-name last-name]

OWNER `approx@gauss.technion.ac.il` (Allan Pinkus)

9379 `aus.mathematics` Mathematics research in Australasia. *Newsgroup*

9380 Banach Space Theory Papers Index: Index of archive of papers on Banach Space Theory.

`gopher://math.okstate.edu`

`wais://math.okstate.edu/banach.src`

INFO `banach-owner@math.okstate.edu`

➤ **BEATCALC:** For mental math exercises. (See entry 6550 for full listing.)

9381 Cellular-Automata: On cellular automata and lattice gases, including theory, applications, and available software packages. *Mailing List*

± `majordomo@physics.bu.edu` [body = subscribe cellular-automata]

INFO `bruceb@bu.edu` (Bruce Boghosian)

Gated: `comp.theory.cell-automata`

9382 Concurrency Modeling: Papers (LaTeX source and DVI) on modeling concurrent behavior written by members of the Boole Group, c/o Prof. Vaughan Pratt, Computer Science Department, Stanford University.

`ftp://boole.stanford.edu`

INFO `pratt@cs.stanford.edu`

Comments: Almost all papers are stored in their TeX, DVI, and PostScript forms, in the respective directories `/pub/TEX`, `/pub/DVI`, and `/pub`. All are compressed using gzip and hence all must be retrieved using binary mode. For example the paper "jelia" appears three times, as `/pub/TEX/jelia.tex.gz`,

`/pub/DVI/jelia.dvi.gz`, and `/pub/jelia.ps.gz`. The PostScript versions are placed at the top (`/pub`) level for convenience on the assumption that PostScript viewers are more widely available than either DVI viewers or LaTeX. U.S. 8.5"x11" letter size is assumed rather than A4.

9383 **DMANET:** On the mathematical analysis of discrete structures and the design of discrete algorithms and their applications in operations research, computer science, and engineering. *Newsletter*

± **POST** `dmanet@math.utwente.nl`

INFO `u.faigle@math.utwente.nl` (Ulrich Faigle)

ARCHIVE `listserv@hearn.nic.surfnet.nl`

9384 **e-MATH:** This is the American Mathematical Society's World Wide Web site. It serves as a gateway to subscription-based products and free services·offered by the AMS for the mathematics community. It includes content-searching electronic journals in mathematics, a preprint server, employment information, access to AMS-TeX macros and fonts, and more.

`http://www.ams.org/`

INFO `ams@ams.org`

9385 **Electronic Journal of Combinatorics:** A refereed journal of discrete mathematics that welcomes submissions of papers in all branches of combinatorics, graph theory, discrete algorithms, etc. *E-Journal, moderated*

`ftp://ftp.math.gatech.edu/pub/ejc/Journal`

`gopher://ejc.math.gatech.edu:8081`

`http://ejc.math.gatech.edu:8080/Journal/journalhome.html`

± `calkin@math.gatech.ed`

INFO `calkin@math.gatech.edu` (Neil Calkin)

ARCHIVES

`ftp://ftp.math.gatech.edu/pub/ejc/Journal`

`gopher://ejc.math.gatech.edu:8081`

`http://ejc.math.gatech.edu:8080/Journal/journalhome.html`

Frequency: about twice monthly

9386 **Electronic Journal of Differential Equations (EJDE):** Dedicated to the rapid dissemination of original, high-quality research in all aspects of differential and integral equations. *E-Journal, moderated*

`ftp://ftp@ejde.math.swt.edu/pub/`

`gopher://ejde.math.swt.edu`

`telnet://ejde@ejde.math.swt.edu`

`http://ejde.math.swt.edu/`

± `subs@ejde.math.swt.edu`

INFO EDITOR `editor@ejde.math.unt.edu` (Alfonso Castro)

Frequency: irregular

9387 **European Mathematical Information Service:** This site is the information system of the European Mathematical Society (EMS). It includes the Electronic Library of the EMS (ELibEMS)—a collection of electronic journals and conference proceedings, information about the EMS, information on happenings in the field of mathematics, and science-related information from Brussels.

`http://www.emis.de/`

`ftp://ftp.emis.de/`

`gopher://gopher.emis.de/`

INFO `wegner@math.tu-berlin.de` (B. Wegner)

INFO `jo@zblmath.fiz-karlsruhe.de` (M. Jost)

MIRRORS

`http://cirm.univ-mrs.fr/EMIS/` (Marseille)

`http://www.maths.soton.ac.uk/EMIS/` (Southampton)

`http://alf1.cc.fc.ul.pt/EMIS/` (Lisboa)

9388 `fj.sci.math` Mathematical discussions and pursuits. *Newsgroup*

9389 GRAPHNET: For discussions of graph theory by mathematicians, including Hamiltonian problems, extremal graph theory, coloring problems, factorization, and enumeration problems. Also for announcements concerning graph theory. *Mailing List*

± `listserv@vm1.nodak.edu` [body = SUBSCRIBE GRAPHNET first-name last-name]

INFO `shreve@plains.nodak.edu` (Warren Shreve)

ARCHIVE `listserv@vm1.nodak.edu`

Gated: `bit.listserv.graphnet`

9390 Impulsiv: A German e-journal on math, physics, and computer science. Entertaining. *E-Journal*

`http://www.fachschaften.tu-muenchen.de/FSMPI/Impulsiv/index.html`

± `http://www.informatik.tu-muenchen.de/cgi-bin/nph-gateway/hp3/~impulsiv/`

INFO OWNER `impulsiv@fachschaften.tu-muenchen.de`

INFO OWNER `fsmpi@fachschaften.tu-muenchen.de` (Stefan Zehl)

Language: German

Frequency: irregular (approx. 4 times a year)

9391 MATHDEP: For notices on mathematical science seminars in Ireland, and mathematics with some Irish connection. *Mailing List*

INFO `wsulivan@irlearn.ucd.ie` (UCD Maths Department)

9392 MAW-LIST: On Mathematics Awareness Week, April 21-27. The 1996 topic is "Mathematics and Decision Making." *Mailing List*

± `majordomo@maa.org` [body = SUBSCRIBE MAW-LIST]

INFO `kholmay@nas.edu` (Kathleen Holmay)

OWNER `rickey@falcon.bgsu.edu` (Fred Rickey)

POST `maw-list@maa.org`

9393 MCRIT-L: On multi-criteria analysis, a discipline that helps to formulate decisions in the face of (sometimes) conflicting criteria. *Mailing List*

± `listserv@hearn.nic.surfnet.nl` [body = SUBSCRIBE MCRIT-L first-name last-name]

INFO `mcrit@sjaan.fbk.eur.nl`

9394 MIDWPDE: Information on the Midwest Partial Differential Equations Seminar, a semiannual meeting on recent developments in partial differential equations. *Mailing List*

± `listserv@uicvm.uic.edu` [body = SUBSCRIBE MIDWPDE first-name last-name]

INFO `midwpde-request@uicvm.uic.edu`

ARCHIVE `listserv@uicvm.uic.edu` [body = INDEX MIDWPDE]

9395 Morphology Digest: The Morphology Digest is an electronic newsletter for workers in the field of mathematical morphology, stochastic geometry, random set theory, image algebra, etc. *Newsletter*

`http://www.cwi.nl/projects/morphology/`

± `morpho@cwi.nl` [subject = subscribe]

INFO `henkh@cwi.nl` (Henk Heijmans)

ARCHIVES

`http://www.cwi.nl/projects/morphology/`
`ftp://ftp.cwi.nl/pub/morphology/digest`

Frequency: about every six weeks

9396 PDG: On game theory, especially Prisoner's Dilemma-type problems. *Mailing List*

± `majordomo@ifi.uio.no` [body = subscribe pdg]

INFO OWNER `thomasg@ifi.uio.no` (Thomas Gramstad)

FAQ `majordomo@ifi.uio.no` [body = info pdg]

➤ **PSYSTS-L:** On statistical techniques used in psychology, with particular emphasis on multiple regression, path analysis, structural equation modeling, factor analysis, and configural frequency analysis. (See entry 9528 for full listing.)

➤ **QNTEVA-L:** On the theory and design of quantitative methods to evaluate social, educational, psychological, and other forms of programs and policies. (See entry 5364 for full listing.)

9397 **SAMATH:** For the Saudi Association for Mathematical Sciences. *Mailing List*

± `listserv@saksu00.bitnet` [body = SUBSCRIBE SAMATH first-name last-name]

INFO OWNER `f40m001@saksu00.bitnet` (Dr. Omar Hamed)

➤ `sci.crypt`: Different methods of data en/decryption. *Newsgroup*

➤ `sci.crypt.research`: Cryptography, cryptanalysis, and related issues. *Moderated newsgroup*

➤ `sci.logic`: Logic—math, philosophy, and computational aspects. *Newsgroup*

9398 `sci.math` Mathematical discussions and pursuits. *Newsgroup*

9399 `sci.math.research` Discussion of current mathematical research. *Moderated newsgroup*

➤ **Society for Mathematical Biology Digest:** From the Society for Mathematical Biology. Containing items of current interest submitted by readers, including scientific queries, announcements of publications, meetings and job opportunities, news items, etc. (See entry 9021 for full listing.)

9400 **Society for Industrial and Applied Mathematics (SIAM) Gopher Server:** An electronic magazine and information service of the Society for Industrial and Applied Mathematics. It includes an online book catalog, employment information, mathematics TeX information, and more.

`http://www.siam.org/`

INFO `gray@siam.org`

9401 **TECHMATH:** About mathematical activity in Israel. *Mailing List, moderated*

± `listproc@gauss.technion.ac.il` [body = SUBSCRIBE TECHMATH first-name last-name]

OWNER `hershkow@techunix.technion.ac.il` (Danny Hershkowitz)

ARCHIVE `listproc@gauss.technion.ac.il`

9402 **Theory and Applications of Categories:** Peer-reviewed electronic journal on category theory. *E-Journal*

`http://www.tac.mta.ca/tac/`

± `tac@mta.ca`

± `ftp://ftp.tac.mta.ca/pub/tac/`

INFO OWNER `rrosebrugh@mta.ca` (Robert Rosebrugh)

ARCHIVE `ftp://ftp.tac.mta.ca/pub/tac/volumes`

Language: English abstracts required

Frequency: irregular

9403 `tnn.math` Discussions about mathematics. *Newsgroup*

9404 **University of South Carolina Department of Mathematics:** A multi-topic information service hosted at the University of South Carolina's Department of Mathematics in Columbia, South Carolina. It includes information on wavelet-related mathematical materials and archives of *Wavelet Digest*.

`http://www.math.sc.edu/`

INFO `mathwww@math.sc.edu`

9405 **University of Southampton Faculty of Mathematical Studies:** This gopher is designed to provide a resource for the faculty of mathematical studies at Southampton University.

`gopher://gopher.maths.soton.ac.uk`

INFO `jhr@mir.maths.soton.ac.uk`

9406 **University of Southampton, Faculty of Mathematical Studies:** The WWW server for the faculty of mathematical studies, University of Southampton, England.

`http://www.maths.soton.ac.uk/homepage.html`

INFO `enquiry@maths.soton.ac.uk`

MATHEMATICS—ALGEBRA

9407 **AXIOM:** Information about and resources for users of the AXIOM Computer Algebra System, published by Numerical Algorithms Group, Ltd. (NAG), running on a range of workstations and personal computers.

http://www.nag.co.uk:70/symbolic/AX.html

INFO infodesk@nag.co.uk

Comments: Some areas of the bulletin board are only accessible to AXIOM developers or users who have purchased support.

9408 **Contributions to Algebra and Geometry:** Research articles on algebra, geometry, algebraic geometry, and related fields. *E-journal*

http://www.zblmath.fiz-karlsruhe.de/e-journals/BAG/index.html

INFO wegner@math.tu-berlin.de (B. Wegner)

Frequency: twice a year

9409 **Journal of Lie Theory:** Journal of Lie Theory is a journal for speedy publication of information in the following areas: Lie algebras, Lie groups, algebraic groups, and related types of topological groups such as locally compact and compact groups. Applications to representation theory, differential geometry, geometric control theory, theoretical physics, and quantum groups are considered as well. The principal subject-matter areas according to the Mathematics Subject Classification are 14Lxx, 17Bxx, 22Bxx, 22Cxx, 22Dxx, 22Exx, 53Cxx, and 81Rxx.

http://www.emis.de/journals/JLT/

ftp://ftp.emis.de/pub/EMIS/journals/JLT/

INFO hofmann@mathematik.th-darmstadt.de (Prof. Dr. Karl H. Hofmann)

INFO jo@zblmath.fiz-karlsruhe.de (M. Jost)

MIRRORS

http://www.maths.soton.ac.uk/EMIS/ljournals/JLT/

http://alf1.cc.fc.ul.pt/EMIS/journals/JLT/

http://cirm.univ-mrs.fr/EMIS/journals/JLT/

Comments: The journal's ISSN is 0940-2268 and the Electronic Edition Managing Editor is K. H. Hofmann (Darmstadt)

9410 **sci.math.symbolic** Symbolic algebra discussion. *Newsgroup*

MATHEMATICS—GEOMETRY

➤ **Contributions to Algebra and Geometry:** Research articles on algebra, geometry, algebraic geometry, and related fields. (See entry 9408 for full listing.)

9411 **geometry.announcements** Geometry Announcements. *Newsgroup*

➤ **geometry.college:** Geometry at the College Level. *Newsgroup*

9412 **geometry.forum** Geometry Forum Discussion and Information. *Newsgroup*

9413 **geometry.institutes** Institutes for Geometry Study. *Newsgroup*

➤ **geometry.pre-college:** Geometry for Secondary Education. *Newsgroup*

9414 **geometry.puzzles** Recreational Geometry Problems. *Newsgroup*

9415 **geometry.research** Geometry Research. *Newsgroup*

9416 **geometry.software.dynamic** Discussion of Dynamic Geometry Software. *Newsgroup*

MATHEMATICS—NUMERICAL ANALYSIS

9417 **NA-net:** Numerical analysis discussions. *Mailing List*

http://www.netlib.org/na-net/na_home.html

± na.join@na-net.ornl.gov [body = Firstname: your-first-name /Lastname: your-last-name /Email: your-e-mail-address (please note that each of these must be on a separate line)]

INFO na.help@na-net.ornl.gov (infobot)

OWNER dongarra@cs.utk.edu (Jack Dongarra)

9418 `sci.math.num-analysis` Numerical analysis. *Newsgroup*

MATHEMATICS—SOFTWARE

➤ <u>Centre for Experimental and Constructive Mathematics (CECM):</u> Collection of Internet resources and tools for mathematics and computers. (See entry 9371 for full listing.)

➤ <u>Netlib:</u> A collection of mathematical software, papers, and databases. (See entry 9373 for full listing.)

➤ <u>Cellular-Automata:</u> On cellular automata and lattice gases, including theory, applications, and available software packages. (See entry 9381 for full listing.)

9419 `comp.soft-sys.math.mathematica` Mathematica discussion group. *Moderated newsgroup*

9420 `comp.soft-sys.matlab` The MathWorks calculation and visualization package. *Newsgroup*

➤ `geometry.software.dynamic:` Discussion of Dynamic Geometry Software. *Newsgroup*

9421 **Mathematica World:** An online Mathematica user service. Mathematica World encourages users to develop their skill and expand their use of Mathematica.

`http://www.wri.com/MW/`

INFO `mw_forward@wri.com` (Dr. Stephen Hunt)

Frequency: monthly

Price: varies by subscription type

➤ **National Institute of Standards & Technology (NIST):** Information about NIST programs, products, and activities. The site includes GAMS (Guide to Available Mathematical Software) and a computer security bulletin board. (See entry 5520 for full listing.)

➤ **RS1-L:** For users of RS/1, a research and data-analysis software package running on VMS, Unix, and MS-DOS. (See entry 9558 for full listing.)

9422 **THEORIST:** For users of the Theorist math software program. *Mailing List*

± `majordomo@presby.edu` [body = SUBSCRIBE THEORIST]

INFO `jtbell@presby.edu`

ARCHIVE `majordomo@presby.edu`

MATHEMATICS—STATISTICS & PROBABILITY

➤ **The Chance Project:** Database and information on a course for teaching probability and statistics. (See entry 4299 for full listing.)

9423 `comp.soft-sys.sas` The SAS statistics package. *Newsgroup*

9424 `comp.soft-sys.spss` The SPSS statistics package. *Newsgroup*

9425 **Electronic Journal of Probability:** For high-quality research articles in all areas of probability. Sister publication to Electronic Communications in Probability, which publishes survey articles, research announcements, and short notes. *E-journal*

INFO `ejpecp@math.washington.edu`

INFO `jose@math.duke.edu` (Greg Lawler)

INFO `rcarmona@princeton.edu` (René Carmona)

INFO `burdzy@math.washington.edu` (Chris Burdzy)

ARCHIVE `http://www.math.washington.edu/~ejpecp/`

Frequency: irregular (articles posted as soon as they are accepted)

9426 **A Guide to Statistical Computing Resources on the Internet:** Listing of the most valuable and useful resources pertinent to statistical computing. It includes: resources dealing specifically with two of the most commonly used statistical packages, SAS and SPSS; information resources related to statistical computing in general, including such statistical packages as BMDP, S, and LISREL; and information resources on statistics in general.

`http://asa.ugl.lib.umich.edu/chdocs/statistics/stat_guide_home.html`

`ftp://una.hh.lib.umich.edu/inetdirsstacks/statistics:varnweise`

`gopher://una.hh.lib.umich.edu/00/inetdirsstacks/statistics:varnweise`

INFO `stat-guide@umich.edu` (Ken Varnum & John Weise)

➤ **PSYSTS-L:** On statistical techniques used in psychology, with particular emphasis on multiple regression, path analysis, structural equation modeling, factor analysis, and configural frequency analysis. (See entry 9528 for full listing.)

➤ **QUANHIST.RECURRENT:** On comparative approaches to history and economic history. (See entry 5208 for full listing.)

9427 **SAS-L:** On SAS, a statistical analysis package. *Mailing List*

± `listserv@vm.marist.edu` [body = SUBSCRIBE SAS-L first-name last-name]

± `listserv@uga.cc.uga.edu` [body = SUBSCRIBE SAS-L first-name last-name]

± `listserv@vm.akh-wien.ac.at` [body = SUBSCRIBE SAS-L first-name last-name]

INFO `harold@uga.cc.uga.edu` (Harold Pritchett)

INFO `harry@marist.edu` (A. Harry Williams)

ARCHIVES

`listserv@vm.marist.edu` [body = INDEX SAS-L]

`listserv@uga.cc.uga.edu` [body = INDEX SAS-L]

Gated: `bit.listserv.sas-l`

➤ **SASPAC-L:** For users of the SAS software package to access census and other public data files. (See entry 5365 for full listing.)

9428 `sci.stat.consult` Statistical consulting. *Newsgroup*

➤ `sci.stat.edu:` Statistics education. *Newsgroup*

9429 `sci.stat.math` Statistics from a strictly mathematical viewpoint. *Newsgroup*

9430 **StatLib:** StatLib is an archive of statistical software, data sets, and general information. The archive contains macros for statistical packages, complete statistical systems, subroutine libraries, and a large collection of useful data sets.

`http://lib.stat.cmu.edu/`

`ftp://lib.stat.cmu.edu`

`gopher://lib.stat.cmu.edu`

INFO `mikem@stat.cmu.edu`

MUSEUMS & EXHIBITS

➤ **ARGUS-L:** For users of ARGUS, a Unix-based collections-management system used in art, ethnographic, and natural history museums. (See entry 720 for full listing.)

9431 **The Chicago Academy of Sciences:** Founded in 1857, the Chicago Academy of Sciences is dedicated to increasing the understanding and appreciation of science through exhibits and educational programs that focus on the natural environment. This site contains pertinent information related to the Nature Museum, exhibits, and educational programs.

`http://www.chias.org/`

INFO `cas@chias.org`

➤ **CIDOC-L:** On documentation and information management at museums. (See entry 721 for full listing.)

9432 `dc.smithsonian` Smithsonian Institute-related events in the Washington, D.C. area. *Newsgroup*

➤ **Exploratorium:** A collection of 650 interactive exhibits in the areas of science, art, and human perception. (See entry 4301 for full listing.)

➤ **Los Alamos National Laboratory:** This is the central information server for the Los Alamos National Laboratory, located in Los Alamos, New Mexico. (See entry 9550 for full listing.)

➤ **Mark Dewell's Railway Preservation Pages:** A guide to all preserved railways, locomotives, societies, and museums in the U.K. The guide includes full timetables and details of special events on the railways featured. An online database of preserved railway locomotives is also available. (See entry 6644 for full listing.)

➤ **Museum-L:** Discussion group about museums. (See entry 724 for full listing.)

➤ **The Smithsonian Institution:** Online guide and tour to the museums and programs of the Smithsonian Institution in Washington, D.C. (See entry 725 for full listing.)

➤ **UVa Computer Science Museum:** This page contains a growing collection of historical computers and computer-related artifacts. (See entry 9209 for full listing.)

NANOTECHNOLOGY

9433 **Nanotechnology on the WWW:** The Web page includes a list of Internet resources (e.g., Web sites, mailing lists, electronic journals) on nanotechnology and related subjects (such as molecular modeling and nanoscopy). "Nanotechnology is a (projected) technology of design and fabrication of mechanisms at the molecular level."

`http://www.lucifer.com/~sean/Nano.html`

INFO `sean@lucifer.com` (Sean Morgan)

MIRROR `http://galaxy.einet.net/galaxy/Engineering-and-Technology/Mechanical-Engineering/Nanotechnology/Nano.html`

9434 `sci.nanotech` Self-reproducing molecular-scale machines. *Moderated newsgroup*

NEWS

9435 **cc:Browser:** A newsmagazine dedicated to converging technologies, published by Faulkner Information Services. *E-Journal*

`http://www.faulkner.com/`

9436 `chile.revistas.xxi` *XXI Ciencia & Tecnologia*, science and technology magazine. *Newsgroup*

9437 `clari.tw.misc` General technical industry stories. *Moderated newsgroup*

9438 `clari.tw.top` Top technical stories. *Moderated newsgroup*

➤ **Digital Media *Perspective:** Brief, concise version of in-depth reports and analysis in *Digital Media*, a paper newsletter covering high-tech industries with the digital technology itch. (See entry 3342 for full listing.)

9439 **gina:** gina, the global Internet news agency, is a convenient source for high-tech product news and announcements. gina offers a daily summary via e-mail, or you can simply visit the site for daily postings. News releases are mostly from the computer and entertainment industries.

`http://www.earthlink.net/gina/`

INFO `ginainfo@gina.com`

9440 **INNOVATION:** Summary of trends, strategies, and innovations in business and technology. *Newsletter*

± `innovation-request@newsscan.com` [body = `subscribe`]

INFO `comments@newsscan.com` (John Gehl)

Frequency: weekly

Price: $15/year

9441 **Novice-MZT (News from MZT):** News from the Ministry for Science and Technology of the Republic of Slovenia. *Distribution List, moderated*

`http://www.mzt.si/scientia/`

± **INFO** `novice-mzt@krpan.arnes.si`

± **INFO** `novice.mzt@uni-lj.si`

Language: Slovene

Frequency: published twice a month

9442 **Science On-Line:** Science On-Line includes: *Science* magazine, current and back issues; Science's Next Wave, an electronic network for young scientists; Classified Advertising, including career opportunities; Beyond the Printed Page, interactive projects and additional data; and Electronic Marketplace, with the latest new product information.

`http://science-mag.aaas.org/science/`

INFO `science-feedback@forsythe.stanford.edu`

OCEANOGRAPHY

9443 **Oceanography Information Servers:** A collection of oceanography information on the Internet.
http://www-ccs.ucsd.edu/src_oceanography.html
INFO webmaster@coast.ucsd.edu

9444 `bionet.biology.deepsea` Research in deep-sea marine biology, oceanography, and geology. *Moderated newsgroup*

9445 **The Data Zoo:** A collection of data sets from various physical oceanographic experiments conducted off the California coast by various institutions.
http://www-ccs.ucsd.edu/zoo/
ftp://coast.ucsd.edu/zoo/
gopher://gopher-ccs.ucsd.edu/11/zoo/
INFO zookeeper@coast.ucsd.edu

➤ **Marine-L:** On marine-related topics: education, navigation, ships, industry, meterology. (See entry 1970 for full listing.)

9446 **Scripps Institution of Oceanography:** This site contains extensive information on the institute, including information on its programs, ships, databases, and the holdings of its library.
http://sio.ucsd.edu/
INFO www@sio.ucsd.edu

➤ **Virginia Coast Reserve Information System (VCRIS):** This site includes weather and ecological data for Virginia coast sites. The site is operated by the Virginia Coast Reserve Long-Term Ecological Research Project (VCR/LTER). (See entry 9047 for full listing.)

9447 **Woods Hole Oceanographic Institution (WHOI):** This site contains information on the institution, its library and research laboratories, and pointers to other oceanographic resources on the Internet.
http://www.whoi.edu/
INFO webmaster@whoi.edu
INFO information@whoi.edu

ORGANIZATIONS

9448 **CISTI:** Canada Institute for Scientific and Technical Information—worldwide scientific, technical, and medical information.
http://www.cisti.nrc.ca/cisti/cisti.html
INFO telnet://cat@cat.cisti.nrc.ca
INFO danielle.langlois@nrc.ca

9449 **American Association for the Advancement of Science:** General information about AAAS as well as information on *Science* magazine and other programs of the AAAS.
http://www.aaas.org/
INFO webmaster@aaas.org

9450 **CNET-OP:** Information about CINECA (Italian research organization) and its networks (CINECAnet/GARR). *Mailing List*
± listserv@icineca.cineca.it [body = SUBSCRIBE CNET-OP first-name last-name]
INFO anr0@icineca.bitnet (Gabriele Neri)
ARCHIVE http://www.cineca.it/
Language: Italian

PALEONTOLOGY

9451 **University of California Museum of Paleontology:** Online exhibits and collections databases from the University of California Museum of Paleontology, the fourth largest paleontological museum in the United States. Also includes information on geology, phylogeny, or evolutionary biology and the history of science.
http://ucmp1.berkeley.edu/
http://ucmp1.berkeley.edu/FAQ/faq.html

INFO webmaster@ucmp1.berkeley.edu

➤ **On-line Resources for Earth Scientists (ORES):** Earth-science resources, including digital documents, news sources, software, data sets, and public online services. Subjects include the environment, forestry, geography, geology, geophysics, GIS, GPS, geodesy, mapping, paleontology, remote sensing, space, meteorology, wildlife, and jobs in earth sciences. (See entry 9333 for full listing.)

9452 **The Paleolimnology Home Page:** A central Web resource for scientists and others working on the science of pale-olimnology: the past ecology of freshwater systems as illuminated by investigations of sediment cores and other means.

http://www.indiana.edu/~diatom/paleo.html

INFO sweets@ucs.indiana.edu (P. Roger Sweets)

9453 **sci.bio.paleontology** Life of the past (but no creation vs. evolution!). *Newsgroup*

PHYSICS

9454 **AIP History of Physics Newsletter:** Reports activities of the Center and its Niels Bohr Library, and other information on work in the history of physics and allied sciences. *E-journal*

http://aip.org/history/newsletters.html

INFO nbl@aip.org

INFO sweart@aip.org

Frequency: semiannual

9455 **alt.sci.physics.acoustics** The soundness of the science of sound. *Newsgroup*

9456 **alt.sci.physics.new-theories** Scientific theories you won't find in journals. *Newsgroup*

9457 **ANEMO-L:** Anemometry in turbulent fluid flow. *Mailing List*

± listserv@nic.surfnet.nl [body = SUBSCRIBE ANEMO-L first-name last-name]

OWNER j.m.bessem@wbmt.tudelft.nl (J.M. (Hans) Bessem)

OWNER p.j.groot-de@research.dsmnet.unisource.nl (P.J. (Hans) de Groot)

9458 **Applied Physics Letters Online:** Online journal of the American Institute of Physics. *E-Journal*

INFO aplonline@aip.org (Tim Ingoldsby, Director of New Product Development)

ARCHIVE http://www.ref.oclc.org:2000/

Frequency: weekly

Price: varies with membership category

9459 **BURG-CEN:** On fluid mechanics—mainly for Ph.D. students attached to J. M. Burgers Centre for Fluid Mechanics. *Mailing List*

± listserv@hearn.nic.surfnet.nl [body = SUBSCRIBE BURG-CEN first-name last-name]

INFO r.e.g.poorte@wb.utwente.nl (Edwin Poorte)

INFO d.f.delange@wb.utwente.nl (Frits de Lange)

ARCHIVE listserv@hearn.nic.surfnet.nl [body = INDEX BURG-CEN]

Language: English, Dutch

➤ **Cellular-Automata:** On cellular automata and lattice gases, including theory, applications, and available software packages. (See entry 9381 for full listing.)

9460 **cern.alice** A Large Ion Collider Experiment. *Newsgroup*

➤ **Concurrency Modeling:** Papers (LaTeX source and DVI) on modeling concurrent behavior written by members of the Boole Group, c/o Prof. Vaughan Pratt, Computer Science Department, Stanford University. (See entry 9382 for full listing.)

9461 **Currents:** The weekly newspaper of Lawrence Berkeley National Laboratory (Berkeley Lab). *Newsletter*

http://www.lbl.gov/Publications/Currents/

INFO mbbodvarrson@lbl.gov (Mary Bodvarrson, LBL Public Information)

ARCHIVE http://www.lbl.gov/Publications/Currents/

9462   **FISICA-L:** For scholarly discussion of physics. *Mailing List*
± `listserv@listserv.rl.ac.uk` [body = SUBSCRIBE FISICA-L first-name last-name]
INFO EDITOR OWNER `gweber@ifi.unicamp.br` (Gerald Weber)
INFO `mcohenca@if.usp.br` (Joseph Max Cohenca)

9463   `fj.sci.physics` Discussion on physics. *Newsgroup*

9464   **FSVS-L:** On using freeware, shareware, and public-domain software in university education and research, particularly for nuclear sciences and physical engineering. *Mailing List*
± `listserv@earn.cvut.cz` [body = SUBSCRIBE FSVS-L first-name last-name]
INFO `fsvs-l-request@earn.cvut.cz`
ARCHIVE `listserv@earn.cvut.cz` [body = INDEX FSVS-L]

9465   **Fusion:** On cold and hot nuclear fusion. *Mailing List*
+ INFO `fusion-request@zorch.sf-bay.org` (Scott Hazen Mueller)
ARCHIVE `listserv@vml.nodak.edu` [body = INDEX FUSION]
Gated: `sci.physics.fusion`

9466   `hepnet.announce` Announcement of general interest. *Newsgroup*

9467   `hepnet.conferences` High Energy Physics conference & workshops. *Newsgroup*

9468   `hepnet.freehep` The freehep High Energy Physics archives. *Newsgroup*

9469   `hepnet.general` General interest items for High Energy Physics. *Newsgroup*

9470   `hepnet.jobs` High Energy Physics job announcements and discussions. *Newsgroup*

➤   **IACIS:** The International Association of Colloid and Interface Scientists (IACIS) is a voluntary, nonprofit organization of individuals who are actively interested in promoting the field of colloid and interface science. (See entry 9141 for full listing.)

➤   **IARPE-L:** On radiation protection. (See entry 5053 for full listing.)

➤   **Impulsiv:** A German e-journal on math, physics, and computer science. Entertaining. (See entry 9390 for full listing.)

9471   **INTERF-L:** The Israeli interest group on interfacial phenomena and complex fluids. *Mailing List, moderated*
± `listserv@taunivm.tau.ac.il` [body = SUBSCRIBE INTERF-L first-name last-name]
INFO `andelman@taunivm.tau.ac.il` (David Andelman)

9472   **NEXUS—National Network of Physics Societies:** This is the information service for physics students and societies connected to the Institute of Physics. It includes job information, events, Ph.D. and M.Sc. positions, society programs, and contact addresses and past copies of NEXUS News, the society's newsletter.
`http://www.qmw.ac.uk/NEXUS/home.html`
INFO `p.k.guinnessy@qmw.ac.uk`

➤   **Oak Ridge Laboratory Review:** The latest and greatest research and development activities at the Oak Ridge National Laboratory. (See entry 9552 for full listing.)

➤   **Omega-Point-Theory:** On Omega Point Theory in Frank J. Tipler's book, *The Physics of Immortality*. (See entry 5338 for full listing.)

9473   **PHYS-STU:** For discussion of physics and related topics by physics students. *Mailing List*
± `listserv@uwf.cc.uwf.edu` [body = SUBSCRIBE PHYS-STU first-name last-name]
INFO `phys-stu-request@uwf.cc.uwf.edu`
ARCHIVE `listserv@uwf.cc.uwf.edu` [body = INDEX PHYS-STU]

9474   **PHYSHARE:** Resource sharing on high-school physics. *Mailing List*
± `listserv@psuvm.psu.edu` [body = SUBSCRIBE PHYSHARE first-name last-name]
INFO `jdp115@psuvm.psu.edu` (Dave Popp)
ARCHIVE `listserv@psuvm.psu.edu`

9475 **Physics and Astronomy Department, University of Oklahoma:** This site provides information on the Department of Physics and Astronomy at the University of Oklahoma.
http://www.nhn.uoknor.edu/
INFO feldt@phyast.nhn.uoknor.edu

9476 **Physics Education News (PEN):** On physics and science education. From the education division of the American Institute of Physics (AIP). *Newsletter*
gopher://pinet.aip.org/00/pen.archive/
± listserv@aip.org [body = SUBSCRIBE PEN first-name last-name]
INFO EDITOR tschwab@aip.org (Mr. Tracy Schwab)
ARCHIVES
gopher://pinet.aip.org
http://www.aip.org/pinet/listserv/PEN.info.html

9477 **Physics News Update:** A digest of physics news items by Phillip F. Schewe, American Institute of Physics. *Newsletter*
gopher://pinet.aip.org/00/physnews.archive/
± gopher://pinet.aip.org
INFO physnews@aip.org (Phillip F. Schewe)
ARCHIVE gopher://pinet.aip.org

9478 **sci.physics** Physical laws, properties, etc. *Newsgroup*

9479 **sci.physics.accelerators** Particle accelerators and the physics of beams. *Newsgroup*

9480 **sci.physics.computational.fluid-dynamics** Computational fluid dynamics. *Newsgroup*

9481 **sci.physics.cond-matter** Condensed matter physics, theory and experiment. *Newsgroup*

9482 **sci.physics.electromag** Electromagnetic theory and applications. *Newsgroup*

9483 **sci.physics.fusion** Information on fusion, especially "cold" fusion. *Newsgroup*

9484 **sci.physics.particle** Particle physics discussions. *Newsgroup*

9485 **sci.physics.plasma** Plasma science and technology community exchange. *Moderated newsgroup*

9486 **sci.physics.research** Current physics research. *Moderated newsgroup*

➤ **sci.techniques.mag-resonance:** Magnetic resonance imaging and spectroscopy. *Newsgroup*

9487 **sci.techniques.mass-spec** All areas of mass spectrometry. *Moderated newsgroup*

9488 **sci.techniques.spectroscopy** Spectrum analysis. *Newsgroup*

9489 **sci.techniques.xtallography** The field of crystallography. *Newsgroup*

9490 **SPS:** For the Society of Physics Students (SPS). *Mailing List*
± autoshare@rip.physics.unk.edu [body = SUB SPS first-name last-name]
OWNER price@rip.physics.unk.edu
OWNER price@platte.unk.edu (Robert I. Price)

9491 **SUP-COND:** On superconductivity research in Israel. *Mailing List, moderated*
± listserv@taunivm.tau.ac.il [body = SUBSCRIBE SUP-COND first-name last-name]
INFO jo@most.gov.il

9492 **tnn.physics** Discussions in physics. *Newsgroup*

9493 **UNK Department of Physics and Physical Science:** Web site of the department of Physics and Physical Science at the University of Nebraska at Kearney.
http://rip.physics.unk.edu/
INFO price@rip.physics.unk.edu

9494 **Warsaw University Physics Department:** Information on the physics department, local tourism, and other Polish resources.
http://www.fuw.edu.pl/

INFO www@fuw.edu.pl

PHYSICS—OPTICS

9495 `co.ocs` Discussion on optoelectronic computing at CU and CSU. *Newsgroup*

9496 **CONFOCAL:** On all aspects of confocal microscopy and confocal microscope design. *Mailing List*
± `listserv@ubvm.cc.buffalo.edu` [body = SUBSCRIBE CONFOCAL first-name last-name]
INFO `summers@ubmed.buffalo.edu` (Robert Summers)
ARCHIVE `listserv@ubvm.cc.buffalo.edu` [body = INDEX CONFOCAL]

9497 **OPT-PROC:** On holography and optical computing. *Mailing List, moderated*
± `listserv@taunivm.tau.ac.il` [body = SUBSCRIBE OPT-PROC first-name last-name]
INFO `feglaser@weizmann.bitnet` (Shelly Glaser)
INFO `feglaser@weizmann.weizmann.ac.il` (Shelly Glaser)

9498 **OPTICS-L:** News on optics, electro-optics, and lasers in Israel. *Mailing List, moderated*
± `listserv@taunivm.tau.ac.il` [body = SUBSCRIBE OPTICS-L first-name last-name]
INFO `jo@most.gov.il`
Please Note: Subscription by approval only.

➤ **Optoelectronic Computing Systems Laboratory at Colorado State University:** This site contains information on digital optical computing. It includes an archive of the lab's publications and technical reports on optical computing, plus GIFs from optical computing experiments. (See entry 2676 for full listing.)

9499 `sci.optics` Discussion relating to the science of optics. *Newsgroup*

9500 `sci.optics.fiber` Fiber optic components, systems, applications. *Newsgroup*

9501 `sci.techniques.microscopy` The field of microscopy. *Newsgroup*

PRIMATOLOGY

9502 **LPN-L:** For scientists doing research on or with nonhuman primates, including care and breeding, research news, requests for information or materials, and conservation. *Mailing List, moderated*
± `listserv@brownvm.brown.edu` [body = SUBSCRIBE LPN-L first-name last-name]
INFO `primate@brownvm.brown.edu` (Judith E. Schrier)
ARCHIVE `listserv@brownvm.brown.edu` [body = INDEX LPN-L]

9503 **primatology:** On primatology: monkeys, apes, and social anthropology. *Mailing List*
± `mailbase@mailbase.ac.uk` [body = join primatology first-name last-name]
OWNER `tonyd@castle.ed.ac.uk` (Tony Dickinson)

PSYCHOLOGY

➤ **AAGT:** On Gestalt therapy: philosophy, theory, practice, and research. (See entry 5029 for full listing.)

➤ `alt.dreams:` What do they mean? *Newsgroup*

9504 `alt.dreams.lucid` What do they *really* mean? *Newsgroup*

9505 `alt.human-brain` A delicacy in some corners of the planet. *Newsgroup*

9506 `alt.hypnosis` When you awaken, you will forget about this newsgroup. *Newsgroup*

9507 `alt.mindcontrol` Are you sure those thoughts are really your own? *Newsgroup*

9508 `alt.psychology.jung` Discussion of works and theories of Carl Jung. *Newsgroup*

➤ `alt.psychology.nlp:` Neuro-linguistic programming. *Newsgroup*

9509 `alt.psychology.personality` Personality taxonomy, such as Myers-Briggs. *Newsgroup*

9510 `alt.psychology.transpersonal` Transpersonal psychology. *Newsgroup*

9511 **APASD-L:** On research and funding opportunities for psychologists. *Mailing List, moderated*

± listserv@vtvm1.cc.vt.edu [body = SUBSCRIBE APASD-L first-name last-name]
INFO apasddes@gwuvm.bitnet (Deborah Segal or Lara Frumkin)

9512 BGUBS-L: For the Behavioral Sciences Department at Ben Gurion University in Israel. *Mailing List*
± listserv@bguvm.bitnet [body = SUBSCRIBE BGUBS-L first-name last-name]
INFO chermesh@bgumail.bgu.ac.il (Ran Chermesh)
Please Note: Subscription by approval only.

9513 bit.listserv.envbeh-1 Forum on environment and human behavior. *Newsgroup*

9514 bit.listserv.ioob-1 Industrial psychology. *Newsgroup*

9515 BLISS-L: On the Barus Lab Interactive Speech System, DOS software for psychological subject testing using speech and visual displays. *Mailing List*
± listserv@brownvm.brown.edu [body = SUBSCRIBE BLISS-L first-name last-name]
INFO mertus@brown.edu
ARCHIVE listserv@brownvm.brown.edu [body = INDEX BLISS-L]

9516 Bowlby: On attachment theory: research on early childhood development and parent-infant affectional-cognitive bonds. *Mailing List, moderated*
± listserv@sjuvm.stjohns.edu [body = SUBSCRIBE BOWLBY first-name last-name]
OWNER garelli@attach.edu.ar (Juan C. Garelli)

9517 CHARTER: For organizing GlobalPsych: human nature, human futures, and the Internet. *Mailing List*
± listserv@sjuvm.stjohns.edu [body = SUBSCRIBE CHARTER first-name last-name]
OWNER i.pitchford@sheffield.ac.uk
Please Note: Subscription by approval only.

9518 CSGnet: For discussion among the Control Systems Group Network (CSGnet), a behavioral-science group interested in perceptual control theory (PCT). *Mailing List*
ftp://postoffice.cso.uiuc.edu/csgnet/
http://www.ed.uiuc.edu/csg/
± listserv@postoffice.cso.uiuc.edu [body = SUBSCRIBE CSGNET first-name last-name]
INFO garyc@prairienet.org (Gary Cziko)
Gated: bit.sci.purposive-behavior

9519 DEBONO: On the work of Edward de Bono on lateral thinking and practical creativity. *Mailing List*
± listserv@sjuvm.stjohns.edu [body = SUBSCRIBE DEBONO first-name last-name]
OWNER i.pitchford@sheffield.ac.uk

➤ **EMPATHY:** For teachers of interpersonal communication courses. (See entry 5173 for full listing.)

➤ **EVALTEN:** On evaluation methodology and statistics in mental health. (See entry 4947 for full listing.)

➤ **fj.sci.human-factors:** Discussion about human factors and ergonomics. *Newsgroup*

9520 fj.sci.psychology Discussion and pursuit of psychology. *Newsgroup*

➤ **FLN:** For scholarly discussion of figurative language—discussion is international and interdisciplinary (psychology, linguistics, AI, computational linguistics, literary studies). (See entry 5294 for full listing.)

➤ **FreudNet: The A.A. Brill Library :** Information on Sigmund Freud from the A. A. Brill Library. (See entry 5031 for full listing.)

➤ **HYPNOSIS:** On hypnosis, suggestion, and suggestibility: for researchers and clinicians. (See entry 5014 for full listing.)

9521 Man, Neuron, Model: Preprints of Russian articles on neuroscience and psychophysiology translated into English. *E-Journal*
http://www.hku.hk/psycho/abstracts1.html
INFO OWNER balaban@ivnd.msk.su (BALABAN, P.)
ARCHIVE http://www.hku.hk/psycho/abstracts1.html

9522 **MPSYCH-L:** Announcements from the Society for Mathematical Psychology. *Mailing List*
http://www.socsci.uci.edu/smp/index.html
± listserv@brownvm.brown.edu [body = SUBSCRIBE MPSYCH-L first-name last-name]
INFO metzger@umbc.edu (Mary Ann Metzger)
INFO bi599088@brownvm.brown.edu (Bob Stout)

➤ **NUVUPSY:** Points of view critical of the "therapeutic state" and institutional psychiatry. (See entry 5017 for full listing.)

9523 **PSYART:** On the psychological study of the arts, especially literature. *Mailing List, moderated*
http://nermv.nerdc.ufl.edu/~psyart
± listserv@nervm.nerdc.ufl.edu [body = SUBSCRIBE PSYART first-name last-name]
INFO nnh@nervm.nerdc.ufl.edu (Norm Holland)
INFO psychoanalysis|of

9524 **PSYCGRAD:** Discussion forum for psychology graduate students. *Digest & Reflector*
ftp://aix1.uottawa.ca
gopher://panda1.uottawa.ca:4010
± listserv@acadvm1.uottawa.ca [body = SUBSCRIBE PSYCGRAD first-name last-name]
INFO simpson@aix1.uottawa.ca (Matthew Simpson)
ARCHIVE listserv@acadvm1.uottawa.ca [body = INDEX PSYCGRAD]

➤ **Psych-DD:** For psychologists and allied professionals on mental retardation. (See entry 9883 for full listing.)

9525 **PSYCHE-D:** Discussions on the electronic journal PSYCHE. *Mailing List*
± listserv@iris.rfmh.org [body = SUBSCRIBE PSYCHE-D first-name last-name]
INFO psyche-d-request@iris.rfmh.org
ARCHIVE listserv@iris.rfmh.org [body = INDEX PSYCHE-D]

9526 **PSYCHOSYNTHESIS:** Psychosynthesis Discussion Group. *Mailing List*
± listproc@robles.callutheran.edu [body = SUBSCRIBE PSYCHOSYNTHESIS]
OWNER cullen@robles.callutheran.edu (John Cullen)

9527 **PSYCOLOQUY:** Brief reports of new ideas and findings in all areas of psychology and its related fields (biobehavioral, cognitive, neural, social, etc.). *E-Journal, moderated*
ftp://cogsci.ecs.soton.ac.uk/pub/harnad/Psycoloquy
ftp://ftp.princeton.edu/pub/harnad/Psycoloquy
ftp://princeton.edu/pub/harnad/
gopher://gopher.cic.net
gopher://gopher.princeton.edu/11/.libraries/.pujournals
http://www.princeton.edu/~harnad/psyc.html
http://cogsci.ecs.soton.ac.uk/~harnad/
± listserv@pucc.princeton.edu [body = SUBSCRIBE PSYC first-name last-name]
INFO psyc@pucc.princeton.edu (Stevan Harnad)
ARCHIVE listserv@pucc.princeton.edu [body = GET PSYC FILELIST]
Gated: sci.psychology.journals.psycoloquy
Frequency: irregular (items posted upon acceptance)

9528 **PSYSTS-L:** On statistical techniques used in psychology, with particular emphasis on multiple regression, path analysis, structural equation modeling, factor analysis, and configural frequency analysis. *Mailing List*
± listserv@mizzou1.missouri.edu [body = SUBSCRIBE PSYSTS-L first-name last-name]
INFO wood@psysparc.psyc.missouri.edu (Phil Wood)
Comments: Discussion is generally in response to graduate statistics classes taught by the list owner. Other participants welcome, but be advised a certain proportion of the discussion is always rather elementary in nature.

9529 **Q-Method:** On Q methodology, a general approach to the scientific study of subjectivity. *Mailing List*

± `listserv@kentvm.kent.edu` [body = SUBSCRIBE Q-METHOD first-name last-name]

INFO OWNER `sbrown@kentvm.kent.edu` (Steven R. Brown)

9530 RatioLab - Interactive Decision Laboratory: A computerized laboratory at the Hebrew University, dedicated to behavioral reaserch related to game-theoretic models.

`http://pluto.mscc.huji.ac.il/~msratio/`

INFO `msratio@pluto.mscc.huji.ac.il`

INFO `yish@cs.huji.ac.il`

9531 RATION-L: For academic discussions of theories of rational behavior. *Mailing List*

± `listserv@vm.tau.ac.il` [body = SUBSCRIBE RATION-L first-name last-name]

INFO `ration-l-request@vm.tau.ac.il`

9532 Research Psychology Funding Bulletin: An index of funding announcements; lists each funding announcement by title and a one-line description of contents. *Newsletter*

± `listserv@vtvm1.bitnet` [body = SUBSCRIBE APASD-L]

INFO `apasddes@gwuvm.bitnet` (Deborah Segal or Lara Frumkin)

Frequency: monthly

9533 `sci.psychology` Topics related to psychology. *Newsgroup*

9534 `sci.psychology.announce` Psychology-related announcements. *Moderated newsgroup*

9535 `sci.psychology.consciousness` On the nature of consciousness. *Moderated newsgroup*

9536 `sci.psychology.journals.psyche` E-journal on consciousness. *Moderated newsgroup*

9537 `sci.psychology.misc` General discussion of psychology. *Newsgroup*

9538 `sci.psychology.personality` All personality systems and measurement. *Newsgroup*

9539 `sci.psychology.psychotherapy` Practice of psychotherapy. *Newsgroup*

9540 `sci.psychology.research` Research issues in psychology. *Moderated newsgroup*

9541 `sci.psychology.theory` Theories of psychology and behavior. *Newsgroup*

9542 SELF-HELP-RESEARCH: Academic discussion of self-help research.

± `listserv@postoffice.cso.uiuc.edu` [body = SUBSCRIBE SLFHLP-L first-name last-name]

INFO `self-help-research-request@postoffice.cso.uiuc.edu`

INFO `b-dienes@uiuc.edu` (Bruce Dienes)

ARCHIVES

`ftp://postoffice.cso.uiuc.edu/slfhlp-l`

`listserv@postoffice.cso.uiuc.edu` [body = GET SLFHLP-L LOG*yymm* where *yy* is the year and *mm* is month]

FAQ `listserv@postoffice.cso.uiuc.edu` [body = INFO SLFHLP-L]

➤ **SOCIOBIO:** On the evolution of social behavior. (See entry 9022 for full listing.)

➤ **SPORTPSY:** On exercise and sport psychology. (See entry 6699 for full listing.)

➤ **STUTT-X:** On the research of fluency disorders. (See entry 9874 for full listing.)

9543 Subject Specific Resource List in Psychology: Includes mailing lists, libraries and departments, software, newsgroups, e-journals, and virtual reality.

`http://www.lib.umich.edu/chouse/inter/267.html`

`ftp://una.hh.lib.umich.edu/psych%3Aalvoeiro`

`gopher://una.hh.lib.umich.edu/00/inetdirsstacks/psych%3Aalvoeiro`

INFO `j.alvoeiro@psychology.hull.ac.uk` (Jorge Alvoeiro)

MIRROR `gopher://ukoln.bath.ac.uk:7070/00/Link/Tree/Psychology/1501_-_Subject_Specific_Resource_List_in_Psychology`

➤ **Transcultural-Psychology:** On the delivery of mental health services to diverse cultures. (See entry 5026 for full listing.)

➤ **VALIDATA:** On psychological measure development, testing, and validation. (See entry 2037 for full listing.)

RESEARCH

➤ **CISTI:** Canada Institute for Scientific and Technical Information—worldwide scientific, technical, and medical information. (See entry 9448 for full listing.)

9544 `alt.inventors` People with new ideas. *Newsgroup*

➤ `be.science:` About science and scientific research in Belgium. *Newsgroup*

9545 **Berkeley Lab Home Page:** Home page of the Ernest Orlando Lawrence Berkeley National Laboratory (also known as the Berkeley Lab).

`http://www.lbl.gov/`

INFO `jbkahn@lbl.gov` (Jeff Kahn, LBL Public Information)

➤ `bionet.sci-resources:` Information about funding agencies, etc. *Moderated newsgroup*

9546 `bit.listserv.qualrs-l` Qualitative research of the human sciences. *Newsgroup*

➤ **CNET-OP:** Information about CINECA (Italian research organization) and its networks (CINECAnet/GARR). (See entry 9450 for full listing.)

➤ **Cochlear Fluids Research Laboratory:** All about your inner ear. Includes a pictorial guide, and information on inner-ear research programs. (See entry 4830 for full listing.)

9547 **Community of Science Web Server:** This site is designed to help scientists identify and locate researchers with interests and expertise similar to their own. It also contains a series of databases that provide information about research funded by the federal government.

`http://cos.gdb.org/`

INFO `cw3@bestpl.hcf.jhu.edu` (Charles Wise)

INFO `evd@bestpl.hcf.jhu.edu` (Edwin Van Dusen)

Comments: As an electronic publishing firm, COS offers other stand alone databases such as the Commerce Business Daily, the Federal Register, and the U.S. Patent Citation Database. COS will continue to offer fresh interfaces for research oriented subject matter, and plans to offer several new funding and medically oriented databases in 1996.

9548 **CONICIT—VENEZUELA:** This site, sponsored by CONICIT (Consejo Nacional de Investigaciones Cientificas y Tecnologicas), the National Council of Science and Technology Rresearch in Venezuela, provides news and events in science and technology in Venezuela.

`gopher://gopher.conicit.ve`

INFO `jrivas@conicit.ve`

9549 **DANTE IN PRINT:** Publication series containing all papers and articles published by or on behalf of DANTE (Delivery of Advanced Network Technology to Europe, Ltd.). It includes an overview of developments in DANTE services and other activities, all in the area of European research networking.

`http://www.dante.net/`

INFO `dante@dante.org.uk`

Comments: All papers published in DANTE IN PRINT have been published before. Mostly in Conference proceedings and journals or magazines. There is always a reference to the occasion or original source.

➤ **Fitzroy:** A listing of undergraduate research experiences, which can serve as starting points or sources of advice for other undergrads looking for summer research opportunities. (See entry 4302 for full listing.)

➤ **GTRTI-L:** On research and teaching in global information technology. (See entry 9366 for full listing.)

9550 **Los Alamos National Laboratory:** This is the central information server for the Los Alamos National Laboratory, located in Los Alamos, New Mexico.

`http://www.lanl.gov/`

INFO `www@lanl.gov`

➤ **Molecular Biology Computational Resource at Baylor College of Medicine:** Information for biological and biomedical research. (See entry 9071 for full listing.)

➤ **National Institutes of Health (NIH):** This site provides health and biomedical information useful to the NIH intramural research community in Bethesda, Maryland, and biomedical researchers around the world. (See entry 5057 for full listing.)

9551 **National Science Foundation (NSF):** Information from the NSF, including programs, grants and funding guidelines, other NSF publications, and links to results of NSF-funded research.
   http://www.nsf.gov/
   INFO webmaster@nsf.gov

9552 **Oak Ridge Laboratory Review:** The latest and greatest research and development activities at the Oak Ridge National Laboratory. *E-Journal*
   http://www.ornl.gov/ORNLReview/rev26-2/text/home.html
   INFO krausech@ornl.gov
   Frequency: quarterly, more or less

9553 **RAND:** Website of RAND, a nonprofit institution that helps improve public policy through research and analysis. The site includes RAND publications, a wide range of information on its projects, and initiatives.
   http://www.rand.org/
   INFO correspondence@rand.org

9554 **RedIRIS, CSIC, Spain:** RedIRIS is the Spanish Academic and Research Network
   http://www.rediris.es/
   http://x500.rediris.es/ (X.500 server)
   ftp://ftp.rediris.es
   gopher://gopher.rediris.es
   INFO infoiris@rediris.es

9555 **Research Funding Agencies :** A list of WWW sites containing information of interest to researchers in all fields of science and technology that may be helpful in assisting faculty, students, and companies in identifying research funding opportunities.
   http://www.cs.virginia.edu/~seas/resdev/sponsors.html
   INFO webman@cs.virginia.edu

9556 **Research Funding Opportunities and Administration (TRAM):** This site contains searchable research funding sources available from one location. The funding information is updated daily. TRAM also contains a set of grant application forms collected from various sources, as well as standard agreements for subcontracts, nondisclosures, licenses, and links to other servers related to research funding and administration.
   http://tram.rice.edu/TRAM/
   INFO sdc@rice.edu
   FAQ http://tram.rice.edu/TRAM/faq.html

9557 **Research Horizons:** On research at the Georgia Institute of Technology. *Newsletter*
   gopher://gopher.gatech.edu/11/Horizons
   INFO lea.mclees@gtri.gatech.edu (Lea McLees)
   ARCHIVE gopher://gopher.gatech.edu/11/Horizons
   Frequency: three times per year

9558 **RS1-L:** For users of RS/1, a research and data-analysis software package running on VMS, Unix, and MS-DOS. *Mailing List*
   ± listserv@vm1.nodak.edu [body = SUBSCRIBE RS1-L first-name last-name]
   INFO rs1-l-request@vm1.nodak.edu
   ARCHIVE listserv@vm1.nodak.edu [body = INDEX RS1-L]

➤ **The Salk Institute for Biological Studies:** A private, nonprofit research organization in La Jolla, California. Scientists there do fundamental research in biology and its relation to health, studying such problems as the organization and operation of the brain, the control of gene activity, and the molecular origins of disease. (See entry 4900 for full listing.)

9559 **sci.comp-aided** The use of computers as tools in scientific research. *Newsgroup*

9560 `sci.research` Research methods, funding, ethics, and whatever. *Newsgroup*

9561 `sci.research.careers` Issues relevant to careers in scientific research. *Newsgroup*

9562 `sci.research.postdoc` Anything about postdoctoral studies, including offers. *Newsgroup*

9563 `sci.techniques.testing.misc` General testing techniques in science. *Newsgroup*

9564 `sci.techniques.testing.nondestructive` Nondestructive tests in science. *Newsgroup*

➤ **Scout Report:** Weekly publication of InterNIC Information Services of resources and news primarily of interest to the research and education community. (See entry 4530 for full listing.)

➤ **U.S. Office of Scientific and Technical Information (OSTI):** The Office of Scientific and Technical Information (OSTI) manages the Department of Energy's (DOE) program for the collection, processing, and availability of scientific and technical information (STI) generated and acquired by the Department of Energy. (See entry 9231 for full listing.)

ROBOTICS

9565 `alt.culture.electric-midget` The "culture" of little robots. *Newsgroup*

9566 **AutomationNET:** A forum for anyone who makes automation products, integrates automation systems, needs automated systems, or for anyone who just wants to learn more about the automation industry.
http://www.automationnet.com/
INFO azure@automationnet.com

➤ **CMU Libraries CS, Robotics and Electrical Engineering Resources:** Pointers to Web resources in computer science, robotics and electrical engineering including reference tools, bibliographies, books, journals, patents, standards, technical reports, and more. (See entry 9166 for full listing.)

9567 `comp.home.automation` Home automation devices, setup, sources, etc. *Newsgroup*

9568 `comp.robotics.misc` All aspects of robots and their applications. *Newsgroup*

9569 `comp.robotics.research` Academic, government, and industry research in robotics. *Moderated newsgroup*

9570 `fj.engr.robotics` Topics about robotics. *Newsgroup*

9571 **Internet Robotics Sources:** An extensive collection of robotics resources on the Web. Covers business, government, and research robotics pages among many others.
http://www.cs.indiana.edu/robotics/world.html
INFO jla@cs.indiana.edu (Jason L. Almeter)

9572 **Robotics Internet Resources Page:** This page is a collection of robotics-related resources on the Internet. It includes pointers to Web pages, FTP sites, software, and robotics video demonstrations.
http://piglet.cs.umass.edu:4321/robotics.html
INFO connolly@ai.sri.com (Christopher I. Connolly)

9573 `tnn.robot` Discussions about robot technology. *Newsgroup*

SOCIAL ISSUES

9574 `alt.technology.obsolete` Outdated or outmoded technology. *Newsgroup*

➤ **C+Health:** About the health effects of computer use. (See entry 3706 for full listing.)

➤ **DO-IT News:** An electronic newsletter about increasing the representation of people with disabilities in science, engineering, and mathematics fields. (See entry 9863 for full listing.)

➤ **Economic Democracy Information Network (EDIN):** A project dedicated to expanding the voice of community organizations on the information superhighway. (See entry 9646 for full listing.)

➤ **ENVSEC_D:** On environment, population, and security. (See entry 10108 for full listing.)

➤ **FEED:** An online-only magazine of politics, culture, and technology. (See entry 646 for full listing.)

9575 `fj.soc.tech` Topics on society and technology. *Newsgroup*

➤ **futurework:** This list focuses on ways for communities worldwide to deal with economic globalization and technological change. (See entry 9761 for full listing.)

➤ **ICGEBnet:** This is the information server of the International Center for Genetic Engineering and Biotechnology, Trieste, Italy. It carries molecular biology and biotechnology-related information. This site also contains information on safety aspects of biotechnology and of genetically modified organisms. (See entry 9113 for full listing.)

➤ **Impact ONLINE:** Impact Online promotes community involvement by offering information on nonprofits and on volunteer opportunities nationwide. Impact Online even offers "virtual volunteer" opportunities that can be done entirely online. The site also offers a complete online course for nonprofits interested in using technology for social change. (See entry 9671 for full listing.)

➤ **The League for Programming Freedom:** The League for Programming Freedom is a grassroots organization of professors, students, businessmen, programmers, and users dedicated to bringing back the freedom to write programs. Their aim is to reverse the recent changes that prevent programmers from doing their work by fighting software patents and "look and feel" interface copyrights. (See entry 3727 for full listing.)

9576 **New Technology in the Human Services:** Besides providing subscription information for the journal *New Technology in the Human Services*, this site also provides a free indexing and abstracting service to publications on new technology in the human services, and a directory of software for the field.

    `http://www.fz.hse.nl/nths/`
    INFO `j.steyaert@fz.hse.nl`
    INFO `annw@chst.soton.ac.uk`

9577 **POPPER:** Discussions on philosophy of science and Sir Karl R. Popper's views on rationalism and humanitarianism. *Mailing List*

    ± `listserv@sjuvm.stjohns.edu` [body = SUBSCRIBE POPPER first-name last-name]
    OWNER `garelli@attach.edu.ar` (Juan C. Garelli)

➤ **RISKS:** On risks to the public in the use of computers and related systems—across all application areas, and including problems with security, reliability, safety, and human well-being. (See entry 3733 for full listing.)

9578 `sci.skeptic` Skeptics discussing pseudoscience. *Newsgroup*

9579 **SCIFRAUD:** On fraud in science. *Mailing List*

    ± `listserv@cnsibm.albany.edu` [body = SUBSCRIBE SCIFRAUD first-name last-name]
    INFO `ach13@cnsvax.albany.edu` (A. C. Higgins)

9580 `soc.culture.scientists` Cultural issues about scientists and scientific projects. *Newsgroup*

➤ **SPEED:** SPEED: An Electronic Journal of Technology, Media, and Society provides a forum for the critical investigation of technology, media, and society. (See entry 6097 for full listing.)

➤ `talk.origins`: Evolution versus creationism (sometimes hot!). *Newsgroup*

9581 **Technology Review Magazine:** MIT's National Magazine of Technology and Policy. *E-Journal*

    `http://web.mit.edu/techreview/www/`
    ± `trsubscriptions@mit.edu`
    INFO `mconnors@mit.edu` (Martha Connors)
    Frequency: eight times a year
    Price: $30/year

9582 **Women in Technology Directory:** A professional directory for women in technological fields designed to facilitate and encourage women's ability to network with one another via e-mail.

    `http://www.sdsu.edu/wit`
    INFO `wit@sciences.sdsu.edu`

➤ **YSN:** The Young Scientists' Network: activism on employment issues for scientists just beginning their careers. (See entry 8903 for full listing.)

SPACE

➤ **Astronomy and Earth Sciences Archive at Stanford:** Astronomy/earth science-oriented material for Unix users. Includes Earth topography data, the CIA World Map II vector outline database in a compressed binary Unix/C-readable format, software and data of interest for amateur astronomers, and information of general usefulness or interest for earth scientists. Also contains some generic utilities for Unix machines, including C source for a Morse code practice program for Unix machines. (See entry 9310 for full listing.)

9583   **Astronomy Scape:** Hubble images, NASA images, satellite images, digitally enhanced for ultrafast loads, 3-D navigation, live forums, and interesting reviews.

http://www.onworld.com/AS/

INFO submit@onworld.com

9584   **Brazilian National Institute of Space Research (INPE):** Meteorology, astrophysics, image processing, and other space-related research.

http://yabae.cptec.inpe.br/

http://www.inpe.br/

ftp://grid.inpe.br/pub/

INFO danton@dpi.inpe.br (D. Nunes) (D.Nunes)

9585   **CANSPACE:** On space geodesy, including Navstar Global Positioning System (GPS), Glonass, Transit, very long baseline interferometry, satellite laser ranging, satellite altimetry. *Mailing List*

± listserv@unb.ca [body = SUBSCRIBE CANSPACE first-name last-name]

INFO lang@unb.ca (Richard Langley)

ARCHIVE listserv@unb.ca [body = INDEX CANSPACE]

9586   **clari.tw.space**   NASA, astronomy, and spaceflight. *Moderated newsgroup*

9587   **Educational Space Simulations Project:** ESSP is all about Educational Space Simulations, an exciting way to teach mathematics and space science.

http://chico.rice.edu/armadillo/Simulations/simserver.html

INFO chris@tenet.edu (Chris Rowan)

➤   **EUVE Observatory Newsletter:** On NASA's Extreme Ultraviolet Explorer satellite (EUVE). (See entry 8929 for full listing.)

9588   **The Galileo Spacecraft Home Page:** Photos and information on the Galileo spacecraft on its mission to Jupiter.

http://www.jpl.nasa.gov/galileo

INFO askgalileo@gllsvc.jpl.nasa.gov

9589   **International Space Station Bulletin Board:** An overview of Space Station Alpha as it is developed. Much of the data on this site requires a password for access, but the Technical Data Book, a fairly detailed description of the station and its development phases, is viewable by the public.

http://issa-www.jsc.nasa.gov/ss/SpaceStation_homepage.html

INFO josephine.j.juel@jsc.nasa.gov

INFO don.f.erwin1@jsc.nasa.gov

FAQ http://issa-www.jsc.nasa.gov/ss/faq.html

9590   **Jonathan's Space Report:** Summary of spaceflight activity—satellite launches, space shuttle and *Mir* space station program activity. *E-Journal*

http://hea-www.harvard.edu/QEDT/jcm/space/jsr.html

± INFO mcdowell@urania.harvard.edu (Jonathan McDowell)

ARCHIVE ftp://sao-ftp.harvard.edu/pub/jcm/space/news/

Frequency: Approximately weekly

9591   **The NASA Home Page:** Information about the National Aeronautics and Space Administration. Includes NASA news, and information on space sciene, aeronautics, the Mission to Planet Earth, human space flight, all of NASA's centers, space technology, and a gallery of photos, sounds and movies.

http://www.gsfc.nasa.gov/

INFO comments@www.hq.nasa.gov

FAQ http://www.hq.nasa.gov/office/pao/QandA/subject.html

9592   **NSSDC News:** Newsletter describing mainly activities at, and new data products and services available from, NASA's National Space Science Data Center (NSSDC). *Newsletter*

```
http://nssdc.gsfc.nasa/gov/nssdc_news/toc.html
```
± `http://nssdc.gsfc.nasa.gov/`
± `request@nssdca.gsfc.nasa.gov`
INFO `king@nssdca.gsfc.nasa.gov` (Joseph H. King)
EDITOR `mrobinson@nssdca.gsfc.nasa.gov` (Miranda Robinson)
ARCHIVE `http://nssdc.gsfc.nasa.gov/`
Frequency: trimonthly

➤ **On-line Resources for Earth Scientists (ORES):** Earth-science resources, including digital documents, news sources, software, data sets, and public online services. Subjects include the environment, forestry, geography, geology, geophysics, GIS, GPS, geodesy, mapping, paleontology, remote sensing, space, meteorology, wildlife, and jobs in earth sciences. (See entry 9333 for full listing.)

9593 `sci.space.news` Announcements of space-related news items. *Moderated newsgroup*

9594 `sci.space.policy` Discussions about space policy. *Newsgroup*

9595 `sci.space.science` Space and planetary science and related technical work. *Moderated newsgroup*

9596 `sci.space.shuttle` The space shuttle and the STS program. *Newsgroup*

9597 `sci.space.tech` Technical and general issues related to spaceflight. *Moderated newsgroup*

9598 **SEDSNEWS:** This list is an echo of `sci.space.news` for those without Usenet. *Distribution List*
± `listserv@tamvm1.tamu.edu` [body = SUBSCRIBE SEDSNEWS first-name last-name]
INFO `fhd@tamvm1.tamu.edu` (H. Alan Montgomery)
ARCHIVE `listserv@tamvm1.tamu.edu`
Gated: `sci.space.news`

➤ **Spacesim:** An electronic newsletter for space-simulation enthusiasts. (See entry 3700 for full listing.)

TECHNICAL COMMUNICATIONS

➤ **EST-L:** On teaching English for scientific and technical writing. (See entry 4545 for full listing.)

9599 **Society for Technical Communications:** From the largest professional organization serving the technical communication profession.
```
http://www.clark.net/pub/stc/www/
http://stc.org/
```
INFO `stc@tmn.com`
FAQ `http://www.clark.net/pub/stc/www/faq.html`

9600 **TECHWR-L:** For technical writers on all technical communication issues. *Mailing List*
± `listserv@vm1.ucc.okstate.edu` [body = SUBSCRIBE TECHWR-L first-name last-name]
INFO `ejray@galaxy.galstar.com`
ARCHIVE `listserv@vm1.ucc.okstate.edu`
Gated: `bit.listserv.techwr-l`

TELECOMMUNICATIONS

9601 `alt.cable-tv.re-regulate` Debating regulation of cable television. *Newsgroup*

9602 `alt.cellular` Cellular telephone technology. *Newsgroup*

9603 `alt.cellular-phone-tech` Brilliant telephony mind blows net-news naming. *Newsgroup*

9604 `alt.cellular.oki.900` A whole group for a telephone model. *Newsgroup*

9605 `alt.dcom.telecom` Unmoderated discussion of telecommunications technology. *Newsgroup*

9606 `alt.dss` Discussion of the new Digital Satellite Systems. *Newsgroup*

9607 `alt.satellite.tv.crypt` Satellite signal decryption techniques. *Newsgroup*

9608 `alt.satellite.tv.europe` All about European satellite TV. *Newsgroup*

9609 `alt.satellite.tv.forsale` TV satellite systems wanted or for sale. *Newsgroup*

9610 `aus.comms` Discussion about communications in general. *Newsgroup*

9611 `aus.comms.fps` Fast Packet Switching. *Newsgroup*

9612 `aus.radio.wicen` Wireless Institute Civil Emergency Network (WICEN). *Newsgroup*

9613 `bit.listserv.radio-l` Digital audio broadcasting list. *Moderated newsgroup*

9614 **CCMI-L:** From *411* newsletter, on operation and tech issues for telecom managers. *Mailing List*
± `listserv@usa.net` [body = SUBSCRIBE CCMI-L first-name last-name]
OWNER `philk@ucg.com` (Phil Kemelor)

9615 `clari.nb.telecom` Newsbytes: telecom and online industry news. *Moderated newsgroup*

9616 `clari.tw.telecom` Phones, satellites, media, and general telecom. *Moderated newsgroup*

9617 `clari.tw.telecom.cbd` Telecommunications equipment and materials. *Moderated newsgroup*

9618 `clari.tw.telecom.misc` Satellites, telecommunications. *Moderated newsgroup*

9619 `clari.tw.telecom.phone_service` Long-distance, local, cell service. *Moderated newsgroup*

9620 `clari.tw.telecom.releases` Press releases: the telecommunications industry. *Moderated newsgroup*

9621 `comp.dcom.isdn` The Integrated Services Digital Network (ISDN). *Newsgroup*

9622 `comp.dcom.telecom` *Telecommunications Digest. Moderated newsgroup*

9623 `comp.dcom.telecom.tech` Discussion of technical aspects of telephony. *Newsgroup*

9624 **DASP-L:** On digital acoustic signal processing. *Mailing List*
± `listserv@earn.cvut.cz` [body = SUBSCRIBE DASP-L first-name last-name]
INFO `dasp-l-request@earn.cvut.cz`
ARCHIVE `listserv@earn.cvut.cz` [body = INDEX DASP-L]

9625 **dld:** Discount Long Distance Digest: marketing info on selling long distance telecom. *Digest, moderated*
`http://www.webcom.com/~longdist/digest.html`
± `dld-request@webcom.com` [body = subscribe]
INFO EDITOR OWNER `vantek@northcoast.com` (William Van Hefner)
ARCHIVES
`dld-request@webcom.com`
`ftp://ftp.webcom.com/pub1/longdist/digest`
FAQ `http://www.webcom.com/~longdist/dldfaq.html`

9626 `essug.misc` Esoteric telephony. *Newsgroup*

9627 `essug.telco` Local and long distance telephone companies. *Newsgroup*

9628 **EUEARN-L:** On eastern European telecommunications. *Mailing List*
± `listserv@ubvm.cc.buffalo.edu` [body = SUBSCRIBE EUEARN-L first-name last-name]
INFO `euearn-l-request@ubvm.cc.buffalo.edu`
ARCHIVE `listserv@ubvm.cc.buffalo.edu` [body = INDEX EUEARN-L]
Gated: `bit.listserv.euearn-l`

9629 `fj.net.modems` Modem hardware, software, and protocols. *Newsgroup*

9630 `fj.net.phones` Telephone networks. *Newsgroup*

9631 `iijnet.dcom.isdn` Discussion of ISDN. *Newsgroup*

9632 **ISDN:** On the emerging telephone ISDN standard. The primary focus is on social issues related to ISDN deployment. *Mailing List*
± `isdn-request@dumbcat.sf.ca.us`

INFO marc@dumbcat.sf.ca.us

POST isdn@dumbcat.sf.ca.us

9633 **Long Distance Digest:** Discusses the long-distance telephone service industry—information on long-distance resellers, carriers, aggregators, wholesalers, their agents, and others involved in the business of selling long-distance services. *Newsletter*

http://www.webcom.com/longdist/digest.html

INFO vantek@aol.com (Van Hefner)

INFO vantek@northcoast.com (William Van Hefner)

ARCHIVE ftp://ftp.webcom.com/pub1/longdist/digest subdirectory

Frequency: weekly

9634 **Masters in Telecommunications Management:** Information on the master of science in telecommunications management program at Oklahoma State University.

http://orcs.bus.okstate.edu/mstm/mstm.html

INFO mstm-osu@okway.okstate.edu

9635 **pdx.telecom** Issues regarding telecommunications. *Newsgroup*

9636 **RADIO-L:** On developing digital audio broadcasting (DAB) standards. *Mailing List, moderated*

± listserv@vm1.spcs.umn.edu [body = SUBSCRIBE RADIO-L first-name last-name]

OWNER ston0030@gold.tc.umn.edu (Ronald L. Stone)

OWNER ah617@freenet.carleton.ca (Ted Ledingham, Moderator)

ARCHIVES

listserv@vm1.spcs.umn.edu [body = IND RADIO-L]

ftp://vm1.spcs.umn.edu/radio-l.601/

FAQ listserv@vm1.spcs.umn.edu [body = GET RADIO-L FILES RADIO-L]

Gated: bit.listserv.radio-l

9637 **Telecommunications Electronic Reviews:** Provides reviews of and pointers to print and electronic telecommunications and networking resources. Resources include books, articles, serials, discussion lists, software, training materials, and more. *Newsletter*

± listserv@uicvm.uic.edu [body = SUBSCRIBE LITA-L first-name last-name]

INFO linda.knutson@ala.org (Linda Knutson)

INFO twilson@uh.edu (Thomas C. Wilson)

ARCHIVE listserv@uicvm.uic.edu [body = INDEX LITA-L]

Frequency: irregular

9638 **TELECOMREG:** On telecommunication regulation. *Mailing List*

± listserver@relay.doit.wisc.edu

OWNER borton@macc.wisc.edu (Barry Orton)

9639 **TELECOMWORLDWIRE:** TELECOMWORLDWIRE is a daily international newsletter covering telecommunications and IT news and developments, delivered to a diverse global readership of industry participants, users, buyers, consultants, researchers, sector groups, and educators.

http://www.m2.com/

INFO tww-edit@m2.com

9640 **TELXCH-L:** On telecomunications in the state of New York and national telecommunications and policy issues related to digital infrastructure. *Mailing List*

± listserv@albnydh2.bitnet [body = SUBSCRIBE TELXCH-L first-name last-name]

INFO pbachman@skidmore.edu (Peter Bachman)

ARCHIVE listserv@albnydh2.bitnet

Comments: Messages for listowner should have the keyword TELXCH-L in the subject header.

9641 **tnn.dcom.satellite** Discussions about communications via satellite. *Newsgroup*

9642 **TOUCHTON:** On Touch-Tone/Voice Response Systems. *Mailing List*

± `listserv@sjsuvm1.sjsu.edu` [body = SUBSCRIBE TOUCHTON first-name last-name]

INFO `touchton-request@sjsuvm1.sjsu.edu`

ARCHIVE `listserv@sjsuvm1.sjsu.edu` [body = INDEX TOUCHTON]

9643   `uk.telecom`   Discussion of U.K. telecommunications. *Newsgroup*

9644   **xpress-list:** For discussion of the X*Press X*Change data service, which is available on some cable television systems in the U.S. and Canada and on some satellite television channels. *Mailing List*

`http://www.grot.com/xpress/`

± `majordomo@best.com` [body = subscribe xpress-list e-mail-address]

INFO OWNER `owner-xpress-list@lists.best.com` (Brian Smithson)

INFO `brian@grot.com` (Brian Smithson)

ARCHIVE `ftp://ftp.grot.com/xpress/`

TELECOMMUNICATIONS—ACCESS

9645   `ak.bushnet.thing`   Alaskan Public Access Networking. *Newsgroup*

➤   **Arlington Community Television's Homepage:** Home page for Channel 33—Arlington, Virginia's community access cable station. This home page offers information about ACT and access in general, contact information, and examples of the type of progams produced through the facilities. (See entry 1487 for full listing.)

➤   **Devmedia:** On the democratization of media and communication: radio, TV, video. (See entry 6104 for full listing.)

9646   **Economic Democracy Information Network (EDIN):** A project dedicated to expanding the voice of community organizations on the information superhighway.

`http://garnet.berkeley.edu:3333/`

INFO `newman@garnet.berkeley.edu`

9647   **The Network Startup Resource Center:** This site contains information about: networking in the developing world, low-cost networking tools, general computer networking information, and networking tips and frequently asked questions. You can search for networking solutions and information by country.

`http://www.nsrc.org/`

`gopher://gopher.nsrc.org`

INFO `nsrc@nsrc.org`

➤   **SEA: the society for electronic access.:** A New York City-based organization that promotes civil liberties and access in cyberspace. (See entry 9751 for full listing.)

➤   **Voters Telecomm Watch (VTW):** A volunteer organization, concentrating on legislation as it relates to telecommunications and civil liberties. (See entry 9752 for full listing.)

VETERINARY

9648   `alt.med.veterinary`   Veterinary medicine and animal health. *Newsgroup*

9649   **BSE-L:** On bovine spongiform encephalopathy (BSE, "mad cow disease"). *Mailing List, moderated*

± `listserv@rz.uni-karlsruhe.de` [body = SUB BSE-L first-name last-name]

INFO `bse-l-request@rz.uni-karlsruhe.de`

EDITOR `siegfried.schmitt@rz.uni-karlsruhe.de`

OWNER `je04@ibm3090.rz.uni-karlsruhe.de` (Siegfried Schmitt)

ARCHIVE `listserv@rz.uni-karlsruhe.de` [body = GET BSE-L LOGxx where xx is the year for which you want archives]

9650   **VETCAI-L:** On computer-assisted instruction in veterinary medicine. *Mailing List*

± `listserv@ksuvm.ksu.edu` [body = SUBSCRIBE VETCAI-L first-name last-name]

INFO `michaels@ksuvm.bitnet` (Wayne Michaels)

ARCHIVE `listserv@ksuvm.ksu.edu`

9651   **VETINFO:** On veterinary informatics. *Mailing List*

± `listserv@wulist.wustl.edu` [body = SUBSCRIBE VETINFO first-name last-name]

INFO ken@wudcm.wustl.edu (Ken Boschert)
INFO jcase@cvdls.ucdavis.edu
(Jim Case, DVM)
ARCHIVE http://netvet.wustl.edu/vetinfo.htm
Please Note: Subscription by approval only.

9652 **VETLIB-L:** On veterinary-medicine library issues and information. *Mailing List*
± listserv@vtvm2.cc.vt.edu [body = SUBSCRIBE VETLIB-L first-name last-name]
INFO kok@vtvm1.bitnet (Vicki Kok)
ARCHIVE listserv@vtvm2.cc.vt.edu

VIDEO

9653 **alt.video.dvd** Discussion of Digital Video Disk hardware and software. *Newsgroup*

9654 **alt.video.laserdisc** LD players and selections available for them. *Newsgroup*

9655 **aus.comms.videocon** Videoconferencing—compressed video. *Newsgroup*

9656 **comp.dcom.videoconf** Video conference technology and applications. *Newsgroup*

9657 **comp.os.ms-windows.video** Video adapters and drivers for Windows. *Newsgroup*

9658 **Desktop Video:** A guide to the basic concepts of desktop video production, from preproduction to distribution.
http://godzilla.inre.asu.edu/~guy/Video1.html

9659 **DIGVID-L:** On digital video: formats, platforms, distribution. *Mailing List*
± listserv@ucdavis.edu [body = SUBSCRIBE DIGVID-L first-name last-name]
OWNER jpgorrono@ucdavis.edu (Jon Gorrono)
OWNER dengelman@cetis.hut.nl (Danny Engelman)

9660 **DVI-list:** On Intel's DVI (Digital Video Interactive) system. Covers both applications and programming with DVI. *Mailing List*
± listserv@calvin.dgbt.doc.ca [body = subscribe dvi-list first-name last-name]
INFO server@calvin.dgbt.doc.ca
ARCHIVE ftp://debra.dgbt.doc.ca/pub/dvi

9661 **HDTVNewsList:** On high-definition television (HDTV). *Distribution List, moderated*
OWNER sysop@teletron.com (Howard Barton)

9662 **hepnet.videoconf** Video conferencing High Energy Physics researchers. *Newsgroup*

9663 **rec.video** Video and video components. *Newsgroup*

9664 **rec.video.desktop** Amateur, computer-based video editing and production. *Newsgroup*

9665 **rec.video.production** Making professional-quality video productions. *Newsgroup*

9666 **rec.video.professional** Professional video, technical and artistic. *Moderated newsgroup*

9667 **rec.video.satellite.dbs** DBS systems and technologies. *Newsgroup*

9668 **rec.video.satellite.misc** Non-TVRO and non-DBS satellite information. *Newsgroup*

SOCIAL ISSUES

9669   **HandsNet:** HandsNet is a national, nonprofit network that promotes information sharing, cross-sector collaboration, and advocacy among individuals and organizations working on a broad range of public interest issues. The site includes action alerts, forums, and information on the various social programs that HandsNet is involved with.

http://www.handsnet.org/
INFO hninfo@handsnet.org

➤   **Nonprofit Resources Catalogue:** A collection of resources of interest to nonprofit organizations. Covers: business and work, fundraising and giving, general nonprofit resources, general reference, health and human services, news sources, United States government, weather and disasters, and more. (See entry 2056 for full listing.)

9670   **Resources Nonprofit:** An extensive collection of Internet resource of interest to nonprofit organizations. As well as including listings on specific nonprofits and resources relating to specific social issues that nonprofits are often involved in, the site includes information on funding opportunities, nonprofit management issues, nonprofits and technology, philanthropy, volunteer activities, and business, corporate and government information.

http://www.sils.umich.edu/~nesbeitt/nonprofits/nonprofits.html
INFO public-services@umich.edu

9671   **Impact ONLINE:** Impact Online promotes community involvement by offering information on nonprofits and on volunteer opportunities nationwide. Impact Online even offers "virtual volunteer" opportunities that can be done entirely online. The site also offers a complete online course for nonprofits interested in using technology for social change.

http://www.impactonline.org/
INFO info@impactonline.org

9672   `soc.misc` Socially oriented topics not in other groups. *Newsgroup*

ABORTION & REPRODUCTIVE RIGHTS

9673   **Abortion Clinics Online:** A listing of abortion clinics and other pro-choice Internet resources.

http://www.realpages.com/abortion/
INFO annrose@randomc.com

9674   **The Abortion Rights Activist:** News and information on abortion rights activism.

http://www.cais.com/agm/
INFO agm@cais.com

9675   `alt.abortion.inequity` Paternal obligations of failing to abort unwanted child. *Newsgroup*

9676   `alt.support.abortion` Pro-choice advocates. *Newsgroup*

9677   **California Abortion and Reproductive Rights Action League (CARAL):** Information on abortion and reproductive rights activism: comprehensive.

http://www.matisse.net/politics/caral/caral.html
INFO caral@aol.com

9678   `clari.news.issues.reproduction` Abortion, fertility, reproduction. *Moderated newsgroup*

9679   `clari.news.reproduction` Abortion, contraception, fertility. *Moderated newsgroup*

9680   **Life Communications:** News and comment on pro-life issues, mainly abortion and euthanasia. *Newsletter*

http://www.netcentral.net/lists/wli.html
± http://www.netcentral.net/lists/wli.html
INFO OWNER plnews-mod@netcentral.net
INFO frezza@ee.gannon.edu (Steve Frezza)
ARCHIVE plnews-mod@netcentral.net
Frequency: bimonthly

9681   **LifeLinks:** For right-to-life information and resources.

```
http://www.nebula.net/~maeve/lifelink.html
```
INFO maeve@nebula.net

➤ **SNUFFIT-L:** The Church of Euthanasia. (See entry 528 for full listing.)

9682 **talk.abortion** All sorts of discussions and arguments on abortion. *Newsgroup*

9683 **Ultimate Pro-Life Resource List:** The Ultimate Pro-Life Resource List is the most comprehensive listing of right-to-life information on the Internet.
```
http://www.prolife.org/ultimate
```
INFO ertelt@netcentral.net

ABUSE & VICTIMS' RIGHTS

➤ **Marriage Resources:** This page provides information about marriage, codependency, and friendships. (See entry 6026 for full listing.)

9684 **alt.abuse.offender.recovery** Helping abuse offenders to recover and heal. *Newsgroup*

9685 **alt.abuse.recovery** Helping victims of abuse to recover. *Newsgroup*

9686 **alt.abuse.transcendence** Nonstandard ways to deal with all forms of abuse. *Newsgroup*

➤ **alt.sex.incest:** Discussing the issues of intra-familial sexual relations. *Newsgroup*

9687 **alt.sexual.abuse.recovery** Helping others deal with traumatic experiences. *Newsgroup*

➤ **INTVIO-L:** On intimate, or family, violence. (See entry 9931 for full listing.)

➤ **Kathy's Resources on Parenting, Domestic Violence, Abuse, Trauma & Dissociation:** Friendly and exhaustive index to resources that foster interpersonal respect and nonviolence. (See entry 9932 for full listing.)

➤ **NCS-L:** For discussing the design and use of the National Crime Survey to produce national estimates of criminal victimization. (See entry 9805 for full listing.)

➤ **Support Coalition & Dendron News:** Dendron News is the voice of Support Coalition, a nonprofit alliance of 30 grass-roots advocacy, human rights, and support groups. "Breaking the silence about psychiatric oppression!" "Heal Normally, Naturally!" These are some of the slogans from a little-known, diverse 25-year-old social change movement: The psychiatric surivors liberation movement, sometimes known as "mad lib." Stop forced drugs and forced electroshock! (See entry 4711 for full listing.)

ADOPTION

9688 **adoption:** On adoption. *Mailing List*
± listserv@sjuvm.stjohns.edu [body = SUBSCRIBE ADOPTION first-name last-name]
OWNER dih1@cornell.edu (Diane I. Hillmann)
OWNER myers@ab.edu (Roger Myers)

9689 **alt.adoption** For those involved with or contemplating adoption. *Newsgroup*

9690 **alt.adoption.agency** Licensed nonprofit adoption agency information. *Newsgroup*

9691 **BRTHPRNT:** For birth parents of adoptees. *Mailing List*
± listserv@win95.dc.lsoft.com [body = SUBSCRIBE BRTHPRNT first-name last-name]
OWNER nathan@ubvm.cc.buffalo.edu (Nathan Brindle)

➤ **clari.news.childrn+family:** Children and families, adoption, marriage. *Moderated newsgroup*

AFRICAN-AMERICANS

9692 **African American Web Connection:** For Web links of interest to people of African American descent.
```
http://www.wp.com/wrjones/african.html
```
INFO wrjones@acm.org

9693 **Afronet:** For net resources of interest to African-American communities: good, clear design and business emphasis. Also, a source for information on the movie *Waiting to Exhale*.

http://www.afronet.com/
INFO afronet@earthlink.net

9694 **The Universal Black Pages:** For a complete and comprehensive listing of African diaspora-related Web pages.
http://www.gatech.edu/bgsa/blackpages.html
INFO bgsa@www.gatech.edu
FAQ http://www.gatech.edu/bgsa/blackpages/essential.html

➤ **alt.rodney-king:** Riot catalyst. *Newsgroup*

9695 **The Black Information Network:** For data gathered from entities that have concerns rooted within the black community.
http://www.bin.com/
INFO ejenkins@bin.tca.com [Eric Jenkins]
INFO csmith@bin.tca.com [Clara Smith]

➤ **SEBSEL:** For international networking of black engineers and scientists (no discussion, information only). (See entry 9236 for full listing.)

➤ **BLK Homie Pages:** News and information about the black lesbian and gay communities. (See entry 9954 for full listing.)

9696 **clari.news.blacks** Black news. *Moderated newsgroup*

9697 **ONE:** A chronicle of progressive Black politics and culture that will fuse a diverse body of thought into one cohesive agenda: freedom of expression. *E-Journal*
http://www.clark.net/pub/conquest/one/home.html
INFO ekeone@aol.com (Eric Easter)
INFO conquest@clark.net (Richard Landry—Webmaster)

AGE

9698 **Internet and E-mail Resources on Aging:** Includes commercial services, Freenets, online library catalogs, BBSs, mailing lists, e-journals, newsgroups, gopher sites, Web sites, and selected e-mail addresses.
http://www.aoa.dhhs.gov/aoa/pages/jpostlst.html
http://www.lib.umich.edu/chouse/inter/645.html
INFO post@hslc.org (Joyce Post, Phila. Geriatric Center)

9699 **clari.news.aging** News of senior citizens and aging. *Moderated newsgroup*

9700 **Elders:** On elders: social and political issues, electronic grandparents, and mentors. *Mailing List*
gopher://gopher.etext.org/11/Zines/CyberSenior
± listserv@sjuvm.stjohns.edu [body = SUB ELDERS first-name last-name]
OWNER edabbs@extro.ucc.su.oz.au (Elaine Dabbs)
OWNER patd@chatback.demon.co.uk (Pat Davidson)
Please Note: Subscription by approval only.

9701 **soc.retirement** Retirement, aging, gerontology issues. *Newsgroup*

ANIMAL RIGHTS

9702 **AR-News:** A public news wire for items relating to animal rights and welfare. Informational postings only. *Distribution List*
http://www.cygnus.com/~ian/ar-charter.html
± ar-news-request@cygnus.com (Ian Lance Taylor or Chip Roberson)
INFO ar-news-owner@cygnus.com (Ian Lance Taylor)

9703 **AR-Views:** An unmoderated list for the discussion of animal rights. *Mailing List*
http://www.cygnus.com/~ian/ar-charter.html
± ar-views-request@cygnus.com

INFO `ar-views-owner@cygnus.com` (Ian Lance Taylor)

➤ **EARTHSAVE:** On personal food choices and the ecology of the planet. (See entry 5836 for full listing.)

➤ **LPN-L:** For scientists doing research on or with nonhuman primates, including care and breeding, research news, requests for information or materials, and conservation. (See entry 9502 for full listing.)

9704 `talk.politics.animals` The use and/or abuse of animals. *Newsgroup*

ASIAN-AMERICANS

9705 **Chinese Community Information Center (CCIC):** The CCIC site is the Chinese Community Information Center set up by IFCSS (Independent Federation of Chinese Students and Scholars in the U.S.) to serve its community and its friends. Includes news, information for Chinese expatriates, information on Chinese & computers, and more.

`http://www.ifcss.org/`
`ftp://ftp.ifcss.org`
INFO `www-admin@ifcss.org`

Comments: Software uploaded must be accompanied by a description. To upload other data, please write to contact address.

➤ `pgh.org.uccp`: The University Chinese Club of Pittsburgh. *Newsgroup*

BIRTH

➤ <u>Midwifery Internet Resources:</u> Contains information about and instructions for accessing Internet resources for midwives. (See entry 5113 for full listing.)

9706 `misc.kids.pregnancy` Pre-pregnancy planning, pregnancy, childbirth. *Newsgroup*

9707 `sci.med.midwifery` The practice of obstetrics by midwives. *Moderated newsgroup*

BODY SIZE

9708 `alt.fan.skinny` Fat fetishes have no place here. *Newsgroup*

9709 `alt.support.big-folks` Sizeism can be as awful as sexism or racism. *Newsgroup*

9710 `alt.support.diet` Seeking enlightenment through weight loss. *Newsgroup*

9711 `alt.support.diet.rx` Discussion of the use of anorectic drugs in obesity. *Newsgroup*

9712 `alt.support.dwarfism` Support for unusually short people. *Moderated newsgroup*

9713 `alt.support.eating-disord` People over the edge about weight loss. *Newsgroup*

9714 `alt.support.obesity` Support/resources to treat obesity. *Moderated newsgroup*

9715 `alt.support.short` Short people commiserate. *Newsgroup*

9716 `alt.support.tall` Issues of interest to tall people. *Newsgroup*

9717 `soc.support.fat-acceptance` Self-acceptance for fat people. No diet talk. *Newsgroup*

CHILDREN

➤ **adoption:** On adoption. (See entry 9688 for full listing.)

9718 `alt.activism.children` Open discussion of political issues about children. *Newsgroup*

9719 `alt.child-support` Raising children in a split family. *Newsgroup*

9720 `alt.kids-talk` A place for the pre-college set on the net. *Newsgroup*

9721 `alt.parenting.twins-triplets` The issues of raising twins and other multiples. *Newsgroup*

9722 `alt.parents-teens` Parent-teenager relationships. *Newsgroup*

9723 `alt.support.breastfeeding` Discussion and support for breastfeeding. *Newsgroup*

9724 `alt.support.foster-parents` People who are foster parents. *Newsgroup*

➤ **alt.support.househusbands:** men who tend the home (See entry 0 for full listing.)

9725 **alt.support.single-parents** Single parenting solutions and support. *Newsgroup*

➤ **Bowlby:** On attachment theory: research on early childhood development and parent-infant affectional-cognitive bonds. (See entry 9516 for full listing.)

9726 **csn.ml.kids** Mailing list gatewayed by Colorado SuperNet. *Newsgroup*

9727 **csn.ml.kidsnet** Mailing list gatewayed by Colorado SuperNet. *Newsgroup*

9728 **Cyber Kids:** Online magazine for kids and by kids containing stories, artwork, puzzles, and more. *E-Journal*
http://www.woodwind.com/cyberkids/index.html
INFO cyberkids@mtlake.com (Mountain Lake Software, Inc.)
Comments: Site also includes interactive bulletin board and database of links to other Web sites.

➤ **ECPOLICY-L:** On early childhood policy. (See entry 4145 for full listing.)

9729 **fj.life.children** Children, childcare, and parenting. *Newsgroup*

➤ **INTVIO-L:** On intimate, or family, violence. (See entry 9931 for full listing.)

➤ **Kathy's Resources on Parenting, Domestic Violence, Abuse, Trauma & Dissociation:** Friendly and exhaustive index to resources that foster interpersonal respect and nonviolence. (See entry 9932 for full listing.)

9730 **The KID List:** Lists for children.
http://www.cais.com/makulow/kid.html
INFO john@trainer.com

9731 **Kid's Window:** A multimedia resource for children to learn about Japanese language and culture.
http://jw.nttam.com/KIDS/kids_home.html
http://jw.stanford.edu/KIDS/kids_home.html
INFO jw@fuji.stanford.edu

9732 **MEALTALK:** On child nutrition programs.
± majordomo@nalusda.gov [body = subscribe mealtalk first-name last-name e-mail-address]
OWNER jgladsto@nalusda.gov (John Gladstone)
ARCHIVE majordomo@nalusda.gov [body = INDEX MEALTALK]

9733 **misc.kids** Children, their behavior and activities. *Newsgroup*

9734 **misc.kids.consumers** Products related to kids. *Newsgroup*

9735 **misc.kids.health** Children's health. *Newsgroup*

9736 **misc.kids.info** Informational posts related to misc.kids hierarchy. *Moderated newsgroup*

9737 **misc.kids.vacation** Discussion on all forms of family-oriented vacationing. *Newsgroup*

9738 **National Child Care Information Center (NCCIC):** Information and resources on child care.
http://ericps.ed.uiuc.edu/nccic/nccichome.html
INFO cesarone@uiuc.edu

➤ **ParentsPlace.com:** Resource for parents. Includes discussion groups, articles on parenting, and a shopping mall. (See entry 9935 for full listing.)

➤ **QUAKER-K:** Discussion group for Quaker children ages 5 to 12. (See entry 8763 for full listing.)

9739 **relcom.kids** About kids. *Newsgroup*

9740 **SAC-L:** On school-age care. *Mailing List*
± listserv@postoffice.cso.uiuc.edu [body = SUBSCRIBE SAC-L first-name last-name]
INFO cesarone@uiuc.edu

➤ **scot.bairns:** Scottish newsgroup for or about children. *Newsgroup*

➤ **Triplets:** The Triplets list is for discussions of issues concerning triplets and other multiples. It is an open forum in which parents, relatives, doctors, nurses, researchers, and others can discuss a wide range of topics pertaining to multiples. (See entry 9939 for full listing.)

➤ **twins:** Forum on twins/triplets/etc. Topics include research on twin-related issues and parenting issues as well as issues concerning adult twins. (See entry 9940 for full listing.)

CIVIL RIGHTS & CIVIL LIBERTIES

9741 `alt.discrimination` Quotas, affirmative action, bigotry, persecution. *Newsgroup*

9742 `alt.freedom.academic` Meaning of, threats to, and defenses for academic freedom. *Newsgroup*

9743 `alt.freedom.of.information.act` All about the FOIA. *Newsgroup*

9744 `alt.gov.foi-legislation` Freedom of information laws on all levels. *Newsgroup*

➤ `alt.rodney-king`: Riot catalyst. *Newsgroup*

9745 `alt.society.civil-liberties` Same as alt.society.civil-liberty. *Newsgroup*

9746 `clari.news.civil_rights` Freedom, civil rights, human rights. *Moderated newsgroup*

9747 **CLSPEECH:** On free speech law, intended mainly for legal academics. *Mailing List*
± `listserv@ftplaw.wuacc.edu`
OWNER `volokh@law.ucla.edu` (Eugene Volokh)
Please Note: Subscription by approval only.

9748 **CYBER-RIGHTS:** Campaign for cyber rights: "Don't let the grinch steal cyberspace!" *Mailing List, moderated*
± `listserv@cpsr.org` [body = SUBSCRIBE CYBER-RIGHTS first-name last-name]
EDITOR `andyo@ora.com` (Andy Oram)

9749 **Electronic Frontier Foundation:** The Electronic Frontier Foundation is a 501(c)3 nonprofit organization "working in the public interest to protect privacy, free expression, and access to online resources and information." The site includes very important information on the interaction between our government and the Internet, as well as an extensive archive with documents on a wide range of topics, including activism, censorship, cryptography and computer security, net culture and cyber-anthropology, intellectual property, law, privacy, and more. It also archives various e-journals related to its mission.
`http://www.eff.org/`
`ftp://ftp.eff.org`
`gopher://gopher.eff.org`
INFO `webmaster@eff.org`

9750 **EFFector Online:** For the Electronic Frontier Foundation (EFF). *Newsletter*
`http://www.eff.org/pub/EFF/Newsletters/EFFector/`
`gopher://gopher.eff.org/11/EFF/Newsletters/EFFector/`
± `listserv@eff.org` [body = SUBSCRIBE effector-online first-name last-name]
INFO `info@eff.org`
ARCHIVE `ftp://ftp.eff.org/pub/EFF/Newsletters/EFFector/`
Gated: `comp.org.eff.news`
Frequency: roughly biweekly

➤ **EPIC Alert:** Online newsletter of the Electronic Privacy Information Center in Washington, D.C. Focuses on privacy and civil-liberties issues in the information age. (See entry 3723 for full listing.)

➤ **GovAccess:** On computer-assisted citizen participation in—and protection from—government. (See entry 5381 for full listing.)

➤ **PRIVACY:** Discussion and analysis of issues relating to the general topic of privacy (both personal and collective) in the "information age." (See entry 3731 for full listing.)

➤ **The Red Rock Eater News Service:** All the news that Phil Agre, media and communications professor at UCSD, thinks fit to print on the subject of how technology affects peoples' lives. (See entry 3732 for full listing.)

➤ **ReligionLaw:** On religion and the law; technical orientation. (See entry 5528 for full listing.)

➤ **RIGHTS-L:** For persons interested in the ongoing effort to create a bill of rights and responsibilities for electronic citizens. (See entry 5612 for full listing.)

9751 **SEA: the society for electronic access.:** A New York City-based organization that promotes civil liberties and access in cyberspace.

http://www.sea.org/

INFO sea@sea.org

INFO clay@sea.org (Clay Irving)

➤ **Sonoma State University Computer Science Department:** This is the WWW server for the computer science department at Sonoma State University, Rohnert Park, California. Includes information for computer-science majors at Sonoma State, and Project Censored (a media research project on censorship) "Top Ten Censored Stories" lists. (See entry 9206 for full listing.)

➤ **Stormfront:** A collection of resources on white nationalism. (See entry 5673 for full listing.)

➤ **Support Coalition & Dendron News:** Dendron News is the voice of Support Coalition, a nonprofit alliance of 30 grass-roots advocacy, human rights, and support groups. "Breaking the silence about psychiatric oppression!" "Heal Normally, Naturally!" These are some of the slogans from a little-known, diverse 25-year-old social change movement: The psychiatric surivors liberation movement, sometimes known as "mad lib." Stop forced drugs and forced electroshock! (See entry 4711 for full listing.)

9752 **Voters Telecomm Watch (VTW):** A volunteer organization, concentrating on legislation as it relates to telecommunications and civil liberties.

http://www.vtw.org/

INFO vtw@vtw.org

COMMUNITY DEVELOPMENT

9753 `alt.community.intentional` Some spinoff from `alt.co-ops`. *Newsgroup*

9754 `alt.community.local-money` LETS and other local money systems. *Newsgroup*

➤ `alt.housing.nontrad`: Communes, co-housing, and alternative living arrangements. *Newsgroup*

➤ **Arlington Community Television's Homepage:** Home page for Channel 33—Arlington, Virginia's community access cable station. This home page offers information about ACT and access in general, contact information, and examples of the type of progams produced through the facilities. (See entry 1487 for full listing.)

9755 **BIDS4NYC:** On business improvement districts. *Mailing List*

± listserv@sjuvm.stjohns.edu [body = SUBSCRIBE BIDS4NYC first-name last-name]

OWNER sunsetrest@aol.com (Tony Giordano, registrar)

➤ `bit.org.peace-corps`: Peace Corps. *Newsgroup*

9756 **CD4URBAN:** This list deals with all topics involving community development in urban areas. Common discussion subjects include enterprise communities and empowerment zones, other zoning regulations, and low-income housing development. *Mailing List*

http://www.infoanalytic.com/cds

± listproc@u.washington.edu [body = subscribe cd4urban]

OWNER alboss@scn.org (Al Boss)

ARCHIVE listproc@u.washington.edu

9757 **CED-NET:** Discussion on the trends, opportunities, and changes in community economic development. The list's goal is to focus on what communities can do for themselves in terms of programs and funds, among other things. *Mailing List*

± majordomo@sfu.ca [body = subscribe ced-net]

INFO OWNER jjespers@sfu.ca (John Jespersen)

ARCHIVE http://www.sfu.ca/cedc

➤ **The Center For Civic Networking:** Included in this site is information on developing a sustainable information network, policy issues regarding electronic development, and information regarding municipalities and local governmental information networks. The Center for Civic Networking is a nonprofit organization whose goal is to help develop models of beneficial uses of the Internet for local, regional, and national organizations and governments. (See entry 2422 for full listing.)

9758 CNET: On community network building in remote and rural Canadian communities. *Mailing List*

http://cnet.unb.ca/

± listserv@unb.ca [body = SUBSCRIBE CNET first-name last-name]

EDITOR ryana@unb.ca (Anne Ryan)

Language: French, English

9759 Community Development Society: The international Community Development Society (CDS), founded in 1969, is a dynamic professional association offering a global perspective on community development.

http://www.infoanalytic.com/cds

INFO alboss@scn.org (Al Boss)

9760 CommunityDevelopmentBanking-L: On community reinvestment. *Mailing List*

± listproc@cornell.edu [body = SUBSCRIBE COMMUNITYDEVELOPMENTBANKING-L first-name last-name]

EDITOR alternatives@pobox.com (William Myers)

ARCHIVE ftp://ftp.lightlink.com/pub/afcu

➤ **Economic Democracy Information Network (EDIN):** A project dedicated to expanding the voice of community organizations on the information superhighway. (See entry 9646 for full listing.)

9761 futurework: This list focuses on ways for communities worldwide to deal with economic globalization and technological change. *Mailing List*

http://csf.colorado.edu/FW

± listserv@csf.colorado.edu [body = SUBSCRIBE FUTUREWORK first-name last-name]

INFO OWNER lerner@watserv1.uwaterloo.ca (Sally Lerner)

POST futurework@csf.colorado.edu

Comments: There is also a moderated list, FW-L, that serves as a "bulletin board." Subscribe as for futurework, but substitute FW-L.

➤ **Minnesota Extension Service:** The official electronic information service for the Minnesota Extension Service, St. Paul campus of the University of Minnesota. (See entry 8917 for full listing.)

9762 The National Association of Regional Councils (NARC): Included on this site are reports from NARC task forces, news bulletins, and general information about NARC and its affiliates.

gopher://narc.org/11/.NARC

INFO epling@narc.org

➤ **North Carolina Cooperative Extension Gopher:** This is the NC Cooperative Extension WWW server located at North Carolina State University, Raleigh, North Carolina. (See entry 8918 for full listing.)

➤ **OICISNET:** Network project to support the developmental activities of Organization of Islamic Conference (OIC) member countries and their institutions. (See entry 8795 for full listing.)

9763 PRA: PRA (Participatory Rural Appraisal) is devoted to the topic of participatory community development. *Mailing List*

http://tdg.uoguelph.ca/~pi

± listserv@uoguelph.ca [body = SUB PRA first-name last-name]

OWNER srimkus@uoguelph.ca (Susan Rimkus)

ARCHIVE http://tdg.uoguelph.ca/~pi

POST pra@uoguelph.ca

9764 RURALDEV: On community and rural economic development. *Mailing List*

± listserv@ksuvm.ksu.edu [body = SUBSCRIBE RURALDEV first-name last-name]

INFO rcyoung@ksu.ksu.edu (Ron Young)

ARCHIVE listserv@ksuvm.ksu.edu

➤ **uk.org.community:** U.K. CommUnity matters. *Newsgroup*

➤ **uk.org.community.committee**: U.K. CommUnity committee matters. *Moderated newsgroup*

➤ **URBWLF-L**: For the interchange of ideas and experiences among researchers, managers, planners, and educators concerned with wildlife habitats, urban ecosystems, and the quality of life in urban areas. (See entry 4686 for full listing.)

➤ **USDA Cooperative State Research, Education, and Extension Service**: This site is set up to provide access to information from the USDA Extension Service, other USDA agencies, and other federal agencies as it relates to the Cooperative Extension System. (See entry 8922 for full listing.)

CONSPIRACY

9765 **The Conspiracy Page**: Well-rounded guide to net resources on conspiracy and secret histories.
http://rock.san.uc.edu/~taylorrm/
INFO conspira@one.net
INFO taylorrm@ucbeh.san.uc.edu

9766 **alt.conspiracy** Be paranoid—they're out to get you. *Newsgroup*

9767 **alt.conspiracy.area51** The U.S. government has a secret they're not telling you. *Newsgroup*

9768 **alt.conspiracy.jfk** The Kennedy assassination. *Newsgroup*

9769 **alt.conspiracy.retards** For those not impressed with the conspiracy-minded. *Newsgroup*

➤ **alt.illuminati**: See alt.cabal. *Newsgroup*

9770 **alt.jfk.assassination** JFK assassination conspiracy discussion. *Moderated newsgroup*

9771 **Fair Play**: Devoted exclusively to the JFK case. It is oriented toward research and journalism, but previous issues have included JFK-related fiction and poetry. *Magazine*
http://rmii.com/~jkelin/fp.html
INFO jkelin@rmii.com (John Kelin)

➤ **Stormfront**: A collection of resources on white nationalism. (See entry 5673 for full listing.)

CONSUMERS

9772 **alt.consumers.free-stuff** Free offers and how to take advantage of them. *Newsgroup*

9773 **alt.coupons** /koo pahns/, not /kew pahns/. Try it. *Newsgroup*

9774 **alt.culture.openair-market** Discussing open-air markets around the world. *Newsgroup*

9775 **ba.consumers** Bay Area (USA) group for consumer topics. *Newsgroup*

9776 **civil-justice**: On measures aimed at restricting victims' rights and weakening liability laws. *Newsletter*
± listproc@essential.org [body = SUBSCRIBE CIVIL-JUSTICE first-name last-name]
OWNER jbelluck@essential.org (Joseph Belluck)

9777 **clari.living.consumer** Consumer issues and products. *Moderated newsgroup*

9778 **ieee.ces.broadcast-cable** Consumer Electronics Society—broadcast/cable. *Newsgroup*

9779 **ieee.ces.home-automation** Consumer Electronics Society—home automation. *Newsgroup*

9780 **ieee.ces.personal-communications** Personal Communications. *Newsgroup*

9781 **MaxLife-L**: Towards a positive, healthy lifestyle without consumerism. *Mailing List*
± listserv@listserv.unc.edu [body = SUBSCRIBE MAXLIFE-L first-name last-name]
OWNER gordonse@iris.uncg.edu (Sharon Gordon)

9782 **McSpotlight**: An online library of detailed, accurate, up-to-date information about the McDonald's Corporation, its business practices, and its effects on the world. Everything you could ever need to know about the "McLibel Trial" and worldwide opposition and resistance to the company (and others like them) can be found on this Web site. Possibly the most comprehensive and damning collection of material on a multinational corporation ever assembled.
http://www.mcspotlight.org/

INFO `mclibel@europe.std.com`
INFO `info@mcspotlight.org`
MIRRORS
`http://muu.lib.hel.fi/McSpotlight/` (Finland)
`http://www.envirolink.org/mcspotlight`
`http://www.ch.planet.gen.nz/~mcspot/` (New Zeland)

9783 **misc.consumers** Consumer interests, product reviews, etc. *Newsgroup*

9784 **relcom.consumers** Consumer information on products and services. No ads. *Newsgroup*

CRIME

9785 **alt.crime** Crime in general, not just the crimes in `alt.*`. *Newsgroup*

9786 **alt.rodney-king** Riot catalyst. *Newsgroup*

9787 **alt.true-crime** Criminal acts around the world. *Newsgroup*

9788 **biz.stolen** Postings about stolen merchandise postings. *Newsgroup*

➤ **CJUST-L:** Criminal justice discussion list. (See entry 5459 for full listing.)

9789 **clari.news.crime.abductions** Kidnappings, hostage-taking. *Moderated newsgroup*

9790 **clari.news.crime.fraud+embezzle** Fraud, embezzlement, white-collar crime. *Moderated newsgroup*

9791 **clari.news.crime.hate** Hate crimes. *Moderated newsgroup*

9792 **clari.news.crime.issue** The social issue of crime. *Moderated newsgroup*

9793 **clari.news.crime.misc** Other crimes. *Moderated newsgroup*

9794 **clari.news.crime.murders** Murders and shootings. *Moderated newsgroup*

9795 **clari.news.crime.murders.misc** Murders and shootings. *Moderated newsgroup*

9796 **clari.news.crime.murders.political** Political murders and shootings. *Moderated newsgroup*

9797 **clari.news.crime.organized** Organized crime. *Moderated newsgroup*

9798 **clari.news.crime.sex** Sex crimes, child pornography. *Moderated newsgroup*

9799 **clari.news.crime.theft** Thefts and robberies. *Moderated newsgroup*

9800 **clari.news.crime.top** Well-known crimes. *Moderated newsgroup*

9801 **clari.news.crime.white_collar** Insider trading, fraud, embezzlement. *Moderated newsgroup*

9802 **clari.news.issues.death_penalty** Death penalty, executions. *Moderated newsgroup*

9803 **clari.news.punishment** Prison conditions, torture, death penalty. *Moderated newsgroup*

➤ **CRIMPROF:** On the substantive and pedagogical issues in teaching criminal law and procedure. (See entry 5556 for full listing.)

9804 **Death Penalty Information:** Information on the death penalty. Includes general information and statistics, papers on capital punishment, wrongful convictions, and links to other death penalty pages. This page is part of the home page of the American Criminology Society's Critical Criminology Division.
`http://sun.soci.niu.edu/~critcrim/dp/dp.html`
INFO `critcrim@sun.soci.niu.edu`

➤ **Forensic-psychiatry:** For scholarly discussion of forensic psychiatry. (See entry 5012 for full listing.)

➤ **INFAQ Criminal History Research Page:** INFAQ, a criminal history research firm, offers criminal history checks to the general public through this Web site. Order online and get results through e-mail. (See entry 1915 for full listing.)

➤ **Journal of Criminal Justice and Popular Culture:** Reviews of movies with a criminal-justice theme, and refereed papers on criminal justice and popular culture. (See entry 704 for full listing.)

9805 **NCS-L:** For discussing the design and use of the National Crime Survey to produce national estimates of criminal victimization. *Mailing List*

± `listserv@umdd.umd.edu` [body = SUBSCRIBE NCS-L first-name last-name]
INFO `brianw@umdd.bitnet` (Brian Wiersema)
ARCHIVE `listserv@umdd.umd.edu`

CYBERCULTURE

9806 `alt.culture.internet` The culture(s) of the Internet. *Newsgroup*

9807 `alt.culture.net-viking` Norsemen on the net. *Newsgroup*

9808 `alt.cybercafes` Cyber/computer/Internet cafes or coffee shops. *Newsgroup*

9809 `alt.cyberpunk` High-tech lowlife. *Newsgroup*

9810 `alt.cyberpunk.chatsubo` Literary virtual reality in a cyberpunk hangout. *Newsgroup*

9811 `alt.cyberpunk.movement` A little laxative might help. *Newsgroup*

9812 `alt.cyberpunk.tech` Cyberspace and cyberpunk technology. *Newsgroup*

9813 `alt.cyberspace` Cyberspace and how it should work. *Newsgroup*

9814 `alt.geek` To fulfill an observed need. *Newsgroup*

9815 `alt.life.internet` This may be the answer to "get a life" for some. *Newsgroup*

9816 `alt.privacy` Privacy issues in cyberspace. *Newsgroup*

9817 `alt.virtual-adepts` Cybermagick and related issues. *Newsgroup*

9818 `alt.wired` *Wired* magazine. *Newsgroup*

➤ **Biohazard:** A site ostensibly designed to foster collaboration among Bay Area artists, its front page is introduced by a collage made from text and links that betray Biohazard's unique aesthetic and nonlinear sense of humor. (See entry 1636 for full listing.)

➤ **Computer Underground Digest (CuD):** Discussion of legal, ethical, social, and other issues regarding computerized information and communications. Readers are encouraged to submit reasoned articles relating to computer culture and communication. (See entry 3719 for full listing.)

➤ **cwd-l:** Brock Meeks' CyberWire Dispatch List. (See entry 2876 for full listing.)

9819 **Cyberpunk:** Texts for understanding technology and culture, from the English Server at CMU.
`http://english-www.hss.cmu.edu/cyber.html`
INFO `webmaster@english.hss.cmu.edu`
MIRROR `http://english.hss.cmu.edu/cyber.html`

9820 **Cybersphere:** French magazine on cyberculture: corporate philosophical bent. *Magazine*
`http://www.quelm.fr/CybersphereU.html`
INFO `info@c-sphere.quelm.fr`
EDITOR `http://www.quelm.fr/`
OWNER `cfievet@quelm.fr` (Cyril Fievet)
ARCHIVE `http://www.quelm.fr/CybersphereU.html`
Language: French & English
Frequency: monthly

9821 **Cyborganics:** The first step in a grand plan to build a funky, friendly place that exists on both sides of the screen.
`http://www.cyborganic.com/`
INFO `gardener@cyborganic.com`

➤ **Electronic Frontier Foundation:** The Electronic Frontier Foundation is a 501(c)3 nonprofit organization "working in the public interest to protect privacy, free expression, and access to online resources and information." The site includes very important information on the interaction between our government and the Internet, as well as an extensive archive with documents on a wide range of topics, including activism, censorship, cryptography and computer security, net culture and cyber-anthropology, intellectual property, law, privacy, and more. It also archives various e-journals related to its mission. (See entry 9749 for full listing.)

9822   `eunet.cyberrights`   European perspective of rights of people in cyberspace. *Newsgroup*

9823   **Extropians:** Spin-off of *Extropy* magazine—advanced technology, self-transformation, futurist philosophy, life extension, voluntarism. *Mailing List*
     `http://www.extropy.org/`
     ± `extropians-request@extropy.org` [body = e-mail-address]
     INFO `extropians-request@extropy.org`
     FAQ `http://www.c2.org/~arkuat/extr`

➤   **FEED:** An online-only magazine of politics, culture, and technology. (See entry 646 for full listing.)

➤   **The Foresight Exchange (FX):** The Foresight Exchange is a market that is designed to ascertain the probabilities of specific advances in science and technology. It is a "futures" market about the future. The subject matter dealt with by this market varies from politics and current events to science and technology to popular culture. (See entry 1225 for full listing.)

9824   **FringeWare:** Fringe culture dispersed through design and undesign, community, humor, the marketplace, the net.
     `http://www.fringeware.com/`
     INFO `email@fringeware.com`
     FAQ `http://www.fringeware.com/HTML/what.html`

➤   **George Jr. magazine:** A monthly magazine (with daily updates) of culture, books, art, music, and software for the wired. (See entry 511 for full listing.)

9825   **Globetrotter Magazine:** A WWW-based magazine covering all areas of popular science, technology, and techno-culture. *E-Journal*
     `http://www.dungeon.com/~globe`
     Frequency: bimonthly

9826   **HotWired:** Online sister of *Wired* magazine. Contains articles, discussion forums, and lots more for net hipsters and newbies alike. "Mainstream Culture for the 21st Century."
     `http://www.hotwired.com/`
     INFO `hotwired-info@hotwired.com` (response from a live being)
     INFO `info-rama@hotwired.com` (infobot)
     FAQ `hotfaq@hotwired.com` (infobot)

➤   **INDIE-BRASIL:** From Brazil, a list on indie pop rock culture. (See entry 996 for full listing.)

➤   **info-gnu:** Software development for social change: progress reports from the GNU Project and requests for help. Ask `info-gnu-request@prep.ai.mit.edu` for a list of other mailing lists and resources of all the GNU Project mailing lists and newsgroups. (See entry 3726 for full listing.)

9827   **Inquisitor Mediarama:** The adjunctive Web site to *Inquisitor* magazine, a quarterly journal of art, technology, and culture. *E-Journal*
     `http://mosaic.echonyc.com/~xixax/Mediarama/`
     `gopher://echonyc.com`
     INFO EDITOR `inquisitor@echonyc.com` (Dany Drennan, Editor)
     ARCHIVES
     `http://mosaic.echonyc.com/~xixax/Mediarama/`
     `gopher://echonyc.com`
     Frequency: quarterly to irregular
     Price: $5 per copy. $16 per 4-issue subscription

9828   **Line Noiz:** Line Noiz is a cyberpunk-related e-zine featuring articles on cyberpunk, cyberpunk science fiction, the Internet, and other associated themes. *E-Zine*
     INFO `ae687@freenet.carleton.ca` (Billy Biggs)
     ARCHIVE `http://www.magi.com/~vektor/linenoiz.html`
     Frequency: irregular

➤ **McLuhan-List:** To revitalize and update the work of the late media guru (Marchall McLuhan). (See entry 6094 for full listing.)

9829 **MEME:** On cyberspace and its social impact from a historical point of view. *Distribution List*
http://www.reach.com/matrix
± listserv@sjuvm.stjohns.edu [body = SUBSCRIBE MEME first-name last-name]
OWNER davidsol@panix.com (David S. Bennahum)
ARCHIVES
http://www.reach.com/MATRIX/MEME.HTML
http://www.reach.com/MATRIX
Frequency: twice monthly

9830 **NetDynam:** On online group dynamics. *Mailing List*
± listserv@sjuvm.stjohns.edu [body = SUBSCRIBE NETDYNAM first-name last-name]
OWNER mcrkley@databank.com (Matthew Merkley, M.D.)
ARCHIVE listserv@sjuvm.stjohns.edu [body = INDEX NETDYNAM]

➤ **Processed World Wide Web:** Web site of *Processed World* magazine, the notorious "magazine with a bad attitude." Antiauthoritarian misfits go to work and and bite the hand that bores them. (See entry 2013 for full listing.)

➤ **rec.games.frp.cyber:** Discussions of cyberpunk-related role-playing games. *Newsgroup*

➤ **The Red Rock Eater News Service:** All the news that Phil Agre, media and communications professor at UCSD, thinks fit to print on the subject of how technology affects peoples' lives. (See entry 3732 for full listing.)

➤ **RIGHTS-L:** For persons interested in the ongoing effort to create a bill of rights and responsibilities for electronic citizens. (See entry 5612 for full listing.)

➤ **SEA: the society for electronic access.:** A New York City-based organization that promotes civil liberties and access in cyberspace. (See entry 9751 for full listing.)

9831 **soc.net-people** Announcements, requests, etc. about people on the net. *Newsgroup*

9832 **TNC:** On technoculture, or the broad and complex relationships between technology and culture. *Mailing List*
± majordomo@ucet.ufl.edu [body = SUBSCRIBE TNC]
INFO OWNER true@english.ufl.edu (Anthony Rue)
INFO wleric@showme.missouri.edu (Eric Crump)
ARCHIVE http://www.ucet.ufl.edu/writing/mail-archives/tnc

9833 **The Virtual Journal (Le Journal Virtuel):** The Associated Humans' Electronic Journal a news e-zine on ecology, social, humanitarianism, sciences, poetry, art, and cyberspace. *Magazine*
http://www.ina.fr/CP/HumainsAssocies/JournalVirtuel/HA.JV.HomePage.html
INFO OWNER humains@iway.fr (Tatiana Faria)
ARCHIVE http://www.ina.fr/CP/HumainsAssocies/JournalVirtuel/HA.JV.HomePage.html
Language: French
Frequency: bimonthly

DEATH

9834 **GriefNet:** A collection of resources for those who are experiencing any type of major loss: death, major illness, life changes, etc. This site is sponsored by Rivendell Resources, a nonprofit foundation based in Ann Arbor, Michigan.
http://rivendell.org/
gopher://gopher.rivendell.org
INFO griefnet@rivendell.org

9835 **alc.suicide** Discussions and methods. *Newsgroup*

9836 **alt.basement.graveyard** Another side of the do-it-yourself movement. *Newsgroup*

9837 **alt.consciousness.near-death-exp** Discussion of near-death experiences. *Newsgroup*

9838 **alt.obituaries** Notices of dead folks. *Newsgroup*

9839 `alt.suicide.holiday` Talk of why suicides increase at holidays. *Newsgroup*

9840 **DeathNET:** This site is an archive specializing in all aspects of death and dying. DeathNET houses a number of self-contained Web sites such as: The Living Will Center (about living wills, advance directives, and patients' rights), The Garden of Remembrance (online obituaries), Life's End (shopping center for "end of life" needs), and DeathTALK (for discussions on death and dying).
`http://www.rights.org/~deathnet/`
INFO `rights@islandnet.com`

9841 **Euthanasia World Directory:** Collection of resources and information on the "right-to-die" movement and its related organizations.
`http://www.efn.org/~ergo/`
INFO `ergo@efn.org`
MIRROR `http://www.rights.org/~deathnet/`

9842 **Index and Glossary of the Scottish Voluntary Euthanasia Society:** Very good collection of materials relating to euthanasia; includes local information and pointers to other related sites on the net.
`http://www.netlink.co.uk/users/vess/a_z.html`
INFO `didmsnj@easynet.co.uk`

9843 **The Obituary Page:** Online obituaries.
`http://catless.ncl.ac.uk/Obituary`
INFO `lindsay.marshall@newcastle.ac.uk`

➤ **SNUFFIT-L:** The Church of Euthanasia. (See entry 528 for full listing.)

9844 **The Suicide Information and Education Centre (SIEC):** This site has information on how to access information on suicide prevention, postvention, intervention, and caregiver training.
`http://www.igw.ca/sie/`
INFO `siec@nucleus.com`

9845 `talk.euthanasia` All aspects of euthanasia. *Newsgroup*

9846 **Widow Net:** A site for support and information for widows and widowers.
`http://www.fortnet.org/~goshorn/`
INFO `widownet@fortnet.org`

9847 **World Wide Cemetery:** An online cemetery. You can construct a text or multimedia "monument" to commemorate a loved one at this site. Visitors can leave flowers at monuments.
`http://www.io.org/cemetery/`
INFO `cemetery@io.org`

DISABILITIES

9848 **Cornucopia of Disability Information:** Broad range of disability-related information and resources.
`gopher://val-dor.cc.buffalo.edu`
INFO `leavitt@ubvms.cc.buffalo.edu`

9849 **DO-IT and the Internet: Disability-Related Resources:** Internet resources of potential interest to people who have disabilities or are interested in disability-related issues. Creation and maintenance of the list are funded largely by the University of Washington and the National Science Foundation.
`http://weber.u.washington.edu/~doit/Brochures/internet_resources.html`
`ftp://una.hh.lib.umich.edu/inetdirsstacks/disability:martineau`
`gopher://hawking.u.washington.edu`
INFO `doit@u.washington.edu` (Sheryl Burgstahler)
Comments: Ink-print copies, updated at least quarterly, are available from the DO-IT office e-mail; `doit@u.washington.edu`, or call (206) 685-3648.

➤ **Special Education Resources:** A comprehensive list of resources relating to special education including information on learning disabilities, gifted children, behavioral and emotional disorders, mental retardation, health and physical impairments, autism and communication disorders, sensory impairments, and early childhood. (See entry 4378 for full listing.)

9850 ABLE-JOB: Discussion of disabilities and employment. *Mailing List*

± `listserv@sjuvm.stjohns.edu` [body = SUBSCRIBE ABLE-JOB first-name last-name]

EDITOR `rbanks@uwstout.edu` (Dick Banks)

9851 ADA Attorneys List: For lists of attorneys whose specialties include Americans with Disabilities Act (ADA) law. *Distribution List*

`gopher://sjuvm.stjohns.edu`

INFO OWNER `anndell@rdz.stjohns.edu` (Ann Dellarocco)

ARCHIVES

`gopher://sjuvm.stjohns.edu`

`http://www.rdz.stjohns/~anndell`

Frequency: monthly

➤   **ADAPT-L:** On library adaptive technology. (See entry 5718 for full listing.)

9852 ADVOCACY: On the rights of people with disabilities. *Mailing List*

± `listserv@sjuvm.stjohns.edu` [body = SUBSCRIBE ADVOCACY first-name last-name]

OWNER `rbanks@uwstout.edu` (Dick Banks)

9853 AECUDEP-L: On universal design in education, practice, or advocacy. *Mailing List*

± `mailserv@admin.aces.k12.ct.us` [body = SUBSCRIBE AECUDEP-L first-name last-name]

OWNER `aecudep-moderator@admin.aces.k12.ct.us`

ARCHIVE `gopher://gopher.aces.k12.ct.us/11gopher_root:[_aec]`

9854 alt.support.disabled.artists To promote creativity among disabled artists. *Newsgroup*

➤   **alt.support.learning-disab:** For individuals with learning disabilities. *Newsgroup*

9855 Amputee: On amputee issues: amputees, relatives, friends, health professionals. *Digest & Reflector*

± `listserv@sjuvm.stjohns.edu` [body = SUBSCRIBE AMPUTEE first-name last-name]

EDITOR OWNER `igregson@wimsey.com` (Ian Gregson)

ARCHIVE `listserv@sjuvm.stjohns.edu` [body = INDEX Amputee]

Frequency: daily

9856 AWD: On acts and legal decisions regarding people with disabilities. *Mailing List, moderated*

± `majordomo@counterpoint.com` [body = subscribe awd]

OWNER `hal@counterpoint.com` (Hal P. Kingsley)

➤   **bit.listserv.axslib-1:** Library access for people with disabilities. *Newsgroup*

9857 bit.listserv.dsshe-1 Disabled student services in higher education. *Newsgroup*

9858 bit.listserv.easi Computer access for people with disabilities. *Newsgroup*

9859 bit.listserv.l-hcap Handicap list. *Moderated newsgroup*

9860 clari.news.disabilities News of the disabled. *Moderated newsgroup*

9861 Disability Resources, Products, Services, and Communication: Evan Kemp Associates' (a corporation providing products and services to the disability community) Web page contains numerous links to other disability resources on the net, descriptions of their products, and the opportunity to obtain a complimentary 1-year subscription to their newspaper.

`http://disability.com/`

INFO `webmaster@eka.com` (Evan Kemp Associates)

9862 DISPORT: On sports and athletics for disabled people, especially amputees. *Mailing List, moderated*

± `listserv@sjuvm.stjohns.edu` [body = SUBSCRIBE DISPORT first-name last-name]

EDITOR `igregson@wimsey.ca` (Ian Gregson)

ARCHIVE `http://www.wimsey.ca/~igregson/index.html`

9863 DO-IT News: An electronic newsletter about increasing the representation of people with disabilities in science, engineering, and mathematics fields. *Newsletter*

`http://weber.u.washington.edu/~doit/`

± INFO `doit@u.washington.edu` (Sheryl Burgstahler)

± `listproc@u.washington.edu`

ARCHIVE `gopher://hawking.u.washington.edu`

Frequency: irregular, four to six times a year

9864 Families and Disability Newsletter: Contains disability-related information for families, service providers, policy makers, and people with disabilities. *Newsletter*

`http://kuhttp.cc.ukans.edu/cwis/units/lsi/b/beachhp.html`

± INFO `cindy@dole.lsi.ukans.edu` (Cindy Higgins)

OWNER `beach@dole.lsi.ukans.edu`

Frequency: triannual

9865 `fj.misc.handicap` Interest for/about the handicapped. *Newsgroup*

9866 GW-INFO: On GW Micro products for computer access by the blind and learning disabled. *Mailing List*

± `listserv@gwmicro.com` [body = SUBSCRIBE GW-INFO first-name last-name]

OWNER `mdlawler@gwmicro.com` (Michael Lawler)

9867 Lanugage Based Learning Disability:Remediation Research: This site presents information related to remediation research efforts for language-based learning disability. Information related to dyslexia is also provided. Multiple forums and a live chat room are provided for parents, teachers, clinicians, and researchers.

`http://www.ld.ucsf.edu/`

`http://www-ld.ucsf.edu/`

INFO `wmjenk@phy.ucsf.edu`

Comments: The Web site is very dynamic and interaction between all users and the site organizers is encouraged.

► **MADNESS:** MADNESS is an electronic action and information discussion list for people who experience mood swings, fright, voices, and visions. (See entry 4950 for full listing.)

9868 `misc.handicap` Items of interest for/about the handicapped. *Moderated newsgroup*

9869 National Institute on Life Planning for Persons with Disabilities (NILP): NILP is a national clearinghouse for persons with disabilities, families, and professionals on all aspects of life planning.

`http://www.sonic.net/nilp/`

INFO `rfee@sonic.net` (Richard W. Fee)

► **St. John's University:** This site serves as the university's CWIS, and hosts the SJU Electronic Rehabilitation Resource Center and the SJU Learning Styles Network. This site also contains some resources for K–12 teachers. (See entry 4450 for full listing.)

9870 WebABLE!: An information repository for people with disabilities and accessibility solution providers. WebABLE! is dedicated to promoting the interests of adaptive, assistive, and access technology researchers, users, and manufacturers.

`http://www.webable.com/`

INFO `mpaciello@webable.com` (Mike Paciello)

DISABILITIES—COMMUNICATION DISORDERS

9871 Net Connections for Communication Disorders and Sciences: List of resources for professionals and students in the fields of speech-language pathology, audiology, and speech science, and persons with communication disabilities or differences and their support persons.

`http://www.lib.umich.edu/chouse/inter/114.html`

`ftp://una.hh.lib.umich.edu/inetdirsstacks/commdis:kuster`

`gopher://una.hh.lib.umich.edu/inetdirs/`

INFO `kuster@vax1.mankato.msus.edu` (Judith Maginnis Kuster)

9872 `alt.support.stuttering` Support for people who stutter. *Newsgroup*

9873 **CDMAJOR:** On communication disorders, primarily for students and faculty in speech-language pathology, audiology, speech science, or hearing-science programs. *Mailing List*

± `listserv@kentvm.kent.edu` [body = SUBSCRIBE CDMAJOR first-name last-name]

INFO `acaruso@kentvm.kent.edu` (Anthony J. Caruso)

ARCHIVE `listserv@kentvm.kent.edu`

9874 **STUTT-X:** On the research of fluency disorders. *Mailing List*

± `listserv@asuvm.inre.asu.edu` [body = SUBSCRIBE STUTT-X first-name last-name]

INFO `atdnm@asuvm.inre.asu.edu` (Don Mowrer)

ARCHIVE `listserv@asuvm.inre.asu.edu`

9875 **Stuttering Home Page:** Dedicated to providing information about stuttering for people who stutter (PWS), parents and others who interact with PWS, speech-language pathologists, researchers, educators, and students. It is the joint project of John Harrison, National Stuttering Project program director, and Judith Kuster, associate professor at Mankato State University.

`http://www.mankato.msus.edu/dept/comdis/kuster/stutter.html`

INFO `kuster@vax1.mankato.msus.edu` (Judith Maginnis Kuster)

DISABILITIES—DEAFNESS

9876 `alt.support.hearing-loss` Support group for hearing impaired. *Newsgroup*

9877 `bit.listserv.deaf-l` Deaf list. *Newsgroup*

9878 **Deaf-Magazine:** Deaf-Magazine: for everyone. *E-journal, moderated*

± `listserv@listserv.deaf-magazine.org` [body = SUBSCRIBE DEAF-MAGAZINE first-name last-name]

INFO `root@deaf-magazine.org` (Mr. Nathan R. Prugh)

Gated: `alt.soc.deaf.magazine`

Frequency: monthly

➤ **Sign Linguistics Resource Index:** An index of resources of interest to people researching sign languages (See entry 5306 for full listing.)

9879 `uk.people.deaf` Discussion group for the deaf in the UK. *Newsgroup*

DISABILITIES—MENTAL RETARDATION

9880 `bit.listserv.down-syn` Down's syndrome discussion group. *Newsgroup*

9881 **The Down Syndrome Home Page:** This page contains information on Down Syndrome and links to other related resouces on the net.

`http://www.nas.com/downsyn/`

INFO `trace@nas.com`

9882 **Fragilex:** On Fragile X Syndrome Single-Gene Disorder, the most common cause of inherited mental retardation. *Mailing List, moderated*

± `majordomo@counterpoint.com` [body = subscribe fragilex e-mail-address]

INFO `http://www.counterpoint.com/`

OWNER `hal@counterpoint.com` (Hal P. Kingsley)

9883 **Psych-DD:** For psychologists and allied professionals on mental retardation. *Mailing List*

± `listserv@vm1.nodak.edu` [body = SUBSCRIBE PSYCH-DD first-name last-name]

OWNER `plaud@badlands.nodak.edu`

DISABILITIES—VISUAL IMPAIRMENT

9884 `alt.comp.blind-users` Computer technology for the visually impaired. *Newsgroup*

9885 The Audio Description Home Page: Provides information and resources for audio description techniques for people who are seeing-impaired.

http://www.tmn.com/Artswire/www/ad/home.html
gopher://gopher.tmn.com/11/Artswire/ad
INFO jsnyder@tmn.com

9886 bit.listserv.blindnws Blindness issues and discussions. *Moderated newsgroup*

9887 BlindFam: On blindness and how it affects family life. *Mailing List*

± listserv@sjuvm.stjohns.edu [body = SUBSCRIBE BLINDFAM first-name last-name]
OWNER patt@squid.tram.com (Patt Bromberger)
OWNER myers@ab.edu (Roger Myers)
ARCHIVE listserv@sjuvm.stjohns.edu [body = INDEX BlindFam]
Comments: Blindness is meant to include everyone with a visual impairment. Subscription by children, parents, and students are encouraged.

9888 BLINDNWS: On blindness and visual impairment. *Digest & Reflector, moderated*

± listserv@vm1.nodak.edu [body = SUBSCRIBE BLINDNWS first-name last-name]
INFO wtm@sheldev.shel.isc-br.com (Bill McGarry)
ARCHIVE listserv@vm1.nodak.edu [body = INDEX BLINDNWS]
Gated: bit.listserv.blindnws

➤ **Education of the Visually Impaired:** Description of curriculum issues related to education of blind and visually impaired students and links to related resources. (See entry 4382 for full listing.)

9889 IBM-SRD: For users of the IBM-SRD screen reader. *Mailing List*

± listserv@vm1.nodak.edu [body = SUBSCRIBE IBM-SRD first-name last-name]
INFO ibm-srd-request@vm1.nodak.edu
ARCHIVE listserv@vm1.nodak.edu [body = INDEX IBM-SRD]
Gated: bit.listserv.IBM-SRD

DISASTER RELIEF

➤ **ca.environment.earthquakes:** Same as ca.earthquakes. *Newsgroup*

9890 clari.news.trouble.disaster Disasters. *Moderated newsgroup*

9891 Emergency Management/Planning Newsletter: The journal is used to discuss events and programs in the emergency management and planning community. *Newsletter*

INFO EDITOR kanecki@cs.uwp.edu (David H. Kanecki, Editor)
INFO scs@sdsc.edu
ARCHIVE kanecki@cs.uwp.edu (David H. Kanecki, Editor)
Frequency: monthly and biweekly, as information is received

DIVERSITY & MULTICULTURALISM

892 DIVERSITY-FORUM: On human resource management of diversity in business, education & social work. *Mailing List*

± majordomo@igc.apc.org [body = subscribe diversity-forum]
INFO OWNER nadm@europa.com (National Association for Diversity Management)
ARCHIVE gopher://gopher.nadm.org:7012
FAQ gopher://gopher.nadm.org:7012

EDEQUITY: On education equity in multiculturalism contexts. (See entry 4322 for full listing.)

➤ **POS302-L:** Seminar-based college level discussion on race, ethnicity, and social inequality. (See entry 10064 for full listing.)

➤ **soc.culture.intercultural:** People of mixed "culture", "ethnicity", "race". *Newsgroup*

➤   **Transcultural-Psychology:** On the delivery of mental health services to diverse cultures. (See entry 5026 for full listing.)

DRUGS

9893   `alt.drugs`   Use `rec.drugs.misc` instead. *Newsgroup*

9894   `alt.drugs.culture`   Entertainment while under the influence. *Newsgroup*

9895   `alt.drugs.hard`   Heroin, cocaine, and friends. *Newsgroup*

9896   `alt.drugs.leri`   I'm a little leary of drugs too. *Newsgroup*

9897   `alt.drugs.pot`   Use `rec.drugs.cannabis` instead. *Newsgroup*

9898   `alt.drugs.pot.cultivation`   Use `rec.drugs.cannabis` instead. *Newsgroup*

9899   `alt.drugs.psychedelics`   Use `rec.drugs.psychedelic` instead. *Newsgroup*

9900   `alt.drugs.usenet`   Repeatedly pushing the button for a fix. *Newsgroup*

9901   `alt.hemp`   It's about knot-tying with rope. Knot! *Newsgroup*

➤   `alt.music.psychedelic`   All types of psychedelic music. *Newsgroup*

9902   `alt.psychoactives`   Better living through chemistry. *Newsgroup*

9903   `clari.news.alcohol+drugs`   News of alcohol and drugs, use and abuse. *Moderated newsgroup*

9904   `clari.news.drugs`   Drug abuse and social policy. *Moderated newsgroup*

9905   **High Times:** On hemp, marijuana, and psychedelic drugs such as LSD and Ecstasy. Industrial uses of hemp (paper, cloth, food, oil) are extensively covered.
`http://www.hightimes.com/~hightimes/`
INFO `htwebman@hightimes.com`
INFO `hteditor@hightimes.com`

9906   **Hyperreal Drugs Archive:** Includes information on recreational drugs, including subjective reports from users and research into safety issues, as well as items related to drug policy.
`http://hyperreal.com/drugs`
FAQ `http://hyperreal.com/drugs/faqs`

9907   **LSD-51:** An interactive hypertext zine that originally comemmorated the 50th anniversary of the accidental discovery of LSD with fiction, archive, and testimonials submitted from all over the net. *E-Zine*
± `ftp://ftp.brown.edu/pubs/bobby_rabyd`
INFO `rabyd@brownvm.brown.edu` (Vera Rabyd)
ARCHIVE `ftp://ftp.brown.edu/pubs/bobby_rabyd`
Frequency: annual

9908   **MAPS Webpage:** This site contains publications and other information of the Multidisciplinary Association for Psychedelic Studies (MAPS). This organization, chartered in 1986, studies various therapeutic applications of psychedelic drugs and marijuana, including pain relief. Various materials on ketamine also appear in these publications.
`http://www.maps.org/`
INFO `sylvia@maps.org`

9909   `rec.drugs.cannabis`   The drug cannabis (marijuana). *Newsgroup*

9910   `rec.drugs.misc`   Stimulants, sedatives, smart drugs, etc. *Newsgroup*

9911   `rec.drugs.psychedelic`   LSD, Ecstasy, magic mushrooms, and the like. *Newsgroup*

➤   `sdnet.hemp`   San Diego hemp legalization discussions. *Newsgroup*

9912   `talk.politics.drugs`   The politics of drug issues. *Newsgroup*

➤   **TAO:** As "freedom and independent consciousness face the threat of cyber-design and virtual reality," this site provides a wise and impassioned response. (See entry 5594 for full listing.)

FAMILIES & PARENTING

➤ <u>Jon's Home-School Resource Page</u>: Extensive collection of home-schooling resources and information. Includes a lists of home-schooling mailing lists and newsgroups, pointers to FAQs on home-schooling topics, and a collection of many practical documents for to help home schoolers in their work. (See entry 4205 for full listing.)

9913 `alt.dads-rights` Rights of fathers. *Moderated newsgroup*

9914 `alt.dads-rights.unmoderated` Unhindered discussion of the rights of fathers. *Newsgroup*

9915 `alt.flame.parents` Going off about perceived parental injustices. *Newsgroup*

9916 `alt.parenting.spanking` Discussion about punishment methods for children. *Newsgroup*

9917 `alt.sex.incest` Discussing the issues of intra-familial sexual relations. *Newsgroup*

9918 `alt.support.househusbands` Men who tend the home. *Newsgroup*

9919 `alt.support.step-parents` Dealing with stepparents. *Newsgroup*

9920 **At-Home Dad Newsletter Online:** At-Home Dad is a new quarterly newsletter written to provide connections and resources for the 2 million fathers who stay home with their children. Sections include At Home Dad Network with e-mail addresses of dads to help connect at-home dads across the country, home business section, and inteviews and stories of fathers who are the primary caregiver for their children.
`http://www.parentsplace.com/readroom/athomedad/index.html`
INFO `athomedad@aol.com`

➤ **California Homeschool Network (CHN):** CHN exists to provide resources and information about home schooling; to protect the right of the family to educate its children at home in the manner it deems appropriate without regulation; and to foster community among home educators in California. (See entry 4207 for full listing.)

9921 `clari.news.childrn+family` Children and families, adoption, marriage. *Moderated newsgroup*

9922 `clari.news.crime.abuse` Spouse and child abuse. *Moderated newsgroup*

9923 `clari.news.family` Families, adoption, marriage. *Moderated newsgroup*

9924 **FACE:** Central Ohio Fathers and Children for Equality newsletter. Contains articles on visitation, custody, child support, poverty, parenting, propaganda, feminism, justice, equality, etc. *E-Journal*
± `air@mailer.fsu.edu`
INFO `tr@cbnea.att.com` (Aaron L. Hoffmeyer)
ARCHIVE `ftp://cwgk4.chem.cwru.edu/face`
Frequency: monthly
(See also mailing list: FREE-L)

9925 **FAMLYSCI:** For the Family Science Network: marriage, therapy, sociology, and behavioral-science aspects of family medicine. *Mailing List*
`http://www.uky.edu/HumanEnvironmentalSciences/FamilyNetwork/fam.html`
± `listserv@ukcc.uky.edu`
INFO OWNER `gwbrock@ukcc.uky.edu` (Greg Brock, Ph.D.)
ARCHIVE `http://www.uky.edu/HumanEnvironmentalSciences/FamilyNetwork/fam.html`

9926 **Fathers And Children for Equality (FACE) Newsletter:** Advocates noncustodial and nonresidential parents' rights and reform in domestic relations law. Topics are related to the domestic relations and custody of children for divorced parents. *Newsletter*
± `listserv@iupui.edu` [body = `SUBSCRIBE FREE-L` first-name last-name]
± `listserv@indycms.iupui.edu` [body = `SUBSCRIBE FREE-L` first-name last-name]
INFO `tr@cbnea.att.com` (Aaron L. Hoffmeyer)
Gated: `alt.dads-right`
Frequency: monthly

9927 **Fathers' Forum:Resosurce for expectant and new fathers:** The Fathers' Forum is a resource for expectant and new expectant fathers. It includes articles by Bruce Linton, Ph.D., author and researcher on men's development as fathers, list of programs for fathers and resource links to other parenting/fatherhood sites.

http://www.fathersforum.com/

INFO mblarts@slip.net

9928 Fathers' Resource Center: The Fathers' Resource Center is a nonprofit 501(c)3 family-service agency located in and serving the Twin Cities. Services include: fathers' parenting classes, family law clinics, fathers' support groups, understanding-abuse program, dealing with male anger program, father-to-father mentoring, quarterly newsletter, lending library, and a speakers bureau.

http://www.parentsplace.com/readroom/frc/index.html

INFO stafford@winternet.com

9929 FREE-L: On fathers' rights and equality, including parenting, divorce law, mediation, child support, false charges of sex abuse, and child custody. *Digest & Reflector*

± listserv@indycms.iupui.edu [body = SUBSCRIBE FREE-L first-name last-name]

INFO free-l-request@indycms.iupui.edu

ARCHIVE listserv@indycms.iupui.edu [body = INDEX FREE-L]

Please Note: Subscription by approval only.

Gated: bit.listserv.free-l

9930 Full-Time Dads Magazine: *Full-Time Dads* is the international magazine for caring fathers. FTD offers support, connection, and community for at-home dads.

http://www.parentsplace.com/readroom/fulltdad/index.html

INFO fulltdad@aol.com

9931 INTVIO-L: On intimate, or family, violence. *Mailing List, moderated*

± listserv@uriacc.uri.edu [body = SUBSCRIBE INTVIO-L first-name last-name]

EDITOR famviol@uriacc.uri.edu (Amy Silverman)

9932 Kathy's Resources on Parenting, Domestic Violence, Abuse, Trauma & Dissociation: Friendly and exhaustive index to resources that foster interpersonal respect and nonviolence.

http://www.mcs.net/~kathyw/home.html

INFO kathyw@mcs.net

➤ **MANIC MOMS "A humorous newsletter for crazed mothers.":** The purpose of this newsletter is to find the humor in daily struggles with children (or the people who behave like children) and to comfort manic moms everywhere that they are not alone. (See entry 518 for full listing.)

➤ **The Men's Issues Page:** On the full range of men's concerns: health, parenting, justice, self-awareness, and growth. (See entry 10056 for full listing.)

9933 National Parent Information Network (NPIN): Information and resources for parents and for those who work with parents.

http://ericps.ed.uiuc.edu/npin/npinhome.html

INFO cesarone@uiuc.edu

9934 PARENTING-L: On parenting. *Mailing List*

± listserv@postoffice.cso.uiuc.edu [body = SUBSCRIBE PARENTING-L first-name last-name]

INFO cesarone@uiuc.edu

9935 ParentsPlace.com: Resource for parents. Includes discussion groups, articles on parenting, and a shopping mall.

http://www.parentsplace.com/

INFO jackie@parentsplace.com

9936 Single Parenting In The Nineties: Single Parenting in The Nineties is a monthly newsletter written primarily by and for single parents. The Web site allows you to preview a sampling of their articles and subscribe to the newsletter.

http://www.parentsplace.com/readroom/spn/index.html

INFO pilotpub@execpc.com

9937 Single Parents Association: Web site of Single Parents Association (SPA), a nonprofit organization devoted to providing educational opportunities and fun family activities for single parents and their children.

http://www.neta.com/~spa

INFO spa@neta.com

Comments: Outside of Arizona call 1-800-704-2102 for a free, 8 page newsletter and information on joining the SPA. If you live in Arizona, please call (602) 788-5511.

➤ `soc.culture.jewish.parenting`: Issues about raising Jewish children. *Moderated newsgroup*

9938 **Stepfamily Association of Illinois, Inc. (non-profit):** The Stepfamily Association of Illinois is a nonprofit organization to support co-parents and kids living in multi-home stepfamilies.

http://www.parentsplace.com/readroom/stepfamily/index.html

INFO pilgrim27@aol.com

➤ **TAGFAM:** For mutual help and support for TAG families, and providing stimulating environments for talented and gifted children. (See entry 4181 for full listing.)

9939 **Triplets:** The Triplets list is for discussions of issues concerning triplets and other multiples. It is an open forum in which parents, relatives, doctors, nurses, researchers, and others can discuss a wide range of topics pertaining to multiples. *Mailing List*

± majordomo@tripcom.com [body = subscribe triplets first-name last-name e-mail-address (the e-mail address is optional)]

INFO OWNER owner-triplets@tripcom.com (Adam Horwitz)

POST triplets@tripcom.com

9940 **twins:** Forum on twins/triplets/etc. Topics include research on twin-related issues and parenting issues as well as issues concerning adult twins. *Mailing List*

± twins-request@cup.hp.com [body = subscribe]

OWNER owner-twins@cup.hp.com

Comments: Owner also maintains lists on adult twins and twins research.

➤ **WME-L:** On the Worldwide Marriage Encounter workshops: sacrament of matrimony and holy orders. (See entry 8734 for full listing.)

GAY, LESBIAN, BISEXUAL & TRANSGENDERED

➤ **Domestic Partnerships and Same Sex Marriages:** Pointers to net-wide information on domestic partnerships and same-sex marriages. (See entry 6025 for full listing.)

9941 **Queer Infoservers:** The most complete listing of queer WWW, gopher, WAIS, FTP, and telnet-based services in existence.

http://www.infoqueer.org/queer/qis/

INFO queer@infoqueer.org

9942 **Queer Resources Directory:** Massive archive of files about everything queer—*the* place, and it has been since 1991.

http://www.qrd.org/QRD

INFO staff@qrd.org

FAQ http://www.qrd.org/QRD/QRD-faq.html

9943 **Queernet.Org:** Queernet hosts some of the most interesting and friendly LGBT mailing lists on the net. Send for their list of lists.

http://www.queernet.org/

± majordomo@queernet.org [body = lists]

INFO info@queernet.org

9944 `alt.lesbian.feminist.poetry` Everyone has their niche. *Newsgroup*

➤ `alt.personals.motss`: Romance for gay people. *Newsgroup*

➤ `alt.personals.transgendered`: People seeking TV/TS friends. *Newsgroup*

9945 `alt.politics.homosexuality` As the name implies. *Newsgroup*

➤ `alt.sex.bears`: Hairy homosexual men. *Newsgroup*

➤ `alt.sex.homosexual`: Homosexual relations. *Newsgroup*

➤ **alt.sex.motss:** Jesse Helms would not subscribe to this group. *Newsgroup*

➤ **alt.sex.stories.gay:** Erotic tales involving homosexuals. *Newsgroup*

9946 **alt.shoe.lesbians** A discussion for shoe lesbians and their friends. *Newsgroup*

9947 **alt.support.boy-lovers** Peer support for boy lovers. *Newsgroup*

9948 **alt.transgendered** Boys will be girls, and vice versa. *Newsgroup*

9949 **ARENAL:** For international communication among Spanish-speaking gays, lesbians, and bisexuals. *Mailing List*
http://www.indiana.edu/~arenal/Homepage.html
± listserv@mx.gw.com [body = SUBSCRIBE ARENAL first-name last-name]
INFO dsoto@mx.gw.com (Daniel Soto)
Language: Spanish, English, and others

9950 **aus.culture.lesbigay** Discussion group for non-heterosexual people. *Newsgroup*

9951 **AvMail:** On aviation issues from a gay & lesbian perspective. *Mailing List, moderated*
± avmail@aol.com
EDITOR OWNER fyetka@aol.com (Peter J. Lehman)

9952 **ba.motss** Newsgroup for Bay Area MOTSSers. *Newsgroup*

➤ **Bisexual Spouse Support Mailing List (SSML):** The Spouse Support Mailing List (SSML) is an Internet mailing list in both standard and digest formats for monogamous, straight spouses and their bisexual partners who are trying to make their marriages survive and thrive. Membership is moderated and confidential. (See entry 6028 for full listing.)

9953 **bit.listserv.gaynet** GayNet discussion list. *Moderated newsgroup*

9954 **BLK Homie Pages:** News and information about the black lesbian and gay communities.
http://www.blk.com/blk/
INFO newsroom@blk.com

9955 **can.motss** Gay/lesbian/bi issues in Canada. *Newsgroup*

9956 **cd-forum:** For the support of cross-dressing, transsexuality, and other gender issues. *Digest & Reflector, moderated*
± INFO cd-request@therev.losalamos.nm.us
Please Note: Subscription by approval only.

9957 **clari.news.gays** Homosexuality and gay rights. *Moderated newsgroup*

9958 **The CyberQueer Lounge:** A comprehensive guide to and collection of lesbian, gay, bisexual, transgendered, and AIDS resources.
http://www.cyberzine.org/html/GLAIDS/glaidshomepage.html
INFO tomh@cyberzine.org

9959 **Gay Male S/M Activists:** GMSMA is the world's largest organization of men seriously interested in safe, sane, consensual sadomasochism.
http://www.ability.net/gmsma/
INFO gmsma@ability.net

9960 **glb-bookshops:** For those involved with the gay and lesbian bookstore and gift-shop trade. *Mailing List, moderated*
± majordomo@vector.casti.com [body = subscribe glb-bookshops]
INFO OWNER lambda@clark.net (Deacon Maccubbin)
Please Note: Subscription by approval only.
Comments: This is a trade list and *only* those connected in some way with the gay and lesbian bookstore and gift-shop trade are invited to subscribe.

9961 **GLB-DISCUSS:** For GLBT* Community Discussion. *Mailing List*
± listserv@listserv.aol.com [body = SUBSCRIBE GLB-DISCUSS first-name last-name]
OWNER atropos@aol.net (David B. O'Donnell)
OWNER julie@drycas.club.cc.cmu.edu (Julie Waters)

9962 glb-medical: On homosexuality and the medical profession. *Mailing List, moderated*
± `mailserv@ac.dal.ca` [body = `sub glb-medical`]
OWNER `kevinsp8@ac.dal.ca` (Kevin Speight)

9963 GLB-NEWS: For news clippings and information of interest to the gay/bi/lesbian/transgender community. *Distribution List, moderated*
± `listserv@listserv.aol.com` [body = `SUB GLB-NEWS` first-name last-name]
INFO `listserv@listserv.aol.com` [body = `INFO GLB-NEWS`]
INFO EDITOR OWNER `atropos@aol.net` (David B. O'Donnell)
INFO `julie@drycas.club.cc.cmu.edu` (Julie Waters)
ARCHIVE `listserv@listserv.aol.com` [body = `INDEX GLB-NEWS`]
POST `glb-news@listserv.aol.com`
FAQ `listserv@listserv.aol.com` [body = `SEND GLB-NEWS GUIDELINES`]

9964 GLB-PRESS: Press releases of interest to the Gay/Bi/Lesbian/Trans community. *Mailing List*
± `listserv@listserv.aol.com` [body = `SUBSCRIBE GLB-PRESS` first-name last-name]
OWNER `atropos@aol.net` (David B. O'Donnell)
OWNER `julie@drycas.club.cc.cmu.edu` (Julie Waters)

9965 LGBPSYCH: For lesbian/gay/bisexual psychology grad students *Mailing List*
± `listserv@vm1.mcgill.ca` [body = `JOIN LGBPSYCH@VM1.MCGILL.CA` e-mail-address first-name last-name]
OWNER `neil@psych.mcgill.ca`

9966 Mariposa's Wings: The take-off point for the gay-pagan Internet.
`http://www.mcs.net/~deanm/index.html`
INFO `deanm@mcs.com`

➤ **MEDGAY-L:** On gay-lesbian medieval studies—official list of the Society for the Study of Homosexuality in the Middle Ages. (See entry 5218 for full listing.)

9967 ne-social-motss: Announcements of social and other events, and other happenings in the northeastern United States of interest to lesbian, gay, bisexual, and transgendered people. *Mailing List*
± `majordomo@plts.org` [body = `subscribe ne-social-motss`]
INFO `ne-social-motss-approval@plts.org`

9968 ne.motss Issues pertaining to homosexuality in New England. *Newsgroup*

9969 nv.bi Talk for bisexually natured persons. *Newsgroup*

➤ **The Official Nicola Griffith Page:** Information on Nicola Griffith, author of the novels *Ammonite* and *Slow River* and the collection *Women and Other Aliens* (forthcoming). (See entry 604 for full listing.)

9970 oh-motss: The Ohio Members Of The Same Sex mailing list is for open discussion of lesbian, gay, and bisexual issues in and affecting Ohio. *Mailing List*
± `majordomo@dmshome.youngstown.oh.us` [body = `subscribe oh-motss`]
INFO `oh-motss-request@dmshome.youngstown.oh.us`

➤ **pa.motss:** Gay, lesbian, and bisexual people and issues in Pennsylvania. *Newsgroup*

➤ **Partners Task Force for Gay & Lesbian Couples:** This site provides extensive information on issues of concern to same-sex couples, including legal marriage and sources of support. (See entry 6030 for full listing.)

9971 Pen and Sword: Imaginative art and writing for the gay, lesbian, and diverse community. *Magazine*
`http://www.rahul.net/jag/`
ARCHIVE `http://www.rahul.net/jag/`
Frequency: quarterly

➤ **Penpal Connection!:** Free pen-pal service for the gay community. (See entry 5949 for full listing.)

➤ **pgh.motss:** Lesbian, gay, and bisexual issues in Pittsburg. *Newsgroup*

9972 Planet Q: Interactive multimedia services for, by, and/or about the queer community: gay, lesbian, bisexual, transgendered, and HIV+ people and their supporters.
http://planetq.com/
INFO info@planetq.com

➤ **pnw.motss:** Issues about homosexuality in the Pacific Northwest. *Newsgroup*

9973 RAINBOW-L: Announcements of gay, lesbian, bisexual, and transgender authors appearing in conference on America Online. *Distribution List*
± lambdamac@aol.com [body = subscribe rainbow-l]
INFO lambdamac@aol.com
Comments: While the list is of primary interest to America Online members, others are welcome to subscribe.

9974 SACS: For gay and lesbian Anglicans interested in leather sex and spirituality. *Mailing List*
± majordomo@vector.casti.com [body = SUBSCRIBE sacs]
OWNER sacs-owner@vector.casti.com

9975 sappho: A discussion group for gay and bisexual women. All women are invited to join, but only women may join. *Digest & Reflector*
http://www.apocalypse.org/pub/sappho
± INFO sappho@apocalypse.org

➤ **sdnet.motss:** San Diego gay, bi, lesbians, and friends. *Newsgroup*

9976 soc.bi Discussions of bisexuality. *Newsgroup*

9977 soc.motss Issues pertaining to homosexuality. *Newsgroup*

9978 soc.support.transgendered Transgendered and intersexed persons. *Newsgroup*

9979 soc.support.youth.gay-lesbian-bi Gay youths helping each other. *Moderated newsgroup*

9980 soc.women.lesbian-and-bi Lives of lesbian and bisexual women. *Moderated newsgroup*

9981 spouse-support: For monogamous heterosexual spouses of bisexual partners. *Digest & Reflector, moderated*
http://www.qrd.org/qrd/electronic/email/spouse-support
± majordomo@texsys.com [body = SUBSCRIBE spouse-support or spouse-support-digest]
INFO spouse-support-owner@texsys.com
OWNER majordom@texsys.com
Please Note: Subscription by approval only.

9982 TRANSGEN: For and about people who are transsexual, transgendered, and/or transvestites. *Mailing List*
http://drycas.club.cc.cmu.edu/~julie/transgen.html
± listserv@brownvm.brown.edu [body = SUBSCRIBE TRANSGEN first-name last-name]
INFO transgen-request@brownvm.brown.edu
OWNER julie@drycas.club.cc.cmu.edu (Julie Waters)
Please Note: Subscription by approval only.

9983 triangle.motss Issues pertaining to homosexuality in the Triangle area. *Newsgroup*

➤ **triangle.personals.bi:** Personal ads for the bisexual crowd. *Newsgroup*

➤ **triangle.personals.m-seeking-m:** Personals for men seeking men. *Newsgroup*

➤ **triangle.personals.motss:** Personal ads for the same-sex crowd. *Newsgroup*

➤ **triangle.personals.w-seeking-w:** Personals for women seeking women. *Newsgroup*

9984 uk.gay-lesbian-bi Forum for bisexuals, lesbians, and gays in the U.K. *Newsgroup*

9985 vegas.bi Talk for bisexually natured persons. *Newsgroup*

9986 vegas.motss MOTSS community talk. *Newsgroup*

GENEALOGY

► **Butler County (Ohio) Pioneers:** Add your own or contact others who had ancestors living in Butler County, Ohio, in the early 1800s. Genealogy site. (See entry 8340 for full listing.)

9987 **Interactive Genealogy:** Genealogy research on the Internet can lead to new contacts with others just an e-mail away who share your same ancestors.

http://history.cc.ukans.edu/heritage/heritage_main.html

http://falcon.cc.ukans.edu/~nsween/inter-gen.html

INFO nsween@falcon.cc.ukans.edu

Comments: Interactive Genealogy is a part of Kansas Heritage, a history and genealogy site especially for Kansas research.

9988 **soc.genealogy.benelux** Genealogy in Belgium, the Netherlands, and Luxembourg. *Newsgroup*

9989 **soc.genealogy.computing** Genealogical computing and net resources. *Newsgroup*

9990 **soc.genealogy.french** Francophone genealogy. *Newsgroup*

9991 **soc.genealogy.german** Family history including a German background. *Newsgroup*

9992 **soc.genealogy.hispanic** Genealogy relating to Hispanics. *Newsgroup*

9993 **soc.genealogy.jewish** Jewish genealogy group. *Moderated newsgroup*

9994 **soc.genealogy.marketplace** Genealogy services and products. *Newsgroup*

9995 **soc.genealogy.medieval** Genealogy in the period from roughly A.D. 500 to A.D.1600. *Newsgroup*

9996 **soc.genealogy.methods** Genealogical methods and resources. *Moderated newsgroup*

9997 **soc.genealogy.misc** General genealogical discussions. *Newsgroup*

9998 **soc.genealogy.nordic** Genealogy in the Scandinavian countries. *Newsgroup*

9999 **soc.genealogy.surnames** Surnames, queries and tafels. *Moderated newsgroup*

10000 **soc.genealogy.uk+ireland** Genealogy of Britain, Ireland and offshore isles. *Newsgroup*

GUN CONTROL

10001 **alt.politics.org.batf** Politics of the U.S. firearms (etc.) regulation agency. *Newsgroup*

10002 **ba-firearms:** Announcement and discussion of California firearms legislation and related issues. *Mailing List*

± ba-firearms-request@shell.portal.com

INFO ba-firearms-approval@shell.portal.com

10003 **ca-firearms:** On California firearms legislation and related statewide issues. *Mailing List*

± ca-firearms-request@shell.portal.com

INFO ca-firearms-approval@shell.portal.com

10004 **can.talk.guns** Flames about Canadian gun owners, nonowners, and laws. *Newsgroup*

10005 **clari.news.guns** Gun control and other gun news. *Moderated newsgroup*

10006 **clari.news.issues.guns** Gun control and other gun news. *Moderated newsgroup*

10007 **Handguns & Accessories for Women & Southpaws:** Handguns as a self-defense tool. Solid information and arguments.

http://www.io.com/~cortese/resources/guns.html

INFO cortese@netcom.com

10008 **info.firearms.politics** Political firearms discussions (firearms-politics@ns1.rutgers.edu). *Moderated newsgroup*

10009 **National Rifle Association:** On firearm safety, firearms training, law enforcement programs, junior shooting activities, women's issues, hunter services, recreational shooting, competitions, gun collecting, and defense of the Second Amendment.

http://www.nra.org/

ftp://ftp.nra.org

INFO www@nra.org

10010 **rec.guns** Discussions about firearms. *Moderated newsgroup*

10011 **talk.politics.guns** The politics of firearm ownership and (mis)use. *Newsgroup*

HISPANICS/LATINOS/CHICANOS

10012 **Hispanic Online:** Interactive magazine for Hispanics featuring sections on business, career, education, art, community, and news.

http://www.hisp.com/

INFO aestrada@hisp.com

10013 **CHICLE:** For Chicano literature and culture exchange—includes music, dance, art, theater, film, sports. *Mailing List moderated*

± listserv@unmvma.unm.edu [body = SUBSCRIBE CHICLE first-name last-name]

INFO tmarquez@unm.edu (Teresa Marquez)

Comments: Has a rules of ethics code.

10014 **LatinoLink Magazine:** Stories, photos, and essays by Latino journalists in the U.S. and Puerto Rico.

http://www.latinolink.com/

INFO lavonne@latinolink.com

10015 **Texas Hispanic Business Journal:** Directed primarily to small, Hispanic-owned business; providing resource profiles, how-to information, and focusing on issues that impact the Hispanic business community. *E-Journal*

http://rampages.onramp.net/~thbj/

± INFO OWNER thbj@onramp.net (Rick Zahn)

Language: English, Spanish

Frequency: monthly

HOMELESSNESS

10016 **Comm-Act:** On community-based solutions for hunger and homelessness. *Mailing List*

± listserv@soundprint.org [body = SUBSCRIBE COMM-ACT first-name last-name]

OWNER beth@soundprint.org (Beth Lewand)

ARCHIVE gopher://soundprint.org

10017 **HOMELESS:** For a variety of viewpoints on homelessness. *Mailing List*

± listserv@csf.colorado.edu [body = SUBSCRIBE HOMELESS first-name last-name]

INFO schaper@csf.colorado.edu

OWNER southard@oregon.uoregon.edu (Dee Southard)

ARCHIVE http://csf.colorado.edu/homeless

Comments: csf.colorado.edu/homeless

HUMAN RIGHTS

➤ **Virtual Library on International Development:** A very well-organized collection of pointers to international development resources. Resources are well categorized and accessible by region, type of organization, and resource theme. (See entry 10047 for full listing.)

➤ **ACTIV-L:** Information for activists involved in peace, empowerment, human rights, and justice. (See entry 5580 for full listing.)

10018 **aimembers-l:** For members of Amnesty International. *Digest & Reflector*

http://www.derechos.org/amnesty/aim-l.html

± aimembers-l-request@lists1.best.com [body = subscribe (for digest) or subsingle (for reflector)]

INFO OWNER marga@derechos.org (Margarita Lacabe)

Please Note: Subscription by approval only.

10019 `alt.activism.death-penalty` For people opposed to capital punishment. *Newsgroup*

10020 Amnesty International Online: News, press releases, and more from Amnesty International. It also includes pointers to other human rights and Amnesty Internation chapters worldwide.

    `http://www.amnesty.org/`

    INFO `rmitchellai@gn.apc.org` (Ray Mitchell)

    INFO `blackie@io.org` (Mike Blackstock)

10021 AMNESTY-L: For news releases from Amnesty International's International Secretariat and distribution of Amnesty International documents. *Mailing List*

    ± `majordomo@io.org` [body = SUBSCRIBE AMNESTY-L]

10022 ASYLUM-L: On legal aspects of asylum and refugee status. *Mailing List*

    ± `majordomo@ufsia.ac.be` [body = SUBSCRIBE asylum-l]

    INFO OWNER `cgr.vanheule.d@alpha.ufsia.ac.be` (Dirk Vanheule)

    FAQ `majordomo@ufsia.ac.be` [body = SUBSCRIBE asylum-l]

10023 Chechnya: On Chechnya: especially human rights and humanitarian aid. *Mailing List*

    `http://www.smns.montclair.edu/~chechen`

    ± `listserv@plearn.edu.pl` [body = SUBSCRIBE CHECHNYA first-name last-name]

    INFO `http://mercury.ci.uw.edu.pl/public/dilan/wiench`

    OWNER `wiench@plearn.edu.pl` (Piotr Wiench)

➤ **Chile Information Project (CHIP News):** News on economics, especially mining, and human rights and democratization in Chile. (See entry 7635 for full listing.)

10024 `clari.news.issues.human_rights` Freedom, civil rights, human rights. *Moderated newsgroup*

10025 derechos-l: On human rights, esp. in Spanish-speaking countries. *Digest & Reflector*

    `http://www.derechos.org/ddhh/derechos.html`

    ± `derechos-l-request@lists1.best.com` [body = subscribe (for digest) or subsingle (for reflector)]

    INFO OWNER `marga@derechos.org` (Margarita Lacabe)

    ARCHIVE `http://www.derechos.org/nizkor`

    Language: Spanish

    Please Note: Subscription by approval only.

10026 East Timor Action Network News: Regular newsletter of the East Timor Action Network—United States consiting of current news, reports, and calls to action regarding human rights and self-determination for East Timor. *Newsletter*

    `gopher://gopher.igc.apc.org/11/peace/timor.gopher`

    ± **INFO** `cscheiner@igc.apc.org` (Charles Scheiner)

    ± **INFO** `fbp@igc.apc.org`

    ARCHIVE `gopher://gopher.igc.apc.org/11/peace/timor.gopher`

    Frequency: quarterly, with urgent action alerts approximately monthly

    Price: $10/year paper

10027 `fj.soc.human-rights` Discussion about human rights, bioethics, and discrimination. *Newsgroup*

➤ **The Fourth World Documentation Project:** An electronic library containing over 400 primary texts on political struggles waged by indigenous peoples worldwide for sovereignty, self-determination, and human rights. (See entry 10070 for full listing.)

10028 Human Rights Gopher: Host of a variety of human-rights organizations.

    `gopher://gopher.humanrights.org:5000`

    INFO `hrwatchnyc@igc.apc.org`

➤ **International Security Network (IntSecNet):** A one-stop virtual library and information network for security and defense studies, peace and conflict research, and international relations. The International Security Network is a joint effort of diverse research institutions, financially supported by the Swiss government. (See entry 10110 for full listing.)

➤ **MADNESS:** MADNESS is an electronic action and information discussion list for people who experience mood swings, fright, voices, and visions. (See entry 4950 for full listing.)

10029 The Occupation of Kuwait: Legacy of Pain: A site documenting in words, pictures, and video the human-rights violations and environmental tragedy suffered by Kuwaitis during Iraq's occupation of Kuwait.

```
http://www.cs.cmu.edu/~anwar/legacy-kuwait.html
http://www.kuwait.org/legacy-kuwait.html
```
INFO anwar+@cs.cmu.edu

➤ **OneWorld Online:** This site has an extensive amount of information on global issues. The site is indexed and includes documents on global justice, conflict, aid, trade, education, health, human rights, population, and sustainable human development, as well as daily news summaries. It also hosts information for numerous international development and relief organizations. (See entry 10052 for full listing.)

➤ **People's Tribune:** Devoted to the proposition that an economic system that can't or won't feed, clothe, and house its people ought to be changed. (See entry 5666 for full listing.)

➤ **reg.easttimor:** E-mail distribution of postings from the Alliance for Progressive Communications (APC) conference on East Timor and Indonesia. Includes reports from a wide range of advocacy and support groups, as well as reports and translations from the international press, and official documents and statements from the UN, national governments, and other sources. (See entry 7698 for full listing.)

10030 soc.rights.human Human rights and activism (e.g., Amnesty International). *Newsgroup*

HUNGER

➤ <u>**Virtual Library on International Development**</u>**:** A very well-organized collection of pointers to international development resources. Resources are well categorized and accessible by region, type of organization, and resource theme. (See entry 10047 for full listing.)

10031 alt.org.food-not-bombs The Food Not Bombs homeless aid organization. *Newsgroup*

IMMIGRATION

10032 alt.politics.immigration All issues related to immigration. *Newsgroup*

10033 American Immigration Report: Though part of this page describes a subscription-based service, it provides other useful immigration information free of charge, including articles (up to date) on current immigration law, a guide to the Senate's proposed immigration reform, and a bulletin summarizing immigrant numbers, among other things.

```
http://www.xmission.com/~seer/uslawyer/index.html
```
INFO uslawyer@inforamp.ca (Mark Carmel, Attorney at Law)

10034 clari.news.immigration Refugees, immigration, migration. *Moderated newsgroup*

10035 clari.news.immigration.misc Immigration, migration. *Moderated newsgroup*

10036 clari.news.refugees Refugees, involuntary migrations. *Moderated newsgroup*

10037 Migra-List: All about international migration issues. *Mailing List*

± INFO migra-list-request@cc.utah.edu

10038 Migration News: Summary of the most important immigration and integration developments during the preceding month. *Newsletter*

```
http://migration.ucdavis.edu/
```
± INFO migrant@primal.ucdavis.edu

ARCHIVE http://migration.ucdavis.edu/

10039 misc.immigration.canada Canada immigration issues. *Newsgroup*

10040 misc.immigration.misc Miscellaneous countries' immigration issues. *Newsgroup*

10041 misc.immigration.usa USA immigration issues. *Newsgroup*

➤ **OneWorld Online:** This site has an extensive amount of information on global issues. The site is indexed and includes documents on global justice, conflict, aid, trade, education, health, human rights, population, and sustainable human development, as well as daily news summaries. It also hosts information for numerous international development and relief organizations. (See entry 10052 for full listing.)

10042 Siskind's Immigration Bulletin: Monthly newsletter focusing on U.S. immigration law and procedures. *Newsletter*
http://www.visalaw.com/~gsiskind/
± INFO gsiskind@telalink.net (Greg Siskind)
Frequency: monthly

10043 U.S. Immigration and Naturalization Service: An official U.S. government site, the INS Web page (and gopher) includes the following: general information on the INS, a table of immigration to the U.S. in 1994, INS press releases, regulations from the CFR, and the full text of the Immigration and Nationality Act.
http://gopher.usdoj.gov/offices/ins.html

10044 USA-GREENCARDLOTTERY: To clarify the law pertaining to the annual green-card lottery. *Mailing List, moderated*
± OWNER uslawyer@inforamp.net (The Law Office of Mark Carmel)

10045 USA-IMMIGRATION: A discussion of U.S.A. immigration laws moderated by Mark Carmel, attorney at law. *Mailing List, moderated*
± OWNER uslawyer@inforamp.net (The Law Office of Mark Carmel)
ARCHIVE http://www.xmission.com/~seer/uslawyer/index.html

10046 VISALAW: Siskind's Immigration Bulletin: on U.S. immigration law. *Newsletter*
± majordomo@listserv.telalink.net
INFO majordomo-owner@listserv.telalink.net (technical questions)
OWNER gsiskind@telalink.net (Greg Siskind)
ARCHIVE http://www.visalaw.com/~gsiskind/

INTERNATIONAL DEVELOPMENT

10047 <u>Virtual Library on International Development</u>: A very well-organized collection of pointers to international development resources. Resources are well categorized and accessible by region, type of organization, and resource theme.
http://www.synapse.net/~acdi03/indexg/welcome.htm
INFO ycontami@synapse.net

10048 alt.peace-corps The works of the Peace Corps. *Newsgroup*

10049 bit.org.peace-corps Peace Corps. *Newsgroup*

10050 CARE: Information about the international development organization CARE, whose humanitarian programs include emergency relief, micro-enterprise, the environment, population, AIDS prevention, girls' education, agriculture, primary health care, and food security.
http://www.care.org/
INFO info@care.org

➤ **Communications for a Sustainable Future:** An interdisciplinary effort to facilitate more rapid change in social thought toward a viable future. This resource provides a collection of archives and mailing lists on sustainability. (See entry 5191 for full listing.)

10051 Multinational Monitor: Founded by Ralph Nader in 1980; tracks the activities of multinational corporations, covering environment, labor, indigenous, consumer, health, and safety issues, mostly in the Third World. *Newsletter*
± gopher://essential.org
INFO EDITOR monitor@essential.org (Aaron Freeman, Associate Editor)
ARCHIVE ftp://essential.org
Frequency: monthly (ten times per year)
Price: varies with subscription type

➤ **The Network Startup Resource Center:** This site contains information about: networking in the developing world, low-cost networking tools, general computer networking information, and networking tips and frequently asked questions. You can search for networking solutions and information by country. (See entry 9647 for full listing.)

10052 OneWorld Online: This site has an extensive amount of information on global issues. The site is indexed and includes documents on global justice, conflict, aid, trade, education, health, human rights, population, and sustainable human development, as well as daily news summaries. It also hosts information for numerous international development and relief organizations.

```
http://www.oneworld.org/
```
INFO feedback@oneworld.org

10053 PCORPS-L: For international volunteers, especially the Peace Corps. *Mailing List*

± listserv@cmuvm.csv.cmich.edu [body = SUBSCRIBE PCORPS-L first-name last-name]

INFO OWNER 3zlufur@cmuvm.csv.cmich.edu (Elliott Parker)

ARCHIVE listserv@cmuvm.csv.cmich.edu [body = INDEX PCORPS-L]

Gated: bit.org.peace-corps

10054 U.S. Agency for International Development: This site provides access to information on USAID programs, as well as to some interesting databases including a famine early warning system, and more. USAID is an independent federal government agency that conducts foreign assistance and humanitarian aid to advance the political and economic interests of the United States.

```
http://www.info.usaid.gov/
ftp://ftp.info.usaid.gov
gopher://gopher.info.usaid.gov
```
INFO webmaster@info.usaid.gov

➤ **United Nations Development Programme Information System:** This site contains information related to the United Nations Development Program and other United Nations agencies. (See entry 5445 for full listing.)

➤ **The World Bank:** This site contains information about the World Bank, its press releases, country and project Information, regional information, publications, and research studies. (See entry 5446 for full listing.)

MEN'S ISSUES

➤ `alt.feminazis:` For people who hate radical feminists. *Newsgroup*

10055 `alt.mens-rights` We hold these truths to be self-evident. *Newsgroup*

➤ `alt.support.househusbands:` men who tend the home (See entry 0 for full listing.)

➤ **Fathers' Forum:Resosurce for expectant and new fathers:** The Fathers' Forum is a resource for expectant and new expectant fathers. It includes articles by Bruce Linton, Ph.D., author and researcher on men's development as fathers, list of programs for fathers and resource links to other parenting/fatherhood sites. (See entry 9927 for full listing.)

➤ `fj.soc.men-women:` Fairness, right, etc. between women and men. *Newsgroup*

➤ **Full-Time Dads Magazine:** *Full-Time Dads* is the international magazine for caring fathers. FTD offers support, connection, and community for at-home dads. (See entry 9930 for full listing.)

➤ **gender:** A mailing list for discussing all aspects of gender and (biological) sex issues. (See entry 10118 for full listing.)

➤ **Married Man Home Page:** This page was created by Ritchie White and Dan Starks, who created it out of their realization that they both have wives. It is is meant as encouragement to those men who are or will be married someday. The site also includes links to other marriage-related Web sites. (See entry 6029 for full listing.)

10056 The Men's Issues Page: On the full range of men's concerns: health, parenting, justice, self-awareness, and growth.

```
http://www.vix.com/men
```
INFO throop@vix.com

10057 `soc.men` Issues related to men, their problems, and relationships. *Newsgroup*

MINORITIES

10058 `alt.left-handed` For left-handed folks. *Newsgroup*

10059 `alt.lefthanders` How gauche. *Newsgroup*

10060 **Arab-American:** For fostering and building community among Americans of Arabic descent. *Mailing List*

± mailserv@carleton.edu [body = SUBSCRIBE ARAB-AMERICAN first-name last-name]

OWNER cabdullh@freenet.columbus.oh.us (Cheryl Abdullah)

OWNER anixon@carleton.edu (Andrea Nixon)

➤ **Black Graduate Student Association at Massachusetts Institute of Technology:** Support and social group for black graduate students at M.I.T. (See entry 4397 for full listing.)

10061 **clari.news.ethnicity** Ethnicity issues. *Moderated newsgroup*

10062 **clari.news.minorities.misc** Ethnicity issues, news of minorities. *Moderated newsgroup*

➤ **Minority Bank Monitor:** The site provides information on every women- or minority-owned financial institution in the U.S. (See entry 1666 for full listing.)

10063 **PAP:** For the Association of Polish-American Professionals (APAP). *Mailing List*

± majordomo@cloud9.net

INFO miszczak@ids2.idsonline.com (Martin Miszczak)

OWNER miszczak@cloud9.net (Martin Miszczak)

Please Note: Subscription by approval only.

Comments: E-mail contact before subscribing.

10064 **POS302-L:** Seminar-based college level discussion on race, ethnicity, and social inequality. *Mailing List, moderated*

± listserv@ilstu.edu [body = SUBSCRIBE POS302-L first-name last-name]

OWNER gmklass@ilstu.edu (Gary Klass)

Please Note: Subscription by approval only.

10065 **soc.culture.intercultural** People of mixed "culture", "ethnicity", "race". *Newsgroup*

➤ **Thrace:** For Turkish-minority members of West Thracia (a province of Greece). (See entry 7318 for full listing.)

MISSING PEOPLE

10066 **alt.missing-adults** Locating missing adults. *Newsgroup*

10067 **alt.missing-kids** Locating missing children. *Newsgroup*

➤ **The Investigative Resource Center:** Provided by Investigative Resources International, a professional investigation firm, this site offers pointers to many private investigators and legal and reference resources on the Web, including a good list of searchable databases helpful in locating people and unusual information. (See entry 1917 for full listing.)

NATIVE AMERICANS & INDIGENOUS PEOPLES

10068 **NativeWeb:** For indigenous peoples' resources on the World Wide Web. *Mailing List*

http://web.maxwell.syr.edu/nativeweb

± listserv@thecity.sfsu.edu [body = SUBSCRIBE NATIVEWEB first-name last-name]

OWNER mandell@thecity.sfsu.edu (Al Mandell)

ARCHIVE listserv@thecity.sfsu.edu [body = INDEX NATIVEWEB]

10069 **alt.native** People indigenous to an area before modern colonization. *Newsgroup*

➤ **Arctic Circle:** The purpose of Arctic Circle is to stimulate among viewers a greater interest in the peoples and environment of the Arctic and Subarctic region. This "electronic circle" has three interrelated themes: natural resources, history and culture, and social equity and environmental justice. New material is being added on a regular basis. (See entry 4630 for full listing.)

➤ **EARAM-L:** On early American literature and history, i.e., before circa 1820, including Native Americans, "discovery" documents, colonial and federal materials. (See entry 615 for full listing.)

10070 **The Fourth World Documentation Project:** An electronic library containing over 400 primary texts on political struggles waged by indigenous peoples worldwide for sovereignty, self-determination, and human rights.

http://www.halcyon.com/FWDP/fwdp.html

```
ftp://ftp.halcyon.com/pub/FWDP/
```
INFO `jburrows@halcyon.com`
MIRRORS
```
ftp://ftp.etext.org/pub/Politics/Fourth.World
gopher://gopher.etext.org/11/Politics/Fourth.World
gopher://server.gdn.org/11/FWDP
http://www.gdn.org/gdn.html#FWDP
```

➤ **Homelands:** About national and regional autonomy and independence movements in America and around the world. (See entry 5587 for full listing.)

10071 INDKNOW: For indigenous knowledge systems, traditional ecological knowledge and development. *Mailing List*
```
http://csf.colorado.edu/
gopher://csf.colorado.edu
```
± `listproc@u.washington.edu` [body = SUBSCRIBE INDKNOW first-name last-name]
INFO `pdh@u.washington.edu` (Preston D. Hardison)

10072 IROQUOIS: For discussion on the Iroquois language. *Mailing List*
± `listserv@utoronto.bitnet` [body = SUBSCRIBE IROQUOIS first-name last-name]
INFO `cdyck@epas.utoronto.ca` (Carrie Dyck)
ARCHIVE `listserv@utoronto.bitnet`

10073 NAT-LANG: On the languages of aboriginal peoples. *Mailing List*
± `listserv@tamvm1.tamu.edu` [body = SUBSCRIBE NAT-LANG first-name last-name]
INFO `gst@gnosys.svle.ma.us` (Gary S. Trujillo)
ARCHIVE `listserv@tamvm1.tamu.edu`

10074 NAT-WORK: On Native American employment: culture, barriers, solutions. *Mailing List*
± `listserv@vm1.cc.uakron.edu` [body = SUB NAT-WORK first-name last-name]
INFO `r2jsq@vm1.cc.uakron.edu` (Joe Quickle)

10075 NATCHAT: Discussion of issues pertaining to aboriginal peoples. *Mailing List*
± `listserv@tamvm1.tamu.edu` [body = SUBSCRIBE NATCHAT first-name last-name]
INFO `gst@gnosys.svle.ma.us` (Gary S. Trujillo)
INFO `mkkuhner@genetics.washington.edu`

10076 NATIVE-L: News and information on issues pertaining to aboriginal peoples. *Mailing List*
± `listserv@tamvm1.tamu.edu` [body = SUBSCRIBE NATIVE-L first-name last-name]
INFO `gst@gnosys.svle.ma.us` (Gary S. Trujillo)
ARCHIVE `listserv@tamvm1.tamu.edu`

10077 NativeWeb: A cyber-place for the world's indigenous peoples. Includes an electronic store, an native events calendar, and pointers to other native Internet resources.
```
http://web.maxwell.syr.edu/nativeweb/
```
INFO `decole@maxwell.syr.edu` (David Cole)
FAQ `http://web.maxwell.syr.edu/nativeweb/nativeweb/listserv.html`

10078 `soc.culture.native` Aboriginal people around the world. *Newsgroup*

➤ **Zapatistas in Cyberspace:** For net sources of information and news on Chiapas and the Zapatistas. (See entry 7523 for full listing.)

PARANORMAL PHENOMENA

10079 `alt.alien.research` Extraterrestial body snatching for fun and profit. *Newsgroup*

10080 `alt.alien.visitors` Space aliens on Earth! *Newsgroup*

10081 `alt.bible.prophecy` Discussion of the Bible and its prophecies. *Newsgroup*

10082 `alt.bigfoot` Dr. Scholl's gone native. *Newsgroup*

10083 `alt.bigfoot.research` Serious discussion by Bigfoot researchers. *Moderated newsgroup*

10084 `alt.folklore.ghost-stories` Boo! *Newsgroup*

10085 `alt.life.afterlife` The warm light at end of the tunnel is a locomotive. *Newsgroup*

10086 `alt.magick.tyagi` Magick as revealed by Mordred Nagasiva. *Newsgroup*

10087 `alt.misc.forteana` Charles Fort, his books, and general weird happenings. *Newsgroup*

10088 `alt.out-of-body` Out-of-body experiences. *Newsgroup*

10089 `alt.parallel.universes` Perpendicular universes hurt more. *Newsgroup*

10090 `alt.paranet.abduct` "They replaced Jim-Bob with a look-alike!". *Newsgroup*

10091 `alt.paranet.paranormal` "If it exists, how can supernatural be beyond natural?". *Newsgroup*

10092 `alt.paranet.psi` "How much pressure can you generate with your brain?". *Newsgroup*

10093 `alt.paranet.science` "Maybe if we dissect the psychic . . .". *Newsgroup*

10094 `alt.paranet.skeptic` "I don't believe they turned you into a newt.". *Newsgroup*

10095 `alt.paranet.ufo` "Heck, I guess naming it 'UFO' identifies it.". *Newsgroup*

10096 `alt.paranormal` Phenomena that are not scientifically explicable. *Newsgroup*

10097 `alt.paranormal.channeling` Spiritual mediumship, channeling, and channelers. *Newsgroup*

10098 `alt.paranormal.spells.hexes.magic` And Rolaids.spells.relief. *Newsgroup*

10099 `alt.psychology.synchronicity` Interdisciplinary discussion of synchronicity. *Newsgroup*

10100 `alt.sci.time-travel` Theory of time travel. *Newsgroup*

➤ **APAR-L:** On apparitions approved by the Catholic Church. (See entry 8742 for full listing.)

10101 **PSI-L:** Discussion on the nature of parapsychology, not its existence. Topics include ESP, out-of-body experiences, dream experiences, altered states of consciousness, etc. *Mailing List*
± `listserv@vm.its.rpi.edu` [body = SUBSCRIBE PSI-L first-name last-name]
INFO `lnaqc@cunyvm.cuny.edu` (Lusi N. Altman)
ARCHIVE `listserv@vm.its.rpi.edu` [body = INDEX PSI-L]

PEACE & DISARMAMENT

➤ **ACTIV-L:** Information for activists involved in peace, empowerment, human rights, and justice. (See entry 5580 for full listing.)

➤ `alt.fan.noam-chomsky`: Noam Chomsky's writings and opinions. *Newsgroup*

10102 `bit.listserv.disarm-l` Disarmament discussion list. *Newsgroup*

10103 **CAVEAT-L:** To stop interpersonal violence: discussion, information, activism. *Mailing List*
± `listproc@fhs.mcmaster.ca` [body = SUBSCRIBE CAVEAT-L first-name last-name]
OWNER `caveat@fhs.csu.mcmaster.ca` (CAVEAT Administrator)

10104 `clari.news.conflict` War, conflict, peace talks. *Moderated newsgroup*

10105 `clari.news.conflict.misc` War and conflict. *Moderated newsgroup*

10106 `clari.news.conflict.peace_talks` Peace talks and cease-fires. *Moderated newsgroup*

➤ **Communications for a Sustainable Future:** An interdisciplinary effort to facilitate more rapid change in social thought toward a viable future. This resource provides a collection of archives and mailing lists on sustainability. (See entry 5191 for full listing.)

10107 **DISARM-L:** On disarmament, including military and political strategy; technology; sociology; peace activism; conventional, chemical, and biological weapons; superpower intervention and exploitation of the Third World; economic disruption; and nonaggression. *Digest & Reflector*
± `listserv@cnsibm.albany.edu` [body = SUBSCRIBE DISARM-L first-name last-name]

INFO OWNER `dfp10@cnsibm.albany.edu` (Donald F. Parsons, M.D.)

ARCHIVE `listserv@cnsibm.albany.edu` [body = `INDEX DISARM-L`]

Frequency: monthly

10108 ENVSEC_D: On environment, population, and security. *Distribution List, moderated*

± `majordomo@aaas.org` [body = `SUBSCRIBE ENVSEC_D`]

EDITOR `bsmith@aaas.org` (Brian Smith)

Please Note: Subscription by approval only.

10109 Global_Ed: From British Columbia Teachers for Peace and Global Education (PAGE): educators on peace, justice, freedom, and sustainability. For the exchange of information, ideas, and issues to further the development of global education. *Mailing List*

± `global_ed-request@bbs.sd68.nanaimo.bc.ca` [body = `SUBSCRIBE GLOBAL_ED`]

OWNER `msilverton@bbs.sd68.nanaimo.bc.ca` (Mike Silverton)

10110 International Security Network (IntSecNet): A one-stop virtual library and information network for security and defense studies, peace and conflict research, and international relations. The International Security Network is a joint effort of diverse research institutions, financially supported by the Swiss government.

`http://www.fsk.ethz.ch/isn/`

INFO `postmaster@sipo.reok.ethz.ch`

➤ **OneWorld Online:** This site has an extensive amount of information on global issues. The site is indexed and includes documents on global justice, conflict, aid, trade, education, health, human rights, population, and sustainable human development, as well as daily news summaries. It also hosts information for numerous international development and relief organizations. (See entry 10052 for full listing.)

➤ **QUAKER-P:** On Quaker concerns related to peace and social-justice issues. (See entry 8765 for full listing.)

PHILANTHROPY

10111 CharitiesUSA: This site includes a list of charities, news flashes on natural disaster or other emergency relief efforts, and more.

`http://www.charitiesusa.com/charitiesusa`

INFO `mharding@charitiesusa.com`

➤ **The Robert Wood Johnson Foundation:** Information about The Robert Wood Johnson Foundation—the nation's largest private philanthropy devoted to health care. (See entry 5059 for full listing.)

10112 `tnn.interv.corp` Corporate philanthropy activities. *Newsgroup*

POVERTY

➤ **Virtual Library on International Development:** A very well-organized collection of pointers to international development resources. Resources are well categorized and accessible by region, type of organization, and resource theme. (See entry 10047 for full listing.)

10113 `clari.news.issues.poverty` Poverty, homelessness, hunger. *Moderated newsgroup*

10114 `clari.news.poverty` Poverty, homelessness, hunger. *Moderated newsgroup*

➤ **United Nations Development Programme Information System:** This site contains information related to the United Nations Development Program and other United Nations agencies. (See entry 5445 for full listing.)

RAPE & SEXUAL HARASSMENT

➤ **INTVIO-L:** On intimate, or family, violence. (See entry 9931 for full listing.)

➤ **Kathy's Resources on Parenting, Domestic Violence, Abuse, Trauma & Dissociation:** Friendly and exhaustive index to resources that foster interpersonal respect and nonviolence. (See entry 9932 for full listing.)

➤ **The Men's Issues Page:** On the full range of men's concerns: health, parenting, justice, self-awareness, and growth. (See entry 10056 for full listing.)

10115 SASH-L: For discussion on forming policy and organizing against sexual harassment. *Mailing List*

± listserv@asuvm.inre.asu.edu [body = SUBSCRIBE SASH-L first-name last-name]

INFO phoebe.stambaugh@nau.edu (Phoebe Stambaugh)

INFO melssen@aznvx1.azn.nl (Fred Melssen)

10116 **talk.rape** Discussions on stopping rape; not to be cross-posted. *Newsgroup*

SEXUALITY

➤ **alt.magick.sex:** Pursuing spirituality through sexuality and vice versa. *Newsgroup*

➤ **ASC-L:** On academic sexual correctness: privacy, consent, and institutional encroachment. (See entry 4091 for full listing.)

10117 **clari.news.sex** Sexual issues, sex-related political stories. *Moderated newsgroup*

➤ **Gay Male S/M Activists:** GMSMA is the world's largest organization of men seriously interested in safe, sane, consensual sadomasochism. (See entry 9959 for full listing.)

10118 **gender:** A mailing list for discussing all aspects of gender and (biological) sex issues. *Mailing List*

± gender-request@ifi.uio.no [body = subscribe]

± majordomo@ifi.uio.no [body = info gender]

INFO OWNER thomasg@ifi.uio.no (Thomas Gramstad)

FAQ majordomo@ifi.uio.no [body = info gender]

➤ **The Men's Issues Page:** On the full range of men's concerns: health, parenting, justice, self-awareness, and growth. (See entry 10056 for full listing.)

10119 **Safer Sex: Your Online How-To Guide:** On safe sex: methods, news, views.

http://www.safersex.org/

INFO ss-admin@safersex.org

➤ **SEXADD-L:** On sexual addiction: clinical and research focus—*not* a recovery group. (See entry 4709 for full listing.)

10120 **SHS:** The Society for Human Sexuality mailing list. Intended for general discussion of human sexuality and as a way to distribute information about events put on by the Society for Human Sexuality (a sex-positive registered student organization at the University of Washington). *Mailing List*

ftp://ftp.u.washington.edu/pub/user-supported/sfpse

http://weber.u.washington.edu/~sfpse/

OWNER sfpse@u.washington.edu

Comments: Disclaimer: Discussion is often frank and sexually explicit. To subscribe to this mailing lists, you must be over 18 years of age; by subscribing, you are certifying that you are over the age of 18, that it is legal for you to read sexually explicit material in your area, and that you freely wish to read such material.

10121 **The Society for Human Sexuality:** Sober and enlightened information on all aspects and phases of human sexuality.

http://weber.u.washington.edu/~sfpse/

ftp://ftp.u.washington.edu/pub/user-supported/sfpse

INFO sfpse@u.washington.edu

➤ **WomenSpace:** An area for young women and girls full of fun, uninhibiting information about health, relationships, sexuality, and a host of other information of special interest to young women and girls. (See entry 5120 for full listing.)

SOCIAL WORK

10122 **CSOCWORK:** For Canadian social workers: social policy, services, professional networking. *Mailing List*

± listserv@pdomain.uwindsor.ca [body = SUBSCRIBE CSOCWORK first-name last-name]

OWNER bobgc@uwindsor.ca (Prof. Bob Chandler, MSW)

ARCHIVE listserv@pdomain.uwindsor.ca [body = INDEX CSOCWORK]

➤ **DIVERSITY-FORUM:** On human resource management of diversity in business, education & social work. (See entry 9892 for full listing.)

➤   **EMPATHY:** For teachers of interpersonal communication courses. (See entry 5173 for full listing.)

10123 MDSW: A discussion list on topics of social-work interest for people in Maryland and surrounding areas. *Mailing List*

   ± `listproc@list.ab.umd.edu` [body = `SUBSCRIBE MDSW` first-name last-name]

   INFO OWNER `hchaikli@ssw02.ab.umd.edu`

   INFO `jblumenf@ssw02.ab.umd.edu`

10124 SOCSEC-L: On the Dutch social services sector. *Mailing List*

   ± `majordomo@knoware.nl` [body = `subscribe socsec-l`]

   OWNER `janvds@knoware.nl` (Jan van der Sluis)

   OWNER `rdeklein@knoware.nl` (Ronald de Klein)

   OWNER `r.deklein@nizw.nl` (Ronald de Klein)

   Language: Dutch

10125 SOCWORK: On social work and related areas of interest. *Mailing List*

   `http://comp.uark.edu/~social`

   ± `listserv@uafsysb.uark.edu` [body = `SUBSCRIBE SOCWORK` first-name last-name]

   INFO `socwork-request@uafsysb.uark.edu`

   OWNER `cljones@comp.uark.edu` (Cindy L. Jones)

   OWNER `cljones@uafsysb.uark.edu` (Cindy L. Jones)

   ARCHIVE `listserv@uafsysb.uark.edu` [body = `INDEX SOCWORK`]

   FAQ `http://comp.uark.edu/~social/socquest.html`

10126 SWCO: On social work in the state of Colorado. *Mailing List*

   `http://lamar.colostate.edu/~mcmurray/swco.html`

   ± `listserv@colostate.edu` [body = `SUBSCRIBE SWCO` first-name last-name]

   OWNER `mcmurray@lamar.colostate.edu`

TERRORISM

10127 `alt.current-events.amfb-explosion` Terrorism in America's heartland. *Newsgroup*

10128 `alt.fan.unabomber` Fans of the mystical and awe-inspiring Unabomber. *Newsgroup*

10129 `clari.news.terrorism` Terrorist actions and related news around the world. *Moderated newsgroup*

10130 `clari.news.usa.terrorism` Terrorism within the USA. *Moderated newsgroup*

10131 `clari.usa.terrorism` Terrorism in the United States. *Moderated newsgroup*

10132 `clari.world.terrorism` Terrorist actions and related news (non-U.S.). *Moderated newsgroup*

UTOPIA, DYSTOPIA & FUTURISM

10133 `alt.culture.virtual.oceania` Oceania project discussion and news. *Moderated newsgroup*

10134 `alt.future.millennium` For the discussion of all millennium matters. *Newsgroup*

10135 `alt.gathering.rainbow` For discussing the annual Rainbow Gathering. *Newsgroup*

➤   `alt.housing.nontrad:` Communes, co-housing, and alternative living arrangements. *Newsgroup*

10136 `alt.society.futures` Musing on where we're all headed. *Newsgroup*

10137 `alt.society.neutopia` A place to further the cause of peace and love. *Newsgroup*

10138 `bit.listserv.xtropy-l` Extropian list. *Newsgroup*

➤   **CHARTER:** For organizing GlobalPsych: human nature, human futures, and the Internet. (See entry 9517 for full listing.)

➤   **Extropians:** Spin-off of *Extropy* magazine—advanced technology, self-transformation, futurist philosophy, life extension, voluntarism. (See entry 9823 for full listing.)

10139 La Revue Intemporelle - The timeless magazine: Publishing since 1988, once a year, a free magazine treating fundamental themes such as human dignity, the planet Earth, consciousness, love and the creation of a planetary federation. *Magazine*
http://www.ina.fr/CP/HumainsAssocies/HA.Revues.intemporelles.html
± humains-fr@univ-rennes1.fr (mailing list)
INFO humains@iway.fr (Tatiana Faria)
ARCHIVE http://www.ina.fr/CP/HumainsAssocies/HA.Revues.intemporelles.html
Language: French
Frequency: annual

10140 Les Humains Associes - The Associated Humans: The Associated Humans is a nongovernmental and nonprofit organization, founded in 1984. It comprises psychologists, journalists, scientists, and artists. As a cultural and artistic movement, it unifies humanity and environment through the social aspect.
http://www.ina.fr/CP/HumainsAssocies
INFO humains@iway.fr (Tatiana Faria)

10141 misc.survivalism Disaster and long-term survival techniques and theory. *Newsgroup*

10142 tnn.interv.alt-info Information exchange on alternative society. *Newsgroup*

UTOPIA, DYSTOPIA & FUTURISM—WHOLE SYSTEMS

10143 alt.co-evolution The Whole Earth Review and associated lifestyles. *Newsgroup*

10144 alt.co-ops Discussion about cooperatives. *Newsgroup*

10145 bit.listserv.geodesic List for the discussion of Buckminster Fuller. *Newsgroup*

10146 well.general Local news for and about the Whole Earth 'Lectronic Link. *Newsgroup*

10147 WHOLESYS-L: On envisioning "whole systems": it's all connected . . . *Mailing List*
± listserv@netcom.com [body = SUBSCRIBE wholesys-l]
OWNER ffunch@netcom.com (Flemming Funch)
ARCHIVE http://www.newciv.org/worldtrans/whole.html

10148 WHOLEINFO-L: Edited digest of WHOLESYS-L. *Digest, moderated*
± listserv@netcom.com [body = SUBSCRIBE wholeinfo-l]
INFO http://www.newciv.org/worldtrans/whole.html
OWNER ffunch@netcom.com (Flemming Funch)
ARCHIVE http://www.newciv.org/worldtrans/whole.html

WOMEN'S ISSUES & FEMINISM

➤ **PEG, a Peripatetic, Eclectic Gopher:** A collection of pointers to all sorts of Internet resources. Especially strong are its virtual reference desk, Internet assistance, politics and government, medicine, and women's studies resource lists. (See entry 2726 for full listing.)

➤ **WWW Women's Sports Page:** A comprehensive collection of links to women's sports pages around the net, compiled by Amy Lewis. (See entry 7022 for full listing.)

10149 alt.feminazis For people who hate radical feminists. *Newsgroup*

10150 alt.feminism.individualism Discussions about feminism and individualism. *Newsgroup*

10151 alt.women.attitudes The different attitudes that women have. *Newsgroup*

10152 alt.women.supremacy Women's social status and general gender wars. *Newsgroup*

10153 Amazons International: On the image of the female hero in fiction and in fact, as it is expressed in art and literature, in the physiques and feats of female athletes, and in sexual values and practices. *Newsletter*
± amazons-request@ifi.uio.no [body = subscribe]
EDITOR thomas@math.uio.no (Thomas Gramstad)
ARCHIVE gopher://gopher.etext.org/11/Politics/Amazons.Intl

FAQ `majordomo@ifi.uio.no` [body = `info amazons`]

➤ **bionet.women-in-bio:** Discussions about women in biology. *Newsgroup*

10154 **clari.news.women** Women's issues: sexism, harassment. *Moderated newsgroup*

➤ **COE:** Circles of Exchange: 10 years' mail exchange on women's spirituality goes cyber. (See entry 8780 for full listing.)

10155 **EE-WOMEN:** On women's issues in central and Eastern Europe, and in the NIS. *Mailing List*

± `listproc@cep.nonprofit.net` [body = `SUBSCRIBE EE-WOMEN first-name last-name`]

OWNER `cep@minerva.cis.yale.edu` (Civic Education Project)

10156 **FeMiNa:** According to maintainers, this is the only searchable database for woman- and girl-oriented sites on the Web. Very good women's health coverage.

`http://www.femina.com/`

INFO `asherman@interport.net`

10157 **FEMINIST:** American Library Association's Feminist Task Force. On all aspects of feminism, but especially on how it relates to the tasks and work of librarians. *Mailing List*

± `listserv@mitvma.mit.edu` [body = `SUBSCRIBE FEMINIST first-name last-name`]

INFO `feminist-request@mitvma.mit.edu`

ARCHIVE `listserv@mitvma.mit.edu` [body = `INDEX FEMINIST`]

➤ **Feminist-Theology:** On Jewish and Christian feminist theology. (See entry 8781 for full listing.)

10158 **fj.soc.men-women** Fairness, right, etc. between women and men. *Newsgroup*

10159 **geekgirl:** Women and technology: irreverent, smart, fun, committed. One of the best uses of the Web, now or in the future.

`http://www.next.com.au/spyfood/geekgirl/`

INFO `gg@geekgirl.com.au`

➤ **gender:** A mailing list for discussing all aspects of gender and (biological) sex issues. (See entry 10118 for full listing.)

➤ **GEOGFEM:** On feminism in geography. (See entry 9321 for full listing.)

➤ **International Directory of Women Web Designers:** The Web's only comprehensive international directory of Web design and related Internet consultancy firms that are owned and operated by women. Inside, you will find businesses that specialize in Web page design, server setup and maintenance, Internet training and consulting, and more. Companies have been broken down geographically to help you find a consultant or designer in your area. Links to company sites and contact information about the company are included. (See entry 3025 for full listing.)

➤ **INTVIO-L:** On intimate, or family, violence. (See entry 9931 for full listing.)

➤ **Isis Pages:** Isis is a Web site devoted to the art and culture of women of African descent. (See entry 5139 for full listing.)

➤ **Minority Bank Monitor:** The site provides information on every women- or minority-owned financial institution in the U.S. (See entry 1666 for full listing.)

10160 **NrrdGrrl!:** A site for women who like to do things their own way.

`http://www.interport.net/~ameliaw/nrrd.html`

INFO `ameliaw@interport.net`

➤ **The Official Nicola Griffith Page:** Information on Nicola Griffith, author of the novels *Ammonite* and *Slow River* and the collection *Women and Other Aliens* (forthcoming). (See entry 604 for full listing.)

10161 **Paglia-L:** On the writings and ideas of Dr. Camille Paglia. *Mailing List, moderated*

± `mailserv@ac.dal.ca` [body = `SUBSCRIBE PAGLIA-L e-mail-address`]

INFO `paglia-l-request@ac.dal.ca`

EDITOR `damion001@aol.com` (Damion Doohan)

EDITOR `kevinsp8@ac.dal.ca` (Kevin Speight)

EDITOR `bpholmes@ac.dal.ca` (Boyd Holmes)

10162 `soc.feminism` Discussion of feminism and feminist issues. *Moderated newsgroup*

10163 `soc.women` Issues related to women, their problems and relationships. *Newsgroup*

10164 `tnn.interv.women` Information exchange on women's issues. *Newsgroup*

10165 `uk.wic` Discussion of women in computing. *Newsgroup*

➤ **WH-NEWS:** A newsletter about women's health. (See entry 5118 for full listing.)

➤ **WIG-L:** On the feminist study of German literature. (See entry 622 for full listing.)

➤ **WISHPERD:** On women in sports, health, physical education, recreation, and dance. (See entry 7023 for full listing.)

➤ **WMST-L:** For scholarly discussion of women's-studies teaching, research, and program administration. (See entry 5219 for full listing.)

10166 WOMEN: On women's issues in Turkey and in other developing countries. *Mailing List*

± `listproc@bilkent.edu.tr` [body = `SUBSCRIBE WOMEN` first-name last-name]

OWNER `kubra@hun.edu.tr` (Hatice Kubra Bahsisoglu)

OWNER `msan@hun.edu.tr` (Mujgan San)

Language: Turkish & English

Comments: Administrators also run another list, Kadin, that is is on the same topic but in the Turkish language only.

➤ **Women in Technology Directory:** A professional directory for women in technological fields designed to facilitate and encourage women's ability to network with one another via e-mail. (See entry 9582 for full listing.)

YOUTH

➤ **KIDLINK:** KIDLINK is a global networking project for youths 10-15. The KIDLINK list is for official news and information about the KIDLINK series of projects, which span many other lists and services. KIDLINK coordinates the worldwide dialog of thousands of youth 10-15 in scores of countries. Other KIDLINK lists are RESPONSE, KID-PROJ, KIDFORUM, the KIDCAFE family of lists, the KIDLEADER family of lists, KIDPLAN, and a family of project COORDination lists. (See entry 4480 for full listing.)

10167 `alt.org.jaycees` Junior Chamber of Commerce. *Newsgroup*

10168 `alt.politics.youth` Discussions about youth politics. *Newsgroup*

10169 `alt.skinheads` The skinhead culture/anti-culture. *Newsgroup*

10170 `alt.skinheads.moderated` The skinhead culture/anti-culture. *Moderated newsgroup*

10171 `alt.society.generation-x` Lifestyles of those born 1960-early-1970s. *Newsgroup*

10172 `alt.teens` Teenagers. *Newsgroup*

➤ **Child-Psychiatry:** On child and adolescent psychiatry: treatment issues, psychopharmacology, inpatient/outpatient care plans, emergency child/adolescent psychiatry, et cetera. (See entry 5008 for full listing.)

10173 `clari.news.crime.juvenile` Crimes by children and teenagers. *Moderated newsgroup*

➤ **CM:** An electronic viewing journal of Canadian materials for young people. Reviews and articles about Canadian books, videos, and materials for young people. (See entry 7139 for full listing.)

10174 GANGTM: On gangs and gang-related problems. *Mailing List*

± `gangtm-request@dhvx20.csudh.edu`

OWNER `lpress@dhvx20.csudh.edu` (Larry Press)

10175 Internet Herald: A magazine of news, commentary, and a little something else by Generation X. *E-Journal*

`http://server.berkeley.edu/herald/`

± `herald@server.berkeley.edu`

INFO OWNER `aurenhof@server.berkeley.edu` (Auren Hoffman)

ARCHIVE `http://server.berkeley.edu/herald/`

Frequency: monthly

➤   `mex.joven:`   Mexican newsgroup on youth issues. *Newsgroup*

10176 `rec.scouting` Scouting youth organizations worldwide. *Newsgroup*

10177 **Shadow:** Fiction/nonfiction magazine for teens. (Adults too . . .) *Magazine*
   `http://nermal.santarosa.edu/~tmurphy/shadow.html`
   ± INFO OWNER `brianwts@aol.com` (Brian Murphy)
   ARCHIVE `http://nermal.santarosa.edu/~tmurphy/shadow.html`
   Frequency: quarterly

10178 `soc.religion.christian.youth-work` Christians working with young people. *Moderated newsgroup*

10179 **T@P Online:** College and young-person-oriented mega-site, including extreme sports, music, travel, film, and more (over 17 sections). *Magazine*
   `http://www.taponline.com/tap/new.html`
   INFO EDITOR OWNER `editor@taponline.com` (Joshua Fruhlinger, editor)
   ARCHIVE `http://www.taponline.com/`
   Frequency: daily

10180 **Y-RIGHTS:** On kid/teen rights. *Mailing List*
   ± `listserv@sjuvm.stjohns.edu` [body = SUBSCRIBE Y-RIGHTS first-name last-name]
   INFO `y-rights-request@sjuvm.stjohns.edu`
   ARCHIVE `listserv@sjuvm.stjohns.edu` [body = INDEX Y-RIGHTS]

10181 **YES-LIST:** On youth in entertainment and sports: problems with fame. *Mailing List*
   `http://www.eskimo.com/~satterwh/yes.html`
   ± `majordomo@eskimo.com` [body = subscribe yes-list]
   OWNER `satterwh@netcom.com` (Michael Satterwhite)

10182 **Youth Activity Center of Boca Raton, Florida:** The Youth Activity Center in Boca Raton, Florida, is a nonsectarian corporation established to provide an alternative positive social environment for youth and their parents. YAC differs from other youth centers because it gives youth and parents a safe place to play, learn, and socialize.
   `http://www.bocanet.com/yac`
   INFO `webmaster2@bocanet.com`

➤   **Youth Ministry Forum:** On ministry to teenagers. (See entry 8735 for full listing.)

LIBRARY CATALOGS (OPACS)

Over one thousand five hundred libraries around the world have card catalogs that are accessible via the Internet, and the number increases weekly. You can use online card catalogs to examine the holdings of libraries, browse for books by topic for a research project, and in some cases examine special databases.

To log onto an OPAC (Online Public Access Catalog), you will need to use telnet or TN3270, an enhanced version of telnet that emulates the IBM terminals many online library catalogs require. (For more information on connection services, see "An Internet Refresher" at the beginning of this book.)

Entry Format:
>**OPAC or Library Name:** Country *Software Type*
>>**TELNET/TN270** `host.domain` Login instructions, if any
>>Alternate access routes, if any
>or
>**Library Name:** Country (Access via **Name of OPAC from which library is accessible**)

Where to Find It: The entries in this chapter were taken from the database of a program called Hytelnet, written by Peter Scott. Hytelnet is a powerful program that provides hypertext access to OPACs and other telnet-reachable resources. For more information on Hytelnet, including PC and Unix versions of the software, point your web browser to `http://library.usask.ca/hytelnet`. There is also a mailing list associated with Hytelnet that distributes updates and information on new OPACs. To subscribe to this mailing list, send e-mail to `listserv@library.berkeley.edu` with SUB-SCRIBE HYTEL-L in the body of your message.

The entries in this chapter were verified to make sure that access is indeed possible following the instructions listed. A small number of the OPACs listed in Hytlenet could not be verified, so I have not listed them. This does not mean, however, that the OPACs don't exist. OPACs are often unreachable for a number of reasons: libraries sometimes limit access to certain hours, international links go down, host computers crash, etc. A number of the entries listed required many login attempts before access was finally gained.

Comments: Logging in to some of the OPACs in this list can be a bit tricky. No instructions are listed here for OPACs with easy-to-follow online instructions. If the login process is not so easy, instructions are given, and I have tried to make them as clear as possible. Each step in the login process is separated by the ▶ symbol. Text in the `Courier` font is the text that you should type, or, in the case of "wait for the prompt" instructions, text that you will see on your screen. The ↵ symbol indicates that you need to press the return key at a point where you would not automatically do so (for example, before you are presented with a prompt, or at a prompt instead of entering information). Type <control>-C (when using TN3270) or <escape>-<shift>-] to exit from almost any OPAC (the first screen of the OPAC should give you the exit command if it is neither of these two). If you encounter a "clear the screen" instruction and are not using an IBM terminal with a <clear screen> key, type <escape>-O-M. Similarly, if you are prompted to press a PF key and are not using a terminal with PF keys, type <escape> and then the number of the PF key (i.e., if prompted to press PF6, type <escape>-6). Access addresses are listed in order of preference; try the top one first.

OPACSs are probably the most confusing resource online. The many OPAC systems were designed by different organizations, use different structures, yet are often linked to one another. It is sometimes difficult to find the particular library catalog you want, even after you've logged on correctly to the OPAC that contains it, and when using some of the larger OPACs it is far too easy to go around in circles without coming across what you're looking for. The instructions given with the entries below should at least get you past the first hurdles and allow you to explore. Keep in mind that many OPACs have help files online; refer to them if you are having problems finding the catalog you want.

OPAC Software Types: A number of OPAC software packages are used by more than one library. Comments and brief instructions on how to use the more common ones are given below. The format of these entries is:

TYPE
Comments, explanations, or special instructions, if any.

Help command: what to enter to access help
Searching:
>   **by author:** instructions on searching by author
>   **by title:** instructions on searching by title
>   **by subject:** instructions on searching by subject
>   **by key word:** instructions on searching by key word
>   **by other data:** instructions on searching by other data
>   **additional search information:** more ways to search, if any

Navigating:
>   **desired location:** navigation keystrokes
>   **other:** navigation keystrokes

Other actions:
>   **actions:** keystrokes

BLCMP

Help command: H

Searching:
>   **by author:** Select A from the menu. Then enter the author's name at the : prompt
>   **by title:** Select T from the menu. Then enter the title at the : prompt
>   **by subject:** Select S from the menu. Enter the subject at the : prompt
>   **by key word:** Select K from the menu and enter the key word at the : prompt

BuCAT

Help command: HELP

Searching:
>   **by author:** find a=author
>   **by title:** find t=title
>   **by subject:** find s=subject
>   **by author, title, and subject indexes at once:** find key word/phrase
>   **additional search information:** You can combine words or phrases using symbols for the boolean operators "and" (symbols "&", "/") "or" (symbol "|"), and "not" (symbol "~"). (example: find united nations & peace)

CATS

Every CATS system has its own site-specific menu system, which is different from that of every other CATS system. All of them are extremely easy to use, so no instructions are provided here.

CLSI

No information available.

DOBIS/LIBIS

No information available.

DRA

Help command: ??.

Searching:
>   **by author:** a=author's last-name first-name
>   **by title:** t=title
>   **by subject:** s=subject
>   **by call umber:** c=call number (example: c=f1897.5)
>   **by ISBN:** i=ISBN (example: i=449908984)
>   **by ISSN:** n=ISSN (example: n=0010-0285)
>   **by LCCN:** l=LCCN (example: l= 9390457)
>   **by Music Publishers Number:** r=MPN (example: r=CD 80096 telarc)
>   **by key word:** Enter k=key word (Some DRA sites use the Z39.58 standard for the key word search. See the section on "Using Z39.58.")

DYNIX

The Dynix library package is an entirely different product from the Dynix Operating System used on Sequent Computers.

Searching:

by author: Choose the appropriate number from the main menu

by title: If the exact title is known, select the "Title Alphabetical list" option on the menu. If the exact title is not known, select the "Title Words" option

by subject: Choose the appropriate number from the main menu

by key word: Choose the appropriate number from the main menu. Some systems will look for terms in the subject field, some in the title field, as indicated on the menu

by call number: Choose the appropriate number from the main menu

GEAC

Help command: HELP

Searching:

by author: AUT Author (example: AUT Haring)

by title: TIL Title (example: TIL The Animal Folktales of Africa)

by subject: SUB Subject (example: SUB Folktales)

by key word: KEY Key word/string (example: KEY Animal Folktales)

Navigating:

previously displayed screens: BAC

next screen: FOR

Other actions:

to select an item in a list of items: enter the number to the right of the item

GvB

No information available.

INLEX

Help command: HE= and the desired command (example: HE=AU for author help)

Searching:

by author: au= Author

by title: ti= Title

by subject: su= subject

by call number: ca= call number

Navigating:

next page: NP

previous page: PP

first page: FP

last page: LP

step back: SB

exit: EX

Other actions:

to display titles: dt= line number

to display call numbers: DC

to display full record: DF
for instructions: IN
for bulletin board: BB

INNOPAC

INNOPAC is very easy to use. Just press the letter or number next to the item that you want. There is no need to press the <enter> or <return> key when choosing one of the menu options.

Searching:
by author: select A on the main menu
by title: select T on the main menu
by subject: select S on the main menu
by key word: select either K or W, as listed on the menu

Other actions:
to show items with the same subject when looking at a single record: select S
to show items nearby on the shelf when looking at a single record: select Z

LIBERTAS

Every Libertas system has its own site-specific menuing system, which is different from that of every other Libertas system. All of them are extremely easy to use, so no instructions are provided here.

LS/2000

Searching:
by author: enter the number for heading search; when prompted, enter the author name (last-name, first-name)
by title: enter the number for heading search; when prompted, enter the title
by key word: enter the number for key word search; when prompted, enter as much of the *beginning* of the heading as you are sure of

Other actions:
to go one step backward in your search: ^
to see more of a list ending with more: a
to see previous pages of a list ending with more: /B

MultiLIS

MultiLIS is menu/prompt driven and is not difficult to use. Status and error messages are usually displayed in the lower right-hand corner of the screen. Press the <return> key to acknowledge these messages.

Help command: press the <help> key or KeyPad7
Searching:
by author: enter author's last-name first-name (example: haring leigh, haring, leigh, or haring l)
by title: enter one or more words from the title (in any order)
by subject: enter one or more words that describe the subject (in any order) (example: folktales african animal)

Navigating:
previous menu/screen: press PF1

> **previous screen or record:** press PF2
> **next screen or record:** press PF3
> **exit:** press PF1

Other actions:

> **to see the titles listed as the result of a search:** enter the number or range of numbers next to the particular title(s). (Once you have selected items from this display, you cannot return to this display without redoing the search)
>
> **to start a new search:** press PF1
>
> **to print a record:** press PF4
>
> **to limit a search by date or language when a list of titles is displayed:** press PF5 or KeyPad5
>
> **to display a search history from the searching screen:** press PF2 or KeyPad2

NOTIS

Help command: h or HELP for help

Searching:

> **by author:** a= author
> **by title:** t= title
> **by subject:** s= subject
> **by key word:** k= string (example: k=folktales)
> **by subject:** SU 4-word heading (example: SU Folktales of Africa)
> **by call number:** enter CA call-number (example: CA QA76.8.I294 1988)
> **by combination of fields:** CO Author last-name Title firstword (example: CO Haring Animal for Leigh Haring's *The Animal Folktales of Africa*)
> **additional search information:** You may use the logical operators (and, or, not) and parentheses to group the operators. Also, $ is a wildcard character. (Examples: k=folktales and Anansi; k=folktales and not American; k=folk$ and (Africa or Anansi))

Other actions:

> **to pick an item in a list of items:** enter the number to the right of the item

OCLC

Help command: <esc>-H-<return>

Searching:

> **by author:** A
> **by title:** A
> **by key word:** K
> **by classmark:** C
> **by ISBN (International Standard Book Number):** I
> **by LBN (Library Book Number):** L

Navigating:

> **exit:** <esc>-Q-<return>

UNICORN

No information available.

URICA

URICA is menu-driven and very easy to use. However, there are a few things to note.

Help command: \
Other actions:
> **to exit from a menu and return to the last menu:** .

UTCAT

Some terminal packages remap the keypad <enter> key to other keys. For example, in Procomm the equivalent to Keypad <enter> is Shift-F10. Keypad <enter> is equivalent to <escape>-O-M.

Help command: HEL or press PF6
Searching:
> **by author:** a author last-name, first-name (example: a haring, leigh)
> **by title:** t title (example: t the animal folktales of africa)
> **by subject:** s subject (example: s folktales)
> **by key word:** tk key word/string (example: tk animal africa)

Navigating:
> **previous screen:** BAC (or press PF1)
> **from brief or full records to the corresponding index:** IND (or press PF3)
> **Search Choices Menu:** MEN (or press PF7)
> **exit:** STO (or press PF8)

Other actions:
> **to repeat the last search:** REP (or press PF2)
> **to see the index of authors:** AI name of the first author you wish to see (last-name, first-name) (example: ai haring, leigh)
> **to see the index of titles:** TI followed by the first title you wish to see (example: ti animal folktales of africa)
> **to view general information about the Online Catalog:** EXP (or press PF4)
> **to view current information about Online Catalog developments:** NEW (or press PF5)
> **to send comments to library staff:** COM
> **to select an item from a list:** enter the number of the desired item

VTLS

VTLS features a Novice User Search System that can be accessed at any time by entering ?. This novice mode is an easy-to-use menu-driven method of searching. In addition, the novice mode also offers training on using the Advanced User Search System. Advanced User Search System commands may be entered at any novice level prompt.

Help command: /HELP
Searching:
> **by author:** A/Author last-name, first-name (example: A/Haring, Leigh)
> **by title:** T/title (omit initial articles like "the," "a," and "of") (example: T/animal folktales of africa)
> **by subject:** S/ subject (example: S/folktales)
> **by key word:** W/key word (example: W/africa)
> **additional search information:** To search for key words with boolean operators, use the B/ search command followed by a key word, then an operator, and then the

second key word. (example: `B/folktales and africa; B/folktales or anansi`)

Navigating:

previous screen: `PS`
next screen: `NS`
Novice User Search System: `?`

Z39.58

Z39.58 is a standard from NISO known as the Common Command Language standard. Basic searches are in the form FIND [index name] [search terms].

Help command: `HELP`
Searching:

by author: `FIND AU` author (example: `FIND AU Haring`)
by title: `FIND TI` title (example: `FIND TI The Animal Folktales of Africa`)
by subject: `FIND SU` subject (Harvard only) (example: `FIND SU folktales`)
by topic: `FIND TO` topic (Dartmouth only) (example: `FIND TO africa`)

Other actions:

to display results of search: `DISPLAY`

LIBRARY CATALOGS

Aarhus School of Business: Denmark *custom*

TELNET merkur.bib.dk ◗ wait for the prompt Username ◗ enter MERKUR

Aarhus University: Denmark *custom*

TELNET helios.aau.dk ◗ wait for the prompt login ◗ enter rc9000 ◗ press the ESC key ◗ wait for the prompt att ◗ enter sol

Aberdeen University: United Kingdom *DYNIX*

TELNET library.abdn.ac.uk ◗ wait for the prompt login ◗ enter library

Abilene Christian University: United States (Access via **Abilene Library Consortium**)

Abilene Library Consortium: United States *DRA*

TELNET alcon.acu.edu ◗ wait for the prompt Username ◗ enter alcpac

Abo University: Finland *VTLS*

TELNET bo.abo.fi ◗ wait for the prompt BO> ◗ enter HELLO userid,REF.CLAS01

Academia Sinica: Taiwan *INNOPAC*

TELNET las.sinica.edu.tw ◗ wait for the prompt login ◗ enter library

Acadia University: Canada *custom*

TELNET auls.acadiau.ca ◗ wait for the prompt login ◗ enter opac

Ada Community Library—Idaho: United States ID *INNOPAC*

TELNET 192.207.186.1 ◗ wait for the prompt login ◗ enter library

Adams State College: United States (Access via **MARMOT Library Network**)

Adelphi University: United States *INNOPAC*

TELNET alicat.adelphi.edu ◗ wait for the prompt login ◗ enter alicat

Agawam Public Library: United States (Access via **CARL**)

Agnes Scott College: United States *INNOPAC*

TELNET library.scottlan.edu ◗ wait for the prompt login ◗ enter library

Agnes Scott College—Decatur: United States (Access via **Georgia On-Line Library Information System**)

Agricultural Bibliographic Information System of the Netherlands (AGRALIN): The Netherlands *custom*

TELNET agralin1.bib.wau.nl ◗ wait for the prompt AGRALIN> ◗ enter hello opac.bas

Air Force Institute of Technology: United States *DRA*

TELNET sabre.afit.af.mil ◗ wait for the prompt Username ◗ enter AFITPAC

Albert Einstein College of Medicine: United States *custom*
    TELNET `lis.aecom.yu.edu` ◗ press ↵ ◗ press ↵

Albion College: United States *INNOPAC*
    TELNET `library.albion.edu` ◗ wait for the prompt `login` ◗ enter `library`

Albuquerque Academy: United States NM *INNOPAC*
    TELNET `libros.aa.edu` ◗ wait for the prompt `login` ◗ enter `library`

Allegan Public Library: United States (Access via **KELLY**)

Allegheny College: United States *INNOPAC*
    TELNET `allecat.alleg.edu` ◗ wait for the prompt `login` ◗ enter `library`

Allentown College of St. Francis de Sales: United States *INNOPAC*
    TELNET `trexler.allencol.edu` ◗ wait for the prompt `login` ◗ enter `library`

Alma College: United States *DYNIX*
    TELNET `mark.alma.edu` ◗ wait for the prompt `Username` ◗ enter `dynixpac`

American International College: United States (Access via **CARL**)

American University: United States (Access via **Washington Research Library Consortium**)

Amherst—Jones Library: United States (Access via **CARL**)

Anderson University: United States *UNICORN*
    TELNET `bones.anderson.edu` ◗ wait for the prompt `login` ◗ enter `guest`

Andrews University: United States *INNOPAC*
    TELNET `library.libr.andrews.edu` No login required

Anna Maria College: United States (Access via **CARL**)

Anne Arundel County Public Library, Maryland: United States *DRA Gateway*
    TELNET `axp.aacpl.lib.md.us` ◗ wait for the prompt `Username` ◗ enter `DIALPAC`

Anoka County Library: United States *DRA*
    TELNET `anoka.lib.mn.us` ◗ wait for the prompt `Username` ◗ enter `LIBRARY`

Appalachian State University: United States *INNOPAC*
    TELNET `library.appstate.edu` ◗ wait for the prompt `login` ◗ enter `library`

Araphoe Community College: United States (Access via **CARL**)

Arizona Health Sciences Center: United States *UNICORN*
    TELNET `medlib.arizona.edu` ◗ wait for the prompt `login` ◗ enter `remote` ◗ wait for the prompt `Password` ◗ enter `remote` ◗ press ↵

Arizona State University: United States AZ *custom*
    TELNET `victor.umd.edu` ◗ wait for the prompt `Enter Choice>` ◗ enter `PAC`
    TELNET `192.153.23.254` No login required
    TELNET `carl.lib.asu.edu` ◗ wait for the prompt `Enter Choice>` ◗ enter `CARL`

Arkansas State University: United States AR *VTLS*
    TELNET `apache.astate.edu` ◗ wait for the prompt that ends in `HELLO USER.CLAS01` ◗ enter `hello user.clas01`

Armstrong State College: United States *DRA*
    TELNET `library.armstrong.edu` ◗ wait for the prompt `Username` ◗ enter `LIBRARY`

Art Institute of Chicago: United States *INNOPAC*
  TELNET `innopac.artic.edu` No login required

Asian Institute of Technology: Thailand *INNOPAC*
  TELNET `rccvax.ait.ac.th` ◗ wait for the prompt `Username` ◗ enter `LIBRARY`
  TELNET `clair.ait.ac.th` ◗ wait for the prompt `login` ◗ enter `library`

Aspen Schools: United States CO (Access via **MARMOT Library Network**)

Aston University: United Kingdom *custom*
  TELNET `library.aston.ac.uk` ◗ wait for the prompt `login` ◗ enter `library`

Athabasca University: Canada *BUCAT*
  TELNET `aucat.athabascau.ca` ◗ wait for the prompt `Username` ◗ enter `aucat`

Atlanta—Fulton Public Library: United States GA *custom*
  TELNET `pac.carl.org` ◗ wait for the prompt `Enter Choice>` ◗ enter `PAC`

Atlantic County Library System, New Jersey: United States NJ *DYNIX*
  TELNET `library.atlantic.edu` ◗ wait for the prompt `login` ◗ enter `book`

Atlantic School of Theology: Canada *GEAC*
  TELNET `novanet.dal.ca` ◗ wait for the prompt `login` ◗ enter `opac` ◗ press ⏎

Auburn Public Library: United States (Access via **CARL**)

Augsburg College: United States *DYNIX*
  TELNET `host.clic.edu` ◗ wait for the prompt `login` ◗ enter `apac`

Augusta College: United States *DRA*
  TELNET `library.gsu.edu` No login required
  TELNET `acvax.ac.edu` ◗ wait for the prompt `Username` ◗ enter `acpac`

Augusta-Ross Township: United States (Access via **KELLY**)

Augusta/Mckay Library: United States (Access via **KELLY**)

Auraria University: United States (Access via **CARL**)

Aurora University: United States (Access via **ILLINET On-line Catalog**)

Australian Bibliographic Network: Australia *custom*
  TELNET `abn.nla.gov.au` ◗ wait for the prompt `login` ◗ enter `vt100`

Australian National University: Australia *INNOPAC*
  TELNET `library.anu.edu.au` ◗ wait for the prompt `login` ◗ enter `library`

Austrian Academic Library Network: Austria *custom*
  TELNET `opac.univie.ac.at` No login required

Ayer Public Library: United States (Access via **CARL**)

Azusa Pacific University: United States *GEAC ADVANCE*
  TELNET `apu.edu` ◗ wait for the prompt `login` ◗ enter `public`

Bangor Public Library: United States (Access via **University of Maine Library System**)

Bank Street College of Education: United States *DYNIX*
  TELNET `149.70.1.181` ◗ wait for the prompt `login` ◗ enter `dialin`

Bar-Ilan University: Israel *custom*
  TELNET aleph.biu.ac.il ◗ wait for the prompt Username ◗ enter aleph

Barat College: United States (Access via **ILLINET On-line Catalog**)

Bard College: United States *INNOPAC*
  TELNET library.bard.edu ◗ wait for the prompt login ◗ enter internet

Barnes College Library: United States (Access via **Washington University of St Louis Medical Library**)

Barry University: United States *DRA*
  TELNET bliss.barry.edu ◗ wait for the prompt Username ◗ enter PUBLIC

Bates College: United States *INNOPAC*
  TELNET ladd.bates.edu No login required

Baylor University: United States *MULTILIS*
  TELNET library.baylor.edu ◗ wait for the prompt Username ◗ enter baylis ◗ press ⏎

Baystate Medical Library: United States (Access via **CARL**)

Beaumont Public Library: United States (Access via **CARL**)

Beaumont Royal Oak Hospital Library: United States (Access via **Detroit Area Library Network**)

Belmont Technical College: United States *INNOPAC*
  TELNET 199.218.105.50 ◗ wait for the prompt login ◗ enter library ◗ wait for the prompt Password ◗ enter library

Belmont University: United States *DRA*
  TELNET adelicia.belmont.edu ◗ wait for the prompt Username ◗ enter library

Beloit College: United States *DRA*
  TELNET lib.beloit.edu ◗ wait for the prompt Username ◗ enter belcat

Ben-Gurion University: Israel (Access via **Hebrew University**)

Bergen County Cooperative Library System, New Jersey: United States NJ *DRA Gateway*
  TELNET bergen.bccls.org ◗ wait for the prompt Username ◗ enter PUBLICPIX

Berkeley Public Library: United States *INNOPAC*
  TELNET library.ci.berkeley.ca.us ◗ wait for the prompt login ◗ enter library

Berrien Springs Community Library: United States (Access via **KELLY**)

Bethel College: United States *DYNIX*
  TELNET host.clic.edu ◗ wait for the prompt login ◗ enter apac

Biblioteca Nacional: Venezuela *NOTIS*
  TELNET iabn.ve ◗ wait for the prompt login ◗ enter biblio

Biblioteca Nacional—National Library of Spain: Spain *custom*
  TELNET ariadna.bne.es ◗ wait for the prompt TERMINAL TYPE ◗ enter 2 for VT100 ◗ wait for the prompt APPLICA-TION NAME ◗ enter 3

Bibliothek St. Gabriel: Austria (Access via **Austrian Academic Library Network**)

Bibliotheque Publique et Universitaire de Neuchatel: Switzerland *GEAC*
  TELNET bpu.unine.ch No login required

Bibliotheque Universitaire d'Angers: France *DYNIX*

TELNET `buangers.univ-angers.fr` ◗ wait for the prompt `login` ◗ enter `buangers` ◗ wait for the prompt `Password` ◗ enter `plessis`

BIBSYS: Norway *custom*

TELNET `castor.bibsys.no` ◗ wait for the prompt —> ! `vt100n1,3278` ◗ press ↵ ◗ wait for the prompt that ends in (F.eks. VM aa02abcd) ◗ enter `vm xx00bi01` ◗ wait for the prompt `ENTER PASSWORD` ◗ enter `BIBSYS`

Birkbeck College: United Kingdom (Access via **London University Central Libertas Consortium**)

Birmingham (AL) Public Library and Board of Education: United States AL *CLSI*

TELNET `athena.bham.lib.al.us` ◗ wait for the prompt `login` ◗ enter `library`

Birmingham-Southern College: United States *UNICORN*

TELNET `panther.bsc.edu` ◗ wait for the prompt `login` ◗ enter `library`

Bishop's University: Canada *GEAC ADVANCE*

TELNET `library.ubishops.ca` ◗ wait for the prompt `login` ◗ enter `lib` ◗ wait for the prompt `Password` ◗ enter `bishops`

Boise State University: United States *GEAC ADVANCE*

TELNET `catalyst.idbsu.edu` ◗ wait for the prompt `login` ◗ enter `catalyst`

Bond University: Australia *URICA*

TELNET `library.bond.edu.au` ◗ wait for the prompt `login` ◗ enter `opac`

Borgess Health Information Library: United States (Access via **KELLY**)

Boston College: United States MA (Access via **Boston Library Consortium**)

Boston Library Consortium: United States MA *INNOPAC*

TELNET `tulips.tufts.edu` ◗ wait for the prompt `Username` ◗ enter `BLC`
TELNET `library.bu.edu` ◗ wait for the prompt `login` ◗ enter `blc`

Boston Public Library: United States MA *custom*

TELNET `bpl.org` ◗ wait for the prompt `Username` ◗ enter `BPL`

Boston University: United States MA *INNOPAC*

TELNET `bupac.bu.edu` ◗ wait for the prompt `login` ◗ enter `library`
TELNET `library.bu.edu` ◗ wait for the prompt `login` ◗ enter `library`

Botsford Hospital Library: United States (Access via **Detroit Area Library Network**)

Boulder, Carnegie—Manuscripts & Photographs: United States CO (Access via **Boulder, Colorado, Public Library System**)

Boulder, Colorado, Public Library System: United States CO *custom*

TELNET `victor.umd.edu` ◗ wait for the prompt `Enter Choice>` ◗ enter `PAC`
TELNET `pac.carl.org` ◗ wait for the prompt `Enter Choice>` ◗ enter `PAC`
TELNET `192.153.23.254` No login required
TELNET `161.98.1.68` No login required

Bowdoin College: United States *INNOPAC*

TELNET `library.bowdoin.edu` ◗ wait for the prompt `login` ◗ enter `library`

Bowie State University: United States (Access via **University of Maryland Library System**)

Bowling Green State University: United States *INNOPAC*

TELNET `cat.ohiolink.edu` ◗ wait for the prompt `login` ◗ enter `ohiolink`
TELNET `bglink.bgsu.edu` ◗ wait for the prompt `login` ◗ enter `library`

Bowman Gray School of Medicine—Wake Forest University: United States *INNOPAC*
  TELNET 152.11.242.245 ▶ wait for the prompt login ▶ enter opac

Bradford University: United Kingdom *URICA*
  TELNET library.brad.ac.uk ▶ wait for the prompt Logon please ▶ enter library

Bradley University: United States (Access via **ILLINET On-line Catalog**)

Brandeis University: United States *DRA*
  TELNET library.brandeis.edu ▶ wait for the prompt Username ▶ enter LOUIS

Brandon University: Canada *BUCAT*
  TELNET library.brandonu.ca ▶ wait for the prompt Username ▶ enter libcat

Brevard Community College—Florida: United States FL *NOTIS*
  TELNET luis.nerdc.ufl.edu ▶ wait for the prompt login ▶ enter luis

Briar Cliff College: United States *DYNIX*
  TELNET lib.briar-cliff.edu ▶ wait for the prompt login ▶ enter library ▶ wait for the prompt Password ▶ press ↵

Bridgewater College: United States *INNOPAC*
  TELNET alex.bridgewater.edu ▶ wait for the prompt login ▶ enter library

Bridgman Public Library: United States (Access via **KELLY**)

Brigham Young University: United States *NOTIS*
  TELNET library.byu.edu ▶ wait for the prompt that ends terminal type ▶ enter 2 for vt100 ▶ wait for the prompt => ▶ enter a

British Geological Survey and Institute of Terrestrial Ecology: United Kingdom *LIBERTAS*
  TELNET kwvs.nkw.ac.uk ▶ wait for the prompt Username ▶ enter LIBRARY

Brock University: Canada *INNOPAC*
  TELNET 139.57.128.23 No login required

Bronson Hospital Health Sciences Library: United States (Access via **KELLY**)

Brookhaven National Laboratory: United States *custom*
  TELNET suntid.bnl.gov ▶ wait for the prompt login ▶ enter brookhaven
  TELNET inform.bnl.gov ▶ wait for the prompt login ▶ enter brookhaven

Brooklyn Law School: United States NY *INNOPAC*
  TELNET brkl.brooklaw.edu ▶ wait for the prompt login ▶ enter brkl

Broomfield Public Library: United States (Access via **Boulder, Colorado, Public Library System**)

Broward Community College, Florida: United States FL *NOTIS*
  TELNET luis.nerdc.ufl.edu ▶ wait for the prompt login ▶ enter luis

Brunel University: United Kingdom *UNICORN*
  TELNET lib.brunel.ac.uk ▶ wait for the prompt [] ▶ press ↵
  TELNET library.brunel.ac.uk ▶ wait for the prompt [] ▶ press ↵

Brunswick College: United States (Access via **Georgia On-Line Library Information System**)

Bryn Mawr College: United States *INNOPAC*
  TELNET tripod.brynmawr.edu ▶ wait for the prompt login ▶ enter library

Buchanan Public Library: United States (Access via **KELLY**)

Bucknell University: United States *DRA*
  TELNET quartz.bucknell.edu ▶ wait for the prompt Enter class ▶ enter library ▶ press ↵ ▶ press ↵
  TELNET library.bucknell.edu ▶ wait for the prompt Username ▶ enter LIBRARY

Bud Werner/Steamboat Public: United States (Access via **MARMOT Library Network**)

Budapest University of Economics: Hungary *custom*
  TELNET pernix.bke.hu ▶ wait for the prompt Username ▶ enter EGO

Bur Oak Library System: United States (Access via **ILLINET On-line Catalog**)

Butler University: United States *DRA*
  TELNET ruth.butler.edu ▶ wait for the prompt Username ▶ enter iliad

C*O*N*N*E*C*T: Libraries in the Greater Hartford Area: United States *custom*
  TELNET pac.carl.org ▶ wait for the prompt Enter Choice> ▶ enter PAC

C.S.I.R.O: Australia *GEAC*
  TELNET library.its.csiro.au ▶ wait for the prompt login ▶ enter library

C/W MARS, Inc.: United States *custom*
  TELNET pac.carl.org ▶ wait for the prompt Enter Choice> ▶ enter PAC

C/W MARS: Central and Western Massachusetts: United States *custom*
  TELNET 134.241.70.1 ▶ wait for the prompt Enter Choice> ▶ enter PAC

Cabrillo College: United States *INNOPAC*
  TELNET 198.94.144.4 ▶ wait for the prompt login ▶ enter library

Cal Poly State University: United States *custom*
  TELNET library.calpoly.edu No login required

California Academy of Sciences: United States CA *DRA*
  TELNET sfpl.lib.ca.us ▶ wait for the prompt Username ▶ enter CASPAC

California Institute of the Arts (CalArts): United States *DRA Gateway*
  TELNET vax1.calarts.edu ▶ wait for the prompt Username ▶ enter CALIS

California State Polytechnic University—Pomona: United States CA *INNOPAC*
  TELNET opac.lib.csupomona.edu No login required

California State Polytechnic University—San Luis Obispo: United States CA *INNOPAC*
  TELNET poetry.lib.calpoly.edu ▶ wait for the prompt login ▶ enter library

California State University—Bakersfield: United States CA *GEAC ADVANCE*
  TELNET csublib.lib.csubak.edu ▶ wait for the prompt login ▶ enter library

California State University—Chico: United States CA *custom*
  TELNET libcat.csuchico.edu ▶ wait for the prompt login ▶ enter libcat

California State University—Dominguez Hills: United States CA *GEAC ADVANCE*
  TELNET opac.csudh.edu ▶ wait for the prompt login ▶ enter opac

California State University—Fresno: United States CA *GEAC ADVANCE*
  TELNET alis.csufresno.edu ▶ wait for the prompt login ▶ enter remote

California State University—Fullerton: United States CA *INNOPAC*
  TELNET opac.fullerton.edu ▶ wait for the prompt login ▶ enter library

California State University—Hayward: United States CA *INNOPAC*

TELNET `library.csuhayward.edu` ❯ wait for the prompt `login` ❯ enter `library`

California State University—Long Beach: United States CA *NOTIS*

TELNET `coast.lib.csulb.edu` ❯ press ↵

California State University—Los Angeles: United States CA *INNOPAC*

TELNET `opac.calstatela.edu` No login required

California State University—Sacramento: United States CA *INNOPAC*

TELNET `eureka.lib.csus.edu` ❯ wait for the prompt `login` ❯ enter `library`

California State University—San Marcos: United States CA *INNOPAC*

TELNET `pac.csusm.edu` ❯ wait for the prompt `login` ❯ enter `library`

California State University—Stanislaus: United States CA *GEAC ADVANCE*

TELNET `ollie.csustan.edu` ❯ wait for the prompt `login` ❯ enter `lib`

California University of Pennsylvania: United States CA *custom*

TELNET `carmen.cup.edu` ❯ wait for the prompt `Username` ❯ enter `VULCAT` ❯ wait for the prompt `Continue >` ❯ enter OK

Cambridge University: United Kingdom *CATS*

TELNET `ipgate.cam.ac.uk` ❯ wait for the prompt `->` ❯ enter `uk.ac.cam.ul`

TELNET `ul.cam.ac.uk` No login required

Camosun College: Canada *BuCAT*

TELNET `camcat.camosun.bc.ca` ❯ wait for the prompt `Username` ❯ enter `catinq`

Canada Centre for Mineral and Energy Technology: Canada *MULTILIS*

TELNET `canlib.emr.ca` ❯ wait for the prompt `login` ❯ enter `opac`

Canadian Forces Command and Staff College: Canada *DYNIX*

TELNET `library1.cfcsc.dnd.ca` ❯ wait for the prompt `login` ❯ enter `irc`

Canisius College: United States *INNOPAC*

TELNET `138.92.8.41` ❯ wait for the prompt `login` ❯ enter `cando`

Canterbury Public Library: New Zealand *DRA*

TELNET `library.ccc.govt.nz` ❯ wait for the prompt `Username` ❯ enter `OPAC`

Canton Public Library: United States *INNOPAC*

TELNET `lis.ca.metronet.lib.mi.us` No login required

Capilano College: Canada *INNOPAC*

TELNET `library.capcollege.bc.ca` ❯ wait for the prompt `login` ❯ enter `library`

Carleton College: United States *INNOPAC*

TELNET `muse.library.carleton.edu` ❯ wait for the prompt `login` ❯ enter `muse`

Carleton University: Canada *custom*

TELNET `library.carleton.ca` No login required

CARL—Colorado Alliance of Research Libraries: United States CO *custom*

TELNET `victor.umd.edu` ❯ wait for the prompt `Enter Choice>` ❯ enter PAC

TELNET `192.153.23.254` No login required

TELNET `161.98.1.68` No login required

TELNET `pac.carl.org` ❯ wait for the prompt `Enter Choice>` ❯ enter PAC

Carnegie Library of Pittsburgh: United States *custom*
  TELNET clp2.clpgh.org ◗ wait for the prompt Username ◗ enter CATALOG

Carnegie Mellon University: United States *custom*
  TELNET library.cmu.edu ◗ wait for the prompt login ◗ enter library

Carver County Public Library: United States *DRA*
  TELNET carver.lib.mn.us ◗ wait for the prompt Username ◗ enter SEARCH

Case Western Reserve University: United States *INNOPAC*
  TELNET cat.ohiolink.edu ◗ wait for the prompt login ◗ enter ohiolink
  TELNET catalog.cwru.edu No login required

CASLIN Czech and Slovak Library Information Network: Czech Republic *custom*
  TELNET alpha.nkp.cz ◗ wait for the prompt login ◗ enter visitor ◗ Enter your Internet address

Castleton State College, Vermont: United States (Access via **Middlebury College**)

Catholic Theological Union: United States (Access via **ILLINET On-line Catalog**)

Catholic University of America: United States (Access via **Washington Research Library Consortium**)

Catholic University of America Law Library: United States *INNOPAC*
  TELNET columbo.law.cua.edu ◗ wait for the prompt login ◗ enter library

Cayuga Community College: United States *MULTILIS*
  TELNET caylib.cayuga-cc.edu ◗ wait for the prompt Username ◗ enter OPAC1

Cedar Crest College: United States *DRA Gateway*
  TELNET ccclib.cedarcrest.edu ◗ wait for the prompt Username ◗ enter GATEWAY

Cedar Rapids Public Library: United States *DRA*
  TELNET crpl.cedar-rapids.lib.ia.us ◗ wait for the prompt Username ◗ enter CATALOG

Cedarville College: United States *INNOPAC*
  TELNET library.cedarville.edu ◗ wait for the prompt login ◗ enter library

Center for Research Libraries: United States (Access via **ILLINET On-line Catalog**)

Central College of Iowa: United States *INNOPAC*
  TELNET lib.central.edu No login required

Central Florida Community College—Florida: United States FL *NOTIS*
  TELNET luis.nerdc.ufl.edu ◗ wait for the prompt login ◗ enter luis

Central Mass Regional Library: United States (Access via **CARL**)

Central North Carolina Library Consortium: United States NC *INNOPAC*
  TELNET sheba.library.ncat.edu ◗ wait for the prompt login ◗ enter library

Central Washington University: United States *custom*
  TELNET cluster.cwu.edu ◗ wait for the prompt Username ◗ enter LIBRARY

Centre College: United States *INNOPAC*
  TELNET innovative.centre.edu ◗ wait for the prompt login ◗ enter library

Centre for Newfoundland Studies: Canada (Access via **Memorial University—Newfoundland**)

Centro Informatico Cientifico de Andalucia: Spain *custom*
  TELNET sevax2.cica.es ◗ wait for the prompt Username ◗ enter ALEPH

Centro Universitario Ramon Carande: Spain *LIBERTAS*

TELNET 147.96.201.150 ◗ wait for the prompt Username ◗ enter BIBLIOTECA

CERN Scientific Information Service: Switzerland *custom*

TELNET vxlib.cern.ch ◗ wait for the prompt Username ◗ enter ALICE

Chalmers University of Technology: Sweden *LIBERTAS*

TELNET cthlib.lib.chalmers.se ◗ wait for the prompt Username ◗ enter CHANS ◗ wait for the prompt Password ◗ enter INCHANS

Chandler Gilbert Community College Center Library: United States (Access via **Maricopa Community Colleges Libraries and Media Centers**)

Chapman University: United States *INNOPAC*

TELNET clarke.chapman.edu ◗ wait for the prompt login ◗ enter library ◗ wait for the prompt Password ◗ enter library

Charing Cross & Westminster Medical School—Serials: United Kingdom (Access via **London University Central Libertas Consortium**)

Chatham College: United States *GALAXY*

TELNET libra.chatham.edu ◗ wait for the prompt Username ◗ enter ABBI

Chemeketa Cooperative Regional Library Service, Oregon: United States OR *DYNIX*

TELNET ccrls.chemek.cc.or.us ◗ wait for the prompt login ◗ enter ccrls

Chicago Public Library: United States (Access via **ILLINET On-line Catalog**)

Chicago State University: United States IL (Access via **ILLINET On-line Catalog**)

Chicopee Library: United States (Access via **CARL**)

Chipola Junior College—Florida: United States FL *NOTIS*

TELNET luis.nerdc.ufl.edu ◗ wait for the prompt login ◗ enter luis

Christian Brothers University: United States *DRA*

TELNET bucs.cbu.edu ◗ wait for the prompt Username ◗ enter OPAC

Christopher Newport University: United States *VTLS*

TELNET library.cnu.edu ◗ wait for the prompt that ends in John Smith Library ◗ enter hello cnu.lib

Chung Yuan Christian University: Taiwan *INNOPAC*

TELNET cycul.cycu.edu.tw ◗ wait for the prompt login ◗ enter library

Citadel, the Military College of South Carolina: United States SC *DRA*

TELNET cit1.citadel.edu ◗ wait for the prompt Username ◗ enter CITLIB

City College of San Francisco: United States CA *DYNIX*

TELNET surf.ccsf.cc.ca.us ◗ wait for the prompt login ◗ enter mpub

City Library of Antwerp: Belgium (Access via **University of Antwerp**)

City of Abilene Public Library System: United States (Access via **Abilene Library Consortium**)

City Polytechnic of Hong Kong: Hong Kong *custom*

TELNET peking.cityu.edu.hk ◗ wait for the prompt Username ◗ enter LIBCATALOG

City University: United Kingdom *INNOPAC*

TELNET library.city.ac.uk ◗ wait for the prompt login ◗ enter library ◗ wait for the prompt Password ◗ enter library

City University of New York: United States NY *NOTIS*

TN3270 `cunyvm.cuny.edu` ◗ tab to `COMMAND   ===>` ◗ enter `dial vtam` ◗ wait for next screen ◗ tab to `APPLICA-TION =>` ◗ enter `CUNYPLUS` ◗ wait for next screen ◗ clear screen ◗ enter `LNAV`

Clackamas Community College—Oregon: United States OR *DYNIX*

TELNET `198.153.201.218` ◗ wait for the prompt `login` ◗ enter `libr`

Claremont Colleges: United States *INNOPAC*

TELNET `library.claremont.edu` ◗ wait for the prompt `Username` ◗ enter `LIBRARY`

Clarion University of Pennsylvania: United States PA *GEAC*

TELNET `vaxa.clarion.edu` ◗ wait for the prompt `Username` ◗ enter `LIBRARY`

Clark University: United States (Access via **CARL**)

Clayton State College—Morrow: United States (Access via **Georgia On-Line Library Information System**)

Cleveland State University: United States OH *INNOPAC*

TELNET `scholar.csuohio.edu` ◗ wait for the prompt `login` ◗ enter `library`

Climax-Scotts Schools: United States (Access via **KELLY**)

Climax/Lawrence Memorial Library: United States (Access via **KELLY**)

Clinton—Bigelow Public Library: United States (Access via **CARL**)

Coe College: United States *DYNIX*

TELNET `library.coe.edu` ◗ wait for the prompt `login` ◗ enter `lib`

Colby College: United States *INNOPAC*

TELNET `library.colby.edu` No login required

Colgate University: United States *INNOPAC*

TELNET `library.colgate.edu` ◗ wait for the prompt `login` ◗ enter `library`

College of Charleston: United States *DRA*

TELNET `ashley.cofc.edu` ◗ wait for the prompt `Username` ◗ enter `LIBRARY`
TELNET `library.cofc.edu` ◗ wait for the prompt `Username` ◗ enter `LIBRARY`

College of Lake County, Illinois: United States IL *INNOPAC*

TELNET `lrc.clc.cc.il.us` No login required

College of Mount St. Joseph: United States *INNOPAC*

TELNET `199.18.195.1` No login required

College of New Caledonia: Canada *BUCAT*

TELNET `cncacm.cnc.bc.ca` ◗ wait for the prompt `Username` ◗ enter `CALCAT`

College of Physicians of Philadelphia Library: United States PA (Access via **HSLC HealthNET Health Sciences Information Network**)

College of St. Catherine—Main Campus: United States *DYNIX*

TELNET `host.clic.edu` ◗ wait for the prompt `login` ◗ enter `scpac`

College of St. Catherine—St. Mary's Campus: United States *DYNIX*

TELNET `host.clic.edu` ◗ wait for the prompt `login` ◗ enter `scpac`

College of the Holy Cross: United States *DRA*

TELNET `hcacad.holycross.edu` ◗ wait for the prompt `Username` ◗ enter `LIBRARY`

College of William & Mary, Virginia: United States VA *UNICORN*
TELNET lion.swem.wm.edu ◗ wait for the prompt login ◗ enter lion

College of Wooster: United States *INNOPAC*
TELNET woolib.wooster.edu ◗ wait for the prompt login ◗ enter library

Coloma Public Library: United States (Access via **KELLY**)

Colorado Alliance of Research Libraries: United States CO (See **CARL**)

Colorado Christian University: United States CO *GALAXY*
TELNET ruth.ccu.edu ◗ wait for the prompt Username ◗ enter LIBRARY

Colorado College: United States CO *INNOPAC*
TELNET tiger.cc.colorado.edu ◗ wait for the prompt login ◗ enter library

Colorado Mountain College: United States CO (Access via **MARMOT Library Network**)

Colorado Northwestern CC: United States CO (Access via **MARMOT Library Network**)

Colorado School of Mines: United States CO (Access via **CARL**)

Colorado State University: United States CO (Access via **CARL**)

Colorado University Health Sciences Center Library: United States CO (Access via **CARL**)

Columbia College: United States (Access via **ILLINET On-line Catalog**)

Columbia Seminary—Decatur: United States (Access via **Georgia On-Line Library Information System**)

Columbia University: United States NY *NOTIS*
TELNET columbianet.columbia.edu No login required
TELNET clio.cul.columbia.edu ◗ wait for the prompt TERM = (unknown) ◗ enter vt100

Columbia University—Law Library: United States NY *INNOPAC*
TELNET pegasus.law.columbia.edu ◗ wait for the prompt login ◗ enter pegasus

Columbia University—Teachers College: United States NY *INNOPAC*
TELNET educat.tc.columbia.edu ◗ wait for the prompt login ◗ enter educat

Columbus State Community College: United States *INNOPAC*
TELNET cslink.colstate.cc.oh.us No login required

Communications Research Centre: Canada *MULTILIS*
TELNET hazel.dgcp.doc.ca ◗ wait for the prompt login ◗ enter library

Community College of Allegheny County, Pittsburgh: United States PA *DYNIX*
TELNET library.ccac.edu ◗ wait for the prompt logname ◗ enter alleycat

Community College of Rhode Island: United States RI (Access via **Rhode Island Higher Education Library Information Network**)

Community College of Southern Nevada: United States NV (Access via **Nevada Academic Libraries Information System**)

Comstock Township Library: United States (Access via **West Michigan Information Network**)

Concordia College: United States *DYNIX*
TELNET host.clic.edu ◗ wait for the prompt login ◗ enter scpac

Concordia University: Canada *INNOPAC*
TELNET mercury.concordia.ca ◗ wait for the prompt login ◗ enter clues

Concordia University—Canada: Canada *INNOPAC*
TELNET `mercury.concordia.ca` ◗ wait for the prompt `login` ◗ enter `clues`

Concordia University—Illinois: United States (Access via **ILLINET On-line Catalog**)

Connecticut State University: United States CT *INNOPAC*
TELNET `csulib.ctstateu.edu` No login required

Consejo Superior de Investigaciones Cientificas: Spain *custom*
TELNET `cti.csic.es` ◗ wait for the prompt `Username` ◗ enter `aleph`

Coppin State College: United States (Access via **University of Maryland Library System**)

Corn Belt Library System: United States (Access via **ILLINET On-line Catalog**)

Cornell: United States NY *NOTIS*
TN3270 `cornellc.cit.cornell.edu` ◗ tab to COMMAND ◗ enter `library` ◗ wait for next screen ◗ press ↵

Cornell College—Iowa: United States IA *NOTIS*
TELNET `library.cornell-iowa.edu` ◗ wait for the prompt `login` ◗ enter `library`

Cornell University: United States NY *NOTIS*
TN3270 `notis.library.cornell.edu` ◗ press ↵
TELNET `ez-cornellc.cit.cornell.edu` ◗ wait for the prompt ENTER TERMINAL TYPE ◗ enter `vt100` for vt100 ◗ ◗ wait for the prompt USERID　===> ◗ press ↵ ◗ wait for the prompt that ends in `following commands:` ◗ enter `LIBRARY`

Cornell University—Medical College: United States NY *custom*
TELNET `lib.med.cornell.edu` ◗ wait for the prompt `Username` ◗ enter `guest`

Cortez Public Library: United States (Access via **MARMOT Library Network**)

Cranfield Institute of Technology: United Kingdom *LIBERTAS*
TELNET `libvax.ccc.cranfield.ac.uk` ◗ wait for the prompt `Username` ◗ enter `EXTERNAL`

Creighton University: United States *PALS*
TELNET `owl.creighton.edu` ◗ wait for the prompt TELNET: ENTER ATTACH COMMAND ◗ enter `attach pals`

CRSBP Monteregie: Canada *MULTILIS*
TELNET `crsbp.qc.ca` ◗ wait for the prompt `login` ◗ enter `public`

Cumberland College of Health Sciences—University of Sydney: Australia *VTLS*
TELNET `library.cchs.su.oz.au` ◗ wait for the prompt that ends in (SNAPPO.CCHS.SU) ◗ enter `hello ref.clas01`

Cumberland Trails Library System: United States (Access via **ILLINET On-line Catalog**)

Curry College: United States *INNOPAC*
TELNET `artemis.curry.edu` ◗ wait for the prompt `login` ◗ enter `library` ◗ wait for the prompt `Password` ◗ enter `library`

Curtin University of Technology: Australia *custom*
TELNET `cc.curtin.edu.au` ◗ wait for the prompt `Username` ◗ enter `guest`

Daemen College, New York: United States NY *INNOPAC*
TELNET `205.232.33.202` ◗ wait for the prompt `login` ◗ enter `library` ◗ wait for the prompt `Password` ◗ enter `library`

Dakota County Public Library: United States *DYNIX*
TELNET `dakota.lib.mn.us` ◗ wait for the prompt `login` ◗ enter `library`

Dalhousie University: Canada *GEAC*

TELNET novanet.dal.ca ◗ wait for the prompt login ◗ enter opac ◗ wait for the prompt Password ◗ press ↵

Danbury Public Library, Connecticut: United States CT *INNOPAC*

TELNET 199.79.138.10 No login required

Danish Natural and Medical Science Library: Denmark *custom*

TELNET cosmos.dnlb.bib.dk ◗ wait for the prompt Username ◗ enter cosmos ◗ wait for the prompt Skriv kommando> ◗ enter dia eng

Danish Veterinary and Agricultural Library—AGROLINE: Denmark *custom*

TELNET agroline.bib.dk ◗ wait for the prompt login ◗ enter agroline ◗ wait for the prompt Password ◗ enter agroline

Dartmouth: United States *Z39.58*

TELNET lib.dartmouth.edu ◗ wait for the prompt -> ◗ enter CONNECT MELVYL ◗ wait for the prompt TERMINAL? ◗ enter VT100 for VT100 ◗ wait for the prompt that ends in MELVYL System -> ◗ press ↵

David Lipscomb University: United States *GALAXY*

TELNET dlu.edu ◗ wait for the prompt Username ◗ enter LINIS

Dayton & Montgomery County Public Library, Ohio: United States OH *DRA*

TELNET dayton.lib.oh.us No login required

De La Salle University: Philippines *custom*

TELNET isis.dlsu.edu.ph ◗ wait for the prompt login ◗ enter isis

Deakin University: Australia *INNOPAC*

TELNET mips1.lib.deakin.oz.au No login required

TELNET library.deakin.edu.au No login required

DeKalb College—Clarkston/Decatur/Dunwoody: United States (Access via **Georgia On-Line Library Information System**)

Denison University: United States *INNOPAC*

TELNET dewey.library.denison.edu No login required

TELNET dewey2.library.denison.edu No login required

Denver Medical Library: United States CO (Access via **CARL**)

Denver Public Library: United States CO (Access via **CARL**)

Denver University: United States CO (Access via **CARL**)

DePaul University: United States (Access via **ILLINET On-line Catalog**)

Des Moines Area Community College: United States *INNOPAC*

TELNET library.dmacc.cc.ia.us No login required

Desert Research Institute Libraries: United States NV (Access via **Nevada Academic Libraries Information System**)

Detroit Area Library Network (DALNET): United States *NOTIS*

TELNET pluto.acs.oakland.edu No login required

Detroit Public Library: United States MI (Access via **Detroit Area Library Network**)

Diablo Valley College: United States *INNOPAC*

TELNET alice.dvc.edu ◗ wait for the prompt login ◗ enter library

Dickinson School of Law: United States *INNOPAC*

TELNET library.dsl.edu ◗ wait for the prompt login ◗ enter library

Dixie University: United States *DYNIX*
TELNET lib.dixie.edu ◊ wait for the prompt login ◊ enter pub

Douglas Public Library District: United States *DYNIX*
TELNET 198.59.43.1 ◊ wait for the prompt login ◊ enter ac

Dowagiac Public Library: United States (Access via **KELLY**)

Drake University: United States *DRA*
TELNET lib.drake.edu ◊ wait for the prompt Username ◊ enter LIBRARY

Drew University: United States *DRA*
TELNET forest.drew.edu ◊ wait for the prompt Username ◊ enter LIBRARY

Drexel University: United States *DRA*
TELNET library.drexel.edu ◊ wait for the prompt Username ◊ enter pac

Drury College: United States *DYNIX*
TELNET lib.drury.edu ◊ wait for the prompt login ◊ enter drury

Dublin City University: Ireland *DYNIX*
TELNET library.dcu.ie ◊ wait for the prompt login ◊ enter opac

Dudley—Pearle L. Crawford Mem: United States (Access via **CARL**)

Duke University: United States *DRA*
TELNET ducatalog.lib.duke.edu ◊ wait for the prompt Username ◊ enter LIBRARY ◊ press ↵

Duke University Library: United States (Access via **Triangle Research Libraries**)

Dundee Institute of Technology: United Kingdom *DYNIX*
TELNET library.dct.ac.uk ◊ wait for the prompt login ◊ enter library

DuPage Library System: United States (Access via **ILLINET On-line Catalog**)

Duquesne University: United States *DRA*
TELNET main.library.duq.edu ◊ wait for the prompt Username ◊ enter library

Durango Public Library: United States (Access via **MARMOT Library Network**)

Eagle County Public Library: United States (Access via **MARMOT Library Network**)

East Carolina University: United States *custom*
TELNET marquis.lib.ecu.edu ◊ wait for the prompt login ◊ enter library

East Central University: United States *INNOPAC*
TELNET library.ecok.edu ◊ wait for the prompt login ◊ enter opac

East Longmeadow Public: United States (Access via **CARL**)

East Stroudsburg University: United States *DYNIX*
TELNET kemp02.admin.esu.edu ◊ wait for the prompt login ◊ enter library

East Tennessee State University: United States TN *NOTIS*
TELNET library.east-tenn-st.edu ◊ wait for the prompt that ends in and press enter ◊ enter magellan ◊ press ↵

East Texas State University: United States TX *DRA*
TELNET etsulb.etsu.edu ◊ wait for the prompt Username ◊ enter pac

Eastern Illinois University: United States IL (Access via **ILLINET On-line Catalog**)

Eastern New Mexico University: United States NM *DRA*

TELNET `golden.enmu.edu` ▶ wait for the prompt `Username` ▶ enter `callup1`

Eastern Oregon State College: United States OR *INNOPAC*

TELNET `eos.eosc.osshe.edu` ▶ wait for the prompt `login` ▶ enter `eos`

Eastern Virginia Medical School: United States VA *custom*

TELNET `picard.evms.edu` ▶ wait for the prompt `Username` ▶ enter `GOLIS`

Eau Claire District Library: United States (Access via **KELLY**)

Ecole des hautes etudes commerciales de Montreal: Canada *MULTILIS*

TELNET `biblio.hec.ca` ▶ wait for the prompt `login` ▶ enter `biblio`

Ecole Polytechnique: France *custom*

TN3270 `frpoly11.polytechnique.fr` ▶ tab to Commande ▶ enter `dial vtam` ▶ wait for the prompt that ends in Commande ▶ enter `BI`

Ecole Polytechnique—Montreal: Canada *GEAC ADVANCE*

TELNET `cat.biblio.polymtl.ca` ▶ wait for the prompt `login` ▶ enter `cat`

Edinburgh University: United Kingdom *GEAC ADVANCE*

TELNET `geac.ed.ac.uk` No login required

TELNET `eulib.ed.ac.uk` ▶ press ↵

Edison Community College: United States *INNOPAC*

TELNET `elink.edison.cc.oh.us` ▶ wait for the prompt `login` ▶ enter `library`

Edith Cowan University: Australia *custom*

TELNET `library.cowan.edu.au` ▶ wait for the prompt `login` ▶ enter `library`

Edmonton Public Library: Canada *DRA*

TELNET `dewey.publib.edmonton.ab.ca` ▶ wait for the prompt `Username` ▶ enter `MNAF`

Eidgenoessiche Technische Hochschule Zuerich: Switzerland *custom*

TELNET `ethics.ethz.ch` No login required

Eidgenoessiche Technische Hochschule Zuerich (Swiss Federal Institute of Technology, Zurich): Switzerland *custom*

TELNET `ethics.ethz.ch` ▶ wait for the prompt `COMMAND ===>` ▶ press ↵

El Colegio de Mexico: Mexico *custom*

TELNET `opac.colmex.mx` ▶ wait for the prompt `login` ▶ enter `opac`

Elgin Community College, Illinois: United States IL *INNOPAC*

TELNET `greens1.elgin.cc.il.us` ▶ wait for the prompt `login` ▶ enter `library` ▶ wait for the prompt `Password` ▶ enter `library`

Elizabeth City State University: United States *DYNIX*

TELNET `marquis.lib.ecu.edu` ▶ wait for the prompt `login` ▶ enter `library`

Elmhurst College: United States (Access via **ILLINET On-line Catalog**)

Elms College: United States (Access via **CARL**)

Elon College: United States *DRA*

TELNET `vax1.elon.edu` ▶ wait for the prompt `Username` ▶ enter `LIBRARY`

Embry-Riddle Aeronautical University: United States *CLSI*

TELNET `orville.db.erau.edu` ◗ wait for the prompt `login` ◗ enter `library` ◗ wait for the prompt `Password` ◗ enter `library`

Emerson College: United States (Access via **Fenway Libraries Online, Inc.**)

Emory University: United States *UNICORN*

TELNET `library.gsu.edu` No login required
TELNET `euclid.cc.emory.edu` ◗ wait for the prompt that ends `login` ◗ enter `euclid`

Environmental Protection Agency National Online Library System: United States *custom*

TELNET `epaibm.rtpnc.epa.gov` No login required

Erasmus University of Rotterdam: The Netherlands *custom*

TELNET `eurbib.eur.nl` ◗ wait for the prompt `Username` ◗ enter `OPC`

Estes Park Public Library: United States (Access via **CARL**)

Eugene Public Library, Oregon: United States OR *ULISYS*

TELNET `euglib.ci.eugene.or.us` ◗ wait for the prompt `Username` ◗ enter `CATALOG`

Europa-Universitaet Viadrina Frankfurt: Germany *custom*

TELNET `oder.euv-frankfurt-o.de` ◗ wait for the prompt `Benutzerkennung` ◗ enter `katalog`

European Southern Observatory—La Silla: Italy *UNICORN*

TELNET `ac4.hq.eso.org` ◗ wait for the prompt `login` ◗ enter `lslib`

European University Institute—Florence, Italy: Italy *INNOPAC*

TELNET `149.139.6.100` No login required

Evergreen Valley College: United States *INNOPAC*

TELNET `library.sjeccd.cc.ca.us` No login required

Fachbibliothek für Biologie an der Universitaet Wien: Austria (Access via **Austrian Academic Library Network**)

Fachbibliothek für Mathematik, Statistik, Informatik Universitaet Wien: Austria (Access via **Austrian Academic Library Network**)

Fachhochschule Coburg: Germany *custom*

TELNET `lemmi.fh-coburg.de` ◗ wait for the prompt `login` ◗ enter `opac`

Faculty of Agriculture Library—Gembloux: Belgium *custom*

TELNET `midas.biblio.fsagx.ac.be` ◗ wait for the prompt `login` ◗ enter `midas`

Fairfield University: United States *DRA*

TELNET `fair1.fairfield.edu` ◗ wait for the prompt `Username` ◗ enter `LIB`

Fairleigh Dickinson University: United States *DYNIX*

TELNET `alpha.fdu.edu` ◗ wait for the prompt `login` ◗ enter `tricat` ◗ wait for the prompt `Password` ◗ press ↵

Fairmont State College: United States (Access via **West Virginia University**)

Fakultaetsbibliothek für Medizin an der Universitaet Wien: Austria (Access via **Austrian Academic Library Network**)

Fanshawe College: Canada *DRA Gateway*

TELNET `lib.fanshawec.on.ca` ◗ wait for the prompt `Username` ◗ enter `FCLINK`

Farmington Community Library: United States *DYNIX*

TELNET `lis.fh.metronet.lib.mi.us` ◗ wait for the prompt `login` ◗ enter `library`

Fashion Institute of New York: United States NY *MULTILIS*

  TELNET slscva.ca.sunycentral.edu ◗ wait for the prompt Username ◗ enter FIT_NETOPAC

Fenway Libraries Online, Inc.: United States *DRA*

  TELNET flo.org ◗ wait for the prompt Username ◗ enter guest

Ferguson Library, Stamford, Connecticut: United States CT *DRA Gateway*

  TELNET flvax.ferg.lib.ct.us ◗ wait for the prompt Username ◗ enter GUEST

Fermi National Accelerator Laboratory: United States *custom*

  TELNET fnlib.fnal.gov ◗ wait for the prompt Username ◗ enter LIBRARY

Ferris State University: United States *PALS*

  TELNET pals.ferris.edu ◗ wait for the prompt CATALOG-SYS=> ◗ enter BE

Finnish National Bibliography (FENNICA): Finland *VTLS*

  TELNET hyk.helsinki.fi ◗ wait for the prompt MPE XL: ◗ enter hello,user.clas01

Finnish National Library (HELKA): Finland *VTLS*

  TELNET hyk.helsinki.fi ◗ wait for the prompt MPE XL ◗ enter HELLO,USER.CLAS02

Fitchburg Public Library: United States (Access via **CARL**)

Fitchburg State College: United States (Access via **CARL**)

Five-College Library System, Massachusetts: United States MA *INNOPAC*

  TELNET fclibr.library.umass.edu No login required

Flint Area Library Cooperative Online Network: United States *DYNIX*

  TELNET hp.falcon.edu ◗ wait for the prompt login ◗ enter gdpub

Florida A&M University: United States FL (Access via **Florida State University**)

Florida Atlantic University: United States FL (Access via **Florida State University**)

Florida Community College Jacksonville: United States FL *NOTIS*

  TELNET luis.nerdc.ufl.edu ◗ wait for the prompt login ◗ enter luis

Florida International University: United States FL (Access via **Florida State University**)

Florida Keys Community College—Florida: United States FL *NOTIS*

  TELNET luis.nerdc.ufl.edu ◗ wait for the prompt login ◗ enter luis

Florida State University: United States FL *NOTIS*

  TELNET luis.nerdc.ufl.edu ◗ wait for the prompt login ◗ enter luis

Fordham University Law School: United States NY *INNOPAC*

  TELNET lawpac.fordham.edu ◗ wait for the prompt login ◗ enter fullpac

Forschungsinstitut Brenner-Archiv—Innsbruck: Austria (Access via **Austrian Academic Library Network**)

Fort Collins Public Library: United States *DYNIX*

  TELNET libsys.ci.fort-collins.co.us ◗ wait for the prompt login ◗ enter library

Fort Lewis College Library: United States (Access via **MARMOT Library Network**)

Fort Morgan Public Library: United States (Access via **CARL**)

Fort Vancouver Regional Library: United States *DYNIX*

  TELNET fvrl.lib.wa.us ◗ wait for the prompt login ◗ enter catalog

Franklin and Marshall College: United States *DRA*
  TELNET `library.fandm.edu` ❯ wait for the prompt `Username` ❯ enter `libcat`

Free Library of Philadelphia: United States PA *DRA Gateway*
  TELNET `philly.flp.lib.pa.us` ❯ wait for the prompt `Username` ❯ enter `FLPNET`

Front Range Community College: United States (Access via **CARL**)

Frostburg State University: United States (Access via **University of Maryland Library System**)

Fundacion Romulo Gallegos (CELARG): Venezuela (Access via **Biblioteca Nacional de Venezuela**)

Furman University: United States *INNOPAC*
  TELNET `library.furman.edu` No login required

Gainesville College: United States (Access via **Georgia On-Line Library Information System**)

Galesburg Memorial Library: United States (Access via **West Michigan Information Network**)

Galien Township Public Library: United States (Access via **KELLY**)

Gallaudet University: United States (Access via **Washington Research Library Consortium**)

Gardner, Colorado Library: United States CO (Access via **CARL**)

Garfield County Public Library: United States (Access via **MARMOT Library Network**)

Gateway Community College Library: United States (Access via **Maricopa Community Colleges Libraries and Media Centers**)

Gdansk University: Poland *VTLS*
  TELNET `koala.bg.univ.gda.pl` ❯ wait for the prompt MPE XL ❯ enter `hello user.clas01`

Geomatics Information Centre/Centre d'Information en GÈomatique: Canada *MULTILIS*
  TELNET `casu.pps.emr.ca` ❯ wait for the prompt `Username` ❯ enter `OPAC`

George Fox College: United States *INNOPAC*
  TELNET `198.106.64.75` ❯ wait for the prompt `login` ❯ enter `library`

George Mason University: United States (Access via **Washington Research Library Consortium**)

George Washington University: United States (Access via **Washington Research Library Consortium**)

George Washington University—Law Center: United States *INNOPAC*
  TELNET `jacob.nlc.gwu.edu` ❯ wait for the prompt `login` ❯ enter `library`

Georgetown University: United States (Access via **Washington Research Library Consortium**)

Georgetown University Law Library: United States *INNOPAC*
  TELNET `gull.ll.georgetown.edu` ❯ wait for the prompt `login` ❯ enter `gull`

Georgia College—Milledgeville: United States GA (Access via **Georgia On-Line Library Information System**)

Georgia On-Line Library Information System—OLLI: United States GA *PALS*
  TELNET `library.gsu.edu` No login required

Georgia Southern University: United States GA *DRA*
  TELNET `gsvms1.cc.gasou.edu` ❯ wait for the prompt `Username` ❯ enter `LIBRARY`
  TELNET `gsvms2.cc.gasou.edu` ❯ wait for the prompt `Username` ❯ enter `INFO`

Georgia Southern University—Statesboro: United States GA (Access via **Georgia On-Line Library Information System**)

Georgia Southwestern College: United States GA (Access via **Georgia On-Line Library Information System**)

Georgia State Department of Archives & History: United States GA (Access via **Georgia On-Line Library Information System**)

Georgia State Instructional Resource Center—Atlanta: United States GA (Access via **Georgia On-Line Library Information System**)

Georgia State Law Library—Atlanta: United States GA (Access via **Georgia On-Line Library Information System**)

Georgia State Pullen Library—Atlanta: United States GA (Access via **Georgia On-Line Library Information System**)

Georgia Tech Gilbert Library—Atlanta: United States GA (Access via **Georgia On-Line Library Information System**)

Getty Center for the History of Art and the Humanities: United States
TELNET opac.pub.getty.edu ▶ wait for the prompt login ▶ enter library

Glasgow University: United Kingdom *INNOPAC*
TELNET eleanor.lib.gla.ac.uk No login required

Glen Grove School Learning Center (4-6): United States *custom*
TELNET gg.ncook.k12.il.us ▶ wait for the prompt login ▶ enter library

Glen Oaks Community College: United States (Access via **KELLY**)

Glendale Community College Library: United States (Access via **Maricopa Community Colleges Libraries and Media Centers**)

Glenview Public Library: United States *custom*
TELNET gpl.glenview.lib.il.us ▶ wait for the prompt login ▶ enter library ▶ press ↵ ▶ wait for the prompt CLSN3046 login ▶ enter library ▶ wait for the prompt Password ▶ press ↵

Goldsmiths' College: United Kingdom (Access via **London University Central Libertas Consortium**)

Gonzaga University: United States *custom*
TELNET foley.gonzaga.edu ▶ wait for the prompt Enter Choice ▶ enter PAC

Gordon Technical College: Australia *INNOPAC*
TELNET mips1.lib.deakin.oz.au No login required
TELNET library.deakin.edu.au No login required

Goucher College: United States *INNOPAC*
TELNET library.goucher.edu ▶ wait for the prompt login ▶ enter library

Governors State University: United States (Access via **ILLINET On-line Catalog**)

Grambling State University: United States *DRA*
TELNET gopac.gram.edu ▶ wait for the prompt Username ▶ enter library

Granby Public Library: United States (Access via **CARL**)

Graz—Universitaetsbibliothek: Austria (Access via **Austrian Academic Library Network**)

Great Neck Public Library: United States *INNOPAC*
TELNET gneck.greatneck.lib.ny.us ▶ wait for the prompt login ▶ enter internet

Great River Library System: United States (Access via **ILLINET On-line Catalog**)

Greene County Public Library: United States *DRA*
TELNET gcpl.lib.oh.us ▶ wait for the prompt Username ▶ enter PUBLIC

Greenfield Public Library: United States (Access via **CARL**)

Greenville Technical College: United States *DRA*
   TELNET appnet.gvltec.edu ◖ wait for the prompt Username ◖ enter GTCLIB

Grenfell College: Canada (Access via **Memorial University—Newfoundland**)

Griffith University: Australia *GEAC ADVANCE*
   TELNET library.gu.edu.au ◖ wait for the prompt login ◖ enter library

Guilford College: United States *DRA*
   TELNET pals.guilford.edu ◖ wait for the prompt Username ◖ enter hegepac

Gulf Coast Community College—Florida: United States FL *NOTIS*
   TELNET luis.nerdc.ufl.edu ◖ wait for the prompt login ◖ enter luis

Gull Lake Community Schools: United States (Access via **KELLY**)

Hackett Catholic Central High School: United States (Access via **KELLY**)

Hahnemann University: United States *custom*
   TELNET hal.hahnemann.edu ◖ wait for the prompt Username ◖ enter hal

Haifa University: Israel (Access via **Hebrew University**)

Halifax Public Library: Canada *DYNIX*
   TELNET library.nsh.library.ns.ca ◖ wait for the prompt login ◖ enter pac

Halton Hills Public Library, Ontario: Canada *DYNIX*
   TELNET dickens.hhpl.on.ca ◖ wait for the prompt login ◖ enter library

Hamilton College: United States *VTLS*
   TELNET hamlib.hamilton.edu ◖ wait for the prompt that ends in to logon ◖ enter HELLO USER.LIB

Hamline University: United States *DYNIX*
   TELNET host.clic.edu ◖ wait for the prompt login ◖ enter scpac

Hamline University—Law Library: United States (Access via **Hamline University**)

Hampden—Sydney College: United States *INNOPAC*
   TELNET lion.hsc.edu ◖ wait for the prompt login ◖ enter library

Handelshogeschool—Antwerp: Belgium (Access via **University of Antwerp**)

Hardin Simmons University: United States (Access via **Abilene Library Consortium**)

Harding University: United States *DRA Gateway*
   TELNET library.harding.edu ◖ wait for the prompt Username ◖ enter OPAC

Harris County Public Library: United States (Access via **CARL**)

Hartford Public Library: United States CT (Access via **KELLY**)

Hartwick College: United States *INNOPAC*
   TELNET 147.205.85.30 ◖ wait for the prompt login ◖ enter library

Harvard Public Library: United States (Access via **CARL**)

Harvard University: United States *custom*
   TN3270 hollis.harvard.edu ◖ wait for the prompt ===> ◖ enter HOLLIS

Haverford College: United States *INNOPAC*

TELNET `tripod.brynmawr.edu` ▶ wait for the prompt `login` ▶ enter `library`

Hawaii State Public Library System: United States HI *DRA*

TELNET `starmaster.uhcc.hawaii.edu` ▶ wait for the prompt `enter class` ▶ enter `hspls` ▶ press ↵

Hebrew University (Automated Library Expandable Program—ALEPH): Israel *custom*

TELNET `aleph.huji.ac.il` ▶ wait for the prompt `Username` ▶ enter `aleph`

HELIN (Higher Education Library Information Network): United States *INNOPAC*

TELNET `library.uri.edu` ▶ wait for the prompt `login` ▶ enter `library`

Henderson State University, Arkansas: United States *DRA Gateway*

TELNET `aspen.hsu.edu` ▶ wait for the prompt `Username` ▶ enter `LIBRARY`

Hendrix College: United States *DRA*

TELNET `alpha.hendrix.edu` ▶ wait for the prompt `Username` ▶ enter `PAC` ▶ wait for the prompt `Password` ▶ enter PAC

Henking School Learning Center (K-3): United States *custom*

TELNET `he.ncook.k12.il.us` ▶ wait for the prompt `login` ▶ enter `library`

Hennepin County Library, Minnesota: United States MN *DYNIX*

TELNET `hennepin.lib.mn.us` ▶ wait for the prompt `login` ▶ enter `library`

Heriot-Watt University: United Kingdom *CLSI*

TELNET `x25-pad.ja.net` Connect to: hw.lib

Herkimer County Community College: United States *MULTILIS*

TELNET `slscva.ca.sunycentral.edu` ▶ wait for the prompt `Username` ▶ enter `HCC_NETOPAC`

Hershey Medical Center/Penn State University George T. Harrell Library: United States PA (Access via **HSLC HealthNET Health Sciences Information Network**)

Heythrop College: United Kingdom (Access via **London University Central Libertas Consortium**)

High Plains Regional Libraries: United States (Access via **CARL**)

Hillsborough Community College—Florida: United States FL *NOTIS*

TELNET `luis.nerdc.ufl.edu` ▶ wait for the prompt `login` ▶ enter `luis`

Hillsdale College: United States *INNOPAC*

TELNET `library.hillsdale.edu` ▶ wait for the prompt `login` ▶ enter `library`

Hiram College, Ohio: United States OH *INNOPAC*

TELNET `hiraml.hiram.edu` ▶ wait for the prompt `login` ▶ enter `library`

Hochschulbibliothek der Hochschule für kuenstlerische und industrielle Gestaltung in Linz: Austria (Access via **Austrian Academic Library Network**)

Hoffman School Learning Center (4-6): United States *custom*

TELNET `ho.ncook.k12.il.us` ▶ wait for the prompt `login` ▶ enter `library`

Hofstra University: United States *DRA*

TELNET `vaxa.hofstra.edu` ▶ wait for the prompt `Username` ▶ enter `LIBRARY`

Hogeschool Rotterdam & Omstreken: The Netherlands *custom*

TELNET `hrovx6.hro.nl` ▶ wait for the prompt `Username` ▶ enter `OPC`

Holden—Gale Free Library: United States (Access via **CARL**)

Holyoke Community College: United States (Access via **CARL**)

Hong Kong Academy for Performing Arts: Hong Kong *INNOPAC*
TELNET 202.40.151.2 No login required

Hong Kong Institute of Education: Hong Kong *INNOPAC*
TELNET edlis.ied.edu.hk No login required

Hong Kong Polytechnic: Hong Kong *DRA*
TELNET library.hkp.hk ◗ wait for the prompt Username ◗ enter LIBRARY

Hong Kong University of Science & Technology: Hong Kong *INNOPAC*
TELNET ustlib.ust.hk No login required

Hood College: United States (Access via **Maryland Interlibrary Consortium**)

Houston Area Library Automated Network (HALAN): United States *custom*
TELNET pac.carl.org ◗ wait for the prompt Enter Choice> ◗ enter PAC
TELNET jesse.hpl.lib.tx.us ◗ wait for the prompt Enter Choice> ◗ enter PAC

Houston Public Library: United States TX (Access via **CARL**)

HSLC HealthNET Health Sciences Information Network: United States *DRA*
TELNET shrsys.hslc.org ◗ wait for the prompt Username ◗ enter sal

Hudson Public Library: United States (Access via **CARL**)

Hull University: United Kingdom *INNOPAC*
TELNET geac.hull.ac.uk No login required
TELNET libsys.lib.hull.ac.uk No login required

Humboldt State University: United States *custom*
TELNET alexvon.humboldt.edu ◗ wait for the prompt login ◗ enter library

Humboldt-Universitaet zu Berlin: Germany *custom*
TELNET mx500.unibib.hu-berlin.de ◗ wait for the prompt Benutzerkennung ◗ enter opac

Hungarian Academy of Sciences: Hungary *custom*
TELNET vax.mtak.hu ◗ wait for the prompt Username ◗ enter ALEPH

Idaho State University: United States ID *VTLS*
TELNET csc.isu.edu ◗ wait for the prompt MPE XL ◗ enter hello user.clas01

ILLINET On-line Catalog: United States *custom*
TELNET illinet.aiss.uiuc.edu ◗ wait for the prompt Press b and <RETURN> to login ◗ enter b

Illinois Benedictine College: United States IL (Access via **ILLINET On-line Catalog**)

Illinois Institute of Technology: United States IL (Access via **ILLINET On-line Catalog**)

Illinois Institute of Technology—Chicago Kent Law Library: United States IL *INNOPAC*
TELNET clark.kentlaw.edu ◗ wait for the prompt login ◗ enter library

Illinois Math and Science Academy: United States IL (Access via **ILLINET On-line Catalog**)

Illinois State Library: United States IL (Access via **ILLINET On-line Catalog**)

Illinois State University: United States IL (Access via **ILLINET On-line Catalog**)

Illinois Valley Library System: United States IL (Access via **ILLINET On-line Catalog**)

Illinois Wesleyan University: United States IL (Access via **ILLINET On-line Catalog**)

Ilsley Public Library—Middlebury, Vermont: United States VT *DRA*
   TELNET `myriad.middlebury.edu` ◗ wait for the prompt `Username` ◗ enter `IPL`
   TELNET `lib.middlebury.edu` ◗ wait for the prompt `Username` ◗ enter `lib`

Imperial College—University of London: United Kingdom *LIBERTAS*
   TELNET `vaxa.lib.ic.ac.uk` ◗ wait for the prompt `Username` ◗ enter `LIBRARY`

Incarnate Word College: United States *DYNIX*
   TELNET `the-college.iwctx.edu` ◗ wait for the prompt `login` ◗ enter `library`

Indian River Community College—Florida: United States FL *NOTIS*
   TELNET `luis.nerdc.ufl.edu` ◗ wait for the prompt `login` ◗ enter `luis`

Indiana Institute of Technology: United States IN *NOTIS*
   TELNET `iuis.ucs.indiana.edu` ◗ wait for the prompt `User ID` ◗ enter `guest`

Indiana State Library: United States IN *DRA*
   TELNET `statelib.lib.in.us` ◗ wait for the prompt `Username` ◗ enter `PUBLIC`

Indiana State University: United States IN *NOTIS*
   TELNET `library.indstate.edu` No login required

Indiana University: United States IN *NOTIS*
   TELNET `iuis.ucs.indiana.edu` ◗ wait for the prompt `User ID` ◗ enter `guest`

Indiana University of Pennsylvania: United States PA *custom*
   TELNET `opac.lib.iup.edu` ◗ wait for the prompt `login` ◗ enter `library`

INLAN Library System—Spokane, Washington: United States WA (Access via **University of Maryland Library System**)

Innsbruck—Universitaetsbibliothek: Austria (Access via **Austrian Academic Library Network**)

Institut Fourier: France *custom*
   TELNET `ifbibli.grenet.fr` ◗ wait for the prompt `login` ◗ enter `bib`

Institut Jozef Stefan: Slovenia *custom*
   TELNET `ijslib.ijs.si` ◗ wait for the prompt `Username` ◗ enter `OPAC` ◗ wait for the prompt that ends in E – English ◗ enter E for English

Instituto de Altos Estudios de la Defensa Nacional: Venezuela (Access via **Biblioteca Nacional de Venezuela**)

Instituto Tecnologico y de Estudios Superiores de Monterrey: Mexico *INNOPAC*
   TELNET `academ02.mty.itesm.mx` ◗ wait for the prompt `login` ◗ enter `itesmcat`

International Centre for Theoretical Physics—Trieste: Italy *custom*
   TELNET `library.ictp.trieste.it` ◗ wait for the prompt `Username` ◗ enter `OPAC`

International Development Research Center: Canada *custom*
   TELNET `ddbs.idrc.ca` ◗ wait for the prompt `login` ◗ enter `guest`

Iowa State University: United States IA *NOTIS*
TELNET `isn.iastate.edu` ♦ wait for the prompt DIAL ♦ enter LIB

Istituto e Museo di Storia Della Scienza Firenze: Italy *custom*
TELNET `galileo.imss.firenze.it` ♦ wait for the prompt `login` ♦ enter `easypac`

Jagiellonian University: Poland *VTLS*
TELNET `fridge.bj.uj.edu.pl` ♦ wait for the prompt that ends in `hello user.clas02` ♦ enter `hello user.clas02`

James Cook University: Australia *DYNIX*
TELNET `jculib.jcu.edu.au` ♦ wait for the prompt `login` ♦ enter `opac`

James Madison University: United States *INNOPAC*
TELNET `newleo.jmu.edu` ♦ wait for the prompt `login` ♦ enter `library`

Jewish Hospital Medical Library: United States (Access via **Washington University of St Louis Medical Library**)

Jewish Hospital School of Nursing Library: United States (Access via **Washington University of St Louis Medical Library**)

Jewish Theological Seminary of America: United States *custom*
TELNET `jtsa.edu` ♦ wait for the prompt `Username` ♦ enter `aleph`

Joensuu University: Finland *VTLS*
TELNET `joyk.joensuu.fi` ♦ wait for the prompt `(JOYK.JOENSUU.FI)` ♦ enter `hello,user.clas01`

John Brown University: United States *GALAXY*
TELNET `library.jbu.edu` ♦ wait for the prompt `Username` ♦ enter `LIBRARY`

John Carroll University: United States *DRA*
TELNET `jcvaxc.jcu.edu` ♦ wait for the prompt `Username` ♦ enter `JCU_OPAC` ♦ wait for the prompt `Password` ♦ enter `grasselli`

John Marshall Law School: United States *INNOPAC*
TELNET `catalog.jmls.edu` ♦ wait for the prompt `login` ♦ enter `catalog`

Johnson And Wales University: United States *INNOPAC*
TELNET `johnw.jwu.edu` ♦ wait for the prompt `login` ♦ enter `student`

Johnson State College—Vermont: United States VT (Access via **Middlebury College**)

Joliet Junior College: United States (Access via **ILLINET On-line Catalog**)

Judson College: United States (Access via **ILLINET On-line Catalog**)

Juniata College: United States *GALAXY*
TELNET `juncol.juniata.edu` ♦ wait for the prompt `Username` ♦ enter `JCLIB`

Jyvaskyla University: Finland *VTLS*
TELNET `jyk.jyu.fi` ♦ wait for the prompt `JYKHPXL` ♦ enter `hello,user.clas01`

Kalamazoo Christian High School: United States (Access via **KELLY**)

Kalamazoo College: United States *INNOPAC*
TELNET `146.113.52.1` No login required

Kalamazoo Regional Psychiatric Hospital: United States (Access via **KELLY**)

Kankakee Community College: United States (Access via **ILLINET On-line Catalog**)

Kansas City Public Library: United States *custom*
>   TELNET vax1.kcpl.lib.mo.us ◗ wait for the prompt Username ◗ enter KACEY

Kansas City, Kansas Public Library: United States KS *INLEX*
>   TELNET otto.kckpl.lib.ks.us ◗ wait for the prompt KCKPL ◗ enter hello visitor.library

Karolinska Institute: Sweden *LIBERTAS*
>   TELNET kibib.kib.ki.se ◗ wait for the prompt Username ◗ enter LIBRARY

Kaskaskia Library System: United States (Access via **ILLINET On-line Catalog**)

Katholieke Universiteit Nijmegen: The Netherlands *custom*
>   TELNET kunlb1.ubn.kun.nl ◗ wait for the prompt Username ◗ enter opc
>   TELNET opc.ubn.kun.nl ◗ wait for the prompt Username ◗ enter OPC

Keele University: United Kingdom *custom*
>   TELNET potter.cc.keele.ac.uk ◗ wait for the prompt login ◗ enter library ◗ wait for the prompt Password ◗ enter library

Keene State College/Keene Public Library: United States *INNOPAC*
>   TELNET ksclib.keene.edu ◗ wait for the prompt login ◗ enter library

KELLY: Regional Online Catalog for WESTNET: United States *NOTIS*
>   TELNET public.library.wmich.edu ◗ wait for the prompt login ◗ enter w

Kennesaw State College: United States *PALS*
>   TELNET library.gsu.edu No login required
>   TELNET ksclib.kennesaw.edu ◗ wait for the prompt login ◗ enter library ◗ wait for the prompt library's Password ◗ enter library

Kent County—Delaware Automated Library System (KENTNET): United States DE *DYNIX*
>   TELNET kentnet.dtcc.edu ◗ wait for the prompt login ◗ enter library

Kent State University: United States *INNOPAC*
>   TELNET catalyst.kent.edu No login required
>   TELNET kentlink.kent.edu No login required

Kenyon College: United States *DRA*
>   TELNET kcvax2.kenyon.edu ◗ wait for the prompt Username ◗ enter niso
>   TELNET library.kenyon.edu ◗ wait for the prompt Username ◗ enter LIBRARY

King County Library System—Washington: United States WA *DYNIX*
>   TELNET 198.104.1.63 ◗ wait for the prompt login ◗ enter kcls

Kirkwood Community College: United States *VTLS*
>   TELNET library.kirkwood.cc.ia.us ◗ wait for the prompt login ◗ enter library

Kitsap Regional Library, Washington State: United States WA *DYNIX*
>   TELNET linknet.kitsap.lib.wa.us ◗ wait for the prompt login ◗ enter guest

Kuopio Reserve Library: Finland *VTLS*
>   TELNET varasto.uku.fi ◗ wait for the prompt VARASTOKIRJASTO ◗ enter hello,user.clas01

Kutztown University: United States *PALS*
>   TELNET kutztown.edu ◗ wait for the prompt login ◗ enter bearcat

La Salle University: United States *INNOPAC*
  TELNET connelly.lasalle.edu ◗ wait for the prompt login ◗ enter library

La Sierra University: United States *INNOPAC*
  TELNET libris.lasierra.edu ◗ wait for the prompt login ◗ enter library

Labrador Institute of Northern Studies: Canada (Access via **Memorial University—Newfoundland**)

Lafayette College: United States *INNOPAC*
  TELNET 139.147.42.4 ◗ wait for the prompt login ◗ enter library

Lake City Community College—Florida: United States FL *NOTIS*
  TELNET luis.nerdc.ufl.edu ◗ wait for the prompt login ◗ enter luis

Lake Forest College: United States (Access via **ILLINET On-line Catalog**)

Lake Sumter Community College—Florida: United States FL *NOTIS*
  TELNET luis.nerdc.ufl.edu ◗ wait for the prompt login ◗ enter luis

Lakehead University: Canada *custom*
  TELNET think2.lakeheadu.ca ◗ wait for the prompt Username ◗ enter faculty

Lakeland Community College: United States *INNOPAC*
  TELNET 198.30.230.3 No login required

Lakeland Library Cooperative, Michigan: United States MI *CLSI*
  TELNET lakeland.lib.mi.us ◗ wait for the prompt login ◗ enter public

Lamar Community College: United States (Access via **CARL**)

Lancaster Town Library: United States (Access via **CARL**)

Lapin University: Finland *VTLS*
  TELNET 128.214.30.51 ◗ wait for the prompt MPE XL ◗ enter hello,user.clas01

Latrobe University Bendigo: Australia *GEAC ADVANCE*
  TELNET ucnvlib.ucnv.edu.au ◗ wait for the prompt login ◗ enter library ◗ wait for the prompt Password ◗ press ↵

Laurentian University: Canada *MULTILIS*
  TELNET laulibr.laurentian.ca ◗ wait for the prompt Username ◗ enter netlib
  TELNET libr.laurentian.ca ◗ wait for the prompt Username ◗ enter NETLIB

Laval University: Canada *MULTILIS*
  TELNET ariane.ulaval.ca ◗ wait for the prompt Username ◗ enter ariane

Lawrence Livermore National Laboratory: United States *custom*
  TELNET library.llnl.gov ◗ wait for the prompt login ◗ enter patron

Lawrence University: United States *DRA*
  TELNET lucia.lib.lawrence.edu ◗ wait for the prompt Username ◗ enter lunet

Lawton Public Library: United States (Access via **KELLY**)

Le Moyne College: United States *INNOPAC*
  TELNET 192.231.122.50 ◗ wait for the prompt login ◗ enter library

Lee Library Association: United States (Access via **CARL**)

Leeds Metropolitan University: United Kingdom *LIBERTAS*
  TELNET library.lmu.ac.uk ◗ wait for the prompt Username ◗ enter LIBRARY

Lehigh: United States *UNICORN*
TELNET `asa.lib.lehigh.edu` ▶ wait for the prompt `login` ▶ enter `public`

Leiden University: The Netherlands *custom*
TELNET `rulub3.leidenuniv.nl` ▶ wait for the prompt `Username` ▶ enter OPC3

Leominster Public Library: United States (Access via **CARL**)

Lesley College: United States (Access via **Fenway Libraries Online, Inc.**)

Lewis & Clark College: United States *INNOPAC*
TELNET `innopac.lclark.edu` ▶ wait for the prompt `login` ▶ enter `library`

Lewis & Clark Library System: United States (Access via **ILLINET On-line Catalog**)

Lewis University: United States (Access via **ILLINET On-line Catalog**)

LIBLINK: Access to New South Wales Libraries: Australia *custom*
TELNET `unilinc.edu.au` ▶ wait for the prompt `login` ▶ enter `liblink`

Library and Information Service of Western Australia: Australia *INNOPAC*
TELNET `innopac.liswa.wa.gov.au` No login required

Library Cooperative of Macomb—Michigan: United States MI *DYNIX*
TELNET `macomb.lib.mi.us` ▶ wait for the prompt `login` ▶ enter `library`

Library Information Network for Community Colleges (LINCC), Florida: United States *DRA*
TELNET `lincc.ccla.lib.fl.us` ▶ wait for the prompt `Username` ▶ enter TBLC

Library of Virginia and Virginia State Archives: United States VA *VTLS*
TELNET `hp3000.vsla.edu` ▶ wait for the prompt `login` ▶ enter `hello gopher,user.clas52` ▶ press ↵

Limburgs Universitair Centrum: Belgium (Access via **University of Antwerp**)

LINCC—Florida Community Colleges: United States FL *NOTIS*
TELNET `luis.nerdc.ufl.edu` ▶ wait for the prompt `login` ▶ enter `luis`

Lincoln Township Public Library: United States (Access via **KELLY**)

Lincoln Trail Libraries System: United States (Access via **ILLINET On-line Catalog**)

Linfield College: United States *INNOPAC*
TELNET `library.linfield.edu` ▶ wait for the prompt `login` ▶ enter `wildcat`

Linz—Universitaetsbibliothek: Austria (Access via **Austrian Academic Library Network**)

Littleton, Colorado Reuben Hoar Library: United States CO (Access via **CARL**)

Liverpool John Moores University: United Kingdom *DYNIX*
TELNET `libb.livjm.ac.uk` ▶ wait for the prompt that ends in `please login as lion` ▶ enter `lion`

LOCIS: Library of Congress Information System: United States *custom*
TELNET `locis.loc.gov` No login required

Lock Haven University: United States *DYNIX*
TELNET `owl.lhup.edu` ▶ wait for the prompt `owl login` ▶ enter `slpac`

London University Central Libertas Consortium: United Kingdom *LIBERTAS*
TELNET `consull.ull.ac.uk` ▶ wait for the prompt `Username` ▶ enter LIBRARY

London University, School of Advanced Study: United Kingdom *INNOPAC*
TELNET `library.sas.ac.uk` ▶ wait for the prompt `login` ▶ enter `library`

London University—British Library of Political and Economic Science: United Kingdom *LIBERTAS*
TELNET blpes.lse.ac.uk ❯ wait for the prompt Username ❯ enter LIBRARY

London University—Imperial College: United Kingdom *LIBERTAS*
TELNET vaxa.lib.ic.ac.uk ❯ wait for the prompt Username ❯ enter LIBRARY

London University—Institute of Education: United Kingdom *LIBERTAS*
TELNET library.ioe.ac.uk ❯ wait for the prompt Username ❯ enter LIBRARY

London University—Kings College and United Medical Schools: United Kingdom *LIBERTAS*
TELNET lib.kcl.ac.uk ❯ wait for the prompt Username ❯ enter LIBRARY

London University—Queen Mary and Westfield College: United Kingdom *LIBERTAS*
TELNET lib.qmw.ac.uk ❯ wait for the prompt Username ❯ enter LIBRARY

London University—Royal Holloway and Bedford New College: United Kingdom *LIBERTAS*
TELNET lib.rhbnc.ac.uk ❯ wait for the prompt Username ❯ enter LIBRARY

London University—School of Oriental and African Studies: United Kingdom *LIBERTAS*
TELNET lib.soas.ac.uk ❯ wait for the prompt Username ❯ enter LIBRARY

London University—University College: United Kingdom *LIBERTAS*
TELNET lib.ucl.ac.uk ❯ wait for the prompt Username ❯ enter LIBRARY

Longmeadow—Storrs Library: United States (Access via **CARL**)

Lorain County Community College: United States *INNOPAC*
TELNET 192.232.30.17 No login required

Los Alamos National Laboratory: United States NM *GEAC Advance*
TELNET admiral.lanl.gov No login required

Loughborough University: United Kingdom *BLCMP*
TELNET liba.lut.ac.uk No login required

Louisiana State University: United States LA *NOTIS*
TN3270 lsumvs.sncc.lsu.edu ❯ wait for the prompt Select ==> ❯ enter L

Louisville Public Library: United States (Access via **Boulder, Colorado, Public Library System**)

Loyola College/Notre Dame: United States (Access via **Maryland Interlibrary Consortium**)

Loyola Marymount University: United States *INNOPAC*
TELNET linus.lmu.edu ❯ wait for the prompt login ❯ enter library

Loyola University: United States *NOTIS*
TELNET luccpua.it.luc.edu ❯ wait for the prompt that ends in LOGON ID ❯ enter guest ❯ wait for the prompt that ends in ENTER PASSWORD ❯ enter LUIS

Lund University: Sweden *VTLS*
TELNET lolita.lu.se ❯ wait for the prompt that ends in to logon ❯ enter HELLO TELNET.LOLITA

Luther College: United States (Access via **CARL**)

Lynchburg College: United States *DYNIX*
TELNET leo.lion.edu ❯ wait for the prompt login ❯ enter lclib

Lynchburg Public and College Libraries: United States *DYNIX*
TELNET lion.edu ❯ wait for the prompt login ❯ enter sblib

Lynchburg Public Library: United States *DYNIX*

TELNET `leo.lion.edu` ◗ wait for the prompt `login` ◗ enter `lpdial`

Lyndon State College—Vermont: United States VT (Access via **Middlebury College**)

Lyon School Learning Center (K-3): United States *custom*

TELNET `ly.ncook.k12.il.us` ◗ wait for the prompt `login` ◗ enter `library`

M.A.I.N.: Morris Automated Information Network—New Jersey: United States NJ *DRA*

TELNET `main.morris.org` ◗ wait for the prompt `Username` ◗ enter `PUBLIC`

Macalester College: United States *DYNIX*

TELNET `host.clic.edu` ◗ wait for the prompt `login` ◗ enter `scpac`

Macomb Community College: United States (Access via **Detroit Area Library Network**)

Macon College: United States (Access via **Georgia On-Line Library Information System**)

Maharasakham University: Thailand *INNOPAC*

TELNET `202.44.240.5` ◗ wait for the prompt `login` ◗ enter `library` ◗ wait for the prompt `Password` ◗ enter `library`

Maharishi International University: United States *DRA*

TELNET `vax1.miu.edu` ◗ wait for the prompt `Username` ◗ enter `LIBRARY`

Maine State Law and Legislative Reference Library: United States ME (Access via **University of Maine Library System**)

Maine State Library: United States ME (Access via **University of Maine Library System**)

Malaspina College: Canada *BuCAT*

TELNET `mala.bc.ca` ◗ wait for the prompt `Username` ◗ enter `macat`

Mallinckrodt Institute of Radiology Library: United States (Access via **Washington University of St Louis Medical Library**)

Manatee Community College—Florida: United States FL *NOTIS*

TELNET `luis.nerdc.ufl.edu` ◗ wait for the prompt `login` ◗ enter `luis`

Mansfield University: United States *DYNIX*

TELNET `matloc1.mnsfld.edu` ◗ wait for the prompt `login` ◗ enter `library`

Marcellus/Wood Memorial Library: United States (Access via **KELLY**)

Maricopa Center for Learning & Instruction: United States (Access via **Maricopa Community Colleges Libraries and Media Centers**)

Maricopa Community Colleges (Libraries and Media Centers): United States *custom*

TELNET `lib.maricopa.edu` ◗ wait for the prompt `Username` ◗ enter `LIB`

Maricopa County Library District: United States *DRA*

TELNET `library.maricopa.gov` ◗ wait for the prompt `Username` ◗ enter `LIBRARY`

Marietta College: United States *INNOPAC*

TELNET `mclib.marietta.edu` ◗ wait for the prompt `login` ◗ enter `library`

Marin County, California, Public Library System: United States CA *INNOPAC*

TELNET `marinet.lib.ca.us` ◗ wait for the prompt `login` ◗ enter `marinlib`

Marist College: United States *DOBIS/LIBIS*

TN3270 `vm.marist.edu` ◗ wait for the prompt `dobis` ◗ enter `?`

Marlborough Public Library: United States (Access via **CARL**)

MARMOT Library Network—Colorado Western Slopes: United States CO *custom*
  TELNET victor.umd.edu ▶ wait for the prompt Enter Choice> ▶ enter PAC
  TELNET pac.carl.org ▶ wait for the prompt Enter Choice> ▶ enter PAC
  TELNET 192.245.61.4 No login required

Marquette University: United States *INNOPAC*
  TELNET libus.csd.mu.edu No login required

Maryland Interlibrary Consortium: United States MD *custom*
  TELNET 144.126.176.78 No login required

Marylhurst College: United States *DYNIX*
  TELNET molli.marylhurst.edu ▶ wait for the prompt login ▶ enter library

Marymount University: United States (Access via **Washington Research Library Consortium**)

Marywood College: United States *DYNIX*
  TELNET @marywood1.marywood.edu ▶ wait for the prompt Username ▶ enter LIBPAC ▶ wait for the prompt Password ▶ enter PAC ▶ wait for the prompt login ▶ enter libpac

Massachusetts College of Art: United States MA (Access via **Fenway Libraries Online, Inc.**)

Massachusetts College of Pharmacy: United States MA (Access via **Fenway Libraries Online, Inc.**)

Massachusetts General Hospital: United States MA *INNOPAC*
  TELNET magic.mgh.harvard.edu ▶ wait for the prompt login ▶ enter magic

Massachusetts Institute of Technology: United States MA *GEAC Advance*
  TELNET library.mit.edu ▶ wait for the prompt login ▶ enter library ▶ wait for the prompt Password ▶ press ↵

Mattawan Consolidated Schools: United States (Access via **KELLY**)

Maynooth College: Ireland *custom*
  TELNET library.may.ie ▶ wait for the prompt login ▶ enter opac

McKendree College: United States (Access via **ILLINET On-line Catalog**)

McMurry University: United States (Access via **Abilene Library Consortium**)

Medical College of Georgia: United States *custom*
  TELNET merlin.mcg.edu ▶ wait for the prompt login ▶ enter merlin

Medical College of Ohio: United States OH *INNOPAC*
  TELNET cat.ohiolink.edu ▶ wait for the prompt login ▶ enter ohiolink
  TELNET osler.mco.edu No login required

Medical College of Pennsylvania Eastern Pennsylvania Psychiatric Institute Library Florence A. Moore Library of Medicine:
United States PA (Access via **HSLC HealthNET Health Sciences Information Network**)

Medical Research Library of Brooklyn: United States NY *DRA*
  TELNET medlib.hscbklyn.edu ▶ wait for the prompt Username ▶ enter MEDLIB

Mediterranean Agronomic Institute of Chania: Greece *GEAC ADVANCE*
  TELNET zorbas.maich.gr ▶ wait for the prompt login ▶ enter opac

Melbourne City Libraries: Australia *DYNIX*
  TELNET library.slv.vic.gov.au No login required

MELVYL—University of California: United States CA *custom*

TELNET lib.dartmouth.edu ◗ wait for the prompt -> ◗ enter CONNECT MELVYL

TELNET victor.umd.edu ◗ wait for the prompt Enter Choice> ◗ enter PAC

TELNET melvyl.ucop.edu No login required

Memorial University—Newfoundland: Canada *custom*

TELNET mungate.library.mun.ca ◗ wait for the prompt login ◗ enter mungate

Mercer Law Library: United States (Access via **Georgia On-Line Library Information System**)

Mercer University: United States *INNOPAC*

TELNET mainlib.mercer.peachnet.edu No login required

Mercer University—Law School: United States *INNOPAC*

TELNET lawcat.mercer.peachnet.edu No login required

Meredith College: United States *DRA*

TELNET carlyle.meredith.edu ◗ wait for the prompt Username ◗ enter PAC

Merrimack Valley Library Consortium: United States *CLSI*

TELNET mvlc.lib.ma.us ◗ wait for the prompt login ◗ enter library

Mesa Community College Library: United States (Access via **Maricopa Community Colleges Libraries and Media Centers**)

Mesa County Public Library: United States (Access via **MARMOT Library Network**)

Mesa County Schools Library: United States (Access via **MARMOT Library Network**)

Mesa State College Library: United States (Access via **MARMOT Library Network**)

Messiah College: United States *NOTIS*

TELNET mcis.messiah.edu ◗ wait for the prompt login ◗ enter opac

Metro Boston Library Network: United States MA *DRA*

TELNET mbln.bpl.org ◗ wait for the prompt Username ◗ enter LIBRARY

Miami University Library: United States FL *INNOPAC*

TELNET cat.ohiolink.edu ◗ wait for the prompt login ◗ enter ohiolink

TELNET watson.lib.muohio.edu ◗ wait for the prompt login ◗ enter library

Miami University of Ohio: United States OH *INNOPAC*

TELNET miamilink.lib.muohio.edu ◗ wait for the prompt that ends in [delete]=history list ◗ enter 1 for SHERLOCK

Miami-Dade Community College—Florida: United States FL *NOTIS*

TELNET luis.nerdc.ufl.edu ◗ wait for the prompt login ◗ enter luis

Michigan State University: United States MI *NOTIS*

TELNET thorplus.lib.purdue.edu ◗ wait for the prompt login ◗ enter catnet

TELNET merit-telnet-gw.msu.edu ◗ wait for the prompt Which Host? ◗ enter HELP

TELNET ibmgate.msu.edu ◗ wait for the prompt Enter selection ◗ enter magic ◗ wait for the prompt USERID ===> ◗ press ↵ ◗ wait for the prompt that ends in following commands ◗ enter DIAL MAGIC

Mid-York Library System: United States *DRA*

TELNET libvax1.midyork.lib.ny.us ◗ wait for the prompt Username ◗ enter GUEST

Middle Georgia College: United States GA (Access via **Georgia On-Line Library Information System**)

Middle Tennessee State University: United States TN *PALS*

TELNET `acad1.mtsu.edu` ♦ wait for the prompt `Username` ♦ enter `LIBRARY` ♦ wait for the prompt `(Y/N)` ♦ enter `Y`

Middlebury College: United States *DRA*

TELNET `lib.middlebury.edu` ♦ wait for the prompt `Username` ♦ enter `lib`

Milford Town Library: United States (Access via **CARL**)

Millbury Public Library: United States (Access via **CARL**)

Millersville University: United States *DYNIX*

TELNET `ville.millersv.edu` ♦ wait for the prompt `login` ♦ enter `library`

Millikin University: United States (Access via **ILLINET On-line Catalog**)

Mills College: United States *DYNIX*

TELNET `millslib.mills.edu` ♦ press ↵ ♦ wait for the prompt `Logon` ♦ enter `library`

Ministry of Education—Taiwan: Taiwan *custom*

TELNET `lib.ntit.edu.tw` ♦ wait for the prompt `login` ♦ enter `library` ♦ wait for the prompt `Select` ♦ enter E for English

Minneapolis Public Library: United States *GEAC*

TELNET `mpls.lib.mn.us` No login required

Minuteman Library Network—Massachusetts: United States MA *DRA*

TELNET `mln.lib.ma.us` ♦ wait for the prompt `Username` ♦ enter `LIBRARY`

Mississippi College: United States MS *INNOPAC*

TELNET `mical.mc.edu` ♦ wait for the prompt `login` ♦ enter `library`

Mississippi State University: United States MS *custom*

TELNET `libserv.msstate.edu` ♦ wait for the prompt `Username` ♦ enter `msu`

Missouri Western State College: United States MO *VTLS*

TELNET `monet.mwsc.edu` ♦ wait for the prompt `INLEX_LOGON` ♦ enter `hello gtc.library`

Monash University: Australia *PALS*

TELNET `library.monash.edu.au` No login required

Monmouth College: United States *CLSI*

TELNET `goals.monmouth.edu` ♦ wait for the prompt `login` ♦ enter `goals`

Monson Free Library: United States (Access via **CARL**)

Montana College of Mineral Science and Technology: United States MT *DYNIX*

TELNET `digger.mtech.edu` ♦ wait for the prompt `login` ♦ enter `mtlib` ♦ press ↵

Montana State University: United States MT *INLEX*

TELNET `catalog.lib.montana.edu` ♦ wait for the prompt `:` ♦ enter `hello msu.library`

Montclair State University: United States *DRA*

TELNET `alpha.montclair.edu` ♦ wait for the prompt `Username` ♦ enter `LINC`

Montefiore Medical Center: United States NY *custom*

TELNET `lis.aecom.yu.edu` ♦ press ↵ ♦ press ↵ ♦ wait for the prompt `( '?' for HELP)` ♦ enter 0 for Change Locations

Monterey Institute of International Studies: United States *INNOPAC*
TELNET monti.miis.edu No login required

Montgomery County Department of Public Libraries—Rockville, MD: United States MD (Access via **University of Maryland Library System**)

Montgomery County—Rockville, MD: United States MD (Access via **CARL**)

Montrose Public Library: United States (Access via **MARMOT Library Network**)

Moravian College and Theological Seminary: United States *DYNIX*
TELNET proxy.moravian.edu ◗ wait for the prompt tn-gw-> ◗ enter library ◗ wait for the prompt login ◗ enter library

Morehead State University: United States *UNICORN*
TELNET unicorn.morehead-st.edu ◗ wait for the prompt login ◗ enter library

Morehouse School of Medicine: United States *custom*
TELNET library.msm.edu ◗ wait for the prompt Username ◗ enter PUBCAT

Morgan Community College: United States (Access via **CARL**)

Morningside College: United States *DYNIX*
TELNET chief.morningside.edu ◗ wait for the prompt login ◗ enter library

Mount Allison University: Canada *DRA Gateway*
TELNET bigmac.mta.ca ◗ wait for the prompt Username ◗ enter CATALOG ◗ press ↵ ◗ press ↵
TELNET library.mta.ca ◗ wait for the prompt Username ◗ enter CATALOG ◗ press ↵ ◗ press ↵

Mount Angel Abbey—Oregon: United States OR *NOTIS*
TELNET 199.2.113.200 ◗ wait for the prompt type 'library' and press enter ◗ enter library

Mount Saint Vincent University: Canada *GEAC*
TELNET novanet.dal.ca ◗ wait for the prompt login ◗ enter opac ◗ wait for the prompt Password ◗ press ↵

Mount Sinai School of Medicine: United States *UNICORN*
TELNET levy.library.mssm.edu ◗ wait for the prompt login ◗ enter guest ◗ wait for the prompt Password ◗ enter guest

Mount St. Mary's College: United States (Access via **Maryland Interlibrary Consortium**)

Mount Vernon Nazarene College: United States *INNOPAC*
TELNET 149.143.2.2 ◗ wait for the prompt login ◗ enter library

Mt. Wachusett Community College: United States (Access via **CARL**)

Murdoch University: Australia *INNOPAC*
TELNET library.murdoch.edu.au ◗ wait for the prompt login ◗ enter library

Museum of Fine Arts—Boston: United States MA (Access via **Fenway Libraries Online, Inc.**)

Nanyang Technological University: Singapore *DRA*
TELNET ntuix.ntu.ac.sg ◗ wait for the prompt login ◗ enter libopac

Napier University: United Kingdom *DYNIX*
TELNET dns1.napier.ac.uk ◗ wait for the prompt login ◗ enter spcpac

Nashville Public Library: United States TN *INNOPAC*
TELNET waldo.nashv.lib.tn.us ◗ wait for the prompt login ◗ enter lib ◗ wait for the prompt Password ◗ enter guest

Nashville State Technical Institute: United States TN *UNICORN*

TELNET `library.nsti.tec.tn.us` ▶ wait for the prompt `login` ▶ enter `guest`

National and University Library—Zagreb: Croatia *custom*

TELNET `nsb2.nsb.hr` ▶ wait for the prompt `login` ▶ enter `opac1` ▶ wait for the prompt `Password` ▶ press ↵

National Cancer Institute, Frederick Cancer Research & , Development Center: United States *INNOPAC*

TELNET `library.ncifcrf.gov` ▶ wait for the prompt `login` ▶ enter `library`

National Center for Atmospheric Research: United States *UNICORN*

TELNET `library.ucar.edu` No login required

National Cheng Chi University: Taiwan *INNOPAC*

TELNET `cculais.nccu.edu.tw` ▶ wait for the prompt `login` ▶ enter `library` ▶ wait for the prompt `Password` ▶ enter `library` ▶ wait for the prompt `(A,T,S,K,C,G,N,R,I,L,V,X,Q)` ▶ enter X for English

National Chiao Tung University: Taiwan *custom*

TELNET `lib1.nctu.edu.tw` ▶ wait for the prompt `login` ▶ enter `library` ▶ wait for the prompt `Internal Code ? [1,2,3]` ▶ enter 3 for NON-CHINESE terminal

National Chung Cheng University: Taiwan *INNOPAC*

TELNET `libauto.lib.ccu.edu.tw` ▶ wait for the prompt `login` ▶ enter `library`

National Chung Hsing University: Taiwan *custom*

TELNET `mainlib.nchu.edu.tw` ▶ wait for the prompt `login` ▶ enter `library` ▶ wait for the prompt `Select` ▶ enter E for English

National Institutes of Health: United States *INNOPAC*

TELNET `nih-library.nih.gov` No login required

National Kaohsiung Institute of Technology: Taiwan *INNOPAC*

TELNET `140.127.112.201` ▶ wait for the prompt `login` ▶ enter `library`

National Kaoshiung Normal University: Taiwan *INNOPAC*

TELNET `140.127.53.11` ▶ wait for the prompt `login` ▶ enter `library` ▶ wait for the prompt that ends in `(A,T,S,W,N,V,R,C,I,X,Q)` ▶ enter X for English

National Library of Australia: Australia *DYNIX*

TELNET `janus.nla.gov.au` No login required

National Library of Medicine Locator: United States *custom*

TELNET `locator.nlm.nih.gov` ▶ wait for the prompt `login` ▶ enter `locator`

National Library of Scotland: United Kingdom *VTLS*

TELNET `opac.nls.uk` No login required

National Sun Yat—Sen University: Taiwan *INNOPAC*

TELNET `lib.nsysu.edu.tw` No login required

National Tainan Teachers College: Taiwan *DYNIX*

TELNET `192.192.96.16` ▶ wait for the prompt `login` ▶ enter `library` ▶ wait for the prompt that ends in (øÔæ‹ ©Œ øÈ$J<OFF>¬˜∂}) ▶ enter 4 for English VT100

National Taiwan Institute of Technology: Taiwan *custom*

TELNET `m8640.ntit.edu.tw` ▶ wait for the prompt `login` ▶ enter `library`

National Tsing Hua University: Taiwan *custom*

TELNET `140.114.72.2` ▶ wait for the prompt `login` ▶ enter `search` ▶ wait for the prompt `Select` ▶ enter E for English mode

National University of Singapore: Singapore *custom*
  TELNET `linc.nus.sg` ▶ wait for the prompt `login` ▶ enter `opac`

National-Louis University: United States (Access via **ILLINET On-line Catalog**)

Natural Resources Canada: Canada *MULTILIS*
  TELNET `hqlib.emr.ca` ▶ wait for the prompt `login` ▶ enter `opac`

Nazareth College Of Rochester: United States NY *INNOPAC*
  TELNET `libra.naz.edu` ▶ wait for the prompt `login` ▶ enter `library`

Nebraska Independent College Library Consortium (NICLC): United States *custom*
  TELNET `library.ccsn.edu` ▶ wait for the prompt `Username` ▶ enter `LIBRARY`

Neu-Technikum Buchs: Switzerland *custom*
  TELNET `buch.ntb.ch` ▶ press ↵ ▶ wait for the prompt `login` ▶ enter `buch`

Nevada Academic Libraries Information System (NALIS): United States NV *INNOPAC*
  TELNET `library.nevada.edu` No login required

New Buffalo Public Library: United States (Access via **KELLY**)

New England Conservatory: United States (Access via **Fenway Libraries Online, Inc.**)

New England School of Law Library: United States NE *INNOPAC*
  TELNET `portia.nesl.edu` ▶ wait for the prompt `login` ▶ enter `library`

New Hampshire State Library: United States NH *GALAXY*
  TELNET `lilac.nhsl.lib.nh.us` ▶ wait for the prompt `Username` ▶ enter `GUEST`

New Jersey Institute of Technology: United States NJ *DRA*
  TELNET `libsys.njit.edu` ▶ wait for the prompt `Username` ▶ enter `WWW_L`

New Mexico State Library: United States NM *DYNIX*
  TELNET `is.state.nm.us` ▶ wait for the prompt `login` ▶ enter `salsa` ▶ wait for the prompt `Password` ▶ press ↵

New Mexico State University: United States NM *VTLS*
  TELNET `library.nmsu.edu` No login required

New Orleans Public Library: United States *DYNIX*
  TELNET `sequent.gno.lib.la.us` ▶ wait for the prompt `login` ▶ enter `nopline`

New South Wales Libraries (LIBLINK): Australia *custom*
  TELNET `unilinc.edu.au` ▶ wait for the prompt `login` ▶ enter `liblink`

New York Academy of Medicine: United States NY *INNOPAC*
  TELNET `library.nyam.org` ▶ wait for the prompt `login` ▶ enter `library`

New York Botanical Garden Library: United States NY *INNOPAC*
  TELNET `librisc.nybg.org` ▶ wait for the prompt `login` ▶ enter `library`

New York Public Library: United States NY *custom*
  TELNET `nyplgate.nypl.org` ▶ wait for the prompt `login` ▶ enter `nypl`

New York Public Library—Branch Libraries Catalog: United States NY *custom*
  TELNET `nyplgate.nypl.org` ▶ wait for the prompt `login` ▶ enter `nypl`

New York State Library: United States NY *UNICORN*
  TELNET `nysl.nysed.gov` ▶ wait for the prompt `login` ▶ enter `catalog`

New York University: United States NY *GEAC ADVANCE*
TELNET bobcat.nyu.edu ◗ at the first prompt enter bobcat
TELNET mclib0.med.nyu.edu ◗ at the first prompt enter library

New York University Law Library (JULIUS): United States *INNOPAC*
TELNET mclib0.med.nyu.edu ◗ wait for the prompt login ◗ enter library

New York University Library BOBCAT System: United States *GEAC*
TELNET mclib0.med.nyu.edu ◗ wait for the prompt login ◗ enter library ◗ wait for the prompt Choose one ◗ enter A
TELNET bobcat.nyu.edu ◗ wait for the prompt login ◗ enter bobcat

New York University Ehrman Medical Library, Waldmann Dental Library, and Environmental Medicine Library: United States *INNOPAC*
TELNET mclib0.med.nyu.edu ◗ wait for the prompt login ◗ enter library

North Adams Public Library: United States (Access via **CARL**)

North Adams State College: United States (Access via **CARL**)

North Carolina State University: United States NC *DRA*
TELNET lib.lib.ncsu.edu ◗ wait for the prompt Username ◗ enter library ◗ press ⏎

North Carolina State University Library: United States NC (Access via **Triangle Research Libraries**)

North Central College: United States (Access via **ILLINET On-line Catalog**)

North East Wales Institute: United Kingdom *INNOPAC*
TELNET library.bangor.ac.uk No login required

North Florida Junior College: United States FL *NOTIS*
TELNET luis.nerdc.ufl.edu ◗ wait for the prompt login ◗ enter luis

North Georgia College—Dahlonega: United States GA (Access via **Georgia On-Line Library Information System**)

North of Boston Library Exchange: United States *CLSI*
TELNET college.noble.mass.edu ◗ wait for the prompt login ◗ enter library

North Olympic Library System—WA: United States WA *DYNIX*
TELNET nols.lib.wa.us ◗ wait for the prompt login ◗ enter library

North Suburban Library System: United States (Access via **ILLINET On-line Catalog**)

North York Public Library: Canada NY *DRA*
TELNET 198.231.94.1 ◗ wait for the prompt Username ◗ enter NYPL

Northampton, Colorado, Library: United States CO (Access via **CARL**)

Northborough Free Library: United States (Access via **CARL**)

Northeastern Illinois University: United States IL (Access via **ILLINET On-line Catalog**)

Northeastern Ohio Universities College of Medicine (NEOLINK): United States OH *INNOPAC*
TELNET library.neoucom.edu ◗ wait for the prompt login ◗ enter library

Northeastern University: United States *custom*
TELNET victor.umd.edu ◗ wait for the prompt Enter Choice> ◗ enter PAC
TELNET pac.carl.org ◗ wait for the prompt Enter Choice> ◗ enter PAC
TELNET library.lib.northeastern.edu ◗ wait for the prompt Enter Choice> ◗ enter CATALOG

Northeastern University—Law Library: United States *custom*
  TELNET `library.lib.northeastern.edu` ♦ wait for the prompt `Enter Choice>` ♦ enter CATALOG

Northern Arizona University: United States AZ (Access via **University of Maryland Library System**)

Northern Illinois Library System: United States IL (Access via **ILLINET On-line Catalog**)

Northern Illinois University: United States IL (Access via **ILLINET On-line Catalog**)

Northern Lights Cooperative System, Minnesota: United States MN *DRA Gateway*
  TELNET `aurora.northernlights.lib.mn.us` ♦ wait for the prompt `Username` ♦ enter NORTHERN

Northern Nevada Community College: United States NV (Access via **Nevada Academic Libraries Information System**)

Northern Territory University: Australia *DYNIX*
  TELNET `lib2.ntu.edu.au` ♦ wait for the prompt `login` ♦ enter `libnet`

Northwest College: United States (Access via **CARL**)

Northwest Missouri State University—Maryville: United States MO *DRA*
  TELNET `northwest.missouri.edu` ♦ wait for the prompt `Username` ♦ enter GUEST

Northwestern University: United States *NOTIS*
  TELNET `thorplus.lib.purdue.edu` ♦ wait for the prompt `login` ♦ enter `catnet`
  TN3270 `lib.cc.purdue.edu` ♦ wait for the prompt `Database Selection` ♦ enter `remote`
  TELNET `illinet.aiss.uiuc.edu` ♦ wait for the prompt that ends in `to login` ♦ enter b

Norwich University—Vermont College: United States VT *DRA*
  TELNET `lib.middlebury.edu` ♦ wait for the prompt `Username` ♦ enter LIB

Nottingham University: United Kingdom *LIBERTAS*
  TELNET `library.nott.ac.uk` ♦ wait for the prompt `Username` ♦ enter LIBRARY

Nova Scotia College of Art and Design: Canada *GEAC*
  TELNET `novanet.dal.ca` ♦ wait for the prompt `login` ♦ enter `opac` ♦ wait for the prompt `Password` ♦ press ⏎

Nova Scotia Provincial Library: Canada *MULTILIS*
  TELNET `rs6000.nshpl.library.ns.ca` ♦ wait for the prompt `login` ♦ enter `liscat`

Nova Southeastern University: United States *INNOPAC*
  TELNET `novacat.law.nova.edu` ♦ wait for the prompt `login` ♦ enter `library`

Oakland University: United States (Access via **Detroit Area Library Network**)

Oakland, Michigan, Community College: United States MI (Access via **Detroit Area Library Network**)

Oakton Community College: United States (Access via **ILLINET On-line Catalog**)

Oberlin College: United States *INNOPAC*
  TELNET `obis.lib.oberlin.edu` No login required

Occidental College: United States *INNOPAC*
  TELNET `oasys.lib.oxy.edu` No login required
  TELNET `oasys.oxy.edu` No login required

Oesterreichische Nationalbibliothek: Austria (Access via **Austrian Academic Library Network**)

Oesterreichische Phonothek: Austria (Access via **Austrian Academic Library Network**)

Oesterreichisches Bundesinstitut für d. wissenschaftl. Film: Austria (Access via **Austrian Academic Library Network**)

Oglethorpe University—Atlanta: United States GA (Access via **Georgia On-Line Library Information System**)

Ohio Northern University: United States OH *INNOPAC*
  TELNET `polar.onu.edu` No login required

Ohio State University: United States OH *INNOPAC*
  TELNET `thorplus.lib.purdue.edu` ◗ wait for the prompt `login` ◗ enter `catnet`
  TN3270 `lib.cc.purdue.edu` ◗ wait for the prompt `Database Selection` ◗ enter REMOTE
  TELNET `oscar.us.ohio-state.edu` No login required

Ohio State University—Jewish and Middle Eastern Studies: United States OH *INNOPAC*
  TELNET `aleph.lib.ohio-state.edu` ◗ wait for the prompt `Username` ◗ enter ALEPH
  TELNET `innopac.usc.edu` No login required

Ohio University: United States OH *INNOPAC*
  TELNET `alice.library.ohiou.edu` ◗ wait for the prompt `login` ◗ enter `library`

Ohio Wesleyan University: United States OH *INNOPAC*
  TELNET `libra.owu.edu` ◗ wait for the prompt `login` ◗ enter `library`

OhioLink: United States *INNOPAC*
  TELNET `cat.ohiolink.edu` ◗ wait for the prompt `login` ◗ enter `ohiolink`

Okaloosa-Walton Community College—Florida: United States FL *NOTIS*
  TELNET `luis.nerdc.ufl.edu` ◗ wait for the prompt `login` ◗ enter `luis`

Old Colony Library Network: United States MA *DYNIX*
  TELNET `ocon.ocln.org` ◗ wait for the prompt `login` ◗ enter `library`

Old Dominion University: United States *INNOPAC*
  TELNET `iii.lib.odu.edu` No login required

Olivet Nazarene University: United States *GEAC ADVANCE*
  TELNET `panther.olivet.edu` ◗ wait for the prompt `login` ◗ enter `library`

OLLI: the University System: United States *PALS*
  TELNET `library.gsu.edu` No login required

Ontario Institute for Studies in Education: Canada *MULTILIS*
  TELNET `eloise.oise.on.ca` ◗ wait for the prompt `login` ◗ enter `eloise`

Orange, Colorado, Library: United States CO (Access via **CARL**)

Orbis: An Oregon Academic Union Catalog: United States OR *INNOPAC*
  TELNET `orbis.uoregon.edu` No login required

Oregon Health Sciences University: United States *VTLS*
  TELNET `ohsu.edu` ◗ wait for the prompt `login` ◗ enter `catalog` ◗ wait for the prompt `Password` ◗ enter `catalog`

Oregon Institute of Technology: United States OR *INNOPAC*
  TELNET `hedgehog.oit.osshe.edu` ◗ wait for the prompt `login` ◗ enter `library`

Oregon State Library: United States OR *DRA*
  TELNET `opac.osl.or.gov` ◗ wait for the prompt `Username` ◗ enter `catalog`

Oregon State University: United States OR *GEAC ADVANCE*
TELNET `oasis.kerr.orst.edu` ◗ wait for the prompt `login` ◗ enter `oasis`

Otero Junior College: United States (Access via **CARL**)

Otsego District Public Library: United States (Access via **KELLY**)

Ottawa Public Library: Canada *DRA*
TELNET `ottlib.carleton.ca` ◗ wait for the prompt `Username` ◗ enter `freenetcat`

Oulu University: Finland *VTLS*
TELNET `kirjasto.oulu.fi` ◗ wait for the prompt `KIRJASTO` ◗ enter `hello,user.clas01`

Outagamie Waupaca Library System (OWLS), Wisconsin: United States WI *CLSI*
TELNET `owls.lib.wi.us` ◗ wait for the prompt `login` ◗ enter `owlsnet`

Oxford Brookes University: United Kingdom *BLCMP*
TELNET `opac.brookes.ac.uk` No login required

Oxford Free Public Library: United States (Access via **CARL**)

Oxford University: United Kingdom *DOBIS/LIBIS*
TELNET `library.ox.ac.uk` ◗ press ↵

Pacific Lutheran University: United States *DYNIX*
TELNET `library2.plu.edu` ◗ wait for the prompt `login` ◗ enter `library`

Pacific University: United States *DYNIX*
TELNET `harvey.pacificu.edu` ◗ wait for the prompt `login` ◗ enter `catalog`

Palm Beach Community College—Florida: United States FL *NOTIS*
TELNET `luis.nerdc.ufl.edu` ◗ wait for the prompt `login` ◗ enter `luis`

Palmer Public Library: United States (Access via **CARL**)

Paradise Valley Community College Library: United States (Access via **Maricopa Community Colleges Libraries and Media Centers**)

Parchment Community Library: United States (Access via **KELLY**)

Parchment Public Schools: United States (Access via **KELLY**)

Parmly-Billings Public Library: United States *DYNIX*
TELNET `billings.lib.mt.us` ◗ wait for the prompt `login` ◗ enter `library`

Pasadena Public Library: United States (Access via **CARL**)

Pasco-Hernando Community College—Florida: United States FL *NOTIS*
TELNET `luis.nerdc.ufl.edu` ◗ wait for the prompt `login` ◗ enter `luis`

Pathfinder System: United States (Access via **MARMOT Library Network**)

Paw Paw District Library: United States (Access via **KELLY**)

Paw Paw Public Schools: United States (Access via **KELLY**)

Pennsylvania State University: United States PA *NOTIS*
TELNET `thorplus.lib.purdue.edu` ◗ wait for the prompt `login` ◗ enter `catnet`
TN3270 `lib.cc.purdue.edu` ◗ wait for the prompt `Database Selection` ◗ enter `REMOTE`
TELNET `lias.psu.edu` ◗ wait for the prompt that ends in `[enter]` ◗ enter `Y` ◗ wait for the prompt that ends in `(not displayed)` ◗ press ↵

Peoria Public Library: United States *custom*

  TELNET `universe.rsa.lib.il.us` No login required

Pepperdine University: United States *VTLS*

  TELNET `lib.pepperdine.edu` ◗ wait for the prompt that ends in `to access library` ◗ enter HELLO USER.CLAS01

Pepperell, Colorado, Library: United States CO (Access via **CARL**)

Petra Christian University: *custom*

  TELNET `library.petra.ac.id` ◗ wait for the prompt `login` ◗ enter `catalog`

Philadelphia College of Osteopathic Medicine O.L. Snyder Memorial Library: United States PA (Access via **HSLC HealthNET** Health Sciences Information Network)

Philadelphia College of Pharmacy and Science Joseph W. England Library: United States PA (Access via **HSLC HealthNET** Health Sciences Information Network)

Philipps-Universitaet, Marburg: Germany *custom*

  TELNET `vaxub1.ub.uni-marburg.de` ◗ wait for the prompt `Username` ◗ enter OPC

Phillips Laboratory Technical Library—Kirtland Air Force Base: United States *UNICORN*

  TELNET `library.plk.af.mil` ◗ wait for the prompt `login` ◗ enter `mosaic`

Phoenix Community College Library: United States AZ (Access via **Maricopa Community Colleges Libraries and Media Centers**)

Phoenix Public Library, Arizona: United States AZ *DYNIX*

  TELNET `pac.lib.ci.phoenix.az.us` No login required

Pikes Peak Community College: United States (Access via **CARL**)

Pikes Peak Library District: United States *custom*

  TELNET `victor.umd.edu` ◗ wait for the prompt `Enter Choice>` ◗ enter `pac`
  TELNET `pac.carl.org` ◗ wait for the prompt `Enter Choice>` ◗ enter `PAC`
  TELNET `192.245.61.4` No login required
  TELNET `192.153.23.254` No login required

Pima Community College: United States *INNOPAC*

  TELNET `libcat.pima.edu` No login required

Pitkin County Public Library: United States (Access via **MARMOT Library Network**)

Pittsburg State University: United States PA *DYNIX*

  TELNET `psuaxe.pittstate.edu` ◗ wait for the prompt `login` ◗ enter `library`
  TELNET `library.pittstate.edu` ◗ wait for the prompt `login` ◗ enter `library`

Pittsfield, Colorado, Library: United States CO (Access via **CARL**)

Plainwell/Charles A. Ransom Public Library: United States (Access via **KELLY**)

Plateau Valley Schools Library: United States (Access via **MARMOT Library Network**)

Pleasant Ridge School Learning Center (4-6): United States *custom*

  TELNET `pr.ncook.k12.il.us` ◗ wait for the prompt `login` ◗ enter `library`

Plymouth State College: United States *INNOPAC*

  TELNET `lola.plymouth.edu` No login required

Point Loma Nazarene College: United States *INNOPAC*

  TELNET `192.147.249.103` ◗ wait for the prompt `login` ◗ enter `public1`

Politecnico di Torino: Italy *custom*

TELNET `pico.polito.it` ◗ wait for the prompt : ◗ enter HELLO XQ.BIB

Polk Community College—Florida: United States FL *NOTIS*

TELNET `luis.nerdc.ufl.edu` ◗ wait for the prompt login ◗ enter luis

Port Arthur Public Library: United States (Access via **CARL**)

Port Neches Public Library: United States (Access via **CARL**)

Portland Community College: United States *DYNIX*

TELNET `zeus.cc.pcc.edu` ◗ wait for the prompt login ◗ enter library ◗ wait for the prompt Password ◗ enter catalog

Portland Public Library, Maine: United States ME *INNOPAC*

TELNET `porpl.portland.lib.me.us` ◗ wait for the prompt login ◗ enter library

Portland State University: United States OR *UNICORN*

TELNET `psulib.cc.pdx.edu` ◗ wait for the prompt login ◗ enter dialin

Presbyterian College: United States *INNOPAC*

TELNET `library.presby.edu` ◗ wait for the prompt login ◗ enter library

Prince George's County Memorial Library System: United States *CLSI*

TELNET `198.76.216.1` ◗ wait for the prompt login ◗ enter pgcat

Princeton Manuscripts Catalog: United States *NOTIS*

TN3270 `pucc.princeton.edu` ◗ tab to COMMAND ===> ◗ enter FOLIO

TELNET `catalog.princeton.edu` ◗ wait for the prompt that ends in SELECT AN OPTION ◗ enter 8 ◗ wait for the prompt that ends in SELECT AN OPTION ◗ enter 4

Princeton University: United States NJ *NOTIS*

TELNET `catalog.princeton.edu` No login required

Private Academic Library Network of Indiana (PALNI): United States IN *DRA*

TELNET `maple.palni.edu` ◗ wait for the prompt Username ◗ enter PALNI

Providence College: United States (Access via **Rhode Island Higher Education Library Information Network**)

Providence Public Library—Rhode Island: United States *DYNIX*

TELNET `198.115.231.11` ◗ wait for the prompt login ◗ enter library

Providence University: Taiwan *custom*

TELNET `luking.pu.edu.tw` ◗ wait for the prompt login ◗ enter library ◗ wait for the prompt Password ◗ press ↵ ◗ wait for the prompt Choose (E, C, Q) ◗ enter E for English

Provo Public Library, Utah: United States UT *DYNIX*

TELNET `univ.provo.lib.ut.us` ◗ wait for the prompt login ◗ enter library

Public Library of Cincinnati and Hamilton County: United States OH *custom*

TELNET `plch.lib.oh.us` No login required

Pueblo Community College: United States (Access via **CARL**)

Purdue University: United States *NOTIS*

TELNET `thorplus.lib.purdue.edu` ◗ wait for the prompt login ◗ enter catnet

TN3270 `lib.cc.purdue.edu` ◗ wait for the prompt Database Selection ◗ enter REMOTE

Queen Elizabeth II Library: Canada (Access via **Memorial University—Newfoundland**)

Queen's College Library: Canada (Access via **Memorial University—Newfoundland**)

Queen's University: Canada *NOTIS*
TN3270 `qucdnadm.queensu.ca` No login required
TELNET `qlineascii.queensu.ca` No login required

Queensland University of Technology: Australia *URICA*
TELNET `library.qut.edu.au` No login required

Ramsey County Public Library: United States *DYNIX*
TELNET `ramsey.lib.mn.us` ◗ wait for the prompt `login` ◗ enter `library`

Randolph—Macon Woman's College: United States *DYNIX*
TELNET `leo.lion.edu` ◗ wait for the prompt `login` ◗ enter `rmlib`

Rechenzentrum Der Universitaet Zuerich (University of Zurich): Switzerland *DOBIS*
TELNET `nuz.unizh.ch` ◗ wait for the prompt `#` ◗ enter `tso`

Red Academica Universitaria: Venezuela (Access via **Biblioteca Nacional de Venezuela**)

Red Rocks Community College: United States (Access via **CARL**)

Reed College: United States *INNOPAC*
TELNET `hauser.library.reed.edu` No login required

Regent University: United States *INNOPAC*
TELNET `regen.regent.edu` ◗ wait for the prompt `login` ◗ enter `library`

Regina Public Library: Canada *DYNIX*
TELNET `opc.rpl.regina.sk.ca` ◗ wait for the prompt `login` ◗ enter `public`

Regis College/Teikyo Loretto University: United States (Access via **CARL**)

Rensselaer Polytechnic Institute: United States *custom*
TELNET `infotrac.rpi.edu` No login required

Research and Reference Centers: United States (Access via **ILLINET On-line Catalog**)

Rhode Island College: United States RI (Access via **Rhode Island Higher Education Library Information Network**)

Rhode Island Higher Education Library Information Network (HELIN): United States RI *INNOPAC*
TELNET `library.uri.edu` ◗ wait for the prompt `login` ◗ enter `library`

Rhodes College: United States *DRA*
TELNET `vax.rhodes.edu` ◗ wait for the prompt `Username` ◗ enter `LIBCAT`

Rice University: United States *UNICORN*
TELNET `alexandria.rice.edu` ◗ wait for the prompt `login` ◗ enter `guest` ◗ wait for the prompt `Password` ◗ press ↵

Richland Community Library: United States (Access via **KELLY**)

Richland County Public Library, South Carolina: United States SC *DYNIX*
TELNET `rcpl.richland.lib.sc.us` ◗ wait for the prompt `login` ◗ enter `public`

Rijksuniversteit Limburg: The Netherlands *custom*
TELNET `ihol02.rulimburg.nl` ◗ wait for the prompt `Username` ◗ enter `OPC1`

Rio Salado Community College Library/Media Services: United States (Access via **Maricopa Community Colleges Libraries**

and Media Centers)

River Bend Library System: United States (Access via **ILLINET On-line Catalog**)

Riverside City & County Public Library, California: United States CA *DRA Gateway*
TELNET `rivlib.riverside.lib.ca.us` ♦ wait for the prompt `Username` ♦ enter `CATALOG`

Roanoke College: United States *INNOPAC*
TELNET `fintel.roanoke.edu` ♦ wait for the prompt `login` ♦ enter `campus`

Robert Gordon University: United Kingdom *URICA*
TELNET `193.63.232.51` ♦ wait for the prompt `login` ♦ enter `LIBRARY` in all caps

Rochester Institute of Technology: United States *INNOPAC*
TELNET `ritvax.isc.rit.edu` ♦ wait for the prompt `Username` ♦ enter `LIBRARY`

Rockefeller University: United States *custom*
TELNET `library.rockefeller.edu` ♦ wait for the prompt `login` ♦ enter `library`

Rockingham County Public Library, North Carolina: United States NC *INNOPAC*
TELNET `199.72.201.62` ♦ wait for the prompt `login` ♦ enter `library`

Roger Williams University: United States (Access via **Rhode Island Higher Education Library Information Network**)

Rolling Prairie, Illinois, Library System: United States IL (Access via **ILLINET On-line Catalog**)

Roosevelt University: United States (Access via **ILLINET On-line Catalog**)

Rosary College: United States (Access via **ILLINET On-line Catalog**)

Roskilde University: Denmark *custom*
TELNET `find.uni-c.dk` ♦ wait for the prompt `login` ♦ enter `find`

Rowan College of New Jersey: United States NJ *DRA*
TELNET `namor.rowan.edu` ♦ wait for the prompt `Username` ♦ enter `LIBRARY`

Royal Institute of Linguistics and Anthropology, Leiden: The Netherlands *custom*
TELNET `rultlv.leidenuniv.nl` ♦ wait for the prompt `Username` ♦ enter `OPC3`

Royal Institute of Technology—Stockholm: Sweden *LIBERTAS*
TELNET `kthbib.lib.kth.se` ♦ wait for the prompt `Username` ♦ enter `tekline`

Royal Library (Koninklijke Bibliotheek): The Netherlands *custom*
TELNET `kbnlb4.konbib.nl` ♦ wait for the prompt `Username` ♦ enter `OPC` ♦ wait for the prompt `Vul in` ♦ enter `eng` for English

Royal Melbourne Institute of Technology: Australia *GEAC ADVANCE*
TELNET `library.rmit.edu.au` ♦ wait for the prompt `jaguar login` ♦ enter `library`

Royal Military College of Canada: Canada *DYNIX*
TELNET `library.rmc.ca` ♦ wait for the prompt `login` ♦ enter `library`

Royal Observatory—Edinburgh: United Kingdom *custom*
TELNET `library.roe.ac.uk` ♦ wait for the prompt `login` ♦ enter `opac` ♦ wait for the prompt `Enter User Identifier` ♦ enter `EASY` in all caps ♦ wait for the prompt `Enter Password` ♦ enter `EASY` in all caps

Royal Postgraduate Medical School: United Kingdom (Access via **London University Central Libertas Consortium**)

Royal Roads Military College: Canada *DYNIX*
TELNET `library.royalroads.ca` ♦ wait for the prompt `login` ♦ enter `library`

Royal Veterinary College: United Kingdom (Access via **London University Central Libertas Consortium**)

Rutgers University: United States *GEAC*
 TELNET `library.rutgers.edu` ▶ press ↵ ▶ press ↵ ▶ press ↵

Rutgers University Law Library—Newark: United States NJ *INNOPAC*
 TELNET `law-new.rutgers.edu` ▶ wait for the prompt `login` ▶ enter `library`

Ryerson Polytechnical Institute: Canada *DRA*
 TELNET `hugo.lib.ryerson.ca` ▶ wait for the prompt `Username` ▶ enter RYERSON

Saint Bonaventure University: United States *DYNIX*
 TELNET `cat.sbu.edu` ▶ wait for the prompt `login` ▶ enter `mpac`

Saint Joseph Hospital Library: United States (Access via **CARL**)

Saint Mary's College—Moraga, California: United States CA *INNOPAC*
 TELNET `albert.stmarys-ca.edu` No login required

Saint Mary's University: Canada *GEAC*
 TELNET `novanet.dal.ca` ▶ wait for the prompt `login` ▶ enter `opac` ▶ wait for the prompt `Password` ▶ press ↵

Saint Vincent College and Archabbey, Pennsylvania: United States PA *INNOPAC*
 TELNET `biblio.stvincent.edu` ▶ wait for the prompt `login` ▶ enter `library`

Saint Xavier University: United States (Access via **ILLINET On-line Catalog**)

Salford University: United Kingdom *BLCMP*
 TELNET `saiso.salford.ac.uk` No login required

Salisbury State University: United States (Access via **University of Maryland Library System**)

Salt Lake City Public Library: United States UT *custom*
 TELNET `slcpl.slcpl.lib.ut.us` ▶ wait for the prompt `login` ▶ enter `citycat`

Salve Regina University: United States *INNOPAC*
 TELNET `salve2.salve.edu` ▶ wait for the prompt `login` ▶ enter `library`

Salzburg—Universitaetsbibliothek: Austria (Access via **Austrian Academic Library Network**)

Sam Houston State University: United States *DRA*
 TELNET `niord.shsu.edu` ▶ wait for the prompt `Username` ▶ enter `saminfo` ▶ wait for the prompt `Selection` ▶ enter A for Newton Gresham Library

San Diego State University: United States *INNOPAC*
 TELNET `library.sdsu.edu` ▶ wait for the prompt `login` ▶ enter `library` ▶ press ↵ ▶ press ↵

San Francisco Public Library: United States CA *DRA*
 TELNET `sfpl.lib.ca.us` ▶ wait for the prompt `Username` ▶ enter TELPAC

San Francisco State University: United States CA *GEAC ADVANCE*
 TELNET `opac.sfsu.edu` ▶ wait for the prompt `login` ▶ enter `sfsu` ▶ wait for the prompt `Password` ▶ press ↵

San Jose City College: United States CA *INNOPAC*
 TELNET `library.sjeccd.cc.ca.us` No login required

San Jose State University: United States *INNOPAC*
 TELNET `sjsulib1.sjsu.edu` No login required

San Miguel County Public Library: United States (Access via **MARMOT Library Network**)

Sangamon State University: United States (Access via **ILLINET On-line Catalog**)

Santa Clara University: United States CA *INNOPAC*
   TELNET sculib.scu.edu No login required

Santa Fe Community College—Florida: United States FL *NOTIS*
   TELNET luis.nerdc.ufl.edu ◗ wait for the prompt login ◗ enter luis

Saskatchewan Provincial Library: Canada *DYNIX*
   TELNET provlib.gov.sk.ca ◗ wait for the prompt login ◗ enter public

Saskatoon Board of Education: Canada *MULTILIS*
   TELNET library.sbe.saskatoon.sk.ca ◗ wait for the prompt Username ◗ enter OPAC

Saskatoon Public Library: Canada *DRA*
   TELNET charly.publib.saskatoon.sk.ca ◗ wait for the prompt Username ◗ enter PUBLIC

School of the Art Institute: United States (Access via **ILLINET On-line Catalog**)

Scott County Public Library: United States *DRA*
   TELNET scott.lib.mn.us ◗ wait for the prompt Username ◗ enter library

Scottsdale Community College Library: United States (Access via **Maricopa Community Colleges Libraries and Media Centers**)

Scottsdale Public Library, Arizona: United States AZ *DRA*
   TELNET lib.ci.scottsdale.az.us ◗ wait for the prompt Username ◗ enter DIALUP

Scuola Normale Superiore di Pisa: Italy *custom*
   TELNET vaxsns.sns.it ◗ wait for the prompt Username ◗ enter bib

Seattle Pacific University: United States WA *DRA*
   TELNET jerome.spu.edu ◗ wait for the prompt Username ◗ enter pac

Seattle Public Library: United States *DYNIX*
   TELNET spl.lib.wa.us ◗ wait for the prompt login ◗ enter library

Seattle University Law Library: United States WA *INNOPAC*
   TELNET simon.ups.edu ◗ wait for the prompt login ◗ enter library

Seminole Community College—Florida: United States FL *NOTIS*
   TELNET luis.nerdc.ufl.edu ◗ wait for the prompt login ◗ enter luis

Seton Hall University: United States *GEAC ADVANCE*
   TELNET shucat.shu.edu ◗ wait for the prompt login ◗ enter opac

Seton Hall University—School of Law: United States *INNOPAC*
   TELNET laws13.shu.edu ◗ wait for the prompt login ◗ enter library ◗ wait for the prompt Password ◗ enter library

Shawnee Library System: United States (Access via **ILLINET On-line Catalog**)

Shawnee State University: United States *INNOPAC*
   TELNET beartrack.shawnee.edu No login required

Sheffield Hallam University: United Kingdom *URICA*
   TELNET opac.shu.ac.uk ◗ wait for the prompt login ◗ enter opac ◗ wait for the prompt Password ◗ press ↵

Shepherd College: United States (Access via **West Virginia University**)

Shippensburg University: United States *PALS*
   TELNET `ellis.ship.edu` No login required

Shirley, Colorado, Library: United States CO (Access via **CARL**)

Shrewsbury, Colorado, Public Library: United States CO (Access via **CARL**)

SIBIL: Swiss-French Network Catalogue: Switzerland *custom*
   TELNET `sibil.switch.ch` ❥ press ↵ ❥ wait for the prompt that ends in FOR MENU ❥ enter 02

Simmons College: United States *INNOPAC*
   TELNET `lib.simmons.edu` No login required

Simon Fraser University: Canada *INNOPAC*
   TELNET `library.sfu.ca` ❥ wait for the prompt Username ❥ enter `sfulib`

Simpson College: United States *INNOPAC*
   TELNET `dunnlib.simpson.edu` ❥ wait for the prompt login ❥ enter `library`

Sinclair Community College: United States *INNOPAC*
   TELNET `kong.sinclair.edu` No login required

Singapore Polytechnic: Singapore *VTLS*
   TELNET `library.sp.ac.sg` ❥ wait for the prompt MPE XL ❥ enter `hello internet,user.clas01`

Sioux City Public Library: United States *DYNIX*
   TELNET `scity.sc.lib.ia.us` ❥ wait for the prompt login ❥ enter `library`

Skagit Valley Community College: United States *INNOPAC*
   TELNET `svclib.ctc.edu` ❥ wait for the prompt login ❥ enter `library`

Skidmore College: United States *DYNIX*
   TELNET `lucy.skidmore.edu` ❥ wait for the prompt login ❥ enter `pac`

Smithsonian Institution: United States *NOTIS*
   TELNET `siris.si.edu` ❥ wait for the prompt TS> ❥ press ↵

Sno-Isle Library System—Marysville, Washington: United States WA (Access via **University of Maryland Library System**)

Sodus Township Library: United States (Access via **KELLY**)

Sonoma County Library: United States *DYNIX*
   TELNET `sonoma.lib.ca.us` ❥ wait for the prompt login ❥ enter `public`

Sonoma State University: United States *DRA Gateway*
   TELNET `vax.sonoma.edu` ❥ wait for the prompt Username ❥ enter `opac`
   TELNET `sonoma.edu` ❥ wait for the prompt Username ❥ enter `OPAC`

South Bank University: United Kingdom *DYNIX*
   TELNET `sbulib.sbu.ac.uk` ❥ wait for the prompt login ❥ enter `lrlib`

South Carolina State Library: United States SC *DRA*
   TELNET `leo.scsl.state.sc.us` ❥ wait for the prompt Username ❥ enter `LION`

South Dakota Library Network: United States SD *PALS*
   TELNET `204.52.252.131` No login required

South Florida Community College—Florida: United States *NOTIS*
TELNET `luis.nerdc.ufl.edu` ◗ wait for the prompt `login` ◗ enter `luis`

South Hadley, Colorado, Library System: United States CO (Access via **CARL**)

South Haven, Michigan, Libraries: United States MI (Access via **KELLY**)

South Mountain Community College Library: United States (Access via **Maricopa Community Colleges Libraries and Media Centers**)

Southampton University: United Kingdom *URICA*
TELNET `lib.soton.ac.uk` ◗ wait for the prompt `login` ◗ enter `library`

Southbridge, Colorado, Libraries: United States CO (Access via **CARL**)

Southeastern Libraries Cooperating, Minnesota: United States MN *DRA*
TELNET `selco3.selco.lib.mn.us` ◗ wait for the prompt `Username` ◗ enter `LIBRARY`

Southern Adirondack Library System/Mohawk Valley Library Association: United States *DRA*
TELNET `sallib.sals.edu` ◗ wait for the prompt `Username` ◗ enter `GUEST` ◗ press ↵ ◗ press ↵

Southern Alberta Institute of Technology: Canada *custom*
TELNET `library.sait.ab.ca` ◗ wait for the prompt `Username` ◗ enter `SAITLIBRARY`

Southern Illinois University: United States IL (Access via **ILLINET On-line Catalog**)

Southern Illinois University—Law Library: United States *INNOPAC*
TELNET `solopac.c-lawlib.siu.edu` ◗ wait for the prompt `login` ◗ enter `guest`

Southern Methodist University: United States *NOTIS*
TN3270 `vm.cis.smu.edu` ◗ tab to COMMAND   ===> ◗ enter `dial vtam`

Southern Oregon State College: United States OR *INNOPAC*
TELNET `lib.sosc.osshe.edu` ◗ wait for the prompt `login` ◗ enter `library`

Southern State Community College, Ohio: United States OH *INNOPAC*
TELNET `soucc.southern.cc.oh.us` ◗ wait for the prompt `login` ◗ enter `library` ◗ wait for the prompt `Password` ◗ enter `library`

Southern Tech—Marietta: United States (Access via **Georgia On-Line Library Information System**)

Southern Utah University: United States UT *DYNIX*
TELNET `lib.li.suu.edu` ◗ wait for the prompt `login` ◗ enter `public`

Southfield Public Library, Michigan: United States MI *INNOPAC*
TELNET `198.111.68.10` No login required

Southwest Baptist Theological Seminary: United States *DRA*
TELNET `lib.swbts.edu` ◗ wait for the prompt `Username` ◗ enter `LIB`

Southwest Baptist University: United States *DYNIX*
TELNET `bearcat.sbuniv.edu` ◗ wait for the prompt `login` ◗ enter `literacy`

Southwest System: United States (Access via **MARMOT Library Network**)

Southwest Texas State University: United States TX *DRA*
TELNET `panam2.panam.edu` ◗ wait for the prompt `Username` ◗ enter `PACKEY`
TELNET `admin.swt.edu` ◗ wait for the prompt `Username` ◗ enter `SWTLIBRARY`
TELNET `leela.swt.edu` ◗ wait for the prompt `Username` ◗ enter `SWTLIBRARY`

Southwestern Michigan College: United States MI (Access via **KELLY**)

Southwestern University: United States *DYNIX*
   TELNET `library.txswu.edu` ◗ wait for the prompt `login` ◗ enter `library`

Southwick Library: United States (Access via **CARL**)

Spokane Public Library, Washington: United States WA *DRA Gateway*
   TELNET `spokpl.lib.wa.us` No login required

Spring Hill College, Alabama: United States AL *UNICORN*
   TELNET `library.shc.edu` ◗ wait for the prompt `login` ◗ enter `public` ◗ wait for the prompt `Password` ◗ enter `public`

Springfield, Colorado City Libraries: United States CO (Access via **CARL**)

Springfield-Greene County Library: United States *DYNIX*
   TELNET `main.sgcl.lib.mo.us` ◗ wait for the prompt `login` ◗ enter `public`

Springman Jr. High School Learning Center (7-8): United States *custom*
   TELNET `sp.ncook.k12.il.us` ◗ wait for the prompt `login` ◗ enter `library`

St Bartholomew's and The Royal London School of Medicine and Dentistry: United Kingdom *UNICORN*
   TELNET `138.37.242.10` ◗ wait for the prompt `login` ◗ enter `library`

St. Ambrose University, Iowa: United States *CLSI*
   TELNET `ql.rbls.lib.il.us` ◗ wait for the prompt `login` ◗ enter `ql`

St. Andrews University: United Kingdom *custom*
   TELNET `saul.st-and.ac.uk` ◗ wait for the prompt `Username` ◗ enter `SAULCAT`

St. Boniface General Hospital Libraries: Canada *DRA Gateway*
   TELNET `umopac.umanitoba.ca` ◗ wait for the prompt `Username` ◗ enter `BISON`
   TELNET `bison.umanitoba.ca` ◗ wait for the prompt `Username` ◗ enter `BISON`

St. George's Hospital Medical School: United Kingdom (Access via **London University Central Libertas Consortium**)

St. John's Mercy Medical Center Library: United States (Access via **Washington University of St. Louis Medical Library**)

St. Johns River Community College—Florida: United States FL *NOTIS*
   TELNET `luis.nerdc.ufl.edu` ◗ wait for the prompt `login` ◗ enter `luis`

St. Joseph County Public Library, Indiana: United States *INNOPAC*
   TELNET `stjos.sjcpl.lib.in.us` No login required

St. Joseph's University: United States *GEAC ADVANCE*
   TELNET `biblio.sju.edu` No login required

St. Joseph/Maud Preston Palenske Memorial Library: United States (Access via **KELLY**)

St. Lawrence University: United States *INNOPAC*
   TELNET `ody.stlawu.edu` ◗ wait for the prompt `login` ◗ enter `library`

St. Louis Children's Hospital Library: United States MO (Access via **Washington University of St. Louis Medical Library**)

St. Louis College of Pharmacy Library: United States MO (Access via **Washington University of St. Louis Medical Library**)

St. Mary's Health Center Library: United States MO (Access via **Washington University of St. Louis Medical Library**)

St. Mary's University: United States *DYNIX*
   TELNET `vax.stmarytx.edu` ◗ wait for the prompt `Username` ◗ enter `dynix`

St. Michael's College: United States *DRA*
TELNET `smclib.smcvt.edu` ▶ wait for the prompt `Username` ▶ enter `PUBLIC`

St. Norbert College: United States *INNOPAC*
TELNET `snclib.snc.edu` ▶ wait for the prompt `login` ▶ enter `library`

St. Paul Public Library: United States *custom*
TELNET `stpaul.lib.mn.us` ▶ wait for the prompt `login` ▶ enter `library`

St. Petersburg Junior College—Florida: United States FL *NOTIS*
TELNET `luis.nerdc.ufl.edu` ▶ wait for the prompt `login` ▶ enter `luis`

Stadsbibliotheek van Antwerpen: Belgium (Access via **University of Antwerp**)

Staffordshire University: United Kingdom *DYNIX*
TELNET `horizon.staffs.ac.uk` ▶ wait for the prompt `login` ▶ enter `library`

Stanford University: United States *custom*
TELNET `forsythetn.stanford.edu` ▶ wait for the prompt `Account?` ▶ enter `socrates` ▶ wait for the prompt `OK to proceed?` ▶ enter `YES`

Starved Rock Library System: United States (Access via **ILLINET On-line Catalog**)

State Library of Florida: United States FL *DRA*
TELNET `stafla.dlis.state.fl.us` No login required

State Library of Massachusetts: United States MA (Access via **Boston Library Consortium**)

State Library of Ohio: United States OH *INNOPAC*
TELNET `slonet.ohio.gov` No login required

State Library of Pennsylvania: United States PA *NOTIS*
TELNET `copa.prepnet.com` ▶ press ⏎

State Library of South Australia: Australia *INNOPAC*
TELNET `ferrari.slsa.sa.gov.au` ▶ wait for the prompt `login` ▶ enter `library`

State Library of Tasmania: Australia *DYNIX*
TELNET `talis.tased.edu.au` ▶ wait for the prompt `login` ▶ enter `opac` ▶ wait for the prompt `Password` ▶ press ⏎

State Library of Victoria: Australia *DYNIX*
TELNET `library.slv.vic.gov.au` No login required

State Technical Institute: United States (Access via **KELLY**)

Stephen F. Austin State University: United States TX *custom*
TELNET `horizon.sfasu.edu` ▶ wait for the prompt `login` ▶ enter `guest`

Sterling and Francine Clark Art Institute: United States *INNOPAC*
TELNET `francine.williams.edu` ▶ wait for the prompt `login` ▶ enter `library`

Sterling, Colorado, Libraries: United States CO (Access via **CARL**)

Stockholm University: Sweden *GEAC*
TELNET `bib10.sub.su.se` ▶ wait for the prompt `Login` ▶ enter `SUB`

Stonehill College, Massachusetts: United States MA *INNOPAC*
TELNET `lib.stonehill.edu` ▶ wait for the prompt `login` ▶ enter `library`

Strathclyde University: United Kingdom *GEAC*
TELNET `wwwx25.niss.ac.uk` `20008` No login required

Sturbridge, Colorado, Libraries: United States CO (Access via **CARL**)

Sturgis Public Schools: United States (Access via **KELLY**)

Suburban Library System: United States (Access via **ILLINET On-line Catalog**)

Suffolk Cooperative Library System, New York: United States NY *INNOPAC*
TELNET 199.173.91.40 ❱ wait for the prompt login ❱ enter public

Suisse Union Catalogue of Foreign Serials: Switzerland (Access via **Swiss-French Network Catalogue**)

Sul Ross State University: United States *UNICORN*
TELNET lobopac.sulross.edu ❱ wait for the prompt login ❱ enter wml

Summit County Public Library: United States (Access via **MARMOT Library Network**)

SUNY Alfred College of Technology: United States NY *MULTILIS*
TELNET slscva.ca.sunycentral.edu ❱ wait for the prompt Username ❱ enter ALF_NETOPAC

SUNY College—Cortland: United States NY *MULTILIS*
TELNET slscva.ca.sunycentral.edu ❱ wait for the prompt username ❱ enter CORTL_NETOPAC

SUNY College—Oswego: United States NY *MULTILIS*
TELNET slscva.ca.sunycentral.edu ❱ wait for the prompt username ❱ enter OSWEGO_NETOPAC

SUNY Farmingdale: United States NY *MULTILIS*
TELNET snyfarve.cc.farmingdale.edu ❱ wait for the prompt Username ❱ enter FARM_OPACN

SUNY Health Science Center—Syracuse: United States *MULTILIS*
TELNET slscva.ca.sunycentral.edu ❱ wait for the prompt Username ❱ enter CORTL_NETOPAC

SUNY Hudson Valley Community College: United States NY *MULTILIS*
TELNET splavd.cc.plattsburgh.edu ❱ wait for the prompt Username ❱ enter HVC_OPACX

SUNY Institute of Technology—Utica/Rome: United States NY *UNICORN*
TELNET unicorn.sunyit.edu ❱ wait for the prompt login ❱ enter remote

SUNY Maritime Academy: United States NY *MULTILIS*
TELNET slscva.ca.sunycentral.edu

SUNY—Albany: United States NY *GEAC ADVANCE*
TELNET library.albany.edu ❱ wait for the prompt login ❱ enter opac ❱ wait for the prompt Password ❱ press ↵

SUNY—Brockport: United States *DYNIX*
TELNET acspr1.acs.brockport.edu ❱ wait for the prompt Login ❱ enter library ❱ wait for the prompt Password? ❱ enter drake ❱ enter ? for Help

SUNY—College at Buffalo: United States NY *INNOPAC*
TELNET snybufac.cs.snybuf.edu ❱ wait for the prompt login ❱ enter library

SUNY—Fredonia: United States NY *PALS*
TELNET library.fredonia.edu No login required

SUNY—Stony Brook: United States NY *NOTIS*
TN3270 ccvm.sunysb.edu ❱ tab to COMMAND ===> ❱ enter STARS

Susquehanna University: United States *INNOPAC*
TELNET ben.susqu.edu ❱ wait for the prompt login ❱ enter library

Swarthmore College: United States *INNOPAC*
TELNET tripod.brynmawr.edu ❱ wait for the prompt login ❱ enter library

Swedish Medical Center Library: United States (Access via **CARL**)

Swedish University of Agricultural Sciences Libraries (LUKAS): Sweden *custom*

TELNET lukas.slu.se ◗ wait for the prompt login ◗ enter slubib

TELNET upnod.slu.se ◗ wait for the prompt Enter address ◗ enter lr

Sweet Briar College: United States *DYNIX*

TELNET leo.lion.edu ◗ wait for the prompt login ◗ enter sblib

Swinburne University of Technology: Australia *DYNIX*

TELNET ollie.xx.swin.oz.au ◗ wait for the prompt login ◗ enter pacnet

Swiss National Library: HELVETICAT: Switzerland *VTLS*

TELNET helveticat.snl.ch ◗ wait for the prompt HELVETICAT ◗ enter hello internet,user.clas01 ◗ wait for the prompt that ends in Passwort eingeben ◗ enter SNL

SWITCH Consortium—Milwaukee: United States *INNOPAC*

TELNET aslan.stritch.edu ◗ wait for the prompt login ◗ enter library

Taiwan Provincial Library—Taichung: Taiwan *DYNIX*

TELNET 192.192.47.120 ◗ wait for the prompt login ◗ enter library ◗ wait for the prompt Select or type <OFF> ◗ enter 4 for English VT100

Tata Institute: India *custom*

TELNET library.tifr.res.in ◗ wait for the prompt login ◗ enter library

Technical University of Budapest: Hungary *custom*

TELNET tulibb.kkt.bme.hu ◗ wait for the prompt Username ◗ enter ALEPH

Technical University of Nova Scotia: Canada *GEAC*

TELNET novanet.dal.ca ◗ wait for the prompt login ◗ enter opac ◗ wait for the prompt Password ◗ press ↵

Technion: Israel (Access via **Hebrew University**)

Technische Universitaet Berlin: Germany *custom*

TELNET wd0ko.ww.tu-berlin.de ◗ wait for the prompt login ◗ enter wiwidok ◗ press ↵

Technische Universiteit Eindhoven: The Netherlands *custom*

TELNET vb2.libr.tue.nl ◗ wait for the prompt Username ◗ enter INTERVUBIS

Technischen Universitaet Braunschweig: Germany *custom*

TELNET allegro-x.biblio.etc.tu-bs.de ◗ wait for the prompt login ◗ enter opac ◗ wait for the prompt Password ◗ enter opac

Technischen Universitaet Wien: Austria (Access via **Austrian Academic Library Network**)

Tel Aviv University: Israel (Access via **Hebrew University**)

Temple University Dental/Allied Health/Pharmacy/Health Sciences Center Library: United States (Access via **HSLC HealthNET Health Sciences Information Network**)

Tennessee Technological University: United States TN *DRA*

TELNET atlas.tntech.edu ◗ wait for the prompt Username ◗ enter PAC

Terra Community College, Ohio: United States OH *INNOPAC*

TELNET info.terra.cc.oh.us ◗ wait for the prompt login ◗ enter library ◗ wait for the prompt Password ◗ enter library

Texas A&M University: United States TX *NOTIS*

TELNET panam2.panam.edu ◗ wait for the prompt Username ◗ enter PACKEY

TN3270 `tamvm1.tamu.edu` ◗ tab to COMMAND ===> ◗ enter `dial vtam` ◗ wait for next screen ◗ enter `NOTIS`

TELNET `venus.tamu.edu` ◗ wait for the prompt `Username` ◗ enter `vtam`

Texas A&M University—Corpus Christi: United States TX *INNOPAC*

TELNET `portal.tamucc.edu` ◗ wait for the prompt `login` ◗ enter `library`

Texas Christian University: United States TX *DRA*

TELNET `lib.is.tcu.edu` ◗ wait for the prompt `Username` ◗ enter `TCUCAT`

Texas Health Science Libraries Consortium: United States *UNICORN*

TELNET `ils.library.tmc.edu` ◗ wait for the prompt `login` ◗ enter `texmed`

Texas Southern University: United States TX *GEAC*

TELNET `library.tsu.edu` ◗ press ↵

Texas State Agencies: United States TX *CLSI*

TELNET `panam2.panam.edu` ◗ wait for the prompt `Username` ◗ enter `packey`

TELNET `gabi.tsl.texas.gov` ◗ wait for the prompt `login` ◗ enter `PUBLIC`

Texas Tech University: United States TX *DRA*

TELNET `panam2.panam.edu` ◗ wait for the prompt `Username` ◗ enter `PACKEY`

TELNET `ttacs3.ttu.edu` ◗ wait for the prompt `Username` ◗ enter `PACKEY`

Texas Woman's University: United States TX *GEAC ADVANCE*

TELNET `twu.edu` ◗ wait for the prompt `Username` ◗ enter `iris`

Thames Valley University: United Kingdom *BLCMP*

TELNET `tvutalis.tvu.ac.uk` ◗ wait for the prompt `login` ◗ enter `opac` ◗ wait for the prompt `Password` ◗ enter `library`

Three Oaks Township Library: United States (Access via **West Michigan Information Network**)

Three Rivers System: United States (Access via **MARMOT Library Network**)

Tilburg University: The Netherlands *custom*

TELNET `kublib.kub.nl` ◗ wait for the prompt `Username` ◗ enter `KUBGIDS`

Tompkins—Cortland Community College: United States *MULTILIS*

TELNET `slscva.ca.sunycentral.edu` ◗ wait for the prompt `username` ◗ enter `TCC_NETOPAC`

Touro College School of Law: United States *INNOPAC*

TELNET `library.touro.edu` ◗ wait for the prompt `login` ◗ enter `library`

Towson State University: United States (Access via **University of Maryland Library System**)

Trent University: Canada *DRA*

TELNET `babel.trentu.ca` ◗ wait for the prompt `Username` ◗ enter `TOPCAT`

Trevecca Nazarene College: United States *DRA*

TELNET `maclib.trevecca.edu` ◗ wait for the prompt `Username` ◗ enter `MACKEY`

Triangle Research Libraries: United States *custom*

TELNET `librot1.lib.unc.edu` ◗ wait for the prompt `Username` ◗ enter `LIBRARY`

Trinidad State Jr. College: United States (Access via **CARL**)

Trinity Christian College: United States (Access via **ILLINET On-line Catalog**)

Trinity College—Dublin: Ireland *DYNIX*

TELNET `lib1.tcd.ie` ◗ wait for the prompt `login` ◗ enter `opac`

Triton College: United States (Access via **ILLINET On-line Catalog**)

Truckee Meadows Community College: United States (Access via **Nevada Academic Libraries Information System**)

Tulane University, Louisiana: United States *NOTIS*
TELNET rs1.tcs.tulane.edu ◗ wait for the prompt login ◗ enter tulanet

Tulane University—Law Library: United States *INNOPAC*
TELNET library.law.tulane.edu ◗ wait for the prompt login ◗ enter library

Turners Falls, Colorado, Public Library: United States CO (Access via **CARL**)

Twente University: The Netherlands *custom*
TELNET utbiv3.civ.utwente.nl ◗ wait for the prompt Username ◗ enter PCTO ◗ wait for the prompt Vul in: ◗ enter ENG for English

Union College: United States *DRA*
TELNET conan.union.edu ◗ wait for the prompt Username ◗ enter minerva

United States Air Force Academy: United States *DYNIX*
TELNET kestrel.usafa.af.mil ◗ wait for the prompt login ◗ enter library

United States Government Printing Office: United States (Access via **Georgia On-Line Library Information System**)

United States Military Academy: United States *INNOPAC*
TELNET library.usma.edu ◗ at the first prompt enter library

United States Naval Academy: United States *INNOPAC*
TELNET library.nadn.navy.mil No login required

Universidad Autonoma de Madrid: Spain *LIBERTAS*
TELNET olmo.bibcen.uam.es ◗ wait for the prompt Username ◗ enter BIBLIOTECA

Universidad Autonoma de Mexico: Mexico *custom*
TELNET serlunam.dgbiblio.unam.mx ◗ wait for the prompt login ◗ enter opac ◗ wait for the prompt Password ◗ enter opac

Universidad Carlos III: Spain *custom*
TELNET sauron.uc3m.es ◗ wait for the prompt login ◗ enter ebla ◗ wait for the prompt Password ◗ enter uc3mes

Universidad Catolica Andres Bello: Venezuela (Access via **Biblioteca Nacional de Venezuela**)

Universidad Central de Venezuela: Venezuela (Access via **Biblioteca Nacional de Venezuela**)

Universidad Complutense de Madrid: Spain *LIBERTAS*
TELNET eucmvx.sim.ucm.es ◗ wait for the prompt Username ◗ enter biblioteca

Universidad de Alcala: Spain *LIBERTAS*
TELNET alcala.alcala.es ◗ wait for the prompt Username ◗ enter BIBLOS

Universidad de Concepcion: Chile *DYNIX*
TELNET cisne.bib.udec.cl ◗ wait for the prompt login ◗ enter opac

Universidad de Los Andes: Venezuela *custom*
TELNET gallego.bieci.ula.ve ◗ wait for the prompt login ◗ enter sari

Universidad Nacional de Colombia: *custom*
TELNET biblioteca.campus.unal.edu.co ◗ wait for the prompt login ◗ enter un

Universidad Nacional Experimental de Tachira: Venezuela (Access via **Biblioteca Nacional de Venezuela**)

Universidad Pompeu i Fabra: Spain *VTLS*

TELNET `sahara.upf.es` ❿ wait for the prompt `login` ❿ enter `biblio`

Universidade de Sao Paulo: Brazil *custom*

TELNET `bee08.cce.usp.br` ❿ wait for the prompt `login` ❿ enter `dedalus`

Universidade Federal do Rio Grande do Sol: Brazil *custom*

TELNET `asterix.ufrgs.br` ❿ wait for the prompt `login` ❿ enter `sabibib`

Universita de Lecce: Italy *custom*

TELNET `siba1.unile.it` ❿ wait for the prompt `login` ❿ enter `isis`

Universitaet Bamberg: Germany *custom*

TELNET `ubgx2.unibib.uni-bamberg.de` ❿ wait for the prompt `login` ❿ enter `opace`

Universitaet Clausthal: Germany *Pica*

TELNET `opac.ub.tu-clausthal.de` ❿ wait for the prompt `login` ❿ enter `opc`

Universitaet des Saarlandes: Germany *custom*

TELNET `mars.rz.uni-sb.de` ❿ wait for the prompt `login` ❿ enter `opac`

Universitaet Duesseldorf: Germany *custom*

TELNET `opac.ub.uni-duesseldorf.de` ❿ wait for the prompt `login` ❿ enter `opac`

Universitaet Essen: Germany *custom*

TELNET `opac.bibl.uni-essen.de` ❿ wait for the prompt `login` ❿ enter `opac`

Universitaet Freiburg: Germany *custom*

TELNET `opac.ub.uni-freiburg.de` ❿ wait for the prompt `login` ❿ enter `opacvt` ❿ wait for the prompt `Password` ❿ enter `opacvt`

Universitaet für Bildungswissenschaften, Klagenfurt: Austria (Access via **Austrian Academic Library Network**)

Universitaet für Bodenkultur: Austria (Access via **Austrian Academic Library Network**)

Universitaet Goettingen: Germany *custom*

TELNET `opac.sub.gwdg.de` ❿ wait for the prompt `Username` ❿ enter `OPC`

Universitaet Koeln: Germany *custom*

TELNET `hardthuegel.ub.uni-koeln.de` ❿ wait for the prompt `login` ❿ enter `opac`

Universitaet Marburg: Germany *custom*

TELNET `vaxub1.ub.uni-marburg.de` ❿ wait for the prompt `Username` ❿ enter `OPC`

Universitaetsbibliothek Erlangen-Nuernberg: Germany *custom*

TELNET `faui43.informatik.uni-erlangen.de` ❿ wait for the prompt `login` ❿ enter `gi`

TELNET `elis:elis.uni-erlangen.de` ❿ wait for the prompt `login` ❿ enter `elis`

Universitaetsbibliothek Tuebingen: Germany *custom*

TELNET `opac.ub.uni-tuebingen.de` ❿ wait for the prompt `login` ❿ enter `opac` ❿ wait for the prompt `Password` ❿ enter `opac`

Universitaire de Nice: France *GEAC ADVANCE*

TELNET `pharos.unice.fr` ❿ wait for the prompt `login` ❿ enter `bunsa`

Universitaire Fakulteiten St. Ignatius Antwerpen: Belgium (Access via **University of Antwerp**)

Universitaria de Cordoba: Spain *DOBIS/LIBIS*

TELNET `lucano.uco.es` ◗ wait for the prompt `login` ◗ enter `libis`

Universitat Autonoma de Barcelona: Spain *VTLS*

TELNET `babel.uab.es` ◗ wait for the prompt `Entreu HELLO UAB.BIB` ◗ enter `HELLO UAB.BIB`

Universitat de Barcelona: Spain *VTLS*

TELNET `tieta.bib.ub.es` ◗ wait for the prompt `Entreu HELLO BUB.BIB` ◗ enter `hello bub.bib`

Universitat de les Illes Balears: Spain *LIBERTAS*

TELNET `vx4000.uib.es` ◗ wait for the prompt `Username` ◗ enter `BIBLIOTECA1`

Universitat de Lleida: Spain *VTLS*

TELNET `biblio.udl.es` ◗ wait for the prompt `Entreu HELLO BIBLIO.UDL` ◗ enter `hello biblio.udl`

Universitat de Valencia: Spain *DOBIS/LIBIS*

TN3270 `mvs.ci.uv.es` ◗ wait for the prompt `Application` ◗ enter `bluv` ◗ enter Function Key PF1

Universitat Jaume I: Spain *VTLS*

TELNET `violant-telnet.uji.es` ◗ wait for the prompt `MPE XL` ◗ enter `hello,user.clas01`

Universitat Politecnica de Catalunya: Spain *VTLS*

TELNET `tahat.upc.es` ◗ wait for the prompt `Username` ◗ enter `biblioteca`

Universitat Pompeu Fabra: Spain *VTLS*

TELNET `sahara.upf.es` ◗ wait for the prompt `login` ◗ enter `biblio`

Universitat Rovira i Virgili: Spain *VTLS*

TELNET `biblio.urv.es` ◗ wait for the prompt `MPE XL` ◗ enter `hello gopher,ref.clas01`

Universite de Moncton—Bibliotheque Champlain: Canada *GEAC*

TELNET `139.103.2.2` ◗ wait for the prompt that ends in `SERVICE?` ◗ enter `champ`

Universite de Montreal: Canada *GEAC ADVANCE*

TELNET `atrium.bib.umontreal.ca` ◗ wait for the prompt `login` ◗ enter `public`

Universite de Pau et des Pays de l'Adour: France *custom*

TELNET `crisv2.univ-pau.fr` ◗ wait for the prompt `login` ◗ enter `grace`

Universite de Sherbrooke: Canada *MULTILIS*

TELNET `catalo.biblio.usherb.ca` ◗ wait for the prompt `login` ◗ enter `biblio`

Universite Libre de Bruxelles: Belgium *DOBIS/LIBIS*

TELNET `bib1.ulb.ac.be` ◗ wait for the prompt `login` ◗ enter `cible`

Universiti Teknologi Malaysia: Malaysia *DYNIX*

TELNET `psz.utm.my` ◗ wait for the prompt `login` ◗ enter `opac`

University Center—Tulsa: United States *DRA*

TELNET `192.234.12.3` ◗ wait for the prompt `Username` ◗ enter `LIBRARY`

University College of Cape Breton: Canada *GEAC*

TELNET `novanet.dal.ca` ◗ wait for the prompt `login` ◗ enter `opac` ◗ wait for the prompt `Password` ◗ press ↵

University College of London: United Kingdom *LIBERTAS*

TELNET `lib.ucl.ac.uk` ◗ wait for the prompt `Username` ◗ enter `LIBRARY`

University College of Swansea: United Kingdom *LIBERTAS*
TELNET `lib.swan.ac.uk` ◗ wait for the prompt `Username` ◗ enter `LIBRARY`

University College of the Cariboo: Canada *BUCAT*
TELNET `cariboo.bc.ca` ◗ wait for the prompt `Username` ◗ enter `CARCAT`

University College of the Fraser Valley: Canada *BUCAT*
TELNET `sumas.ucfv.bc.ca` ◗ wait for the prompt `Username` ◗ enter `FVCBUCAT`

University College—Cork: Ireland *DOBIS/LIBIS*
TELNET `vax1.ucc.ie` ◗ wait for the prompt `Userid` ◗ enter `LIBRARY`

University College—Dublin: Ireland *custom*
TELNET `pacx.ucd.ie` ◗ wait for the prompt `Which service do you require please?` ◗ enter `library`

University College—Galway: Ireland *DYNIX*
TELNET `library.ucg.ie` ◗ wait for the prompt `login` ◗ enter `library`

University Library of Limburg: Belgium (Access via **University of Antwerp**)

University of Abertay Dundee: United Kingdom *DYNIX*
TELNET `library.dct.ac.uk` ◗ wait for the prompt `login` ◗ enter `library`

University of Akron: United States OH *INNOPAC*
TELNET `library.uakron.edu` No login required
TELNET `mercury.lib.uakron.edu` No login required

University of Alabama: United States AL *NOTIS*
TN3270 `ua2mvs.ua.edu` ◗ wait for the prompt that ends in `desired application` ◗ enter `library`

University of Alabama, Birmingham, Lister Hill Health —Sciences Library: United States AL *DYNIX*
TELNET `medicus.lhl.uab.edu` ◗ wait for the prompt `login` ◗ enter `lpub`

University of Alabama—Birmingham: United States *NOTIS*
TELNET `uabdpo.dpo.uab.edu` ◗ wait for the prompt `enter your terminal id` ◗ enter `56` ◗ wait for the prompt `LOGONID  ===>` ◗ press ↵

University of Alabama—Huntsville: United States *PALS*
TELNET `library.uah.edu` ◗ wait for the prompt `>` ◗ enter `HE` for Help

University of Alaska: United States AK *VTLS*
TELNET `gnosis.alaska.edu` ◗ wait for the prompt `:` ◗ enter `hello,user.gnosis`

University of Alberta: Canada *DRA*
TELNET `dra.library.ualberta.ca` ◗ wait for the prompt `Username` ◗ enter `GATE`

University of Antwerp: Belgium *custom*
TELNET `main.bib.uia.ac.be` No login required

University of Arizona: United States AZ *INNOPAC*
TELNET `sabio.arizona.edu` No login required
TELNET `sabio.library.arizona.edu` No login required

University of Arkansas—Fayetteville: United States *INNOPAC*
TELNET `library.uark.edu` ◗ wait for the prompt `login` ◗ enter `library`

University of Arkansas—Little Rock: United States AR *DRA Gateway*
TELNET `library.ualr.edu` ◗ wait for the prompt `Username` ◗ enter `LIBRARY`

University of Arkansas—Little Rock/Pulaski County Law Library: United States *INNOPAC*
 TELNET `themis.law.ualr.edu` No login required

University of Arkansas—Medical Sciences Library: United States AR *CLSI*
 TELNET `uamslib.uams.edu` ▶ wait for the prompt `login` ▶ enter uams ▶ wait for the prompt `Password` ▶ enter `lib-cat`

University of Arkansas—Monticello: United States *DRA Gateway*
 TELNET `library.uamont.edu` ▶ wait for the prompt `Username` ▶ enter PAC

University of Auckland: New Zealand *NOTIS*
 TELNET `aucat.auckland.ac.nz` ▶ wait for the prompt `Username` ▶ enter AUCAT

University of Baltimore: United States MD (Access via **University of Maryland Library System**)

University of Baltimore Law: United States MD (Access via **University of Maryland Library System**)

University of Bath: United Kingdom *URICA*
 TELNET `solomon.bath.ac.uk`

University of Birmingham: United Kingdom *BLCMP*
 TELNET `lib.bham.ac.uk` No login required

University of Brighton: United Kingdom *BLCMP*
 TELNET `wwwx25.niss.ac.uk` No login required

University of Bristol: United Kingdom *LIBERTAS*
 TELNET `lib.bris.ac.uk` ▶ wait for the prompt `Username` ▶ enter LIBRARY

University of British Columbia: Canada *custom*
 TELNET `library.ubc.ca` ▶ wait for the prompt that ends in `Enter your Library id (or HELP)` ▶ press ↵

University of Bucharest: Romania *custom*
 TELNET `bcub.ro` ▶ wait for the prompt `Username` ▶ enter OPAC

University of Buffalo: United States *NOTIS*
 TELNET `bison.cc.buffalo.edu` No login required

University of Calabria: Italy *custom*
 TELNET `unical.fis.unical.it` ▶ wait for the prompt `Username` ▶ enter UTENTI

University of Calgary: Canada *custom*
 TELNET `develnet.ucalgary.ca` ▶ wait for the prompt `Request` ▶ enter `library`

University of California (MELVYL): United States CA *custom*
 TELNET `melvyl.ucop.edu` ▶ wait for the prompt `TERMINAL?` ▶ enter VT100 if VT100 ▶ press ↵

University of California and California State: United States CA (See **MELVYL**)

University of California—Berkeley: United States CA *custom*
 TELNET `gopac.berkeley.edu` ▶ wait for the prompt `Enter Choice` ▶ enter GOPAC

University of California—Berkeley Boalt Hall Law Library: United States CA *INNOPAC*
 TELNET `lawcat.law.berkeley.edu` ▶ wait for the prompt `login` ▶ enter `library`

University of California—Davis, Law Library: United States CA *INNOPAC*
 TELNET `innopac.ucdavis.edu` ▶ wait for the prompt `login` ▶ enter `guest` ▶ wait for the prompt `Password` ▶ enter `guest`

University of California—Irvine: United States CA *INNOPAC*
TELNET `antpac.lib.uci.edu` ▶ wait for the prompt `login` ▶ enter `library`

University of California—Santa Cruz: United States CA *INNOPAC*
TELNET `library.ucsc.edu` ▶ wait for the prompt `login` ▶ enter `library`

University of Canberra: Australia *URICA*
TELNET `library.canberra.edu.au` ▶ wait for the prompt `login` ▶ enter `uclid`

University of Canterbury: New Zealand *URICA*
TELNET `cantva.canterbury.ac.nz` ▶ wait for the prompt `Username` ▶ enter `opac` ▶ wait for the prompt that ends in Connected ▶ press ↵

University of Central Florida: United States FL (Access via **Florida State University**)

University of Central Lancashire: United Kingdom *DYNIX*
TELNET `lib.uclan.ac.uk` ▶ wait for the prompt `login` ▶ enter `opac`

University of Central Oklahoma: United States OK *NOTIS*
TELNET `aix0.ucok.edu` ▶ wait for the prompt `TS>` ▶ press ↵

University of Chicago: United States IL *custom*
TELNET `illinet.aiss.uiuc.edu` ▶ wait for the prompt that ends in `to  login` ▶ enter `b`

University of Cincinnati: United States OH *INNOPAC*
TELNET `cat.ohiolink.edu` ▶ wait for the prompt `login` ▶ enter `ohiolink`
TELNET `uclid.uc.edu` No login required

University of Colorado—Boulder: United States CO (Access via **CARL**)

University of Colorado—Health Sciences Center: United States CO *INNOPAC*
TELNET `library.hsc.colorado.edu` ▶ wait for the prompt `login` ▶ enter `library`
TELNET `library.uchsc.edu` ▶ wait for the prompt `login` ▶ enter `impulse`

University of Colorado—Law Library: United States CO *INNOPAC*
TELNET `lawpac.colorado.edu` No login required

University of Connecticut—Health Center Library: United States CT *NOTIS*
TELNET `lyman.uchc.edu` ▶ wait for the prompt `login` ▶ enter `library`

University of Connecticut—Law School Library: United States CT *INNOPAC*
TELNET `137.99.202.99` ▶ wait for the prompt `login` ▶ enter `library`

University of Crete: Greece *custom*
TELNET `triton.iesl.forth.gr` ▶ wait for the prompt `login` ▶ enter `library`

University of Dallas: United States TX *DYNIX*
TELNET `library.udallas.edu` ▶ wait for the prompt `login` ▶ enter `dial`

University of Dayton: United States *INNOPAC*
TELNET `library.udayton.edu` No login required

University of Delaware: United States DE *NOTIS*
TELNET `delcat.udel.edu` No login required

University of Dundee: United Kingdom *DYNIX*
TELNET `libb.dundee.ac.uk` ▶ wait for the prompt `login` ▶ enter `library`

University of Electro-Communications: Japan *custom*

TELNET `baloo.cc.uec.ac.jp` ◗ wait for the prompt `login` ◗ enter `limepub` ◗ wait for the prompt `BHV9f` `=` ◗ enter 9 for English

University of Essex: United Kingdom *INNOPAC*

TELNET `serlib0.essex.ac.uk` ◗ wait for the prompt `login` ◗ enter `library`

University of Exeter: United Kingdom *LIBERTAS*

TELNET `lib.ex.ac.uk` ◗ wait for the prompt `Username` ◗ enter `LIBRARY`

University of Florida: United States FL (Access via **Florida State University**)

University of Georgia and Georgia College: United States GA *custom*

TELNET `gsvms2.cc.gasou.edu` ◗ wait for the prompt `Username` ◗ enter `INFO`

TN3270 `uga.cc.uga.edu` ◗ tab to COMMAND `===>` ◗ enter `dial vtam` ◗ wait for the prompt `===>` ◗ enter `L`

University of Georgia—Athens: United States GA (Access via **Georgia On-Line Library Information System**)

University of Georgia—Law Library: United States *INNOPAC*

TELNET `lawlib.lawsch.uga.edu` No login required

University of Gothenburg: Sweden *VTLS*

TELNET `gunda.ub.gu.se` No login required

University of Groningen: The Netherlands *custom*

TELNET `129.125.19.10` ◗ wait for the prompt `Username` ◗ enter `OPC`

University of Guam: United States *DYNIX*

TELNET `uog9.uog.edu` ◗ wait for the prompt `login` ◗ enter `ocean`

University of Guelph: Canada *custom*

TELNET `searchme.uoguelph.ca` ◗ wait for the prompt `login` ◗ enter `searchme`

University of Hanover: Germany *custom*

TELNET `has12.tib.uni-hannover.de` ◗ wait for the prompt `Username` ◗ enter `OPC`

University of Hartford: United States CT *DRA*

TELNET `ipgate.hartford.edu` ◗ wait for the prompt `login` ◗ enter `netvax::`

University of Hawaii—Honolulu: United States HI *custom*

TELNET `victor.umd.edu` ◗ wait for the prompt `Enter Choice` ◗ enter `pac`

TELNET `pac.carl.org` ◗ wait for the prompt `Enter Choice` ◗ enter `PAC`

University of Hong Kong: Hong Kong *DRA*

TELNET `hkulbr.hku.hk` ◗ wait for the prompt `Username` ◗ enter `HKULOPAC`

University of Houston: United States TX *INNOPAC*

TELNET `uhopac.lib.uh.edu` No login required

TELNET `library.uh.edu` No login required

University of Huddersfield: United Kingdom *BLCMP*

TELNET `library.hud.ac.uk` ◗ wait for the prompt `login` ◗ enter `library`

University of Iceland: Iceland *LIBERTAS*

TELNET `saga.rhi.hi.is` ◗ wait for the prompt `Username` ◗ enter `BOKASAFN`

University of Idaho: United States Idaho *CARL*

TELNET `ida.lib.uidaho.edu` ◗ wait for the prompt `destination?` ◗ press ↵

University of Illinois—Champaign/Urbana: United States IL *custom*
TELNET `illinet.aiss.uiuc.edu` ❱ wait for the prompt that ends in `to login` ❱ enter b

University of Illinois—Medical: United States IL (Access via **ILLINET On-line Catalog**)

University of Illinois—Urbana: United States (Access via **ILLINET On-line Catalog**)

University of Iowa: United States *NOTIS*
TELNET `oasis.uiowa.edu` ❱ wait for the prompt that ends in `'?' for MENU` ❱ enter ?

University of Kansas Medical Library System: United States MO *INNOPAC*
TELNET `kumclib.mc.ukans.edu` No login required

University of Kentucky: United States KT *custom*
TN3270 `ukcc.uky.edu` ❱ wait for the prompt that ends in `TO BEGIN SESSION` ❱ press ↵

University of Kent—Canterbury: United Kingdom *CATS*
TELNET `cats.ukc.ac.uk` No login required

University of Kings College: Canada *GEAC*
TELNET `novanet.dal.ca` ❱ wait for the prompt `login` ❱ enter `opac` ❱ wait for the prompt `Password` ❱ press ↵

University of Lethbridge: Canada *INNOPAC*
TELNET `eureka.uleth.ca` ❱ wait for the prompt `login` ❱ enter `library`

University of Liege: Belgium *custom*
TELNET `bibli.ulg.ac.be` ❱ wait for the prompt `login` ❱ enter `bibli`

University of London Serials Database: United Kingdom *LIBERTAS*
TELNET `flcs.ull.ac.uk` ❱ wait for the prompt `Username` ❱ enter `LIBRARY`

University Of Lowell: United States *DRA*
TELNET `libvax.ulowell.edu` ❱ wait for the prompt `Username` ❱ enter `LIBRARY`

University of Macau: Macau *DYNIX*
TELNET `umaclib1.umac.mo` ❱ wait for the prompt `login` ❱ enter `netpub`

University of Maine Library System: United States ME *INNOPAC*
TELNET `ursus.maine.edu` No login required

University of Maine—Augusta: United States ME (Access via **University of Maine Library System**)

University of Maine—Farmington: United States ME (Access via **University of Maine Library System**)

University of Maine—Fort Kent: United States ME (Access via **University of Maine Library System**)

University of Maine—Machias: United States ME (Access via **University of Maine Library System**)

University of Maine—Presque Isle: United States ME (Access via **University of Maine Library System**)

University of Maine—School of Law: United States ME (Access via **University of Maine Library System**)

University of Manchester Institute of Science and Technology: United Kingdom *BLCMP*
TELNET `joule.li.umist.ac.uk` ❱ wait for the prompt `login` ❱ enter `joule` ❱ wait for the prompt `Password` ❱ enter `library`

University of Manitoba Libraries: Canada *DRA Gateway*
TELNET `BISON:umopac.umanitoba.ca` ❱ wait for the prompt `Username` ❱ enter `BISON`
TELNET `bison.umanitoba.ca` ❱ wait for the prompt `Username` ❱ enter `BISON`

University of Maribor: Slovenia *custom*

TELNET rcum.uni-mb.si ▶ wait for the prompt Username ▶ enter OPAC ▶ wait for the prompt that ends in E — English ▶ enter E for English

University of Maryland Library System: United States MD *custom*

TELNET victor.umd.edu ▶ wait for the prompt Enter Choice ▶ enter PAC

University of Maryland—Baltimore County: United States MD (Access via **University of Maryland Library System**)

University of Maryland—College Park: United States MD (Access via **University of Maryland Library System**)

University of Maryland—Eastern Shore: United States MD (Access via **University of Maryland Library System**)

University of Maryland—Health Sciences Library: United States MD *DRA*

TELNET hsl.ab.umd.edu ▶ wait for the prompt Username ▶ enter PAC

University of Maryland—Law Library: United States MD (Access via **University of Maryland Library System**)

University of Maryland—University College: United States (Access via **University of Maryland Library System**)

University of Massachusetts—Amherst: United States (Access via **Boston Library Consortium**)

University of Massachusetts—Boston: United States MA *ULISYS*

TELNET libra.cc.umb.edu ▶ wait for the prompt Username ▶ enter CATALOG
TELNET libra.cc.umb.edu ▶ wait for the prompt Username ▶ enter CATALOG

University of Massachusetts—Dartmouth: United States MA *MULTILIS*

TELNET library.umassd.edu ▶ wait for the prompt Username ▶ enter LIBRARY

University of Massachusetts—Medical Center Library: United States MA (Access via **CARL**)

University of Medicine and Dentistry of New Jersey: United States NJ *custom*

TELNET library.umdnj.edu ▶ wait for the prompt Username ▶ enter LIBRARY

University of Melbourne: Australia *INNOPAC*

TELNET cat.lib.unimelb.edu.au ▶ wait for the prompt login ▶ enter library

University of Miami: United States FL *INNOPAC*

TELNET stacks.library.miami.edu No login required

University of Miami—Medical Library: United States FL *INNOPAC*

TELNET callcat.med.miami.edu ▶ wait for the prompt login ▶ enter library

University of Michigan: United States MI *NOTIS*

TELNET thorplus.lib.purdue.edu ▶ wait for the prompt login ▶ enter catnet
TN3270 lib.cc.purdue.edu ▶ wait for the prompt Database Selection ▶ enter REMOTE
TELNET mirlyn.merit.edu No login required

University of Michigan—Business School: United States MI *INNOPAC*

TELNET lib.bus.umich.edu ▶ wait for the prompt login ▶ enter mentor

University of Michigan—Dearborn: United States *INNOPAC*

TELNET wizard.umd.umich.edu ▶ wait for the prompt login ▶ enter library

University of Michigan—Flint: United States MI *NOTIS*

TELNET mirlyn.merit.edu ▶ wait for the prompt that ends in to continue ▶ press ↵ ▶ wait for the prompt Database Selection ▶ enter FLNT

University of Michigan—Law Library: United States MI *INNOPAC*

TELNET lexcalibur.lib.law.umich.edu No login required

University of Minnesota: United States MN *NOTIS*

TN3270 `lib.cc.purdue.edu` ◗ wait for the prompt `Database Selection` ◗ enter REMOTE

TELNET `thorplus.lib.purdue.edu` ◗ wait for the prompt `login` ◗ enter `catnet`

TN3270 `pubinfo.ais.umn.edu` No login required

TELNET `pubinfo.ais.umn.edu` No login required

TELNET `lumina.lib.umn.edu` No login required

University of Minnesota—Duluth: United States MN *UNICORN*

TELNET `lib.d.umn.edu` ◗ wait for the prompt `login` ◗ enter `libpub` ◗ wait for the prompt `Password` ◗ enter `library`

University of Miskolc: Hungary *custom*

TELNET `gold.uni-miskolc.hu` ◗ wait for the prompt `login` ◗ enter `miko`

University of Mississippi: United States MS *INNOPAC*

TELNET `lib1.lib.olemiss.edu` ◗ wait for the prompt `login` ◗ enter `olemiss`

University of Missouri—Columbia: United States MO *custom*

TN3270 `umcvmb.missouri.edu` ◗ tab to COMMAND ===> ◗ enter `dial vtam` ◗ wait for the prompt that ends in to disconnect ◗ enter `libcics`

University of Missouri—Rolla: United States MO *custom*

TN3270 `umrvmb.umr.edu` ◗ tab to COMMAND ===> ◗ enter `dial vtam` ◗ wait for the prompt `Enter Application Name` ◗ enter LUMIN

University of Missouri—St. Louis: United States MO *custom*

TN3270 `umslvma.umsl.edu` ◗ tab to COMMAND ===> ◗ enter `dial vtam` ◗ wait for the prompt that ends in ENTER VTAM LOGON ◗ enter `libcics`

University of Montana: United States MT *DYNIX*

TELNET `lib.umt.edu` ◗ wait for the prompt `login` ◗ enter `griznet` for UM Mansfield Library and IMS

University of Natal—Durban: South Africa *URICA*

TELNET `library.und.ac.za` ◗ wait for the prompt `login` ◗ enter `lib` ◗ wait for the prompt `Password` ◗ press ↵

University of Nebraska: United States *INNOPAC*

TELNET `iris.unl.edu` ◗ wait for the prompt `login` ◗ enter `library`

University of Nebraska—Kearney: United States *INNOPAC*

TELNET `rosi.unk.edu` ◗ wait for the prompt `login` ◗ enter `library`

University of Nebraska—Lincoln: United States *INNOPAC*

TELNET `iris.unl.edu` ◗ wait for the prompt `login` ◗ enter `library`

University of Nebraska—Medical Center: United States NE *custom*

TELNET `library.unmc.edu` No login required

University of Nebraska—Omaha: United States *INNOPAC*

TELNET `genisys.unomaha.edu` ◗ wait for the prompt `login` ◗ enter `genisys`

University of Nevada—Las Vegas: United States NV (Access via **Nevada Academic Libraries Information System**)

University of Nevada—Reno Library: United States NV (Access via **Nevada Academic Libraries Information System**)

University of New Brunswick: Canada *UNICORN*

TELNET `quest.unb.ca` ◗ wait for the prompt `login` ◗ enter `quest`

University of New England: Australia *VTLS*

TELNET `opac.une.oz.au` ◗ wait for the prompt `login` ◗ enter `pac`

TELNET `pac.une.edu.au` ▶ wait for the prompt `login` ▶ enter `pac`

University of New England—Northern Rivers: Australia *GEAC*

TELNET `unilinc.edu.au` ▶ wait for the prompt `login` ▶ enter `unilinc`
TELNET `pac.une.edu.au` ▶ wait for the prompt `login` ▶ enter `unilinc`

University of New England—Orange Agricultural College: Australia (Access via **New South Wales Libraries**)

University of New Hampshire: United States NH *INNOPAC*

TELNET `library.unh.edu` No login required

University of New Mexico: United States NM *custom*

TELNET `tome.unm.edu` ▶ wait for the prompt `login` ▶ enter `library`

University of New Mexico—Law School: United States NM *INNOPAC*

TELNET `library.unm.edu` ▶ wait for the prompt `login` ▶ enter `library`

University of New Mexico—Law School Library: United States NM *INNOPAC*

TELNET `libros2.unm.edu` ▶ wait for the prompt `login` ▶ enter `library` ▶ wait for the prompt `Password` ▶ enter `library`

University of New Mexico—Medical Center Library: United States *INNOPAC*

TELNET `biblio.unm.edu` ▶ wait for the prompt `login` ▶ enter `library`

University of New South Wales: Australia *custom*

TELNET `unilinc.edu.au` ▶ wait for the prompt `login` ▶ enter `UNILINC`

University of New South Wales—College of Fine Arts: Australia (Access via **New South Wales Libraries**)

University of Newcastle: Australia *INNOPAC*

TELNET `bliss.newcastle.edu.au` ▶ wait for the prompt `Username` ▶ enter `LIBRARY`

University of Newcastle—Upon Tyne: United Kingdom *GEAC ADVANCE*

TELNET `library.ncl.ac.uk` ▶ wait for the prompt `login` ▶ enter `netopac`

University of North Carolina Coastal Library Consortium: United States NC *INNOPAC*

TELNET `uncclc.coast.uncwil.edu` No login required

University of North Carolina—Asheville: United States NC *INNOPAC*

TELNET `uncavx.unca.edu` ▶ wait for the prompt `Username` ▶ enter `HIDENSEEK`

University of North Carolina—Chapel Hill: United States *DRA*

TELNET `unclib.lib.unc.edu` ▶ wait for the prompt `Username` ▶ enter `LIBRARY`

University of North Carolina—Charlotte: United States *VTLS*

TELNET `aladdin.uncc.edu` No login required

University of North Carolina—Greensboro: United States NC *DRA*

TELNET `steffi.uncg.edu` ▶ wait for the prompt `Username` ▶ enter `JACLIN`

University of North Florida: United States FL (Access via **Florida State University**)

University of North Texas: United States TX *VTLS*

TELNET `library.unt.edu` ▶ wait for the prompt that ends in `to logon to system` ▶ enter `HELLO USER.LIB`

University of North Wales—Bangor: United Kingdom *INNOPAC*

TELNET `library.bangor.ac.uk` No login required

University of Northern British Columbia: Canada *DRA Gateway*

TELNET `library.unbc.edu` ▶ wait for the prompt `Username` ▶ enter `LIBRARY`

University of Northern Colorado: United States CO (Access via **CARL**)

University of Northern Iowa: United States IA *INNOPAC*

TELNET `starmaster.uni.edu` ◗ wait for the prompt `Choose SERVICE` ◗ enter 1 for UNISTAR

University of Notre Dame: United States *NOTIS*

TELNET `thorplus.lib.purdue.edu` ◗ wait for the prompt `login` ◗ enter `catnet`

TELNET `irishmvs.cc.nd.edu` ◗ wait for the prompt `Enter Command` ◗ enter `library`

University of Oklahoma: United States *NOTIS*

TN3270 `uokmvsa.backbone.uoknor.edu` ◗ tab to `APPLICATION` ◗ enter `olin`

University of Oregon: United States OR *INNOPAC*

TELNET `janus.uoregon.edu` No login required

University of Osnabrueck: Germany *custom*

TELNET `opac.ub.uni-osnabrueck.de` ◗ wait for the prompt `Username` ◗ enter OPC

University of Otago: New Zealand *DYNIX*

TELNET `libcat.otago.ac.nz` ◗ wait for the prompt `login` ◗ enter `libcat`

University of Ottawa: Canada *DYNIX*

TELNET `lib.uottawa.ca` ◗ wait for the prompt `==>` ◗ enter `pubmrt`

University of Pennsylvania: United States PA *NOTIS*

TELNET `pennlib.upenn.edu` No login required

University of Pennsylvania—Law School Library: United States PA *INNOPAC*

TELNET `lola.law.upenn.edu` ◗ wait for the prompt `login` ◗ enter `lola`

University of Pittsburgh: United States PA *NOTIS*

TELNET `gate.cis.pitt.edu` ◗ wait for the prompt `Service` ◗ enter PITTCAT

University of Plymouth: United Kingdom *LIBERTAS*

TELNET `lib.plym.ac.uk` ◗ wait for the prompt `Username` ◗ enter LIBRARY

University of Portland, Oregon: United States OR *INNOPAC*

TELNET `lib.uofport.edu` ◗ wait for the prompt `login` ◗ enter `search`

University of Puerto Rico: United States PR *NOTIS*

TELNET `136.145.2.10` ◗ wait for the prompt that ends in `TO BEGIN SESSION` ◗ press ↵

TELNET `ocsrisc.upr.clu.edu` ◗ wait for the prompt `TS` ◗ press ↵

University of Queensland: Australia *PALS*

TELNET `libsys.campus.uq.oz.au` ◗ wait for the prompt that ends in `type BE [return]` ◗ enter BE

TELNET `libsys.library.uq.oz.au` ◗ wait for the prompt that ends in `type BE [return]` ◗ enter BE

University of Redlands: United States *INNOPAC*

TELNET `library.uor.edu` ◗ wait for the prompt `login` ◗ enter `library`

University of Rhode Island: United States RI (Access via **Rhode Island Higher Education Library Information Network**)

University of Richmond: United States *DYNIX*

TELNET `whiz.urich.edu` ◗ wait for the prompt `login` ◗ enter `dupub`

University of Rochester: United States NY *GEAC*

TELNET `128.151.226.71` ◗ press ↵

TELNET `chester.cc.rochester.edu` ◗ press ↵

University of San Diego: United States CA *INNOPAC*
TELNET `sally.acusd.edu` ▶ wait for the prompt `login` ▶ enter `library`

University of Saskatchewan: Canada *INNOPAC*
TELNET `sundog.usask.ca` No login required

University of Scranton: United States *DRA*
TELNET `library.uofs.edu` ▶ wait for the prompt `Username` ▶ enter `LIBRARY`

University of South Florida: United States FL (Access via **Florida State University**)

University of Southern California Law Library: United States CA *INNOPAC*
TELNET `innopac.usc.edu` No login required

University of Southern Colorado: United States CO *DYNIX*
TELNET `starburst.uscolo.edu` ▶ wait for the prompt OK ▶ enter `Login Publ` ▶ wait for the prompt `Password?` ▶ enter USC

University of Southern Maine: United States ME (Access via **University of Maine Library System**)

University of Southern Mississippi: United States MS *GEAC ADVANCE*
TELNET `library.lib.usm.edu` ▶ wait for the prompt `login` ▶ enter `oscar`

University of Southern Queensland: Australia *VTLS*
TELNET `library.usq.edu.au` ▶ wait for the prompt MPE XL ▶ enter `hello libbie.vtls`

University of St. Thomas—Chaska Center: United States *DYNIX*
TELNET `host.clic.edu` ▶ wait for the prompt `login` ▶ enter `apac`

University of St. Thomas—O'Shaughnessy-Frey Library: United States *DYNIX*
TELNET `host.clic.edu` ▶ wait for the prompt `login` ▶ enter `apac`

University of Sunderland: United Kingdom *DYNIX*
TELNET `dynix.sunderland.ac.uk` ▶ wait for the prompt `login` ▶ enter `library` ▶ wait for the prompt `Password` ▶ enter `library`

University of Surrey: United Kingdom *custom*
TELNET `lib-serv.surrey.ac.uk` ▶ wait for the prompt `login` ▶ enter `library`

University of Sussex: United Kingdom *GEAC*
TELNET `library.sussex.ac.uk` No login required

University of Sydney: Australia *INNOPAC*
TELNET `lib7.fisher.su.oz.au` ▶ wait for the prompt `login` ▶ enter `library`

University of Sydney—Conservatorium of Music: Australia (Access via **New South Wales Libraries**)

University of Sydney—Sydney College of the Arts: Australia (Access via **New South Wales Libraries**)

University of Technology—Sydney: Australia (Access via **New South Wales Libraries**)

University of Teesside: United Kingdom *custom*
TELNET `libsun.tees.ac.uk` ▶ wait for the prompt `login` ▶ enter `library` ▶ wait for the prompt `Password` ▶ enter `library`

University of Tennessee—Chatanooga: United States *VTLS*
TELNET `library.utc.edu` No login required

University of Tennessee—Knoxville: United States TN *GEAC*
TELNET `txhl01.lib.utk.edu` No login required

University Of Tennessee—Martin: United States TN *INNOPAC*

TELNET library.utm.edu No login required

University of Tennessee—Memphis Health Science Library: United States TN *custom*

TELNET utmem1.utmem.edu ❯ wait for the prompt Username ❯ enter HARVEY

University of Texas-Pan American: United States TX *DRA*

TELNET panam2.panam.edu ❯ wait for the prompt Username ❯ enter PACKEY

University of Texas-Permian Basin: United States *DRA*

TELNET panam2.panam.edu ❯ wait for the prompt Username ❯ enter PACKEY

University of Texas—Arlington: United States TX *NOTIS*

TELNET admin.uta.edu ❯ press ↵

University of Texas—Austin: United States TX *UTCAT*

TELNET panam2.panam.edu ❯ wait for the prompt Username ❯ enter PACKEY

TELNET utcat.utexas.edu ❯ press ↵ ❯ wait for the prompt GO ❯ press ↵

TELNET utxuts.dp.utexas.edu ❯ wait for the prompt login ❯ enter utcat

University of Texas—Austin Tarlton Law Library (TALLONS): United States TX *INNOPAC*

TELNET tallons.law.utexas.edu ❯ wait for the prompt login ❯ enter library

University of Texas—Dallas: United States TX *NOTIS*

TN3270 vm.utdallas.edu ❯ tab to COMMAND ===> ❯ enter LIBRARY ❯ enter Function Key Clear

TELNET ibm.utdallas.edu No login required

University of Texas—Medical Branch, Galveston Moody Medical Library Automated Catalog: United States TX *custom*

TELNET panam2.panam.edu ❯ wait for the prompt Username ❯ enter PACKEY

University of Texas—Pan American Library: United States TX *DRA*

TELNET panam2.panam.edu ❯ wait for the prompt Username ❯ enter PACKEY

University of Texas—Permian Basin Library: United States TX *DRA*

TELNET panam2.panam.edu ❯ wait for the prompt Username ❯ enter PACKEY

University of Texas—San Antonio: United States TX *custom*

TELNET utsaibm.utsa.edu No login required

University of Texas—Southwestern Medical Center: United States TX *UNICORN*

TELNET library.swmed.edu ❯ wait for the prompt login ❯ enter tlntutsw ❯ wait for the prompt tlntutsw's Password ❯ enter library

TELNET medcat.library.swmed.edu ❯ wait for the prompt login ❯ enter tlntutsw ❯ wait for the prompt tlntutsw's Password ❯ enter library

University of the Aegean—Mytilene: Greece *GEAC ADVANCE*

TELNET library.libuam.ariadne-t.gr ❯ wait for the prompt login ❯ enter lib

University of the Aegean—Samos: Greece *GEAC ADVANCE*

TELNET hera.aegean.ariadne-t.gr ❯ wait for the prompt login ❯ enter lib

University of the District of Columbia: United States (Access via **Washington Research Library Consortium**)

University of the Pacific: United States *INNOPAC*

TELNET pacificat.lib.uop.edu ❯ wait for the prompt login ❯ enter library

University of the Witwatersrand: South Africa *custom*

TELNET delphi.wits.ac.za ❯ wait for the prompt login ❯ enter intopac

University of Tokyo: Japan *custom*

TELNET `opac.cc.u-tokyo.ac.jp` ◗ wait for the prompt that ends in `terminal identification number` ◗ enter `01` for VT100 ◗ wait for the prompt `ENTER USERID` ◗ enter `library`

University of Toledo: United States OH *INNOPAC*

TELNET `utmost.cl.utoledo.edu` No login required

University of Toronto: Canada *DRA Gateway*

TELNET `vax.library.utoronto.ca` ◗ wait for the prompt `Username` ◗ enter `UTLINK`

University of Tsukuba: Japan *custom*

TELNET `anzu.cc.tsukuba.ac.jp` No login required

University of Ulster: United Kingdom *custom*

TELNET `library.ulst.ac.uk` ◗ press ⏎

University of Uppsala: Sweden *VTLS*

TELNET `disa.ub.uu.se` ◗ wait for the prompt that ends in `to logon` ◗ enter `hello disa.telnet`

University of Vermont: United States VT *NOTIS*

TELNET `luis.uvm.edu` No login required

University of Victoria: Canada *NOTIS*

TELNET `mpg.uvic.ca` ◗ wait for the prompt `Enter SERVICE Name` ◗ enter `UVVM` for UVVM Full Screen Access

University of Waikato: New Zealand *DRA*

TELNET `library.waikato.ac.nz` ◗ wait for the prompt `Username` ◗ enter `OPAC`

University of Wales—Aberystwyth: United Kingdom *LIBERTAS*

TELNET `lib.aber.ac.uk` ◗ wait for the prompt `Username` ◗ enter `LIBRARY`

University of Wales—College of Cardiff: United Kingdom *LIBERTAS*

TELNET `liby.cf.ac.uk` ◗ wait for the prompt `Username` ◗ enter `LIBRARY`

University of Wales—Lampeter: United Kingdom *LIBERTAS*

TELNET `wwwx25.niss.ac.uk` No login required

University of Warwick: United Kingdom *BLCMP*

TELNET `opac.warwick.ac.uk` No login required

University of Washington: United States WA *custom*

TELNET `uwin.u.washington.edu` No login required

University of Washington—Gallagher Law Library: United States WA *custom*

TELNET `uwin.u.washington.edu` No login required

University of Waterloo: Canada *GEAC*

TELNET `watcat.uwaterloo.ca` No login required

University of West Florida: United States FL (Access via **Florida State University**)

University of Western Ontario: Canada *GEAC*

TELNET `geac.lib.uwo.ca` ◗ press ⏎

University of Western Sydney Libraries: Australia (Access via **New South Wales Libraries**)

University of Westminster: United Kingdom *LIBERTAS*

TELNET `lib.wmin.ac.uk` ◗ wait for the prompt `Username` ◗ enter `LIBRARY`

University of Windsor: Canada *NOTIS*
  TELNET `library.uwindsor.ca` No login required

University of Winnipeg: Canada *DRA Gateway*
  TELNET `bison.umanitoba.ca` ◗ wait for the prompt `Username` ◗ enter `BISON`

University of Wisconsin—Eau Claire: United States *NOTIS*
  TELNET `lib.uwec.edu` ◗ wait for the prompt `login` ◗ enter `library`

University of Wisconsin—Green Bay: United States *NOTIS*
  TELNET `notis.uwgb.edu` ◗ wait for the prompt `login` ◗ enter `library`

University of Wisconsin—La Crosse: United States WI *LS/2000*
  TELNET `library.acs.uwlax.edu` ◗ wait for the prompt `login` ◗ enter `library`

University of Wisconsin—Madison: United States WI *custom*
  TELNET `thorplus.lib.purdue.edu` ◗ wait for the prompt `login` ◗ enter `catnet`
  TN3270 `lib.cc.purdue.edu` ◗ wait for the prompt `Database Selection` ◗ enter `REMOTE`
  TELNET `lego.adp.wisc.edu` No login required

University of Wisconsin—Milwaukee: United States *custom*
  TELNET `nls.lib.uwm.edu` No login required

University of Wisconsin—Oshkosh: United States *NOTIS*
  TELNET `notis.llr.uwosh.edu` ◗ wait for the prompt `login` ◗ enter `library`

University of Wisconsin—Parkside: United States WI *LS/2000*
  TELNET `library.uwp.edu` ◗ wait for the prompt `login` ◗ enter `library`

University of Wisconsin—Platteville: United States WI *NOTIS*
  TELNET `lib.uwplatt.edu` ◗ wait for the prompt `login` ◗ enter `library`

University of Wisconsin—River Falls: United States WI *LS2000*
  TELNET `davee.dl.uwrf.edu` ◗ wait for the prompt `login` ◗ enter `library`

University of Wisconsin—Stevens Point: United States WI *LS2000*
  TELNET `lib.uwsp.edu` ◗ wait for the prompt `login` ◗ enter `library`

University of Wisconsin—Stout: United States *NOTIS*
  TELNET `lib.uwstout.edu` ◗ wait for the prompt `login` ◗ enter `library`

University of Wisconsin—Whitewater: United States WI *LS/2000*
  TELNET `lib.uww.edu` ◗ wait for the prompt that ends in `TO BEGIN SESSION` ◗ press ↵

University of Wollongong: Australia (Access via **New South Wales Libraries**)

University of Wuppertal: Germany *custom*
  TELNET `wzunix.bib.uni-wuppertal.de` ◗ wait for the prompt `login` ◗ enter `guest`

University of Wyoming: United States (Access via **CARL**)

University or Warwick: United Kingdom *BLCMP*
  TELNET `opac.warwick.ac.uk` No login required

University System of Georgia On-Line Library Information System: United States (Access via **Georgia On-Line Library Information System**)

Ursinus College: United States *DRA*
  TELNET `lib.ursinus.edu` ◗ wait for the prompt `Username` ◗ enter `LIBRARY`

Utah State University: United States UT *NOTIS*
TELNET `library.usu.edu` No login required

Utah Valley State College: United States UH *DYNIX*
TELNET `library.uvsc.edu` No login required

Vaasan University: Finland *VTLS*
TELNET `kustaa.uwasa.fi` ◗ wait for the prompt MPE XL ◗ enter `hello,user.clas01`

Vail Public Library: United States (Access via **MARMOT Library Network**)

Valdosta State University: United States *DRA*
TELNET `vsc1.valdosta.peachnet.edu` ◗ wait for the prompt Username ◗ enter LIBRARY

Valencia Community College—Florida: United States FL *NOTIS*
TELNET `luis.nerdc.ufl.edu` ◗ wait for the prompt login ◗ enter `luis`

Valley Library Consortium—Michigan: United States MI *DYNIX*
TELNET `vlc.svsu.edu` ◗ wait for the prompt login ◗ enter `valcat`

Vancouver Public Library: Canada *DYNIX*
TELNET `goliath.vpl.vancouver.bc.ca` ◗ wait for the prompt login ◗ enter `netpac` ◗ wait for the prompt Password ◗ enter `netpac1`

Vanderbilt University: United States *NOTIS*
TELNET `ctrvax.vanderbilt.edu` ◗ wait for the prompt Username ◗ enter ACORN

Vassar College: United States *INNOPAC*
TELNET `vaslib.vassar.edu` ◗ wait for the prompt login ◗ enter `library`

Vatican Library (Biblioteca Apostolica Vaticana): Italy *GEAC ADVANCE*
TELNET `librs6k.vatlib.it` ◗ wait for the prompt login ◗ enter `opac`

Vermont College: United States VT *custom*
TELNET `lib.middlebury.edu` ◗ wait for the prompt Username ◗ enter LIB

Vermont Law School: United States VT *INNOPAC*
TELNET `library.vermontlaw.edu` ◗ wait for the prompt login ◗ enter `library`

Vermont Regional Libraries: United States VT (Access via **Middlebury College**)

Vermont State Colleges: United States VT *custom*
TELNET `lib.middlebury.edu` ◗ wait for the prompt Username ◗ enter LIB

Vermont State Library—Montpelier: United States VT (Access via **Middlebury College**)

Vermont State—Department of Libraries: United States *DRA*
TELNET `dol.state.vt.us` ◗ press ↵
TELNET `lib.middlebury.edu` ◗ wait for the prompt Username ◗ enter LIB

Vermont Technical College: United States VT (Access via **Middlebury College**)

Veterinaermedizinischen Universitaet Wien: Austria (Access via **Austrian Academic Library Network**)

Vicksburg Community Library: United States (Access via **KELLY**)

Vicksburg Community Schools: United States (Access via **KELLY**)

Victoria University of Manchester: United Kingdom *custom*
TELNET `library.man.ac.uk` ◗ wait for the prompt login ◗ enter `library` ◗ press ↵

Victoria University of Technology: Australia *INNOPAC*

TELNET `zebra.vut.edu.au` ◗ wait for the prompt `login` ◗ enter `library`

Victoria University of Wellington: New Zealand *DYNIX*

TELNET `library.vuw.ac.nz` ◗ wait for the prompt `login` ◗ enter `opac`

Villanova University Law Library: United States *INNOPAC*

TELNET `153.104.15.249` No login required

Vilnius University: LIthuania *custom*

TELNET `munin.vu.lt` ◗ wait for the prompt `What is your terminal type?` ◗ enter `6` for VT100 ◗ wait for the prompt `Enter YOUR name, please` ◗ enter `opac` ◗ wait for the prompt `Enter password , please` ◗ enter `opac`

Virginia Commonwealth University: United States VA *NOTIS*

TN3270 `vcuvm1.ucc.vcu.edu` ◗ tab to COMMAND `===>` ◗ enter `dial vtam`

Virginia Military Institute: United States VA *DRA*

TELNET `vax.vmi.edu` ◗ wait for the prompt `Username` ◗ enter `LIBRARY`

Virginia Tech: United States VA *VTLS*

TELNET `vtls.vt.edu` ◗ wait for the prompt that ends in `Terminal Server ****` ◗ press ↵

Vrije Universiteit: The Netherlands *CLSI*

TELNET `ubvucat.vu.nl` ◗ wait for the prompt `login` ◗ enter `cat`

Waitakere Libraries: New Zealand *DRA Gateway*

TELNET `pollux.dslak.co.nz` ◗ wait for the prompt `Username` ◗ enter `WPLOPAC`

Wake Forest University: United States *DYNIX*

TELNET `lib.wfunet.wfu.edu` ◗ wait for the prompt `login` ◗ enter `wake`

Waseda University: Japan *DOBIS/LIBIS*

TELNET `wine.wul.waseda.ac.jp` ◗ wait for the prompt `===>` ◗ enter `1`

Washburn University: United States *INNOPAC*

TELNET `lib.wuacc.edu` ◗ wait for the prompt `login` ◗ enter `lib`

Washington and Lee University: United States *INNOPAC*

TELNET `iii.library.wlu.edu` ◗ wait for the prompt `login` ◗ enter `library`

Washington College: United States WA *INNOPAC*

TELNET `library.washcoll.edu` ◗ wait for the prompt `login` ◗ enter `library`

Washington College of Law: United States *INNOPAC*

TELNET `leagle.wcl.american.edu` ◗ wait for the prompt `login` ◗ enter `Library`

Washington County Public Library: United States *DYNIX*

TELNET `wcm.washington.lib.mn.us` ◗ wait for the prompt `login` ◗ enter `library`

Washington Research Library Consortium: United States WA *NOTIS*

TN3270 `gmuibm.gmu.edu` No login required

TELNET `xlibris.wrlc.org` ◗ wait for the prompt that ends in `the library catalog` ◗ press ↵

Washington State University and Eastern Washington University: United States WA *custom*

TN3270 `wsuvm1.csc.wsu.edu` ◗ tab to COMMAND `===>` ◗ enter `dial vtam`

Washington University Libraries—St. Louis (WorldWindow): United States *NOTIS*

TELNET `library.wustl.edu` ◗ wait for the prompt `TERM = (vt220)` ◗ enter `VT100` if VT100 ◗ press ↵ ◗ press ↵

Washington University of St. Louis: United States MO *NOTIS*
    TELNET `library.wustl.edu` ◗ wait for the prompt `Username [` ◗ press ↵

Washington University of St. Louis Medical Libraries: United States MO *NOTIS*
    TELNET `library.wustl.edu` ◗ wait for the prompt `Press <Enter> to see list of libraries>` ◗ press ↵

Watervliet District Library: United States (Access via **KELLY**)

Wayne County Community College: United States (Access via **Detroit Area Library Network**)

Weber State University: United States *DYNIX*
    TELNET `lib.weber.edu` ◗ wait for the prompt that ends in `login` ◗ enter `pac`

Webster University: United States *DYNIX*
    TELNET `library1.websteruniv.edu` ◗ wait for the prompt `login` ◗ enter `opac`

Webster, Colorado, Library: United States CO (Access via **CARL**)

Weizmann Institute of Science: Israel (Access via **Hebrew University**)

Wellesley College: United States *INNOPAC*
    TELNET `luna.wellesley.edu`

Wentworth Institute: United States (Access via **Fenway Libraries Online, Inc.**)

West Bloomfield Public Library: United States *INNOPAC*
    TELNET `lis.wb.metronet.lib.mi.us` ◗ wait for the prompt `login` ◗ enter `library`

West Boylston, Colorado, Library: United States CO (Access via **CARL**)

West Georgia College: United States GA *UNICORN*
    TELNET `library.isil.westga.edu` ◗ wait for the prompt `login` ◗ enter `public`

West Georgia College—Carrollton: United States GA (Access via **Georgia On-Line Library Information System**)

West Michhhigan Information Network (WESTNET): United States (See **KELLY**)

West Springfield Public Library: United States (Access via **CARL**)

West Virginia University: United States VA *NOTIS*
    TELNET `e3270.wvnet.edu` No login required

Westborough Public Library: United States (Access via **CARL**)

Westbrook School Learning Center (K-3): United States *custom*
    TELNET `wb.ncook.k12.il.us` ◗ wait for the prompt `login` ◗ enter `library`

Western Illinois Library System: United States IL (Access via **ILLINET On-line Catalog**)

Western Illinois University: United States IL (Access via **ILLINET On-line Catalog**)

Western Iowa Tech Community College: United States IA *DYNIX*
    TELNET `iq.witcc.cc.ia.us` ◗ wait for the prompt `login` ◗ enter `library`

Western Kentucky University: United States *NOTIS*
    TELNET `topcat.wku.edu` ◗ wait for the prompt `Command` ◗ enter `TOPCAT`

Western Mass Regional Library: United States MA (Access via **CARL**)

Western Michigan Regional Online Catalog: United States MI (See **KELLY**)

Western Michigan University: United States MI *NOTIS*
    TN3270 `library.wmich.edu` No login required

TELNET `public.library.wmich.edu` ❱ wait for the prompt `login` ❱ enter `w`

Western Nevada Community College: United States NV (Access via **Nevada Academic Libraries Information System**)

Western New England College: United States NE (Access via **CARL**)

Western New Mexico University: United States NM *GALAXY*
TELNET `silver.wnmu.edu` ❱ wait for the prompt `Username` ❱ enter `ACCESS`

Western North Carolina Library Network: United States NC *INNOPAC*
TELNET `ncwes.appstate.edu` ❱ wait for the prompt `login` ❱ enter `ramsey`

Western Oregon State College: United States OR *INNOPAC*
TELNET `140.211.118.20` No login required

Western State College: United States *DRA*
TELNET `192.101.138.5` ❱ wait for the prompt `Username` ❱ enter `AC`

Western Washington University: United States *INNOPAC*
TELNET `lis.lis.wwu.edu` No login required

Westfield State College: United States (Access via **CARL**)

Westminster College: United States *DYNIX*
TELNET `libr.wcslc.edu` ❱ wait for the prompt `login` ❱ enter `pac`

Westminster Public Library, Colorado: United States CO *DYNIX*
TELNET `198.243.1.1` ❱ wait for the prompt `login` ❱ enter `ac`

Westmont College: United States *DYNIX*
TELNET `westmx.westmont.edu` ❱ wait for the prompt `login` ❱ enter `public`

Wheaton College: United States *DYNIX*
TELNET `titus.wheaton.edu` ❱ wait for the prompt `login` ❱ enter `dpac`

Wheaton College—MA: United States *INNOPAC*
TELNET `155.47.2.2` ❱ wait for the prompt `login` ❱ enter `Library`

Wheelock College: United States (Access via **Fenway Libraries Online, Inc.**)

Whitinsville Social Library: United States (Access via **CARL**)

Whitman College: United States *INNOPAC*
TELNET `library.whitman.edu` No login required

Wichita State University: United States *NOTIS*
TN3270 `twsuvm.uc.twsu.edu` ❱ tab to COMMAND `===>` ❱ enter `dial menu` ❱ wait for the prompt `===>` ❱ enter `Library`

Widener University School of Law: United States *INNOPAC*
TELNET `lawcat.widener.edu` ❱ wait for the prompt `login` ❱ enter `library`

Wien, Universitaetsbibliothek: Austria (Access via **Austrian Academic Library Network**)

Wilbraham, Colorado, Public Library: United States CO (Access via **CARL**)

Wilfrid Laurier University: Canada *custom*
TELNET `mach1.wlu.ca` ❱ wait for the prompt `login` ❱ enter `public`

Willamette University: United States *INNOPAC*
TELNET `library.willamette.edu` No login required

William Paterson College: United States *DRA*
TELNET `wpc.wilpaterson.edu` ◗ wait for the prompt `Username` ◗ enter `ASK_Q`

William Woods University, Missouri: United States *DRA Gateway*
TELNET `micro.wcmo.edu` ◗ wait for the prompt `Username` ◗ enter `CLIO1`

Williams College: United States *INNOPAC*
TELNET `library.williams.edu` No login required

Williamstown Public Library: United States (Access via **CARL**)

Wilmington Library—Delaware: United States *DYNIX*
TELNET `wilmnet.dtcc.edu` ◗ wait for the prompt `login` ◗ enter `library`

Winchendon, Colorado, Library: United States CO (Access via **CARL**)

Winnefox Library System, Wisconsin: United States WI *DRA*
TELNET `axp.winnefox.org` ◗ wait for the prompt `Username` ◗ enter `OSHKOSH`

Winnipeg Public Library: Canada *DYNIX*
TELNET `winpuli.city.winnipeg.mb.ca` ◗ wait for the prompt `login` ◗ enter `wplpac`

Winthrop University: United States *INNOPAC*
TELNET `library.winthrop.edu` No login required

Wirtschaftsuniversitaet Wien: Austria (Access via **Austrian Academic Library Network**)

Wittenberg University: United States *INNOPAC*
TELNET `lib.wittenberg.edu` ◗ wait for the prompt `login` ◗ enter `library`

Worcester Polytechnic Institute: United States (Access via **CARL**)

Worcester Public Library: United States (Access via **CARL**)

Worcester State College: United States (Access via **CARL**)

Wright State University: United States *INNOPAC*
TELNET `cat.ohiolink.edu` ◗ wait for the prompt `login` ◗ enter `ohiolink`
TELNET `wsuol2.wright.edu` No login required

Wye College: United Kingdom (Access via **London University Central Libertas Consortium**)

Xavier University: United States *INNOPAC*
TELNET `xulas.xu.edu` ◗ wait for the prompt `login` ◗ enter `library`

Yale University Law Library: United States *INNOPAC*
TELNET `ringding.law.yale.edu` ◗ wait for the prompt `login` ◗ enter `library`

Yavapai Library Network, Arizona: United States AZ *DYNIX*
TELNET `prescott.lib.az.us` ◗ wait for the prompt `login` ◗ enter `yavacat`

Youngstown State University: United States *INNOPAC*
TELNET `library.ysu.edu` ◗ wait for the prompt `login` ◗ enter `library`

Zentralbibliothek für Physik in Wien: Austria (Access via **Austrian Academic Library Network**)

Zentralbibliothek Zurich: Switzerland *GEAC*
TELNET `nuz.unizh.ch` ◗ press ⏎ ◗ wait for the prompt `#` ◗ enter `tso`

INDEX

history of: 5249
international development: 10050
Middle Eastern: 4616
news: 8915
pesticide and herbicide manufacturer: 1905
resource collections: 2735
software and document archives: 8895
supplies, news: 1865
sustainable: 4658, 8910
U.S. and Canada patterns: 4654
agroforestry: 8914
AHL: see American Hockey League
AI: see artificial intelligence
AIB-CUR [Mailing List]: 5744
AICS-L [Mailing List]: 2131
AIDS: 4689, 4889, 4893, 4896, 4897, 9958
aids [Mailing List]: 4897
AIDS
daily news summary: 4968
prevention: 10050
stories: 4891
AIDS Information Newsletter [Newsletter]: 4888
AIDSBKRV [Mailing List]: 4889
AIDSLINE (medical database): 4691
aikido: 6590
AIKIDO-L [Mailing List]: 6590
aimembers-l [Digest & Reflector]: 10018
AIntAcc-L [Mailing List]: 1658
AIP History of Physics Newsletter [E-journal]: 9454
Air Cadet Gliding Program: 6263
Air Force ROTC, discussion: 5485
air medical practice: 5077
air pollution: 4623
control: 9255
air transportation: 1971
air travel: 6286, 7833
Air Warrior (computer game): 6394
AIRCRAFT [Mailing List]: 6259
aircraft
aeronautics: 8946
components: 1821, 1822
Kitfox: 6266
ownership: 6276
piloting: 6277
radio-controlled: 7001
show: 6259
airlines
airfare discounts: 7850
complaints: 1815
industry news: 1819
airports, industry news: 1819
Airwaves Radio Journal [E-Journal]: 1270
AIX operating system: 3944, 3983, 3985
users: 3982
AJAX Military and Intelligence Agencies Access [Resource]: 5480

AJN Network [Resource]: 4969
Akademische Software Kooperation [Resource]: 4481
Akademische Software Kooperation Software Information System: 4481
Akihabara, Japan: 7437
Akron, OH, Freenet: 2420
al-stewart [Mailing List]: 1162
ALA-PLAN [Mailing List]: 5691
Alabama [Subject]: 7884-7887
Alabama Research and Education Network: 3807
Alabama Supercomputer Authority: 3807
Alabama, news: 7884
ALACRO-L [Mailing List]: 5745
Alamo Community College District CWIS [Resource]: 4142
Alaska [Subject]: 7888-7890
Arctic Circle: 4630
culture: 7889
network news: 7888
news: 7890
Public Access Networking: 9645
Albania: 7268, 7282
Albert A. List College of Jewish Studies, alumni: 4128
Alberta, Canada [Subject]: 7149-7156
employment: 7150
politics: 7151
alchemy: 5236
alcohol: 5858
Japanese discussion: 5879
news: 9903
Alcoholics Anonymous: 4700
alcoholism: 4707
research: 9553
ALCTS Network News (AN2) [Newsletter]: 5692
Aldus: 2296
Aldus Freehand: 2449, 2460, 2460
Alesis Quadraverb effects boxes: 771
ALF-L [Mailing List]: 5760
alfalfa: 8907
alfrednorth [Mailing List]: 5318
algae, blue-green: 9035
algebra [Subject]: 9407-9410
group theory: 9409
help: 4278
Lie: 9409
Algeria: 7542
Alias Research 3-D graphics software: 2457
Alice in Chains: 1005
Alien (film series): 1403
aliens: 10079, 10080
sexual contacts with: 371
The ALISE Home Page [Resource]: 5693
ALL networks, sysop issues: 2174
All The Best Locations! [Resource]: 2993
All-in-One Search Page [Resource]: 2754

Allegis Investment Management [Resource]: 1737
Allen, Woody: 483
allergies: 4762
coincident intolerances: 4799
self-care and prevention: 4761
wheat and gluten: 4799
Allergy [Mailing List]: 4761
Alliance of Higher Education: 5752
ALLIANCE-MA [Mailing List]: 6062
Alliant computers, discussion: 3400
Alligator Online [Resource]: 4469
allman [Mailing List]: 1006
Allman Brothers: 1006, 1007
ALLMUSIC [Distribution List]: 727
Alpha AXP architecture: 4067
Alpha Phi Omega, Pittsburgh, PA: 4174
ALPHA-IDS [Mailing List]: 4060
Alpine region, news: 7271
Alpine skiing: 6663, 6672
Alta Vista [Resource]: 2727
alteration, construction industry: 1847
alternate futures: 4474
alternate histories: 1345
alternative energy industries, news: 9223
alternative education [Subject]: 4110-4112
alternative health care: 4725
alternative medicine [Subject]: 4712-4727
The Alternative Medicine Hompage [Resource]: 4719
alternative music [Subject]: 797-801
female: 799
reviews: 756
rock: 996
Alternative News Collective, MIT: 4474
alternative society: 10142
Alternative Transients Program: 9261
alternative zines: 1633
ALTLEARN [Mailing List]: 4111
altruism: 9022
ALUMNET [Digest & Reflector]: 4125
alumni: 7262
Bronx Science High School: 4113
Choate-Rosemary Hall: 4116
Cranbrook school: 4117
Deerfield Academy: 4118
Earlham College: 4126
Glenbrook Academy: 4127
Groton: 4119
ITC: 4115
Jewish Theological Seminary of America: 4128
Milton Academy: 4121
Occidental College: 4129, 4130
Phillips-Andover Academy: 4122
Phillips-Exeter Academy: 4123
prep schools: 4114
St. Paul's School: 4124
Stuyvesant High School: 4131

midgets: 338
pantyhose: 361
pinups, nonphotographic: 311
pregnant women: 343
preteen: 342
redheads: 344
S&M: 317
sounds: 364
spanking: 345
teen, female: 348
teen, male: 350
teenage: 349
teens: 346
teens, discussion: 347
urine: 352
voyeurism: 353
fashion magazine: 5790
fine-art: 455, 456
 computer-generated: 249
 discussion: 454
fonts: 2380
fractals: 250
furniture: 6034
games, executable: 6389
gardens: 5894
GEOS: 3379
girlfriends: 354, 6000
gothic: 248
IBM PC: 2531
Japanese animation: 16
lesbian: 357
lingerie: 358
Macintosh: 3050, 3081
Microsoft Windows: 2624
MIDI: 848
MOD/669 format music samples: 728
MODs and related sound formats: 849
Moss, Kate: 5791
MS-DOS: 2576
MS-DOS, discussion: 2577
multimedia: 3187
multimedia, discussion: 3188
nudes: 360
OS/2 ABI: 2586
PCBoard systems: 2196
personal pictures: 5953
photographic, fine arts: 1236
pictures composed of ASCII characters: 2434
porn stars: 341
Psion computers: 3145
railroad: 6640
SHARP X68000: 3155
sounds
 discussion: 3189
 erotica: 364
 from animated shows: 19
 television: 1511
 utilities: 3190
sounds (movies): 668

sounds and pictures of J. R. "Bob" Dobbs: 535
sports: 6674
Star Trek: 1351
Star Wars: 1459
supermodels: 362
tasteless pictures: 476
teen idols: 176
teen starlets: 177
transvestite: 351
utilities, pictures-related: 2439
vehicles: 6221
voyeur pictures: 363
BIND server, Berkeley: 3901
binding: 1910
Bingaman, Jeff, Senator: 5465
biochemical research: 4851
biochemistry: 9007
BIOCONTROL-L Biological Control List [Mailing List]: 4621
biodiversity [Subject]: 4561-4565, 8949, 8952
 electronic publishing in: 8954
Biodiversity Information [Mailing List]: 4563
Biodiversity Information Network [Resource]: 4564
biodynamic agriculture: 5348
biofeedback: 4944
Biohazard [Resource]: 1636
bioinformatics: 8952, 8953, 9007, 9057, 9131
 electronic publishing in: 8954
Bioinformatics at the Weizmann Institute of Science [Resource]: 8953
Bioline Publications [Resource]: 8954
BIOLINE-L [Mailing List]: 9085
biological conservation: 4591
 and geographical information systems: 9317
biological hazards: 4854
biology [Subject]: 8949-9083
 aging: 9056
 computational: 8959, 9069
 databases: 9008, 9057
 discussion: 9006
 electromagnetic field effects: 4847
 employment: 8972, 8973
 funding: 8991
 grasses: 9026
 information theory: 8971
 journal contents: 8974
 journals, writer's advisory: 8977
 marine: 9444
 mathematical: 9021
 molecular: 9054
 resource collections: 2735
 Sequence Retrieval System (SRS) software: 9100
 software and document archives: 8895, 9008, 9069

software sources: 8993, 9008
software sources, WWW: 8994, 9008
software, information about: 8992
teachers, secondary, enhancement: 8999
technologies: 4665
tropical: 8961
undergraduate research opportunities: 4302
women in: 8998
yeast: 9062
bioluminescence: 9061
Biomch-L [Mailing List]: 8955
biomechanics and human/animal movement: 8955
biomedical engineering: 5101, 5109
Biomedical Library Acquisitions Bulletin (BLAB) [Newsletter]: 4904
Biomedical Market Newsletter [Resource]: 4901
Biomedical Multimedia Unit [Resource]: 4827
Biomedicine and Health in the News [Resource]: 4964
Bionet announcements: 8956
Biophysical Society, announcements: 8985
biophysics: 8962
BIOPI-L [Mailing List]: 8999
biosafety: 9113
bioscience: 9007
biostatistical software: 4858
biosym [Mailing List]: 9000
Biosym Technologies software: 9000
BIOTECH [Mailing List]: 9102
BioTech [Resource]: 9103
Biotechniques (journal), discussion: 8975
biotechnology: 8949, 8952, 9007, 9084, 9102, 9118
 activists: 9110
 business and: 9104
 dictionary of terms in: 9103
 electronic publishing in: 8954
 high school teaching: 9109
 news: 9105
 safety issues: 9113
biotechnology & genetics [Subject]: 9084-9121
bird-watching: 4588, 4683, 6626
birds: 7742
 conservation: 4588
 domesticated: 6195
 pet: 6206
 pet, exotic: 6196
birth [Subject]: 9706-9707
birth parents: 9691
birthdays: 548
bisexual: see also gay, lesbian, bisexual & transgendered

Bisexual Spouse Support Mailing List (SSML) [Mailing List]: 6028
bisexuals: 9963, 9969, 9976
  heterosexual partners of: 9981
  Las Vegas, NV: 9985
  personals: 5959
  Spanish-speaking: 9949
  women: 9980
  youth: 9979
BitGraph terminals: 3461
Bitnet
  discussion about: 2931
  help: 2687
  link failure announcements: 2856
  news about: 2872
BIZ-BIOTECH [Digest & Reflector]: 9104
biz.marketplace discussion: 1705
Bizarro: 149
BizOpList [Distribution List]: 2064
BizWeb [Resource]: 2755
Bjordahl, Hans: 150
Bjork: 1018
black
  culture: 9697
  engineers and scientists: 9236, 9237
  news: 9696
  politics: 9697
Black Graduate Student Association at Massachusetts Institute of Technology [Resource]: 4397
The Black Information Network [Resource]: 9695
black metal (music): 970
Black Sabbath: 1019
Black, Clint: 830
Blackadder: 225
blackjack: 6369
Blackstone Press: 5569
Blade Runner: 1407
Blake [Mailing List]: 599
Blake, William: 599
BLAST.famy [E-Journal]: 2499
BlindFam [Mailing List]: 9887
blindness
  computer screen readers: 9889
  family life and: 9887
  issues and discussions: 9886, 9888
blindness, computer use by the blind: 9884
BLINDNWS [Digest & Reflector]: 9888
BLISS-L [Mailing List]: 9515
Blitz Basic: 3519
BLK Homie Pages [Resource]: 9954
Bloomfield Hills Model High School [Resource]: 4215
Blue Oyster Cult: 1022, 1023
The Blue Penny Quarterly [E-Journal]: 566
blue-green algae: 9035
bluegrass: see also country western & bluegrass

bluegrass music: 831, 835
  radio hosts: 872
blues music[Subject]: 802-804, 925
Blues Brothers: 673
Blues Traveler: 1020
BluFire Model & Talent Registry [Resource]: 1809
Blur (music group): 1021
bmt-talk [Mailing List]: 4797
board games [Subject]: 6344-6363
  buying and selling: 6354
  shogi: 6362
  United Kingdom: 6363
Board of Governors of State Colleges and Universities, Illinois [Resource]: 4412
boats: 6651
  building: 6652
  cruising: 6653
  for sale, Portland, OR: 8379
  marketplace: 6654
  paddle driven: 6655
  racing: 6656
  radio controlled: 7001
  small: 6650
Bobs [Mailing List]: 964
Bobs, The (singing group): 964
BOB©WEB [Resource]: 1263
boc-l [Mailing List]: 1022
body art [Subject]: 94-98
  binaries: 95
Body Modification ezine (BME) [Resource]: 96
body painting, temporary: 94
body size [Subject]: 9708-9717
bodyboard surfing: 6990
bodybuilding [Subject]: 6799-6800, 96
BODYGUARD-101-L [Mailing List]: 1960
BODYGUARD-L [Mailing List]: 1961
bodyguards: 1961
  training: 1960
Bolen Books [Resource]: 116
Bolivia: 7647
Bolo (networked war game): 6469
Bolton, Michael: 944
Bon Jovi, Jon: 1093
Bond, James: 4
bondage: 375
  personals: 5961
bonding (insurance), building industry: 1835
bone marrow transplants: 4797
BONSAI [Mailing List]: 5898
bonsai: 5895, 5898, 5905, 5911
book discussion
  Okinawa, Japan: 7440
Bookport [Resource]: 104
BookRead Project: 4336
books [Subject]: 99-121
  Canadian, youth oriented: 7139
  discussion: 109

  Australia: 7060
  San Diego, California: 7953
  for sale
    Portland, OR: 8380
  marketplace: 111
  mystery genre: 1218
  new releases: 115
  news: 106, 107
  online, directory of: 5677
  rare: 5772
  reviews: 99, 102, 112
    K-12: 4216, 4217
    science fiction: 1342
  technical: 108
  technical, discussion: 103
Books That Work [Resource]: 6040
bookstores [Subject]: 116-121, 99, 100
  Christian: 8700
  gay and lesbian: 9960
  how to start one: 105
BookWeb [Resource]: 105
BookWire [Resource]: 99
boomerangs: 6961
bootleg music: 736
BOP [Mailing List]: 5876
The Borderline Humor Netazine [E-Journal]: 495
boredom, remedies: 537
Borland C++: 3551
Borland Delphi
  database aspects: 3579
  discussion: 3580
  writing components: 3578
Borland Pascal: 3551, 3577
BosNews [Distribution List]: 7805
Bosnia and Herzegovina: 5633, 7800, 7805, 7814
  news: 7802, 7808
Boston Book Review, The: 99
Boston Bruins: 6869
Boston Celtics: 6755
Boston Computer Society: 4021, 4031
  activist issues: 4017
  announcements: 4018, 4019
  FAQs: 4020
  Macintosh users: 4023
  Online Services Committee: 4022
  users groups: 4024
Boston Red Sox: 6707
Boston University
  College of Communication: 5176
  CWIS: 4413
Boston University CWIS [Resource]: 4413
Boston.Com [Resource]: 6107
botany [Subject]: 9025-9040
  cell walls: 9034
  databases: 8906, 8952
Bottom Line, The: 892
Boulder, CO, general interest: 8044
Bounty Hunters Online [Resource]: 122?

L

software for: 9069
Molecular Biology Computational Resource at Baylor College of Medicine [Resource]: 9071
Molecular Evolution & Organelle Genomics Site [Resource]: 9116
molecular libraries: 9065
molecular modeling: 9063, 9131, 9433
molecular modelling
 software: 1907
mollusc DNA: 9095
Molson (beer): 5861
Monaco, news: 7304
money: 1668
 discussion: 6049
 -making schemes: 1984
Money Issues [E-Magazine]: 6052
Mongolia: 7052
Monitor [Resource]: 5107
monitors, buy and sell: 3653
Monkees [Mailing List]: 1105
Monkees (music group): 1105
Monkees, The: 1106
monkeys: 9503
monopolies, software: 3727
monster movies: 1310
Mont Blanc pens: 555
Montana [Subject]: 8223
Montana, news: 8223
Montgomery County, MD, news: 8182
Montreal
 Freenet: 7209
Montreal Canadiens: 6878
Montreal Expos: 6722
Montreal, Canada
 for sale: 7211
 general interest: 7210
Monty Python: 1522
MOO Papers [Resource]: 3180
mood: 4950
mood disorders: 4959
mood swings: 4950
Moody Blues: 1107, 1108
Moorcock, Michael: 1398
Moore, Alan, comics: 123
Moore, Kenya: 192
MOOs: see also MUDs & MOOs
Morbidity and Mortality Weekly Report (MMWR) [Resource]: 4860
Moria (game): 6485
Mormonism: 8690
Morning Star PPP: 2912
MORPHMET [Mailing List]: 9011
Morphology Digest [Newsletter]: 9395
morphometrics: 9011
Morrison, Van: 1109
Morrissey: 1110
Mortal Kombat: 6409
Mortal Kombat III: 6410
mortgage, online calculator: 1942
Moss, Kate: 5795
Moss, Kate, binaries: 5791

Mother Jones magazine: 641
motherboards: 3662
mothers, stress relief for: 518
moths: 9049
Motif GUI: 4010
 X-Windows: 4003
Motley Crue: 1111
motor boats
 racing: 6657
motor sports: 3343, 6610
 Australian: 7082
 rally: 6252
 United Kingdom: 7791
motorcycles & motorsports [Subject]: 6594-6612
motorcycling: 6598, 6600, 6605, 6609
 Kentucky: 6601
 New England: 6602
 New York City, NY: 6603
 off-road riding: 6606
 Ottawa, Canada: 6604
 racing: 6608
 San Francisco Bay Area, CA: 6599
 Texas: 6612
 two-stroke, and life: 6611
MOTORDEV [Mailing List]: 9012
MOTSS: 7969, 8494, 8524, 9977
 Las Vegas, NV: 9986
 Nevada: 8244
 San Francisco Bay Area, CA: 9952
mountain biking, in Austin, TX: 9358
MouseTracks [Resource]: 2027
movement science: 8955
movement therapy: 5072
movers, Portland, OR: 8467
MovieLink [Resource]: 706
movies
 Branagh and Thompson: 680
 Burton, Tim: 689
 Chile: 695
 cult films: 669
 digital, Internet: 2679
 discussion: 703, 711
  North Carolina: 719
 Evil Dead: 670
 independent: 682
 Indian: 683, 7340
 Joe vs. the Volcano: 684
 Kubrick, Stanley: 685
 lists and surveys: 710
 monsters: 1310
 movie people: 714
 moviegoing: 712
 music: 786
 new films: 709
 news: 708
 past films: 713
 Persian: 7538
 Portland, OR: 8399
 Raimi, Sam: 676
 reviews: 704, 705, 716, 2703
  San Diego, CA: 7970

Rocky Horror: 671
 science fiction: 674
 Scorsese, Martin: 686
 self-referential: 707
 sex: 691
 silent: 687
 Spielberg, Steven: 688
 Spinal Tap: 678
 Tank Girl: 1422
 Tarantino, Quentin: 679
 technical aspects: 717
 visual effects: 690
movies & films [Subject]: 666-719
Movies-seivoM [Mailing List]: 707
Moxy Fruvous: 1112
Mozart, Wolfgang Amadeus: 816
Mozilla (Web browser): 3028
MPSYCH-L [Mailing List]: 9522
MS-Access [Mailing List]: 2341
MS-DOS: see Microsoft MS-DOS
MSP-L [Mailing List]: 2908
MSX computer system: 3370, 3410
MTMM studies: 2037
MTN [Mailing List]: 4100
MTV: 1573, 1573
MTV European top 20 charts: 991
MUD info [Resource]: 3174
MUDs: 3185, 9358
 administration: 3181
 and MOOs, directories to: 6330
 announcements: 3182
 criticism: 6508
 Island: 3176
 programming: 3177
MUDs & MOOs [Subject]: 3174-3186, 4039
Mule text editor: 3834
MULTC-ED [Mailing List]: 4323
multi-user dungeons: see MUDs
multicriteria analysis: 9393
Multics: 3100
multiculturalism
 art gallery: 72
 education [Subject]: 4321-4323
 education equity: 4322
 nursing: 4972
multiculturalism: see also diversity & multiculturalism
multifaith communities: 8855
multilevel marketing: 2028
MultiMax computers: 3405
multimedia [Subject]: 3187-3206
 Amiga computers: 3199
 authoring software: 3198
 binaries: 3187
 binaries, discussion: 3188
 binaries, erotica: 304
 education: 4520
 journal citations: 5725
 magazines, Trinity College: 5281
 press releases: 6103
 sounds: 3203

Norwegian, language learning: 4262
NorWord [Distribution List]: 4262
NOSC Page [Resource]: 2767
NOSMOKE [Mailing List]: 4708
Nostradamus: 8770
Not Just Bibles [Resource]: 8675
Not Just Cows [Resource]: 8904
not-for-profit [Subject]: 2054-2060
Notes From The Edge [Newsletter]:
    1180
Notes from the Windowsill (Formerly
    The WEB Online Review)
    [Newsletter]: 222
notices, Portland, OR: 8401
Notre Dame
    football: 6802
    sports: 6954
Nouvelles de la Bibliotheque nationale:
    5756
Nova Scotia, Canada [Subject]: 7168-
    7169
    announcements: 7168
    general interest: 7169
Novato, CA, news: 8028
Novell: 3295, 3477
    Groupwise products, WordPerfect
        Office: 3267
    interest group, Israel: 4030
    LAN Interest Group: 3290
    Netware: 3291, 3292, 3294
novels, online: 585
novelty music: 778
Novice-MZT (News from MZT)
    [Distribution List]: 9441
Nowhere Man: 1581
NPPA-L [Mailing List]: 6095
NPR: see National Public Radio
NRCH [Mailing List]: 4881
NRLib-L [Mailing List]: 4592
NrrdGrrl! [Resource]: 10160
NRSOCSCI [Mailing List]: 4659
NSSDC News [Newsletter]: 9592
NT: see Microsoft Windows NT
NT-INFO [Mailing List]: 2671
NTP: 2910
ntp [Mailing List]: 2910
NUC-OPS [Mailing List]: 9227
nuclear energy: 9224
    plant operators: 9227
    research: 9553
nuclear fusion: 9465
nuclear magnetic resonance (NMR):
    9067
nuclear medicine: 4918
nucmed [Mailing List]: 4918
nudism: see also naturists
nudism: 6613-6615
    binaries: 360
numerical analysis [Subject]: 9417-9418
numismatics, literature: 5238
NuRPG: 6513
NURSENET [Mailing List]: 4974

NurseRes [Mailing List]: 4975
nursing [Subject]: 4969-4978
    cultural issues: 4972
    intravenous (IV) therapy: 4973
    practitioners: 4970
    research: 4975
    school: 4977
    traveling RNs: 4976
NUTEPI [Mailing List]: 4861
nutrition [Subject]: 4979-4984, 6700
    awareness: 4655
    children: 9732
    epidemiology: 4861
NUVUPSY [Mailing List]: 5017
NWHQ [E-Journal]: 573
NWP [Mailing List]: 3295
nwu-sports [Mailing List]: 6959
NYCKayaker [Mailing List]: 6650
Nye, Bill: 1512, 1536
NYHIST-L [Mailing List]: 5254
NYPD Blue: 1582
NYSLAA-L [Mailing List]: 5757
NYSO-L [Mailing List]: 5776
nz.* hierarchy, network status: 7568
nz.* newsgroups, software announce-
    ments: 7563

O

O'Boingo Electronic Newsletter (OBEN)
    [Newsletter]: 1119
O'brien, Conan: 184
O'Connor, Sinead: 1117
O'Donnell, Peter: 158
O'Reilly & Associates
    new products announcements: 1924
    Unix book archives: 3753
O'Rourke, P. J.: 196
O-Hayo Sensei [Newsletter]: 4151
Oak Ridge Laboratory Review [E-
    Journal]: 9552
Oakland Athletics: 6725
Oakland Raiders: 6806, 6828
OANDP-L [Mailing List]: 5080
Oasis: 1118
oats, genome: 9111
OB-GYN-L [Mailing List]: 5116
Oberon programming language: 3616
obesity: 9717
    anorectic drug treatment: 9711
    support: 9714
obituaries: 6115, 9838, 9840, 9843
The Obituary Page [Resource]: 9843
object-oriented
    3-D graphics: 2454
    databases: 2375
    programming [Subject]: 3630-3646
        BETA: 3633
        C++: 3540
        Macintosh: 3066
        teaching: 3642
    technology, CERN forum: 3631

Objective-C programming language:
    3636
objectivism: 5323, 5352, 5626
ObjectPAL: 2362
OBJECTPAL-L [Mailing List]: 2362
Oblomov [Mailing List]: 4951
oboes: 895
The Observer [Newsletter]: 9158
obsessive-compulsive disorder: 4936,
    4952
obstetrics: 5116
obstetrics and gynecology, journal: 511
Occ-Env-Med-L [Mailing List]: 4985
Occidental College: 4130
Occidental College, alumni: 4129
occult
    history: 5236
    sciences: 8835
The Occupation of Kuwait: Legacy of
    Pain [Resource]: 10029
occupational health: 4987, 4988
occupational medicine: 4985
occupational safety & health [Subject]:
    4985-4988
occupational therapy: 5078
OCD-L [Mailing List]: 4952
oceangoing vessels: 1983
Oceania [Subject]: 7578-7581
    news: 7579
oceanography [Subject]: 9443-9447,
    1970, 4647
    radiocarbon dating: 9313
Oceanography Information Servers
    [Resource]: 9443
oceans: see also river, ocean & water
OFFCAMP [Mailing List]: 5767
office equipment: 1683
office management: 2016
Office of Arid Lands Studies, Universi
    of Arizona: 4631
Office of Senator Bob Kerrey [Resourc
    5464
Office of U.S. Senator Jeff Bingaman
    [Resource]: 5465
office space, Portland, OR: 8402
The Official Nicola Griffith Page
    [Resource]: 604
The Official Online Guide to Canada's
    West Coast Music Industry
    [Resource]: 767
OFFSHORE [Mailing List]: 1774
offshore business: 1728
offshore investment structures: 1774
OGRE [Mailing List]: 6348
oh-motss [Mailing List]: 9970
Ohio [Subject]: 8340-8356
    commercial advertising: 8349
    education, K-12: 4236
    employment: 8353
    for sale: 8351
    general interest: 8352
    news: 8341

Psychology in Daily Life Page
[Resource]: 5069
psychopathology: 4954
language and: 5018
psychopharmacology: 4954, 5020, 5023
psychophysiology: 4944, 9521
psychosocial health: 9517
PSYCHOSYNTHESIS [Mailing List]:
9526
psychosynthesis: 9526
psychotherapy [Subject]: 5029-5033,
5020, 9539
PSYCOLOQUY [E-Journal]: 9527
PsyNetUSA [Mailing List]: 5033
PSYSTS-L [Mailing List]: 9528
Ptolemy simulation/code generation
environment: 3699
PUBLABOR [Mailing List]: 2014
public access
archives, computer: 3738
television: 1486
television, Eugene, OR: 8370
public broadcasting: 4945
Soundprint radio documentaries:
1289
Public Broadcasting Service: 6067, 6071
public domain, electronic texts: 5676
public education, restructuring: 4370
public financial managers: 5417
public health
economics of: 4688
NIS: 7599
public health & safety [Subject]: 5034-
5043
public policy: 4184
Minnesota: 8199
research: 9553
public radio: 1283
public safety, research: 9553
public-access computer system forum:
3705
The Public-Access Computer Systems
Review [E-Journal]: 4524
publication offices, educational and
nonprofit: 1930
publications, educational: 4213
Publishers Weekly: 99
Publishers' Catalogues Home Page
[Resource]: 1929
publishing [Subject]: 1921-1935
academic: 1933
desktop: see also desktop publishing
electronic: 2417
electronic: see also electronic publishing
developer tools: 2415
end-user tools: 2416
industry news: 1925
software: see also software publishing
systems, supplier industry: 1926
PUBPOL-L [Mailing List]: 4184

PUBS-L [Mailing List]: 1930
Puerto Rico: 7232, 10014
Pulitzer Prize: 6093
Pulp (music group): 1134
pulp, fiction: 1322
Punjabi culture: 7349
punk: 976
European: 977
straight edge: 978
puns: 485
puppetry: 1625
Purdue CS Information Service
[Resource]: 9203
Purdue University: 4443, 6950
Pure Software: 3491
PURTOPOI [Mailing List]: 4549
Putnam, Hilary: 5317
puzzles: 6562
computer-based: 6476
PV-Wave programming language: 3609
PVM system: 3798
Pyramid 90x computers: 3878
pyrotechnics: 7021
Python [Mailing List]: 3645
Python programming language: 3618
python, object-oriented programming
language: 3645

Q

Q methodology: 9529
Q-Method [Mailing List]: 9529
QNTEVA-L [Mailing List]: 5364
QNX operating system: 3394
Quadralay C++ Archive [Resource]:
3550
Quadralay's Cryptography Archive
[Resource]: 3691
Quadraverb [Mailing List]: 771
Quake, game: 6546
QUAKE-L [Digest & Reflector]: 9334
QUAKER-K [Digest & Reflector]: 8763
QUAKER-L [Digest & Reflector]: 8764
QUAKER-P [Digest & Reflector]: 8765
Quakerism [Subject]: 8763-8767
Quakers: 5584, 8766, 8767
qualitative research: 5129
human sciences: 9546
quality control management: 2025
quality management system, ISO 9000:
5312
Quality Resources Online [Resource]:
2025
QUALRS-L [Mailing List]: 5129
QUANHIST.RECURRENT [Mailing
List]: 5208
quantitative methods: 5364
quantum cosmology: 5338
Quantum Leap (television series): 1449
creative fiction: 1528, 1586
QUARKXPR [Mailing List]: 2385
QuarkXPress, Macintosh: 2385
Quarterly Black Review, The: 99

Quayle, Dan: 5399
Queatre [Mailing List]: 1624
Quebec & Montreal, Canada [Subject]:
7209-7214
Quebec Nordiques: 6885
Quebec, Canada: 7214
employment: 7213
general interest: 7212
politics: 5651
sports: 7132
theater: 1624
Queen: 1135
Queensland University of Technology,
Brisbane [Resource]: 4444
Queensryche: 1136, 1137
Queer Infoservers [Resource]: 9941
Queer Resources Directory [Resource]:
9942
Queernet.Org [Resource]: 9943
Quick Information About Cancer for
Patients and Their Families
[Resource]: 4733
QUILTART-LIST [Mailing List]: 1268
quilting [Subject]: 1266-1269
art: 1268
Quine, Willard Van Orman: 5317
Quipu: 2893
quotations: 489
famous people: 512
Quote-Page [Distribution List]: 1776
Quote.Com [Resource]: 1777

R

r a z o r f i s h [Resource]: 3038
rabbis: 8777
women: 8826
rabbits: 6188
pet: 6203
raccoons: 4672
race, social inequality and: 10064
Rachel's Environment & Health Weekly
[Newsletter]: 4853
racing
animal: 6328
go-karts: 6594
sport rally: 6220
sports: 6226
racism, white nationalism: 5673
racquet sports [Subject]: 6911-6916
racquetball: 6911
radiation
in medicine, physics of: 5044
protection from: 5053
safety: 4854
radical left: 5661
radio [Subject]: 1270-1292
amateur: 6156, 6158, 6163, 6167, 61?
amateur: see also amateur, shortwa
& pirate radio
Australian: 7080
broadcasting: 1282
Canadian Broadcasting Corp.: 710€

news, miscellaneous: 4573
reports: 4576, 6146
  Antarctica: 7049
  British Columbia, Canada: 7162
  Germany: 4568
  Philadelphia, PA: 6150
  San Francisco and California: 4577
  San Francisco Bay Area, CA: 8014
  South America: 9584
  United States: 2703, 4575
  worldwide: 4572
  satellites: 4585
Weather Scape [Resource]: 6151
The Weaver [Magazine]: 8847
Web Journal of Current Legal Issues [E-journal]: 5569
Web of Addiction [Resource]: 4697
Web Training [Resource]: 2920
Web Travel Review [Magazine]: 7853
Web Weavers [Resource]: 3018
Web4Lib [Mailing List]: 5736
WebABLE! [Resource]: 9870
WebCrawler [Resource]: 2749
Webcutter [Resource]: 9121
The Webfoot's Travel Guide [Resource]: 7854
WebGod (World Wide Web server): 2997
webNews [Resource]: 2886
webpersonals.com [Resource]: 5999
weddings: 6027
  Islamic: 8799
  planning: 6031
Weddings Online [Resource]: 6033
weddings, marriage & domestic partnership [Subject]: 6024-6033
Ween: 801
weight loss: 9710
weights [Mailing List]: 4870
weights
  and weight training: 4870
  lifting: 6799, 6800
!Weird Online World! [E-Zine]: 2867
Weird Science: 1605
Weird Usenet: 529
WEIRD-L [Mailing List]: 532
welfare, corporate welfare reform: 5421
Well of Souls (book series): 1414
WELL, The: 2821
Wellfleet routers and bridges: 3255
wellness: 4866
Welsh
  culture: 7235
  language: 4266
WELSH-L [Mailing List]: 4266
werewolves: 1309
Wesleyan/holiness perspective: 8762
West Bank, news: 7536
West Marin County, CA
  news: 8029
West Virginia [Subject]: 8634
  news: 8634

WESTCANALTER [Mailing List]: 1001
Westerberg, Paul: 1142
Western Australia Internet Association: 7077
Western canon: 616
Western European stock markets: 1762
Western European Union (WEU): 5444
western United States, real estate listings: 1956
wetlands: 4632, 4640
Wey South: The WWW page of the Wey & Arun Canal Trust [Resource]: 5271
WH-NEWS [Newsletter]: 5118
What is the Internet? [Resource]: 2852
What's new in Italy [Resource]: 7397
What's New Too! [Resource]: 2887
wheat: 8907
  allergy: 4798
  genome: 9111
Whisper [E-Zine]: 75
White House: 5384, 5411
  news: 5408
white nationalism [Subject]: 5671-5673
white pages: 2741
white pages: see also search services & white pages
white supremacy: 5671-5673
White Wolf, games: 6518
white-collar crime: 9801
white-water kayaks: 6661
Whitehead, Alfred North: 5318
whitehouse, alt.dear: 5398
Whitewater scandal: 5397
WhiteWolf, games: 6517
WHNT 19 News [Resource]: 6139
Who's Who Online [Resource]: 2769
Who, The: 1179
Who-RPG-L [Mailing List]: 6522
Whois Servers List [Resource]: 2770
whois servers, list of: 2770
Whole Earth 'Lectronic Link (WELL): 10146
Whole Earth Review, coevolution: 10143
whole systems [Subject]: 10143-10148
whole systems theory: 10147, 10148
whole systems theory and science fiction: 1455
WHOLEINFO-L [Digest]: 10148
WHOLESYS-L [Mailing List]: 10147
Wicca: 8852, 8853
Wicca and Women's Spirituality [Resource]: 8857
Wide Area Information Server (WAIS): 2897, 2897, 2904
wide area networks [Subject]: 3318-3319
Widow Net [Resource]: 9846
WIG-L [Mailing List]: 622
Wildcat! BBS (Mustang Software): 2194
WILDCAT-L [Mailing List]: 2206
wilderness: 6630
  preservation: 6661

wildlife [Subject]: 4668-4686, 9333
  college and university education: 4680
  photography: 1259
  urban areas: 4686
Willoughby, Doug: 3343
wills, living: 9840, 9842
Wilson, E. O.: 9022
WIN-TCP TCP/IP software: 3316
Wind Energy Weekly [Newsletter]: 92
WindoWatch [Magazine]: 2660
windowing systems: 3426, 3436
Windows: see Microsoft Windows
Windows NT: see Microsoft Windows NT
windsurfing: 6659
wine: 5859, 5870
  Australia and New Zealand: 5883
  Japan: 5880
  making: 5881, 5885
  Niagara region: 8294
Wing Commander (game): 6422
Wings (television series): 1606
Winnie the Pooh: 582
Winnipeg Jets: 6891
Winnipeg, Canada, politics: 7148
Winsock [Subject]: 3320-3325
  e-mail applications: 2403
  miscellaneous applications: 3323
  news applications: 2946
  programming: 3321
  programming, tools: 2646
  software archive: 3325
  Trumpet news reader: 2928
  users: 4029
  voice communication: 3322
WINSOCK-L [Mailing List]: 3324
WinSock-L-Announce [Distribution List]: 3325
WINTCP-L [Mailing List]: 3317
winter sports, Australia: 6676
winvn news reader: 2963
WIOLE-L [Mailing List]: 4535
Wired magazine: 9818, 9826
Wireless Institute Civil Emergency Network: 6159
wireless network technology standards: 3774
Wisconsin [Subject]: 8635-8642
Wisconsin
  for sale: 8639
  general interest: 8640
  news: 8635
Wisconsin Primate Center Software Archive [Resource]: 3753
Wiseguy: 1607
WISHPERD [Mailing List]: 7023
witches: 5236
Witches Trine: 8855
WITSENDO [Mailing List]: 4818
Wittgenstein, Ludwig: 5317
WME-L [Mailing List]: 8734

ABOUT THE AUTHOR

Eric Harris-Braun has no home page. He usually writes software for a living, but couldn't resist the opportunity to once again undergo large amounts of stress doing something other than programming. He is also the author of Snap Mail, an easy-to-use e-mail package for Macintosh networks that is published by Casady & Greene.

THE INTERNET DIRECTORY ONLINE

Your purchase of this book gives you access to the online version and any future updates and enhancements. The home page for the online *Internet Directory* is:

`http://www.randomhouse.com/tid/`

In the center of the CD-ROM, you will find a serial number. After an initial period of open promotional access, you will need your serial number to use the online version.